The

RISE

of

AMERICAN
DEMOCRACY

Books by Sean Wilentz

The Rise of American Democracy: Jefferson to Lincoln (2005)

The Rose & the Briar: Death, Love and Liberty in the American Ballad (ed., with Greil Marcus, 2004)

David Walker's Appeal to the Coloured Citizens of the World (ed., 1995)

The Kingdom of Matthias (with Paul E. Johnson, 1994)

The Key of Liberty: The Life and Democratic Writings of William Manning, "A Labourer," 1747–1814 (with Michael Merrill, 1993)

Major Problems in the History of the Early Republic, 1789–1848 (ed., 1992)

Rites of Power: Symbolism, Ritual, and Politics since the Middle Ages (ed., 1985)

Chants Democratic: New York City & the Rise of the American Working Class, 1788–1850 (1984)

The

RISE

of

AMERICAN
DEMOCRACY

—

JEFFERSON TO LINCOLN

Sean Wilentz

W. W. Norton & Company
New York London

For information about permission to reproduce selections from this book, write to
Permissions, W. W. Norton & Company, Inc., 500 Fifth Avenue, New York, NY 10110

ISBN 0-393-05820-4

W. W. Norton & Company, Inc.
500 Fifth Avenue, New York, NY 10110

W. W. Norton & Company Ltd.
Castle House, 75/76 Wells Street, London W1T 3QT

To P.B. and L.W.
& to all my dearest

CONTENTS

III. SLAVERY AND THE CRISIS OF AMERICAN DEMOCRACY

LIST OF ILLUSTRATIONS

THE CRISIS OF THE OLD ORDER

(The following illustrations appear between pages 102 and 103.)

1. Thomas Jefferson inauguration banner, 1801. Believed to be one of the earliest partisan banners in America. The streamer in the eagle's mouth reads: "T. JEFFERSON President of the United States of AMERICA/JOHN ADAMS is no MORE."
2. John Singleton Copley, *Paul Revere*, ca. 1768.
3. Charles Willson Peale, *George Washington at Princeton*, 1779.
4. Charles Willson Peale, *Timothy Matlack*, ca. 1780.
5. Attributed to Rembrandt Peale, *Timothy Matlack*, ca. 1802.
6. Gilbert Stuart, *Thomas Jefferson*, 1805.
7. James Sharples, *James Madison*, 1797.
8. Charles Balthazar Julien Févret de Saint-Mémin, *William Duane*, 1802.
9. *Journal & Rules of the Council of Sachems of St. Tammany's Society*, New York, 1789.
10. Amos Doolittle, *A New Display of the United States*, 1799. A patriotic portrait of President John Adams, engraved during the rupture within the Federalist Party.
11. John Trumbull, *Alexander Hamilton*, ca. 1792.
12. Gilbert Stuart, *William Loughton Smith*, ca. 1790. A South Carolina Federalist, Smith delivered a speech in the House in 1790 strongly defending slavery as a benevolent institution.
13. Gilbert Stuart, *John Randolph*, 1804–05.
14. Tally of Electoral College votes, February 11, 1801. The official tally, leaving Jefferson and Burr tied. The right-hand column shows that one Rhode Island elector voted for John Jay.
15. "Speech of Mr. Jefferson at His Inauguration," 1801. Jefferson's speech was widely reprinted in Republican newspapers, and as broadsides such as this.

DEMOCRACY ASCENDANT

(The following illustrations appear between pages 486 and 487.)

SLAVERY AND THE CRISIS OF AMERICAN DEMOCRACY

(The following illustrations appear between pages 710 and 711.)

MAPS

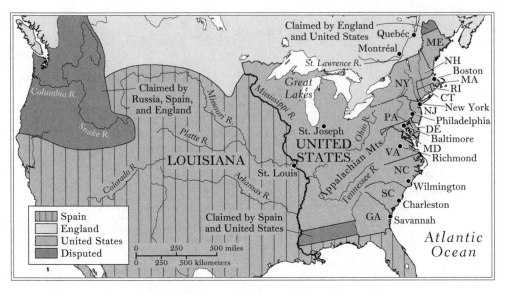

NORTH AMERICA, 1783

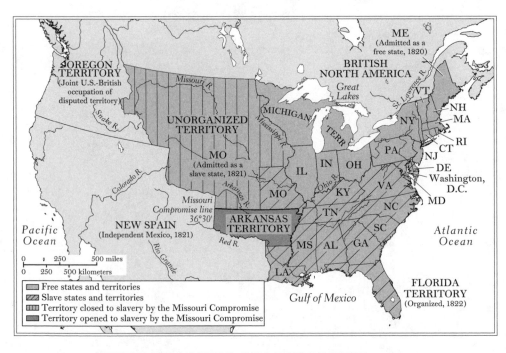

THE MISSOURI COMPROMISE, 1820

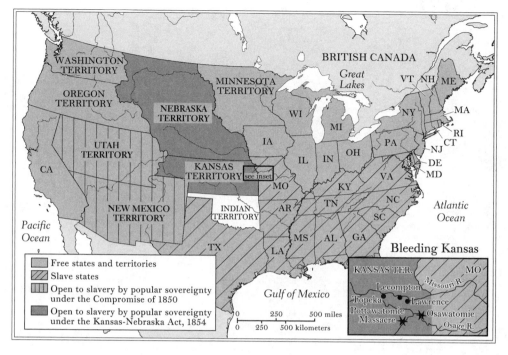

THE KANSAS-NEBRASKA ACT, 1854

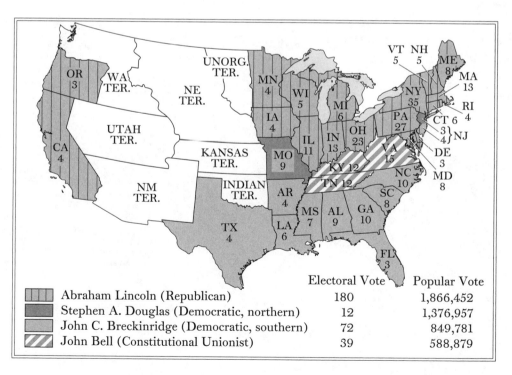

	Electoral Vote	Popular Vote
Abraham Lincoln (Republican)	180	1,866,452
Stephen A. Douglas (Democratic, northern)	12	1,376,957
John C. Breckinridge (Democratic, southern)	72	849,781
John Bell (Constitutional Unionist)	39	588,879

THE ELECTION OF 1860

PREFACE

This book's simple title describes the historical arc of its subject. Important elements of democracy existed in the infant American republic of the 1780s, but the republic was not democratic. Nor, in the minds of those who governed it, was it supposed to be. A republic—the *res publica*, or "public thing"—was meant to secure the common good through the ministrations of the most worthy, enlightened men. A democracy—derived from *demos krateo*, "rule of the people"—dangerously handed power to the impassioned, unenlightened masses. Democracy, the eminent Federalist political leader George Cabot wrote as late as 1804, was *"the government of the worst."*[1] Yet by the 1830s, as Alexis de Tocqueville learned, most Americans proclaimed that their country was a democracy as well as a republic. Enduring arguments had begun over the boundaries of democratic politics. In the 1840s and 1850s, these arguments centered increasingly on slavery and slavery's expansion and led to the Civil War.

The changes were astonishing, but neither inevitable nor providential. American democracy did not rise like the sun at its natural hour in history. Its often troubled ascent was the outcome of human conflicts, accommodations, and unforeseen events, and the results could well have been very different than they were. The difficulties and the contingencies made the events all the more remarkable. A momentous rupture occurred between Thomas Jefferson's time and Abraham Lincoln's that created the lineaments of modern democratic politics. The rise of American democracy is the story of that rupture and its immediate consequences.

Democracy is a troublesome word, and explaining why is one of my book's goals. A decade before the American Revolution, the early patriot James Otis defined democracy in its purest and simplest form as "a government of all over all," in which "the votes of the majority shall be taken as the voice of the whole," and where the rulers were the ruled.[2] As fixed descriptions go, this is as good as any, but its abstractness, of course, begs explication. Since the Revolution, citizens, scholars, and political leaders have latched onto one or another aspect of government or politics as democracy's essence. For some, it is a matter of widened political rights, usually measured by the extent of the suffrage and actual voting; for others, democracy means greater opportunity for the individual pursuit of happiness; for still others, it is more a cultural phenomenon than a political one, "a habit of the heart," as de Tocqueville put it, in which deference to rulers and condescension for the ruled give way to the ruder conventions of equality.

All these facets are important, but I think we go astray in discussing democracy simply as a form of government or society, or as a set of social norms — a category or a thing with particular structures that can be codified and measured. Today, democracy in America means enfranchisement, at a minimum, of the entire adult citizenry. By that standard, the American democracy of the mid-nineteenth century was hardly a democracy at all: women of all classes and colors lacked political and civil rights; most blacks were enslaved; free black men found political rights they had once enjoyed either reduced or eliminated; the remnant of a ravaged Indian population in the eastern states had been forced to move west, without citizenship. Even the most expansive of the era's successful democratic political reforms encompassed considerably less than half of the total adult population, and at best a bare majority of the free adult citizenry.* But to impose current categories of democracy on the past is to block any understanding of how our own, more elevated standards originated. It is to distort the lives of Americans who could barely have anticipated political and social changes that we take for granted. It is to substitute our experiences and prejudices for theirs.

By democracy, I mean a historical fact, rooted in a vast array of events and experiences, that comes into being out of changing human relations between governors and the governed. Stopping history cold at any particular point and parsing its political makeup negates that historical flow and stifles the voices and activities of actual people attempting to define the operations of government. Only over an extended period of time is it possible to see democracy and

---

* This is based on the figures gathered in the federal census for 1850, which show that 44.5 percent of the adult population (twenty years and older) and 51.0 percent of the free adult population were white males. Noncitizens and Indians are not included in the calculations.

democratic government grow out of particular social, intellectual, and political contexts.

Democracy appears when some large number of previously excluded, ordinary persons—what the eighteenth century called "the many"—secure the power not simply to select their governors but to oversee the institutions of government, as officeholders and as citizens free to assemble and criticize those in office. Democracy is never a gift bestowed by benevolent, farseeing rulers who seek to reinforce their own legitimacy. It must always be fought for, by political coalitions that cut across distinctions of wealth, power, and interest. It succeeds and survives only when it is rooted in the lives and expectations of its citizens, and continually reinvigorated in each generation. Democratic successes are never irreversible.

Since de Tocqueville, there has been a long tradition of scholarship devoted to understanding the democratic rupture that this book describes. The rise of American democracy engaged the attention of great historians now forgotten by the general reading public (Dixon Ryan Fox, J. Franklin Jameson), as well as such acknowledged giants as Henry Adams, Charles and Mary Beard, Frederick Jackson Turner, Richard Hofstadter, and, most recently, Gordon S. Wood. But modern study of the subject owes the most to Arthur M. Schlesinger Jr.'s *Age of Jackson*, published in 1945. Before Schlesinger, historians thought of American democracy as the product of an almost mystical frontier or agrarian egalitarianism. *The Age of Jackson* toppled that interpretation by placing democracy's origins firmly in the context of the founding generation's ideas about the few and the many, and by seeing democracy's expansion as an outcome of struggles between classes, not sections. More than any previous account, Schlesinger's examined the activities and ideas of obscure, ordinary Americans, as well as towering political leaders. While he identified most of the key political events and changes of the era, Schlesinger also located the origins of modern liberal politics in the tradition of Thomas Jefferson and Andrew Jackson, and in their belief, as he wrote, that future challenges "will best be met by a society in which no single group is able to sacrifice democracy and liberty to its interests." Finally, Schlesinger examined and emphasized the shattering moral and political dilemmas that an expanding southern slavery posed to American democracy, leading to the Civil War.[3]

Since *The Age of Jackson* appeared, a revolution in historical studies has focused scholars' attentions on groups of Americans and aspects of American history that held minor interest at best in the historical profession in 1945. That revolution has altered historians' views of every detail of our past. The tragedy of Indian removal; the democratic activities of ex-slaves and other free blacks, and the political impact of slaves' resistance; the ease and sometimes the viciousness with which some professed democrats, North and South, championed white racial supremacy; the participation of women in reform efforts (and, in time, in electoral campaigns), along with the ridicule directed at the fledgling woman suffrage movement; the liberal humanitarian impulses of supposedly "conservative," pro-business politics; the importance of ethnicity and religion in shaping Americans' political allegiances—each of these, either ignored or slighted sixty years ago, has generated its own scholarly literature.

Yet if the social history revolution has profoundly changed how historians look at the United States, it has not diminished the importance of the questions *The Age of Jackson* asked about early American democracy. On the contrary, it has made those questions—especially about democratic politics, social class, and slavery—all the more pertinent to our understanding of the dramatic events that led from the American Revolution to the American Civil War. Some important recent works have attempted to raise those questions anew, and combine the so-called new style of history with the older. The most ambitious of them have reinterpreted the connections between society and politics before 1860 as part of a larger market revolution that swept across the country. But these admirable studies have generally submerged the history of politics in the history of social change, reducing politics and democracy to by-products of various social forces without quite allowing the play of politics its importance. *The Rise of American Democracy* offers a different interpretation, with a greater emphasis on the vagaries of politics, high and low.[4]

The subtitle, *Jefferson to Lincoln*, reaffirms the importance of political events, ideas, and leaders to democracy's rise—once an all-too-prevalent assumption, now in need of some rescue and repair. Thomas Jefferson, more than any other figure in the early republic, established (and was seen to have established) the terms of American democratic politics. Abraham Lincoln self-consciously advanced an updated version of Jefferson's egalitarian ideals, and his election to the presidency of the United States caused the greatest crisis American democracy has yet known. By singling out Jefferson and Lincoln, I certainly do not mean to say that presidents and other great men were solely responsible for the vicissitudes of American politics. One of the book's recurring themes is how ordinary Americans, including some beyond the outermost reaches of the country's formal political life, had lasting influence on the exercise of power. But just as political leaders did not create American democracy out of thin air, so the masses of Americans did not simply force their way into the corridors of power. That Jefferson and not John Adams was elected president in 1800–01—a fact that nearly did not come to pass—made a great difference to later political developments. So did the presence of other public officials, elected and unelected, from the top of American public life to the bottom. Featuring Jefferson and Lincoln in the subtitle is a shorthand way of insisting on what ought to be a truism: that some individuals have more influence on history than others. The title, by referrring to a broader history, insists that they cannot make history just as they please, constrained as they are by a host of forces, persons, and popular movements beyond their control and anticipation.

The book can be read as a chronicle of American politics from the Revolution to the Civil War with the history of democracy at its center, or as an account of how democracy arose in the United States (and with what consequences) in the context of its time. Either way, the book has a few major themes. One, given special attention in the opening chapters, is that democracy, at the nation's inception, was highly contested, not a given, and developed piecemeal, by fits and starts, at the state and local as well as the national level. A second theme is that social changes barely foreseen in 1787—the rapid commercialization of the free labor North and the renaissance of plantation slavery in the South—deeply affected how democracy advanced, and retreated, after 1815.

Third, Americans perceived these social changes primarily in political terms and increasingly saw them as struggles over contending ideas of democracy. Americans of the early nineteenth century lived in a different mental universe from ours with regard to politics. Above all, they inherited from the Revolutionary era a republican perspective that regarded political institutions as the foundation of social and economic relations, and not the other way around. Certain kinds of societies appeared more conducive than others to a just and harmonious government. Americans sharply disagreed about which societies were superior. But if order and happiness abounded, they believed it was because political institutions and the men running them were sound: disorder and unhappiness stemmed from unsound institutions or from the corruption of sound institutions by ambitious and designing men. Across the chasm of the Civil War, the era of high industrialism, and the conflicts of the twentieth century, we are more likely to see economic power and interests as the matrix for politics and political institutions. For Americans of the early republic, politics, government, and constitutional order, not economics, were primary to interpreting the world and who ran it—a way of thinking that can wrongly look simplified, paranoid, and conspiracy-driven today.[5]

A fourth theme concerns the constancy of political conflict: democracy in America was the spectacle of Americans arguing over democracy. If the word became a shibboleth for new and emerging political parties and movements, it did not on that account become degraded and bland. Precisely because opposing groups claimed to champion the same ideal, they fought all the harder to ensure their version would prevail. There was no end to the possible qualifying labels Americans could devise to illustrate exactly what sort of democrats they were—not just with separate major- and third-party labels (Democratic, Whig, State Rights, Know-Nothing, and so on) but with the blizzard of names for factions within the parties that always bemuse uninitiated readers: Loco Foco,

Barnburner, Hunker, Silver Gray.* In part, these labels connoted patronage connections for political insiders. But in an age when elections came to be conducted more or less year-round, they also reflected beliefs and deep commitments above and beyond partisan machinations—while for a radical such as William Lloyd Garrison they were craven and sinful, and for a corrosive skeptic such as Herman Melville they inspired ambivalence and dread.

Fifth, the many-sided conflicts over American democracy came, in the 1840s and 1850s, to focus on an issue of recognized importance since the republic's birth: the fate of American slavery. Throughout the decades after the Revolution, but with a hurtling force after 1840, two American democracies emerged, the free-labor democracy of the North and the slaveholders' democracy of the South—distinct political systems as well as bodies of thought. Although they often praised identical values and ideals, and although they were linked through the federal government and the national political parties, the two were fundamentally antagonistic. The nation's political leaders suppressed those antagonisms, sometimes in the face of powerful protests and schismatic movements, from the 1820s through the early 1850s. By 1860, the conflict could no longer be contained, as a democratic election sparked southern secession and the war that would determine American democracy's future.

The book's final theme is implied in the others: the idea of democracy is never sufficient unto itself. Since the Second World War, and even more since the great democratic revolutions of 1989–91, the world has witnessed the continuing resilience and power of democratic ideals. So swiftly have former tyrannies turned into self-declared democratic governments that the danger has arisen of taking democracy for granted, despite its manifest fragility and possible collapse in large parts of the globe. As the early history of the United States shows, the habits and the institutions of modern democracy are relatively new in the larger span of history. Their breakthrough, even in the most egalitarian portions of the New World, required enormous reversals of traditional assumptions about power and legitimacy. As those habits and institutions began taking hold, different American social orders produced clashing versions of democracy, generating enmities so deep that they could only be settled in blood. Thereafter, democratic

---

* From 1856: "Thus every party and sect has a daily register of the most minute sayings and doings, and proceedings and progress of every other sect; and as truth and error are continually brought before the masses, they have the opportunity to know and compare. There are political parties under the names of Whigs, Democrats, Know-nothings, Freesoilers, Fusionists, Hunkers, Woolly-heads, Dough-faces, Hard-shells, Soft-shells, Silver-greys, and I know not what besides; all of them extremely puzzling to the stranger, but of great local significance." Isabella Lucy Bird, *The Englishwoman in America* (London, 1856), 422–3.

ideas, both in the United States and elsewhere, have had to be refreshed, fought over, and redefined continually. The rise of American democracy, from Jefferson's era to Lincoln's, created exhilarating new hopes and prospects, but also fierce conflicts and enormous challenges about what democracy can be and should be. Democracy's hopes and prospects, its conflicts and challenges, persist. So do its vulnerabilities.

The

RISE

of

AMERICAN
DEMOCRACY

PROLOGUE

O n pleasant evenings in the middle of the 1830s, Noah Webster, nearing
his eighties, would return home from his daily walk around New
Haven, sit in his front-porch rocker, pick up his newspaper, and moan.
The latest political dispatches told Webster that the republic he had loved and
fought for had gone to the devil, a democratic devil in the shape of Andrew Jackson, and the future looked bleak. Webster's wife, upon hearing his sighs, knew
what was coming: a monologue on mob rule, the death of Christian virtue, and
the savagery of strange doctrines and slogans ("rotation in office," "the rich
oppress the poor," *"the spoils belong to the victors"*) that had taken the country by
storm. Later in the evening, a few of Webster's professor friends from Yale might
stop by to listen and nod their heads, forming a mutually admiring circle of dyspeptic learned men. On these occasions, Webster would brighten momentarily.
But many of his companions, like himself, had grown old, and the number of
Americans like them was too small, Webster feared, to save the republic now.[1]

When the professors did not appear, Webster would rouse himself, scratch
down his opinions, and mail them to a few agreeable editors and elected officials.
He was still a well-known figure, a veteran political controversialist, die-hard
nationalist, and self-made man, a Founding Father of sorts. Although the great
dictionary he had published years earlier had not yet found its market, his blue-
backed speller had been a rousing success, and trustworthy critics had hailed
him as the man who had literally defined the American language. Perhaps his
countrymen would heed his wisdom after all. And so he composed his didactic
letters, denouncing President Jackson and Jackson's fanatical democratic principles. Webster devised a plan to check the egalitarian tide by raising the voting

age to forty-five, dividing the electorate into two classes according to age and wealth, and letting each class choose one house of Congress—an Americanized gerontocratic version of the British Lords and Commons. But his ideas impressed few readers and caused many to snicker, and the old man sank into acrid reveries about his days as a boy soldier during the American Revolution. Had he foreseen what would follow, he told an associate, he never would have enlisted in the patriot cause.[2]

Webster was a political relic in the 1830s, yet around the country, other Americans were also pessimistic. In the summer of 1837, James Kent, the nation's most distinguished legal commentator, journeyed to the spa at Saratoga Springs and joined other gentlemen in discussing the destructiveness of what Kent called "the democracy of numbers and radicalism." In Manhattan, the affluent parvenu and former mayor of New York, Philip Hone, recoiled with horror from the unkempt Jacksonian supporters who ran wild in the streets on election days, and who on one dismal occasion besieged him in his own house with catcalls. Further south, slaveholding planters and officeholders who thought Jackson a turncoat despaired at his popularity with the plain people and voters. "The old 'Warrior Chief' has kicked up a h-ll of a dust throughout the nation," a Tennessean wrote to a North Carolina planter, in 1834, adding that while "most of our friends of N. Carolina are against [Jackson's] 'experiments,' I should suppose that the people of the State were for him." Other southerners despaired that the masses of farmers and the anti-Jacksonians were like aliens in blood.[3]

Jackson's critics were prone to see the sum of the new democratic order in the president's craggy face, and in what Kent called "the horrible doctrine and influence of Jacksonism." But men with longer experience such as Noah Webster knew there was more to it than that. For Webster, Jackson was a reborn Thomas Jefferson, accomplishing what Jefferson had only imagined accomplishing when the philosophizing mood was upon him. Jackson himself, not known for philosophizing, called his political beliefs an extension of "good old jeffersonian Democratic republican principles." And if Jackson came to symbolize a fulfillment of Jeffersonian desires, his path had been cleared long before he took office. The kind of political charisma (and, for many, scariness) he emanated could not have been produced by his military glory and personal fortitude alone. For more than half a century, Americans of all persuasions had been preparing the way for Jackson, or some democratic leader like him.[4]

The mysterious rise of American democracy was an extraordinary part of the most profound political transformation in modern history: the triumph of popular government and of the proposition—if not, fully, the reality—that sovereignty rightly belongs to the mass of ordinary individual and equal citizens.[5] For centuries, throughout the Western world, such political arrangements had seemed utterly unnatural. Since Plato, doctrines of hierarchical authority had dominated political thought, whether classical (favoring the rule of the wise), Christian (favoring the rule of the holy), or some mixture of the two. According to these doctrines, most of humanity was unsuited for public duties more elevated than the drudgery of farm animals. History seemed to support hierarchical theory. The fate of popular government in the ancient Greek city-states and the Roman republic had been tragic. Periodic peasant uprisings and urban disorders, from the late fourteenth century on, persuaded the articulate classes of Britain and Europe that the "people" were dangerously unstable and incapable of rational thought. "The beast," "the rabble," "th' idiot multitude" reappeared with contemptuous regularity in the learned treatises, poems, and plays of the early modern West.[6]

Rebellion, civil war, and regicide in England after 1640 set the beast stirring, allied as never before (albeit testily) with its social betters among the Puritan and Parliamentarian insurgents. Entrenched inside Oliver Cromwell's army and in the London trades—"the hobnails, clouted shoes, the private soldiers, the leather and woolen aprons," the preacher and radical hero John Lilburne said—so-called Leveller agitators proposed not simply the abolition of the monarchy and the House of Lords, but the establishment of a government truly representative of the people, based on an equitably distributed franchise. In smaller pockets of rebellion, more outlandish plebeian prophets—Ranters, Diggers, Seekers—announced diverse visions of communal heavens on earth. But the revolution's leaders kept radical dissenters on the political margins. At the famous army debates at Putney in 1647, Cromwell and his lieutenants squelched any possibility of popular suffrage. Over the ensuing chaotic decade, the propertied and educated few closed ranks against the unreasonable many. With the restoration of the English monarchy in 1660, plebeian radical politics plunged underground, to reappear sporadically in conspiracies, riots, and revels over the century to come.[7]

When democracy broke through again, in the 1770s, it was in the New World, not the Old, as a beleaguered force within the American Revolution. The combustion was not spontaneous. Even before the outbreak of the English Civil War, religious sectarians who preferred flight to New England to life under Tudor monarchy established at least a nominal conception of self-rule by compact, to which some dissenters (such as a group of four Rhode Island towns in 1647) attached the word "democracy." In 1644, the schismatic Roger Williams declared that "the *Soveraigne, originall,* and *foundation* of *civill power* lies in the people." Bits and pieces of the English plebeian radicalism of the 1640s and 1650s crossed the Atlantic and survived to help inspire the American revolutionaries and frighten their opponents over a century later. As the independence struggle with Britain reached a crisis in 1774, the more radical of the Massachusetts towns excoriated George III for aspiring, as the selectmen of Billerica put it, to "the unlimited Prerogative, contended for by those arbitrary and misguided Princes, *Charles* the First and *James* the Second, for which One lost his Life, and the Other his Kingdom." The most popular antimonarchical pamphlet of the Revolution, Thomas Paine's *Common Sense*, contained numerous allusions to old English democratic themes.[8]

The radicalism of the seventeenth century belongs to the genealogy of American democracy. And there were important differences between the colonies and the mother country in political practice. Colonial charters installed property requirements for voting, usually landed freeholds, but in newly settled colonial areas where land was cheap, anywhere from 70 to 80 percent of white adult men could meet the qualification. It was far easier for an American man of middling means than for his British counterpart to hold local and even legislative office. The colonies lacked Britain's encrustation of civil bureaucracies, church sinecures, and military commands. Americans' experience of town meetings (where, in New England, humble men won election to local offices) and of independent, parish-run dissenting churches gave them a strong taste of direct political engagement. Some British visitors and American royalists regarded the colonies as wild egalitarian outposts. A writer in *Rivington's New York Loyal Gazette* flatly blamed the Revolution on the Americans' "democratic form of government." Some later historians, with no royalist motives, have even described eighteenth-century America as a "middle-class democracy" long before the Revolution.[9]

Yet the evidence of colonial democracy, and especially of the differences with Britain, can be highly deceiving. In older settled rural areas of the colonies, as in coastal towns and early cities, the proportion of eligible voters among white men was much smaller than elsewhere, as little as two in five. Those proportions probably declined during the years immediately preceding the Revolution, when the rate of property ownership in the colonies was falling. The famous town-meeting democracies of New England were often run as means to ratify decisions already made by local leaders, and to give the air of amicable consensus. In the mid-eighteenth century, more than previously, the British monarchy was the wellspring of American political authority, the bestower of favor and fortune through royal appointment to the competing "interests" or "connections" of America's premier gentry families. Within this monarchical setting, rival families or factions might mobilize ordinary voters on election days, through treats or barbecues or more raucous, even violent gatherings—but the royalist favorites always remained in charge. Outside elections, the everyday gulf between noble patricians and the beastlike people was deep, even among those fortunate men who had risen out of the rabble. No less than the established grandees, up-and-coming patriot leaders respected elaborate codes of social deference. The young George Washington beheld the lesser farmers of Virginia as "the grazing multitude." The ambitious John Adams, perhaps in order to set himself apart from his humble background, spoke offhandedly of the "common Herd of Mankind."[10]

Philosophically, the assumption prevailed that democracy, although an essential feature of any well-ordered government, was also dangerous and ought to be kept strictly within bounds. The word itself appeared rarely in pamphlets, newspapers, and sermons before the Revolution, most often alongside "monarchy" and "aristocracy," as one of the three elements of government, tied to specific social orders, that needed to be mixed and balanced in accord with the British model. On the other occasions when either the word or the concept of democracy appeared, the context was usually pejorative, connoting, at best, a ridiculous impracticality, especially in large countries. At midcentury, the historian William Smith wrote that "[i]n proportion as a Country grows rich and populous, more Checks are wanted to the Power of the People." John Adams deeply feared that although "the prospect of free and popular Governments" might be pleasing, "there is great Danger that these Governments will not make Us happy," and would be undone by noise, meanness, and ignorance. Even the radical Thomas Paine took care, during and long after the Revolution, to reject the idea of a pure or simple democracy in favor of representation grafted on democracy.[11]

The major claims on democracy's behalf before the Revolution rested on the rising power, in many colonies, of the lower houses of the colonial legislatures, in imitation of the rising power of the Commons in England after the Glorious Revolution of 1688–89. In principle, these assemblies represented the common middling sort, the small farmers, artisans, and petty merchants who made up the great bulk of the colonial free male population. According to one North Carolinian, the assemblies were supposed to act as "Eyes for the Commonality, as Ears for the Commonality, and as Mouths for the Commonality." Yet even though a few members of the Commonality actually sat in the assemblies, the legislators were generally out of touch with their own constituents between elections, and ran their affairs much like the oligarchies that commanded the early eighteenth-century House of Commons under Robert Walpole. Colonial assemblymen would receive petitions and letters from their localities, but did with them whatever they pleased. Otherwise, the people had no formal voice of their own in government. And that was exactly how it was supposed to be—for once the electors had chosen their representatives, they ceded power, reserving none for themselves until the next election. As one New England divine wrote, the electorate did not "surrender so much their right or liberty to their Rulers, as their Power."

There was no sense of any continued exercise of political power by the "people out-of-doors." The people, as a political entity, existed only on election days.[12]

If the unelected had any other political voice, it came in the form of extrale-gal mob violence and crowd disturbances—forms of protests condoned and even instigated by established political leaders when it suited their political advantage. "Popular commotions," as John Adams called them, could be dangerous, espe-cially when led by unscrupulous private factions of the insider leadership, but they were tolerable "when Fundamentals are invaded." Whether commanded from above or organized on their own, these tumults affirmed that the mass of ordinary citizens had no regular, legal, permanent involvement in the making of decisions, the actual stuff of government and politics. They also reinforced the traditional image of the people as the rowdy multitude, not to be entrusted with formal power.[13]

Only when the gathering American revolutionary impulses reached the brink of independence in the 1770s did they begin to look discernibly democratic in any sense that the Puritan radicals would have understood. At stake were the Revolution's central claims about sovereignty and representation. On the one hand, the patriot movement argued that because Americans had neither elected representatives of their own in Parliament nor any transcendent common inter-ests with the mother country, the imperial connection was oppressive. Tradi-tional Tory claims that the colonists enjoyed virtual representation, with their interests protected by members of Parliament who embodied the good of the entire realm, dissolved before American contentions that those very M.P.'s (as a Georgia clergyman wrote) had no "right to represent and lay on taxes on those who never invested them with any such power, and by whom they neither would nor could be elected." Without popular consent, there could be no just or legiti-mate representation. Without that legitimacy, Parliament had no sovereignty over America.[14]

On the other hand, patriot leaders were dedicated to building a polity gov-erned by the wisest and best among themselves, who would selflessly devote themselves to securing the unified public good. Outside the imperial context, they clung tenaciously to the idea of virtual representation when it came to their own ordinary people. Products of the British constitutional system, they shared an assumption that men who lacked an independent estate had "no will of their own," as Sir William Blackstone had written in his authoritative *Commentaries on the Laws of England*. Dependent men were politically unreliable because they could be easily manipulated by their patrons—or, alternatively, might use political power to plunder their patrons. Even Thomas Jefferson, who would emerge as one of the most democratic of the Revolution's leaders, was reflexively suspicious at first. "A choice by the people themselves," he complained to a friend in 1776, "is not generally distinguished for it's wisdom."[15]

The Revolution, by destroying the old forms of monarchical government and virtual representation, opened up lines of argument and ways of thinking that severely undermined hierarchical assumptions. The most hard-headed of the revolutionary leaders understood this and, for the most part, found it frightening. Taken too literally, the axiom that government should rest on the people's consent—especially when mingled with the assertion, made most forcefully in Jefferson's Declaration of Independence, that all men were endowed with equal and natural rights—could provoke disorder and give undue influence to the less-than-wise and the less-than-good. John Adams predicted, with prescience, that loosening voting requirements would mean "new claims will arise; women will demand a vote; lads from twelve to twenty-one will think their claims not closely attended to; and every man who has not a farthing will demand an equal voice with any other, in all acts of state."[16]

To the horror of Adams and others, their fears came to pass, as ordinary Americans, organized in independent committees, conventions, and other associations, raised a democratic clamor even before independence from Britain had been secured. "The people are now contending for freedom," one Massachusetts pamphleteer declared in 1776, "and would to God they might not only obtain, but likewise keep it in their own hands." From all across Revolutionary America, cities and countryside alike, came appeals for a widened suffrage, equalized representation, unicameral legislatures, overhauled judiciaries, and a seemingly endless list of other egalitarian demands.[17]

It was one thing, these city and country democrats pointed out, to speak of establishing a kingless republican government and of vaunting the public good. It was quite another to specify what kind of republics the new American governments, state and national, would be. The *philosophe* Montesquieu, read widely in translations of his *L'Esprit des Lois*, had observed that republics could be of different types, in which either "the body, or only a part of the people, is possessed of the supreme power." (As a Massachusetts writer would put it more bluntly a few years after independence, "Republicks are divided into democraticks and aristocraticks.") And so, in an exuberant exchange of ideas, popular spokesmen, and a small portion of the patriot leadership, argued that the new American governments ought to be as "democratick" as possible—and that any government which lacked the full approval of the people, as one New York committee of radical artisans put it, was guilty of "promoting the selfish views . . . of oligarchy." Faced with this pressure chiefly from below, patriot leaders, embroiled in worsening conflict with the British Crown and its functionaries, found themselves backed into a dilemma that would bedevil Americans long after they won their independence.[18]

How "democratick" the governments produced by the American Revolution actually were was open to dispute then, and still is. But between 1776 and the ratification of the Federal Constitution in 1788, a shift certainly occurred in the ways Americans, at every level of political society, talked and thought about democracy. At the outbreak of the Revolution, the necessity of a mixed government of the different social orders remained a widespread article of faith, except among the most radical patriots. As one of Thomas Paine's critics wrote, "[N]o government was ever purely aristocratical or democratical—owing probably to the unavoidable evils incident to each." Eleven years later, when the Framers met in Philadelphia to design a new federal government, fears of democratic government, or of too much democratic government, were still palpable. Yet when they settled down to repair what James Madison called the "vices of the political system" under the Articles of Confederation, and even more when they defended the new constitution they had written, the leading delegates gravitated to ideas very different from the conventional wisdom of 1776. The new federal edifice would not be a mixed government. Nor would it lodge sovereignty in the newly independent state governments, as the Articles had done. Instead, the people of the United States would be sovereign. In the new plan, according to James Wilson (Madison's kindred spirit at the Federal Convention), "[A]ll authority of every *kind is derived by* REPRESENTATION *from the* PEOPLE *and the* DEMO-CRATIC *principle is carried into every part of the government.*" Therefore, the Constitution, "in its principles," was "purely democratical"—the very phrase that, before the Revolution, had seemed absurd and treacherous. In words and in feelings, the unthinkable was becoming the desirable.[19]

"**A** fundamental mistake of the Americans," Noah Webster, not yet a relic, wrote in 1789, "has been that they considered the revolution as completed when it was just begun." Webster's judgment would be borne out over the next few years, when new convulsions hastened the emergence of new forms of democratic politics. As Webster understood, those convulsions and fresh departures were continuations of the upheaval that had started in earnest in 1776.[20]

I.

THE CRISIS OF
THE NEW ORDER

1

AMERICAN DEMOCRACY IN A REVOLUTIONARY AGE

In the summer of 1776, three different assemblages of revolutionaries worked in Philadelphia. The famous one, the Second Continental Congress, having sat in continuous session for ten months, voted to dissolve ties with Britain on July 2, and two days later signed a formal Declaration of Independence, written chiefly by Thomas Jefferson. In late June, a Pennsylvania Provincial Conference also set up nearby. The delegates had just been chosen by their extralegal local committees of correspondence and, with the approval of the Continental Congress, displaced the dilatory colonial assembly. Under the Provincial Congress's aegis, and while the Continental Congress was declaring the nation's independence, elections were held for delegates to the Pennsylvania Convention to devise a state constitution. This third group assembled on July 8, and spent the summer at the State House, steps away from the rooms where the Continental Congress was working, inventing a new Pennsylvania commonwealth.[1]

One famous delegate, Benjamin Franklin, was elected to all three bodies and played a leading role in shaping both the Declaration of Independence and the new Pennsylvania constitution. At seventy, Franklin was among the older patriot leaders, and the oldest to sign the Declaration. He was also the most renowned, thanks to his scientific discoveries and "Poor Richard" writings, as well as his long political service. And he was proving to be, in some respects, among the most democratic. Franklin's work at the Continental Congress—as an esteemed delegate, a member of the select committee that helped Jefferson draft the Declaration, and a major contributor to the debates over the new Articles of Confederation—is well known. After independence was declared, he pushed to create a strong federal government run by a popularly elected legislature based on proportional representation. (Few of those ideas got far.) Much less familiar is Franklin's contribution as president of the now-obscure State Convention that drafted and approved the most egalitarian constitution produced anywhere in Revolutionary America.[2]

Under the new state plan, Pennsylvanians would be governed by a legislature with a single house and a twelve-man executive council elected by a broad franchise of taxpaying freemen. Representation of different parts of the state in the legislature would be more equitable than in the past. The Council of Censors would be elected every seven years to evaluate the government and censure any constitutional violations. A formal declaration of rights proclaimed "[t]hat all men are born equally free and independent," and that the state's government would exist for the "common benefit, protection and security of the people, nation, or community, and not for the particular emolument or advantage of any single man, family, or set of men, who are only part of that community." It is unclear how much of a hand Franklin had in actually writing the new constitution. But his ideas and, at times, his style were plainly in evidence, so much so that many people thought he was the sole author. With Franklin presiding, the Convention adopted the new framework at the end of September and put it immediately into effect.[3]

It is not surprising that Franklin's more egalitarian leanings prevailed in the Pennsylvania Convention and not in Congress. The planters, merchants, and professional men who signed the Declaration of Independence—including John Hancock, John Adams, and Edward Rutledge, as well as Franklin and Jefferson—were notables of wealth and standing, with reputations of high degree, at least in their respective provinces. The group's views on government and democracy varied widely, with Franklin, although hardly a thoroughgoing democrat, standing at the more democratic end. The leaders of the Pennsylvania Convention were very different. Most were Philadelphia artisans and intellectuals of a radical democratic bent, many of them disciples of Thomas Paine, with names unfamiliar to most Americans, then and now: George Bryan, James Cannon, Thomas Young, Timothy Matlack. The majority of the delegates were humble farmers from the rural interior, chosen by the radical leadership because of their adherence to democratic political ideals. "They are mostly honest well meaning Country men, who are employed," the Rev. Francis Allison observed with some disdain, "but intirely unacquainted with . . . high matters." The Convention also had strong political ties to the lower sort in the rank and file of Philadelphia's militia companies.[4]

Franklin was one of the few Americans who could feel perfectly comfortable taking a leading role simultaneously inside the Continental Congress and the Pennsylvania Convention—one group defining a nation, the other defining a state; one with a patrician tone, the other decidedly plebeian. Likewise, he may have been the only Pennsylvanian with the prestige, wit, and political skill to bring together the disparate elements within the Pennsylvania State Convention—men from the city and the country, men who agreed on certain egalitarian principles but were otherwise divided by clashing backgrounds, educations, temperaments, and expectations. A similar pattern appeared in the other new states. American democratic politics originated in both the country and the city, from New England through the South. Democratic hopes, which the Pennsylvanians temporarily fulfilled in 1776, would depend on whether these two political milieux could be united—and on how much influence the country democrats and the city democrats would then have in shaping the new republican order.

THE COUNTRY DEMOCRACY

Land forms "the true and the only philosophy of the American farmer," the French immigrant (and self-styled "American Farmer") J. Hector St. John Crève-coeur observed in 1782. Speaking as if he were an ordinary native tiller of the soil, Crèvecoeur dissembled shamelessly—at the time he wrote, he owned an estate in the Hudson River Valley—but his appreciation of everyday rural political thought was acute. "This formerly rude soil has been converted by my father into a pleasant farm," he wrote of his home, "and in return it has established all our rights; on it is founded our rank, our freedom, our power as citizens, our importance as inhabitants in such a district." At the end of the eighteenth century, land, and the labor applied to it, provided the ordinary farmer's basis for social respect and civic participation. Getting and protecting claims to the land and its products was the pervasive political imperative of the country democracy.[5]

Country democracy arose from a disparate white rural majority of farmers, whom the Pennsylvania gentleman democrat George Logan referred to collectively as "the Yeomanry of the United States." From affluent incipient commercial farmers who lived near cities or river towns to hardscrabble settlers living just beyond the frontier line, these farmers and their households shared certain broad characteristics. They subsisted primarily on the produce of their own farms and on what they could obtain from exchange with neighbors, although a growing number were engaged in some sort of cash-crop production (chiefly wheat, flax, and livestock in the northern states, tobacco and wheat in the southern states). With land plentiful and cheap labor in short supply, theirs were family-centered operations in which fathers directed the work of legally dependent wives and children—and on some farms, most commonly but not yet exclusively in the South, perhaps a slave or two. Contrary to still-persistent

American myths of rural rugged individualism, the yeoman households were tightly connected to each other—and, increasingly, to the outside world.[6]

Descended from transatlantic victims of religious persecution and rural dispossession, large numbers of whom had arrived as indentured servants, the American yeomanry had ample reason to celebrate life in the New World. Compared to anything they could have expected in Britain or Europe, America was a wide-open place of cheap and bountiful land and lightly enforced government—"the poor man's best country," in one commonly used phrase.[7] But all was not flourishing tranquility. Especially in backcountry areas, conflicts between and among yeomen, would-be yeomen, great proprietors, and government officials, as well as combat with Indians, led to continual wrangling and sporadic violence, all of which worsened after the Revolution.

Much of the conflict concerned access to the land, as farmers seeking independent land titles found themselves squeezed out by gentlemen who had exploited their political connections to gain large (sometimes huge), loosely defined land grants. Tensions between debtors and creditors were also endemic. During hard times, indebted farmers fell back on the forgiving ethic of a complex barter system and demanded stay laws and other forms of legal relief, while government officials enacted restrictive fiscal policies and creditors demanded the immediate payment they believed rightfully theirs.[8] Excessive judicial fees, burdensome taxes, and the failure of colonial (and later state) governments to keep order against bandits and Indians posed severe dangers to would-be independent householders.

Yeomen battled back, with a vehemence born of fear, prejudice, and insular hatreds—as well as an admixture of egalitarian ideals. The largest of the yeoman rebellions before the Revolution, the so-called North Carolina Regulation, began in 1764. Led by, among others, a mystical preacher and landowner named Hermon Husband, the uprising turned into full-scale war against autocratic eastern gentry rule that ended only when the rebels were crushed by combined colonial and British forces at the Battle of Alamance (near present-day Burlington) in 1771. Earlier, New Jersey yeomen defied land laws that favored their proprietors, and New York settlers rebelled unsuccessfully to gain rights over land that, as one of them put it, they had worked "for nearly 30 years past and had manured and cultivated." Farmers in the Granville District of North Carolina, and the Rocky Mount District of South Carolina, obstructed surveyors and rioted against land speculators. Also in South Carolina, propertied vigilantes, frustrated at government indifference to backcountry brigandage, took matters into their own hands in 1767 and 1768. In central Pennsylvania, the "Paxton Boys," furious at the lack of military backing from the colonial assembly against Indian raids, massacred some government-protected Indians and undertook a menacing march on Philadelphia. (Government officials led by Benjamin

Franklin met with the protesters and quelled the unrest.) After the Revolution "Liberty Men" in central Maine, "Wild Yankees" in northeastern Pennsylvania, and "Green Mountain Boys" in western Vermont all challenged local landlords and the courts. The most notorious of these struggles culminated in the New England Regulation of 1786–87 associated with Daniel Shays.[9]

The yeoman disturbances occurred in tension with peaceable efforts to obtain redress from colonial and state governments. Before the Revolution, the worst-afflicted backcountry areas occasionally sent petitions to their legislators on matters other than local grievances, humbly pointing out (as the self-styled "poor industrious peasants" of Anson County, North Carolina did in 1769) that unlike the great men of the colony, "great numbers of poor people" had to "toil in the cultivation of bad Lands whereon they can hardly subsist." But during the Revolution, when yeoman households furnished the bulk of the manpower and the supplies to fight the patriot cause, ordinary farmers exerted political leverage on the new Revolutionary governments as they had never done under colonial rule. Petition campaigns continued, as did the sending of instructions to representatives, but with broad political themes and in plainer, more assertive language. The upsurge in the newly established Commonwealth of Virginia was typical of what happened in other states: after 1776, yeomen farmers swamped the Virginia Assembly with petitions that called for reforms ranging from the easing of debt payments to (in Baptist districts) disestablishing the official Anglican Church.[10]

Owing to larger numbers of ordinary farmers in the state legislatures, the petitioners could reasonably expect their demands would at least receive a hearing. The shift in representation was most pronounced in the northern states, yet even in the planter-led South, the proportion of ordinary farmers doubled from one-eighth of the total in the 1760s to one-fourth in the 1780s. These country democrats also participated in the constitutional state-building process, determined to ensure that they would not succumb to the permanent domination of eastern plantation and mercantile elites.[11]

Nowhere were they more vocal or persistent on constitutional issues than in Massachusetts. Months before hostilities between redcoats and patriots broke out in Lexington and Concord in April 1775, crowds of western Massachusetts farmers shut down the courts in Berkshire and Hampshire Counties in an angry response to the passage of the British Intolerable Acts in 1774. Later in 1775, the eastern Massachusetts patriot leadership, with the hurried advice of the Continental Congress, adopted a revolutionary state charter that was a revamped version of the old colonial charter, but did so without consent from the people. The westerners duly rebelled again, now against their new leaders, reshutting the courts and keeping them closed until 1778 in Hampshire County and until 1781 in Berkshire County.[12]

The Massachusetts rebels—dubbed the Berkshire Constitutionalists and led by the Reverend Thomas Allen, the eloquent, Harvard-educated pastor of Pitts-field's Congregational church—were especially incensed at the continuation of the appointive judicial system. With its arbitrary licensing practices and fee gouging, the system had ruled for many years, according to one Pittsfield peti-tion, "with a rod of Iron." The new patriot legislature tried to ease the situation by sharply reducing legal fees, but by the time the offer arrived, larger demo-cratic concerns had come into play. Above all (as a second Pittsfield petition declared in May 1776), the backcountrymen now upbraided the doctrine "that the Representatives of the People may form Just what fundamental Constitu-tion they please & impose it upon the people." Here was a significant shift, from demands for judicial reform to a call for drafting a wholly new constitu-tion to submit for approval to the voters. After two years of official stalling in Boston and renewed protests in the western counties, the call was finally heeded—first in 1778, when the town meetings rejected a constitution drafted by the legislature, and then in 1780, when they approved a constitution framed by a special state convention.[13]

The final constitution fell short of what the Berkshire Constitutionalists desired, and it did not end extralegal rural unrest against the courts and creditors. The Berkshire men did, however, help establish the proposition that any new American constitution required popular approval, an idea of democratic sover-eignty realized nowhere outside Massachusetts until the ratification of the new Federal Constitution in 1787–88. What is more significant, the country demo-crats articulated a coherent egalitarian politics, prickly about power imposed from afar, insistent on equal legislative representation for all parts of the state, and opposed to property requirements in politics. The only qualifications required for any officeholder (let alone a voter), one town meeting stated, ought to be personal merit and fidelity to liberty's cause: "Pecuniary Q[u]alifications can never give a good understanding or good Heart."[14]

At the center of these country democratic claims were those concerns about the land and control of the land, cited by Crèvecoeur. Before the Revolution, there had been periodic outbreaks of popular apprehension that a designing class of royal officials, lawyers, and monied speculators was out to build up its own power and bring the yeomanry, as one phrase had it, "into lordships." Similar fears arose on the eve of the Revolution, as they did whenever country democrats felt insecure in the face of increased political centralization, and the imminent possibility of biased legislation and oppressive fiscal policies. The fears persisted into the 1780s and well beyond. In 1786, a Massachusetts writer charged that "the wealthy men of this state"—adherents of the "aristocratical principle"— hoped to "drive out that hardy and independent spirit from among us, and forge the chains for our liberties so strong, that the greatest exertions and convulsions will not break them." One backcountry Pennsylvanian noted in 1788 that his neighbors remained frightened they might yet be turned into "dependents . . . who will be reduced to a sort of vassalage."[15]

Evangelical religion added a spiritual basis to these fearful egalitarian politics. Out of the postmillennialist stirrings of New England's rural Great Awakening—as well as the ministrations of evangelizing Separate Baptists, Methodists, so-called New Side Presbyterians, and untold numbers of more idiosyncratic preachers elsewhere—came a growing cultural divide between the backcountry and the seaboard, where more staid, rationalist Anglicans (later Episcopalians), Congregationalists, and Unitarians held sway. Converts to the evangelical gospel found themselves in a new, direct, and individual relation with God that sliced across hierarchies of wealth and standing but insisted on humankind's utter dependence on the Lord. By contrast, the gentry and urban mercantile elite were apt to regard the evangelical effusions of the countryside, with their strange gestures and ardent prayer, as ignorant, degraded, and dangerous to civic order. James Madison, while fighting to end the persecution of Baptists in Virginia in the mid-1770s, reported with alarm the stories he heard from his fellow gentry about the "monstrous effects of the enthusiasm prevalent among the Sectaries."[16]

The spiritual divisions between the elite and the yeomanry showed up in various ways. The most direct conflicts involved country evangelical efforts to end the formal establishment of religion. (In Massachusetts, for instance, the town of Ashby in rural Middlesex County denounced draft provisions in the 1780 Constitution requiring public financial support for the Congregational churches, citing the past "Rivers of blood which has run from the Veins of Marters" as a consequence of "the authority of Legeslature over religeous Society.") Religious vernacular, as well as religious leadership, also appeared in country democracy's strictly secular fights, involving evangelicals and nonevangelicals alike. Hermon Husband, the North Carolina Regulation commander, had been born in 1724 on a small farm in Maryland, where, under the spur of the Great Awakening, he had a religious conversion that led him first to the Presbyterians, then to the Quakers, and finally to a mystical, ascetic faith all his own. Husband drenched his secular political declarations in evangelical language both original and borrowed, appealing to "King Jesus" on behalf of oppressed North Carolinians. The Congregationalist Reverend Allen, leader of the Berkshire Constitutionalists, invoked Jesus and the Disciples in his political lectures, and called for a new constitution settled on a broad basis of civil and religious liberty. Religious men reappeared prominently among the distressed yeomanry, from the Baptist minister Valentine Rathbun of Pittsfield (Thomas Allen's lieutenant during the Berkshire agitation), to the Baptist New Yorker Melancton Smith, an upstater who had moved to Manhattan, who spoke in the 1780s as a self-styled "Plebeian" and tribune of New York's "respectable" yeomanry, and who had been named in honor of Philip Melancthon, coworker with Martin Luther and German Protestant peacemaker.[17]

THE CITY DEMOCRACY

If land formed the basic philosophy of the country democracy, then philosophy—a mastery of abstract ideas as well as arcane manual arts—formed, in effect, the "land" of the urban democrats, the basis for its civic claims and social status. The city democracy rank and file consisted chiefly of skilled artisans and mechanics, as well as petty merchants, shopkeepers, and other tradesmen—what Thomas Jefferson distinguished as "[t]he *yeomanry* of the city (not the fashionable people nor paper men)." Their intellectual and political leaders included a mixture of Enlightenment-smitten professionals (most conspicuously physicians, clergymen, teachers, and lawyers) and men from undistinguished backgrounds whose skills as political writers and organizers blossomed during the Revolutionary years and after. Beneath both the rank and file and the leadership, sometimes pushing the city democrats to take more forceful positions, were lesser tradesmen, the lower grades of sailors and mariners, and unskilled day laborers; beneath them were the free laboring poor and then the slaves.[18]

The urban population of late-eighteenth-century America was proportionally miniscule. Yet the major seaports were commercially dynamic and growing fast, at a rate far greater than the nation as a whole, and a few of them were emerging as economic powerhouses. Even before the outbreak of the Revolution, Boston, once North America's premier entry port, had slipped behind New York and Philadelphia (now the colonies' leading port) in terms of ship tonnage cleared. This trend deepened after Independence, as the latter two became the shipping centers for their prosperous and rapidly growing agricultural hinterlands, far more productive than New England's rocky, worked-over farming areas. To the south, Baltimore and Charleston also picked up considerable economic ground.[19]

Artisans and mechanics, although of secondary social standing in the mercantile cities, were essential to growth. They supplied the seaport merchants and their households with everything from ships to shoe buckles. They also created local manufacturing economies to supply nearby regional markets with necessities as well as luxury goods. Artisan firms—in most cases tiny, with perhaps one or two employees and a live-in apprentice—were roughly analogous to the yeomen's rural homesteads: headed by an authoritarian father, the master craftsman, who oversaw the labor of his wife, children (including any apprentices), and journeymen employees. The proportion of slaves and other unfree adult laborers, an important segment of the urban artisan workforce as late as the 1750s, dwindled sharply north of Baltimore after the Seven Years' War, as rising city populations opened up new markets in artisan wage labor. Without replicating the elaborate guild systems of Europe, the American artisans cultivated an extended familial sense of what they called "the Trade," of reciprocal rights and obligations among masters, journeymen, and apprentices in a particular craft that would open the way to economic independence to any individual who mastered the requisite manual and business skills.[20]

Artisan realities did not always match the ideal. At the top of the trades, master craftsmen often found themselves entangled in credit arrangements with their merchant customers that belied their supposed independence. At the bottom, a large number of lesser artisans, including shoemakers and clothing workers, eked out a scant living and, in hard times, fell into destitution. Just as there was stratification among the trades, there were early signs of divisions within trades between masters and journeymen employees, exacerbated by the growth of readily available pools of cheap wage labor. A handful of craft strikes and other job actions broke out in other seaports over the next quarter century, presaging greater labor conflicts to come.[21]

The main source of plebeian discord in the eighteenth-century cities, however, was not between or within trades, but between artisans of all ranks and the merchant elite. For several decades before the Revolution, propertied enfranchised artisans played significant and at times crucial roles in deciding urban elections. Stifling their deep prejudices about laboring men as "the rabble," competing factions of merchants reached out for their support, and thereby invented many of the tools and techniques that would later become essential to democracy's expansion: the naming of political "tickets"; organizing political caucuses, through taverns and volunteer fire companies; substituting public nomination meetings for private nominations; using a growing seaport newspaper press for (increasingly vitriolic) political appeals; political pamphleteering and the rise of a new subclass of pamphleteers. All these innovations contributed to a curious transformation of urban politics well before the Revolution, popularizing existing techniques of electioneering, but still under the firm control of the mercantile elite.[22]

A more fundamental transformation began during the Stamp Act crisis, and developed with a growing intensity from 1774 to 1776, when the artisans began nominating and electing their own men to office. Invigorated by their involvement in extralegal committees and demonstrations, and dismayed by the hesitation of some merchants and the opposition of others, anti-British artisans and tradesmen developed a sense of themselves as a distinct political interest. "If we have not the Liberty of nominating such Persons whom we approve," a Philadelphian who called himself "A Brother Chip" advised his "Brethren the Trades-men, Mechanics. &c." in 1770, "our Freedom of voting is at an End." In other seaports, large and small, artisans and their allies made their presence felt either in the patriot movement or in electoral politics or both, despite what one Philadelphia merchant called the "Many Threats, Reflections, Sarcasms, and Burlesques" aimed against them.[23]

The artisans' political fortunes varied from place to place. Ironically, in Boston, where laboring people defied British authority in the streets as nowhere else in America, mechanics made the least impact as a distinct interest, in part because the British military occupation from 1768 to 1776 muted social divisions among the patriots even after the redcoats departed. In New York City, by con-trast, artisans won a substantial number of local offices and controlled the extralegal committees, although they were unable, until the very eve of the Rev-olution, to wrest political control from the merchants and lawyers. The New York Mechanics' Committee, which in 1774 superseded the local Sons of Liberty as the head of the local resistance movement, ceased to be the predominant voice in city affairs only when the British occupied Manhattan in 1776. (The occupa-tion may have been a major reason why New Yorkers failed to produce a state constitution anywhere near as democratic as Pennsylvania's.) Similar artisan groups spearheaded radical activity in Baltimore and Charleston (before the British occupied the latter in 1780).[24]

The city democracy truly flourished in Philadelphia, where radical artisans joined forces with the lowest classes of mechanics and unskilled laborers. The year 1770 was the turning point. Craftsmen, infuriated by the attempts of some local merchants to evade the patriots' nonimportation agreements against British goods, formed the first mechanics' committees. In that year's assembly elections, a radical local anti-British slate (including a tailor, one Joseph Parker) triumphed at the polls. Two years later, the Mechanics' Committee demanded publication of assembly debates and the opening of public galleries in the legislatures, as well as a variety of economic reforms, including abolition of the provincial excise taxes on liquor. Then, between 1773 and 1776, radical artisans steadily replaced moderates on the city's Committee of Inspection and Observation, which over-saw local resistance efforts. By the time Congress signed the Declaration of Inde-pendence in the Pennsylvania State House (since renamed Independence Hall), artisans occupied almost half the committee's seats.[25]

Confronted by a Quaker-controlled state assembly that refused to vote for independence from Britain, the Inspection and Observation Committee held its own open-air town meeting in May 1776, with more than four thousand persons in attendance. The committee called for the convening of a patriot Provincial Conference to draft a new state constitution—"the Coup de Grace to the King's authority in this province," wrote one young militia captain. And at this point, the mechanics' constituency became closely allied with another important political stratum: radical democratic professionals and writers, many of modest wealth and little previous political influence. This group included Timothy Matlack, a debt-ridden hardware retailer, schismatic Quaker, champion cockfighter, militia battalion commander, and excellent penman (who probably handwrote the officially engrossed version of the Declaration of Independence signed by Congress); the deist Thomas Young, a self-educated physician to the poor and (said John Adams) "eternal fisher in troubled waters"; Benjamin Rush, the College of New Jersey (now Princeton) graduate and evangelical Presbyterian, who likewise served Philadelphia's poor (and, as a delegate to the Second Continental Congress, signed the Declaration of Independence); and James Cannon, a Scots-trained professor of mathematics at the College of Philadelphia. Above all, they included the most gifted democratic writer in the English-speaking world, Thomas Paine.[26]

Although he had emigrated from England only two years earlier, Paine (a former corset maker, sailor, shopkeeper, and excise official) had already won renown as the most uncompromising and effective advocate for American independence, on the basis of his immensely popular pamphlet, *Common Sense*, published in January 1776. With his limpid logic and acidulous sarcasm (calling William the Conqueror "[a] French bastard landing with an armed banditti"), Paine took the polemical style of earlier political pamphleteers, stripped it of its pretense, and rendered it accessible to those readers and unlettered listeners who gathered in the plebeian taverns and debating clubs that he himself habituated. In the span of a single sly statement—"Male and female are the distinctions of nature, good and bad the distinctions of heaven, but how a race of men came into the world so exalted above the rest, and distinguished like some new species, is worth inquiring into"—Paine could kindle ordinary Americans' accumulated sense of personal insult at monarchical society into revulsion and revolution.[27] His democratic ideas were no less disturbing to many leading patriots than they were to Loyalists. Believing in the basic harmony of reasonable individuals—and thus society if left to its own devices—Paine considered aristocratic government, established by a parasitic caste of the pedigreed and privileged, as the chief author of human misery.

> Society is produced by our wants, and government by our wickedness; the former promotes our happiness *positively* by uniting our affections, the latter *negatively* by restraining our vices. The one encourages intercourse, the other creates distinctions. . . . Society is in every state a blessing, but government, even in its best state, is but a necessary evil.

For Paine, government was rife with opportunities for the privileged few to oppress the many. Accordingly, *Common Sense* offered some egalitarian fundamentals for benign republican rule: unicameral state legislatures elected by a broad franchise; a national legislature; frequent elections; and a written constitution securing individual rights, including rights to property and religious freedom. In Massachusetts, a scandalized John Adams replied to what he would later call Paine's "yellow fever" by writing a brief defense of mixed government, *Thoughts on Government*. A Philadelphia patriot worried that Paine's proposals would stir "the multitude in a perpetual ferment like the ocean in a storm." But in mid-1776, Paine and his radical friends held the initiative in Pennsylvania.[28]

The radicals' position in that critical year was bolstered, and further radicalized, by the presence of the thirty-one companies of the Philadelphia militia, headed by their Committee of Privates. Led by mechanics and tradesmen of modest means, the committee provided its rank and file, known as "Associators," with something of a political education, not unlike what the English agitators in Oliver Cromwell's New Model Army had attempted in the 1640s and 1650s. (The militiamen did not hesitate to speak up, through the committee, on matters ranging from unrestricted manhood suffrage to "equal consultation" about the design of uniforms.) Several radical leaders had close ties to the militia: James Cannon was secretary of the Committee of Privates, while Thomas Young and Timothy Matlack were militia officers. This gave the Associators a direct connection to the constitution-making process. And in a memorial to the Continental Congress, issued nine days before the open-air meeting on the obdurate assembly, the committee members vented their antagonism to the British and the patriot elite as well, declaring their "sense of being oppressed by the very men whose liberties and estates they are called out to defend."[29]

With assembly conservatives in disgrace, the moderate assembly majority leaderless, and the Continental Congress on record calling for new state governments where none "sufficient to the exigencies of their affairs" existed, the Philadelphia radicals stepped into the breach. (Paine served as their adviser.) Closely controlling the nominations and elections to both the proposed Provincial Conference and its constitutional convention, they packed the groups with sympathetic delegates, including a disproportional number of country democrats from the discontented western parts of Pennsylvania. The drafters met, with Benjamin Franklin as their president, and the final product was that remarkable new state constitution. Some of the provisions, such as the unicameral legislature, extended institutions already in place; others, including the broadened suffrage and the more equal representation plan, were brand new. An even more radical provision, outlawing "an enormous proportion of property invested in a few individuals," narrowly failed to win approval. The greatest controversy occurred in the Provincial Conference, where the rural democrats, aided by the more pious of their Philadelphia counterparts, won a requirement that all delegates to the constitutional convention affirm the divinity of Jesus Christ and the divine inspiration of the Bible—a measure hotly contested by delegates James Cannon and Thomas Young, who called it "bigoted."[30]

Time would prove unkind to the Pennsylvania Constitution of 1776, and to the coalition that created it. It attracted criticism as soon as it was approved, even from radicals like Benjamin Rush. (Among the constitution's numerous defects, Rush argued, was the unicameral legislature, which he thought would be more vulnerable to corruption from above than a two-tiered body, where democrats could concentrate their power in the lower house.) Alarmed moderate and conservative notables from around the state, seeing democracy boiling over, quickly regrouped as the Republican faction, and they capitalized on some overbearing miscalculations by the radicals. Unlike the Berkshire democrats of Massachusetts, the Pennsylvania radicals failed to seek approval of the new constitution through a popular referendum, fearing that, though they had united the country and the city, they were more advanced in their democratic views than the people at large. The decision ensured their constitution went into effect, but at the cost of alienating a considerable portion of the moderate citizenry. The new legislature also enacted a series of test laws between 1777 and 1779 that demanded oaths of allegiance to the revolutionary government, and were deeply offensive to Quakers. By 1789, the anticonstitution forces built a base of public support that included some of the better-off mechanic elements. Finally, in September 1790, the Republicans won ratification of a new state constitution that eradicated most of the democratic provisions of its predecessor (although not the liberal suffrage), installed a bicameral legislature, and created a governorship with sweeping appointive powers.[31]

The story was nearly the reverse in New York. Subject to British occupation after 1776, New York's artisan democrats never seized power as the Philadelphians did, but they forcefully resumed their political activities as soon as the British evacuated in 1783. Late in that year, they elected a radical Whig ticket to the state assembly by a 4 to 1 margin. Thereafter, they organized the Committee of Mechanics, which pressed for the exclusion of ex-Tories from politics, formed an umbrella group for master craftsmen called the General Society of Mechanics and Tradesmen, nominated and elected several craftsmen to the state assembly, and agitated for democratic reforms, including popular election of the mayor. In 1786, numerous mechanics joined with professionals and merchants as members of the fraternal Society of Saint Tammany or Columbian Order, led by their "Grand Sachem," an upholsterer named William Mooney. The businessman and philanthropist John Pintard, a Tammany officer, described the society as "a political institution . . . whose democratic principles will serve in some measure to correct the aristocracy of our city."[32]

In their successes as well as failures, the city democrats' experiences of the Revolution pointed out some of their connections and differences with country democrats. Both groups vaunted themselves as productive, independent citizens—"honest Laborious husbandmen and machanicks," in the words of a New Hampshire petition in 1783. Both groups were wary of political operations dominated by, in their eyes, well-connected but nonproducing gentry and merchants, on the principle (as one Connecticut shoemaker put it) that "*Might* generally overcomes *Right*." Both groups saw government's chief proper function as the promotion of equal access to opportunity and personal independence.[33]

But there were differences that played out at many levels. Country democrats, especially in places where they were underrepresented in state legislatures, were more isolated than their urban counterparts from the operations of government and from the dynamics of economic power—so much so that even after the Revolution, the basic legitimacy of the state and (after 1789) federal governments would be less assured in some troubled rural areas than it was in the cities. Like the North Carolina Regulators in the 1760s or the participants in the New England Regulation twenty years later, country men, in their insularity and frustration, were quicker to turn violent when they found more regular channels blocked or unresponsive. Until the late 1790s, they would show far less reluctance than city democrats to oppose and violate federal laws, sometimes aggressively. Moreover, city democrats, still for the most part seaport dwellers, were men of commerce—"American Commerce; unfettered by the influence of tyrants," ran one later celebratory toast—interested in getting their fair share of oceanic and coastal trade and gaining access to their own banking facilities, as well as encouraging internal commercial routes. Government aid to such projects did not disturb them, so long as the projects were for the general welfare and did not favor monied insiders. Many country democrats, by contrast, were distant from extensive commercial contacts and tended to distrust public projects as inherently biased. There were, to be sure, some country democrats who wanted to develop closer links to eastern markets and (especially in boom times) acquire as much bank credit as they could. But any downturn in the business cycle could easily stoke their hostility against the instruments of economic improvement and the well-connected men who ran them.[34]

The two democracies also differed in cultural tone. Religion, including evangelical religion, played an important role in the lives of many city democrats; indeed, by the end of the eighteenth century, the seaport cities were the largest centers of Methodist and Baptist worship in the country. Paine's *Common Sense*, although the product of a quintessentially skeptical urban intelligence, was thick with biblical allusions and millennial language, instantly recognizable to its city and country readers alike. Some of the leading Philadelphia city democrats, including Benjamin Rush and Christopher Marshall, were devout believers. Yet the cities also displayed great spiritual variety, ranging from the more rationalist forms of Protestant worship such as Universalism to non-Christian freethinking deist sects, and also including Jews, Roman Catholics, and nonbelievers, the last group the largest of all. Ethnically and linguistically as well, the cities were more diverse than the rural settlements, which forced city democrats to pay close attention to integrating different constituencies, and also attracted fresh waves of ambitious and talented political émigrés from overseas, especially from England and Ireland. Although rural settlements, especially in the North, were coming increasingly within the orbit of Enlightenment culture and high political debate (through the diffusion of newspapers, almanacs, magazines, and, via early town lending libraries, books), the country democracy had nothing to compare with the philosophical societies, colleges, and debating clubs, high and low, of its urban counterpart. If the unpolished country democrats harbored prejudices against what one of them called, suspiciously, "men of learning," the city democracy's faith in reason bred a certain naive and, in retrospect, self-defeating intellectual arrogance, evident in the Philadelphia radicals' political overreaching. That overreaching, and the arguments over Christian religious tests in the Pennsylvania Provincial Congress in 1776, also showed that religion could divide democratic partisans.[35]

The alliance of country and city that forged the Pennsylvania Constitution of 1776 proved these tensions could at least temporarily be contained. But the eventual breakdown of that alliance, and the more common distancing between country movements and city ones in other states, showed how difficult that containment could be. Those difficulties and divisions would recur in the years immediately after independence, when political turmoil led to the creation of a new national government.

THE REVOLUTION AND "PROPER *DEMOCRACY*"

How successful, overall, was the democratic impulse that arose during the Revolution? Narrowly defined, the results, as inscribed in the state constitutions, can appear modest. As of 1790, fewer than half of the original thirteen states provided an approximation to white manhood suffrage by replacing freehold qualifications with minimal taxpaying requirements. (Massachusetts actually stiffened property requirements in its 1780 constitution.) None, except Pennsylvania, broke completely with the ancient ideal of mixed and balanced government whereby distinct branches of the state were supposed to correspond to ranks in society. To the extent they did shift, at least in theory, it was often toward sharpening the distinction between persons and property, linking the upper houses of the new legislatures to the representation of propertied interests—on the presumption, stated most starkly in Massachusetts, that "men possessed of property are entitled to a greater share in political authority than those who are destitute of it." Revolutionary state-builders hedged in the democratic element by establishing bicameral legislatures (except in Pennsylvania and Georgia); by approving property requirements, sometimes quite severe, for officeholding; by retaining powerful appointive state and local offices not elected by the people; and by continuing malapportionment of the legislatures to favor the wealthier and more settled districts.[37]

The very fact, though, that the patriots won American independence deprived an entrenched monarchical interest of wealth and power. Although not confined to royal officials or rich and well-born colonists, the Loyalists, who would now be replaced by rebels, included some of the country's most powerful families. The reversal was particularly wrenching in New York, where the Revolution devastated the colonial ruling class of Loyalist mercantile and seigneurial families centered in Manhattan and the Hudson Valley, and where power shifted to relative newcomers, led by Governor George Clinton, who drew their power from upstate middling farmers. Similar sharp transitions occurred in New Jersey and North Carolina, but every new state felt the shift to a greater or lesser degree. Exclusion from the franchise, by provincial congresses and state legislatures, of identified resident Tories and all who refused to swear oaths of allegiance to American independence further tied political loyalties to political rights.[38]

Democratic interests and ideas also made considerable headway within the patriot movement, quite apart from the singular developments in Pennsylvania. In Maryland, armed uprisings by militiamen precipitated a significant reduction in property requirements for voting and won an expansive Declaration of Rights as part of the new state's constitution (one of seven such declarations adopted around the country). New York, New Jersey, New Hampshire, North Carolina, and South Carolina also significantly liberalized their suffrage laws. (Massachusetts and Maryland, as well as New York, nearly adopted a minimal taxpaying requirement.) Religious tests that excluded all but Protestants from the franchise, common throughout the colonies, were dropped everywhere except in South Carolina. In North Carolina, Georgia, and (in some counties) New Jersey, as well as Pennsylvania, voting by written ballots became the norm, and the New York convention proposed trying the system since some had claimed it "would tend more to preserve the liberty and equal freedom of the people."[39]

Other important changes accompanied suffrage reforms. Outside the Chesapeake region, lawmakers undertook serious efforts to reduce malapportionment in their legislatures. North Carolina's constitution provided equal representation for every county in both houses of the legislature; New York, New Jersey, and South Carolina stipulated periodic changes in representation to help ensure continued equity and proportionality. Constituents became bolder in instructing and petitioning their representatives, a right explicitly endorsed by four of the seven state declarations of rights. Although many important state offices stayed appointive, the new constitutions took the power of appointment out of the hands of the governors and gave it to the legislatures, or to some combination of the executive and legislative branches—a mark of the Revolution's bedrock antimonarchialism.

Officeholding democratized markedly. "[S]ince the war," one disgusted Massachusetts conservative remarked in 1786, "blustering ignorant men, who started into notice during the troubles and confusion of that critical period, have been attempting to push themselves into office." In the lower legislative houses, a much-expanded number of representatives in the mid-1780s included far greater proportions of ordinary farmers, artisans, and other men of middling wealth and station than had sat in the colonial assemblies—even in the states that retained property-holding requirements for lawmakers. In the upper houses in most states, places were found for ambitious men of unassuming background and modest attainments, such as the upwardly mobile Scots immigrant farmer Alexander Webster of New York's rural Washington County, or John Birdsong of Chatham, North Carolina—a man so obscure that his name does not survive on any tax list or census recording. Everywhere, electioneering and undisguised competition for legislative office intensified. Thanks to state constitutional provisions for annual legislative elections, secured in every state except South Carolina, the glacier-like pace of office turnover prevalent in the provincial assemblies became a break-neck scramble, with half or more of the representatives in any given legislature changing in any given year.[40]

The Revolution's democratic impact was not confined to voting qualifications, representation arrangements, and election results. Nothing like the articulate democratic outburst that gripped America in 1776 had occurred anywhere in the world since the days of the Levellers and Diggers. Speaking with special warmth for "the poorer sort, who are perhaps nine tenths of the useful part of mankind," democratic partisans demanded any and every sort of political innovation in order to secure what one called "Proper *Democracy* . . . where the people have all the power in themselves." There were calls to abolish the posts of governor and lieutenant governor, along with the legislative upper houses (where, a Pennsylvanian declared, "a small number of grandees . . . thirst for power at the expense of the people"), and there were calls for rotation in office, simplified legal codes, and popular ratification of specific laws, as well as for annual elections and a widened suffrage. The din was so loud, conventional republicans observed, that the patriot leadership found itself fighting on two fronts, against "*popular licentiousness, anarchy, and confusion*" as well as against the British monarchy.[41]

The explosion forever changed the context of American politics and culture.

Revolutionary committees of correspondence, Sons of Liberty, mechanics' electoral tickets, county conventions, as well as the patriot militia and Continental
Army—all had had the effect of announcing the end of the old deference and
sporadic mob violence of the "people out-of-doors" and the beginning of a new
abiding presence of ordinary Americans in public and political life. No matter
how troublesome it might be, that presence had to be recognized and taken into
account, as the shrewder patriot leaders understood. Failing to do so (Jefferson's
friend Edward Pendleton acknowledged) was "disagreeable to the temper of the
times." With politics thrust to the forefront of Americans' minds, the Revolution's democratic strivings fundamentally altered how they perceived themselves
and each other.[42]

Consider the formal portraiture of the age. Shortly before the Revolution, John
Singleton Copley, the most accomplished painter in New England, and a Loyalist, could depart from his upper-class patrons and execute a plain but respectful
portrait of a highly successful Boston silversmith and devoted patriot. Paul Revere
looks out with a pensive expression, his shirt neck open, the tools of his trade by
his side—a portrait of the artisan as a thoughtful man of substance. A bit later, in
the work of a younger, less expert artist, the patriot Charles Willson Peale (a volunteer in George Washington's army, veteran of Valley Forge, and officer in the
radical Philadelphia militia), the democratic sensibility deepened greatly. In his
famous depiction of the Battle of Princeton, Peale presented a victorious but less-
than-godlike, bottom-heavy General Washington, one waistcoat button missing,
standing against a backdrop that in one version pointedly included a marching
line of ordinary American soldiers and their redcoat prisoners.[43]

After independence, Peale also painted one of the chief Philadelphia radicals, Timothy Matlack, who went on to become Pennsylvania's secretary of state
and keeper of its great seal. The picture shows Matlack in his full political glory,
a self-made new man of power dressed in flashy buff-blue trousers with matching waistcoat, surrounded by statute books and revolutionary charters. More
than a decade later, the factional struggles in Pennsylvania had cost Matlack his
secretaryship, but he had won a patronage job as the state's master of the rolls,
and Peale's son Rembrandt painted him again, a reflective public servant and
patriot who lived by his pen. Ordinary people not only were present; they had
begun, as the conservative Gouverneur Morris said about the New York mob,
"to think and reason"—and to help run political affairs. What painters
expressed on canvas, gentry political leaders understood as a public sensibility
that could not be ignored.[44]

Even amid the acute internal crises that followed independence, the new revolutionary governments managed to heed and incorporate popular discontent,
although in rough and incomplete ways. The sharpest conflicts surrounded the
so-called New England Regulation, a string of rural uprisings best known for the

Massachusetts rebellion led by an ex-army captain from Berkshire County, Daniel Shays, in 1786. Following the adoption of the new state constitution, the Massachusetts legislature, in order to repay its Revolutionary War debt, adopted stringent financial policies, which prompted distressed country towns to hold popular conventions demanding debtor relief. When these demands fell on deaf ears, Shays and his compatriots in other parts of the state took up arms and disrupted local courts, only to be crushed by a privately funded militia organized by Governor James Bowdoin.[45]

The Shays affair dramatized not only the rawness and limitations of American democracy in the aftermath of independence, but also its possibilities. Under sharp duress, and unable to organize a timely, effective, and legitimate political opposition, the Shaysites loaded their muskets, scaring gentlemen of property and standing all across the new republic. Yet the affair did not end with the dispersal and indictments of Shays's bedraggled recruits. Sympathetic with the rebels' plight (if not their tactics), and horrified by the ham-handed repression, Massachusetts voters turned out in extraordinary numbers in the statewide elections the following spring, removed Bowdoin and his most adamant allies from office, and elected a government that reached an accommodation with the rebels (including a pardon of Captain Shays). In all, one democratic Massachusetts farmer recalled years later, "everything appeared like the clear and pleasant sunshine after a most tremendous storm . . . a striking demonstration of the advantages of a free elective government."[46]

DEMOCRACY AND THE FEDERAL CONSTITUTION

Not every American greeted the outcome in Massachusetts, or the turbulent politics elsewhere during the 1780s, with such sanguinity—and these more pessimistic reactions helped lead directly to the Philadelphia Constitutional Convention in 1787. In addition to the Shays scare, political developments at the state level shocked patriot leaders who had hoped the Revolution would bring calm and enlightened government. With the democratization of the state legislatures, licentiousness seemed to be running rampant. Narrow-minded men, suspicious of government power and fiercely protective of their local interests— lacking what James Madison called "liberality or light"—started pressing for punitive legislation against former Loyalists, as well as for stay laws and other forms of debtor relief that would soon destroy the new governments' finances. Worse, the national government, under the loosely knit Articles of Confederation, was so feeble that it had become nearly impossible to conduct a foreign policy, secure the nation's defense, and complete commercial treaties, let alone settle the leftover debts from the Revolution.[47]

When, in 1787, with the Shays Rebellion fresh in their minds, fifty-five delegates assembled in Philadelphia to discard the Articles summarily in favor of a
new federal plan, fears of a tyrannical *demos* were pervasive. Above all else, the
delegates wished to create a new, more perfect union that would promote an
enlightened class of rulers who would think continentally instead of in straitened, self-interested terms. Delegates spoke openly of the need to restrain what
one Virginian called "the turbulence and follies of democracy," and what a New
York delegate had called "popular phrenzy." Yet the majority of the convention,
as of the country, also believed that sovereignty belonged, ultimately, to the citizenry. Once the delegates convened in secret session, the temper of the times
seeped into the room.[48]

The delegates' antidemocratic assumptions were voiced most cogently three
weeks into their deliberations, when the brilliant young nationalist from New
York, Alexander Hamilton, broke his silence and proposed some guiding principles. "All communities," he said, "divide themselves into the few and the many.
The first are the rich and well-born, the other the mass of the people." Because
the latter, Hamilton claimed, were "turbulent and changing" and "seldom judge
or determine right," it was vital to give the former—the rich—"a distinct permanent share in the government." Hamilton then proposed creating a federal political hierarchy that would come as close as possible to the British state, with an
executive elected for life and an upper legislative chamber elected to serve on
good behavior.[49]

A few of the delegates, including Gouverneur Morris, thought Hamilton's
speech the most profound and best argued of the entire convention. Yet after
listening respectfully to his advice, the delegates basically ignored it. Instead,
the Framers' final document reflected James Madison's idea that the creation of
an extended republic with large electoral districts would favor the selection
of "men who possess the most attractive merit," while inhibiting the formation of
an "unjust and interested majority" out to subvert the rights of others, especially property rights. Instead of aligning the government directly with the rich
and wellborn, the convention favored strong institutional filters on the powers
of the ordinary citizenry. The executive would not be elected directly by the
voters but in the Electoral College, by electors chosen by the states. Neither
would the Senate, the powerful upper house of the national Congress, be
elected directly, unless the states so dictated, which none of them would. A
national judiciary, headed by the Supreme Court, would be appointed by the
indirectly chosen executive with the advice and consent of the indirectly
selected Senate. The only national office for which the Constitution stipulated
popular elections was for members of the House of Representatives, to be chosen by the same electorate that voted for "the most numerous branch" in each
of the state legislatures.[50]

Power would indeed shift to the advantage of the enlightened few over the impassioned many. But still, there were concessions: it would do so without establishing a formally class-based government, abrogating popular sovereignty, or forsaking the Revolutionary contributions of ordinary Americans. "A dependence on the people is, no doubt, the primary control on the government," Madison would write in defending the Constitution in *Federalist 51*. The design for the Senate, a hotly contested issue, was an excellent case in point. As the writer who called himself "A Democratic Federalist" conceded, the proposal for the Senate had an appearance of aristocracy that was alarming. But in fact, the new body was formally just as representative and democratic as the House "without one distinction in favor of the birth, rank, wealth or power of the senators or their fathers." Depending on what the states decided, there were no fixed property qualifications for electing a senator, and none at all for serving as one. Senators were not supposed to represent a social class, estate, or interest; rather, they represented their respective states, gave small states a check on the larger states' advantages in the House, and provided an important mediating force between encroachments by the Executive and "the precipitation and inadvertence of the people"—all without impeding on "the real principles of liberty." So it went throughout the new federal plan. If designed to restrain and guide democracy, the Constitution hardly repudiated it, no matter how much some of the Framers might have wanted to do so. Instead, the delegates constructed a stable and energetic but properly classless national government.[51]

Occasionally, one delegate or another sounded a more Hamiltonian note. A particularly tense exchange occurred in response to the proposed linkage of the suffrage eligibility for the House of Representatives to those for elections to the state assemblies. Gouverneur Morris, proclaiming himself unafraid of being labeled an aristocrat, charged that this franchise would be much too broad, and called instead for a freehold property qualification to vote for all federal officers. Give the votes to people with little or no property, Morris said, restating the traditional conservative wisdom, "and they will sell them to the rich who will be able to buy them." James Madison basically agreed, noting that, although Morris's plan might be imprudent, "the freeholders of the country would be the safest depositories of republican liberty."[52]

The most eloquent rebuttal came from Benjamin Franklin—now eighty-one and so weakened in body, though not in mind, that he sometimes had to be carried to the convention's meetings in a sedan chair. "It is of great consequence that we should not depress the virtue and public spirit of our common people," Franklin began, noting how much of both qualities the people had displayed during the Revolutionary War. That spirit, he contended, was a direct result of "the different manner in which the common people were treated in America and Great Britain." To insist on a freehold suffrage requirement would risk opening the door to further restrictions in the future. At all events, Franklin insisted, the elected had no right to narrow the privileges of the electors. Morris's proposal was overwhelmingly defeated. To advance further the popular legitimacy of their work, the delegates then decided to submit the Constitution for approval not to the state legislatures (whose interests might conflict with those of the proposed national government) but to specially elected state ratifying conventions.[53]

A more divisive conflict at the Philadelphia convention, carefully submerged in the final document, concerned slavery. At the Revolution's commencement, slavery existed in all thirteen of the colonies, but a combination of moral revulsion and economic marginality had led to its decline in the North. By 1787, Massachusetts, Pennsylvania, Connecticut, and Rhode Island had undertaken formal emancipation, and the institution was crumbling in New Hampshire. Delegates to the Philadelphia convention included some of the most stalwart antislavery men in the country (among them Franklin, a slaveholder himself until 1781), who had treated southern demands on slavery-related issues with an ironic contempt. Yet delegates from the southern states, above all South Carolina and Georgia, made it clear that they would not approve of the more perfect union unless it gave some positive protections to slavery.[54]

The result was a series of compromises that, during coming decades, would loom large. The final draft avoided mentioning slavery explicitly. (It would, James Madison said, be "wrong to admit in the Constitution the idea that there could be property in men.") But the delegates effectively barred the federal government from taking any action against slavery in the states, counted slaves as three-fifths of full citizens for the purposes of representation in the House of Representatives and the Electoral College (as well as for direct taxation), and included a provision guaranteeing slaveholders return of their runaway slaves. In a bitterly debated measure, they also barred congressional interference with the transatlantic slave trade for twenty years. Some in the lower South thought the concessions too wispy, but voices of compromise prevailed. "In short," Charles Cotesworth Pinckney told the South Carolina convention called to debate the Constitution's ratification, "considering all circumstances, we have made the best terms for the security of this species of property it was in our power to make. We would have made them better if we could; but, on the whole, I do not think them bad."[55]

There was little room to accommodate Americans who, in the various state ratification conventions, denounced what they regarded as the Constitution's deeply antidemocratic features. Some of the milder critics, including Thomas Jefferson (who was away in Paris as the American minister to France), fixated on the original document's lack of a declaration or bill of rights—a complaint overcome when, at the most sharply divided ratification conventions, Madison and

others gave informal assurances that the Constitution would be amended to provide such protections. (Although dubious about the worth of such "parchment
barriers" to tyranny, Madison single-handedly codified and then pushed hard for
rapid approval of the first ten amendments, the Bill of Rights, which the states
would finally ratify at the end of 1791.) Other, sterner critics ripped into what they
considered the Constitution's aristocratic, centralizing bias. "[I]t appears that the
government will fall into the hands of the few and the great," declared Melancton
Smith in New York. "This will be a government of oppression." More colorfully,
the Massachusetts war veteran and farmer Amos Singletary charged that under
the new Constitution, "they will swallow up all us little folks, like the great
Leviathan . . . just as the whale swallowed up *Jonah*."[56]

Slavery was also an issue at the state conventions. While southerners railed
against the Constitution's provision permitting Congress to halt the international
slave trade after 1808, some northerners objected to the clause counting three-
fifths of the slave population as a basis for federal representation—a measure
(Melancton Smith again) that would "give certain privileges to those people who
were so wicked as to keep slaves." These criticisms failed to halt the ratification of
the new federal plan by state conventions that, by design of the state legislatures,
were elected with a purposely broad set of franchise qualifications—the broadest
in the history of the infant republic. Objections to the rule of a supposedly
enlightened, disinterested elite would continue, though, to inform democratic
undertakings for decades to come.[57]

The most immediate consequences of the debates over the Constitution for
democratic politics were the divisions they caused between country and
city democrats. Pro-Constitutionalists and Anti-Federalists alike recognized that
opposition to the new federal plan would be greatest in rural areas distant from
seaboard towns and cities. "I dread the cold and sour temper of the back counties," the conservative Framer Gouverneur Morris told George Washington.
Rural anti-Federalism was, however, a complicated phenomenon. Prominent
gentry critics such as the Virginia slaveholders George Mason and Richard
Henry Lee objected mainly to what they considered the Constitution's over-
centralized structure and to the lack of a written bill of rights. Drawn from the
same ranks of cultivated, cosmopolitan notables as the delegates to the Philadelphia convention—Mason had been a delegate, one of three who stayed to the
end but refused to sign the final document—these gentry Anti-Federalists
asserted that the nation's leaders should be drawn from a gentlemanly elite, and
they shared the disquiet about democracy that drove some of the Framers. But in
line with thinking dating back to British Whig oppositionist writings of the
1720s, they also worried that no group of men could be trusted with too much

power. In Mason's words, the new federal design would "commence in a moderate Aristocracy" and probably wind up as either a monarchy or an "oppressive Aristocracy."[58]

A much harsher anti-aristocratic animus emanated from the yeomanry. Unconvinced that any group of uniquely virtuous natural leaders existed, these men beheld the Federalists' claims to disinterested patriotism as camouflage for their pursuit of wealth and domination. The "lawyers, and men of learning, and moneyed men, that talk so finely, and gloss over matters so smoothly," the farmer Singletary charged, would "get into Congress themselves" and place "all the power and all the money into their own hands." Writing under the pseudonym "Aristocrotis," the backcountry Pennsylvanian William Petrekin mocked the wellborn and "the full blooded gentry" who believed they monopolized the "necessary qualifications of authority; such as the dictatorial air, the magisterial voice, the imperious tone, the haughty countenance" that were necessary to run the government "upon true despotic principles."[59]

These country democrats were not simply challenging natural aristocracy's claims to disinterestedness; they were asserting their own interests. By virtue of their numbers and their control of productive land, they argued, they themselves ought to dominate government. Rejecting completely the theory of virtual representation, they insisted that representatives ought to be direct agents of their constituents, and resemble them closely. And there was a moral dimension to the backcountry argument, which cast the yeomanry, neither rich men nor poor men, as the best rulers. Melancton Smith told the New York ratifying convention that "those in middling circumstances . . . are inclined by habit, and the company with whom they associate, to set bounds to their passions and appetites . . . hence the substantial yeomanry of the country are more temperate, of better morals, and less ambition, than the great," who resembled "a hereditary aristocracy." Smith concluded that "a representative body, composed principally of the respectable yeomanry is the best possible security to liberty." Backcountry evangelical preachers and laymen, hundreds of whom served as delegates to the state ratifying conventions, also objected to the Constitution's centralizing thrust, much as they did efforts to centralize ecclesiastical authority, as a threat to "the glorious liberty of the children of God." Some, especially Methodists, also complained about the Constitution's accommodations to slavery.[60]

By contrast, the artisans and mechanics in all the seaboard cities enthusiastically supported the new Constitution. With their livelihoods tied to foreign trade, local artisan suppliers as well as mechanics faced competition at the war's end from British imports. They saw the new federal plan, with its promise of a coherent national commercial policy, including a tariff, as a blow for American economic nationalism and a direct benefit to themselves. At the height of the ratification debates, masters and journeymen in all of the major ports mounted their largest public demonstrations since the end of the Revolution, marching craft by craft and holding aloft emblems of their trades and patriotic pro-federal banners. There were, to be sure, some urban naysayers, such as Philadelphia's "Montezuma," who, much like the backcountry democrats, denounced the Constitution's friends as "the Aristocratic Party of the United States," out to create a new "*monarchical, aristocratical democracy.*" But dissenters were in the minority among the city democrats in 1787–88. The alliance between the city democracy and the mercantile elite played a crucial part in securing adoption of the new federal Constitution.[61]

The differences between the country and city democrats would persist long after the Constitution debates, causing difficulties for Americans with egalitarian beliefs and loyalties at every level of political society. Yet the differences sometimes diminished. Rural estrangement from the new federal plan, and the state political elites that backed it, remained strong, and occasionally turned violent, after 1788. Shortly after Pennsylvania's state convention ratified the Constitution, anti-Federalist yeomen rioted in Carlisle, in scenes that reminded some fearful Federalists of the Shaysite uprisings. In rural districts throughout the state, resistance to farm foreclosures and tax collection dating back over years turned increasingly desperate and ferocious. In western Virginia and North Carolina, secession movements arose, uneasily uniting planters, backwoodsmen, and land speculators, to win independence from, respectively, their states' Tidewater and central-valley political elites. (Their efforts would achieve admission to the Union for Kentucky in 1792 and for Tennessee four years later.)[62]

Policies initiated by the new federal government after 1789, under President George Washington, further inflamed the situation, prompting showdowns that involved, among thousands of others, the aging North Carolina mystic and former Regulator Hermon Husband. But by then, objections to Washington administration policies had inflamed city democrats as well. In the early 1790s, as prosperity stalled and tariff protection wore thin, urban democrats complained that import merchants seemed to prize their commercial connections to Britain above republican solidarity, and that haughty, well-connected financial interests were manipulating the government to enrich themselves at the expense of the common citizenry. Although respect for the Constitution did not decline, the seaport alliance of merchants and mechanics that had backed the Constitution's ratification disintegrated. The elements emerged for a re-creation of the kind of democratic insurgency combining city and countryside that had once succeeded in Pennsylvania, but now on a national instead of merely a statewide basis. What remained unclear was who might organize such an insurgency—and whether, under the terms of the new national Constitution, it could even establish its political legitimacy.

FRANKLIN'S DEATH

In April 1790, Benjamin Franklin died at age eighty-four. He had spent most of his time since 1776 in Paris, arranging for vital trade treaties and government loans for the Revolutionary War effort, while he enjoyed the city's cosmopolitan pleasures and basked in his reputation as the premier American *philosophe*. After negotiating the conclusive Treaty of Paris in 1783, he stood second only to George Washington as America's foremost hero.

Recalled home to Philadelphia in 1785, Franklin turned to a number of philanthropic, educational, and reform endeavors. In 1787, he advised a group of local journeymen printers when they struck their employers over wage cuts. The same year, he helped reorganize a disbanded abolition society founded by the Quaker humanitarian Anthony Benezet. Also in 1787, Franklin agreed to serve as a delegate to the Federal Constitutional Convention. Although he had misgivings about specifics in the new national plan, he refrained from airing them in public, remarking that the new government would not turn into a despotism unless "the people shall become so corrupted as to need despotic Government." His last public act, two months before he died, was to sponsor a petition to the new Congress advocating the gradual abolition of slavery.[63]

Strange things began happening to Franklin's reputation during these final years. He had always elicited distrust in the elevated ranks of Philadelphia society, as a shrewd, humble man made good, a wealthy outsider who had challenged the power of the province's old proprietary party, the demiurge behind the democratic constitution of 1776. Now, after his sojourn in Paris and his participation in unsettling reform projects back home, his social cachet in select circles sharply declined. A friend, Deborah Norris Logan, later recalled "the remark of a fool, though a fashionable party-man at the time, that it was by no means 'fashionable' to visit Dr. Franklin." And after his death, when Franklin's name became linked posthumously to a new upsurge of democratic politics, his memory became deeply suspect among the well-to-do and politically conservative. Some friends of the new Washington administration began ridiculing the departed statesman—the son of a Boston candlemaker—as an upstart soapboiler, a "fawning mob orator," and "a whoremaster, a hypocrite and an infidel."[64]

The American Revolution had proved more egalitarian in its outcome than many of its leaders had hoped or expected it would be in 1776. At the state and local levels, portions of the *demos* once largely excluded from the exercise of power were now among the people's governors. Efforts to rein in the egalitarian impulse had faltered. When those efforts finally succeeded, with the ratification of a new federal constitution in 1788, the Framers had felt compelled to bend to what James Wilson called "the genius of the people."[65]

A tiny group of state and national leaders, hoping to enlarge the influence of a disinterested natural aristocracy, had invented a national government that would not permit those natural aristocrats to speak only with each other. Yet the structures of American politics, at every level, were still highly uncertain. The federal convention had established the basic framework for a classless republic, but no more than that. Questions abounded, not least over the fate of the democratic presence that the Revolution had created. How would elections to the new government be conducted? Would what James Madison once called the "arts of Electioneering which poison the very fountain of Liberty" clog the Constitution's carefully designed filtration of talent? Would efforts to restrict those baneful arts intrude on the public's liberty? Of what, exactly, did that liberty consist?[66]

Democracy had happened in America between 1776 and 1787. But as the mounting attacks on Franklin's memory thereafter suggested, democracy's achievements were fragile, its institutions only barely formed, and its future far from guaranteed.

2

THE REPUBLICAN INTEREST
AND THE SELF-CREATED
DEMOCRACY

The framers of the federal Constitution tried to balance the imperatives of popular sovereignty against the fear of excessive democracy. They could not, even with the addition of the Bill of Rights. Within five years of the Constitution's ratification, new forms of democratic politics emerged, alarming many of the nation's leaders and perplexing others. Thomas Jefferson would eventually become the head and chief beneficiary of this democratic resurgence. But its most striking early manifestations came from well outside Jefferson's world of gentry politics.

In April 1793, a few weeks into George Washington's second term as president, a group calling itself the German Republican Society announced its formation in Philadelphia. Led by a printer and state representative, Henry Kammerer, a physician, Michael Leib, and an ex-army officer and former congressman, Peter Muhlenberg, the members acknowledged their common ethnic background but addressed the republic at large, as American citizens, on issues of national importance. Declaring that "there is a disposition in the human mind to tyrannize when cloathed with power," the new society expressed its disenchantment with federal policies and promised to watch elected officials with an eagle eye. Several weeks later, also in Philadelphia, a larger group, the Democratic Society of Pennsylvania, with no particular ethnic connection, organized itself on the same principles. Its leaders included Benjamin Franklin's favored grandson, the editor of the democratic *Aurora General Advertiser*, Benjamin Franklin Bache.[1]

By the end of 1794, more than thirty of these so-called Democratic-Republican societies (each had a distinctive name, but most included either the word *Democratic* or *Republican*) arose from upper Vermont to South Carolina, and as far west as Kentucky. They mounted elaborate dinners and Fourth of July celebrations; they extolled the French Revolution (in progress since the year of Washington's inauguration), erected tricolored liberty poles, and listened to orations on mental liberty and freedom of the press. They debated current political affairs, published addresses and resolutions criticizing the Washington administration, and agitated for social reforms. They corresponded with each other. Popular democratic politics reappeared everywhere—and quickly came under suspicion as illegitimate and possibly subversive, unfit for a postrevolutionary republic. Each society, one disgusted Virginian wrote, was an "odious conclave of tumult."[2]

The Democratic-Republican societies appeared alongside a growing opposition, inside the government, to the Washington administration. Divisions surfaced in the nation's first capital, New York City, as soon as the First Congress convened in March 1789. Representatives from backcountry districts railed against what they deemed the administration's pompous and monarchical public manner—what one Pennsylvanian called "all the faulty finery brilliant scenes and expensive Trappings of Royal Government."[3] Beginning in 1790, Treasury Secretary Alexander Hamilton's accomplished and audacious reports on the public credit, funding the national debt, and establishing a national bank stirred sharp debate inside President Washington's cabinet and the Congress. Over the next two years, the first semblance of a formal political opposition, led by Secretary of State Thomas Jefferson and Congressman James Madison, spread across the countryside through networks of dissident editors and notables. In 1793, as American opinion began to divide sharply over the French Revolution and American foreign policy, the opposition, known as the Republican interest, stepped up its efforts to halt what it perceived as the government's accelerating Anglophilic, antirepublican drift.

The rise of the Democratic-Republican societies, just when international tensions began to worsen, presented an opportunity and a challenge to Jefferson, Madison, and their allies. On the key national issues, ranging from Hamilton's financial program to foreign affairs, the societies and the mostly patrician Jeffersonian opposition agreed. The societies made no pretense about their support for the Republican interest, and they greatly amplified public criticism of the administration and its supporters. Their activities could be a valuable reinforcement, out-of-doors, to the opposition's efforts inside the cabinet and in Congress. The problem, though, was that the societies were also a self-consciously anomalous force, without any obvious place within the frame of the new Constitution, working independently of the lines of interest and influence where the opposition leaders operated. The societies intended not simply to support certain positions and political leaders, but to become the vehicles for a continuing independent expression of the popular will. With an ebullient grandiosity befitting the age, they hoped to destroy systems of social and political deference that had survived the Revolution. They wanted to create new networks of intelligence and enlightenment that would help emancipate all humanity.

To their opponents in the administration, who appropriated the name Federalists, the societies exemplified unbridled democracy at its worst, and posed a clear and present danger to the republic. The societies' friends in the Republican opposition were not always so sure what to make of them—an uncertainty that turned into acute uneasiness when some of the rural societies appeared to cross over from protests to active disloyalty. Finally, under the withering assaults of the Federalists, the Republican interest and the societies came to understand that they could not do without each other. A democratic widening of American politics ensued, not as great as the society men originally envisaged, but greater than anything Jefferson, Madison, and their fellow gentry oppositionists could have imagined in 1789.

AGAINST MONOCRACY: JEFFERSON, MADISON, AND THE VIRGINIA IDEAL

Jefferson and Madison were born eight years apart and raised roughly thirty miles from each other in neighboring counties of the Virginia Piedmont. Scions of leading planter families, both were well educated (Jefferson at William and Mary and with the great law teacher George Wythe at Williamsburg, Madison at Princeton); both were imbued with the rationalist values of the Enlightenment; and both were drawn to politics despite their indifferent public personae. They would enjoy a long and productive friendship and collaboration.[4]

Yet Jefferson and Madison were also very different men, and their differences were particularly evident at the new federal government's founding. Jefferson, the charming, rangy, elusive polymath, displayed the greater intellectual ambit of the two, and a penchant in private for flights of political fantasy. Madison, half a foot shorter, nervous, and achingly shy, had the more systematic mind, one capable, as Jefferson's was not, of building grand and nuanced practical designs out of his political principles. A tireless committeeman and preeminent member of the Second Continental Congress from 1779 until 1783, Madison had acquired from the Revolution a broad view of American government that vaunted the nation's well-being over sectional or local interests. With that view, he became the chief theorist of the Federal Constitution, favoring a large republic with a strong central government and an energetic executive. Jefferson, who in 1779 began the first of two disastrous terms as wartime governor of Virginia, believed in American nationalism, but also had a greater fear of government's coercive abuses. Hence his wariness, which he conveyed to Madison from his minister's post in Paris in 1788, of approving the Constitution without a bill of rights—the "principal defect," he wrote, in the Framers' work.[5]

Their differences were philosophical as well as temperamental. Madison, with more than a trace of Calvinist pessimism, was drawn to inventing reasoned political institutions in order to quiet what he saw as mankind's innate passion for destructive conflict. Jefferson, in his more haphazard yet sanguine way, preferred proposing plans to liberate individual reason, and enhance what he saw as mankind's potential for harmony and order. Far more instinctively than Madison, Jefferson viewed political turbulence as beneficial: "It prevents the degeneracy of government," he wrote, "and nourishes a general attention to the public affairs."[6] Those disagreements began to recede, however, in 1790, after Secretary of the Treasury Hamilton announced the first portion of his ambitious financial program and Congressman Madison attacked it.

Madison and Hamilton had been friends and colleagues since they first met in the Continental Congress in 1782—and were closer in their politics, it seemed, than were Madison and Jefferson (who had never laid eyes on Hamilton until he joined Washington's cabinet). Madison and Hamilton's shared nationalism and their mounting frustration at the ascendancy of the state governments under the Articles of Confederation outweighed their other political considerations in the mid to late 1780s. Both men attended the Annapolis Conference, a failed effort to alter the Articles, in 1786. Both were, in different ways, outstanding advocates of a strong central government during the federal convention at Philadelphia. Above all, over the winter of 1787–88, using the joint pseudonym "Publius," they composed the most powerful of *The Federalist* papers to defend the convention's work, eloquently expressing their distrust of majorities, their fear of faction, and their belief that robust central government could be an antidote to selfish human frailty and divisiveness. "Hearken not to the unnatural voice which tells you that the people of America . . . can no longer live together as members of the same family," declared Madison in *Federalist 14*.[7]

Yet when Hamilton, secretary of the Treasury, sought to improve upon the Framers' work, his friendship with Madison abruptly ended. Hamilton, the ingenious, West Indies–born New York lawyer and former army officer, was convinced that the Constitution could not guarantee greatness—or even survival—for the new republic. History taught him that no matter how they were governed, agrarian societies like America's produced little more than what was needed to sustain their people in modest comfort. Contrary to the then-fashionable classical and contemporary poets' portrayal of idyllic pastoral life so dear to Jefferson's heart, Hamilton was convinced that such conditions were morally enervating and politically dangerous. Uninspired to improve their circumstances, individuals would lapse into habits of public indifference and brutish self-regard. Lacking a substantial material surplus on which to draw, the government would have a difficult time raising a credible military force to ward off hostile nations. "[O]ne of two evils must ensue," Hamilton wrote in *Federalist 30*, "either the people must be subjected to continual plunder, as a substitute for a more eligible mode of supplying the public wants, or the government must sink into a fatal atrophy, and, in a short course of time, perish."[8]

Alternatively, an America that mobilized its boundless material resources through public and private credit would, in Hamilton's view, protect both commerce and the nation, and encourage an intensified, urbane sociability. "Industry is increased," he wrote to Robert Morris in 1781, about the benefits of public debt and a national bank, "commodities are multiplied, agriculture and manufacturers flourish, and herein consist the true wealth and prosperity of a state." In order to secure this, Hamilton looked instinctively to Great Britain, both as a model and as an irreplaceable commercial ally. The immense increase since 1750 of Britain's funded debt—the system of mortgaging government revenues by selling public securities in order to finance recurrent wars—had been accompanied by an extraordinary growth of the British economy. By imitating that system with a privately directed national bank, foreign impost revenues, and internal excise taxes, Americans could establish their own government securities as a stable currency while giving their merchants access to the large pools of capital required to develop the country. Because those monies would be used chiefly for economic improvement and presumably not for wars, the consequent expansion of national wealth would help to fund the debt. Finally, Hamilton argued that the United States would have to sustain cordial relations with the British government, lest the nation lose the enormous public revenues as well as private profits received from its commerce with Britain. Without those revenues, he was certain, America could not honor its national obligations.[9]

Hamilton released his plans to Congress in stages, beginning in January 1790 with his report on public credit, followed almost a year later by a report on establishing a national bank (accompanied with a request for an excise tax on whiskey), followed a year after that by a report on manufacturing. In order to restore public confidence in American finances, Hamilton's opening report called, first, for the repayment at face value of all national securities from the Revolutionary and Confederation periods to the current holders of those securities and, second, for the federal government to assume all state debts left over from the Revolution. The latter proposal came with the understanding that each state would be compensated for its donation once the total debt was retired. As Hamilton saw it, the plan offered a simple solution to the tangled problems of uniting and repaying the state and national public creditors, as well as the means to offer generous federal relief to indebted states. Not coincidentally, the plan would also create a large federal debt whose funding, supported by imposts and excise taxes, would be the key to achieving Hamilton's vision of American prosperity and power—"the price of liberty," he wrote.[10]

To Madison, the debt funding and assumption schemes reeked of oppressive favoritism. By paying only the current holders of national securities—monied speculators who had purchased the securities at cut-rate prices in the 1780s—Hamilton would completely ignore the claims of the original holders—ordinary citizens of limited means who had accepted or bought their securities in good faith but who had been forced by the uncertain postwar economic climate to sell their paper at a fraction of its face value. "[T]here must be something wrong, radically & morally & politically wrong," Madison observed, "in a system which transfers the reward from those who paid the most valuable of all considerations, to those who scarcely paid any consideration at all."[11] Federal assumption of state debts under Hamilton's program, meanwhile, would benefit those states, above all Massachusetts and South Carolina, that were still heavily in arrears far more than it would those (including Virginia and all the other southern states) that had largely retired their debt.

Jefferson would level similar charges against Hamilton's larger financial program, but initially he was more cautious than Madison and remained publicly noncommittal. His long journey home from his posting in France and his indecision about joining Washington's cabinet as secretary of state delayed his arrival in New York until late March 1790—more than a month after Congress had already defeated Madison's effort to block Hamilton's plan to compensate the current holders of government paper. Once he had settled in, Jefferson helped arrange what he described as a compromise meeting, in which Madison agreed to permit approval of a revised version of Hamilton's assumption proposal in exchange for establishing the federal government's permanent capital at a site well to the south of New York, on the Potomac River bordering Maryland and Virginia.[12]

Jefferson later told President Washington, a bit defensively, that in 1790 he had no clear idea of what Hamilton's financial system entailed and that the quick-tongued New Yorker had duped him. Whatever the truth in that, Jefferson certainly was alarmed at the depth of the disagreements in Congress and hoped to find some middle ground. (If Hamilton and his foes were not reconciled, he wrote to his fellow Virginian, James Monroe, the arguments over the debt would cause "our credit . . . [to] burst and vanish," and the nation would disintegrate.) Only in January 1791, after Hamilton unveiled his bank proposal and Congress approved it, did Jefferson take the full measure of Hamilton's plans and assume a firmer adversarial stance. In private (and on strict constructionist constitutional grounds that Madison had already explained in the House), Jefferson futilely tried to persuade Washington to veto the bank bill. Thereafter, until the end of 1793, Jefferson would help lead the attack on Hamilton and Hamilton's proposals, but he would do so behind closed doors and in personal letters, lest he appear a disloyal cabinet member or the leader of a faction—anathema in a political atmosphere that despised parties as corrupt fomenters of division and enemies to the government itself. It fell to Madison, the younger and shyer man, to serve as chief public spokesman for the embryonic opposition, on the floor of the House and, writing anonymously, in the fledgling, outnumbered opposition press.[13]

The early congressional clashes over Hamilton's policies had a strong sectional character, pitting the North against the South. Nearly two-thirds of the House votes in favor of Madison's failed discrimination proposal came from Virginia; when the assumption plan finally passed the House, more than half the southern congressmen stubbornly cast negative votes, despite the prearranged compromise about moving the capital to the Potomac. The House tally approving the bank bill was even more dramatic: northern representatives nearly unanimously backed the bill but the southerners voted heavily against it. Slavery, the most obvious difference between the sections, cannot explain the emerging partisan divide. Northerners, some of whom were still squabbling about emancipation in their own states, did not perceive an antislavery agenda behind Hamilton's proposals. On slavery issues, Virginians in the First Congress commonly voted with the North. Narrower local self-interest played a larger role, especially with respect to Hamilton's assumption plan, which appeared unfavorable to every southern state except South Carolina. But there were also more profound social and ideological issues at stake for Jefferson, Madison, and their southern allies.[14]

Hamilton's unembarrassed Anglophilia offended some southerners, especially Virginia planters hit hard by British military depredations during the Revolution and still uncompensated for their losses, including losses of slaves. More important, Hamilton's economics, founded on his reported claim that "a public debt is a public blessing," confirmed his treachery in the minds of southern planters and farmers. On the eve of the Revolution, Virginians, many of whom had unwisely refused to retrench in the face of weakening tobacco markets, owed more money to British creditors than the inhabitants of any other colony, and nearly as much as all of the other colonists combined. It was a miserable situation, not simply because it offended what were supposed to be gentlemanly norms about insolvency, but because it left the indebted planters lashed in a terrible dependence to distant British merchants.[15]

The more forward-looking planters acknowledged that they would have to mend their ways if they were to keep from repeating the cycle of debt dependency. But no amount of agricultural self-improvement could undo what Jefferson and others considered the corrosive and degrading effects of Hamilton's debt-based finance system. That system, they contended, blatantly favored certain classes of Americans, generally northerners (speculators in government stock, residents of states with large debts), to the exclusion, and at the expense, of everyone else. Speaking in the House against the proposed bank, James Jackson of Georgia called it an unconstitutional monopoly, "calculated to benefit a small part of the United States, the mercantile interest only; the farmers, the yeomanry will derive no advantage from it." Instead of increasing the store of national wealth available to all, Hamilton's plans would replace the old imperial debt system with a pernicious new one, run by well-connected men who produced nothing yet who lived handsomely off the proceeds gained from other men's products.[16]

Jefferson and others could also not help detecting royalist designs in Hamilton's economic policies. In restrospect, that suspicion was unfair. Hamilton's admiration for British government and political economy no more made him a crypto-monarchist than his opponents' later enthusiasm for the French Revolution made them incipient Jacobin terrorists. Moreover, as some of Hamilton's northern friends tartly pointed out, it ill behooved Americans, including Jefferson and Madison, who lived off the unrequited labor of human chattel to call any other group of Americans exploiters. Yet having lived for most of their lives under monarchy, it was understandable that royalism became the chief point of reference for Hamilton's foes, who appreciated certain American social and political principles that the Treasury secretary detested. Those principles— which the opposition would soon pit against a somewhat more measured anti-Hamilton epithet, *monocracy*—formed the elements of what would become a distinct Virginia political ideal.[17]

Jefferson was especially prone to wrap his political judgments, including those about Hamilton, inside praise of rural virtues, while condemning large cities. "Those who labor in the earth," he wrote famously in 1783, "are the chosen people of God, if ever he had a chosen people." In drawing this distinction, he did not mean to dismiss the cultural and intellectual amenities of urban life (which, during his extended residences in New York, Philadelphia, and, especially, Paris, he enjoyed to the hilt). Nor did he despise urban commerce, including the transoceanic commerce that helped enrich American farmers. Rather, he was registering a Virginian's suspicions of urban speculators who contributed nothing to the production and distribution of goods, as well as of what he called "the mobs of great cities"—the hordes of hangers-on and impoverished persons who, because they were reliant on the goodwill of employers and patrons, could never be trusted to arrive at virtuous, independent political judgments. To protect the republic from being corrupted by these dependent men, Jefferson looked to expanding the influence of America's free majority of self-reliant planters and yeomen (he never really distinguished between the two)—honest, moderately prosperous, and productive toilers whose reason, supposedly, was not clouded by

servility to others. Encouraging these men would ward off what he called in a letter to Madison in 1785 the enormous inequality in property that produced
"much misery to the bulk of mankind"—inequality that Hamilton's plans would
ratify and exacerbate.[18]

Madison echoed his friend's somewhat static pastoral republicanism from
time to time. "'Tis not the country that peoples either the Bridewells or the Bed-
lams," he wrote in 1792. "These mansions of wretchedness are tenanted from the
distresses and vices of overgrown cities." But Madison added his own nationalist
vision of effective, harmonious government, as he had propounded it in *Federalist 10* and 55. In the 1780s, that vision had alarmed many prominent Virginians
as too centralizing; but in the 1790s, Madison showed that his nationalism was at
odds in several ways with his ex-friend Hamilton's. In doing so, Madison
achieved a degree of reconciliation with portions of the gentry that had opposed
the Constitution, and solidified a new coalition of former Federalists and anti-
Federalists from 1787 to 1788 against Hamilton's plans.[19]

Breaking with Hamilton involved no intellectual inconsistency on Madison's
part (although Hamilton would bitterly claim it did). Contrary to Madison's vision
of the new constitutional order, Hamilton's fiscal plans would, he believed, ally
the federal government to a particular class of speculators, create (through the
national bank) a means to dispense bounties to political favorites and bribes to
opponents, and introduce what Madison called the "corrupt influence" of "substituting the motive of private interest in place of public duty." More generally,
Madison observed, the funding system would enlarge "the inequality of property,
by an immoderate, and especially an unmerited, accumulation of riches." The
delicate balance of social forces so vital to Madisonian popular sovereignty would
be destroyed—and with it, Madison's design for an enlightened republic.[20]

Over the course of the 1790s, Jefferson and Madison would help turn their
objections to Hamilton's project into a coherent alternative vision of America,
influenced by Virginia aspirations and prejudices but capable of appealing to
other groups, including the reemerging urban democrats of Philadelphia, New
York, and other cities. In 1791, however, Jefferson, Madison, and their allies in
Congress were struggling, not very successfully, to keep Hamilton's proposals
from sweeping aside all opposition. Despite the advantages in congressional representation given to the southern states under the three-fifths clause of the Constitution, Hamilton appeared able, at will, to push his bills through the House as
well as the Senate. And Hamilton had the trust of his old commanding officer, a
Virginian far more imposing than Thomas Jefferson—President Washington,
who, in politics, surmounted all local connections and came as close any American ever would to an elected Patriot King. "Congress may go home," the country democrat Congressman William Maclay wrote. "Mr. Hamilton is all
powerful and fails in nothing which he attempts."[21]

Opposing Hamilton inside the government without appearing to defy Washington was a major problem confronting the Virginians. A related, larger difficulty was to find political tools that could rally and unify voters and officeholders from around the country without seeming to disrupt the spirit of national harmony. Grappling with both problems forced Jefferson, Madison, and their disgruntled allies in the political elite to stretch their ideas about democracy.

FIRST STIRRINGS OF REPUBLICAN ORGANIZATION

At the end of February 1791, three days after President Washington signed the bill establishing Hamilton's bank, Jefferson contacted Madison's old Princeton classmate, the journalist and poet Philip Freneau, and offered him a lowly translator's clerkship in the State Department at an annual salary of $250—a pretext for persuading Freneau to come to Philadelphia and edit a new, nationally distributed opposition newspaper. The project was perilous, financially and politically, and all parties concerned had to move gingerly, but to Freneau, the prospect of leading the attack on Alexander Hamilton was too tantalizing to pass up.[22]

After two short, unsuccessful postcollege stints as a schoolteacher, Freneau, an adventuresome young man with literary ambitions, had sailed on a privateer during the Revolution, fallen captive to the enemy, and suffered terribly aboard one of the Royal Navy's notorious prison ships. His memories of that suffering forever smoldered in his writing. Politically close to Thomas Paine—whom Jefferson also, briefly, considered trying to lure into the administration in 1791—Freneau established his reputation in Philadelphia after the war as both poet and polemicist, then moved to New York City, where, as editor of the *Daily Advertiser*, he gained additional notice in 1790 with vituperative attacks on Hamilton's debt-funding and banking proposals. Recommended not just by Madison but by another prominent Princeton graduate and Virginian, Henry ("Light Horse Harry") Lee, Freneau seemed the ideal choice to counter John Fenno, the editor of the quasi-official administration newspaper, the *Gazette of the United States*—the purveyor, in Jefferson's excited view, of "doctrines of monarchy, aristocracy, and the exclusion of the influence of the people." After dickering for five months about business arrangements, Freneau accepted both the clerkship and the editorial post. At the end of October 1791, he put through the press the first issue of his twice-weekly *National Gazette*.[23]

By establishing a national newspaper, the leaders of the emerging Republican opposition displayed their growing coherence and self-confidence as a political force, but they also displayed a limited conception of democracy and dissent. Freneau would bring to the Republicans the slashing, egalitarian style of the Revolutionary-era city democracy. At a time when newspapers were just beginning to reach the more remote corners of the country, the *National Gazette* promised to stimulate sympathetic opinion as no existing newspaper could. Yet in Freneau, Jefferson and Madison had also found someone whose instincts and loyalty they thought they could trust—an ink-stained democrat, yes, but also one who could work well with the opposition's gentry leadership. ("With Mr. Freneau I have been long and intimately acquainted," Madison reassured another Republican.)[24] More generally, the *National Gazette* would be instrumental in helping those leaders (particularly Madison, who would write several important articles for the paper in 1792) to connect with their notable friends and subscribers around the country, and who would in turn influence their own friends and neighbors. If, as Jefferson put it, Freneau's paper was to serve as an anti-administration "whig-vehicle of intelligence" with a democratic edge, it was a vehicle that traveled from the top down, closely watched by men who thought of themselves as the country's natural leaders.[25]

This style of organizing through the ministrations of a political elite dominated Republican national efforts through the elections of 1792. When Jefferson and Madison embarked in the late spring of 1791 on what would become a famous "botanizing tour" of New York and New England, rumors flew about how they were actually establishing closer political contacts with friendly local powers, especially Robert R. Livingston and Aaron Burr in New York City. The rumors had merit; but whatever occurred, the tour bespoke what were still the Republicans' limited views of what constituted a legitimate opposition.[26] Inside and outside Congress, political dissent would mainly involve the cooperation of a few leading gentlemen who would handle their affairs discreetly, more like diplomats than like grubby politicians. Newspapers and pamphlets written by trustworthy allies would shape public opinion. And nothing would be said or done that might be construed as unfriendly to President Washington.

Ideas about building permanent electoral machinery that might fuse the national leadership with the voters were nearly as alien to the Republican leaders as they were to Federalists. James Madison, writing in the *National Gazette*, asked his readers to face the fact that something he called "parties" had come to exist in American politics, and that there were not several of these parties (as he had said there might be in *Federalist 10*) but only two. Yet Madison made it clear that only one of those two parties, his own,—the "friends to republican policy . . . in opposition to a spirit of usurpation and monarchy"—was the legitimate legatee of the Revolution and the Constitution. Once that legitimate party prevailed, Madison and his allies believed, the "monocratic" crisis would end, parties would be rendered unnecessary, and the high-minded decisions of enlightened natural leaders would, at last, guide the nation.[27]

The structure of politics at the state level further discouraged partisan electioneering. In virtually all of the southern states, neither the governor, congressional representatives, state legislators, nor presidential electors were selected by a statewide vote. Elections had a localist character, centered around individual candidates, that made them almost impervious to national organizing. In New England, where statewide elections were much more common, a haphazard multiplicity of election tickets, with some candidates appearing on several lists for the same election, made it almost impossible to build coherent political organizations. Only in New York and Pennsylvania were electoral procedures more favorable to would-be Republican and Federalist organizers. Yet, even in those states, major candidates eschewed party labels.[28]

Intrigue, deception, and bungling in high places, befitting a late-eighteenth-century *opera buffa*, overshadowed popular organizing—such as it was—on the national political stage. One little scandal began innocently enough in April 1791, when Madison gave Jefferson a copy of Thomas Paine's latest work from London, the first part of Paine's defense of the French Revolution, *Rights of Man*. (Madison had borrowed the copy belonging to John Beckley, the clerk of the House of Representatives and an admirer of Paine.) After reading the book with delight, Jefferson, following Beckley's instructions, forwarded it to the printer in charge of preparing an American edition, but he unwisely included a note praising the book as an antidote to certain "political heresies which have sprung up among us"—an unmistakable reference to some recently published political writings by Vice President Adams. Not thinking to ask Jefferson's permission, the printer included the note as a preface, and all hell broke loose. Hamilton severed relations with Jefferson for good. The embarrassed Jefferson wrote a hurried explanation to Washington and later apologized to Adams. Under the pseudonym "Publicola," Adams's twenty-four-year-old son, John Quincy, leapt to his father's defense in the newspapers. For years thereafter, the elder Adams would have little to do with Jefferson, who, despite their political differences, had been a long-standing friend, collaborator, and correspondent.[29]

A few months later, Hamilton strayed into an even wilder and juicier scandal of his own that would take much longer to come to light. One summer day, Maria Reynolds, outwardly a respectable lady in much distress, introduced herself out of the blue to the Treasury secretary, told him her husband had abandoned her, and requested funds to enable her to stay with friends in New York. Much affected by the woman's story, Hamilton, a married man, gave her some money—and then commenced an affair with her that continued for over a year. In time Mrs. Reynolds, working in collusion with her all-too-present husband, James, ensnared Hamilton into paying hush money. The liaison continued, until the husband and an accomplice, awaiting trial on charges of fraud stemming from a different matter, began spreading rumors that they had proof, written in Hamilton's hand, of financial misconduct at the very highest levels of the Treasury Department. Three concerned congressmen (including Senator James

Monroe), accompanied by clerk of the House John Beckley, confronted Hamilton in private with notes he had written Mrs. Reynolds; Hamilton told his visitors the whole story. Satisfied that no public monies had been involved, the congressmen decided to drop the matter. For the time being, nothing seemed amiss, at least publicly—but Beckley, angry at Hamilton's attacks on Jefferson, held on to the Hamilton-Reynolds letters, in case they might some day prove politically useful. It would take a few years, but that day would come.[30]

The scandals and the skulduggery marked the persistence of an older form of elite politics, revolving around personal character, honor, and gentlemanly reputation. Another episode unfolded during the vice presidential contest in 1792. Early in the year, Republican leaders, not wanting to challenge President Washington, concocted a plan to run the popular governor of New York, George Clinton, against Vice President John Adams, and thereby register the electorate's displeasure with the administration. In the spring, Clinton was narrowly reelected governor over John Jay—but only because of flagrant voter fraud by some of his upstate supporters. Jefferson, alarmed at the possible fallout from the fraud revelations, counseled Clinton to resign from office. New York's hyperambitious young U.S. Senator Aaron Burr confused matters further when he allowed friends in New York and Pennsylvania to circulate his name as a possible alternative challenger for the vice presidency. Madison and Monroe wanted nothing to do with Burr; fortuitously, Hamilton, who also loathed Burr, bid his fellow New York Federalists to go easy on Clinton, while he threw his wholehearted support (complete with unsolicited campaign advice) to John Adams. The Republicans wound up sticking with Clinton, who kept his New York job and ran a respectable second to Adams in the Electoral College, carrying nearly all of the South, including Virginia. Burr, meanwhile, blamed the Virginians for thwarting his candidacy and began quietly nursing his disappointments.[31]

After 1792, Republican leaders, driven as much by confusion and fear as by principle, began enlarging their views about political organization. Although candidates aligned with the Republican interest ran well enough in the congressional races to gain a majority in the House, the majority was small, and the Federalists still controlled both the presidency and (by a wide margin) the Senate. The results posed a difficult puzzle: if the Republicans truly represented, as Madison claimed in an essay for the *National Gazette,* the interests and the ideals of "the mass of people in every part of the union, in every state, and of every occupation," why did every opposition candidate not win every election by a landslide?[32]

The problem involved two distinct but related matters: Why was voter turnout, especially in national elections, so low—often less than one in four eligible voters, considerably less than in local and state elections? And why did the active voters elect congressional representatives who, once in office, gravitated disproportionately to the Federalists? The influential John Taylor of Caroline (known by the Virginia county where he resided, and speaking on behalf of his fellow Virginians in Congress) blamed a conniving "paper interest" consisting of roughly five thousand of Hamilton's friends, who had gained "an irresistible *influence* over the Legislature" and over the electorate through propaganda and the granting of personal favors. Under the circumstances, it was easy to understand why the electorate had grown lethargic while what Taylor called "the artificial interest" controlled the federal government.[33]

One possible corrective, proposed by Taylor in 1794 and followed up years later by Jefferson, was to embolden state legislatures to assume a more active role in governing the nation. Because the state legislatures elected U.S. senators, their collective influence over the direction of the federal government could well prove decisive. But Republican leaders also decided they would have to redouble their efforts to educate and mobilize the virtuous but misinformed citizens. Establishing Freneau's *National Gazette* had been an important step; so, later, had been Taylor's call to elect representatives who shared a "similarity of interests" with their constituents. But the *Gazette* was doomed to fold in 1793, the victim of a yellow fever epidemic that swept through Philadelphia.[34] And before the *Gazette*'s demise, the national returns in 1792 showed that the gentry Republicans needed to innovate further if they were to overthrow the "paper interest." They would end up taking instruction from men with more democratic instincts than their own, organized in the Democratic-Republican societies.

"THE CAUSE OF *EQUAL LIBERTY* EVERY WHERE"

The Democratic-Republican societies were conceived in response to domestic political problems and beholden to the examples of 1776. But they also looked to the revolution in Paris for examples and solidarity—and in the societies' early months, it seemed that foreign affairs would dominate everything else. In April 1793, right after the German Republicans had organized in Philadelphia, a British packet arrived in New York with the first news of the execution of Louis XVI and France's declaration of war on Britain and Holland. Two days later, the new French minister to the United States, "Citizen" Edmond Charles Genet, arrived in Charleston to a rousing reception, then set off on his problematic mission: to whip up American support for the regicide republic. The Washington administration, which had quickly proclaimed the nation's neutrality, requested Genet's recall to France a mere four months later. During the summer, the headstrong, bombastic envoy thoroughly alienated even his best American friends in high places, including the pro-French Secretary of State Thomas Jefferson. The political fallout hastened Jefferson's decision to retire from the cabinet late in 1793, and Jefferson warned his ally James Madison that Genet's American friends would "*sink the republican* interest."[35]

Those friends included, most conspicuously, the new Democratic-Republican societies, who saw Genet as a besieged apostle of revolutionary defiance. A few weeks after his arrival, a committee from the German Republican Society waited on Genet in Philadelphia and urged "the perpetual union and freedom of our respective republics." Genet was the man who came up with the suggestion that the larger Philadelphia group look to the future and name itself the Democratic Society instead of the Sons of Liberty. Certain societies in the Carolinas and Kentucky, with Genet's encouragement, aided French plans for insurrections against Spanish-held Louisiana and Florida, and for securing rights to navigate the Mississippi River. Longer than most pro-French Americans, the societies stood by Genet against what one club called "the most indecent calumnies" directed against him.[36]

Some administration supporters seized on the connections and battered both the Republican opposition and the societies as (in the Massachusetts conservative Fisher Ames's words) "the impure off-spring of Genet."[37] But the Genet affair obscured how principled dissent over the Washington administration's policies, at home and abroad, had triggered the societies' rise — dissent far more important than the exhortations of Citizen Genet. There was no need, the societies insisted, to look across the Atlantic to see liberty besieged by tyranny: "the peaceful Temple of Liberty is threatened in this Western hemisphere," the Philadelphia society declared. Disgust at Hamilton's financial programs had been growing for three years, among city and country democrats alike. The alliance between Federalists and urban mechanics over the Constitution had broken down over popular fears that Hamilton's paper system was designed to enrich a few speculators and merchants at the expense of the many. Similar anxieties gripped rural areas that had never been enamored of the new federal plan.[38]

In local fights as well, there was mounting alienation over perceived Federalist favoritism toward the wealthy and well connected. One telling battle unfolded in New York City, where master mechanics had to wage a long battle against Federalist state legislators to gain a charter for their General Society of Mechanics and Tradesmen. "Those who assume the airs of 'the well born,'" wrote one self-styled "Friend to Equal Rights," "should be made to know that the *mechanics* of the city have *equal rights* to the merchants, and that they are as important a set of men as any in the community." Another city democrat asked why monied interests like banks could easily win official incorporation while more democratic ones could not. The New Yorkers finally won their charter in 1792, but the damage was done.[39]

The societies' outrage at Hamiltonian finance and Federalist elitism would always be at the core of their protests against the Washington administration. Their complaints repeated those of Jefferson, Madison, and the Virginia opposition, but in a very different key. Hamilton's innovations augured an accumulation of power in the hands of the federal government that the society men thought would pervert commerce and introduce, the Democratic Society of New York proclaimed, "the corrupt principles and abandoned polity of foreign climes." Mainly, Hamilton's program promised to set one class above all others: the insider monied men and speculators who manipulated government to gain special favors and advantages at the direct expense of ordinary citizens—and who then expected ordinary citizens to regard them as their superiors. "Our councils want the integrity or spirit of republicans," one western Pennsylvania society asserted, because of "the pernicious influence of stockholders or their subordinates." An eighteenth-century sense of class injustices and insult pervaded the societies' meetings. "Less respect to the consuming speculator, who wallows in luxury, than to the productive mechanic, who struggles with indigence," ran one New York society toast. Jefferson and his gentry allies saw the struggle before them in terms of urban corruption and rural virtue. The societies saw themselves embattled by arrogant parasites who demanded they defer.[40]

The administration's foreign policy, and the way it was promulgated, brought popular malaise to a head and sealed the link of domestic concerns to international politics. By refusing to side with revolutionary France against Britain and Holland, President Washington (with Secretary Hamilton's concurrence and over Secretary Jefferson's strenuous objections) in effect declared that the Franco-American mutual defense treaty of 1778, so vital to winning American independence, had died along with Louis XVI. The administration saw no favorite in the cataclysmic conflict between beleaguered republicanism and rampant monarchy, its critics claimed. And the president had proclaimed the nation's neutrality without consulting the Senate, the first such independent executive action on a major foreign policy matter. Not only had America deserted an old friend (now a republican friend) at war against the rotten old regime; it had done so, some charged, by an act of presidential usurpation on behalf, the Democratic Society of Pennsylvania said, of "the aristocratical faction among us."[41]

The protests and related activities of the city-based societies, especially Philadelphia's Democratic Society, attracted the greatest initial public attention. With more than three hundred members (making it the largest urban society of all), and meeting in the nation's temporary capital (which had been relocated from New York in 1791), the Philadelphia group resembled the city's democratic movement from the Revolution.[42] Thomas Paine, ever on the international front lines of political upheaval, was himself in Paris, where, as an elected member of the revolutionary National Assembly he voted against the king's execution on humanitarian grounds and wound up, rather ironically, spending most of 1794 in a Jacobin prison, expecting to be executed. But many of Paine's political associates and admirers from Philadelphia's radical intelligentsia were prominent members of the Democratic Society, including the watchmaker-turned-astronomer David Rittenhouse, Dr. Benjamin Rush of both the Continental Congress and the Pennsylvania Provincial Congress of 1776, and Benjamin Franklin Bache, whose Philadelphia *Aurora General Advertiser* had become the leading anti-administration newspaper.[43] Apart from some conspicuous self-made men of wealth (including the banker Stephen Girard), as well as professionals and minor public officials among its officers, the majority of the members were ordinary artisans, including journeymen as well as master craftsmen. The rank and file may have included some of the lower class of laborers of the kind who had filled the militia companies in 1776, but primarily they were from the aspiring yet humble middling sort, the self-designated "productive" classes. The same membership pattern appears to have prevailed in the other seaport societies. The rural clubs, likewise, brought together a leadership of prominent landed locals with lowlier farmers, land renters, and artisans.[44]

The Philadelphia society and the rest of the seaport groups linked America's fate to that of the new French republic and adapted the approved French rhetorical styles of revolutionary correctness. On May 1, 1794, about eight hundred members and supporters of the Philadelphia group, addressing each other as "Citizen," gathered at a grand festivity to celebrate, in part, the armies and government of France. A few weeks earlier, New York's Democratic Society had honored the momentous French military victory against the British at Toulon (taking the time to toast Thomas Paine and his *Rights of Man*). Early in 1795, the Boston society, replying to some Federalist name-calling, announced that "if to advocate the right of Free Enquiry and Opinion, and to wish success to the cause of *equal Liberty* every where, compose the character of *Jacobins*, we avow ourselves JACOBINS."[45]

Such passionate pronouncements fooled those who would be fooled by them. Rather than start a new American revolution and execute George Washington, the revived city democrats wanted to secure the Revolution they had believed was already won, against resurgent aristocracy and even monarchy. If, at times, the urban Democratic-Republicans could sound gullible and sometimes callous in their enthusiasm for *la révolution*, they themselves were no terrorists or Robespierreists. The city societies repeatedly affirmed their loyalty to orderly government and the federal Constitution. Their own constitutions and bylaws were models of democratic decorum, providing for annual elections of officers by secret ballot, open participation by the membership, and regular monthly meetings. Just after they declared themselves "Jacobins," the Boston Democratic-

Republicans qualified themselves: if the term meant violent opposition to the constituted authorities of the United States, or efforts to suppress free inquiry and expression, then "we detest the appellation."[46]

The groups' primary task was to provide a continuing forum to prevent American liberty's downfall, and to express that dissent in the name of the people. Lacking, under the Constitution, any institutional popular safeguard, between elections, against the perceived aristocratic revival, each society assumed that role for itself, combining the functions of a public observation committee, a tool for political education, and a fraternal order. Allied with independent radical editors—Bache and his successor, William Duane, as well as Eleazer Oswald in Philadelphia, Thomas Greenleaf in New York—they released ever-more pointed, occasionally vicious commentary on political events and administration actions, with language steeped in the apocalyptic furor of the time. It was, the society leaders freely admitted, a civic role unspecified in the Constitution—but only aristocrats and monarchists, they insisted, would claim that the Constitution's internal checks and balances were sufficient guarantees against tyranny. "Let us keep in mind," the Pennsylvania society declared, "that supineness with regard to public concerns is the direct road to slavery, while vigilance and jealousy are the safeguards of Liberty."[47]

The societies interpreted "public concerns" broadly and pursued humanitarian as well as political causes. Much of their activity involved creating a new public space for discussion of controversial political topics, and the dissemination of circulars and memorials, as well as remonstrances to the president and Congress. Like the Republican opposition, the societies were convinced that the Federalists secured their rule in part through a combination of purposeful misinformation and public ignorance. They aimed to build from the bottom up—just as the gentry Republicans did from the top down—new networks of political intelligence that would challenge the prevailing Federalist point of view. This required full freedom of assembly and the press. "It is the unalienable right of a free and independent people to assemble together in a peaceable manner," one North Carolina society resolved, in a typical pronouncement, "to discuss with firmness and freedom all subjects of public concern, and to publish their sentiments to their fellow citizens."[48]

Freedom of expression was, of course, the basis for further reforms. Some societies demanded fairer representation in state legislatures, in part, a South Carolina club observed, because impartial distribution of seats would prove "a means of disseminating political knowledge among the inhabitants." Other society men called for reductions in legal fees, the abolition of imprisonment for debt, and reform of criminal codes to eliminate capital punishment for minor offenses. The most imposing efforts involved establishing public libraries and library companies and demanding legislative aid to free public schooling to break down class privileges and cultivate an enlightened free citizenry. "The progress of education—," one society proclaimed at a Fourth of July celebration. "May it cause a speedy abolition of every species of dangerous distinction, and render every American a patriot from principle." Memorials and resolutions from Democratic-Republican groups proved instrumental in getting two states, New York and Delaware, to establish rudimentary public-school funding laws.[49]

In attacking ignorance, the societies' efforts at public enlightenment, including their parades and festivities, were part of a larger assault on deference. Popular habits of subordination to, and even reverence of, what one society called "aristocratical finesse" were essential to sustaining the Federalists' rule, the democrats argued. Too many ordinary citizens, even in republican America, still felt awe, resignation, and even shame in the presence of their alleged superiors— men with better educations, finer speech and more elegant clothing, smoother hands and smoother manners than theirs. This sense of inferiority was demoralizing, and it bred apathy and worse. "As ignorance is the irreconcilable enemy of Liberty it is also the immediate parent of guilt," the New York society declared. "[I]t poisons every pure fountain of morals in a state, and generates the greater proportion of crimes, that infest and disturb the peace of society." Demoralization and criminality, in turn, justified and reinforced the basic elitist presumption that the lower orders were savages who needed oversight by their benign, gentlemanly superiors.[50]

Overthrowing the Federalists' aristocracy required erasing that sense of embarrassment and inferiority. The escalating fervor in the denunciations of the societies indicated that the societies' refusal to defer was upsetting their foes deeply, as they had intended. And the rapid growth of the societies around the country in 1793 and 1794, even in the face of fierce attacks, suggested that popular submission might finally be breaking down. "In fine," the New York society observed, "the splendid frippery, the pompous sophistry, with which the bands of slavery have been tinselled over, are now found like a species of rotten wood."[51]

At their most visionary, the societies foresaw the triumph of what Tunis Wortman, of the New York Democratic Society, called "social virtue." With an enthusiasm that was becoming common among Enlightenment writers, high and low, the members celebrated men's capacities to enlarge the sphere of happiness once aristocracy had fallen. Their cause, as they saw it, was the democratic cause of 1776, but it was also the cause of humankind—a cause they believed, with dead seriousness, that fate had entrusted to them and their fellow democrats in the Old World. Their final goal was nothing less than the universal victory of egalitarian government. "When once that happy aera dawns upon the world," Wortman wrote, luxury, wealth, and sumptuous dissipation will give place to the charms of public spirit, and to the solid delights of a general and expanded philosophy: no distinctions will be known but those which are derived from a happy combination of virtue with talents. . . . The arts of civilized life will then be esteemed and cherished: Agriculture and manufactures will flourish; commerce, unrestrained by treaties and unshackled by partial provisions, will become as extensive as the wants and intercourse of nations. Philosophy, the sciences, and the liberal arts will advance in a continued and accelerated progression. Sanguinary punishments will then be forgotten and unknown. Persecution and superstition, vice, prejudice, and cruelty will take their eternal departure from the earth.

Out of free inquiry and political equality would come a euphoric new order of the ages.[52]

In directing the attentions and exertions of the citizenry toward these various missions, great and small, the societies declared it essential that they operate, as the Philadelphia group put it, "regardless of party spirit or political connection"— statements which have helped persuade some historians that the societies were public pressure groups and not incipient political parties. In fact, the lines between the societies and the Republican interest were extremely blurry, especially in the larger seaboard cities. Intimate contacts existed between prominent Republicans—including, from Pennsylvania, Albert Gallatin and Jefferson's fellow political plotter John Beckley—and local figures with knowledge of the societies' activities (among them the president of the New York society, Gallatin's father-in-law James Nicholson). Societies would sometimes pay tribute to individual Republicans—and, on at least one occasion in Philadelphia, the entire Republican congressional delegation. Some Democratic-Republicans, like the Philadelphians Henry Kammerer and Peter Muhlenberg, had served as elected government officials even before the societies began. According to the *Aurora*, in 1795 all of Philadelphia and New York City's congressional representatives were society members, as were two Philadelphia representatives to the Pennsylvania state assembly. Beginning in 1794, members of the New York City society quietly enlisted to canvass their neighborhoods and solicit votes for Republican candidates.[53]

Republican leaders, meanwhile, without trusting the Democratic-Republican societies enough to embrace them publicly, certainly noticed their political activities and sometimes worked with them, informally and behind the scenes. Madison, who along with Beckley always kept close tabs on local politics, was impressed by the New York and Philadelphia societies' festivities and protests, and with their sub-rosa efforts around election times. "It is said," he wrote warmly to Jefferson late in 1794, concerning a close congressional race in New York City, "that if Edwd. Livingston, as is generally believed, has outvoted Watts, . . . he is indebted for it to the invigorated exertions of the Democratic Society of that place, of which he is himself a member." The techniques of the city democrats to gain and consolidate support were particularly effective. As early as 1794, James Monroe helped initiate through his New York friends a pro-Republican town meeting in Manhattan on foreign affairs, attended chiefly by mechanics. The assembled appointed a committee that prepared resolutions (later endorsed by the city's Democratic Society). A week later, a reconvened town meeting of "on moderate estimate 2000 citizens" approved the committee's resolutions; and a week after that, the Democratic Society sponsored a large pro-Republican, pro-French parade and celebration.[54]

Yet if the Republicans and the societies had similar politics and common members, and if they sometimes worked hand in glove, they were not identical; nor were the societies creatures of the Republican interest. Every society member may have been a Republican, but not every Republican was a society member, or even completely happy with the societies' existence. As their actions during the Genet affair had shown, the clubs could be unruly and take positions that were politically untenable. Their status, as unelected bodies who claimed to speak directly for the people, was disquieting to some Republicans. "[T]he middling class of people about the country . . . generally reprobate Democratic Societies," a self-described plebeian and "old whig of 1775" wrote in a leading New York Republican newspaper. The Republicans would never relinquish to the societies the management of nominations and campaigns. The societies, for their part, had strong partisan interests and ties but operated as independent organizations, believing they were directly expressing the popular will through their activities—assuming a voice of their own that provoked Federalist outrage.[55]

The administration's friends possessed their own lines of political influence to counter the Democratic-Republican clubs. The Society of the Cincinnati, the ex-army officers' group founded in 1783, was widely perceived as a political auxiliary of the Washington administration. During the storm over Citizen Genet, Federalist forces (organized in part by Alexander Hamilton) exploited their close contacts with pro-British merchants and other notables around the country in order to mount local protest meetings and circulate anti-Genet petitions. It was one thing, though, for gentlemen to band together with no official political motives or to encourage their fellow leading citizens, in an ad hoc way, to express their views on public matters. It was quite another, in the Federalists' eyes, for ordinary citizens to organize overtly political clubs, complete with their own constitutions and officers and regular private meetings. The Democratic-Republicans' repudiation of that principle struck Federalists as popular usurpation. The groups were "unlawful," the prominent Federalist Oliver Wolcott Jr. insisted, "as they are formed for the avowed purpose of a general influence and control upon the measures of government."[56]

Reasoned, elitist constitutional objections like Wolcott's were overwhelmed by the apparent determination of other antisociety critics to prove that they were precisely the supercilious snobs the Democratic-Republican groups accused them of being. William Cobbett, the young, émigré conservative English editor, disparaged the Democratic Society of Pennsylvania as a bunch of "butchers, tinkers, broken hucksters, and trans-Atlantic traitors." One "Acquiline Nimble Chops, Democrat," contributed a mock epic poem, *Democracy*, lambasting society supporters as demagogues who had stirred up the thoughtless multitude of artisans, "the greasy caps." The city democrats reveled in such insults, happy to have provoked their enemies into showing just how hateful they really were.[57]

Outwardly, and somewhat deceptively, the Democratic-Republicans appeared to have effaced the old distinctions between the city and country democracies. The rural societies, along with their urban counterparts, disapproved of Federalist policies, foreign and domestic, and openly criticized pro-administration congressional candidates; they proclaimed the equal rights of man (including their own right to associate); and from time to time, they praised the French Revolution. But the differences between city and country democrats, visible during the Revolution, quietly persisted. The rural societies' public statements lacked the elaborate Enlightenment defenses of mental freedom that were common in the city groups' addresses. Although formally secular, the country democrats occasionally revealed their deep religious attachments. (One Pennsylvania group, the backcountry Republican Society at the Mouth of Yough, took it upon itself "to introduce the Bible and other religious books into their schools.") The rural meetings were also much less regular than the city groups' monthly gatherings, and when they did meet, it was as often to agitate over purely local concerns—protection from Indians, opening the Mississippi to American commerce—as it was to discuss the neutrality proclamation or other national issues.[58]

Above all, the rural societies were less prone to acknowledge (let alone extol) the soundness of the U.S. Constitution and the legitimacy of federal rule, and more prone to turn to direct resistance, including violence, to government authority. "[A] Democracy by representation is the best mode of Government, which the wisdom of man hath devised," was as far as the Democratic Society of Kentucky would go in endorsing the new federal system. "[P]atriotism, like every other thing, has its bounds," one circular from west of the Alleghenies remarked; loyalties "to government cease to be natural, when they cease to be mutual." In

Pennsylvania, the Republican Society at the Mouth of Yough paid lip service to the authority of the state of Pennsylvania and the United States, but also tried to claim exclusive authority over four counties.[59]

The differences between the seaboard cities and rural districts to the west accompanied another separate set of sectional divisions, between northern and southern democrats over slavery. The northern societies included several outspoken antislavery men, among them James Nicholson and Alexander McKim, the presidents, respectively, of the Democratic Society of the City of New York and the Republican Society of Baltimore. In a defense of the societies, Duane of the Philadelphia *Aurora* charged that President Washington had never truly been a supporter of America's revolutionary ideals, as "twenty years after the establishment of the Republic" he was still "possessed of FIVE HUNDRED of the HUMAN SPECIES IN SLAVERY." Conservative propagandists attempted, in word and in picture, to portray the societies as friendly to blacks as well as hostile to slavery, noting at one point that their French ally Genet was a member of the antislavery Société des Amis des Noirs in Paris. But antislavery views were decidedly inconspicuous among Democratic-Republican planters and farmers in Virginia and states southward. Some of the more mainstream heroes of the societies, above all Jefferson, were as vulnerable, if not more, to criticism over slavery as Washington was, and some society leaders—Alexander Smith in Virginia, John C. Breckinridge in Kentucky, among others—were strongly proslavery. As a consequence, Duane notwithstanding, even the northern societies refrained from saying much about slavery, preferring to focus on the common Federalist foe (which itself included slaveholders in its ranks and was hardly an antislavery force).[60] The more consequential split within the society movement was between the seaboard and rural societies, as would become obvious by the end of 1794.

THE FEDERALIST COUNTERATTACK

The Whiskey Rebellion of 1794, centered in western Pennsylvania, came to exemplify the refractory post-Revolutionary country democracy, and it caused the Democratic-Republican societies their first major emergency. In 1791, in a vote that sharply divided eastern urban mercantile districts from the backcountry, Congress approved an excise tax on distilled liquor as part of Secretary Hamilton's fiscal program. Westerners objected on many counts: the tax was inequitable, it was aimed at rural men distant from power; and it revived a particularly obnoxious Old World means of gathering revenue. Whiskey was a barter medium as well as an item for sale in cash-poor regions; taxing it would interfere with the most mundane exchanges between ordinary farmers. As soon as the law went into effect, angry backcountry men tarred and feathered would-be federal tax collectors, and, here and there, they destroyed the houses and barns of neighbors who cooperated with the government. In August 1792, four western Pennsylvania counties organized committees of correspondence, which pledged to use every legal measure "that may *obstruct operation of the* [excise] *Law*, until we are able to obtain its total repeal."[61]

Hamilton reasonably called the Pennsylvanians' pledge self-contradictory, and counseled using military force to enforce collection. In September 1792, the Washington administration issued a warning against noncompliance. After two years of a jittery impasse, however, in which noncompliance became the rule among distillers from Pennsylvania down through Kentucky, President Washington decided to make an example of the Pennsylvanians. In the summer of 1794, a federal marshal rode west with writs ordering sixty nontaxpaying dis-tillers into court in Philadelphia. In response, an armed mob, after beating back federal troops, destroyed the home of the region's federal excise inspector and began planning to seize the federal garrison in Pittsburgh. The Whiskey Rebel-lion had begun.[62]

The eastern urban Democratic-Republicans sympathized with the back-country rebels' cause, but not at all with their tactics. The New York society called upon all the other groups to petition Congress for repeal of the excise, yet also condemned "the too hasty and violent resistance of our brethren in the west of Pennsylvania." In Philadelphia, Bache's *Aurora* denounced both the Washington administration's hard line and the westerners' resort to violence. In western Pennsylvania, however, there were problematic ties between the rebels and the local societies. In Washington County, a group of dissidents founded what they called the Society of United Freemen (better known as the Mingo Creek Society), assumed local electioneering and judicial functions, and operated as an extralegal court of equity for its members. As the tax rebel-lion spread, the Mingo Creek group seemed to be (as one local put it) "the cra-dle of the insurrection." And although it appears that the group was not formally a Democratic-Republican club, at least seven members of the neigh-boring Democratic-Republican Society of the County of Washington (includ-ing its president, James Marshall) later admitted to being deeply involved in the uprising. In the furor that followed, distinctions between one club and another became irrelevant to the forces of order.[63]

Cooler heads persuaded the rebels to abandon their plan against Pittsburgh, but the continuing resistance finally convinced Washington to assemble an army of approximately thirteen thousand state militiamen and volunteers—a combined force roughly as large as the entire Continental Army that defeated the British in the Revolution. With a minimum of violence, the troops restored order. Among the first of the rebels apprehended was old Hermon Husband, now seventy-three and still preaching about the imminence of the New Jerusalem. Albert Gallatin, the leading opposition congressman from western Pennsylvania, called Husband a madman because of his biblical sermons on political reform. In fact, Husband took a moderate position in the whiskey excise affair, counseling the rebels to abjure violence—but he was arrested nevertheless and held in a Philadelphia jail until May 1795, when the charges against him were dropped. (His health ruined, Husband died soon after, traveling the road back to his Pennsylvania farm.) The most radical of the rebels escaped farther inland; westerners promised to obey the law; and the Washington administration turned more conciliatory. The president eventually pardoned the two rebels found guilty of treason.[64]

The political repercussions of the rebellion were nevertheless severe, especially for the Democratic-Republican societies. Even more disturbed by the Pennsylvanians' uprising than by the Washington administration's response, the urban societies (and a few rural ones, in Vermont, New York, and North Carolina) amplified their repudiation of the insurgents. Not only had the rebels violated regular democratic principles; they had given the Federalists both the means to smear all democrats as traitors and the pretext to suppress the Democratic societies. And this was precisely what the Federalists had in mind. "[T]hey may now, I believe, be crushed," Washington's secretary of state Edmund Randolph told the president, barely containing his delight.[65]

In late September 1794, President Washington issued his proclamation that called up the state militias and blamed the disorder on "combinations against the Constitution and laws of the United States" in western Pennsylvania. Two months later, after the Republicans scored some key electoral victories in Federalist congressional districts, Washington, at Hamilton's urging, devoted a large portion of his annual message to Congress to attacking "certain self-created societies" that had "assumed the tone of condemnation." No one doubted that he was referring to the Democratic-Republican clubs. The president's fears were sincere enough. From long experience, he had never trusted the loyalty of the backcountry yeomen. He was perfectly convinced, as he wrote privately, that the societies' agenda was "to sow among the people the seeds of jealousy and distrust of the government by destroying all confidence in the administration of it." Because all the societies, not just those in rebellion, were extraconstitutional, Washington believed, they were a clear threat to public order and republican principles. Left unchecked, they would "shake the government to its foundation."[66]

Given Washington's enormous prestige, his condemnations were heavy blows. They did not, however, knock out the societies. Quite the opposite: Washington's blanket condemnation shifted the onus of overreaction away from the clubs and toward the administration. At least six new Democratic-Republican societies sprang up in smaller towns and rural areas, from New York to South Carolina, during the weeks after Washington's attack. Privately, even political moderates such as the Virginian Garritt Minor averred that the president's constitutional opinions were "improper, erroneous, and subversive of our liberties." Far from cowed, several of the groups blasted back at the claim that they were illegitimate because they were self-created. The class bitterness that permeated the societies exploded, as ordinary citizens faced presidential excoriation for speaking their minds and bringing pressure to bear on government—things any gentleman felt perfectly free to do. "The government is *responsible* to its sovereign the people for the faithful exercise of its entrusted powers," the president of the New York Democratic Society hotly affirmed, "and *any part of the people* have the right to express their opinions on the government." The Philadelphia and New York societies expanded their agendas after Washington's address, the former stepping up its campaign for public school funding, the latter issuing detailed circulars on civil liberties and Americans' rights to free enquiry and association. In Manhattan, pro-administration members of the Tammany Society failed to get the membership formally to endorse Washington's message, whereupon they resigned from the society en masse, leaving Tammany a full-fledged ally of the Republican opposition.[67]

The societies also escaped official censure by the House of Representatives, after a three-day debate that illuminates the uncertain state of American democracy in the mid-1790s. Following Washington's attack, the Senate, dominated by friends of the administration, approved a report that praised the suppression of the Whiskey Rebellion and replicated Washington's formula, singling out "certain self-created societies" that had been "founded in political error." In the House, where opposition forces held a slim majority, administration men went ahead with a censure motion, describing the societies as lethal sores on the body politic. Fisher Ames, in a fiery speech, claimed the societies had "arrogantly pretended sometimes to be the people, and sometimes the guardians, the champions of the people" with "more zeal for a popular Government, and . . . more respect for Republican principles, than the real Representatives are admitted to entertain."[68]

The Republican leadership saw where this was headed. "The game," wrote Representative James Madison (Jefferson had retired the previous year, which left Madison as the chief of the anti-administration forces), "was to connect the Democratic Societies with the odium of insurrection, to connect the Republicans in Congress with those Societies," and to place President Washington "in opposition to both."[69] Wary of attacking Washington directly or endorsing the societies, the House opposition objected to the censure motion on the narrow grounds that there was insufficient evidence linking the societies to the Pennsylvania outrages, and that any such evidence should be assessed by the courts, not by Congress. One Republican congressman, Gabriel Christie of Maryland, did praise the Republican Society of Baltimore by name, as "a band of patriots, not the fair-weather patriots of the present day, but the patriots of seventy five," who, when apprised of the Whiskey Rebellion, "offered their personal services to go and help to crush this commotion in the bud." Madison and a few others also raised serious questions about Washington's denunciation of the societies. Too energetic an effort to correct abuses of the rights of popular expression, Madison told the House, would threaten liberty and freedom of speech and of the press. The beleaguered societies, he insisted, presented no threat—but a congressional censure *would* present such a threat. "It is in vain to say that this indiscriminate censure is no punishment . . . ," Madison declared. "If we advert to the nature of Republican Government, we shall find that the censorial power is in the people over the Government, and not in the Government over the people." Infractions of law by ordinary citizens were punishable through the courts, but "not censurable through the Legislative body."[70]

Madison did little to clarify, let alone defend, the role of extraconstitutional associations as part of the regular business of American politics. As of 1794, the Republican interest remained hazy about the proper mechanisms for democratic politics. But Madison and the Republicans succeeded in removing any mention of the societies from the House's condemnation of the Whiskey Rebellion. Their success emboldened society members and supporters to assert more boldly the groups' legitimacy. "After having set up a government, citizens ought not to resign it into the hands of agents—" the pro-society *Independent Chronicle* of Boston had observed months earlier, "whither does this tend but toward despotism?" In a Paineite vein, the German Republican Society of Philadelphia declared that "associations of some sort are necessary . . . to keep up the equipoise, between the people and the government." Thus encouraged, the remaining societies took up, in 1795, their last great effort: fighting against the Jay Treaty.[71]

As soon as President Washington had announced his appointment in April 1794 of John Jay, chief justice of the Supreme Court, as special envoy to Great Britain—to settle disputes left over from the Revolution, exacerbated by recent British interference with American shipping to France and the French West Indies—the Democratic-Republican clubs protested. Not only (the societies argued) did the appointment of a judicial officer to an executive post violate the constitutional theory of separated powers—Jay himself was so flagrantly pro-British and anti-French, the Pennsylvania Democratic Society charged, that it would be "a sacrifice of the interests and the peace of the United States to commit a negociation to him." These criticisms would seem gentle fourteen months later, when the secret terms of the treaty—signed the previous November and taken up by the Senate, meeting in closed session, in early June 1795—leaked out to the opposition press.[72]

The Democratic-Republicans insisted that the treaty was both pro-British and antidemocratic. That the Senate decided to debate the treaty in secrecy was bad enough. Worse, the treaty's terms amounted to virtually complete capitulation. Jay had failed to secure various items he had been instructed to obtain, including full confirmation of America's neutral shipping rights, the end of the impressments of American sailors into the Royal Navy, and compensation for American slaveholders for slaves seized by the British during the war. Only on the issue of British evacuation of its military posts in the western United States did Jay deliver. The treaty's supporters, above all Alexander Hamilton and his ally Rufus King of Massachusetts, defended the pact as a reaffirmation of American sovereignty that strengthened the nation's commercial relations with its most important trading partner. On the basis of those arguments, the Senate approved the treaty by a 20 to 10 margin, and in mid-August 1795, President Washington signed it. But at every step along the way, public disapproval, stoked by Republican sympathizers, mounted. There were calls to impeach Jay, whose effigy, along with copies of the hated treaty, was burned in several towns and cities. In New York, according to Hamilton, "the leaders of the clubs were seen haranging in every corner of the city, to stir up the citizens." When Hamilton and his friends tried to take over a huge antitreaty public meeting, and Hamilton declared that the people had full confidence in the wisdom of the president, oppositionists drove them away with coarse catcalls. (Allegedly, one angry Republican threw a rock that hit Hamilton in the head; in the heated arguments that followed, Hamilton challenged Democratic Society leader James Nicholson to a duel, later averted.) Some critics even demanded Washington's removal from office.[73]

The Democratic-Republican societies pitched in with their own protests, but in a telling sectional pattern. In the northern seaport cities, the treaty's paltry concessions on neutral trading rights, along with the methods by which it was debated and approved, was cause for the utmost alarm—and for praising the resistant congressional Republicans. The southern societies, urban and rural, objected even more loudly, with the additional complaint (absent up North) that, in the words of one South Carolina society, Britain's refusal to compensate "the value of the Negroes and other property carried away" was reason enough to scuttle the agreement.[74]

In sharp contrast, the northern rural and backcountry groups said almost nothing. Many, perhaps most, of these groups, particularly in western Pennsylvania, had fallen by the wayside after the Whiskey Rebellion. But for those that survived, from Vermont through rural New York State, the eventual recovery of the western posts, the granting of commercial concessions to Americans trading with Lower and Upper Canada, and the fear of war should the treaty be rejected greatly softened any hostility. In all, the country democracy split over the Jay Treaty, as the southerners (galvanized by the slavery issue) joined forces with the city democracy in opposition, while northern country democrats backed off.[75]

Washington's signing of the Jay Treaty would have appeared to settle the issue, but the Republican interest, its numbers enlarged in the newly elected Fourth Congress, made a last-ditch effort to block the appropriations necessary to implement it. A minor constitutional crisis arose when President Washington dragged his feet in sending the official treaty papers to the House. Pro-treaty forces then organized their own petition campaign, which drowned out the opposition efforts. Finally, the House vote on treaty appropriations ended in a 49–49 tie that would have to be decided by the Speaker of the House, Frederick Muhlenberg. Ordinarily, Muhlenberg, a convert to the opposition and brother of Peter Muhlenberg, who had helped found the very first Democratic-Republican society, could have been counted on to kill the appropriations. But pro-treaty men exerted enormous pressure on him, including (according to family tradition) a threat from his son's prospective father-in-law, a stalwart Federalist, that "[i]f you do not give us your vote, your son shall not have my Polly." Muhlenberg hesitated, then voted in favor of the appropriations, handing the Washington administration a crucial victory.[76]

Once again, the combined efforts of the executive and the Senate had thwarted the congressional opposition and the Democratic-Republican societies. The first target of the opposition's frustration was Frederick Muhlenberg. Five days after casting his tie-breaking vote, Muhlenberg was accosted by his own brother-in-law, Bernard Schaefer, an all-too-rabid Republican, who called him a rank deserter and stabbed him. Poor Muhlenberg more or less recovered physically, but he was dead politically, failing to stand in 1796 for his House seat.[77] Yet by the time he left the Congress, the greatest victim of the debates over the Jay Treaty was neither himself nor any of the congressional Republicans, but the Democratic-Republican societies.

THE FALL AND LEGACY OF
THE SELF-CREATED SOCIETIES

Five months after President Washington signed the Jay Treaty, a conservative Connecticut newspaper mordantly rejoiced that the Pennsylvania Democratic Society had dissolved: "the various germs which have sprouted from that root of anarchy, will wither and die." The prediction was generally true. The Democratic Society of New York lasted for another three years, while reports of sporadic activities by other local groups (including the formation of new ones) appeared as late as 1800. But the losing fight against the Jay Treaty was the last gasp of the Democratic-Republican societies as a force in American politics. Eight months after the Philadelphia group disbanded, the semiofficial administration newspaper, the *Gazette of the United States*, happily noted that "the Demo societies are dead," and the opposition and the surviving societies did not attempt to deny it.[78]

There had been a great deal of determined activity, but in strictly political terms, the groups had failed. All of their major protest campaigns had been fruitless. Neither they nor their congressional friends could make much of a dent against an energetic executive—the great Revolutionary War hero—backed by a strong majority in the Senate. Sectional strains among the self-declared democrats, particularly those between the seaboard societies and the rural societies, showed with costly results during the Whiskey Rebellion and the fight over the Jay Treaty. Although the societies did escape congressional censure, the Republicans' arguments on their behalf still fell short of vindicating their right to exist.

Yet conventional standards are seldom the best for judging the effects of fledgling political movements. By reviving and updating the country and the city democracies in the idiom of post-Revolutionary politics, the Democratic-Republican societies had expanded the debates about politics and democracy in America. They had challenged assumptions about deference to political leadership that prevailed among many Republican leaders as well as among the Federalists. The intellectual and emotional core of the societies' case was wonderfully presented early in 1794 by an Irish-born Vermont editor, Matthew Lyon, an army veteran who would go on to a legendary career as an irrepressible Republican politician and manufacturing entrepreneur:

> These . . . Democratic societies . . . are laughed at and ridiculed by men who consider the science of government to belong naturally only to a few families, and argue, that their families ought to be obeyed & supported in princely grandure; that the common people ought to give half their earnings to these few, for keeping them under, and awing the poor commonality from destroying one another, which their savage nature would lead to, were it not for the benignity and good sense of the few superiors Heaven has been pleased to plant among them.

A privileged few had taken it upon themselves to serve as the nation's leaders; these men used their privileges to sustain themselves in grandeur at the expense of "the poor commonality"; and they subdued the rest of the people with pretension, ridicule, and false noblesse as well as with political force. By puncturing that pretension and defying the ridicule and noblesse, the societies showed that the science of government fell well within the comprehension of ordinary citizens. And they called the only proper republican system, one which respected and unleashed that comprehension, "democracy." A New York City society member wrote that "the words Republican and Democratic are synonymous." A Massachusetts writer proclaimed that "he that is not a Democrat is an aristocrat or a monocrat."[79]

To conservative and even moderate upholders of Washington and Hamilton, such claims sounded heretical or even traitorous, as if some of the people had forgotten their proper passive and obedient place between elections. In New York, the pro-administration members of the Tammany Society, before their walkout, hastily passed a resolution in January 1795 insisting that public political associations, though "excellent as revolutionary means, when a government is to be overthrown," created "phrenzy" that had no place in the free and happy United States. To Hamilton's friend Nathaniel Chipman, the societies and their "dictators" threatened political order and responsible representation with "all precipitation, all the heat and ungovernable passions of a simple democracy."[80]

The Republican interest understood the societies' motivations far better than the administration did, and considered President Washington's cold attempt to crush them as, in Madison's words, "perhaps the greatest error of his political life."[81] Still, by mid-decade, opposition leaders were unsure what role, if any, the rude democracy might play in their own political efforts and in the life of the nation. The Democratic-Republican societies left behind a changed political landscape, but their brief history had failed to resolve some crucial questions. How could a popular majority redress its grievances under the prevailing theories of separated and divided powers and of federal checks and balances? Was a majority in the House of Representatives sufficient to carry that electoral majority's wishes, or might new institutions be necessary? The Democratic-Republicans' solution to the last problem—forming political organizations outside the government—had come to naught. And in 1796—the year of the nation's first contested presidential election—American democracy, city and country, seemed more than ever on the defensive, whereas Federalist-style deference seemed regnant and vindicated.

Those circumstances would change utterly over the next four years, as the political crisis of the fragile new order worsened, nearly to the verge of civil war. They changed chiefly because too many Federalists learned too little about what a growing number of citizens now believed were their essential democratic prerogatives. But they also changed because opposition organizers—mainly in the middle Atlantic states, and in service to the Republican slaveholders of Virginia—learned some lessons from the "self-created" democracy and joined forces with what was left of it. Thus expanded, the Republican opposition would fight to validate the proposition framed by James Madison during the House debate over the societies—that in a republic, "the censorial power is in the people over the Government, and not in the Government over the people."

3

THE MAKING OF
JEFFERSONIAN DEMOCRACY

O n the last day of 1793, as the Democratic-Republican societies were trying to recover from their entanglement with Citizen Genet, Secretary
of State Thomas Jefferson resigned his post, retired from politics, and
returned to his epicurean estate-in-eternal progress, Monticello. Sick of the
polemical fray (which he had never enjoyed), Jefferson retreated to his books,
gadgets, French wines, and slaves, expecting to clear up some heavy financial
debts, shake a nagging case of rheumatism, and finish his house, all in splendid
ignorance—"the softest pillow" he called it, quoting Montaigne—of politics. At
age fifty, a widower for eleven years, Jefferson had spent most of his adult life at
the center of great public events, and he had already earned historical immor-
tality as the author of America's Declaration of Independence. Now hopeful
that the citizenry would confound the political heresies of Alexander Hamilton,
he handed the reins of opposition over to James Madison and Madison's congressional allies, and slipped away to his and Madison's native rural Virginia—
relieved, he said, that "the length of my tether is now fixed for life from
Monticello to Richmond."[1]

After an uneventful winter, perturbing news and irritating Federalist criticism
began to reach him through the mails and the Virginia newspapers. In April,
word arrived of John Jay's impending mission to Britain—an announcement
made only slightly less offensive to Jefferson by reports of Hamilton's mortification at not getting the assignment. Over the late summer and autumn, Jefferson
came to share Madison's view that Hamilton was shamefully seizing on the
Whiskey Rebellion to advance his personal political fortunes and disgrace the
Republican interest. President Washington's denunciation of the Democratic-

Republican societies was, he wrote to Madison, "one of the extraordinary acts of boldness of which we have seen so many from the faction of Monocrats." At Hamilton's instigation, the Revolution's greatest man had "permitted himself to be the organ of . . . an attack on the freedom of discussion, the freedom of writing, printing, and publishing."[2]

In 1795, when the controversy over the Jay Treaty escalated, Jefferson, although avowedly still on the sidelines, could not help weighing in with old friends. He approved of the popular protests against the treaty, including a public meeting in his own Piedmont county of Albemarle. After those protests failed, he wrote an indignant letter to his Florentine associate from Revolutionary days, Philip Mazzei, which would eventually come back to haunt him. An "Anglican, monarchical, and aristocratical party," he told Mazzei, had seized the federal government, along with certain unnamed apostates, "men who were Samsons in the field and Solomons in the council, but who have had their heads shorn by the harlot England"—a slanderous reference, Jefferson's enemies would later charge, to the incorruptible Washington.[3]

At the close of the summer of 1796, Washington publicly confirmed what had been long been suspected: he would not seek another term. He thus turned the upcoming election into the first contested race for the presidency. Opposition leaders, consulting loosely as a congressional caucus of the Republican interest, decided that Jefferson would be their strongest candidate against the president's heir presumptive, Vice President John Adams. The remnants of the Democratic-Republican societies decided the same thing. "It requires no talent at divination to decide who will be candidates for the chair," the Philadelphia *Aurora General Advertiser* declared in mid-September, a week before Washington's announcement:

> THOMAS JEFFERSON & JOHN ADAMS will be the men, & whether we shall have at the head of our executive a steadfast friend to the Rights of the People, or an advocate for hereditary power and distinctions, the people of the United States are soon to decide.

Jefferson, gripped by a mixture of restiveness and fatalism, acquiesced in his own candidacy, and came within three Electoral College votes of defeating Adams after a bruising campaign. And so, under the existing constitutional rules, Jefferson was named the nation's new vice president. In February 1797, he departed Monticello to take up his duties in Philadelphia, leaving his debts unresolved and the new walls to his house unbuilt.[4]

The elections of 1796 sent a confusing message. Despite Washington's anointing of Adams, the Republican interest ran strong in the South, controlling Virginia, the largest and most powerful state, and winning a large majority in the

Georgia legislature. Republican tickets also carried Philadelphia (previously a Federalist stronghold) and ran better than expected in New York City. Pennsylvania broke narrowly for Jefferson, and had Adams not picked up two isolated electoral votes in Virginia and North Carolina, he would have lost the election.[5]

The Pennsylvania race was especially important for the Republicans, who merged their election machinery with what was left of the most imposing of the failed Democratic-Republican societies, and turned the politics of protest over the Jay Treaty into a presidential campaign. With the resourceful Republican operative, House clerk John Beckley, overseeing matters, veterans of the Democratic Society of Pennsylvania—most auspiciously Benjamin Bache, Michael Leib (who had been elected to the state assembly in 1794), and a Philadelphia hatter and friend of Beckley's, Major John Smith—geared up a sophisticated statewide campaign. Handbills with the names of the Republican electors appeared in every district. A campaign staff produced fifty thousand Republican ballots (written out by hand, as the election laws demanded) and delivered them to local partisans a week before the election. Major Smith and others crisscrossed the state, holding public meetings and arousing the voters wherever they found them gathered. Torrents of campaign broadsides poured from the presses of Philadelphia, many of them appealing directly to the artisans and small tradesmen who had been the Democratic Society's membership base, urging them to decide "whether the Republican JEFFERSON, or the Royalist ADAMS, shall be President of the United States." The statewide results were more than encouraging: a 25 percent turnout of eligible voters and a narrow Republican majority, strong enough to give Jefferson fourteen of Pennsylvania's fifteen electoral votes. But the results in Philadelphia, where the former society leaders had concentrated their efforts, were staggering: more than two in five eligible Philadelphians showed up at the polls and handed the Republican slate more than 60 percent of the vote—a landslide in what been a solidly Federalist city.[6]

The top-down opposition politics of the Jeffersonians had linked up with the bottom-up politics of the Democratic-Republican societies. The Republicans remained very much in charge, with the humbly born, hard-nosed Beckley serving as their overseer and go-between. Still, Beckley, Leib, Bache, Smith, and their friends—political professionals of indifferent backgrounds—brought a more democratic style and substance into what was fast becoming an enlarged Republican coalition that stretched into the middle Atlantic states. (Similar efforts in New York City raised hopes that it too might soon move to the Republican column.) The Federalists, meanwhile, had new problems to contend with. Accusations about a plot supposedly hatched by Alexander Hamilton to maneuver Thomas Pinckney of South Carolina into the presidency instead of John Adams—high-level intrigue of a more customary sort—dominated the last-minute electoral jockeying and further clouded the results. Nationwide, though, the Federalists were the winners, retaining the presidency and gaining what in time became a solid majority in the House of Representatives to go along with their majority in the Senate. They also won substantial legislative majorities in New York and Massachusetts.[7]

Early in 1797, some observers interpreted the closeness of the presidential election as a portent of an amiable Adams administration, reinforced by what the incoming president called his "ancient friendship" with Jefferson. Hamilton was, for the moment, out of the picture—he had retired to his New York City law practice in 1795. Jefferson, who saw Adams as the only sure barrier against Hamilton among the Federalists, was relieved at the outcome, and graciously professed that neither his second-place finish nor the prospect of serving under Adams had injured his pride. ("I am his junior in life," he told Madison, "was his junior in Congress, his junior in the diplomatic line, his junior lately in our civil government.") The vice presidency might even be preferable given the conflicts that surely lay ahead. "This is certainly not a moment to covet the helm," Jefferson wrote Edward Rutledge late in December. Jefferson did have pestering doubts about what he thought of as Adams's English bias in government, made worse when Adams decided to retain every member of Washington's cabinet, including Treasury Secretary Oliver Wolcott Jr., Secretary of State Timothy Pickering, and Secretary of War James McHenry—all close political friends and followers of Hamilton's. Nevertheless Jefferson remained confident that the great mass of the citizenry was Republican, and hopeful that Adams could be persuaded to oversee the government "on it's true principles."[8]

All the upbeat auguries proved utterly wrong. The nation was entering a new and more dangerous phase of its political crisis; 1796 would prove the Federalists' last great political hurrah; and consolidated forms of democratic protest and politics would emerge under Jefferson's and Madison's leadership. The breakdown of comity, and the Republicans' eventual success, was in large measure due to Hamilton's headstrong persistence, Adams's sometimes muddled patriotic stubbornness, and Jefferson's great good fortune. More broadly, it was caused by the Federalists' incapacity to square their politics with the democratic ideas unleashed in the 1790s.

JOHN ADAMS AND THE REIGN OF WITCHES

The striver John Adams was as unlikely an aristocrat as any leading official in the early federal executive branch, despite what his opponents charged. Raised twelve miles south of Boston, the son of a pious middling farmer who made shoes part-time, Adams had hoped to become a farmer himself. His father, however, wanted him to become a minister, paid for the proper preparatory schooling, and sent him to Harvard. There, Adams became a tireless bookworm, but his interests ran to the law, not religion, and three years after graduating from college, he was admitted to the Suffolk County bar. A patriot from the very beginning of the imperial crisis, he was selected as one of Massachusetts's delegates to the First Continental Congress in 1774. Thereafter, he served his state and his country with impressive diligence in a variety of important civilian posts at home and abroad (including, from 1785 to 1788, a stint as the first American minister to Great Britain).[9]

Garrulous, pudgy, short, and prone to anxious, self-absorbed outbursts, Adams climbed to the top chiefly because he exercised his lawyerly skills with undivided assiduity and ambition. He admitted that he was "but an ordinary man" and "not like the Lion."[10] Yet Adams, apart from fulfilling his public duties, also wrote several formal treatises on political theory, which (although inferior to Madison's writings in originality, Jefferson's in style, and Hamilton's in both) amounted to the only extended effort by any Founding Father to formulate a comprehensive science of politics.

Adams's political philosophy is difficult to pin down. For the most part, he stated conventional republican themes in conventional terms—the need to control passion through selfless virtue, for example, and to keep political power from becoming concentrated in any individual or in any branch of the government. Like Madison and other Framers, he did not flinch at what he saw as society's natural hierarchies and at the special influence exercised by what he called America's aristocracy—an aristocracy, he duly noted, founded not simply on birth and marriage, but on education, wealth, and merit as well (and that therefore included him). With his rage for political equilibrium, however, Adams never quite grasped that under the Constitution, a new theory of popular sovereignty had replaced the traditional ideal of balancing the different social orders. After 1788, Madison, who understood the new regime perfectly, could see that the few instead of the many had become the chief threat to the American republican experiment. Adams moved in the opposite direction, pronouncing in his ponderous *Discourses on Davila* in 1790 that the genius of America lay in its mixed government, which checked *"the legislation of confusion"* by upholding decency, honesty, and order against an unstable democracy. After American independence, Adams's social views took a sharper elitist turn, away from the idea that merit was randomly distributed among all classes and toward his claim, in 1787, that "gentlemen will ordinarily, nothwithstanding some exceptions to the rule, be the richer, and born of the more noted families." Yet his affection for aristocracy did not, finally, define his political allegiances. While his conservative fears, heightened by the French Revolu-

tion, made him a stalwart Federalist in the early 1790s, his fixation on balanced government and his hatred of partisanship alienated him from other
Federalists after he assumed the presidency.[11]

President Adams's difficulties began less than a month after he took office,
when he learned that France's latest revolutionary government, the Directory,
had refused to receive the newly appointed American minister to Paris, Charles
Cotesworth Pinckney, and had declared that henceforth all American ships carrying British goods would be liable to seizure. Enraged by the Jay Treaty, the
French had been attacking American merchantmen on the high seas for
months. Now the two nations seemed on the brink of war, which Adams wanted
to avoid. Hoping to rise above domestic political divisions and show his good
faith to the French, the president tried to name his trustworthy friend from Massachusetts, the Republican Elbridge Gerry, along with James Madison, as special
commissioners, charged with joining Pinckney in Paris and resolving the crisis.
But cabinet members Wolcott, Pickering, and McHenry insisted that only loyal
Federalists be allowed to represent the United States, and forced Adams to back
down. After one of the substitute Federalist nominees, Francis Dana, declined to
serve for personal reasons, Gerry was eventually reinstated to the commission,
joined by the moderate Virginia Federalist John Marshall. By then, however, the
political haggling had created considerable bad feeling, ending the rapprochement between Adams and Jefferson (who believed he had been frozen out of the
decision-making process despite his contacts in France, and truly feared an
impending war) and emboldening Hamilton's friends.[12]

Once the American commissioners arrived in Paris, the French government,
marinated in corruption and flushed by the recent military successes of its young
general, Napoleon Bonaparte, unintentionally gave Adams and the Federalists a
huge political gift. After granting the three envoys a pro forma fifteen-minute
audience, the French foreign minister, Talleyrand, handed them over to some
French agents, who, during the ensuing days, demanded under-the-table bribes
and an official American subsidy to France as preconditions for any further talks.
The negotiations got nowhere (although the Republican Gerry lingered in
Paris, trying to string them along, to the great displeasure of his Federalist colleagues). Finally, in the spring of 1798, Adams released to Congress the diplomatic dispatches describing what had occurred, referring to the would-be
bribers as "X," "Y," and "Z." War fever, combined with Federalist righteousness,
quickly overwhelmed all but the most staunchly Republican parts of the country. The people, it seemed, were far more friendly to Federalist rule than the old
Democratic-Republican clubs had imagined, at least when the nation's honor
was at stake. The diminutive, anxious Adams suddenly became, for the only
time in his life, the focus of popular enthusiasm as the heroic American
commander-in-chief.[13]

Temporarily catching the delirium himself, Adams took to delivering militant speeches, and appeared in public in military regalia, a sword strapped to his side. He also gained authorization from Congress to build up the navy, establish a new cabinet-level department of the navy, and enlarge the regular army with the addition of what came to be called the Provisional Army. Adams stopped just short of asking for a formal declaration of war against France, but a "quasi-war" ensued on the high seas. Congressional Federalists, meanwhile, were eager to give the president even more than he had requested and passed four additional measures to help create what Hamilton, in a letter to Rufus King, called *"national unanimity"*—that is, to crush domestic political dissent that they believed was out to destroy the government. Long concerned about the growing numbers of immigrants to America since the Revolution—the vast majority of whom supported the Republicans—the Federalists narrowly pushed through Congress three anti-alien bills that toughened naturalization requirements, established a registry and surveillance system for foreign nationals, and empowered the president to deport summarily any alien he deemed a threat to the nation's security. Even more ominously for the Republicans, Congress passed a loosely worded sedition bill that outlawed a wide range of statements, written and unwritten, including any that could be construed as bringing either the president or the Congress (but, pointedly, not the vice president) "into contempt or disrepute"—and made them punishable by up to five years' imprisonment and five thousand dollars in fines.[14]

Some Republican leaders, including James Monroe, thought the Federalist onslaught was suicidal, and they counseled their colleagues to lie low. Vice President Jefferson also tried to keep his friends and allies calm. "[A] little patience," he wrote to John Taylor, "and we shall see the reign of witches pass over, their spells dissolve, and the people recovering their true sight, restore their government to it's true *principles*." Jefferson was less sanguine than he sounded. He had become a pariah inside the administration, having suffered through the publication the previous year of what he thought was the private letter of 1796 to Philip Mazzei about the former Samsons and Solomons who were now monarchists. He had no doubts that the Federalists' new laws shredded the Constitution and the Bill of Rights, and that their purpose was the "suppression of the whig presses." With the Federalists firmly in control of all three branches of the federal government, and with a vastly enlarged army soon to be placed at the federal government's disposal, the possibility loomed that they could wipe out the opposition with prison terms and bayonets before the next presidential election, which still lay two years ahead. Jefferson did propose one democratic remedy, the popular election of federal juries, to restrain the Federalist juggernaut, but the proposal got nowhere. Thereafter, he and his lieutenants turned to the alternative line of defense that Taylor had discussed years earlier and had arisen at earlier moments of crisis—interposing the state governments against oppressive federal laws.[15]

Proposing that the states could help negate the alien and sedition acts was a desperate move, undertaken during what the Republican leaders and rank and file reasonably considered a political emergency. (Even as Jefferson and Madison were writing what would become known as the Kentucky and Virginia Resolutions, local Republican newspapers and meetings were calling for Congress to repeal the new laws.) It was also, at least in Jefferson's unrevised formulations, a constitutionally dangerous step that proved politically ineffective. Jefferson secretly drafted an initial set of resolutions at Monticello sometime in the late summer or early autumn of 1798, with the idea that some friendly state legislature would adopt them as its own. In October, at the suggestion of his Virginia ally and confidante, Wilson Cary Nicholas, he agreed to allow John Breckinridge—a former resident of Albemarle County and, more recently, president of the Lexington branch of the Kentucky Democratic Society—to arrange for the Kentucky legislature to act on the resolutions, while pledging silence about the vice president's role in the matter. On November 13, the Kentucky legislators, with little discussion and in almost unanimous votes, passed the resolutions as Breckinridge presented them, with Jefferson's most controversial claims about state rights removed, and three days later, Governor James Garrard gave his approval. One month later, after a lengthy debate, the Virginia legislature passed a milder set of resolutions that Madison had drafted. Jefferson, with the help of John Taylor, tried to revise Madison's moderate statement, but the legislature rejected his new language and approved Madison's original.[16]

The resolutions argued that the alien and sedition acts exceeded the federal government's delegated authorities, revisiting the ground laid out by Jefferson and Madison seven years earlier during the debate over Hamilton's bank. The resolutions also returned to past precedents in which state legislatures had questioned the constitutionality of federal laws, notably an official challenge by Pennsylvania's lawmakers to the excise law in 1791 and Virginia's resolutions against Hamilton's assumption policies and the Jay Treaty. What was new—and, particularly in Jefferson's presentations, unsafe—concerned the state legislatures' powers to decide for themselves when specific federal laws were usurpations of authority. Since the Supreme Court's power of judicial review had not yet been firmly established, there was certainly room for argument about how the sovereign people could challenge the constitutionality of federal laws, and by what procedures. But Jefferson's belief, stated in his draft of the Kentucky Resolutions, that "nullification" was the rightful remedy for unconstitutional laws, and that the members of an individual state legislature could unilaterally declare such laws "void, and of no effect" within its borders, undercut the Constitution and would have neutered the federal government. Jefferson's own thinking on the matter fluctuated. But his draft resolutions had alarming implications, especially in their ambiguity about whether the Constitution was a compact of the several state governments or, in line with the Framers' thinking, a national compact formed outside the state governments.[17]

The final texts of both the Kentucky and Virginia Resolutions avoided these pitfalls, thanks to Breckinridge's and Madison's interventions. Yet even the more temperate versions failed to gain support from the other state legislatures. Several states followed Maryland's House of Delegates in rejecting the idea that any state government could, by legislative action, even claim that a federal law was unconstitutional, and suggested that any effort to do so was treasonous. A few northern states, including Massachusetts, denied the powers claimed by Kentucky and Virginia and insisted that the Sedition Law was perfectly constitutional, as it banned not truth but "licentiousness, in speaking and writing, that is only employed in propagating falsehood and slander." Ten state legislatures with heavy Federalist majorities from around the country censured Kentucky and Virginia for usurping powers that supposedly belonged to the federal judiciary. Northern Republicans supported the resolutions' objections to the alien and sedition acts, but opposed the idea of state review of federal laws. Southern Republicans outside Virginia and Kentucky were eloquently silent about the matter, and no southern legislature heeded the call to battle.[18]

A more potent counterattack came from city and country democratic editors once the Federalists, fiercely but also clumsily, began putting the Sedition Law into effect. Jefferson had correctly predicted that Bache's *Aurora* would be one of the Federalists' primary targets. Bache was indicted for seditious libel under the common law, weeks before the Sedition Law indictments began, but died in early September 1798, a victim of the latest outbreak of yellow fever in Philadelphia. Other prominent figures formerly tied to the Democratic-Republicans— including Thomas Adams, the editor of Boston's *Independent Chronicle,* and the spirited Matthew Lyon of Vermont (who, as a newly elected congressman, had enhanced his notoriety in the House by spitting in the face of a Federalist colleague who insulted him)—were also rounded up. Philip Freneau escaped indictment only because he was temporarily out of an editorship, but the Irish-born John Daly Burk, one of his successors as editor of the New York *Time-Piece* (which Freneau had founded after the *National Gazette* folded), was tried on a common-law indictment. Also on the prosecutors' lists were Freneau's close collaborator, David Frothingham of the *New York Argus,* and Lyon's loudest defender, Anthony Haswell of the *Vermont Gazette* in Bennington. Other victims included James Callender and Thomas Cooper, a pair of radical British émigrés who had become prominent in America after 1796. But the main objects of attack were well-known city and country democrats who, since mid-decade, had been outspoken Republican supporters and, in some cases, strategists and organizers.[19]

By displaying an undeferential defiance instead of panic, the editors registered more effective protests against the new laws than did Jefferson and Madison's controversial resolutions. William Duane, Bache's successor at the *Aurora*, practically begged to be arrested in 1799, when he tried to circulate petitions calling for the repeal of the Alien Friends Law and flatly charged in the *Aurora* that the American government had become the corrupt creature of Great Britain. (Born in upstate New York in 1760, Duane had lived most of his life in Ireland until returning to America in 1796; yet while he considered himself no alien at all, he opposed the law on constitutional grounds.) Duly indicted under the very law he had protested, and freed on bail, Duane published his newspaper while his trial dragged on. Suddenly, as his editor's luck would have it, he surreptitiously obtained an advance copy of a bill, proposed by a Pennsylvania Federalist senator, James Ross, that would have replaced the Electoral College in the next presidential election with a thirteen-member committee, consisting of the chief justice of the Supreme Court, Federalist Oliver Ellsworth, plus six members from each (Federalist-dominated) house of Congress. Duane allowed the bill's unauthorized publication in the *Aurora*, thereby publicizing a Federalist plot to steal the election, and brought down the wrath of the Senate, which had him indicted under the Sedition Law. At this point, Duane decided that discretion was the better part of valor and went into hiding until Congress adjourned. He had more than made his point about the vengefulness and high-handed chicanery of his Federalist foes.[20]

Elsewhere, as well, the Federalist repression backfired. In upstate Otsego County, New York, Jedediah Peck, a surveyor, farmer, and Baptist minister, had begun his political life as a loyal member of William Cooper's locally dominant Federalist connection, but set himself apart, oddly, as a populist, antilawyer (and antislavery) country democrat. Elected as a Federalist to the state legislature in 1798, Peck's objections to the Sedition Law led to a final break with his party and, in 1799, earned him an indictment for circulating supposedly seditious petitions. Yet instead of public censure, Peck gained instant celebrity as a political hero, thronged by supporters as he traveled down the Hudson Valley to his trial in Manhattan. Across the border in Vermont, Matthew Lyon, the first man indicted and convicted under the Sedition Law, had already made a mockery of his accusers, blasting the law and its makers from his jail cell and winning reelection to Congress by a healthy margin in 1798. Friends paid off Lyon's one-thousand-dollar fine, and he too enjoyed an elaborate victory procession, all the way from the jail in Vergennes near Lake Champlain to the House of Representatives in Philadelphia.[21]

There were additional embarrassments for the Federalists, none more comical than the prosecution of one Luther Baldwin, a Newark, New Jersey, toper who was sent to federal prison for having told a tavern-keeper that he would not

care if President Adams were to get shot "thro' his arse." In Dedham, Massachusetts, the trial of David Brown, occasioned by the raising of a Republican liberty
pole, suggested that even in strongly pro-Federalist New England, there was
growing restiveness at the Federalists' regime.[22] The Federalists, while throwing a
scare into the Virginia Republican gentry, had aroused the anger and the
resourcefulness of the Republicans' potential political base, from New England
down through Virginia—and in doing so, helped redirect the public's fury away
from France and toward the Adams administration.

In 1799 and 1800, that fury, later celebrated by Jeffersonian loyalists as "the
Spirit of '98," would help crack open the fissures among the Federalists that the
war frenzy had hidden. It would also contribute greatly to the national political
might of the resurgent Republican opposition. Yet it would be shortsighted to
interpret these events as marking the inexorable rise of a new Jeffersonian
democracy. There was nothing inexorable about the political tendencies of these
years, as the strange presidential election of 1800 would prove. And, despite the
Republicans' growing unity of purpose, there were important hidden fissures
inside their ranks as well, closely connected to issues born of democracy, race,
and slavery. All but invisible in national debates, these divisions had cropped up
in state constitutional struggles of the 1790s.

Over the dozen years after the Federal Constitutional Convention in
Philadelphia, several states either passed legislation or made adjustments to their
own constitutions on important matters ranging from emancipation to voting. In
New York, antislavery efforts, led by the Republicans Erastus Root and Aaron
Burr as well as by the Federalist John Jay, finally won a state gradual emancipation law in 1799 that would see the institution's end in the late 1820s. (New Jersey was more recalcitrant, and would not enact its own gradual abolition law
until 1804.) Regarding suffrage, representation, and related matters, the most
dramatic change came in Pennsylvania with the fall, in 1790, of the democratic
constitution of 1776. Elsewhere, especially in the North, the trend was toward
more incremental changes that expanded popular control of government, at
both the state and the local level. In 1788, for example, New York finally authorized the use of written ballots for the election of most state officials, and made
polling places more accessible by establishing the township as the basis for elections. New Jersey enacted similar reforms in the same year.[23]

In some states, notably Pennsylvania and New York, groups perceived as
among the more democratic forces in state matters also were allied with the
Republican opposition—battling, as one rural democrat argued, the "prevalent
idea, that representation is a representation of property and not of the people:—
an idea the legitimate offspring of feudal despotism." But the link between
Republicanism and democratic reform was far cloudier in the slaveholding

states. In heavily Federalist South Carolina, for example, Republican reformers gained a widened suffrage and moved the capital from Charleston to Columbia to make it more accessible to backcountry representatives—but the legislature also sharply increased property requirements for state officeholders. In Maryland, Federalists and Jeffersonians allied and successfully resisted calls for suffrage reform—while the reformers, also including Federalists and Jeffersonians, began picking up ground only when they explicitly restricted the franchise to white men. In Kentucky, rival factions of Jeffersonians—one concentrated in the yeoman-dominated Green River district, the other a so-called Aristocratic planter faction—battled hard over democratic reforms. The more conservative forces prevailed in part out of fear that the reformers aimed to undermine slavery. (Among the more eloquent of the reformers was an idealistic, twenty-year-old Lexington lawyer, freshly arrived from Virginia, named Henry Clay, who, writing under the pseudonym "Scaevola," proposed a new state constitution that provided for gradual emancipation.)[24]

The outcome of the state reform politics of the 1790s contained important hints and portents about the emerging Republican opposition, especially concerning democracy, slavery, and the links between the two. The resulting tensions—between northern and southern Republicans, as well as among southern Republicans—would persist and affect the course of democratic development for decades. They would have a more immediate impact in 1800 when a group of bondsmen living in and around Richmond, Virginia, heard antislavery messages in the gentry Republicans' and city democrats' egalitarian pronouncements and plotted a rebellion that proved a factor in the presidential election.

Little of this was evident, however, in 1799, amid the continuing Federalist repression. Sedition charges, and not slavery or the suffrage, galvanized political debates. Although they stirred only opposition with their Kentucky and Virginia Resolutions, Jefferson, Madison, and the rest of the Republican gentry remained hopeful that the crisis would pass and that responsible, truly republican leaders would reclaim the country. But the Federalists believed just as strongly that the future belonged to them.

"THE 'RALLYING POINT'"

Conservative Federalists, led semiclandestinely by Alexander Hamilton, were unfazed—indeed, they were emboldened—by public reactions to Congress's war measures. Hamilton had suffered through personal disgrace in 1797 when John Beckley leaked to the scandalmonger-journalist James Callender the long suppressed news about the Maria Reynolds affair. (Hamilton publicly confessed and salvaged his honor, but the exposé virtually destroyed any future chance of his winning high elective office.) Larger political developments, in the conservative Federalists' eyes, appeared to be moving in their favor. In addition to the alien and sedition acts, Congress had approved the first direct federal tax on dwellings, land, and slaves to pay for military preparations against France. The failed Kentucky and Virginia Resolutions provoked persistent and credible rumors that the Virginia legislature had begun stockpiling arms against an attack by the national government. In the off-year congressional elections held between April 1798 and March 1799, Federalist candidates fared extremely well, especially in the South (where criticism of the Resolutions was severe), and won a commanding 60 to 46 majority in the House to go along with its large majority in the Senate. Early in 1799, a brief uprising in the heavily German areas of Bucks and Northampton Counties in eastern Pennsylvania—led by a local cooper and Revolutionary militia captain named John Fries, and directed chiefly against federal land-tax assessors—reanimated the specters of Daniel Shays and Hermon Husband. It all seemed to confirm the Federalist view that the Republican opposition had become a reckless enemy of the United States—intent, one Virginian wrote to Hamilton, on gaining "[n]othing short of DISUNION, and the heads of JOHN ADAMS and ALEXANDER HAMILTON; & some others perhaps." Hamilton—who through pressure from his allies in the cabinet and ex-President Washington was named inspector general of the Provisional Army, second in command to Washington himself—would see to it that law and order prevailed, in part by screening the names of proposed new army officers in order to guarantee their political reliability.[25]

President Adams was in a much gloomier mood, genuinely worried over the growing bellicosity and self-confidence of his fellow Federalists (above all Hamilton, whom he had never trusted), and how they might ruin his chances for re-election. He only grudgingly gave way over Hamilton's Provisional Army commission. He grew suspicious of the large fortunes made by military contractors and well-connected speculators, and fretted about the new taxes *"liberally laid on"* that might be more than the people could bear. He stewed, at his family home in Quincy and in Philadelphia, about the widespread fears that Hamilton intended to use the army first to crush legitimate political activities in the South and then to make himself military chieftain of the nation. More a diplomat than a warrior, the president put away his sword and, in the autumn of 1798, began earnestly following up diplomatic hints from Paris, conveyed by Elbridge Gerry and others, that the French were eager to end the quasi-war crisis.[26]

Over the ensuing year, the breach between Adams's and Hamilton's supporters threatened the viability of the newly reenergized Federalist national coalition. In the spring state legislative elections in 1799, held before the full impact

of the Sedition Law prosecutions hit the country, Federalist candidates continued to benefit from the protracted anti-French fervor and actually increased their
majority in the House. Thereafter, however, Adams's decision, originally
announced in February, to reopen negotiations with France, followed by his
decision to withdraw to Quincy for several months, sent Federalist leaders into a
whirl of retribution and behind-the-scenes plotting against both the Republicans
and Adams. Hamilton was especially active, scheming to expand the military
even further, to deploy the army and quell Virginia's supposedly imminent insurrection, and even to amend the Constitution in order to break up the larger states
into smaller units, thereby crippling Virginia's political power. By the opening of
the new year, with the presidential election only months away, Hamilton was
musing in letters to his friends about whether it made more sense for the Federalists to dump Adams and thereby risk a serious schism, or to "annihilate themselves and hazard their cause by continuing to uphold those who suspect or hate
them." Adams, for his part, decided to suspend further enlistments in the Provisional Army, which emboldened congressional moderates, in the spring of 1800,
to kill the new army altogether.[27]

The Republicans united behind Vice President Jefferson — "the 'rallying
point,' the head quarters, the everything" of the opposition, one Virginia Federalist wrote, and the virtually certain candidate for president. Jefferson himself,
although determined to keep out of the public eye, did all that he could
behind the scenes, arranging for the Kentucky and Virginia legislatures to
restate their objections to the alien and sedition acts and encouraging the circulation of friendly pamphlets among individual citizens in the various states.
Jefferson's political friends made even more decisive preparations for the 1800
campaign. Especially in the middle Atlantic states and the upper South,
Republicans learned the organizing lessons of 1796 and began putting them
into practice early in 1800. In Virginia, Maryland, and New Jersey, where there
had been little in the way of a statewide Republican electoral organization,
elaborate local committees and networks of correspondence quickly appeared.
In Pennsylvania, where Republicans were already well organized, county committees took over the jobs of framing local Republican tickets and directing the
campaign in their respective districts. In the teeth of the Sedition Law, Republicans around the country banded together to support local, unabashedly partisan newspapers. And in what proved to be the election's signal state, New York,
a highly sophisticated and effective electioneering operation arose in Manhattan, overseen by the man who had run with Jefferson in 1796 and would run
with him again, Aaron Burr.[28]

Burr was as charming and politically talented as he was proud and personally ambitious. Both his grandfather, the renowned evangelist Jonathan
Edwards, and his father, Aaron Sr. (who succeeded Edwards as president of the

new college at Princeton), died while he was an infant. Raised by relatives, Burr graduated from Princeton with honors at age sixteen, then briefly read law at his brother-in-law Tapping Reeve's prestigious school in Litchfield, Connecticut, until the outbreak of the Revolution in 1775, when he volunteered to fight. After serving with distinction as an officer on the Continental line, he established a law practice in New York City and rose quickly in politics, winning a seat in the New York assembly in 1784, getting appointed state attorney general in 1789, and gaining election by the legislature to the U.S. Senate in 1791. An outsider to New York family politics—and thus intellectually and temperamentally drawn to the Republican opposition—Burr was not a city democrat, let alone an agrarian ideologue, but a well-schooled epicurean and political adventurer whose taste for political intrigue, brilliant women, fine wine, and even finer conversation was outstripped only by his hatred of boredom. He did, however, understand the political possibilities opened by the city democracy.[29]

Not fully trusted by Jefferson and the other Virginia Republicans (who considered him vulgar, if politically useful), Burr was still smarting over his thwarted effort to contest John Adams for the vice presidency in 1792, as well as over the national elections four years later, in which, as Jefferson's running mate, he had finished a humiliating fourth in the Electoral College balloting. (Federalist victories in the 1796 New York legislative elections also cost him his Senate seat.) Falling back on election to the state assembly, he took an interest in antislavery and led the successful effort to pass New York's gradual emancipation law in 1799, only to lose his reelection bid at the height of the quasi-war with France. In 1800, he appears to have had his eye on winning the governor's race a year later, but before that, he worked hard to ensure a Republican victory in the hotly contested New York legislative elections in April. Because they were held months before most other states' legislative races, and because they would decide which side would receive New York's Electoral College votes, the elections were a crucial early test of the presidential field. Normally pro-Federalist New York City, Burr's base of operations, loomed as the key battleground. "[I]f the *city* election of N York is in favor of the Republican ticket, the issue will be republican," an apprehensive Jefferson (briefed by Burr) wrote to Madison in March. Burr's interests and Jefferson's were once again intertwined.[30]

Burr performed his political tasks brilliantly, enlarging on the mass electioneering methods pioneered by city democrats in 1796. Months in advance of the April balloting, he made the rounds among his numerous contacts in Manhattan; he opened his home to provide entertainment, meals, and even sleeping quarters for party workers; and he arranged regular party organizational meetings at Abraham "Bram" Martling's Tavern on downtown Chatham Street, now Park Row, the site of the Tammany Society's gatherings. Behind the scenes, he worked closely with his ally, Matthew L. Davis (an auctioneer and Tammany stalwart) to concoct a Republican ticket of prominent names from all the state's leading Republican factions. Then he helped keep the nominees' names secret until after the divided Federalists had patched together their list of candidates, a collection of unrenowned businessmen and master artisans. Coordinating their efforts with separate committees in each of the city's seven wards as well as with a citywide general committee, Burr and his lieutenants toiled ceaselessly to distribute handbills and address as many bodies of assembled voters as they could. Hamilton's Federalist friends tried to match the Republicans' efforts, but the final tally showed an unexpected Republican victory in the city, based on huge margins in the poorer wards, and a narrow Republican victory statewide. "That business [that is, the campaign] has been conducted and brought to issue in so miraculous a manner," enthused James Nicholson, the former head of the New York Democratic Society, "that I cannot account for it but from the intervention of a Supreme Power and our friend Burr the agent."[31]

The New York results severely demoralized the Federalist leadership. Taking the outcome as a personal and political blow, Hamilton tried, unavailingly, to talk his old colleague, Governor John Jay, into calling a special session of the lame-duck Federalist legislature to enact a new election law guaranteeing the Federalists enough of New York's electoral votes. President Adams believed Hamilton was the chief cause of all his political troubles. He took the occasion of his renomination by a secret Federalist congressional caucus in early May to force out two of Hamilton's allies in the cabinet, Secretary of State Timothy Pickering and Secretary of War James McHenry, whom he was certain, correctly, had plotted against him. The Republican congressional leaders, for their part, smelled victory and at their own sub-rosa nominating caucus, held at a Philadelphia boardinghouse, named Burr, the season's political genius, as their vice presidential candidate once again. Assured that he would receive the full support of Jefferson's men in Virginia and South Carolina, Burr assented.[32]

The most distressing piece of news for Republicans was from Virginia and involved not the elections but what Governor James Monroe described to Jefferson in April as rumors of "a Negro insurrection" in their home state. Since the Revolution, when the British had offered freedom to rebellious slaves, the possibility of some sort of slave uprising had loomed as all too real to southern slaveholders. Here and there, after American independence, runaway slaves managed to escape recapture and establish their own maroon communities, a potential threat to local stability. Even more troubling was the revolutionary example of Saint Domingue (present-day Haiti), where slaves and free blacks overthrew and massacred much of the resident French planter elite in 1791, and then established, under the leadership of the ex-slave general Toussaint L'Ouverture, the first black-controlled country in the New World. "The scenes which are acted in St. Domingo," a nervous Monroe observed, speaking for all his fellow slaveholders, "must produce an effect on all the people of colour in this and the States south of us, more especially our slaves, and it is our duty to be on our guard to prevent any mischief resulting from it."[33]

At the end of August, Monroe learned that the rumors had merit. A major revolt, involving hundreds of slaves in and around Richmond, had only narrowly been averted days earlier. The mastermind of the foiled plot, still at large, was a literate blacksmith named Gabriel, owned by Thomas Henry Prosser, a wealthy Richmond merchant and tobacco planter with land holdings in Henrico County, about six miles from the city. Born into slavery in 1776, Gabriel had served a blacksmith's apprenticeship as a boy, attaining sufficient physical power and skill to be hired out to other masters in Richmond. A tall young man (standing six feet, two or three inches), prized by his master and mistress (who were likely the ones who taught him to read and write), he enjoyed the unusual privileges of an urban, hired-out slave, including the relative freedom of working beside free black and white artisans. What Gabriel read and with whom he conversed then is unknown. But it is clear that he imbibed much of the egalitarian political rhetoric that made the rounds in the mechanics' shops and tavern haunts, along with news and gossip about Virginia and Richmond politics.[34]

Gabriel's plans, as he explained them to his recruits, were audacious, clever, and, in places, purposely vague in order to prevent their betrayal. Upward of one thousand slaves, as well as a small number of free blacks and white artisans, carefully picked for their loyalty, discretion, and fighting abilities, would march on Richmond and divide into three columns. The central column, armed with weapons converted from farm tools, would seize guns that the rebels understood were stored at the state capitol, then take Governor Monroe hostage. (Knowing Monroe to be friendly to the French Revolution, Gabriel actually thought he might accede to the rebels' demands.) The other two columns would set diversionary fires in the warehouse district, capture the main bridge leading to the city, and await the arrival of rebel reinforcements, recruited from Virginia towns as distant as Charlottesville.[35]

Despite Gabriel's precautions to keep the plan secret, two slaves told their masters on the morning of August 30, roughly twelve hours before the rising was to commence. A torrential rain that evening led the rebels to hold off for an extra day, which gave the alerted authorities enough time to react in force. Governor Monroe called out units of the state militia, while irregular bands of white patrollers hunted for Gabriel and the conspiracy's other implicated leaders. Dozens of suspects were jailed over the following weeks, of whom more than sixty were tried in connection with the conspiracy. Twenty-six slaves (including Gabriel, who eluded capture for nearly a month) were convicted and hanged. One other died in captivity, allegedly a suicide.[36]

Although it ended disastrously for the plotters, the Richmond insurrection conspiracy came close to catching the city and state off guard—far too close to allow its intended victims to rest comfortably. And it caused problems for Governor Monroe and Vice President Jefferson. Virginia Federalists predictably tried to turn the events to their political advantage, blaming their adversaries for inciting the slaves to rebel. (The editor of the Fredericksburg *Virginia Herald* stated flatly that the Republicans' talk of "Liberty and Equality has been infused into the minds of the negroes.") Northern Federalists similarly blamed what President Adams's son Thomas Boylston Adams called the Jeffersonians' "seducing theories about equality," expressed no sympathy for the rebels, and echoed the *Boston Gazette*'s smug observation that "[i]f any thing will correct & bring to repentance old hardened sinners in Jacobinism, it must be an insurrection of their slaves." Early in the investigation, Richmond officials discovered that two French émigrés had indeed aided Gabriel, a fact that, had Monroe not moved to suppress it, could have fueled even more effective Federalist propaganda. Then, in mid-September, the continuing roundups, trials, and executions of slaves began to embarrass the Virginia Republicans further, seeming to confirm the extent of the plot while also making the authorities look like the truly bloodthirsty ones.[37]

The Republicans tried their best to contain the issue until the elections were over. Finally, in October, in part because of Jefferson's advice to avoid the further embarrassment of obeying "a principle of revenge," Monroe adopted a policy of deporting convicted rebels outside the United States, a punishment that would also give the slaves' owners the chance of receiving compensation by selling their difficult property abroad.[38]

Gabriel and his men did not come close to destroying the institution of slavery. Their insurrection scare made little difference, if any, in deciding the outcome of the autumn elections in most states. But the foiled rebellion had badly frightened Virginia's slaveholders, and caused some, including Monroe and Jefferson, to feel certain pangs of conscience once the plot had been crushed. Republican efforts to minimize the political damage became, in turn, vitally important once the state-by-state results started piling up and showed that, despite the New York election, the Federalists were running better than had been expected. It soon became evident that the selection of electors by the South Carolina legislature, held in December, would decide the national outcome. And in South Carolina, slave insurrections were taken very seriously indeed.

A TORTUOUS REVOLUTION:
THE ELECTIONS OF 1800 AND 1801

The election of 1800 would turn out to be two elections—one held by the voters and state legislatures, the other, in 1801, by the House of Representatives. In a strange series of twists and turns, a combination of popular campaigning and high-level political intrigue left the result hanging in the balance for months. Old-style elite politics and newer forms of democracy inspired both intense passions and cool, hard-nosed calculations. Political leaders and rank-and-file voters alike came to believe, with the utmost conviction, that victory for their side was essential to the nation's survival. The crisis of the new American order came to a head, exposing the fragility of the republic's political institutions.[39]

By September 1800, relations between John Adams and Alexander Hamilton had sunk so low that Hamilton started writing, originally for private circulation, a lengthy pamphlet denouncing the president—"a man of an imagination sublimated and eccentric"—for nearly destroying the Union. Late in October, a copy of Hamilton's caustic remarks fell into William Duane's hands, and the *Aurora* reprinted the best portions. At the very highest echelons, plainly, Federalist solidarity had collapsed. "Mr. Adams ought not to be supported," Oliver Wolcott Jr. wrote, insisting that the president was "incapable of supporting any political system," and doubting whether his reelection would be "a less evil to the country than to incur any risque of the promotion of Mr. Jefferson." Yet at the state level, outside New York, the Federalists managed to hold on to what had previously been their strongest electoral redoubts.[40]

Throughout the summer and early fall, the harsh ideological as well as personal tone of the campaign hardened partisan loyalties and turned the contest into a democratic outpouring. Republican speakers and editors endlessly excoriated their opponents over the alien and sedition acts, the Provisional Army, and their Anglo-monarchical proclivities. Some southern Republicans raised the issue of state rights, but generally Jefferson's supporters, fearing continued unease at the Kentucky and Virginia Resolutions, stressed their attachment to the Constitution and the spirit of 1776, now endangered by the Federalists' repression. The Federalists countered that the Republicans were bloodthirsty, godless Jacobins in disguise, who had roused up "discontented hotheads" and would reduce the country to a "land of *groans*, and *tears*, and *blood*." The Federalists' abuse of Jefferson was especially severe, his alleged disloyalty to his country "proved" by his letter of 1796 to Philip Mazzei—damning evidence cited endlessly by the Federalist press.[41]

The attacks and counterattacks churned public interest to the point where in the most hotly contested states, upwards of 70 percent of the eligible voters in some counties turned up at the polls. The enthusiasm did not, however, automatically translate into electoral votes for Jefferson. The heat of the campaign blurred the divisions among the Federalists, and that newfound unity, in combination with the antidemocratic biases of state election laws—by which state legislatures selected presidential electors in eleven of the sixteen states—held Jefferson's electoral totals to a minimum outside his southern base.

Although the Republicans put up a spirited, long-shot fight in New England (and nearly captured the Massachusetts statehouse), they did not win a single electoral vote in the region. Worse, in New Jersey, voters in Newark and a strong organization statewide gave the Republicans a small majority of the overall popular vote, but the Federalists, holding a two-to-one majority in the state assembly, gained all seven of the state's electoral votes. In Maryland, where the voters directly chose presidential electors, the Republicans scored a marginal popular victory but could only manage an even split between Jefferson and Adams in the electoral vote tally because the electors were chosen by district. In Pennsylvania, a continuing impasse over the state's election districting laws, prompted by partisan maneuvering in the Federalist-controlled upper house, made it seem likely that neither candidate would receive any of the state's votes, which would harm Jefferson far more than Adams. (Jefferson had won the state in 1796, and Republican congressional candidates would nearly sweep it in 1800. The legislature eventually awarded eight of the state's electoral votes to Jefferson and seven to Adams—better, for the Republicans, than no votes at all, but a clear inflation of Adams's total that might well have tipped the election.) "Pensva. stands little chance of a vote . . . ," Jefferson wrote to Thomas Mann Randolph at the end of November. "In that case, the issue of the election hangs on S. Carol[in]a." And the outcome in South Carolina, the most Federalist of all the southern states, wound up depending on a peculiar political split inside the Pinckney family.[42]

Senator Charles Pinckney was second cousin to Adams's vice presidential candidate, Charles Cotesworth Pinckney. Both men had been born into the political elite of the South Carolina low country; both had been prominent delegates to the federal convention in 1787; but by the end of the 1790s, they were not on speaking terms. While "C.C.," along with his brother Thomas (Adams's failed running mate in 1796) were stalwart Federalists, Charles, elected governor as a Federalist in 1789, grew alienated from the Washington administration—initially (it appears) because he was passed over for the ministry to Britain in favor of Thomas in 1792, and more profoundly after 1795, when he took strong exception to the Jay Treaty. Casting his lot with the Republican planters of South Carolina's interior counties, Charles, a man of eminent self-regard, won a third term as governor in 1796. Two years later

(although denounced by his former low-country friends as a corrupt class traitor, "Blackguard Charlie"), he was elected to the U.S. Senate. In 1800, having
established his Republican bona fides, he managed Jefferson's presidential
campaign in South Carolina.[43]

Hamilton's maneuverings complicated Blackguard Charlie's tasks. His ties
with Adams now completely cut, Hamilton tried to succeed where he had failed
in 1796, by securing all of South Carolina's electoral votes for C.C. Pinckney
and thereby elevating Pinckney to the presidency. Although the Republicans, by
winning lopsided victories outside Charleston, commanded a majority in the
new legislature, many of the Republican lawmakers were also devoted to Pinckney. And Republican standing in the state had momentarily plummeted in the
wake of Gabriel's plot, forcing James Monroe to write reassuringly to South Carolina's panicked Republican lieutenant governor, John Drayton—remarks that
calmed but could not completely quell suspicions that the Republican appeal to
equality was too dangerous in a slave society. Seeing what was hapzpening,
Charles Pinckney delayed his arrival in the Senate and, he told Jefferson, took a
"post with some valuable friends in Columbia," where he meant to remain "until
the thing is settled." The details of his labors within the legislature—promises
made, deals cooked up—are lost to us; what is clear is that Blackguard Charlie
held the Republican caucus firmly in line behind both Jefferson and Burr. "The
Election is just Finished," Pinckney wrote to Jefferson, "and We Have, thanks to
Heaven's Goodness, carried it." He did not neglect to add that he, Charles Pinckney, and not just Heaven, deserved credit, as "it would have been almost death to
our cause for me to quit Columbia."[44]

In fact, by thwarting his cousin and Alexander Hamilton, Pinckney succeeded
too well—although given the formally secret results of the state-by-state electoral
balloting, he had no way of knowing that. Prior to the presidential balloting in
South Carolina, both Adams and Jefferson had secured 65 electoral votes each.
(All state electors cast their votes on the same day, December 3, although the
results were not officially made public until February.) Thanks to the South Carolinians' discipline, Jefferson and Burr each received the state's 8 available votes,
seemingly putting Jefferson over the top. But through a fluke in the voting, Jefferson had not defeated Burr, who also now had 73 votes. Most observers, including
Jefferson and (probably) Burr, expected that one of the South Carolinians and
one or two of the Georgia electors would cast a pro forma vote for some other
Republican, thereby making Jefferson president and Burr vice president—but,
none did, leaving Jefferson and Burr deadlocked. Under the Constitution, the
House of Representatives would now have to decide the election, with each state
delegation casting one vote. And to make the situation all the more perverse, the
House members who voted would not be the Republican majority that the 1800
elections had produced, but the lame-duck Federalist majority elected in 1798 at

the height of the XYZ crisis with France. Requiring the support of nine state delegations to elect the new president, the Republicans controlled only eight, and the Federalists six. The Maryland and Vermont delegations were evenly divided.[45]

This issue would be decided in the new national capital, the District of Columbia, where the federal government had finally relocated earlier in 1800. The mood there were panicky. Around the country, rival groups of unofficial Republican and Federalist militia had reportedly begun to drill, in preparation for a possible civil war. Southerners, already shaken by the Gabriel conspiracy, traded rumors about Federalist plots to block Jefferson's election as president, while Federalists suspected that Virginians were willing to impose Jefferson on the nation at bayonet point if necessary. Albert Gallatin drafted a memorandum which insisted that any Federalist effort to usurp the election would have to be "resisted by freemen wherever they have the power of resisting." Soon, Jefferson himself would be warning of armed resistance. Adding to the atmosphere of chaos and impending doom, a mysterious fire in early November that destroyed the building housing the War Department was followed ten weeks later by an equally mysterious fire that destroyed portions of the Treasury Department.[46] Amid the ruins and the inevitable partisan charges about who set the fires, the House settled down inside the north (or Senate) wing of the new Capitol, the only part of the building as yet completed, to decide who would be the next American president.

Aaron Burr could have instantly ended the crisis by removing his name from consideration for anything but the vice presidency. But he refused, despite making all sorts of statements of fealty to Jefferson—and by late December, when he fully realized that he had a credible chance to win the presidency, he decided to play out the string, come what may. Of course, as Burr knew well, any victory margin in his favor would come from Federalists who preferred someone they saw as a corrupt northern opportunist to the satanic Thomas Jefferson. The House, amid round-the-clock intrigue, began its voting on February 11. On the first ballot, Jefferson won the support of eight states, Burr of six, with the two divided states, Vermont and Maryland, so badly split that they cast no votes. Twenty hours and twenty-six ballots later, the results remained the same.[47]

Ironically, it was Hamilton who, having already made John Adams's life miserable, would help decide the matter in Jefferson's favor. Jefferson, with his Gallic enthusiasms, was bad enough to Hamilton, but had more of a temporizing than a violent temperament, whereas the profligate, ambitious Burr would be infinitely worse. A plan cooked up by Federalist intransigents to continue the stalemate until Adams's term expired, and then elevate the Federalist president pro tempore of the Senate to the Executive Mansion, struck Hamilton as wrongheaded. A far wiser course, he told associates, would be to allow Jefferson's election, but only on condition that the Virginians agree to various political concessions, which would include sustaining both the existing fiscal system and the Federalists' neutral foreign policy.[48]

One of Hamilton's correspondents, James Bayard of Delaware, broke the deadlock. Bayard was his state's lone congressman and could decide everything by switching from Burr to Jefferson. After discussions with two of Jefferson's supporters — though not with the candidate himself — Bayard was persuaded that Jefferson had made specific concessions about preserving the public credit. Bayard was also bemused by Burr's odd behavior — refusing to seek the presidency actively, while also refusing to eliminate himself as a candidate. And so Bayard helped worked out an arrangement: he would withdraw his support for Burr by voting a blank ballot, Vermont's and Maryland's Federalists would absent themselves and thereby hand their respective states to Jefferson, and South Carolina's Federalists would, like Bayard, vote a blank ballot. After the thirty-sixth ballot, with ten states voting for Jefferson, four for Burr, and two abstaining, the Virginian was declared the nation's third president, and Burr its third vice president.[49]

Jefferson's friends were elated. Jefferson, however, who had won the presidency by the skin of his teeth, serenely kept his own counsel. With barely two weeks to go before his swearing-in as president, he withdrew to his boardinghouse. There he would make sense of his victory and then try to convey that sense to the nation the best way he knew how, in a carefully composed inaugural address.

MARCH 4, 1801

Before daybreak on inauguration day, a heartbroken and sullen John Adams departed the Executive Mansion and began the long coach ride to Quincy, his public career finished. In December, hours before the presidential electors met to confirm his defeat, Adams had received from home the devastating news of the death, at age thirty, of his second son, Charles, a troubled alcoholic whom he had renounced as a worthless rake. Fighting with grief and guilt, Adams pulled himself together and dutifully completed his last ten weeks in office, working on treaty negotiations with France and filling vacancies in the bureaucracy and the army with reliable moderate Federalists and personal friends. He signed into law the sweeping Judiciary Act of 1801, a parting shot from the lame-duck Federalist Congress, which reorganized the federal judiciary, reduced the size of the Supreme Court (depriving Jefferson of adding his own selection when the next seat came open), and created sixteen new federal judgeships to which Adams named steadfast Federalists.

Trying to put the best face on his defeat, Adams blamed Hamilton, but not just Hamilton. "No party that ever existed knew itself so little, or so vainly overrated its own influence and popularity, as ours," he later wrote to his friend Benjamin Stoddert.

> None ever understood so ill the causes of its own power, or so wantonly destroyed them. If we had been blessed with common sense, we should not have been overthrown by Philip Freneau, Duane, Callender, Cooper, and Lyon or their great patron and protector. A group of foreign liars, encouraged by a few ambitious native gentlemen, have discomfited the education, the talents, the virtues, and the property of the country. The reason is, we have no Americans in America. The Federalists have been no more Americans than the anties.

From the start of his administration, Adams mused bitterly, he, the man of balance, had tried to keep the extremists at bay, but he (and, he implied, the country) had been overmatched. "Jefferson had a party, Hamilton had a party, but the commonwealth had none," Adams concluded.[50]

Six hours after Adams left the city, Thomas Jefferson—dressed in a plain suit, his graying red hair unpowdered—walked with little fanfare in a brief militia procession from his lodgings to the Capitol, took the presidential oath of office, and delivered the speech on which he had worked the previous fortnight. Some of those who crowded the Senate chamber could barely hear his thin, high-pitched voice, but Jefferson had given an advance copy to a new and friendly local paper, the *National Intelligencer*, edited by Samuel Harrison Smith, so that the entire city of Washington could know his words before day's end.[51]

What Jefferson said was directly at odds with what Adams was thinking. In the most important speech of his life, Jefferson displayed his singular ability to mold the political situation before him with his words, turning democratic hopes and assumptions into political facts. He began by acknowledging the rancor of the recent election, but suggested it was nothing more than the normal to-and-fro of a people able "to think freely and to speak and to write what they think." Now that the citizenry had voted, "according to the rules of the Constitution," all Americans would "of course, arrange themselves under the will of the law, and unite in common efforts for the common good."[52]

As political rhetoric, this was a risky but brilliant combination of disingenuousness and indirection. Not only had the recent election been full of high-level intrigue; it had been fought so fiercely in part because Jefferson's supporters believed (with good reason) that Americans could no longer think, speak, and write freely. Jefferson insisted on the legitimacy of his selection, no matter how close it had been, by pointing to the very document, the Constitution, that the Federalists had charged he wished to undermine. There was no reason to assume, less than three weeks after the electoral fracas had ended, that Americans would unite behind his leadership as a matter of course. (It is impossible to imagine the Republicans extending such great goodwill had either of the "monocrats," Adams or Pinckney, prevailed.) But by saying it was so, Jefferson dared to think he could make it so.

Eager to promote reconciliation, Jefferson blamed the recent electoral tumults mainly on the political struggles in Europe, and on Americans' disagreements over the proper "measures of safety" to take in response. He then sounded what many took as the address's unifying keynote, that "every difference of opinion is not a difference of principle," and that, finally, however divided Americans' opinions might be, "[w]e are all republicans: we are all federalists." Reading those words as they appeared in print—as *Republicans* and *Federalists*—helped persuade numerous leading Federalists to retract their past doubts and predict that, as Hamilton wrote several weeks later, "the new President will not lend himself to dangerous innovations, but in essential points will tread in the steps of his predecessors." It may also have affirmed their belief that the assurances made to James Bayard during the last days of the election in the House were both authentic and sincere.[53]

Yet if Jefferson planned nothing dangerous, he had no intention of sustaining his predecessors' policies, as far as he could help it. Understood fully as he wrote them, without capital letters, his remarks about republicans and federalists may only have meant that Americans shared a commitment to a republican government under the Federal Constitution—not that Republicans and Federalists were equally legitimate contenders for power. In a wonderfully tempered passage, Jefferson repudiated the Federalist claim that the national government lacked what Hamilton liked to call "energy":

> I know, indeed, that some honest men fear that a republican government can not be strong, that this Government is not strong enough; but would the honest patriot, in the full tide of successful experiment, abandon a government which has so far kept us free and firm on the theoretic and visionary fear that this Government, the world's best hope, may by possibility want energy to preserve itself? I trust not. I believe this, on the contrary, the strongest Government on earth.

If Jefferson was willing to call his adversaries "honest"—elsewhere in the speech he referred to those "whose positions will not command a view of the whole ground"—he also quietly called them deluded.[54]

Against the Federalists, Jefferson reiterated the democratic principle that public honor and confidence should result "not from birth, but from our actions." And as "the sum of good government," he described qualities that promised basic departures from the previous administrations' policies, specifically, "a wise and frugal government, which shall restrain men from injuring one another, shall leave them otherwise free to regulate their own pursuits of industry and improvement, and shall not take from the mouth of labor the bread it has earned." Whatever concessions his supporters may have made to Bayard over the public credit in order to get Jefferson elected, major portions of the Federalist edifice of internal taxes, a standing army, and regulation of speech and opinion were about to fall.[55]

Jefferson revealed his truest intentions a year and a half into his presidency, when, after facing stiff resistance from Federalists in Congress, he told Levi Lincoln that by establishing republican principles, he would "sink federalism into an abyss from which there shall be no resurrection for it." He undertook that mission with the backing, as he told the British radical émigré and scientist Joseph Priestley just after the inauguration, of "a mighty wave of public opinion" that had arisen against the Federalists' encroaching tyranny. The change would be dramatic. A popular song sung in anticipatory celebration of Jefferson's election made clear what the new president himself later announced, with calm finesse, in his inaugural address:

> THE gloomy night before us flies,
> The reign of terror now is o'er;
> Its gags, inquisitors, and spies,
> Its herds of harpies are no more!
>
> Rejoice! Columbia's Sons, rejoice!
> To tyrants never bend the knee,
> But join with heart and soul and voice,
> For *Jefferson and Liberty*.

Looking back as an old man, Jefferson would speak of the election as the "revolution of 1800," remarking that it was "as real a revolution in the principles of our government as that of 76 was in its form," one "not effected indeed by the sword . . . but by the rational and peaceable instrument of reform, the suffrage of the people." His moderation, in leading this democratic revolution, consisted mainly of his recognition of Solon's ancient wisdom, that (as he put it) "no more good must be attempted than the nation can bear."[56]

Jefferson's "revolution of 1800" did leave open some major questions about the democratization of American politics. The egalitarian fundamentals of his appeal, along with the democratic electioneering efforts undertaken by his supporters, surpassed anything seen before in national affairs. The Republicans' absorption of the techniques and the constituency of the city democracy—most notably under Beckley's direction in Philadelphia and Burr's in New York

City—had created both a Republican infrastructure of newspapers, public events, and loyal operatives, and a national coalition of planters, yeoman, and urban workingmen allied against a Federalist monocracy. In four of the five states where the voters directly chose presidential electors—Virginia, Kentucky, North Carolina, and Maryland—Jefferson won a popular majority.[57] Yet various structural factors, along with partisan maneuvering, limited the scope of Jefferson's victory and created some large historical ironies. In three of the states decided by the popular vote, the electors were chosen by district and not statewide, which deprived Jefferson of twelve electoral votes. In two other states where the legislatures chose electors, New Jersey and Pennsylvania, the Republicans also won statewide victories not reflected in the electoral voting, costing Jefferson upward of fourteen additional electoral votes. Except for southern slavery, and the inflation of southern vote by the three-fifths clause in the Constitution, Adams, aided by the split electoral votes in pro-Jefferson states—especially the split caused by the successful obstructionist Federalists in Pennsylvania—would have won reelection.[58] And for all of Jefferson's reliance on democratic principles and tactics, he might never have gained the presidency without the insider wire-pulling of a renegade South Carolina low-country aristocrat—along with later help from, of all people, Alexander Hamilton.

The Republicans did win a smashing victory in the congressional elections, picking up twenty-three seats in the House (enough to seize a formidable majority) and seven seats in the Senate (giving them a majority of two, the first time ever they controlled the upper chamber). Coupled with Jefferson's narrow victory, it was enough to justify claims that a seismic shift had occurred. Yet Federalism was far from dead, at least in the northern states. And the Republican coalition of city and country democrats, built in part out of the elements of the Democratic-Republican societies, was still commanded by Virginian gentry slaveholders. Traditional political arrangements, conducted by elected officials—gentlemen for the most part, well removed from the voters—still largely determined national political affairs. It remained far from clear that the patrician Republican leaders considered partisan popular politics—described by Jefferson as recently as 1789 as "the last degradation of a free and moral agent"—as anything more than an unfortunate and temporary expedient to ward off monocracy.[59]

Jefferson and his allies had achieved an accession to national power that removed the Federalists from power in two of the three branches of the federal government. Considering the alarming state of American politics after 1796, that achievement was not small. But the tensions within the emerging Jeffersonian order, including those provoked by Gabriel Prosser's plot, were strong enough to ensure renewed and bitter battles over what, exactly, was the sum of good government.

4

JEFFERSON'S TWO PRESIDENCIES

The first thing that Thomas Jefferson saw as president was the dark face of John Marshall, the chief justice of the Supreme Court, who had just sworn him into office. The two were second cousins, related through the august Randolph family of Virginia—and they intensely disliked each other's politics. Marshall was now the country's preeminent moderate Federalist, one of John Adams's few trustworthy political friends, confirmed (in the waning days of Federalist rule) as his handpicked chief justice. He regarded Jefferson as a self-important dreamer—"the grand lama of the mountain"—blind to the practical imperatives of national government. Jefferson thought Marshall a hypocrite and a sophist, dominated by "the plenitude of his English principles." Yet on this day, shared political fears and desires overrode the Virginians' mutual suspicions.[1]

Shortly before the noontime ceremony, Marshall began writing a letter to Adams's running mate, Charles Cotesworth Pinckney, expressing his cautious hope that "the public prosperity and happiness may sustain no diminution under democratic guidance." Marshall explained that, though "[t]he democrats are divided into speculative theorists and absolute terrorists: With the latter I am not disposed to class Mr. Jefferson." After breaking off to officiate at the inauguration, Marshall returned to his letter, still wary but encouraged. Jefferson's speech, he said, was "well judged and conciliatory" even though "strongly characteristic of the general cast of his political theory." Marshall found little to admire in that theory, but he and Jefferson had overseen a peaceful transit of power, despite the turmoil of the previous two years. "The changes of administration, which in every government and in every age have most generally been epochs of confusion, villainy and bloodshed, in this our happy country, take place without any species of distraction, or disorder," one spectator at the inauguration wrote. This cheerful result was due largely to the capacity for moderation of men like Jefferson and Marshall.[2]

Even as they staked out moderate ground, the president and the chief justice were destined to clash before long. Some days earlier, while completing the last-minute Federalist expansion of the federal judiciary, Marshall (in his plural capacity as secretary of state) had affixed the official seals on the commissions of more than three-dozen so-called midnight judgeship appointments, including one for a Georgetown lawyer named William Marbury. Amid the distractions of Jefferson's election and inauguration, Marshall failed to have the commissions delivered. While Marshall was giving Jefferson the oath of office, the documents sat forgotten on a desk at the State Department, where President Jefferson would discover them, accidentally, two days later. Already infuriated at the Federalists' judicial maneuverings, Jefferson pondered over whether the undelivered documents were now dead letters. From this incident would issue a memorable skirmish in the continuing struggle between Republicans and Federalists—a struggle that would now turn on battles over the fledging federal judiciary.

The larger struggle over democracy created fresh difficulties for the new Republican leadership. Having ousted their common enemy from national power, the Republicans began to divide into moderate, radical, and so-called Old Republican factions, with very different conceptions of democracy—differences that threatened Republican unity at the state and local levels as well as in Washington. "I confess I do not like tampering with established systems or forms of government," wrote Pennsylvania's preeminent moderate Republican Thomas McKean. ". . . I never desire to see any more Revolutions, and pant after tranquility, peace and sociability."[3] Other Republicans thought McKean and those like him were Federalists in disguise. Blessed by a sudden outbreak of peace in Europe, and by a stroke of enormous good luck in the Caribbean, Jefferson, leaning to the moderates, proved remarkably successful at carving out a middle Republican course during his first administration, while holding the Republicans together and reducing the active Federalist threat. But during his second term, stresses at home and abroad grew so intense that Jefferson would leave office in 1809 frustrated and exhausted—and with the nation's survival, let alone American democracy's, far from assured.

MONOCRACY ATTACKED

Even before he finally moved into the cavernous new president's house in late March, Jefferson began implementing a two-track strategy for destroying Federalism: reconciling moderate Federalists to his own administration while extirpating the excesses of Federalist rule. Accordingly, he appointed his cabinet and chief envoys with care, trying to appear as nonconfrontational as possible. As expected, he chose his old collaborator James Madison as secretary of state, and, to intense Federalist displeasure, named the Genevan émigré Albert Gallatin as secretary of the treasury. But he balanced the group geographically and politically by appointing the moderate New Englanders Levi Lincoln, Henry Dearborn, and Gideon Granger as, respectively, attorney general, secretary of war, and postmaster general. The Federalist Rufus King was given the crucial post of minister to Great Britain, while the ex-Federalists Robert R. Livingston and Charles Pinckney (the proud "Blackguard Charlie") took up similar assignments in France and Spain. In the continuing press wars with the Federalists, Jefferson turned to the *National Intelligencer* as the quasi-official administration organ, edited by the reliably fair-minded Republican Samuel Harrison Smith. Jefferson, one Federalist opponent observed, did his best to surround himself with "mild and amiable men," in contrast to the sorts of designing ideologues who had helped make his predecessors' cabinet a torment.[4]

With this political camouflage in place, Jefferson began to dismantle the Federalists' chief legacies. Although the Sedition Law had expired on inauguration day, ten of its victims were still in legal trouble. David Brown remained behind bars in Massachusetts, unable to pay his fine; twice he had written clemency petitions to President Adams, who ignored them. Eight days after the inauguration, Jefferson, who had always considered the law a nullity, pardoned Brown in full, along with all others still in prison for sedition when he assumed office; four days after that, he agreed to remit a sedition fine assessed against the Virginia journalist James Callender. Later, Jefferson discontinued the Sedition Law prosecution still pending against William Duane of the *Aurora* and lifted all other penalties and prosecutions. In his first annual message, delivered on December 8, he bid the incoming Republican Congress to repeal the Federalists' naturalization laws of 1798, asking, "[S]hall oppressed humanity find no asylum on this globe?" Congress duly complied.[5]

On fiscal policy, Jefferson frontally attacked the Hamiltonian system by initiating the complete elimination of federal internal taxation, including the land tax and the hated whiskey excise. Secretary Gallatin initially balked at removing the duties, not because he approved of them but because his first priority was to cut the huge debt inherited from the Federalists. Jefferson insisted that ending the excise, an enormous political symbol as well as a public burden, be included as part of Gallatin's plans. Gallatin, and then Congress, assented in no uncertain terms: "let them all go," Gallatin said, "and not one remain on which sister taxes may be hereafter engrafted."[6]

Patronage questions caused Jefferson greater difficulty. Faced with a federal establishment monopolized by Federalist appointees, he could hardly avoid fir-

ing some officeholders and substituting his supporters. But lacking any precedents, eager to calm partisan tensions, and appalled at the politics of spoilsmanship practiced at the state level, Jefferson at first attempted to minimize
patronage replacements, except for replacing "midnight" appointees or those
accused of official misconduct.[7] He modified his policy in July, in part because of
complaints from office-hungry local Republicans and, even more, because hard-
line Federalists rejected his olive branch. After trying to replace Adams's midnight appointee Elizur Goodrich with the aging but committed Republican
Samuel Bishop as port collector in arch-Federalist New Haven, Jefferson
received an angry remonstrance from a group of eighty powerful New Haven
merchants, complaining that his choice was incompetent and that they, the merchants, were "a class of citizens" who deserved special favor in the matter. The
president, affronted, publicly defended Bishop and asked the merchants some
barbed questions of his own: "Is it *political intolerance* to claim a proportionate
share in the direction of the public affairs? Can they [that is, the Federalists] not
harmonize in society unless they have every thing in their own hands?" Jefferson
claimed that his call for unity at the inauguration and later had "been quoted
and misconstrued into assurances that the tenure of offices was to be undisturbed." Appointees, he reiterated, would be judged not by their birth or standing
but by their achievements and actions.[8]

Jefferson's response pleased his more partisan backers in New England and
the middle Atlantic states, and infuriated the Federalists. In retrospect, it
appears that the Federalists overreacted. Jefferson actually had fairly elevated
ideas about staffing the upper branches of the civil service with respectable,
well-educated men. Although he moved outside the clusters of wealthy families
that Adams had favored, he still believed, as he would later write, that most citizens were "unqualified for the management of affairs requiring intelligence
above the common level." All told, during his eight years in office, he removed
109 of the 433 federal officials with presidential appointments; of the removed,
more than one-third were midnight appointments by Adams. But Jefferson
came increasingly to believe that the Federalists had drawn the circle of eligible
appointees much too tightly, favoring eastern urban gentlemen with business
and family connections at the exclusion of rural men and westerners, humble-
born citizens of accomplishment, and (as he put it) men of "every shade of
opinion which is not theirs."[9] Without endorsing partisanship for its own sake,
Jefferson challenged the Federalists' standards of political preferment and
staked out the limits of conciliation.

Patronage battles were linked to the momentous contest over the federal judiciary. The federal bench was thoroughly Federalist, and the Judiciary Act of 1801
had opened the way for many of Adams's late appointments and curtailed future

THE CRISIS OF
THE NEW ORDER

1. Thomas Jefferson, inauguration banner, 1801

2. John Singleton Copley's portrait of
Paul Revere, ca. 1768

3. Charles Willson Peale's 1779
portrait of George Washington at
the Battle of Princeton in 1777

4. Charles Willson Peale's portrait of
Timothy Matlack, ca. 1780

5. Portrait of Timothy Matlack attributed to Rembrandt Peale, ca. 1802

6. Thomas Jefferson, 1805

7. James Madison, 1797

8. William Duane, 1802

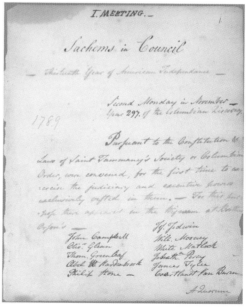

9. *Journal & Rules of the Council of Sachems of St. Tammany's Society, New York, 1789*

10. John Adams, 1799

11. Alexander Hamilton, ca. 1792

12. William Loughton Smith, ca. 1790

13. John Randolph, 1804–05

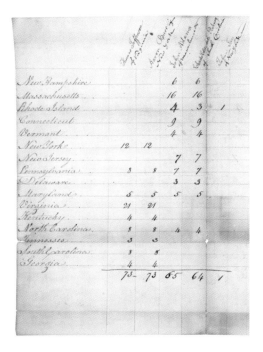

14. Tally of Electoral College votes,
February 11, 1801

15. Broadside of Thomas Jefferson's first
inaugural address, 1801

16. Abraham Bishop, ca. 1790

17. John Marshall, 1808

19. Federalist satire of Jefferson and
Sally Hemings, 1804

18. Federalist cartoon of Napoleon
stinging Jefferson into the Louisiana
Purchase, 1803

20. Federalist cartoon of Liberty nursed by Mother Mob, 1807

21. Anti-British cartoon on alleged bribery of the northwestern Indians, 1812

22. Tenkswatawa, 1823

23. Republican satire of the Hartford Convention as traitorous, 1814

Near the City of **NEW ORLEANS**, on the

A CORRECT VIEW of the **BATTLE** Gen.! And.' Jackson, Over 10,000 British Troops, in

Eighth of January 1815, Under the Command of several wounded and upwards of 3,000 of their choisest

which 3 of their most distinguished Generals were killed & and made Prisoners, &c.

Soldiers were killed; wounded.

24. The Battle of New Orleans, ca. 1815–20

Jeffersonian influence by reducing the size of the Supreme Court by one justice. Yet while the president favored vacating the midnight appointments, he rejected an all-out partisan attack on the independence of the judicial branch. As late as December 1801, Jefferson declared that although the judiciary, "and especially that portion of it recently erected," would "of course present itself to the contemplation of Congress," he had in mind no reforms greater than a reduction in the size of the federal court system.[10]

The affair of the undelivered judicial commissions eventually moved Jefferson to seek sterner measures. After discovering John Marshall's forgetfulness, Jefferson quickly decided to grant appointments to twenty of the forty-two names selected by Adams, exclude the others, and add five Republican appointments of his own—an exemplary act, in his mind, of moderate leadership. The Federalists, however, would not be placated by what they considered an underhanded maneuver that exploited a technical error. In December, four of the Adams appointees excluded by Jefferson, including William Marbury, petitioned the Supreme Court for a writ that would require Secretary of State Madison to deliver their commissions. Chief Justice Marshall granted the petitioners' preliminary motion and scheduled hearings. In private, Jefferson exploded. The Federalists, he wrote on the day Marshall ruled, "have retired into the Judiciary as a stronghold . . . and from that battery all the works of republicanism are to be beaten down and erased."[11] He would now try to destroy the Federalists' domination of the courts, beginning with repeal of the Judiciary Act of 1801.

Led by Kentucky Senator John Breckinridge, Jefferson's old co-conspirator from the Kentucky Resolutions effort four years earlier, congressional Republicans charged their adversaries with judicial tyranny and introduced a bill to repeal the act in January 1802. The Federalists replied that the new administration was seeking to subvert the Constitution and destroy the independence of the federal courts. The Republicans prevailed narrowly in the Senate and more convincingly in the House, then took the additional step of passing a law delaying the next Supreme Court term for over a year, lest the Court invalidate the repeal before it took effect. Some indignant justices threatened to strike down the meddlesome legislation and cause a full-blown constitutional crisis. "I believe a Day of severe trial is fast approaching for the friends of the Constitution," Samuel Chase wrote, "and I fear we must be principal actors and may be sufferers therein." Chief Justice Marshall, after considering resistance, heeded the calmer heads on the Court, and the justices decided to bide their time.[12]

The measured, temperate side of much of Jefferson's public rhetoric during his early months in office, even when he was replying to Federalist rebukes, has lulled some later writers into regarding him, wrongly, as an accommodating trimmer, and his attacks on the Federalists as half-hearted. To be sure, Jefferson never went as far as some of his supporters wished, nor as far as the more highly strung Federalists predicted. On some important matters he stopped short of his own political and constitutional principles. Above all, regarding Hamilton's bank, Jefferson did nothing, heeding Secretary Gallatin's advice that the institution, if stripped of its political favoritism, had its potential benefits, while recognizing that to destroy it outright before its charter elapsed in 1811 would throw the nation's economy into chaos. Jefferson understood that, given his lack of an electoral mandate, too sudden or too hostile an effort at reform might well backfire. "What is practicable must often control what is pure theory," he wrote Pierre du Pont de Nemours in January 1802. Within the constraints of existing political circumstances, Jefferson believed, he was doing his utmost to destroy the Federalists' unrepublican perversions—and that issues requiring compromise could be laid aside for another time.[13] But when Federalists pushed him, he pushed back hard, even if he retained his outwardly temperate mien.

The outstanding feature of Jefferson's first two years as president was the rapidity with which the harmonious tone of inauguration day soured—as a result, chiefly, of the bitter opposition to his presidency mounted by the Federalists. Initially, over the winter and spring of 1801, many of even the most caustic Federalist writers expressed a fatalistic resignation to the Republican victory and remained hopeful that the Jeffersonians' downfall would be swift once they tried to implement their policies.[14] By late summer, the Federalists' strategic highmindedness had curdled, while their political unity held. Every new replacement appointment by Jefferson became the subject of intense criticism and purported exposés from the Federalist newspapers. The courts became a special focus of Federalist outrage. Having already condemned Jefferson's early decision to hold back a few of the undelivered judicial commissions, the Federalist press seized on his involvement in the outstanding Sedition Law cases, interpreted it in the direst conspiratorial light, and assailed the administration for unconstitutional tampering with the judicial process. While the press attacks unsettled some moderate Federalist leaders, most were persuaded that the Republicans had begun a Jacobinical persecution of the wealth and talent of the country. By the time the new Congress assembled in December and heard the new president's first annual message, some Federalist editors had already called for his impeachment, on the flimsy grounds that his involvement in the Duane and Callender cases amounted to a high crime against the Constitution. The subsequent congressional debate over repeal of the Judiciary Act, in which Federalist spokesmen cast Jefferson as diabolically ambitious and vengeful, further pushed the opposition toward claiming his very election had been tainted and lacked legitimacy.[15]

Much subtler now, but nearly equal in eventual importance, were growing strains within the victorious Republican coalition. Some years later, Jefferson claimed he "had always expected that when the republicans should put down all things under their feet, they would schismatize among themselves . . . into moderate and ardent republicanism."[16] The Republicans had barely begun to put all things under their feet when schisms cracked open.

Vice President Aaron Burr, a faction unto himself, presented personal as well as political problems. Jefferson suspected that Burr had been an intriguer during the election crisis of 1800–01, and kept his distance. Late in 1801, Burr tried unsucessfully to capitalize on Federalist alienation and enhance his own stature by helping to stall repeal of the Judiciary Act. The feint failed, leaving Burr, according to one Federalist congressman, "a completely isolated man." But though he was down, Burr was not out.[17]

Of greater political and ideological significance were the signs of division between Jefferson and a knot of southern agrarian slaveholder ideologues, most conspicuously the twenty-eight-year-old Virginia representative John Randolph. Pallid, beardless (due to a childhood illness), and fonder of his hunting dogs than of most men and all women, Randolph was the best orator and wittiest insulter in the Congress, and the Republicans' floor leader in the House. A fearsome defender of state rights and hater of Federalist New England, Randolph had already raised doubts about unnamed moderate supporters of Jefferson's "whose Republicanism has not been the most unequivocal." Once Jefferson began preaching and, even worse, practicing conciliation, Randolph grew bitter, as did a number of his important southern agrarian Republican patrons and friends, among them the Speaker of the House, Nathaniel Macon of North Carolina.[18]

Jefferson also faced suspicious city and country democrats, sometimes aligned with the agrarian ideologues, who pushed him to undertake more dramatic political, economic, and judicial reforms. They included some familiar veteran agitators with careers dating back to the Revolution, among them the Berkshire clergyman Thomas Allen and his Baptist itinerant ally John Leland, the Boston artisan radical Benjamin Austin, and the still-feisty sixty-five-year-old Thomas Paine (whom Jefferson officially welcomed back to America as a hero in 1802). Younger democrats of rising importance included the country Pennsylvanians Simon Snyder and Nathaniel Boileau, the radical British émigré editor John Binns, and the Kentucky Green River yeoman leader Felix Grundy. A few of the country democrats, such as John Bacon of western Massachusetts, actually managed to gain a voice in Congress. Most imposing of all, though, were the collaborative efforts of the Philadelphia city democrats William Duane (back to editing the *Aurora* and safe from prosecution) and Michael Leib, formerly of the Democratic Society of Pennsylvania, who had been elected to Congress in 1798. At the *Aurora,* Duane commanded the country's most trenchant and influential independent Republican newspaper; together, Duane and Leib had turned their Philadelphia Republican machine of the 1790s into an electoral force to be reckoned with by national as well as Pennsylvania politicians.[19]

Like the planter ideologues, the city and country democrats spoke of the dangers that excessive official power posed to American principles, especially what the *Aurora* called "the *arbitrary power* assumed by the courts." Like the planters, they recycled the republican rhetoric of the Revolution against those Republicans they believed were insufficiently vigilant against crypto-monarchism — acting as, in Jefferson's words, radical "high-fliers" against the mainstream "moderates." Yet the planters and the democrats were quite distinct. Apart from Michael Leib, who struck up a working connection with John Randolph in Congress, the leading city and country democrats never displayed special solidarity with the slaveholders. The planters were generally unsympathetic to the kinds of judicial reform, including the popular election of judges and the eradication of British common-law precedents, favored by the democrats. City democrats such as Duane, Paine, and Austin were hospitable to a dynamic, expanding commerce; the planter ideologues opposed further commercialization and (at least rhetorically) detested the entrepreneurial ethos. Above all, northern city and country democrats were generally hostile to the planters' chief property interest, chattel slavery—a difference graphically portrayed early in 1802 when virtually all of the northern Republicans broke ranks and defeated a bill imposing a five-hundred-dollar fine on anyone caught "harboring, concealing, or employing" a fugitive slave, proposed by Joseph Hopper Nicholson of Maryland.[20]

The moderate Republican faction might well be called the Madisonians. Not only was James Madison the greatest political figure among them; most were Republicans who had originally favored ratification of the U.S. Constitution only to become estranged, like Madison, by the policies of George Washington, John Adams, and, above all, Alexander Hamilton. Unlike the planter ideologues and country democrats (most of whom had Anti-Federalist backgrounds), the moderates did not abhor strong national government, but only what they considered specific abuses of power epitomized by Hamilton's funding program and the alien and sedition acts. On the state as well as the national level, they were friendlier than other Republicans were to government efforts at encouraging economic development, including the chartering of state banks and preserving a reformed Bank of the United States. They were far less committed than either the city or the country democrats were to constitutional and judicial reform. And the moderates were willing to risk alienating the other Republican factions in order to win over moderate Federalists. "[I]t would be better to displease many of our political friends," Gallatin wrote, "than to give an opportunity to the irreconcilable enemies of a free government of inducing the mass of Federal citizens to make a common cause with them."[21]

And what of the president? Although he was basically a moderate, in private, particularly in his personal correspondence, and occasionally on public issues, Jefferson's chronic impulsiveness and his irritated distaste for his stubborn Federalist foes could shatter his measured demeanor. One can read the inaugural address and other declarations of harmony as, in part, the thin-skinned Jefferson's attempt to change the tone of politics and forestall the kinds of vicious political and personal attacks that abounded in 1800. But those attacks came anyway, and at times they threw Jefferson into such a fury that he would veer toward more militant Republicans. Years later, recalling his friend's outbursts against "monarchists" and all who tolerated them, Madison would write of how "allowances ought to be made for a habit in Mr. Jefferson as in others of great genius of expressing in strong and round terms, impressions of the moment." But Jefferson often made no such allowances for himself and his adversaries.[22]

Publicly, Jefferson tried to remain friendly with all Republican camps, preserving harmony while remaining personally in command. He saw clearly the risk that pursuing conciliation with the Federalists too ardently might, as he told Gallatin, "absolutely revolt our tried friends." Intellectually, Jefferson was too much the experimenter and Enlightenment visionary to dismiss unorthodox democratic ideas, or their proponents, out of hand. It is difficult to imagine any other moderate Republican helping to arrange for the return to the United States of Tom Paine, infidel and calumniator of George Washington. Yet Jefferson not only arranged the trip; he arranged it at government expense and greeted Paine with a warm public address in the autumn of 1802, commending him to live long and "continue your useful labors"—a severe provocation to the Federalists, and a momentary alarm to moderate Republicans. Likewise, Jefferson refused to disengage from talented combative democrats like William Duane, despite complaints from moderate Republicans. Duane might be "over zealous," he told Madison, but he was an honest Republican who reflected the views "of a great portion of the republican body."[23]

And so the Republican attack on monocracy advanced in 1801 and 1802, enraging the Federalist opposition but failing to convince many Republicans that the administration was acting with sufficient vigor. Once the Republican divisions appeared, the Federalists took courage. The repeal of the Judiciary Act early in 1802—achieved only by a tiny margin in the Senate—looked like it might be a turning point. "[W]e plainly discern that there is no confidence nor the smallest attachment prevails among [the President's party]," House minority leader James Bayard wrote to Hamilton in April. "The spirit which existed at the beginning of the Session is entirely dissipated. A more rapid and radical change could not have been anticipated."[24]

A little more than two years later, Bayard would be out of office, Jefferson's Republicans would reign supreme, and Hamilton would be dead.

JEFFERSON ASCENDANT

Early in his presidency, in his more placid moods, Jefferson was apt to minimize the clash between Republicans and Federalists as the product of disputes over international diplomacy. Those disputes seemed to abate in 1801 and 1802. The rise to political supremacy of Napoleon Bonaparte, whom Jefferson despised and feared, sapped the Republican leadership's fervor for France and narrowed the differences between Jeffersonians and Federalists. ("[A] gigantic force has risen up which seems to threaten the world," Jefferson would write to an English friend two years later.) The pause in European hostilities following the signing of the Anglo-French peace treaty of Amiens in 1802 further tranquilized America's foreign relations with France and Britain. Yet the lull was deceptive, and proved only that the interests of the United States were inextricably bound up with the desires and designs of the two great Atlantic powers, regardless of the situation in Europe. Remarkably, amid the lull, Jefferson completed the most auspicious act of his presidency, the Louisiana Purchase.[25]

The continuing entanglements among the United States and the Old World powers were partly the result of rapid American movement and settlement westward. Prior to Jefferson's election, two new trans-Appalachian states, Kentucky and Tennessee, had been added to the Union. Following "Mad" Anthony Wayne's victory over the Shawnees, Ottowas, and other tribes at the Battle of Fallen Timbers in 1794, settlers flocked to Ohio, which was admitted as the seventeenth state in 1803. Politically, all three new states leaned toward the Jeffersonians. Commercially, their interests led them to place additional pressure on the administration to sustain Americans' rights to free navigation on the Mississippi River, as well as their rights to free deposit of goods in New Orleans as guaranteed by Thomas Pinckney's treaty with Spain signed in 1795. So long as feeble Spain, on its last legs as an imperial power, controlled New Orleans, and with it the expansive Louisiana Territory to the west and north, western American flatboats could expect no interruption in supplying eastern and international shippers with ample agricultural goods. European power politics, however, complicated by the revolutionary stirrings of the age, intervened.

In 1800, Bonaparte, envisaging a revival of the French empire in North America after nearly half a century of decline, secretly arranged with Spain for a retrocession of the Louisiana Territory, including New Orleans, to France— an arrangement to be formally announced at a later date. Also in secret, he plotted the overthrow of Toussaint L'Ouverture. Some leading northern Federalists, including John Adams—who as president appointed a consul general to Saint Domingue in 1799 and instructed him to emphasize amity as well as trade—had encouraged the insurgents. Jefferson, however, was deeply concerned, even prior to the Gabriel Prosser scare, about the effects L'Ouverture's revolution might have in the United States. Although he tolerated commerce with Saint Domingue when it seemed likely to offset French designs for a New World empire, too much trade with the rebels, he wrote to Madison, would bring "black crews, supercargoes & missionaries thence into the Southern states." To the pleasure of arch New England Federalists such as Timothy Pickering, Jefferson's embrace of egalitarianism was selective. The president even dropped hints that he was willing to aid in L'Ouverture 's demise if it would help persuade France to make a lasting peace with Britain. "[N]othing would be easier," he reportedly told the French chargé Louis-André Pichon in the summer of 1801, "than to furnish your army and fleet with everything, and to reduce Toussaint to starvation."[26]

A French takeover of Louisiana was an entirely different matter. That would turn the most belligerent European power into America's western neighbor. News of the retrocession agreement inevitably leaked out. Jefferson abruptly changed course, telling the French that, were Bonaparte to grab Louisiana, the United States would ally with Great Britain against France.

Two developments later in 1802 deepened the western crisis. In June, news arrived in Paris that a French expeditionary force under Napoleon's brother-in-law, General Charles Leclerc, had routed the Saint Domingue revolutionaries and, by trickery, taken L'Ouverture prisoner. (The black Jacobin would die of cold and starvation, in April 1803, in a dungeon-room jail in the French Jura Mountains.) Then, in mid-October, the Spanish suddenly closed New Orleans to international commerce and revoked the Americans' right to deposit their goods in the port. Spain's motives remain obscure; interfering with deposit rights was a clear violation of Pinckney's treaty. In Congress, outraged Federalists and some western Republicans, certain that France was responsible for the closure, began talking of forcibly seizing New Orleans. Jefferson made some preliminary preparations for war but decided to hold off until he had received word from Robert Livingston, his minister in Paris, who had instructions to purchase New Orleans and the Florida territories from Napoleon and end the crisis peacefully.

The Louisiana Purchase was one of the luckiest strokes in the history of American diplomacy. Livingston was an experienced politician, but no match for Napoleon's supremely cynical foreign minister Talleyrand, who, as ever, held the Americans in contempt. (That the self-assured Livingston was deaf, irritable, and unable to speak French did not help the American effort.) Early in 1803, alarmed by the closing of New Orleans, Jefferson officially recognized the retrocession of Louisiana to France and nominated James Monroe (who knew France well and was trusted by western Republicans) to bolster Livingston's mission. But Jefferson, working closely with Secretary of State Madison, also sent word across the Atlantic restating America's objections to France's planned takeover of Louisiana. And after hours at the White House the French envoy Pichon, attending one of the president's famous informal dinners, noticed that Jefferson, seasoned in drawing-room diplomacy, "redoubled his civilities and attentions to the British chargé."[27]

Monroe arrived in France authorized to offer Bonaparte upwards of ten million dollars to purchase New Orleans and the Floridas. When he met with Livingston, he learned to his astonishment that, in the interim, Bonaparte had renounced Louisiana, and Talleyrand had inquired about the possibility of America's purchasing the whole of Louisiana Territory, the enormous uncharted expanse that lay between the Mississippi River and the Rocky Mountains. Livingston, stupefied by Talleyrand's proposal, had restated his original offer, but when he and Monroe finally comprehended what the French were saying, they quickly concluded a treaty that went well beyond their official instructions. At a total cost of fifteen million dollars—about three cents an acre—the United States would end the French imperial threat, secure New Orleans and the Mississippi River Valley, and more than double its own land area. "We have lived long," Livingston remarked at the treaty-signing ceremony, "but this is the noblest work of our whole lives."[28]

In reality, the Louisiana Purchase was the result of many factors and the work of many people, including the ex-slaves of Saint Domingue. Conquering the island for France and reinstating slavery proved much more difficult than capturing Toussaint L'Ouverture, in part because of the locals' continued armed resistance and in part because an outbreak of yellow fever began killing off the French invaders by the hundreds. When Bonaparte learned in January 1803 that General Leclerc himself had died of the fever, the first consul's imperial enthusiasm faded quickly. Fed up with his American adventures, in need of fresh revenues for future military campaigns, and eager to forestall an Anglo-American alliance, he solved three problems at one stroke: the bargain-rate sale of Louisiana.[29]

In the context of the Napoleonic struggle for world supremacy, the Louisiana Purchase was a minor episode. Yet for most American citizens, it marked a virtual second Declaration of Independence. Excited talk of peace and commerce—and not of territorial acquisition—dominated the celebrations. "We have secured our rights by pacific means: truth and reason have been more powerful than the sword," the *National Intelligencer* exulted. Jefferson saw the Purchase as vindication of his preference for diplomacy over armed conflict. "Peace is our mission," he wrote to his English friend Sir John Sinclair, "and though wrongs might drive us from it, we would prefer trying every other just principle of right and safety before we would recur to war."[30]

The New England Federalists took the greatest notice—balefully—of the vastness of the territory suddenly acquired, feeding the partisan rancor. "We are to give money of which we have too little for land of which we already have too much," exclaimed one writer in the Boston *Columbian Centinel*—a wasteland "unpeopled with any beings except wolves and wandering Indians." The Virginians, and not the nation, would benefit by carving out innumerable new states and securing their political dynasty. Yet these fears made little impact, either in Congress (which quickly approved the Purchase treaty and related enabling legislation by large majorities) or in the country at large. Shrewder Federalists conceded that the purchase would heighten the administration's popularity, particularly among eastern commercial interests who well understood the importance of securing control of the Mississippi. "[O]n the whole," Rufus King wrote, "it seems agreed on all sides that the measure will operate in favour of the new administration, whose authority and popularity extend in every quarter."[31]

Actually, Jefferson's strict-constructionist scruples, and his suspicions that the Constitution did not grant the executive explicit power to acquire new territory, did more to delay the matter than the Federalist opposition did. But his most forceful advisers, ranging from Treasury Secretary Gallatin to Thomas Paine, thought that the constitutional issue was wispy, and urged Jefferson to go ahead. "It appears to me one of those cases with which the Constitution has nothing to do . . . ," Paine wrote. "[T]he idea of extending the territory of the United States was always contemplated, whenever the opportunity offered itself." Bonaparte was restless—war with Great Britain had resumed only two weeks after the signing of the Purchase treaty—and the amendment process was cumbersome and time-consuming. Jefferson backed off his objections, secure in his view that the Purchase would provide sufficient land to keep the United States an agrarian yeoman's republic for all time. But, typically, Jefferson also expressed his general view against "broad construction," lest any Federalist—or John Randolph—think he was abandoning principle. In the long run, he wrote, "the good sense of our country" would correct any evils that might arise from the Purchase.[32]

Over the coming decades, the consequences of the Purchase would indeed disturb public opinion over constitutional issues connected to the expansion of slavery—and help rip the country to pieces. But in 1803 those far-off cataclysms were hard to imagine. Instead, the chief short-term political effect of Jefferson's diplomacy was to advance the political decline of the Federalists—a decline so precipitous that some ineffectual New England hard-liners like Timothy Pickering, who despaired of ever seizing the national government back from the Virginia Jacobins, spoke of seceding from the Union. "[T]here is no time to be lost, lest [Federalism] should be overwhelmed, and become unable to attempt its own relief," Pickering wrote to George Cabot. "Its last refuge is New England; and immediate exertion, perhaps, its only hope."[33]

The expedition into Louisiana led by Jefferson's private secretary, Meriwether Lewis, and William Clark helped consolidate the Jeffersonians' fortunes. Even before he had the chance to purchase the whole territory, Jefferson had obtained a secret congressional appropriation to enable the explorers to find a path to the Pacific, study the geography of Upper Louisiana, and learn the customs of local Indian trade and diplomacy. In May 1804, with the unexplored vastness now part of the United States, Lewis and Clark's "Corps of Discovery," nearly fifty in number, embarked from the settlement of St. Louis and headed up the Missouri River. Eighteen months later, the group reached the Pacific, and in September 1806, it returned to St. Louis bearing amazing stories along with specimens of exotic flora and valuable furs.[34] As a feat of well-planned and well-executed daring, and an exercise in Enlightenment mapmaking and taxonomy, the Lewis and Clark expedition was an extraordinary success, which solidified Americans' imaginative hold on their new domain. Politically, Lewis and Clark's triumph further wounded the opposition. "The Feds alone treat it as philosophism, and would rejoice of its failure," the president wrote to Lewis over the winter of 1804–05 — but eighteen months later, the "philosophism" had plainly paid off.[35]

Political issues predating the Purchase, above all the lingering affair of the judiciary commissions, also played out to the Republicans' short-term advantage — or, more precisely, to the Federalists' disadvantage. The battle over repeal of the Judiciary Act had led congressional Federalists over the edge. "We are standing at the brink of that revolutionary torrent which deluged in blood one of the fairest countries of Europe," Minority Leader Bayard asserted at the close of his floor speech opposing repeal. ". . . The meditated blow is mortal, and from the moment it is struck, we may bid a final adieu to the Constitution." After failing to persuade the Supreme Court to kill the repeal immediately, some of the more conservative congressional Federalists continued the fight by publishing philippics, getting friends to petition the Congress, and planning test cases to help reinstate the act. But their efforts went nowhere, even in the Federalist courts. The Federalist George Cabot complained of "how little dependence there is, even on good men, to support our system of policy and government."[36]

The Supreme Court's now-famous ruling in *Marbury v. Madison*, delivered by the moderate Chief Justice Marshall in February 1803, halted the Federalist counteroffensive, much to the surprise of Republican and Federalist alike. For more than a year, the case had loomed as a showdown between the judiciary and the executive — and specifically between Marshall and Jefferson. And, indeed, in a detailed but taut decision, the Court lambasted Jefferson and his administration for withholding the disputed commissions from Marbury and his colleagues, calling it "not warranted but violative of vested legal right." Without holding Jefferson personally responsible, Marshall made it clear that he thought the grand lama had squandered the people's trust. No Federalist campaign pamphlet could have presented a more cogent case against Jefferson's reelection in 1804.[37]

But Marshall's attack also misled, for it came coupled to a cleverly convoluted ruling against Marbury. The plaintiff, Marshall asserted, certainly deserved his writ, and under the Judiciary Act of 1789, the Supreme Court had the power to grant it. However, Marshall went out of his way to declare that that power expanded the Court's jurisdiction in ways that ran afoul of Article III of the Constitution, and was therefore null and void. Marshall's long and fearsome prologue tossed the Federalists a bone and allowed their press to rejoice that the Court had determined that "Mr. Jefferson, the idol of democracy, the friend of the people, had trampled upon the charter of their liberties."[38] But in cold political terms, the *Marbury* decision turned back the Federalists' campaign over the judiciary and averted a potentially explosive constitutional crisis pitting the Court against the executive—and it left poor Marbury without his judgeship. The Jeffersonians appreciated as much. The major Republican newspapers, Smith's *National Intelligencer* and Duane's *Aurora*, as well as the vexed Jefferson let the case pass without comment.

The *Marbury* ruling contained a keynote principle for which it has since become famous—the idea that the Court has ultimate constitutional authority to overrule acts of Congress as well as the states, commonly referred to as judicial review. Yet *Marbury* hardly established the principle of judicial review of state laws, a power the Constitution had already invested in the Supreme Court. And it was, and is, far from clear that Marshall intended the *Marbury* decision to establish the Supreme Court as the final arbiter on federal legislation. He never claimed such power outright during his remaining thirty-three years on the Court, although he would have several opportunities to do so; indeed, he was always cautious whenever discussing the Court's powers. Although expansive ideas on judicial review—amounting more exactly to judicial supremacy— gained numerous champions over the coming years, in practice the principle would lie dormant for more than two decades after Marshall's death, until advanced by a Court with a very different political outlook, and in a much more politically inflammatory case concerning the legal status of an obscure black man named Dred Scott.

Marshall's genuine achievement was to fend off efforts to politicize further the national judiciary in the immediate wake of the repeal of the 1801 Judiciary Act—and thereby contribute to a beleaguered but evolving politics of moderation. He managed to attack the Republicans and remind them of the principle of judicial review without forcing a showdown with Jefferson. But he also confuted those Federalists who had hoped to use the case to cripple Jefferson and his administration. "Let such men read this opinion and blush, if the power of blushing still remains with them," declared the pro-Marshall *Washington Federalist.* "It will remain as a monument of the wisdom, impartiality and independence of the Supreme Court, long after the name of its petty revilers shall have sunk into oblivion."[39] Temporarily, at least, Marshall's ruling helped consolidate a middle ground between judicial supremacists and antijudicial Republican dogmatists, based on a de facto compromise: Federalists would accept the repeal act and cease their partisan maneuverings, provided Republicans curtailed their own assaults on Federalist control of the judiciary.

Federalist irreconcilables, concentrated in New England, were neither placated by Marshall's denunciation of Jefferson nor capable of compromise. Worse still, the acquisition of Louisiana and the apparent rising popularity of the president seemed to augur the Federalists' total defeat in national politics. The midterm elections of 1802 had gone badly for the Federalists, who, despite their early hopefulness about divisions among their opponents, lost ground to the Republicans in some supposedly safe districts, including the Delaware seat of House minority leader Bayard. The coming presidential election, with Jefferson running once again at the head of the Republican ticket, looked like a certain rout. The Federalists, many of whom inclined naturally to pessimism in the best of times, were most alarmed by the growing signs that unchecked democracy, what George Cabot called *"the government of the worst,"* was not collapsing under the weight of its own incompetence. For that, they chiefly blamed the unscrupulous, demagogic Virginia Republicans—above all, Timothy Pickering wrote, "[t]he cowardly wretch at their head," who "while, like a Parisian revolutionary monster, prating about humanity, would feel an infernal pleasure in the utter destruction of his opponents."[40]

Quietly, Pickering and his cabal of Federalists continued their plotting to get New England, along with New York and New Jersey, to secede. By contemplating separation, the plotters displayed less regard for the federal union than had the backers of the Kentucky and Virginia Resolutions of 1798. By homing in on the political advantages handed Virginia and the rest of the slaveholding South by the Constitution's three-fifths clause, they at once hit the Virginians at their sorest ethical point, as the preachers of liberty and owners of slaves, and reaffirmed the underlying sectional differences in national affairs. But the Federalists, even those who considered slavery an evil, were no abolitionists. ("Without a separation," Pickering wondered, "can those States [i.e., New England, plus New York and New Jersey] ever rid themselves of negro Presidents and negro Congresses, and regain their just weight in the political balance?") The immense irony of erstwhile nationalists advocating secession was not lost on such leading Federalists and Unionists as Alexander Hamilton and Rufus King, and the secession conspiracy faded for lack of support. Instead, Pickering and company turned their attention to the ever-fractious nominal Republican, Vice President Aaron Burr.[41]

By 1804, Burr, thoroughly distrusted by Jefferson and Jefferson's friends in Congress, no longer seemed as indispensable as he had four years earlier to secure the Republicans' crucial electoral base in New York. Jefferson had long relied on the aging New York governor George Clinton for advice about policy and patronage, and in February 1804, the Republican congressional caucus duly dumped Burr and named Clinton as its nominee for vice president. Immediately, Burr set his sights on winning the New York governorship, a prospect that intrigued some Federalist hard-liners. "Were New York detached (as under [Burr's] administration it would be), from the Virginia influence, the whole Union should be benefited," an excited Timothy Pickering wrote in early March. "Jefferson would then be forced to observe some caution and forbearance in his measures." But in 1804, as in 1801, Burrite Federalists faced the stern opposition of Alexander Hamilton, who despised Vice President Burr even more than he did President Jefferson.[42]

For years, despite public displays of mutual cordiality, Hamilton had hated and pursued Burr with a passion that, if not necessarily "pathologic" as one biographer has concluded, certainly bordered on the obsessive. To Hamilton, Burr was an undistinguished and mendacious self-promoter, a man of "an irregular ambition" and "prodigal cupidity." Hamilton's opposition made little difference to the New York governor's race, which Burr lost by a landslide, thanks in part to slanderous attacks on the candidate by George Clinton. But Burr blamed Hamilton anyway, making much ado over a particular alleged slight, and the stage was set for an "interview" with pistols at Weehawken, New Jersey, just across the Hudson from Manhattan, on the morning of July 11. The next day, Hamilton, a bullet lodged near his spine, died in agony. Burr, indicted for murder by courts in both New York and New Jersey, fled to South Carolina, ever thereafter an object of vilification. From New York, Secretary Gallatin wrote to Jefferson after Hamilton's funeral that "much artificial feeling, or semblance of feeling," worked up by the anti-Burr and Federalist interests, had mingled with the public's sincere shock and grief at what occurred. Gallatin failed to mention a riper irony: that in encouraging an alliance with Burr, certain Federalists had set in motion events that led to the killing of Hamilton, the greatest Federalist mind of all.[43]

Following the momentous duel, the presidential election of 1804 came as something of an anticlimax. However, in sharp contrast to the contest four years earlier, it ended in one of the most lopsided outcomes in all of American history. The Federalists, overcome by their loss of the presidency four years earlier, held no nominating caucus; instead, Federalist leaders and electors privately conferred with each other and, insisting they would only choose the best man after the electoral votes had been cast, settled on Charles Cotesworth Pinckney of South Carolina and Rufus King, now of New York, as their nominees. In effect, the party ran no campaign, except for their electoral slates in the states. Pinckney and King did not lack experience, talent, or high reputation. But the Republicans, having built up their state-level organizations, stifled their internal differences, profited from peace, prosperity, and Jefferson's popularity, and rendered Pinckney and King forgotten also-rans—or, more properly, never-rans. The Republicans lost only two states and won 162 electoral votes to 14 for their adversaries. Even in the Federalist citadel of Massachusetts, the Republicans not only carried the presidential tally but increased their vote for state and local offices, completing, as John Quincy Adams told his father, a revolution in the commonwealth's politics. "The new century opened itself by committing us on a boisterous ocean," Jefferson rejoiced, taking special pleasure in the Massachusetts result. "But all this is now subsiding, peace is smoothing our paths at home and abroad, and if we are not wanting in the practice of justice and moderation, our tranquility and property may be preserved, until increasing numbers shall leave us nothing to fear from without."[44]

Nothing to fear from without—but from within? Political developments were further solidifying the Republican ascendancy over the Federalists, but also contained some disturbing divisions and paradoxes, with greater ramifications than the Burrite schism for the Jeffersonians. Growing tensions between city and country democrats, on the one hand, and Republican moderates, on the other, intensified divisions within the party. Sectional differences presaged far fiercer national conflicts to come. And these divisions arose directly from complicated struggles, concentrated in state politics, to define a democratic polity.

FEDERALISTS, CLODHOPPERS, AND TERTIUM QUIDS: DEMOCRACY IN THE STATES

In 1806, Jefferson's favorite American architect, Benjamin Latrobe, ventured some thoughts on politics, writing that "[a]fter the adoption of the Federal Constitution, the extension of the right of suffrage in the States to a majority of all the adult male citizens, planted a germ which [has] gradually evolved and has spread actual and practical democracy and political equality over the whole union."[45] Latrobe exaggerated. The Jeffersonian ascendancy, by repudiating the Federalists' hidebound elitism, greatly encouraged democratic ferment. After 1800, formal petitions and newspaper articles flooded state capitals demanding widened suffrage and fairer representation for rapidly growing cities and backwoods settlements. Overall, however, democratic reformers, urban and rural, won only a few solid victories. In some places, especially in the slaveholding South, even the successful reforms in the decade after 1800 achieved less than met the eye. And although Republicans were usually at the forefront of change, pressure for democratization divided moderate and radical Republicans against each other.

One set of pressures for democratic reform came from the organization of new territorial and state governments west of the Alleghenies. As fresh settlers swelled the Old Northwest population, constitutional and political organization became an issue of primary importance. Settlers in the northern territories objected primarily to the fifty-acre freehold qualification for voting in the western territories, a restriction inherited from the Northwest Ordinance of 1787. Newly established western newspapers, North and South, railed against all vestiges of aristocracy, quoting from the work of various British and American democratic reformers. In Ohio, radical Republican democrats defended the rights of "laboring men" and farmers, and demanded a constitution "that will set the natural rights of the meanest African and the most abject beggar upon an equal footing with those citizens of the greatest wealth and equipage." Other democrats were less egalitarian, notably on racial issues, but still insisted that the landholding upper class—"a kind of Noblesse," one Jeffersonian called it—should relinquish any claims to formal political supremacy. Although they did not win all they wanted, the democrats created a new state government, and after that a Republican-dominated party system, far more egalitarian than their Federalist adversaries had desired.[46]

Practical considerations also advanced western democracy. Above all, the legal complications of surveying western land and granting freehold titles often were too cumbersome to accommodate any propertied voting requirement. In Kentucky, freehold suffrage, established in 1776 while the area was still part of Virginia, was useless given the state's Byzantine land laws and constant litigation over land titles. Hence, the state's relatively conservative state constitution of 1792 conceded universal free manhood suffrage, with no property or taxpaying requirement. In Ohio, delays in granting freehold land titles so restricted the territorial electorate that in 1798, even before statehood, the federal government enfranchised owners of town lots that were worth as much as fifty-acre freeholds. By 1815, Kentucky was the only western state that matched Vermont's complete elimination of property requirements for voting, but Ohio's constitution of 1803 established virtual adult male suffrage by imposing a minimal taxpaying requirement (while also restricting the vote to whites, as Kentucky had done in its revised constitution of 1799). Tennessee sustained a freehold requirement that would last until 1834, but provided as an alternative a trivial six-month residency requirement that was tantamount to granting adult manhood suffrage.[47]

Kentucky, with its wide-open suffrage for white men, was the site of the most dramatic western reform clash of the Jeffersonian years. Picking up where they had left off after the disappointing constitutional struggle of 1799, Kentucky's country democrats, still strongest in the state's rapidly growing yeoman Green River district, turned back to legislative matters, and to a radical version of Jeffersonian-style judicial reform. Led by a resourceful political newcomer full of home-spun eloquence, the twenty-two-year-old lawyer Felix Grundy, the reformers undertook replacing Kentucky's centralized and (to remote settlers) inaccessible court system with circuit courts that would meet three times a year in each county for six-day terms. Demanding an "equal and impartial distribution of advantages and privileges," Grundy and his allies lambasted their opponents as an alliance of parasitic lawyers, lazy judges, and greedy land speculators who feared having local juries decide on their land titles. More moderate Republicans, including Henry Clay, replied that the proposed reforms would destroy the uniform and independent judiciary that was vital to continued economic growth. But Grundy's forces won a compromise reform in 1802 that enlarged the existing court system.[48]

East of the Alleghenies, southern reformers won a few triumphs. Maryland reformers, supported by Baltimore's city democrats, secured an adult male suffrage law and, in time, additional concessions including popular election of the governor and the elimination of property and religious tests for public officeholders. A revision of South Carolina's constitution in 1808 partially rectified the state's gross malapportionment by giving the state's up-country counties a majority of the seats in the lower house of the legislature. A year later, the city democracy of Charleston joined with backcountry planters (including a young Yale graduate named John C. Calhoun) to secure the franchise for all white male adults who had resided in the state for two years. The Carolina up-country, where politics had been comparatively open and competitive even before the revisions, greatly increased its power in the legislature, with the promise of it increasing even further with future reapportionment now scheduled every ten years. But the reforms also left the state senate securely in the hands of the low-country grandees and did nothing to alter the state's high property requirements for officeholding. The lower-house reapportionment wound up benefiting a new class of up-country cotton planters more than it did the pineywoods yeomanry. The state's suffrage debate turned on the claim that enfranchising all adult white men would further entrench popular loyalty to the institution of slavery. In all, democratization in South Carolina ironically went hand in hand with consolidating the power of the state's expanding slaveholder elite.[49]

Democratic reformers gained the most momentum during the first decade of the new century in the northeastern and middle states. A detailed look at events in these states shows the complexity of democratic reform as it actually proceeded during Jefferson's presidency, including the divisions reform efforts provoked among Republicans. It also reveals a pattern. Where Federalists and Federalism remained strong, the democrats' greater coherence created a viable Jeffersonian opposition and prepared the way for more successful reform efforts in later years. Where Federalists and Federalism were weakest—notably in Pennsylvania—growing pressure for democratic reform helped widen the gap between radical Republicans and moderate Republicans.

Federalist Connecticut was the most conservative northeastern state, its political institutions still governed largely on the terms of its original royalist charter of 1662. A virtual oligarchy of Federalist notables and prominent Congregational clergymen (leaders of what remained the state's formally established church) ran local affairs. Under the circumstances, state politics inspired little public interest. (In the 1790s, as few as 5 percent of Connecticut's eligible voters actually cast ballots in gubernatorial elections.) "The advancement of political science, generated by our revolution," one New York Republican paper observed, "has neither changed her constitution nor affected her *steady habits*." As the Massachusetts Federalist Fisher Ames put it, "folly"—that is, democracy—was not a fashion in Connecticut.[50]

In these straitened circumstances, the reform leader was an idealistic renegade of the Connecticut establishment. Abraham Bishop, graduate of Yale in 1778, came from a background "respectable for order and religion," one Federalist editor observed with chagrin. In 1787, Bishop traveled to Europe and returned home nearly two years later a red-hot enthusiast for *liberté, egalité,* and *fraternité*. Over the next ten years, as one of the few outspoken critics of Federalism in the state, he became a genuine political force. Bishop denounced the Hamiltonian funding system as "the Political Baal," described Federalism as a sort of miasma that addled the brains of the voters, and ridiculed the union of church and state. When he was not taunting his opponents, Bishop was busy behind the scenes organizing editors and dissenters that one pro-Federalist newspaper grumbled about as "the democratic literate, so often, at houses of public entertainment [chiefly, taverns] who harangue the mob." Although they could not carry Connecticut for Jefferson, Bishop and his allies established the Connecticut Republicans as a distinct party organization, directed by a statewide Republican general committee that appointed county committees, which in turn oversaw town and district committees.[51]

Just as important as the Bishop Republicans' strictly partisan efforts were their attempts to reform Connecticut politics and government. Bishop himself proposed to write a new state constitution that would totally separate church and state, provide for genuine checks and balances among the three branches of government, and widen the franchise. Federalists moved quickly and surely to crush these and other "Jacobinical" heresies by enacting a complicated and intimidating new measure, soon dubbed the "Stand Up Law," that required *viva voce* polling in all elections except those for governor or town representative. It would take another fifteen years before the Connecticut reformers gained the initiative. Yet the Republicans had rattled the Federalist establishment and provoked the electorate out of its political slumbers. Between 1804 and 1806 the number of voters who participated in the state's gubernatorial election would increase by 70 percent.[52]

In Massachusetts, never a one-party state, Republican organization and pressure for democratic reform developed more successfully. The state's Federalists were just as fearful of Jeffersonian extremism as were their Connecticut counterparts—but having survived Shays' Rebellion and weathered the turmoil of the 1790s, Massachusetts conservatives shrank from the sorts of intense counterdemocratic activities undertaken by Connecticut's conservatives. Republican organizers accordingly built a political organization even more sophisticated than the Connecticut machine, headed by the party's legislative caucus, which chose the statewide central committee. County and town committees had the chief responsibility for widening popular support, circulating campaign materials, and getting Republican voters to the polls. The Massachusetts Republicans also introduced democratic procedures within the party, including countywide conventions that nominated candidates for Congress; passed resolutions on sundry public matters; and conducted, as one convention announced in 1808, "such other business as might be deemed necessary for the support of the Republican cause."[53]

The major political battles in Massachusetts concerned the state's antiquated judiciary—not over whether to reform it but over how thoroughly it should be reformed. Between 1803 and 1805, the Federalist-controlled state legislature enacted several reforms outlined by Theodore Sedgwick, the former Speaker of the U.S. House of Representatives who had been appointed to the Massachusetts Supreme Court. Massachusetts Republicans accepted most of Sedgwick's proposals, but objected fervently to two of them: increasing judges' salaries and limiting juries' powers to interpret the law, which the reformers believed would permit the solidly Federalist state bench to continue its blatantly partisan domination.[54] Between 1803 and 1806, the Republican legislators, although in the minority, killed every proposal to increase the salaries of the state supreme court justices. They remained equally vocal about allowing juries to interpret the law as they saw fit, sometimes reaching the point of endorsing what today would be called jury nullification.[55] But after 1806, when the Republicans actually gained control of the legislature, the terms of debate over the judiciary and state politics lurched leftward—and the Republicans began to factionalize into moderates and democratic radicals. Country democrats, including the remainders of the old Berkshire Constitutionalist movement, demanded complete elimination of the common law, further simplification of court procedures, and the popular election of all judges. (The claim that voters lacked sufficient wisdom to choose judges, the Baptist itinerant John Leland contended, "saps the foundation of all representative government, and supports the monarchical.") Boston's city democrats, led by Benjamin Austin, also agitated on the matter. Moderate Republicans reacted with alarm and, led by the lawyer Joseph Story of Salem, moved quickly to thwart them.[56]

The breach opened in 1806 when, with moderate Federalist support, Story chaired a special committee that insisted on maintaining the judiciary's independence and recommended, among other reforms, an increase in judicial salaries, which the legislature enacted. The radicals denounced the new law, in the apoplectic mixed metaphors of the *Pittsfield Sun*, as "nothing short of a premeditated blow at the *root of Democratic Government*, and a *Chief Corner Stone* of the great *Fabric of Aristocracy*."[57] But the radicals lacked the legislative muscle required to repeal the law, or to get rid of Story, who, with Federalist backing, was reelected head of the lower house's judiciary committee in 1807 and 1808. With the Republican majority now sorely split, Story did not manage to complete any further moderate judicial reforms, but the radicals, too, were stymied, which created lasting divisions among Massachusetts Republicans.

The middle Atlantic states, where sophisticated party organizations had developed before 1800, presented their own peculiarities with respect to democratic politics, often closely tied to voter fraud. The one major New York reform of the period came after New York City Federalist election inspectors, in 1801, refused to allow Republican voters who had been issued temporary freehold deeds to cast their ballots. Under the city charter, dating back to colonial times, voting in local elections was restricted to freemen of the corporation or male twenty-pound freeholders. (Voting was also *viva voce*.) Most ordinary New Yorkers could not meet the financial requirements, and Federalists, in control of the corporation, refused to grant freemanships to any but their merchant friends. Consequently, in 1800, although 13 percent of the city's total population was qualified to vote in state elections, only 5 percent could vote in municipal elections. Republican operatives got around the exclusion by issuing the temporary freeholds. Incensed at their exclusion in 1801, a group of cartmen petitioned the mayor and alderman. Republicans, in and out of the city, supported them, and in 1804, the state legislature passed a law that overrode the city charter, established written ballots in city elections, and gave the vote in assembly elections to all adult male citizens who rented a tenement worth twenty-five dollars a year.[58]

Across the Hudson River, in New Jersey, intense partisanship and lax enforcement of voting requirements bred concern among Republicans and Federalists alike. In 1802, numerous complaints arose after a Trenton election in which, critics claimed, ineligible minors, Philadelphians, slaves, married women, and others were permitted to vote. Five years later, a vigorous contest in Essex County, to determine whether Newark or Elizabeth would be the county seat, caused so many irregularities—including, allegedly, trooping scores of women, eligible and ineligible, to the polls—that the total vote in Newark alone was greater than had ever been recorded for the county as a whole. The legislature duly clarified the regulations and granted the vote to free white males who paid any state or county tax—an approximation of universal white manhood suffrage. But the new law also barred blacks and noncitizens from voting and ended the state's singular enfranchisement of propertied widows, purposefully included in the state constitution of 1776. Supporters of female disenfranchisement justified it as a response to the Essex County fiasco: the new regulations simplified matters by making it easier to determine, at a glance, who was an eligible voter.[59]

The reform struggles in Pennsylvania were the most ferocious of any in the nation. The suffrage was not at issue, as the drafters of the state constitution of 1790 took care to preserve the relatively mild taxpaying requirement stipulated in the original radical 1776 constitution. Instead, politics revolved chiefly around judicial reform, as in Kentucky and Massachusetts. But Pennsylvania was also a very special case. After 1802, when the Federalists lost in a crushing statewide defeat, the state's chief political battles pitted against each other, as nowhere else, powerful rival Jeffersonian factions of moderates, city radicals, and country radicals. These contests would eventually spill over into federal affairs and affect the brand-new national Republican coalition.[60]

The nominal leader of the moderates, Governor Thomas McKean, had, prior to his election in 1799, served for more than twenty years as the first chief justice of Pennsylvania's Supreme Court, and had been active in drafting the 1790 constitution. More politically gifted than the aloof and arrogant McKean was his secretary and staunch ally, Alexander J. Dallas. A brilliant immigrant from the West Indies, Dallas had risen quickly in Philadelphia oppositionist politics after the Revolution—including a stint as a member of the Democratic Society of Pennsylvania—and had considerable influence and power throughout the state. Two other veterans of the political wars of the 1790s, Peter Muhlenberg and Albert Gallatin, were also leading moderates. Bitterly opposed to the Federalists' organic conceptions of hierarchical privilege and order, they nonetheless found some common ground with the Federalists about the courts. Above all, the moderates believed that through prudent economic development, ordinary men would seize upon the ample opportunities the nation had to offer and rise in the world. One prerequisite for that development was an efficient, independent judiciary, which would permit the widening of economic growth free of political connections.[61]

To the left of the McKean-Dallas faction stood the still-vibrant Philadelphia city democracy, led by William Duane of the *Aurora* and his longtime collaborator Michael Leib. Together, Duane and Leib had built a powerful local Republican electoral machine, especially strong in the city suburbs heavily populated by laboring men. On national issues, they sided with those who wanted President Jefferson to purge the government of Federalists and overhaul the federal judiciary from top to bottom. Closer to home, they attacked the application of arcane common law by state courts, demanded the creation of arbitration courts elected by the people to decide contract and title disputes, pushed to reduce the power of trained lawyers, and sought to expand the power of the lower legislative house at the expense of the governor and the senate. The city democrats viewed McKean, Dallas, and their moderate friends as backsliders, and even traitors, to the Republican cause, and the principles of the Revolution. The contest was "no longer that of resistance to foreign rule," the *Aurora* declared, "but *which of us shall be the rulers?*"[62]

A third group of Pennsylvania Republicans consisted of country-based insurgents who came to be known, memorably (after a derisive remark by McKean), as the Clodhopper Democrats. Their foremost figure was the future governor Simon Snyder, an exemplar of how ambitious country democrats of modest backgrounds could attain the highest state offices. Born in Lancaster, Snyder had moved to southeastern Northumberland County in 1784, a partially schooled twenty-four-year-old. By working as a journeyman tanner and as a scrivener, Snyder made enough money to purchase some land, build a mill, and open a store. His neighbors elected him justice of the peace, chose him as a delegate to the state constitutional convention in 1790, and elected him to the state legislature in 1797. After arriving in Lancaster, the state capital, Snyder befriended another freshman legislator, Nathaniel Boileau, the son of a Montgomery County farmer, who had matriculated at the College of New Jersey in Princeton and was then admitted to the Pennsylvania bar. Rounding out the Clodhopper leadership was the remarkable Irish-born émigré printer John Binns, whose activities across the Irish Sea as a young member of the radical London Corresponding Society landed him in prison on several occasions before he fled to America in 1802. Lured to Northumberland County by his fellow British radical exiles, Joseph Priestley and Thomas Cooper, Binns established a newspaper in 1802, the Northumberland *Republican Argus*, which, as the Clodhoppers' chief political organ, quickly became the most important rural newspaper in the state, a counterpart to the *Aurora*.[63]

The court struggle began in 1802, and it culminated, briefly, in a statewide coalition of city and country democrats that frightened moderate Republicans and Federalists alike. Initially, Republicans of all persuasions could agree on the need to reform the judiciary and check the most blatantly partisan Federalist justices—above all, the chief judge of the western circuit, Alexander Addison, whom Governor McKean denounced as "the transmontane Golia[t]h of federalism," and whom the moderates impeached and removed from office. But Duane and the Philadelphia radicals wanted more—a clean sweep of Federalist justices from the state supreme court and a complete overhaul and simplification of the state's legal code to place it more in line with what one critic called "the plain and simple nature of a Republican government." Deriding the McKean moderates as the Tertium Quid—literally, the "third thing," standing between Federalism and genuine Republicanism—Duane, Leib, and the city democrats forged an alliance with Snyder, Boileau, and their country counterparts and founded a mass organization, complete with country committees, called the Democratic Society of the Friends of the People, an echo of the 1790s. They pressed for additional removals and managed to impeach (though not convict) three more Federalist justices. They also proposed a new state convention to overhaul the state's judiciary.[64]

In 1805, the coalition of the Snyderites and the Philadelphia radicals, with the elderly Thomas Paine's benediction, managed to persuade the Republican legislative caucus to dump McKean as its gubernatorial candidate, in favor of Snyder. Horrified, a coalition of moderate Republicans and Federalists endorsed McKean's reelection. The ensuing campaign was one of the nastiest in Pennsylvania history, filled with Snyderite charges that McKean had systematically ignored the will of the people and McKeanite counterblasts that a victory for Snyder would plunge the state into the "pristine imbecility" of a pure democracy. Drawing his support chiefly from older, commercialized agricultural regions as well as from the major cities (other than the Duane-Leib–controlled parts of Philadelphia County), McKean eked out a five-thousand-vote majority— but, as Albert Gallatin noted, he owed "his re-election to the Federalists." Tensions arose thereafter between country and city democrats, in part because the country democrats favored various moderate Republican proposals to widen access to bank credit and promote road-, canal-, and bridge-building projects that the *Aurora* group believed favored established Philadelphia vested interests. Yet under the pressure of a sudden Federalist revival, the Clodhoppers effected a rapprochement with both the Quids and the *Aurora* democrats, succeeded in electing the Clodhopper Simon Snyder as governor in 1807, and commenced a Republican regime that would last for a decade.[65]

The vicissitudes of Pennsylvania politics expose the shortcomings of the many interpretations that cast the politics of the Jeffersonian era as a straightforward battle between sharply demarcated partisan interests: agrarian versus commercial, or pro-capitalist versus anticapitalist, or backward-looking Federalists versus forward-looking Jeffersonians (or vice versa). For the men who lived through these politics on the ground, as well as for those who shaped them at the top, the Republican coalition, in particular, was much more complex and fractious than such interpretations allow.

What we can see, in Pennsylvania and the other states, is the emergence of a diverse new generation of democratic political leaders, ranging from the Yale apostate Abraham Bishop to self-made men such as Felix Grundy and Simon Snyder. Their vehemence against both Federalist elitism and what they deemed the tepidness of some Republicans stirred up politics in their respective states and offered portents of democratic outbursts to come. The actual achievements of these men and their followers was limited. Even where reform succeeded, the results were not always uniform or lasting. (One, little noticed at the time, was the decision by Pennsylvania, after the electoral crisis of 1800, to switch to the direct popular selection of presidential electors in time for the 1804 campaign. By 1804, a total of eight of the seventeen states provided for direct election, beginning a trend that, by 1824, would leave only six of the twenty-four states where legislatures still did the choosing.) "Democratization" chiefly marked growing differences between the somnolent slaveholding South—where, at least in South Carolina, democratization of a kind became, ironically, a bulwark for slavery—and the more agitated North—where democratization accompanied both the enactment of gradual emancipation laws in the last holdout states and the emergence of a viable Republican opposition to the Federalist political establishment. In the long run, these differences would cause the breakdown of the Union. In the short run, they highlighted the persisting divisions within American politics at the state as well as the national level, despite the formation of a successful new party and the decline of an old one—even as the newly reelected president savored his crushing triumph in the 1804 election.[66]

THE SECOND PRESIDENCY

In contrast to the exquisite care with which he wrote his first inaugural address, President Jefferson had the chance to be loose and expansive when he came to write his second. "The first was from the nature of the case all profession & promise," he boasted to a young Virginian, John Tyler, whereas the second was "performance." The optimism was misplaced. In part because of his own political overreaching, Jefferson would leave Washington in 1809 feeling like a released prisoner. His new troubles became manifest already during the months between his reelection and his second swearing-in.[67]

The administration's struggle against the judiciary had not ended with *Marbury*. Emboldened by the Pennsylvania Republicans' ouster of Judge Alexander

Addison, Jefferson and his lieutenants decided to use the weapon of impeachment to attack their most obnoxious foes on the Federalist bench. Their choicest target was a deranged and allegedly alcoholic federal district judge, John Pickering of New Hampshire. Impeached by the House for drunkenness and unlawful rulings, Pickering was tried by the Senate, and removed from office in March 1804 by a bare two-thirds' majority. But Pickering's was to prove only a warm-up case. On the very same day that the Senate removed him, the House passed a resolution, introduced weeks earlier by John Randolph, calling for the impeachment of a far more formidable figure, the doctrinaire yet resourceful associate justice of the Supreme Court, Samuel Chase.[68]

Chase was, in 1804, the most powerful conservative Federalist in the federal government, and the Republicans' loathing for him ran deep. Confirmed by the Federalist-controlled Senate in 1795, he turned into a single-minded enforcer during the alien and sedition crisis. He presided belligerently over several of the most sensational sedition trials and punished those convicted to the limits the law allowed. Moderate Federalists, including President Adams, abjured his behavior, and the more radical of the Republican editors demanded his impeachment. Jefferson, in his early conciliatory phase, decided against assailing him. But Chase's bitterness and recklessness increasingly got the better of him, especially after the repeal of the Judiciary Act of 1801. In May 1803, while riding circuit in his native Maryland, he delivered, as a charge to a Baltimore grand jury, a polemic against various signs of what he called impending "mobocracy," including the administration's judicial policies and Maryland's recent adoption of universal white manhood suffrage. "The modern doctrines by our late reformers, that all men in a state of society are entitled to enjoy equal liberty and equal rights have brought this mighty mischief upon us," he raged to the jurors, his massive frame shaking, "and I fear that it will rapidly progress until peace and order, freedom and property, shall be destroyed." Jefferson immediately (and impulsively) wrote Congressman Joseph Hopper Nicholson of Maryland, broadly hinting that Chase ought to be impeached and removed from the Court, while adding that "for myself, it is better that I should not interfere."[69]

Although Chase had plainly disgraced his position, Jefferson would have been wiser, politically and constitutionally, had he heeded his own caution and said nothing. Impeaching the incompetent Pickering, though itself of questionable constitutional correctness, was one thing; impeaching Chase, who was harshly partisan but patently fit to serve, was quite another. Chase's courtroom speech, construed by Jefferson as "seditious," hardly amounted to a self-evident high crime or misdemeanor, the sole grounds for impeachment as stipulated by the Constitution. Although the Republican press, including the *National Intelligencer*, attacked Chase repeatedly over the summer of 1803, most Republican leaders, including Congressman Nicholson, seemed unwilling to test either

Chase or the Constitution—and even Jefferson in time calmed down and took no official action. Suddenly, however, in January 1804, John Randolph, the least reliable of the congressional Republicans, rose in the House and introduced his resolution. It required nearly an additional year of discussions and debate, but in the end, Randolph and his allies prevailed and the House passed eight articles of impeachment. One of the articles singled out Chase's charge to the Baltimore jury as "an intemperate and inflammatory political harangue" intended "to excite the fears and resentment of said grand jury, and the good people of Maryland" against the governments of Maryland and the United States.[70]

The irony, for Jefferson, was that by the time he took up the Chase issue, the troublesome Randolph was on the verge of breaking with the administration over another matter entirely, the so-called Yazoo compromise, involving alleged administration corruption in a long-standing Georgia land-fraud dispute.[71] Randolph's motives for pursuing the Chase and Yazoo matters combined ideological rectitude, personal hurts, and his sense that his influence was on the decline. Randolph and his allies were powerful enough to delay a settlement of the Yazoo case until after President Jefferson left office. The Chase impeachment, however, proceeded more swiftly, and, for the Republicans, more dangerously. There is no evidence that Jefferson, as much as he wanted Chase ousted, approved of Randolph's taking the lead in the effort. Several leading northern Republicans, in both the House and the Senate, tried to slow down the impeachment process. But in 1804, most Jeffersonians in the House of Representatives still detested Samuel Chase far more than they distrusted John Randolph. With some misgivings, they sent the articles of impeachment on to the Senate.[72]

Chase's trial, presided over by Vice President Burr, back from his exile, and conducted with great pomp and solemnity in the Senate chamber, was a debacle. Chase, a seasoned lawyer, assembled a superb defense team, including the southern Federalists Robert Goodloe Harper and Luther Martin. In contrast to Chase's meticulous and unflappable defenders—especially Martin, a notorious drunk but a courtroom bulldog—Randolph and the House impeachment managers looked amateurish. Randolph's final summation, a rambling affair that lasted more than two hours, was described by one listener, the admittedly biased John Quincy Adams, as "without order, connection, or argument; consisting altogether of the most hackneyed commonplaces of popular declamation, mingled up with panegyrics and invectives upon persons, with a few well-expressed ideas, a few striking figures, much distortion of face and contortion of body, tears, groans, and sobs, with occasional pauses for recollection, and continual complaints of having lost his notes."[73] The show concluded, mercifully, on March 1, 1805, three days before Jefferson's second inauguration. A majority of the senators found Chase guilty on only three of the eight impeachment articles, and just one article—the eighth, covering Chase's charge to the Baltimore jury—came within five votes of winning the two-thirds' majority required to convict and remove the accused. Six of the twenty-five Republican senators, all but one of them northerners, voted against all of the articles.*

By rejecting a constitutionally dubious impeachment drive, the Chase acquittal established practical limits on the congressional impeachment power, while it reinforced judicial independence. These were vital steps in the continuing battle over the shape of the nation's democratic institutions, and the principles they established would be respected for decades. Yet the case did stigmatize the kind of blatantly partisan behavior that Chase had assumed was his privilege. (Victorious but humbled, old Chase served out his term politely and without controversy until his death in 1811.) For Jefferson, the entire affair had proved an embarrassment, though nowhere nearly as great an embarrassment as it was for Randolph, who never fully recovered politically and who forever suspected, with good reason, that Jefferson had quietly hung him out to dry. Embittered by the outcome, Randolph and his friends, their revolt against the administration broken, would become known as Old Republicans or as Tertium Quids, neither Federalist nor Jeffersonian (but not to be confused with the Pennsylvania moderate Republicans given the same nickname by their radical foes).

The only national figure who emerged from the affair with his reputation enhanced was the outgoing vice president, Aaron Burr. When, after the clamor over his killing of Hamilton subsided, Burr had resurfaced in Washington, some northern Federalists wondered if he ought to be impeached as well, since he was still under indictment for murder in New York and New Jersey. But neither Republicans nor southern Federalists agreed. Instead, as president of the Senate, Burr oversaw the proceedings against Chase with widely acknowledged fairness and dignity. The day after Chase's acquittal, Burr delivered a stirring valedictory speech to the Senate that reduced some listeners to tears. Soon enough, though, Burr was embroiled in his customary intrigues, which caused Jefferson's next major round of political headaches.[74]

All the mysteries of the Burr conspiracy will probably never be revealed, but enough is known that it must be judged an authentic threat, not just to Jefferson but to the republic. This can be difficult to grasp, for in retrospect the drama easily looks like a convoluted farce, featuring a huge cast of unlikely characters. But wrapped inside the farce was a near disaster. Even before he had finished his vice presidency, Burr began plotting with the money-hungry Brigadier General James Wilkinson, who was the commanding officer of the U.S. Army and governor of

---

* Two of the articles, concerning Chase's alleged disregard of Virginia procedures in the sedition trial of James Callender, won not a single vote in the Senate. See AC, 8th Congress, 2nd session, 664–9.

the new Louisiana Territory (and, secretly, an agent for the Spanish Crown). The two conspirators' plans were mutable; new ideas kept coming to them as they boastfully tried to inveigle various American politicians, military leaders, and rich, would-be power brokers, as well as foreign diplomats, into supporting their scheme. At the very least, it seems, they expected to launch military attacks on Mexico, persuade the western states to secede, and create a new nation on the North American mainland. Only Wilkinson's defection late in 1806 halted the planned attacks.[75]

The real threat the conspiracy posed to American democracy concerned the uncertain political allegiances of the nation's military leadership. When he took office in 1801, Jefferson, reacting to the Federalists' partisan military buildup, moved to depoliticize and reduce drastically the size of the army. (The latter effort led to the establishment of the United States Military Academy at West Point in 1802.) But the process—which curtailed opportunities for career advancement for all existing officers—took time to promulgate, leaving a disgruntled officer corps intact just as Jefferson, after the Louisiana Purchase, needed the U.S. Army more than ever to command western military posts. Then, Jefferson's unmilitary reactions to a series of British provocations on the high seas after 1805 added to the discontent among officers with state as well as national commissions. Burr tried to exploit these weaknesses as he traveled among the officer corps, feeding on the resentments against the president and promising a stirring and patriotic military adventure. Burr was convinced he owned General Wilkinson's loyalty. To his new recruits, including a Tennessee militia commander in Nashville, Andrew Jackson, whom he personally courted, he applied his full powers of charm and persuasion. "[Y]our country is full of fine Materials for an Army," he told Jackson, "and I have often said that a Brigade could be raised in West Ten[nessee] which would drive double their Number of frenchmen off the Earth." Thousands of miles to the west of Washington, the possibility of domestic military interference in internal American politics, raised by Hamilton in 1799 and 1800, loomed once again—led, this time, by Hamilton's slayer.[76]

Finally, and fortunately, General Wilkinson's sole loyalties were to himself. Fearing that Burr's military plans had become preposterous and hoping to sustain his standing with both the American and Spanish governments, Wilkinson betrayed Burr to Jefferson. Even before Burr was apprehended and transferred to Richmond for trial on charges of treason, Jefferson, in one of his rash moments, publicly proclaimed Burr's guilt and then plunged into trying to ensure his conviction. The trial—in which Burr retained a team that included none other than Samuel Chase's defender, Luther Martin—became a political imbroglio. Federalists, including presiding Justice Marshall, used the occasion to embarrass Jefferson, going so far as to issue a subpoena to the president. (Jefferson, on straight constitutional grounds, correctly refused to reply, and from here on, his contempt for Marshall was unequivocal.) Aided by the chief justice's peculiarly narrow construction of the Constitution's treason clause, Burr won a "not proven" verdict, which Marshall recorded as "not guilty." The government tried then to have Burr sent to Ohio to face new treason charges, but Marshall granted Burr bail—which Burr, in character, jumped. He then sailed to Europe and attempted in vain to gain an audience with Bonaparte to essay yet another intrigue.[77]

Amid Burr's trial, and while still facing Marshall's subpoena, President Jefferson confronted a realized military threat. On June 22, 1807, HMS *Leopard*, one of a squadron of British ships stationed off the coast of Virginia, intercepted USS *Chesapeake*, on the suspicion that the American frigate was harboring four British deserters. The American commander, Commodore James Barron, rightly refused the request to search his ship—such searches were permissible on merchantmen, but not on warships—then temporized, without calling his men to their battle stations. The *Leopard* opened fire on the Americans, killing three and wounding eighteen. After the Americans struck their colors, the British boarded and seized the alleged deserters, all of whom claimed to be Americans. The *Chesapeake* then limped back to Norfolk a splintered wreck.[78]

The *Chesapeake* incident had been long in coming. The collapse of the Peace of Amiens in 1803, followed in 1805 by the British naval victory at Trafalgar and the French army's triumph at Austerlitz, had left Britain the commander of the Atlantic, France the commander of the European continent, and the United States a neutral with no military leverage whatsoever. In the spring of 1806, a single British warship, HMS *Leander*, stationed off New York Harbor, halted as many as twenty merchantmen at a time, pending searches for deserters. In April, one of *Leander*'s shots across the bow of another vessel killed an American sailor, which touched off a riot in Manhattan and furious indignation around the country. The attack on the *Cheapeake* a year later, followed by fresh British Orders in Council banning neutrals from trading with France and its colonies, poured oil on the fire. The nation was furious; Jefferson shared that fury but was more ironic: "I suppose our fate will depend on the successes or reverses of Bonaparte," Jefferson wrote some weeks after the attack. Two weeks later, he sounded angrier—"It is really mortifying that we should be forced to wish success to Bonaparte," he told John Taylor—but after initially favoring a military response, he detached himself from the war fever. Instead, he would try to mobilize the public's outrage toward a policy of peaceful compulsion.[79]

Jefferson's philosophy of international conflict directly challenged the bellicose expediencies of raison d'état that had driven Old World diplomacy for centuries. Jefferson was no pacifist. He thought the British attacks deserved a forceful response, and rejected the idea (which many Federalists and foreigners ascribed to him) that he should pursue peace at any price. ("This opinion must be corrected when just occasion arises," he wrote in 1806, "or we shall become the plunder of all nations.") But he knew that, in part because of his own policies to reverse the Federalist debts and taxes, the country was in no position to take on Great Britain. And his Enlightenment principles led him to regard war, with its ghastly cost in lives and property, as the absolute final resort in international disputes. European powers held him in contempt for this, but that much was to be expected. Instead, with the strong backing of Secretary of State Madison (and despite the personal opposition of Treasury Secretary Gallatin) he favored commercial coercion, a form of economic warfare that had been tested and proved at least partially effective—though far less so, in retrospect, than Jefferson and others believed they had—since the agitation against the Stamp Act in 1765.[80]

And so, in December 1807, Jefferson replied to the British with what amounted to a boycott in reverse—a proposed embargo that would prohibit all oceanic trade with foreign nations, later extended to cover land and water commerce with Canada. Given a choice of evils, war or a radical embargo, Jefferson decided to pick, as a test, what he called, in a letter to Gallatin, the *"least bad."* Both houses of Congress swiftly passed the embargo bill. Aghast when voluntary compliance with the measure quickly abated, Jefferson personally and relentlessly sought to enforce it, requesting supplementary laws to halt smuggling across the Canadian border and across the Atlantic. These culminated in the draconian Giles's Enforcement Bill, enacted in January 1809. Disobedience of the law, sometimes flagrant, continued, prompting Jefferson to approve mobilizing troops in upstate New York and deploying revenue ships off the Atlantic coast and on inland waters. When challenged over the embargo's severity, the president privately denounced his critics, centered in maritime New England, as disloyalists, inflamed, he wrote, by "the monarchists of the North." Yet, outside of his annual messages in 1807 and 1808, and a calm but unyielding reply to a round of anti-embargo petitions from Massachusetts, he made inadequate efforts to explain the policy to the public or to understand the public's grievances, which he believed the Federalists were exaggerating.[81]

The embargo was certainly a roll of the dice, but it was not a witless exercise in "Quaker-gun diplomacy," as it came to be ridiculed by Federalists. By embracing neutrality, Jefferson and Madison thought they could counter the duke of Portland's Tory ministry by influencing British as well as American public opinion. British oppositionists, especially those tied to manufacturing and American trade, could be counted on to blast the Portland ministry for advocating an oppressive imperial system disguised as a necessary exigency of war. Robbed of their best customer, Britain's sensible businessmen would, presumably, come to their senses and demand respect for American neutral rights. Jefferson also thought that, at the very least, the embargo would give the United States enough breathing room to get its own house in order. "Till they return to some sense of moral duty," Jefferson wrote of the Old World belligerents, "we keep within ourselves. This gives time. Time may produce peace in Europe. Peace in Europe removes all causes of differences till another European war, and by that time our debt may be paid, our revenues clear, and our strength increased."[82]

Neither time nor fortune aided Jefferson's experiment. Although the British opposition came to the Americans' defense, they lacked the political muscle to budge the Portland ministry. In the United States, the embargo's effects hit quickly and hard, cutting American shipping by as much as 80 percent and causing severe hardship among craftsmen and laborers in the seaport cities and neighboring farmers. Yet the embargo, although severe, was not quite the economic disaster its harshest critics claimed it to be, in part because the prosperity of recent years gave most merchants and farmers a cushion, and in part because the federal Treasury, which ran up an extraordinary total surplus of $17 million from 1805 to 1807, could withstand a cutoff of import duties. Those hardest hit by falling commodity prices—cotton and tobacco prices plunged by 40 to 50 percent in 1808—were southern planters, who were not among the leading complainers. In the Northeast, where the coastal trade appears to have thrived, resourceful merchants found ways to circumvent the laws and get goods shipped abroad, often with the connivance of local officials, including Republicans.[83]

The magnitude of the successful violations of the embargo, and, at times, violent resistance to it, deepened the pathos of Jefferson's situation. In New London, Connecticut, the collector of customs—a Federalist so powerful that local Jeffersonians did not wish to obstruct him—allowed dozens of ships to leave port and pick up cargoes on order before the embargo began. Massachusetts federal juries acquitted more than four out of five accused offenders brought up on charges of violating the embargo law. At least one customs house official was murdered, in coastal Maine, as a result of local resistance to the law. Smuggling was rampant across the Canadian border; newspapers and letter writers actually reported more ship activity than usual on Lake Champlain. The longer the embargo continued, the quicker public support evaporated. The quicker Jefferson lost favor, the more recalcitrant he became.[84]

New England led an all-out personal attack on the president. Yankee coastal towns and cities condemned the "dambargo"—also known in its reverse spelling as the cursed "o grab me"—from the moment it came into effect. As Jefferson became increasingly stubborn about enforcement, his personal correspondence, which always included hate mail, filled up with assassination threats and poison-pen letters. ("I have agreed to pay four of my friends $400 to shoat you if you don't take off the embargo by the 10th of Oct 1808 which I shall pay them, if I have to work on my hands & nees for it," ran one of many.) By late 1808, the Massachusetts legislature threatened to disregard the law, while looser tongues revived talk of New England secession.[85]

As if gathering together all of their frustrations of the past eight years, Federalist propagandists let loose, portraying Jefferson (much as they portrayed democracy itself) as at once feeble and despotic. One precocious poet, the thirteen-year-old William Cullen Bryant (whose politics later changed dramatically), composed a bit of nastiness, "The Embargo," that touched on every bit of scurrility ever aimed at President Jefferson, including the charge about Jefferson's secret love affair with his mulatto slave, Sally Hemings:

> Go, wretch, resign the president's chair
> Disclose secret measures foul or fair,
> Go, search with curious eye, for horned frogs,
> 'Mongst the wild wastes of Louisiana bogs;
>
> Go scan, philosophist, thy ****** [Sally's] charms,
> And sink supinely in her sable arms;
> But quit to abler hands the helm of state,
> Nor image ruin on the country's fate.

Jefferson's supporters, like the president himself, reacted with hurt and indignation. "We are nearly all in favor of the embargo," Governor John Langdon of New Hampshire reassured him, "and . . . would not suffer a few enemies and speculators to make their fortunes." William Plumer, a New Hampshire Federalist, left his party over the embargo, and attributed the New England uproar to "designing men" out to influence the coming elections. But if Republicans could dismiss the propaganda, they could not ignore that the embargo fight had refreshed the flagging Federalist opposition and emboldened the administration's southern Old Republican foes.[86]

Early in 1809, as Jefferson prepared to leave office, New England's congressional Republicans broke ranks with the administration over the embargo, joined by the New York friends of Vice President Clinton and the southern clique surrounding John Randolph. Jefferson admitted in his final annual message that the "candid and liberal experiment" had failed to coerce the Old World powers, but he still believed that the British would back down and hoped Congress would extend the measure in some form. The House refused the extension, then stipulated that the policy end on March 4, the day Jefferson was to step down. A "sudden and unaccountable revolution of opinion, chiefly among the New England and New York members," had led to the experiment's demise, Jefferson remarked bitterly. Instead, Congress passed a weaker substitute, the Non-Intercourse Act, allowing exports to all countries except Britain and France and permitting a renewal of trade with whichever of the belligerents showed respect for neutral rights. An undisguised appeal to mercantile self-interest, the new policy virtually ensured that both Britain and France would obtain all they wanted of American goods, and that British goods would be smuggled with impunity across American borders. "Thus we were driven from the high and wise ground we had taken," Jefferson wrote.[87]

Approaching the age of sixty-six and eager to retire to Monticello, Jefferson had firmly rejected supporters' entreaties that he seek a third term. Now he lacked the will to fight back over the embargo. But he battled hard to elect his secretary of state and political heir, James Madison, to the presidency. It was not a sure thing. John Randolph and other anti-administration Republicans persuaded James Monroe to allow his name to be placed before the Republican congressional nominating caucus as an alternative. Then Federalist state leaders, meeting secretly in a self-assembled conclave in New York, renominated their still-respected ticket of Charles Cotesworth Pinckney and Rufus King, claiming that they would restore the prosperity and national honor squandered by Jefferson's disastrous embargo. Younger Federalists, learning lessons from the Republicans and frustrated by their elders' antipolitical elitism, organized several state committees and geared up a disciplined electioneering machinery to promote their own brand of political elitism with populist trappings.[88]

Finally, the ancient Vice President Clinton, nudged along by his up-and-coming nephew DeWitt, presented himself as a candidate for both president and vice president, strongly attacking the congressional caucus system for nominations. Jefferson unflinchingly stood by Madison, tried to convince Monroe to back off, and proved the chief of the Republican coalition, winning over skeptics such as William Duane and the *Aurora* group and forcing Clinton to accept the second spot. The Federalists' turn to popular electioneering, meanwhile, could not overcome the Republicans' political machinery, especially in the southern and middle states. Madison defeated Monroe with ease in the congressional nominating caucus (which the Quids did not even bother to attend), and he and Clinton crushed the Federalist ticket in the Electoral College. With his administration given a vote of confidence, and his legacy secured, Jefferson virtually handed over command at that moment, weary of the fight, knowing that his successor was in a terrible bind. "Our situation is truly difficult," he wrote in November. "We have been pressed by the belligerents to the very wall & all further retreat [is] impraticable."[89]

On March 4, 1809, with the wounds from the embargo fight still bleeding, Jefferson declined Madison's offer to ride with him in his carriage to the inauguration ceremonies. Instead, he rode to the Capitol on horseback with his grandson, Thomas Jefferson Randolph, tied up his mount, and joined the assembly within. "[N]ever did [a] prisoner, released from his chains, feel such relief as I shall on shaking off the shackles of power," he wrote two days before. "[N]ature intended me for the tranquill pursuits of science, by rendering them my supreme delight. [B]ut the enormities of the times in which I have lived, have forced me to take a part in resisting them, and to commit myself on the boisterous ocean of political passions. I thank god for the opportunity of retiring from them without censure, and carrying with me the most consoling proofs of public approbation." A week later, after winding up some final pieces of personal business, he joined a small caravan of wagons and headed, at last, back to Monticello. Never again would Thomas Jefferson set foot in the city of Washington.[90]

THOMAS JEFFERSON, JEFFERSONIAN DEMOCRACY, AND DEMOCRACY

The once-revered Jefferson and his presidency have suffered a long-term decline in historical reputation that would have delighted any conservative Federalist snob or fractious southern Quid. Historians have accused Jefferson of betraying his principles once he reached office by expanding federal power and outfederalizing the Federalists, chiefly through the Louisiana Purchase and the embargo. Others view Jefferson as a hopeless visionary who became entangled with great historical forces that he did not understand. Some have condemned Jefferson as a hypocrite who vaunted human equality and at the same time dispossessed Indians, owned slaves (and sired children with one of them), did nothing to benefit free blacks (while himself benefiting politically from the extra representation and electoral votes given the slave South), and held what have since become distasteful views about women. Still others depict him as a wild-eyed utopian revolutionist who (according to one variation on the theme) was a Jacobin fellow traveler and prototerrorist or (according to another) was a sentimental agrarian who tried to block America's destined transformation into a modern commercial society. Some of these critics wrench a handful of Jefferson's more intemperate or grandiose private remarks out of context in order to sustain the Federalist plotter Timothy Pickering's judgment that he was a "Parisian revolutionary monster." Others, with a preference for perfect consistency over political dexterity, turn Jefferson's virtues as a pragmatic leader into vices. Still others indict him as a foe of civil liberties.[91]

These critics fail to recognize that Thomas Jefferson, although a fervent advocate of his principles, never thought he had to live up to some idealized abstraction of "Jeffersonian democracy" in the real political world. They seem to assume that time stood still from March 4, 1801, until March 4, 1809. The alleged grand inconsistencies of Jefferson's presidency were flexible responses to unforeseen events, responses to contingencies undertaken against fierce New England Federalist opposition—all the while in pursuit of ideals ranging from the enlargement of opportunities for the mass of ordinary, industrious Americans to the principled avoidance of war. The most significant of these, the Louisiana Purchase, was an outcome of luck more than design—but Jefferson smartly seized the opportunity.

Jefferson made serious blunders and miscalculations, especially in his anticlimactic second term. Ironies abounded, not least when Yankee Federalist obstruction of his boldest political experiment, the embargo, led the foremost champion of limiting federal power to try to impose federal power on almost every American community. And there were also victims of the Jeffersonians' success, quite apart from the Federalists. Although the great showdowns with the surviving eastern woodland tribes occurred after 1809, Jefferson's Indian treaties were predicated on his abiding faith that the white yeoman empire would—and should—supplant the Indians' hunting grounds. Regarding blacks, slave and free, Jefferson had abandoned the antislavery idealism of his youth as politically impractical. He believed that slavery was evil and that it was doomed—"interest," he wrote in 1805, "is really going over to the side of morality"—but he had no expectation that the end would come any time soon, and was ever fearful that precipitate emancipation would lead to race war and economic ruin. He had also reached the conclusion that blacks and whites could never peacefully inhabit the same country. His envisaged empire of liberty was for whites, with the inclusion of peaceable Indians who uplifted themselves and assimilated as idealized, virtuous yeomen farmers.[92]

The fashion to demonize Jefferson and Jeffersonian democracy, however, badly distorts the record. On slavery, for example, Jefferson and his party left an ambiguous but largely positive legacy. His own evolving views were ambivalent, summed up in his later famous remark that he would go to great lengths to end slavery "in any *practicable* way." As things stood, he wrote, "we have the wolf by the ear, and we can neither hold him, nor safely let him go. [J]ustice is in one scale, and self-preservation in the other." If he became maddeningly circumspect about slavery, with the fear of black insurrection always in the back of his mind—and, with respect to Saint Domingue, on the front of his mind—Jefferson always considered racial bondage a threat to white liberty and equality, contrary to the growing view among slaveholders that slavery made white equality possible. And although issues connected to slavery did not bulk large in national politics during Jefferson's presidency, when they did arise, the Republicans divided against each other along sectional lines. Against strong opposition from Deep South slaveholders, Federalist and Republican, Jefferson backed the earliest possible closing of the transatlantic slave trade, with its "violations of human rights which have been so long continued on the unoffending inhabitants of Africa, and which the morality, the reputation, and the best interests of our country have long been eager to proscribe."[93]

On other issues, ranging from the expansion of slavery into the western territories to slavery's future in the District of Columbia, northern Republicans, in and out of Congress, took outspoken antislavery positions on explicitly Jeffersonian grounds—proclaiming, in the words of one Massachusetts representative, that slavery negated "a proper respect for the rights of mankind." Basing his remarks on the Declaration of Independence and Paine's *Common Sense*, Abraham Bishop welcomed the insurrection in Saint Domingue and threw a challenge at his countrymen: "We have firmly asserted, *that all men are free*. Yet as soon as the poor blacks . . . cried out, *It is enough*, . . . we have been the first to assist in riveting their chains!" This northern Jeffersonian antislavery impulse would come into its own only after Jefferson left office. Yet even while Jefferson was president, antislavery Jeffersonians offered an alternative to Jefferson's own gloominess, discretion, and paralysis, and to the obdurate pro-slavery views of other southern Republicans. And Jefferson never tried to disown these antislavery men.[94]

Nor, despite Jefferson's repeated paeans to rural life, were he and his party monolithic, unyielding agrarians. Even before he became president, Jefferson noted that the costs of the country's remaining "merely agricultural," and whether "such a state is more friendly to principles of virtue and liberty," were matters "yet to be solved." The embargo, and then the developments that led to the War of 1812, would finally settle the matter, causing Jefferson to change his mind and advocate great manufactories. Before then, the northern Republican press was more supportive of manufacturing than the Federalists, who eschewed both manufacturing and government support for it as violations of "free trade"— that is, the continued domination of ocean-borne commerce and mercantile interests in the northeastern economy.[95]

It is extraordinary how much Jefferson and his collaborators did achieve in eight years. All of Jefferson's original legislative agenda became law. Thereafter, until the abandonment of the embargo in 1809, not a single important piece of Jeffersonian legislation failed to pass Congress. After 1801, the federal government ran a deficit in only one year before 1809, and accumulated a net surplus of more than $20 million. Although Jefferson resisted radical pressure to purge the government of Federalists and generally appointed accomplished men to office, he chose them on the basis of their records of intelligence and virtue, departing from the Federalists' preference for men of wealth and pedigree. Inside of four years, President Jefferson managed to turn the Republican majority of 1800–01—accompanying his own razor-thin victory—into the dominant force in national politics. He was the first American president to lead his party to triumph and, for nearly eight years, keep the momentum of that triumph going, while sustaining his immense personal reputation. (Even proud John Randolph, after his break with the administration, admitted that "[t]he colossal popularity of the President seemed to mock all opposition.")[96] Jefferson is also the only national leader in history ever to achieve the vast expansion of his country—more than doubling its physical size—while at the same time professionalizing and curtailing its military. He accomplished all this while enduring the most venomous sorts of personal and political attacks, originating from inside his own party as well as from conservative Federalists.

The links among Jefferson, Republicanism, and democratic reform were less straightforward. By beating back Federalist presumption, the Jeffersonian ascendancy opened up the political system, encouraging and enabling self-made plebeians such as Simon Snyder to reach for and attain high political office. Here was the greatest political achievement of Jefferson's two presidencies. Against Federalism's immense condescension and determined obstructionism, Jefferson and his party vindicated the political equality of the mass of American citizens—those ordinary men whom Jefferson's supporter Bishop described, in a tart reply to Federalist taunts, as the "poor ragged democrats" who would no longer defer to "ye well-fed, well-dressed, chariot-lolling, caucus-keeping, levee-reveling federalists."[97] In those regions and states, such as Bishop's Connecticut, where Republicanism initially was weakest, a substantial opposition arose and took the first steps toward democratic reform.

Popular participation in politics grew apace, in some places (especially in New England and the middle Atlantic states) exploding to levels unimaginable in the 1790s. In Massachusetts, the percentage of eligible white males who actually voted nearly doubled, reaching roughly 70 percent by 1808. In Pennsylvania, where turnouts of about 25 percent were typical for much of the 1790s, the proportion of free adult men voting for governor jumped from 56 percent in 1799 to 70 percent in 1808, a level not surpassed until after 1840. In some counties of North Carolina, turnouts reached beyond 80 percent. To be sure, voting for presidential electors still generally lagged behind that for state and local offices. (In

Pennsylvania, for example, there was a 32 percent turnout for the presidential voting in 1808, less than half that for the governor's race.) But even these figures marked a substantial increase over the norm before Jefferson's election. And in some places—notably New Jersey, where more than 70 percent of eligible voters cast ballots for president in 1808—rising participation in national elections matched or even exceeded that in state and local elections. Only in states, especially in the South, where party competition was minimal, notably Virginia, did participation fall—although this may have been a factor of the unusual interest in the 1800 contest as well as the lack of a credible Federalist opposition. The heightened involvement elsewhere also mattered more as states began to shift from choosing presidential electors by legislative vote to direct elections by the voters. The filters on democracy created by the Framers were proving porous, while the suppression of democracy sought by the Federalists in the 1790s was thoroughly discredited.[98]

Yet if democratic power and participation were expanding, politics and Republican Party affairs continued to operate at the national level largely from the top down. The congressional caucus held firm control over presidential and vice presidential nominations and the formulation of party policy. In the states where Republicanism was strongest, especially the South, reform was far less conspicuous than in other regions. Where reform did occur in the South, as in South Carolina, it paradoxically strengthened the power of the dominant slaveholder elite. If Federalism was badly weakened, the factions within the Republican coalition—urban radicals, rural Clodhoppers, schismatic Randolphite Quids, and dominant moderates—held very different views about democracy. The future of democratic reform depended on which of these Republican views prevailed.[99]

That outcome in turn depended on the leadership of the new president, James Madison—exacting, self-effacing, and the greatest proponent of republican constitutionalism in the nation. Madison was a more rigorous political thinker than Jefferson, yet he lacked the intellectual breadth and the personal prestige that helped Jefferson hold together the querulous Republicans and sink Federalism into the abyss. He also lacked his old friend's disarming shrewdness and charm. On the evening of his inauguration, Madison attended a crowded celebration ball accompanied by his vivacious wife, Dolley. Jefferson, no longer in charge, arrived at the festivities buoyant but a little unsure of how he should act. He managed to corner John Quincy Adams—who, strikingly, had supported Jefferson over the Louisiana Purchase and the embargo, and had now broken with his party—for a learned and lively discussion of Homer, Virgil, and various minor later classical poets before making his polite farewells.[100] Madison stayed on grimly, bored to distraction. Earlier in the day, he had mumbled through an unremarkable inauguration address, stating what he would repeat to visitors and friends in the coming weeks as his administration's basic posture in the wake of the embargo's failure: peace before war, war before submission.

Less than three years later, Madison would lead the country into the war that his predecessor had tried so hard, and at such great political cost, to avoid. The war's effects would startle the ultradoctrinaire Republicans, especially the surviving southern Quids, who assumed that military expenditures and wartime coercion inevitably destroyed public liberty. In some respects, in the ideologues' view, the war did just that. But in other ways, war generated fresh democratic forces with cruel ironies of their own.

5

NATIONALISM AND
THE WAR OF 1812

The coming of the war with Britain, and the war itself, permanently altered the structure of American politics. Internationally, the United States faced new tests of its will as a sovereign republic, secure in its rights to trade and sail the seas unencumbered. President Madison's exertions to find an honorable settlement short of war proved just as time-consuming and ineffective as had President Jefferson's. And domestic politics, connected as always to international politics, also remained troublesome, reopening debates over democracy and the scope of federal power.[1]

On his first full day in office, the new president found himself not yet entangled either with Napoleon Bonaparte or British Foreign Secretary George Canning, but with a leading country democrat, the Clodhopper governor of Pennsylvania, Simon Snyder, and the Olmstead affair. The dispute involved a meandering court case dating back more than thirty years. One Captain Gideon Olmstead, having heroically commandeered a British sloop to Philadelphia during the Revolution, demanded his fair share of the prize money due him from the state of Pennsylvania. In early 1809, the U.S. Supreme Court ruled in Olmstead's favor and ordered Pennsylvania to pay. But Governor Snyder stood fast against what he called unjust federal interference, and declared that he would call out the state militia to defy the Court's ruling. He was not bluffing. In late March, in Philadelphia, state troops, with bayonets fixed, forcibly prevented a U.S. marshal from serving the Court's writ.[2]

Snyder quickly backed down after federal authorities intervened, and Olmstead eventually got his prize money. The militia commander and eight of his men were convicted for resisting the service of the writ, but swiftly pardoned by

President Madison. The truly significant moment in the affair came when Snyder pleaded his case to Madison, railed against the Court's "usurpation of power and jurisdiction," and paraphrased the Virginia Resolutions of 1798 as if they endorsed the doctrine of state nullification. Madison's reply was at once conciliatory and firm, stating that the Constitution compelled him to enforce the Court's decree, and suggesting that Snyder give way.[3]

Few would recall for long the Olmstead affair, overtaken as it quickly was by momentous events at home and abroad. Yet Madison, in his handling of Governor Snyder, made it clear he did not believe that the Republicans' "Spirit of 1798" countenanced nullification—or any hint of state autarchy. As president, Madison would endorse a new and consistent but controversial Republican nationalism—too Republican to suit the persistent Federalists and too friendly to expanding federal power to suit many Republicans. In defending his position, Madison would eventually find himself leading the nation into war, while warding off domestic adversaries less pliable than Simon Snyder.

The war exposed the nation's internal rifts and military weaknesses. Although the Americans won some significant victories, they would be fortunate to conclude the conflict in a diplomatic impasse with the British. The war also pushed forward powerful paradoxes and omens about national development and democratic politics. Despite terrible embarrassments, Madison and the Republican nationalists, and their reconfiguration of Jeffersonian democracy, emerged politically supreme. Challenges to federal authority and even talk of secession abounded—but, ironically, these came chiefly from the erstwhile champions of strong central government, the New England Federalists. By sealing the fate of the Federalist Party as a national force, the conflict with Britain ended up affirming the Jeffersonian "revolution" of 1800–01, even though some Republicans thought that revolution had lost its way. Few democratic reforms of consequence occurred during Madison's presidency, but the war, by crushing Indian insurgencies in the South and Northwest, widened western expansionists' ambitions, which cleared the way for new permutations of American democracy. And the war's extraordinary final battle made a national hero out of a strange western slaveholding democrat who would dominate American politics over the decades to come.

THE RISE OF THE REPUBLICAN NATIONALISTS

The road to war ran unbroken from Jefferson's second administration. Instead of bringing Britain and France to heel, the Non-Intercourse Act irritated the British into sustaining the Orders in Council and impressing additional American sailors, and it led the French to seize American ships. In May 1810, the

Republican-controlled Congress, trying to tether a drifting foreign policy, passed an act stating that should either of the belligerents cease violating neutral rights, the president could punish the other one by suspending trade. The French, contemptuous as ever of the Americans, ambiguously promised to lift their own decrees against American shipping if Washington broke off trade with London. Madison agreed. But Napoleon did not immediately call off his ship seizures, leaving Madison vulnerable to criticism from the British and Anglophile Federalists. By the autumn of 1811, the three-way estrangement of Britain, France, and the United States was complete, with Federalists opposing a war with Britain, Republicans favoring one, and Madison caught in the middle. For a time, it seemed that the United States might enter an almost-certainly catastrophic triangular war with both of the great powers.[4]

Two domestic factors tipped the balance toward war with Britain, and Britain alone, in 1812. The first was the emergence of a new generation of aggressive, anti-British Republican nationalists, who saw the spirit of 1776 endangered. The second was the appearance of a prophecy-driven Indian resistance to white encroachment.

During the first eighteen months of Madison's presidency, Republican faction fighting flared, all the more intensely now that Jefferson was no longer in charge. Divergent domestic and foreign policy aims defined the various camps. The leading city and country democrats, including William Duane and Simon Snyder, as well as some alienated moderate Jeffersonians from Virginia and Maryland, were furious at Madison's decision to retain Albert Gallatin as secretary of the Treasury, especially after they had scared Madison off from appointing Gallatin as secretary of state. Not only was Gallatin tied to the most moderate of Pennsylvania Republicans; under Jefferson, and even more under Madison, he became increasingly bold in calling for federal spending on canal- and road-building projects that the city and country democrats feared would favor the monied few. In direct conflict with Jefferson, although with Madison's tacit approval, Gallatin also prepared the way to gain, in 1811, a rechartering and enlargement of the Bank of the United States. To critics like Duane, these actions made Gallatin nothing less than "the evil genius of this nation, more pernicious and corrupt than Hamilton was and much more dangerous because insidious, frigid, and profound in artifice."[5]

Duane and his fellow democrats were additionally enraged by Madison's foreign policy of commercial coercion—a policy they also blamed on Gallatin. When Jefferson's embargo failed, the democrats believed, the time had come for tougher measures, including preparations for a possible war against Great Britain. Gallatin—the "Genevan Secretary," Duane snorted—had unpatriotically intervened, counseling "base submission" to Britain's outrageous violations of American maritime rights to ensure that the treasury would continue to fatten on customs receipts. Only Gallatin's dismissal, and a new policy of armed neutrality and retaliation against the British, could vindicate the nation's honor and independence, Duane and the others declared.[6]

Another group, consisting of John Randolph and the eternally discontented southern Old Republicans, abhorred the idea of a war with Britain but also disdained Gallatin, and harbored even deeper suspicions of the president, even though he was a Virginian. Randolph and his friends had long despised Madison for his involvement in framing, defending, and ratifying the Constitution. As president, Madison's acquiescence in Gallatin's banking and internal improvement schemes, and his supportive stance over rechartering the BUS in 1811, deepened their alienation. Worse, in 1810 and early 1811, what looked like the increasingly anti-British drift of administration policy offended planter ideologues who feared war and a consolidation of federal military power, and who, in any event, were devout Anglophiles. Madison tried to placate the Old Republicans in 1811 by naming the orthodox Jeffersonian James Monroe as his new secretary of state—but by 1812, even Monroe would begin looking unreliable to the Randolphites.[7]

The younger Republican nationalists rejected what they considered Madison's appeasement of Britain as forcefully as did Duane. Yet to sustain, as historians have generally done, Randolph's polemical nickname for these nationalists, the "War Hawks," is to honor an eccentric source while reducing the group's outlook to bellicosity. Bellicose they were, especially toward Britain—but they also developed an expansive view of government and federal power, exceeding Madison's, that helped shape the nation's politics for the next forty years. Their foremost leader, now and later, was the young Kentucky lawyer Henry Clay.

Clay had come far since his reformist entry into Kentucky politics. After the pro-slavery Republicans' victory at the state constitutional convention in 1799, he tempered his egalitarianism and focused on his lucrative law practice. A gifted litigator, he gained special recognition for his talents in navigating Kentucky's arcane land-tenure laws and for his persuasive forensics in capital cases. He also married well, winning the daughter of one of Lexington's most prominent families. In 1803, Clay entered the state legislature, where he led the counterattack on the efforts by downstate yeomen to reform the state's court system. By 1805, Clay had become, at age twenty-eight, the leading spokesman for the Bluegrass Republicanism he had once battled so hard.[8]

After he went to Washington (initially to serve out two other men's separate unexpired terms in the U.S. Senate), Clay made a strong impression there too, though not solely for his legislative skills. "He is a great favorite with the ladies . . . ," his fellow senator William Plumer remarked, "gambles much here—reads but little." Clay's unfeigned gregariousness helped make him a political powerhouse. During elections, he not only joined in the required stump-side fraternizing and drinking, he genuinely enjoyed it. A vivid conversationalist who could swear like a sailor, he would sit around for hours, with friends and voters, backslapping, joking, snorting snuff. John Quincy Adams, who did read much, thought Clay's public and private morals loose, yet he conceded that Clay had all the virtues required in a popular leader and was "a republican of the first fire." In 1810, his Kentucky fortune secure, Clay announced his candidacy for the House of Representatives, claiming to prefer the "turbulence" of the lower house to "the solemn stillness of the Senate Chamber."[9]

Clay thought of himself as a devout Jeffersonian, and in some respects he still was. In the Senate, he staunchly opposed the pro-Gallatin moderate efforts to recharter the BUS, attacking the institution as a monopolistic, unconstitutional abomination, its stockholders mainly British and its officers and beneficiaries "a splendid association of favored individuals." Commerce and credit, he thought, were best expanded by local elites and the wildly proliferating state banks, most of them in the hands of friendly Republicans. Under his leadership, the Senate defeated the bank recharter bill.[10]

But Clay's days as a mere local improver were nearly over. In Washington, he declared that the West required nationally funded internal improvements and tariff protection. Just as urgently, he argued that the region needed the federal government to take firm action against Great Britain to ward off Indian attacks, Canadian competition, and naval interference with ships bearing western produce on the high seas. In 1810, he raised the roof of the Senate with a speech that pilloried the administration's policy of commercial coercion and called on "a new race of heroes" to vindicate the sacrifices of their patriot fathers. Clay's foreign policy pronouncements won him the most attention, but they were linked to a fresh view of American economic and political development, western in inspiration but national in its implications—the embryo of what would become known in later years as the American System.[11]

A distinct but related southern pro-nationalism also arose in and around 1810, advanced most brilliantly by John Caldwell Calhoun of South Carolina. Born in 1782 to a successful Scots-Irish backcountry family, Calhoun was only thirteen when he lost his father, Patrick Calhoun, an immigrant who had played a leading role in South Carolina's variety of the early country democracy. Breaking off his formal education, John helped work his father's twelve-hundred-acre plantation (with about thirty slaves) for five years to support his mother. When his older brothers agreed to take over, Calhoun returned to school with a vengeance, mastering Latin and Greek at his brother-in-law Moses Waddell's soon-to-be-famous backwoods academy. He then headed north to Yale, where he enrolled as a junior in 1802 and where his intellectual exploits remain legendary to this day. After graduating, Calhoun attended Judge Tapping Reeve's law academy in Litchfield,

Connecticut, then returned to South Carolina—not to the backcountry, but to aristocratic Charleston, where he read law in the office of the grandee Federalist attorney Henry William De Saussure. In 1808, he entered politics, winning election to the South Carolina House of Representatives. He arrived in the state capitol in Columbia in time to participate in revising the state constitution.[12]

Calhoun's rise bespoke social changes as well as his personal achievements. With an iron will molded by his indomitable father and by his Presbyterian upbringing, he plotted his self-improvement precisely and became something of a celebrity wunderkind in South Carolina—severe, even priggish, and totally lacking a sense of humor, but with a correct and cultivated charm and a powerful mind. Calhoun's was a special case, but it was not an utterly isolated one. South Carolina, with its abundant waterways connecting hill piedmont to tidewater, was open to the spread of plantation agriculture to the backcountry, especially in the early years of the nineteenth century, when short-staple cotton cultivation became practicable thanks to Eli Whitney's invention of the cotton gin. In 1800, Governor John Drayton proclaimed the state's exploding cotton production, in the backcountry as well as the low country, "a matter of National joy." By 1808, even distant portions of the piedmont were absorbed into the plantation economy. With that absorption came the emergence of a unique statewide planter elite, composed increasingly of former outsiders like John Calhoun but united in its endorsement of established low-country interests, above all slavery.[13]

The intermingling of South Carolina's backcountry and low-country slaveholders was a cultural and political as well as an economic phenomenon. Education was crucial: Moses Waddell's academy was one of several rural schools that arose after the Revolution to help prepare the sons of prosperous inlanders for the elite. Statewide improvements of bridges, ferries, and roads accelerated the backcountry cotton boom and lifted inland planters out of their social isolation from Charleston's high society. Intermarriage linked Charleston and piedmont fortunes. (In 1811, Calhoun married a low-country second cousin, Floride Colhoun, the daughter of a deceased Cooper River grandee and one-time U.S. Senator.) In state politics, the rising inland slaveholders, allied in national politics with the Republicans, eroded the Federalist low country's long-standing supremacy without threatening the solidarity of the slaveholders' regime—a process officially ratified by the reform of the state constitution in 1808.[14]

Calhoun embodied the persisting divisions as well as the overriding unity of the evolving South Carolina slavocracy. Despite his prolonged sojourn in Charleston, his sense of propriety always made him uncomfortable with what he called the low country's "intemperance and debaucheries." After he established himself in politics, he resettled permanently at Fort Hill plantation, about twenty-five miles from his backcountry boyhood home. Yet Calhoun's support for internal improvements and his intensifying association with long-established political families helped him assimilate in the highest political circles. Yankee-trained, Calhoun was also more cosmopolitan than many of his better-born low-country peers. If his worldliness did not enamor him of New England politics, it helped make him a fervent nationalist during his early days in Columbia and, after his election to the House of Representatives in 1810, in Washington.[15]

Anglophobia became for Calhoun, as for Clay, the chief initial outlet for his nationalist passions. British warships were blocking cotton shipments to Europe and had sent prices tumbling. Scorning both the Jeffersonian policy of peaceable coercion and the Yankee Federalists' friendliness to Great Britain, Calhoun concluded that the British had humiliated the new republic, and that only a rebirth of the old revolutionary spirit could vindicate the country. "It is the commence[ment] of a new era in our politicks," he wrote self-confidently shortly after his arrival in Congress, one that would end the "commercial arrangiments and negotiations" of the current regime, and dispel the chimera that the country could "avoid and remove difficulties by a sort of political management." That new era would advance deeper nationalist assumptions. "There is, sir, one principle necessary to make us a great people—," Calhoun declared, "to produce, not the form, but the real spirit of union, and that is to protect every citizen in the lawful pursuit of his business. . . . Protection and patriotism are reciprocal. This is the way which has led nations to greatness." Economic improvement with government backing had, in South Carolina, promoted statewide unity and prosperity. For Calhoun, it was essential to national unity and prosperity as well.[16]

Henry Clay and John C. Calhoun, arrivistes from the West and the South, gravitated to each other shortly after they entered the House of Representatives. The elections had brought a reshuffling across the country, stemming from popular resentment at American acquiescence to Great Britain. When the new House finally assembled, in November 1811, almost half of its 140 old members had been replaced, leaving Republicans in charge by a margin of three to one, with younger militants in the forefront. Clay, having already won notice in the Senate, was immediately elected to fill the vacant House Speakership. After welcoming Calhoun to join his informal boardinghouse caucus, he helped arrange for the South Carolinian's appointment to the powerful Foreign Affairs Committee. Other young newly elected members with similar backgrounds shared their views, including Langdon Cheves and William Lowndes of South Carolina, and Clay's old antagonist, Felix Grundy, who, having moved to Tennessee and married a second cousin of Calhoun's, had become an outspoken advocate of western commercial expansion. Key northeastern congressmen were also sympathetic, including Calhoun's old associate from Yale and Reeve's academy, Peter B. Porter of New York, now chairman of the Foreign Affairs Committee, who hoped that with a quick thrust across the border, the United

States might annex Upper Canada. All told, the militant younger men composed a bloc of around sixty representatives in the Twelfth Congress.[17]

To John Randolph and the other die-hard Old Republican agrarians, the new-style nationalist Jeffersonian Republicans, with their love of tariffs and armies, came to look like neo-Federalists. But there were enormous differences between Federalism and the kind of pro-development Republicanism the younger men espoused. Federalists remained skeptical about rapid western settlement; the young Republicans promoted orderly growth and development of the West, linked to ambitious internal improvements. Federalists clung to their belief that American prosperity required close and special connections with Great Britain, but the young Republicans favored developing the nation's internal markets as well as its agricultural exports. Above all, the new Republicans advanced a more democratized conception of economic development, opening opportunity, as Calhoun put it, "to every capitalist, however inconsiderable."[18]

On foreign affairs, the divergence between the younger nationalist Republicans and President Madison narrowed in 1810 and 1811. By the summer of 1811, Madison broadly agreed with Clay that war with Great Britain was almost inevitable. In November, the president greeted the new Twelfth Congress by announcing that it was time for "putting the United States into an armor and an attitude demanded by the crisis." He called for expanding the regular army and raising a volunteer corps.[19]

HOSTILE INCURSIONS: THE PROPHET, TECUMSEH, AND INDIAN RESISTANCE

Fed by Madison's new militance, hatred of England mounted, spiked by the second key factor in leading America to war—a continuing political and spiritual revival among the displaced western Indian tribes. Although the Republicans entirely blamed the British, the insurgency was more a product of long-standing bitterness between the Indians and American settlers. It was led by a charismatic one-eyed Shawnee prophet who called himself Tenskwatawa, and his older brother, the warrior Tecumseh.

During Jefferson's second term, the governor of Indiana Territory, William Henry Harrison, a son of the Virginia Tidewater elite, wrote repeatedly to the president about an alarming new Indian cult and its shaman leader, the Prophet—"an engine set to work by the British for some bad purpose." Harrison insisted that sinister forces lay behind the spreading cult: "[T]he Prophet is a tool of British fears or British avarice, designed for the purpose of forming a combination of the Indians, which in case of war between that power and the United States may assist them in the defense of Canada." Jefferson, who considered the Indian seer merely a "transient enthusiasm," ordered Harrison to find some way to buy him off. Dismissive of the Indians' religion and wary of the British, both men reacted with the paternalism and the callousness that guided federal Indian policy.[20]

In 1800, an estimated 600,000 Indians lived in what is now the continental United States, most of them west of the Mississippi. They were a mere remnant of the native American population, in excess of five million, before European arrivals brought devastating disease and displacement. The devastation had been particularly severe among the eastern woodland Indians, but the survivors still posed a problem for would-be American settlers. In the 1780s and early 1790s, raiding parties and combined forces of Shawnees, Ojibwas, and others success-fully resisted American expansion into Ohio Territory. The decisive American victory at the Battle of Fallen Timbers in 1794 and the ensuing Treaty of Greenville gained the Americans enormous tracts of Indian land—and threw much of the Indian remnant, now pushed farther west, into demoralized poverty. Thereafter, Republican policy toward the survivors combined complaisant respect for the Indians' potential for uplift with resolve that they take up yeoman-style agriculture.[21]

"I consider the business of hunting as already having become insufficient to furnish clothing and subsistence to the Indians," President Jefferson wrote to Benjamin Hawkins, his Indian agent for all of the tribes south of the Ohio River, in 1803. "The promotion of agriculture, therefore, and household manufac-ture"—by which Jefferson meant simple spinning and weaving—"are essential in their preservation, and I am disposed to aid and encourage it liberally." Jeffer-son projected an idyllic future yeoman republic in which "our settlements and theirs [would] meet and blend together, to intermix, and become one people." But Jeffersonian idealism about the Indians had a coercive side. One way to ensure that the natives would cede their hunting grounds on the cheap, Jefferson privately advised Governor Harrison, would be to ensnare them in debt for the cost of farming goods and other necessities. Active resistance could be punished by removal and resettlement across the Mississippi, as "an example to others, and a furtherance of our final consolidation."[22]

Jefferson thus injected an ethos of uplift into his policy of manipulation. In the territories, other Americans—Indian-hating farmers, impatient land specula-tors, ambitious politicians—were less benevolent. Harrison served those more aggressive interests as much as he served Jefferson. Only twenty-seven when he became governor of Indiana Territory in 1800, Harrison had fought at Fallen Timbers and later served as a delegate from the Northwest Territory to Congress. Like his fellow gentry paternalist Jefferson, he bore no particular hatred toward the Indians. But as Jefferson's local lieutenant, he became the chief agent for the expropriation of Indian land, by means fair and foul. Between 1802 and 1805, he completed treaties with nearly a dozen tribes to gain title to southern Indiana, most of Illinois, and parts of Wisconsin and Missouri for two and a half cents or less per acre. Harrison was a sharp bargainer, bribing Indian leaders, striking side deals with renegade splinter groups, and plying negotiators with liquor. The treaties provoked protests from Indians caught up in the vicious cycle of distress, who charged, with reason, that they violated the Greenville Treaty. "The white people . . . ," one Shawnee chief complained, "destroyed all that God had given us for our support."[23]

The Indians' discontent acquired powerful spiritual dimensions in 1805. A Shawnee healer named Lalawethika (or "the Rattle")—known among his fellows as a drunken idler—fell into a graphic dream-vision of the souls of the damned, their howls of suffering rising out of Eternity, "roaring like the falls of a river." Awakened, the healer swore off alcohol and began relating prophecies about the impending doom of the white invaders and sinful Indians. Americans, he declared, were children of the evil Great Serpent who had come from the sea to emasculate and conquer the Indians. To thwart them, Indians must ban alcohol, reduce their dependence on trade, and curtail social contacts with whites. From now on, he said, he would be known as Tenskwatawa (or "the Open Door"), the portal through which the regenerated Indians would gain salvation. By 1806, Tenkswatawa, also known as the Prophet, had enough of a following to build a new center for his religion—pointedly at Greenville, site of the despised treaty.[24]

For decades, shamans of different eastern tribes had envisaged apocalyptic scenes and bid their fellows to repent. Tenskwatawa was special for two reasons. Although an ugly, off-putting man, he was eloquent in a trance, "expressive of a deep sense and solemn feeling of eternal things," according to a group of wandering American Shakers who witnessed one of his performances. And Tenkswatawa's brother Tecumseh (or "Shooting Star") would soon embark on efforts that gave the Shawnee prophet's warnings additional force.[25]

Tecumseh had grown up in the Ohio River Valley to become an accomplished hunter and warrior. With his older brother, Chiksika, he participated in a number of bloody frontier raids in Kentucky and Tennessee in the late 1780s and early 1790s. He also fought at Fallen Timbers and, in its aftermath, refused to sign to the Treaty of Greenville. A respected chief by the time he reached his late twenties, Tecumseh led a small Shawnee band (including his wife and newborn son) to a permanent summer settlement in Indiana Territory in 1798. There he kept the peace and concentrated on the hunt.[26]

During the uneasy winter of 1805–06, as Lalawethika spoke of the holy Open Door, Tecumseh changed his clothes and bearing. He abjured the beads and ribbons and linen shirts sold by American traders, donned the Shawnees' traditional simple deerskin suits, and renounced whiskey forever. Although not a thoroughgoing convert to the Prophet's religion, Tecumseh was strongly affected by the antisettler vision. He drew political conclusions. Much as his brother updated old religious themes, so Tecumseh drew on secular precedents, including Shawnee efforts at building an Indian confederacy that dated back to the 1740s. As members of far-flung tribes made their pilgrimage to Greenville to see Tenskwatawa—probably the greatest religious awakening among the woodland tribes to date—so Tecumseh's political, and military, plans grew more ambitious.[27]

Heightened tensions between the British and Americans also pushed him. The British in Canada, defending a long and vulnerable border with the United States, were always looking for Indian support. The Americans, however, took any signs of goodwill between the British and the Indians—or, for that matter, of any change in Indian habits—as proof of an imminent Anglo-Indian offensive. Americans' fears worsened in the face of the Prophet's growing prominence. The senior British agent at Fort Malden, the chief British outpost in western Canada, could see clearly what was happening in 1806: "The discontent of the Indians arises principally from unfair purchases of their lands, but the Americans ascribe their dissatisfaction to the machinations of our government." In the late summer of 1807, President Jefferson, although still convinced that Tenskwatawa was more of a fool than a danger, ordered western governments to take military precautions.[28]

The brothers Tecumseh and Tenskwatawa, hoping to consolidate their resources and preserve a fragile peace with both sides, retreated from Greenville with their people back into Indiana Territory in 1808, settled near the lush confluence of the Wabash and Tippecanoe rivers, and built a new village that the whites would come to call Prophetstown. With its two hundred bark houses set along neat rows and lanes, its council house and medicine lodge, and more than one hundred acres of cultivated fields, Prophetstown was an imposing, busy site, visited by white traders and travelers as well as by Indian pilgrims. For the Indians, it would be the headquarters for spiritual renewal. So powerful were the Prophet's visions that even Governor Harrison (with whom Tenkswatawa met in August 1808) temporarily revised his opinion and declared the cult a positive influence for reform and peace. Tecumseh dickered with the British as well as the Americans, and shored up professions of mutual respect and nonaggression.[29]

The calm proved illusory. West of Prophetstown, the situation remained disturbed, as old complaints and new ones against the Americans, chiefly from the Sac, Fox, and Winnebago tribes, led to a brief war scare in the spring of 1809. Governor Harrison, his ambitions fixed on gaining Indiana statehood, continued his inflammatory bargaining and obtained nearly three million more acres of Indian land at about one-third of a cent per acre. Criticized even by some local American land officials, Harrison's acquisitions enraged Tenkswatawa and Tecumseh. Wearing a British military uniform, Tecumseh threatened village chiefs with death for their accommodations. In 1810 and 1811, he organized an Indian confederation based on the doctrine of pantribal common land owner-ship, and leaned toward a formal alliance with the British.[30]

"No difficulties deter him . . . ," Governor Harrison wrote of Tecumseh in 1811. "You see him today on the Wabash and in a short time you hear of him on the shores of Lake Erie or Michigan, or on the banks of the Mississippi, and wherever he goes he makes an impression favorable to his purposes." In fact, Tecumseh's aim extended far beyond the Great Lakes region, from New York all the way to Florida. Harrison recognized this and moved to check him. While Tecumseh, after a testy meeting with Harrison at Vincennes, was proselytizing among the Muskogees, Cherokees, and Chickasaws to the south in November 1811, Harrison made a decisive strike against Prophetstown.[31]

In violation of President Madison's express orders to prepare for war but keep the peace, Harrison gathered a force of nearly one thousand regulars and militia-men, marched them north, and camped provocatively close to Prophetstown atop a high plateau. Assured by Tenkswatawa's visions of the Americans' gunpow-der turning to sand and of the Indians becoming bulletproof, a force of between three and five hundred Indian converts—including Kickapoos and Winnebagos as well as Shawnees—attacked the Americans and inflicted heavy casualties in close-quarter combat. But the Open Door's visions came to naught. (He later blamed the failure on his wife's menstruation, which, he said, had weakened his spirit and sullied his medicine.) Despite heavy losses, Harrison's troops repelled the Indian attack. They then marched into Prophetstown, which the Indians had abandoned the night before, burned it to the ground, destroyed its food supplies, and opened and emptied Indian graves. Harrison claimed a great victory at what the Americans called the Battle of Tippecanoe.[32]

In December 1811, five weeks after Prophetstown's destruction and shortly after Tecumseh completed his journey south, an enormous earthquake, centered in what is now northwestern Arkansas, shook Indian villages and American towns as far east as South Carolina. Thousands of severe aftershocks felt from Canada to the Gulf of Mexico followed over the next four months. Sand and water spewed as high as treetops, birds perched on people's heads, and the Mississippi River temporarily reversed its flow. Indians everywhere drew dire, even apocalyp-tic conclusions. In Ohio, an Indian told Moravian missionaries that the Great Spirit was sorely displeased by what had happened at Prophetstown. Among the Creeks, whom Tecumseh had recently visited, young prophets known as Red Sticks proclaimed the earthquake a sign of the Great Spirit's decree that land ces-sions had to stop and the tribes had to unite. There were reports that Tecumseh had predicted the devastation, and in some variants, that he had actually caused it by stamping the earth until it trembled.[33]

Tecumseh was in Missouri, remarkably close to the quake's epicenter, making unsteady progress convincing local Shawnees and Delawares to join his confederation. In late January 1812, he returned to Prophetstown, which Tenkswatawa and the desolate survivors had reoccupied. While he tried to placate the Americans, Tecumseh edged ever closer to allying with the British. News of Harrison's attack arrived in Washington, to mixed reactions, just as the newly elected Twelfth Congress was assembling. John Randolph and the Anglophilic southern Old Republicans condemned the action as reckless. Western Federalists, thin though their ranks were, called Harrison a worthless busybody and condemned him for exceeding his orders and butchering the Indians purely to advance his personal ambitions. One Ohio Republican lamented the "melancholy affair" and wished it had never happened. Worse, reports began coming to Washington that contradicted Harrison's self-serving account of the battle, and claimed that the general had won only because the Indians had staged a strategic retreat. But younger, belligerent Republicans, especially from the South and West, hailed Harrison as a hero.[34]

The latter view prevailed at the Executive Mansion, at least initially. Madison sent a jubilant special message to Capitol Hill about the Battle of Tippecanoe, expressing his confidence that all "hostile incursions" would now cease. Over the coming months, he backed away from his enthusiasm, persuaded by reports that Harrison had attacked the Indians needlessly. But the administration acted hesitantly, and too late; Tippecanoe touched off further Indian attacks, and soon Tecumseh allied with the British, turning the belligerent Republicans' presumptions into self-fulfilled prophecy. The Indians' goal of checking American westward expansion became closely intertwined with the British goal of defending their interests in Canada. So long as American relations with Britain deteriorated, the likelihood of a full-scale war with the Indians grew. And the more the Indians resisted after Tippecanoe, the faster American relations with Britain deteriorated.[35]

1812

As war fever intensified in America, opposition to the Orders in Council also mounted in Britain, chiefly among trade-starved manufacturers. But the dismissive British government only sent its haughty envoy, Sir Augustus John Foster, to lecture the Americans about the imperatives of imperial security. The victory of the U.S. ship *President* over a much weaker British sloop *Little Belt* off the Chesapeake coast in the spring of 1811 stimulated American outrage and overconfidence. "[F]orbearance has become a crime, and patience ceased to be a virtue," wrote the Baltimore editor Hezekiah Niles in his new *Weekly Register*. By January 1812, President Madison completely changed his mind about

France presenting a greater threat to the republic than Britain. By April, he had decided for war.[36]

The charge, endorsed by subsequent generations of historians, that Congress dragged a bumbling, weak-kneed Madison into war is highly overstated. Madison, to be sure, was a less effective president than his predecessor. He had spent his entire career, before 1809, either as a legislator or as a diplomat, and was better suited to backstairs committee work and negotiations than to any executive position. Colorless, shy, bookish, and prone to nervousness, he often seemed indecisive. Long after the Non-Intercourse Act proved a failure, Madison's continued, principled search for a diplomatic solution short of war, his naïveté in dealing with Napoleon, and his persistent underestimation of the British will made his administration look rudderless. The failure of the bank rechartering effort early in 1811 made it look as if it was sinking.[37]

Yet Madison needed no prodding to change course and begin preparing resolutely for war. Like Jefferson, he rejected the Old World ideas of raison d'état and hated warfare, but he was no pacifist—especially so far as Great Britain was concerned. By the autumn of 1811, when he asked Congress for ten thousand additional troops, he began to see that no degree of commercial persuasion would force the British to back down. It was the supposedly warlike Congress, and not the White House, that then vacillated and avoided raising the taxes necessary to fulfill Madison's military requests until after war had actually been declared. Old Republicans and pro-British Federalists mocked the administration and the pro-war Republicans—"Go to war without money, without men, without a navy!" John Randolph sneered—which only stiffened the president's resolve. By the following spring, Madison was certain that the conservative British prime minister, Spencer Perceval, wanted war with the United States. "We have nothing left therefore, but to make ready for it," he wrote to Jefferson in early April 1812.[38]

On April 1, Madison forced the issue by sending a terse one-sentence request to Congress asking for a new sixty-day embargo, which would give American ships time to return to port and await diplomatic news from Britain about the status of the Orders in Council. The imperial dispatches stating that the Orders stood finally arrived in Washington on May 22. Nine days later, Madison sent a war message to Congress citing British impressment, goading of the Indians, blockades, and spurned diplomacy, and concluding that Britain was already "in a state of war against the United States." The House formally declared war by a decisive margin on June 4. The Senate concurred, by a much narrower majority, two weeks later.[39]

Had the British and the Americans been better informed about each others' political situation—or had communications across the Atlantic simply been speedier—war might have been averted. Misreading Madison's early caution as passivity, the British ambassador did not recognize that by the time the Americans implemented their new embargo, they fully expected war would follow. Likewise, Foster's American counterpart in London, Jonathan Russell, could not see how British economic difficulties, beginning with a depression in late 1810 and exacerbated by Napoleon's blockade of Europe, were quickly sapping the Orders of political viability. Ironically, just as Madison was committing himself and the country to war, his peaceable coercion policies were beginning to hurt the British badly. Fate then intervened, to make war even less likely. On May 11, a madman in London assassinated Perceval. The new British ministry, headed by the earl of Liverpool, put aside American affairs for several weeks, and by the time it recovered, Parliamentary opposition to the Orders prevailed. The Foreign Office reversed itself and announced that on June 23 the Orders would be suspended for one year. But by the time the news of that decision reached Washington in August, Congress had already declared war.[40]

Even had the news arrived earlier, however, pro-war Republicans might have considered a one-year suspension of the Orders too little, too late. And well before they learned of the diplomatic paradox, New England Federalists and southern Old Republicans were outraged at the war vote. The Federalists, having undermined Jefferson's embargo, had tried to obstruct all subsequent efforts at peaceful coercion, and flatly endorsed British arguments, even over impressment. Pseudopatriotic Republicans, they claimed, were attempting to turn American ships into a refuge for low-life deserters from the Royal Navy. Jefferson's old foe Timothy Pickering wrote in all seriousness that he believed Napoleon Bonaparte himself had bribed the congressional majority. John Randolph denounced the pro-war Republicans as fools who lusted after Canada. "I know that we are on the brink of some dreadful scourge," he said.[41]

In truth, the victorious majority represented the triumph of neither treachery nor cupidity, but the consolidation of the new nationalists, strongest in the West and the South, with crucial supporters from the middle Atlantic states. No single influence, political or economic, can explain this convergence. Economically, congressional support for the war tended to come from areas, now badly depressed, more involved in rural production for export than in the maritime transport trade. Anger at assumed British responsibility for Indian unrest—in which Americans conveniently overlooked their own mistreatment of the Indians—reinforced war fever in the West and Deep South. The pro-war Republicans' basic motives in seizing Canada were to deprive Britain of important naval bases and help quiet the Indians.[42]

The crisis shows that, when push came to shove, the Republicans' shared patriotic fervor against the British Empire and concerns about Federalist treachery could overcome the factionalism of the Madison years. In the House, outside of the New York delegation (where anti-Madison feeling ran high), approximately nine out of ten Republicans voted in favor of war. In the Senate, where Federalists and Republicans were more evenly matched, a slender majority of members probably wished to avoid war. Ultimately, however, most of the wavering Republican Senate fell into line, including the veteran city democrat and longtime Madison antagonist Michael Leib of Philadelphia. So did the majority of country and city democrats outside Washington, their abiding contempt for Madison and Gallatin now put aside.[43]

Fears that the republic was endangered bound the pro-war Republicans together. Ever since the completion of independence, they believed, the great ideal of republicanism had been threatened, by the British from without and the Federalists from within. The British, by exerting their naval might, had dominated the American economy and unjustly seized dozens of ships and thousands of American citizens. Those degrading arrangements might be tolerable for (mostly Federalist) Yankee shipmasters, who stood to make handsome profits under the British aegis and could write off the impressments as one of the costs of doing business. The arrangements might also be tolerable for anti-Jeffersonian Anglophiles. But they were anathema to economically stressed producers everywhere, who blamed their plight on the arrogant British and their loyal Yankee Federalist friends. Add to that the widespread belief that the British were responsible for subverting the Indians, and the fate of the republic seemed to be at stake. John Adams's son John Quincy—who, having quit his father's party, had become a new star of the Republican diplomatic corps, now as minister to St. Petersburg—contended that "something besides dollars and cents is concerned," and there was "no alternative left but war or the abandonment of our right as an independent nation."[44]

As Madison prepared the country for combat, he also readied himself for his reelection campaign. Due to the war crisis, April passed without the customary nominating caucus of congressional Republicans. The president looked to be strongly positioned, though he still had powerful Republican opponents—above all, in Pennsylvania, William Duane, who hotly supported the war but preferred DeWitt Clinton of New York, the nephew of Madison's ailing vice president, George Clinton, to Madison. But Duane could not persuade Governor Simon Snyder and the Clodhopper country democrats, who on the eve of the Republican caucus announced their support for the president.[45]

DeWitt Clinton, whose uncle finally died in mid-April, refused to give up. Long the leader of New York's Republicans and now the most powerful figure in the state's politics, Clinton, at age forty-three, was ready to carry on his family legacy, push aside the aging Revolutionary generation, and advance to national leadership. He and his fellow New York Republicans were also eager to challenge the Virginians' domination of their party. Shortly after Madison won the congressional caucus's endorsement, New York's Republican legislators nominated Clinton, who quickly accepted. Clinton then courted the Federalists, hoping to fuse them with the anti-Madisonian Republicans into a victorious coalition—what Duane, who had reconciled himself to Madison's reelection, called "a group more oddly consorted than the assemblage in the ark."[46]

The early fighting against Britain improved Clinton's prospects. The war did not go well. American military strategy was straightforward: hit the British hard in Canada, gather support from anti-British Canadians (a group that amounted mostly to wishful thinking on the Americans' part), and seize the crucial river port of Montreal. But Madison had at his disposal only a small regular army scattered across the country, a larger but disorganized militia still under the official control of the individual states, a tiny navy, and virtually no military command structure whatsoever. In mid-August, the surrender of Detroit without a shot to a combined force of British troops and Indians by the frightened and quite possibly drug-addled General William Hull was a devastating military and emotional blow. Adding greatly to Hull's fear, and to the subsequent American disgrace, was the presence at Detroit of Tecumseh at the head of one thousand warriors.

By the end of 1812, the British controlled nearly half the Old Northwest. The small but stirring victory of the American ship *Constitution* (dubbed, thereafter, "Old Ironsides") over HMS *Guerrière* off the Massachusetts coast revived American spirits, as did, a few weeks later, the news that Captain Stephen Decatur's *United States* had captured the British frigate *Macedonian* off the coast of Africa. Even some of the most sanguine hawks were worried, though. "Our executive officers are most incompetent," John C. Calhoun despaired to a friend.[47]

Amid the setbacks, Federalist organizers, especially the younger men, continued to retool the Republican techniques they had once maligned. Federalist state delegates from around the country met in New York at a "peace convention," a rudimentary version of a national nominating convention. Unable to agree on a candidate, the group decided to leave the way open for state Federalist parties to support Clinton. Most of them did so; but even more important, local and national organizations (led by scores of "popular" groups called Washington Benevolent Societies) arose to campaign, at times rambunctiously, for Federalist candidates, and to make sure that supporters got to the polls. In New England, pro-Clinton Federalists proclaimed that their man was a peace candidate; their counterparts in the middle Atlantic states and the South suggested that Clinton would conduct the war with greater skill and fortitude than Madison; and everywhere, Federalist partisans denounced Madison's Republicans as complacent officeholding elitists—lackeys of Napoleon Bonaparte who cared nothing about the well-being of the American people.[48]

By late summer, although Clinton had his hands full creating his bipartisan coalition, Madison's reelection was no longer guaranteed. Four years earlier, Madison had won all but five of the seventeen states, and the Republicans retained two-thirds of the House. In the off-year balloting for Congress in 1810, the Republicans actually picked up seats, cutting the size of the Federalist House caucus in half. But under the strain of a divisive war—with New York Republicans chafing under the domination of the Virginians, and Federalists learning the virtues of grassroots political organization—Madison became vulnerable. Assured of solid support from New England (apart from Republican Vermont), Clinton needed only to hold on to his home state's electoral votes and win Pennsylvania's to gain the White House.

New York did stay loyal to Clinton, largely (and, in retrospect, ironically) because of the labors of a young upstate legislator, Martin Van Buren. The son of a tavern-keeper from the sleepy Hudson River Valley town of Kinderhook, Van Buren, at age thirty, had enjoyed a swift rise. Admitted to the New York State bar in 1803, he became known as the ablest Republican lawyer in rural, Federalist Columbia County, and in 1812, with Clinton's support, he narrowly won election to the state senate. Van Buren took up his seat in Albany as the new legislature decided to whom it would award the state's twenty-nine electoral votes. He was torn, he later recalled, between his personal loyalty to Clinton and his desire to support "a vigorous prosecution of the War." What tipped him was the legislature's earlier endorsement of his patron Clinton and "the wishes of my immediate constituents." Already Van Buren was an effective backstairs politician, crafting and then helping to ram through the senate a resolution binding the caucus to an exclusively Clintonian electoral ticket. The state assembly, where the Federalists were strong, followed suit. Van Buren had won New York for his patron, rather than his president.[49]

Pennsylvania saved Madison's presidency. The Clintonians inundated the state with propaganda pitched directly at nominal Republicans. They appealed much more quietly to Pennsylvania Federalists. Clinton, it appears, styled himself in Federalist circles an "American Federalist," who, as president, would make immediate peace with Britain. But among most Republicans, patriotic unity over the war outstripped the abiding distrust of President Madison. When news of Clinton's negotiations with the Federalists leaked out, lukewarm Republicans, offended, turned against him. Despite the persistent factionalism, the president still won a large statewide victory, which gave him, barely, the electoral margin he needed to win reelection.[50]

The politics of 1812 are supposed to have brought a continued rejuvenation and democratization of the Federalist Party—what one historian has described as nothing less than "a revolution of American conservatism." The claims are inflated. Outside New England and portions of New York, Federalism was too weak to accomplish much of anything, let alone revolutionize conservatism.

DeWitt Clinton was a fusion candidate, not a Federalist, and his supporters made sure to call him a pro-war man wherever it would gain him votes. Many of Clinton's key backers, from Michael Leib to Martin Van Buren, were not conservatives and certainly not Federalists. Federalist candidates did sweep congressional districts in New England and upstate New York, doubling their strength in the new Congress. But that still left them with only one-third of the total membership in the House, roughly what they had in 1809—and that membership, more than ever, hailed from a small portion of the Northeast, chiefly Massachusetts and Connecticut. Federalists in 1812 were a narrow sectional party, powerless outside their surviving strongholds. Younger conservatives may have started to come to terms with democratic politics, but they could not complete that revolution until they had abandoned Federalism.[51]

The politics of 1812 instead highlighted the shifting dynamics within the Republican Party. Potentially damaging divisions persisted, but the younger militant nationalists, now allied with Madison, had won the political initiative. A new generation of Republican moderates had come to the fore—friendly to government-backed economic development, opposed to Federalist political principles, and eager for war with Britain. Simultaneously, up-and-comers like Martin Van Buren were staking out their own political careers, firmly within the Republicans' ranks. The war itself would prove extremely difficult, and stir heated dissent in New England. Finally, though, it would solidify the nationalist Republicans' control of national politics—and their ascendancy over the contending forces within their own party, including southern Quids, country Clodhoppers, pro-Clinton schismatics, and fiery urban democrats like William Duane.

WAR, POLITICS, AND THE FEDERALISTS IN DISSENT

In 1813, Britain's exasperated reaction to Congress's declaration of war turned into outrage as the war against Napoleon reached its climactic phase. New England Federalists' attacks turned accordingly vitriolic, at once sympathetic to the British and contemptuous of their own government's unfortunate early war efforts. "Utterly astonished at the declaration of war, I have been surprised at nothing since," observed the freshman representative Daniel Webster, elected to Congress in the Federalists' New England sweep of 1812. "Unless all history deceives me, I saw how it would be prosecuted when I saw how it was begun. There is in the nature of things an unchangeable relation between rash counsels and feeble execution."[52]

So long as Britain remained chiefly concerned with France, the Americans did not suffer as greatly as they might have. (Thanks to the British, New England merchants suffered the least of all. At the end of 1812, the Royal Navy clamped down a blockade that would eventually stretch from New York to New Orleans—but the friendly New Englanders were permitted maritime access to the lucrative Canada trade they had cultivated during the embargo and nonimportation.) Neither side was able to break through against the other in 1813. Indeed, the Americans could actually claim some important victories. American naval forces under Commodore Isaac Chauncey deployed enough warships on Lake Erie, the crucial waterway of the northern theater of action, to keep the British from capturing it. In September, a small newly built American fleet, under Captain Oliver Hazard Perry, defeated the enemy off South Bass Island at the lake's western end in the deadliest naval battle of the entire conflict. Perry's success opened the way for William Henry Harrison, now the senior American officer in the Northwest, to prosecute one of the most important campaigns of the war.[53]

For nearly a year, Harrison had tried and failed to break the British and their Indians allies' hold on the land approaches to Detroit. Once he received word of Perry's victory, Harrison shipped twenty-seven hundred troops westward from Ohio across Lake Erie. This compelled the British and the Indians to withdraw their main force, including fifteen hundred Indians under Tecumseh, from Fort Malden, near Detroit. The British brigadier marched his men eastward toward Niagara; the Americans—most of them militiamen from Kentucky—pursued on horseback and finally caught up with them on October 5 at a Canadian settlement along the Thames River. Losing only twelve dead and nineteen wounded, Harrison's troops killed or wounded forty-eight of the British and Canadian soldiers, captured six hundred, and killed thirty-three Indians. The British retreated ingloriously, never again to threaten from the Northwest. And among the dead Indian warriors in the riverside brush was Harrison's nemesis, Tecumseh.[54]

Nearly forgotten today, the Battle of the Thames had an enduring significance only slightly smaller than that of the renowned Battle of New Orleans fifteen months later. Harrison's triumph added not an acre of conquered land to the American dominion. Its chief immediate result was a grisly rampage of Indian hating. (The Kentuckians reportedly skinned the bodies of Indian victims and tanned the skin into leather for trophies.) But the battle's long-term effects were manifold. Harrison's triumph virtually settled the northwestern boundary and Indian questions. With Tecumseh dead and the major Indian opposition crushed, American settlers could now safely move into all of Indiana and Michigan Territories and farther west. The British would soon abandon their idea, first broached in the 1770s, of creating an Indian buffer state between the United States and Canada.

None of these larger results could have materialized had the United States lost the war, which at times in 1814 seemed genuinely possible. In April, after his disastrous retreat from Moscow and more than a year of crushing reversals, Napoleon abdicated his throne. Battle-tested British troops now came to America. Out to avenge the setbacks of the previous year, they planned to retake the key northern lakes and rivers and hand Michigan Territory over to the Indians. They also hoped to seize enough of the Maine district to secure Canada's southeastern border. Between July and September, the British occupied coastal Maine, where many antiwar locals reportedly welcomed them with open arms.

In July, British Major General Robert Ross, commanding forty-five hundred veterans of the Napoleonic wars, joined forces with Vice Admiral Alexander Cochrane in Bermuda. Cochrane's assignment was to distract the Americans and exact retribution short of killing civilians. He sailed north to hit the Chesapeake. After chasing a small American naval force up the Patuxent River, the British dispersed a combined force of competent regular artillery and poorly trained militia, reached Washington, and set fire to the Capitol. President and Mrs. Madison fled the White House just before the arrival of local looters and His Majesty's army, leaving behind, one memoirist wrote, "an elegant and sumptuous past and a table set for forty." The British commanding officers, Ross and Admiral George Cockburn, entered the executive residence with their hungry men and enjoyed the presidential meal. Cockburn, who despised America and Americans, raised a facetious toast to Madison, swiped a cushion and one of the president's hats, and delivered ribald remarks about the country and its First Family. Then the two commanders personally set fire to the Executive Mansion. The next morning, British troops burned the building housing the State, War, and Navy Departments, as well as all nonmilitary public buildings except for the combined General Post Office and Patent Office. After departing Washington, of the mud-splattered exiles of the Madison administration regrouped as best they could across the Potomac at the Reverend William Moffit's estate in Little Falls, Virginia, four miles from the city, which for a night became the closest thing there was to a capital of the United States.[55]

The destruction in Washington and the temporary removal of the government proved more a psychological than a military setback for the Americans. Washington was strategically valueless: the British abandoned the city as soon as they had burned it. Because the Americans' chain of command remained dispersed, with considerable discretion still left to state militias, the gutting of the national capital did not unduly interfere with their military capabilities. Two weeks after they set fire to Washington, the self-confident British, under Cochrane, Ross, and Cockburn, attacked Baltimore and were repulsed by the heavily entrenched Maryland militia. An intense British rocket bombardment on Fort McHenry in Baltimore harbor failed utterly, inspiring the Maryland lawyer and eyewitness Francis Scott Key to write his defiant anthem, "The Star Spangled Banner." Then, in early September, American naval forces under Captain Thomas Macdonough thrashed a major enemy offensive near Lake Champlain, decisively checking the latest British effort to grab American territories on the northern front and sending the redcoats scurrying back to Canada.

The British could not vanquish the Americans, and the Americans could not vanquish the British. Neither the Madison administration (which returned to what was left of Washington) nor Congress could expect to accomplish any of the high-flown war aims proclaimed two years earlier. In January 1814, Madison entered diplomatic negotiations, and in early August, in the Flemish town of Ghent, an American delegation that included John Quincy Adams and Henry Clay met the British. The British initially took a hard line, demanding conces- sions that included the creation of an Indian nation north of the Ohio River. The American envoys threatened to break off negotiations if the British did not drop their Indian demands. Thereafter, both sides moved closer to a peace agreement, if only because neither side had much hunger to prolong the war.[56]

For the American delegation, ending the war was imperative. Embittered New Englanders had detached from the rest of the country more than at any time since Jefferson's election. By December 1814, obdurate New England Fed- eralists were talking openly of secession and a separate peace with the British, and popular unrest had sporadically turned violent. The dissent, among seces- sionists and nonsecessionists alike, focused on foreign affairs but was rooted in the Yankee Federalists' undiminished resistance to Jeffersonian ideas and poli- tics. In Connecticut, Rhode Island, and, especially, Massachusetts, the war offered the Federalists a new lease on political life. Massachusetts Republicans, alarmingly, had taken control of the General Court in 1806 and won the gover- norship. But outrage at the embargo, the enforcement acts, and the war drove a successful Federalist resurgence.[57]

In 1812, Congress's declaration of war immediately led the newly reelected Federalist Massachusetts governor, Caleb Strong, to call for a public fast to express outrage about the conflict, in sympathy with "the nation from which we are descended." Strong later refused to call up the state's militia to serve, as did three other New England Federalist governors. President Madison's difficult reelection, and the British occupation of Maine in 1814, deepened dissent. One round of memorials, collected from at least forty towns early in 1814, called for a New England antiwar convention, to seek remedies for the federal govern- ment's unconstitutional abuses. Some carried plain seccessionist implications. "The history of the late administration of the national Government," wrote the townsmen of Wendell, in words that both sarcastically and ominously para- phrased Jefferson's Declaration of Independence, is "a history of repeated injuries and usurpations, having a direct tendency to the Establishment of an Absolute Tyranny over these States."[58]

The politics of the Massachusetts Federalist leadership, like those of the rest of the region, varied from the hatred of democracy spewed by the self-described "raving" Fisher Ames and the hard-line Essex Junto, to the more practical elitism of the elegant Bostonian Harrison Gray Otis. Their differences of tone and strategy did not disrupt the Federalists' basic unity over fundamental principles. Old and young, secessionist and antisecessionist—all agreed that the Revolution had been won to replace the British monarchy with a natural American aristocracy of moral, well-educated property holders, the rightful governors over a licentious and disorderly populace. They shared an a priori respect for the past, upholding "the good old *school*" of their fathers against "the insidious encroachments of *innovation.*" Since the Revolution, supposedly, agrarian Virginia Jacobin slaveholders had taken advantage of the Constitution's three-fifths rule and stirred up the ignorant democratic populace (including hateful recent immigrants), thus undermining balance and order. In 1801, they seized the reins of national government. Once in power, the levelers attacked all that was sound and conservative, and despoiled the mercantile interests of New England. "From the peace to this time," Stephen Higginson wrote in 1803, "it has been [Virginia's] main object, to depress the northern States, to secure the influence & safety of the south." New England Federalists argued the same points even more fervently after more than a decade of Jeffersonian democracy.[59]

Curiously, it has become fashionable in more recent times to cast the Federalists' apprehensions and antiwar protests as part of a broader Federalist antislavery humanitarianism—one that was egalitarian when compared to the glaring contradictions of the Republican slaveholders, Jefferson above all, about human liberty. By these lights, opposition to the War Hawks was in part an effort to halt the growth of slavery. Rarely has any group of Americans done so little to deserve such praise. Several members of the older Federalist cohort could boast of authentic antislavery activities in the 1770s and 1780s (along with, it should be added, some northern Republicans). Through the 1820s some Yankee Federalist lawmakers and clergymen expressed sincere moral repugnance at human bondage. But the antislavery currents in Federalism were always restrained, and they virtually dried up after 1800. The Federalists' chief aim was the removal of the three-fifths clause, without any true representation for blacks— that is, the political aggrandizement of northern Federalism. Although public attacks on the planters for their immorality and hypocrisy added to the Yankee Federalists' treasury of moral virtue, those attacks often expressed little concern about the slaves, or about slavery as an institution. The Federalists did not hate the Jeffersonians out of antislavery conviction; rather, they sometimes took antislavery positions because they hated the "Jacobin" Jeffersonians.[60]

Beneath the surface, the Federalists' views on the South and slavery were perfectly in keeping with their broader antidemocratic politics and their parti-

san interests. To have any right to interfere with southern institutions and property would have contradicted their own insistence on property's inviolability
and their region's rights to freedom from outside interference. It also would
have killed off what remained of southern Federalism, which was positively
pro-slavery, foreclosing any possibility that the party could regain a national
presence, let alone national power. Charging the Jeffersonians with duplicity,
on the other hand, permitted the Federalists to evade the fact that northeastern
Republicans had greatly increased their strength from 1800 through 1809,
thanks largely to city and country democrats who had no stake in slavery and
whose ranks included many outspoken antislavery men. It also cloaked how
traditionalist ideas about order and station left open no room to equality for
freed slaves. Even authentically antislavery Federalist clerics bid northern
blacks to "be contented," as Jedidiah Morse put it, "in the humble station in
which Providence has placed you."[61]

In the end, the war's democratic repercussions contradicted the Federalists'
antidemocratic assumptions and accentuated their political isolation from the
rest of the country. Those repercussions originated not in politics but in how the
Americans fought the war. For better and for worse, the Jeffersonians' long-
standing opposition to a large standing army meant that militiamen and volunteers bore much of the burden of fighting on land after 1812. Barely trained and
poorly supplied, the militias earned a reputation among the officer corps for
uselessness. Yet some outfits acquitted themselves as gunmen, creating a myth
of the brave and patriotic citizen-soldier. The imagery stimulated demands for
widening the franchise, above all in Virginia, where property qualifications
remained steep. Across the state, militiamen mustered into the service signed
petitions protesting their disenfranchisement. At the war's end, the exclusion
seemed all the more outrageous. How, some democrats asked, could men be
expected to fight and die for their country if they could not vote? "A Representative Democracy is the Ordinance of God," declared one protest meeting of
backcountry democrats and militia veterans that gathered in Harrisonburg in
June 1815.[62]

The war also produced a new crop of military heroes whose authentic and
invented glory became a democratic political resource waiting to be tapped.
During and after the Revolution, most of this sort of political capital had flowed
to the austere Federalist George Washington. But during the War of 1812, when
military leadership was more fragmented, many more commanders gained
renown for the respect they had earned from the rank and file of ordinary soldiers
as well as for their triumphs in the field. The politically ambitious victor of the
Battle of the Thames, William Henry Harrison, was one of these commanders;
so, in a smaller way, was Colonel Richard Mentor Johnson of Kentucky, who
would later claim, dubiously but to great effect, that he had personally slain

Tecumseh. And among the new heroes was a general barely known to the citizenry before the war—Andrew Jackson of Tennessee.

None of the new popular military men were Federalists, and none came from New England. And so the War of 1812 further hastened the Federalists' final crisis, in ways that even the gloomiest among them could not have fully anticipated. In retrospect, the ironies are poignant, even painful. In their own minds, the Federalists were bravely defending the political spirit and substance of 1776 against southern planters and the deluded democratic hordes. Yet with their antiwar activities, they turned their political movement—originally organized by some of the most determined anti-British and anti-Tory leaders in America—into a pro-British American Tory party. The sons of New Englanders who had once defied the British Empire now seemed, at best, equivocal in the face of British coercion. The confident, nationalist party of Washington, Hamilton, and Adams had shriveled into the phobic sectional party of Otis, Pickering, and Ames. And the Federalists themselves dealt their party its coup de grace.

The end would come suddenly and, for the Federalists, by surprise. In 1814, New England Federalism was still riding high. In the Massachusetts governor's race, the incumbent Caleb Strong ridiculed complaints about his indiscriminate opposition to the war and won roughly 55 percent of the vote. In the legislative elections, the Federalists gained control over the lower house with a gargantuan majority. Federalist leaders remained on the antiwar barricades in the autumn, as the British blockade of the coast, now expanded to include New England, remained unbroken. Governor Strong ordered the Massachusetts General Court to consider what steps to take amid the crisis. In mid-October, both houses of the Court approved a report, written by a joint committee chaired by Harrison Gray Otis, summoning a convention of delegates from the New England states to consider the expediency of proposing "a radical reform in the national compact." Connecticut and Rhode Island heeded the call and chose delegations, as did a handful of commercial Connecticut River Valley counties in New Hampshire and Vermont. On December 15, twenty-six eminent Federalists, mostly lawyers, convened at the State House in Hartford, Connecticut.[63]

By assembling in an extralegal convention, the Federalists at once underscored their self-conscious links to the Revolution and built on their own more recent partisan precedents, including the thinly veiled pro-Clinton "peace convention" of 1812. Various plans were afoot. One group (including Noah Webster) in Hampshire County, Massachusetts, revived Webster's proposal for a convention to recommend amendments to the Constitution. Hard-liners demanded even bolder action. John Low, a representative from coastal Maine, called for a deputation of Massachusetts leaders to travel to Washington, inform President Madison of New England's displeasure, and demand that he resign.

Another dissenter devised a plan to prohibit collection of federal internal duties. But the relatively moderate complexion of the Hartford group—which, within New England Federalism, was more a matter of degree than philosophy—portended a calibrated outcome, mild in its rhetoric if not its final intentions. Under the control of practical party men like Harrison Gray Otis, the convention included none of the most prominent Federalist recalcitrants like Fisher Ames or Timothy Pickering. On the eve of the gathering, Josiah Quincy asked George Cabot, who had been named the convention's president, to predict what would happen. Cabot replied that he knew exactly what the result would be: "A GREAT PAMPHLET!" He proved correct.[64]

On January 3, after nearly a month of disputation behind closed doors, the convention adopted its final report, largely the work of Otis. The report began with the convention's hope to reconcile everyone "to a course of moderation and firmness." Yet what, to Otis, seemed moderate still represented a drastic program. A section on the South was meant to sound conciliatory, predicting that a new nationalist solidarity would soon arise, but only with the disappearance of the South's "visionary theorists"—old Federalist code words for the Jeffersonian democrats. The bulk of the writing recited New England's familiar wartime grievances—the conscription of state militiamen, the inequitable political power of the slaveholding states—and proposed seven "essential" constitutional amendments as nonnegotiable demands. These included the repeal of the three-fifths clause, a requirement that two-thirds of both houses of Congress agree before any new state could be admitted to the Union, limits on the length of embargoes, and the outlawing of the election of a president from the same state to successive terms, clearly aimed at the Virginians. Finally, the report authorized future conventions. Although the delegates endorsed neither New England secession nor the pursuit of a separate peace with Britain, they did not foreclose either should the war drag on and their resolutions fail.[65]

From a Federalist angle, it all looked like a triumph of prudent but stern good sense. Some of the "warm bloods" grumbled, but most Connecticut and Massachusetts partisans—including the normally irreconcilable Pickering—praised the report for what Pickering called its "high character of wisdom, fairness, and dignity." Federalist newspapers from New Hampshire to New York extolled the document. For all of January, Federalists were optimistic that they might at last have some effect again on national policy. With the approval of his legislature, Governor Strong of Massachusetts appointed a three-man commission to present the gist of the convention's grievances, in his state's name, to President Madison. The trio left Boston on February 3. Only on February 14, the day after they arrived in Washington, did the commissioners learn, with the rest of the capital, that the negotiators at Ghent had signed a peace treaty six weeks earlier, on Christmas Eve.[66]

At Ghent, American bargaining depended largely on the disposition of Henry Clay. Madison had included Clay in the peace delegation not because of his negotiating prowess—Clay was known as a fearsome debater and organizer, not a suave diplomat—but because he could be counted on to defend western interests and because he had enormous influence in Congress. At the peace table, Clay's directness of speech, along with his taste for rambling late-night conversations and card-playing sessions featuring plenty of liquor and cheap cigars, surprised his British counterparts and offended his American colleague, the correct professional John Quincy Adams. More than the other Americans, Clay remained brightly optimistic about his country's fortunes in the field and in the negotiations. He dismissed the rising dissent in New England as "a game of swaggering and gasconade." He also encouraged his fellow Americans, as the negotiations wore on, to adopt a cardsharp's calculating spirit of "brag"—what is known today as bluffing. "He asked me if I knew how to play *brag*," Adams wrote in his diary. "I had forgotten how. He said the art of it was to beat your adversary by holding your hand with a solemn and confident phiz, and out bragging him."[67]

Clay nearly overdid it. Once news of the American victories in Baltimore and upstate New York reached Ghent, the British backed off from their tough demands and followed up an American suggestion that a treaty be negotiated based on the complete restoration of the status quo as of July 1812. Clay would have liked to get more out of the enemy, but he checked his disappointment and agreed to go along—only to put his foot down, to Adams's consternation, over the matter of British navigation rights on the Mississippi River. James Bayard, one of the American delegates, despaired at Clay's stubborness and accused him of "bragging a million against a cent." Fortunately for the negotiations, all sides eventually agreed to omit the Mississippi question from the treaty, leaving it, along with several other outstanding issues, to be settled at some future date. Otherwise, the prewar status was restored.[68]

Intrepid gambler though he was, it would require even more of Clay's bluffing skills to make the Treaty of Ghent look like a great American victory. After two and a half years of war, the United States was left with a few heroes such as Harrison, Perry, and Johnson, a few disgraces such as William Hull, a government with its finances in disarray, a federal capital that partially lay in ashes, and nearly seven thousand killed or wounded—almost two-thirds the number of casualties incurred during the Revolutionary War, which had lasted nearly three times as long. The republic had survived, a patriotic vindication. Otherwise, the best that could be said was that American military triumphs of late summer had staved off defeat and helped push the British into serious negotiations—a genuine, but modest, achievement.

At year's end, in Ghent, Clay, ignorant of events back home, was assembling his arguments to prove that the diplomatic stalemate was in fact a glorious affirmation of American independence. In frigid Hartford, Harrison Gray Otis was drafting the Federalist manifesto whose sentiments would later be officially delivered to James Madison. And nearly fifteen hundred miles to the southwest, in the parlor of a makeshift headquarters on Royal Street in New Orleans, an American general, Andrew Jackson, was scrambling to thwart a British invasion—an engagement whose outcome would cinch Clay's brag and complete the Federalists' ruin.

VENGEANCE AND GLORY:
THE EMERGENCE OF JACKSON

Jackson looked like a man cut away from the stake, erect but gaunt and pallid after more than a year of nearly continuous combat, capped by repeated attacks of dysentery. At age forty-seven, he was wrinkled and his auburn hair gone gray. His head and left fingers bore jagged livid reminders of a sword blow struck by a British officer during the Revolution, when he was a boy.[69]

Jackson had been in New Orleans for three weeks, pulling together the city's defenses and awaiting an enormous British expeditionary force. Early on the afternoon of December 23, three Creole gentlemen appeared with important information. The visitors, sweaty and winded from a hard ride, were duly ushered in to see the general. One of them, a young M. Villère, stammered that the British had just encamped at his family's plantation nine miles away. Jackson invited his guests to share a glass of wine. "I will smash them, so help me God!" Jackson supposedly said of his old enemy.[70]

Jackson was a skilled general, not a great one. Although he had built a career in the military, it was not his first profession. His father, also named Andrew, arrived in the Carolina backcountry from Ireland with his wife Elizabeth and their two sons in 1765. Subsistence farmers, the Jacksons settled along the disputed border between the two Carolinas in the Waxhaw area, near Elizabeth's five married sisters and another family of in-laws. Andrew built a small log cabin and cleared enough land to support Elizabeth and the boys, but in the late winter of 1767, he died—killed, according to one account, by a falling log while he was clearing timber. A few days later, with the clan deep in mourning, Elizabeth gave birth to her third son, whom she named in honor of her dead husband.

Elizabeth, a pious Presbyterian, wanted young Andrew to train for the ministry, one of the chief paths to social advancement for a poor Scots-Irish boy. She put aside enough money to provide him with the best possible schooling with local ministers, which by Waxhaw standards was exceptional. But the Revolution and its chance for patriotic adventure intervened. At age thirteen, Andrew joined in ferocious irregular backwoods fighting against the British. One of his brothers died of exposure after the Battle of Stono Ferry in 1779; Andrew and his surviving brother, Robert, were betrayed by a Waxhaw Tory and captured. When Andrew refused to polish a British officer's boots, the officer slashed him, scarring him for life. Jailed in Camden, the brothers contracted smallpox, whereupon Elizabeth arranged to have them released as part of a prisoner exchange. Robert died; Andrew's fever broke; and (before Andrew fully recovered) Elizabeth journeyed to British-occupied Charleston to nurse two nephews held on a disease-ridden prison ship. There she died of cholera, her body placed in an unmarked grave. "I felt utterly alone," Jackson recalled years later, "and tried to recall her last words to me."[71]

Jackson fell back on the largess of his Waxhaw kinfolk, but found them, to one degree or another, disagreeable. They found him obstreperous. He took work as a saddler's helper, then traveled on his own to liberated Charleston to receive a four-hundred-pound inheritance from one of his Irish grandfathers. Only fifteen, he remained in Charleston and acted out the role of a high-living, low-country gentleman, squandering his inheritance on a binge of drinking, gambling, and women. He returned to the Waxhaw district, shamed and somewhat chastened, taught school, went back to work for the saddler, and saved his wages. In 1784, he left for good and traveled north to Salisbury, North Carolina, a growing county seat, to study law. He could not persuade the best lawyer in town to take him on as a clerk, but he picked up enough training from local attorneys to qualify for the bar in 1787. When the position of first public prosecutor in newly settled middle Tennessee opened up, Jackson got the job. On his way west, he fought the first of what would be several duels (this one bloodless) and purchased his first slave—minimum requirements for any true southern gentleman. Lawyer Jackson arrived in Nashville in October 1788. He was only twenty-one.

There has been, in recent decades, abundant psychological theorizing on how Jackson's youthful traumas accounted for his later vengeful personality.[72] The prenatal loss of his father, his "abandonment" by his mother, his testy relations with his Waxhaw kin—all could well have accounted for the grown man's propensity for violent language (and violent actions), his abrupt mood swings, and a "slobbering" speech impediment that curtailed his ability to address crowds. A drawback to these arguments is that there is no evidence whatsoever that Jackson harbored any resentments toward either of his parents. The estrangement between Jackson and the rest of his family was hardly unusual for ambitious young men in the insular backcountry. But whatever the familial sources of his rage may have been, two important and exhaustively documented facets of that rage plainly resulted from Jackson's boyhood tribulations. One was a mighty drive to gain honor and respect, according to the prickly mores of southern manhood. The other, rooted in his Scots-Irish heritage but scorched into his body and soul by the Revolution, was his hatred of the British and their empire.

Jackson's rapid rise had social and political as well as personal origins, not unlike Henry Clay's in Kentucky and John C. Calhoun's in South Carolina. The uprooting of the old Tory elite of the colonial North Carolina bench and bar had opened up a vocation much better suited to Jackson's talents and tastes than the ministry or saddle making. Among the first lawyers to arrive in the Cumberland River region, Jackson quickly became one of Nashville's leading citizens in the years before Tennessee statehood. His marriage in 1791 to Rachel Donelson, from a prominent local family, added to his political stature, which then helped elect him as a delegate to the state constitutional convention in 1795 and, the following year, as the new state's first congressman. In Philadelphia, Congressman Jackson aligned himself with the backcountry opposition, supporting western military preparedness, opposing direct federal taxation, and voting against an effusive House resolution in praise of the departing President Washington. But Jackson had no patience for the backstairs plotting and purely rhetorical combat of national politics. Soon after being elevated to the Senate, he resigned, spent a few years as a circuit-riding justice on the Tennessee Supreme Court, and then quit government affairs, apparently forever, in favor of moneymaking and a career in the military.

The moneymaking was a matter of utmost necessity. While advancing in law and politics, Jackson had also plowed his energies into planting, merchandising, and land speculation, only to lose nearly everything when a business associate whose notes he had endorsed went bankrupt. Forced to start over outside Nashville, Jackson recouped his losses by buying slaves and cashing in on the boom market for short-staple cotton. In time, his new enterprise, the Hermitage, would become one of the most successful plantations in Tennessee. But the master (who always referred to the Hermitage as his "farm") would permanently harbor a raging distrust of debt, banks, and the entire paper-money credit system.

Jackson's passion for the military reignited soon after he arrived in the Cumberland region, when he joined fellow settlers' counterattacks against Muskogee and Chickamauga raiding parties. He angled for the post of commander of the Tennessee militia, a job he captured in 1802. Thereafter, his political involvement dwindled to nothing and his military ambitions soared, though there were new frustrations. For ten years, he leaped at the first sign that war might be declared, if not against the British, then against their allies, the Spanish and the Indians. (Jackson took a kinder view of Britain's greatest enemies, the French, including Napoleon, whom he admired for his bravura and energy.) But there was little need for Jackson's military services. In 1806, he fell in with the wandering adventurer Aaron Burr and played a direct if minor role in provisioning Burr's western conspiracy (only to discover to his horror that at least some of the conspirators were plotting treason). Jackson returned to the Hermitage, purchased more land

and slaves, gambled on his gamecocks and racehorses, and endlessly quarreled with his detractors, at times with pistols drawn: a self-made southern planter, restlessly awaiting a war.

When war finally came, it was against Jackson's mightiest enemies, the British, along with the major fifth column in the southern theater, the rebellious Muskogee Indians of the upper Alabama region around the Coosa and Tallapoosa rivers. "*Who are we? and for what are we going to fight,*" Jackson proclaimed in a handwritten call for enlistments. "[A]re we the titled Slaves of George the third? the military conscripts of Napoleon the great? or the frozen peasants of the Russian Czar? No—we are the free born sons of america; the citizens of the only republick now existing in the world."[73]

After he led his troops on a mission (eventually aborted by Secretary of War John Anderson) to defend the lower Mississippi Valley, Commander Jackson's troops, in recognition of his toughness, gave him the nickname "Hickory," which soon became "Old Hickory." In the autumn of 1813, he received another chance at glory when ordered to clear up a persisting Indian threat in northern Alabama Territory. Upwards of four thousand discontented Muskogees (called "Creeks" by the Americans, because of their skill in navigating and settling in their heavily creek-crossed terrain) emerged as the southern branch of Tecumseh's pantribal confederacy. Led by the half-Creek, half-Scots chief Red Eagle—called, in English, William Weatherford—these Red Sticks (they painted their bodies and war clubs bright red) alienated both the neighboring Chickasaws and a large faction of their fellow Creeks, thus precipitating a civil war.

News that the Red Sticks had massacred hundreds of white Americans, adults and children, at the fortified Alabama River home of a part-Creek, part-white merchant, Samuel Mims, led Jackson and the Americans to intervene directly. The Fort Mims massacre struck all of Jackson's sore points about rebellious Indians, gallant southern manhood, and (through the Red Sticks' connection to Tecumseh) the perfidious British. Ordered by Tennessee's governor to go on the offensive, Jackson assured friendly Creeks and their leaders that he would defend them, but vowed personal revenge against all others, and swore to his own troops that he would fight by their side. At a hostile Creek village south of Huntsville, Alabama, one thousand of Jackson's soldiers encircled nearly two hundred Creek fighters, killed every one of them, and took the women and children as captives. (American losses totaled only five dead and forty-one wounded.) "We have retaliated for the destruction of Fort Mims," Jackson reported curtly to Tennessee governor Willie Blount. "We shot them like dogs," a then-obscure Tennessee soldier and marksman named David Crockett later recollected.[74]

After another smashing victory in November at the village of Talladega, Jackson's fortunes soured when his supplies ran low and his men threatened to desert. Only the fortuitous arrival of replacements permitted him to remain in the field. At the end of March 1814, the augmented forces, now numbering close to four thousand men including friendly Creeks and Cherokees, overwhelmed nearly a thousand Red Sticks at Horseshoe Bend, in another lopsided bloodbath. Three weeks later, Red Eagle surrendered, and virtually the entire Creek Nation submitted to Jackson's authority.

As the price of peace, Jackson imposed a treaty that ceded twenty-three million acres of Creek land to the United States—more than half of the Creeks' total holdings, representing approximately three-fifths of present-day Alabama and one-fifth of Georgia. The forfeited lands included territories held by friendly Creeks who had fought alongside Jackson as well as territories held by Red Sticks. Jackson forced his allies, as well as those he had defeated, to submit. In doing so, he completed a land grab that opened up immense tracts of fertile land to speculators and settlers, and foreclosed the doom of the entire Creek Nation. Although the rigors of the campaign permanently broke his already damaged health—struck down by his chronic dysentery and unable to digest food, he sometimes subsisted on diluted gin—Jackson was rewarded with a commission as major general in the U.S. Army.

In strictly military terms, his reputation was exaggerated. The enemy, although formidable, was far less so than the British army and navy. Lacking ordnance and sufficient musketry, the rebels could not match the Americans' firepower. Jackson did perform well on the field for an inexperienced commander, designing simple but effective stratagems for confusing the Creeks, deploying his men skillfully, and redeploying them swiftly. His indomitable will, displayed both in suppressing mutiny among the militia and in dictating peace to the surrendering Creek chiefs, overcame his own torments. Given the delicate balance of American wins and losses in the War of 1812, his victories made him look like a military genius. But the reality was more prosaic: Jackson, when aroused, was an accomplished and unforgiving killer.

Jackson turned his fury against his greatest foe of all. "I owe to Britain a debt of retaliatory vengeance," he wrote to his wife. "[S]hould our forces meet I trust I shall pay the debt." After repulsing a British attack on Mobile, he made war on the Spanish in West Florida, who with the British (he told Rachel) were "arming the hostile Indians to butcher our women & children." The only snag in his plan was the inconvenient fact that the United States was not formally at war with Spain. Jackson, caring little for technicalities, threatened to invade Florida, provoking the Spanish governor to invite the British to land at Pensacola, a clear violation of Spanish neutrality. Fully justified in his own mind, Jackson invaded in October 1814, seized Pensacola from a combined force of Spanish, British, and Indians, and then handed the town, rendered militarily useless, back to its Spanish governor. A week later, while still in Pensacola, Jackson learned that the

British had launched an enormous invasion from Jamaica—sixty ships carrying more than ten thousand troops—aimed at New Orleans, and that he had been ordered to crush it.[75]

New Orleans was the gateway to what Thomas Jefferson had envisaged as the empire of liberty. If the British could seize it, they would control the entire lower Mississippi Valley and, once joined by forces sent from Canada, effectively control all of what was then the American West. Since the British had never formally recognized the Spanish retrocession of western lands to the French in 1800, there would have been strong grounds for them to claim that the Louisiana Purchase was illegitimate and, by right of conquest, the entire area would belong to them. Even short of such schemes, possession of New Orleans was vital to the outcome of the current fighting. Should the Americans lose the city, everyone realized, they would almost certainly lose the war. Although New Orleans, surrounded by lakes and bayous, enjoyed daunting natural protections against invasion, the British had the navy and the men.

Louisiana had been admitted to the Union in 1812, but the state's loyalties and those of its city were uncertain. In New Orleans, the long-resident Creole French and Spanish populations could not be counted on to support the American cause. South of the city, the bayous around Barataria Bay belonged to a large band of well-armed privateers and smugglers commanded by a fiercely independent, Haitian-born former blacksmith, Jean Lafitte. There were also fears of slave unrest. In January 1811, the territorial governor had savagely suppressed a rebellion of five hundred slaves, who burned several sugar-cane plantations north of New Orleans and briefly menaced the city itself. Now, with a British armada at Louisiana's doorstep, there was every reason to fear that the invaders would try to mobilize the slaves.[76]

Jackson arrived with his troops on December 1, and with his slim force (numbering, at best, seven hundred), he hastily pieced together an auxiliary army and navy. He had insulted Lafitte and the Baratarians as "hellish banditti," but now he struck a deal that secured their supplies and skills (including their expertise at cannoneering). Over the objections of skittish slaveholders, Jackson also organized two battalions of free black soldiers, ordering one reluctant assistant district paymaster to respect all of the enlistees on the muster rolls "without inquiring whether the troops are white, black or tea." Finally, in late December, contingents from Tennessee, Kentucky, and Mississippi arrived, brought by General John Coffee, General William Carroll, and Major Thomas Hinds. Although still outnumbered, the swarming Americans at least resembled a credible fighting force.[77]

Once he had learned that the British were closing in, Jackson redeployed his main force behind an old millrace five miles outside the city and dug in behind mud ramparts reinforced with cotton bales and wooden platforms. There, for three weeks, the Americans withstood repeated bombardments and ground attacks. By January 8, with four thousand men on his frontline and another thousand in reserve, Jackson faced, less than a mile to the east, ten thousand British, most of them veterans of the Napoleonic wars, under the command of Lieutenant General Sir Edward Pakenham. At dawn, the British began an all-out assault on the Americans.

Pakenham's original plan of attack had called for widening a canal to allow British-controlled barges to ferry troops across the Mississippi and blister the Americans with crossfire. Fortune wound up favoring the Americans. A hastily built British dam containing the river collapsed, delaying and nearly ruining the canal effort. The next morning, a British regiment was supposed to spearhead the British attack using ladders and sugar-cane bundles to bridge the ditches that lay in front of the American position, and then to scale Jackson's breastworks. Only when the men were in attack position did they realize that they had left the ladders and cane bundles to the rear. By the time they retrieved their equipment, the battle was well underway. Protected behind their barricades, the Americans poured volley after volley of grape, canister, and rifle fire into the advancing British line.*

By eight in the morning, the shooting had stopped. Jackson walked from position to position, congratulating the soldiers, as the army's band (which had been playing "Yankee Doodle" throughout the battle) struck up "Hail Columbia." The men cheered for General Jackson. Then the Americans climbed up and over their embankments to see what they had done.

Not even the most gruesome scenes of backwoods Indian fighting could prepare them for the aftermath of this kind of battle, fought with a heavy complement of cannons against thousands of uniformed troops. The British dead and wounded lay in scarlet heaps that stretched out unbroken for as far as a quarter mile. Maimed soldiers crawled and lurched about. Eerily, while the battle smoke cleared off, there was a stirring among the slain soldiers, as dazed redcoats who had used their comrades' bodies as shields arose and surrendered to the Americans. Jackson, who had seen hard combat and not flinched, was shaken: "I never had so grand and awful an idea of the resurrection as on that day," he later recalled.[78] In two hours of combat (and, perhaps, only five minutes of truly decisive shooting) the British had lost, by their own accounting, almost

---

* The British might also have gained an advantage when, despite the canal fiasco, five hundred troops managed to cross to the opposite banks of the Mississippi. Easily dispersing the token American defense force—a major deployment error by Jackson—the men rushed to the American batteries where they could rake Jackson's men undisturbed. But the detachment had landed well south of where it intended, and by the time the men were ready to unleash their crossfire, the main British assault had become a shambles.

three hundred killed, over a thousand wounded, and almost five hundred captured or missing—roughly 40 percent of their main attack force of five thousand. American casualties totaled only thirteen killed, thirty-nine wounded, and nineteen missing. It was a stunning disparity, greater than even the most one-sided of Jackson's triumphs over the Creeks.

If the battle's scale was difficult to comprehend, the outcome was still in many ways a typical Jackson victory, brutal, lucky, and finally overwhelming. Two weeks later, all of the British sailed away. Then began the exaltation of Andrew Jackson. President Madison sent a special commendation. Congress unanimously passed a lengthy resolution of thanks, and ordered a gold medal struck. The city of Washington, still recovering from the fires of August, erupted with delight, as did Philadelphia and New York. Newspapers ran encomiums from Jackson's men talking of his shrewd leadership and his bravery under fire. Parades were organized, songs and fiddle tunes composed, illuminations lit.

Jackson did nothing to discourage the ecstatic homage. "[T]he 8th of January," he wrote to one associate a month after the battle, "will be ever recollected by the British nation, and always hailed by every true american."[79] Vengeance and glory were his.

THE WAR OF 1812 AND THE TRANSFORMATION
OF AMERICAN POLITICS

When the news from Ghent came just over a week after the news from New Orleans, Washington's jubilation redoubled—but three visitors from Boston walked glumly past the throngs of revelers. Harrison Gray Otis, Thomas H. Perkins, and William Sullivan, the Massachusetts commission sent to relay the Yankee Federalist complaints to President Madison, knew their effort was now pointless. Perkins and Thompson did drop in at the president's lodgings, a large house formerly occupied by the French minister, where they paid their respects to Madison. Otis, embittered, stood on ceremony and refused to enter because he and his delegation had received no formal invitation. Otis also reported that Madison was now claiming that the New Englanders' efforts had been bound to fail all along, no matter the circumstances. "I believe however we should have succeeded," the unrepentant Otis wrote to his wife, "and that the little Pigmy shook in his shoes at our approach."[80]

The pygmy was now elated. The undertaking begun at Hartford, so mild and purposeful in the Federalists' own minds, had placed not just Otis and his colleagues but Federalists everywhere in an awkward position that lent itself cruelly to ridicule. In New England, self-righteousness died hard: there alone, Federalism persisted as a credible force over the coming years, especially in

Massachusetts, where Federalists retained control of the state government until 1823. Elsewhere, Federalists finally fell outside the ken of respectability, reviled as disloyalists who had wanted to end the war on Britain's terms, and lumped together with the traitorous "blue-lights" who had signaled at night to British warships anchored off the Connecticut shore. The quasi–Federalist Republican jurist Joseph Story enthused to a friend that the war's conclusion presented a "glorious opportunity for the Republican party to place themselves permanently in power."[81]

Posterity's judgment on the War of 1812 has been more severe. Ever since Henry Adams wrote his enormous and misunderstood study of the Jefferson and Madison administrations, the war has generally been viewed as a needless and costly conflict, instigated by predatory War Hawk Republicans and bungled by an inept president. Such accounts usually minimize the British offenses to American independence, and not just to commercial interests. Impressments, above all, struck at the lowest and most vulnerable of free Americans, and even such ex-Federalists as John Quincy Adams viewed them as intolerable. The critics often slight the active and purposeful efforts by the New England Federalists to undermine the war effort while New England merchants cheerfully traded with British and American forces alike. They slight Madison's remarkable calm in the face of those efforts. They disregard how, simply by fighting the Royal Navy to a standoff, the American navy performed better than any of Britain's other foes of the era. They dwell on how the war's expenses deranged the country's public finances—true enough—but they neglect how (thanks to bonds floated by Gallatin's protégé and successor, Alexander J. Dallas) the U.S. Treasury, at the end of 1815, boasted the largest credit balance in the young nation's history. They miss the fact that apart from the symbolic embarrassment at Washington, the worst American defeats came early in the war—and that, by mid-1814, Madison had found generals like Jackson who measured up to their assignments. They forget that although the Treaty of Ghent failed to end impressment, it did stipulate the repatriation of nearly four thousand Americans, classified as prisoners of war, who had been press-ganged into the British service.[82]

Even without Jackson's victory, Madison and the Republicans could have mounted the strained but plausible case that they had defied the dire early predictions of the Federalists and the Old Republicans. At the very least, they would have ceded nothing to the mighty British. On the eve of the signing of the Ghent Treaty, John Quincy Adams wrote to his wife that he had had the privilege of helping in "redeeming our union." His fellow negotiator, James Bayard, spoke of how Europeans regarded the Americans with a newfound respect. But with the Battle of New Orleans, what had ended as a kind of proud stalemate had the look and feel of an enormous American victory.[83]

The United States was the war's emblematic winner, but there were also very real losers in America. The biggest losses of all were suffered by Indians, North and South, whose power to resist expansion east of the ninety-fifth meridian was forever destroyed. Next came the disgraced New England Federalists, and then the southern Quids and the city and country democrats (including fervently pro-war democrats) who, for different reasons, had opposed the moderate Republicanism of the Jefferson years and, later, the nationalist Republicanism advanced by Henry Clay and John C. Calhoun. "Let us extend the national authority over the whole extent of power given by the Constitution," Joseph Story exclaimed. "Let us have great military and naval schools; an adequate regular army; the broad foundations laid of a permanent navy; a national bank." What had begun as the congressional nationalist faction in 1811, a pro-war version of moderate Republicanism, now commanded a seemingly unbeatable Republican Party.[84]

The war's end also marked a watershed in the rise of American democracy. Between 1801 and 1815, a Jeffersonian democracy that had once rightly feared for its own existence became the nation's preeminent political power. Presumptions about the natural superiority of well-born and well-bred gentlemen, challenged during the American Revolution, now fell. A new generation of Republicans, including men of humble origins, attained high government and military office. The proportion of eligible voters who participated in American elections grew substantially, as did (though less substantially) the proportion of American men who were eligible to vote. Party competition was the major reason, as political involvement grew most intense and widespread in areas where the rivalry between Republican and Federalists sharpened most, above all in the middle Atlantic states. Republican political organization, foreshadowed by the Democratic-Republican societies of the 1790s, had become increasingly sophisticated, producing statewide organizations that, again chiefly in the middle Atlantic states, opened up more participation by the rank-and-file party faithful and moved away from the top-down organization through state caucuses. These democratic alterations forced the more realistic of the Federalists to adapt to increasingly democratic American realities. Yet despite those adjustments, the Federalist realists could not sustain Federalism. The truly dynamic force in American politics after 1809 was not a rejuvenated Federalism, learning from the Jeffersonians' successes and exploiting their mistakes. It was a nationalist Republicanism, promoted by westerners and southerners who rejected the Federalists' political ideas and their Anglophilic economics as inimical to the character of the country.[85]

Compared to the American polity of the founding era, the change was, in retrospect, extraordinary. When the country and city organizers of the Democratic-Republican societies of the 1790s dared to speak out, between elections, on sensitive public issues, the president of the United States and the U. S. Senate (and, nearly, the House of Representatives too) formally censured them as fomenters of disorder and tyranny. Even the societies' friends in the early Republican opposition did not quite know what to make of the rambunctious, undeferential democrats. At the end of the War of 1812, this kind of hauteur and such confusion were unimaginable outside the most hidebound conservative circles. In one of the greatest paradoxes of all, the most inflammatory criticisms of the government during the war had came from conservative New England Federalists—with no Sedition Law raining down on their heads.

The pressures for democratic reform had not come even close to exhausting themselves in 1815. "The spirit of our country is doubtless more democratic than the form of our government," the Massachusetts Federalist George Cabot ruefully acknowledged after Thomas Jefferson's election in 1801.[86] Fifteen years later, although much had changed, the form had still not kept pace with the growing spirit. Despite Federalism's retreat, there were powerful Americans who wanted to restrain that change, and keep the boisterous influence of popular politics to a minimum. Even within the triumphant Republican coalition, the congressional caucus system, although under increasing pressure, still governed the selection of national candidates and the formulation of programs. And even among Republicans, there remained fundamental differences, cloaked during the war, about the definition of democratic government.

Despite the wishful thinking of some Republican leaders, the end of Federalism as a national power did not bring the end of fundamental political conflicts. Affirming the republic's independence in the war against Britain actually had the unforeseen effect of spurring action among ordinary Americans for even wider democracy—action that would meet with resistance from quondam Federalists and some Republicans alike. Those conflicts would become intertwined with divisions at the political top that, within a decade, would shatter the deceptive harmony and single-party ascendancy of the immediate postwar years. One of those divisions, over the future of American slavery, would set northern and southern Republicans—and the constituencies they represented—on a fateful collision course. The other major division, over the proper instruments and democratic direction of national development, would pit both Clay and Calhoun against a new—and, to many, frightening—popular political force. At the head of that force would stand Andrew Jackson.

II.

DEMOCRACY ASCENDANT

6

THE ERA OF BAD FEELINGS

A s 1815 ended, James Madison was jubilant. During the summer and
autumn, off the coast of Africa, Commodore Stephen Decatur had subdued the plundering corsairs of Tunis, Tripoli, and Algiers, ending once
and for all their sporadic attacks on American shipping. After reporting on this
latest military triumph in his seventh annual message to Congress, Madison was
free to concentrate on domestic matters for the first time during his presidency.
His rhetoric lacked fire, but his postwar plans were lofty.[1]

Madison's speech affirmed that the war had reinforced the evolution of mainstream Republicanism, moving it further away from its original agrarian and localist assumptions. The war's immense strain on the treasury led to new calls from
nationalist Republicans for a national bank. The difficulties in moving and supplying troops exposed the wretchedness of the country's transportation links, and
the need for extensive new roads and canals. A boom in American manufacturing
during the prolonged cessation of trade with Britain created an entirely new class
of enterprisers, most of them tied politically to the Republicans, who might not
survive without tariff protection. More broadly, the war reinforced feelings of
national identity and connection. "The people have now more general objects of
attachment with which their pride and political opinions are connected," Albert
Gallatin wrote to his old associate, the fiery democrat-turned-manufacturer
Matthew Lyon. "They are more Americans."[2]

Madison and the moderate Republican nationalists did not advance unchallenged. The war's conclusion brought a resumption of the tensions between pro-
development Republicans and country and city democrats, notably William
Duane of Philadelphia. Southern Old Republicans were incensed at what they

considered Madison's neo-Federalism. In 1814, the most thoughtful of the Virginia Quids, John Taylor of Caroline, published his *Inquiry into the Principles and Policy of the Government of the United States*—an informed if rambling attack on the Hamiltonian system, more than twenty years in the writing, that registered Taylor's disgust at Madison's apostasy. Over the next five years, Taylor's criticisms turned into a more exacting argument that federal consolidation threatened the private property rights of ordinary citizens, including the rights of southern planters to their peculiar property in black people. In back of that sharpening lay a renascence of plantation slavery.[3]

The South's deepened commitment to slavery accompanied (and was aggravated by) growing antislavery sentiment in the North. By 1804, every state north of the Mason-Dixon Line had taken some step toward the eventual elimination of slavery. Emancipation, in turn, sharpened northern resistance to the spread of slavery into the territories and newly admitted western states. That resistance, and the furious southern reaction to it, threatened, for a time, to dissolve the Republican coalition along sectional lines, and left behind a rupture that would never fully mend. And political leaders in both the North and the South also faced another, very different set of provocations. After 1815, democratic reformers in various states seized upon the wartime services and sacrifices of ordinary soldiers and pressed for an expansion of suffrage rights and an equalization of political representation. At the height of that agitation, in 1819, the American economy, red hot with postwar expansion, melted down, leading to the first national depression in American history. Quickly, outcries for widened democracy became attached to collisions of class caused by the economic disaster—and to fresh attacks by city and country democrats on banks, paper money, and the Republican nationalists.[4]

Except for a few apprehensive souls such as Taylor, it was nearly impossible for Americans to foresee this turbulence amid the celebrations of 1815. For the moment, the nation's sections and classes seemed more tightly knit than at any time since the Revolution. The fading of Federalism left only one party, the Republicans, to run the nation's affairs. "Discord does not belong to our system," Madison's successor James Monroe declared upon entering the restored and freshly whitewashed Executive Mansion—forever after known as the White House—in 1817. A Boston Federalist newspaper surveyed the harmony and proclaimed the commencement of an "ERA OF GOOD FEELINGS."[5]

That era would last less than four years before giving way to a much longer Era of Bad Feelings.

DEMOCRATIC STRUGGLES IN NEW ENGLAND

Aside from the quasi-feudal polity of Rhode Island, no state in the nation was formally more undemocratic in 1815 than Connecticut. The Royal Charter of 1666 remained the basic plan of state government. Political innovations since 1800, including the notorious *viva voce* Stand-Up Law of 1801, had reinforced Connecticut's theocratic establishment, dubbed the Standing Order. Although Abraham Bishop and his allies had created a viable Republican opposition, Connecticut's elections remained dominated by a Federalist-Congregationalist autocracy. Church ministers, in consultation with party leaders, helped dictate policy and control Federalist nominations. Anglophilia was so intense and overt that in March 1815, immediately after the cessation of the war, the high society of Hartford—described by one writer as "the metropolitan see of Federalism"—warmly hosted British Vice Admiral Henry Hotham and his officers, fresh from serving the Crown in the waters outside New London.[6]

Connecticut Federalism grew so reactionary that it wound up offending some Connecticut Federalists. Religious divisions ran especially deep, as Episcopalians, Baptists, and Methodists (along with smaller numbers of Unitarians, deists, and nonbelievers) chafed under persisting indignities, including the legal requirement that they deposit with the state a formal declaration of dissent. In 1801 and 1802, the sojourning Virginia Baptist John Leland denounced "the mischief of Connecticut religion," and he called on dissenters to demand a new constitution that secured religious liberty. Leland's appeal produced no rapid results, although, as in other states, Connecticut's Methodist and Baptist minority did ally with the new Republican Party. More strikingly, over the ensuing decade, large numbers of Federalist Episcopalians also gravitated to the Jeffersonians.[7]

Connecticut's evolving political economy produced additional political rifts. Between 1800 and 1815, a manufacturing sector began to emerge in the eastern and southern portions of the state, aided by the embargo, the Non-Intercourse Act, and the wartime cessation of trade. In 1820, only Rhode Island could claim an appreciably larger percentage of its population engaged in manufacturing. The new manufacturers, in turn, had closer affinities with the Republicans than with the Federalists. Federalist leaders did not oppose early industrial development, and some even encouraged it. But the combination of Federalist Anglophilia and mercantile priorities conflicted with the interests of the state's manufacturers, who wanted to block imports of British manufactured goods. Alert Republicans appealed for the manufacturers' support (as well as for the support of their employees) by backing special protective legislation and by celebrating them as the creators of a new form of national economic independence—"truly gratifying," one Republican paper noted, "to every true American."[8]

The Federalists' antiwar politics, which had culminated in the Hartford Convention, also raised questions about the Standing Order's patriotism. Even some nominal pro-Federalists regarded the convention as "synonymous with *treachery and treason.*" Members of the stiff-necked clerical wing of the state's Federalist party, led by Governor John Cotton Smith, aggravated matters by claiming that the prestige of the delegates' names alone vindicated the convention's proceedings. Republicans hit back hard, denouncing the Hartford gathering as "the foulest stain upon our escutcheon."[9]

In February 1816, a meeting of Republican and Episcopalian citizens from around the state assembled in New Haven to unite all elements opposed to the Federalist-Congregationalist establishment. Several issues arose, including the state's obsolete suffrage laws, but the participants united behind challenging religious intolerance. In an effort to reinforce the group's credibility, the meeting unanimously nominated the impeccable ex-Federalist Oliver Wolcott Jr. for governor in the upcoming state elections, under the banner of the American Toleration and Reform Ticket.[10]

The patrician Wolcott was an improbable tribune for democratic reform, which helps explain why he was so effective. Alexander Hamilton's successor as Treasury secretary, and a tormentor of President John Adams, Wolcott had made his national reputation in the 1790s as a stalwart conservative Federalist, a "representative of Mr. Hamilton," in one admiring Hartford editor's words. But Wolcott became estranged from the Federalists over foreign policy, and he broke with the party completely when he backed the war effort in 1812. On religious questions, he had become more broad-minded as he grew older. Having invested in a cloth manufactory, he was also sensitive to the interests of Connecticut's manufacturers. Wolcott's mellowed moderate conservatism made him a pariah in the state's Federalist press, which turned him into something of a hero to reformers.[11]

In the May elections, Wolcott garnered an impressive 47 percent of the vote, while his Tolerationist running mate, ex-Federalist Judge Jonathan Ingersoll, won the race for lieutenant governor. A year later, Wolcott won the governorship by a razor-thin margin, and in the autumn legislative elections of 1816, the Tolerationists took control of the lower chamber, the General Assembly. Although they still controlled the upper house, the Federalists were in retreat, and the Tolerationists broadened their attack to include a wide range of antiquities and defects in the state's political structure. Under the new name of the Constitutional and Reform Party, the reformers forced a repeal of the Stand-Up election law and broached the question of calling a state constitutional convention.

Grassroots agitation emboldened the insurgents, pushing them well beyond the moderate reformism favored by Governor Wolcott. In conservative Litchfield County, one "Solyman Brown" bid his "benighted section" to at last face up to democratic realities. A widely publicized essay, "The Politics of Connecticut," by the ex-Federalist Republican George H. Richards of New London, demanded a new constitution that would establish political as well as religious equality. "The Charter of King Charles II contains principles obnoxious to a Republican government," the town meeting of Wallingford declared in a memorial to its state representatives. At least sixteen other town meetings issued similar memorials between November 1817 and April 1818, and thereafter a deluge of petitions hit Hartford from towns all across the state.[12]

Wolcott responded to the protests evenly, praising the old charter as sound for its time, but acknowledging the need for a more precise definition of government power and a declaration of the people's rights. Conservative Federalists vehemently counterattacked. Jonathan Edwards Jr. proclaimed the existing charter the best constitution in the world. Lyman Beecher fretted that the reformers intended to install a dictatorship of the dissenting sects and the rest of the hoi polloi. But the conservatives were now outnumbered. (To make matters worse, some New Haven Federalists defected to the opposition, attracted by a Reform Party proposal to alternate General Assembly meetings between their city and the state capital in Hartford.) After enacting a number of new reforms — including a suffrage act that granted the vote to free adult white males who paid taxes or served in the militia — the Reform Party legislators secured a call for a statewide election, to be held under the expanded suffrage law, that would select delegates to a constitutional convention. Even before the results were known, the tumultuous scenes at the polls on election day, July 4, were enough to cause Federalists to despair. ("The Universal suffrage law is horrible," the Reverend Thomas Robbins of Scantick wrote in his diary.) The reform coalition won a majority at the convention of nearly two to one.[13]

The final draft of the new constitution, hammered out in Hartford over three weeks in late summer, was a moderate document that displeased some Republicans almost as much as it did the hard-liners of the Standing Order. Now led by the outspoken lawyer, Jeffersonian organizer, and customs collector of Middletown, "Boss" Alexander Wolcott (a cousin of the governor), the state's Republicans formed only a left-wing minority within the larger reform alliance. At the convention, the Republicans pressed for provisions that would have weakened the independence of the state judiciary, ended at-large voting for state senate representatives in favor of districted voting, and reapportioned town representation. All were democratic reforms; all would have enhanced the electoral prospects of Republican candidates; but all were turned aside by a centrist coalition of restrained Republicans, liberal Federalists, and cautious reformers like Governor Wolcott. "Boss" Wolcott, along with several of his allies, wound up voting against the final draft, saying it was "founded on no basis of republican equality."[14]

One reform that stirred only passing debate but would later have great signifi-cance outside the state was the complete disenfranchisement of black voters. The numbers of free blacks had been negligible in eighteenth-century Connecti-cut, and the numbers of black freeholders even smaller—and no effort had ever been made to exclude otherwise qualified blacks from voting. By the close of the War of 1812, however, small but concentrated black communities had grown up, especially in and around the port cities of New Haven and New London, and were causing some consternation. In 1802, one self-styled "White Freeman" in Wallingford noted that his town included two black freeholders, "both demo-crats and free," and wondered whether, if they were ever elected to the legisla-ture, they would actually be permitted to take office. In 1814, the Federalist-dominated legislature passed a law restricting freemanship to free white males. When the Reform Party legislators passed their expanded suffrage law four years later, they retained the racial exclusion.[15]

The constitutional convention moved back and forth on the issue. An early resolution came out of a drafting committee restricting the vote to "white male citizens of the United States" with minimal property requirements. The aging Federalist judge Stephen Mix Mitchell proposed an amendment striking the word *white*, but after what was reported simply as "some debate," the amendment failed, and the draft language was approved by a vote of 103 to 72. From this dis-tance and given the spotty sources, the politics behind the exclusion are difficult to discern. Federalists as well as Republicans appear to have been on both sides of the issue, yet the debate in the constitutional convention also appears to have been brief and to have stirred little interest outside the convention hall (apart, no doubt, from the state's black communities). What is clear is that when the oppor-tunity first presented itself, the majority of the state's moderate political leaders though it prudent to exclude the state's small but growing free black population from the polity—making Connecticut the second of the original northern states, after New Jersey, to draw a racial line in its suffrage laws. The action would pro-vide an important precedent.[16]

Too tame for some, and regressive for the state's free blacks, the new constitu-tion nevertheless brought substantial reform to Connecticut—a belated end to old colonial structures and a local completion of the American Revolution. One key shift involved property and the suffrage. Connecticut Federalists still clung to the traditional argument that wage earners and other nonfreeholders, no matter how industrious, were so dependent on their employers and patrons that they should not be permitted to vote. Moderate reformers as well as Republicans rejected this argument out of hand, and countered that payment of taxes was suf-ficient economic proof of an individual's qualifications as a virtuous citizen. In slightly modified form, the convention upheld the legislature's earlier rule, open-ing the vote to white men "of good moral character" who had resided in their towns six months and were either freeholders worth seven dollars, militiamen, or state taxpayers.[17]

Most dramatically, the new constitution overthrew the Congregationalist establishment by securing to all Christian denominations equal powers, rights, and privileges. Federalists fought the change furiously at the convention and gained some minor concessions regarding tithing responsibilities of church members, but could not prevent the majority from winning what, for two years, had been their chief raison d'être. With their insistence on religious toleration, the reformers guaranteed themselves sufficient popular support to carry the ratification vote in October. Moderate though the new constitution was, the fracturing of Connecticut's union of church and state would be long remembered as an overdue but momentous revolution—and, in the state's former ruling circles, as a catastrophe, when Connecticut, one minister asserted decades later, repudiated "[t]he ancient spirit which had . . . linked her . . . to the throne of the Almighty for almost two hundred years."[18]

A similar political dynamic—involving democratic agitation, divisions within Federalism, and restrained reform—appeared in the less oligarchic commonwealth of Massachusetts. As in Connecticut, an unlikely figure led the reformers. Josiah Quincy was a former congressman and self-declared "raving Federalist" whose extreme anti-Jeffersonianism in Washington had led Henry Clay to declare that he "shall live only in the treasonable annals" of American history. After he quit Congress in 1813 and returned home to a country estate outside Boston, Quincy emerged as the leader of a third force in the city's politics, still hostile to the Republicans but also alienated from the old-line Federalist Central Committee because of its unshakable disdain for popular politics. Within Boston, Quincy aligned himself with a "Middling Interest" of artisans and petty merchants, led by the self-made printer Joseph T. Buckingham, who had been hit hard by the Panic of 1819 and were now seeking reform of laws governing debt and militia service. Elsewhere, especially in the old country democratic counties of Hampshire and Berkshire, reformers agitated for reapportionment of the state legislature and continued changes in the state judiciary. In 1820, the district of Maine's decision to seek separate statehood necessitated an overhaul of Massachusetts representation. And so, in a move instigated by Quincy (who had won election to the state legislature), voters approved a state referendum calling for a new convention in Boston, to suggest revisions of the 1780 constitution.[19]

The convention's dramatic highpoint involved an extremely subtle but significant clash—not between reformers and antireformers but between two Federalist delegates, the aging antimajoritarian John Adams and the young conservative Daniel Webster. At issue was a plan devised by democratic reformers to apportion both houses of the state legislature, and not just the lower house, on the basis of population and not property. Adams, pallid and shriveled at age eighty-five, arose to deny that all men were born free and equal, to announce that government's "great object is to render property secure," and to denounce any effort to end property-holding qualifications for voters and officeholders. Government by "mere numbers," Adams argued, would lead the many to pillage the propertied few in scenes reminiscent of the French Revolution. Webster broadly agreed with Adams—"We have no experience that teaches us, that any other rights are safe, where property is not safe," he declared—but he believed that the majority actually held property and respected property rights. While for the present he would keep the existing arrangements for the upper house, Webster also urged government to encourage a wide diffusion of property "as to interest the great majority of society in the protection of the government." To Adams, imprisoned in his eighteenth-century orthodoxies, democracy directly threatened property. To Webster, property ownership could be sufficiently widespread among the many, and opportunity to gain additional property sufficiently wide, that democracy and property rights were compatible. Over the years to come, Webster's more benign and dynamic vision would expand and encourage a genuine revolution of American conservatism.[20]

The political agility of the Massachusetts conservatives, young and old, spared them from any sweeping changes for the moment, but could not fully defeat reform. In the contests for convention delegates, the Federalist Central Committee gained a majority for its own loyalists, along with friendly moderate and conservative Republicans who were wary of the most determined democrats. The coalition of antireformers and moderate reformers repeatedly thwarted what Joseph Story later derided as "a pretty strong body of radicals" inside the convention. As in Connecticut, the reformers made their greatest gains in proposing expanded religious liberties, recommending an end to the existing religious test for officeholders and equalization in the distribution of local tax monies to Unitarians and Congregationalists. The convention also proposed abolishing the existing freehold suffrage and giving the vote to all adult male taxpayers who had been resident in the state for twelve months and in their towns or districts for six months. Concerning the structures of government, the convention recommended stripping public prosecutors of the common-law right to indict citizens on their own, revising the structure of the governor's advisory executive council, and providing for the future amending of the constitution by approval of the legislature and a public referendum. The voters duly approved most of the proposed reforms, including the liberalized suffrage and the elimination of the test oath.[21]

Compared to what had happened in Connecticut, the Massachusetts revisions seemed minor, if only because Connecticut's existing colonial-era charter had demanded much more reform than Massachusetts's revolutionary constitution of 1780. Compared to what the most emphatic Massachusetts democrats had hoped to achieve—universal manhood suffrage, complete separation of church and state, senate representation based on population not property, substantially diminishing of the independence of the state judiciary—the convention's reforms looked negligible. "What has the convention done?" the frustrated Boston Middling Interest leader Joseph Buckingham asked. "Nothing—absolutely nothing." Among Federalists, the mood was one of quiet satisfaction. "We have got out as well as we expected," Webster confided to a friend. Still, the convention had reformed the old connection between property and power with regard to voting. More important, with its amendment provision, the revised constitution created the means for approving reforms without having to reconsider the entire constitution, thereby creating the possibility of more dramatic changes in the future.[22]

DEMOCRATIC STRUGGLES IN NEW YORK

Months after the Massachusetts movement ran its course, a more consequential uprising overhauled New York's constitution, in the greatest reform convention held anywhere in the country during the decade after 1815. New York's existing constitution of 1777, with its elaborate two-tier property qualifications for voting and its highly centralized arrangements for appointing state officials and vetoing legislative acts, was nearly as obsolete as Connecticut's old royal charter.* But because New York's society and politics were more complex and fractious than those of any New England state, the combination of democratic agitation and constitutional reformism achieved far more.

Popular pressure for reform arose quickly after the conclusion of the War of 1812, focused on liberalizing the state's stiff property requirements for voting as well as on altering the appointment process. In New York City and in Albany, where the number of workingmen and laborers excluded from the franchise was growing rapidly, newspapers reported on developments in Connecticut and Massachusetts, as well as on the suffrage agitation as far away as Britain. In the state's rapidly growing western and northern rural areas, large-scale emigration from New England—where even before the latest round of reformism, the newcomers had enjoyed suffrage requirements more liberal than New York's—increased the pressure for constitutional revision. A growth in rural tenancy,

---

* Under the 1777 state constitution, renters of tenements worth 40 shillings annually, freeholders worth £20, and freemen—merchants, prominent artisans, and like citizens—of the cities of New York and Albany could vote for members of the state assembly, but only freeholders worth £100 could vote for members of the state senate and for governor. Under the 1804 statutory revision for New York City, voting for the assembly was revised to enfranchise adult men who rented a tenement worth $25 per year. The £100 freehold requirement for senator electors had been translated into a $250 requirement by the time of the 1821 convention.

whereby farmers remained ineligible to vote until they had paid off in full their installment mortgages, added to the ferment in the countryside. In 1817 and 1820, reform conventions assembled in Washington County and Montgomery County; another reform meeting, called by a group of "Republican Young Men," convened in Saratoga in January 1821. By then, following the constitutional conventions in Connecticut and Massachusetts, New York had come to look like an undemocratic oddity, its politics dominated by provisions like the freehold suffrage that were relics of British feudalism. "In this enlightened age, and in this republican country," one critic declared in the early summer of 1821, the rights of free citizens "should not be tested by the refinements and subtleties of Norman jurisprudence."[23]

Factionalized party politics, exacerbated by the imperious leadership of DeWitt Clinton (who was elected governor in 1817), also helped turn constitutional reform into a potent issue. Clinton's dalliance with the Federalists in 1812 had stretched the personal loyalty of some upstate Republicans almost to the breaking point. (That point had already been passed in New York City, where anti-Clintonians, calling themselves City Democrats, had seized command of the local Republican organization and its Manhattan headquarters, Tammany Hall.) As governor, Clinton's unreliable patronage policies, support for various Federalist projects (including a Federalist bank charter, obtained through legislative bribery), and arrogant, almost patrician style led to a full-scale revolt. The anti-Clintonians took as their distinguishing political insignia the bucktail worn by New York City's Tammany democrats. And from the upstate Bucktails' ranks emerged a capable and disciplined new leadership, headed by Clinton's erstwhile ally, Martin Van Buren.[24]

Ideology as well as political self-interest propelled the Bucktails. Clinton's collaboration in the temporary revival of New York Federalism after 1812 struck the Van Buren Republicans as nearly treasonous. The new Clintonism, which effaced the Jeffersonian principles of the 1790s, needed purifying. Once approved by the Republican caucus, party decisions had to be upheld to the letter. "The "cardinal maxim . . . ," one Bucktail legislator said in 1824, "[should be] always to seek for, and when ascertained, always to follow the will of the majority." Any who wavered would be cut down as a matter of practical expediency and in deference to what Van Buren called "the democratical spirit." And while they preached party regularity, Van Buren's Bucktails accommodated to the electorate's will. On some issues—support for reform of the militia system, for example—they took up matters that appealed strongly to their own urban artisan base as well as to small farmers. On others, they learned how to tack with the prevailing winds. In his successful run for governor in 1817, Clinton had struck a strong popular chord with the latest version of his visionary proposal to build a canal across almost the entire breadth of the state, connecting the port of New

York with the agricultural riches of the Great Lakes region. The Van Buren Republicans initially rejected it as a neo-Federalist attempt to align the established rich and wellborn behind Clinton's political fortunes. When Van Buren learned of the proposal's popularity upstate, he switched his position at the last minute, and brought along enough anti-Clintonian votes in the state senate to pass the canal bill. Clinton won the election for governor anyway—a signal defeat for Van Buren—but the switch was a sign of the Van Burenites' growing pragmatic flexibility.[25]

Clinton managed to retain enough popularity to win re-election in 1820, but the tightly organized Bucktails took control of the state legislature and of New York's peculiar Council of Appointments, which was empowered to select scores of state and local officials, high and low. (The Bucktail legislature also elected Van Buren to the U.S. Senate.) Van Buren's men wielded power ruthlessly, replacing Clintonians with their own loyalists throughout state government in what one newspaper called a "bloody inquisition." The Bucktails also looked for ways to forestall any Clintonian recovery. One sure method—that, paradoxically, might threaten the appointive weapons they now exercised freely—was to back the popular demands for constitutional reform. A convention bill had come before the legislature in 1818, but Clinton and his supporters had blocked it. A year later, amid rising popular protests, Clinton agreed to hold a convention limited strictly to changing the appointment power, but the Bucktails refused to take the bait. A bill calling for an unrestricted convention finally passed in 1820, after the Bucktails had captured the legislature, but the Council of Revision, controlled by Governor Clinton, vetoed it—delaying matters by claiming (perfectly correctly) that only the people at large had the power to call a constitutional convention. Unfazed, the Bucktails passed yet another bill early in 1821, creating a convention contingent on approval by a popular referendum. The Clintonians, not wanting to look like enemies of popular sovereignty, grudgingly went along. In a special election, with a widened suffrage that allowed virtually all adult males to vote, the convention proposal passed by a three to one margin.[26]

The convention delegates, elected by the same widened suffrage, were, as a group, more diverse, more rural, and more liberal than their earlier counterparts in Connecticut and Massachusetts. Over half of the New York delegates were farmers, ranging from large landholders in Dutchess and Columbia Counties to small producers from the northern and western parts of the state. Nearly half were migrants from other states, chiefly in New England. Above all, the vast majority—98 of the 126 delegates—were either Bucktails or men friendly to Van Buren. Although a few old-line Federalists and Clintonians, including the eminent jurist Chancellor James Kent and the great patroon Stephen Van Rensselaer, made their presence felt on various issues, their numbers were marginal. The major lines of conflict pitted a feisty band of radical Bucktails, including the popular George Clinton Republican and antislavery man Erastus Root and Samuel Young of Genesee County—chiefly representing small farmers and rural townsmen from west of the Hudson—against a large and at times uneasy coalition of liberal and moderate Bucktails led by Van Buren.[27]

Van Buren's side prevailed on every important issue. Easily overcoming Kent and the conservatives, the convention toppled the existing two-tiered freehold voting arrangement—yet replaced it not with universal white manhood suffrage, as favored by the radicals, but with a modest taxpaying requirement, which could also be met with membership in the militia or work on public roads. The convention eliminated both the Council of Revision (which controlled legislative vetoes) and the Council of Appointments (regarding patronage offices), giving much of the latter's power to county-court judges and new county boards of supervisors (which, not coincidentally, Bucktail Republicans controlled). The delegates made thousands of formerly appointive offices, ranging from sheriffs and county clerks to militia officers, open to popular election. Radical efforts to remake completely the state judiciary stalled, and the respected high conservative Kent was allowed to keep his job as chancellor of the old court of chancery—but the convention created a new supreme court to replace the existing Federalist-dominated body, and established a new system of circuit judges. Senatorial representation, now to be based on persons not property, was altered to create eight senatorial districts instead of the existing four—a defeat for the Federalists and Clintonians, who had wanted even more districts in order to favor their little pockets of strength in Albany and Columbia Counties.[28]

The moderate and liberal Bucktails also carved out a victory on black suffrage and representation. New York was home to the largest number of blacks of all the northern states, including nearly thirty thousand "free persons of color" and some ten thousand slaves, due to be freed in 1827 under the state's gradual emancipation law. The concentration of blacks, slave and free, in the five counties of what is now New York City and in the lower and mid Hudson Valley represented the largest such concentration anywhere in the country outside Charleston, South Carolina. (One-third of the state's free black population lived in Manhattan.) Black adult males, enfranchised on equal terms with whites under the 1777 constitution, were overwhelmingly loyal to the Federalists, in part because of alienation from the party of the slaveholders Jefferson and Madison and in part because of Federalist influence in the Hudson Valley small towns and countryside. In close elections, the black vote, although a small portion of the total, could swing key districts and even (or so it was alleged in 1813) decide the balance of power in the state assembly. For surviving Federalists, scrambling for whatever voting blocs they could find, black support was a vital resource. Now, with the imminent enlargement of the free black citizenry, the numbers of black voters would increase by about one-third. Moreover, if blacks were counted as part of the population on which the legislature would be apportioned, new advantages would go to New York City and its neighboring counties. Even more than in Connecticut, white fears of enlarged black political power pervaded the New York convention.[29]

On the representation question, rural radical Bucktails like Samuel Young and Federalists like Rufus King could agree that direct representation was meant to be restricted to free white citizens, to the exclusion of blacks as well as paupers and white unnaturalized immigrants. "It was not the intention of the committee," King reported for the Committee on the Legislature, "to have free people of colour, or aliens, taken into account." Limiting the political power of New York City and its supposedly degrading influence was the ostensible reason for the exclusion, but so, too, most delegates appear to have assumed that only resident citizens deserved representation, and that free blacks were not truly full citizens. The delegates finally settled on a provision whereby "persons of color" (but not aliens) who paid taxes would be counted for purposes of representation and apportionment.[30]

The suffrage issue was more divisive. In their reports to the convention on the legislative committee's recommendations, Nathan Sanford of New York City and John Ross of rural Genesee County declared that only resident white male citizens should be eligible to vote. This quietly affirmed the exclusion of unnaturalized immigrants who, under the 1777 constitution, had been permitted to vote if they met the stringent property requirements. The patrician Federalist Stephen Van Rensselaer then offered an amendment to exclude what he called "the wandering population," but his amendment's language, by accident or design, omitted the word "white." The radical Bucktail Young immediately moved that the word be added. Like Connecticut, presumably, New York would eliminate property requirements for white male citizens while also eliminating the black electorate. The proposal sparked a heated debate.[31]

Federalist conservatives, including Chancellor Kent and Abraham Van Vechten, supported a motion by their antislavery colleague Peter Jay to strike the word *white*, while they also hoped to retain the $250 freehold qualification for all voters, white and black, in elections for state senators. Whatever their partisan motives may have been, these conservatives believed that class and property superseded color as a qualification for voting. "The landed interest of the state, on account of its stability and importance," Van Vechten told the convention, "is . . . entitled to distinct weight in the choice of at least one branch of the legislature."

A minority of the Bucktail radicals, most vociferously a firebrand physician from Delaware County, Robert Clarke, dissented and insisted on universal suffrage for black and white men alike in all elections. (Denying blacks a vote in a government they were bound to obey, the Jeffersonian Clarke said, was "repugnant to all the principles and notions of liberty, to which we have heretofore professed to adhere, and to our declaration of independence.") Most of the radical Bucktails, however, demanded democracy for white men only and the disfranchisement of all blacks—reversing the conservative idea by insisting that color, and not property, should govern suffrage qualifications. "The minds of the blacks are not competent to vote," Samuel Young, the most outspoken, asserted. ". . . Look to your jails and penitentiaries. By whom are they filled? By the very race, whom it is now proposed to cloth[e] with the power of deciding upon your political rights."[32]

Partisanship and rural distaste for New York City cannot fully explain the vehemence of Young's racism. Among the conservatives, lingering patrician ideas of hierarchy placed all of the middling and lower orders in a naturally subordinate position, regardless of color—a subordination to be marked by property distinctions in political rights. (The exceptions were a group of even more conservative delegates who voted both to ban black voting and to sustain the freeholder requirement for whites in senate elections.) But for some of the most vocal Bucktail democrats, Young above all, the political equality they sought could not be squared with social inequality—and the conservatives' effort to oppose the first while glossing over the second was infuriating. For the racist democrats, as for most white Americans, free blacks were an inferior people who did not fully share in the burdens of the state. "The distinction of colour," Young said, "is well understood": relatively few free blacks were taxpayers; all were barred, by federal law, from militia service; a disproportionate number were illiterate and thus, Young charged, easily manipulated. To recognize these and other obvious inequalities in everyday life but to ignore them in politics was, to the racist democrats, a sinister absurdity, one that cheapened the franchise they were fighting to enlarge and that played into the hands of the white aristocratic few. Noting that Connecticut had recently banned black voting, Young insisted that "[w]e ought to make a constitution adapted to *our* habits, manners, and state of society." For Young and his allies—one of whom explicitly affirmed his own antislavery convictions—black disenfranchisement was the corollary of emancipation.[33]

The majority of the convention took a more temperate anti-black position. Van Buren was loath to disenfranchise all propertied, taxpaying blacks who had heretofore voted. He thus joined with a coalition consisting of moderate and radical Bucktails and most of the Federalists to support Jay's proposal, and the convention by a narrow margin reinstated black suffrage. But neither could Van Buren, who himself had owned a slave as a young man, imagine keeping blacks on the same footing as whites. He backed a compromise put together by a select committee of thirteen that limited black male suffrage for all elections to those who owned freeholds worth $250—the same property qualification the conservatives wanted to retain for the entire electorate in senatorial contests. (Black voters would also have to meet a special three-year residency requirement, three times longer than for whites.) The compromise left the existing minuscule electorate for governor and state senators intact, but it disenfranchised the overwhelming majority of free blacks previously eligible to vote for assembly candidates, as well as adult male slaves who would be free after 1827. Van Buren insisted that the principle of black suffrage had been sustained, and added with bland condescension that the property restrictions "held out inducements to industry." New York's racial exclusions were less severe than Connecticut's. But the New Yorkers still affirmed that the conservative idea of a responsible freehold franchise, obnoxious to white male voters, made sense regarding blacks.[34]

Politics prevailed at the New York convention—not simply the opportunistic politics of Bucktail supremacy, but a vision of party democracy that foreshadowed later developments at the state and national level. With their constitutional revisions, Van Buren and his allies all but ensured their command of New York politics for nearly a generation, under the semi-ironic title of the Albany Regency. In shifting a great deal of the appointive power to the county level, where his forces were strongest, Van Buren also candidly acknowledged that political parties were not only compatible with but necessary to an orderly democratic regime. "The republican party [was] predominant in the state," Van Buren told the convention, according to one recorder's notes, "and he did not believe that magnanimity, or justice, required that they should place themselves under the dominion of their opponents. While they continue to be in the majority, it was no more than right that they should exercise the powers of the government. That the majority should govern, was a fundamental maxim in all free governments."[35]

To portray the New York convention only as a partisan affair, though, run by and for merely operational democrats, is to miss the deeper ideological issues at stake and to slight the convention's democratic achievements. At the time, the more cynical view prevailed among archconservative delegates like Abraham Van Vechten, who charged that the push for reform had "arisen more from violent party collisions, than from any real dissatisfaction" with the existing constitution. Later historians have endorsed Van Vechten's claim. Yet popular agitation to revise the constitution had begun before the "collisions" Van Vechten described, and had taken on a life of its own before 1821. After repeated rebuffs by the Clinton Republicans, pro-reform sentiment carried the popular referendum on calling a convention by a huge majority. Van Buren and his allies exploited this sentiment, but they also created a polity and state government that, for white male citizens, were far more democratic in spirit and in form than anything New Yorkers had ever known.[36]

In trying to protect the status quo, conservative delegates turned to two contradictory lines of argument about what Chancellor Kent called the terror of democratic principles: either the poor would, as Kent said, "share the plunder of the rich," or the propertied few would manipulate the masses. By defeating these chimeras—contemptuous, they believed, of ordinary citizens—the Bucktails won a major victory against what they saw as a resurgent Federalism in a political war that dated back to the 1790s. As Van Buren put it in a private letter before the convention to Rufus King—not a man to be impressed by populist claptrap—the war pitted the "yeomanry of the State" against a "nefarious band of speculators" that had "preyed upon the very vitals of government." If the War of 1812 had vindicated American independence and the Revolution of 1776, then, in the eyes of the Van Burenites and their followers, the convention of 1821 vindicated, in New York, the Jeffersonian revolution of 1800–01.[37]

The vindication was substantive as well as symbolic. True, the Van Burenites shied away from backing universal manhood suffrage, even for whites; and for most black voters, the convention of 1821 was a disaster. In opposing those delegates whom Van Buren derided as the "Map-caps among the old democrats," the Bucktails could sometimes sound as conservative as James Kent. But more than any other group of reformers in the older states in the years after 1815, the Bucktails also won dramatic democratic victories. They reduced the term of the governor from three years to two, making the chief executive more responsible to the electorate as well as to his party. Under the new constitution, most state positions were elective, while the rest were appointed not by the now-defunct Council of Appointments but by order of the governor and the state senate. Above all, the number of New Yorkers eligible to vote for the state assembly rose from roughly 200,000 to roughly 260,000, and those eligible to vote for governor and state senate rose from roughly 100,000 to roughly 260,000. Whereas previously about two-thirds of all white males could vote in assembly elections and only about one-third could vote as well for governor and state senators, now more than 80 percent could vote in all elections. No revision of an existing state constitution had enfranchised anywhere near so many citizens in a single stroke. It was close enough to universal white manhood suffrage that, a mere five years later, New York amended its new constitution to remove the last, difficult-to-enforce taxpaying requirements for white male voters.[38]

DEMOCRATIC STRUGGLES IN THE WEST AND THE SOUTH

Between 1816 and 1820, four western states—Indiana, Mississippi, Illinois, and Alabama—joined the Union. The conclusion of the War of 1812, by removing the threat of the woodland Indians in the North and the Creeks in the South, accelerated both the white settlement of these areas and the alacrity with which Congress acted to incorporate them as states. Formally, their constitutions were democratic in comparison to most of the original state constitutions back East. But contrary to persisting myth, developed most powerfully by Frederick Jackson Turner, no "wind of Democracy" blew from the Mississippi Valley back to the long-settled regions of the seaboard. In fact, the West borrowed heavily from eastern examples. And although the arrivistes who settled in the West chose—and in some cases were forced to adopt—democratic institutions, their actions did not spring from democratic mores unique to a frontier setting. They arose out of a combination of self-interest on the part of the more prominent settlers and political pressure from below.

Westerners did exert some indirect democratic influences in the East when eastern reformers asserted that unless they heeded democratic pressures, capable residents would migrate west in droves. "By rendering it the interest and happiness of our population to stay at home," the Republican editor of the New York *Columbian* wrote in 1817, "is the only way to check the [emigration] rage." Western constitution makers, meanwhile, relied heavily on the precedents of neighboring states from which the majority of new settlers had come, which in turn had built on earlier precedents. Thus, Illinois and Indiana drew on the constitutional structures of Ohio, which had earlier drawn on the examples of Kentucky, Tennessee, and Pennsylvania. One Massachusetts newspaper, reviewing the Mississippi constitution of 1817, remarked that it was so similar to those "of many of the other states that its perusal does not excite much interest." Alabama took Mississippi's constitution as its model when it framed its own constitution two years later.[39]

The wealthier and more politically connected residents of the new states certainly sounded more democratic than many of their eastern counterparts. In Alabama's plantation-dominated black belt, Georgia émigrés from the Tidewater Broad River region established themselves early as a social elite but espoused broadly democratic ideas for the white male citizenry. "[T]he fundamental principle of all our institutions," John W. Walker of the Broad River group wrote on the eve of Alabama's first constitutional convention, "supposes [the Constitution] to be an act of the People themselves." Yet self-interest, as well as democratic idealism, had shaped westerners' views well before statehood was in the offing. Under the fifty-acre freehold requirement for voting in the territories established by Congress, only a tiny proportion of western settlers qualified—including many who actually owned sufficient land but had difficulty establishing their titles. In Mississippi in 1804, only a little more than two hundred out of a total of nearly forty-five hundred residents were entitled to vote. Similar circumstances in Indiana led to petitions calling the voting requirements, as one put it, "subversive of the liberties" of the people at large. Congress reluctantly gave way in a series of reforms that eventually established a small taxpaying suffrage requirement for adult white males.[40]

Territorial leaders, particularly in the Old Northwest states, saw liberalized voting laws as an important incentive to attract enough new settlers to qualify for statehood. Thereafter, leading residents in sparsely populated areas saw even further liberalization as a means to encourage settlement, raise land values, hasten economic development, and expand the tax base. In the southwestern states, full citizenship and enfranchisement of all white men enlisted in the militia would ensure full participation in policing patrols, which would help minimize the possibility of slave revolts. It would also, in time, become a powerful means of blurring the class lines between slaveholders and nonslaveholders, by appealing to their basic equality as white citizens regardless of property—creating a Master Race democracy.[41]

Self-interested sagacity, however, goes only so far in explaining the trend toward expanded democracy in the new states. In some places, notably Alabama, plain settlers and their champions pushed more conservative men further than they wanted to go. At the 1819 Alabama constitutional convention, an exclusive Committee of Fifteen offered a draft constitution that included the absence of any property or taxpaying qualifications for voting and officeholding. Overall, the Alabama Committee's draft plan offered the new state's white male adults the most liberal state constitution in the country. But even that was too limited for the delegates from the "upper counties" in the northern part of the territory, populated mainly by nonslaveholding yeomen. With timely aid from a few of the more prominent delegates—including the convention's president, Princeton-educated John W. Walker—the upper-county delegates forced the convention to base representation in both the upper and lower houses of the legislature strictly on the basis of white population. The upper-county men also secured a provision abolishing imprisonment for debt, and they defeated efforts to prevent the popular election of county sheriffs, the most important state officials at the local level.[42]

In other western states, the more democratic forces prevailed from the outset. The election of delegates to the Indiana state constitutional convention in 1816 was thrown open to all adult white male citizen taxpayers. The convention, dominated by farmers and lawyers who had resettled from the Virginia backcountry, in turn approved a constitution that provided white manhood suffrage and voting by written ballot, and established a decentralized judiciary with term limits of seven years for judges. Soon after Alabama completed its constitution, Mississippians began raising the issue of revising their own constitution in order to catch up. In Illinois, no taxpaying requirement was required at any stage.[43]

The major obvious difference among the western state constitutions concerned slavery, although the politics behind that difference were complicated. In Indiana, a faction of resident slaveholders known as the Virginia Aristocracy, backed by William Henry Harrison and his so-called Vincennes Junto, was losing its sway to an antislavery faction, called the Parvenues, concentrated in the southeastern parts of the territory. When the constitutional convention met in 1816, antislavery opinion mobilized itself, and the Parvenues and their allies got the upper hand. After a bitter debate, the convention adopted a provision which declared that "the holding of any part of the human creation . . . can only originate in usurpation and tyranny" and outlawed slavery and involuntary servitude in perpetuity—but the delegates also excluded blacks from the franchise. The Illinois constitution of 1818 likewise banned both slavery and black suffrage. But under pressure from the state's large southern-born white population, it also sustained existing black employment indentures on terms close to slavery. In 1819, the new Illinois legislature would pass a series of draconian black codes strictly regulating black settlement and employment, and in 1822 the antislavery governor Edward Coles—a native of Albemarle County, Virginia, and protégé of Thomas Jefferson—would have to organize furiously to stave off an effort to introduce slavery. In Mississippi and Alabama, egalitarianism for whites became in part a means for protecting slavery. In Illinois and Indiana, it helped to prevent slavery from taking root—although not without a fight and not without the total exclusion of blacks from the polity. As in Connecticut and New York, political rights for men in the new northwestern states would stop sharply at the color line.[44]

The stongest resistance to any egalitarian trends, including those that purportedly enhanced slavery, appeared in the seaboard South. South Carolina's broad suffrage and quasi-aristocratic governance, installed in 1808, sustained the state's basic conservative character, and neither North Carolina nor Georgia (where white manhood suffrage had been established in 1789) generated significant reform activity between 1800 and 1820. By contrast, in Virginia, the largest and economically most diverse of the southern states, the slaveholding Tidewater political establishment confronted demands for constitutional revision quite similar to those that arose in New England and New York. But conservative Virginians killed off calls for a new state convention, partly by granting piecemeal concessions and partly by remaining united.

Much as in the northeastern states, Virginia's democratic movement originated from below. On June 21, 1815, a meeting of nonfreeholders assembled in Harrisonburg in Piedmont Rockingham County to protest "the inhibitions to the elective franchise," chiefly Virginia's fifty-acre freehold requirement. The group also appointed a committee to draft a petition that would be circulated throughout the state, signed by other nonfreeholders and their supporters, and forwarded to the legislature in Richmond. Issued on July 4, the petition demanded that militiamen recently "coerced into military service" as well as all male taxpayers be given the franchise, and that the state assembly call "a CONVENTION of the PEOPLE" to revise the 1776 constitution.[45]

Signed copies of the circular poured into the legislature from the western counties, populated mainly by nonslaveholding small farmers and commercial wheat growers. The legislature, dominated by eastern slaveholders, took no action, which prompted a new round of formal western protests during the summer of 1816, now led by moderate gentleman reformers. In early August, delegates from eleven western counties met in Winchester to demand equalized representation in the state legislature. An even larger meeting, consisting of men from thirty-five counties, assembled later that month in Staunton—and, when taken over by more insistently democratic reformers, issued a call for a state convention with an unlimited scope that would consider suffrage reform as well as equal representation. The democrats' passion left even some of the genteel western reformers worried that "the idle and vicious & worthless" were about to overthrow the rights of property.[46]

From his Albemarle County aerie, Thomas Jefferson viewed the agitation with approval. In June 1816, he received a pamphlet from its author, one H. Tompinkson—actually Samuel Kercheval, a freethinking Piedmont writer and reformer—endorsing the convention movement, along with a note inquiring about his reactions. Begging that his opinions be kept out of "the gridiron of the public papers," Jefferson delivered a lengthy affirmation that actually went much further than the radical Virginia democrats had dared to go. Jefferson supported a "general suffrage" (that is, giving the ballot to all taxpayers and militiamen) as well as equal representation, but he also proposed a complete overhaul of the county court system and a revamping and democratization of local government to resemble more closely the townships of New England. "I am not among those who fear the people," Jefferson emphasized. "They, and not the rich, are our dependence for continued freedom."[47]

Among the great majority of Virginia's Republican landed gentry, however, Jefferson's democratic views were anathema. Schooled in the traditional conventions of advancement through honor, talents, and connections, slaveholders of all partisan persuasions had little use for the rude democracy being foisted on them by the nonfreeholders. If few were as allergic to democracy as John Randolph—who, in his acidulous way, would later remark that Jefferson had no authority on any subject, even "in the mechanism of a plough"—most believed that apart from electioneering days, politics ought to be left in the hands of virtuous gentleman-masters like themselves, and that men of property, especially slaveholders, deserved a larger voice in the legislature than others.[48]

An instinct for political self-preservation did open the way for some concessions to the more moderate of the westerners. Thomas Ritchie, a friend of Jefferson's and now the editor of the influential *Richmond Enquirer*, gave considerable coverage to the reformers' activities. At Ritchie's urging, a few eastern Republicans pushed a convention proposal through the lower house of the legislature in 1816. Thereafter, a coalition of western Republicans, Federalists, and eastern moderate Republicans passed legislation extending internal improvements and new bank charters to western areas and reducing the disproportional representation of the eastern counties in the senate—thereby conciliating the more temperate and well heeled of the western reformers. But the senate killed the convention bill. "Enough was done at the last session," one conservative wrote, hopefully, after the legislature adjourned, "to quiet the Western counties and to prevent any mischief at the next." Virginia's Republican old guard had, for the moment, thoroughly contained the democratic challenge.[49]

The reformers' defeat in Virginia affirmed emerging patterns in the state-level efforts at constitutional liberalization after 1815. Several factors contributed to the pressure for change—religious tensions, the search for partisan advantage, economic self-interest, as well as the growth of portions of the population either ineligible to vote or badly underrepresented under the existing rules. But in no state did reform come easily, or without agitation and pressure from below. In the older states, the task of calling state conventions proved extremely difficult, resisted by establishment leaders until they had no choice but to accede. Once assembled in conventions, conservatives and moderates proved highly capable of limiting reform. The greatest exception, outside the new states, came in New York, and even there, moderate and not radical reformers prevailed. Local political elites, as in Virginia, might forestall major reforms with concessions, but in no instance did reforms occur simply because of the calculations of the existing ruling groups. The success of the state movements depended, in turn, on the solidarity, homogeneity, and political will of the respective local elites, leaving the southeastern slave states the most impervious to change.

The result was a highly uneven pattern of democratization. By the end of 1821, twenty-one of the twenty-four states had approved something approaching a divorce of property-holding and voting—a major shift since the nation's founding. But of the four original states that lay below the Potomac, two, Virginia and North Carolina, still had significant property restrictions on the suffrage, and a third, South Carolina, placed severe property limits on officeholding that helped keep political power firmly in the hands of the slaveholder elite. Only six states, all but one of them in the free North, had approved manhood suffrage, regardless of property, for blacks as well as whites; conversely five of the original thirteen states—Connecticut, Delaware, Maryland, New Jersey, and New York—had either withdrawn or sharply curtailed black voting rights. The new states admitted to the Union after 1789, from Maine to Louisiana, had generally liberal constitutions, but outside the New England states and Tennessee, they too excluded blacks from the polity. In the only state where women had enjoyed the franchise, New Jersey, that right had been removed. And in every state but four, aliens were formally banned from the polls.[50]

Democracy for white men had come a long way since the Revolution, but it had also had to overcome resistance, sometimes intense, in much of the country—and it still had far to go in most of the older portions of the South. For those white men left out, as well as for free black men newly excluded, the sight of democratization for others stoked deep resentments. The full ramifications of these trends, and of the passions that lay behind them, would not, however, become fully apparent until the mid-1820s. By then, two national political crises, both of which began in 1819, had destroyed the optimistic spirit of patriotic unity proclaimed by President James Monroe and had greatly altered the context of democratic reform. The first crisis involved the sudden collapse of the economy—a catastrophe caused, many believed, by the reborn Bank of the United States.

THE PANIC OF 1819

James Monroe was a model of dignified and somewhat dim perseverance—an unlikely promoter of vigorous postwar economic expansion and improvement. A son of Virginia's lesser tobacco gentry, he had studied law with Jefferson, attached himself to his mentor's political fortunes, and doggedly risen the political ladder to the highest reaches of national affairs, winning appointment (at Jefferson's urging) as Madison's secretary of state. Fluent in French but less than brilliant—"a mind neither rapid nor rich," William Wirt noted in one widely quoted remark—Monroe was by nature more of an ideological purist than either Jefferson or Madison, and he remained one well after 1801. In 1808, when some doctrinaire Virginians bridled at Jefferson's selection of Madison as his successor, Monroe let it be known that he would allow himself to be advanced as an alternative—backing off only at the last minute, and thereby saving his political career. Under Madison, Monroe directed the State Department with admirable energy. He displayed particular fortitude during the British destruction of Washington when, while the rest of the administration scattered into the Virginia night, he organized what meager defenses he could. The Republican congressional caucus duly gave him its presidential nomination in 1816, and he won the election handily over Rufus King, losing only in the die-hard Federalist strongholds of Delaware, Massachusetts, and Connecticut. Yet Monroe came to the presidency generating a sense of solid and unexciting entitlement—a gray-haired worthy of fifty-nine, at the tag end of the Revolutionary generation, whose penchant for wearing old-fashioned knee breeches and silk stockings on ceremonial occasions signaled a certain strangeness in the rapidly rebuilding capital.[51]

Monroe turned out to be more of a combination of old and new than a throwback to the 1790s. Catching up with the Republican mainstream, he had shifted toward nationalist views since 1808, a shift that became more pronounced during the war. "The nation has become tired of the follies of faction," the Philadelphia ex-Federalist and man of letters Nicholas Biddle wrote with relief to an associate shortly after Monroe won the White House, "and the ruling party has outgrown many of the childish notions with which they began their career 20 years since." For Monroe, ending factionalism also meant fulfilling Jefferson's old dream of incorporating the remnants of Federalism into a grand national party. He did not appoint Federalist holdouts to office, lest his own friends denounce him for treachery, but he made a point of reaching out to the surviving Federalists in Congress and generally won their backing. As for rejecting old dogma, Monroe began his presidency by vigorously supporting government encouragement to industry, trade, commerce, and national defense—sentiments that led the newly selected attorney general, Richard Rush, to wonder if Mr. Monroe had moved too far in the Federalists' direction.[52]

Other observers, with longer memories than Rush, also viewed Monroe's embrace of consensus and nationalist improvement with misgivings. Although the new president had no visible enemies in Washington, he also had no fervent friends. He was an old man's young man, whose career had thrived thanks to alliances with his elders, above all Jefferson, now all but passed from the political scene. Moreover, Rufus King wrote in 1818, "strong passions" lurked just beneath the surface of nationalist amity on Capitol Hill, "waiting only for an occasion to show themselves." By the end of Monroe's first term, those passions had men shouting all across the political nation—the result, in part, of the moderate nationalist Republicans' rejection of the formerly preternatural Jeffersonian hatred of a national bank.[53]

Republican reconciliation with Hamilton's bank idea had taken place by fits and starts, and was never monolithic. In 1811, when the charter for the Bank of the United States (BUS) came up for renewal, the Madison administration, goaded by Secretary of the Treasury Gallatin, supported it. (Madison, the anti-BUS scourge of twenty years earlier, allowed that "expediency and almost necessity" now required rechartering the bank.) In Congress, a coalition of Republican southerners and westerners, seeing the bank as an instrument for economic development in their respective regions, led the recharter effort. But they were checked on three different fronts, which led to the bank's downfall by a single vote in both the House and the Senate. Old-line Jeffersonians, ranging from the Virginia planter William B. Giles to the veteran city democrat Michael Leib of Pennsylvania, resurrected the constitutional antibank arguments originally advanced by Jefferson and Madison. More interestingly, some of the most commercially oriented Republicans, including Henry Clay, opposed recharter on the grounds that the national bank unfairly constrained the operations of state banks, which had proliferated throughout the country (rising in number from three in 1791 to eighty-eight in 1811). Finally, some of the nation's leading capitalists—above all, in New York City, John Jacob Astor, the immigrant mercantile magnate, and the speculator Jacob Barker—had fallen out with the national bank's directors and (with plenty of state bank stock in their coffers) lobbied hard to kill the recharter bill.[54]

Five years later, the disasters of wartime, plus the intervention of leading financiers, turned the tide yet again. In 1813, the Treasury Department, facing imminent federal bankruptcy due to military expenditures and the wartime loss of revenue, floated sixteen million dollars' worth of government paper. Astor and Barker invested heavily, along with Secretary Gallatin's fellow Pennsylvanian, the longtime pro-Republican financier Stephen Girard, in concert with Hamburg-based merchant David Parish, who represented European capital. No one in this tiny group, including Secretary Gallatin, had been born in the United States, yet they could claim, justly, to have patriotically rescued the nation's credit at a perilous moment.

Patriotism was not altruism. The bonds promised the investors a triple profit, and in 1814, Girard, Astor, and Parish, looking to guarantee their investment, tendered an undisguised Hamiltonian proposal to the Madison administration— to enhance the value of their investment by making government bonds exchangeable for stock in a new BUS. The proposal faltered when Treasury Secretary Gallatin, privy to the deal, departed for Ghent as part of Madison's peace commission. When Pennsylvania's senators, Michael Leib and Abner Laycock, blocked the appointment of their nemesis (and Gallatin's favorite) Alexander Dallas as Gallatin's replacement at the Treasury Department, the bank plan looked dead. But after the burning of Washington, and following direct intervention by what Dallas called an anonymous "deliberate concert among the Capitalists," the Pennsylvanians gave way, Dallas was confirmed, and the bank proposal was back on track. After a few legislative false starts, the pro-bank forces in Congress, now led by the repentant Speaker of the House Henry Clay and his nationalist comrade John C. Calhoun, won enough support from hitherto wary southerners and westerners to prevail in April 1816.[55]

Monroe fully supported the bank's rebirth. As secretary of state during the darkest days of the war, he had come to understand the Hamiltonian imperatives of wartime finance, and he extended those imperatives to the postwar situation. A national bank, he wrote to Madison in May 1815, would "attach the commercial part of the community in a much greater degree to the Government; interest them in its operations. . . . This is the great desideratum of our system." Monroe's change of heart was eased by the fact that some of the most prominent figures in the "commercial part" were now self-made Republican parvenus, exemplified by Astor and Girard.[56]

As immigrant outsiders-made-good, both Astor and Girard found the Republicans more socially and politically congenial than the Federalists. And their expanding influence added a fresh dimension to Republican politics to go along with the young national Republicans of the South and the West: an eastern monied group that strongly advocated the creation of a stable and efficient national system of money and credit. Their idea was to Republicanize Hamiltonian bank policy—understanding, as their congressional ally Calhoun boasted, that the Republicans had the support of "the yeomanry, the substantial part of our population," who would now "share in the capital of the Bank."[57]

The chief financial rationale for re-creating the BUS was to ensure that this democratized expansion proceeded soundly. Under the financial stresses of the war, state-chartered banks had suspended specie payments, which meant that they could issue the equivalent of paper money in bank notes to borrowers without regard to the amount of gold or silver coin the banks actually held in their vaults. The suspension continued after peace returned, allowing established banks to make large dividends by extending loans and note issues far in excess of their specie reserves, and permitting new private banks to open with only tiny amounts of borrowed specie on hand and indulge in profligate lending of their own notes. With so much bank paper of dubious value forced into general circulation, the nation's economic health was threatened by a large and growing bubble of speculation. A new BUS, however, serving as the federal government's depository, could curb the inflation by reinstating specie payments—that is, by regularly presenting the state bank notes it received back to the state banks and demanding specie in return, thereby compelling the banks to reduce their vastly inflated loans and note issues. Acting as a financial balance-wheel, the national bank would, in principle, keep currency values and capital markets stable, and prevent national economic expansion from turning into an orgy of overspeculation and runaway inflation.[58]

The main office of the Second BUS opened in Philadelphia on January 7, 1817, with Girard and four other Republicans serving as its government-appointed directors, and with another Republican, Dallas's friend William Jones, serving as its president. In the short run, all went swimmingly, despite some initial resistance from state and private banks. "We oppened here our office and agreed to take Bills on Baltimore Virginia & Phila," Astor wrote to Gallatin from New York, in his still-unsteady English, of the resumption of specie payments on February 20. "[I]n half an hour all was at par & on a level." By enforcing discipline over state and private bank emissions of paper, Astor and his friends had seemingly created what Astor called "a national blessing." Yet February 20, 1817, would prove the zenith of the "Era of Good Feelings" as far as the bank and American enterprise were concerned. A year later, Astor warned Gallatin that redoubled speculation, goaded by the BUS, now threatened "a general Blow up" among the state banks. A year after that, the American economy collapsed from top to bottom.[59]

The bank's directors were both financially and morally culpable, but their offenses involved making a bad situation worse. The downfall originated in much larger shifts in the Atlantic economy, initiated in 1815 by Napoleon's final defeat at Waterloo. Britain's warehouses were bulging with manufactured goods, which, with the coming of peace, the British dumped on the American market, overwhelming the protectionist tariff measures enacted by Congress in 1816 and threatening American manufacturers who had sprung up in the hot-house wartime economy. Those difficulties were masked by a dizzying climb in agricultural export prices, sparked by European crop failures and by a seemingly limitless British demand for American short-staple cotton, now easily grown throughout the American South. A speculative boom in American land and cotton ensued, fueled by the riotous proliferation of new state-chartered banks prior to the national bank's reinstallation. Unnoticed at the time, however, was a growing shortage in available specie due to political unrest in Mexico and Peru, the major sources of supply for gold and silver, which in turn put a downward pressure on wholesale commodity prices. That pressure, coupled with the recovery of European agriculture and increased British imports of East Indian cotton, sent prices of American goods tumbling in 1818, and burst the speculative bubble. American staple prices and land values dropped by anywhere from 50 to 75 percent; and backward the dominos fell, from ruined speculator to merchant to farmer.[60]

The national bank badly exacerbated the situation. At direct fault was its president, William Jones. A deft political self-promoter, Jones had won the confidence of both Monroe and Madison as well as Alexander Dallas, even though his Philadelphia mercantile firm had recently limped through bankruptcy proceedings and despite his uneven record in government service at the Navy and Treasury Departments. Stephen Girard, now a bank director, scorned Jones as an adventurer, and Gallatin was so aghast at Jones's elevation that he never thereafter spoke to Alexander Dallas. But Jones had the support of the majority of bank directors as well as of the White House, and his style of cheery indifference came to dominate the bank's policies, both in Philadelphia and at its branch offices. The original BUS, Jones wrote to Secretary of the Treasury William Crawford in July 1817, had been too conservative in its credit operations, "circumscribed by a policy less enlarged, liberal, and useful than its powers and resources would have justified." Backed by his board, Jones would Republicanize the bank by feeding the postwar rage to get rich quick.[61]

Rather than force state banks to curtail their inflated emissions of notes and loans, Jones approved lavish lending, especially by its new branches on the western urban frontier. By putting so many BUS notes into circulation, Jones abdicated the leverage he had had over the state banks early in 1817—for no longer could the national bank demand specie payments without being pressed for such payments in return. Compounding the problem, the Baltimore branch directors, with Jones's connivance, forced other BUS branches to redeem notes they had issued to themselves and various insider friends, expecting that the speculative boom would know no end. By 1819, the fraud netted the Baltimoreans three million dollars, half of which was never recovered. Finally, in 1818, Jones sharply reversed course, and began calling in loans—but too late to save his own skin. Early in 1819, pushed by Astor and Girard, the bank's directors finally dismissed Jones and replaced him with the South Carolinian Langdon Cheves. The new president further tightened the screws, reducing the bank's liabilities by more than half, sharply cutting back the total value of bank notes in circulation, and more than tripling the bank's specie reserves.[62]

Without question, Cheves's decision to contract instinctually made sense, both in halting the runaway inflation and in doing right by his stockholders. Not only had Jones accelerated the speculation he was supposed to control; he had allowed the Baltimore swindlers to create what Nicholas Biddle (who joined the BUS board of directors in 1819) called "that solecism—a monied institution governed by those who had no money." For reversing that trend and restoring the bank's credibility, many historians have given Cheves high marks. Yet for the national economy, his timing and the extent of his actions could not have been worse. By the time Cheves took over the BUS, Jones's all-too-late contraction had already begun to right the situation. In clamping down even harder through 1820, Cheves accumulated a huge horde of specie in the BUS—and, in the process, contributed to turning what might have been a sharp recession into a prolonged and disastrous depression. Just as the bank intensified its deflationary pressure, commodity prices for American staples on the world market collapsed. Coupled with the bank's brutal deflation, the free fall of agricultural prices prevented state banks from either collecting from their debtors or meeting their obligations to the BUS—leading to a tidal wave of bank failures, business collapses, and personal bankruptcies. As the financial writer and bank critic William Gouge later observed, "[T]he Bank was saved and the people were ruined."[63]

The panic appeared, at first, to hit hardest in the nation's cities. New England bore the least suffering, in part because its conservative state banks had resisted the bubble and retained their specie reserves, and in part because postwar competition from British manufacturers had checked speculation. But farther South and West, from the older seaboard ports to the growing commercial centers in the newly settled interior, the effects were catastrophic. In New York, the public almshouse, already under strain, could not handle the hundreds of new cases. In Philadelphia, three-fourths of the workforce was reported idle in 1820, and hundreds were imprisoned for nonpayment of debts. The larcenous Baltimore commercial firm Smith and Buchanan fell, John Quincy Adams recorded in his diary, "with a crash which staggered the whole city," causing the failure of more than a hundred major merchants and throwing thousands out of work. From Pittsburgh, Lexington, and Cincinnati came dolorous dispatches of unremitting commercial annihilation. (Lexington, briefly the center of Kentucky's cordage manufacturing, would never really recover, and the lion's share of Cincinnati's commercial real estate wound up in the hands of the forecloser of last resort— the Second BUS.)[64]

The panic was just as damaging—and its effects would last longer—in rural America. "[A]ffairs are much deranged here . . . ," one British traveler wrote from Jeffersonville, Indiana. "Agriculture languishes—farmers cannot find profit in hiring labourers. . . . Labourers and mechanics are in want of employment. I think that I have seen upwards of 1500 men in quest of work within eleven months past, and many of these declared, that they had no money." Back in Virginia, the aged ex-president Jefferson reported that "lands cannot now be sold for a year's rent." Among the victims was Jefferson himself, who, having cosigned a number of bank loans for his friend Wilson Carey Nicholas, was overwhelmed "by a catastrophe I had never contemplated." Right away, he wrote a "Plan for Reducing the Circulating Medium," in which he called for "the eternal suppression of bank paper," the transfer to a specie currency, and a prohibition on bank charters by any government, state or federal. He asked his friend William C. Rives to introduce the proposal to the Virginia legislature without disclosing the author, but it got nowhere. Jefferson would spend the few remaining years of his life scrambling to keep his beloved Monticello from defaulting into the hands of his and Nicholas's creditors.[65]

In Washington, responses to the disaster ranged from denial to rumblings about restricting bank credit. In his annual message in 1819, President Monroe took only passing notice of currency problems and the downturn in manufacturing, and said that the difficulties were lifting on their own accord. A year later, when the crisis had worsened, Monroe noticed that "an unvaried prosperity is not to be seen in every interest of this great community," but generally saw "much cause to rejoice in the felicity of our situation." Secretary of the Treasury William Crawford, on the contrary, issued a report that lamented the BUS's expansion of credit, criticized the excess number of state banks, and called for a sharp curtailment of the paper-money system, including the prohibition of small-denomination note issues.[66]

In the immediate crisis, however, with the BUS charter not due to expire until 1836, banks and finance as well as debt laws were mainly state responsibilities— and the political fury over the panic shook state politics even more broadly and severely than the continuing campaigns for constitutional reform (and sometimes precipitated new ones). In Boston, the hardest-hit city in New England, popular anger at an alarming rise in imprisonment for debt helped consolidate the Middling Interest and pave the way for the calling of the 1820 Massachusetts convention. Debtor-relief laws were enacted in Vermont and Maryland, and came close to passage in North Carolina, Virginia, Delaware, and New Jersey. New York and Rhode Island approved milder forms of debt relief. More dramatically, several eastern states intervened to restrict state banks. New York State's Bucktail reformers, their constituents reeling from the panic, included a provision in their new constitution requiring a two-thirds' legislative majority to approve any new state banking charter. In 1820, the Pennsylvania legislature commanded all state banks to resume specie payments. Vermont passed similar legislation and forced the closure of every bank in the state. Other eastern states tightened regulations governing existing state banks. In the West, Ohio, Indiana, Illinois, Kentucky, Tennessee, Louisiana, and Missouri passed debtor-relief laws, while Illinois, Missouri, and Alabama issued state paper money aimed at aiding small debtors. And more radical popular outrage against commercial banking—sometimes directed against banks generally, sometimes simply against the BUS—spread like wildfire. "All the flourishing cities of the West are mortgaged to this money power," exclaimed Thomas Hart Benton of the nation's newest state, Missouri, inventing an antibank phrase that would loom large in national politics over the decades to come. Virtually every western state passed legislation restricting bank charters and credit; only Louisiana and Mississippi escaped the antibank wrath.[67]

Some of the attacks on the BUS came from the same state bankers that state legislatures were trying to regulate. These banks had always resented the BUS's power to restrain their operations, and their solution to the crisis was to expand greatly the issuance of state bank paper in order to end what they called a scarcity of money. But across the country, the antibank revulsion also brought appeals, similar to Jefferson's, for the partial or total elimination of the paper-money system—what, in future years, would become known as a "hard-money" politics. By facilitating the spread of credit, the argument went, both the BUS and the state banks had created a dangerous new speculative economy, prone to illusory breakneck booms followed by busts that left the great mass of the population strapped or destitute. To correct matters, hard-money advocates demanded the virtual elimination of bank paper except for certain kinds of commercial transactions, and for its replacement with metal currency, whose value would not wildly fluctuate. Numerous antibanking schemes appeared from the pens of newspaper editors (including Thomas Ritchie of the *Richmond Enquirer*), legislators and political leaders (including the Grand Sachem of New York City's Tammany Hall), fledgling political economists, and committees of local citizens. The greatest political effect was to reinvigorate the city and country democracies, with a renewed focus on economic and financial issues.[68]

The revived city democracy appeared most dramatically in the eastern seaports, above all in Philadelphia. Although no longer the nation's largest city, and with its mercantile sector in decline, Philadelphia had begun experiencing rapid new growth as a manufacturing center at the end of the eighteenth century. The growth accelerated during Jefferson's embargo, the War of 1812, and after. Philadelphia master craftsmen and merchants began investing in scores of new enterprises, running the gamut from highly mechanized gun manufactories and printing firms to small outwork proto-sweatshops turning out cheap shoes and clothing for the expanding western and southern markets. Along with this diverse urban manufacturing base emerged a new and polyglot class of manufacturing wage earners, ranging from highly skilled overseers to poor, barely skilled women and children pieceworkers.[69]

The early industrialization of Philadelphia—similar, if less dramatic transformations also unfolded in Boston, New York, and Baltimore—had, by 1819, already brought to America class tensions of a sort familiar in the Old World. The established customs, hierarchies, and solidarities of craft—based on the presumption that all honest and sober skilled tradesmen would some day earn their independent competence—crumbled under the rearrangement of work and a spreading permanent dependence on wages. The surest sign of new troubles was the evolution of journeymen's friendly associations into something closer to trade unions, a step first taken by the city's shoemakers in 1794. An especially bitter shoemakers' strike over the winter of 1805–06—initiated when master shoemakers tried to cut wages—concluded in the conviction of the union leaders on common-law restraint-of-trade conspiracy charges and signaled a sharpening of class lines. Something, it seemed, had gone terribly awry amid the city's rapid industrial progress. "[T]he time before long will come," one local petty craftsman observed, dolefully, "when we shall tread in the steps of Old England."[70]

Leading the charge against the new industrial inequities was the editor of the venerable *Aurora*, the indefatigable William Duane. Duane's red hair, close-cropped in front in the "radical" French style known as the Brutus cut, had faded to light amber—but his devotion to Paineite radical democratic principles remained undiminished. Virtually alone among Philadelphia's democrats, Duane defended the striking shoemakers in 1805, claiming that were their union suppressed, then "the constitution is a farce and the bill of rights is only a satire upon human credulity." He bitterly opposed the effort to recharter the BUS in 1811. More generally, Duane brought his English experience to bear in warning that America was, indeed, treading the same path as its former imperial ruler—allowing "the *paper money*, the *mercantile*, and the *banking* system" to enrich the few, while creating an Anglicized society where "poverty, stupidity, disease, and vice have superseded industry, intelligence, health, and innocence."[71]

Pennsylvanians did, of course, enjoy political rights only dreamed of by British radicals, and Duane clambered into the electoral arena to help rally the city's working classes. In addition to his work at the *Aurora*, he organized Republican election committees, public meetings, and reading groups, mobilizing the artisans' autodidact pride and their renewed sense of injury against both the Federalists and the pro-banking Republicans. Yet through the prewar boom years, Duane's radical Republicans (who included a newcomer, an idealistic young army veteran and ex-clerk at the BUS named Stephen Simpson) found that good times had fractured the workingmen's vote. By 1810, the moderate Republicans had gained a decided edge even in the Duanite's city stronghold, the plebeian Northern Liberties district. The patriotic demands of wartime in turn inspired an uneasy truce between the major Republican factions. In 1813, Duane, serving as adjutant general of the state militia, organized thousands of workingmen to serve as volunteers manning the city's rickety defense works.[72]

After the war, a combination of political estrangement and an uneven economic boom that bypassed manufacturing, followed by the devastation of 1819, reinflamed the Duanites. A new, even more aggressively pro-business group of "New School" Republicans had, in the meantime, emerged from among the moderate Republicans. Buoyed by the nationalist promise of the Era of Good Feelings, and devoted to rapid expansion of banking facilities, the New Schoolers won the governorship for their most prominent leader, William Findlay, in 1817. Knit closely by kinship and business ties—so much so that they also became known as "the Family Party"—the New Schoolers took a firm grip on the machinery of Pennsylvania politics, largely thanks to their control of the state Republican caucus. But they acted too swiftly in trying to remake the party in their own image, which led to grumbling about how the state was under the thumb of "a few lawyers of *questionable* character" and "a host of bank stock holders and bank directors." And Findlay hurt himself when he quietly joined in various shady operations, including an extortion scheme involving the awarding of auctioneers' licenses.[73]

Writing for the *Aurora* under the pseudonym "Brutus," Stephen Simpson became the scourge of the New Schoolers, moving beyond the old radical democratic politics with fresh explications of political economy. The caucus system, long a blight to the Duanite radicals, came in for fresh attack. But Simpson also ripped into the favoritism and oppression of the New Schoolers' banks. He demanded not just reform but "the total prostration of the *banking* and *funding* system" by the elimination of all bank charters, the reliance on specie as the circulating medium, and the confinement of paper to commercial operations. The Panic of 1819 turned the protests into an uproar. Duane's son, William John

Duane, who had won election to the state legislature, joined an officeholders' revolt in Harrisburg in 1820. After calling for a constitutional amendment to ban the BUS, the reformers managed to pass a law requiring forty-two so-called village banks that had been chartered all at once in 1814 to return to specie payments by the first of August or forfeit their charters. Reviving the old country-city alliance, Duanite sympathizers in rural counties as well the cities circulated mass petitions declaring that (in the words of one circular from Huntingdon County) "the industrious are impoverished whilst the speculating part of the community are growing daily more wealthy." The younger Duane chaired a special investigative committee whose official report confirmed that "[d]istress is general," and then thwarted Governor Findlay's efforts to relieve public distress by expanding paper-money loans. Findlay's attempts to obstruct the return to specie payments worsened the political crisis.[74]

The depth of the *Aurora* group's antibank, hard-money fervor marked the culmination of a gradual ideological and political switch of considerable importance. Early in Jefferson's presidency, Duane, like other city democrats, had considered commercial banking a useful tool for general prosperity so long as it was not concentrated in a few private hands and so long as ordinary mechanics and farmers had access to its loans. But Duane's own overly optimistic use of bank credit over the following years had nearly ruined him, and he shifted toward the idea of a national paper currency issued by the federal government, which would serve as a check on irresponsible bankers and provide a sound currency. By 1819, he had shifted again, taking Simpson's position that only a carefully administered, specie-based currency system, free from the baneful influence of chartered commercial banks, could spare the country an entrenched plutocracy and mass misery. The chartering of the Second BUS in 1816 had increased his worries that privileged private investors had once again seized control of the public interest, and that the new mammoth institution would "overdo the system of banking." The New Schoolers, in Duane's eyes, had created a rage for paper money and easy credit that could only bring moral and financial catastrophe. And amid the panic, Duane's supporters, now known as the Old School faction, came generally to regard the banking and paper-money system as a monstrous engine of oppression.[75]

The immediate political results of the Old School upsurge were mixed. Statewide, the backlash following the panic cost William Findlay reelection in 1820, but the New Schoolers were able to regroup and retake the governorship in 1822 with a compromise candidate acceptable to both urban and rural dissidents. Duane, Simpson, and the reborn city democracy, meanwhile, fared far less well in Philadelphia than they did, briefly, statewide. Factionalism plagued the radicals: in 1820, Philadelphia voters were presented with a baffling list of candidates claiming Federalist, moderate Federalist, Old School, New School, and a variety of no-school family allegiances—"a perfect chaos of small factions," Nicholas Biddle wrote. The Old Schoolers ran weakly even in the workingmen's wards. Although William Duane still emanated charisma, the most effective Old School officeholder, Michael Leib, was on his last legs (he would die in 1822, the same year that Duane, saddled with debts, finally abandoned the *Aurora*). The up-and-coming radicals and reformers, including Simpson and the younger Duane, lacked the connections, electoral shrewdness, and practical skills of their elders. Still, Philadelphia's Old Schoolers (some of whom had taken up the name City Democrats) had begun to establish themselves as a political force. And, thanks to the *Aurora* and especially to the writings of Simpson (soon to begin his own paper, the *Columbian Observer*), they had emerged as an intellectual force as well, promoting a workingman's critique of the banking system and the early industrial order.[76]

Country dissidents in other states also generated their own antibanking political ideas. The most developed rural critiques appeared in the writings of surviving southern Old Republicans, notably John Taylor. After the depression hit, Taylor's *Inquiry* of 1814 began to look prophetic. The entire "paper system" of bank notes, bonds, bills, and stocks that Taylor had claimed was robbing honest producers seemed, amid the foreclosures and bankruptcies of 1819 and 1820, to be fulfilling its appointed piratical role. Worse, in Taylor's eyes, that system won a unanimous official endorsement in 1819 from Chief Justice John Marshall and the Supreme Court in the case of *McCulloch v. Maryland*.

The *McCulloch* decision was the latest in a series of Supreme Court rulings that struck down state laws interfering with corporate charters and protecting bankrupt debtors—and there would be many more to come. Marshall, Jefferson's old nemesis, had outlasted his state-rights critics and, in a concerted campaign, had talked dubious Republican associate justices into joining a judicial phalanx to enlarge federal power and enhance its instruments of economic development. The *McCulloch* ruling was especially rich in neo-Hamiltonian implications. Maryland had passed a law levying a severe—some said prohibitive—fifteen-thousand-dollar annual tax on the operations of the Baltimore branch of the BUS. In upholding a suit by Baltimore bankers protesting the Maryland law, Marshall and the Court also pronounced an interpretation of the Constitution that seemed to explode what was left of Jeffersonian restraint of federal power. Declaring that "[t]he power to tax involves the power to destroy," Marshall's opinion basically rephrased Hamilton's broad interpretations of Article I, Section 8 as the law of the land. "Let the end be legitimate, let it be within the scope of the constitution, and all means which are appropriate, which are plainly adapted to that end, which are not prohibited, but consist with the letter and spirit of the constitution, are constitutional." The bank, in short, was fully constitutional—and the states could do nothing to impede its operations.[77]

Taylor responded with a hastily written tract, *Construction Construed and Constitutions Vindicated*, probably the most influential thing he ever wrote. Recapitulating his earlier attacks on exploitative "artificial" property, Taylor ripped into the rechartering of the BUS and the *McCulloch* decision as the final corruptions overthrowing the American Revolution. The heretic Marshall and his fellow justices had at last enshrined the federal government as a new "sovereign power," completing an effort first undertaken (but, originally, thwarted) in 1787 and then doggedly advanced by Hamilton and his successors in an unholy genealogy of oppression: "The great pecuniary favour granted by congress to certificate-holders, begat banking; banking begat bounties to manufacturing capitalists; bounties to manufacturing capitalists begat an oppressive pension list." All of that had created "a perfect aristocracy, exercising an absolute power over the national currency."[78]

Taylor's was a voice from the past, reflecting the deepening anxieties of the old Chesapeake Tidewater planter elite amid the devastation that followed the Panic of 1819. Never a democrat (in sharp contrast to William Duane), Taylor had no use for the kinds of constitutional reforms advocated by his nonslaveholding fellow Virginians. *Construction Construed* was as much concerned with preserving slaveholders' rights against a potentially intrusive federal government as it was with resisting the BUS. Yet if detached from its pro-slavery moorings, Taylor's arguments on capitalist consolidation and federal complicity carried force with more thoroughgoing egalitarians. In Philadelphia, Duane, a committed antislavery man who also detested the *McCulloch* decision, echoed and even printed the relevant anticapitalist portions of Taylor's writings, simply ignoring the portions on slavery. Elsewhere, alliances of up-and-coming planters and country democrats turned Taylor's arguments against the resident gentry and their banker friends as well as against the BUS.[79]

One of the loudest of the rural movements—and, in the end, the most consequential—arose in Tennessee. After Tennessee gained statehood in 1797, an ambitious entrepreneurial gentry, led by the affluent lawyer, speculator, and jurist John Overton, emerged in and around Nashville, controlling, among other assets, the state's two banks. Unlike Henry Clay and his Bluegrass friends in Kentucky, who came to welcome the rechartering of the Second BUS, the Overton forces continued to regard the national bank as a threat to their local interests. When the panic struck in 1819, Overton's men moved rapidly to protect those interests, passing what they billed as a relief act that was actually designed to shield the two state banks and the state's large debtors. The blatant favoritism aroused the public against what one editor called the banking "horse-leeches of the country" who had "produced a monied aristocracy." On the defensive, the legislature, goaded by the tempered ex-radical Felix Grundy, established stay laws, began a program for the cheap sale of public lands, and established a new loan-office "bank" to lend state paper to poor debtors—moves that mitigated the suffering, but mainly in middle Tennessee and not in the poorer regions. They did not calm the growing revolt. Representatives from mountainous, yeoman-dominated East Tennessee, in particular, denounced Grundy's loan office as an "untried and dangerous experiment" and called all paper institutions disastrous for the nation's well-being.[80]

The insurgency soon found a leader from among the younger self-made heroes of the War of 1812. William Carroll, an unschooled migrant from rural Pennsylvania, had joined Andrew Jackson's state militia staff in 1812, risen quickly to succeed Jackson as general of the Tennessee militia, and played a major role at the Battle of New Orleans. Returning to Nashville after the war, Carroll also returned to his mercantile pursuits, made a good deal of money, and established a popular reputation above and beyond anything the Nashville grandees had to offer. In 1821—having been nearly ruined in the depression and having decided that the banks and their gentry friends were responsible—the ex-shopkeeper challenged the Overton candidate for governor, the planter Henry Chase (who took a somewhat milder pro-specie position), and crushed him. Soon after Carroll took office, his backers in the state legislature—including another veteran of Jackson's command, the semiliterate rifleman David Crockett—opposed the stay laws and loan bank as biased and forced the old state banks out of business by demanding that they resume specie payments. Carroll would go on to become (save for his old commander) the most popular politician in Tennessee, winning reelection to five more terms as governor.[81]

In Tennessee, as in the rest of the shaken country, commercial banks, and especially the Second BUS, became the scapegoats for the nation's economic ills. The charges against the BUS were not completely justified. If before and after the panic the bank looked to some like a grasping and devouring monster, its policies were in fact a sign of weakness as well as strength. The bank could not be blamed for the drastic modifications in the Atlantic economy that occurred after the end of the Napoleonic Wars. Nor could it be blamed for initiating the reckless proliferation of unsound chartered and unchartered banks around the country, especially in the South and West, and for the unwise borrowing by investors. As an official inquiry by the Pennsylvania state senate concluded, the problem lay "*first* in the excessive number of banks, and secondly in their universal bad administration."[82] Yet many of these same state and local bankers had no trouble evading their responsibilities and joining in the public condemnations of the BUS.

The BUS, mismanaged from the start, played an important role in hastening and then deepening the economic crisis, loosening credit when it should have been tightened and then tightening credit for far too long. The incompetence (and, in some instances, larceny) of its directors understandably made the bank the focus of public anxiety at a fundamental turning point in American life, with profound political repercussions. Americans may always have been an enterprising people, but amid the transforming spread of commerce that accelerated after 1815, the structures and rules of enterprise were changing dramatically. As the business historian Bray Hammond, no enemy to banks and banking, once observed, "[A]n economy in which barter has been important and financial transactions had been wholly subordinate to the exchange of goods was giving way to an economy concerned more and more with obligations, contracts, negotiable instruments, equities, and such invisible abstractions. . . . Later generations that contemplate an America which is miraculously productive in a myriad of ways, from sea to sea, can understand only with an effort the terrible cost to their progenitors of settling and improving it."[83] Countless small farmers, tyros in this new economy, had relied on unending credit only to be undone by plunging prices, rising costs, and implacable creditors. Countless urban artisans and shopkeepers had either been thrown into complete idleness or seen the value of their wages and incomes plummet amid a flood of notes no longer worth the paper they had been printed on.

For these ordinary Americans at the bottom of a chain of debt that they only vaguely understood, the panic and depression cracked open huge questions about who was to be the chief beneficiary of the new business order—and about its implications for political democracy. Would those who actually produced useful goods, ordinary men like themselves, accumulate the full fruits of their labor and enterprise? Or would their fruits be stolen, as they saw it, by unelected monied men and their political allies who had promised, falsely, to provide prosperity everlasting? And would those men continue to be permitted to wield such enormous power unchecked by the sovereign people?

THE BUBBLE BURSTS

The Panic of 1819 and the ensuing depression came as little surprise to some older political heads. "[T]he paper bubble is then burst," Thomas Jefferson wrote in November 1819 to his old foe John Adams, with whom he had reconciled in recent years. "[T]his is what you & I, and every reasoning man, seduced by no obliquity of mind or interest, have long foreseen."[84] Always distrustful of the paper system, even when he had deferred to Albert Gallatin over the first BUS, Jefferson took no pleasure in the suffering the panic caused—he was among the sufferers—but did feel a measure of vindication.

What remained to be seen was who, in national politics, might turn the politics of depression and the democratic outrage it inspired to his advantage.

Nationalist Republicanism had been dealt a severe blow, but neither the southern Old Republicans nor the city democrats nor the country democrats appeared capable of creating a credible national alternative. Under the stress of economic collapse, the regnant Republican coalition looked increasingly fractured, yet with no one national figure an obvious claimant to the presidential succession after Monroe (who, lacking a serious challenger from either his own party or the Federalists, won reelection without opposition in 1820). And by the time political leaders began adapting to the effects of the panic, its implications had been clouded by a distinct though related political crisis over slavery that also began in 1819—a crisis originally confined to Washington City but that quickly assumed national significance.

7

SLAVERY, COMPROMISE, AND DEMOCRATIC POLITICS

Despite the compromises at the federal convention in 1787, conflicts over slavery had never completely disappeared from national politics. Hardly a year passed without some discussion that touched on the matter. The First Congress argued over whether to include a special tariff on imported slaves, and whether to accept petitions for regulating the "debasing" and "abominable" slave trade and for gradual emancipation. (Both proposals were scuttled.) In 1798, there was a sharp contest over outlawing slavery in the newly formed Mississippi Territory, followed six years later by a failed effort, led by the Federalist James Hillhouse of Connecticut, to ban slavery in the newly acquired Louisiana Territory. The movements to abolish slavery in New York and New Jersey helped prompt James Sloan, a New Jersey Republican, to propose unsuccessfully in 1804 the gradual abolition of slavery in the District of Columbia. Slavery, and southern slaveholders' fears over its future, were also latent concerns in foreign policy questions from the adoption of the Jay Treaty to extending diplomatic recognition to the black republic in Haiti. In 1807, with President Jefferson's firm support, Congress formally abolished the transatlantic slave trade, at the earliest possible date under the Constitution, but only over the stern objections of both Federalists and Republicans from the Deep South.[1]

Sectional divisions worsened after 1815. Contrary to the enlightened hopes of the Revolutionary generation, including slaveholders such as Jefferson, slavery flourished in the South, even as it died in the North. Southern defensiveness over slavery as an unfortunate burden gave way to assertions of the institution's basic benevolence. Northerners, including egalitarian Jeffersonian Republicans as well surviving Yankee Federalists, grew increasingly embittered at having to make repeated political concessions to the unapologetic planters. The rapid inclusion of new states carved out of the Louisiana Purchase lands raised the critical question of whether the nation would permit human bondage to expand even farther or would begin, once and for all, to commence its elimination. Between 1819 and 1821, with Americans already reeling from economic catastrophe, congressional debates over that question focused on the future of Missouri Territory and boiled over—further dissipating illusory invocations of an Era of Good Feelings and creating a fearsome specter of the nation's collapse.

BACKGROUND TO CRISIS

The recurrent struggles over slavery during the decades preceding the Missouri crisis indicated some important political facts and shifting dynamics that lay just beneath the surface of the early republic's politics. First, contrary to the tangled ambivalence of many Jeffersonian slaveholders, lawmakers from the Deep South, Republicans and Federalists alike, expressed a powerful commitment to slavery during the new nation's earliest days. Their justifications anticipated almost every theme of what would later be called the "positive good" pro-slavery argument. Southern slaves, the Republican senator James Jackson of Georgia declared in 1789, had exchanged African barbarism for American ownership by masters "bound by the ties of interest and law, to provide for their support and comfort in old age or infirmity." William Loughton Smith, the South Carolina Federalist, addressed the House a year later and called slavery the ideal status for blacks—a race deficient in intellect, "indolent" and "improvident," but well suited physically for labor on southern plantations. "If, then, nothing but evil would result from emancipation," he concluded, "why should Congress stir at all in the business, or give any countenance to such dangerous applications."[2]

Through Jefferson's first administration, the pro-slavery southerners could usually count on the support of conservative northern Federalists. Although several leading Federalists were conspicuously involved in manumission societies and other antislavery efforts, Federalism showed its more traditional face in Congress, intent on sustaining party solidarity across sectional lines against the common Republican foe. Vaunting, as ever, the inviolability of private property, Federalists were swift to denounce antislavery agitation as a threat to social peace, derived from the vicious French egalitarianism advanced by Jefferson and his party. To the Massachusetts Federalist Senator George Cabot fell the honor of introducing the fugitive slave bill in 1793, which implemented the Constitution's guarantee that masters could cross state lines to retrieve their runaways. Harrison Gray Otis declared, typically, in 1798 that he would not "interfere with the Southern states as to the species of property in question" and that "he really wished that the gentlemen who held slaves might not be deprived of the means of keeping them in order."[3]

Virginia Republicans, by contrast, sometimes aligned with moderate northern Federalists and northern Republicans against the Deep South on matters relating to slavery, at least through 1800. Well into the post-Revolutionary era, the assumption prevailed among many Virginians, slaveholders and nonslaveholders, that human bondage was a moribund abomination. Thomas Jefferson had famously written, in his *Notes on the State of Virginia* of 1785, that "[t]he whole commerce between master and slave is a perpetual exercise of the most boisterous passions, the most unremitting despotism on the one part, and degrading submissions on the other. . . . I tremble for my country when I reflect that God is just." Jefferson would never tremble enough to free more than a handful of his own slaves. Neither he nor most other first-rank southern political leaders took up the antislavery cause too publicly or too vociferously. When pushed hard by the Deep South slaveholders—as they were in 1790, over a House committee report giving Congress wide powers over slavery—the Virginians chose expediency over idealism. Still, the Enlightenment and religious humanitarian impulses that helped bring emancipation to the northern states were there in Virginia and the upper South. Manumissions rose markedly after 1790. (A greater number of Virginia slaves were freed between the Revolution and the War of 1812 than at any time until 1865.) A persistent glut and depressed prices in world tobacco markets further augured a shift in southern agriculture toward wheat production, highly profitable without slave labor. To some Virginians, including Jefferson, it appeared as if morality and self-interest might actually converge in the not-too-distant future.[4]

That future never came, and by 1815, the politics of slavery had acquired an entirely different political charge. The closer Congress verged on legislation concerning the institution directly, the more southerners recoiled, and the more pro-slavery views hardened. More important, slavery experienced a renaissance after 1790 that forever changed the course of southern history—and American history. A rapid rise of world demand for sugar and, even more, for cotton; the decline of many Caribbean plantation economies in the wake of the Saint Domingue revolution and the reduction of the Spanish empire during the Napoleonic Wars; the expansion, with the Louisiana Purchase, of American territory suited to plantation-based economies; the boom in short-staple (or upland) cotton production enabled by the introduction of Whitney's cotton gin—all gave Americans extraordinary advantages in reviving their own plantation system. For some southerners, the combination of new opportunities and revived fears of slave revolts led to a new vision of an American slavery spreading steadily westward, no longer dependent on freshly imported (and possibly troublesome) slaves from

Africa but on a growing domestic slave population, beautifully situated to cash in on the production of sugar and cotton.[5]

Suddenly, the liberal blandishments of the post-Revolutionary years either faded away, fell on the defensive, or turned, ironically, into their opposites. In border states like Henry Clay's Kentucky and in portions of the lower South where slavery was scarce, the Jeffersonian view of slavery as a necessary evil— degrading to master and slave alike, but not amenable to any safe and practical immediate solution—still held powerful sway. But elsewhere, pro-slavery opinion became more widespread and bolder. Some Deep South slaveholders paradoxically came to support antislavery efforts to end the transatlantic slave trade in 1807, seeing in western expansion a more secure basis for slavery's future. More generally, the lower South became even more outspoken in its view of slavery as benevolent. In a speech to the House late in 1806, a young, ardently pro-slavery Republican, Peter Early of Georgia, revealed how southern sensibilities were changing. Noting that he had earlier described slavery as an "evil," Early begged to explain that he had only meant to say that "[r]eflecting men" in the South apprehended slavery as a "political evil" that might "at some future day" cause great troubles, but "that few, very few, consider it a crime." As if affirming that former heresy was becoming southern orthodoxy, Early then added, "I will tell the truth. A large majority of people in the Southern states do not consider slavery as even an evil."[6]

Northern hostility to slavery grew apace, for opportunistic as well as principled reasons. With the decline of southern Federalism after 1800, northern conservatives had less reason to attach themselves to Deep South slaveholders—and additional political reasons to try to restrict slavery's expansion while attacking the three-fifths clause and other pillars (as they saw them) of Jeffersonian power. Now it was the Republicans who had the most to worry about in preserving intersectional party unity, leading some northern Republicans to back southern positions. Yet northern Republicans still formed a core of antislavery opinion in Congress. In one telling House vote during Jefferson's first term, rejecting the proposed abolition of slavery in the District of Columbia in 1804, southern Republicans voted with the majority by a margin of 40 to 1, as did northern Federalists by a margin of 13 to 5. Northern Republicans voted in favor of abolition, 25 to 16.[7]

The sectional cleavage deepened after 1815, as cotton became the most valuable staple commodity in the Atlantic world. The end of the war with Britain and the reopening of the cotton trade with the Lancashire mills vastly stimulated the American cotton boom, and with it the spread of slavery. Between 1815 and 1820, the amount of baled cotton produced by the southern states doubled, and it would double again between 1820 and 1825. Before the war, the boundary to cotton cultivation ran as far north as the backcountry of South Carolina and as far east as central Georgia; thereafter, cotton slavery swept into Alabama and then into Mississippi and Louisiana. In the older states of the upper South, the Deep South cotton boom sent the price of redundant slaves soaring, giving slave-holders there a strong material incentive to support slavery's expansion. In the North, however, despite the mercantile fortunes to be won by shipping cotton across the Atlantic, there arose a new determination to check any further west-ward expansion of slavery, especially when evidence began to mount that smug-glers were successfully evading the ban on the transatlantic slave trade. Northern concern about expansion—and disgust at the southerners' truculence over slavery—heightened when the acquisition of Florida from Spain under the terms of the Adams-Onís Treaty of 1819 raised the issue of admitting another new slave state.[8]

Five days before the treaty was formally signed in Washington, the House of Representatives completed debate over a bill approving admission of the territory of Missouri to the Union. Given that the territory was already home to thousands of slaves, most observers might have safely assumed that it would enter with slav-ery intact. But two alarmed northern Republicans would take nothing for granted—and, drawing the line at Missouri, they revealed how forceful northern antislavery opinion had become.

THE MISSOURI CRISIS IN CONGRESS

James Tallmadge caught his fellow congressmen off guard on February 13. A Poughkeepsie, New York, lawyer and former secretary to Governor George Clin-ton, Tallmadge had served in Congress for just twenty months (and would leave the House, by choice, after serving a single term). He had, so far, made two mildly auspicious congressional contributions: joining an unsuccessful effort to obstruct Illinois statehood because its new constitution was "insufficiently" anti-slavery; and giving an eloquent speech in defense of General Andrew Jackson, who stood accused of exceeding his authority and executing civilians in connec-tion with his postwar military command in East Florida. Mainly, Tallmadge was considered an ambitious, personable, odd-duck backbencher, nominally a Clin-tonian (and therefore detested by Van Buren's Bucktails), but also distrusted by DeWitt Clinton as well as the surviving Federalists.

Tallmadge's behind-the-scenes ally in his surprise attack, his fellow New York congressman John W. Taylor of Ballston Springs, was very different, a well-known Clintonian and shrewd politician who, in 1820, would succeed Henry Clay as Speaker of the House. Taylor had an established record as an antislavery man, and in that same session of Congress, he led a narrowly defeated effort to ban extension of the institution into Arkansas Territory. Tallmadge, too, was staunchly antislavery—before coming to Congress, he had helped craft and enact New York's final emancipation law in 1817—but his personal political motivations for initiating the crisis remain a puzzle. It is equally puzzling why the unknown Tallmadge instead of Taylor took the lead on the Missouri issue. What is certain is that the two New York Republicans—working on their own—started an uproar that would rattle the already strained Jeffersonian coalition.[9]

At stake, formally, were the terms of Missouri's admission to the Union, but the implications were much graver. In the flurry of state admissions since 1815, the numbers of new states that allowed slavery and those that did not had been equal, leaving the balance of slave and free states nationwide, and thus, in the Senate, equal as well. But that balance was deceptive. Prior to Illinois's admission to the Union in 1818, antislavery forces, fortified by the exclusion of slavery in the territory under the Northwest Ordinance, found themselves challenged by downstate settlers from the South. The antislavery men managed to gain a state constitution that formally barred slavery, but at the cost of including an apprenticeship system regulating the lives of free blacks—the focus of Tallmadge and others' effort to block Illinois's admission—as well as the selection of two southern-born pro-slavery senators. In practical terms, there was an argument to be made that by admitting neighboring Missouri as a slave state, the pro-slavery bloc in the Senate would enjoy not a two-vote majority but a four-vote majority. And among some northerners, there was a mounting determination to prevent Missouri from having a constitution as bluntly racist as Illinois's.[10]

Southerners saw the situation completely differently. With discussions already underway for the creation of Maine as a new state, Missouri's admission as a slave state was essential to preserve the sectional balance. Moreover, Missouri was to be the second state carved out of the Louisiana Purchase, and the first whose land lay entirely west of the Mississippi River. The precedent for Purchase land, though slight, was pro-slavery.[11] Although Missouri, unlike Louisiana, was not suited to cotton, slavery had long been established there, and its western portions were promising for growing hemp, a crop so taxing to cultivate that it was deemed fit only for slave labor. Accordingly, southerners worried that if slavery were banned in Missouri—with its ten thousand slaves, comprising roughly 15 percent of its total population—there would be a precedent for doing so in all the states from the trans-Mississippi West. When the territorial citizens of Missouri applied for admission to the Union, most southerners—and probably, at first, most northerners as well—took it for granted that slavery would be allowed. All were in for a shock.

Tallmadge rose in the House near the end of the week's business and offered a resolution containing two amendments to the Missouri enabling bill then pending before the Committee of the Whole, banning further introduction of slavery into the new state and freeing all slaves born in the state after its admission when they reached the age of twenty-five. The ensuing debate in the House lasted but a few days—the Fifteenth Congress would expire on March 4—but it was blistering. Opponents of the amendments, including the territorial delegate from Missouri, harshly attacked them and threatened disunion were they ever approved. Let it come, Tallmadge spat back: "Sir, if a dissolution of the Union must take place, let it be so!" ("I hope that a similar discussion will never again take place in our walls," wrote one shaken representative from New Hampshire.) Northern House members, strikingly, united across party and factional lines to support Tallmadge. Despite virtually unanimous opposition from the slaveholding states, the lopsided margins in favor of the amendments by free-state congressmen—84 to 10 on the first amendment, 80 to 14 on the second—were sufficient for Tallmadge's proposals to prevail narrowly in the House. In the Senate, five northern members, including both senators from Illinois, provided the margin to defeat the amendments, but the House antislavery northerners (now called restrictionists) would not cower. By a twelve-vote margin, the House, voting once again on sharp sectional lines, reapproved Tallmadge's proposals, thereby killing the statehood bill and handing the dispensation of Missouri over to the Sixteenth Congress, which was not due to assemble for another nine months. And when the new Congress met, the divisions proved to be just as deep as before.[12]

The debate over Missouri in both Congresses stimulated northern Federalists as well as Republicans. Senator Rufus King of New York expressed the Federalist view with a special wintry eloquence. At sixty-four, King was the last of the original Federalists still on the national stage, a point that rankled the Republican southern delegations. At Philadelphia in 1787, King had argued strongly against the three-fifths clause as an ignominious sop to the slaveholders. Now, more than thirty years later, he warmly supported keeping slavery out of Missouri, restating the persisting Yankee Federalist fear of southern political dominance. The issue, for King, was not chiefly moral, at least not in his early speeches on the matter. Asked by a southerner, at one point during the crisis, about his views on slavery, he replied that he was only imperfectly informed on the subject, and was interested in it only as it had a bearing on "great political interests." For King, that meant protecting the free white majority, objecting once more to the three-fifths rule, and rejecting state rights—securing what he called "the common defence, the general welfare, and [the] wise administration of government." In his early pronouncements on Missouri, the embers of northern Federalism flared one last time.[13]

Southern Republicans saw all this as a deliberate and desperate power play on behalf of discredited Federalist heresy. To Thomas Jefferson, the Missouri controversy amounted to a reckless effort by the Federalist "Hartford convention men" to resurrect their political fortunes by seizing on the slavery issue and then salvaging Federalism by creating a new northern sectional party. Andrew Jackson called Tallmadge's maneuver part of the "wicked design of demagogues, who talk about humanity, but whose sole object is self agrandisement regardless of the happiness of the nation." John Taylor of Caroline, at work on his refutation of *McCulloch v. Maryland*, added a closing section on how the Missouri debates foreshadowed the unlawful assumption by a neo-Federalist general government of the power to abolish slavery. And fair-minded northerners could understand the southerners' fears, even if their sympathies about slavery lay elsewhere. Restriction, John Quincy Adams wrote in his diary, "disclosed a secret," unanticipated by its proponents, that the North could be united upon halting any further extension of slavery: "[H]ere was a new party ready formed, . . . terrible to the whole Union, but portentously terrible to the South—threatening in its progress the emancipation of all their slaves." Yet contrary to what Jefferson and others charged, the "new party," in the House, were not the Yankee Federalists and crypto-Federalist Clintonians, but a bloc of between forty and fifty northern Republicans.[14]

Like every other party to the Missouri controversy, the Republican restrictionists were a mixed lot in almost everything except their sectional origins. But unlike the others, they boasted no great figure who had achieved the celebrity of their Federalist ally King, or their numerous Republican opponents from the South. They included experienced ex-Federalists such as Joseph Hemphill of Pennsylvania and Clifton Clagett of New Hampshire (who first came to Congress in, respectively, 1800 and 1803), as well as Jeffersonian veterans such as Peter Hercules Wendover of New York City—a successful artisan who, in 1799, had won the first of his two terms as president of the city's Republican-friendly General Society of Mechanics and Tradesmen. They also included younger men such as William Plunkett Maclay of Pennsylvania, the nephew and namesake of the prickly country Republican member and diarist from the First Congress, William Maclay; and Marcus Morton of Massachusetts, an idealistic lawyer who had become a Jefferson devotee. Roughly two-thirds of the antislavery Republicans came not from Federalist New England but from the middle Atlantic states, although their leading spokesmen on the House floor included the little-known but forceful Republican lawyers Arthur Livermore of New Hampshire, Timothy Fuller of Massachusetts, and John Wilson Campbell of Ohio. Their contentions in favor of restriction advanced an antislavery Jeffersonian reading of politics and the Constitution that overlapped but was quite distinct from the antislavery arguments of King and the Federalists. That reading prefigured arguments that in later years would become the foundations of the political antislavery platforms of the Liberty, Free Soil, and Lincoln Republican Parties.[15]

At the heart of the Republicans' reasoning was their claim that the preservation of individual rights, and strict construction of the Constitution, demanded slavery's restriction. The claim was rooted in humanitarian morality, not expediency—the firm belief, as Fuller declared, that it was both "the right and duty of Congress" to halt the spread "of the intolerable evil and the crying enormity of slavery." Individual rights, the Republicans asserted, had been defined by Jefferson himself in the Declaration of Independence—"an authority admitted in all parts of the Union [as] a definition of the basis of republican government." If all men were created equal, as Jefferson said, then slaves, as men, were born free and entitled to life, liberty, and the pursuit of happiness under any truly republican government. The Constitution had, in turn, explicitly made the guarantee of republican government in the states a fundamental principle of the Union. Thus, the extension of slavery was, by any strict reading of the national compact, not only wrong but unconstitutional.[16]

The Founding Fathers, the Republicans conceded, had permitted slavery to persist as a purely local, not a national, right. Given the social and political practicalities of 1787, they had had no other choice, as no feasible plan existed for ending slavery in the southern states without creating even greater evils. But the local exception, the Republicans argued, should not be confused for a permanent national rule. The Founders, as Tallmadge pointed out, had not committed the "original sin" of inventing slavery. Rather, as Hemphill claimed, "a certain kind of rights" had "grown out of original wrongs"—a set of rights that the Founders expected would fade away, not proliferate. Not only did the Constitution studiously, even tortuously avoid the words *slave* and *slavery*. The Founders had also taken steps, as William Plumer Jr. of New Hampshire put it, "leading gradually to the abolition of slavery in the old States," above all by explicitly allowing for the eventual abolition of the foreign slave trade and by prohibiting slavery in the Northwest Territory under the Northwest Ordinance. Furthermore, the Republicans insisted, Article IV, Section 3 of the Constitution authorized Congress to admit new states as it saw fit, without any stipulated limitations. "The exercise of this power, until now, has never been questioned," John Taylor charged in debate. Once again, the Republicans averred, the proslavery side was attempting to rewrite the explicit letter of the Constitution, as well as to denigrate its spirit.[17]

As all southerners immediately understood, these were intensely dangerous arguments. Bits and pieces of them had turned up earlier, in Congress as well as in the speeches of Republicans like Tallmadge advocating emancipation in the northern states. As early as 1798, the Massachusetts Republican Joseph Varnum declared his hope that "Congress would have so much respect for the rights of humanity as to not legalize the existence of slavery any farther than it at present exists." The democratizing forces unleashed in the northern states, privileging persons over property, also rendered the Constitution's three-fifths clause ever more an anachronistic, quasi-aristocratic embarrassment—one which if spread to new states would mean, contrary to the Framers' intentions (a Pennsylvania Republican remarked), that "[t]he scale of political power will predominate in favor of the slaveholding States." But it took the cotton boom and the Missouri crisis for northern Republicans to mount a truly threatening Jeffersonian anti-slavery critique in national affairs. By making Jefferson's Declaration, as one antislavery proponent called it, the great "national covenant" from which the Constitution proceeded virtually as a legal and spiritual instrument, the pro-restrictionist Republicans affirmed a new form of nationalist loyalty. Firmly planted in Jeffersonian writ, this nationalism would not seek to expand the pow-ers of the federal government one whit beyond the strictest construction, yet neither would it endorse the idea, dear to John Taylor and the Virginia Old Republicans, that the Union was a mere compact of the several states. It would not fall into the Federalist trap of inventing a new national good; rather, it would restrict an old national evil.[18]

The nation, said the antislavery northern Republicans (in agreement with the Federalists), preceded the states as a historical fact. Therefore, preserving the self-evident rights of equal individual citizens—which they took to be the essence of republicanism—must take precedence over honoring the rights of individual states. The aim of that federal Union had been eventually to remove the injus-tice of slavery, not to perpetuate it. The Constitution, strictly interpreted, gave the sons of the founding generation the legal tools to hasten that removal, including, in the case of Missouri, barring the admission of additional slave states. Republican principle—what one antislavery representative called "the good old Republican doctrines"—as well as constitutional mandate gave them no choice but to keep slavery out of Missouri.[19]

To do otherwise would bring the condemnation of future generations—and, John W. Taylor suggested, even worse condemnation still. "History will record the decision of this day as exerting its influence for centuries to come . . . ," Tay-lor declared in the first set speech of the House debate; then he delivered an extended sentence-long blast:

> If we reject the amendment and suffer this evil, now easily eradi-cated, to strike its roots so deep in the soil that it can never be removed, shall we not furnish some apology for doubting our sincer-ity, when we deplore its existence—shall we not expose ourselves to the same kind of censure which was pronounced by the Saviour of Mankind upon the Scribes and Pharisees, who builded the tombs of the prophets and garnished the sepulchres of the righteous, and said, if they had lived in the days of their fathers, they would not have been partakers with them in the blood of the prophets, while they

manifested a spirit which clearly proved them the legitimate descen-
dents of those who killed the prophets, and thus filled up the measure of their fathers' iniquity?

Not only did the pro-slavery men lack patriotism—they were pharisaic
blasphemers.[20]

The slave-state representatives reacted to the charges by banding together
with a unity even more impressive than the northerners'. Most of their arguments took a straightforward state-rights position: as Congress had no power to
interfere with slavery in the states where it already existed, so it was powerless to
do so in new states just gaining admission. "Can any gentleman contend," John
Scott, the delegate from Missouri asked, "that, laboring under the proposed
restriction, the citizens of Missouri would have the rights, advantages, and
immunities of other citizens of the Union? Have not other new states, in their
admission, and have not all the states in the Union, now, privileges and rights
beyond what was contemplated to be allowed to the citizens of Missouri?" Precedent, as well as constitutional principle, demanded that Missourians decide the
slavery question for themselves. States were the essential units in federal affairs,
and each new state possessed the same power to decide its own constitution as
the original thirteen states had enjoyed. Equality for all meant, in this instance,
allowing Missouri to retain slavery as it wished to do.[21]

Had Tallmadge and the restrictionists merely followed their Federalist allies'
reasoning, the sectional argument might have remained pitched at this abstract
legalistic and constitutional level. But the antislavery Republicans also attacked
slavery head-on as an immoral institution, whose very existence in any new states
would deny those states a truly republican government. By condemning slavery
while abjuring broad construction of the Constitution, the Republicans less-
ened their vulnerability to charges, plausible enough when delivered against
the Federalists, that they were using the slavery issue as a pretext to enlarge federal power and their own political advantage. And they exposed the southerners
to countercharges that *they* were simply twisting constitutional issues as a means
to expand slavery.

The result was a rupture within the Republican camp, between antislavery
northerners who embraced egalitarian Jeffersonian ideals and hard-core, pro-
slavery southerners who rejected those ideals—leaving in the middle Republican
nationalists such as Henry Clay, who like Jefferson considered slavery a necessary
evil. As debate wore on, the southern antirestrictionists, particularly in the Deep
South, found it difficult to cling to the antislavery shibboleths that had prevailed
among the enlightened slaveholders of Jefferson's generation. Some did so, like
the Georgia representative Robert Reid, who called slavery "a dark cloud which
obscures half the luster of our free institutions." But increasingly, in and out of

Congress, these high-minded pronouncements sounded ritualistic and pale beside angry southern objections that only fanatics would seek to eliminate or even check slavery anytime soon.[22]

The soft antirestrictionist line, voiced most eloquently by Speaker Clay and a young Virginia congressman named John Tyler, held that diffusing slavery across a wider geographic area would actually benefit the slaves and encourage the institution's eventual demise. "Slavery has been represented on all hands as a dark cloud [and] . . . in this sentiment I completely concur . . . ," Tyler told the House. "How can you otherwise disarm it? Will you suffer it to increase in its darkness over a particular portion of this land until its horrors shall burst upon it?" This had become Jefferson's and Madison's view as well—that a dispersion of the slaves would reduce racial anxieties and the threat of slave revolts, dilute the institution of slavery, and afford the slaves better food, clothing, and shelter than if they remained confined to the existing slave states. Defeating Tall-madge's proposals, Tyler contended, would "ameliorate the condition of the slave, and . . . add much to the prospect of emancipation and the total extinc-tion of slavery."[23]

At one level, the diffusion argument was a rhetorical fallback for the tortured enlightened slaveholders of the older generation who genuinely believed slavery an evil but who could not imagine getting rid of it peacefully except by highly deliberate and time-consuming means. At another level, diffusionism was in line with efforts by younger men concentrated in the border states—above all, those of the American Colonization Society, founded in Washington in 1816 with Clay presiding—to promote the voluntary colonizing of free blacks to Africa and provide a spur for humane and gradual emancipation. "No man is more sensible of the evils of slavery than I am, nor regrets them more," Clay would write a few years after the Missouri crisis. To restrict slavery's spread would only hurt the chances for eventual tranquil emancipation—or so Clay and many of his south-ern colleagues had convinced themselves. Yet even the soft antirestrictionists insisted that the North had no business at all interfering with slavery. And they sometimes cast aspersions on the northern Republicans' egalitarianism, likening it (in Tyler's words) to the radical leveling doctrines of the Jacobins, who pro-claimed liberty and equality "at the very moment when they were enriching the fields of France with the blood of her citizens." Behind these attacks lay the ever-present fear that too much talk of equality might cause the slaves to revolt.[24]

A harder southern line also emerged during the Missouri crisis, expanding on the contention, long-established in the Deep South, that slavery was essentially benevolent. As sectional bitterness spiked, so did the southerners' militancy over slavery—as well as their threats that if decided wrongly, the Missouri controversy would have cataclysmic results. Thomas W. Cobb of Georgia allowed, but only for the sake of argument, that slavery might involve "moral impropriety." But he would not bother to dignify with a direct reply the "slander" heaped on "the character of the people of the Southern States in their conduct towards, and treatment of, their black population," and warned that unless the slandering ceased, a fire of southern resistance would arise that "could be extinguished only in blood!" In the Senate, the esteemed Old Republican Nathaniel Macon of North Carolina, as orthodox a Jeffersonian as could be found anywhere, not only defended slavery but also denied that the egalitarian sentiments once written down by his gloried mentor had any binding force whatsoever. "A clause in the Declaration of Independence has been read," Macon said, calmly and simply, "declaring that 'all men are created equal;' follow that sentiment and does it not lead to universal emancipation?" Macon would not have it so: just as the Declaration "is not part of the Constitution or of any other book," so there was, he proclaimed, "no place for the free blacks in the United States."[25]

The most passionate defense of slavery, by Old Republican Senator William Smith of South Carolina, actually annoyed many of Smith's fellow southerners in its frankness, but it showed where hard-line southern Republican thinking was headed all along. The "venerable patriot" Jefferson had been wrong, Smith said, to claim in *Notes on the State of Virginia* that some basic antagonism pitted master against slave: "The master has no motive for this boisterous hostility. It is at war with his interest, and it is at war with his comfort. The whole commerce between master and slave is patriarchal." Likewise, northerners were completely wrong to say that slavery was sinful. Had not "the only living and true God" specifically condoned slaveholding in the laws He gave to Moses, as recorded in Leviticus? By substituting their own religion of nature for the Bible, the antislavery restrictionists were endorsing the same intoxicating pagan beliefs "preached up in the French Convention in the days of Robespierre" that had led to the Reign of Terror. By maligning slavery as a moral and political evil, ambitious rabble-rousers, "like the praetorian guards of the Romans," hoped "finally [to] take the Government in their own hands, or bestow it on the highest bidder." Stirred by misguided humanity, the traducers of the South were in fact the traducers of benevolence, order, and all that was holy, led by reckless partisans who would unleash on the nation a torrent that none but the Lord could quell.[26]

Harsh though they were, these congressional thrusts and counterthrusts did not necessarily mark a general national political crisis. When the first stage of the Missouri debates ended in deadlock in March 1819, hopes had run high among moderates, led by Henry Clay, that after the recess, a new Congress would take up the matter with greater detachment—a possibility that filled Tallmadge and other restrictionists with "fearful anxiety." Yet those hopes and fears proved illusory, for antislavery northerners decided to take their cause to the people, in the first American antislavery political campaign of its kind. By the next winter, of 1819–20, that campaign, and southern reactions to it, had turned the controversy in Congress into a desperate situation, demanding every bit of shrewdness that Speaker Clay and his moderate allies could muster.[27]

THE DEBATE OVER SLAVERY: AGITATION, COMPROMISE, REPERCUSSIONS

The northern agitation leading up to the Sixteenth Congress began in late August 1819. Public meetings, organized by local luminaries, assembled in virtually every major town and city from Maine to New Jersey and as far west as Illinois, to cheer pro-restrictionist speakers, pass antislavery resolutions, draft circular letters demanding a free Missouri, and instruct their representatives to stand fast. On November 16, more than two thousand citizens gathered in New York City, headquarters of the movement, where they established their own committee of correspondence and arranged for the printing of an antislavery circular for wide distribution. By December, according to William Plumer, it had become "political suicide" for any free-state officeholder "to tolerate slavery beyond its present limits." The agitation cut across partisan lines. Some of the most prominent organizers of the popular protests were Federalists and Clintonians, and the crusade began with a meeting in Burlington County, New Jersey, a traditional Federalist stronghold—all of which lent superficial credence to the southerners' charges of a political conspiracy. But antislavery fervor gripped northern Jeffersonian supporters as well. "[Slavery's] progress should be arrested, and means should be adopted for its speedy and gradual abolition—and for its ultimate extinction," William Duane wrote in the Philadelphia *Aurora*. One prominent Maine Republican noted that "in most of the states which contend for restriction, federalist and republican are scarcely known."[28]

Nearly as striking as the bipartisanship of the northern opposition was the virtual absence of any similar agitation in the South. "The people do not yet participate in the unhappy heat of zeal and controversy, which has inflamed their Senators and Representatives," the *Baltimore Patriot* remarked at the height of the crisis. The economic devastation of the Panic of 1819 seems to have cast a greater pall on the planters and farmers of the South than did the debates about Missouri. More important, in the unreformed court-dominated southern polities, there was little to be gained and much to be risked by stirring up the populace over slavery issues. That populace, after all, included a white majority with uncertain loyalties to slavery, and a large black minority that, as far as the South's rulers were concerned, would be better off hearing as little as possible, even secondhand or thirdhand, about the lunatic Yankee agitators in Congress. "Our people do not petition much," Nathaniel Macon remarked, "we plume ourselves on not pestering the General Government with our prayers. Nor do we set the woods on fire to drive the game out." The wisdom of that restraint, from the slaveholders' viewpoint, would be confirmed during the years to come.[29]

James Tallmadge did not return to Washington for the new Congress in December (having already decided to seek a state senate seat in Albany), but the ruckus he kicked up resumed even more intensely than before. Maine was now officially applying for admission to statehood, separate from Massachusetts. Antirestrictionists were quick to assert that if Congress had the power to ban slavery in Missouri, so it had the power to make Maine's admission contingent on Missouri coming in as a slave state. ("The notion of an equivalent," Speaker Clay agreed, had guided commonwealths and states "from time immemorial.") The House passed a new Maine statehood bill after a bruising debate, only to have the Senate Judiciary Committee add an amendment admitting Missouri without restriction. After decisively rejecting efforts led by the Republican Jonathan Roberts of Pennsylvania to recommit the bill to committee, the Senate united the Maine and Missouri statehood bills, then heard an additional amendment from one of the Illinois antirestrictionists, Jesse B. Thomas—the germ of a possible compromise. As newly amended, the Senate bill would admit Maine as a free state and Missouri as a slave state, and bar slavery from all additional states carved out of the Louisiana Purchase territory that lay north of latitude 36°30'. Sectional balance would be sustained: the North would give way on the admission of Missouri as a slave state and be rebuffed in its meddling, but the South would give way on the principle that Congress had the authority to regulate slavery in the territories, something southerners had successfully resisted since the ratification of the Constitution.[30]

On February 17, the Senate passed compromise measures with the Thomas amendment, 24 to 20—only to have the House, which had been debating its own Missouri statehood bill, dismiss the Senate proposals in a sharply sectional vote. John W. Taylor, now the sole leader of the antislavery congressmen, offered a strengthened version of the Tallmadge amendments that freed all children of slaves at birth, and as amended, the bill passed the House by a wide margin. The Senate remonstrated with the lower house, demanding passage of its own bill— and, once again, the House flatly refused.[31]

The political will and parliamentary skill of the compromisers, most conspicuously Henry Clay, finally broke the impasse, or so it appeared. Clay's major weapon as Speaker, apart from his rhetorical skills and stamina, was his power over committee appointments. On February 29, the House consented to hold a joint conference with the Senate over the outstanding issues, and Clay chose reliably pro-compromise members for the conference committee. Keeping the restrictionists momentarily happy, Clay, the next day, allowed the House to pass its own Missouri bill, even as the conference committee met. The day after that, the Senate returned the House bill once more, with the restrictionist amendment stricken and the Thomas amendment restored—and at virtually the same hour, the conference committee issued a quickly drafted statement urging passage of the Senate version. Clay knew that he could never get a majority in the House if he presented his compromise in a single bill, so the House considered Missouri statehood and the 36°30' questions separately. With the South voting as a bloc and with eighteen northerners either going along or absenting themselves, the House agreed, by a mere three votes, to remove its slavery restriction provision. The outcome was touch and go until the final tally was counted. ("One hour before & one hour after, we should have lost the vote," the pro-compromise Maine congressman John Holmes remarked soon after.) With Missouri now opened to slavery, the House approved the Thomas amendment, over strong opposition from seaboard southern Old Republicans, centered in Virginia, and Deep South hard-liners who rejected any federal interference with slavery. On March 6, President Monroe signed the Missouri statehood bill.[32]

It all happened so quickly that it seemed to have been scripted in advance, a script that has never been and may never be recovered in full. Certainly Clay's wizardry, formidable as it was, cannot completely explain what transpired. Pressure for compromise in fact came from many imposing sources. At the White House, even before Thomas offered his amendment to the Senate, President Monroe, who fervently favored allowing slavery in Missouri—and believed that the controversy was a power play by his old foe DeWitt Clinton—kept close tabs on the Virginia delegation. He also quietly conferred with friendly northern congressmen, using patronage promises to seal their loyalty. ("[T]he influence of the Palace, which after all is heavier than the Capitol," Representative William Plumer Jr. wrote his father at the end of February, "[has] produced a considerable change here.") John C. Calhoun, on solid nationalist grounds, publicly calmed southerners' fears—expressed most vociferously by the influential Richmond editor Thomas Ritchie—that compromise over Congress's power to ban slavery in the territories was capitulation. Outside of government, Monroe mobilized influential allies—chief among them the banker Nicholas Biddle—to line up support. "Rely upon it you have nothing to fear at home," Biddle assured one wavering Pennsylvania congressman, who eventually voted with the pro-compromise side.[33]

One ferocious antirestriction participant, John Randolph, crowed soon after the vote that the southerners had so frightened their antagonists that the compromisers could have rounded up as many northern backsliders (whom he dubbed "dough faces") as they needed to admit slavery into Missouri. As was his custom, he wildly exaggerated. It would be just as accurate—and in some respects more accurate—to say that the southerners, led by the border South, gave way over the Thomas amendment, in their frustration at the antislavery northerners' obduracy. "[I]t has been ascertained by several votes in the House of Representatives that a considerable majority of that body are in favor of restriction as to all the country purchased from France under the name of Louisiana," a weary Senator Montfort Stokes of North Carolina wrote as the compromise took shape. "All that we from the slave holding states can do at present is to rescue . . . a considerable portion of Louisiana, including all the settled parts of that extensive country." Better to settle for Missouri (and probably, in the more distant future, Arkansas Territory) than for nothing at all. Of far greater consequence numerically to the outcome than northern defections over slavery in Missouri was the compromisers' effort to seize on this sense of angry frustration and rally southern support for both ends of the compromise. In 1819, when Tallmadge proposed his amendment, thirteen southern congressmen were absent. A year later, all but three southerners were present and voted against restriction (as did the representative from the newly admitted slave state of Alabama). This eleven-vote pickup from the South represented the lion's share of the fourteen votes added to the antirestrictionist column between 1819 and 1820. But the hard part was winning enough southern votes to pass the Thomas amendment, which Clay managed by holding onto a majority, albeit slender, of 39 to 37 among House southerners, the great bulk of the votes in favor coming from the border states. In the end, the compromise involved winning over a tiny minority of northerners and a small majority of southerners.[34]

At the critical margins, a deficit of solidarity and of leadership did show up on the northern antislavery side. John W. Taylor, in charge of the antislavery restrictionist cause, lacked Speaker Clay's power and presence. Many in Congress perceived the New Yorker, who harbored higher political ambitions, as growing more tepid the longer the fight continued. Additional difficulties for the northerners stemmed from the always intricate factional fighting in New York. Martin Van Buren's Bucktails remained lukewarm about restriction, suspicious that their archenemy DeWitt Clinton stood to profit politically from a restrictionist victory, and vulnerable to patronage pressure from the Monroe administration. The Bucktails were also, in general, more hostile than other northern Republicans to the idea of racial equality, as they would soon affirm at the New York State constitutional convention. One of the six northern freshmen who voted to open Missouri to slavery was Henry Meigs, a Bucktail close to Van Buren, and three of the absentees, including the erstwhile pro-restrictionist Caleb Tompkins, were also Bucktails. Although no evidence of any prearrangement has come to light, those four New York votes, colored by local considerations quite distinct from the slavery issue, did represent the antirestrictionists' miniscule margin of victory. The compromising Bucktail votes bespoke Van Buren's willingness to ignore northern antislavery opinion (and, some would say, truckle to the slaveholders) in order to reach political accommodation with the South—something that would come to typify Van Buren's politics over the next twenty years.[35]

Still, responsibility for opening Missouri to slavery cannot be placed solely or chiefly on the Van Buren Bucktails, let alone on northern acquiescence. Northern support for nonrestriction and compromise in 1820 came from a small, motley group from various states, Federalists as well as Republicans. The great majority of New York Republicans, including Bucktails as well as Clintonians, voted for restriction in 1820. Only one of the northern representatives who voted for restriction in 1819 voted against it a year later. Compared to the southerners' close vote endorsing the Thomas amendment, the northern vote against slavery in Missouri—a division of 87 to 14—was unyielding.[36]

Unfortunately for Clay and the compromisers, die-hard antislavery northerners and the pro-slavery citizens of Missouri proved less malleable than the House of Representatives. Over the late winter and spring of 1820, Federalist and Republican restrictionists in Pennsylvania and Ohio—joined by a radical Irish immigrant editor in Washington, Baptist Irvine—urged northern congressmen to reject the compromise by refusing to approve Missouri's new constitution when Congress reassembled. Then the Missourians, faced with the seemingly straightforward task of writing a pro-slavery state constitution in compliance with the statehood bill, gratuitously inserted a clause requiring the new state government to enact legislation that barred "free negroes and mulattoes" from entering the state. An apparent violation of the U.S. Constitution's guarantee that the rights of citizens in any state would be respected by all states, the clause deeply offended northerners, who proclaimed that the compromise was now dead. Compounding the difficulty, Clay had retired as Speaker, prefatory to retiring from the House, and was succeeded (after a lengthy sectional struggle) by John W. Taylor. By the time Clay arrived in Washington in January 1821 for what he had hoped would be a brief second session, the House was in chaos. While northerners declared that Missouri was still a territory, southerners insisted that Missouri was now a state and that no additional conditions could be attached to its admission.

The making of the so-called second Missouri Compromise was even more convoluted than the making of the first—and it demanded even more of Clay. The Senate adopted a resolution accepting the Missouri constitution with a proviso that withheld congressional consent to "any provision" that contravened Article IV, Section 2 of the Constitution. Revived restrictionist House Republicans, however, defeated a resolution admitting Missouri—only to fail to pass a subsequent resolution, offered by Republican William Eustis of Massachusetts, that would have struck the offensive clause from the Missouri constitution. Like punch-drunk brawlers, the contestants threw rhetorical haymakers at each other for weeks to come, in one wild round after another, each side standing its ground, neither side able to put the other away. Clay, now working through a chastened Speaker Taylor, did his best to stack committees, undermine the southern hotheads and northern hotheads alike, and cajole a compromise out of the House. Finally, in late February, a joint House and Senate committee, headed by Clay, hammered out the wording of a resolution admitting Missouri provided that the state legislature solemnly pledge not to pass any law in violation of the U.S. Constitution. By a six-vote margin, the House assented; two days later the Senate approved the measure; and on August 10, 1821, President Monroe officially proclaimed that Missouri was the Union's twenty-first state. "I was exhausted," Clay later recalled, "and I am perfectly satisfied that I could not have borne three weeks more of such excitement and exertion."[37]

It has been said that had the Civil War broken out over the Missouri controversy, it would have amounted to a brawl on the floors of Congress, with the rest of the nation looking on perplexed. Certainly by 1821, the nation, in its second year of unprecedented hard times, welcomed the end of the congressional quarreling over slavery and the preservation of the Union. So did virtually all of the major figures who would dominate national politics over the coming two decades: Henry Clay, John C. Calhoun, John Tyler, William Crawford, John Quincy Adams, Nicholas Biddle, Martin Van Buren, and Andrew Jackson, all of whom either helped achieve the compromise or supported it with varying degrees of enthusiasm. Divided over other important issues—especially the questions of banking and economic development raised by the Panic of 1819—they would prove effective at keeping the slavery issue out of national debates, at least until the early 1830s.

The issues debated, and the charges leveled, from 1819 to 1821 were, however, of far more than passing interest. Once a resurgent southern slavery had been attacked and defended as directly as it had been during the Missouri crisis, it would prove impossible to restore completely any fiction of sectional amicability, either in Washington or around the nation. Even Thomas Jefferson, normally the sanguine apostle of reason, grew pessimistic. "This momentous question, like a fire bell in the night, awakened and filled me with terror," he wrote in a famous letter to Congressman John Holmes of Maine in April 1820, at a moment when it seemed, mistakenly, that the controversy had been settled. "I considered it at once as the knell of the Union." Jefferson, who had no use for the emerging pro-slavery ideology expressed by the likes of William Smith, would never abandon his belief that the Missouri affair had been manufactured by a failed Federalist monarchical plot. (It must have pained him to hear northern Republicans cite his beloved Declaration and southern Republicans slight it, although characteristically he left no direct comment on the matter.) Yet Jefferson also apprehended that the inflammatory issues at hand would outlast any political cabal.[38]

Clay's brokered bargain bought national political peace, but the Missouri crisis hardened northern and southern positions on slavery, in and out of Congress. What occurred in 1820 and 1821 was not a genuine compromise so much as it was a cleverly managed political deal, patched together by moderate leaders frightened by the depth of sectional antagonisms, yet unable to achieve genuine sectional accord. By pushing the two halves of the compromise through the House on separate votes, Clay helped to create an exaggerated sense of amity. Antislavery Republican representatives had not at all been cowed by a recalcitrant South, as John Randolph claimed, and neither had their constituents. Whereas virtually all of the Republicans who voted for the original Tallmadge amendments voted against opening Missouri to slavery a year later, the majority of those northern congressmen who either voted against restriction or absented themselves in 1820 found themselves out of office after the next election in 1822.

In the South, meanwhile, opinion moved in the opposite direction. Missouri had been opened to slavery, but the Thomas proviso affirmed in law the northern antislavery Republican argument that Congress had the power to interfere with slavery's expansion, and to set aside forever a large portion of national territory as free soil. This, the pro-slavery Republican Nathaniel Macon wrote, was "acknowledging too much." Clay was fortunate to get a bare majority of southern congressmen to back the 36°30' restriction. Those who went along with him were not quite as fortunate: more than two-thirds of the congressmen who took a hard line and voted against the Thomas proviso won reelection in 1822, compared to about two-fifths of those who supported it. And reinforcing southern fears and resentments was a very different kind of agitation, one that followed the Missouri upheaval by more than a year but that was closely linked to it in the public mind.[39]

In 1781, a slave ship captain, Joseph Vesey, had carried a young slave, perhaps born in Africa, from St. Thomas in the Danish Virgin Islands to work in the sugarcane fields of Saint Domingue. Captain Vesey bought him back after a year, renamed him Telemaque, and, in 1783, settled in Charleston, South Carolina, where he arranged to have the young slave trained as a carpenter. The slave, with another new name, Denmark, grew into a powerful man, married a slave woman (and, thereafter, took at least one other wife), and fathered at least three children. His life changed forever in 1799 when he won a fifteen-hundred-dollar jackpot in the East Bay Charleston lottery—enough to buy his freedom, though not his family's, and establish his own carpentry shop. Thereafter, Denmark Vesey became a mainstay of Charleston's rapidly growing free black community—a class leader in the much-harassed local African Church whose shop on Bull Street became an informal meeting place for freedmen and slaves alike.[40]

On June 16, 1822, white Charlestonians awoke in panic. Some weeks earlier, a slave had told his master's family that the city's blacks were planning an insurrection—improbable, and therefore all the more frightening for the city's slaveholding families, who prided themselves on the relative mildness of their local variant of human bondage. Governor Thomas Bennett, whose own trusted house servants were implicated, had investigated and, to his great relief, heard one slave after another scoff at the reported conspiracy. But on June 14, another slave stepped forward to confirm an imminent uprising, which he said was due to begin at midnight the following Sunday, when slaves from outlying plantations would be crowded into the city to sell their masters' produce. Bennett ordered the military to secure the city, then proceeded prudently, tracking down the origins of the latest scare while trying to keep his fears under control.

Claiming they were fed up with Bennett's caution, Charleston city authorities led by the mayor, James Hamilton Jr., stepped in, arrested scores of suspected conspirators, and extracted information from them in secret special court sessions. The tales the authorities uncovered were blood-curdling—of a plot involving up to nine thousand slaves and free blacks from Charleston and its hinterlands who would seize the city arsenal, exterminate the white male population, and ravage the white women, before escaping by ship to the black republic of Haiti. All roads from the confessions and testimony seemed to lead back to the African Church, to an associate of Vesey's named Gullah Jack Pritchard (who had concocted a mystical faith and had supposedly given recruits amulets to ward off bullets), and to Vesey, the plot's alleged mastermind. With a minimum of judicial safeguards, the authorities duly convicted and hanged Vesey and five of his confederates on July 2. Gullah Jack, apprehended on July 5, was hanged one week later. Nearly two dozen more convicted rebels were put to death in a mass execution on July 26, and over the next two weeks eight more blacks were convicted and one executed. Finally, their thirst for revenge and deterrence slaked, the local judges halted the carnage and, in August, published an official account of the proceedings as an exemplar of fair-minded slaveholders' justice.[41]

The surviving evidence, most of it obtained under coercion, forms an interpretive house of mirrors. Read one way, it shows a sophisticated and widespread conspiracy, the largest insurrectionary plot ever by U.S. slaves, that was detected only at the last minute. Read another way, it shows a frantic white population manipulated by ambitious politicians, obtaining false or greatly exaggerated testimony before sending innocent men to their deaths—leading to the largest number of executions ever handed out by a civilian court in the nation's history. Much depends on the reader's preferences for seeing slavery as an institution that did more to stir the revolutionary passions of the oppressed or the cruel and even murderous passions of the oppressors. Apart from what might have been idle boasting (or frightened invention), there is little to support the idea that thousands had been recruited for an uprising, and various inconsistencies in the testimony suggest that some of it was fabricated to suit the captors' suspicions and their intentions to inflame white fears. Yet there is also sufficient evidence of a plot—not least the words of the original betrayer blacks—to conclude that *something* dangerous was afoot in Charleston in the summer of 1822.[42]

In a more important sense, the mere fact that most of white Charleston, and then the rest of the country, believed there had been a slave conspiracy was enough to make the Vesey affair a major event. Charleston commanded attention—the premier southern city in that part of the South where the density of the black population was the greatest, a seaport vulnerable to the sort of uprising that appeared to have been in the works. It was made all the more vulnerable by the access its black population had to easily diffused newspaper reports and pamphlets about the Yankee troublemakers and the Missouri crisis. For white Charleston—and in turn, the white South—few passages in the official account were more chilling than the reported confession of the slave Jack Purcell just before he was hanged:

> If it had not been for the cunning of that old villain Vesey, I should not now be in my present situation. He employed every stratagem to induce me to join him. He was in the habit of reading to me all the passages in the newspapers that related to Santo Domingo, and apparently every pamphlet he could lay his hands on, that had any connection with slavery. He one day brought me a speech which he told me had been delivered in Congress by a Mr. King on the subject of slavery; He told me this Mr. King was the black man's friend, that Mr. King had declared that he would continue to speak, write, and publish pamphlets against slavery as long as he lived, until the Southern States consented to emancipate their slaves, for that slavery was a disgrace to the country.

Simply allowing public airing of antislavery views seemed to provide fodder for bad elements like Vesey and his friends, who would rise up and slit their masters' throats. "Our Negroes," the Charlestonian Edwin C. Holland reflected, "are truly the *Jacobins* of the country." The fears of slave rebellions aired during the congressional debates over Missouri appeared to have been alarmingly accurate.[43]

And so the repercussions of the Missouri controversy spread into the deepest recesses of the institution of slavery, opening up the possibility (or, just as important, a specter of the possibility) of a popular uprising at the regime's foundations. Those repercussions inflamed sectional arguments that, over the next four decades, would sear the American political system—a dialectic of northern outrage and southern repressive self-protection that proved every bit as destructive as Thomas Jefferson had feared it would. And Missouri had an additional, more immediate repercussion that went utterly unnoticed at the time—the passing presence, in Vesey's own church, of a free black migrant from North Carolina named David Walker, who would in time make his own fateful revolutionary plans.

Still, the bargain over Missouri achieved its immediate goal of pushing aside the slavery issue under a deceptive nationalist truce so that Americans could concentrate on even more pressing matters of economic survival. For all of the portents provoked by the Missouri crisis and resulting sectionalism, the politics of panic, depression, and democracy proved even more riveting in the early 1820s, dividing against each other the national political leaders who had rallied to the compromise over slavery. A permanent realignment of congressional politics along North-South sectional lines—welcomed by some, feared by most—had failed to materialize, thanks to Clay and the compromisers. A different realignment was underway, one strongly affected by sectionalism but influenced even more by the hard times and democratic ferment of Monroe's second term—a realignment that would revive, with new labels and updated ideas, the party divisions of the 1790s. The first indications of this political transformation surfaced during the contest to decide which Republican would succeed Monroe to the White House—a contest from which the least likely of the contenders, Andrew Jackson, emerged as the most popular of all.

JACKSON REEMERGES: THE ELECTION OF 1824

For nearly a quarter-century, one or another Virginia gentry Republican with his political roots in the American Revolution had occupied the American presidency. That tradition, everyone knew, would end after the election of 1824. A new generation of political leaders had come to the fore, many of whom were born after Thomas Jefferson drafted the Declaration of Independence. The leading presidential prospects hailed not from the Old Dominion but from more energized areas of the country, including reinvigorated commercial New England, the cotton-enriched slave states of the lower South, and the rapidly expanding West. All but one could point to long and distinguished careers of service in Congress, the cabinet, or the diplomatic corps. Their respective chances would hinge on the factional fallout from the prolonged depression, the Missouri debates, and the wave of democratic reform that had swelled since 1815.

John Adams's son John Quincy was in many ways the most remarkable of the lot. His public service stretched back to 1781, when at age fourteen, thanks to his father (and with a fluency in French), he traveled to St. Petersburg as secretary of the American legation. After service as the American envoy to the Netherlands and then Berlin, he was elected to the U.S. Senate in 1802, where he broke with his father's party over Jefferson's embargo, resigned his seat in 1808, and instantly became Federalism's best-known apostate. Under President Madison, Adams served as minister to Russia and, in 1814, as commissioner (and calming influence over Henry Clay) at the Ghent treaty negotiations. Above all, as Monroe's secretary of state, he moved from triumph to triumph, arranging with England for the joint occupation of the Oregon country, obtaining from Spain the cession of the Floridas, and formulating the basic principles of what became known as the Monroe Doctrine—accepting the balance of power in Europe and British dominance on the high seas while committing the British to accept American dominance of the Western Hemisphere. Given the past Republican practice of having secretaries of state succeed their presidents, Adams had a strong presumptive claim to the White House.[44]

The economic depression and, even more, the Missouri crisis clipped Adams's wings. His comparatively limited experience in domestic affairs proved increasingly disadvantageous amid the nation's economic difficulties. Many thought him a pampered novice in the cut-and-thrust of congressional politics. Although he publicly supported the Missouri Compromise as the only possible solution under the constraints of the Constitution, privately he regretted not having pushed harder for restriction. Adams had friends and admirers outside New England—among them Andrew Jackson—but the debates over Missouri turned southerners against any nonslaveholding candidate, much less the son of the very last Yankee Federalist president. Adams's candidacy would rise or fall on the basis of how well he could run in the free states outside his New England base, above all in New York and Pennsylvania with their large blocs of electoral votes.

Two southerners presented themselves as a possible alternative to Adams. Secretary of the Treasury William Henry Crawford of Georgia was the main beneficiary of the Old Republican revival provoked by the panic. A gregarious, outsized political intriguer and successful cotton planter, Crawford was not a Quid ideologue, having cultivated a strong alliance with the Second Bank of the United States and having come to endorse moderately protectionist tariff legislation. But when the economy collapsed in 1819, Crawford turned the Treasury Department into the headquarters for neo-Jeffersonian efforts to slash federal expenditures and curb the alleged financial profligacy of the postwar nationalists. Calhoun, whose War Department suffered more than most, despised him; John Quincy Adams called him "a worm preying upon the vitals of the Administration within its own body." Crawford and his so-called Radical supporters took the slurs as a badge of honor and waged war from within the Monroe administration and in Congress, cutting federal expenditures and hoping to sweep into the White House in 1824 by re-creating a sense of rectitude among the Republican faithful. "He is called the 'radical' candidate, by way of derision," one of Crawford's northern admirers wrote. "Jefferson was called the democratic or jacobinical candidate in '98 & '99 & by the same sort of people who now talk about 'radicals.'"[45]

Jefferson himself thought Crawford the best choice, as did Madison, although they would not declare themselves openly. The Georgian also had some important and influential younger friends from New York, Van Buren and the ascendant Albany Regency. Elected to the Senate in 1820, Van Buren took his seat in the session after the second Missouri Compromise, determined to purge national politics of the factionalism rampant in his own state and the sectionalism that had erupted over Missouri. He blamed Monroe's consolidation policy, above all, and worked tirelessly in Washington, he wrote, "to commence the work of a general resuscitation of the old democratic party" with "a radical reform in the political feelings of this place." Reviving the Jeffersonian New York–Virginia political axis was Van Buren's first goal, which prompted him to help House allies unseat the Clintonian John W. Taylor from the Speaker's chair in favor of the more reliable Virginian Philip Barbour. Then, by joining Virginia and New York's votes in the Republican congressional nominating caucus to those of Crawford's base in Georgia and North Carolina, Van Buren hoped to create an unstoppable momentum on the Georgian's behalf. With Crawford in the White House and "regular" Republicans elected nationwide, Van Buren calculated, Clintonian-style treachery and its crypto-Federalist abettors would crumble.[46]

Bad feelings and worse fortune, however, haunted Crawford's campaign. In September 1823, he succumbed to what appears to have been a massive stroke, which left him a partially paralyzed, semi-blind hulk who had to be hoisted out of bed in order to make occasional public appearances. Crawford's friends, including Van Buren, gamely insisted that he would recover, and in a fierce act of will, Crawford forced himself to return to his duties at the Treasury Department in time for the 1824 elections, despite a relapse in May. But Crawford's political recovery was hampered by the late-in-the-game candidacy of a second southern presidential contender, Secretary of War John C. Calhoun. Until the summer of 1821, the South Carolinian might have seemed most likely to support his friend and fellow nationalist in the cabinet, John Quincy Adams. But a political sojourn through the northern states had convinced Calhoun that although Adams could not win outside New England, a broad-minded slaveholder could save the Republic from the clutches of the retrenchment Radical Crawford. Never one to slight his own abilities, Calhoun entered the lists, concentrating his initial efforts on converting the business-friendly, pro-BUS, New School Republicans of Pennsylvania to his cause.[47]

Henry Clay, putatively the western candidate, also enjoyed widespread celebrity as "The Great Compromiser" who had saved the Union in 1820 and 1821. Urged by friends and political cronies to return to the center of political action, he abandoned his lucrative retirement (spent in part collecting fees as the BUS's favorite lawyer), regained his House seat in 1822, and was triumphantly reinstalled as Speaker the following year. Back in power, he assembled ideas about vigorous federal action to bolster internal economic development, which he had been musing over and speaking about for several years, and integrated them as a comprehensive program to combat hard times and sectional divisions. "Is there no remedy within the reach of the Government?" he asked the House. "Are we doomed to behold our industry languish and decay yet more and more? But there is a remedy, and that remedy consists in . . . adopting a genuine American system." Federally sponsored internal improvements, combined with responsible sale of the public lands and a high tariff wall to protect American manufacturers would, Clay proclaimed, benefit all Americans and strengthen the bonds of Union. Quickly dubbed "the American System," it was a western enterpriser's agenda of federal aid—but it was also, Clay insisted, a national vision of improvement and unity.[48]

Clay's gregarious personality and legislative record distinguished him immediately from the rest of the field. In the Eighteenth Congress, he built on those advantages, pushing successfully for the General Survey Bill to plan federal internal improvements and, in 1824, for the first explicitly protectionist tariff in the nation's history. But Clay had his weaknesses, not least his unswerving faith in his own greatness. According to John Quincy Adams (admittedly no friend to the Kentuckian), Clay in conversation would become "warm, vehement, and absurd upon the tariff," making it "extremely difficult to preserve the temper of friendly society with him." In fact, as Clay the brag artist knew well, his political situation was tricky. Adams had sewn up New England, and either Crawford or Calhoun would almost certainly carry the Southeast. To succeed, Clay would have to pick up a bloc of electoral votes from either New York or Pennsylvania, while carrying Ohio, Illinois, Indiana, Missouri, Kentucky, and Tennessee—too little to win outright, but enough to deprive any other candidate of an electoral majority and throw the election into the House of Representatives, where his personal influence would prevail. All of which seemed eminently possible, except for the curious candidacy of another western slaveholder with virtually no presidential credentials whatsoever.[49]

Andrew Jackson, although still a national idol, had receded into a knot of resentments. During the winter of 1817–18, an incident along the border of Spanish Florida had led the Monroe administration to unleash the man now lionized as "the Hero of New Orleans," and still major general of the U.S. Army, against the Spanish authorities. Jackson, familiar with the area from his Pensacola campaign during the late war, proved as ruthless as ever, pursuing across the border Seminole Indians who stood in his way, summarily executing two British citizens whom he found among the Indians, and (greatly exceeding his

orders) expelling the Spanish from Pensacola and installing an American government there. A diplomatic row ensued, along with a humiliating formal congressional investigation into Jackson's behavior. In time, Jackson survived the charges
of insubordination and witnessed an infuriated but enfeebled Spanish Crown
give way in negotiations with the United States and cede the Floridas to American control. But Jackson could not forgive those in the administration and Congress—virtually everyone of importance, as far as he knew, other than Calhoun
and Adams—who had criticized his Florida exploits. Crawford became his special nemesis when the Radicals in Congress cut the army in half and forced Jackson's resignation as the junior of the nation's two major generals. Jackson took
little comfort when President Monroe, in 1821, named him governor of the new
Florida territory. After eleven tempestuous weeks mainly spent fighting departing
Spanish grandees, he quit the post and returned to the Hermitage, where he
would brood and nurse his latest hurts.[50]

Most of official Washington hoped that the old soldier would now finally fade
away, and except for several ironic twists of fortune, he might have. His comeback
began in Tennessee, supported by the bank-friendly Overton faction. After turning aside an offer to run for governor, Jackson acceded to his stalking-horse nomination for the presidency, solely as a means to keep Tennessee's Radicals, led by
his old protégé Governor William Carroll, in check. Few, including Jackson, took
his presidential aspirations seriously, given his small experience in elective office.
(Jackson himself actually favored Adams, his most outspoken friend in the cabinet
during the Florida contretemps; most of his Tennessee backers actually favored
either Adams or Clay.) Had everything proceeded as planned, Andrew Jackson
might be remembered today as minor footnote to presidential history.

Strangely, however, Jackson's candidacy, made formal by his nomination by
the Tennessee legislature in the autumn of 1822, elicited interest not only in
neighboring Alabama and Mississippi but as far east as North Carolina and New
Jersey. More ominously, Jackson, no obedient pawn, began thinking and acting
for himself on the issues related to Tennessee banking. His alliance with Overton
and opposition to the Tennessee Radicals had not led him to abandon his distrust
of banks and bankers, dating back to his near ruin due to bad paper two decades
earlier. In 1820, at the height of the state's postpanic banking controversy, he had
helped draft a memorial that denounced Felix Grundy's paper-money loan office
bill and blamed the depression on "the large emissions of paper from the banks."
(Indeed, it had been temporary endorsement by some of the Radicals of inflated
state-issued paper money, as well as their friendliness with Crawford, that convinced Jackson to keep his distance from them.) Yet if, at the time, he stayed loyal
to his old patrons, the Overton machine's efforts to protect large debtors and the
state banks had always offended Jackson—and the offense deepened when, in
1823, Overton and his allies got the legislature to pack the state supreme court

with justices favorable to expanded land speculation. Jackson, enraged, began putting it about that he opposed all banks on principle, which prompted Overton to demonstrate Jackson's political weakness by secretly backing the reelection of one of his (and Jackson's) old enemies to the Senate by the state legislature in 1823. Jackson's friends, awakening late to the scheme, hurriedly nominated their man, and with the candidate himself showing up outside the legislature the night before the balloting, he won by a scant ten-vote margin. Senator-elect Jackson's presidential campaign was very much alive.[51]

An even greater shock came over the following autumn and winter from Pennsylvania, thanks principally to William Duane, Stephen Simpson, and the revived antibanking Philadelphia city democracy. As soon as John C. Calhoun had begun courting the state's New School Republicans and emerged as almost certain to win the state's backing, Duane and company began casting about for a candidate of their own. Adams, Clay, and Crawford were out of the question, not least because each was connected to the discredited incumbent administration. But Simpson had served under Jackson at New Orleans and thought he was one of the greatest living Americans—a second George Washington and a reformist leader who would create a genuinely democratic party, free of corrupt old uses like the caucus system, to protect what Simpson called "the productive classes."[52]

In January 1822, Duane's *Aurora* floated the long-shot Jackson's name for the presidency. Simpson then started his own pro-Jackson weekly, the *Columbian Observer*, and a pro-Jackson movement began making headway all across the state. Calhoun's lieutenants and pro-Calhoun New Schoolers dismissed Jackson's supporters as an agglomeration of "giddy young men," "the dregs of society," and "grog shop politicians of the villages & the rabble of Pittsburgh and Philadelphia"—only to discover at the state party's nominating convention in March 1823 that the rabble was numerous enough to thwart them. Sensing an impending Jacksonian rout, the New Schoolers managed, just barely, to postpone the nomination process for a year, but disaster delayed was not disaster averted. During the autumn and winter of 1823–24, Old School Jacksonians held mass meetings and rallies across the state, deploying all of the methods of public agitation that Duane's and Michael Leib's City Democrats had inherited from the Democratic Society of the mid-1790s and refined in support of Jefferson. In Philadelphia, Simpson, Duane, and the *Aurora* democrats at last managed to rip control of the local party machinery away from the New Schoolers. With the city's delegation secure for Jackson, the New Schoolers, facing certain defeat, gave up on Calhoun and grudgingly backed the Tennessean. Calhoun's backers managed to win him the convention's nomination for vice president, which Calhounites elsewhere now focused on securing.[53]

The Pennsylvania outcome left a presidential field of four. It also bolstered Jackson's supporters in North Carolina, where pro-Crawford Quids had alienated popular support in the interior of the state by opposing a campaign for democratic reform of the state constitution. Anti-Crawford sentiment had initially gravitated to Calhoun, but by the spring of 1824, the North Carolina "People's Ticket" switched to Jackson. Suddenly, even in Washington, Jackson's presidential bid had genuine credibility. After visiting John Quincy Adams, Congressman William Plumer Jr. wrote to his father that "I was surprised to find that he (& I find many other people talk in the same way) considered Jackson as a very prominent & formidable candidate. And what was more, he not only considered him as strong, but also as meritorious—He had, he said, no hesitation in saying that he preferred him decidedly to any other candidate—." Jackson's chances improved even more when Crawford's political lieutenants, led by the political magician from New York, Martin Van Buren, played by the old rules and gained their man an orthodox victory that proved disastrous.[54]

Since 1796, all Republican presidential and vice presidential candidates had secured the backing of their respective party's congressional caucus, a practice that had always struck some democratic writers as open to abuse. In 1816, Crawford had refrained from allowing his name to be placed before the caucus, and in 1824, Senator Van Buren believed that this earlier forbearance had earned Crawford the nomination, which a revived New York–Virginia axis could secure. But a forced display of party discipline, of the sort Van Buren found so appealing, proved to be political poison. The early challenges to the caucus system, notably George Clinton's in 1808, had obvious personal motivations, augmented by the desires of northern Republicans to break the Virginians' domination of the party. But after 1812, Federalists (who had abandoned the system in favor of conclaves of state party leaders) as well as Republicans charged that the caucus embroiled presidential politics in "*aristocratic* intrigue, cabal and management." In 1817, with the Federalist threat virtually gone, local anticaucus stirrings began in earnest, most conspicuously in Pennsylvania. Republicans of all stripes wondered whether the caucus system—originally designed to keep the party leadership in touch with the wishes of its rank and file—had become a usurping anachronism. In 1820, amid the Missouri crisis, the caucuses met but then adjourned without even going through the formalities of making nominations, and President Monroe was reelected virtually without opposition. The elder William Plumer, among many others, approved of how the caucus system had reached "a low ebb," and complained that it involved "too much regard for private, & too little respect for the public interest."[55]

Four years later, the end of the system was nigh—and the harder that Van Buren cracked the caucus whip for Crawford, the less it hurt his adversaries. Adams told associates that, on principle, he would never consent to receive a nomination for any office from a congressional caucus; Jackson and Clay likewise stayed on the sidelines; and on the eve of the meeting, all but eighty congressmen, fewer than one-third of the total, had publicly pledged not to attend. Van Buren insisted on going through with the gathering, but only sixty-six actually showed up, to hand Crawford a lopsided and thoroughly Pyrrhic victory. Less than a month later, the Senate debated, without coming to a vote, what Rufus King attacked as the "self-created central power" of the caucus, and the system was quietly buried. Poor Crawford, insensibly bearing the onus of the last official caucus nomination, lost whatever slim chances for the presidency still remained.[56]

Pennsylvania proved to be Jackson's breakthrough. With Calhoun now knocked out of the contest, Jackson inherited his large following in New Jersey and Maryland as well as in both of the Carolinas. In Washington, where he unexpectedly found himself in the Senate, he played the charming, socially correct gentleman, putting the lie to his reputation as an impetuous barbarian. Without compromising the protocol of appearing not to be actively campaigning, he also reassured supporters from clashing parts of his embryonic alliance. His Tennessee friends Major William Lewis and Senator John Eaton arranged for Stephen Simpson's *Columbian Observer* to publish a series of letters—signed "Wyoming" but written by Eaton—spelling out the case for Jackson as a virtuous keeper of the Revolutionary heritage against corrupt privilege, and as a genuinely national candidate in a field of sectional favorites. On specific issues like the tariff, Jackson carefully explained his position to his close advisers and the public alike. To a protectionist Pennsylvanian (in a letter he was fully aware would be published), he claimed that "*a fair protection*"—which he believed the pending tariff bill did too little to provide—"would place the american labour in a fair competition with that of [E]urope." The letter matched his position in the Senate, where he consistently voted against amendments that would have lowered rates. But when an antitariff North Carolinian expressed his concern, Jackson replied (in another letter he knew would be published) that he favored a "judicious examination and revision" of the tariff, not an oppressive one.[57]

Jackson's opponents leapt on the statements and charged him with being two-faced. (In response to the North Carolina letter, Henry Clay is reputed to have said, "Well by ——, I am in favor of an *in*judicious tariff.") In fact, the statements were perfectly consistent, if artfully constructed. Instead of trapping himself by taking a dogmatic stance one way or the other, Jackson stuck to a middle ground, singling out certain products (like Pennsylvania iron) as articles of our "national independence, and national defence" in need of protection, while he refrained from naming others (including New England cotton goods). He also found a way to link tariff protection to the cause of populist Jeffersonian simplicity, arguing that tariff revenues were required to eliminate the accursed national debt that, if left standing, would "raise around the administration a moneyed aristocracy, dangerous to the liberties of the country."[58]

Jackson's shifts in tone and unorthodox combinations of ideas were astute political moves, designed to solidify his disparate coalition. He had become a politician for whom, as for any army general, there is nothing without victory. But by confounding expectations—another military virtue—Jackson also defied what were becoming the pat categories of political thinking on specific policies while offering his own synthesis, and tying it to the people's cause. It was a trait that would become more pronounced as Jackson's political experience grew. Older Republicans—including the man Jackson called his political hero, Thomas Jefferson—could not fully grasp the appeal of the violent, passionate Old Hickory. (Jefferson, reportedly, thought he was "a *dangerous man*.") But younger Republicans who knew him, including the convert John Quincy Adams, understood that what many mistook for Jackson's intellectual confusion and emotional rashness hid what Adams called his "profound calculation."[59]

Jackson's managers were single-minded in promoting their candidate as a national and not merely a sectional figure, a crucial appeal in the aftermath of the Missouri struggles and the Vesey affair. "The union is no longer activated by one soul, and bound together by one entirety of interest," the Pennsylvania Jacksonians declared at their Harrisburg nominating convention: Jackson would correct that, an Alabama paper proclaimed, by being "the President of the whole people, the enlightened ruler of an undivided empire, and not a sectional magistrate devoted to the 'universal Yankee nation' of the East or the mixed, mingled and confused population of the South." The other aspirants tried to build similar messages—Crawford by stressing his orthodox Jeffersonian loyalties, Adams by stressing his long and distinguished record in the nation's service, and Clay by playing up his ideas for national economic improvement—but none was as persuasive as the Hero of New Orleans.[60]

The Jacksonians also invited mass participation in the campaign. Voters and spectators turned out on short notice for frequent rallies and parades, staged to invigorate the faithful and display that Jackson was the outsider candidate whose legitimacy could only come from the people at large, and not from any club of Washington fixers. Jackson benefited from other campaign innovations, including taking straw votes at militia musters and grand jury meetings. No doubt the pro-Jackson press inflated the enthusiasm these efforts generated—but more conventional observers, used to a smaller deployment of treating and stumping during campaigns, were shocked and dismayed at the Jacksonians' display. Some called the shows meaningless stagecraft. "Mere effervescence . . . can accomplish nothing," one pro-Calhoun New School Pennsylvanian sniffed, before Jackson knocked his man out of the race. Others sounded genuinely worried, as if these audacious tactics would carry away the thoughtless multitude, and they questioned the very legitimacy of Jackson's campaign.[61]

With Jackson's candidacy surging, the center of intrigue moved to New York, one of only six states where the state legislature still chose presidential electors.

As ever, the place was a hornet's nest. Van Buren and the Albany Regency, loyal to Crawford to the bitter end, had decided to resist public sentiment in favor of popular choice of electors in order to ensure that the Bucktail-controlled Albany legislature would hand Crawford the state's bonanza of thirty-six electoral votes. New York business interests friendly to John C. Calhoun tried to take the high ground, demanding that the Regency allow the people at large to choose the state's presidential electors—and portrayed Crawford and his friends as democracy's foes. When Calhoun's campaign collapsed in Pennsylvania in March 1824, so did his friends' efforts in New York—but Van Buren's Clintonian enemies, already organizing a reform crusade, rallied to what they called the People's Party and campaigned hard for the new Election Bill, which would give to the voters the direct power to select presidential electors.[62]

Van Buren had badly outsmarted himself. To accede to the new bill would mean placing his slaveholder candidate, Crawford, at the mercy of New York's manifestly antislavery voters—a risky proposition in the wake of the Missouri Compromise. Worse, it might actually open the way for the hated Clinton himself to run as a favorite-son candidate, a contest Clinton would almost certainly win. Over the previous half-dozen years, work had proceeded steadily on the astounding canal-building project that Clinton had first proposed in 1808. With the new Erie Canal now nearing completion (and with Clinton serving as unpaid chief of the Canal Board), the ex-governor "Magnus Apollo" had become a hero all over again in the western part of the state. Even his political enemies had to grant that the canal was a marvel. Were Clinton to win New York, he could easily jump to the front of the presidential pack as the one man who could unite the anti-Crawford forces outside the South—a prospect that frightened Martin Van Buren even more than the prospect of being labeled undemocratic.[63]

One Bucktail blunder led to another. As the price for suppressing their democratic principles on the Election Bill, radical Bucktails demanded that the Regency inflict some sort of punishment on Clinton. On the very last day of the legislative session, without consulting Van Buren (who was away in Washington), Regency bosses led by one aging Judge Roger Skinner gave the go-ahead, and Clinton was summarily removed, for no stated reason, from his Canal Board post. Van Buren exploded with rage, understanding immediately that the gratuitous disgracing of Clinton would give his enemy, as he put it, "what he had never before possessed—the sympathies of the people." ("[T]here is such a thing in politics," Van Buren later snapped at Judge Skinner, "as *killing a man too dead!*") Clinton, for his part, did not miss a beat. Unable to break the Regency's lockhold over the Election Bill, he wrapped himself in the populist garb of the People's Party, ran for governor, and, in October, swept back into power. Three-quarters of the new state assembly would be anti-Regency men.[64]

Luckily for Van Buren, it would be the lame-duck legislature that would allocate the state's electoral votes, but for once he seemed to have lost his touch. After a prolonged series of Byzantine negotiations, the battered Buck-tails mustered only four electoral votes for Crawford—three fewer than Clay received, with the rest going to Adams. Van Buren, one Adams supporter exulted, "looks like a wilted cabbage, and poor Judge Skinner has quite lost his voice." Yet Van Buren managed to salvage a victory of sorts from the Regency's sorry performance.[65]

By the time the New York legislature assembled formally to choose its electors, the popular rush for Jackson had secured sixty-six electoral votes; Adams had fifty-one votes, Crawford thirty-nine, and Clay thirty-three. The election seemed destined, as Clay had hoped, to end up in the House of Representatives. But the Twelfth Amendment to the Constitution, approved in 1804 after the Jefferson-Burr deadlock, stipulated that only the top three candidates would be considered, and Clay was running fourth. If Clay's backers fared as expected in the New York machinations, Clay might have gained hope that he would make the short list and then, in all likelihood, win the White House. But as the New York electors prepared to meet and cast their ballots, Van Buren maneuvered to suppress Clay's total. One elector pledged to Clay, under great pressure, switched to Jackson; two other Clay electors failed to appear and were replaced by Adams men; and the Regency persuaded one Adams elector to vote for Crawford. The final revised New York total was Adams twenty-six, Crawford five, Clay only four, and Jackson one. Had the original New York totals stood, the Electoral College result would have left Crawford and Clay in a tie for third place—but Van Buren, having failed to win his state for Crawford, at least made sure that his man, and not Clay, made it to the next round. The Great Compromiser was finished, in this election anyway, and New York had made the difference.[66]

The biggest story of the election, however, unfolded in Pennsylvania and New Jersey (where the voters, and not the legislatures, now chose presidential electors) as well as in North Carolina, Illinois, Indiana, and the new states of the Southwest. Jackson won them all and, except in New Jersey, did so by landslide margins. In several states where he did not win—Maryland, Ohio, Missouri—Jackson finished a strong second. All told, he won 42 percent of the vote in the eighteen states that allowed voters to choose presidential electors—nearly 10 percentage points better than his nearest competitor, Adams. Outside Adams's New England base (where he and Clay were completely shut out), Jackson was the plain preference of the large majority of the voters. If those states where he ran second to Clay added their congressional votes to those of the states Jackson won outright, Jackson would have had the backing of fourteen congressional delegations—two more than necessary to win the election in the House of Representatives. (John C. Calhoun, meanwhile, had prevailed overwhelmingly in his quest for the vice presidency, having won the support of both the Adams and the Jackson forces.)

Considering where Jackson had stood only two years earlier, it was an extraordinary achievement, the sharpest ascent by any man in the young republic's political history. Out of the depths of his postwar difficulties, Jackson, a man of humble origins and minimal formal education, had risen to capture the imagination of a broad cross-section of the electorate. "The Giant Augean Stable at Washington wants cleansing," a group of Stephen Simpson's Old Schoolers had proclaimed over the winter of 1822–23, "and we know of no other Hercules." Tapping into the democratic frenzy unleashed by the Era of Bad Feelings, Jackson had become that frenzy's great symbol.[67]

Now, only two rivals stood between him and the presidency, one a purported political lightweight, the other a virtual corpse. Yet despite all that Jackson had accomplished, his fortunes hung on the deliberations of the resourceful also-ran, Henry Clay, who was not quite finished after all.

"SOMETHING RADICALLY WRONG"

Late in May 1820, two of the most learned public men of their time boarded a carriage in Washington, took a long ride into the Maryland countryside and conversed freely about politics. Secretary of War John C. Calhoun was gloomy about what he called "a general mass of disaffection to the Government, not concentrated in any particular direction, but ready to seize upon any event and looking out anywhere for a leader." The alarming Missouri question and the tariff debates, he said, were "merely incidental" to the crisis—one born of "a general impression that there was something radically wrong in the administration of the Government." His companion, Secretary of State John Quincy Adams, although more sanguine, was inclined to agree that the long-time "scourge of the country . . . speculations in paper currency," coupled with political demagogy, had hurt the Monroe administration. Unfortunately, Adams reflected, although "the disease is apparent, the remedy [is] not discernible." All he could do was to place his faith in Time, Chance, and Providence. "I have but one formula suited to all occasions—," he wrote in his diary, "'Thy will be done.'"[68]

Five years later, Adams would have reason to believe that a merciful deity had answered his prayers. But as the campaign of 1824 proved, the disaffection ran far deeper than either Adams or Calhoun had feared. Worse, some of the ambitious men whom Adams loathed helped change the fundamentals of national politics forever—and, in the process, secured for their leader, Andrew Jackson, a powerful claim on the presidency.

The panic, as Adams perceived, was pivotal. Not only did the hard times of

1819 and the early 1820s revive, in new forms, the city and country democracies, they also raised fundamental questions about the nationalist economic policies of the new-style Republicans under Madison and Monroe, and focused inchoate popular resentments on the banks, especially the Second BUS. The critics were diverse, socially as well as ideologically, ranging from local monied interests, planters, and enterprisers angry chiefly at the BUS, to radicals like Stephen Simpson, for whom all commercial banking was a crime. The hostility was far from universal, as the strong northwestern popular vote for Henry Clay amply proved in 1824. But the panic persuaded a large portion of the electorate that something was terribly awry in the national government, and that (as one Pennsylvanian, appalled by "moonstruck madness" of the Jacksonians, observed) there "must be a new order of things."[69]

The Missouri controversy, meanwhile, proved far more important than a "merely incidental" outburst. All four of the presidential contenders in 1824 (as well as Calhoun, before he backed out) publicly supported the congressional compromises. The northern restrictionists could not force the national debate their way, but neither could the southern die-hards. Each man tried to depict himself as the only true national candidate, with broad patriotic appeal, while disparaging his opponents as sectional favorites. Yet resentments over slavery did not disappear. John Quincy Adams, the sole nonslaveholder in the race, managed to win some support, but was badly beaten in the South and Southwest. William Crawford, the candidate of the southeastern slaveholders and Van Buren–style northern "regulars," ran poorly outside of his southeastern base. Henry Clay, the western slaveholding compromiser, lost the support of southerners who thought him too hard on slavery and from northerners who thought him too soft. He wound up winning, barely, only one state, Ohio, apart from his native Kentucky and a grateful Missouri.[70]

Both the panic and the Missouri debates underscored in different ways the overriding question of democracy as Americans perceived it. In economic matters, the questions arose primarily as a matter of privilege. Should unelected private interests, well connected to government, be permitted to control, to their own benefit, the economic destiny of the entire nation? Or should the manifest public good, for rich and poor alike, be pursued no matter what the majoritarian democrats believed and demanded? Regarding slavery, the questions were a matter of justice. Did the federal government have the constitutional power to control the expansion of slavery? Were blacks as well as whites endowed with certain inalienable rights that slavery destroyed? Should settler-citizens, slaveholders and nonslaveholders, have the right to decide slavery's fate for themselves? Should the nation's leaders abide by the Missouri Compromise's spirit and keep slavery issues out of national politics? Or did justice demand a sectional showdown over slavery?

Amid these debates, politicians tried to adapt to the broader shift in political sensibilities that emerged out of the War of 1812. At the state level, that required either accommodating, co-opting, or (as in Virginia) squelching surging demands for expanding democracy. At the national level, it required at least appearing to be in league with an enlarged popular sovereignty. "We must be democratic, we must be on the side of the people," one New York Clintonian wrote to another in 1821. "[I]f our adversaries are republicans, we must be democratic; if they are democratic, we must be jacobinal." The debacle over the nominating caucus in 1824 symbolized all that had changed. Those who heeded convention—above all, Martin Van Buren and his pro-Crawford Radical allies—painted themselves into a political corner. The more one did not play by the old rules, the better.[71]

All of which accounts for the phenomenal emergence of Andrew Jackson. As a newcomer to national politics, Jackson had none of the insider connections with Van Buren–style "regular" northern Republicans that Crawford had; as a westerner (like Clay) and as a slaveholder (like Calhoun and Clay), he was unable to build an independent following east of the Hudson River. But elsewhere, Jackson's outsider status and his military glory made him the exceptional man, the only candidate untainted by the Monrovian political establishment in Washington, the only one who could convincingly portray himself, outside New England, as a national figure, the only one who could win credible followings outside his regional base. Only Jackson, as his backers insisted, seemed to possess the combination of heroism and independence required to offset sectional prejudices, prevent the entrenchment of what he called a "moneyed aristocracy," and, in the pro-Jackson Pennsylvania convention's words, vindicate "the durability of our free institutions."[72]

Jackson became, in sum, the leader whose ascendance Calhoun had predicted in 1820. According to the later reflections of one of his supporters, Thomas Hart Benton, Jackson should therefore have been elected president in 1824, in line with what Benton called "the *demos krateo* principle."[73] But as the events of the following winter proved, the meaning of *demos krateo* was far from self-evident, at least in Washington City.

8

THE POLITICS OF MORAL
IMPROVEMENT

As Congress assembled in January 1825 to select a new president, Henry Clay reveled in the machinations. Having finished fourth in the Electoral College voting, he knew he would not be elected. But none of the other candidates had anything close to the simple majority of state delegations in the House required for election under the Twelfth Amendment. Clay, having carried three states and with a toehold in New York, could come close to deciding the matter. The Speaker played along with delight as representatives of Jackson, Crawford, and Adams buttonholed him, paid him florid compliments, and then pleaded the case for their man. "How can one withstand all this disinterested homage & kindness?" Clay wrote wryly to his Kentucky neighbor Francis P. Blair.[1] Clay knew the choice was virtually his to make, and that Adams would be his beneficiary.

Clay had disliked Adams ever since Ghent, and later the two had disagreed sharply over the Spanish treaty that obtained Florida, but they shared broadly nationalist views. Crawford was impossible, a retrenchment Radical who seemed to be at death's door. Jackson was even worse, a backwoods Napoleon who, in Clay's view, had proved his unfitness to lead during the Florida affair. Jackson's election, Clay told friends, would "be the greatest misfortune that could befall the country" and "give the strongest guaranty that the republic will march in the fatal road which has conducted every other republic to ruin." So Clay would support Adams, an intention he announced to his closest associates in mid-December, nearly nine weeks before the House was scheduled to gather. In Washington, on the evening of January 9, the two met privately, at Adams's instigation, mainly, it appears, to smooth over their personal differences. It was all over but the shouting, although there would still be plenty of that.[2]

Less than two weeks before the House gathered, Stephen Simpson's *Columbian Observer* published a sensational anonymous letter, from Washington, claiming that "the friends of Mr. Clay have hinted that they, like the Swiss, would fight for those who pay best," and charging that they had struck a secret deal to make Adams president. The price? "[S]hould this unholy coalition prevail," the letter said, "Clay is to be appointed Secretary of State." Clay whipped off a reply published in the quasi-official Washington *National Intelligencer*, pronouncing the author, whoever he was, a liar, and challenging him to a duel. Two days later, also in the *Intelligencer*, George Kremer, a flamboyant, democratic House backbencher from Pennsylvania unmasked himself as the accuser and declared he was ready to prove his charges.[3]

Embarrassed to be entangled with the eccentric Kremer, Clay backed away from his challenge but demanded that Kremer offer proof. Kremer dodged.[4] Finally, on February 9, the House began selecting the president of the United States. The three states Clay had won—Ohio, Missouri, and Kentucky—had already announced they would vote for Adams, leaving the New Englander two states short of his goal. Maryland, too, would back Adams, but only on the first ballot; after that, all bets were off. New York, split down the middle, became the key to victory. Adams and Daniel Webster went to work to secure the crucial vote of the old patroon Stephen Van Rensselaer, and the squire congressman came through, handing New York's vote to Adams. "May the blessing of God rest upon the event of this day!" the president-elect wrote in his diary.[5]

Henry Clay then committed one of the greatest errors in American political history. During the weeks leading up to the House vote, Adams and his lieutenants had given what they discreetly called "assurances" to various potential supporters in Congress. Among the least questionable of these understandings was reached with Clay. Both Adams and Clay were too sophisticated to strike any explicit bargain, either during their private meeting on January 9 or at any other time. None was needed. Clay brought with him congressional influence, charm, and geographical balance, all things that the New Englander required. Two days after the House voted, President-elect Adams duly informed President Monroe that he had offered the State Department to Clay; three days later, he returned to the White House to tell Monroe that Clay had accepted. Washington exploded. Suddenly, George Kremer's bluff looked like prophecy. "So you see," Andrew Jackson roared in private, "the *Judas* of the West has closed the contract and will receive the thirty pieces of silver. his end will be the same."[6] Clay would never rid himself of the taint of this alleged "corrupt bargain" for the rest of his long public life.

If, in politics, a blunder is worse than a crime, then Clay, along with Adams, was guilty indeed, of a complete failure of political intelligence and imagination. That Clay only gradually came to understand what went wrong only proved the failure's magnitude. By his own lights, he had acted with patriotic correctness, even statesmanship. The Constitution's stipulations about procedures had been followed to the letter. By joining his supporters to those of the national candidate most like himself, Clay was promoting what he considered a credible divination of the democratic will as endorsing nationalist programs. The only display of bad faith had been the smear campaign mounted by the low Kremer and company, which he, the Speaker, had manfully foiled.[7]

Clay disregarded the cardinal political maxim that the appearance of wrongdoing can be just as damaging as actual wrongdoing. More important, while playing by the established patrician rules of high politics, Clay did not comprehend how much and how quickly the rules were changing in the 1820s along majoritarian lines. To Clay, there was nothing wrong with commandeering for Adams the congressional vote of his home state of Kentucky (where he had trounced Jackson by nearly a three to one margin), even though Adams had won not a single popular vote in Kentucky and even though the state legislature had pointedly instructed its congressmen to vote for Jackson. Clay dismissed the national popular vote (which Jackson had won decisively, and in which the combined total of Jackson and Crawford was more than 50 percent), the Electoral College plurality (which Jackson had also won decisively), and the combination of first- and second-place finishes in the states (by which Jackson would have won easily in Congress). Adams, supposedly the lesser political calculator of the two, actually understood the situation far better than Clay, noting some months later in his diary that the election had not transpired "in a manner satisfactory to pride or just desire; not by the unequivocal suffrages of a majority of the people; with perhaps two-thirds of the whole people adverse to the actual result."[8]

On March 4, Adams, after two sleepless nights, took the oath of office at the Capitol. John C. Calhoun, deeply offended by what he saw as Clay's selfish maneuvers, was sworn in as vice president. Clay, flushed with success, won a hotly contested confirmation as secretary of state from the Senate. Andrew Jackson suppressed his fury, graciously attended Adams's inauguration, voted against Clay's confirmation, and returned to a hero's homecoming in Nashville. But on the day that Adams was sworn in, a pro-Tammany New York City newspaper published a letter that Jackson had written days earlier to a local supporter, blasting Henry Clay for his insults and intrigues of recent months:

> To him thank god I am in no wise responsible, there is a purer tribunal to which in preference I would refer myself—to the Judgment of an enlightened patriotic & uncorrupted people—to that tribunal I would rather appeal whence is derived whatever reputation either he or I are possessed of.

In October, with the Adams presidency only seven months old, the Tennessee legislature in a nearly unanimous vote advanced Jackson's name for the presidency in 1828, the earliest such nomination by far in any presidential season to that time. Jackson gratefully accepted and retired from the Senate, lest he be seen as using his office "for selfish consideration."[9]

President Adams's morally inspired, ambitious vision of the nation would help set the terms for the battles of the next four years. But far from Washington, popular movements, old and new, with their own moral, religious, and political concerns, complicated local and, eventually, national politics—some in broad agreement with Adams's views, others in sharp contrast. Always there was the certainty that in 1828 Andrew Jackson would fight to reclaim what he believed was rightfully his. The Era of Bad Feelings had entered a new and furious phase.

A "SACRED" DUTY AND TRUST: JOHN QUINCY ADAMS IN THE WHITE HOUSE

"You come into Life with advantages which will disgrace you, if your success is mediocre," Vice President John Adams wrote his son in 1794. ". . . [I]f you do not rise to the head not only of your Profession, but of your Country, it will be owing to your own *Laziness Slovenliness* and *Obstinacy*." The younger Adams, at age twenty-seven, had already achieved much at the time, most recently as an essayist and orator defending the Washington administration and attacking the "political villainy" of Edmond Genet. Left to his own devices, he would have preferred a tranquil, bookish life as a Boston lawyer or, perhaps, a Harvard scholar. But his father's monumental expectations, as ever, overruled young Johnny's preferences, filling him with the mixture of determination and corrosive self-doubt that would torment him for most of the rest of his life.[10]

Few Americans of such great accomplishment and distinction have left behind so revealing a record of inner affliction as Adams did in his great lifelong diary. Alongside the notations of his diplomatic triumphs, there are constant self-beratings. He repeatedly fretted that he suffered from "imbecility of will," a tendency to distraction that he feared would drive him mad. Even after his demanding father and his meddlesome mother, Abigail, were dead, their spirits haunted Adams, feeding his drive for eminence but also chastising him lest he fall prey to the sin of pride. Adams devoted mind, body, and soul to keeping his demons at bay. As president, he followed a strict daily regimen, awaking well before dawn, walking up and down Pennsylvania Avenue for two hours no matter the weather, and swimming in the Potomac during bathing season. To soothe his nerves he drank quinine and valerian root tea. For spiritual uplift, he read two or three chapters of scripture each morning, along with the corresponding sections in biblical commentaries. After hours, he enjoyed billiards as "a resource both for exercise and amusement." His diary was his greatest refuge, except when fatigue or distraction kept him from writing, which left "another chasm in the record of my life."[11]

Among those he trusted, Adams was witty, chatty, and passionate, but he preferred solitude to most forms of Washington socializing. With strangers and most acquaintances, he adopted a protective reserve, masking his emotions with an austere gravitas. Behind the mask, Adams was a man of enormous learning, piety, and ambition, all of which shaped his political outlook. No president, including Jefferson, contributed more to American scholarship. Fluent in seven languages, sometime Boylston Professor of Rhetoric at Harvard, Adams was conversant in current debates in mathematics and the natural sciences, as well as in theology. With his translation of Christoph Martin Wieland's romance *Oberon* (completed while he served his father as ambassador to Prussia), he established the serious study in the United States of German language and literature. His religious devotions, described constantly in his diary, were of the liberalizing post-Calvinist Unitarian stamp, blending rationalism and enthusiasm in a creed of human elevation. "Progressive improvement in the condition of man," he would observe many years later, "is apparently the purpose of a superintending Providence." As Adams did God's will by improving himself, so he would improve the nation.[12]

Adams harnessed his intellectual and emotional drives—and kept himself from going to pieces—with an intensely competitive political resolve. His adversaries underestimated him as a spoiled, book-smart dauphin; his maneuvers to win the presidency over the winter of 1824–25 amply showed him as a resourceful politician. (Many years later, Ralph Waldo Emerson would shrewdly describe Adams as "no literary gentleman" but "a bruiser," "an old roué who cannot live on slops, but must have sulphuric acid in his tea.") Yet Adams, like Clay, followed political rules that, in the 1820s, were quickly becoming outdated. A throwback, in some ways, to his father's generation, he imagined that national politics was an arena for the resolution of regional differences by like-minded men of virtue and education. He disdained public display of competitive striving as undignified. He despised mass party politics of the sort now associated with Andrew Jackson, and firmly favored government of and by the best men—"the most able and the most worthy," he told Henry Clay. He was a partisan who hated what was coming to be known as partisanship, a Federalist-turned-Republican who thought nominal affiliations counted for little and personal integrity counted for nearly everything—a politician who was not so much without a political party as he was opposed to the very idea of a political party.[13]

As president, Adams hoped to usher in an era of great spiritual and intellectual as well as material improvements. His first annual message to Congress, delivered in December 1825, spelled out his goals exactly. He would have Congress fund the construction of extensive new roads and canals; he wanted to complete an old proposal of George Washington's and establish a great university in the city that now bore Washington's name; he would build at public expense an astronomical observatory, of which Europe could boast more than one hundred but of which in all of the Western Hemisphere there were none. "In assuming her station among the civilized nations of the earth," Adams declared, "it would seem that our country had contracted the engagement to contribute her share of mind, of labor, and of expense to the improvement of those parts of knowledge which lie beyond the reach of individual acquisition."[14]

Adams's vision was moral as well as political—nothing less, he said, than a "sacred" duty and trust. Although his means would be very different from theirs, Adams wanted to mobilize the resources of the federal government to increase what the old Democratic-Republican societies had championed as "social virtue." Henry Clay, like other Republican nationalists, had described the ethical and patriotic benefits of active government and the American System as a byproduct of economic expansion. Adams took a larger view. What was the use of popular sovereignty in a post-Federalist world, he asked, if government lacked the authority to advance the spiritual as well as the material conditions of the nation at large, for the weak and the middling as well as the strong? Must the nation be forever hamstrung by its old fears from the 1790s—fears, he explained, that had been scattered in a new era where "[t]he spirit of improvement is abroad upon the earth"? Who could call the federal government's energetic use of its enumerated powers a return to monocracy, so long as it aimed to work directly "for the benefit of the people themselves." Had not Jefferson himself laid aside the neat formulas of antigovernment convention when he believed strong executive action necessary to the public good, above all in the Louisiana Purchase? Might reflexive suspicion of government power disable such action, making us a lesser and not a greater nation than we could be?[15]

Adams was neither an old-fashioned Federalist nor, strictly, a Republican economic nationalist. Neither, however, was he a "positive" liberal prophet of the modern democratic state. His energetic view of government, summarized in his first annual message's famous declaration that "liberty is power," held that only the federal government had the authority and the resources required to undertake his grand improvement projects. Yet through his presidential years, there was nothing democratic in the actual politics of Adams's liberality. Although he celebrated what he called, in his inaugural address, "a confederated representative democracy," he detested even the limited ideas of party and party loyalty that had arisen from the crises of the 1790s. He portrayed his administration as a patrician return to the rule of "talents and virtue alone." Especially in the aftermath of the corrupt-bargain episode, Adams's more attractive side was occluded

by his utter failure to adjust to the democratic ferment of the 1820s. He appeared
as if he wanted to impose his benevolent will on the people, instead of heeding
the people's will. More than any other prominent American leader, he resembled a cosmopolitan liberal aristocrat, a type far more common in Britain and
Europe than in America, his politics resembling those of his admirer, Alexis de
Tocqueville.[16]

Which is to say that Adams's program was doomed from the start. The spe-
cious allegations that he had struck a sordid gentleman's deal with Henry Clay
hurt Adams badly even before his inaugural. Once in the White House, his
antiparty stance on federal appointments, and his determination to unite all factions, including those that wished him ill, would have crippled him even had his
policies proved popular. More important, those expensive federal policies were
anathema to most Americans—and most of their elected representatives—who
were still recovering from the economic and political crises of the Monroe years.
While they were trying to make ends meet, the president wanted to spend the
people's money to build a university and an observatory—an extravagant waste, it
seemed, proposed by a Harvard elitist who had connived his way into the presidency. For southerners, there was the special fear, in the wake of the Missouri
crisis, that the Yankee Adams's idea of improvement also meant renewed attacks
on slavery and its expansion.[17]

The new president certainly had the courage of his convictions. Instead of
cloaking his overriding purpose, Adams at the conclusion of his first message to
Congress, dared the representatives not "to slumber in ignorance or fold up our
arms and proclaim to the world that we are palsied by the will of our constituents." Yet for all its bravery, that majestic line—delivered by a president who
had run a clear second in the popular vote—survives as one of the most politically ruinous in the history of American presidential rhetoric. Adams took what
encouragement he could from a few friends (including Edward Livingston, the
former New York Democratic Society member, now a congressman from
Louisiana) who told him they agreed with the message's every word. But the
advance private reviews from his own cabinet members, including Secretary of
State Clay, were negative. The intramural warnings appear only to have hardened the pugnacious Adams's resolve, but the public's jeering proved devastating. Alternatively mocked as an effete dreamer and denounced as a would-be
Caesar, Adams suffered through what he called in his diary a "protracted agony
of character and reputation." Less than a year into his presidency, he began to
realize that Congress would enact none of his improvement projects.[18]

Foreign affairs, Adams's forte, proved no happier, and for reasons that had
much to do with domestic politics. The major debacle involved the spread of
republicanism in Latin America, and the elaboration of the Monroe Doctrine

barring European interference in Western affairs, of which Adams, as secretary of state, had been the chief author. By 1825, revolutions in the Argentine, Chile, Peru, Colombia, and Mexico had changed the face of Atlantic politics, and raised new concerns. Belligerent factions in newly independent Colombia and Mexico harbored designs on wresting the slave colony of Cuba away from the tottering Spanish government as soon as the last traces of Spanish rule departed from their own shores. Adams and Clay persuaded the Mexican and Colombian governments to back off, but Adams, with his penchant for ambitious projects, and with Clay's support, also wanted to foster stronger commercial and political ties among all of the Western republics. In his first annual message he announced plans to dispatch ministers to a conference scheduled to be held the following year in Panama, "to deliberate upon objects important to the welfare of all." Three months later, the Senate consented to Adams's plenipotentiary nominations—but the American mission, like the conference itself, was doomed.[19]

In light of the recent abolition of slavery in Chile and Central America, and its impending abolition in much of the rest of formerly colonized Latin America outside Brazil and Cuba, southern Republicans feared that the Panama conference would raise the specter of emancipation. They were also repelled by the idea that American officials would have to mix as equals with a black Haitian envoy. Northern Republicans aligned with Senator Martin Van Buren of New York (who was still a Crawford-style Radical) saw an opportunity to build southern support and harass the administration by objecting to a possible surrender of American sovereignty in any agreements made in Panama. Debates on the matter became intensely personal, at times turning the House of Representatives into what one member called "a perfect Scene of Confusion," with "no one addressing the Chair, the Chairman crying out Order Order, Order, hurly burly, helter skelter, Negro states and yankies." John Randolph, still the most stinging voice of southern Old Republicanism, delivered a rambling speech in the Senate insinuating that Secretary Clay had forged the invitations to the Panama meeting, and denouncing the president and his Kentucky ally as a sordid combination "of the puritan and the black-leg." (Randolph's remarks prompted a duel with Clay, which drew no blood.) More costly, to the administration, was the fuss kicked up by the publication, with Adams's approval, of a pseudonymous letter attacking Vice President Calhoun for failing to speak up during Randolph's rant. Calhoun assumed, mistakenly, that Adams himself was the author and he sent a bristling pseudonymous reply. The clerk who actually wrote the first letter anonymously fired back, and the Adams administration's Panama policy looked like it had degenerated into warfare between the president and the vice president.[20]

The denouement was pathetic. Apart from the United States, only four other countries wound up sending officials to the Panama meeting, which gathered in

June 1826. The two American delegates never actually arrived: John Sergeant, the Pennsylvania Federalist, refused to suffer through the Panamanian summer; and Richard Anderson of Kentucky died of a mysterious tropical disease en route. The actual conference was reduced to drafting hastily some common defense treaties, none of which would ever come into effect. Another grand design shattered.

On a different diplomatic front, dealing with the surviving Creek and Cherokee tribes in Georgia, the Adams administration became embroiled with the state government in what would prove to be a momentous shift in southern politics, and responded in a way that ultimately looked pusillanimous. Politics in Georgia since 1819 had pitted established planter and financier interests from the coast and piedmont, in a faction led by the pro-Crawford Radical governor George Michael Troup, against backcountry small farmers and debtors led by a semiliterate former Indian fighter, John Clark. Georgia's backcountry democrats, having elected Clark governor in 1819 and 1821, fought for constitutional reforms, most auspiciously in a campaign that, in 1824, transferred election of the state governor from the legislature to the electorate. But Troup, who had displaced Clark in a close vote in the legislature in 1823, managed to hold the governor's mansion in the first popular election and staved off democratic opposition by harping on issues designed to unite the planters and the backcountry. Clark and his supporters had generally agreed with the planters on Indian removal. And so, as John C. Calhoun, still a leading nationalist, saw it, Troup, like other "mad and wicked" Crawford men, began blending "the Slave with the Indian question, in order, if possible, to consolidate the whole South" as a sectional political force under the Radicals' command.[21]

Of special interest to land-hungry Georgians, planters and backcountry farmers alike, were nearly five million acres of rich cotton lands, lying between the Chattahoochee and Flint rivers in the northwestern part of the state, legally occupied by Creeks and Cherokees. Since 1802, the Indian tribes had lost huge tracts of land in extortionate federal treaties. By the 1820s, the Indians were fed up, and the Monroe administration, led by Secretary of War Calhoun, agreed to let them stay put. But Governor Troup, working with a part-Creek cousin of his named William McIntosh, arranged for a total cession of Creek lands with paltry compensation in the so-called Treaty of Indian Springs, signed on February 12, 1825. Amid the confusion following Adams's election as president, the Senate quickly approved the treaty, and Adams agreed to it—but after learning about its fraudulence, he suspended the cession. Governor Troup forced a crisis by ordering a survey of the lands in question preparatory to their distribution by lottery. On the Indian question, Troup insisted, the federal government was now powerless to interfere with the State of Georgia.

The Creeks reacted to the Indian Springs cession by closing ranks and executing the traitor McIntosh and his Indian co-conspirators. The Adams administration was more uncertain. Secretary Clay, in contrast to Calhoun, thought the Indians ineluctably inferior to Anglo-Saxons. Adams agreed, remarking that there was "too much foundation" for Clay's assertion that the Indians were "destined to extinction" and "not worth preserving." Embarrassed by the Indian Springs treaty, the administration tried to save face by negotiating a second agreement, the Treaty of Washington, which restored to the Creeks a tiny portion of their original lands and which the Senate duly ratified. But Governor Troup and the Georgia legislature, smelling blood, refused to recognize the new agreement, then ordered the commanders of two Georgia militia divisions to prepare to repel a hostile federal invasion.[22]

In an inflammatory declaration sent to Secretary of War James Barbour, Troup scorned federal authority:

> From the first decisive act of hostility, you will be considered and treated as a public enemy; and, with the less repugnance, because you, to whom we might constitutionally have appealed for our own defense against invasion, are yourselves the invaders, and, what is more, the unblushing allies of the savages whose cause you have adopted.

Troup's constitutional presumptions were veering toward what would soon be an even more radical theory of undivided state sovereignty. "The governor's roughness and violence," the nationalist *Niles' Weekly Register* observed, amounted to a "desperate effort to . . . bring about a political scramble," reminiscent of the Hartford Convention and contemptuous of the Union. Yet after the White House announced it would, if necessary, meet force with force, first the Senate and then President Adams yielded to the Georgians and allowed them to regain the entirely of the Creek lands and commerce the Creeks' final expulsion. In the first menacing assertion of what came to be known as southern state-rights sectionalism, Adams permitted the nation to surrender to a state.[23]

The ironies of the situation—and for Adams, the political humiliation—deepened over the months to come. Vice President Calhoun, who had seen his "civilizing" Indian policy rejected, hastened his own dramatic shift from nationalism to southern sectionalism, under political pressure from South Carolina's equivalents of the Troup Radicals. Emboldened by their victory, Troup's men, having narrowed the breach between themselves and the backcountry, turned their sights against the Cherokees, hoping to remove them as well. Adams, although now formally as well as personally committed to Indian removal, did not follow up with any practical plan to achieve it, which only hardened the surging Radical South against him.

From a long-term perspective, the debacle offers a glimpse at a political process that would soon dominate southern politics. In Indian removal, Troup and the Georgia planters found a winning issue that, by appealing to land hunger, racial antagonisms, frontier fears, and suspicion of Yankees, undercut the backcountry forces led by John Clark. By then attaching to that issue the slogan of "state rights," and pitting local prerogatives—"the sovereignty of Georgia," Troup proclaimed—against a meddlesome, outsider federal government, the planters consolidated local support. State and sectional loyalty, buttressed by racism and desire for land, supplanted the democratic agitation that had been exacerbated by the Panic of 1819—and raised troubling implications about the nation's future.[24]

One of the planters not at all impressed by Troup's state-rights vehemence was Andrew Jackson. Watching the affair from the Hermitage, still furious at Adams and Clay, Jackson fully approved of Indian removal. On the Georgia matter, however, he thought the president was acting in good faith, if weakly, while Troup and his accomplices were demagogically abetting their personal ambitions. Troup's behavior, he observed in 1825, "has afforded evidence of derangement from some cause." The entire affair, he wrote, was "produced by designing Whitemen" who wanted to distract attention from the fraud used to extract the "fictitious" original Indian Springs treaty from the Creeks. "State rights and military despotism are themes where eloquence can be employed, and the feelings of the nation aroused," he added some months later, but he hoped that "both these themes will slumber for some other occasion." Jackson had no respect for the administration's empty threats—nobody was silly enough, he wrote, to believe that men like Adams and Clay "who so oft have denounced mil[itary] chieftains" would "raise the sword against a sover[e]ign State"—but his contempt for the administration did not change his mind about the limits of state sovereignty. In due course, he himself would battle against even more extreme versions of the themes he wished would slumber, as developed by the transformed ex-nationalist, John C. Calhoun.[25]

More immediately, the developments in Georgia dramatized the dangerous drift of the administration's policy. Had Adams summoned the nerve to call Troup's bluff and send troops to Georgia, it is likely that the other southern states (save, perhaps, South Carolina) would have supported or at least acquiesced in federal action. Instead, Troup's triumph encouraged Alabama and Mississippi to adopt extreme state-rights positions regarding Indian tribes within their own borders, and set the stage for new and even more worrisome collisions between the federal government and the states over the tariff of 1824. Adams, who displayed little enough concern for the Indians, bears responsibility for allowing the southern bullies to have their way.

Adams's weakness must be understood not as a personal failing—in politics, he was normally anything but weak—but in the context of his deteriorating political situation. He well might have called up troops to force Troup to back down, but would have thereby risked the outbreak of a bloody civil conflict. And he would have done so in the teeth of intense opposition from within his own cabinet, above all from Henry Clay, as well as from the Senate, where one committee advised him to complete the Creeks' relinquishment of Georgia land. Trapped, Adams bowed to political circumstances, which only made those circumstances grimmer.

The consequences of Adams's political slide would not become fully apparent until the final year of his presidency. Until then, events in Washington—and, indeed, conventional political events—receded in importance. As Adams failed to revive national harmony, popular movements redirected public loyalties and unleashed fresh ideas and programs. Many of these movements emerged from outside electoral politics, but they would all have dramatic political effects on both the theory and the practice of American democracy. The most profound of them involved the greatest explosion of evangelical religious fervor yet in the nation's history.

RAPTURES OF JOY AND DEVOTION: PIETY, POLITICS, AND THE SECOND GREAT AWAKENING

In 1771, when the Regulator country democrats of North Carolina squared off against the royal governor William Tryon, a backwoods Prebysterian minister, David Caldwell, tried unsuccessfully to mediate between his plebeian flock and the imperial British government. Caldwell became an active patriot in 1776 and, after independence, a leading participant in North Carolina politics. He left legacies in both politics and religious life. His grandson, John Caldwell Calhoun, would become one of the leading American nationalists—and then the leading southern sectionalist—of his day. And at the turn of the nineteenth century, several young ministers whom Caldwell had helped train headed west to sanctify the newly settled farmers and planters of Kentucky.[26]

Among the most successful of Caldwell's students was a tall, awkward Pennsylvania-born minister of Scots-Irish extraction, James McGready. What McGready lacked in elegance he made up for with eloquence and homiletic fervor. In 1797 (and thereafter for three years running) his sermonizing sparked a remarkable excitement and religious revival in the still-raw settlements of Logan County, in southwestern Kentucky near the Tennessee border. Then, in August 1801, in a clutch of cabins called Cane Ridge in Bourbon County near Lexington, another of David Caldwell's pupils, Barton Stone, hosted an ecumenical three-day communion service that turned into a week-long explosion of ecstatic devotion, involving more than twenty preachers (Presbyterian and Methodist, white and black) and upwards of twenty thousand worshippers. The roar of raucous piety at Cane Ridge sounded like Niagara: "Sinners dropping down on every hand," one participating minister wrote, "shrieking, groaning, crying for mercy, convoluted; professors [of religion] praying, agonizing, fainting, falling down in distress, for sinners, or in raptures of joy!"[27]

One year after Cane Ridge, hundreds of miles away in New Haven, Connecticut, a more sedate but still remarkable revival of religion gripped the undergraduates of Yale College. In 1795, Timothy Dwight, grandson of the great New England evangelist Jonathan Edwards, had ascended to the presidency of Yale in place of Thomas Jefferson's friend Ezra Stiles, hoping to rid the place of its reputation for irreligion and pro-French radical politics. Dwight's stern hand did not work immediate wonders—in 1800, there was only one church member in the college's graduating class—but in 1802, a revival hit the campus. "Wheresoever students were found," remarked one participant, the future minister Noah Porter, "in their rooms, in the chapel, in the hall, in the college-yard, in their walks about the city—the reigning impression was, 'surely God is in this place!' The salvation of the soul was the greatest subject of conversation, of absorbing interest."[28]

Fifteen more revivals would break out at Yale over the next forty years. Under Dwight's spur, Yale became the intellectual seedbed of the so-called New Haven Theology, formulated by Dwight's student, professor of theology Nathaniel W. Taylor, which recast and energized received Calvinist doctrine. And although "Pope" Dwight could not save the Connecticut Standing Order (which finally collapsed one year after his death in 1817), his students, above all the great organizing cleric Lyman Beecher, spread revised versions of the New Haven revival out into the rest of New England, and then into upstate New York, Ohio, and points west—wherever New Englanders and their children settled in large numbers.

The concurrent events at Cane Ridge and Yale were in no way the result of a coordinated effort. Their differences—in denominational origins, liturgy, and social setting—outweighed their similarities. Likewise, the so-called Second Great Awakening—of which these revivals were harbingers, and which would last into the 1840s—was a diverse movement, generated by impulses too unruly and doctrines too contradictory to be contained by any one organization. It was a movement that, at its outermost edges, saw farmers and factory workers talk directly with Christ Jesus, angels appear in remote villages bearing wholly new dispensations and commandments from the Lord, and women of all ages and backgrounds commune with the spirits of the dead. Closer to its core, the Awakening saw rival denominations (especially Methodists and Baptists) denounce each others' beliefs and practices nearly as much as they denounced sin and Satan.[29]

A few recurring and overriding themes are detectable through the furor. First, the sheer scale of religious conversions was astounding, in every part of the

nation. Although the figures are sketchy, it appears that as few as one in ten
Americans were active church members in the unsettled aftermath of the American Revolution. The evangelizing that ensued proceeded, at first, in fits and
starts, but gathered tremendous momentum after 1825. By the 1840s, the preponderance of Americans—as many as eight in ten—were churched, chiefly as
evangelizing Methodists or Baptists (in the South) or as so-called New School
revivalist Presbyterians or Congregationalists (in the North). What was, in 1787,
a nation of nominal Christians—its public culture shaped more by Enlightenment rationalism than Protestant piety—had turned, by the mid-1840s, into the
most devoted evangelical Protestant nation on earth.

Second, although it is better understood as a movement of the heart and the
spirit than of the mind, the Awakening asserted a hopeful, crisis-driven, post-
Calvinist theology. The awakeners' devotions contrasted sharply both with the
hyper-Calvinism of the Edwardseans and the Old School Presbyterians (with
their strict belief in predestination and God's inscrutable will) and with the laxity
about salvation promoted by well-heeled Unitarians and more plebeian Universalists. The degree of departure from Calvinist orthodoxy varied: whereas the
Methodists and New School churches largely abandoned the central Calvinist
doctrines of election and predestination, the Baptists, at least formally, retained
them. (Some Baptists, objecting to what they perceived as even the slightest
backsliding, formed their own more fiercely traditional Calvinist connections.)
But in all of the largest denominations, there was a fresh emphasis placed on
individual rejection of personal sin and on the struggle to attain God's merciful
grace, through His Son, the Redeemer Jesus Christ—an intense process that culminated in a wrenching moment of spiritual rebirth.

Emotional display reached a deafening intensity in the camp-meeting style
that prevailed in the South. Drawing heavily on the "new measures" of the Wesleyan Methodists, the camp-meeting phenomenon shattered the unity of the
largely Presbyterian clerisy of the southern and southwestern backcountry,
prompting some church leaders to back off in disapproval and others (including
the Cane Ridge preacher, Barton Stone) to reject their own Calvinist orthodoxy.
The communal camp-meeting uproars (commonly attended, on their outskirts,
by scoffers, drinkers, and prostitutes, drawn by the mere presence of a throng) in
turn solidified the believers' faith that they truly had gained redemption and a
holy discipline that set them apart from the rest of the world (not least from the
sinners at the edges of the crowd). For the preachers, meanwhile, the camp
meetings' aftermath helped institutionalize the revival, binding the fresh harvests
of souls into local congregations that could be linked to other congregations,
within regular, regionally organized denominations.[30]

Socially and spiritually, the southern revivals paradoxically challenged and
confirmed existing structures of authority. In contrast to the Episcopal and old-

line Presbyterian connections, and the smaller but influential deistic currents among the enlightened gentry, the revivals bred a devotional upsurge from the lower and middle strata of southern life that can only be described as democratic. In place of refined, highly trained ministers, young Methodist circuit riders and unschooled Baptist farmer-preachers became cynosures of religious life, preaching a gospel of holiness open to the most degraded and forlorn of God's children. Simplicity and directness in all things were signs of grace, in contrast to ornament and artifice. Among the truest believers, restraint in all but love of Christ was the only way to escape hellfire. "Therefore avoid the allurements of Voluptuousness," one self-reproving Methodist preacher wrote in his diary, "and fly every temptation that leads to her banquet as you would the devil himself."[31]

Most unsettling of all, in the southern revival's opening stages, was the announced indifference of some evangelicals to race and their outright hostility to slavery. Methodist circuit riders were particularly aggressive in seeking out black converts, slave and free. In the 1780s, conferences of Methodists and Baptists condemned slaveholding as, in the words of one Methodist assembly, "contrary to the laws of God, man, and nature, and hurtful to society, contrary to the dictates of conscience and pure religion." (In 1784, the Methodists actually moved to excommunicate slaveholders, although they quickly retreated into less coercive methods of moral suasion.) At least one black minister preached to a separate throng of blacks at the Cane Ridge meeting in 1801. In the first wave of conversions, African Americans accounted for as much as one-third to one-quarter of the membership in individual evangelical churches. And into the 1820s, evangelical egalitarianism among whites helped make the mountainous areas of the upper southern states, notably Tennessee, home to the largest number of antislavery societies in the nation.[32]

By 1830, however, the more egalitarian and antislavery implications of the southern revivals had adapted to the resurgent slaveholders' regime. Middling evangelical farmers who cashed in on the cotton boom and became small slaveholders had little use for imprecations against African bondage. Established planters mostly ignored antislavery preaching with a cold contempt—although, from time to time, they took firmer action, as in Charleston where, in 1800, authorities publicly burned Methodist antislavery pamphlets. In 1816, the Methodists formally gave up on trying to end slaveholding, while still pronouncing it "contrary to the principles of moral justice." Over the next thirty years, southern evangelicalism, among whites, transformed itself into a doctrine of Christian mastery, no longer troubled by human bondage but providing slaveholders with a set of religious and moral imperatives to treat the slaves, as they would all subordinates, on the highest moral level, in accord with scriptural injunctions. While instilling order and benevolence, the churches also reinforced the slaveholders' claims to supremacy. "We who own slaves," the well-known South Carolina Baptist clergyman James C. Furman wrote to a master suspected of wrongdoing, "honor God's law in the exercise of our authority."[33]

More broadly, the southern evangelicals' spiritual egalitarianism centered increasingly on inculcating personal holiness to the exclusion of all else—an ethos of individual sanctification that precluded wider secular campaigns or benevolent reform. Older social distinctions between elite nonevangelicals and plebeian evangelicals blurred, as successful Methodists and Baptists began striving for their own sort of refinement, signaled by the building of several denominational academies and colleges, like the Virginia Baptist Education Society of Richmond, all across the region. Simultaneously, the color line grew darker, creating a southern revivalist piety that, among whites, fully accommodated itself to the slaveholders' regime. Slaveholders did spearhead the spread of Christian devotion in rural areas, especially in the 1830s and 1840s, but did so with an eye to provide their property with the kind of moral uplift that would make them better slaves (and make the masters better Christian stewards). Black evangelical churches, with their own preachers and proselytizers, held their own services, most conspicuously in seaboard cities like Charleston with large free black populations. But these segregated houses of worship came under close scrutiny from officials as possible breeding grounds of sedition—scrutiny that intensified following Charleston's allegedly church-based Denmark Vesey affair in 1822. Among the slaves as well as free blacks, despite their masters' intentions and surveillance, Christianity became what they made it, a source of communal solidarity, pride, and endurance, with a millennial edge of impending liberation. But among whites, slaveholder and nonslaveholders, the Second Great Awakening became a pillar of the reborn slaveholding order.[34]

The northern awakening involved dramatic adaptations by the declining patrician Yankee establishment. Pressured on one side by the passing popularity of anticlerical "Jacobin" skeptics and, even more, by dissenting evangelicals and liberalizing Unitarians who opposed their political privileges, the old-line Calvinist clergy had embraced Federalism with unsurpassed fervor. The election of the deist and secularist Jefferson in 1801 and the rise of a viable northern Republican party further sapped the clerics' dominance. But Timothy Dwight's reclamation of Yale from the infidels energized the orthodox by borrowing the evangelicals' voluntarist organizing methods—above all, the formation of the Moral Society to effect and enforce what one of his acolytes called a "reformation" among students and faculty. When Dwight's student Nathaniel Taylor loosened Calvinist doctrine and argued that salvation was a matter of individual regeneration as well as God's will, fresh opportunities opened to expand the flock of the faithful. Looking back, Taylor's accomplice, Lyman Beecher, would even call the Connecticut Standing Order's destruction in 1818, paradoxically, "*the best thing that ever happened*," because it forced the more complacent congregations to evangelize. "By voluntary efforts, societies, missions, and revivals," Beecher observed, "[ministers] exert a deeper influence than ever they could by queues and shoe buckles, and cocked hats and gold-headed canes."[35]

Beecher was the most vigorous and ambitious of the Yankee missionaries. Born and raised in New Haven, well outside the local patriciate—both his father and his grandfather were blacksmiths—Beecher was an eminently practical and blunt man of God, more a polemicist and organizer than a theologian. Ordained a Presbyterian minister in 1799, he took up his first ministry in East Hampton, Long Island, where he gained notice in 1804 for a sermon, following Alexander Hamilton and Aaron Burr's fatal interview, that denounced dueling and its sinful code of "honor." In 1810, he moved to Litchfield, Connecticut, and burnished his reputation with Dwight-inspired sermons on the gloomy state of the nation's soul. Everywhere, Beecher charged, "[t]he name of God is blasphemed; the bible is denounced; the Sabbath is profaned; the worship of God is neglected; intemperance hath destroyed its thousands . . . while luxury, with its diversified evils, with a rapidity unparalleled, is spreading in every direction, and through every class."[36]

Beecher's solution was to encourage circuit-riding ministers to spark revivals and establish local lay moral reform groups. In 1813, Beecher organized the Connecticut Society for the Promotion of Good Morals, which quickly boasted dozens of branches and several thousand members. Three years later, he helped launch the Domestic Missionary Society for Connecticut and Vicinity, sending young reformist Congregational and "New Side" Presbyterian ministers to convert the soaring numbers of Yankee migrants in upstate New York and northern New England. At about the same time, like-minded churchmen opened a branch of the New England Tract Society. By 1817, Beecher and his allies had established a mass-circulation religious magazine and, in Hartford, a charitable school for the deaf and dumb, the first of its kind in the country. Quicker than many of his colleagues, Beecher came to understand how the successful voluntarist innovations of the revivals had rendered formal state support unnecessary. "[T]ruly," he wrote, "we do not stand on the confines of destruction. The mass is changing. We are becoming another people."[37]

Methodist circuit riders and Baptist exhorters also crisscrossed the North with growing success, but it was the allied front of evangelized Presbyterians and Congregationalists, the so-called Presbygationals, who left the strongest spiritual, cultural, and, in time, political mark in the northern states. The Presbygationals' influence redoubled in the 1820s when, backed by pious businessmen in the seaboard cities, they confederated various state and local efforts to form the American Sunday-School Union (claiming fifty thousand students), the American Tract Society, the American Home Missionary Society, and the American Society for the Promotion of Temperance (a special interest of Lyman

Beecher's). And by the latter years of John Quincy Adams's presidency, Presbygationals were contemplating political efforts to shape public morality. Like their
southern counterparts, Yankee evangelicals eschewed parties and formal electoral politics as profane and divisive. Yet far more than most southerners, the
northerners believed that proper moral stewardship demanded direct participation in secular affairs, including the promotion of what the Philadelphia pastor
Ezra Stiles Ely described in 1827, a bit rashly and vaguely, as a "Christian party
in politics."[38]

The first notable evangelical political campaign focused on ending desecra-
tion of the Sabbath. Despite local ordinances enforcing the restriction of commerce on Sundays, Sabbath breaking had increased across the country during
the early years of the nineteenth century. Most egregiously, in the eyes of the
pious, the Jeffersonian Congress, in 1810, had passed a postal regulation requiring postmasters to conduct business on Sunday whenever mail arrived on that
day. Already perturbed by the Jeffersonians' adamant hostility to any merging of
church and state, evangelicals saw the Sunday postal law as an assault, both real
and symbolic, on proper Christian order. By compelling Sunday mail operations, the government not only forced thousands of postal workers to violate the
Sabbath, but also invited townsmen and farmers from surrounding districts to
defile the Lord's Day, which in turn invited local businessmen to do the same
and encouraged local officials to ignore Sunday closing laws. That so many
local postmasters (political appointees all) were also petty merchants and
"greengrocers"—meaning that they sold liquor—only worsened the blasphemous rowdiness. Reestablishing the Sabbath was as "necessary to the health of
the state," one evangelical observed, as enforcing "laws against murder and
polygamy."[39]

Sabbatarian efforts gained little notice until Lyman Beecher and his friends
formed the General Union for Promoting the Observance of the Christian Sabbath in May 1828. Thanks to the financial backing of numerous, newly successful businessmen-converts with Yankee backgrounds—above all the flour
merchant Josiah Bissell of Rochester, New York, and the silk merchant Lewis
Tappan of Manhattan—the Union deployed all of the organizing and proselytizing techniques familiar to the northern revivalists, including tract distribution,
public rallies, and prayer concerts. Bissell supplied the money to back a six-day,
blue-law stagecoach service. A similar Sabbatarian boat line was established to
travel (liquor-free) along the Erie Canal from Albany to Buffalo, but never on
Sundays. Along with Tappan, Bissell toured the friendly Presbygational churches
of the Northeast to drum up support for the cause. Over the summer and
autumn of 1828, while most of the political nation was embroiled in a presidential campaign, the Sabbatarian machine promoted a national petition campaign
directed at Congress. By year's end, Bissell was predicting imminent triumph,

telling Tappan that the "petitions were flowing in well," and actually welcoming displays of anti-Sabbatarian opinion in the West as "just enough . . . to give a zest to the Sabbath measures."[40]

With their new emphasis on inner sanctification, moral choice, and benevolent stewardship, the proponents of what came to be known as the New School transformed a staid New England Protestant devotionalism into a vital evangelizing creed, distinct from rationalist Unitarians and traditional Calvinists and from southern camp-meeting Methodists and Baptists. Agitation in turn created the institutional basis of what would become an entirely new kind of political power, democratic in tone and sophisticated in its organizational tactics, but very different from the main forms of democratic politics that had emerged since the Revolution. The full meaning of those efforts would only become clear when new coalitions in secular politics displaced the disarray of the 1820s. And those new political alignments would be shaped by yet another enthusiasm that arose from the Yankee areas of western New York during John Quincy Adams's presidency—one that began with an abduction and a rotting corpse.

ANTI-MASONRY AND "A SECOND INDEPENDENCE"

On October 7, 1827, in the settlement of Lewiston, a drowned man's body washed up at Oak Orchard Creek, where the creek joins Lake Ontario. Although the body was badly decomposed, many people in the neighborhood were certain that it had been one William Morgan, who had disappeared more than a year earlier after being snatched from the Canandaigua town jail. Morgan's widow came out to Lewiston and confirmed that the putrid mass looked like her vanished husband; Morgan's dentist inspected the corpse's teeth and affirmed the identity; and the body was duly buried with grand obsequies in Morgan's adopted hometown, Batavia. Others were not so sure. After several disinterments, and amid charges that certain interested parties had tampered with the body to make it look more like Morgan, the local coroner officially ruled that the dead man could not be named. But by then, the mysterious corpse had become a cause célèbre, deepening the popular outrage against Morgan's kidnappers—the members, allegedly, of a vast murder and cover-up conspiracy involving the Order of Ancient Free and Accepted Masons.[41]

Morgan had been a perfect nobody until a few weeks before his disappearance. A native of Virginia, he had wandered around upstate New York as an itinerant bricklayer and stonemason. Upon settling in Leroy, New York, outside Rochester, he claimed membership in the Masonic Order, and his new neighbors admitted him to the local lodge. At some point in the early 1820s, however, Morgan relocated to nearby Batavia and was denied Masonic membership there by a lodge that took a dim view of his dubious social standing and inability to land a job. Enraged—and, quite possibly, seeing an opportunity to make some easy money—Morgan enlisted the aid of a Batavia printer, David Miller, and published a purported full-scale exposé of the lower-degree Masonic rituals and lore. Morgan's tract circulated widely around the country. Incensed loyal Masons tried to burn down Miller's printshop and harassed both Miller and Morgan with petty legal charges. Morgan was twice remanded to the Canandaigua jail, the second time for an alleged unpaid debt, but suddenly was released to two men who paid his debt, shunted him into a waiting carriage, and carted him off westward to Fort Niagara—where he disappeared forever.

Within a month of Morgan's disappearance, western New York State was awash in broadsides and newspaper articles describing the events, which touched off a wave of protest meetings. Governor DeWitt Clinton, himself a Mason, offered a reward for apprehending the kidnappers. Grand juries in five counties investigated suspect Masons, including the sheriff in Canandaigua, who was convicted for complicity in Morgan's disappearance. But most of the accused and the suspected escaped punishment, either by fleeing the state or by finding the charges against them summarily dropped by judges and juries believed to be dominated by Masons. At many of the trials that did take place—legal proceedings continued for four years after Morgan's disappearance—Masonic witnesses refused to testify, placing their obligations to the secret fraternity above those to society. The Masonic lodges, meanwhile, insisted on the Order's innocence and took no disciplinary actions whatsoever. Some Masons tried to blame Morgan for his own misfortunes because he had broken his oath of secrecy about Masonic rituals; a few even charged that Morgan had collaborated in his own kidnapping, to enlarge his notoriety and sell more pamphlets. The Mason's ripostes only deepened suspicions that Morgan had been murdered, and that the Order was conspiring to protect the evildoers. The appearance of the corpse in Oak Orchard Creek came as belated but positive proof to the growing Anti-Masonic movement that they had been correct all along. If not the murdered man himself, one leader of the agitation said, the body was "a good enough Morgan," unless and until he turned up alive.[42]

The continuing intrigues of New York politics turned the affair into a major political event. Following the disputed presidential election of 1824–25, Martin Van Buren had switched his national allegiance to the cheated Andrew Jackson, and by the summer of 1827, Van Buren was cultivating a pro-Jackson alliance with his old enemy, Governor Clinton. But both Jackson and Clinton were high-degree Masons, and Jackson was a slaveholder to boot, which offended transplanted Yankees in the strongest Anti-Masonic districts—all of which caught the notice of Van Buren's political opponents. With Van Buren's allies shouting about phony issues, so-called Anti-Masons nominated candidates in the 1827 legislative elections who pledged to uproot the secret order's malevolent influence. The Oak Orchard corpse controversy was still raging when New Yorkers went to the polls and elected fifteen Anti-Masons from several western counties to the state assembly. A strange and unpredictable political movement had been born—one that would soon be afoot from Pennsylvania to Maine, and particularly in New England and areas, like western New York, settled heavily by migrants from New England.[43]

The rise of Anti-Masonry has often been linked, at times facilely, to a species of extremist lower-class paranoia supposedly peculiar to American democracy. The Anti-Masons' claims that a gigantic conspiracy had seized control of the nation's institutions were, to be sure, overwrought and ripe for political manipulation. But fears of all-powerful conspiratorial secret societies—including, prominently, the Freemasons—were rife throughout the revolutionized Atlantic world at the end of the eighteenth and beginning of the nineteenth century. Those fears cut across class lines: prior to the Anti-Masonic outbursts of the 1820s, the greatest American conspiracy theory had come not from the easily deluded unwashed but from the highly educated New England Federalist clergy, who blamed both the French Revolution and the appearance of the Jeffersonian opposition on secret cabals, including the European-based, so-called Bavarian Illuminati. The Anti-Masons' thinking was perfectly in keeping with the broader American republican outlook, inherited from the Revolutionary era, which blamed social disorder on political corruption by select and malign factions or cabals. There was, moreover, justified outrage at the New York lodges' efforts to suppress Morgan's publication and reasonable suspicion that some sort of cover-up had taken place. The Masons' refusal to cooperate with public authorities threw fuel on the fire. That so many of the judges and other authorities were themselves Masons made Anti-Masonry an intelligible response to events.[44]

The Morgan excitement fed long-growing popular resentments originating in the rapid commercialization of the northeastern states. The Masonic Order had enjoyed a long history in America when the outburst against it began. Especially popular in New England, Freemasonry flourished among upper- and middling-class men throughout the early republic, counting within its fraternity such patriots as George Washington, Benjamin Franklin, and at least eleven other Framers of the Constitution. Dedicated to spreading their own blend of latitudinarian Christian virtue and crypto-Enlightenment reason, Masons performed a panoply of ceremonial rituals and symbols, including the wearing of their famous white aprons, which offered members an elaborate, esoteric nondenominational aesthetic absent in most Protestant churches—and that was open to men of lukewarm religious devotion. The public appearance of the Masonic lodges in full regalia at civic events gave the Order an air of importance. The intense secrecy that shrouded other lodge rituals from view made Freemasonry all the more

charismatic and high-minded among its brotherhood. "[E]very character, figure, and emblem, depicted in a lodge," Thomas Smith Webb, the early-
nineteenth-century Masonic organizer, wrote in 1821, "has a moral tendency,
and inculcates the practice of virtue."[45]

Freemasonry's looming crisis was rooted in its success, as well as in its
worldly, meritocratic ethos. At the end of the eighteenth century, the lodges had
a distinctly Federalist air about them, a by-product partly of Freemasonry's popularity in New England. After 1800, however, increasing numbers of Jeffersonian and Republican partisans and officeholders gained admission to the
Order—including, in New York, not a few of Van Buren's Bucktails—in keeping with Freemasonry's openness to successful men of influence and virtue,
regardless of social background, religious affiliation, or political connections.
The Order also grew phenomenally, especially in the middle Atlantic states,
where the number of lodges rose from 327 to 525 over the decade from 1810 to
1820. In the developing cities and towns along the widening thoroughfares of
northern commerce, above all the Erie Canal, young men of the commercial
and professional classes, separated from their kin back East, gained from the
lodges fraternal connections and an instant badge of social distinction and
acceptance. These, in turn, bred a mixture of power, exclusiveness, and self-
satisfaction that, to outsiders, could look like arrogance—the kind of arrogance
that, as in the Morgan case, set itself above the law. "In the foundation of every
public building we have beheld the interference of these mystic artisans with
their symbolic insignia," one Anti-Mason complained, "in every public procession, we have seen their flaunting banners, their muslin robes, and mimic
crowns." The Masons replied that they were, indeed, a special set of men, the
natural leaders of the community.[46]

The Morgan case ripped away that perceived complacency and exposed rising
moral and political anxieties about Freemasonry's proliferation—and about how
the Masons, with their unfair advantages, had established what amounted to a
hidden unelected government, run by and for themselves, that could manipulate
the government elected by the people. With men of power in their secret ranks,
one Anti-Masonic article explained, the Masons could rule wherever and whenever they liked: "in the desk—in the legislative hall—on the bench—in every
gathering of business—in every party of pleasure—in every enterprise of government—in every domestic circle—in peace and in war—among enemies and
friends—in one place as well as another." To older, Federalist-oriented elites,
Freemasonry seemed to have fallen into the hands of aggressive upstarts who,
although successful in business, lacked the proper education and breeding
required of civic leaders. To poorer, less-connected farmers and rural shopkeepers, the Masons looked like an incipient self-created nobility, based on mysterious principles known only to the favored few. What, they wanted to know, was

going on behind the thick barred doors of those Masonic temples? What private business arrangements were being hatched; what political deals were being cut? Even worse: What debauched revelries did the Masons indulge in once freed from the obligations of the hearthside and the restraints of public scrutiny?[47]

As the lurid speculation mounted amid the Morgan affair, propagandists and opportunists threatened to commandeer the Anti-Masonic movement. To compete with local newspaper editors—who included a substantial number of Masons and kept the excitement out of their columns—an Anti-Masonic "free press" appeared in every county of western New York. Former Masons organized mock lodges and performed the Order's secret rituals in public view. Hair-raising accusations and confessions, along with suspect solicitations on behalf of William Morgan's bereft widow, began circulating in cheap pamphlet form much like the religious tracts of the revivalists. Yet the men who made the most of the Anti-Masonic excitement were not profiteers but capable pro-Adams politicians with genuine Anti-Masonic allegiances. Their leader was the Rochester editor and printer, Thurlow Weed.

Born in 1797, in a log cabin near the town of Catskill, New York, Edward Thurlow Weed was a thoroughly self-made man. Raised in an economically marginal and peripatetic household, he had entered the printer's trade as a thirteen-year-old apprentice in Onondaga in central New York (whence his father, Joel, chronically in debt, had moved the family two years earlier). As a tramp journeyman printer, he held jobs in various localities from Cooperstown to Albany, joined an early trade union, the New York Typographical Society, eventually married, and acquired a little weekly newspaper of his own, which he called *The Republican Agriculturalist*, in the Chenango County town of Norwich. Weed made his name, though, farther west in Rochester, where, after selling the *Agriculturalist* in 1820, he became junior editor of the anti–Van Buren *Evening Telegraph*. A supporter of DeWitt Clinton and of the Erie Canal project that promised to make Rochester a boomtown, Weed coarsely lit into the Bucktails as a corrupt cabal of wire-pullers interested only in exploiting the spoils of office. ("Van Buren's pimps," he called them at one point.) In 1823, Weed was one of the local leaders of the Clintonian People's Party, and the following year (while supporting John Quincy Adams for the presidency and after lobbying with state legislators in Albany on behalf of local banking interests), he was elected state assemblyman on the People's Party ticket. A tall, darkly handsome young man, Weed cut an impressive figure in Albany, but he remained financially strapped. When his old *Telegraph* boss put the paper up for sale, though, he obtained a twenty-five-hundred-dollar loan from a wealthy Clintonite friend, snapped up part-ownership of the paper, energetically increased its paid advertising base, and, in September 1826—the month that William Morgan disappeared—shifted it from a weekly to a semiweekly publication schedule.[48]

Like most of his anti-Bucktail neighbors, many of whom were Masons or familiar with members of the Order, Weed initially regarded the tumult over the Morgan affair skeptically. (Morgan had approached Weed about publishing his exposé, but Weed wanted nothing to do with it.) After visiting Lewiston early in 1827, however, Weed became persuaded that Morgan had been murdered, and he joined with those calling on the Masons to denounce the crime and help identify the perpetrators. The lodges' silence pushed him over the line. By the start of the autumn election campaign, Weed had allied himself with the Anti-Masonic crusade, even though, as a consequence, subscriptions to the *Telegraph* dropped sharply.

The Anti-Masons' surprisingly strong showing in the 1827 elections vindicated Weed's political shrewdness as well as his sense of outrage. In purely political terms, Anti-Masonry not only inflamed public sensibilities; it offered a wonderful solution to what had become several serious difficulties for the anti-Bucktail partisans. To their chagrin, DeWitt Clinton, hoping to improve his own future, had recommitted himself to Andrew Jackson's presidential candidacy, in alliance with Martin Van Buren. The Adams administration and its supporters, now known as National Republicans, already tainted by the alleged corrupt bargain, showed a singular ineptness in handling local patronage and seemed, on their own, a weak alternative to the Van Burenites. With the Erie Canal completed, there was a dearth of issues with which to inflame local anti-Bucktail voters. Suddenly, an independent popular movement arose, pledged to the protection of republican liberty against corrupt insiders—a movement, based in heavily Yankee western counties, that appealed, for different reasons, to evangelicals, temperance men, and ordinary farmers put off by eastern elitists and their smug imitators. Organized in politics, under Weed's careful hand, the Anti-Masons of 1827 preached democracy against the entrenched self-styled democrats, Van Buren's Bucktails, much as Clinton's People's Party had three years earlier.

After the 1827 elections, Weed traveled to Washington, where he opened negotiations to complete a quiet formal alliance between the administration and the politicized Anti-Masons. Upon his return to Rochester early in 1828, he did what he had done best, establishing a new paper, *The Anti-Masonic Enquirer*, while helping to found, with his Clintonian, anti-Bucktail friends, a formal Anti-Masonic party. The day before the *Enquirer*'s first issue appeared, DeWitt Clinton suddenly died, clearing the way for a thorough reorganization of Clintonian voters under new leadership. Through the *Enquirer*, Weed became one of those leaders, as he stoked the fires of Anti-Masonry by ridiculing Masonic pretensions—holding off, for the moment, from backing Adams for reelection, but with every intention of doing so once the presidential campaign began in earnest later that year.[49]

While Weed plotted, a passing acquaintance of his, William Henry Seward, was following a similar political course, attempting to ally the National Republicans and the Anti-Masons. Seward had first encountered the editor by chance in Rochester three years earlier, when, on an excursion to Niagara Falls, his wagon got mired in a patch of mud and Weed came to his assistance. The two men were strikingly different: Weed, the poor man's son, well over six feet tall, hard-bitten and calculating; Seward, a Phi Beta Kappa college graduate and lawyer, the son of an affluent Republican officeholder, red-haired, slight, and with a penchant for idealism. Their common interests were political. Seward, although raised in a Bucktail household, had broken ranks, along with his father, in 1824, persuaded that Van Buren and his allies had, as he wrote a friend, "sunk into cunning and chicanery." John Quincy Adams was far more to his liking, a man hobbled by what Seward described as "pedantry," but a champion of the moral, educational, and economic improvements that Seward thought essential to local and national development.[50]

When Anti-Masonry spread to Seward's home in Auburn over the winter of 1827–28, Seward formally remained a National Republican, but also quietly helped draft Anti-Masonic speeches and proclamations. The Anti-Masons of Cayuga, after agreeing to form a coalition ticket with the Adams men, then nominated Seward for Congress without first notifying him. The nomination offended National Republicans, who thought Seward had become too clever by half; Seward, embarrassed, withdrew from the race, which ensured the election of the Bucktail candidate. Thereafter, convinced that National Republicanism was dead in the water, Seward threw himself into political Anti-Masonry, proclaiming it the true cause of the common man—all of which led him to renew and deepen his connection to the man who had helped pull him out of the Rochester mud years earlier.

Grafting Anti-Masonry to National Republicanism, as Weed and Seward were attempting to do as early as 1828, would require major political and ideological adjustments. The grassroots outrage and vulgar appeals of the Anti-Masons offended National Republican worthies, who preferred that government be left to gentlemen of education and virtue. The demonization of Freemasonry had no appeal at all for those self-made allies of the administration who had joined the Order on their way up the social ladder—most conspicuously Grand Master Mason Henry Clay. What one Adamsite called "this demon of Antimasonry" expressed a distrust of conniving politicians that in time would lead Anti-Masons to condemn Adamsites as well as Van Burenites. National Republicans, meanwhile, took numerous positions, above all supporting internal improvements, which, although popular in Anti-Masonry's western New York strongholds, had nothing to do with the Anti-Masons' one great cause.[51] Still, in its raw, conspiracy-obsessed form, Anti-Masonry made fresh problems for Martin Van Buren and the anti-Adams Republicans. Picking up where the Clintonian People's Party had left off, but without the imperious DeWitt Clinton, the Anti-Masons revived the antiaristocratic animus that had stunned the Bucktails in 1823, especially in western New York, and invested it with greater authenticity and passion. The transition from the ranks of the people's men to Anti-Masonry was a smooth one for Yankee farmers—and for rising politicians like Thurlow Weed—who were thoroughly convinced that the Masonic Order threatened the rule of law.

More broadly, in terms fitted to the rapidly commercializing Northeast, Anti-Masonry revamped moralistic and egalitarian themes that had once been the mainstays of the old country democracy. Exactly fifty years after America had declared its independence of the British monarchy—a coincidence lost on nobody—new forms of privilege and exclusiveness now seemed to threaten the land. Insidiously, that threat had wormed its way into the very heart of the commercializing countryside, proclaiming its ethical and intellectual superiority, all the while plotting secret power grabs and protecting kidnappers and murderers. Masonry may once have included such great men as Washington and Franklin, but that legacy had been corrupted by a new class of power-hungry, virtueless men—a brotherhood of sharpsters sworn to aid each other, in business and politics, to the exclusion of the democratic majority. The fate of the republic hung in the balance, emboldening Anti-Masons to fight for what they called "a *Second Independence*," to "hand down to posterity unimpaired the republic we inherited from our forefathers."[52]

MORALITY, DEMOCRACY, AND
THE POLITICS OF IMPROVEMENT

At a glance, the evangelical revivals and the Anti-Masonic movement shared little, intellectually or spiritually, with each other, or with the rationalist sacred elevation proclaimed by President John Quincy Adams. Both the evangelicals and the Anti-Masons had a rougher, more democratic edge than the patrician progressive Adams. Both deployed the kinds of direct emotional appeals that Adams found coarse. Neither particularly prized the bookish life of the mind or the men who pursued it. Some prominent evangelicals, notably the outspoken Philadelphian Ezra Stiles Ely, regarded Adams as a poor Christian or, even worse, a deist in disguise. And, although they railed against the Masons for their immorality and expressed sympathy for Sabbatarianism and other evangelical causes, Anti-Mason leaders like Thurlow Weed could not have cared less about saving anybody's soul.[53]

Yet even as Adams suffered through his presidency, lines of convergence became visible, at least to political operatives like Weed and Seward. Anti-Masonry appealed, across denominations, to traditional Yankee moral virtue and mistrust of secular slackness, as well as to insistence on equality before the law—and the upright Adams happened not to be a Mason. Directed against the wily partisan Van Buren, and his new favorite, the slaveholding Mason Andrew Jackson, Anti-Masonry had enormous potential for reviving anti-Bucktail politics as a popular democratic movement. Evangelical religion had similar political potential in western New York and the rest of greater New England. With the Yankee revivalist rejection of Calvinist orthodoxy came a new emphasis on individual moral choices and stewardship of the fallen as the source of social as well as individual well-being. Out of the democratized spirituality of the revivals arose a panoply of voluntary efforts to spread the gospel—and to encourage others to live righteously and find Christ's salvation. Although based on religious precepts very different from Adams's—a difference that meant everything to the likes of Reverend Ely—those efforts to encourage self-improvement were in line with the idea of National Republicanism as, in Adams's formulation, a "sacred" cause, dedicated to using government power to uplift the nation in mind and spirit.

Events outside greater New England after 1825 made these potential convergences seem more striking—and, for men like Weed and Seward, made their success all the more imperative. Like the Anti-Masons, urban workingmen, led by the democratic radicals of Philadelphia, continued their agitation, raising issues that neither the Adamsites nor any other Republican faction were prepared to handle. Similar movements gathered strength in portions of the rural South and West, most strikingly in Kentucky. By the late 1820s, these reborn city and country democracies were politically active and vibrant as never before, with ideas very different from those of the Yankee moralizers, Anti-Masons, and National Republicans—and they were looking for a national leader very different from either John Quincy Adams or Henry Clay.

9

THE ARISTOCRACY AND
DEMOCRACY OF AMERICA

Andrew Jackson and his political supporters read President Adams's ambitious first annual message with indignant disbelief. As they saw it, a president whose election lacked democratic legitimacy had brazenly bid the Congress to disregard the will of the electorate, expand its own powers, and legislate on behalf of the favored few at the expense of the many. "When I view the splendor & magnificence of the government" that Adams proposed, Jackson wrote, "together with the declaration that it would be criminal for the agents of our government to be palsied by the will of their constituents, I shudder for the consequence — if not checked by the voice of the people, it must end in consolidation & then in despotism."[1]

Jackson, already looking to a rematch in the 1828 elections, was confident that "the intelligence, and virtue, of the great body of the American people" would defeat Adams's plans. Instead of extravagant programs enlarging the federal government's authority, Jackson proposed that Congress should pay off the national debt and apportion whatever surplus remained to the states for the education of the poor. At such moments, when he stressed retrenchment, Jackson sounded much like his old foe William Crawford and the other state-rights southern Radicals. Although they had some things in common, Jackson's evolving politics were more complex. And although Jackson would welcome, indeed court, the state-rights Radicals, including Crawford, he knew that they provided an insufficient political base for a national victory.

The fragmented results of 1824 had shown clearly that success at the national level required building disparate coalitions that cut across the lines of class and section. To defeat Adams, Jackson needed to find a message that conveyed his thinking above and beyond state rights, and build a winning national combination. He needed, in particular, to expand beyond his connections to William Duane and Steven Simpson and impress city and country democrats who had not backed him in 1824. That would not be simple. Conceptions of American democracy were, as ever, in flux in the late 1820s, appearing in new variations to suit altered social circumstances. And by 1828, democratic movements were forming new minor parties and raising new issues about equality, the Constitution, and economic justice.

THE CITY DEMOCRACY REBORN

The sudden revival of Philadelphia's radical Old School Democracy in 1824, in support of Andrew Jackson, faded once John Quincy Adams became president. Even before Jackson lost in the House, the pro-banking and erstwhile pro-Calhoun New School Democrats had taken over the pro-Jackson movement and reconsolidated their command over Pennsylvania's political machinery. With William Duane's *Aurora* defunct, Michael Leib dead, and their supporters virtually locked out of office and influence, Philadelphia's Old School—and with it, America's city democracy, dating back to the Revolution—seemed to have reached the end of the line. Only three years later, however, early in 1828, it reemerged, transformed, as the Philadelphia Working Men's Party, based in the city's trade unions and dedicated to raising what its chief spokesman, the shoemaker William Heighton, called a new standard in politics, "the banner of equal rights."[2]

Although closely connected to the Duanite democrats, the new party formed along fresh lines, taken in response to economic and social changes long evident in all of the northern cities, especially the major seaports, but that had accelerated after the recovery from the Panic of 1819. Manufacturers and master craftsmen, with widened access to mercantile capital, expanded the subdividing and rearranging of the work process in order to hire cheap, relatively unskilled labor (including women and children) and cut their own costs. Small master craftsmen, clinging to an insecure independence, found their prospects shakier than ever. Skilled journeymen, their job security and incomes threatened, faced becoming, as one of their number put it, "journeymen through life." Craft wage-earners began insisting that, as one printer's group put it, "the interests of the journeymen are separate and in some respects opposite of those of their employers."[3]

Philadelphia, still the nation's leading manufacturing center, was home to the most prominent working-class dissent, from which the Working Men's Party would grow. Journeyman wage-earners in a least a dozen trades formed new societies, joining the eight surviving unions in other crafts. Strikes became increasingly common, numbering no fewer than ten in the year 1821 alone. In 1827, when the city's journeyman carpenters went on strike, demanding a limitation of their workday to ten hours, the other trade societies rallied to their support. After a series of public meetings in the working-class stronghold of Southwark, a new organization arose, the Mechanics' Union of Trade Associations (MUTA)—the first citywide organization of journeymen in America.[4]

Echoing the opening paragraphs of Jefferson's Declaration of Independence, the MUTA turned its support for the carpenters into a broader assertion that "[w]hen the disposition and efforts of one part of mankind to oppress another, have become too manifest to be mistaken and too pernicious in their consequences to be endured," it was right and proper for the oppressed to organize for mutual protection. The membership left no doubt about the cause of their collective misery: "an unequal and very excessive accumulation of wealth and power into the hands of a few." Soon thereafter, the carpenters won their strike; the emboldened MUTA supported the creation of a new workingmen's newspaper, the *Mechanics' Free Press*; and early in 1828, the MUTA established the Working Men's Party as its formal political arm. Looking to the autumn elections, the new party pledged to defend the unions and secure various reforms, from expanding public education to restricting bank charters, while electing "men of our own nomination, *whose interests are in unison with ours.*"[5]

Heighton, the foremost organizer of both the MUTA and the Working Men's Party and later editor of the *Mechanics' Free Press*, is a mysterious, meteoric figure. Born around 1800, the son of a poor tradesman in the English Midlands, he emigrated to America with his family about 1812 and settled in Southwark. He appears to have been apprenticed to the shoemakers' trade in his native Northamptonshire town of Oundle, an early industrial shoemaking center; in any event he became a wage-earning shoemaker in Philadelphia, turning out cheap footwear for merchants and middle-man masters in exchange for meager pay. During the five years he led the city's labor movement, Heighton said a great deal about what he was thinking and what he had read, and in the taverns and meeting rooms of Southwark he was something of a celebrity. Yet when he departed Philadelphia sometime in the early 1830s, he virtually vanished. We do not even know what he looked like.[6]

Heighton exemplified the self-taught working-class radical appearing all across the Atlantic world in the opening decades of the nineteenth century. Although his ideas were rooted in the democratic egalitarianism of Thomas Paine and the elder William Duane, Heighton also updated it to fit with the changed social circumstances of the early industrializing world, above all the fracturing of the urban artisan crafts. Borrowing heavily from the writings of other contemporary radical political economists—his favorites included the Englishman John Gray's *Lecture on Human Happiness*—he began with the proposition that the value of all property was based on the labor expended to produce it, the so-called labor theory of value. The theory was so expansive that it could justify the new industrializing order or condemn it. Critics like Gray and, later, Heighton, adopted a strict view of labor as the actual production of goods by human effort, and divided society into what Gray called the exploited "productive many" and the unproductive few, including landlords, moneylenders, merchants ("mere *distributors of wealth*"), and manufacturers. Only by suppressing the unproductive few and abolishing capitalist wage labor—what Gray labeled the "competitive system"—would the deserving many receive their just reward and gain "as much wealth as we have the power of CREATING!!!"[7]

Inspired by Gray, Heighton adapted his radical critique to the social and economic antagonisms of working-class Philadelphia, and in 1827 he began proclaiming his ideas at mass public meetings in Southwark. A "system of competition," he declared, had ground down the mass of the city's producers while enriching a privileged elite. Heighton offered a taxonomy of the nonproducing exploiters, naming six distinct groups—legislative, judicial, theological, commercial, independent, and military—that earned their collective luxuries from the labor of the many. If these parasites were not overthrown, he charged, then the producers' prospects—"as a class," he wrote—would be "a gloomy one of endless toil and helpless poverty." To win what was rightly theirs, Heighton said, workingmen had to educate themselves and establish both libraries and "a POOR MAN'S PRESS," all "appropriated to the interests and enlightenment of the working class and supported by themselves." Duly enlightened, the workers would then have to organize.[8]

The chief difference between Heighton's thinking and his British counterparts' concerned politics. In Britain, where large portions of the urban middle class, let alone workers, were disenfranchised, and where all species of plebeian radicalism had been routinely crushed since the French Revolution, political organizing seemed a hopeless enterprise—and, in any case, an irrelevant one. Reversing the eighteenth-century radical assumptions of Paine and the city democrats, Gray and others claimed that economics, and not politics, was the true matrix of exploitation. Heighton, building on work of the Old School democrats and writing in a country where the franchise for white men was expanding, took the opposite view, in line with ideas about the primacy of politics that Americans generally shared. "Surely we, the working class, who constitute a vast majority of the nation . . . ," he asserted, "have a right to expect an improvement in our *individual condition* will be the natural result of legislative proceedings." Class injustices enforced at law—the entire range of what Heighton called "monopolistic legislation"—could be undone at law as well. With the trade unionists organized into their own political party, Heighton saw nothing "which can materially impede their progress or prevent their success."[9]

Heighton and other workingmen radicals built on other aspects of the

Paineite legacy as well, above all in their religious beliefs. Although hardly uniform in its devotions, Philadelphia's old city democracy had always had strong connections with small but lively rationalist currents outside either the city's Quaker meetings or its Anglican or Presbyterian churches—skeptical about the divinity of Christ, dubious about human damnation and the existence of hell, and endlessly inquisitive about the mysteries of creation and nature. At the more radical end of this spectrum, deists (or, as they preferred to call themselves, freethinkers or free enquirers) dispensed with all clergy and upheld the frankly anti-Christian, Enlightenment benevolence elaborated most famously (and, among Christians, notoriously) by Paine's *Age of Reason*. Benjamin Franklin Bache, the elder Duane's mentor and one of the most prominent Philadelphia freethinkers, had, in the 1790s, distributed hundreds of cheap copies of Paine's tract from the *Aurora's* printing shop, and the Paineite freethinking current persisted into the 1820s.[10]

Slightly more conventional, and more numerous, were the artisans who dominated the congregation at the First Universalist Church on Lombard Street in the heart of Southwark, originally founded by the late ex-Baptist minister Elhanan Winchester in 1781. The Universalists were devout Christians who looked to the Bible for spiritual and moral instruction, but they also believed human nature inherently good and altruistic, not sinful and self-interested. Their God revealed Himself through the handiworks of nature, to be comprehended by humanity with scientific inquiry. And through Jesus Christ, their God had guaranteed salvation to all His children, poor and rich, lazy and diligent, drunken and sober. "GOD loves all his Creatures without Exception . . . ," the Reverend Winchester had taught, "his tender Mercies are over all his works." In the mid-1790s, nearly two in five of the subscribers to the First Universalist Church were also members of the Pennsylvania Democratic Society; thirty years later, numerous important trade union and MUTA leaders, including William Heighton, were also Universalists. Universalist clergy, in turn, opened their churches to mass meetings and other workingmen's activities, including at least one of the assemblies where Heighton delivered a major organizing speech prior to the MUTA's foundation.[11]

These continued links assumed special importance alongside efforts by the evangelical sects and, in time, Presbygational revivalists and Sabbatarians to proselytize among the city's workers. Universalism directly rebuked the evangelical focus on individual sin as the sole source of workers' distress—a precept, they charged, that acclimated workers to inequalities rooted in politics and economics. The same view was pervasive among the leadership of the workingmen's movement. "When you have complained of oppression," one correspondent for the *Mechanics' Free Press* exclaimed, "they have told you that such was the dispensation of Providence, and you must be obedient." It was not (as some evangelicals contended) that the radicals encouraged libertinism: Heighton, in particular, inveighed against workers wasting their money and their minds in the city's taverns and gaming rooms. Instead, the MUTA sought to create an alternative to both the evangelical chapels and the dram shops, raising the moral and intellectual standards of the producers with rational enlightenment and not hellfire moralism.[12]

There were some glaring limits to the radicals' inclusiveness. Although geared chiefly to the grievances of oppressed wage-earners, the reborn city democracy restricted itself almost entirely to men who worked in the bastardized artisan trades. Cartmen, shop clerks, dock workers, domestics, and day laborers—those who performed what Heighton described as "official" as opposed to "productive" labor—had no societies in the MUTA. The growing numbers of female wage-earners in the debased sweated crafts likewise were excluded—thought by some organized journeymen as more of a threat to their livelihoods than as class allies. Although it is possible that some of Philadelphia's black male workers in the trades, eligible voters all, took part in either the unions or the new party, neither Heighton nor others acknowledged their presence. Neither the MUTA nor the Working Men's Party endorsed the rights of blacks as producers or as citizens, nor did they remark on the expansion of southern slavery. The gaps and the silences, especially over slavery, would soon test the resolve of working-class radicals all across the North.

If, in 1828, the movement and its political party fell far short of proclaiming the cause of all Philadelphia's workers, it still offered a new and effective critique of the inequalities and injustices of the early industrializing city. What remained to be seen was how the Working Men, determined to establish themselves as an independent force, would align themselves in national politics and in the impending presidential election. In contrast to the early Anti-Masons, the transformed city democracy, with its assaults on bankers, manufacturers, and other nonproducers, looked like barren political ground for the pro-improvement, National Republican supporters of Adams and Clay. Despite the dominant New School's conversion to Andrew Jackson's presidential hopes, many MUTA and Working Men loyalists—notably Jackson's Duanite admirer Stephen Simpson—remained fierce Jackson loyalists as well. But like the Anti-Masons, the Working Men had to confront what role a small locally based party with a very specific following and agenda might play in the changing political environment. Would an alliance with Jackson, or any other national opposition leader, betray William Heighton's promise to create a fully independent party of the producers? Alternatively, would a refusal to back any presidential candidate inevitably place the new movement on the political margins in its very first election campaign? If the Working Men declined to throw their full support behind Jackson, might they dampen the anti-administration vote in Philadelphia, where Jackson had received crucial support in 1824, and, in effect, help President

Adams? Finally, looking beyond the autumn elections, would Philadelphia's Working Men inspire workingmen in other cities and towns to form their own political movements, as Philadelphia's Democratic Society had inspired city democrats more than thirty years earlier? Or would the Philadelphians' new departure, for all of its innovations, prove the last gasp of the old city democracy?

COUNTRY POLITICS:
RELIEF WARS AND STATE RIGHTS

While northern city democrats undertook new political ventures, country democrats in the slaveholding states of the West and South continued the struggles over banks, debt relief, and land policy that had broken out after the Panic of 1819. In the newest state, Missouri, panic produced a rebellion at the polls that brought the downfall of the old territorial political establishment just as statehood was gained. With that began a shift in the allegiances of the new state's most popular politician, Thomas Hart Benton. Expelled from the University of North Carolina over an incident involving theft, Benton had moved west with his parents, settled temporarily in Tennessee (where he and his brother Jesse were involved in a nasty tavern brawl and gunfight with Andrew Jackson), and eventually arrived in St. Louis in 1815. Amid the early-postwar boom, Benton prospered as a politician and newspaper editor as well as an attorney, and worked closely with fur-trading and mining interests. After the panic, in 1821, he was named one of the new state's first two U.S. senators. Three years later, he backed the presidential hopes of Henry Clay (who had married Benton's cousin, Lucretia Hart).[13]

Yet Benton, who always thought of himself as something of an outsider, was in political transition. The panic had plunged him into debt, tempering his entrepreneurial enthusiasm. The popular outcry against eastern creditors from his farmer constituents made a powerful impression. And in Washington, Benton, a strong pro-slavery man during the Missouri admission controversy, had gravitated toward the Virginia Quids, especially John Taylor and John Randolph, and their denunciations of the Second Bank of the United States and the Hamiltonian "paper" system. Even as he supported Clay in 1824, Benton was devising a new agrarian policy for distributing the public lands of the West to poor settlers by drastically reducing the price once the lands had been on the market for five years, a proposal that appalled pro-development Clay supporters. In the final presidential showdown in 1825, Benton backed Jackson instead of Clay's anointed Adams, completing his break with the nationalist Republicans. Adding acerbic attacks on the national bank to his cheap-land proposals, he transformed himself into the spokesman for Missouri's small-farm settlers—and of western opposition to Clay's American System.[14]

A greater battle—involving issues and personalities of singular importance to later national developments—unfolded in Clay's Kentucky, where disputes over legislative reforms led to a full-blown constitutional crisis over the state courts. Like the rest of rural America, Kentucky, once the richest state west of the Alleghenies, had been hit hard by the panic and rendered a virtual creditors' protectorate. The downturn's effects lingered into the early 1820s. A so-called Relief Party, after winning a commanding legislative majority in 1819, enacted several pro-debtor measures: abolition of imprisonment for debt, laws greatly extending the time granted to repay creditors, and, above all, replacement of the Bluegrass-dominated Bank of Kentucky with a special relief bank, the Bank of the Commonwealth, empowered to issue massive amounts of inflationary paper money. Creditor interests, aghast, appealed to the state judiciary, which, after the hard times lifted in 1823, declared the laws unconstitutional—moves that the aroused legislature denounced as both economically ruinous and an attack on the electorate, "subversive of their dearest and most valuable political rights." Relief issues dominated the 1824 state elections, in which another pro-relief majority was returned to the legislature. The pro-relief candidate for governor, an admired former officer from the War of 1812, Joseph Desha, trounced his pro-court opponent by a margin of nearly two to one. The new legislature, led by a rugged, self-made ex-congressman named John Rowan—who had once killed a man in a duel over who was the greater master of classical languages—passed a reorganization bill that created an entirely new court of appeals, friendlier to the state's hard-pressed small farmers. But the members of the established court refused to stand down, creating a dual court system and a constitutional crisis of the first order.[15]

The political alignments over Kentucky relief and the court issue fit the basic patterns found throughout the South and West after 1819, pitting the more settled, economically developed areas against the rest of the state. Antirelief sentiment, and support for the old court, clustered in the commercializing Bluegrass areas in Lexington and the south-central counties. This was Henry Clay's Kentucky: pro-improvement, friendly to banking and financial institutions, home to Kentucky's finest plantations and largest manufacturing enterprises. The mountainous and knob-hill counties to the east, along with the western and southern portions along the Tennessee border of the state, were, by contrast, mainly pro-relief—dominated by smaller farmers, including many recent arrivals, unbridled by any established local elite. A clearer demonstration of the class divisions of rural America could not be found, articulated as battles between small farmer and planter-businessmen districts. Yet no section of the state was completely nailed down on the court question, which required both sides to canvass support from every corner of the commonwealth. The most influential arguments on behalf of the country democracy came not from some crossroads hamlet but from the state capital of Frankfort, and were written by a sickly Dartmouth graduate and ex-lawyer, Amos Kendall, who had moved to Kentucky barely a decade earlier.

Straight-laced, shy, and sallow, Kendall was a ferocious polemicist once he had pen and paper in hand. He had been born to a hardscrabble Massachusetts farming family in 1789. A bookish boy afflicted with asthma, he was sent to study at the academies at New Ipswich and Groton, then worked his way through Dartmouth, where he graduated first in his class in 1811. After studying law back in Groton with a Republican congressman, and seeing few opportunities in depressed wartime New England, he decided to move south and west, eventually settling in Lexington, Kentucky. There Kendall befriended a brother of Henry Clay's, which led to a job as tutor to the great man's unruly children, but Kendall, restless, took leave after about a year. With the backing of another congressman—the self-proclaimed slayer of Tecumseh, Richard Mentor Johnson—he decided to get into the newspaper business. In 1816, in Frankfort, he set up shop as part-owner and editor of the *Argus of Western America*, and leapt into the hard-knuckle world of Kentucky political journalism.[16]

Over the following decade, Kendall gradually underwent a conversion not unlike Thomas Hart Benton's. Initially a reluctant supporter of the Second BUS, he changed his mind completely when the bank began contracting credit in 1819. He denounced the bank as an unconstitutional "monied aristocracy," excoriated "paper systems," and upbraided the Marshall Court's decision in *McCulloch v. Maryland*. Initially cool to the pro-relief cause, which he saw as endangering contractual obligations, Kendall turned about again in 1823, when the focus of the relief battle shifted to the courts. Convinced that the antirelief court's rulings embodied the "spirit of monarchy," he became a fierce advocate for the New Court Party formed out of the Relief Party, which led to tremendous strain with his old benefactor, Henry Clay, after the 1824 election. By then, Kendall was the chief articulator of the New Court Party's positions, not simply at the *Argus* but as Governor Desha's ghostwriter—honing a skill he would display to even greater effect in the future.[17]

The New Court Party's other gifted writer, who in time would succeed Kendall at the *Argus*, was the lawyer and pamphleteer Francis Preston Blair. Reared in Frankfort, the son of Kentucky's longtime Republican attorney general James Blair, Preston graduated with honors from Transylvania College the same year that Kendall finished at Dartmouth. Blair, like Kendall, was initially a strong supporter of Henry Clay, only to distance himself after backing Clay for president in 1824. "I never deserted your banner," he wrote to Clay after the fact, "until the questions on which you and I so frequently differed in private discussion—(State rights, the Bank, the power of the Judiciary, &c.)—became the criterions to distinguish the parties, and had actually renewed, in their practical effects, the great divisions which marked the era of 1798." A skilled writer, Blair contributed pamphlets and several open letters (under the pseudonym "Jefferson") to the Relief Party efforts, actually surpassing Kendall in the sting of his invective. But he also took an active role as the clerk of the new court of appeals and (out of step with Kendall's hard-money views) as a director of the state-run, paper-issuing Commonwealth Bank.[18]

While Kendall and Blair, the well-connected New Court supporters, did their utmost in Frankfort, their Relief Party instigated and coordinated activities across the state. Pro-relief leaders—including some, like Rowan and the chief justice of the new court, William Barry, with considerable experience and skill as stump orators—whipped up support for the cause. (Barry, another veteran of the Battle of the Thames who had risen to the top of Kentucky politics, traveled to pro-relief areas and denounced the citizens of his own hometown, Lexington, as "a vile aristocracy.") There was a sublime absurdity to some of the drama, as the two courts jostled for legitimacy. Yet to Kentuckians, it was not a laughing matter but a crucial battle over legislative as against judicial supremacy as well as over economic power. Kendall and his allies declared that they were *republicans of the Jeffersonian school*," reclaiming the spirit of 1798. Their opponents saw them as subversives. "We consider this not only an unconstitutional and high-handed measure," an Old Court Party manifesto proclaimed of the reorganization act, "but one, which if approved, will prostrate the whole fabric of constitutional liberty; *we do consider it a REVOLUTION!*" Determined to wrestle the legislature from the New Court Jacobin demagogues, the Old Court Party men built their own statewide organization, enlisting printers and newspaper editors to circulate their diatribes, and matching the new court's supporters stump speaker for stump speaker.[19]

The fever finally broke in 1826, with the Old Court Party forces victorious. An improving economy had taken the edge off the relief cause's desperation, but equally important, the Old Court Party, with more resources at its disposal, outorganized the insurgents. Yet the results were not as clear-cut as they had been in 1824, the Relief Party's banner year. Whereas the 1824 tally had been a crushing triumph for the New Court men, the next two elections were much closer, with the Old Court Party winning the house but not the senate in 1825, and only capturing both houses the following year. The Old Court forces outlasted their overmatched and exhausted opponents, but did not humiliate them. As the 1828 elections approached, the reforms remained an important factor in Kentucky politics.[20]

Compared to the new city democrats in Philadelphia, the antirelief and pro–new court campaigns, mixing hard-money and inflationist demands, produced little in the way of coherent critiques of the emerging economic order. Much more significant were the Kentuckians' political complaints against the

Old Court Party's flagrant disregard of the people's will, as expressed in the lop-sided mandates of 1823 and 1824. Ironically, in retrospect, Andrew Jackson was not among the movement's early admirers, even though most of its constituents supported his presidential run in 1824. Jackson believed the insurgents' attacks on the duly-constituted judiciary were "alarming and flagi[t]ious," and initially he regarded pro-relief leaders as "the Demagogues of Kentucky." He would even-tually change his mind about the "demagogues," if not about the court struggle. By standing up to Henry Clay's Bluegrass establishment, the New Court Party crystallized a popular majoritarianism attuned to Jackson's own developing democratic ideas. The hard-money currents within the party, expressed most powerfully in Kendall's writings, also converged with Jackson's views on money and banking. After 1826, the New Court men, most conspicuously Kendall and Blair, would expand their grassroots Kentucky democracy into a national politi-cal force. They would do so under Jackson's aegis.[21]

Farther south, planter elites had greater success in establishing their political dominance and in creating a national force very different from either Henry Clay's or Kendall and Blair's. In Georgia, the planter faction headed by George Troup, combining state rights with Indian removal, had already broken the back of John Clark's backwoods democracy and embarrassed the Adams White House. For Troup, echoing John Randolph, virtually any increase in federal power was a danger to the South and especially to slavery, presaging the rise of "a combination of fanatics for the destruction of everything valuable in the south-ern country." In other slaveholding states, planter elites reconsidered their poli-tics in the wake of these events—nowhere more dramatically than in quasi-aristocratic South Carolina.[22]

In the 1820s, South Carolina politics took their own peculiar and dramatic twists and turns. The Panic of 1819, and a subsequent cotton market crash in 1825, crushed many of the state's enterprising planters who had moved up-country to cash in on the cotton boom. With short-staple cotton prices falling through the floor—from twenty-seven cents a pound in 1816 to barely nine cents in 1827—and with competition from large plantations in the Alabama and Mis-sissippi black belts intensifying, thousands of slaveholders moved their families and their chattel westward. The downturn hit the sea-island cotton plantations of the low country hard as well, giving an additional boost to the sort of pro-relief sentiment that elsewhere emanated chiefly from small planters and nonslave-holders. The South Carolinians, however, aimed their criticisms at the Adams administration's high-tariff and internal-improvement policies. Planters per-ceived—incorrectly—that the tariff was the major cause of their misery, forcing them to sell their goods cheap but buy goods dear in protected markets. Addition-ally, more than $1.25 million in federal funds would be spent by decade's end on internal improvements in the northern states, but not a penny would be spent on

South Carolina. Critics charged that South Carolina's pro-nationalist leaders, above all the ambitious Calhoun, were spending "the money of the South to buy up influence in the north."[23]

Slavery, and the fear of slave insurrection, electrified the state's political climate just as dramatically. Lacking the imposing yeoman backcountry of other southern states, and with its formally democratic politics firmly in the grip of the planters, South Carolina was virtually immune from the kinds of powerful country democratic movements that emerged in Kentucky and Georgia after 1819. Any significant uprising from below would come from slaves and free blacks, not white voters—a threat that, after the Vesey insurrection panic of 1822, concentrated white South Carolinians' minds wonderfully. Legal crackdowns on transient free blacks went hand in hand with renewed panics over rumors of imminent uprisings, including a scare in Charleston late in 1825 that touched off six months of reprisals by white lynch mobs and police authorities. Amid the turmoil emerged a sustained body of pro-slavery polemics, defending bondage as an ancient and biblically sanctioned institution, "the step-ladder," one pamphleteer insisted, "by which civilized countries have passed from barbarism to civilization." Coupled with these arguments were claims that by expanding federal power even beyond what the antislavery Republicans had demanded during the Missouri controversy, Adams and his Yankee friends were paving the way to abolishing slavery.[24]

The invigorated antinationalist and pro-slavery strains in South Carolina politics blended with particular power in the speeches and writings of the pro-Crawford Radical, William Smith. A former state circuit court judge, and later John C. Calhoun's fellow U.S. senator, Smith had distinguished himself during the congressional debates over Missouri as the most outspoken defender of slavery in either house, pronouncing it a blessing anywhere it took root. Denied reelection to the Senate by the state legislature, Smith immediately won election to the legislature itself, where in 1825 he revived a set of defeated resolutions directly attacking the tariff and the loose constructionism of President Adams and Vice President Calhoun as unconstitutional. In time, Smith declared, the tariff would either "rend your government asunder, or make your slaves your masters."[25]

Smith and the Radicals gained the political initiative only gradually. As late as 1824, a state legislative committee, dominated by Calhoun's friends, rejected Radicalism outright and declared that any impugning by state authorities of federal laws—including, by implication, the tariff—would be "an act of usurpation." Congressman George McDuffie, Calhoun's follower and confidant, berated, on the House floor, "the extraordinary notion . . . that the State governments are to be considered as sentinels to guard the people against the encroachments of the General Government." But in 1825 and 1826, the South Carolina legislature, under powerful pressure from the planter elite, changed its allegiances, approved Smith's strict constructionist resolutions—and then reelected Smith to the Senate. Smith arrived in Washington to find Calhoun so receptive and pleasant that, he wrote a friend, "I could not hate him as I wished to do." Calhoun had quietly been perturbed by the ferocity of northern antislavery and its connection to expansive federal powers since the Missouri crisis. Now, pulled up short by political developments at home and in Washington, and above all by southern disgust directed at the Adams administration, Calhoun felt the pressure he said "[e]very prominent publick man" now felt, to "reexamine his new position and reapply principles." In time, Calhoun would reapply his own principles so thoroughly that he would become the foremost pro-slavery antinationalist in the nation, surpassing even Smith in his sectionalist thinking. For when Calhoun changed his mind, he changed his whole mind.[26]

The political upheavals of the 1820s, rooted in the Panic of 1819 and the Missouri crisis, left three major forces contending for power in the slaveholding states. Henry Clay and his American System continued to command support among enterprising elites and aspiring businessmen in the border states west of the Virginia Piedmont. A reborn country democracy, distrustful of the nationalizing elites, local and national, gained valuable political experience in the battles over debtor relief and related issues. And in the older eastern states, the antinationalist Radicalism of the disabled William Crawford became the ideological foundation of a planters' resurgence, hoping to reassert authority over the backwoods democrats and to lay the high-tariff nationalists to waste. As the Adams administration ended its second year, it was not yet clear which of these elements would dominate the politics of the slaveholding South and West, and whether any of them would coalesce behind Andrew Jackson's presidential campaign. Without question, however, the balance of forces in slaveholding America was stacked more heavily than ever against John Quincy Adams.

QUINCY ADAMS AT BAY

At ten past one on the afternoon of July 4, 1826, the fiftieth anniversary of the signing of the Declaration of Independence, Thomas Jefferson died at the age of eighty-three. President Adams heard the news two days later (and noted in his diary the "striking coincidence"), but only on July 9 did he learn that his father, too, had died on the Fourth, barely four hours after Jefferson. Although Madison lived on, a generation seemed, finally, to have passed, with providential omens— and for Adams all the signs were bad. In November, his opponents captured majorities in both houses of Congress, dividing the legislative and the executive branches against each other as never before in American history. In his third annual message, delivered to the hostile new Congress, Adams reported failure after failure in foreign affairs but included half-hearted offers for a moderation of land payment requirements and a vague reform of bankruptcy laws. He would not abandon his post without a fight, but privately he thought his position was hopeless. "General Jackson will be elected," he wrote in his diary two weeks later.[27]

Adams's political prospects were so dim that even in Massachusetts an incipient pro-Jackson opposition arose—an unnatural coalition, and not enough to threaten Adams seriously on his home ground, but sufficiently prominent to raise a discomfiting clatter. David Henshaw, the chief Boston organizer of the group, was an unschooled former druggist's apprentice who had made a fortune as a wholesale drug merchant before branching out into banking and insurance. Turning to politics, he won election to the Massachusetts legislature in 1826, and started his own newspaper, the *Statesman*. Never accepted by the Brahmin worthies (whom he blasted as "nabobs" and "Shylocks"), Henshaw gravitated toward less haughty, self-made men (and self-proclaimed democrats) such as the former congressman and current state supreme court judge Marcus Morton. Together Henshaw and Morton formed a new political party, the Friends of Jackson, in anticipation of 1828. Among their fellow Jackson supporters, curiously, were a few of the notables whom Henshaw had found so disdainful, including the impeccable Federalists from Salem, George and Theodore Lyman, and the crusty old veteran of the Hartford Convention, Harrison Gray Otis. Deeply suspicious of John Quincy Adams ever since his apostasy of 1808, these gentlemen may have hoped that a Jackson victory would end the persisting Republican bar against appointing Federalists to office, and they may have found Adams's and Clay's economic nationalism too collectivist and pro-western an experiment. For John Quincy Adams, there seemed to be no completely tranquil political harbor, even in his native state.[28]

The greatest storm brewed on Capitol Hill, where the Twentieth Congress organized itself into a virtual committee for the defeat of the president. On December 2, the House, by a ten-vote margin, replaced Speaker John W. Taylor of New York (of Missouri Compromise fame, who had been reelected Speaker in 1825 and was an Adams ally) with Andrew Stevenson, a Virginian aligned with Jackson. Stevenson duly packed the key standing committees with anti-administration men, including, as chairman of the Ways and Means Committee, the obstreperous John Randolph, whose political antics, among them his recent duel with Henry Clay, had so alienated southside Virginians that he had been turned out of the Senate seat he won in 1825. The Senate, meanwhile, selected as its official printer Duff Green, a Missourian close to Calhoun who had moved to Washington in 1825 and whose *United States Telegraph* had become the capital city's chief scourge of Adams and Clay. Tennessee's newly elected governor, Sam Houston, wrote mordantly to his old friend and military comrade Jackson about the administration's predicament: "[D]esperation is their only hope!!"[29]

At the center of the presidential intrigues was Senator Martin Van Buren, on the verge of being selected by the New York state legislature for a second term. When he was not harassing the Adams White House over the Panama conference, Van Buren spent much of his time after 1825 licking his wounds over Crawford's defeat, reconciling with DeWitt Clinton, reconsolidating his Albany Regency political machine, and (beginning in 1827) fending off the Anti-Masonic uprising in western New York. Yet he was not too distracted to neglect presidential politics—and to undertake a quiet effort, detected by Adams in the spring of 1826, "to combine the discordant elements of the Crawford and Jackson and Calhoun men into a united opposition against the administration." At Christmas in 1826, on a southern trip, Van Buren struck an agreement with Calhoun to promote Jackson's election, with the South Carolinian to continue on as vice president. (Van Buren would keep the compact confidential until after his reelection to the Senate the following February.) In supporting Jackson, Van Buren hoped to build a lasting national party, drawing a line between themselves and Adams's supporters as sharp as the one that had once divided Jeffersonian Republicans from Federalists.[30]

Van Buren understood better than most the imperatives of creating a victorious national coalition—and, more than most, he had both the energy and the political skills to build one. His maneuverings and negotiations over the winter of 1826–27 would prove crucial to the reorganization of national political alliances, and to the birth of what would become known as Jacksonian Democracy. But historians have badly misinterpreted both the intentions and the effects of Van Buren's efforts. Particular attention has focused on a letter Van Buren wrote, mainly to please Calhoun, to the Richmond editor and spokesman of the revived Old Republicans, Thomas Ritchie, on January 13, 1827. The letter solicited Ritchie's support for what Van Buren called a "party," reviving the old Jeffersonian coalition of "the planters of the South and the plain Republicans of the north," in order to squelch the "prejudices between free and slave holding states" that had produced, most dangerously at the time of the Missouri Compromise, a northern "clamour agt. Southern Influence and African Slavery." Here, supposedly, lay a blueprint for the entire political era to come—the formation of a truly professional national party, run by partisans, uniting North and South but fundamentally pro-slavery in its politics, standing in legitimate and enduring opposition to another party.[31]

In fact, although Van Buren did speak (to Ritchie and many others, as early as 1826) about the formation of a new party, and although he observed that "we must always have party distinctions," he was not proclaiming, at this point, any major political innovations beyond a return to the party competition of the Jefferson and Madison years. His main objections were to the amalgamation policies of Monroe, which he believed had artificially admitted Federalists into the

Republican fold, displaced loyalty based on principle with *"personal preference,"* and allowed what he called "local jealousies" to dominate national politics, most ominously in the Missouri crisis. Others had been making the same point for years, including Thomas Jefferson, who, having shifted his views since his presidency, wrote in 1822, "I consider the party division of whig & tory, the most wholesome which can exist in any government, and well worthy of being nourished, to keep out those of a more dangerous character." In devising his alternative, Van Buren chiefly looked backward. His focus was on reviving "the division between Republicans and Federalists" and returning to the "old" solidarities. Those alignments and allegiances, he said, had been papered over by Monroe, but they were never truly obliterated. Better, he said, to face that reality and reconfigure the old Jeffersonian party—with the clear presumption that, this time, the Republicans would stand by their principles and, unless careless, permanently sustain their domination instead of merging with their foes.[32]

The idea that Van Buren was building a pro-slavery or pro-southern party fundamentally distorts his motives and his conception of politics. There was a rising pro-slavery impulse in the South, dating back to the Missouri crisis, and Van Buren certainly wished to incorporate its supporters into his new party—above all his friend Thomas Ritchie, whose blasts against the Missouri Compromise and expanded federal power in the *Enquirer* were among the harshest anywhere. When he approached these southerners, Van Buren naturally emphasized his opposition to the more vociferous antislavery northerners, Republican and Federalist, and blamed them for stirring up sectional trouble (which, in the case of the Missouri crisis, was accurate). But while Van Buren courted the pro-slavery southerners, he neither shared their pro-slavery views nor hoped to build a new party on them. Unlike Ritchie and the others, Van Buren had supported the Missouri Compromise and wished only that it had never been made necessary. As far as possible, he wanted to keep the slavery issue out of national affairs by supplanting sectionalism with party loyalty, a very different proposition from what the increasingly militant pro-slavery men were advocating. While deprecating the antislavery agitation in the North, Van Buren was asking potential allies in both sections—in the South, most delicately, Thomas Ritchie—to honor national political compromise. The South, as well as the North, would have to eschew the politics of slavery.

Van Buren's southern strategizing was only one part of his larger, extremely demanding national effort to unify behind Andrew Jackson a collection of forces that had little in common except their opposition to John Quincy Adams. Personal as well as purely political divisions needed bridging. Relations between Jackson and William Crawford had been sour ever since Crawford's harsh response to Jackson's Spanish Florida expedition in 1818. Crawford passionately hated Jackson's new supporter Calhoun, still known as an ardent nationalist. In the North, there were some anti-Adams men, Bucktails included, who distrusted the South as much as some southerners distrusted the North and who, as one of them wrote to Van Buren, would never accede "the Executive authority to the Slave holding states." Other northerners, especially Bucktails, worried that Jackson would become a creature of Calhoun and DeWitt Clinton—the worst possible combination from a Bucktail point of view. At the end of 1827, it remained uncertain whether Jackson would choose Clinton instead of Van Buren as his chief lieutenant in New York, despite Van Buren's exertions on his behalf. Even worse, there was informed speculation that Jackson might designate Clinton as his favorite for the vice presidency. Reports, direct from the Hermitage, that Jackson was speaking highly of Clinton and was concerned about Van Buren's "reputed cunning" spread a wave of anxiety through the Albany Regency.[33]

Van Buren's situation simplified when, on February 11, 1828, Clinton dropped dead. After the eulogies were over (Van Buren's was one of the most gracious), Regency men who had been put off by Clinton began gravitating toward Jackson's campaign, while Clintonians drifted toward Adams. In Washington, southern and western Jacksonians began praising Martin Van Buren. Gradually, the pieces were falling into place. Crawford, after a personal visit from Van Buren, agreed to back Jackson as vastly preferable to Adams (although Crawford tried, unsuccessfully, to get Van Buren to replace Calhoun with the Old Republican Nathaniel Macon in the ticket's second spot). In New York, Jackson's supporters, with the help of the Regency, swept the legislative elections in 1827 outside the western Anti-Mason districts, carrying New York City by four thousand votes—an excellent early indication that Jackson would win the all-important Empire State a year later. Early in his politicking travels in 1827, Van Buren stopped in Kentucky and made friends with Amos Kendall, who under pressure from local Jackson men had agreed to join Francis Blair and most of the rest of the New Court Party in support of Jackson's candidacy. Encouraged by Van Buren's firmly neo-Jeffersonian views—and later by his help in obtaining a personal loan—Kendall would throw himself into the campaign. Several of the most influential Virginians, including John Randolph's replacement, the newly elected senator John Tyler, also came out for Jackson. The chief remaining business for Van Buren and his allies was to solidify Jackson's support in Pennsylvania and Ohio—an effort that, over the winter and spring of 1828, became entangled with a bewildering congressional tussle over protectionist tariff policy.[34]

While state-rights and pro-slavery advocates were finding their voice in the South, an equally determined school of protectionist writers and propagandists gained a sizable following among the farmers of the middle Atlantic and western states as well as among the manufacturers of New England. The movement had

begun to emerge in 1816, as an assertion of patriotic solidarity. Following the
Panic of 1819, its advocates agitated for higher tariffs as the best means to shelter
American enterprise and bring recovery. After winning a signal victory with the
enactment of the protectionist Tariff of 1824, the movement was emboldened
even further by Adams's victory in 1825. Hezekiah Niles, the self-made printer
and editor of the nationally distributed *Niles' Weekly Register*, held the largest
audience of the protectionist writers. Matthew Carey, an Irish émigré, Jeffersonian, self-taught political economist, and tireless pamphleteer, organized the
Pennsylvania Society for the Promotion of Manufacturers in 1824. Lesser-known
but more systematic political economists, above all Daniel Raymond, gave protectionist doctrine genuine intellectual heft.[35]

The protectionists rejected individualist economic assumptions, already battered by the Panic of 1819, about the beneficence of individual self-interest and
unfettered markets. Individual interest and the national interest, as Raymond
wrote, "are often directly opposed." To augment the nation's wealth and spur
what would now be called economic growth, the protectionists primarily looked
to government to act for the benefit of the whole — "like a good shepherd, who
supports and nourishes the weak and feeble ones in his flock," in one of Raymond's more famous lines. Shielding domestic manufacturers from foreign competition by erecting high tariff walls was, along with federal funding of internal
improvements, the good shepherd's most pressing task.[36]

Frustrated but unchastened by the Senate's rejection, by the narrowest of margins, of higher duties on woolen goods early in 1827, the protectionists and their
friends in Washington (led by the administration's point man, Daniel Webster,
who would soon win election to the Senate) planned an all-out campaign for the
following year. In June 1827, Carey's Pennsylvania Society sponsored a national
convention in Harrisburg of delegates from thirteen states — a remarkable group
of editors, politicians, and political economists as well as businessmen — which
hammered out a comprehensive protective program regarding the woolens
industry and other manufacturers in need. The convention did not back either
Adams or Jackson, hoping to exercise maximum leverage over both men. But the
protectionists' pressure did put the Jacksonians — and especially the coalition
builder Martin Van Buren — in a difficult political bind.[37]

Jackson still held to the moderately protectionist line he had supported as a
senator in 1823 and 1824, although he was beginning to think the importance of
the tariff issue had been greatly exaggerated. But that middle position would not
be good enough for some political blocs whose support Jackson badly needed. To
southern Radicals, any sign of support for a protective tariff by Van Buren and his
friends was a potential deal breaker in the coming presidential election. South
Carolina slaveholders led meetings and petition drives throughout the state,
warning that neither the federal courts nor national elections could protect the

slaveholders' rights and interests over the protective tariff. Thomas Cooper, the ex-Jeffersonian radical turned state-rights ideologue, warned Van Buren, extravagantly, that passage of woolens protection would lead to instant secession by South Carolina. Northern protectionists, in New York as well as Pennsylvania and Ohio, were just as concerned that Van Buren's courting of the southerners would cause him to sell them out over the tariff issue. Those concerns deepened when, during the Senate vote over the woolens bill in 1827, Van Buren absented himself, opening the way for Vice President Calhoun (who denounced the bill as an attack on the South) to cast the tie-breaking, killing vote. All of Van Buren's coalition-building, it seemed, might come to nothing without a congressional deal over the tariff—the one issue over which nobody seemed willing to bargain.[38]

The tariff bill that resulted in 1828 was more political than economic—connected, John Randolph remarked acidly, "to manufactures of no sort, but the manufacture of a President of the United States." Its author, Congressman Silas Wright from northernmost New York State, was one of Van Buren's brightest Regency lieutenants and thus, though only a freshman in the Twentieth Congress, a man of considerable consequence. Inside the House Committee of Manufactures, Wright drafted a bill that levied high duties not only on wool and hemp—appealing to growers and manufacturers in Kentucky, Ohio, and western New York—but also on pig iron and rolled iron, of utmost important in Pennsylvania. Molasses, sail duck, and coarse wool—essential raw materials for New England rum distillers, sailmakers, and clothing manufacturers—likewise were burdened with heavy new duties, a direct attack on pro-Adams Yankees. The economic logic of Wright's bill was utterly whimsical, but its political logic was airtight: offer aid, above all, to the farmers and iron masters of the middle Atlantic and western states, while hitting New England hard. Antitariff southerners, aghast at the very idea of protection, added amendments that would hit the Yankees even harder, hoping to make the bill so obnoxious it would never succeed.[39]

Jackson's friends wanted the protective bill to pass both houses, but could never admit as much to the southern Radicals. And so Van Buren and his agents pulled a bait-and-switch, assuring southerners that even if the House approved the bill, the Senate would kill it—thereby allowing the Jacksonians to tell the middle Atlantic and western state voters that they had fought to protect their manufactures and growers, but without actually forcing higher prices on southern consumers. The bill passed the House. In the Senate, old-line Crawford Radicals, led by Samuel Smith of Maryland, took up the fight to reject it. (It was Smith, speaking on the Senate floor, who gave the measure its notorious title, "a bill of abominations.") But united opposition from New England threatened to ruin everything, so Van Buren presented an amendment calling for upward revision of manufactured woolens duties. The maneuver swayed just enough

New Englanders, including Daniel Webster, to get the bill through the Senate, on the presumption that a bad protectionist bill was better than no bill at all. President Adams, finding no constitutional basis for killing the tariff, signed it into law in mid-May, raising duties overall by about 30 to 50 percent.[40]

In the short term, the tariff of abominations brought Van Buren and the evolving pro-Jackson coalition all they could have desired from what had looked like an impossible situation. Southerners, whose representatives voted almost unanimously against the bill, felt seduced and betrayed—furious Charlestonians lowered shipboard American flags in the harbor to half-staff, burned effigies of Clay and Webster, and organized protest meetings—but were too wary of dividing the ranks against Adams and Clay to vent their anger against the devious Jacksonians. Immediately after the vote, the South Carolina delegation caucused at Robert Hayne's lodging house, where blustery talk erupted about mounting dramatic protest. But at a second meeting, cooler heads—on instruction, almost certainly, from Vice President Calhoun—held sway, and the little rebellion subsided. Calhoun himself reacted philosophically, telling a New York friend that "truth will, in the long run, prevail." Under a Jackson presidency strongly influenced by Calhoun, Radicals consoled themselves, it would be easier to beat back the ignominious new duties; in any case, the southerners had to deal with first things first, namely, ousting Adams and Clay. Meanwhile, among Kentucky hemp growers, Pennsylvania iron makers, and New York wool farmers, the tariff greatly bolstered Jackson's cause, which had been Van Buren's objective all along.[41]

Thoughts about the tariff's long-term repercussions were also taking shape inside John C. Calhoun's obsessive and (on the subject of nationalist politics) thoroughly changed mind. When the Twentieth Congress adjourned, Calhoun returned to his South Carolina plantation where he would spend the duration of the year, playing little part in the election campaign, confident that his election and Jackson's were foregone conclusions. Instead, he brooded over the tariff, and over the larger injustices done to the South. Publicly, he maintained a bland moderation, consistent with his commitments to Jackson and Van Buren. Privately, he filled his correspondence with ruminations about how an oppressive northern majority had gained a permanent ascendancy over the slaveholding states. The fallout from those ruminations would await the outcome of the presidential election. Only in November did Calhoun, at the request of a South Carolina state legislator, start refining his thoughts into a coherent protest.[42]

"UNDER *WHIP & SPUR*":
POLITICS, PROPAGANDA, AND THE 1828 CAMPAIGN

Although he looked like a distinguished old warrior, with flashing blue eyes and a shock of whitening steely gray hair, Andrew Jackson was by now a physical wreck. Years of ingesting calomel and watered gin to combat his chronic dysentery had left him almost toothless. (In 1828, he obtained an ill-fitting set of dentures, but he often refused to wear them). An irritation of his lungs, caused by a bullet he had caught in one of his early duels, had developed into bronchiectasis, a rare condition causing violent coughing spells that would bring up what he called "great quantities of slime." The bullet itself remained lodged in his chest, and another was lodged in his left arm, where it accelerated the onset of osteomyelitis. Rheumatism afflicted his joints, and his head often ached, the effect of a lifetime of chewing and smoking tobacco. He had survived near-total collapse of his health in 1822 and 1825, but for the rest of his life, he enjoyed few days completely free of agony. His outbursts of irascible fury, which sometimes shocked even his old friends and allies, owed partly to his suffering and to his efforts to suppress it.[43] But after the debacle of 1825, they also owed to his determination to vindicate not just his own honor but that of the American people. For Jackson and his admirers, the two had become identical.

Willfulness did not mean rashness. In preparing to wreak his vengeance on Adams (whom he respected) and Clay (whom he despised), Jackson took care not to violate the accepted etiquette of presidential campaigning and appeal directly for the job. He was available to serve his country once more, but to look or sound less elevated than that would have been dishonorable (as well as onerous, given the state of his health). Jackson made only one major public appearance over the months before the election, at a public festivity in New Orleans on January 8, commemorating his great victory thirteen years earlier—an invitation, issued by the Louisiana legislature, that he could not refuse without seeming churlish. Yet while he stuck close to the Hermitage, Jackson threw himself into the fray as no other previous presidential candidate before him had, making himself available for visiting delegations of congressmen, giving interviews to interested parties, and writing letters for newspaper publication. When personal attacks on his character began, he became even more active, his sense of honor on the line. Some of his chief supporters, including Van Buren, asked that "we be let alone" and that Jackson "be *still*," but Jackson would command this campaign just as surely as he had any of his military exploits.[44]

His positions on several key issues were moderate and flexible, replicating much of what he had said in 1824, in generalities that would not upset the national coalition his agents were assembling. On the tariff, the primary political issue in 1828, Jackson remained blandly middle-of-the-road, repeated his support for a "judicious" tariff, and allowed men of different views to imagine that his sympathies lay with them. On internal improvements, Jackson modified his stance somewhat to support a distribution of surplus federal monies to the states for any road and canal projects they wished to undertake, but generally he restated his cautious support for projects that were genuinely national in scope. On the Indian question, he remained persuaded that, for the good of white settlers and natives alike, orderly removal was the only sound solution, but he refrained from saying anything that might be interpreted as an endorsement of the more extreme state-rights removal position.[45]

Instead of a long list of positions and proposals, Jackson's campaign revolved around calls for "reform," a theme broad enough to unite a disparate coalition without merely resorting to platitudes. At one level, "reform" meant undoing what Jackson considered the theft of the presidency in 1825, and ending the political climate that had permitted it. Sometimes, Jackson and his supporters proposed specific changes. Jackson himself said he would exclude from his cabinet any man who sought the presidency—one obvious way to help prevent any future "corrupt bargain." He also called for a constitutional amendment to bar any member of Congress from eligibility for any other federal office (except in the judiciary) for two years beyond his departure from office. Other Jacksonians spoke of the candidate's support for the principle of rotation in office, for limiting presidents to a single term, and for banning the executive from appointing congressmen to civil posts—all means to disrupt insider exclusivity and what Jackson called the "intrigue and management" that had corrupted the government. Otherwise, the Jackson campaign simply reminded the voters of what had happened in 1825—and went further, to charge that "Lucifer" Clay had, during the House negotiations, offered to throw his support to Jackson if Jackson promised he would name him secretary of state.[46]

At another level, "reform" meant returning American government to Jeffersonian first principles and halting the neo-Federalist revival supposedly being sponsored under the cover of the American System. President Adams, Jackson and his men charged, had made the mistake of following his father's footsteps, balancing a "hypocritical veneration for the great principles of republicanism" with artful manipulation of political power. All of "the asperity which marked the struggle of 98 & 1800," Jackson wrote, had returned. Having "gone into power contrary to the voice of the nation," the administration had claimed a mandate it did not possess, and then tried to expand its authority even further. Illegitimate from the start, the new Adams regime raised what Jackson called the fundamental question at stake in the election: "[S]hall the government or the people rule?"[47]

While Jackson and his closest advisors refined this message and called the shots from Nashville, his supporters built a sophisticated campaign apparatus unlike any previously organized in a presidential election, a combination so effective that it obviated the need for either a congressional caucus nomination or a national convention. At the top, Jackson's most capable Tennessee operatives, including John Overton, William Lewis, and John Eaton, concentrated their efforts in a central committee headquarters established in Nashville, where decisions about strategy and tactics could be taken efficiently, in rapid response to continuing events and with Jackson's approval. (A similar, smaller Jackson committee headquarters was established in Washington, to work closely with the pro-Jackson caucus in Congress that met regularly under Van Buren's aegis.) The central committee in turn dispatched its messages to (and received intelligence from) Jackson campaign committees established in each state. Finally, the Jacksonians responded to the reforms in presidential voting around the country— reforms that, by 1828, had included, in all but two states, giving the power to choose presidential electors directly to the voters—by coordinating activities at the local level. The state pro-Jackson committees linked up with local Jackson committees, sometimes called Hickory Clubs, that stirred up enthusiasm with rallies and parades and made sure that their supporters arrived at the polls.[48]

Even more extraordinary than the campaign committees was the dense network of pro-Jackson newspapers that seemed to arise out of nowhere beginning in the spring of 1827. Early in the campaign, Jackson's congressional supporters had caucused and pledged to establish "a chain of newspaper posts, from the New England States to Louisiana, and branching off through Lexington to the Western States." In North Carolina alone, nine new Jacksonian papers had appeared by the middle of 1827, while in Ohio, eighteen new papers supplemented the five already in existence in 1824. In each state, the Jackson forces arranged for one newspaper to serve as the official organ of their respective state committees, refining the broadcast of an authoritative message while promoting a cadre of prominent loyal editors, including Ritchie at the *Enquirer*, Amos Kendall at the *Argus of Western America*, Edwin Croswell at the *Albany Argus*, Isaac Hill at the New Hampshire *Patriot*, and, above all, in Washington, Calhoun's friend Duff Green at the anti-administration *United States Telegraph*.[49]

Funding (as well as copy) for the campaign sheets came directly from Jackson's congressional supporters and their friends, who pioneered numerous fundraising gimmicks, including five-dollar-a-plate public banquets and other ticketed festivities. More substantial sums, including money raised from local bankers and businessmen in the New York–Philadelphia region, were collected and disbursed by Martin Van Buren, who served as the campaign's de facto national treasurer. Some of these monies went to the newspaper editors; others were spent on printing campaign books and pamphlets and producing paraphernalia such as campaign badges. Much of this material made its way to supporters at government cost, thanks to Jacksonian congressmen's liberal partisan use of their personal postal franking privileges.

Jackson's friends made special efforts to solidify their connections to various popular democratic movements, urban and rural, while also winning over more established and politically influential men. The alliances ranged from complete mergers to testy but effective ententes. Kentucky was a special prize for the Jacksonians, having cast its congressional vote for Adams in 1825 at Henry Clay's insistence. The 1828 tariff's high protective rates for hemp growers and manufacturers helped Van Buren offset Clay's advantage among the Kentucky elite, recently aligned with the Old Court Party—but the Jacksonians mainly pinned their hopes on Amos Kendall, Francis Blair, and the revitalized New Court Party machine. In protection-mad Pennsylvania, where the tariff proved extremely popular among the state's ironmongers, the Jacksonians appealed to all of the elements of the old Jeffersonian coalition—including manufacturers, western farmers, and rural Germans—with a propaganda effort headed by the papermaking magnate Congressman Samuel Ingham. In Philadelphia, the presence of numerous New School candidates for state and local office on the Jacksonian ticket alienated the new Working Men's Party, but Jackson's friends reached out to the labor insurgents in various ways, including a direct fifteen-hundred-dollar contribution to rescue Stephen Simpson's financially strapped paper, the *Columbian Observer*. Ultimately, the Workies devised their own Jackson ticket, picking and choosing among the official nominees, offering joint nominations to those they deemed reliable, but running their own candidates for the other slots.[50]

New York, which Jackson had lost in 1824, was a different and, as ever, more difficult story. Under the revised state constitution, voters now chose the state's presidential electors. Unlike in most other states, however, New York's electoral votes would be apportioned on a district-by-district basis, meaning that even if Van Buren's agents carried the overall popular vote, Adams was bound to win a portion of the state's Electoral College total. DeWitt Clinton's death resolved much of the early bickering within the New York pro-Jackson camp, leaving Van Buren in control, but it also raised the possibility that some pro-Clinton Jackson men, who had supported the Tennessean chiefly to promote Clinton, might now drift over to Adams. And then there was the perplexing Anti-Masonic uprising in western New York, an outburst of democratic outrage that could never be won over to Grand Master Mason Andrew Jackson. Even with all of the southern states plus Pennsylvania likely to support Jackson, it would not be enough to elect him president. New York's result would be crucial.

The outlook for Jackson improved when political operatives determined that the Anti-Masonic movement remained, for the moment, localized, and that its chief advocates, Thurlow Weed and William Henry Seward, were having difficulty merging it with the Adams campaign. The outlook improved even more when Jackson's operatives confirmed that Henry Clay was not only a Mason but, as one delighted Manhattan pol put it, "a Mason of rank." Van Buren, meanwhile, decided to make the most of his New York strongholds, above all New York City, where the old Tammany Society, after a history of recurrent factionalism, turned into one of the most united and reliable pro-Jackson organizations in the state. As early as January, Tammany began hosting giant public events touting Jackson, and after the death of DeWitt Clinton—who was hated by the Tammany braves—the way was cleared for an all-out effort to spike the city's vote. Hickory Clubs appeared in every ward, sponsoring hickory tree–planting ceremonies and barroom gatherings to toast the general's success. A clutch of partisan editors in the already well-established New York press churned out reams of pro-Jackson material. "The more he is known," one pro-Jackson paper boasted of its man, "the less and less the charges against him seem to be true."[51]

Against this juggernaut, Adams's supporters—their candidate an awkward public figure who spurned involvement in campaign organization—were badly overmatched. But they tried their best and performed credibly as organizers. Henry Clay, ignoring advice that he resign and let Adams bear the full brunt of defeat, took charge of creating a national campaign and of stumping at dinners and celebrations around the country to make the administration's case. Daniel Webster pitched in as well, overseeing the canvassing of potential financial backers (fully exploiting his ample personal connections to New England capitalists), collecting substantial sums, and keeping track of accounts. Although they could not equal the Jacksonians, the Adamsites created a substantial pro-administration press, headed in Washington by Joseph Gales and William Seaton's *National Intelligencer* and Peter Force's *National Journal*. The Adamsites printed forests' worth of pamphlets, leaflets, and handbills, organized their own state central committees, and sponsored countless dinners and commemorations. In at least one state, New Jersey, the Adamsites probably outorganized their opponents. And everywhere outside of Georgia, where Jackson ran unopposed, there was a genuine contest under way, with both parties, as one Marylander wrote, "fairly in the field, under *whip & spur*."[52]

Adamsite strategic and tactical errors at the state and local level repeatedly undermined whatever enthusiasm the administration's loyalists generated. High-minded stubbornness, linked to an aversion to what looked to some National Republicans like Van Buren–style wheeling and dealing, killed Adams's chances of carrying the middle Atlantic states. In upstate New York, the National Republicans insulted the Anti-Masons by rejecting their nominee for governor, a close friend of Thurlow Weed's, and then bidding the insurgents to show their good faith by adopting the pro-administration slate, ruining any chance of an alliance. In New York City, a protectionist movement, geared to halting the dumping of foreign manufactures on the New York market, arose in the spring; and, by autumn, it had gained a sizable following that cut across class and party lines. But the Adamsites, seemingly unable to believe that their protectionism might appeal to urban workers, held back from the movement. The protectionists ran their own ticket, and the opportunity was wasted. Similar shortsightedness prevailed in Philadelphia, where the Adamsites refused to make common cause with the surviving Federalist establishment, encouraging Jacksonian hopes of taking the city.[53]

The Adamsites did excel in one area, the dark art of political slander. In 1827, a Cincinnati editor and friend of Clay's named Charles Hammond took a fact-finding tour into Kentucky and Tennessee, and unearthed some old stories about alleged legal irregularities in Jackson's marriage (supposedly he was a bigamist), along with charges that Jackson's wife, Rachel, was an adulteress and his mother a common prostitute. The charges were not simply mean-spirited: they evoked broader cultural presumptions that stigmatized Jackson as a boorish, lawless, frontier lowlife, challenging the Christian gentleman, John Quincy Adams. Clay immediately recommended his mudslinger friend to Webster, calling Hammond's paper "upon the whole, the most efficient and discreet gazette that espouses our cause," and suggested that the editor get direct financial support. Hammond, meanwhile, became a fountain of wild and inflammatory charges—that Jackson's mother had been brought to America by British soldiers, that she married a mulatto who was Jackson's father—all of which found their way into what may have been the lowest production of the 1828 campaign, a new journal entitled *Truth's Advocate and Monthly Anti-Jackson Expositor*. Jackson, enraged to the point of tears, held Clay responsible and sent John Eaton to confront the Kentuckian. Clay vehemently denied the charges, though his private correspondence with Hammond contains hints he was lying. Jackson continued to blame everything on Clay.[54]

Character assassination in presidential politics was hardly invented in 1828—recall, for example, the lurid attacks on Thomas Jefferson and "Dusky Sally" Hemings—and Clay could easily and rightly complain of the Jackson campaign's unceasing attacks about the corrupt bargain as the basest sort of slander. But the Hammond affair, beginning more than a year before the 1828 electioneering commenced in earnest, marked the arrival of a new kind of calculated, mass cultural politics, pitting a fervent sexual moralism against a more forgiving, secularist, laissez-faire ethic. Hammond's attacks also ensured that a great deal of the campaign would be fought out in the sewer. The Jacksonians spread sensational falsehoods that President Adams was a secret aristocratic voluptuary who, while minister to Russia, had procured an innocent American woman for the tsar. Clay came in for merciless attacks as an embezzler, gambler, and brothel habitué. The Adamsites responded with a vicious handbill, covered with coffins, charging Jackson with the murder of six innocent American militamen during the Creek War, and labeling him "a wild man under whose charge the Government would collapse." The competition turned largely into a propaganda battle of personalities and politically charged cultural styles instead of political issues. A campaign slogan from four years earlier, coined in support of a possible Adams-Jackson ticket, assumed completely new meaning and summed up the differences, contrasting the nominees as "Adams who can write/Jackson who can fight."[55]

And yet, for all of the vulgarities and slander, the campaign of 1828 was not an unprincipled and demagogic theatrical. Neither was it a covert sectional battle between a pro-slavery southerner and an antislavery New Englander; nor was it a head-on clash between pro-development Adamsite capitalists and antidevelopment Jacksonian farmers and workers, although strong views about slavery and economic development certainly came into play. The campaign pronounced a valediction on the faction-ridden jumble of the Era of Bad Feelings and announced the rough arrival of two distinct national coalitions, divided chiefly over the so-called corrupt bargain and the larger political implications of the American System. It was, above all, a contest over contrasting conceptions of politics, both with ties to the ideals of Thomas Jefferson.

For all of his setbacks and suffering, John Quincy Adams had never abandoned his moral vision of energetic government and national uplift. Protective tariffs, federal road and canal projects, and the other mundane features of the American System were always, to him, a means to that larger end. A fugitive from Federalism, Adams embodied one part of the Jeffersonian legacy, devoted to intellectual excellence, rationality, and government by the most talented and virtuous—those whom Jefferson himself, in a letter to Adams's father, had praised as "the natural aristoi." The younger Adams took the legacy a large step further, seeing the federal government as the best instrument for expanding the national store of intelligence, prosperity, beauty, and light.[56]

Objections to the political ramifications of that vision united the opposition— objections rooted in another part of the Jeffersonian legacy, a fear of centralized government linked to a trust in the virtue and political wisdom of ordinary American voters. Jackson and his polyglot coalition contended that human betterment meant nothing without the backing of the people themselves. Lacking that fundamental legitimacy, Adams, Clay, and their entire administration had, the Jacksonians contended, been engaged from the start in a gigantic act of fraud—one that, to succeed, required shifting as much power as possible to Washington, where the corrupt few might more easily oppress the virtuous many, through unjust tariffs, costly federal commercial projects, and other legislative maneuvers. Were the Adamsites not removed as quickly as possible, there was no telling how far they might go in robbing the people's liberties, under the guise of national improvement, the American System, or some other shibboleth. Hence, the opposition's slogan: "Jackson and Reform."

Jackson himself laid out the stakes in a letter to an old friend, on the omens in what he called the Adamsites' exercise of "patronage" (by which he simply meant "power"):

> The present is a contest between the virtue of the people, & the influence of patronage[. S]hould patronage prevail, over virtue, then indeed "the safe precedent," will be established, that the President, appoints his successor in the person of the sec. of state—Then the people may prepare themselves to become "hewers of wood & drawers of water," to those in power, who with the Treasury at command, will wield by its corrupting influence a majority to support it—The present is an important struggle, for the perpetuity of our republican government, & I hope the virtue of the people may prevail, & all may be well.

Or as one of his New York supporters put it (presuming to speak on behalf of "the sound planters, farmers & mechanics of the country"), the Jacksonians beheld the coming election as "a great contest between the aristocracy and democracy of America."[57]

The balloting began in September and, because of widely varying state polling laws, continued until November. Early returns from New England unsurprisingly gave Adams the lead, although not quite the clean sweep he had expected. (In Maine, a hardy band of ex–Crawford Radicals in and around Portland managed to win one of the state's electoral votes for Jackson.) The trend shifted heavily in mid-October, when Pennsylvania (overwhelmingly, including a strong plurality in Philadelphia) and Ohio (narrowly) broke for Jackson. It remains a matter of speculation how much this news affected the vote in other states, where the polls had not yet opened, but the Jacksonians took no chances, especially in New York, where the three days of voting did not commence until November 3. Holding back until the moment was ripe, the New York Jackson committee suddenly spread the word in late October that Jackson's election was virtually assured, in order to demoralize the opposition. In the end, Jackson carried the state's popular vote, although only by about 5,000 ballots out of 275,000 cast.[58]

The state-by-state reporting of the vote, with news of one Jackson victory after another rolling in, heightened the impression that a virtual revolution was underway. The final tallies showed a more complicated reality. As expected, Adams captured New England, and Jackson swept the South below Maryland. But apart from Jackson's lopsided victory in Pennsylvania, the returns from the key battleground states were remarkably even.[59] If a mere 9,000 votes in New York, Ohio, and Kentucky had shifted from one column to the other, and if New York, with an Adams majority, had followed the winner-takes-all rule of most other states, Adams would have won a convincing 149 to 111 victory in the Electoral College. In other races for federal office the Adamsites actually improved their position. Above all, in the U.S. Senate, what had been a strong six-vote opposition majority in the Twentieth Congress would be reduced to a Jacksonian majority of two when the new Congress assembled in December 1829. Despite all their blunders, and despite Adams's unpopularity, the friends of the administration had not lost future political viability.

These wrinkles in the returns were lost amid Jackson's overwhelming victory nationwide. Jackson won 68 percent of the electoral vote and a stunning 56 percent of the popular vote—the latter figure representing a margin of victory that would not be surpassed for the rest of the nineteenth century. The totals came from a vastly larger number of voters than ever before in a presidential election, thanks to the adoption of popular voting for electors in four states and the bitterness of the one-on-one contest in the middle Atlantic states. More than a million white men voted for president in 1828, roughly four times the total of 1824. Jackson alone won three times as many votes as the total cast for all candidates four years earlier. The magnitude of it all left Adamsites, including the normally sanguine Henry Clay, miserable, and Jacksonians jubilant.

Perhaps the only Jacksonian not thoroughly overjoyed was Jackson himself. Well before the voting was over, he had understood what the outcome would be, and the news confirming his election caused no particular stir at the Hermitage. After all the months of campaigning behind the scenes, and now faced with actually assuming the presidency, the victor reported that "my mind is depressed." Sadness turned to panic and then grief in mid-December, when Rachel Jackson, preparing for the move to Washington, suddenly collapsed and, after five days of violent heart seizures, died. Her husband, who sat up with her throughout her ordeal, would never really recover from the shock. His great biographer James Parton wrote that it henceforth "subdued his spirit and corrected his speech," except on rare occasions when, in a calculated effort to intimidate his foes or inspire his allies, he would break into his customary fits of table pounding and swearing. Yet Rachel's death also steeled Jackson for the political battles to come. Her health had been precarious for several years before she died. Jackson was absolutely certain that the slanders of the 1828 campaign had finally broken her. And for that cruel and unforgivable blow, he would forever blame, above all others, his nemesis, Henry Clay.[60]

"JACKSON AND REFORM"

Jackson's victory marked the culmination of more than thirty years of American democratic development. By 1828, the principle of universal white adult male suffrage had all but triumphed—and accompanying that victory, much of the old politics of deference still left over from the Revolutionary era had collapsed. The country and city democracies of the 1790s had attained a legitimacy only barely imaginable a generation earlier. Once-impregnable political establishments— the Connecticut Standing Order, the Philadelphia Federalist regime, the planter and financier political elites of Georgia and Tennessee and Kentucky—had either fallen or been shaken to their foundations. Even where democratic reformers achieved the least—above all in the seaboard South, and there, above all, in South Carolina—local rulers granted cosmetic changes that permitted them to claim that they fairly represented the citizenry's will.

In building their impressive national organization, the Jacksonians had established once and for all the imperatives of coalition building and party organization following the collapse of the so-called Era of Good Feelings. Capitalizing on the long-term resentments from the Panic of 1819, and insisting on adherence to the Missouri Compromise, they had resolved much of the political confusion by consolidating a popular base that merged the urban mechanics and small farmers of the North with the yeomanry and much of the planter class of the South. Close examination of the 1828 local returns bears out the contention that the Jacksonian electorate, if not necessarily its leadership, was broadly drawn from the less well connected and from the lower (though hardly the lowest) rungs of the social ladder. The pattern was especially striking in the battleground states, where purely regional loyalties to the respective candidates did less to slant the totals than in New England or the South. Whereas Jackson ran strongest in the more isolated districts of small farmers from Pennsylvania on westward, as well as in the lower-class wards of New York City, Philadelphia, Baltimore, and Cincinnati, Adams ran strongest in the rapidly developing small towns along the new canals and transportation routes and in creditor-friendly districts like Kentucky's Bluegrass.[61]

Yet if the Jacksonians' victory in 1828 clarified certain issues pertaining to democracy, it left others open—and opened up still others. Even as the Jacksonians celebrated wildly, the lucubrations of their southern Radical faction (and especially of the converted Vice President Calhoun) threatened one day to tear the alliance apart. In the rural North, the Anti-Masonic movement offered a democratic alternative to Jacksonianism that, in the hands of able men such as Thurlow Weed and William Henry Seward, might yet make its presence felt. In the seaboard cities, it remained to be seen whether the reborn city democracy of the Working Men's Party would spread beyond Philadelphia. Even if they did enlarge their following, the Working Men, along with the Anti-Masons, would have to resolve the place of minor parties in the emerging political order, and how they might advance their views without playing the self-defeating role of spoiler.

Many other open questions presented themselves. The great evangelical revivals and the Reverend Ely's proposed "Christian party in politics" had only barely begun to affect political debates with the Sabbatarian petition campaigns of 1828. What new turns might their politics of moral improvement take now that Andrew Jackson was in the White House? How would the pro-nationalist Supreme Court react to the Jacksonian ascendancy—the branch of the federal government least vulnerable to popular politics, led by an aging but forceful Federalist chief justice? Would Jacksonian party builders like Martin Van Buren and their opponents be able to sustain the Missouri Compromise? How would the defeated but hardly eradicated pro-Adams forces reorganize themselves, and with what new national coalition of their own?

Rather than settling these issues, the democratic triumphs that led to 1828 exposed them to further agitation, from the very top of the political system to the very bottom—even by men and women who stood completely outside the widened ambit of electoral democracy. Very quickly, all sorts of Americans would be wielding the tools of the new political democrats—a mass press, popular conventions, petition campaigns, and other means—to rouse support for demands that neither the Jacksonians nor their opponents were fully prepared to address, including such outlandish things as granting women the vote, banning liquor, restricting immigration, and abolishing slavery.

The antislavery campaign would prove the most unsettling. If the Panic of 1819 had galvanized the popular movements that led to Jackson's victory, the Missouri Compromise had established a shaky political middle ground on the issue that most threatened national unity, the future of what had become the South's peculiar institution. And behind that fact lay the hard, looming paradox of American democracy at the dawn of the Jacksonian age: that the democratizing impulse would in time threaten the very sectional peace on which the new political dispensation was founded. Only as long as Van Buren–style political managers kept alive the spirit as well as the substance of the compromise could they sustain political stability—but by expanding democratic possibilities, they all but guaranteed that their middle ground would come under attack. The nub of the matter was, as ever, political: either American democracy could tolerate slavery or it could not. Or as one Illinois politician—still a humble Indiana farmer's son and part-time ferryman in 1828, surrounded by pro-Jackson relatives but too young to vote—would later put it, "[T]his government cannot endure, permanently half *slave* and half *free*," a house divided against itself.[62]

10

THE JACKSON ERA:
UNEASY BEGINNINGS

Anxious marshals had to stretch a ship's cable across the East Portico of the Capitol to keep Andrew Jackson's inauguration ceremony from being overrun. For weeks, people had been pouring into Washington from hundreds of miles around—job seekers, war veterans, state officials, ordinary Jackson admirers, and the curious, each seemingly determined to shake the new president's hand before inauguration day was over. Now they lined the route from Jackson's lodging house to the Capitol, where late arrivals wedged themselves into every possible space. Never before had an American ceremony of state turned into such a democratic and charismatic spectacle. Francis Scott Key declared the sight beautiful and sublime. But Supreme Court Justice Joseph Story, obliged to attend the swearing in and the reception that followed, thought that "[t]he reign of KING MOB seemed triumphant," and departed as quickly as protocol allowed.[1]

Jackson, in deep mourning for Rachel, was dressed in the blackest black suit, tie, and coat, and looked all the more remarkable for it, his hatless head of now-nearly snow-white hair making him instantly recognizable to the crowds, even at a distance. One eyewitness reported the "electrifying moment" when Jackson appeared at the Capitol and "the color of the whole mass changed, as if by miracle," as all the men suddenly removed their own dark hats and looked upward, exultant. Jackson bowed, a courtly yet popular touch hard to imagine from John Quincy Adams. (Feeling slighted because Jackson had not paid him a courtesy call, Adams avoided the ceremonies, just as his displaced father had in 1801.) As was then the custom, Jackson delivered his inaugural address—a spare speech that took only ten minutes—before taking the oath of office. Jackson announced that his new administration would be dedicated above all to "the task of *reform*" in government. Then the chief justice of the Supreme Court swore Jackson in. Just as it was for Jefferson thirty years earlier, the first face that Jackson saw as president belonged to John Marshall.[2]

The rest of the day's activities—especially the White House reception, where the outpouring of well-wishers, patronage hunters, and glory seekers got out of hand—are set pieces of American political lore, emblematizing, depending on the viewer, either the ebullience or the crass vulgarity of the president's admirers. An impenetrable mass of fancy carriages and country wagons followed Jackson down Pennsylvania Avenue. Thrown open to the public, the rooms on the lower floor of the White House were jammed with people of every age, class, and color, both men and women, and the crowd around the president was so thick and importuning that hundreds of visitors, including Amos Kendall, had to climb in the window of an adjoining room to get anywhere near him. Although not unduly perturbed by the chaos, Jackson had to beat a retreat down a back stairway and return to his lodgings. "What a scene did we witness!" remembered one caller, Margaret Bayard Smith, a fixture of Washington salon society. "*The Majesty of the People* had disappeared, and a rabble, a mob, of boys, negros, women, children, scrambling, fighting, romping. What a pity what a pity."[3]

Jackson's inauguration was not the only sensational political exhibition and portent of 1829. On New Year's Day, Frances Wright, the Scots-born chestnut-haired "Priestess of Beelzebub," disembarked in New York Harbor, determined to capture the city, and especially its workingmen, for her own brand of radical free thought. She began her campaign with a series of lectures, delivered to mixed audiences of men and women numbering upwards of two thousand, denouncing, in brilliantly theatrical presentations, every kind of social inequality. Another sensation took shape in Boston, at the outermost fringes of American politics, where David Walker, a black dealer in used clothes, wrote down and published a mystical prophecy of American slavery's impending downfall. By year's end, Walker's pamphlet would make him, briefly, the most dangerous man in America.[4]

Andrew Jackson, of course, exercised far greater political influence than Wright, Walker, or any other American over the next four years. As he began his administration, the new president said he would eradicate the privilege that had corrupted the federal government. If he had gained a mandate for anything from his rout of Adams, this was it. But exactly *how* Jackson would reform the government was unclear, just as his stance on numerous major issues, including the tariff and internal improvements, remained usefully flexible and, to some critics, singularly vague. By the end of his first term, many of these questions would be resolved, in conflicts involving everything from parlor intrigues in Washington City to Indian removal in the southeastern states. Yet the greatest conflicts, over the Second Bank of the United States and the South Carolina nullification movement, involved fights over money, slavery, the Constitution, and democracy more powerful than anyone could have foreseen in 1829. Their intensity arose in part from agitation by Frances Wright, David Walker, and other frustrated radicals for whom the boisterous democracy displayed at Jackson's inaugural was at best too limited and at worst an utter fraud.

SCANDALS: TREASURY RATS, SPOILSMEN, AND MRS. EATON

The first weeks of the Jackson presidency were marked by scandals—the first involving not the new administration, but the one that had just departed. Immediately, Jackson began clarifying what he meant by reform by investigating and clearing out the old order. Convinced that President Adams's higher civil service appointees had been awash in peculation, he appointed the trustworthy Amos Kendall as fourth auditor at the Treasury Department, with instructions to report directly to the president. Almost instantly, Kendall discovered that his own predecessor, one Tobias Watkins, a Clay man, had embezzled seven thousand dollars, and there were many more discoveries to come, involving fraud by more than a dozen of the former administration's Treasury and customs house agents. "Assure my friends," Jackson wrote to a political associate in April, "we are getting on here *well*, we labour night and day, and will continue to do so, until we destroy all the rats, who have been plundering the Treasury." By the end of the year, close to three hundred thousand dollars turned up missing at the Treasury Department alone. Additional fraud was exposed in virtually every executive department, down to a racket in the awarding of fishing bounties.[5]

The discoveries formed the backdrop for what has become one of the most widely disgraced if also misunderstood of Jackson's political reforms, the implementation of rotation in office. The replacement of one party's appointees with another—so vexing in 1801, the last time control of the White House passed from one party to the other—had become a nonissue during the decades of the Virginia dynasty. John Quincy Adams's Olympian cross-factional approach to appointments disturbed his supporters, but raised no general debate. Now the issue reemerged, forcefully. During the campaign, Jackson's supporters had spoken of introducing rotation in office as a democratic innovation. Friends of Adams and Clay moaned about an imminent Reign of Terror that would replace experienced career government workers with inept, purely partisan appointees. With the revelations at Treasury and elsewhere, and with supporters from around the country pressing for jobs, Jackson was moved to implement quickly what he now called, simply, "rotation."[6]

Rotation in office had some obvious partisan origins. After Jefferson's presidency, wholesale and heavily partisan replacement policies became common in the states, especially in Pennsylvania and in Van Buren's New York. "The old maxim of 'those who are not for us are against us,' you have so often recognized, that its authority cannot be denied," the Bucktail Jesse Hoyt warned Van Buren shortly after Jackson's inauguration. Jackson expanded on that maxim at the national level, rewarding and goading his supporters with the spur of self-interest as well as patriotic service. With his customary wariness, Van Buren himself (who had quit the New York governorship he had just won to serve as Jackson's secretary of state) actually counseled caution in replacing too many men too quickly, lest the administration look arrogant. But Jackson moved aggressively, approving batches of new appointments at a time.[7]

Too often overlooked are the sincere reformist purposes that Jackson attached to rotation in office—part of the larger reform agenda to which he devoted considerable time and thought, and which would dominate his first annual message in 1829. Jackson hoped to destroy the insider political establishment that was responsible for what he believed had been the theft of the presidency in 1825. Stasis bred corruption in the executive, he thought, just as it bred the odious belief that ordinary men lacked the experience necessary to master the mysteries of government service. He wanted, instead, to ventilate and democratize the executive branch by making official duties "so plain and simple that men of intelligence may readily qualify themselves for their performance." Accordingly, he coupled rotation in office to proposals for what today would be called term limits, both for appointed executive officeholders (for whom four-year terminal appointments seemed to him about right) and for the presidents who appointed them (who should be restricted, Jackson suggested, to a single term of either four or six years).[8]

Although he would later face charges of executive despotism, Jackson limited his major rotation reforms to the executive branch. He did not call for terminal limitations for Congress, where fraud or bribery could be punished by the voters, in the most democratic of solutions. Wary of the constitutional separation of powers, Jackson did not propose terminating federal judges, although he later envisaged replacing lifetime appointments with popular election to seven-year terms. Nor did he propose that rotation should be tied to partisan supremacy. Even if a particular party were to remain in the White House year after year, Jackson's rotation idea would have required a regular turnover of executive employees. Its chief aim was to prevent the formation of a permanent government in the executive branch, an aim that won the approval of no less a political thinker than Jeremy Bentham, who wrote Jackson enthusiastically that he too supported rotation in office and had done so for many years.[9]

Jackson's White House replaced roughly one in ten federal appointees during his two terms as president, no greater turnover than Jefferson had overseen. Still, the replacements were unprecedented in their sweep. Among civil officers directly appointed by the president, the removal rate was nearly one-half. Jackson stretched the constitutional limitations on appointing congressmen to civil posts (and broke with one of his campaign's more specific proposals) by naming more than forty sitting members during his first four years. In 1829 and 1830, plummy postmasterships and deputy postmasterships changed hands by the hundreds, particularly in the less politically reliable New England and middle Atlantic states. Especially outrageous to his foes was Jackson's propensity to appoint loyal newspaper editors, among them Amos Kendall, Isaac Hill, and (as commissioner of the General Land Office) the Ohio editor Elijah Heyward—mere "printers," one Virginian sneered—to conspicuous public office. In the first two years of Jackson's presidency, the State Department moved nearly three-quarters of the contracts for printing federal laws from opposition newspapers to pro-Jackson newspapers. To the fastidious—including Jackson supporters like Thomas Ritchie, himself an editor—the policy seemed to endanger the future of a free and independent American press.[10]

Jackson's loftier democratic intentions widened the circle of executive talent and established a principle on appointments that all parties would adopt in decades to come. But democracy was never perfect. Rotation led to some humiliating disasters, as it became bogged down in politics and the president's own misjudgments. Not all of Jackson's confidants and supporters saw the rewarding of political office in the same reformist light he did, least of all the hard-nosed pols of the Albany Regency. When Van Buren's lieutenant, William Marcy, defended Jackson's policy in Congress and declared that "to the victor belongs the spoils of the enemy," he both twisted reform into a defense of the crassest sort of party patronage and handed Jackson's enemies a new rhetorical club—"the spoils system." Jackson's assessment of character, meanwhile, was sometimes flawed. Himself a man of absolute integrity, he too easily assumed the same about others whom he liked and admired. He had a special weakness for men who, sometime in the past, had gone out of their way to defend his honor—not the best standard for choosing civil officers.[11]

A few of those appointees about whom Jackson felt most strongly proved disastrous. The Kentucky relief war veteran William T. Barry, who was appointed postmaster general when the incumbent, John McLean, refused to make patronage replacements, was singularly incompetent at preventing corruption in the awarding of department contracts and had to be replaced in 1835. ("No department of the government had ever before been subject to so severe an ordeal," Martin Van Buren later wrote.) And to Jackson's enduring shame, he made his worst appointment, New York City fixer Samuel Swartwout, to the most lucrative position of all, the collectorship of New York Port, a job rife with opportunities for larceny. Van Buren objected privately to the president, all but calling Swart-wout a crook, but Jackson brusquely ignored him. After ten years on the job, Swartwout would abscond with over one million dollars—more than all of the Adams-appointed thieves combined.[12]

To his credit, Jackson moved to end abuses once he became aware of their extent; and some of the worst embarrassments only came to light after he had left office.[13] Initially, rotation in office distinguished the new administration from Adams's, changing the tone in Washington and providing Jackson's supporters the assurance that corruption was being uprooted and politically reliably men were getting appointed. More immediately trying for the president was the early jockeying for advantage within the administration, especially between Martin Van Buren and John C. Calhoun, both of whom hoped to succeed Jackson as president. The factional lines, based on substantive as well as personal differ-ences, were already clear in 1829. The struggle commenced in a peculiar salon scandal involving the wife of John Eaton, an old political ally whom Jackson had selected as his secretary of war.

Margaret O'Neale Timberlake Eaton was a dark-haired, fine-featured, unashamed beauty who, at thirty, had risen to a dangerously ambiguous position in Washington society. The daughter of a local Irish immigrant tavern-keeper and hotelier, she had grown up amid the new capital's after-hours politicking and carousing at her father's I Street lodging house, a favorite with congressmen, senators, and visiting politicians from around the country. "I was always a pet," she later remarked. A prodigy of sorts (at age twelve, she was taken to the White House to dance for Dolley Madison), Margaret, by the time she reached woman-hood, had little awe for the great and not-so-great lawmakers of Washington, and none at all for their spouses.[14]

Margaret's first husband, John Timberlake, to whom she bore three children, was a naval officer and purser on the USS *Constitution*. The combination of Timberlake's prolonged absences at sea and his wife's close familiarity with so many public officials gave rise to risqué rumors. John Eaton was smitten by Mar-garet when he first came to Washington as a senator in 1818, and the two were spotted together all too often, in New York as well as in the capital. When, ten years later, Timberlake committed suicide aboard ship (distraught, the gossips said, at Margaret's infidelities), and Eaton, in part at Jackson's urging, promptly married her, the stage was set for a social uproar. Not only was the new Mrs. Eaton—known as "Peggy," affectionately by her friends, snidely by her detrac-tors—an allegedly loose woman of low origins. She was a political wife's worst nightmare, an insider darling who had grown into a bewitching predator and who was now, shockingly, the wife of a cabinet member. To uphold their social honor, a group of administration wives, led by the imperious Floride Calhoun, worked up their indignation into a tempest and snubbed Margaret in every way they could, eventually boycotting any function she attended. The ladies' campaign brought social life in the White House to a virtual halt.

Jackson erupted. As a former guest at O'Neale's lodging house, he knew Margaret well and doted on her. The attack on her and her husband not only offended Jackson's paternalist pride; it was a perfect example of aristocratic contempt stoked by Washington's resident insider snobs. Whatever they might or might not have done that was improper, Jackson thought, the Eatons wound up doing the right thing by marrying. Still grieving over Rachel, he immediately likened Mrs. Eaton's persecution to his wife's during the 1828 campaign. He became consumed with the matter, devoting more than half his time to defending Margaret and railing at all who breathed a word against her. In one of the strangest cabinet meetings in all of American history, Jackson tried to quell the affair by making it the only item on the agenda, and thundered, "She is as chaste as a virgin!" The cabinet wives, unmoved, continued to ostracize Peggy.[15]

There is no evidence that what some called "the Eaton malaria" had any factional origins. Calhoun might have seemed a likely protagonist, given his wife's initial prominence in the snubbing. Yet though he later praised the "great victory . . . in favor of the morals of our country, by the high minded independence and virtue of the ladies of Washington," he and Floride were not even in Washington for most of 1829, having returned to his plantation after the inauguration until Congress convened in December. At least in his correspondence, Calhoun paid little attention to the affair. Yet by the end of 1829, Jackson, who initially suspected Henry Clay, had become convinced that Calhoun was secretly directing everything through his Washington hatchet man Duff Green of the *United States Telegraph*—and the scandal opened a schism.[16]

John Quincy Adams, dryly amused at Jackson's difficulties, reported that Washington was filled with rumors about "the volcanic state of the Administration." In what he called the "moral party" were Calhoun (whose wife became so aggrieved she refused to return to Washington for the winter of 1829–30), Attorney General John Berrien, Treasury Secretary Samuel Ingham, and Secretary of the Navy John Branch, as well as the wife of Jackson's nephew and private secretary, Andrew Jackson Donelson, who, in the absence of a first lady, organized the White House social calendar. All save Mrs. Donelson were Washington social mainstays. The pro-Eaton ranks—which Adams called the "frail sisterhood"—included the newcomer politicians: Van Buren (a widower, and exempt from wifely pressures), William Lewis, William T. Barry, and Amos Kendall (who, though he found Mrs. Eaton unsavory, thought she had been slandered and found the continuing fracas absurd). At bottom, it was a cultural divide, pitting pious, self-important Washington fixtures against new arrivals and local commoners whom they deemed vulgar, loose in morals, and uppity. The cultural reverberations, reminiscent of the sexual scandalmongering and clashing masculine styles evident in the 1828 campaign, were powerful. But the Eaton matter also had direct political implications, as most of Eaton's critics were either southerners or close friends of the Calhouns, or both.[17]

Van Buren made the most of the mess. After failing to persuade Mrs. Donelson to give way and invite the Eatons to something—anything—at the White House, he helped organize receptions and dinners for them elsewhere. The loyal secretary of state's stock with the president rose as quickly as the absent Calhoun's fell. Jackson and Van Buren were seen deep in conversation, strolling across the White House grounds and riding together on horseback around Washington. At year's end, Jackson, suffering from what he thought was dropsy and in fear of his life, privately affirmed that Van Buren—"frank open, candid, and manly . . . Republican in his principles"—and not the devious Calhoun should be his successor.[18]

For John C. Calhoun to suffer politically because of a parlor scandal, instigated by his exasperating, politically uninterested wife, was one of the finer ironies of Jackson's early presidency. Although his sense of rectitude made him recoil at Peggy Eaton, Calhoun had little use for drawing-room triviality. Few politicians' letters even to closest friends and family are as devoid of rumor, whimsy, and small talk as Calhoun's. (An apocryphal story made the rounds that Calhoun once tried to compose a poem, wrote down the word "Whereas," and stopped.)[19] There was, in fact, a great and widening divergence between Calhoun and Jackson over fundamental principles of American government, one that originated in the tariff debates of the late 1820s but that had far greater implications. In a world of Calhoun's choosing, those differences, and not the reputation of a cabinet wife, would have been the focus of political struggle. Soon enough they would be.

STATE RIGHTS AND AN ADMINISTRATION ADRIFT

Amid the continuing Eaton distraction, the annoyed Calhoun, once back in Washington, did stick to his last—although, as vice president, he worked behind the scenes, as he had under Adams, lest he appear openly disloyal. His most important work predated the scandal—the report on the tariff he had promised the South Carolina legislature and completed late in 1828, an assignment that Calhoun turned into a brief dissertation on constitutional theory. Released in December 1828 as a revised report by a special committee of the legislature, the document came to be known as the South Carolina Exposition and Protest, and offered, in slightly watered-down form, the first elaboration of Calhoun's doctrine of nullification. Over the decades since 1787, Calhoun argued, a hidden weakness in the Framers' design had surfaced: a national majority could, if built around a privileged sectional interest, oppress a sectional minority. The protective tariff, to Calhoun an unconstitutional perversion of Congress's power to set impost duties, exemplified the oppression, by exceeding the use of tariffs to raise revenues and aiding one sectional interest while exploiting another. To rectify the problem, Calhoun, alluding directly to Jefferson and Madison, insisted, as the Kentucky and Virginia Resolutions had in 1798, that individual states could weigh in on contested points of authority between themselves and the general government. But whereas Jefferson and Madison had appealed to the states in order to check the Federalists, whom they considered a repressive minority faction, Calhoun aimed to secure the interests of a slaveholding minority against the national majority. Although he would claim that he believed in majority rule, he also insisted that majority rights were not "natural" but "conventional"—and, as he explained in his draft of the *Exposition*, that "representation affords not the slightest resistence" to protect minority interests.[20]

The only cure for majority despotism, Calhoun argued, was to recognize the undivided sovereignty of the individual states that, he asserted, was anterior to the Constitution. Just as the federal government could annul any state law ruled binding, so aggrieved states could void, within their borders, any federal law they deemed unconstitutional. Should three-quarters of the states then fail to revise the Constitution, under the amending power, to make the offending law constitutional, the nullifying state would have the option of seceding from the Union. Calhoun would always insist nullification was not secession, which was literally true. But in seizing on the theory of original state sovereignty, he offered a theoretical justification for both nullification and secession.

To Calhoun's chagrin, the *Exposition* actually adopted by the South Carolina legislature sustained his practical steps for nullification but returned to the more traditional state-rights idea that the federal government and the states each enjoyed sovereignty in their separate spheres. The legislature also added a quotation from Thomas Jefferson at odds with Calhoun's thinking, to the effect that it was wrong to consider either the federal or the state governments as superior to one another. Unwittingly, the legislature indicated how Calhoun, although initially a backcountry Republican, had derived his ideas on nullification as much from conservative Federalist legal writings of the early nineteenth century, which he had imbibed at Tapping Reeve's Litchfield academy and Henry De Saussure's law office, as from Jefferson or Madison. In South Carolina, the low-country aristocrat Timothy Ford had anticipated Calhoun's concept of the minority veto as a check on democratic reforms. The first conceptions of a constitutional right to secession had come from Timothy Pickering and the New England plotters of 1804, and then swirled around the deliberations that led to the Hartford Convention ten years later. Both Calhoun's draft and the final exposition invoked Alexander Hamilton's authority as prominently as Jefferson's and Madison's. Out of this undemocratic political strain came Calhoun's defense of the slaveholders' interests in national politics—an innovative combination of Old Republican state-rights theory and Federalism's disdain for the popular majority. And although the *Exposition* ended with Calhoun's call for patience and conciliation given the change in national administrations, it also put the new administration on notice about what would ensue without a drastic reform of the tariff.[21]

Calhoun's name appeared nowhere on the report, but political observers, including Jackson, suspected his authorship—an effort, some thought, to overcome old political rifts and get the Crawfordite Radicals to support his eventual bid for the presidency. Calhoun's direct influence showed, as well, a year later, when, amid a furious Senate debate over a bill to limit the sale of public lands, the vice president's ally, Robert Hayne of South Carolina, rose in opposition as Calhoun sat presiding over the scene in the Senate chamber. Hayne, trying to nourish an intersectional political alliance, argued that the Northeast was now trying to oppress the West over the land question much as it had the South over the tariff. Daniel Webster, in his famous second reply, linked Hayne's remarks directly to the nullifying "Carolina doctrine," charged that the doctrine threatened the Union, and launched into a formidable defense of the federal government, "just as truly emanating from the people as from the states." He concluded with a phrase once engraved in the memories of American schoolchildren: "Liberty *and* Union, now and forever, one and inseparable." Calhoun, the erstwhile nationalist Republican, had melded undemocratic Federalism with state rights to defend a minority, the planters. Webster, the erstwhile Federalist, emphasized the idea of popular sovereignty and repudiated the idea of state sovereignty, while he proclaimed an emboldened democratic nationalism.[22]

For once, the ex-Federalist Webster's thinking converged with the democrat Andrew Jackson's. However sympathetic he might be to state rights—far more so than Webster—Jackson, the national hero, could never countenance heresies like nullification, least of all over a tariff that, by his strict reading of the Constitution, was explicitly a matter delegated to Congress's control. His estrangement from Calhoun worsened when, during the Eaton scandal, the vice president let it be known that he intended to work hard for a sharp downward revision of the tariff, a move Jackson resisted. Push came to shove in April 1830, at a Washington politicos' banquet honoring Thomas Jefferson's birthday. The gathering had been called by southerners and westerners sympathetic to Calhoun, and one toast after another proclaimed state-rights slogans and attacked sectional favoritism by the federal government. Jackson, provoked beyond his careful preparation, raised his glass, glowered directly at Calhoun, and, as if issuing a dueler's challenge, gravely offered his own toast: "Our Union—it must be preserved." (He had planned to say "Our Federal Union," and so the phrase appeared in the newspaper reports the next day—but in the moment, he omitted the softening adjective.) Some in the thunderstruck audience thought they saw the vice president flinch, and though Calhoun's toast in reply was perfectly calm, its wordiness betrayed that he was on the defensive: "The Union—next to our liberty the most dear; may we all remember that it can only be preserved by respecting the rights of the states and distributing equally the benefits and burdens of the Union." The breach was now public, and within weeks would become bitter political warfare, overlapping the continuing struggle over the Eatons.[23]

The cultural rifts apparent in the Eaton affair showed up in other political developments as well. Among them was Jackson's rejection of the Presbygational Sabbatarian movement that had arisen so swiftly in 1828. During the election campaign, Jackson and his strategists had courted the Sabbatarians, including the formidable Philadelphia revivalist Presbyterian Ezra Stiles Ely. When Ely, in 1827, called for "a Christian party in politics," his chief aim, in the short run, had been to round up Presbyterian support for Jackson, whom he preferred to the suspiciously rationalist John Quincy Adams. But Ely's overbearing appeal offended Baptists and Methodists, wary of connecting religion and politics, as well as those in Jackson's coalition with indifferent religious views. The Senate Committee on the Post Office and Public Roads, chaired by the pro-Jackson Richard Mentor Johnson of Kentucky, issued a blazing response to the Sabbatarian petition campaign as a gross intrusion on the constitutional separation of church and state, "fatal . . . to the peace and happiness of the nation." Jackson's loyalty to Margaret Eaton, in turn, infuriated the Sabbatarians. Ely began a personal crusade to uncover every salacious story he could about Margaret, which he then passed on directly to the president. Jackson's reply, though civil, was seething: "Truth shuns not the light; but falsehood deals in sly and dark insinuations, and prefers *darkness*, because its deeds are evil." As far as any alliance between Jackson and the Sabbatarians was concerned, that was that.[24]

The divide between Jacksonians and Presbygationals ran deeper than the fight over Margaret Eaton. The resumption of the Indian removal battle in Georgia greatly exacerbated the conflict and further defined the character of Jackson's administration. Having outmaneuvered John Quincy Adams and cleared out the Creeks, Georgia's governor George Troup and his successors, John Forsyth and George Rockingham Gilmer, were eager to remove the remaining Cherokees. That goal became even more urgent when gold was discovered on Cherokee land in the summer of 1829. In December 1829, the state legislature declared the constitution and laws of the Cherokee Nation null and void as of the following June 1, 1830—leaving the White House and the Congress little more than five months to settle the issue and determine the Cherokees' fate.[25]

The new controversy differed significantly from the earlier Creek removal. With the aid of missionaries from the Boston-based Presbygational American Board of Commissioners for Foreign Missions, the Cherokees had become a model of cultural assimilation—shifting from the hunt to settled agriculture, converting in large numbers to Christianity, adopting a written alphabet (credited to an ex-warrior, Sequoyah, who had fought with Jackson's forces against the Creek Red Sticks at Horseshoe Bend), and approving a tribal constitution that imitated the U.S. Constitution. Yet the Cherokees' adaptations, along with their insistence on constituting themselves as a sovereign nation within Georgia's borders, only heightened the state's resolve to remove them. And President Jackson, who was unashamedly for removal, would not back off from the situation as his predecessors had, even in the face of determined congressional opposition from northern moral reformers, led by Senator Theodore Frelinghuysen of New Jersey.[26]

In his first annual message in December 1829, Jackson asked Congress for funds to remove the remaining southeastern Indians beyond the Mississippi, and touched off a furious reaction from the forces of Presbygational uplift. To the reformers, Jackson's efforts to make uprooting the Indians a federal matter marked the triumph of crass materialism over respect for humanity and the gospel of Christ. They were certain that Jackson, like the Georgians, had no interest in the Indians' welfare and wanted simply to open up valuable new lands for white speculators and settlers. "How long shall it be," one theology student protester, George Cheever, asked in the *American Monthly Review*, "that a Christian people . . . shall stand balancing the considerations of profit and loss on a national question of justice and benevolence?" Men and women, all across the country (including Georgia), joined in massive petition campaigns demanding that Congress defeat Jackson's plans and uphold the Indians' property rights. (In one of the larger campaigns, Lyman Beecher's daughter, Catharine, the head of the Hartford Female Seminary, initiated the nation's first women's petition drive, holding protest meetings in numerous towns and cities, and gathering thousands of signatures.) The American Board's secretary, Jeremiah Evarts, published an antiremoval legal treatise, *The "William Penn" Essays*, that became one of the most talked-about pamphlets since Thomas Paine's *Common Sense*. In their intensity and organizational sophistication—helped by the communication networks of the growing evangelical churches—the protests surpassed the antislavery "Free Missouri" outbursts of 1819. "A more persevering opposition to a public measure had scarcely ever been made," an amazed Martin Van Buren later wrote.[27]

Jackson, unmoved, saw to it that the relevant House and Senate Indian affairs committees were stacked with pro-removal men—including George Troup, whose earlier extremist actions Jackson deplored but who had been elected to the Senate in 1828. The committees produced similar bills that gave the president the power to reserve organized American lands west of the Mississippi from which Indian tribes could "choose" parcels with perpetual title, in exchange for their eastern lands. In addition, Indians who had improved their existing holdings were eligible for individual allotments of eastern lands, which they could either use to stay in the East or sell to obtain funds required to resettle in the West. Although careful to avoid breaching previous treaties, and to appear as if the Indians remained protected, the vaguely worded bills gave the administration enormous power to dissolve tribal government and hasten removal. They spelled out the eastern Indians' doom.[28]

Senator Frelinghuysen's six-hour speech in opposition to the removal bill was so eloquent that it earned him renown as "the Christian Statesman." Closely following the arguments in his friend Evarts's *"William Penn" Essays*, Frelinghuysen attacked the Georgians and their friends in the War Department for repeated violations of treaties with the Indians, and charged that racial prejudice combined with greed motivated the government's efforts to remove the Indians from their lands. ("Do the obligations of justice," he demanded, "change with the color of the skin?") Frelinghuysen's remarks, publicized widely by the American Board, were unavailing in the Senate, where the removal bill passed easily along party lines. But they did help embolden antiremoval forces in the House, especially among the Pennsylvanians who feared retribution from Quaker voters sympathetic to the Cherokees. Only on May 26, after a series of votes decided by tiny margins, did the House approve the bill.[29]

Just as Jackson's rotation-in-office plans were once considered his administration's chief sin, so, in more recent times, has his insistence on Indian removal become the great moral stain on the Jacksonian legacy. Having stirred great public controversy before its enactment, but virtually none among historians and biographers over the ensuing century and a half, Jackson's Indian policy now stands, in some accounts, as the central drama not only of Jackson's first administration but of Jacksonian Democracy itself. The movement's first crusade, aimed, the critics charge, at the "infantilization" and "genocide" of the Indians, removal supposedly signaled a momentous transition from the ethical community upheld by antiremoval men to Jackson's boundless individualism. Jackson's democracy, for these historians—indeed, liberal society—was founded on degradation, dishonor, and death.[30]

Like all historical caricatures, this one turns tragedy into melodrama, exaggerates parts at the expense of the whole, and sacrifices nuance for sharpness. Jackson truly believed that, compared to his predecessors' combination of high-minded rhetoric, treachery, and abandonment, his Indian policy was "just and humane," and would leave the Indians "free from the mercenary influence of White men, and undisturbed by the local authority of the states." Compared to some of his main political adversaries—notably Henry Clay, whose racist contempt for Indians had once prompted him to remark that their annihilation would cause "no great loss to the world"—Jackson was a benevolent, if realistic paternalist who believed that the Indians would be far better protected under federal jurisdiction than under state law. (Having adopted an orphaned Indian boy in 1813, he was literally a paternalist.) Complaints from northern humanitarians sounded, to him, hollow and morally convenient, considering the devastation and dispossession wreaked by their ancestors on the Pequots, the Narragansetts, the Delaware, and the rest of a long list of all but extinct northeastern tribes. The Pennsylvania Quakers alone could point to the alternative benevolent legacy of Jeremiah Evarts's hero, William Penn. Jackson, reflecting on the history of white abuse of Indians, said he wanted "to preserve this much-injured race."[31]

Above all, the Cherokees' demand for full tribal sovereignty was, to Jackson, unconstitutional as well as unrealistic, a view he had developed long before his election. Article IV, Section 3 of the Constitution stated that "no new State shall be formed or erected within the Jurisdiction of any other State" without the approval of that state's legislature. Acceding to the Cherokees' claims, Jackson believed, would violate that clause, giving Congress the illegitimate power to dismember a state while imposing a burden on Georgia and Alabama that other states did not bear. If granted, tribal sovereignty would establish both congressional powers and an Indian *imperium in imperio* that would potentially threaten national integrity and security as much as the Carolina doctrine of interposition and nullification. And unless the Indians relocated to the federal territories, the federal government would be powerless, under the existing constitutional delegation of powers, to help them in any way. "As individuals we may entertain and express our opinions of [the states'] acts," Jackson observed, "but as a Government, we have as little right to control them as we have to prescribe laws for other nations." With clear discomfort, Jackson would follow precedent and negotiate treaties with the tribes to secure their removal, even though doing so contradicted his rejection of Indian sovereignty. The end justified the inconsistent means. To Jackson, removal was the only way to safeguard both the Indians' future and the Constitution of the United States.[32]

Jackson was not a simple-minded Indian hater. His removal policy propounded views on the division of powers between the federal government and the states that fell between the state-rights extremism of Calhoun and George Troup and the nationalism of John Quincy Adams and Henry Clay. Neither was Indian removal, as proposed in 1830, a cornerstone of Jacksonian Democracy, especially among northern Jacksonians. Even Jackson's congressional loyalists were divided over the administration's bill. In the Senate, resistant northern Democrats joined with the opposition and nearly wrecked the bill with amendments. In the House, the Pennsylvania ex-Federalist Jacksonian Joseph Hemphill (who, a decade earlier, had helped lead the fight in the House against the extension of slavery into Missouri) demanded a decent concern for "the moral character of the country," and proposed delaying removal, appointing a commission to inspect the lands to which the Indians were to be sent, and shifting responsibility over the matter from the White House to the Congress. Hemphill closed his remarks with historical observations that blended hardheaded realism about the Indians' fate with a compassionate sense of tragedy:

> Against the aborigines who once possessed this fair country, what complaint have we to make? In what degree are their scalping knives and tomahawks to be compared to our instruments of death by which we have overthrown their once powerful kingdoms, and reduced the whole fabric of their societies, with their kings and queens, to their present miserable condition? How little did they expect, three hundred years ago, that a race of human beings would come from beyond the great waters to destroy them.

Despite intense pressure from Jackson, twenty-four Jacksonians in the House — some angry at the White House over impending internal-improvement matters, others sensitive to the moral outrage of their constituents — voted "nay," while twelve others absented themselves. Sectional loyalties overrode partisanship: northerners broke two to one against the bill and, along with a handful of southerners, nearly defeated it. Only a solid turnout for the administration by Van Buren's New York delegation, along with the recovery of three Pennsylvanians who had begun to waver, saved the measure — a move that Van Buren later said was so unpopular with New York voters that it nearly killed the Albany Regency.[33]

Nothing exculpates Jackson and his pro-removal supporters from the basic truths in the antiremoval arguments. Jackson's paternalism was predicated on his assumption, then widely but not universally shared by white Americans, that all Indians — although Jackson called them his "brothers," he also called himself their "great father" — were "erratic in their habits" and inferior to all whites. His promises about voluntary and compensated relocation, and his assertion that Indians who wished to remain near "the graves of their fathers" would be allowed to do so, were constantly undermined by delays and by sharp dealing by War Department negotiators — actions Jackson condoned. Consigning Indians who resisted removal to live under state law was itself coercive. Jackson tried to head off outright fraud, but the removal bill's allotment scheme invited an influx of outside speculators, who wound up buying up between 80 and 90 percent of the land owned by the Indians who wished to stay at a fraction of its actual worth. At no point did Jackson consider allowing even a small number of Georgia Cherokees who preferred to stay to do so in select enclaves, an option permitted to small numbers of Iroquois in upstate New York and Cherokees in western North Carolina. Above all, Jackson, determined to minimize federal costs and extinguish the national debt, provided woefully insufficient funds for the care and protection of the relocated. Bereft of long-term planning and a full-scale federal commitment, the realities of Indian removal belied Jackson's rhetoric. Although the worst suffering was inflicted after he left office, Jackson cannot escape responsibility for setting in motion an insidious policy that uprooted tens of thousands of Choctaws and Creeks during his presidency, and would cost upwards of eight thousand Cherokee lives during the long trek west on the "Trail of Tears" — an outcome antiremoval advocates predicted in 1829–30.[34]

The politics of Indian removal also reinforced those elements within the Jackson Democracy that presumed the supremacy of whites over nonwhites, and interpreted any challenge to that supremacy as pretended philanthropy disguising a partisan agenda. True, Jackson's opponents, notably Henry Clay, seized on the issue and aided the antiremoval petition effort, whatever their earlier views of the matter. Noticing the divisions among Jacksonians over removal, especially in the swing state of Pennsylvania, Jackson's adversaries sought to exploit them fully, in preparation for the 1832 election. But to reduce all of the critics, as many of Jackson's supporters did, to "factious" politicians who were out to hurt the administration was to confuse the opportunists with sincere humanitarians like Evarts and Frelinghuysen, while making support for removal a matter of strict party orthodoxy. The attacks echoed those against Republican antislavery advocates as designing Federalists during the Missouri crisis in 1819 and 1820. Recast in the political fires of the 1830s and after, this turn of mind would complicate and compromise the Jacksonian variant of political democracy, by rendering all kinds of benevolent reform as crypto-aristocratic efforts to elevate blacks and Indians at the expense of ordinary white men.[35]

Of more immediate importance, however, in the aftermath of the Indian removal debate was a very different conflict over state rights and federal power, involving Jackson's veto of an internal-improvements bill. Like Indian removal, debates over federal aid to road construction and other transportation improvements had a sectional dimension in the Twenty-first Congress's first session. In March and April 1830, Congress debated a bill, introduced by Joseph Hemphill, for a national highway of some fifteen hundred miles that would extend from Buffalo, New York, to New Orleans, via Washington, D.C. By proposing a north-south route connecting the Great Lakes region to the South, the plan envisaged a two-way, man-made alternative to the Mississippi River as a valuable military resource, a concourse for commerce and migration, and a further bond of Union. It also augured large federal expenditures funded by higher tariffs (and possibly a direct tax), while it extended federal power and, its critics charged, benefited certain areas of the country more than others — all anathema to the South. "National objects!" the pro-Jackson Virginian Philip Barbour exclaimed. "Where is the criterion by which we are to decide?" In a sectional vote, the bill was defeated.[36]

More difficult was the fight over the so-called Maysville Road project. Unlike the Hemphill bill, this proposal called only for federal financing, not federal construction, of a road to connect Maysville and Lexington, Kentucky. Although the proposed road would lie entirely within a single state, its advocates claimed that it would one day be a crucial portion of a national road system, and hence deserved federal support. When both the House and Senate approved the bill late in the session, Jackson was torn: although southern Old Republicans were firmly against it, westerners, including Jackson's trusted allies Amos Kendall and Thomas Hart Benton, were friendly to it. Certain to disappoint at least a portion of his coalition, Jackson turned to his new confidante, Martin Van Buren.[37]

In the spirit of Jeffersonian strict construction—but also displaying his propensity to placate the South, especially after the rancor over the tariff in 1828—Van Buren urged a veto. Extravagant federal spending on improvements, he reasoned, would turn elections into corrupt appeals to the voters' narrow self-interest, while opening up new opportunities for congressional logrolling at the public's expense. Jackson, who had been thinking along similar lines, decided to reject not just the Maysville project but a slew of other federal improvement bills. Yet in his Maysville veto message—written chiefly by Van Buren with the help of a young Tennessee congressman, James K. Polk—Jackson also defended the benefits of a "general system of improvement," praised state road and canal projects, and supported judicious federal spending on projects of clearly national importance. Having bolstered his Old Republican southern supporters, some of whom were leaning dangerously toward Calhoun's more extreme state-rights views, the president, his political circumstances precarious, made clear that he did not oppose all government-aided economic development. He would adhere to that position fairly consistently for the rest of his presidency.[38]

"THINGS, THAT HAVE CORODED MY PEACE, AND MY MIND"

Coming at the very end of the new Congress's first session, the passage of the Indian Removal Bill and the announcement of the Maysville Road veto suggested that Jackson had begun to recover from the rocky first year of his presidency. By the middle of 1830, the influence of Calhoun and the incipient nullifiers was on the wane, while that of Van Buren and more moderate state-rights men had increased. The westerners, led by Thomas Hart Benton, although not yet accorded a major role, remained loyal to the president, as did the New Yorkers and (despite the Indian and national road bill debates) the Pennsylvanians, who had been so important in getting Jackson elected. In 1830, the president displayed a successful mixture of deftness and defiance in his dealings with Congress, as well as indifference to the moral objections of the anti-Indian removal movement. Amid persisting conflicts between different portions of the country, he started to chart his own political and constitutional path.

Jackson was not, however, out of the woods. The idea of reform he had announced at his inauguration had not proceeded far except with respect to rotation. The Eaton scandal continued to rage out of control. The alienation of Vice President Calhoun might well lead to the departure of a key element in his successful electoral coalition, the state-rights southern Radicals. Although Jackson got his way on Indian removal, the intense and well-organized public protests — far more impressive, while they lasted, than the Sabbatarian crusade — gave political momentum to his political adversaries and offended many of his northern supporters.

Finding and maintaining his own way, in defense of what he was starting to call "the great task of Democratic reform," was imperative. "[T]here has been, and are things, that have coroded my peace, and my mind, and must cease," he wrote after Congress adjourned, "or my administration will be a distracted one, which I cannot permit." But even as Jackson stumbled to find his footing, developments outside Washington were compounding divisions over slavery and economic development — and creating versions of democracy that sometimes complemented Jackson's, and sometimes attacked its very core.[39]

11

RADICAL DEMOCRACIES

In June 1830, at the very moment that President Jackson pondered how to repair his corroded peace of mind, the free black David Walker, in Boston, put through the press the third and final edition of his *Appeal in Four Articles; Together with a Preamble, to the Coloured Citizens of the World, But in Particular, and Very Expressly, to Those of the United States of America*. Walker was a marked man, and he knew it. He persisted despite his friends' pleas that he flee to Canada.

In the fall of the previous year, Walker had begun sending batches of the pamphlet southward, some on consignment to scattered sympathizers, most smuggled by friendly sailors and ships' stewards, black and white, who on arrival in Charleston, Savannah, or some other southern port would distribute copies to local blacks. Before long, southern authorities began intercepting the *Appeal* and raising a storm. The mayor of Savannah instructed the mayor of Boston, the old Federalist Harrison Gray Otis, to put an end to Walker's mischief, but Otis refused. (Otis agreed that the pamphlet was an piece of "sanguinary fanaticism," but explained that he could do nothing, as Walker had broken no Massachusetts law.) Southern legislatures considered new laws banning "incendiary" publications like Walker's, and rumors circulated that enraged slaveholders had put a price of three thousand dollars on Walker's head—a sum that would rise to ten thousand dollars were he delivered to the South alive. Then, on August 6, Walker suddenly died. No physical evidence of foul play appeared, but word spread that he had been murdered.[1]

The Walker controversy showed that no matter how much conventional politicians tried to abide by the Missouri Compromise, popular agitation over slavery could not be suppressed. Although cut short, Walker's activities would set in motion a chain of events that completely altered the context of American political conflict over slavery. And these events were only part of an efflorescence of reform movements outside the political mainstream—and intense reactions to those movements—that roiled the 1830s. "With this din of opinion and debate, there was a keener scrutiny of institutions and domestic life than any we had known . . . ," Ralph Waldo Emerson observed from the vantage point of the mid-1840s. "The country is full of rebellion; the country is full of kings."[2]

THE BIRTH OF RADICAL ABOLITIONISM

David Walker's effort was the most ambitious black-led campaign in all of American history to incite a general insurrection of southern slaves. The scheme, and the controversy it provoked, marked the emergence of a new, and defiantly radical, abolitionist movement, at first composed almost completely of northern free blacks. Radical abolitionism—which came to be called "immediatism"—arose as a repudiation of the supposedly benevolent antislavery impulses among prominent whites that, in 1816, had led to the creation of the American Colonization Society (ACS). The brainchild of a New Jersey Presbyterian minister, Robert Finley, the ACS was founded in Washington at a meeting of influential national leaders in 1816, led by Henry Clay. It merged two distinct, and in some ways contradictory, points of view: first, a philanthropic antislavery reformism that aimed to eliminate slavery gradually and allow the ex-slaves the chance to return voluntarily to Africa; and, second, a growing fear among slaveholders that the nation's two hundred thousand free blacks were potential fomenters of slave rebellions.[3]

Holding the group together was a deep pessimism about race relations—the long-standing assumption, as Henry Clay observed, that the "unconquerable prejudices" of whites about skin color doomed any effort at racial reconciliation, and that blacks had better be sent back from whence their ancestors were stolen. Clay made clear that, as a slaveholder, he did not see colonization chiefly as a springboard to emancipation, but rather as a way to alleviate the racial tensions in America while providing those blacks who volunteered to go with a chance to start anew "in the land of their fathers." The ACS won a hundred-thousand-dollar grant from Congress in 1819, and in January 1820, the first group of emigrants set sail for Africa, headed for their new home in a settlement called Liberia. After the dispersal of the ad hoc antislavery movement that arose during the Missouri crisis, the ACS stood as the chief mainstream organization at all critical of slavery. Over the next forty-five years, the group would help transport approximately thirteen thousand free blacks across the Atlantic.[4]

Some prominent free blacks, sharing in the ACS's racial pessimism, applauded the effort. But most northern blacks had no intention of leaving the country of their birth. Several mass meetings attacked the ACS campaign as the first step toward forcing them to do so—an opinion reinforced by the spectacle of forced Indian removal. Four separate gatherings in Philadelphia, from 1817 to 1819, denounced the colonizationists as tyrants. "Here we were born, and here we will die," a memorial from a group of New York City's free blacks declared. By the late 1820s, fear and loathing of the ACS had inspired the foundation of new, outspoken black antislavery benevolent associations in the major northern cities, as well as the appearance, in 1827, of the first black American newspaper, *Freedom's Journal*, edited by the New York activists Samuel Cornish and John Russwurm.[5]

The outbursts emanated from a northern free black population too often slighted in considerations of the antislavery movement. Slavery had struck only shallow roots in much of the North, but there were specific locales, notably New York City and the middle and lower regions of the Hudson Valley, where the institution had been strong before the Revolution, and where, by the late 1820s, the numbers of free blacks were substantial. Joined by newly emancipated migrants from the countryside, urban free blacks formed coherent new communities along the seaboard from Baltimore (where slavery remained) up to Boston. Overwhelmingly poor, and held in contempt by the white majority, free blacks mostly occupied the lower rungs of the emerging seaport working class. But in each city, a critical mass of blacks succeeded in business (mainly in service trades such as hairdressing) and formed a small but vibrant and self-educated class. This class created and supported a variety of local institutions, sacred and secular, ranging from the first African Methodist Episcopal (AME) churches to the Prince Hall African Masonic lodge (named for the black Bostonian who helped found the world's first black Masonic lodge in 1775), to the antislavery benevolent societies. Having established themselves against long odds, propertied free blacks led protests over a variety of issues, including disenfranchisement in New York in 1821 and, later, impending disenfranchisement in Pennsylvania. They regarded the colonizationist movement with special anxiety—the "many headed hydra," as one black Boston abolitionist would describe it.[6]

David Walker was a recent arrival to this northern black variation on the city democracy, having spent much of his young adulthood wandering the South. Born in Wilmington, North Carolina, about thirty years earlier to a slave father and free black mother—and hence, under the laws of slavery, born free—he probably obtained at a local AME church the religious instruction that would profoundly shape his later activities and writings. He may also have heard stories of various rumored and attempted slave uprisings in the Wilmington area that had long disturbed local slaveholders. The possibility that Walker had some connection to the Vesey insurrection affair while he was briefly residing in

Charleston early in 1822 is as elusive as everything else connected with that event—although by his own testimony Walker attended services at the African Methodist church where Vesey was a class leader, and which was allegedly one of the plotters' headquarters. After arriving in Boston around 1825, Walker quickly gravitated to the city's leading black institutions and to the interlocking directorate that ran them. An observant member of the May Street AME church (founded in 1818), Walker also rose to the position of secretary in the Prince Hall Masonic lodge and took a leading role in the antislavery Massachusetts General Colored Association. In March 1827, he became the chief Boston fund-raiser and correspondent for *Freedom's Journal* and would later become an agent for a second paper, Cornish's *Rights of All*.[7]

None of these engagements can fully account for the ferocity of Walker's *Appeal*. No doubt Walker read many antislavery proclamations and writings before and after he arrived in Boston. The apocalyptic imagery of his *Appeal* may have owed something to a fiery pamphlet, Robert Alexander Young's *Ethiopian Manifesto*, published in New York early in 1829—although there is little in the *Appeal* that Walker could not have also picked up himself from the Bible, particularly the book of Revelation. Certainly, Walker's work did not come out of the blue. It only seemed that way, hitting antislavery advocates and southern slave-holders like a lightning bolt.[8]

The *Appeal* declared that the subjugation of American blacks—"the most degraded, wretched, and abject set of beings that ever lived since the world began"—could be blamed on four causes: slavery itself; fatalistic submissiveness to whites by blacks, both slave and free; the callousness and inattention of the so-called Christian churches; and the insidious colonization movement. Through-out, Walker indicted white Americans (using the terms *whites* and *Americans* virtually interchangeably) for their racism. Even Thomas Jefferson—the author of the egalitarian Declaration of Independence and, Walker wrote, "one of as great characters as ever lived among the whites"—had expressed hateful opinions about blacks in *Notes on the State of Virginia*. Only a thorough purging of America's heart and soul could, Walker said, redeem the country. To effect that cleansing, America's blacks would have to shrug off their despair-induced feelings of inferiority, improve their own moral condition, and themselves lead the fight for freedom and racial justice.[9]

Written as if it were intended to be read aloud to illiterate blacks, with entire words capitalized and gaggles of exclamation points, the *Appeal* was a deeply alienated piece of work. Yet it still clung to American political principles and the possibility that they might be salvaged from racial oppression. Although Walker condemned Jefferson, he also regarded the Declaration, with its assertion that all men are created equal, as a model of human and political rights. And although Walker also condemned the Christian clergy (specifically exempting black preachers including Richard Allen, one of the founders of the AME church), his logic and his rhetoric were saturated in Christian faith. Walker held out hope that the whites would come to recognize their unrepublican, ungodly errors, repent, and open the way for a glorious new age of racial reconciliation. "What a happy country this will be," he wrote, "if the whites will listen."[10]

Walker's hopes were slender. Even though the *Appeal* did not explicitly call for a slave insurrection, its preamble suggested that God might cause the whites "to rise up one against another . . . with sword in hand," causing slavery's downfall—clairvoyant lines, coming thirty years before the Civil War. And repeatedly, Walker alluded to an impending black rebellion led by some God-sent Hannibal that would overthrow the white oppressors. No strategist or tactician of revolution, Walker wrote more as if he were a Jeremiah or, perhaps, a John the Baptist, rousing his audience to set their sights on liberation and the coming of the Lord.[11]

Walker's message—and his cleverness in actually smuggling it into the South—understandably shocked slaveholders who well remembered the Vesey insurrection scare of 1822. Even before Walker was dead, legislators in Georgia and Louisiana enacted harsh new laws restricting black literacy and rights to assembly. Similar legislation narrowly passed the Virginia House of Delegates but expired in the state senate; North Carolina adopted its own repressive literacy laws in the autumn of 1830. In Walker's hometown of Wilmington, white mobs harassed the free black neighborhoods. In Savannah, vigilantes and police confronted black sailors and prevented them from disembarking. It was bad enough that free blacks and slaves had learned of the loose talk by antislavery northerners during the Missouri debates. Now the idea of a godly slave rebellion was coming down directly from the North, written and published with impunity by the ever-dangerous free blacks, headquartered safely in New England.[12]

Walker's work provoked a different sort of disquiet among the small bands of white antislavery advocates who had repudiated the colonization movement. During the years immediately preceding the Missouri crisis, a few isolated voices, notably the British émigré Reverend George Bourne, exhorted Americans to commence immediately the abolition of slavery. In 1824, the pamphlet *Immediate, Not Gradual Abolition*, by the English Quaker convert Elizabeth Heyrick, shook up antislavery opinion on both sides of the Atlantic. Otherwise, outside of the ACS, a scattering of white antislavery societies—most of them led by Quakers and unreconstructed antislavery Methodists and Baptists, and a majority of them situated in the nonslaveholding districts of the border states—were fighting a losing battle against slavery's revival.[13] Although their presence was dwindling (especially in the upper South), these little groups did produce a few influential authors, editors, and activists. The most important of them was the peripatetic editor and exhorter Benjamin Lundy.

Slight of build and partially deaf, the indefatigable Lundy made his reputation chiefly from his newspaper, the *Genius of Universal Emancipation*. Born in New Jersey in 1789 to a struggling Quaker family, he had headed west at age nineteen to seek his fortune and spent four years apprenticed to a harness and saddle maker in Wheeling, Virginia. There, the sight of slave coffles so offended him ("the iron entered my soul," he later wrote) that he determined to fight the institution, and after moving across river into Ohio, he organized the Humane Society, intended as the first step toward a national abolitionist organization. He also began writing and working for a local Quaker antislavery newspaper, the *Philanthropist*; then, in 1821, he started the *Genius of Universal Emancipation*. After relocating his family once more to the rugged hill country of East Tennessee, Lundy assumed operation (using the *Genius's* title) of one of the livelier border-state antislavery journals, the Quaker Elihu Embree's *Emancipator*. For the next fifteen years, Lundy traveled from New England to Texas like an itinerant preacher, giving lectures, organizing new antislavery societies, and, when a press was handy, printing new issues of the *Genius* (whose column rules, imprint, and heading he kept packed in a small trunk).[14]

Lundy's antislavery program combined a practical sense of political and constitutional limits with the sense of urgency that had marked the "Free Missouri" stirring of 1819–21, and that the colonizationists utterly lacked. Under his plan, the federal government would abolish slavery only where he claimed it had the clear constitutional authority to do so, as in the District of Columbia. No more slave states would be admitted to the Union; the internal slave trade would be banned; and the three-fifths compromise in the Constitution would be repealed. Where slavery currently existed, Lundy favored moral appeals for gradual emancipation. Aid would be provided for free blacks who wished to depart the country (colonization efforts that Lundy himself pushed by trying to resettle blacks in Haiti, Texas, and Canada), but in the free states, free blacks who wished to remain would be accorded the same civil and legal rights as whites. Lundy's unyielding rhetoric as well as his proposals—slaveholders, he proclaimed, ranked among "the most disgraceful whoremongers on earth"—gained him admiration from free blacks, including David Walker, who singled him out for praise. It also impressed a young white writer and printer in Boston, William Lloyd Garrison.[15]

Garrison, aged twenty-two, first ran across the *Genius of Universal Emancipation* early in 1828, on the exchange newspaper pile in the offices of the pro-temperance *National Philanthropist*, where he had been working since the start of the year. A lean, flinty young man, the son of an alcoholic Newburyport, Massachusetts, sailor and his devout Baptist wife, Garrison had been a working printer for nearly a decade, first as an apprentice in his hometown and then for two years as editor of his own paper, the *Free Press*, before he moved to Boston. Although his formal schooling was limited, Garrison had thrived in the world of the self-taught mechanics, gaining a love for literature and poetry as well as for politics. (While at the *Free Press*, he befriended the budding Quaker poet John Greenleaf Whittier and published some of Whittier's early works.) His opinions on public affairs tended toward the uplifting National Republicanism of John Quincy Adams, but Garrison grew impatient with electoral politics and enlisted in the temperance cause—"a great moral influence," he wrote. Under the sway of Lundy's paper—and of Lundy himself, who showed up in Boston on one of his tours in March 1828—Garrison then resigned from his job at the *Philanthropist* and threw himself into antislavery work.[16]

Frustrated by white Bostonians' indifference, Garrison took a brief detour back into partisan politicking as editor of a pro-Adams sheet in Bennington, Vermont—but by the spring of 1829, he was back in Boston, sharing a room with his old friend Whittier and earning his keep with temporary printing jobs. Invited by, of all groups, the local branch of the Colonization Society to deliver a Fourth of July address at the prestigious, all-white Congregationalist Park Street Church, he made the most of the opportunity. Dressed with studied informality, open-necked and spread-collared in the Byronic romantic style, Garrison condemned the Fourth of July as a nauseating spectacle filled with "hypocritical cant about the rights of man." Imagine, he bid his listeners, if the oppressed slaves were ever to rise up in rebellion: would their justifications not fairly replicate Jefferson's Declaration? Was slavery not founded on absurd and immoral racial prejudice— the same prejudice that the slaveholder and charlatan Jefferson had expounded in *Notes on the State of Virginia*? "Suppose that . . . the slaves should suddenly become white," Garrison exclaimed. "Would you shut your eyes upon their sufferings and calmly talk of constitutional limitations?" He implored his audience: "*Let us not shackle the limbs of the future workmanship of God.* Let us, then, be up and doing."[17]

It was as forceful a denunciation of slavery and racism as any white American had ever publicly delivered, and Garrison would soon be making even more radical assertions. Although the exact connections are obscure, there can be little doubt that Garrison's heightened radicalism owed a great deal to his widened contacts with black abolitionists—including, quite possibly, David Walker, who appears to have named a son after him. Garrison also discovered one of Reverend Bourne's old pamphlets, which impressed on him a maxim: "Moderation against sin is an absurdity." When, in August 1829, Garrison took up Lundy's invitation to join him in Baltimore (where Lundy had temporarily settled) as assistant editor of the *Genius*, he, unlike his mentor, had embraced the idea that slavery's demise must commence immediately.[18]

Within weeks, Garrison became a target for repression. After the *Genius* condemned a Massachusetts merchant for allowing one of his ships to be used to transport slaves, Baltimore authorities, possibly at the instigation of pro-Jackson

Maryland officials, tried and convicted Garrison on a seldom-invoked charge of "gross and malicious libel," and sent him to jail for six months. Dramatizing his role as a prisoner of conscience — in fact, he was kept in the kindly warden's own comfortable home — Garrison wrote a pamphlet on intellectual freedom, which Lundy published and which prompted the prominent New York evangelical Arthur Tappan to pay his fine. His notoriety growing, Garrison then lectured up and down the East Coast, drumming up support for a new weekly newspaper he planned to publish in Boston.[19]

"I am in earnest — I will not equivocate — I will not excuse — I will not retreat a single inch — AND I WILL BE HEARD." With the now-famous lines of his first editorial, on January 1, 1831, Garrison announced that his new paper, the *Liberator*, would plant the standard for an uncompromising immediatism on slavery. The paper carried on the work of the *Genius*, collecting news of antislavery efforts and evil complicity with slavery from around the country. But the *Liberator* was pointed in its rejection of gradualism — "a sentiment," Garrison declared, "so full of timidity, absurdity, and injustice."[20]

Garrison's continuing ties with black activists were crucial to his work. Most of the initial financial support for the *Liberator* came from blacks in Boston and other cities, above all the wealthy Philadelphia sailmaker and antislavery leader James Forten. Blacks constituted the majority of the newspaper's subscribers during its first year. Garrison, accordingly, opened the *Liberator*'s columns to black activists, male and female, covering black benevolent and political association activities and publishing work by such formidable figures as Forten and contributors like the former servant Maria Stewart. In July, Garrison published a twenty-four-page pamphlet based on speeches he had delivered to black groups in New York and Philadelphia, reiterating his newspaper's dedication to racial equality and inviting black support from outside of Boston. In his boldest move, Garrison also printed sympathetic appraisals of, and extensive excerpts from, Walker's *Appeal*, deprecating its violent passages but extolling its hatred of slavery and white supremacy. ("It is not for the American people, as a nation," he wrote of the *Appeal* in the second issue of the *Liberator*, "to denounce it as bloody or monstrous.")[21]

In his newfound immediatism, Garrison also forever broke with mainstream American politics. Not surprisingly, in view of his Federalist–National Republican background, he assailed Jackson's administration in Washington — above all the slaveholder at its head who, Garrison declared as early as 1828, ought to be "manacled with the chains he has forged for others and smarting under the application of his own whips." By 1831, however, Garrison had renounced all political parties as hopelessly compromised. No political leader had earned greater admiration from the young Garrison than Henry Clay, the great champion of economic development and uplift. But Clay's support for colonization, and his political fraternization with the slaveholders of his own party, betrayed his moral bankruptcy. Henceforth, Garrison would seek to redeem the nation's soul by agitating outside the political system and renouncing the slightest complicity with slavery and racial discrimination.[22]

Apart from its black supporters—who hailed Garrison as the greatest white man in America—the *Liberator* caused the largest stir among southern slaveholders and their northern political friends. It quickly became a favorite resource for the most outspoken southern pro-slavery papers, which would reprint Garrison's copy as proof positive that fanatics had overrun the northern states. Nearly as contemptuous were northern papers, Jacksonian and anti-Jacksonian alike, that lambasted Garrison as a "mawkish sentimentalist" who was ranting against "imaginary sufferings."[23] But these attacks on Garrison and on radical abolitionism would come to seem gentle after August 1831, when a cataclysmic slave insurrection struck Virginia.

Nat Turner was an unlikely rebel—which made the blood-drenched rampage he helped to lead all the more chilling. Born in rural Southampton County, Virginia, one week before Gabriel Prosser was hanged in Richmond, ninety miles to the north, he was thirty years old at the time of the revolt: shy of company and physically unimposing, broad-shouldered but of medium height, beardless, with thinning hair. As Turner himself would attest, his latest master had treated him kindly, causing Turner, a field worker, no complaints. Turner was a devout Christian, a sometime Baptist preacher who claimed to prefer "devoting [his] time to fasting and praying." Yet it was apparently this piety that bid him into battle.[24]

In 1821, Turner ran away from his overseer, but returned after thirty days. Like many runaways, he may simply have become tired and hungry, and his hunger may have overcome his other senses; in any case, he later reportedly said that he received instruction from a holy vision to "return to the service of my earthly master." Four years later (after his sale to one Thomas Moore), Turner had another vision, of blood drops on ears of corn in the fields, and of hieroglyphs and blood-drawn pictures of men in the leaves in the woods. Three years after that, the heavens roared, and the Spirit appeared to Turner once more, telling him that the Serpent had been loosened, that Christ had laid down the yoke He had borne for men's sins, "and that I should take it on and fight against the Serpent, for the time was fast approaching when the first should be last and the last should be first."[25]

In 1830, Turner was moved to the home of Joseph Travis, the new husband of Thomas Moore's widow. (Formally, Turner was the property of his recently deceased master's infant son, Putnam.) The following February, a solar eclipse signaled to Turner that the appointed time had arrived, and he began making preparations with four close friends for an uprising on July 4, only to fall sick, forcing a postponement. Finally, on August 13, a disturbance in the atmosphere tinctured the sun a bluish green. It was the Spirit's last sign. A week later, Turner and six confederates slipped off into the woods, barbecued and ate a stolen pig, washed it down with stolen brandy, and then made a whole new set of plans. At two the next morning, they hacked to pieces Joseph Travis and his entire household of five, including the baby Putnam Moore, before marching off with some pilfered rifles, old muskets, and powder.[26]

Salathul Francis and his wife, asleep six hundred yards down the road from the Travises, were the next to die, followed by a Mrs. Reese and her son, followed by one household after another, upwards of a dozen, in a winding trail that left every white person who could be found (including the ten children at Levi Waller's place) axed, clubbed, or shot into mangled corpses, their blood sprinkled, according to one account, by Turner on the other rebels. At midday, the slaves—their force now numbering between fifty and sixty, most of them on horseback—headed south to lay to waste the town of Jerusalem, the closest settlement and the site of an armory. They may have intended to hide thereafter in the nearby and virtually uninhabitable Great Dismal Swamp. But the marauders never made it. Alerted to the devastation, a band of white militiamen confronted and scattered the killers only a few miles from their goal. After several skirmishes continuing into the next day, the rebellion was over.

Turner escaped the scene and avoided capture until the end of October. At least fifty-five whites had been slain, and a like number of slaves, including Turner, were tried for the crimes, of whom thirty-two were convicted, twelve transported out of the state and twenty executed (with their masters receiving due financial compensation from the Commonwealth of Virginia). Shortly before his death, Turner gave an extended interview to a profit-minded physician named Thomas Gray, whose rendition of Turner's account, published as *The Confessions of Nat Turner*, remains the fullest (if, perforce, highly questionable) piece of evidence about what transpired. Once he was hanged, Turner's body was dissected, as any eighteenth-century criminal's would have been. If there is any truth to the folk legends, the authorities then grilled down his flesh into grease and ground his bones into dust.

In strictly military terms, the Southampton insurrection amounted to a pin-prick against the slaveholders' regime. Only a tiny portion of an isolated Virginia county had been affected. The terror lasted only a single night and a single morning. Some slaveholders reassured themselves (and tried to reassure others) that although the rebels had wreaked gruesome havoc, most slaves in the surrounding countryside did not rush to join them, and at least a few had helped their masters fight the rebels off—a moment of truth that supposedly proved slavery's basic soundness. One contributor to a Richmond paper saw the occasion as one to pay "tribute to our slaves . . . which they so richly deserve."[27]

A very different perspective comes with the recognition that Turner's rebellion was the deadliest domestic uprising in the nation before the Civil War. If Walker's *Appeal* had offered a pretext for servile mayhem, and Garrison had helped disseminate Walker's ideas, the Virginia episode had made the mayhem real. A panic wave gripped most of the South, as slaveholders began wondering whether beneath the kindly deferent visages of their own bondsmen lurked more Nat Turners, just waiting to strike. Slaves in Virginia and North Carolina were rounded up as suspects in the plot, tried, and executed, while white mobs murdered (and, in some cases, tortured first) upwards of two hundred blacks. Southern editors lashed out at the seditious northerners and their free black southern accomplices whom they blamed for provoking the bloodshed. The *Richmond Enquirer*, quick to detect conspiratorial designs, asked its readers to send information about anyone circulating either Walker's *Appeal* or Garrison's *Liberator*. In Washington, the anti-Jacksonian, pro-colonizationist *National Intelligencer* called on the mayor of Boston to suppress the "diabolical" *Liberator* and punish "the instigator of human butchery" who ran it. The Georgia legislature offered a five-thousand-dollar reward to anyone who brought Garrison down from Boston to stand trial for seditious libel.[28]

The chances that Nat Turner or any of his accomplices, in out-of-the-way Southampton County, knew anything about Walker's and Garrison's writings are unlikely. (By his own testimony, Turner had begun receiving divine instruction a decade before the *Liberator* even appeared.) Garrison, for his part, said that he was "horror-struck" at the first reports of the massacre, his pacifist soul shaken by a nightmare prediction turned "bloody reality." Yet as if to confirm the slaveholders' worst charges, Garrison also refused to condemn the Southampton rebels, noting that their oppression, and not his words, had inflamed the slaves' unholy vengeance. Garrison's stance—as one of a handful of editors to say anything on behalf of the uprising—redoubled the attacks against him, which only stoked Garrison's fury. By the end of 1831, he had increased both the sheet size and the page count of the *Liberator*. At the start of the new year, he was hard at work founding the first American organization of its kind dedicated to immediatist abolitionism, which he hoped would become a model to all righteous Americans, the New England Anti-Slavery Society.[29]

The rise of the abolitionist radicals aggravated divisions within the North and the South as well as between them. The immediate impact was less severe in the North, where, as of 1831, abolitionism remained politically marginal. But in the South, the radical and violent turns in antislavery agitation instantly stirred up abiding differences over slavery—and over the desirability of democracy for white men. Although southerners had united, a decade earlier, around the proposition that slavery should not be barred from the new state of Missouri, there was no consensus over slavery's long-term future. The strains, evident in the Missouri debates, between pro-slavery men like the South Carolinian William Smith and more ambivalent, border-state diffusionists like Henry Clay persisted, as did political and social tensions between slaveholders and nonslaveholders, especially in the upper South. Walker's and Garrison's invective, punctuated by the Southampton massacre, forced a reevaluation on all sides and led to political struggles that quickly became entangled with continuing efforts by plebeian democrats to remove the remnants of patrician domination. In no southern state did these struggles erupt with greater force, or with greater significance, than in Virginia.

SUFFRAGE AND SLAVERY IN VIRGINIA

Democratic reform, for white men only, advanced unevenly in the South after 1825. At one extreme were the western cotton-kingdom states of Alabama and Mississippi, the most democratic in the region—defining the slave-based Master Race democracy. Alabama's constitution of 1819 underwent minor democratic revision in 1830, reducing the terms of state judges from life to six years. Two years later, Mississippians adopted a new constitution that established universal white manhood suffrage, as in Alabama, but that also, surpassing Alabama, eliminated county courts in favor of boards of police (their members elected for two-year terms) and opened all state judgeships to popular election for limited terms of office. At the other extreme was South Carolina, where allied low-country and backcountry planters ruled virtually unchallenged through a centralized system buttressed by high property qualifications for officeholding and selection of the governor by the omnipotent legislature. Reform was almost hopeless in a state whose rulers candidly admitted that they held all power. "The people have none," John C. Calhoun's friend James H. Hammond would later remark, "beyond electing members of the legislature—a power very negligently exercised from time immemorial."[30]

Virginia's Tidewater and Piedmont squirearchy, although nearly as adept as the South Carolinians at deflecting democratic rumblings, faced greater difficulties. The commonwealth's nonslaveholding counties west of the Alleghenies—particularly in the northern region around Wheeling—were expanding rapidly, thanks to continued migration from Pennsylvania, New Jersey, and Delaware. Between 1820 and 1829, the population of the western part of the state rose by nearly 40 percent, compared to a rise of only about 2 percent in the Tidewater counties. With its craggy terrain, ill-suited to slave production of cash crops, and with a populace consisting largely of Pennsylvania Dutch and Scots-Irish, the area was more an extension of the free-labor North than of the slave South. East of the Alleghenies and west of the Blue Ridge Mountains, in the Shenandoah

Valley, slaveholder émigrés from eastern Virginia prospered. Overall, the percentage of slaves in the valley's population, although greater than in the far West, was about half that of the Piedmont and Tidewater counties east of the Blue Ridge. Virginia's borders contained two distinct social orders, with the valley serving as a buffer zone. As the western population continued to swell while the eastern population stagnated, efforts to throw off the East's political domination, secured by the freehold suffrage requirements and an increasingly malapportioned legislature, were bound to revive.[31]

Additional pressure for political reform emanated from the growing cities of eastern Virginia, above all the state capital, Richmond. The city's nonfreeholders, including mechanics and shopkeepers, had long chafed at their exclusion from voting in state elections. By the 1820s, when their numbers had grown to include nearly half of the city's free adult males, they organized as never before to eliminate the freehold suffrage. ("We most earnestly wish that the state . . . would give us some practical proofs of that republican spirit and vigilance that she so much boasts of," said one editorial in 1821.) They were joined in their complaints by leading local editors from opposing political camps, most conspicuously Thomas Ritchie of the *Enquirer* and John Hampden Pleasants of the *Constitutional Whig*, who worried about losing the loyalties of western farmers.[32]

A new round of reform agitation began in 1824, culminating in a popular convention of western counties, held in Staunton in August 1825, which demanded an end to the political monopoly of "the slave owning eastern aristocracy." Conservatives in the eastern-dominated legislature held their ground and rejected, in three successive sessions, bills that would have convened a state constitutional convention. Finally, in 1828, the general assembly approved putting the question to a popular referendum—and with one-fourth of the Tidewater vote (chiefly in the cities) and nearly half of the Piedmont vote breaking in favor of a convention, the reformers won a convincing victory. The old Tidewater and Piedmont regions still held the upper hand: in the subsequent legislative vote over the apportionment of convention delegates, easterners, a slender majority of the state's free population, wound up with two-thirds of the delegates. But the convention's political divisions proved complex, as roughly one in five of the ninety-six delegates ended up supporting reform of certain restrictions and not of others, creating ever-shifting coalitions and uncertain majorities.[33]

The convention met at Richmond in early October, an event as rich in its political symbolism as it was stark in its sectional cleavages. The site, the house chamber of Jefferson's elegantly designed state capitol, was a monument to classical order, reason, and deliberation. The delegates included the greatest living eminences of two generations of Virginians, among them two former U.S. presidents (Madison and Monroe) and the chief justice of the U.S. Supreme Court, John Marshall. In their finery, the easterners, a mixture of Jacksonians, anti-

Jackson National Republicans, and surviving Old Republicans and Federalists, looked every bit as imposing as they hoped to, in what would be their last great collective act as self-appointed guardians of the Revolution's wisdom. The westerners set a very different tone, their ill-cut homespun suits and mud-flecked boots summoning up a rough-hewn democratic future. Their foremost delegate, Philip Doddridge, won grudging admiration from some of the easterners for his breadth of knowledge and command of facts, but he also evoked derision as "a low thick broad shoulder'd uncouth looking man" who spoke with a Scots-Irish brogue and lacked "the bland and polished manner belonging to the South."[34]

The debates themselves featured, from both sides, some of the most direct, informed, and intellectually engaging arguments heard anywhere since the Revolution about the pros and cons of democracy. The most spirited exchanges concerned representation and the freehold suffrage. The westerners argued for apportioning the lower house solely on the basis of white population, making the familiar claim that property owning was no measure of political virtue and that representation based on property was a tyrannical violation of natural rights. Their opponents, including an articulate forty-year-old judge from Northampton County, Abel Upshur, adapted the traditional "stake-in-society" justifications for patrician predominance, including the argument that the propertied, through taxes, did most to support the state. In terms familiar to any reader of Edmund Burke—an influential authority in Virginia—the easterners stressed solidity, permanence, tradition, and the unforeseen consequences of seemingly equitable change. They insisted that the possession of property helped temper the disruptive passions and weaknesses common to all mankind. They also candidly admitted that the struggle involved clashing interests as well as different philosophies, and they backed an amended plan basing representation on a formula that combined population and property. "If the interests of the several parts of the Commonwealth were identical, it would be, we admit, safe and proper that a majority of *persons only* should give the rule of political power," Upshur explained. "But our interests are not identical, and the difference between us arises from property alone."[35]

"Property" was a dazzling abstraction. Everyone knew that it was the easterners' form of property in humans, as well as the greater value of their property, that set them apart from the westerners. Some delegates, including Upshur, forthrightly acknowledged the fact and expanded on it. Easterners agreed that what Upshur called their *"peculiar"* property, "exposed to peculiar impositions, and therefore to peculiar hazards," needed peculiar protection, but they disagreed over how best to achieve it. One faction argued that fairer representation was required to reinforce the westerners' (and nonfreeholder easterners') allegiance to slavery. Chapman Johnson, a Richmond lawyer representing a Piedmont county, said that proper apportionment would reinforce "a feeling of affection and sentiment of justice" between slaveholders and nonslaveholders, curbing any temptations to attack slavery. Others believed exactly the reverse, that adding to the westerners' power would badly undermine the slaveholders' regime.[36]

The antidemocratic arguments held sway among the easterners. The majoritarian rule of "King Numbers," John Randolph insisted (in the last significant public appearance of his life), would create the sort of "Robinhood Society," promoted by the deluded Jefferson, that would lead to a plundering of the slaveholders' property through unfair taxation. Upshur said that easterners could not even count on the cooperation of slaveholders in the West "in any measure calculated to protect that species of property, against demands made upon it by other interests, which to the western slave-holder, are of more important and immediate concern." Others appealed more openly to class presumptions, while also contesting Jefferson's authority. Although intellectual and morally superior to black slaves, the clubfooted conservative Benjamin Watkins Leigh of Chesterfield County charged, the "peasantry of the west" had no more ability to govern than any other peasantry the world over. "I ask gentlemen to say, whether they believe," Leigh asked the convention, "that those who are obliged to depend on their daily labour for daily subsistence, can, or do enter into political affairs? They never do—never will—never can." So "large a dose of French rights of man" as the reformers demanded, Leigh claimed, would plunge Virginia into "fever, frenzy, madness, and death."[37]

Similar divisions appeared over the freehold suffrage. One young reformer from the Piedmont, directly rebutting Leigh, invoked Jefferson and Paine ("whose immortal work, in the darkest days of our revolution, served as a political decalogue") and, with his western allies, attacked the property-based suffrage as a denial of popular sovereignty and free government. Others, from the East as well as the West, defended reform on pro-slavery grounds, citing the urgent need, as one westerner put it, "to call together at least every free white human being, and unite them in the same common interest and Government." Eastern conservatives scoffed at such "visionary" and "theoretical" proposals, and proclaimed their unswerving belief that voting rights belonged only to those who possessed what Philip N. Nicholas of Richmond called the "permanent interest and attachment" that came with owning land, a "durable," "indestructible kind of property." They also argued that expanding the white electorate to include large numbers of nonslaveholders might lead to emancipation, not least, Upshur said, because of the westerners' proximity to Ohio and Pennsylvania, whose "moral sentiment" against slavery would assuredly be felt. "Expediency" (a word the easterners used repeatedly) demanded an unequal suffrage as well as a property-based system of representation.[38]

Defections by Piedmont representatives in the crucial convention votes prevented the eastern conservatives from prevailing outright, despite their disproportionate majority of delegates—but the old guard salvaged a great deal. After the population-property formula for representation was defeated, the conservatives regrouped and narrowly won permanent reapportionment on the basis of the obsolete 1820 census returns, thereby securing for the Tidewater and Piedmont a reduced but still substantial artificial majority in the lower house. The fifty-dollar freehold suffrage requirement was eliminated, but a twenty-five-dollar freehold survived in its place—enough to disenfranchise about one-third of the state's white freemen. The malapportionment of the state senate was left untouched, as was the power of the legislature to select the state's governor and the members of the state judiciary, thus preserving the county-court system that Jefferson had so despised.[39] Westerners hated the results, and in the referendum on ratifying the new constitution, they rejected it by a 5 to 1 margin—but to no avail. Expediency, as understood by the most undemocratic slaveholders, had triumphed.[40] Or so it seemed for a little over a year, when the Southampton insurrection suddenly forced Virginians to reassess what was expedient and what was not.

On January 16, 1832, Thomas Jefferson Randolph of Albemarle County—the dutiful and favored grandson of the departed great man—rose in the House of Delegates chamber and offered up a prophecy as lurid as David Walker's. To Randolph, it was obvious that were slavery perpetuated, troubles far worse than those that had recently hit Southampton County would befall future generations of Virginians. In time, he predicted, the Union would dissolve over the slavery issue. Northern armies, including black soldiers, would invade Virginia and arm the slaves. When the white men of the South marched off to repel the invaders, their women and children would be "butchered and their homes desolated in the rear." The only way to forestall the inevitable was to rid Virginia of slavery and blacks once and for all. And Randolph had a plan. All slaves born after July 4, 1840, would be freed upon reaching adulthood—women at age eighteen, men at twenty-one. All those freed would then be state property and shipped to Africa, their costs covered by the freed slaves themselves once they had earned enough as hired-out workers to finance their passage. By 1861, Randolph calculated, Virginia would be entirely free of slavery, and its population would be virtually lily-white.[41]

Randolph's proposal gained instant approval from the state's leading newspapers, as well as, more surprisingly, from the state-rights extremist Governor John Floyd and some of the key slaveholders in the legislature. The "defenceless situation of the master and the sense of injured right in the slave," James McDowell Jr. from the Shenandoah observed, demanded emancipation and colonization. Western representatives, convinced that slavery was responsible for their continued political subjugation, rallied to the emancipation cause. Eastern defenders of slavery hastily drafted rebuttals, claiming that the dangers of insurrection were small given the overwhelming contentment of the slaves and that, in any event, the legislature had no power whatsoever to abridge slaveholders' property rights.[42]

The two weeks of debate that followed proceeded within well-defined limits. Although a few of the pro-emancipationists talked of extending humanity and justice to the slaves, the majority took more self-interested and, often, racist positions. Slavery, some charged, had shackled the Virginia economy to an outmoded cash crop, tobacco, and hampered the economic diversification that would be the state's only guarantee of future prosperity. Slavery, said others, injured the manners and the morals of the white population, while leaving whites vulnerable to uprisings. Slavery, said still others, would only lead to the spread of what one delegate called the "slothful, degraded African" into the virtuous white western counties. The pro-slavery delegates, for their part, backed off from their endorsements of slavery as benevolent and stressed property rights above all. Even the redoubtable reactionary Benjamin Watkins Leigh remarked that the legislature had no business interfering with the "evil" of slavery.[43]

The outcome of 1830 foretold the outcome of 1832. Rather than choose one of several emancipation proposals, including Randolph's, the reformers drafted a more general proclamation that legislative action against slavery was—the word appeared once more—"expedient." The representatives from the trans-Allegheny West voted unanimously in favor, as did three-quarters of the representatives from the Shenandoah Valley. Had the constitutional convention a year earlier apportioned the lower house of the legislature on the basis of white population, the vote would have come down to the wire. Instead, thanks to the easterners' manipulated majority, the measure was comfortably defeated, 73 to 58—but the controversy was not nailed completely shut. When the pro-slavery men proposed tabling further discussion of emancipation, eleven eastern slaveholders joined with the nine who had backed emancipation to keep the debate roiling. The eastern moderates then helped the western emancipationists pass a resolution to commence slavery's demise by colonizing free blacks as a "first step," to be followed by colonizing slaves once a "more definite development of public opinion" had been achieved. A toothless measure, it gave the emancipationists a small symbolic victory.[44]

With hindsight, historians commonly render the Virginia slavery debates as a thorough and stunning triumph for the most obdurate pro-slavery forces, and a turning point in the rise of pro-slavery politics in the South. Defeated in 1832, gradual abolition would never again be seriously debated in Virginia, and debated only briefly thereafter in Tennessee and Kentucky. Eastern resistance to democratic reform in 1829 and 1830 had helped ensure successful resistance to emancipation two years later. After the debates were over, influential Virginians, above all Thomas Roderick Dew of William and Mary College, chastised the legislature for its loose talk about emancipation, and began hazarding more insistent pro-slavery arguments.[45]

At the time, however, the Virginia debates described a much messier reality in which neither the slaveholders' domination over the Commonwealth nor white solidarity over slavery seemed completely certain. Some observers saw the debates as but a first step toward slavery's eventual removal. The outcome, the Richmond *Constitutional Whig* happily reported, was immediately *"deemed favorable to the cause of abolition,"* which could proceed "when public opinion is more developed . . . and means are better devised."[46] The breach between the state's western emancipationist country democrats and the eastern slaveholder gentry had widened. The old regime, with all its polished manners, had preserved itself only with bothersome political exertions and distasteful concessions. At crucial moments, the old regime had divided against itself and had failed to mount a powerful argument on slavery's behalf. It was a failure of discipline as well as of will that was incomprehensible to slaveholders in other parts of the South, especially the united slaveholders of John C. Calhoun's South Carolina. That failure toughened the South Carolinians' own resolve to resist all encroachments on their prerogatives, whether undertaken by the Yankee oppressors or by backsliding southerners.

The Virginia events also dramatized the growing differences—and, in some respects, similarities—between the slave South and the free North. Apart, perhaps, from Rhode Island, no northern state was ruled by a single class of property owners. The conservative antidemocratic views of John Randolph and Abel Upshur were quickly disappearing on the other side of the Mason-Dixon Line. Yet disputes about labor, property, and democracy also erupted in the burgeoning northern cities during the late 1820s and early 1830s. In part, these arguments arose from the consolidation of a new class of pious urban businessmen, caught up in the moralizing impulses unleashed by the northern version of the Second Great Awakening. They also arose from the spread of the transformed, working-class city democracy that the Philadelphia Mechanics' Union of Trade Associations and Working Men's Party had initiated in 1827—and from some short-lived but spectacular developments in the city of New York, which heightened conflicts over banks, monied power, and political justice. The religious revivals and labor radicalism of the North defined opposing ethics and social outlooks. Both would have deep and lasting effects on national politics.

REVIVALS AND LABOR RADICALISM IN THE NORTH

Nothing better signified the enormous surge of northern commerce and industry after 1815 than the growth of cities.[47] Although the preponderance of the northern population remained rural, an extraordinary rate of urban growth, fed by immigrants and rural migrants—the fastest rate in American history—betokened the emergence of a modern, diversified commercial and industrial northern economy. The resulting stresses and strains astonished observers. New York impressed most of all, supplanting Philadelphia as the seaboard metropolis, its economy fattening off the Erie Canal traffic and the cotton trade connecting New Orleans with Britain and Europe. New York's wharfside forest of masts surrounded a sprawling pandemonium of rich and poor, native-born and newcomers. Two axes were quickly coming to define the distinctly charged poles of New York life: Broadway, slanting north-westward from the Battery, with its fine shops and hotels and churches; and the Bowery, slanting north-eastward, with its groggeries, cheap oyster houses and popular theaters creating what a later writer would call the city's proletarian pandemonium, "in such a condition that Christian men and women are disposed to keep shy." Clustered around these poles, and moving between them, was the most polyglot, minutely stratified population in America, including the nation's largest manufacturing and seaport working class.[48]

Other, smaller cities ranged from the rough-hewn to the spectacular. Alongside the newly constructed roads and canals, settlements arose to process farmers' goods for shipment to the larger cities and abroad, and to distribute goods (from farm tools to ladies' finery) to the western hinterland. "The transition from a crowded street to the ruins of a forest, or to the forest itself, is so sudden" a British traveler noted of Rochester, New York, alongside the Erie Canal, "that a stranger, by turning a wrong corner in the dark, might be in danger of breaking his neck over the enormous stumps of trees." More imposing were the enormous power-loom cotton manufactories and adjacent boardinghouses constructed in East Chelmsford, Massachusetts (now renamed Lowell), by a consortium of capitalists called the Boston Associates, its workforce of young women recruited from the hard-pressed farms of New England. Inside of five years, the Lowell factories had outstripped the family-based Rhode Island cotton mills established by Samuel Slater in the 1790s, as well as the Boston Associates' inaugural venture in Waltham, and they struck visitors as one of the nation's great wonders. Lowell, the Frenchman Michel Chevalier remarked, was nothing like the gloomy factory towns of England but more like a huge brick New World version of "a Spanish town with its convents," where the girls, "instead of working *sacred hearts*, spin and weave cotton."[49]

Lowell was an exception, painstakingly planned by its founders to provide the paternalistic necessities and virtuous monitoring that assured farmers and their wives their mill-worker daughters would be looked after well. Employers in other industrial settings attempted to adapt different kinds of benevolent paternalist regimes for millhands and their families. Most cities, however, large and small, arose with only the lightest of rules and oversight, thereby raising enormous challenges to supply the teeming new neighborhoods with adequate housing, sanitation, and policing. And among leading citizens of property and standing, the pangs of growth posed moral and political dilemmas. How, in the boisterous new urban milieux, could they maintain their own authority as civic leaders? What could be done to instill a proper respect for public order among the growing hordes of poor and ignorant working people? Established secular benevolent institutions—the philanthropic soup kitchens and firewood handouts traditionally afforded the poor—had been overwhelmed by the urban influx since 1815. What, beyond prudent use of the billystick, could uplift as well as restrain those whom one New Yorker regarded as "the multitude of new comers amongst whom are a large portion of the lowest offscourings of Europe . . . improvident, careless, & filthy"?[50]

For many propertied urbanites, above all in the areas newly settled by New England émigrés, the answer appeared in the continuing Second Great Awakening, as recast by a new leader, the charismatic Presbygational evangelist Charles Grandison Finney. Born in Litchfield County, Connecticut, in 1792, but raised in what was then the frontier of Oneida County, New York, Finney had been trained as a lawyer and had professed an indifference to religion until 1821. Prompted by repeated references to the Mosaic code in the British jurist William Blackstone's *Commentaries*, he bought a Bible, started reading, and was suddenly overwhelmed by God's grace. "It seemed as if my heart was all liquid," he later recalled. The next day, he dropped his legal career and began preparing himself for his new calling as an evangelist. Finney soon began gathering ever-larger crowds in the little but growing upstate cities along the Erie Canal, from Troy to Utica, in what he later called his "nine mighty years" of revivals. The roar reached a crescendo in Rochester over the fall and winter of 1830–31.[51]

Finney owed his phenomenal success to his evangelical style and down-to-earth bearing as well as to his liturgical and doctrinal innovations. Most of all, perhaps, he owed his success to his penetrating large blue eyes, set deep in a handsome angular head—eyes that seemed to radiate salvation. Finney was perfectly cognizant of his physical gifts and unapologetically used them to bring sinners to the bosom of Christ. For Finney, a religious revival resulted not from any miraculous visitation but from practical, voluntary human work—"the ordinary rules of cause and effect," he wrote—that, though blessed by God, could be systematized and then taught to other revivalists. Promoting prayer, comprehending (and not simply berating) thoughtless sinners, encouraging a full and unending moral stock-taking by each individual convert—by breaking down the job at hand, Finney was able to offer step-by-step guides on how to promote mass religious awakenings. Not least important, in his own ministry, was his adaptation of a variety of so-called new measures from other sects (notably the Methodists' prayer-inducing "anxious bench" placed directly in front of his pulpit), as well as the attention he paid to his own preaching style, down to divining the line of vision best suited to captivating his audience with his piercing gaze.[52]

Finney's technical feats helped him propound the greatest liberalization yet in America of the doctrine of human agency in salvation. Lyman Beecher and the other pioneers of the northern Second Great Awakening had retained at least a kernel of traditional Calvinism, in their contentions that the ultimate bestowal of grace came only and directly from God. Although Finney would never eliminate God's agency, he pushed it into the background, as a setting of the stage, with the Almighty arranging events (including the appearance of the proper minister) so that sinners would be ready to recognize and receive the Holy Spirit. Otherwise, the preacher, his flock, and the sinners themselves were the true makers of a revival. "Men are not mere *instruments* in the hands of God," Finney declared, abjuring Calvinist orthodoxy more pointedly and thoroughly than his predecessors. "Truth is the instrument."[53]

The fastest-growing city in the nation, Rochester was badly divided. Its rising men of wealth quarreled over politics and religion, and they lived in even greater estrangement from the flour-mill workers, canal boatmen, and immigrant laborers who had flocked to their boomtown. "Rochester was too uninviting a field of labor," Finney later recalled—until a force he referred to simply as "Something" told him that he was needed there all the more. His ministry galvanized the city's families of property as the surest means to restore moral order and unity. Installed at Rochester's Third Presbyterian Church, Finney preached three evenings a week and three times on Sunday, driving himself to the edge of physical breakdown. His sermons were spare and logical—"like a lawyer arguing a case before court and jury," one journalist attendee remarked—filled with everyday examples of how Satan worked his wiles and how all could remake their hearts and receive God's grace. He ended his stay in March 1831 with a five-day protracted meeting that brought the city's business to a halt and left him so exhausted his doctors feared he would soon be dead. In all, Finney had converted between eight and twelve hundred Rochester residents, including a disproportionate number of the city's leading manufacturers, lawyers, and other professionals, and especially their wives and daughters. The fire threw off sparks that lit revivals in nearby towns and villages, converting thousands more.[54]

In capturing Rochester for Christ, Finney proclaimed a cluster of moral imperatives that soon helped the new northern urban middle class define itself. Finneyite theology did not rationalize success or instill complacency; on the contrary, it was a challenge to abandon selfish passions and convert—and then to work ceaselessly spreading the gospel and shepherding others into the flock. In rising to that challenge, the converted learned that life, and receiving life ever-lasting, was a matter of personal moral choices. Bad choices—intemperance, slothfulness, extravagance, dishonesty, violence—blocked the sinner from redemption. Good choices, coupled with prayer, opened the way to personal salvation and hastened the moral perfection of the world that, Finney taught, would precede Christ's Second Coming. That revival-drenched striving in turn sanctified what was becoming the northern middle-class domestic order and offered a way of understanding political discord and social confusion as essentially moral problems. Human suffering, by these lights, could and would be conquered once individuals set themselves sturdily on the road to Christ, one sinner at a time.[55]

The potential political implications of the revivalists' message were enormous, even though politics was not chiefly on Finney's mind. The Finneyite excitement made its greatest stir in the rapidly developing portions of greater New England, and especially in the same so-called Burned-Over District of western New York that had spawned Anti-Masonry. The cities they transformed were boomtowns like Rochester, commanded by families of newfound prosperity searching for spiritual mastery for themselves and their neighbors. The revivalists preached a democratic gospel, at odds with the fatalism and hierarchy of the older Calvinist denominations, and at war with the secularism and indifference they saw closing in all around them. Finneyism offered its adherents a Christ-centered way of life that blamed disorder and degradation on individual decision, not political or social inequality. Here was the basis for yet another variation of the politics of moral improvement in the North—free of hierarchical presumption and over-flowing with benevolence and Christian stewardship, but far more ambitious and better organized than earlier reform efforts stemming from the Second Great Awakening. Sabbatarianism had provided one largely failed model for moralistic politics—several of Finney's most prominent converts were also Sabbatarian leaders—but the evangelical impulse would soon find much sturdier and less narrowly pious political outlets. Among those who would tap into that impulse were anti-Jacksonians ranging from the Anti-Masons Thurlow Weed and William Henry Seward to the abolitionists organized by William Lloyd Garrison.

There were limits to the evangelicals' appeal, though, as Finney and his friends would soon discover. Following the upstate Pentecost, Finney moved his headquarters to Manhattan, where he would be based for three years and preach often thereafter, first in a reconstructed theater and then, beginning in 1835, in a spacious new church, the Broadway Tabernacle, built for him by local evangelical businessmen. Finney's New York years bore fruit, including a proliferation of evangelical missionary societies that turned Manhattan into the center for national evangelical reform. Yet New York, like the other great seaports, was too large, polyglot, and cosmopolitan, even cynical, to be turned upside down like the raw canal cities and towns to the west. Even among the faithful, Finney remarked, "the reason there is so little of the purest kind of piety in New York" was that so many "indulge in some kind of dishonesty, which eats out their religion." Apart from the city's sizable population of prosperous New England émigrés (of whom Arthur and Lewis Tappan were the most conspicuous examples), Finney's crusade made little headway among Manhattan's families of wealth.[56] Equally important, New York's immense and variegated working class mainly evinced hostility for the evangelical crusaders and their mercantile backers—thoughts expressed with a special fierceness by a testy alliance of radicals who, in 1829, created their own version of Philadelphia's Working Men's Party. Although the New York Working Men's independent efforts would come to naught, their critiques of banking and the unrepublican power of concentrated wealth would gain a large following among workers and petty proprietors across the Northeast. Over the coming decade, those critiques would have an enormous influence among the more sympathetic of the Jackson Democrats, including President Jackson.

The freethinker Frances Wright's stormy arrival in January 1829 and her early lectures marked the beginning of the New York radical workingmen's insurgency. Deism and religious skepticism had claimed a small but vocal following in New York since the end of the eighteenth century, when the local skeptic Elihu Palmer made his newspaper, the *Temple of Reason*, the nation's leading exponent of free thought. In reaction to the evangelical resurgence, the movement enjoyed a small comeback in 1825, headed by a talented group of British radical émigrés including George Houston and George Henry Evans. But Wright, the daughter of an enlightened Scots merchant, and her companion Robert Dale Owen, son of the British utopian socialist Robert Owen, electrified the freethinkers' old-time irreligion. They relocated a newspaper they had founded at the Owenite community in New Harmony, Indiana, renamed it the *Free Enquirer*, and hired Evans as their printer. They also bought an abandoned church on the Bowery and turned it into what they called their Hall of Science, which housed their lecture hall, a reading room, a bookstore, a deist Sunday school, and a free medical dispensary. Wright herself took center stage, a scandalous celebrity preaching free love and abolitionism, and ridiculing Christian orthodoxy as the perfect model of mental and political thralldom.[57]

Wright and Owen enriched New York free-thought radicalism intellectually as well as organizationally. There was a mustiness to the extant New York deists' attacks on aristocratic priestcraft, as if the freethinkers had slumbered through the Jeffersonian era of religious disestablishment. Wright and Owen added more pertinent arguments for reform. Both were adherents to the radical interpretation of the labor theory of value that had been proclaimed in Philadelphia by William Heighton. As a corrective to America's plundering by the nonproducing few, they turned chiefly to educational reform and what Owen called his state guardianship plan. Based loosely on liberal schooling experiments in Europe, the scheme called for government-run secular academies, where all children, rich and poor, would be instructed with the most up-to-date methods and freed from sectarian superstition. From these egalitarian barracks of enlightenment would supposedly arise, Owen wrote, a "race . . . to perfect the free institutions of America." Though not without an authoritarian streak of its own, the plan at least recognized the new and growing urban inequalities of the 1820s. "If the divisions of *sect* have estranged human hearts from each other," Wright declared at the Hall of Science, "those of *class* have set them in direct opposition."[58]

Other New York workingmen radicals agreed with Wright and Owen on that point but thought their proposed solution was worse than useless. The harshest and most consequential of these critics was the machinist Thomas Skidmore. The son of a struggling Connecticut farm family, Skidmore had left home at eighteen and wandered along the East Coast as far south as Delaware, picking up odd jobs as a tutor while immersing himself in books on the mechanical arts and political economy. He settled in New York in 1819, set up a small business, and started work on a project to devise an improved form of reflective telescope—all the while continuing his self-education in political theory. As a boy, he had been inspired by the city democratic writings in William Duane's *Aurora*; thereafter, he immersed himself in the works of Locke, Rousseau, Joel Barlow, Jefferson, and Paine, as well as more obscure recent works attacking the competitive-wage labor system. Skidmore first turned up in politics in 1828 as a supporter of John Quincy Adams, drawn to the incumbent president's support for protective tariffs and what Skidmore would later call "necessary and useful Public Works."[59] After Adams's defeat, Skidmore began writing a long treatise of his own, utterly out of step with the ideas of Adamsites and Jacksonians alike—an unremitting attack on the existing system of private property.

Skidmore's self-conscious title—*The Rights of Man to Property!*—placed his work in the Paineite urban democratic tradition but also noted that tradition's limitations. Whereas Paine's *Rights of Man* had blamed social oppression on political inequality, Skidmore blamed the unequal distribution of property, perpetuated from generation to generation by inheritance laws. Even radical interpretations of the labor theory of value were too meek for Skidmore, who charged that individuals' equal rights to property existed independently of human labor. All existing property holdings were illegitimate, based on a primordial violation of the self-evident principle, "engraved on the heart of man," that each had an equal claim on the Creator's endowment. Mocking the comparatively mild plans of "political dreamers" like Robert Dale Owen, Skidmore proclaimed that the rights of labor and the poor would be won only if "we rip all up, and make a full and General Division" of property.[60]

Skidmore never abandoned his attachment to political democracy. His "General Division" would involve, first, the election by the enlightened masses of state legislatures that would call new state constitutional conventions, which would in turn enfranchise all men and women of all races. Thence would begin the process of expropriation and redistribution of existing property. All that could not be divided easily, in particular banks and manufactories, would be retained by the community at large and operated in its name. All else would be thrown into a common pool, with equal shares handed to everyone—men and women, of all colors—upon reaching adulthood. Thereafter, individuals would be permitted to labor as they chose, in cooperative independence. Men and women of superior talent, diligence, luck, and intelligence would, Skidmore allowed, inevitably produce more, to the greater benefit of all—and would therefore accumulate, rightfully, more property than others during their lifetimes. But so long as inheritance was abolished, and all property was returned to the community for redistribution when its owner died, natural differences would not be turned into permanent inequality. Gradually, class oppression would disappear, "till there shall be no lenders, no borrowers; no landlords, no tenants; no masters, no journeymen; no Wealth, no Want."[61]

As political eschatology, Skidmore's tract was just as uncompromising as David Walker's vision of slavery's demise. In some respects, Skidmore was even more audacious than Walker, propounding a nonviolent democratic revolution that would not only abolish slavery but create a new egalitarian regime for all Americans. And as far-fetched as it appears in retrospect, Skidmore's scheme envisaged immediate political organization, to be led not by unreliable men "attached to the cause of a Clay or a Jackson," but by independent "friends of equal rights," chiefly the oppressed small producers and wage earners.[62] Against the backdrop of continuing labor strife, that proposal led to the formation of the New York Working Men's movement.

Labor unrest had broken out repeatedly in New York after 1819. In the spring of 1829, journeymen reacted swiftly when rumors spread that large employers, in unspecified trades, were about to lengthen the workday from ten to eleven hours. At the urging of Skidmore (still at work on his manuscript), a large public gathering of wage earners pledged to refuse to work more than ten hours "well and faithfully employed." Five days later, an even larger crowd, estimated at between five and six thousand, attended a mass meeting in the Bowery, which affirmed the earlier pledge and appointed a committee of fifty small masters and journeymen to coordinate any strikes that followed. Soon after, the suspected employers renounced all plans to extend the workday, but the Committee of Fifty continued to meet and in midsummer decided to run its own independent ticket of candidates in the upcoming legislative elections. That autumn, the committee (joined, somewhat hesitantly, by Robert Dale Owen) announced its platform.

The document showed Skidmore's influence, but it carefully avoided all mention of the General Division. Instead, it attacked private banking and chartered monopolies, and included demands for abolishing imprisonment for debt, reforming the coercive militia system, equal education, and a mechanics' lien law. Egalitarian to the last detail, the meeting then chose its candidate list by lottery, including, as a nominee for state assembly, Skidmore himself.[63]

The 1829 campaign proved the acme of the New York Working Men's independent political efforts. At least one trade society, the painters', backed the movement. Owen, trying to capture the insurgency for himself and his state guardianship plan, assisted George Henry Evans in founding the weekly *Working Man's Advocate*, supposedly as a Working Men's organ. Pro-Jackson papers charged, with some merit, that pro-Clay mechanics and manufacturers, under the guise of "workingmen," were infiltrating and backing the Workies in order to divide the Democratic vote and elect National Republicans. The commercial press, including the Tappans' *Journal of Commerce*, denounced the new "sans-culottes," "Fanny Wright ticket," as a mad "anarchical" enterprise of poor men too ignorant to deserve the franchise. Finally, in November, the Working Men polled nearly one-third of the vote, more than twice the figure won by the National Republicans—enough to elect one of the Workies' state senate candidates and one of their assembly candidates (a journeyman carpenter named Ebenezer Ford), and nearly enough to elect Skidmore (who fell short by a mere twenty-three votes). Flushed with victory, Skidmore's followers formed new political debating societies in at least three workingmen's wards, and Skidmore produced a prospectus for a newspaper loyal to the Committee of Fifty.[64]

Factionalism and manipulation quickly destroyed the fledgling party. As the Democrats had noticed, men friendly to the late administration and to Henry Clay had begun quietly to take over the Workie organization. Emboldened by the returns, they turned first to removing Skidmore, an effort in which they found willing allies among the naive Owenite freethinkers. At a mass meeting in December called ostensibly to debate the movement's future, the Owen and pro-Clay men packed the hall, forcibly prevented Skidmore and the committee from speaking, reconstituted themselves as the Working Men's Party, and purged the Skidmore faction. The next day, a pro-Clay paper rejoiced that the Workies had "wiped away every stigma" of Skidmore's crazed schemes.[65] What had actually happened was that Clay's supporters, using the *Free Enquirer* radicals as their pawns, had seized the movement. Soon after, the Owenites and Clay men turned on each other. Ten months of bitter, at times violent, feuding ensued, after which the Jacksonians regained all of the wards won by the Workies in 1829. Although Owen, Evans, and the other free-thought radicals held out for another year under the name of the Workingmen's Political Association, the New York Working Men's political uprising was effectively dead by the end of 1830.

The New York radicals were not unique in their failings: Philadelphia's Working Men's Party experienced a similar meteoric rise and fall, in a roughly parallel chronology. In 1828, the Philadelphia workingmen's candidates who ran on their own received only a scattering of votes—but all twenty-one Workie candidates who were also on the Jackson ticket were elected, an encouraging sign. A year later, the movement was flourishing. William Heighton's *Mechanics' Free Press* raised numerous specific demands, including the abolition of chartered monopolies, restriction of commercial banks, expansion of public education, and ending imprisonment for debt. Branches of a new Workingmen's Republican Political Association arose in the working-class wards, and city and county conventions, elected by general ward meetings, nominated twelve candidates for the fall elections, some of whom ran as Democrats and some as Adamsites. All of the Working Men's nominees won, leading the *Free Press* to boast that "[t]he balance of power has at length got into the hands of the working people, where it properly belongs." But support began to dwindle in 1830, when conservative papers started linking the movement to the Fanny Wright "infidels" and Skidmore "agrarians" of New York, and when the rank and file divided over whether they should restrict themselves to nominating actual workingmen. The movement's disappointing election totals that autumn, the Democratic *American Sentinel* rejoiced, "consigned *Workeyism* to the tomb of the Capulets; and there is no further nucleus for malcontents to form upon." A year later, the Philadelphia Workie vote was barely half of what it had been in 1829, and the organizers gave up the ghost.[66]

Ironically, the deist and agrarian radicalism that galvanized the New York Workies in 1829 finally proved a fatal liability: it was too radical for most workingmen, and provided a useful foil for more conventional politicians in both Manhattan and Philadelphia. Yet Workeyism's basic criticisms of economic and political inequality proved much more tenacious than the New York and Philadelphia parties did. Individual Philadelphia and New York radicals, including the irrepressible Manhattan editor George Henry Evans, continued their work long after the parties disappeared. Outside Philadelphia and New York, workingmen's parties sprouted up in smaller nearby ports and manufacturing cities, and the movement quickly spread into New England, Delaware, and Ohio. By August 1830, one Delaware paper reported that "not less than twenty newspapers" had "come out fearlessly in the advocacy of the principles of the *Working Men's Party*." Before the agitation was over, the list would expand to include at least fifty newspapers in fifteen states, from Maine to Missouri. Some of the new labor parties were so evanescent that they left mere traces in the historical record; others were pseudo-Workie parties organized by National Republicans. But a few of them, notably the New England Association of Farmers, Mechanics, and Other Workingmen, organized in 1832, became the foundations for even larger labor organizations. And the most important of the newspapers, Evans's *Working Man's Advocate*, lasted well past 1830, as a beacon for every variety of workingmen's reform.[67]

These continuing efforts refocused Workeyism's energies on its more practical critiques of the developing commercial order. Above all, they sustained the radical arguments over monopolies, banking, and the currency that had emerged around the country after the Panic of 1819 and that both the Philadelphia and New York Working Men's movements had amplified. In 1828, the Philadelphians affirmed that the greatest evil they faced was "the legislative aid granted for monopolizing, into a few rich hands, the wealth creating powers of modern mechanism." The original New York Working Men's platform demanded abolition of the existing banking system and of all chartered monopolies. In the very first issue of his *Working Man's Advocate*, Evans promised to fight "the establishment of all exclusive privilege; all monopolies." Workies in the smaller cities seized on the banking issue, proclaiming (in the words of the General Executive Committee of the Farmers, Mechanics and Working Men of the City of Albany) that "at present the laboring classes create the wealth which the bankers and speculators pocket." Even Fanny Wright added currency and banking reform to the deist radicals' education plans as "indispensable" to labor's cause.[68]

The most influential attack on banking appeared in Philadelphia in March 1829, at about the same time that the New York Working Men's movement was getting underway. A protest meeting of workingmen declared that hard times were the result of "too great extension of paper credit," and appointed a committee, not confined to workingmen, to write a report on the evils of the banking system. The committee included both of the Duanes and two trade union leaders, William English and John Robertson, who were also active in the Working Men's Party. It also included an editor and political writer named William Gouge. The report, apparently written chiefly by Gouge, admitted that banks had their uses as institutions of deposit and transfer, but charged that the existing commercial, paper-money banking system had laid "the foundation of *artificial* inequality of wealth, and, thereby, of *artificial* inequality of power," and needed radical reform.[69]

The Workie uprising in turn got the attention of mainstream politicians. Andrew Jackson, who had announced his hostility to all commercial banks as early as 1820, had subscribed for years to the Philadelphia radical Stephen Simpson's *Columbian Observer*. Now Jackson called Simpson "his old friend," and through Thomas Hart Benton received word of Simpson's latest thinking on banking questions. The appearance of the independent Working Men's parties widened the radicals' audience among Jackson's supporters. Heighton's *Mechanics' Free Press* noted proudly in 1830 how the Philadelphia Working Men's campaign had brought "an open acknowledgement of the justice of working people's

attempts to lessen the hours of labor." In New York, Democrats in the state legislature responded to the Workie challenge by abolishing imprisonment for debt
and reforming the militia system, and the Tammany-dominated city council in
Manhattan passed a mechanics' lien law. The lesson, for practical politicians,
was clear: no party could succeed in the newly expanding cities—and, hence,
could not expect to succeed nationally—unless it could appeal to the voters
aroused by the Working Men and address their concerns. If that process of
absorption killed off independent workingmen's politics, it also stimulated the
more liberal and sometimes radical impulses within the Jacksonian coalition—
which, for most of the Workies, quickly became their new political home.[70]

"GET THE WORKIES TO BE UP AND DOING"

Three years after his inauguration, Andrew Jackson had begun asserting control
over his own administration and clarifying its political direction, but Jacksonian
Democracy had yet to come to pass. He had pressed hard, and successfully, for
Indian removal and against expansive federal aid for internal improvements. The
schism between Jackson and John C. Calhoun presaged the president's renunciation of state-rights extremism. Still, much remained to be sorted out, particularly over slavery, the limits of federal power, and the effects of rapid commercial
development. In facing the last of these, Jackson and his closest supporters would
confront the perennial question of how economic power ought to be distributed
and exercised in a democratic republic. And they would find themselves forging
an ever-closer alliance with the workingmen radicals, whose views on some crucial questions were converging with their own.

The Working Men's attacks on monopolies and banks failed, but far more
powerful national Democratic leaders—aided and, in time, goaded further by
the Workies and their friends—would not. One of those leaders, a former bank
director, converted antimonopolist, and crony of Martin Van Buren, New York
Congressman Churchill C. Cambreleng, knew what to expect early in 1832 and
where the former Working Men would fit in. "Get the Workies to be up and
doing on the U.S.B. question," Cambreleng wrote to a Tammany Bucktail.
"They are democrats in principle."[71] The "U.S.B." Cambreleng referred to was
the Second Bank of the United States—against which President Jackson, now
recovered from his early political distractions, was arming for an all-out war.

12

1832:
JACKSON'S CRUCIAL YEAR

By 1832, President Jackson had forcefully resolved the internal disputes that had plagued his administration. The rift with Vice President Calhoun turned into a complete break late in the spring of 1830, after friends began sending Jackson incontrovertible evidence that Calhoun had secretly denounced him during the Florida expedition fracas in 1818—an episode that, like many long past, had never stopped mattering to Jackson. After confronting Calhoun and receiving a supercilious reply, Jackson cut off communication, raging that he had never "expected he would have occasion to say to you, in the language of Caesar, *Et tu Brute*." After his summer vacation, Jackson returned to Washington, where the wearisome Eaton comic opera continued. Still livid over "[t]he double dealing of J.C.C.," he decided to end, once and for all, both the Eaton imbroglio and Calhoun's influence over his administration.[1]

As a first step, Jackson established a reliable party newspaper in Washington to overcome the semiofficial *Telegraph*, edited by Calhoun's loyalist, Duff Green. Jackson summoned to Washington the Kentucky relief war veteran Francis Blair, who had taken over as editor of the *Argus of Western America*. Blair's new semi-weekly paper, the *Globe*—soon to become a daily—would provide an effective counterweight to Green in the capital, while also helping to secure the disciplined attention and loyalty of Jacksonians down the party's chain of command. There would never be any doubt about its standing as, in Amos Kendall's words, "the friend of General Jackson and his administration, having no . . . political views other than the support of his principles."[2]

Purging the cabinet of Calhoun's influence required more patience and finesse, lest it appear that Jackson was acting at the behest of the Eatons—and in retaliation not against Calhoun but against his wife. The pretext he needed finally appeared early in 1831, when Calhoun published a self-serving pamphlet containing his recent correspondence with Jackson, designed to make Van Buren look like an ambitious conniver. (The secretary of state, one overly abrupt opposition observer wrote, "is a gone dog. *he is done.*") For Jackson, this was the final affront, and he axed Calhoun's cabinet allies Samuel Ingham, John Branch, and John Berrien. To keep up political appearances, he also accepted Van Buren's resignation and forced Eaton out of the cabinet. But right away, he nominated Van Buren to serve as the American minister to Great Britain and arranged for Eaton to become governor of Florida Territory, where he and Margaret could settle in honorable exile from Washington's salons. Jackson had precipitously freed himself to start his troubled presidency anew.[3]

The cabinet shake-up—involving the heads of five of the six existing executive departments, excluding only Postmaster General Barry (his incompetence not yet exposed)—was unprecedented. The new cabinet was more distinguished than its predecessor and, above all, untainted by Calhounism. Yet if the new men, particularly the nationalist-inclined Treasury secretary Louis McLane, promised to be personally loyal to the president, they would be cautious about pursuing his reforms. Accordingly, Jackson began to rely on the advice of his closest political friends outside the cabinet—Van Buren, Kendall, Blair, and his old ally from Tennessee, William Lewis—an arrangement that his opponents disparaged as the president's "Kitchen Cabinet" government.

The twelve months following Congress's reassembly in December 1831 proved crucial, to both Jackson and his evolving coalition. The coming elections held everybody's attention. Less obvious were the continuing events in South Carolina that would lead to threatened secession. Jackson, meanwhile, was determined to press forward with what he had decided was the next item on his reform agenda—attacking the hated epitome of monied corruption, the Second Bank of the United States.

DEMOCRACY AND "A *FEW MONIED CAPITALISTS*": ORIGINS OF THE BANK VETO

Jackson's past political allegiances might have signaled that banking, currency, and finance would be near the top of his list of reforms. On the issues of banks and banking, his establishment loyalties had ended long ago. And during the 1828 election, he received word (which he believed) that the Lexington and Louisville, Kentucky, branch offices of the BUS had intervened on Adams's behalf. He then learned of similar charges against the New Orleans branch.

Jackson's opinion of the BUS as a direct threat to American democracy was solidifying.[4]

Banks and banking had not been issues in the 1828 campaign, in part because the debate over the federal tariff took precedence, and in part because raising the matter might upset Jackson's delicately balanced coalition. Jackson later claimed, however, that he had hoped to talk about banks in his inauguration address, only to be dissuaded by his more cautious advisers. And just two months after the inauguration, he was mulling over plans to do something dramatic about the BUS and erect a new institution for holding federal funds. Bringing the strict "hard-money" man Amos Kendall and then Francis Blair (now a hard-money convert) into his administration and giving them important duties was another sign of where Jackson was headed. "Every one that knows me," he later wrote, "does know, that I have always been opposed to the U. States Bank, nay all Banks."[5]

Jackson's complaints about the BUS reaffirmed his long-standing view that it fostered a "corrupting influence . . . upon the morals of the people." His major objections, however, were constitutional and political—objections that affirmed the primacy of politics and political institutions in how Americans thought about the state of the country. On strict Jeffersonian grounds, Jackson believed the bank was constitutionally invalid, an entity that Congress had created by asserting powers not ceded to it by the Framers. Just as important, Jackson perceived that the bank, by its very design, undermined popular sovereignty and majority rule. As a friend and adviser of Van Buren's, the New Yorker James A. Hamilton—ironically, Alexander Hamilton's son—put it in a key early memorandum to Jackson, the bank had concentrated "in the hands of a few men, a power over the money of the country." Unless checked, that power could be "perverted to the oppression of the people, and in times of public calamity, to the embarrassment of the government." But even when well administered, the bank was an enormity, which allowed, Jackson wrote, "a *few Monied Capitalists*" to trade upon the public revenue "and enjoy the benefit of it, to the exclusion of the many." No less worrisome, he added, was the bank's "power to control the Government and change its character," by influencing elections and, if need be, bribing representatives. Preventing a rechartering of the BUS, Jackson told the Tennessean Hugh Lawson White, was essential to his larger reform effort to vindicate "[t]he great principles of democracy."[6]

President Jackson's early thoughts about how to handle the BUS are sketchy. From his correspondence and some recorded conversations, though, it is clear that he was thinking hard—and was receiving a great deal of contradictory advice. His initial preference was to replace the bank with a government-run institution that would serve as a bank of deposit only, severing any connection between public money and the issuance of bank paper. Jackson's partiality for a specie currency was as strong as ever. Yet Jackson also became aware that the BUS performed some valuable services. Above all, the bank reduced the cost of government transactions, and, by checking emissions of state bank paper, restrained speculation. Offered numerous plans for a substitute to the BUS, Jackson showed a willingness to temper his views about how a reformed bank might operate, so long as those operations fell within the limits of his strict reading of the Constitution. By mid-1832, he would write, somewhat disingenuously, that he had always said he would favor "[a] Bank of deposit and Exchange, purely national, without stock holders."[7]

Jackson announced his intention to strike at the BUS in his first and second messages to Congress, although he muted himself at the continued insistence of those advisers, above all Van Buren, who were worried about alienating too many important supporters too soon. In the first message, Jackson made clear that he strongly doubted whether the bank's existing charter was constitutional; he also believed the bank had failed to establish a sound currency. Jackson expanded his criticisms a year later, and proposed a possible replacement for the BUS: a wholly public institution with no private directors or stockholders, shorn of the power to extend loans or purchase property, but capable of retraining state banks from irresponsibly issuing paper. The bank question then receded in Washington for nearly a year, as Jackson recovered from the Eaton scandal and his initial clashes with Calhoun, battled against his recurrent physical ailments, and rebuilt his administration. Outwardly, the president managed to maintain a moderate mien. Privately, he wrote that, once his new cabinet was intact, the "great task of Democratic reform" would recommence—and the bank issue would be "fearlessly me[t]."[8]

In assembling diverse anti-BUS forces, Jackson turned the issue into a matter of principle for his entire party. The major exceptions were inside the new cabinet, where more nationalist members, above all Secretary of the Treasury Louis McLane and Secretary of State Edward Livingston, held to a view that, Jackson wrote privately, "springs from convictions much more favorable than mine" to the bank. McLane and Livingston would prove useful as insider checks on unwisely precipitate actions and as signals to the public that the administration was considering a range of opinions. Otherwise, Jackson's hostility to the BUS meshed well with his reorganized administration party. Among the bank's strongest friends were certain pro-Calhoun slaveholders, including George Poindexter of Mississippi in the Senate and, in the House, the humorless, bombastic, but experienced South Carolina congressman George McDuffie, who had been a Calhoun family protégé since boyhood. Passionate sectionalists on the tariff and state rights, they also sustained parts of Calhoun's old economic nationalism and considered the Second BUS—whose chartering Calhoun had steered through Congress in 1816—as not only benevolent but essential to the nation's prosperity.[9]

With the Calhounites thrown outside the administration, unequivocal antibank southerners, above all Jackson's new attorney general, Roger B. Taney of Maryland, enjoyed enlarged influence. A nearsighted lawyer with repellent features but a soft and persuasive manner, Taney had come to distrust large financiers during his years on the bench and as a state bank director. His anti-BUS animus was so strong that he was the only department head whom Jackson also admitted to his "kitchen cabinet" inner circle. There, Taney joined the Kentuckians Kendall and Blair, who were among the most ferocious antibank men in Washington and who urged Jackson to offer the bank no mercy. "It will come to this," Kendall wrote, "whoever is in favor of that Bank will be against Old Hickory." Both Blair and Kendall used the new *Globe* to denounce the BUS as an unconstitutional creature of "the monied power."[10]

In Congress, Senator Thomas Hart Benton of Missouri—once Jackson's tavern assailant, now his ally—led the antibank forces. Like Kendall and Blair, Benton had completely rejected his early sympathies for Henry Clay's American System and the BUS. Early in February 1831, while Jackson was still grappling with Calhoun and the cabinet, he gave a scorching speech in the Senate on the bank and offered a resolution against renewing its charter, which still had five years to run. He called the bank too powerful for a government based on free and equal laws, an institution that worsened inequality by enriching the already rich and impoverishing the poor. In its place, he would institute a currency based on gold and silver, "the best currency for a republic." If, Benton added, he were "to establish a working man's party"—which was exactly what he wanted the Jacksonian coalition to become—"it should be on the basis of hard money; a hard money party against a paper party." The Senate defeated Benton's resolution, but by only three votes; the great preponderance of the Jackson men backed the Missourian. Blair's *Globe* reprinted Benton's speech in full; party newspaper editors and pamphlet printers around the country picked it up.[11]

Benton's reference to "a working man's party" was purposeful. In the Northeast, former Philadelphia and New York Working Men and their emulators in other cities had strongly influenced and publicized the evolving antibank arguments. They were now primary targets of the Jacksonians' appeals. Apart from a handful of standouts, northeastern congressional support for Jackson's position on the bank was thin. But at the state and local level, particularly in New York, siding with Jackson on the bank question became a mark of party loyalty. (In New York, where Van Buren's men had initially been ambivalent, the state legislature resoundingly passed resolutions against rechartering the bank early in

1831.) And in the cities, large and small, where the Working Men had organized, the administration's antibank efforts won applause for attacking an unrepublican monopoly that, as George Henry Evans wrote, enabled "some men to live in splendor on the labor of operatives."[12]

Benton, Kendall, and Blair, like the Workies, were more thoroughgoing critics of commercial banks and paper currency than were other antibank Jacksonians. The differences replicated those that had distinguished hard-money radicals from anti-BUS state bankers in the aftermath of the Panic of 1819. Taney, for example, although unsurpassed in his detestation for the BUS, objected primarily to the burdens it imposed on state banks. Other enemies of the BUS, including state and local bankers and would-be bankers, east and west, were interested in promoting cheap money, obtaining a share of the federal deposits held by the BUS, or taking over the national bank's functions themselves. David Henshaw, the Massachusetts parvenu, was the most energetic on the latter point. Rewarded for his efforts in the 1828 campaign with the appointment as collector of the port of Boston, Henshaw developed a scheme to replace the BUS with a new and even larger and more powerful bank—with him and his cronies of the so-called Custom House Party in control.[13]

Given their prominence and power, the self-interested anti-BUS men easily created the impression—affirmed by later historians friendly to the bank and antagonistic to the Jacksonians—that the fight was merely one between rival groups of bankers and businessmen. Supposedly, the BUS was trying to uphold its responsible regime against grasping, entrepreneurial outsiders who (with the political aid of ignoramuses like Jackson) wanted to expand their own wealth and power. Jackson himself, so the argument ran, was motivated chiefly by the allegations that certain BUS directors had tried to thwart his election. In his outrage, Alexis de Tocqueville wrote, Jackson decided to "rouse the local passions and the blind democratic instinct of the country" against the bank and its directors. Not surprisingly, this view of the controversy, dismissive of the Jacksonians' political concerns, prevailed within the bank's imposing Greek Revival headquarters on Chestnut Street in Philadelphia. Its main proponent was the bank's president, the enormously capable and self-confident Nicholas Biddle.[14]

Biddle was a wonder, only thirty-seven years old when President Monroe appointed him to run the BUS in 1823. His father, Charles Biddle, was a successful merchant whose own father, though of patrician lineage, had been ruined in business and died young. Charles, after boyhood stints at sea and as a merchant's apprentice, became a leading light in post-Revolutionary Pennsylvania politics. His rise, and his son's even loftier rise, was testimony to how, in the rapidly expanding early republic, the very highest reaches in America could be accessible to men of exceptional talent and drive. The Biddle saga also showed how some of these men, despite their family struggles, could come to think and act as if they had been to the manor born.[15]

A brilliant, urbane graduate of Princeton (where he earned his B.A. at age fifteen), a former Federalist turned Pennsylvania New School Republican, Nicholas Biddle had served in the diplomatic corps (working as Monroe's secretary at the ministry to Great Britain), practiced law, edited a literary journal, and served in both houses of the Pennsylvania legislature—all before he began his career as a banker. Described by one English visitor as "the most perfect specimen of an American gentleman that I had yet seen," Biddle was no amateur dilettante, but a prodigy who seemed capable of mastering whatever vocation he chose. His chief flaws were his hubris and his excitability, both of which proved disastrous in national politics.[16]

As the BUS president, Biddle favored interventionist policies, hoping to check the profligate tendencies of many state and local bankers and provide a sound currency. The bank's charter empowered it to act as the federal government's exclusive fiscal agent: holding its deposits, making interstate transfers of federal funds, and dealing with all federal payments or receipts, including taxes—all in exchange for an annual fee of $1.5 million. Yet although it was linked to the government (which owned one-fifth of its stock), and although it could use public funds interest-free for its own purposes, and although its branches were exempt from taxation by the states, the BUS was a private bank beholden to its directors and its stockholders, an elite group numbering four thousand. Like any other chartered bank, it had the power to issue its own notes and conduct normal commercial bank functions. In 1830, it was responsible for between 15 and 20 percent of all bank lending in the country, and had issued upwards of 40 percent of all the bank notes in circulation nationwide. Its capital of $35 million was more than twice as large as the total annual expenditure of the federal government. Between 1830 and 1832, the BUS expanded further, increasing its notes and loans by 60 percent and its deposits by 40 percent. By issuing orders either to constrict or relax the bank's twenty-five branch offices' demands on state and local banks for specie, Biddle and his bank could regulate the entire economy.[17]

These were enormous privileges and powers for a private institution, beyond anything imaginable today. Biddle commanded his post expertly, salvaging the bank's credibility among business leaders and bolstering the rapid expansion of commerce after the panic depression lifted in 1822. Under Biddle, the BUS was vigilant about issuing notes, holding a specie reserve of one-half their value at a time when other banks held, on average, only between one-tenth and one-quarter of their note values in specie. In the process, Biddle transformed the BUS from a moderately profitable national branch-banking system into something more closely resembling a modern central bank.

Yet if Biddle's skills were unquestionable, the bank's regained prominence and heightened power also deepened misgivings about its anomalous position as a private institution with extraordinary public influence—and of its abuses of that influence, real and potential. Although the White House chose five of the institution's directors, the appointees were kept in the dark about the bank's operations. Biddle was very resistant to public supervision or even official inquiries. Beyond the naming of its five (largely ineffectual) directors, he insisted, "no officer of the Government, from the President downwards, has the least right, the least authority, the least pretense, for interference in the concerns of the bank." Biddle did extremely well by the bank's stockholders. But this fed concerns that Biddle's bank had become an all-powerful institution, accountable to no one but its owners—a monopolistic *imperium in imperio* of a new sort, an unelected fourth branch of government run by and for privileged insiders, exempt from the U.S. Constitution's checks and balances and in flagrant violation of democratic principles.[18]

No argument in the world about the BUS's benefits would have convinced vested interests like Henshaw's crony consortium. At the other end of the ideological spectrum, hard-money men were unmoved by the bank's successes in steadying currency values and in driving worthless state paper out of circulation—for to them, all private commercial banks were suspect. (As Jackson himself told Biddle directly, his hatred was not reserved for the BUS: "I do not dislike your bank any more than all banks.") The bank's role as an engine of commercial development rendered it dubious to those who felt excluded from its power and also among workingmen, farmers, and others who had suffered amid the uncertainties and displacements that commercial development had wrought. The bank made its decisions behind closed doors, and these decisions were made by a man who declared himself beholden to no elected official in the land. Biddle, with his haughty bearing and his presumption that democracy was demagogy, personified the Jacksonians' charges that the bank threatened popular sovereignty.[19]

Offended that anyone would impugn either his integrity or his public spirit, Biddle did not make life easier for himself. He thought nothing of approving dispersal of sizable sums in retainers, personal loans, or both to editors and elected officials, of both parties, in Washington—sometimes violating the bank's own regulations while reinforcing the impression, sensationalized by the *Globe*, that the bank was a fountain of political corruption. Nor, despite his literary skills, did he do a very good job at explaining either his bank or his running of it to the public. One of the main complaints of antibank congressmen concerned a useful reform, introduced by Biddle in 1827, that permitted the

BUS to issue "branch draft" notes without their having to be hand-signed, labo-
riously, by the bank's president and cashier. The need for the notes was straightforward. Yet Biddle never convincingly demonstrated how the branch drafts
facilitated the bank's operations, without creating what Senator Benton called
an "illegal, irresponsible currency." Nor was Biddle politic. When asked, during
public testimony, whether the BUS had ever oppressed any state banks, he
replied it had not, but could also not help noting that "[t]here are very few
banks which might not have been destroyed" had the BUS decided to do so.
While he seemed to expect gratitude for his restraint and generosity, Biddle also
sounded as if he assumed that all future BUS presidents would be just as skilled
and benevolent as he. And there lay the heart of the matter for Jackson and his
allies—that an office as powerful and unchecked as Biddle's was intolerable in a
democratic republic.[20]

THE POLITICS OF THE BANK VETO

The battle over the BUS was a personal clash between Biddle and Jackson as
well as a constitutional struggle, but it began at a moment when a compromise
actually seemed possible. In the autumn of 1831, Treasury Secretary McLane,
the cabinet member friendliest to the BUS, proposed to the president a comprehensive scheme of fiscal reform that would at long last pay off the national debt
but leave the bank standing, though greatly altered. Jackson, jumping at the
chance to pay off the debt and also keep the bank issue out of the upcoming presidential election, bought the plan, so long as the changes removed his constitutional objections to the existing BUS, and so long as the rechartering was delayed
until after 1832. McLane, elated, traveled to Philadelphia to assure Biddle that
all was well. Jackson completed his part of the bargain in the third annual message, where he implied he was willing to go along with chartering a reformed
bank and leave the matter up to Congress. But Secretary McLane overplayed his
hand by calling explicitly in his annual report for rechartering the BUS.

Initially trusting in McLane, Jackson appeared unpersuaded, if defensive,
when some of his supporters objected strenuously to McLane's "ultra federal"
report—"a new version of Alexander Hamilton's," Cambreleng of New York
declared. But when the implacably antibank *Globe* greeted the report by reprinting hostile reactions from other pro-Jackson newspapers, McLane threatened to
resign, then geared up a conspiracy to arrange for Blair's ouster as editor. Disloyalty to Blair was, in Jackson's eyes, tantamount to disloyalty to Jackson himself, as
well as to the larger cause of reform. McLane's influence with Jackson on the
bank declined and Blair remained as the *Globe*'s editor. Compromise over the
BUS was still possible but would depend on whether Biddle was willing to meet

Jackson halfway and allow certain changes in the bank's charter, while also agreeing not to pursue the matter until after the election.[21]

The National Republicans entered the fray in mid-December, when 150 delegates met in Baltimore and nominated Henry Clay for president. Three months earlier, a similar gathering had met in the same city to nominate William Wirt for the presidency on an Anti-Masonic ticket—the first national nominating convention in American history. Since 1828, Thurlow Weed and William Henry Seward had built their little protest party into a substantial organization in several northeastern states. As ever, Weed and Seward were trying to arrange for an alliance with the National Republicans, but the ascendancy of Clay, an unrepentant Mason, made that impossible. The National Republicans, however, were willing to imitate the Anti-Masons and call a nominating convention, in lieu of the congressional caucus of old. And their meeting concluded with a polemical, impossibly long, address warning the nation that if Jackson was reelected, "it may be considered certain that the bank will be abolished."[22]

Behind the scenes, Clay, along with George McDuffie, Daniel Webster, and other pro-BUS men, pressed Biddle to request rechartering of the bank before the election. Confident that a recharter bill would pass Congress, Clay and the others assured him that Jackson would not dare to veto it and face a disastrous public outburst. Such an executive veto of an institution already adjudged constitutional by the Supreme Court would be problematic under any circumstances; and Clay and Webster were also certain that the bank was popular with the voters. Initially, Biddle was more cautious, fearing, as another pro-BUS National Republican remarked, that if he forced "the Chief into a Corner he will veto the bill." But Clay and Webster (who, with their own political calculations in play, quietly hoped to provoke Jackson into a veto) were strong persuaders. In any case, Biddle convinced himself that he would have a stronger chance of winning a showdown with Jackson if it came before the election. Early in January, the nominal Jacksonian George M. Dallas, the son of Alexander J. Dallas, introduced a recharter bill in the Senate, while the South Carolinian McDuffie did so in the House. With Biddle's agreement, the proposals modified the existing charter by placing limits on the bank's powers to hold real estate and establish new branches. They also gave the president of the United States the power to appoint one director at each branch and Congress the power to prevent the bank from issuing small notes. But the reforms were too little, too late. As Biddle had originally feared, the alliance of the bank with Jackson's political opponents ended any hesitancy on Jackson's part to deny the BUS its new charter.[23]

With New York's large congressional delegation divided and Pennsylvania's solidly behind rechartering, Congress's approval of the bank bill was foreordained. But the antibank men made themselves heard, if only for the benefit of the *Globe*. Sometimes they attacked the BUS's supporters as much as the bank itself—reaching out from Capitol Hill to build opposition around the country. ("Why this sudden pressure?" Thomas Hart Benton demanded. "Is it to throw the bank bill into the hands of the President . . . and to place the President under a cross fire from the opposite banks of the Potomac River?") Biddle, meanwhile, coordinated a public pro-BUS campaign and arranged, through his branch bank managers, for scores of petitions from state banks and citizens' groups to arrive on Capitol Hill and make it appear as if the BUS enjoyed massive grassroots support.[24]

There was another drama during this congressional session, closely related to the political machinations surrounding the BUS—the Senate's confirmation vote on Van Buren's nomination as minister to Britain. Clay and Webster managed to maneuver the vote into a tie—leaving Vice President Calhoun, with mock solemnity and great delight, to cast the deciding vote to defeat Van Buren. (Benton later claimed he heard a scornful Calhoun say, "It will kill him, sir, kill him dead. He will never kick sir, never kick.") Having defeated Jackson's chosen successor, the opposition then went to work on outsmarting the president on the bank. When the BUS recharter bill finally came to a vote in July, it passed both houses comfortably. Nicholas Biddle, flushed with victory, appeared in the House to bask in the plaudits of his congressional backers, then hosted a raucous celebration in his lodgings, "sufficiently public," Taney later wrote, "to make sure it would reach the ears of the President."[25]

On the evening of July 8, Van Buren, just returned from his aborted ministry, hurried to the White House and arrived at midnight to find a spectral Jackson, lying on a sick bed but braced for battle. "The bank, Mr. Van Buren, is trying to kill me," the president said quietly, almost matter-of-factly, grasping his friend's hand, *"but I will kill it!"* Jackson's veto message was nearly complete, worked on by Taney, Donelson, Secretary of the Navy Levi Woodbury, and Jackson himself, but drafted and revised by Amos Kendall, whose slashing prose predominated.[26] Signed by Jackson two days later, the document arrived at once at the Senate. It set off a political earthquake.

The bank veto message was a brilliant political document, crafted for wide circulation in order to reach over the heads of Congress, build public support, and unite the disparate Jacksonian factions opposed to the BUS. For the Workies and the western radicals, there were the message's angriest passages, ripping into the "opulent" bank as a despotic monopoly. To reassure Jackson's more moderate allies, the message conceded that "[a] bank of the United States is in many respects convenient for the Government and useful to the people," and remarked that other bank plans had been offered "on terms much more favorable" than the bank bill provided. State bankers, old-line Jeffersonians, and southern state-rights men—including some who backed Calhoun—would kindle to the message's claim that the bank's charter, as proposed, was not "subversive of the rights of the States and dangerous to the liberties of the people." For patriotic, and especially Anglophobic, Americans everywhere, there were discursions, tinged with demagogy, about foreigners who owned a substantial portion of the bank's stock and drained American prosperity.[27]

The message also powerfully elucidated Jackson's political and social philosophy. Some of its strongest statements appeared in its comparatively staid middle section on constitutional issues. Contradicting those who charged that "[m]ere precedent" had settled the constitutionality of the BUS, Jackson beckoned to past congressional and state court opinions against the bank. The Supreme Court's decision in *McCulloch v. Maryland* did not, Jackson asserted, cover every aspect of the bank's charter. Moreover, he claimed, the executive, as a coequal coordinate branch of the government, had the sworn duty to uphold the Constitution as it saw fit, regardless of the Court. On various counts, the message depicted the bank as a privileged private institution that bypassed the authority of the state governments and enjoyed powers exceeding those granted the federal government. But surpassing all discussion of state rights was Jackson's assertion of rightful presidential power within the federal system, especially in relation to the Supreme Court.[28]

The message's concluding passages combined Jackson's constitutional views with his larger democratic vision. "It is to be regretted that the rich and powerful too often bend the acts of government to their selfish purposes," Jackson observed.

> Distinctions in society will always exist under every just government. Equality of talents, of education, or of wealth can not be produced by human institutions. In the full enjoyment of the gifts of Heaven and the fruits of superior industry, economy, and virtue, every man is equally entitled to protection by law; but when the laws undertake to add to these natural and just advantages artificial distinctions, to grant titles, gratuities, and exclusive privileges, to make the rich richer and the potent more powerful, the humble members of society—the farmers, mechanics, and laborers—who have neither the time nor the means of securing like favors to themselves, have a right to complain of the injustice of their Government.

No agrarian leveler, Jackson nevertheless decried artificial inequalities of wealth and power—inequalities he blamed on the ability of privileged men to subvert the Constitution and turn political power, especially federal power, toward enriching themselves further, in defiance of popular sovereignty.[29]

The message was more confused in its economic policy. Perhaps because of Kendall's influence—and apparently contrary to Jackson's own suggestions—it said nothing concrete about establishing a replacement for the bank. This omission fed fears, already rampant, that the president aimed simply to destroy the BUS without installing any substitute. The message's muddled reasoning on the BUS's connection to smaller banks worsened those fears. Early on, the message appeared to support the grievances of the state banks against the BUS monopoly. Yet in a later passage it complained that the BUS's redemption of notes presented by the state banks created "a bond of union" among the banking establishments of the nation that made them "an interest separate from that of the people." The latter remark was in line with Jackson's hostility to all commercial banks, but it contradicted what he had said earlier. The message also argued that the comparatively small amount of bank stock owned by westerners proved that eastern financiers were exploiting the rest of the country. Yet that exploitation consisted chiefly of loans extended by the BUS to western investors, hardly a show of pro-eastern favoritism. Perhaps Jackson was really objecting to western debt and (once again) to the banking system itself. But by refraining from saying so directly, and looking instead to build the strongest coalition against the bank, Jackson's argument was illogical. To uphold its constitutional arguments and democratic vision, and to buttress the antibank coalition, the veto message sacrificed consistency on economics and finance itself.[30]

The National Republicans in Washington reacted sharply, emphasizing, as Jackson had, constitutional issues while proclaiming a very different social outlook. The anti-administration *National Intelligencer* called the veto a proclamation of presidential absolutism. Webster, addressing a packed Senate gallery, rebutted the message's claims about the executive's constitutional powers while charging that the message "attacked whole classes of the people, for the purposes of turning against them the prejudices and resentments of other classes." Clay likened Jackson to a European despot and alleged that an "electioneering motive" lay behind Jackson's act: true enough but risibly hypocritical, given Clay's own electioneering calculations. Back in Philadelphia, Nicholas Biddle, certain that the message would backfire on Jackson, detected the spirit of the French Revolution's Reign of Terror: "It has all the fury of a chained panther biting at the bars of his cage. It really is a manifesto of anarchy—such as Marat or Robespierre might have issued to the mob of the faubourgh St. Antoine." None of which mattered on Capitol Hill, where the bank charter bill again passed the Senate on July 13, this time by a margin of 22 to 19—five votes less than the original tally, and far short of the two-thirds' majority required to override Jackson's veto. In the crunch, Jackson's antibank supporters stood up for the president more consistently than his National Republican opponents stood against him.[31]

The veto message did, however, divide pro- and anti-BUS forces within Jackson's larger coalition around the country. In Boston, the horrified old-line ex-Federalists who had supported him in 1828 dashed over to the National Republicans. In New York, where businessmen's opinions about Biddle's operation were divided, the newly converted pro-BUS editor James Watson Webb assailed the president as a worn-out soldier manipulated by "political gamblers, money changers [and] time-serving politicians." Elsewhere, pro-BUS Jacksonians organized committees of "original Jackson men," heaping scorn on the veto but clinging to Old Hickory's name.[32]

Henry Clay, his mind now completely on his presidential campaign, thought he had Jackson exactly where he wanted him. Told during the initial bank bill debate of Jackson's intentions, Clay had vowed, "Should Jackson veto it, I will veto him!" Now, with stunning éclat, Biddle and Jackson had turned the election into a referendum on the BUS—a contest that, with some timely financial and political help, Clay believed he could win. His friend Biddle threw enormous resources into the campaign, reprinting thirty thousand copies of the veto message—self-evident proof, as far as Biddle was concerned, of Jackson's unfitness for office. (When he learned that the public actually liked Jackson's message, Biddle hastily started printing copies of Webster's speech instead.) National Republican editors, pamphleteers, and cartoonists, making their first widespread appearance in presidential politics, hammered away at Jackson as either a corrupt would-be monarch, King Andrew I, or as the latest revolutionary manipulator. "The spirit of Jacksonianism is JACOBINISM . . . ," the *Boston Daily Advertiser and Patriot* screamed: "Its Alpha is ANARCHY and its Omega is DESPOTISM." Although Clay, the Mason, denounced the Anti-Masons after they nominated William Wirt, some pragmatic National Republicans and Anti-Masons in Ohio, Pennsylvania, and New York did what they could to arrange a working relationship with each other, including forming joint electoral tickets.[33]

The Jacksonians responded by tightening their party organization and surpassing their spectacular electioneering efforts of 1828. Doing so was not simple. In early summer a cholera epidemic ravaged the eastern cities, killing thousands, particularly in the poorer neighborhoods, and unnerving the country. (Among the dead was the radical leader of the New York Working Men, Thomas Skidmore.) Still, the Jacksonians mounted a spirited mass campaign. In late May, the party held its own national convention in Baltimore—a gathering envisioned by Jackson's operatives at least a year earlier—and at Jackson's insistence nominated Van Buren for the vice presidency. Then came the deluge of Jackson processions, hickory-pole raisings, and barbecues (one or two of the latter attended by the president himself), even more boisterous and passionate than four years earlier. Blair oversaw the printing and distribution around the country of huge runs of the *Globe*; Kendall, who managed the campaign, commanded the creation of local Hickory Clubs to augment the state parties' efforts.

Jackson's partisans flung themselves into celebrations of the Old Hero, as a fearless man of spotless honor and indomitable courage unlike the wily degenerate Clay. But the fight over the bank also gave the Jacksonians a popular issue more timely than the long-ago Battle of New Orleans, an issue made sharper because Clay was so closely identified with Biddle. In western New York and eastern Pennsylvania, the veto did, as Clay had hoped, put Jackson's supporters on the defensive, as did Clay's condemnation of the administration's Indian policies. But for the most part, the attack on the BUS captured the public's imagination as proof that Jackson was the intrepid defender of "the humble members of society"—a phrase Jackson's managers repeated endlessly—against the rich and privileged. Of the various issues agitated by the *Globe*, the BUS veto was by far the most popular with local Jacksonian editors, who took their cues from Blair's paper. "It is the final decision of the President," one set of state resolutions cried, "between the Aristocracy and the People—he stands by the People." A North Carolina Jacksonian put the matter squarely: "Who but General Jackson would have had the courage to veto the bill rechartering the Bank of the United States, and who but General Jackson could have withstood the overwhelming influence of that corrupt Aristocracy?"[34]

The outcome was a personal vindication for Jackson and a crushing defeat for Clay. Although the total numbers of votes cast in 1832 rose by more than 100,000 over 1828—roughly 9 percent—Clay actually received 35,000 fewer votes than John Quincy Adams had four years earlier, a decline of nearly 7 percent. In the Electoral College, Jackson garnered 219 votes against 49 for Clay, and broke the National Republicans' lock on New England by carrying Maine and New Hampshire. Few at the time doubted that the veto issue accounted for the lopsided totals. "The Veto is popular beyond my most sanguine expectations," Van Buren wrote. The veto message, the astute and cynical Thurlow Weed later observed, allowed the Jacksonians "to enlist the laboring classes against a 'monster bank' or 'moneyed aristocracy'"—winning "ten electors against the bank for everyone that Mr. Webster's arguments and eloquence secured in favor of it."[35]

The elections also brought some disquieting news for Jackson's supporters. In the congressional races, Jackson had virtually no political coattails. The House of Representatives that convened in 1833 would still have a pro-Jackson majority of forty-six, although it was down from fifty-nine four years earlier. But in the Senate, a pro-Jackson majority of four votes had become a minority of eight. The bank veto, although popular overall, hurt the Jacksonians badly in certain key places, above all the BUS's home, Pennsylvania. Then there was the surprisingly strong showing by William Wirt and the Anti-Masons—less decisive than Clay had hoped it might be, but troublesome enough for northern Jacksonians. By winning nearly 8 percent of the popular vote, almost entirely in New England and the middle Atlantic states, Wirt ensured that Jackson's margin of victory in the popular vote (though not his popular vote total) actually declined marginally compared to 1828—the only such case in history for a president elected to a second term. Were the populist Anti-Masons ever to unite successfully with the National Republicans, the Jacksonian coalition would face a new and formidable threat in the North.[36]

Of even greater immediate concern were the southern results, above all in South Carolina. Outside Maryland and Clay's home state of Kentucky, Jackson swept the South; in Georgia, Alabama, and Mississippi, the National Republicans did not even bother to mount a presidential campaign. But in South Carolina, antitariff nullifiers took charge of state politics and delivered the state's eleven electoral votes to their own breakaway presidential candidate, Virginia's extremist state-rights governor, John Floyd. In seven other southern states, Old Republican state-rights dissenters ran a ticket of electors pledged to the pro-Calhoun Virginian, Philip Barbour, instead of Van Buren, for the vice presidency. These defections were irrelevant to the outcome.[37] Yet the nullifiers' schism and the echoes of sympathy outside South Carolina had enormous implications. In the aftermath of the 1832 election, they would lead to a showdown over the meaning of democracy even more dramatic than the early battles over the BUS.

"A SEPARATE GOVERNMENT": ORIGINS OF THE NULLIFICATION CRISIS

The South Carolina nullifers ostensibly rose to protest the administration-backed tariff of 1832, a mildly protectionist compromise measure passed at the end of the congressional session. The new tariff, prompted by the White House's concern about rising southern discontent, cut the average duties of the 1828 tariff by half. To the tariff-obsessed South Carolina slaveholders, however, this was grossly insufficient and cause enough to rally to Calhoun's nullification doctrines. Yet above and beyond the tariff, nullification was also a political reaction to numerous developments linked to slavery, including the Southampton uprising, the appearance of Garrison's *Liberator*, and the Virginia debates over suffrage and emancipation.[38]

What more would it take, the nullifiers wondered, for the slaveholders en masse to understand the immediate dangers? First Denmark Vesey—at least Charleston knew how to handle its savages!—then David Walker, and then Nat Turner had incited the slaves to insurrection, each more successful in turn. In Boston, Walker's home, a crazed white man was publishing an incendiary abolitionist newspaper with impunity, spreading his hateful message everywhere. The oppressive tariff remained in place, while cotton prices languished at under ten cents a pound for the seventh consecutive year. And in the face of all this, Virginia's squirearchy had actually considered emancipation—proving, one nullifier claimed, that even the Old Dominion had become "infested" with "Yankee influence" and democratic misgivings about slavery. Threatened from without by abolitionists and high-tariff men and from within by the potential of a slave revolt provoked by the North, the slaveholders, Vice President Calhoun said, might "in the end be forced to rebel, or submit." The burden fell on Old Carolina to lead the way and spare the entire South from a state of colonial submission—or utter annihilation.[39]

Rich, snobbish, and arrogant, but anxious about the future, South Carolina's slaveholders had always produced the region's most forceful defenses of slavery's benevolence. And they had no use for the democratic dogma that seemed to be sweeping the rest of the nation. Hugh Swinton Legaré—lawyer, sometime state legislator, and the state's leading literary light—conveyed the tone as well as the thinking of his class: "The politics of the immortal Jefferson! Pish!" Not all of the slaveholding elite, to be sure, saw nullification as the best means to preserve the established order, least of all the old-line merchants and lawyers of Charleston, many of them die-hard Federalists who prized the bonds of Union. (Legaré was among those conservatives whose hearts were with the South but whose traditionalism rejected nullification.) When called on to resist some perceived external threat, as they were during the nullification campaign, South Carolina's antimajoritarian political leaders also proved enormously capable organizers of popular sentiment, among slaveholders and nonslaveholders alike. A peculiar temporary, top-down populism would emerge during the nullification crisis, mobilized by the nullifiers in defense of localist oligarchy against "enslavement" by the federal government.[40]

Yet despite the divisions between pro- and anti-nullifers and despite the nullifiers' tub-thumping popular campaigns, South Carolina swerved outside the mainstream of southern politics. The spread of the cotton economy into its backcountry made South Carolina more uniformly reliant on slave labor—and more solidly dedicated to slavery's preservation—than any other state. Nowhere else were slaveholders so numerous across a wider portion of the state. Nowhere else did slaves comprise a larger portion of the total population, making South Carolina's whites singularly vulnerable to fears of slave insurrection. In no state were the

structures of government (despite the wide suffrage for the legislature) less democratic than in South Carolina. And nowhere else did the defense of slavery and
hostility to majoritarian democracy go hand in hand as they did among South
Carolina's slaveholders. Some of the most fervent nullifiers would present themselves as American revolutionaries, to the point of appropriating carefully selected
bits and pieces of Jefferson's writings in order to align their cause with the patriotic
spirit of 1776. In fact, they were exactly the opposite — nabob counterrevolutionar-
ies, increasingly at war with the democratic forces, identified with Andrew Jackson, that were coming to dominate American politics. They were, above all, the
guardians of an idiosyncratic aristocratic-republican mixture, based on slavery,
that they feared was about to be destroyed by Yankee exploiters, with the aid of
spineless southerners.[41]

Ironically, one of the South Carolinian nullifiers who was slow to rouse himself
was the chief theorist, John C. Calhoun. Having completed his transition from
nationalist to sectionalist, Calhoun was, nevertheless, oddly, a temperate force in
state politics at the opening of the 1830s. Despite his break with Jackson, he was
still trying to maneuver his way into the presidency in 1832 — or, alternatively,
build a political alliance between South and West, based on agreements over liberal land distribution policies, that might help in some later election. There were,
Calhoun still believed, many southerners outside South Carolina who were
restive over the protective tariff and who, united under his leadership, could take
over the seemingly solid pro-Jackson South. The oppressed slaveholder minority
might then be able to build a national majority, under his own command and not
Jackson's, and defeat Yankee despotism. Precipitate advocacy of nullification —
which Calhoun called in "every way imprudent" — might kill such hopes by isolating South Carolina from the other slaveholding states. A few of Calhoun's
closest allies, including Senator Hayne and the young South Carolina editor and
planter James H. Hammond, agreed with him, forming a distinct faction of what
might be called moderate nullifiers, who fully approved of the nullification idea,
yet were unpersuaded that its time had come. But other South Carolinians,
including Calhoun's follower George McDuffie, thought this was all moonshine.
Van Buren's triumph over Calhoun had proved the uselessness of trying to work
from within, they believed — and the rest of the South would never rally around
true state-rights principles unless compelled to do so.[42]

Once again, as in the mid-1820s, Calhoun found himself out of step with the
most vehement elements of South Carolina's ruling class. At first he appeared
willing to let it be so by refusing either to renounce or support what he called
"the ultra measures proposed by the Carolina Hotspurs." But under pressure
from Governor James Hamilton Jr. and Hamilton's radical nullifier allies, Calhoun overcame the divisions in his own mind and composed at his plantation, in

July 1831, what became known as the Fort Hill Letter—an open defense of nullification as a moderate, peaceful, and constitutional check on Yankee oppression.[43]

"Happily," Calhoun wrote, the United States had been spared "artificial and separate classes of society." The disturbing divisions were geographical and required equipoise between the general government and the states. State interposition and removal of offensive federal laws could help preserve that stability and impede the conversion of "the General Government into a consolidated, irresponsible government," without endangering the Union—one of "the great instruments of preserving our liberty, & promoting the happiness of ourselves and our posterity." Although it stopped short of endorsing the radical nullifiers, and explicitly rejected "anarchical and revolutionary" intentions, the letter openly aligned Calhoun for the first time with the nullification idea—disclosing the secret that most political observers had long since guessed, and in effect announcing that he intended to remain South Carolina's premier voice in national politics. Now that his break with Jackson was complete and the nullifying movement seemed unstoppable, Calhoun would leave his lair to help give the movement direction.[44]

Until Calhoun assumed a leading role, Governor Hamilton had been the nullifiers' chief agitator and organizer. He did an excellent job. Having already formed, with McDuffie, the States' Rights and Free Trade Association, Hamilton redoubled his efforts over the winter of 1831–32, overseeing the creation of a formal political party, the staffing of public committees, the writing and printing of pamphlets, and the calling of two statewide antitariff conventions, one in Charleston, the other in the state capital, Columbia. There was significant opposition, strongest among up-country planters and yeomen and Charleston merchants and lawyers. (One of these so-called Unionists, the former envoy to Mexico, Joel R. Poinsett, was in regular contact with a deeply concerned President Jackson, keeping him up-to-date about the nullifiers' latest moves.) But after the passage of the tariff bill in July 1832, Hamilton and the nullifiers, with Calhoun's support, sprang into action. Jackson had believed that by cutting the 1828 rates in half, the new tariff would prove his own free-trade bona fides and silence the extremist protests. "You may expect to hear from So Carolina a great noise . . . ," Jackson wrote to his old friend John Coffee, "but the good sense of the people will put it down." Yet Jackson had badly underestimated both the control that pro-Calhounite slaveholders could exert over South Carolina politics and how much popular support for nullification had grown in the state since 1828. It would have to be Jackson, and not the people of South Carolina, who put down nullification.[45]

Over the summer and early fall of 1832, South Carolinians divided violently over politics: not over the bank veto, nor over Jackson and Clay, but over the state legislature elections, scheduled for October 8 and 9. In Charleston, scene of the worst battles, roving bands of armed Unionists and nullifiers confronted each other nightly. Nullifier rhetoric bristled with attacks on majority rule as oppressive, and with defenses of nullification as (in former U.S. Senator William Harper's words) the best means to "obtain all the good which has resulted from monarchies and aristocracies without any mixture of the evil." The nullifiers left little doubt that they believed the protective tariff was not simply an abstract political wrong but an attack by Yankee outsiders on the planters' prerogatives— and, finally, on slavery itself. In his famous, fanciful "forty bale" theory, McDuffie put the planters' interests foremost, charging that for every hundred cotton bales produced by the South, forty were lost to the tariff. The tariff, the Columbia State Rights and Free Trade Party convention declared, was but a means to effect "the abolition of slavery throughout the southern states."[46]

The Unionists countered with a variety of appeals. In the yeoman-dominated northwestern parishes and among the artisans of Charleston, they attacked the undemocratic slaveholders and slavery itself as an evil. More often, they appealed to the voters' patriotism, insisting that South Carolina's interests were far more secure inside the Union than outside, and that nullification was a dangerous, unrepublican experiment. The Unionists nearly carried Charleston, and won handily in the northernmost, yeoman-dominated parishes. But the nullifiers' lopsided victory margins in the cotton-plantation districts gave them 61 percent of the total vote. Thanks to continued malapportionment of the state legislature, this was sufficient to gain the nullifiers the two-thirds' majority required to authorize the calling of a nullification convention, as laid out in the *South Carolina Exposition and Protest*. Governor Hamilton duly called for a special session of the legislature, which in turn passed a convention bill, setting a date in November for the election of delegates who would convene at Columbia five days later. The Unionists, dejected at their loss, had little fight left in them, and the nullifiers completely controlled the selection of delegates.[47]

After five days of work, the convention, with Calhoun's blessing, approved several documents, the most important of which was the Ordinance of Nullification, written by William Harper. In six dry paragraphs, the Ordinance declared the tariffs of 1828 and 1832 unconstitutional; pronounced them null and void in South Carolina, effective February 1, 1833; and called for the legislature to pass all acts necessary to enforce that nullification. The demand for a nonprotective tariff was nonnegotiable. Should the federal government try to coerce South Carolina into denying the Ordinance, the people of South Carolina would secede from the Union and "forthwith proceed to organize a separate government." Governor Hamilton speedily asked the legislature to revise the state's militia laws and approve the raising of a twelve-thousand-man volunteer army.[48]

Jackson, forewarned by Poinsett, took the precaution of ordering the federal forts in Charleston harbor to prepare for attacks, instructed federal customs officials to move from the city to Fort Moultrie offshore, ordered government revenue cutters to enforce the tariff before ships came close to the harbor, and sent a personal emissary to consult with the Unionist leaders. Jackson determined that if the crisis ever came down to shooting, South Carolina and not the federal government would be forced to be the aggressor. After the Ordinance passed, Jackson tried to isolate the South Carolinians by reinforcing his connections to southern leaders from other states and by offering a variety of concessions.

Firmly convinced that the tariff was constitutional, Jackson believed more than ever that its effects had become greatly exaggerated by protectionists and antitariff men alike. It was even less important, Jackson claimed, now that his policies had paid down the national debt nearly to the point of elimination. Accordingly, and with no great sacrifice on his own part, Jackson devoted a section of his annual message on December 4 to proposing an eventual reduction of tariffs to cover only what was necessary for federal revenue and national defense, in exchange for the exercise of "moderation and good sense" by all concerned. He appeared to have acceded to the Carolinians' low-tariff demands, even though he had acceded nothing that made much difference to him. He ended with an affirmation of traditional Jeffersonian state-rights doctrine—the true doctrine, Jackson implied, and not the disunionist folly of Calhoun and his friends. The annual message contained the president's carrot. Six days later, he pulled out his bludgeon.[49]

"VAIN PROVISIONS! INEFFECTUAL RESTRICTIONS!": JACKSON AND NULLIFICATION

In meeting the nullification crisis, Jackson displayed his style of presidential leadership at its strongest. He had always called on his cabinet members and advisors for help in formulating specific proposals and doctrines. Van Buren and James K. Polk wrote the Maysville Road bill veto; Kendall was the chief author of the bank veto message; others chipped in on these and other major addresses. As the long buildup to the bank veto showed, Jackson was open to persuasion and sometimes wavered before making up his mind. But neither did anything go out under Jackson's name that did not meet with his full approval. The one person always involved was Jackson himself, leaning now toward his more state rights–oriented counselors, then toward those with a more nationalist bent, using them all to fashion what, finally, was his own democratic political philosophy, worked out on the job.

Late in 1832, Jackson turned to Edward Livingston to draft and redraft a stern official response to nullification, a follow-up to his conciliatory annual message. The sudden shift in tone led some of his critics, and has led some historians, to claim that the nullification paper was really Livingston's work, not Jackson's, and that it hopelessly contradicted the annual message. But the president probably labored harder on the nullification paper than on any other message of his presidency, sending Livingston memoranda, inserting his own prose into Livingston's drafts, and otherwise making certain that nothing appeared which did not exactly match his own thinking. (According to one account, Jackson worked so furiously, writing notes with a steel pen, that even when he had finished ten pages the ink on the first was still wet.) As ever, Jackson ran his presidency much as he had run his military and election campaigns, delegating authority, relying on the advice of others, but always in charge. The product was not the contradictory jumble that most observers complained about, containing what even a staunch supporter called "broad errors of doctrine." With the aid of his inner circle, Jackson created a volatile synthesis.[50]

Jackson's declaration—officially titled, simply, "Proclamation"—was a triumph of political and constitutional argument. It opened with a calm but contemptuous restatement of the nullifiers' "strange position" and addressed the Ordinance of Nullification point by point. Then it cut to the heart of the issue: were the artifice of nullification countenanced, then "no federative government could exist" and the United States would simply dissolve. By the strictest reading of the U.S. Constitution, there could be no doubt that Article I, Section 8 granted Congress the power to lay and collect taxes, duties, imposts, and excises. Unlike the case of the BUS, there was no ambiguity about the tariff's constitutional correctness.[51]

By what reasoning, then, did the nullifiers justify their claims that the tariffs of 1828 and 1832 abused the Constitution? They complained that the tariffs were unconstitutionally motivated by a desire to secure protection and not merely to raise revenue. Nonsense! Jackson replied that there was no such thing as unconstitutional motives, only unconstitutional acts. The nullifiers complained that the tariff operated unequally. So what? Jackson noted that a perfect equality in taxes was impossible. In any case, such inequality was no justification for declaring unconstitutional legislation that, unlike internal improvements, the Framers had expressly delegated to Congress. The nullifiers complained that the tariff was higher than necessary, its proceeds utilized to fund unconstitutional expenditures. Ridiculous! Jackson retorted that even though Congress might abuse its discretionary powers, the powers themselves were incontestably constitutional and subject to the popular will at elections. One by one, the nullifiers' alleged constitutional grievances collapsed.[52]

But Jackson was not content to refute the nullifiers' reasoning on the tariff. He wanted to destroy the philosophical and political foundations of nullification itself. Once again he focused on the key issue: Calhoun's theories of the Union and undivided state sovereignty. Those theories, Jackson charged, were recent inventions, unanticipated by the Framers and ratifiers of the Constitution. Laws whose effects were far more controversial than the ones currently at issue—the whiskey excise law in the 1790s, Jefferson's embargo—had been deemed unconstitutional by a majority in one or more states, "but, fortunately, none of those States discovered that they had the right now claimed by South Carolina."[53]

Calhoun's invention, Jackson proclaimed, was nothing more than a fraud wrapped inside an absurdity, produced by "[m]etaphysical subtlety, in pursuit of an impracticable theory." The nation, Jackson instructed, was not created by sovereign state governments when the several states approved the Constitution. In fact, the nation was *older* than both the Constitution and the states. Before 1776, "we were known in our aggregate character as the *United Colonies of America.*" The Declaration of Independence was promulgated by the nation before the state governments (save those of New Hampshire and Virginia) were even organized. Even the highly imperfect Articles of Confederation included a provision that "every State shall abide by the determinations of Congress on all questions which by that Confederation should be submitted to them." When framed and ratified "to form a more perfect union," the Constitution became a new framework for an already existing nation. "The Constitution of the United States . . . forms a *government*, not a league," Jackson concluded. Although the states retained all powers not delegated by the Constitution to the federal government, the federal government retained its complete sovereignty in those delegated areas. Any state's denial of that sovereignty—based on the underlying absurd supposition that "the United States are not a nation"—would injure the entire Union. Thus Jackson smashed the logic behind nullification. The politics of the great Calhoun? Hogwash.[54]

Initial reactions to Jackson's proclamation blended puzzlement and shock. National Republicans applauded the document, but also expressed confusion about how Jackson could have approved it. "One short week," Henry Clay wrote to a political associate, "produced the [annual] message and the proclamation— the former ultra, on the side of State rights—and latter ultra, on the side of Consolodation." Jacksonians asked the same question, but in mortification at what they perceived as Jackson's abandonment of Jeffersonian fundamentals. Some contemporaries came up with explanations which boiled down to a suspicion that the president was now an incompetent old codger, easily manipulated by the nationalist advisers around him like Edward Livingston. And so later historians, equally baffled, have advanced their own explanations for the apparent inconsistencies, ranging from Jackson's alleged pathological rage at John C. Calhoun to the claim that Jackson compensated for his annual message by going too far in a nationalist direction and wound up doing "a poor job of defending the traditional states'-rights position."[55]

Some of these interpretations were and are malicious; others merely misconstrue Jackson's purposes. (It was, for example, not Jackson's aim in the nullification proclamation to defend traditional state rights or a lowered tariff, although he did make clear he supported them.) Many share the inaccurate assumption that Jackson trapped himself in some large contradictions. In fact, Jackson, drawing on long-established beliefs, carved out a coherent and principled democratic nationalism on basic constitutional issues. In his mind, tariff rates and nullification were completely separate matters. The first, as he had said in his annual message, was always subject to negotiation, but the second was not.

Jackson had always objected to extending federal powers beyond what was set forth in the Constitution. He regarded programs like federal internal improvements with deep suspicion. Like Jefferson, he believed that the unchecked growth of federal authority would lead inevitably to new concentrations of power that would benefit the privileged few over the many. But Jackson's guardianship of state rights always allowed that the federal government had legitimate independent powers, in no wise at the whim of the state governments. Contrary to Calhoun's calm assertions, he contended, nullification would lead inexorably to secession and the undoing of all that was won in the Revolution. "There is nothing I shudder at more than the idea of the seperation of the Union . . . ," he wrote to James Hamilton Jr. (not yet a nullifier firebrand) before the 1828 election. "It is the durability of the confederation upon which the general government is built, that must prolong our liberty, the moment it seperates, it is gone." Jackson had seen the ineradicable bonds of Union questioned before, by the blue-light New England Federalists of the Hartford Convention, who had squabbled and made disunionist noises while he was crushing the British at New Orleans. Now Calhoun and the nullifiers were questioning the bonds once again while he was trying to crush the Second BUS.[56]

Jackson's position on nullification arose from his fundamental dedication to democracy and to the idea he expressed in his first message to Congress "*that the majority is to govern.*" It was the very opposite of the neo-Federalist "ultranationalism" seen by so many critics, then and now, in the proclamation. Strict construction of federal power was necessary lest a minority try to advance its own narrow interests with only passing concern for the general welfare. Yet no single state—let alone, Jackson noted in the nullification proclamation, "a bare majority of the voters in any one state"—could be permitted to repudiate laws based on delegated powers and duly enacted by Congress and the president, the people's representatives. The *South Carolina Exposition and Protest* had explicitly rejected majoritarian democracy, claiming that "[c]onstitutional government, and the government of the majority, are utterly incompatible." Jackson denounced such astonishing propositions in the horrified cadences of an American seer: "Vain provisions! ineffectual restrictions! vile profanation of oaths! miserable mockery of legislation!"[57]

Jackson's fury at the nullifiers did owe something to his detestation of John C. Calhoun, but Jackson's personal hatreds alone hardly determined his political reaction to nullification. Long before his break with Calhoun, let alone before the nullification crisis, he had been thinking along the lines spelled out in his proclamation. Those majoritarian nationalist ideas were not uniquely his, but in presenting them as forcefully as he did, and incurring huge political risks, Jackson showed how seriously he took them. "No my friend," Jackson told the characteristically squeamish Martin Van Buren, who had urged he refrain from issuing his proclamation, "the crisis must be now met with firmness, our citizens protected, and the modern doctrine of nullification and secession put down forever."[58]

Ordinary Americans were not as flummoxed as some of the leading national politicians and party editors were by Jackson's hard-line stance. The legislatures of Pennsylvania, Indiana, and Illinois, followed by those of most of the other northern states (and Maryland) passed resolutions affirming the proclamation and condemning nullification as "heretical" and "anti-republican." Large and impassioned public meetings in cities from New York to New Orleans hailed Jackson's message. In Nashville, Governor William Carroll offered to lead a force of ten thousand men to South Carolina. Further east, in the mountainous, small-farmer region of the state, one old Jackson comrade, John Wyly, claimed that the "old chief" would be able to raise enough troops in two weeks' time that they could muster at the state border and "piss enough . . . to float the whole nullifying crew of South Carolina into the Atlantic."[59]

In much of the South, the slaveholder-dominated legislatures responded differently. In Georgia, a powerful minority supported nullification, and although the legislators turned down a proclamation favoring it, they did call for a convention of southern states to discuss the issue. In Virginia, the Tidewater slaveholders were particularly supportive of nullification, but the state assembly, controlled by Jacksonians, refused to endorse South Carolina. The North Carolina legislature condemned South Carolina's "revolutionary" and "subversive" actions, but also denounced the protective tariff as unconstitutional and refrained from endorsing Jackson's proclamation. Alabama called for a federal convention to take up the issues raised by the crisis. But despite these qualms—and despite the quasi-nullifying stances taken by familiar extreme state-rights and antidemocratic leaders, ranging from George Troup in Georgia to Abel P. Upshur in Virginia—no southern legislature backed nullification. South Carolina stood alone. Jackson believed that even that result did not show fully how "the united voice of the yeomanry" despised the nullifiers' doctrines and supported him. South Carolina nullifiers, including Calhoun and James H. Hammond, thought that Georgia and Virginia would have joined their ranks but for the Jacksonians' power.[60]

The president's proclamation was the turning point in the crisis. Jackson had already begun making preparations to aid a volunteer Unionist militia within South Carolina, organized by Poinsett in the northern countries. He ordered federal troops to Castle Pinckney and Sullivan's Island in Charleston harbor, and also sent General Winfield Scott to the city aboard a federal sloop, lest the nullifiers try to seize the customs houses. One week after releasing his proclamation, he ordered Secretary of War Lewis Cass to report on how quickly arms and troops (including three divisions of artillery) could be gathered to "crush the monster in its cradle." The South Carolina legislature, which had reconvened, reshuffled the state's leadership by accepting Governor Hamilton's resignation (he would head the state's new armed forces) and replacing him with Senator Hayne. A red-hot nullifier thus gave way to a more moderate nullifier. Hayne's Senate seat went to the now fully engaged John C. Calhoun, who resigned the vice presidency effective December 28. The legislature—the last in the nation empowered to name presidential electors—also officially handed South Carolina's presidential electoral votes to Virginia's governor John Floyd, who, recovering from his less than stalwart performance during his state's debates over slavery, condemned Jackson for his "warlike" preparations. Yet even as the nullifiers arranged for their showdown with Jackson and railed against federal usurpation, it became apparent that South Carolina was politically isolated. Cooler temperaments began asserting themselves on all sides.[61]

The denouement lasted ten weeks into the new year. Governor Hayne, still hoping against hope to win support from other southern states, ordered the twenty-five thousand volunteers who had answered the call to train at home rather than in Charleston, lest South Carolina look like the aggressor menacing the federal forts in Charleston harbor. Jackson, who all along had wanted to force the nullifiers to back down without sending federal troops, modulated his tone and sent a special message to Congress with some very specific requests. These included permission to call up federal troops and state militia without warning the rebels to disperse, should the nullifiers forcibly confiscate federal property. It was largely a symbolic move—the military request would merely speed up the use of powers the president already possessed under laws passed in 1795 and

1807—and was nowhere near as belligerent as might have been expected. But it was severe enough for all concerned to call the proposal Jackson's Force Bill Message. Calhoun, now back in the Senate, ripped into the Force Bill as soon as it was read in Congress and would do so again in later debates, charging that the administration had issued an "imperial edict" and wished to impose a military despotism. Calhoun's speeches, mixing history and declamation, were brilliant, but they would turn out mainly to be bluster. The forces of compromise, chilled by the specter of civil war, were already at work—and Calhoun, in this crisis, finally, the moderate, was playing his part.[62]

On January 21, with the Ordinance of Nullification due to take effect in ten days, the nullifiers held a mass meeting in Charleston and, in a tactical retreat, voted to postpone the implementation until Congress settled the tariff issue. Calhoun, sticking by nullification as an alternative to disunion, wrote the radical nullifier leaders to say that "we must not think of secession, but in the last extremity," and urged them to suspend the Ordinance for a year. Soon thereafter, an official commissioner from Virginia, the Tidewater grandee Benjamin Watkins Leigh, arrived in Columbia bearing a copy of the state's carefully crafted middle-of-the road resolutions, critical of both Jackson and nullification, and offered to mediate the dispute.[63]

Clay, Webster, and Calhoun then began patching together an agreement. An administration tariff bill, forwarded by Van Buren's ally, the low-tariff New York Congressman Gulian Verplanck, impressed neither the nullifiers nor Clay's pro-tariff men. Clay and Calhoun set about devising an alternative to steal Jackson's thunder. The process was difficult, and not without rhetorical fireworks. First, Congress, cajoled by the master fixer Clay and with Calhoun's accord, hammered out a compromise tariff that lowered rates incrementally until 1842, when they would drop sharply to the levels sought by the nullifiers. At every contested point in the bargaining, Calhoun gave way, assured by the hard-dealer Clay and by Webster that northern protectionists needed gradual adjustment and would go no further—thereby perpetuating for a decade a decidedly protective tariff even as cotton prices remained pathetically low. With the casus belli removed—and with the nullifiers' supposedly nonnegotiable demands negotiated away—the crisis might have appeared over. But Jackson insisted on passing the Force Bill, just as Calhoun insisted on putting on a show of resisting it. In the Senate debate, Calhoun and Webster squared off and rose to their full oratorical powers. Sounding, for once, something like Jackson, Webster declared that "those who espouse the doctrines of nullification reject . . . the first great principle of all republican liberty; that is, that the majority must govern."[64]

The Force Bill debate attracted enormous attention. (John Randolph of Roanoke, who despised John C. Calhoun but despised Daniel Webster even more, excitedly watched the proceedings from the Senate gallery, and told a man seated in front of him to remove his hat, which was blocking his view: "I want to see Webster die, muscle by muscle," he said.) Yet the nullifiers, facing likely defeat in the Senate, quietly agreed to refrain from obstructing the Force Bill's passage, probably in a prearranged deal. The measure carried in the Senate by a 32 to 1 vote, with many slaveholders, including Henry Clay, absenting themselves. Then it passed the House, 149 to 48. Several hours later, the Senate gave its final approval to the compromise tariff. Calhoun claimed the last word and delivered a learned, irrelevant, and attention-getting speech denouncing the Force Bill. He then departed Washington, riding night and day in an open wagon through foul weather to Columbia to make sure that the radical nullifiers stepped down. There was little chance they would not, as what support they had received from the rest of the South evaporated after the compromise tariff passed Congress. A reconvened state convention rescinded the Ordinance of Nullification, but in a final defiant act, the insurgents passed a new ordinance nullifying the Force Bill, salvaging shreds of honor.[65]

Jackson had won a major victory—but a costly one. His losses came from within his own party, especially in the South. Although they spurned nullification, the southern slaveholders, generally, also spurned Jackson's proclamation as much too harsh and much too nationalist. Even staunch southern Jacksonians admitted that, though they thought nullification was madness, the nullifiers had a point. "You can rest assured," one pro-Jackson Mississippian wrote, "S.C. has our sympathies." In Virginia, the cradle of Jeffersonian doctrine, the crisis reopened the rift between the small-farmer, pro-Jackson West and the slaveholder-dominated Tidewater and Piedmont areas, where the nullifiers commanded great support. "I am no nullifier . . . ," one Louisiana planter wrote at the height of the crisis, "but my sympathies are with theirs; and as the nullifiers are contending against laws which are unconstitutional, unjust, oppressive, and ruinous to the South, I will never consent to see them put down by military force, and before I would take part in a crusade by the Yankees to put South Carolina to the sword, I would be hung for treason." In the congressional machinations leading to the compromise, southern Democrats peeled off from the administration and opened up the possibility of an ideologically promiscuous Clay-Calhoun alliance. Others stayed loyal to the party but would seek ways to square white men's democracy with a robust Calhounite idea of state rights. Some southerners who were Unionists in 1832—including a young up-country South Carolina editor, William Lowdnes Yancey—would become secessionists soon enough.[66]

Adverse reactions were far less common in the North, where most of the state legislatures backed Jackson to the hilt on the matter of nullification. Yet many northern Jacksonians found the president's ferocious words and actions disturbing. In Van Buren's New York, orthodox views of state sovereignty and support for the compact theory of the Constitution prevented the Regency, which condemned nullification, from uniting in support of Jackson's proclamation. Van Buren himself opposed the Force Bill. Viewed from a certain angle, this fallout, along with Jackson's fracturing of his southern following, can make it seem as if the nullifiers, and not Jackson, had won the battle. Add in the fact that the nullifiers succeeded in gaining a tariff reduction, albeit a very gradual one, along with the fact that South Carolina Unionism virtually collapsed after 1833, and John C. Calhoun might even look like a triumphant political thinker and strategist. Such, at least, was Calhoun's own assessment. More detached observers saw the long-term outcome as ominous. "Nullification has done its work," the Unionist James Petigru wrote. "It has prepared the minds of men for a separation of the states—and when the question is moved again it will be distinctly union or disunion."[67]

Yet Jackson also was certain that he had won, and with good reason. "I have had a laborious task here," he wrote, "but nullification is dead; and its actors and exciters will only be remembered by the people to be execrated for their wicked designs." With a combination of coercive threats and well-timed moderation, Jackson had scotched the immediate threat. He had vindicated the Union with much of his popular following, if not his Washington following, still intact. Although he got no credit for the compromise tariff, he had helped maneuver events so that Calhoun and his Carolina allies settled for far less than they had demanded—and less than Jackson himself had seemed to offer in his annual message in December 1832. Of all the major figures in the controversy, only Jackson had backed the Force Bill and some sort of tariff reduction, a stand which affirmed his view that nullification and the tariff were completely separate issues. He got his way on both. More broadly, he had articulated a theory of American constitutional democracy that combined Jeffersonian strict construction and respect for state rights with a validation of the American Union. Above all, Jackson had vindicated the idea that had become the keystone of his politics: in the American republic, the majority governs. To uphold that principle, he called on the nation to reject the slaveholder aristocrats, who in their zeal would dismember the Union itself.[68]

The struggle hardly turned the slaveholder Jackson's administration, let alone his intersectional party, into an antislavery force. Jackson did not even see the crisis in those terms. He always ascribed the nullifiers' motivations to sheer political ambition. Now that they had lost, Jackson predicted, they would seize on "the negro, or slavery question" as their "next pretext." The *Globe* agreed, charging that the impulse behind nullification was "a *politician's*, not a *planter's*." Yet the crisis did show that protecting slavery and slaveholders' rights did not lie at the

core of Jackson's political philosophy. Democracy, not pro-slavery, was his animating principle, in the nullification crisis no less than when he vetoed the
rechartering of the BUS. To defend democracy, he would fiercely attack the
most vociferous pro-slavery bloc in the nation.[69]

There was, to be sure, a great deal more to the nullification crisis than met the
eye. As James Petigru sensed, the compromise of 1833 did not settle the deeper
issues at stake any more than had the Missouri Compromises of 1820 and 1821.
The battle between Jacksonian democratic nationalists, northern and southern,
and nullifier sectionalists would resound through the politics of slavery and antislavery for decades to come. Jackson's victory, ironically, would help accelerate
the emergence of southern pro-slavery as a coherent and articulate political
force, which would help solidify northern antislavery opinion, inside as well as
outside Jackson's party. Those developments would accelerate the emergence of
two fundamentally incompatible democracies, one in the slave South, the other
in the free North.

As Calhoun had suggested early on, the struggle involved not simply protective tariffs or state rights but the deeper alienation of the slaveholding South,
whose "peculiar domestick institution" placed it in "opposite relation to the
majority of the Union." Or, as a young, intransigent radical nullifier named
Robert Barnwell Rhett proclaimed at the final gathering of the South Carolina
nullification convention, not just the North but also "the whole world are in
arms against your institutions: . . . Let Gentlemen be not deceived. It is not the
Tariff—not Internal Improvement—nor yet the Force Bill, which constitutes the
great evil against which we are contending." The *Globe*'s prediction, after the crisis had passed, that nullification would give way to an effort to arouse "the fear
and jealousy of the South with regard to their slaves," and push for disunion
would come to seem prescient, even if pro-slavery ideals and not merely ambition would lie behind that effort.[70]

Yet however much Jackson and his supporters misunderstood the deeper
motives and forces, they had presented a powerful and, for the moment, victorious case about the central political issue in the crisis, the legitimacy of nullification. In the final analysis, Jackson declared, devotion to the nation, democracy,
and the will of the majority must take precedence over the nullifiers' allegiance
to region, state, and locality—and to slavery. By stating his ideas as forcefully as
he did, and threatening to take military action, Jackson offended many southern
slaveholders, and even pro–state rights northerners. Yet he still managed to leave
the nullifiers isolated and defeated. He also established a crucial democratic
precedent. Over the decades to come, the southern slaveholders, pushed by Calhoun, his admirers, and his successors, would expand on the pro-slavery and disunionist arguments that underlay nullification. In time, the disunionists would

force a secession crisis far graver than the confrontation over the tariff in 1833. But when that happened—and as Americans fixed their attention, once again, on Charleston harbor—another president, Abraham Lincoln, would turn to Jackson's doctrine for guidance.

"JACKSON CONQUERS EVERY THING"

Thirty-six hours after Congress put the final touches on the compromise that ended the nullification controversy, Jackson took the oath of office for his second presidential term. The ceremony, although surrounded by the usual festivities, was prudent and simple, with little of the exuberance of Jackson's first inaugural and none of the sublime wonder at what sort of president he would be. People now knew. Jackson's second inaugural message, almost exactly the same lean length as his first, noted, with understatement, the "many events" of the previous four years that had "called forth . . . my views of the principles and policy which ought to be pursued by the General Government." Jackson then delivered a concise summary of those views, blending respect for state rights with "the sacred duty of all to contribute to [the Union's] preservation by a liberal support of the General Government in the exercise of its just powers."[71]

The previous four years had brought to a political head social and economic transformations already underway for decades. Jackson had initiated none of these, nor any of the political, social, and religious movements they spawned, including the Working Men, the evangelical moral reformers, the radical abolitionists, and the nullifiers. Toward some of those causes—above all, radical abolitionism and nullification—Jackson was deeply hostile, and would make his hostility even clearer over the years to come. Yet all created political disturbances fed by clashing ideas about democracy that, one way or another, shook the national government as well as the regions and localities where they had originated.

Jackson had entered the White House full of ideas about reforming government and ending the kind of insider corruption that he blamed for his defeat in 1824–25. For two years, scandals and schisms badly distracted his efforts. But on inauguration day in 1833, Jackson could look back with satisfaction at what he had achieved, on the bank veto, nullification, Indian removal, resisting Sabbatarianism—and crushing Henry Clay. In doing all that, Jackson had reshaped the political coalition that had elected him in 1828 to fit his own principles, complete with a chosen successor who would now be his vice president, Martin Van Buren. No longer an ad hoc alliance, his national political operation had begun to resemble a coherent party—what would soon become known simply as the

Democracy. Jackson's supporters had rallied several democratic insurgencies—Workies from the eastern cities, western hard-money men and backcountry democrats, southern yeomen and Unionists—to the Democracy's banner. "General Jackson," wrote John Quincy Adams's son, Charles Francis, as much in awe and candor as in bitterness, "conquers every thing."[72]

Jackson the conqueror still had many powerful enemies to face, though, not least in the Congress of the United States, one house of which now was firmly in the control of his opponents, led by Clay. The outcome of important campaigns, above all the struggle with the BUS, had yet to be settled. Although the nullifiers had been stopped, neither southern misgivings nor the northern antislavery movement that inflamed them would abate simply because of the compromise of 1833. "My opinion is," the defeated Anti-Mason William Wirt wrote after Jackson's reelection, "that he may be President for life if he chooses."[73] The commotions that Jackson and the nation would face during his second term militated otherwise.

13

BANKS, ABOLITIONISTS, AND THE EQUAL RIGHTS DEMOCRACY

O n June 27, 1833, Harvard University granted President Jackson the honorary degree of doctor of laws. Jackson had embarked on a triumphant postelection tour of New York and New England, and Harvard's president, the aging patrician Josiah Quincy of the departed Boston Middling Interest, was persuaded that the nation's oldest university ought to honor Jackson, just as it had honored President Monroe when the latter visited Boston in 1817. John Quincy Adams, a Harvard overseer, boycotted the ceremony, appalled, he wrote, that his alma mater would entertain "a barbarian who could not write a sentence of grammar and hardly could spell his own name." But Josiah Quincy's son, Josiah Jr., the instigator of the degree, had found Jackson "a knightly personage," and the crowds that thronged his route across New England adored the president. "He is amazingly tickled with the Yankees," the humorist Seba Smith's fictional Major Jack Downing chuckled, "and the more he sees on 'em, the better he likes 'em. 'No nullification here,' says he."[1]

Jackson, although delighted by the reception, was in physical agony for the entire trip, as one of his ancient dueling wounds caused bleeding in his lungs. In Concord, New Hampshire, he collapsed, and the tour abruptly ended. After regaining some strength in Washington, Jackson decided to continue his convalescence, accompanied by Francis Blair, at the Rip Raps, a man-made Virginia coastal island owned by the federal government. On the voyage down the Chesapeake, the chop knocked about the steamboat carrying the president's party, and one of the passengers became alarmed. "You are uneasy," Jackson said to him, "you never sailed with *me* before, I see."[2]

Political disquiet was already leading to plots and innovations elsewhere along the eastern seaboard. In New York, divisions between Democrats for and against the Bank of the United States worsened. In Philadelphia as well as New York, trade unionists, picking up where the Working Men ended, launched a series of strikes and organized new citywide union organizations—a prelude to the formation of the National Trades' Union the following year. In December, William Lloyd Garrison and his allies gathered in Philadelphia to form the American Anti-Slavery Society, the first national immediatist organization. In South Carolina, John C. Calhoun, his mind fixed on Jackson's political destruction, interpreted the nullification debacle as a great success that had dealt the tariff system "its death wound blow" and had handed the slavocrats the balance of power in the new Congress.[3]

Another storm was brewing a thousand miles to the southwest, in the northern Mexico state of Coahuila y Tejas, where independence-minded American settlers were squaring off against a new Mexican government headed by Antonio López de Santa Anna. But Tejas was light-years from the Rip Raps during Jackson's month-long stay. After nullification's demise, Jackson had turned his mind to completing the destruction of Biddle's bank. Most of his chief advisers expressed caution, but Jackson had supreme self-confidence. "[I]s it possible that your friends hesitate, and are overawed by the power of the Bank?" he wrote sardonically to Vice President Van Buren, one of the biggest doubters. "[I]t cannot overaw me. I trust in my God and the virtue of the people."[4]

"TO HEAL . . . THE CONSTITUTION": THE BANK WAR AND THE RISE OF THE WHIGS

When he was helping to compose the bank veto message in July 1832, Jackson suggested including some remarks about establishing a new national banking institution in place of the BUS. He wanted to calm the electorate's nerves as well as stand up for constitutional principle. "[N]o inconvenience can result from my veto," he wrote, noting that with four years of the bank's charter still left to run, there would be sufficient time to establish some version of "a national Bank or Banks" that would have the proper restrictions. Jackson's suggestion did not make it into the message's final draft.[5] Nor, amid the distractions of the election and the nullification controversy, did the administration design an alternative to Biddle's bank. By the time Jackson returned to the issue in earnest in 1833, he had decided on a course of action that would cause considerable inconvenience—and lead to an all-out war over banks and banking policy.

Goaded by Amos Kendall and Francis Blair, Jackson began to consider removing the government's deposits from the BUS during the waning days of the 1832 campaign. Four years earlier, he had learned that certain branches of the

BUS were secretly throwing their resources behind John Quincy Adams, but in 1832 the alliance between the bank and the National Republicans was overt—and, in some parts of the country, very effective. The bank, incensed by Jackson's reelection as well as the veto, might now be all the more dangerous to the country. Possessing the government deposits, the BUS could easily flood the country with bank notes, only to squeeze credit prior to the 1836 election and trigger a panic that would help elect pro-BUS men who would reverse Jackson's veto. "[T]he hydra of corruption is only *scotched, not dead*," the president wrote to his young Tennessee congressional loyalist James K. Polk, and its allies intended "to destroy the vote of the people lately given at the ballot boxes." Summarily stripping the bank of its government deposits would dramatically diminish the threat.[6]

Jackson's annual message in December 1832 broached the subject of removal, questioning whether the bank was still a safe depository of the people's money. The Democratic-dominated House of Representatives replied the following March by emphatically rejecting a bill, proposed by Polk, to sell the government's shares in the bank. Convinced that the BUS had thoroughly corrupted Congress, Jackson told both his official cabinet and his Kitchen Cabinet that he was now inclined to remove the deposits on his own and redistribute them to various state banks. Most of Jackson's advisers, in and out of the cabinet, blanched at the prospect. "My first impression is," James Hamilton, no friend to the BUS, said in a brief note, "that the measure proposed was a very questionable one, and must lead to great disturbance in commercial affairs." Kendall, the outstanding exception, sent Jackson a memorandum on why removal was the best course for the country.[7]

Kendall emphasized that the bank now posed a new political threat. Unless destroyed, Kendall charged, this "great enemy of republicanism" would resort to bribery, intimidation, and every other corrupt means to elect its own candidate to the White House in 1836 and regain its charter as soon as Jackson left office. Arousing Jackson's always sensitive manly honor, Kendall claimed that unless he moved decisively, his backers would decide he was "wanting either in the courage or in the good faith" to finish what he had started. Kendall also argued, frankly, that handing the government deposits over to sympathetic state banks would "raise up powerful friends" who would fulfill the bank's fiscal functions and provide a political counterweight to Biddle and the National Republicans.[8]

Plainly, Kendall and Jackson regarded the transfer of the BUS deposits to the state banks with a cold political eye. There is a danger, however, in interpreting these politics too narrowly, as a brazen partisan gambit aimed chiefly at enlarging Jacksonian patronage. Among the chosen state bankers, idealism may well have taken a backseat to opportunism. (As Biddle, quoting Jonathan Swift, had observed, "Money is neither Whig nor Tory.") But Jackson's latest attack on the bank arose from his long-standing objections to the BUS, mixed with his outrage at Biddle's political actions in 1832 and his fears that Biddle would eventually thwart the manifest will of the electorate. Distributing federal monies to selected state banks was hardly an innovation: Jackson was following the precedent set by the Madison administration in 1811. Seeing themselves in a death battle against unconstitutional forces—a "corrupt league," Kendall called it—Jackson and Kendall were not about to take the public funds out of Biddle's control only to place them in the hands of his allies.[9]

More like the Jeffersonians than later generations of American politicians, Kendall and Jackson, reflecting the common party assumptions of the 1830s, still perceived themselves as protectors of the nation against a small, designing, illicit cabal, rallying what Kendall called "the friends of good and pure government"—including, in this case, competent and reliable state bankers. "I have no doubt of the Bank being rechartered unless by the removal of the deposits," Jackson wrote to Vice President Van Buren—a matter, he said, "in which I see the perpetuity of our republican Government involved." That the Jacksonians, like most of their contemporaries, were quick to detect conspiracies against public liberty hardly means that they were engaged in one of their own to fatten their supporters' coffers. The enrichment of loyal state banks was an effect, not a cause, of the Bank War.[10]

Jackson dispatched Kendall to scout out possible recipients of the federal funds in lieu of the BUS. And in June, after a sudden reshuffling of the cabinet, Jackson named the leading son of Philadelphia's city democracy, the lawyer William John Duane, as secretary of the Treasury, a move he would later regret. Over the summer, the president plotted his removal plans with Kendall, Francis Blair, and Roger B. Taney. In August, he received additional support. A report from the government's directors on the BUS board affirmed that the bank had spent eighty thousand dollars on printing campaign materials hostile to Jackson in the 1832 election—and that Biddle himself had spent twenty thousand dollars, with no accounting records whatsoever. Armed with definitive proof of the bank's pollution of American democracy, Jackson presented to the new cabinet a paper, which he himself drafted and Taney redrafted, outlining the cessation of government deposits in the bank effective October 1. In both Jackson's and Taney's versions, the paper restated what, from the very start of the conflict, had been Jackson's central constitutional and political concerns: "The Bank of the United States," Jackson wrote, "is in itself a Government" whose power had only increased; and "the mass of the people" had much to fear from that illegitimate government, run by an "aristocracy" of "the wealthy and professional classes." Removal of the deposits was necessary to undo the aristocracy's insidious efforts at "preventing political institutions however well adjusted, from securing the freedom of the citizen." Secretary Duane's formal approval was all that was required for the removal plan to take effect.[11]

Duane was eminently respectable from a business viewpoint, having worked for the Girard family banking interests in Philadelphia and having won outgoing Treasury Secretary McLane's personal endorsement. But Duane had also been a prominent and outspoken foe of the BUS for fifteen years, first in the Pennsylvania legislature and later as a member of the banking committee of the Philadelphia Working Men's Party. With his father and William Gouge, he had been one of the signers of the well-known Philadelphia report and memorial against the bank in 1829. Here was the perfect choice, a bank lawyer with links to the city democratic tradition. But Duane proved to be, to Jackson, less than his father's son. Conceiving his position as more beholden to Congress than to the president, and offended at Jackson's peremptory tone, the new secretary balked at removing the deposits and forced a showdown when he also refused to resign. "[H]e is either the weakest mortal, or the most strange composition I ever met with," the frustrated president wrote. On September 20, the *Globe* announced the plan to withdraw deposits in the BUS. Five days later, Jackson fired Duane and named the anti-BUS stalwart Taney as his replacement.[12]

By the time the removal of the deposits occurred, its potential effects on the bank had grown. In 1833, thanks to rising surpluses in the federal budget, the government's monies in the BUS had risen to nearly $10 million, about half of the bank's total deposits. As Kendall warned the president, withdrawing those funds precipitously would have a devastating impact on the BUS and therefore on the entire country. By the same token, Biddle could create enormous mischief if he were to meddle with the politically friendly state-chartered banks where the federal funds would now be deposited—soon to be known derisively as the "pet banks." To succeed, Jackson and his men would have to find a way to conduct removal slowly while warding off Biddle's inevitable counterattacks.[13]

Taney, placed in charge of the transit of funds, advanced with care—and with one eye fixed warily on Nicholas Biddle. Three days after the removal order took effect, Taney gave five of the seven state-chartered "pets" a total of $2.3 million in Treasury drafts on the federal deposits at the BUS. Should Biddle try to launch a preemptive strike on any of the pets by suddenly presenting them with notes and demanding payment in specie, the pets could use the drafts to remove federal deposits from the BUS and preserve their own liquidity. But the precaution backfired when, only three days after Taney made his move, one of the state banks presented drafts with a combined value of $100,000 to the BUS, and then endorsed them to a third bank to cover some unsuccessful speculation in stocks by the state bank's director. Over the objections of some of his directors, Biddle immediately reduced the BUS's loans by nearly $6 million. After other state banks presented additional drafts on the federal deposits amounting to $1 million, Biddle contracted credit even further, ordering more than $9 million in reductions by January 1834.[14]

Taney had badly miscalculated. But Biddle was hardly a public-spirited national banker, reacting to events. Long before the state banks began presenting their drafts, the BUS president was planning to take action against an anticipated removal by curtailing bank credit. At the end of July 1833, he warned the New York branch of the BUS that the bank would soon move to "crush the Kitchen Cabinet." Two weeks later, Biddle ordered the branches to demand quicker payment of their bills of exchange. On October 1, when removal went into effect, the bank decided to begin tightening its credit. By January, Biddle's reductions exceeded pet bank withdrawals from the BUS by more than $4 million, and the contraction continued through the summer of 1834. Biddle never wavered in his belief that it was his sworn duty to strike back at Jackson—the sooner and the harder, the better. The timing allowed Biddle and his friends to blame the crisis entirely on what the New Yorker Philip Hone called Jackson's "supererogatory act of tyranny." But in private, Biddle admitted that he was trying to cause general hardship that would agitate state banks other than the pets and force Congress to step in on the BUS's behalf. To business associates, Biddle sounded cool and deliberate. "The ties of party allegiance can only be broken," he wrote one, "by the actual conviction of existing distress in the community." To others, he blustered. "My own course is decided," he wrote to one friendly congressman, "—all the other Banks and all the merchants may break, but the Bank of the United States shall not break." Later, when even sympathetic businessmen grew restive, Biddle snarled that the bank would not be "cajoled from its duty by any small driveling about relief to the country."[15]

The crash resounded throughout the nation. Coupled with the credit crunch it placed on the state banks, the BUS's pressure on individual investors touched off business failures and unemployment that some feared would surpass the disaster of 1819. Businessmen, bankers, and National Republicans howled that the villain was Jackson—Jackson the demagogue, Jackson the spoilsman, Jackson the despot. Daniel Webster, who had been entertaining an entente with Jackson over the preservation of the Union, now led the denunciations with the familiar conservative charge that the Jacksonians were "arraying one class against another." More often, Jackson's opponents took the constitutional high ground, proclaiming the president a power-mad usurper who was using the partisan pet banks to help consolidate his rule. "We are in the midst of a revolution," Henry Clay told the Senate, "hitherto bloodless, but rapidly tending towards a total change of the pure republican character of the Government." Three months later, Justice Joseph Story thought the revolution had been completed: "[T]hough we live under the form of a republic," he wrote, "we are in fact under the absolute rule of a single man."[16]

The firing of Duane and the removal of the deposits, followed by the crash, angered moderate and conservative Democrats nearly as much, just as Van Buren and Jackson's other cautious advisers had feared. Some of the perturbed Jacksonians deserted to the opposition; others stuck with the party but established themselves as so-called Bank Democrats—conservatives who, though they thoroughly approved of killing the BUS charter, thought the removal and deposit bank scheme a thoughtless and possibly unconstitutional act of executive aggression. Complaints from constituents about what seemed to be Jackson's blind vindictiveness weakened the president's position on Capitol Hill. "We cannot resist this tremendous pressure," one congressman cried to an appalled Amos Kendall; "we shall be obliged to yield." A New Hampshire senator remarked that although Jackson remained adamant, "many of his partisans are in much distress under the impression that his lawless and reckless conduct and his obstinacy will prostrate the party."[17]

The threatened defections of antiremoval Democrats opened up fresh opportunities for John C. Calhoun. The bank's supporters might have expected Calhoun to defend the BUS, which had largely been his creation. But for Calhoun, though he would praise the bank's "indispensable" work, attacking Jackson and sustaining his own state-rights doctrine took precedence. In the current conflict, Calhoun claimed, the removal issue was but a pretext for a more fundamental struggle for supremacy between a tyrannical executive and a resistant legislature over who would control the nation's currency—a power, he asserted, that the Constitution expressly granted to Congress. Calhoun's stance was of a piece with nullification, he said. He and the other South Carolina nullifiers—"I am not afraid of the word"—were once again fighting a despotic executive, much as they had over the Force Bill. Just as important, although Calhoun would not say so openly, were the political rewards to be won by opposing removal. As Calhoun's editor Duff Green remarked, "every movement which throws off a fragment from the Jackson party promises to swell our numbers."[18] Nullification was dead for now, but the Bank War might yet make Calhoun president.

Jackson's supporters did not flinch. If the credit and commerce of the country truly were reliant on the monster bank, one New York Jacksonian congressman exclaimed, "I, for one, say perish credit, perish commerce." Opposition claims that Jackson had become an autocrat sparked indignant replies that the bank's backers were trying to divert the voters from the real issue at hand—pretending to be champions of the Constitution and foes of partisan favoritism when they were merely champions of the bank. "It is [Jackson's] measures against the United States Bank, which have excited them to such ferocious political war against him," the contentious pro-Jackson New York editor William Leggett charged.[19]

Jackson himself was immovable, bombastic, and cunning. When groups of concerned businessmen and merchants paid calls on the White House, beseeching him to change course, the president rudely interrupted and dressed them down. "Go to Nicholas Biddle," he told one New York deputation. "We have no money here, gentlemen, Biddle has all the money. He has millions of specie in his vaults, at this moment, lying idle, and yet you come to *me* to save you from breaking. I tell you, gentlemen, it's all politics." The warfare was as much psychological as ideological, and Jackson deployed his vehemence shrewdly. (Once the New York businessmen were safely out of earshot, Jackson was found chortling, "Did n't I manage them well?") The ploy worked, at least in convincing some distinguished men that Jackson was not bluffing and that civilization itself was on the brink of ruin. "The present contest," the Brahmin notable Edward Everett told an English banker, "is nothing less than a war of Numbers against Property."[20]

The retaliation against Jackson peaked during the winter congressional session, thereafter known as "the Panic session." According to the bank's charter, removal of the federal deposits required congressional agreement that the deposits were no longer safe, and Taney duly submitted to the House a report to that effect, blaming Biddle's curtailments. Thanks to the steady work of Congressman Polk, four resolutions passed the House backing Jackson's policies. But in the Senate, Henry Clay, enjoying a commanding National Republican majority as well as the support of John C. Calhoun, won a repudiation of Taney's report. More important, Clay introduced, early in the session, a motion condemning both the removal of Duane and the removal of the deposits, and censuring Jackson for assuming unconstitutional powers "dangerous to the liberties of the people." Thomas Hart Benton attacked the censure move as usurpation by the Senate majority of the House's impeachment power, but Clay and his supporters meant to have their way. For three months, they allowed the resolution to lie open, giving National Republicans repeated chances to denounce Jackson, right under the nose of the president of the Senate, Vice President Van Buren. As the session wore on—one of the most "extraordinary" in memory, Churchill Cambreleng wrote—it became clear that the censure could not be stopped. Finally, at the end of March, the Senate dramatically (if predictably) approved Clay's resolution.[21]

Jackson's lengthy and solemn protest of the censure dwelled on the irregularities of the Senate condemning the executive for committing high crimes and misdemeanors against the state. According to Article II, Section 4 of the Constitution, consideration of such offenses must begin with the House of Representatives, which had the sole power of impeachment. Now, however, the Senate majority had stopped short of impeachment but declared the president had committed impeachable offenses while bypassing the Democratic-dominated House altogether—a process, Jackson declared, that "reverses the whole scheme of this part of the Constitution." Jackson also placed the censure in the larger political context of the Bank War, pointing out that the state legislatures of four pro-censure senators had expressly approved both the recharter veto and the removal of the deposits. Above all, the president used the message to flesh out his conception of democracy and a democratic presidency. Regarding the dismissal of Duane, Jackson insisted that the Senate had the power of advice and consent over cabinet nominations, but no more. Once approved, cabinet secretaries served entirely at the president's pleasure; always the president was in full command of the executive branch. "The President," Jackson intoned, "is the direct representative of the American people"—the only such elected official (apart from the vice president) in the entire government. The Senate's censure attacked democracy by trying to give to Congress—"a body not directly amenable to the people"—a degree of influence and authority that undermined executive power and endangered public liberties. It thereby advanced the consolidation of "a splendid government supported by powerful monopolies and aristocratical establishments."[22]

Senator Poindexter of Mississippi told his colleagues that since Jackson's protest had not been delivered on any official occasion, it was only "a paper with the signature of Andrew Jackson" and should not even be received. But debate continued, in and out of the Capitol, as Jackson's critics compared his response to the edicts of Napoleon, and bid Clay and his friends to go all out and "*impeach* the old *scamp.*" Insofar as traditional republican thinking vaunted legislatures over executives as more directly beholden to the voters, Jackson's assertions did mark a great departure. Yet Jackson's protest reflected the changed political realities of the 1830s, whereby in most states the voters and not the legislatures chose presidential electors. If Jackson's original message went too far in claiming executive power over public monies (requiring a quick corrective postscript message), his aim was not to establish a new executive despotism, or what later generations would call an "imperial presidency." He wanted, instead, to head off Clay's pretensions to establishing an imperial Congress, with the president's powers diluted by some fancied responsibility to the Senate and by the threat of repeated harassment through censure. Jackson sought to sustain and enlarge the American presidency as an independent instrument of the popular will, and ward off the rise of a rough equivalent of a prime ministership at the other end of Pennsylvania Avenue. The argument impressed Clay and the Senate not at all. After two weeks of excoriating rhetoric, the censure motion passed again, by an even wider margin than before, and the Senate refused to place Jackson's protest in its official journal.[23]

It was now almost the middle of May 1834. Clay was in his full glory—or so it seemed to Henry Clay. In fact, on the issue underlying everything, the tide had turned against Nicholas Biddle and the bank's defenders. Disgusted by the continuing recession, business leaders in Boston and New York had shifted their ire away from Jackson and toward the BUS, which, they were now persuaded, was hurting them in order to satisfy Biddle's hatred of Jackson. By the end of 1833, the *Journal of Commerce*, the leading anti-Jackson business paper in the country, was criticizing Biddle's contraction. In March, a concerned Biddle hastened to New York to consult with prominent New York merchants and financiers, led by the venerable Albert Gallatin. With the backing of their friends in Boston, the New Yorkers laid it on the line to Biddle: either relax the bank's policies or face exposure and repudiation.[24]

Biddle played along for a while, but in May resumed the reductions more aggressively than ever. Fed up, the eminent Bostonian manufacturer, business-man, and former opposition congressman Nathan Appleton wrote a long letter to the directors of the Boston BUS branch to be forwarded to Biddle, blaming the bank's arbitrary and "regular system of contraction" for the continuing paralysis of business. Appleton warned Biddle that the direst of consequences would befall him and the country without an immediate change in policy. Biddle hemmed and hawed; Appleton wrote a second and even sterner letter, filled with evidence from the bank's own statements that contraction was neither necessary nor desir-able. Finally, in mid-September, Biddle relented, eventually restoring the bank's loans to the same level as when the contraction began, and placing even more notes into circulation than before. Biddle's counteroffensive was crushed. The panic was over.[25]

The clampdown's economic impact turned out to be milder than had been originally feared. Few banks suffered disastrous runs. State bank emissions of paper currency kept the overall money supply stable. Wholesale prices dipped, but did not collapse. Interest rates and the price of commercial paper rose sharply, but the increases, coupled with a rising surplus of American imports over exports, further stimulated foreign investment in American internal-improvements proj-ects, which restocked both the BUS and the state banks with millions of dollars in needed precious metal. There were numerous accounts, especially in the more commercially developed parts of the country, that the suffering was, as one Democrat observed, "as great as any community can bear." But "Biddle's panic" did more damage to Americans' nerves than it did to their economy.[26]

The Bank War's political impact was much more severe and lasting. Losing the struggle with Jackson plunged Nicholas Biddle into a furious and unsteady gyre. Biddle could never understand the democratic principles behind the attack against him and his beloved bank. With undisguised contempt, he refused to cooperate with a House committee charged with investigating his management of the BUS, thereby deepening the impression that he believed he and his bank were above the law. By the autumn of 1835, Biddle was reduced to deliv-ering a delusional speech to his fellow Nassau Hall alumni, predicting with confidence that the Democratic "banditti" would yet "be scourged back to their caverns," and finally be remembered only because of "the energy with which you resisted and defeated them." A year later, when its federal charter finally ran out, the bank was rechartered as the Bank of the United States of Pennsylvania, a state institution with considerable weight but bereft of its former influence and power.[27]

For Clay and the National Republicans, the Bank War brought a different kind of turning point. The crises of Jackson's first term had stripped away elements of his original coalition but created little basis for the rise of a coherent opposition. On nullification and the Union, Daniel Webster, among many other National Republicans, was more in tune with Jackson than some Jacksonians were. On the tariff, anti-Jackson nullifiers and anti-Jackson friends of the American System were at polar opposites. Clay's refusal to renounce his membership in the Masonic order instantly dashed any hopes of an alliance between the National Republicans and the Anti-Masons.

The Bank War gave these oppositional elements common ground—not in defense of Biddle's bank (which, by the end of 1834, was a lost cause) but against Jackson's assertions of executive power and his creation of pet banks as yet another fountain of partisan corruption. To many later historians, this shared grievance has sometimes seemed, at best, meager and, at worst, an exercise in bad faith, covering deeper political and economic motives—the view expressed by pro-Jackson contemporaries like William Leggett. To be sure, Clay and the National Republicans, the most powerful segment of the opposition, were uniformly favorable to Biddle's bank. Switching from defending the bank to defending the Constitution was in part a calculated tactical move, taken in view of Biddle's tarnished reputation. (Clay told the excitable banker that it was now imperative to keep the question of rechartering the bank "in the rear" and that of executive tyranny "in the front.") But dismissing the attacks on Jackson as diversions from the authentic issues misperceives the opposition's outlook no less than ascribing the Jacksonians' Bank War to narrow economic interests or crass partisan motives.[28]

A belief in the primacy of political structures and institutions had always driven Jackson and his followers in their efforts, as Jackson's protest of the Senate's censure put it, "to heal the wounds of the Constitution and preserve it from further violation." The attacks on Jackson's alleged executive tyranny flowed from the same presumptions. To conservative National Republicans, Jackson's claims were identical to those of the classical Caesars, who had usurped all power by whipping up the mob and handing governance to their corrupt minions. To humanitarian reformers drawn to the opposition, Jackson was a despot who had conspired with southern slaveholders and forced the removal of peaceful American Indians to the West. To nullifiers and their sympathizers, Jackson was the embodiment of the centralizing forces that threatened the slaveholders' liberties. To Anti-Masons, Jackson was an arrogant politician (and a Mason to boot) who had set himself above the rule of law. To a broader troubled populace, including some who had backed Jackson in the past, the events of 1833 and 1834 showed that Jackson had been overcome by what one New Yorker called "an unbridled lust of power, that attacked the very foundation of our free institutions." Whatever the multifarious economic, sectional, or partisan interests beneath them, these were sincere, principled, and potent concerns, strong enough to bind together a powerful anti-Jacksonian coalition.[29]

At every stage of the battle over the deposits, that coalition gained greater coherence, at least in Washington. Henry Clay initiated the process with a series of private dinners over the winter of 1833–34, assembling nullifiers, his own National Republicans, and Anti-Masons (including a recent Anti-Mason convert, John Quincy Adams) to discuss strategy for the presidential contest in 1836. The harmonization became increasingly evident in Congress, as divisions over various issues, including censure, deepened into what looked like unified party blocs. By the spring of 1834, when the emerging opposition won surprising victories in New York City's rough-and-tumble local elections, the new coalition even had a name—the Whig Party, presented as the spiritual progeny of the glorious opponents of King George III, now battling Andrew I's Tory conspiracy against the people's liberties. Under "[t]he happy cognomen of Whigs," a North Carolina anti-Jackson paper exulted soon thereafter, "all the parties opposed to Executive usurpation" could now "rally in defense of LIBERTY against POWER."[30]

It all sounded very different from John Quincy Adams's declaration, in 1825, that liberty *is* power. Some Whigs, like the editors of the Washington *National Intelligencer*, went even further and proclaimed themselves, and not the Tory Jacksonians, "the true Democracy of the Country." In time, other ideological and intellectual currents, above all the anxious, self-improving evangelical fervor of the Presbygational revivals, would reinforce these claims. Whiggery would become a variant of democratic politics just as compelling to its adherents as Jacksonianism had become to Democrats. But that evolution occurred alongside other dramatic developments in the mid-1830's involving radical movements well removed from mainstream party politics. These movements were themselves signs of intensifying social turmoil. Looking back on the upheavals from 1840, the British émigré Thomas Brothers—a one-time Philadelphia labor agitator who turned conservative during these six years—published a book, *The United States of North America as They Are; Not as They Are Generally Described: Being a Cure for Radicalism*. One appendix listed "Miscellaneous Murders, Riots, and Other Outrages, in 1834, 1835, 1836, 1837, and 1838." Several others included the details of additional mob attacks. The bulk of Brothers's

citations concerned violence occasioned, first, by the spread of radical abolitionism and, second, by renewed labor unrest.[31]

"THE ONLY *REAL* DEMOCRACY IN OUR REPUBLIC": ABOLITIONISM AND REACTION

On July 26, 1833, the House of Commons approved the compensated abolition
of slavery throughout the British Empire. Nearly half a century of agitation, in
and out of Parliament, was finally triumphing—and three days later, Britain's
greatest abolitionist leader, William Wilberforce, died, one month short of age
seventy-four. William Lloyd Garrison, on a British sojourn visiting abolitionist
leaders, had met the ailing Wilberforce and received his blessing weeks earlier,
enlarging his own reputation as American abolitionism's great man. Now Garrison joined his British friend, the antislavery campaigner George Thompson, in
the bittersweet funeral procession to Westminster Abbey. Garrison obtained commitments from Thompson and others that they would put themselves and their
financial resources at the disposal of the American immediatists. In October, an
invigorated Garrison sailed back across the Atlantic to Manhattan, where he was
scheduled to give a lecture to the Tappan brothers' New York City Anti-Slavery
Society. But a raucous mob, fifteen hundred strong, prevented the lecture and
forced Garrison to flee for home in Boston. "This young gentleman . . . ," the
New York *Commerical Advertiser* sneered, "will act wisely in never to attempt
addressing a public meeting in *this* country again."[32]

Garrison's odyssey foretold the travails of the radical abolitionist movement in
the mid-1830s. Supported financially by a few wealthy evangelical businessmen,
and propelled by fresh and enthusiastic converts and organizers, abolitionism
became a genuine popular movement. At its peak in 1838, membership in the
American Anti-Slavery Society (AA-SS) rose to three hundred thousand men and
women, enlisted in approximately two thousand loosely affiliated local chapters.
In its most ambitious campaigns, the movement flooded Congress with more
than four hundred thousand separate petitions calling for radical reforms ranging
from the abolition of slavery in the District of Columbia to the repeal of the Constitution's three-fifths clause. Yet despite its rapid growth and impressive organizational skills, abolitionism engendered far more hostility than sympathy in the
northern states, quite apart from the hatred it engendered in the South. By
attacking not merely southern slavery but all forms of racial inequality, the abolitionists appeared to the vast majority of white Americans like fanatics, at war with
all social order and decency. For every convert to the cause, there were hundreds
of northerners who were repulsed by what the New Hampshire anti-abolitionist
writer Thomas Russell Sullivan called the movement's "false zeal and political

aggression." Although the abolitionists successfully reawakened moral concern over slavery, they paid for it by becoming repeated targets for mob violence and official repression.[33]

The organizing assembly of the AA-SS in Philadelphia in December 1833 gave a good indication of how the movement had spread beyond its origins among urban free blacks. Garrison was the preeminent participant. In 1832, partly at the behest of his black supporters, he had published a long but widely read pastiche, *Thoughts on African Colonization*, which exposed the racism of the American Colonization Society and reprinted various black abolitionist speeches and resolutions condemning the society. As Garrison hoped it would, *Thoughts* swayed gradualist antislavery sympathizers into the immediatist camp. Garrison wrote the new association's immediatist Declaration of Principles at the home of the Philadelphia black abolitionist James McCrummell, where he was staying as a house guest. The declaration firmly endorsed nonviolence and the use of moral suasion to eradicate the sin of slavery, while also demanding for blacks "all the rights and privileges that belong to them as men and as Americans."[34]

The other sixty-two official participants and the interested onlookers who attended the meetings represented diverse backgrounds and faiths. Arthur and Lewis Tappan appeared along with other benevolent evangelical businessmen and professionals who had moved from Sabbatarianism and other reform projects into abolitionism. (Arthur was selected as the group's president.) A number of New England Unitarians, including Garrison's Boston associate Samuel May, were present. One-third of the participants were Quakers, among them John Greenleaf Whittier. Black attendance was relatively small, a portent of the AA-SS's future as a largely white-led organization, but a trio of important black leaders—McCrummell and Robert Purvis of Philadelphia, and James Barbadoes of Boston—took an active role. More remarkable was the energetic involvement of a small group of Quaker women, including the outspoken lay preacher Lucretia Mott—a degree of integration in politics across the sex line unheard of in the 1830s outside of Frances Wright's radical platoons, and another portent of where the AA-SS was headed.[35]

Garrison returned to his post at the *Liberator*, and the Tappan brothers and their friends took charge of managing the AA-SS. Right away, they established its headquarters in New York, already the capital of the budding evangelical empire of moral reform. On the model of the temperance and Sunday-law crusades, the Tappans flung together a network for converting the benighted, complete with a newspaper, the *Emancipator* (edited by Elizur Wright on behalf of the New York City abolitionist society, established by the Tappans in 1831), as well as a string of local AA-SS chapters and a company of field agents and itinerant lecturers. AA-SS chapters began sponsoring bazaars, sewing bees, picnics, and other social events to raise money and boost morale. At the movement's height, members could purchase abolitionist newspaper subscriptions, antislavery almanacs, music books, stationery, and pieces of ephemera, including portraits of Garrison priced at one dollar apiece. On the political front, building on the example of the Sabbatarian and anti-Indian removal movements, the abolitionists started their mass petition drives.[36]

Abolitionism's first breakthrough came in Cincinnati, thanks to Arthur Tappan's sponsorship there of the new evangelical Lane Seminary, which he and his brother hoped to turn into a training ground for AA-SS agents. For years, Cincinnati, across the Ohio River from slavery, had been racked by violent racial turmoil and attacks on antislavery advocates, including a rising young editor and ex-slaveholder from bordering Kentucky, James G. Birney—unrest that redoubled the Tappans' determination to make the city an abolitionist center. These efforts began in earnest after the arrival at Lane of a young seminarian, Theodore Dwight Weld. A disciple of Charles Finney's, Weld had graduated from Hamilton College in 1825, already a convert to what he later called "radical abolitionism." He then studied for the ministry and advanced to become a preceptor at the Oneida Institute, an evangelical hotbed in upstate New York supported financially by Lewis Tappan. Weld and Tappan befriended each other, and in 1834, the Tappans sent Weld to Lane, where Lyman Beecher had taken up the presidency two years earlier. Weld brought with him some promising Oneida students, including one Henry B. Stanton, and began holding public meetings and prayer sessions to promote immediatism. Less than three weeks later, to great public notice, Lane's students and faculty endorsed the abolitionist crusade, organized their own antislavery society, and made plans to provide reading and religious instruction to the black residents of Cincinnati.[37]

Leading Cincinnati businessmen pressured the seminary's trustees into ordering the rebels to disband their antislavery society. President Beecher, proclaiming his devotion to free speech and discussion, tried to mediate, but to no avail. "Shall those who are soon to be ambassadors for Christ . . . ," Weld declaimed, "shall *they* refuse to think, and feel, and speak, when that accursed thing . . . wags its impious head, and shakes its blood-red hands at heaven?" Although the abolitionist efforts received wide publicity, the trustees were adamant, and the antislavery seminarians eventually decamped to a new home in the small town of Oberlin, in northern Ohio, where the Tappans founded yet another college and persuaded the charismatic Finney to join the faculty. (Weld turned down a similar offer and became a full-time traveling antislavery lecturer.) The new college became the first American institution of higher learning to open its doors to men and women, blacks and whites—and soon became what Lane was supposed to have become, the nerve center of abolitionism in the Old Northwest.[38]

The uprising at Lane and subsequent abolitionist disturbances marked the emergence of a new kind of American political community. Joining the abolitionists was no rote profession of faith: it was an act of defiance of widely and deeply held social conventions, placing oneself in a position that courted disapproval, ostracism, and even physical attack. Those impelled to do so regarded one another as brothers and sisters in righteousness and sacrifice who had devoted their lives to eradicating slavery—a kind of commitment and identification previously found in religious sects, but now secularized and shifted into radical politics. Like later generations of American radicals, the abolitionists of the 1830s regarded their personal rededication as a life-transforming event, and their participation in the movement as an exhilarating experience of what later generations of dissenters would call "the beloved community." Looking back half a century later, the abolitionist writer Lydia Maria Child remarked that "mortals were never more sublimely forgetful of self than were the abolitionists of those early days"—a nostalgic exaggeration, certainly, but one that captured the movement's animating spirit, setting itself apart from sinful complicity with slavery and racism, and creating a new humane model of equality, freedom, and love.[39]

Two years after the AA-SS's founding, the antislavery radicals had reasons to be encouraged. In the revival-soaked arc of settlement that defined greater New England, from the Erie Canal towns and rural hinterland to Ohio's Western Reserve, support for abolitionism grew steadily. Even in major northeastern cities that were more hostile to the evangelicals, the abolitionist cause made headway among ordinary workingmen and radicals. Paineite urban democrats, beginning with Thomas Paine himself, had always been antislavery: Thomas Skidmore and Frances Wright were outspoken abolitionists, and in 1831, George Henry Evans was the only editor in New York City publicly to defend Nat Turner's rebellion. Some conservatives condemned abolitionism as impious working-class dogma. ("Every one knows," wrote one New York editor, "that [abolition] was one of the original doctrines of the Fanny Wright, no-monopoly, no-property, and no-marriage party.") Abolitionists replied that they did, indeed, represent, in William Goodell's words, "the laboring people of the North," who "*alone* have constituted the only *real* democracy in our republic."[40]

The abolitionists were not merely posing. True, there were some missed connections between the radical abolitionists and the evolving labor movement. In 1831, Garrison, reflecting his National Republican background, attacked the Working Men for inflaming class resentments in a land where, slavery aside, the path to prosperity was open to all. There was a spiritual and political gulf between the evangelical immediatists and the "Fanny Wright" radicals and pro-Jackson workingmen. Some trade union leaders denounced the abolitionists, while others simply held their tongues, not wanting to disrupt the Democracy. The mainstay of abolitionism's white constituency always consisted of modest farmers, small shopkeepers and businessmen, and their wives and daughters, living in and around the smaller cities and towns—not, as some of its critics claimed, a movement of displaced Federalist elites or upper-class monied capitalists, but also not, primarily, a movement of urban wage earners.[41]

It is important, however, not to exaggerate the mutual disdain between white urban labor and the abolitionists in the 1830s, or to minimize labor's involvement as activists and supporters. Although the preponderance of workers (like the preponderance of white northerners) were hostile or indifferent, urban wage-earners and petty proprietors formed a substantial bloc within the abolitionist constituency. In New York, artisans and small shopkeepers signed abolitionist petitions in rising numbers between 1834 and 1837, their ranks including a mixture of well-known evangelical moral reformers and secularist radicals and trade unionists, among them several former Owenite deist veterans of the Working Men's Party. Lynn, Massachusetts, the outwork shoemaking capital, was an abolitionist stronghold, its membership dominated by skilled workers, including officers of the journeymen shoemakers' trade union. Lowell and other New England factory towns had their abolitionist society chapters, which included artisans and mill hands, women as well as men. The abolitionists, for their part, increasingly expressed sympathy for workers and their difficulties. Garrison, challenged over his anti-Workie stand, quickly changed his mind and praised the New England Association of Farmers, Mechanics, and Other Workingmen. Other abolitionists denounced greedy employers and declared that their movement defended "the life, liberty, and happiness of all the lower orders of society in the land, especially at the North."[42]

Black abolitionists, regardless of their wealth, also remained stalwart activists. The AA-SS's original board of managers included half a dozen black leaders, and several others helped establish state affiliates and ladies' auxiliaries. The formidable Forten and Purvis merchant families of Philadelphia were especially prominent, providing leadership to both the AA-SS and the Female Anti-Slavery Society, which was organized soon after the AA-SS. Yet relations between blacks and whites in the movement were strained. Abolitionist polemics about the degraded state of America's people of color, although well intended, rankled their black allies, many of whom had managed to win at least a toehold, and sometimes more, of respectable prosperity. No matter how idealistic they were, few white abolitionists (Garrison being the great exception) could escape sounding patronizing to black abolitionists. Writing to the southern white abolitionist Angelina Grimké, Sarah Forten complained candidly that "even our professed friends have not yet rid themselves" of racial prejudice—although, she added, "when we recollect what great sacrifices to public sentiment they are called upon to make, we cannot wholly blame them." Partly in response to these misgivings, black activists organized their own independent efforts, ranging from groups to promote moral uplift, to the vigilance committees (the most famous of them headed by New York bookseller and printer David Ruggles) that searched out slaves being held in the seaports illegally by their southern masters.[43]

As the abolitionist movement grew larger, more diversified, and more determined, the reactions against it grew fiercer. The mob violence that greeted Garrison in New York, along with an earlier riot in the small town of Canterbury, Connecticut, that destroyed a Garrisonian interracial school, were only the beginnings of a vicious backlash that escalated in 1834 and 1835. Over an eight-day period in early July 1834, New York crowds stormed abolitionist meeting halls, sacked Arthur Tappan's store and Lewis Tappan's house, and besieged black homes and churches. A month later, a briefer but even more destructive series of riots in Philadelphia targeted the homes of forty black families, including the Purvises', and killed at least one black resident. In October 1835, a Boston mob, screaming racist insults, nearly lynched Garrison. (A few weeks earlier, persons unknown, under cover of night, had erected a chilling mock gallows on Garrison's doorstep.) In Hartford, Utica, Washington, Pittsburgh, and Cincinnati, angry whites disrupted abolitionist meetings, wrecked abolitionist press offices, and terrified black neighborhoods. A shower of bricks and exploding firecrackers broke up an appearance by Samuel May in Haverhill, Massachusetts; Theodore Weld, John Greenleaf Whittier, Lydia Maria Child, and other abolitionist lecturers endured volleys of rocks and rotten eggs. One Charleston, South Carolina, newspaper reported cheerfully that a purse of twenty thousand dollars had been set aside in New Orleans for anyone who would kidnap Arthur Tappan and deliver him on the city's levee.[44]

A variety of fears and prejudices, stoked by local political leaders, inflamed the northern mobs. Powerful racist myths and fears—not least the myths of innate black male sexual prowess and depravity, and fears of what some demagogues called the impending "mullatoization" of America—provoked a blind hatred of radical reformers. The great wealth of a few of the movement's most prominent financial backers, including the Tappans, and the antagonism they sometimes expressed toward organized labor, became a pretext for labeling the abolitionists as capitalist snobs who would raise lazy, inferior blacks to the same social level as the hard-working whites—the "limousine liberals" of their day.* The evangelical background of so many abolitionist leaders only deepened their image, among anti-abolitionists, as meddlesome fanatics out to impose their strange views on

---

* Since 1827, the Tappans had been the publishers of the country's leading mercantile newspaper, the pious and adamantly antilabor *Journal of Commerce*. Lewis Tappan would go on, in 1841, to found the successful Mercantile Agency, which would later become the firm of Dun and Bradstreet. More than any other individuals, the Tappans came to symbolize the misleading conception of evangelical reform, and abolitionism in particular, as upper-class efforts.

society at large. Abolitionism's British connections led some to call the movement an Anglo-American aristocratic plot. The acceptance of women as active participants persuaded opponents that the abolitionists were hell-bent on overturning all decorum. "Nothing . . . ," one New England anti-abolitionist pamphleteer wrote of antislavery women, "out-measures the evil that might follow from her political interference in times which try men's souls, when fear of change perplexes the wise."[45]

For all its populist pretensions, however, anti-abolitionism was stoked chiefly by prosperous conservatives of both major political parties who enlisted a slice of the more socially insecure elements of the lower-middle and working classes in their activities. Most of the urban mobs were led not by lower-class rowdies but by local notables—described mordantly by their targets as "gentlemen of property and standing"—who abhorred the abolitionists' challenge to their own social authority. In Cincinnati, the scene of particularly severe rioting, Whig merchants and professionals were represented more heavily in the mobs that broke up abolitionist meetings than they were in the abolitionist constituency. In New York, where the assailants were more likely to be petty tradesmen, artisans, and laborers, the most inflammatory racist verbal attacks on abolitionists (and on "the blubber lips and sooty blood of negroes") appeared in the anti-Jackson, Whig-tinged, so-called Independent Democratic newspapers of James Watson Webb and Mordecai Manuel Noah. Whig prints assailed abolitionism and blamed it on the Jacksonians' hatred of "the rich and intelligent," and their flattering of the ignorant masses with dangerous democratic nostrums. As early as 1831, in the aftermath of the Southampton insurrection, the leading anti-Jacksonian (and later Whig) paper in the country, the National Intelligencer, began calling for the suppression of the abolitionist press, a demand it repeated amid the anti-abolitionist upsurge of mid-decade.[46]

The Jacksonian leadership, for its own part, regarded the antislavery agitation as a distraction from the really important issues of banking and the currency, and as a grievous attack on sectional harmony that menaced the Missouri Compromise. Democratic spokesmen accordingly, and fancifully, denounced the abolitionists as democracy's latest enemies. In league with the pro-bank Whigs, supposedly, the movement wanted to stir up what one editorial in Blair's Globe called "the SLAVE EXCITEMENT" and divide section against section, to the prepare the way for the dissolution of the Democratic Party and the restoration of plutocracy. Some Democratic editors even thought they detected the malefic influence of John C. Calhoun and Duff Green, now trying to achieve with the slavery issue what they had failed to achieve battling the tariff. "Who agitate the slave question?" one editorial asked. "Who seek to produce sectional parties, founded on local jealousies, to obliterate the great landmarks of party founded

on principles?" Who but the nullifiers, along with "[t]he Northern Bank Aristocrats," who saw disrupting the Democratic Party as "their only hope."[47]

President Jackson tried to contain the abolitionists without either endorsing
their attackers or abdicating federal authority. Developments in Charleston,
South Carolina, soon tested his resolve. In 1835, the AA-SS, having already
begun its mass petition drives to Congress, undertook a new campaign, using the
federal postal service, to flood the South with immediatist tracts—an effort to cir-
cumvent the southern restrictions on the distribution of antislavery literature that
had tightened since the David Walker affair. When the AA-SS materials started
turning up in Charleston at the end of July, Alfred Huger, the city's postmaster,
wrote to the newly named but as yet unconfirmed postmaster general, Amos
Kendall, pleading with him to banish the offensive publications and asking him
for instructions on how to proceed. Huger was caught in a bind: he had a sworn
public obligation to deliver the mail, but the abolitionist materials also fell under
South Carolina's ban on "incendiary" publications, and he personally found
them intolerable. While awaiting Kendall's reply, Huger—a planter but also a
Unionist during the nullification struggle, and thus suspect among pro-slavery
extremists—tried to placate state authorities by agreeing to detain all future abolitionist mailings. He duly gathered together the new batches of AA-SS materials,
put them in a separate sack, and locked them away. Word of the latest mailings,
however, spread quickly, and a small band of prominent Charlestonians—known
informally as the Lynch Men—broke into Huger's office, stole the pamphlets,
and staged a raucous public burning of them at the Charleston parade grounds.
Plainly, the seizure was a deliberate violation of federal law—but South Carolina
officials defended it as a sensible effort to keep the inflammatory material from
reaching the ken of ignorant slaves.[48]

Amos Kendall, himself a slaveholder, understood the sensitive political issues
in play and sympathized with the Charleston authorities. In an open letter to
Huger, he said that he could neither sanction nor condemn what had happened,
but affirmed that there were occasional extraordinary circumstances in which
one's obligations to federal law might be superseded by loyalty to one's community. Kendall ordered the Washington, D.C., postmaster not to deliver the abolitionist tracts, told Jackson that he wanted to halt the abolitionists' campaign with
as little commotion as possible, and asked the president for directions. Jackson
had not the slightest doubt that the abolitionists were "guilty of the attempt to stir
up amongst the South the horrors of a servile war." But the president also
detested the anti-abolitionist mobs (and, perhaps especially, the upper-class mob
of nullifying Charleston): "This spirit of mob-law is becoming too common and
must be checked," he told Kendall, "or ere long it will become as great an evil as
a servile war."[49]

As a stopgap measure until Congress reconvened in December, Jackson advised delivering the AA-SS materials only to those who had actually subscribed to them—which would have been few persons, if any, in Charleston—and then to publish the names of any subscribers in the newspapers so that they might be shunned and humiliated. Kendall, however, went his own way, and after scores of southern towns passed resolutions proscribing the abolitionist material, he established a policy of obeying state laws on circulating incendiary publications. Jackson disapproved but did nothing, preferring to allow the situation to cool down until he requested of Congress, in his annual message, a new law banning from the southern mails "incendiary publications intended to instigate the slaves to insurrection."[50]

Jackson's proposal, if enacted, would have amounted to a federal law censoring the mails—another blot on his presidency. Yet even that was insufficient for more obdurate southerners, friend and foe alike. Secretary of State John Forsyth, a Georgian, complained that the administration was coddling the abolitionists, and suggested to Vice President Van Buren, more anxious than ever to placate slaveholder Democrats, that he arrange for a little more "mob discipline" up North. (How directly involved Van Buren became is unclear, but New York Democrats did take the lead in organizing fierce anti-abolitionist demonstrations that sometimes degenerated into violence and that pleased Kendall and Huger.) John C. Calhoun and the other congressional nullifiers objected to Jackson's message and demanded a federal law prohibiting the distribution of abolitionist materials wherever state or territorial laws forbade it. Imposing this degree of state rights over a federal department was, to Jackson, ridiculous, and once again he and Calhoun were at loggerheads.[51]

Finally, in July 1836, through a bipartisan backroom effort led by northern Whigs and Democrats, Congress passed its new postal law. Aimed at correcting the abuses of Postmaster General Barry's corrupt tenure, the law upheld the government's traditional commitment to the inviolability of the mails. A rejection of both the Jacksonian and the Calhounite positions, this portion of the law marked a formal victory for, if anybody, the abolitionists. Yet throughout the South, it went unenforced, and postmasters did as they pleased, with the tacit assumption that federal authority over the mails ended at the post office door. Jackson disapproved of the latest passive resistance to federal authority—but mistrustful of the federal courts, not wanting to stir up further trouble so late in his presidency, and satisfied that he had at least enunciated the principle of federal supremacy, he turned a blind eye. In effect, Kendall's policy prevailed, as it would continue to do until after the Civil War, creating an informal bar that blocked abolitionist writings from the South.[52]

This show of Jacksonian prudence, shaped by hostility to the abolitionists, political expediency, and indifference to civil rights, amounted to a failure of leadership. Jackson's views about the abolitionists and their materials were not the central problem. Those views were commonplace outside the most radical abolitionist circles. John Quincy Adams thought the AA-SS mailings were "inflammatory" and might "kindle the flame of insurrection" among the slaves. Influential Whig editors advocated censorship of the abolitionist literature well before any important Jacksonian paper or spokesman did. Nor was Jackson's position particularly extremist or pro-slavery. Unlike Democrats and Whigs who defended and even sparked anti-abolitionist violence, Jackson specifically denounced it. Caught in his own bind, he was careful to attack what he called particular efforts to foment rebellion, and not the abolitionists per se—overt acts, and not ideas. Unlike Kendall, he never endorsed nonenforcement of federal laws; unlike Calhoun, he would not formally subordinate a federal department, accountable to Congress, to laws and regulations established by the states. Yet by allowing the situation to get out of hand before Congress met, and then by failing to enforce in full the 1836 Post Office Law, Jackson overlooked basic principles about the rule of law that he claimed to be upholding, and left suspended a basic question of jurisdiction between the national and the state governments.[53]

In trying to quiet the problem with a minimum of controversy, Jackson and his administration made the situation worse—and mired the Jackson Democracy in contradictions that would one day prove its undoing. Some northern Democrats viewed both the mob violence and Kendall's actions over the abolitionist mailings as unconstitutional and immoral. "We cannot trample on the charter of our national freedom," New York's *Evening Post* asserted, "to assist the slaveholder in his warfare with fanaticism." Just as ominously, an upstate Jacksonian editor later complained, "the enforcement of *'prudential restrictions'* against the abolitionists" became for some Democratic leaders a measure of party loyalty. With the anti-abolitionist outbursts and the mails controversy appeared the first divisions within the northern Democracy over the compatibility of slavery and Jacksonian equality.[54]

By arousing northern opinion over constitutional rights, the attacks also left the "SLAVE EXCITEMENT" open to continuous agitation in the years to come. During the year that the postal controversy unfolded, the numbers of abolitionist societies more than doubled, in part because of northern outrage at the repression. By seizing on and expanding the democratic techniques of petitioning public officials and mass mailings to the public, the abolitionists forced a crisis that brought them even more attention and support. "Our opposers," said the AA-SS's publishing agent, R. G. Williams, "took the wrong course to accomplish their purpose. Instead of putting us down, they put us and our principles up before the world—just where we wanted to be."[55]

WORKIES, UNIONISTS, AND LOCO FOCOS

While Congress considered the abolitionist mails question, a thin, nervous New York congressman named Ely Moore rose from a sickbed and addressed the House to defend northern labor against southern pro-slavery insults. The rebarbative South Carolina congressman, Waddy Thompson, had described northern workers as overpaid improvident thieves who would raise their wages "by lawless insurrection, or by the equally terrible process of the ballot-box." Moore, the past president of both the New York General Trades' Union (GTU) and the National Trades' Union (NTU), seized on Thompson's slur and composed an ornate but harsh reply. "[I]f it shall be the last act of my life," Moore began, "I will attempt to hurl back the imputations."[56]

It nearly turned out to be Moore's last act. His voice rising with a tremulous rage, he upheld organized labor as honorable and denounced the entire history of aristocracy, especially "moneyed aristocracy," as one "of aggression, of perfidy, sedition, debauchery, and of moral and political prostitution." Moore built toward his closing; one southern congressman muttered to another, "Why, this is the high-priest of revolution singing his war song." When Moore reached his peroration, an attack on Nicholas Biddle, a frightening pallor covered his face: "And let it be remembered, sir, that this enemy of equal rights, this contemner and libeler of the people, is the chief priest, nay, the very Moloch, of the bank-whig aristocracy. No prince better deserves the homage of his subjects; none so well qualified to direct the councils of that political Tartarus, which he has obtained the empire of, and delights to reign over!" Suddenly, Moore stopped and, eyes closed, clutched at the air, pitched forward, and fell to the podium, as his wife, in the gallery, shrieked with horror. Moore later recovered and returned to politics, but this was his finest hour. Northern printers issued special editions of "Moore's Reply to Thompson," by the thousands, and it became a manifesto of the reawakened labor movement.[57]

Labor's revival had begun in New York in 1833, amid the rapid inflation that, apart from the brief downturn caused by Biddle's panic, sent commodity prices soaring far beyond journeymen's wage rates. Following a bitter carpenters' strike in late spring, representatives from nine trades formed the New York GTU, the city's first organization of employees from different crafts. Over the next four years, the GTU led an upsurge that saw New York wage-earners organize more than forty trade unions and conduct nearly as many strikes. A similar citywide federation appeared in Philadelphia in December 1833; then the movement rapidly spread along the seaboard from Boston to Washington and as far west as St. Louis. Delegates from six of the eastern city central unions formed the NTU in 1834; journeymen in individual trades, including the printers and house carpenters, founded their own national organizations; in time, handloom weavers, female factory operatives (including the young women of Lowell), coal heavers, dock hands, day laborers, and other workers outside the artisan trades formed unions and organized strikes in numerous locales. Although exact numbers are impossible to determine, the outbreak certainly led to the organizing of more workers than ever before in American history. "'Tis the only palladium that can protect," Ely Moore proclaimed after his inauguration as NTU president, "'tis the only *Sacred Mount* to which you or your posterity can flee for refuge."[58]

Although not always initially aimed at conducting strikes—"strikes," one New York unionist claimed in 1834, "are scarcely considered by the projectors of Trades' Unions as essential to their purpose"—the unionists' militancy grew as inflation worsened. Most walkouts concerned demands for higher wages or resistance to wage cuts. Shoemakers in Geneva and Hudson, New York, and bricklayers in Pittsburgh struck to establish union-only (or "closed") shops, and Boston's printers union struck to protest the hiring of young women as compositors at cut-rate wages. Otherwise, unions focused on gaining the ten-hour workday. The limitation was already a general rule among private employers in New York, and demanding it became a crusade in Philadelphia and other cities, bringing masses of workingmen into the streets for rallies and torch-light processions as impressive as those mounted by the political parties. "Humanity," one Philadelphia newspaper proclaimed, "requires us not to abuse the brute creation by over-labour, and surely our fellow-man is entitled to as much consideration." Buttressed by claims that excessive work encouraged intemperance and dissipation, the ten-hour movement won repeated victories.[59]

The unions formed their own political community, not only with roots in the evolving city democracy but also with some crucial innovations. A new labor press quickly emerged, to spread the word about union activities and strikes, reprint speeches, and allow rank-and-file union members to have their say on public events. The NTU had its own official organ, the *National Trades' Union*, published weekly under the formal direction of Ely Moore. Local citywide union papers appeared in Boston, New York, Philadelphia, and Washington. Friendly nonunion editors also publicized the cause, above all George Henry Evans's *Man* (published as a union-oriented weekly alongside Evans's continuing *Working Man's Advocate*). Regular union meetings, run according to open democratic guidelines, elected officers to the city-central unions and deliberated over strikes and protests. Processions and festivals enlivened the unionists' efforts, proclaiming to all their public identity and social ideals with banners like the New York GTU's standard of Archimedes lifting a mountain with a lever. "Can you," Moore asked the crowd in a speech following the GTU's first march, "as mechanics and artists, look upon that *banner* without being reminded of your united strength?"[60]

The personnel as well as the ideas of the union movement had some obvious links to the Working Men's upsurge of the late 1820s and early 1830s. William Heighton's Mechanics' Union of Trade Associations (MUTA) in Philadelphia, the parent organization of the city's Working Men's Party, had been a forerunner of the new city unions. Several MUTA leaders, including William English and John Ferrall, turned up again as union leaders after 1833. In New York, the chairmaker John Commerford, Moore's successor as president of the GTU and the editor of the New York labor paper, *Union,* had been an active member of the Owenite faction of New York Workies; two of the Working Men's candidates from 1829, the victorious assemblyman-carpenter Ebenezer Ford and the chairmaker Joseph Parsons, represented their respective trades in the GTU; and the printers' leader, John Windt, had proofread Frances Wright's essays and worked closely with George Henry Evans at the *Working Man's Advocate* in 1829 and 1830. From time to time, reprises of the freethinkers' old campaigns glimmered in the unionists' broadsides, like the demand by one group of striking carpenters to end tax exemptions on clerical property. Always the unionists repeated the by-now familiar Workie denunciations of monopoly and the manipulators of "fictitious capital"—those whom Commerford called the political promoters of "the paper or Hamiltonian scheme."[61]

The union movement, however, was deeper and narrower than the Working Men's had been. Most important, it was specifically a movement of journeymen and wage earners based on a consciousness of class within the various trades and industries that had hardened since the Working Men's demise. Increasingly, the New York unionist John Finch explained, it had seemed that "the *employer* was rapidly running the road to wealth [while] the *employed* was too often the victim of poverty and oppression, bound to the vassalage of inadequate reward for his labor." Without forgetting about bankers, speculators, and monopolists from outside of the trades, the unionists focused on employers as a class, who with "deep and matured design," John Commerford wrote, made their profits by filching from labor. Neither employers nor the blind, abstract market had the right to establish wage rates—"a usurpation of authority," one journeyman shoemakers' group declared.[62]

Some urban democrats objected to this proletarian dividing line and argued, to no avail, that small employers and other sympathizers ought to be included in the journeymen's organizations. Greater problems arose over where to draw lines among different kinds of wage earners—or whether to draw any lines at all. Although women workers organized their own unions, many union men were skeptical of them. The very existence of female wage-labor struck some male journeymen as both a social affront and an economic threat. A woman's "physical organization, natural responsibilities, and moral sensibilities," one unionist argued, "prove conclusively that her labors could only be of a domestic nature." Worse, in a growing number of trades and industries, the employment of low-paid women workers had become a means to cut men's earnings, or dismiss men completely. Unskilled day laborers were similarly problematic, normally kept at arm's length by unionists in the proud skilled artisan trades. This prejudice against the dependent unskilled carried over into racial distinctions. The depressed economic conditions of the vast majority of urban blacks, and the constraints that left the relatively small numbers of upwardly mobile blacks to petty retailing and to service trades such as barbering, put most black workers outside the purview of the trades' unions. Although none of the major unions barred blacks from membership, neither did any black worker assume a position of even minor importance within them.[63]

In time, however, some of the divisions within organized labor softened, and sometimes they disappeared completely. The NTU urged the journeymen in all trades affected by female labor to organize ladies' auxiliaries to their unions. The operatives in the cotton-mill factories of Manayunk, along the Schuylkill River on the outskirts of Philadelphia, went further, organizing a strike over wages in which wives and daughters picketed alongside the men, and in which the committee overseeing management of the strike consisted of three men and two women.[64] Connections between skilled and unskilled workers strengthened most dramatically in the seaboard cities. The New York GTU sponsored a joint meeting of mechanics and laborers in 1836, and its president, John Commerford, called on the unions to support a strike by local stevedores, who had "as good and just" a right to ask what they pleased for their labor as any mechanic or merchant did. Even more remarkably, a coal heavers' strike for the ten-hour day in Philadelphia later in the year prompted journeymen from numerous trades to walk off their jobs in a virtual general strike, and to march alongside the laborers, chanting, "We are all day laborers." The prospect loomed of a more comprehensive movement throughout the country, embracing what Commerford called "the family of labor," "the working classes."[65]

Employers' counterattacks on the movement became a concerted crackdown. In virtually every trade and in every city where labor had organized, employer associations arose as well, denouncing the unions (as the Philadelphia makers of women's shoes put it) for "fostering oppression, tyranny and misrule, and thus obstructing the free course of trade." Blacklists circulated, but these had little impact on the well-organized and, thanks to members' dues, well-funded unions. More effective was the employers' use of the courts to try to break the unions as illegal combinations, either at common law or (in New York) under recently passed legislation that banned associations "injurious to public morals or trade or commerce." Five major prosecutions took place between 1833 and 1836. In three decided by juries—involving carpet-weavers in Enfield, Connecticut, shoemakers in Hudson, New York, and plasterers in Philadelphia—the defendants were acquitted. But a conspiracy case brought against the union shoemakers in Geneva, New York, wound up going all the way to the state supreme court in 1836, where Chief Justice Edward Savage virtually declared trade unions illegal. Armed with the Geneva ruling, Manhattan's employing tailors brought twenty journeymen union strikers up on similar charges. In his charge to the jury, the presiding judge, Ogden Edwards, essentially directed a verdict of guilty, which the jury duly returned.[66]

Within days of the conviction, copies of an ominous handbill, headed by a coffin, appeared all around the city:

> The Rich against the Poor! Judge Edwards, the tool of the Aristocracy, against the People! Mechanics and workingmen! A deadly blow has been struck at your Liberty! The prize for which your fathers fought has been robbed from you! The Freemen of the North are now on a level with the slaves of the South! with no other privileges than laboring that drones may fatten on your life-blood!

Bid by the so-called coffin handbill, a large crowd turned out to hear Edwards pronounce his sentence and began taking up a collection to pay off the convicted unionists' fines. One week later, an evening rally of mechanics and workingmen, estimated at thirty thousand, converged on City Hall Park to hear speakers — "chiefly radicals," the press reported — denounce Edwards, bankers, merchants, employers, and the two major political parties for being "at variance with the spirit and genius of Republican government." After a final cheer, the crowd headed peaceably home, its path lit by the flaming effigies of Justice Savage and Judge Edwards hung from the main gates of the park. Two days after the demonstration, news came from Hudson that a jury had acquitted the shoemakers indicted there, giving the unionists hope.[67]

The giant New York demonstration remained peaceful, but the strikes and protests of the mid-1830s did degenerate into violence. The largest incident involved striking construction workers and diggers along the Chesapeake & Ohio Canal, whose attacks on strikebreakers and local authorities prompted Maryland's governor to call for federal military intervention in 1834. The brutish conditions in the canal-diggers' camps helped explain the violence, but disorder and bloodshed were all too common in the cities as well. In New York alone, violence and the threat of violence arose repeatedly, most notoriously in an affray pitting striking stonecutters against "blacklegs" (or "scabs") in 1834 but also in strikes involving cabinetmakers, piano makers, dockworkers, coal heavers, and tailors. Not surprisingly, the conservative press loudly condemned these incidents as the essence of trade unionism. Yet the remarkable thing was not the use of physical force but that there was not more of it, given the numerous provocations by employers, local marshals, and the courts. The unions tried to play a disciplining role by restraining their members from self-defeating riotous behavior, and by officially repudiating workers who (in the words of the New York GTU) did not act "with that propriety becoming good citizens."[68]

The unions' quest for orderly organization in the economic field still left open, however, the question of whether to organize in elections as well. Questions over participating in politics had bothered the new labor movement from its inception. The examples of the Working Men's parties were discouraging, as was the takeover of local and national politics by insider professionals—those "wire pullers who move the juggling machines of 'the party,'" as the *Union* called them. At the first convention of the NTU, one New England labor leader declared the common view that the workingmen "belonged to no party; they were neither disciples of Jacksonism nor Clayism, Van Burenism nor Websterism, nor any other *ism* but *workeyism*." Yet organized labor never opted out of politics. Although never "intended to interfere in party politics," the *National Trades' Union* observed, the unions granted that "many of the evils under which the workingmen are suffering are of a political origin and can only be reached in that way." On numerous specific issues, ranging from the employment of prison labor to factory work conditions for women and children, unions issued investigative reports and demanded legislative reforms. Some union leaders, most famously Ely Moore, also became deeply involved in electoral politics independently of their unions, most as Jacksonian Democrats. A host of others played important political roles in different party factions that, by 1836, emerged as the northern pro-labor left-wing bloc of the Jackson Democracy.[69]

The first sparks of this more politicized labor Jacksonianism appeared in New England, thrown off by the sputtering embers of the Working Men's movement. In September 1832, the New England Association of Farmers, Mechanics, and Other Workingmen, founded a year earlier by Workies and Workie sympathizers, held its first formal convention in Boston. The presiding officer, Charles Douglas, was the editor of a weekly Rhode Island labor paper, the *New England Artisan*, and among those present was Douglas's "traveling agent," a flamboyant, vociferous organizer named Seth Luther. With Luther supplying lung power, peripatetic energy, and caustic wit, and with Douglas providing the guiding ideas, the *Artisan* and the association stoked existing discontent in the mills of Pawtucket and points north, as well as among hard-pressed small farmers in western Massachusetts. Yet they offered little in terms of practical reform remedies. Douglas, in particular, had a visceral distaste for party politics, which he thought had been thoroughly corrupted by "aristocrats" like the Jacksonian boss and banker David Henshaw.[70]

In 1833, new recruits to the association began to consider mounting an independent challenge against both Henshaw and the dominant National Republican (and later Whig) coalition. Samuel Clesson Allen, a sixty-year-old former congressman, was the least likely convert to the cause. A high-toned Federalist early in his career, Allen had served as a delegate to the Hartford Convention in 1814, then won election to six terms in Congress, leaving office in 1829 disgusted at the ascension of Andrew Jackson, "a man covered with crimes." Yet when he returned to his country home in Northfield, Allen could see that the old rural idyll of his conservative reveries had passed away, transformed from a land of sturdy yeoman into one of dependent tenant farmers, household-bound pieceworkers, and factory hands. At the root of the problem, he gradually concluded, was the monied class, men who "though they produced none of the objects of wealth, of themselves . . . became mighty instruments of accumulation." By 1833, Allen's musings had carried him all the way into Workeyism, and to supporting Jackson's war on the Second Bank of the United States. With the New England Association's endorsement, a committee of Charlestown Working Men persuaded him to be their protest candidate for governor, and did so again in 1834, on a ticket that included another rural Federalist turned Workie, Theodore Sedgwick Jr., the son of the former U.S. Speaker of the House. Neither nominee fared well, but their candidacies commenced a challenge to the state's conservative Democratic leadership.[71]

Another unexpected figure from western Massachusetts joined the Workie crusade during Allen's first campaign in 1833. The greatest American historian of his generation, George Bancroft, a Harvard graduate and failed progressive schoolteacher, had been a literary star since the mid-1820s, best known for his contributions to the eminent *North American Review*. Like all New Englanders of taste and intelligence, Bancroft intensely distrusted Andrew Jackson, yet he was also given to making romantic, liberal democratic public utterances that unsettled his friends and readers. Bancroft's liberalism finally won out over his breeding, and in 1834, the same year he published the first volume of his monumental *History of the United States*, he threw his support to the Working Men and the newly formed Boston Trades' Union, charging that "[t]here is more danger from monopolies than from combinations of workingmen." A year later, he attacked the Whigs as an American Tory party that merged three classes of aristocratic oppressors: commercial monopolists, manufacturing corporations, and southern slaveholders, "the most selfish, the most united, and the most overbearing of all."[72]

Joined by a phalanx of other writers and politicians, including the anticapitalist polemicist Theophilus Fisk, the pro-labor Democratic state legislator Frederick Robinson, and the state supreme court justice and perennial Democratic gubernatorial candidate Marcus Morton, the renegade Bancroft helped push the Workies into a renewed war against the Henshaw Democrats—but this time from within the Democratic fold. Since the inception of the New England Association, radical, hard-money Jacksonians had appealed to the group's members to join the president's crusade against privilege. Shortly after the 1832 election, New England native Amos Kendall spoke in Boston on the brutal effects of the manufacturing monopoly. The following year, the New England Association and its gubernational candidate, Samuel Clesson Allen, endorsed Jackson's war on the BUS and *the power of associated wealth.*" All but the most stubborn anti-political Workies switched to the Democrats, determined to displace the Henshaw machine with one of their own. In 1836, Henshaw, gout-ridden and exhausted, offered to resign the Boston collectorship—and the Democrats stocked their election tickets with Workie leaders and sympathizers, including Bancroft, Allen, and Sedgwick, all of whom ran for Congress. Although the Whigs carried the state, the Democrats for once ran respectably. Having made the Working Men's measures, as one newspaper remarked, "part and parcel of their cause," the Massachusetts Democrats, once a reviled minority, were legitimate contenders for power. Within two years, the new collector of Boston and chief of the Massachusetts Democracy was George Bancroft.[73]

Across the Northeast, a similar dynamic unfolded, pitting moderate and conservative Bank Democrats against more radical Democrats who were partial to the labor movement and supported Jackson's Bank War. In Connecticut, the radical Democrats rallied behind the former Jeffersonian Republican and founding editor of the *Hartford Times*, John Milton Niles, and elevated him to the U.S. Senate in 1835. In Pennsylvania, Thomas Brothers, the English émigré who would later sour on the movement, succeeded William Heighton as Philadelphia's chief labor editor with his newspaper the *Radical Reformer and Working Man's Advocate*. In 1835, an uprising within the Pennsylvania Democracy led to the nomination of Congressman Henry Muhlenberg on a Democratic ticket that also included the veteran Workie and union leader, William English. Although the split handed the gubernatorial election to the Anti-Masonic candidate, himself an ex-Democrat, it served abrupt notice on the state's Bank Democrats that the radicals had arrived.[74]

The most spectacular uprising occurred in New York City. In the autumn of 1834, Tammany Hall announced its opposition to all banks and monopolies in order to flatter the ex–Working Men in its ranks, promote party unity, and help reelect the Van Burenite governor William Marcy. Tammany also nominated four antibank sympathizers for the state legislature and, in his first election, Ely Moore for Congress. Yet in January, as soon as the new Democratic-controlled legislature met in Albany, the members began approving new bank charters to party insiders and their friends, calling it a "judicious" form of attacking monopoly. Antimonopoly newspapers lashed out; the state Democratic committee replied with slurs; and over the ensuing months, the radical Democrats plotted a revolt. In early autumn, the antimonopoly men sponsored a dinner honoring Richard Mentor Johnson, already the national Democrats' designated vice presidential nominee. Congressman Churchill Cambreleng spoke, as did the visiting Boston radical Theophilus Fisk and the printers' union leader John Windt. The event led to a string of crowded meetings of the newly dubbed Equal Rights Democracy.[75]

After sundown on October 29, Democratic officials assembled at Tammany Hall's headquarters, the Wigwam, across from City Hall, for the anticlimactic business of receiving pro-forma approval from the Democratic rank and file for a prearranged slate of candidates. The leadership, with a list of conservative nominees, crept up the backstairs to the spacious meeting room, while outside a dense crowd crammed the front hall staircase and spilled out into Frankfort Street. At seven, the crowd poured in and called Joel Curtis, a veteran Working Man, front and center. A banner was unfurled proclaiming *"Joel Curtis, the Anti-Monopolist chairman."* Then another banner appeared, denouncing the regular party slate, and then several others, while the crowd booed the Tammany regulars and struggled to keep them seated at the podium and prevent an adjournment. The Equal Rights man Alexander Ming Jr. — son of a close associate of Thomas Skidmore's and himself the printer of *Rights of Man to Property!* — clambered atop a table and motioned for silence, when suddenly the room went dark. One of the regular Democrats had escaped and switched off the gaslights, a time-honored Tammany method of stifling rebellion. But the Equal Rights insurgents had come prepared with primitive friction matches, popularly known as "Lucifers" or "loco focos." Holding aloft fifty lit candles and now in total control of the room, they nominated their own ticket.[76]

The conservative Bank Democrats were not to be deterred, and in November their candidate for mayor, the leather manufacturer Gideon Lee, won handily, almost certainly with Whig support. But the Equal Rights Democrats — now mocked as the Loco Focos — won over thirty-five hundred votes, about 15 percent of the total, and established themselves as a viable independent force. Over the next two years, working out of a small, smoky chamber on the second floor of the down-at-heels Military and Civic Hotel on the Bowery, the Loco Focos enlarged their following. Former Workies joined with union men including John Commerford and the journeymen locksmiths' leader Levi Slamm, as well as with radical thinkers such as the currency reformer Clinton Roosevelt, in the hopes of redeeming the Democracy from the bank men and the wire pullers. In the spring of 1836, the Loco Focos ran Ming for mayor and founded their own newspaper, the *Democrat*, edited by Windt and Roosevelt. Following the massive demonstration in support of the convicted journeymen tailors, they called for a new state party convention and sent several delegates to the gathering that eventually met in Utica to nominate yet another Working Men's Party veteran, Isaac Smith, as governor. In the autumn city elections, they struck a marriage of convenience with the Whigs by co-nominating several legislative candidates while also backing the Democrats Cambreleng and Moore—the only two Democrats to win reelection. The Equal Rights Democrats now held the balance of power in New York City politics.[77]

Reporting on the Loco Focos, and inspiring them as well, was the journalist and self-educated intellectual William Leggett. After a knock-about youth that ended with his being cashiered from the navy for insulting an officer, Leggett had washed up in Manhattan, where in the late 1820s he wrote short stories and theater reviews. In 1829, the editor of the *Evening Post*, poet and Jacksonian sympathizer William Cullen Bryant hired him as his assistant, and over the ensuing decade Leggett emerged as the most vehement and most thoughtful of the city's antimonopolist Democratic editors and essayists. Leggett's pugnacious side, and his talent for winning attention, turned up in his slashing verbal assaults on his political and journalistic opponents, as it did in a celebrated brawl with James Watson Webb on Wall Street in 1833. But he was also a serious writer of democratic political theory.[78]

An apostle of Jeffersonian economics, hostile to combinations of government and private enterprise, Leggett turned the free market dogma of propertied conservatives inside out. Proclaiming the cause of labor against capitalist special interests and the paper-money system, Leggett also defended the unions as voluntary and necessary associations of embattled workers. "[L]et us ask," he wrote, "what and where is the danger of a combination of the labouring classes in vindication of their political principles, or in defence of their menaced rights?" Leggett's radicalism went further than that of most, even within the Loco Focos' ranks, notably on slavery and race. Enraged by the mob attacks on the immediatists, and by Amos Kendall's handling of the mails controversy, Leggett converted to abolitionism and the cause of racial equality—leading to the withholding of what looked like a sure nomination to Congress and to what he later called his "excommunication" by the national party. Yet even those radical Democrats who did not share Leggett's views on slavery and the abolitionists never wavered in their affection and admiration for the man; indeed, Leggett's removal from the party helped to trigger the Equal Rights revolt. One of the mutineers' banners displayed the night New York's Loco Focos earned their nickname contrasted a despised Democratic paper with Leggett's: "*The Times must change ere we desert our Post.*"[79]

The labor movement and the radical Democrats would have their greatest influence on the national scene in the realm of political ideas. President Jackson briefly felt the movement's impact in 1834 when, at the request of Maryland authorities, he dispatched federal troops to suppress the violent strike of Irish day laborers along the Chesapeake & Ohio Canal, and, more positively, in 1836, when he approved a federal order to adopt the ten-hour workday at the government shipyard in Philadelphia. Jackson would not tolerate civil disorder, whatever its origin. But his administration's basic sympathies with the labor movement (in contrast with its enmity toward the abolitionists) came across clearly, most explicitly in the *Globe*, which bid "All Democrats or Working Men" to tolerate no proposals that gave "*legal* advantages to *capital*, over *labor*" or otherwise helped harden society into "two distinct classes: namely—masters and slaves." On both practical and ideological grounds, the administration and the more radical wing of the Albany Regency regarded the divisions in the northern Democracy over banking issues with alarm—and viewed the stubbornness of the conservatives, especially in New York, with dismay. It would take a few more years to complete, but an alliance between the Loco Foco Democracy and the Democratic Party's national leadership was already in the making.[80]

JACKSONIAN CONTRADICTIONS

The affinities between the Jackson administration and what John Commerford called the "family of labor" underscored the peculiarities of Jacksonian Democracy as it evolved in the mid-1830s. The removal of the government deposits and Jackson's victory over Nicholas Biddle were completely in line with what the city democrats, now Jackson Democrats, had been demanding about banks and currency for years. In their political efforts, labor leaders naturally gravitated to the Jacksonians. Yet once they did so, they found pro-Jackson politicians who were either offended by the Bank War and not at all friendly to their views or who (like the Tammany "antimonopolists") paid mere lip service to their cause. Radical Democrats were pitted against Bank Democrats. The future of both democracy and Jackson's Democracy would depend on which of these two wings of the party would gain ascendancy in the North.

The politics of antislavery exposed another side of Jackson's coalition. Jackson and his party were decidedly hostile to the antislavery radicals. Without endorsing Calhounite pro-slavery positions, the unapologetic slaveholder Jackson, especially in the postal controversy, tried to silence the immediatist agitators, even if it took a federal censorship law to do so. Those efforts only reinforced the radical abolitionists' conviction that Jackson himself, as well as his party, was no better than any of the other slavocrats, and that their professions to democracy and equality were vitiated by their racism and self-interest. The suppression also alienated some northern Jacksonians as well as Whigs who had had little or nothing to do with the abolitionists.

These contradictory sides of Jacksonianism could not coexist forever. Although still on the defensive—and risking, like William Leggett, political excommunication—some northern Jacksonians were growing uncomfortable at the party's deference to the southern slaveholders, just as larger numbers of

Democrats (including Leggett) were pressing for even more dramatic changes in the banking and currency systems. On the latter issues, the radical Democrats were winning the initiative. But on slavery and antislavery, Jacksonians like Leggett remained the exception through the mid-1830s, their influence hampered not simply by the party's fears about abolitionist disruption but by continuing events in the South and Southwest during the final years of Jackson's presidency. Those events would deepen the Jacksonians' contradictions—and hasten the end of one phase of American democracy's rise, and the beginning of another.

14

"THE REPUBLIC HAS DEGENERATED INTO A DEMOCRACY"

The tumults of the mid-1830s had many causes, but to conservative Whigs, they all boiled down to one—the rise of Andrew Jackson and his demagogic Democratic Party. "They have classified the rich and intelligent and denounced them as aristocrats," the *Richmond Whig* declared, "they have caressed, soothed, and flattered the heavy class of the poor and ignorant, because *they* held the power which they wanted." In pursuit of their selfish ends, the Jacksonians had destroyed the political system designed by the Framers: "*The Republic,*" the Richmond paper cried, "*has degenerated into a Democracy.*" Yet to the Jacksonians, for whom democracy was the fulfillment of republicanism, the transition was far from complete, and the continuing political challenges of Jackson's second term raised difficult questions about how it might be done.[1]

The concept of state rights and its connections to southern politics were especially vexing. When linked to the tariff and nullification, state rights had led Jackson to renounce nullifier extremism in favor of his own democratic nationalism, and fracture his original coalition. But when linked to Indian removal, state-rights claims had helped bind Jacksonians' loyalties to Jackson, especially in the Deep South and Southwest. After the passage of the Indian Removal Bill in 1830, Jackson resettled nearly forty-six thousand Indians west of the Mississippi and cleared the way for moving a like number in the future. In the process, he obtained over a hundred million acres of Indian land for white settlement, preeminently in the nascent cotton kingdoms of Alabama and Mississippi. While he battled the aristocratic slaveholders of South Carolina, Jackson opened up grand new vistas to the West for slaveholders as well as yeoman farmers.[2]

During his last two years in office, Jackson commenced the final removal of the southeastern Indians, ignoring the objections of northern humanitarians and John Marshall's Supreme Court. Southern and sectional politics on other issues remained troublesome for the administration. For years, Anglo-American settlers, a large number of them slaveholders, had been streaming into the Tejas region of Mexico with the encouragement of the newly independent Mexican government. Although exempted from Mexico's abolition of slavery in 1829, the settlers were beginning to chafe at Mexican rule, particularly at a prohibition on further immigration in 1830. By 1835, having drafted their own Texas state constitution two years earlier, the Texans were on the edge of armed revolt, which the Jacksonians fervently supported. But the Texas Revolution also opened up fresh sectional rifts that needed to be handled with care—especially given the rising vociferousness of the northern abolitionists. And while the slaveholders affirmed their control of the region's political system, partisan divisions within the South, chiefly over banking policy, generated a growing and coherent southern anti-Jackson opposition.

Jackson's struggles over economic policy proved just as fractious in the North, and with the approach of the presidential contest of 1836, they continued to dominate national affairs. By all but killing the Second Bank of the United States, Jackson left open how the nation's finances would now operate, which provoked additional divisions inside his own party. The problem became acute when, after the downturn caused by the panic in 1834, the economy entered a period of fevered speculation as bad as any Jackson and his allies had blamed on the BUS. In addition to defections from Democratic ranks, the White House faced resistance from an enlarged and better-organized Whig opposition in Congress, working in concert with John C. Calhoun, who was now consumed by his pro-slavery sectionalism and hatred of Jackson. Yet Jackson, implacable as ever, responded by endorsing new, sometimes drastic experiments in banking policy while implementing a hard-money currency program more radical than any yet proposed.

INDIAN REMOVAL, SOUTHERN POLITICS, AND THE TEXAS REVOLUTION

After 1830, some of the administration's bloodiest encounters with the Indians occurred, paradoxically, outside the areas in the South and Southwest where the removals were heaviest. In 1832, Chief Black Hawk led members of the northwestern Sac and Fox tribes eastward across the Mississippi to reoccupy lands from which they had already been removed. Jackson sent federal troops, which, along with Illinois militia, drove Black Hawk into Wisconsin, where he suddenly halted, turned, and drove off his pursuers. The Black Hawk War, three months in duration, ended in August, when Black Hawk surrendered at Prairie du Chien. Three years later, hostilities broke out with the Seminoles of Florida under Osceola, inaugurating a vicious guerrilla conflict that lasted seven years, at a heavy cost in lives to both sides, before the majority of the surviving Seminoles were removed.[3]

The largest removals involved the Choctaws, Creeks, Chickasaws, and Cherokees. In the summer of 1830, the Choctaws of Mississippi riled Jackson by failing to send representatives to an agreed meeting in Tennessee. Thereafter, Jackson proclaimed the federal government powerless to contravene state law over Indian settlements, and he arranged for an allotment treaty that ultimately sent the majority of the Choctaws, roughly fourteen thousand out of nineteen thousand, to the West, amid horrifying scenes of hardship and death from cholera and malnutrition. The Creeks, living in Alabama, signed an allotment treaty in 1832, only to have speculators move in, buy up their land at a pittance, and push them out. Some displaced Creeks turned to theft and even murder, prompting the War Department to send troops, which forced fifteen thousand Creeks to emigrate west before Jackson left office. The Chickasaws in Mississippi waited two years for western land to be found, then signed an allotment treaty in 1832. Five years later, five thousand were relocated across the Mississippi.[4]

The Cherokees, with the aid of their evangelical allies, put up a stiffer resistance through the courts. As soon as Jackson's removal act went into effect, the Georgia legislature declared all Cherokee laws null and void. The Cherokees hired William Wirt and the prominent ex-congressman John Sergeant, who filed an injunction with the Supreme Court to block the Georgians from executing their laws in Cherokee territory. The case of *Cherokee Nation v. State of Georgia* ended in an apparent defeat for the Indians in 1831 when Chief Justice John Marshall declared in a majority opinion that because the Cherokees were a "domestic dependent nation," they lacked standing to sue. Administration Democrats were elated and claimed that their old nemesis Marshall had affirmed the Cherokees' case was, as Martin Van Buren put it, both "fictitious, not to say factious, and designed for political effect." But the fight over the Cherokees—and by them—was not yet over.[5]

A second Supreme Court ruling a year later, in the *Worcester v. Georgia* case, moved in the opposite direction—and reconnected Indian removal to state rights. A new Georgia law required all white persons to obtain a state license if they wished to live in Cherokee territory. Samuel A. Worcester and Elizur Butler, missionaries from the American Board of Commissioners for Foreign Missions, refused to comply, were sentenced to four years at hard labor, and, with the help of Wirt and Sergeant, appealed their case to the Supreme Court. Interest in the case was high—by this time, Wirt was the Anti-Mason's presidential nominee, while Sergeant was Henry Clay's National Republican running mate—and more than fifty congressmen dropped their business to hear the arguments before the Court. Marshall's decision overturned the Georgia state supreme court, declared Georgia's licensing laws unconstitutional, and directed the state to heed the Court's ruling. The Cherokee Nation, the chief justice declared, was "a distinct community, occupying its own territory," in which the the state of Georgia had no jurisdiction and with whom intercourse was vested solely in the federal government. Georgians immediately complained that the Court had violated their state's sovereign rights.[6]

The outcome created a dilemma for President Jackson. Marshall's court would be out of session until January 1833, which gave Georgia authorities ten months to reply to the Court's mandate. As the deadline approached, however, Jackson's struggle with the South Carolina nullifiers escalated. He did not want to do anything to relieve the pressure on the Cherokees to relocate, and did not want to provoke the Georgians to join the South Carolinians in a state-rights frenzy. Neither, however, did he want to appear as if he were knuckling under to the Georgians—or allowing the missionaries to become anti-administration martyrs. The White House persuaded Georgia Governor Wilson Lumpkin to release the two prisoners, and got the now-defeated presidential candidate Wirt to agree that he would file no further motions when the Supreme Court reconvened. The missionaries Worcester and Butler walked free, and the immediate crisis ended.[7]

The Cherokees' battle against removal continued for another five years. Although Secretary of War Lewis Cass negotiated a removal treaty in the spring of 1834, the majority of the Cherokee chiefs and their followers opposed it. Leading the opposition was John Ross, one-eighth Cherokee by birth. A former army lieutenant who had fought side by side with Jackson during the Creek War in 1814, but who had turned against him over Indian removal, Ross had been elected the Cherokees' principal chief in 1828. Now, as head of the antitreaty National Party, Ross staved off the administration with delay, subterfuge, and, in 1835, an election in which the Cherokees overwhelmingly rejected the proposed treaty. Finally, Governor Lumpkin mobilized the Georgia militia, which rousted and terrorized the antitreaty Indians and temporarily imprisoned Ross. When Ross, upon his release, traveled to Washington to plead for better terms, the pro-treaty party called a rump session and approved a new removal treaty at New Echota that passed the Senate by a single vote in May 1836. Although given two years to prepare for their departure, the Cherokees soon found themselves in need of federal protection. Two antitreaty counselors who had grudgingly signed the new agreement, Major Ridge and his son, John, advised Jackson in 1836 that "[t]he lowest classes of the white people" had begun "flogging the Cherokees with cow hides, hickories, and clubs" to drive them off their allotments. Jackson did nothing.[8]

As ever, Jackson asserted that removal was the best-possible solution for the

Indians themselves. That position may have had merits, but it lacked the crucial one of having the Indians' assent. On the matter of majorities and minorities, the linchpin of Jackson's politics, the majority within the Indians' camp counted for nothing, whereas the white majorities in the specific states counted for everything. Jackson had accomplished his great goal of removing the Indians to what he considered a safe haven—and, in the process, spared them the annihilation that had befallen Indians in the Northeast. But to save the Indians, Jackson's policy also destroyed thousands of them.[9]

Less cruel paradoxes in the Indian removal struggle lay in the area of southern politics. Among those leading the fight against the New Echota treaty (joining Clay, Webster, and a mixture of New England and middle-state Whigs) were three prominent southerners: the veteran Virginia Tidewater conservative Benjamin Watkins Leigh; Alexander Porter, a lawyer and sugar planter from Louisiana; and John C. Calhoun. None was known as an outspoken defender of the Cherokee, although Calhoun had earlier supported "civilizing" missions instead of removal. (Porter opposed Indian removal because he wanted to keep the displaced Indians from crossing through the Southwest.) None had common agendas on other government policies, least of all the protectionist sugar grower Porter and the nullifier Calhoun. All three, however, were devoted pro-slavery men whose devotion was deepening amid the assaults from the abolitionists. And they were passionate opponents of Andrew Jackson and all his works—including, now, the treaty with the Cherokees.[10] Under Calhoun's leadership, this strain of conservative pro-slavery southern politics would, through the mid-1830s, begin to consolidate an anti-Jackson opposition in what, less than a decade earlier, had been a solid Jacksonian South.

Calhoun opposed Jackson at every turn. After trying, and failing, to get the Senate to repeal the Force Bill, Calhoun ripped into the president's protest of the Senate censure with a sharp personal attack: "Infatuated man! Blinded by ambition—intoxicated by flattery and vanity!"[11] On the abolitionist mails controversy, Indian removal, corruption in the post office, and the abuse of executive patronage (about which he prepared an entire report), Calhoun was a single-minded foe. He had ample reason to bear an enormous grudge against Jackson, but he was not a petty man, and his monomania was more philosophical and political than it was personal. Still, in the taut coils of Calhoun's deductive mind, everything Jackson and his supporters did, no matter how innocuous, turned into additional evidence of the president's cancerous ambition and the imminent death of public liberty.[12]

Slavery became Calhoun's other fixation. Prior to the 1830s, even amid the battle over the tariff, Calhoun rarely mentioned slavery, except in direct connection with running his Fort Hill plantation. Early in his congressional career, he registered his shame at witnessing South Carolina oppose the prohibition of the transatlantic slave trade in 1807, perhaps betraying some Yankee influence from his years at Yale and at Tapping Reeve's academy. Slavery was, to be sure, at the bottom of what, during the nullification crisis, Calhoun had called the "opposite relations" between North and South. Yet only when nullification collapsed and the abolitionists began winning a large following did Calhoun begin defending slavery explicitly as a necessary, even preferred way of life. The Calhounite *United States Telegraph* signaled the shift in 1833, crying that it was high time to renounce the "cant" about the evils of slavery. A year later, Calhoun accosted a Philadelphia Whig congressman outside the Capitol and delivered a two-hour tirade about slavery's great advantages, and about how the degraded working masses of the North were bound to use the suffrage to despoil the wealthy. Slavery, Calhoun said, solved this problem "by the denial of all political rights" to the toilers, allowing the whites "to pursue without apprehension the means they think best to elevate their own condition." Slavery, Calhoun concluded, was "indispensable to republican government," a judgment he was soon proclaiming on the floor of the Senate while ridiculing the claims of the abolitionists. "Will our friends of the South," he asked sarcastically after quoting one of the abolitionists' petitions, "agree that they keep shambles and deal in human flesh? . . . Strange language! Piracy and butchery? We must not permit those we represent to be thus insulted on that floor."[13]

Always protective of his political independence, Calhoun did not formally join the Whig Party, keeping his distance by proposing policies of his own on key issues like banking. His chief aims were to sustain the southern nullifier position and, as best he could, his own political ambitions. Other southerners whom Jackson had alienated—state-rights men, up-country improvers, pro-BUS planters, and conservative nationalists—joined the Whig opposition. In Virginia, western pro-improvement men who had supported Clay in 1832 allied with the much larger numbers of state-rights advocates and National Republicans from the Tidewater and Piedmont in angry reaction to Jackson's removal of the deposits. Calling themselves Whigs, engaged in "a struggle between liberty and power," the Virginians forced the Jacksonian William C. Rives to resign from the Senate and replaced him with Benjamin Watkins Leigh, while they also elected a governor and gained control of the state legislature. In North Carolina, nullifiers and the popular state-rights senator Willie P. Mangum struck an alliance with the state's pro-BUS Democracts and its small numbers of National Republicans. In Georgia, Jackson's former attorney general, the Savannah lawyer and attorney for the BUS John M. Berrien, led the new State Rights Party, dominated by men formerly associated with George Troup. Mississippi's state righters, offended by Jackson's actions during the nullification crisis, formed their own association in the spring of 1834 and were almost immediately courted by the state's business-minded former National Republicans to join in a common electoral front.[14]

The rise of a powerful southern Whig opposition to Jackson sharpened some of the class and subregional divisions within southern politics. Southern Whiggery was preeminently a party of commercial development—friendly to the expansion of commercial banking facilities (and offended by Jackson's war on the BUS), partial to internal improvements, and (especially in the hemp-growing areas of the upper South and in the sugar parishes of Louisiana) pro-tariff. The largest planters, ranging from sugar growers in Louisiana to state-rights men in the eastern states, gravitated to the Whigs, taking with them districts where slaveholding was most thickly concentrated. Whigs also drew support, and a good deal of its leadership, from the business and professional classes as well as skilled workers of the coastal and river cities. Rather paradoxically, some of the more remote mountain areas such as western Virginia and East Tennessee also favored the Whigs, drawn to the national party's touting of internal improvements as a means to expand national prosperity. In the rest of the South, especially the Deep South, the Democrats came to depend largely on yeoman farmers in the less developed areas—northern Alabama, eastern Mississippi—who were distrustful of the planters' power, fearful of commercial banks and other monied institutions, and who saw politics, one southern Democrat wrote, as a contest between "*Aristocracy* . . . with the Money Power, Against Democracy or the Will of the People."[15]

Although divided by party, the slaveholders retained their collective domination of the region's political system. Sometimes they did so with carefully calibrated structural reforms that offered minor concessions to nonslaveholders in order to solidify support for slavery—and deflect any hint of antislavery politics. Two sets of state constitutional revisions moved voting requirements and restrictions closer to the Master Race democratic model adopted in the new Deep South states after 1815. In 1835, the North Carolinians extended popular voting for governor to include all male taxpayers over age twenty-one, but sustained the freehold property requirement in voting for members of the state senate and totally eliminated suffrage rights for the state's small numbers of free blacks. A year earlier, a Tennessee state convention completely rewrote the state's constitution. A few delegates from the mountainous eastern portion of the state, where religious antislavery societies had arisen earlier in the century, advanced gradualist abolitionist proposals, claiming that bondage was hampering the state's economic development. But these were bottled up in committee and then voted down. Instead, the convention dropped the symbolic freehold requirement for white male voting (an alternative, minor residency requirement had been in effect since 1796), while closing the suffrage to free blacks except for those men of color who were now "competent witness[es] in a court of justice against a white man."[16]

In less formal ways, slaveholders regardless of party did their utmost to secure the loyalty of the nonslaveholding majority to slavery. As South Carolina's Arthur P. Hayne explained in a paper he sent to Jackson, "a restless feeling" plagued "the South, and not without just cause, in relation to the Question of Property at the South, and unless this feeling be put at rest, who would desire to live in such a community?" One way to keep the lid on was to curtail antislavery talk, with what Hayne called its dangerous "abstract love for liberty." Another—the carrot instead of the stick—was to celebrate the sovereignty of the people, denounce the Yankees, and turn election contests into endless debates over which party or faction was the more loyal to the South—thereby, supposedly, protecting the status and well-being of all southern white men and their households. Southern Jackson Democrats could point to their party's crackdown against the abolitionist menace; Whigs proclaimed that their fights against federal executive tyranny made southern rights more secure than ever, in contrast with the untrustworthy Jacksonians. "Our domestic institutions are threatened with annihilation," one Georgia Whig paper declared.[17]

A third method was to co-opt talented nonslaveholder politicians who looked as if they might pose a political threat to the slavocracy. The case of Franklin Plummer of Mississippi, the most radical southern country democrat of the Jacksonian era, is illustrative. A New Englander who had moved to Mississippi as a young man, Plummer was the political favorite of the impoverished so-called Piney Woods semisubsistence counties in the south-central part of the state. A scabrous, leather-lunged stump-speaker and campaigner—especially effective when he cast his opponents as effete, river-county planter snobs—Plummer won election to the state legislature and then, in 1830, to Congress, over the objections of the local Jackson organization. In Washington, he made his mark as an antibank Jacksonian every bit as radical as any northern Workie or Loco Foco, claiming to stand unterrified for the only principles that could "save our bleeding constitution from destruction." So he remained—until after he left Congress and the bankers and planters of Natchez got hold of him, inviting him to their lavish dinners, fronting him a twenty-five-thousand-dollar loan, and encouraging him to run for the Senate. Plummer, bewitched, bought a fancy carriage, hired liveried servants, and campaigned hard, only to be crushed by fellow Jacksonian Robert J. Walker—a more conventional Democrat, but who could not be accused of betrayal by the yeoman of the Piney Woods. Plummer, his political career over, careened about over the next ten years, finally dying a forgotten drunk in Jackson in 1847. Unimaginable in Calhoun's South Carolina, his meteoric career proved that even in the rough-and-tumble Southwest, plebeian democratic politics would be allowed to rise only so far before being neutered.[18]

Another southern rural democrat seduced by moneyed politicians—but who wound up wrapped in glory—was the Tennessean Colonel David Crockett. Born in 1786 at the confluence of Limestone Creek and the Nolichucky River in what is now northeastern Tennessee, Crockett's renown as a rifleman and Indian fighter under Jackson during the Creek War helped win him election to the Tennessee state legislature in 1821 (where he supported the regime of Governor William Carroll). In 1827, he advanced to Congress as a Jacksonian. "I'm David Crockett, fresh from the backwoods . . . ," he supposedly bragged upon his arrival in the capital, "I can wade in the Mississippi, leap the Ohio, ride a streak of lightning, slip without a scratch down a honey locust, whip my weight in wildcats, hug a bear too close for comfort, and eat any man opposed to Jackson!" Reelected twice more, he had a falling out with the president over some land legislation in 1831 and was eagerly snatched up by the emerging Whigs, who were eager to prove their populist credentials with the electorate. After inventing an entire life of embellished Crockett folklore and publishing it in numerous forms—including a popular biography written by a good friend of Nicholas Biddle's—the Whigs sent him on a tour of the Northeast in 1834, where he praised the BUS, blamed Biddle's panic on Jackson, and performed his disarming king-of-the-frontier act. Eventually, Crockett's political enthusiasm diminished. Defeated for reelection in 1834, and embittered at what he imagined was Martin Van Buren's imminent rise to the White House, he decided to light out, he told a friend, "for the wildes of Texas," where the long-brewing fight between Anglo settlers and the Mexican government had finally become open rebellion.[19]

By the time Crockett crossed the Red River and headed for Nacogdoches, the Texas Revolution had been underway for nearly three months. In November, following a battle between Mexican troops and settlers in Gonzales, a provisional Texan government formed in San Felipe de Austin. Stephen Austin, the great Anglo colonist and landholder (or *empresario*), having been jailed by the new Mexican military government, gave the movement his wholehearted support. On March 2, 1836, fifty-eight delegates, including President Jackson's close friend, the former Tennessee governor and Indian trader Sam Houston, signed a formal declaration of independence in Washington-on-Brazos. The insurgents then fell into squabbling about how to repel the Mexican Army, which was marching northward to crush the rebellion, under the personal command of Mexico's ruler, Antonio López de Santa Anna. One rebel force of about three hundred gathered at Goliad, the gateway to east Tejas, under Colonel James Fannin, while another smaller group, numbering just under two hundred men, held on in San Antonio. On February 23, Santa Anna and his army, eventually reinforced to twenty-five hundred men, laid siege to San Antonio, where the insurgents—commanded by the South Carolina–born William Travis and James Bowie, a frontier drifter, knife designer, and Mexican citizen—holed up in a Spanish mission popularly known as the Alamo. Among them was Crockett.[20]

Rarely has such an overwhelming show of force won so little military advantage. Goliad, not the Alamo, was the real prize. Had the Mexicans simply waited until the arrival of their full artillery, they could have reduced the old mission to rubble with comparatively little sacrifice on both sides. But Santa Anna, humiliated by an earlier defeat suffered by his brother-in-law, General Martín Perfecto de Cos, was inclined to wipe out the San Antonio garrison, and the Texans' stubborn, suicidal resistance only deepened his resolve. "Our commander became more furious," a Mexican lieutenant colonel recalled, "when he saw that the enemy resisted the idea of surrender. He believed as others did that the fame and honor of the army were compromised the longer the enemy lived."[21] Before sunup on March 6, Santa Anna ordered a full assault on the now encircled fortification, his soldiers raising ladders to climb over the mission's old adobe walls. Ninety minutes later, it was over. All but a handful of the rebels were dead, as were approximately six hundred Mexican soldiers, about one-third of the army's assault force. Although Santa Anna spared the insurgents' wives, children, and slaves, he ordered the surviving rebels, including Crockett, bayoneted and shot as "pirates," to serve as an example of the uselessness of the Texans' struggle.[22]

An even worse atrocity was to befall the insurgents near Goliad, who, after surrendering in mid-March to an overwhelming force under General José de Urrea, were imprisoned but then summarily slaughtered on direct orders from Santa Anna. With the Mexican victory at the third major rebel redoubt at San Patricio in early March, the revolution seemed doomed. But in trying to mop up what was left of the Texan rebels—about nine hundred men under Houston's command—Santa Anna divided his armies and left his main force dangerously exposed. On the afternoon of April 21, as screams of "Remember the Alamo" and "Remember Goliad" filled the air, Houston surprised and overran Santa Anna near Lynch's Ferry on the San Jacinto River. After less than half an hour's heavy fighting, followed by an hour or more of vengeful bloodletting by the Texans, Santa Anna's army had been destroyed, and the next day, Santa Anna himself was captured trying to flee, dressed in a common soldier's uniform. At Houston's insistence, the Mexican commander ordered all Mexican forces to depart from Tejas. With the signing of the Treaty of Velasco in mid-May, the Republic of Texas was effectively free and independent—open for recognition and, many Texans hoped, annexation by the United States.[23]

Not since Jackson's victory at New Orleans had Americans been stirred as they were at the news of Houston's startling triumph. "We have barely room to congratulate every man who has Anglo-Saxon blood in his veins," the *Globe* crowed, "on the redemption of our brethren in Texas from Spanish power." The mingling of racial and nationalist themes was no coincidence. To jubilant Americans, the Texans represented Anglo-American freedom and enlightenment, in a war against an inferior political offspring of the rotten, obscurantist Spanish Crown. Although an independent republic, Mexico, under its military chieftain, was at odds with its own liberal democrats (whom, the celebrating Americans usually failed to note, despised the American invaders even more than they did Santa Anna). It was also, supposedly, a clear and present danger to national security, against which the new Texas Republic offered a buffer.[24]

President Jackson, for his part, had long regarded annexing Tejas to the United States—or more properly, he thought, reacquiring it—as an essential element of American expansion. He held the fanciful but sincere view that Tejas rightfully belonged to the United States as part of the Louisiana Purchase, and had been wrongly bargained away by Secretary of State John Quincy Adams in the Adams-Onís Transcontinental Treaty of 1819. By the middle of 1836, however, various considerations forced Jackson to move cautiously on the Texas question. Already suspected of having had a hand in the Texan uprising, Jackson could not afford to act precipitously without making some effort to negotiate with Santa Anna. On the domestic front, noisy abolitionists were beginning the charge that the Tejas uprising was part of a plot to grab a huge new area for the creation of many slave states. The veteran antislavery activist Benjamin Lundy, who had spent considerable time in north Mexico trying to resettle freed American slaves, led the attack, charging that the rebels' rhetoric about "the sacred principles of Liberty, and the natural, inalienable Rights of Man" was utterly bogus, and that they were actually engaged in a "*settled design*" to steal Tejas from Mexico and "*open a vast and profitable* SLAVEMARKET *therein.*" Normally, Jackson might dismiss Lundy and the other abolitionists as fanatics, but a presidential election was approaching, and Lundy had linked up with more prominent sympathizers including John Quincy Adams, who had returned to Congress in 1831. Care had to be given not to allow sectional suspicions from interfering with the victory of Jackson's chosen successor, Martin Van Buren.[25]

The difficulties surrounding Tejas exemplified the paradoxical sectional stresses afflicting the Jacksonian Democrats. Although Jackson secured formal recognition of the Texas Republic, he only did so well after the 1836 presidential election had been decided, and after a personal visit to Washington by Santa Anna. Even then, the Texas question was far from closed, particularly over whether the new republic should be annexed to the United States. And the prolonged battle over annexation would be shaped by both the effects of Jackson's policies and the evolving trends within southern politics. Indian removal had made possible the great expansion of the cotton slave kingdom. The success of the Texas Revolution, and the strong possibility of annexation, opened up even larger possibilities for slavery's spread. And so, Jackson further alienated (if it were possible to do so) antislavery northerners. Simultaneously, however, Jackson's policies on the BUS and nullification had generated a viable southern opposition to his Democracy, from the very planter elite whom the abolitionists accused him of coddling.

The burdens of these cross-pressures would be borne most heavily by Martin Van Buren, first in his presidential campaign in 1836 and then for the rest of his political career. Their full weight would only be felt, however, once the southern and northern anti-Jacksonian forces coalesced—an elusive goal for even the most-determined opposition organizers. Those efforts would unfold amid the last battles between Jackson and his congressional foes over banking and the currency.

"EITHER THE STATE IS SOVEREIGN, OR THE BANKS ARE"

On January 30, 1835, a misty cold morning in Washington, President Jackson attended the funeral services in the House of Representatives chamber for a nullifier congressman from South Carolina. Jackson looked careworn and frail, "scarcely able to go through with the ceremonial," the British traveler and writer Harriet Martineau observed from the gallery. At the end of the funeral, he followed the procession of official mourners onto the East Portico of the Capitol, where a young, thickly bearded man vaulted out of nowhere, aimed a pistol from point-blank range at Jackson's heart, and squeezed the trigger. The pistol cap exploded but failed to ignite the fine powder in the barrel, probably because of the wet weather. Jackson, instead of ducking, cocked his walking cane like a club and charged his assailant, who produced a second pistol, which also misfired. With Jackson still advancing and flailing away, the crowd subdued the would-be assassin and carried him off.[26]

The prisoner turned out to be an unemployed housepainter named Richard Lawrence. When asked, under medical examination, whom he preferred as president, Lawrence replied, "Mr. Clay, Mr. Webster, Mr. Calhoun," but he also claimed that he was the legitimate heir to the British throne and that Jackson had personally prevented his accession by killing his father three years earlier. (The father, it turned out, had been dead for over a decade.) Judged insane, Lawrence was cleared of criminal charges and committed to an asylum. Jackson—who but for the moistness of the morning air almost certainly would have been killed—harbored his conviction that Providence had spared him from a well-laid conspiracy by one of his powerful enemies. Others claimed that the violent mood of the riot-torn nation, and the intense animus that Jackson provoked, helped push the gunman over the edge and into the first attempted presidential assassination in American history. "A sign of the times," Bryant and Leggett's *Evening Post* observed.[27]

The months during and after the congressional Panic session in 1834 had brought Jackson a stressful mixture of gloom and elation. The Senate had censured him for removing the deposits from the BUS and refused to recognize his protest. In the House, the Whigs had bottled up a White House bill for the regulation of the deposits and, at the session's close, combined with Bank Democrats and anti–Van Buren southerners to elect John Bell of Tennessee as Speaker over Jackson's loyalist James K. Polk. In poor health once more, the president enjoyed a short rest at the Hermitage during Congress's summer recess, only to learn after his return to Washington that his estate house had burned nearly to the ground after his departure. And still: the House had approved, during the Panic session, resolutions supporting the BUS veto and backing Jackson's decision to place the removed deposits in a number of friendly state banks. With bipartisan support, the administration won passage of the Coinage Act, which revalued gold upward and led to the minting of vast quantities of gold coins (known as "Jackson eagles" or "Benton gold lozenges") as currency for small transactions. In foreign affairs, tortuous negotiations with France over American spoliation claims left over from the Napoleonic wars had led to a break in relations and the near outbreak of a new war late in 1834. But in February word came that upon receiving a moderately apologetic message from Jackson, the French Chamber of Deputies had backed down, and the crisis was over.[28]

The happiest news for Jackson was the Treasury Department's announcement that, as of January 1, 1835, the federal debt would be completely extinguished. Having peaked at $127 million after the War of 1812, the debt still stood at $58.4 million when Jackson took office. Now, thanks to continuing receipts from the tariff and Jackson's insistence on applying the funds to debt reduction, it was gone. Roger Taney reckoned that it was the first time any major nation had ever succeeded in paying off its debt, which was true then and remains true today. Jackson, whose detestation of financial debt in any form had been born of personal experience as well as Jeffersonian dogma, hailed the impending achievement in his sixth annual message, crediting "the industry and enterprise of our population." The acclaim was nearly universal. To mark the coincidence of the twentieth anniversary of the Battle of New Orleans and the removal of the debt, Jackson's supporters held a gigantic, sparkling celebration in Washington. The *Globe* exulted over its hero's two great victories, "the first of which paid off our scores to *our enemies*, whilst the latter paid off the last cent to *our friends*."[29]

The celebrations masked the appearance of a fresh set of political problems about what should be done with the new federal surplus, which by the end of 1835 would reach an astounding $17 million. That question was, in turn, entangled with the larger issue of what the administration would do about banking and currency policy now that the Second Bank of the United States was all but dead. Although Jackson had committed himself to giving a "full & fair" trial to his "experiment" in state deposit banking, there was still a chance he would support a moderate, constitutional version of a new national bank if the experiment proved in any way deficient. Several plans appeared. The one that got the most attention, formulated by Attorney General Benjamin Butler's brother, Charles, was for a limited deposit and exchange public bank, headquartered in Washington, that would also curtail the issue of bank notes of small denominations and substitute a metallic currency for most transactions. The last element was the most salient, for Jackson had decided that shifting from paper to coin was the best way to ensure that the nation's currency was well regulated. Butler's plan got nowhere, but the idea of gradually prohibiting bank notes up to twenty dollars became the latest object of Jackson's exertions.[30]

Apart from Jackson's Indian policy, nothing in his presidency has attracted more sustained criticism in recent decades than his expansion of the so-called pet bank system and his push for a specie currency after 1834. At worst, historians have ascribed the continuation of the Bank War to Jackson's ignorant antibank rage and his abiding hatred of Biddle, which ambitious state bankers exploited to enrich themselves and create a gigantic speculative bubble in 1835 and 1836. Even some of his most sympathetic biographers and interpreters have conceded that Jackson's understanding of banking and currency was "naive" and even "a little foolish," and that by sponsoring the pet state banks, he removed "a valuable brake on credit expansion" and "accelerated the tendencies toward inflation." Others cite the policies as examples of the rigid laissez-faire ideology—"to liberate business" from government—that supposedly guided the Jacksonians' every move.[31]

There was, without question, a dominant antistatist cast, both symbolic and substantive, to Jacksonian economic politics. The neo-Jeffersonian motto of Blair's Washington *Globe*, later picked up by John O'Sullivan's *Democratic Review*—"That government is best, which governs least"—powerfully expressed the antigovernment creed. Yet as Jackson himself always made clear, the Jacksonians opposed large government not because it burdened business but because they believed it was a creature of the monied and privileged few, constructed in defiance of popular sovereignty, that corrupted democracy. "Experience will show," the New York *Evening Post* said, "that this power has always been exercised under the influence and for the exclusive benefit of wealth." Too rarely have historians understood or even taken seriously the Jacksonians' repeated claims, after as well as during the BUS veto battle, that they aimed not to liberate private business interests from a corrupt government, but to liberate democratic government from the corrupting power of exclusive private business interests. Too rarely have historians appreciated the Democrats' willingness to wield federal power forcefully, over economic issues no less than over nullification, when they thought doing so was necessary to protect the democratic republic.[32]

The administration designed its evolving economic and fiscal policies, including creating a specie currency, as new, fully constitutional means to perform Nicholas Biddle's old job. Those policies, although developed in a piecemeal, halting fashion, originated not in rage or ignorance but in reasoned theories of finance and economic development, as well as in readings of the Constitution in line with Jackson's own. Known, by now, under the general rubric of "hard money," these democratic theories had a long history, from the critiques of the Hamiltonian paper-money system in the 1790s to the writings, forty years later, of the antimonopolist Working Men and western money radicals like Thomas Hart Benton and Amos Kendall. They began to crystallize as a coherent intellectual force in national politics in 1833, with the emergence of what might be called a hard-money intelligentsia, later to be identified with the Loco Focos. Only then did the Jacksonians seize on these theories as a positive justification for their own banking ideas and policies.[33]

The most successful statement was a treatise with an unpromising dry title, *A Short History of Paper Money and Banking in the United States*. Its author, the self-taught printer and journalist William M. Gouge, had been one of the signatories (and probably chief author) of the important Philadelphia Workie memorial against the BUS in 1829. Now, his limpid, massively documented explication became a runaway best-seller, both in its first edition published in 1833 and in a cheap popular edition printed two years later. The *Evening Post*, Blair's Washington *Globe*, and many other newspapers either serialized it or reprinted large excerpts from it. Theophilus Fisk, William Leggett, and other radical Democrats devoured the book, sang Gouge's praises, and became hard-money publicists themselves. Francis Blair made certain that the Kitchen Cabinet members read it, and early in 1835, the Treasury Department, under its new secretary, Levi Woodbury, hired Gouge as an in-house adviser, writing notes and memoranda that would help shape government policy long after Jackson's presidency.[34]

The hard-money men's economic arguments were geared to minimizing the speculative boom-and-bust cycle that plagued all developing commercial economies. Banks, they charged, have a propensity to overissue notes, leading to inflated prices and, in time, to speculative mania. That mania feeds on itself, leading to further expansion of credit and overtrading, a depreciation in the value of currency, and a drain on precious metals. That shortage of metal, in turn, forces banks to contract their credit to borrowers and their emission of bank notes, which has a domino effect on the entire banking and business system, leading to panic and, finally, economic collapse. Thereafter, a few surviving speculators snatch up the property of the prostrate many—and the vicious cycle commences again. To bankers like Nicholas Biddle, the material gains, the transforming improvements, and the sheer adventure of this bold new sort of capitalist commerce were worth the risk of occasional setbacks and even depression. But to Americans with lesser resources, the "humble classes" for whom Jackson presumed to speak, the chronic insecurity was both baffling and hurtful, especially since the lion's share of profits in good times went to others, whereas in hard times they were the ones to suffer most. The surest corrective, the hard-money intellectuals contended, was to remove, as far as possible, bank-issued paper from the day-to-day transactions of the laboring many and replace it with reliable specie—"*real* money," Leggett called it—which would help in "the great work of redeeming this country from the curse of our bad banking system." Suppression of small notes, Roger Taney contended, would end the "fluctuations and disasters" inherent in a paper-based system. With a hard-money currency, the *Globe* agreed, workingmen "would be effectually protected against all the casualties and frauds of paper money."[35]

Hard-money doctrines were not merely economic, nor were they dogmatically laissez-faire. Like Jackson's original justifications for attacking the BUS, they were essentially political and democratic, and they augured, in some respects, increased government authority over the economy, not less. Hard-money men insisted that no institutions independent of the sovereign people ought to be tolerated within the American government. Banks' involvement in extending credit to large borrowers was, by that standard, perfectly legitimate—a purely commercial task that did not encroach on the constitutional powers of the duly elected federal government. To give commercial banks power over the currency itself, however, was a plain encroachment, extending "too great a power," in Benton's words, "to be trusted to any banking company whatsoever." The only remedy was to exclude the banks from control of the currency and reassert the government's responsibilities and oversight—extending "the prerogatives of the Government to the very limits of the Constitution," as Francis Blair's *Globe* put it. Theophilus Fisk stated the matter even more bluntly: "Either the State is Sovereign, or the Banks are."[36]

The implications of these arguments and the policies that they inspired cannot be minimized. The hard-money men explicitly rejected the idea of a commercial system run wholly by and foremost for capitalists. Instead, they favored a different, more modulated commercial system partially regulated by a democratically elected federal government—what might be called "democratic commerce." Sharp periods of rapid growth and intense speculation would be reduced in a hard-money America, but so would sharp bust periods of mass misery. Government would exert, in some important spheres, more power than before to curb speculative frenzies, supplanting what one state Democratic convention called "a great irresponsible monied power . . . permanently fastened upon the country," with a system that was directly accountable to the people.[37]

Although primitive by modern standards, this reasoning was the furthest thing from the kinds of cure-all panaceas churned out by later generations of marginal American money cranks. If anything, the treatises of Gouge and his followers surpassed, in technical rigor and thoroughness, those written by their opponents—including formal political economists like John McVickar, publicists like Willard Phillips and the Reverend Alonzo Potter, and political leaders like Henry Clay and Daniel Webster. Nor, as many historians have charged, were the hard-money men's arguments nostalgic, aimed at turning back the clock to a bygone time of precommercial rustic virtue. Although they often spoke of restoring the values of "plain republicanism" and of curbing the moral corruptions of speculation, the hard-money men did not agitate for a return to a fanciful America of the past. They offered an alternative road to the future, one very different from that proposed by bankers like Nicholas Biddle or political leaders like Henry Clay—a future that was commercial and expansive, but also more democratic, less prone to sharp reversals of individual and collective fortune, and intended to protect the acquisitive interests and prosperity of the industrious many against the political abuses of the privileged few. And, most remarkably, the chief hard-money advocate in America was also the president of the United States—poised yet again, in 1835, to reform the nation.[38]

Jackson and his lieutenants went to work amid rising alarm over the speculation and rising prices that had resumed after the reversal of Biddle's panic in 1834. Several developments contributed to the mania. Jackson's removal of the deposits to the pet banks (whose number would rise to twenty-nine by the end of 1835) inevitably encouraged some irresponsible lending, now that the check once provided by the BUS had been largely removed. But those effects have been exaggerated. Secretary of the Treasury Levi Woodbury—appointed by Jackson after the Senate rejected the anti-BUS man Roger Taney's appointment during the Panic session in 1834—acted to turn his department into what he later called "a central Banking institution," exerting a strong hand over the pet banks, especially in New York, by making new federal deposits contingent on the banks' holding sufficient specie reserves and not overissuing notes.[39]

More decisive were the shocks caused by the skyrocketing federal surplus, a fortuitous (and, for the hard-money advocates, cruelly unlucky) glut in silver caused by international bullion flows, and a speculation boom in the buying of federal lands in the West, encouraged by the silver glut and the rising price of cotton. With the government still accepting paper notes for land-office purchases, the flow of paper westward became a torrent, and eventually filled the treasury's deposits with almost worthless currency. And as long as the circulation of small paper notes nationwide was not actively suppressed, currency values continued to plunge, despite the flood of Jackson eagles into the American market. "[T]his state of things cannot last . . . ," the *Globe* remarked in late spring 1835, reflecting a disquiet felt by hard-money men everywhere. "A reaction is certain to take place as the sun is to continue in its diurnal course."[40]

The administration had already undertaken major efforts to curtail small-denomination paper and to assume the responsibilities formerly met by Biddle and the BUS, most successfully with the Coinage Act and Secretary Woodbury's regulation of the pets. In the face of the speculative boom and accompanying inflation, it continued its incremental reforms. In February 1835, James K. Polk reintroduced a regulatory bill, stifled by the Senate during the Panic session, that would have required deposit banks to hold in precious metal one-quarter the value of notes they had in circulation, and would have banned U.S. receivers from accepting the notes of any bank that issued notes under five dollars. A month later, Woodbury ordered the deposit banks not to issue notes under five dollars or to accept such notes in payment of debts owed the government. The suppression of small bills would continue over the following year until Congress, in April 1836, enacted a ban on notes under twenty dollars effective in March 1837 and required instant convertibility to specie of all notes. Woodbury, in an effort to end "all mystery" in banking, further ordered that the deposit banks issue regular weekly statements, open to public examination. The Treasury Department also expanded the number of state deposit banks to thirty-three, including institutions in North Carolina, South Carolina, Mississippi, and Michigan that were tied to the Whigs. Secretary Woodbury maintained that the primary criteria for selection of deposit banks was a record of sound management. Although political considerations always played a part, they could no longer always govern an expanding system.[41]

Time and politics ran against the administration's reforms. Although several states joined with the federal government in suppressing small bills, the temptations of speculation inspired by the land boom had grown too intense to be denied. Biddle's supposedly responsible Second BUS—which originally touched off the inflationary spiral with its breakneck expansion before Biddle's panic—moved from capricious contraction back to rapid expansion and increased its loans by $15 million during the first six months of 1835; smaller banks followed suit. In 1835, with more than $22 million in federal funds sitting in the state banks, the amount of paper money in circulation rose by nearly one-third to $108 million. A year later, Secretary Woodbury's annual report predicted that there would be "much distress, embarrassment, and ruin" before the hard-money system's moderating effects could be felt. Thomas Hart Benton, speaking in the Senate, foresaw economic collapse: "The revulsion will come, as surely as it did in 1819–'20."[42]

In Congress, the administration faced new resistance within Democratic ranks as well as from the emerging Whigs. If some Democrats had been put off by the removal of the deposits from the BUS, Jackson's hard-money plans sent a shudder of fear and disgust through the ranks. The Tennessean Hugh Lawson White, once a trusted friend of Jackson's, had already defected, less over finance policy than over the president's closeness to Van Buren, whom White despised. At the end of 1834, the Tennessee congressional delegation had caucused and nominated Judge White for the presidency, a shock and surprise for Jackson. So-called paper or Conservative Democrats, led by Senator Nathaniel P. Tallmadge of New York, who had backed Jackson's war on the Second BUS and resisted Clay's censure motion, now balked at Jackson's experiment in hard-money politics and financial regulation, seeking instead to advance the power of the state banks. Later mocked by Jackson as "*all Bankites in desguise*" and "the no party party," Tallmadge and the Conservative Democrats would eagerly pursue the expansion of paper currency. Some would even edge toward supporting a reformed national bank along the lines of Biddle's, assured that national prosperity required, in the words of the Conservative Gideon Lee, "a great moneyed power."[43]

The Whigs, whom the Conservative Democrats increasingly resembled, resisted hard-money policies by reviving an old proposal of Clay's on land policy. As early as 1829, Clay and his followers had proposed a system of distributing a portion of federal monies made from land sales as an alternative to cheap land policies advanced by western Jacksonians—a system that would serve as a roundabout way for state governments to receive federal assistance for new internal-improvement projects. As long as the federal debt remained, the prospects for distribution were dim, but in 1835, with the debt erased, the plan attracted new attention. Clay devised a new version that would offer 15 percent of federal land sale proceeds to the states in which the sales had occurred, with the rest to be divided equally among the remaining states. Ignoring Secretary Woodbury's warnings that the surplus be set aside for federal construction programs and not left open to the states "for reloaning and private gain," congressional Whigs rallied to the plan. After Clay introduced his measure to the Senate, John C. Calhoun introduced a bill of his own on regulating the deposit banks. Over the next several months, the Senate Banking Committee, controlled by Whigs and Conservative Democrats, knit the two proposals together, producing what was called the Deposit Bill—a measure that increased regulation of the state banks and further curtailed the issuance of small bank notes, but that included Clay's distribution plan, obnoxious to the Jacksonians, and more than doubled the number of deposit banks to eighty-one, to include even more banks friendly to the Whigs. Outmaneuvered, the hard-money Democrats tried weakly to separate the regulation and distribution portions of the proposal, but the Whig-Conservative bill passed both houses of Congress in June 1836.[44]

Jackson and his allies were certain that their adversaries were out to destroy the hard-money experiment. Not only had the opposition saddled the administration with a distribution bill it did not like, the addition of forty-eight new deposit banks made Secretary Woodbury's job of restraining speculation much more difficult. Woodbury reported to Congress that the new bill placed enormous pressures on state banks. The *Globe* accused the congressional Whigs of deliberately trying to engineer another financial panic. Jackson had Taney draft a veto message but finally decided against delivering it rather than risk charges that he and his hard-money supporters were playing patronage politics by investing the huge federal surplus entirely in the existing, mostly-friendly deposit banks. Though repelled by the Deposit Bill, Jackson signed it. The land boom, predictably, continued, swelling federal deposits by 50 percent between February and November 1836. The federal land office turned into a gigantic government-sponsored confidence scheme, whereby speculators borrowed large amounts of paper money, used it to buy federal land, then used the land as collateral on further loans—all of which ensnared the federal government, as Benton observed, in "the ups and downs of the whole paper system."[45]

As soon as Congress adjourned, Jackson unilaterally struck down the con game by having Woodbury issue a Treasury Department order (heavily influenced by Benton, and soon known as the Specie Circular) requiring gold or silver coin payments for the purchase of all federal lands—a "tremendous bomb thrown without warning," a contemporary later recalled. The circular's impact was almost immediate, as millions of dollars' worth of paper money was turned away. The Whigs hit the roof at Jackson's latest display of executive tyranny, and the Conservative Democrats joined them. When Congress reconvened in December 1836, the Whigs and Conservatives proposed a bill rescinding the circular and reopening land purchases to paper money. Only five senators, including Wright and Benton, supported the hard-money position. The House added its assent, and the bill reached Jackson's desk the day before the brief session's adjournment. Jackson, who in his last annual message had boasted about the circular and its great advantages to (once again) "the laboring classes," quietly killed the bill with a pocket veto, the final important act of his presidency.[46]

Jackson's Specie Circular, by slamming the brakes on the western land mania and halting the shift of specie from eastern banks to the West, has traditionally received the blame for causing economic disaster. That interpretation now appears simplistic at best. The circular did not halt the land boom as much as had been previously assumed—or as Jackson hoped it would. Continued land sales, now paid for in metallic currency, ended up requiring large transfers of specie from the East, especially the New York City banks, over the winter of 1836–37. (Realizing this, Secretary Woodbury tried frantically to redirect specie eastward late in the autumn of 1836.) More important, supplementary interregional transfers of government funds by the Treasury Department, undertaken in anticipation of the redistribution that the Whigs' and Calhounites' Deposit Act stipulated would begin in 1837, were enormous. The largest New York City banks lost more than $10 million in federal deposits between August 1836 and July 1837. They saw their specie reserves drop from $5.9 million in August 1835 to $3.8 million at the end of 1836 (just before distribution began), and then drop again to $1.5 million by May 1837. Factors outside of American control, based on bullion flows and international trade patterns, also caused British banks to defend their own specie reserves and precipitously raise their interest rates. British demands for payments in metal from depleted New York banks, accompanied by northern crop failures and a sudden drop in cotton prices due to a glut on the world market, sparked the bank failures of early 1837 that were the harbingers of doom.[47] But some sort of blowup had been foreseen by the hard-money advocates, alarmed by the western land speculation, long before the Specie Circular went into effect. The hard-money policies put into place to forestall disaster and change the entire basis of the currency were not so much the triggers for the subsequent distress as they were reforms that came into existence too late—and, thanks in part to the mitigating efforts of the Whigs, western land speculators, and soft-money men, too unevenly—to have much effect. Benton had been correct. In 1837, the crash came.

Jackson realized that his banking experiment had been thwarted, and that the economy had fallen into precisely the kind of speculative boom he had hoped to banish. In the later months of 1836, thoroughly disillusioned with what he now regarded as the irresponsible, unpatriotic state banks, he began thinking about what options remained open to him. He presented Kendall with the outline for a "Third" national bank of exchange and deposit, which would operate out of Washington, report regularly to Congress, and have the power to issue bills worth over twenty dollars. While passing muster, in Jackson's eyes, as a constitutional and democratic institution, the proposed bank could, he believed, provide a "model" to the runaway state banks and "check the paper system and gambling mania that pervades our land." But time had run out: Jackson's presidency was nearly over; the campaign to elect his successor was well underway; and any proposal for a new bank was bound to batter an already weakened Democratic coalition at, politically, the worst possible moment. Although just as worried as Benton and Woodbury were by the inflationary spiral, Jackson kept his proposal confidential, and the economy continued to gallop toward a breakdown.[48]

To critics who blamed the situation on his hard-money policies and the Specie Circular, Jackson could reply that his political opponents, Biddle and Clay, with their obstructions to implementing his experiment in full, were actually the responsible parties. Yet the political impact of Jackson's policies proved greater, in 1836, than their economic and fiscal impact. The fallout from the Bank War and its aftermath united, as never before, the radical antibanking, antimonopoly elements of the Democracy, especially in the Northeast, with the administration. Apart from the singular case of New York City—where the Loco Focos harbored a distrust of Vice President Van Buren as an evasive trimmer on currency and banking issues—the pro-labor, anti-BUS radicals were now fully in the national Democracy's camp, and could be counted on to support it wholeheartedly in 1836. At the same time, the intense divisions between hard-money and Conservative Democrats encouraged the Whigs to believe that Jackson's policies—what Clay called his "ill-advised, illegal, and pernicious" experiment—had proved a political disaster.[49]

In later years, the Whigs would take full advantage of the economic tribulations of Jackson's second term. Yet in 1835 and 1836, as both major parties prepared for the upcoming presidential election, economic disaster lay in the future and the continuing boom times drowned out any complaints about the Jacksonians' handling of the economy. At the state level, Whig candidates fared poorly in the 1835 elections for governorships and state legislatures as well as for federal offices. ("Politically, I am sick at heart," wrote the former Anti-Mason, now a Whig, Thurlow Weed, after he watched the Jacksonians sweep to victory in, of all places, Connecticut. "All looks fearfully, hopelessly black.")[50] John C. Calhoun could be counted on for political mischief but little else, while the southern planters who had bolted from the Jacksonians had only begun to forge a working alliance with northern Whigs. Jackson's opponents had yet to prove themselves capable of doing more than mobilizing against him personally—and he would not be a candidate in 1836. As yet unable to mount a national strategy, they would conduct regional favorite-son campaigns. To fortify themselves and build public appeal, they also would viciously attack the imperial brute Jackson's chosen political heir, Martin Van Buren.

THE DILEMMAS OF MARTIN VAN BUREN: SLAVERY, HARD MONEY, AND A FRACTURED ELECTION

By the time Van Buren was formally named the Democracy's presidential candidate in May 1835, he had been hearing stories about how he would win the nomination for nearly six years. The nation, and its politics, had changed enormously—and in his appearance, if not in his politics, Van Buren had changed nearly as much. His auburn-blond hair had whitened and thinned, making him look less like the dashing pol of his early years than like a dignified, if a bit overripe, statesman. He had toned down his wardrobe, replacing the rakish orange cravats and white duck trousers he once preferred with more somber attire. He was as affable and engaging as ever—"l'ami de tout le monde," John Quincy Adams wrote—although decades of diplomatic dinners and formal receptions had thickened his waistline into a bourgeois gentleman's settled paunch. His prominent forehead, now completely bald, and his broadened features, framed by ample mutton-chop whiskers, had none of Jackson's tortured grimness, and could easily be construed as a visage of pliable complacency. But his deep-set, arresting blue eyes—twinkling at a clever remark, penetrating in discussion—showed that he remained a formidable political presence.[51]

Since returning from his ill-fated brief journey to London as Jackson's designated minister, Van Buren had trod cautiously, always loyal to the administration but trying his utmost to avoid offending important constituencies. The original broker of the Jacksonian coalition—a product of ingenuity, shrewdness, and prudence—Van Buren had tried to contain the coalition through the mid-1830s, out of concern in part for the administration and the nation and in part for his own political future. His break with Calhoun had initiated his rise to becoming Jackson's anointed successor, yet the break and the ensuing battles over the tariff and nullification also caused Van Buren great difficulty because of his close personal and political ties to many South Carolinians, some of whom became nullifiers. He privately disliked Jackson's nullification proclamation because of what he called its "heresies [to the] republican faith," and he counseled the president to show greater forbearance. ("You will say I am on my old track—caution—caution," Van Buren wrote to Jackson, in a tone more loyal than critical.) Initially opposed to the removal of the government deposits from the BUS, Van Buren moved from artful ambiguity to support of the president. In the hard-money controversies that followed, Van Buren did his best to carve out a compromise position within the Albany Regency, which had split into a radical wing and a soft-money wing. In his official duties as vice president, Van Buren performed well, appearing, a friend of Webster's observed, "unruffled in the midst of excitement."[52]

As he geared up for claiming the presidential nomination, Van Buren faced immediate problems in the South, especially in Virginia, where the Bank War and Jackson's resolute stand against nullification had caused massive defections from the Democracy. After the Southampton uprising, the suffrage and slavery debates, and the rise of radical abolitionism, Tidewater Virginians were skeptical of Van Buren for no other reason than that he was a northerner. It was said that he had opposed the War of 1812 (which was untrue) and that he had opposed the spread of slavery into Missouri (when he in fact had supported the Missouri Compromise). Because, in earlier times, he had been on friendly terms with Lewis Tappan, there were even charges that he was a closet abolitionist radical—"an avowed abolitionist in principle," the *Charleston Mercury* asserted. "God knows I have suffered enough for my Southern partialities," Van Buren complained in a rare show of frustration. "Since I was a boy I have been stigmatized as the apologist of Southern institutions, & now forsooth you good people will have it that I am an abolitionist."[53]

Southern misgivings deepened when Van Buren began dealing with the one major obstacle to his nomination—the preference in some western and radical northern circles, including the New York Loco Focos, for Richard Mentor Johnson of Tennessee. Still beloved for his forthright attack on the Sabbatarians and his leadership on abolishing imprisonment for debt, Johnson had been touted for president by George Henry Evans and the *Working Man's Advocate* as early as 1833. Before long, an official campaign biography and pro-Johnson ballad were in mass circulation. A popular play, lionizing Johnson for his supposed slaying of Tecumseh at the Battle of the Thames in 1814, attracted enthusiastic audiences in Baltimore and then in Washington. Struck by Johnson's vigor—along with his ability as a western candidate, Indian-killing war hero, and Kentucky slaveholder to balance the ticket—Van Buren's managers decided to win him over by offering him the vice presidency. Johnson accepted, and his backers' battle cry—"Rumpsey, dumpsey, Colonel Johnson killed Tecumseh"—became attached to the Van Buren campaign.[54]

Johnson's selection caused intense dismay in the South. Some planters regarded him as a coarse braggart who had exaggerated his claims to military fame. More worrisome were his domestic arrangements. Johnson had two daughters, Imogene and Adeline, by his housekeeper, a mulatto ex-slave named Julia Chinn. After Chinn died in 1833, Johnson took up with another woman of partial African descent, and in Washington he accompanied his out-of-wedlock daughters (whom he had provided with excellent private educations) to public functions and festivities, sometimes in the company of their respective white husbands. Johnson's flaunting of his sexual practice was a scandal, far worse than anything charged against John and Margaret Eaton. Johnson, one powerful Tennessee official wrote, was "not only positively unpopular . . . but affirmatively odious." When the Democrats finally convened in Baltimore in May 1835, with Van Buren's nomination a foregone conclusion, the Virginians offered William C. Rives as an alternative to Johnson. Van Buren's men barely assembled the required two-thirds' majority for Johnson, and the Virginia delegation hissed the outcome. In the autumn elections, the Virginia Democracy defiantly substituted Rives's name for Johnson's on the Democratic ticket.[55]

The Whigs' dilemmas were even graver than the Democrats'. Although politically unified as never before, none of the nationally prominent opposition leaders could possibly win, as the ever-astute Thurlow Weed explained: "With Clay, Webster, or Calhoun, or indeed any man identified with the war against Jackson and in favor of the Bank or the Bank's Shadow, the game is up." Although drawn together against Jackson, the Whigs did not yet resemble a national party as much as a coalition of convenience. So heterogeneous was the opposition that there was little point in calling a national convention or even regional conventions. Instead, local editorialists and legislators came up with their own nominees. At best, such a fragmented, multicandidate effort might throw the election into the House; at the very least, it would help oppositionists mount strong fights for state and local offices.[56]

In the South and Southwest, the quondam Jacksonian senator Hugh Lawson White of Tennessee recommended himself to oppositionists wary of the National Republicans with his standing as an "original" Democrat who had backed the bank veto. More important, White's supporters presented him as the only southern candidate in the field, a man of eminence who would stand up to the unsafe Yankee Van Buren and the abolitionist menace. In the North, a combination of midwesterners and mid-Atlantic Anti-Masons advanced the candidacy of William Henry Harrison, the undisputed hero of the Battle of Tippecanoe as well as, Harrison charged, the real hero of the Battle of the Thames. Currently living in obscurity as a court clerk in Cincinnati, Harrison had, in a successful run for a seat in the Ohio state senate in 1819, proclaimed himself a sworn enemy of all banks, above all the BUS, even though he was a director of the local branch of the BUS—a confusing and possibly disabling past that his managers did their best to bury, while Harrison claimed he was "not committed to any course" on the banking issue. But aside from his military glory, albeit somewhat faded, Harrison was a one-man balanced ticket, having been born in Virginia but relocated to Ohio. He was also a man, conveniently, with no recent political record whatsoever other than having been dismissed by Jackson for incompetence as minister to Colombia in 1829—which made him sufficiently anti-Jackson for his supporters' satisfaction. In New England, Daniel Webster refused to step aside in favor of the nonentity Harrison and had his friends continue efforts on his behalf, although finally he would stand as the main Whig standard-bearer only in Massachusetts. In the Southeast, Calhoun, although he would not jump completely into the Whig camp, could be counted on to dampen any remaining enthusiasm for Van Buren.[57]

The Whig campaigners, at their most high-minded, repeated the charge that Jackson's executive tyranny endangered public liberty, and claimed that Van Buren had played a major role in creating that tyranny. The more perspicuous Whigs, including the state party of New York, also proclaimed themselves democrats, declaring that Van Buren and the Democrats were the designers of "a conspiracy, which seeks to promote the interests of the few at the expense of the many" and despoil the "money of the people," and that would eventually destroy all free institutions. Whom the Whigs were referring to as "the few"—political spoilsmen? pet bank stockholders?—was left to the eye of the beholder; the "many," however, were obviously the great honest mass of Americans, including whomever the beholder happened to be. Gradually, but steadily, the Whigs, at least in the North, were learning to befriend His Majesty the People and to cast the Democrats as the People's lethal enemy.[58]

More often, the Whigs indulged in scurrilous personal attacks on Van Buren and his running mate that evoked the broader Whig imagery of the Democrats as parasitic partisans. Whig speakers and editorialists portrayed Van Buren as a cunning and unprincipled politician, out simply to enlarge his own power—"a crawling reptile," the former Anti-Mason William Henry Seward proclaimed, "whose only claim was that he had inveigled the confidence of a credulous, blind, dotard, old man." One slanderous biography of Van Buren, purportedly written by David Crockett before he lit out for Texas, described the vice president as "secret, sly, selfish, cold, calculating, distrustful, treacherous"—the perfect model of a slippery party politician. More elevated in prose but just as damning was a dystopia, *The Partisan Leader*, written by the southern novelist Beverley Tucker and published secretly by Calhoun's ally Duff Green. It depicted a shattered nation in 1849, suffering through the fourth term of Van Buren's presidency, with Virginia trying to decide whether to join the rest of the southern states and secede from the Union. Tucker, like other Whig caricaturists, also smeared Van Buren as an effeminate dandy, with hands "fair, delicate, small, and richly jeweled." Colonel Johnson found himself denounced in the North as a cruel slaveowner, and in the South as a mongrelizer of the white race.[59]

The Democrats countered with testimonials to Van Buren's "cool judgment," "practical wisdom," and "democratic principles." They also placed their candidate within the great democratic tradition, as a loyal Jeffersonian who, like Andrew Jackson, had been born to humble circumstances and had risen by his own merit and not by dint of privilege. Above all, the Democrats proclaimed, Van Buren had stuck by Old Hickory through thick and thin. Yet these encomia betrayed a nervous defensiveness on the Democrats' part, a fear that the Whigs' attacks on Van Buren's character were hitting their mark. As popular heroes went, the unfascinating Martin Van Buren was nothing compared to Andrew Jackson. Many of the virtues that Van Buren embodied and respected—loyalty to party, the ability to compromise, political cunning applied with supreme tact— were easily twisted into the vices of spoilsmanship, flaccidity, and false politesse. Above all, the political strains of the previous eight years caused Van Buren and his managers to worry whether their electoral base was truly secure.[60]

One unexpected issue in the campaign, nativism, had only just begun to surface as a political distemper in the northeastern states. In the 1830s, the numbers of Irish Catholic immigrants to the United States had grown sharply, thanks largely to the falling prices of transatlantic steerage voyages. Protestant native Americans and British immigrants, intensely distrustful of the Papists as a political as well as a cultural threat to the nation's liberties, grew increasingly distressed, and at times, violence broke out. In 1834, a nativist mob stormed and destroyed an Ursuline convent in Charlestown, Massachusetts, stirred by lurid rumors of immoral acts by the nuns. A year later, the celebrated artist and inventor Samuel Finley Breese Morse, a virulent anti-Catholic and sometime Jacksonian, ran for mayor in New York City, and a largely Whig middle-class group, the New York Protestant Association, fell into street battles with Irish mobs. Van Buren ran afoul of nativist opinion when someone unearthed a fairly mild letter he wrote in 1829, as secretary of state, informing the Vatican that Roman Catholics enjoyed the freedom to worship in the United States. Questioned by nativist Whigs about his involvement in a *"popish plot,"* Van Buren demurred and pointed out that he was not, himself, a Roman Catholic—trying his best to evade and defuse the issue without offending Irish-born voters.[61]

Genuinely worried about Hugh Lawson White's candidacy in the South, Van Buren took a firm stand against the abolitionists while eschewing Calhounite pro-slavery. Having already been grilled by the Virginians about his alleged anti-slavery sympathies, Van Buren faced repeated allegations and innuendo that he was soft on abolitionism. The book with Crockett's byline noted Van Buren's past associations with the antislavery "fanatic" Rufus King, and charged that the two "thought, or pretended to think alike on the Missouri question." Rumors persisted through the South that Van Buren was a radical Yankee who planned to free the slaves by act of Congress as soon as he gained the White House. (Overheard and then repeated, the rumors reached slaves' quarters and raised false hopes of imminent emancipation.)[62]

Van Buren denied all of this utterly, as much to reassure the anti-abolitionist majority in the North as to mollify the South. Slaveholders, he wrote to one associate, were "sincere friends to mankind," whereas abolitionists were crypto-Federalists out to undermine the Democracy. When the postal controversy broke out, Van Buren made sure that New York authorities firmly sided with Amos Kendall and pledged that they would no longer forward any objectionable material to the South. In Utica, one Democratic newspaper supported both Van Buren and the abolitionists; but when New York's abolitionists convened in Utica in the autumn of 1835, Jacksonian congressman Samuel Beardsley led a mob that broke up the meeting and destroyed the newspaper's offices, an event then publicized by Van Buren's men as proof positive that their leader had no use for the immediatists. Francis Blair's *Globe* pitched in by reminding readers of the obvious political realities surrounding the slavery issue. "Neither the Whigs nor the Democrats are exclusively confined to the slaveholding or free States," the paper pointed out. "How then can it be the exclusive work of either party?" Tolerating agitation over slavery would destroy the nation's political fabric—and both parties knew it.[63]

Van Buren's most consequential demonstration of his anti-abolitionism—and of his political clout—occurred behind the scenes on Capitol Hill. In 1835, as the mails controversy raged, the American Anti-Slavery Society stepped up its campaign, conducted since 1833, to petition the House of Representatives over a variety of issues related to federal support for slavery. Hundreds of thousands of fresh petitions bombarded Congress, now demanding an end to slavery in Washington, D.C. One of Calhoun's friends, the slaveholder freshman congressman James H. Hammond, saw in the petitions an issue even more incendiary and divisive than the mailings, and in December he proposed a House resolution that would instantly bar the abolitionist entreaties from consideration. Van Buren, seeking to defuse the abolitionist campaign without capitulating to the southern hard-liners, supported a compromise version of the proposal that would refer the petitions to a House committee and keep them off the floor for debate. Such a policy, he said, would give "the abolition question . . . its quietus," and preserve "the harmony of our happy Union."[64]

Luckily for Van Buren, a South Carolina nullifier, Henry L. Pinckney, agreed to propose the milder plan in the House. Although branded a traitor by the most vociferous anti-Jackson southerners, Pinckney stood by his resolution, and Van Buren rallied northern Democrats to support it. On May 26, 1836, a slightly toughened version of Pinckney's plan—which would soon become known as the "gag rule"—was overwhelmingly adopted as a standing rule of the House, over the stifled objections of John Quincy Adams, who declared the proposal unconstitutional, and the loud complaints of southern editors, who considered it a sell-out. The outcome reflected the political realities the *Globe* had talked about. Roughly half of the Whigs and other anti-administration congressman simply abstained, while the rest split on sharply sectional lines, with the vast majority of northerners voting against it—some out of antislavery conviction, others knowing the affair might embarrass Van Buren in northern districts. Nearly four out of five northern Democrats backed the resolution, as a political compromise between the extremes of abolitionism and pro-slavery. Notably, the overwhelming majority of Democrats from Van Buren's New York, ranging from the Radical Churchill C. Cambreleng to the Conservative Gideon Lee, voted aye. The Calhounites and other state-rights extremists, having been outmaneuvered, either cast negative protest votes or, like the Whig Waddy Thompson of South Carolina, abstained.[65]

While simultaneously gagging the abolitionists and isolating the hard-liners, Van Buren also sharpened his position on banking and the currency. In part, he hoped to counter the Whigs (and especially the southerner White) by charging that they were trying to throw the election to the House of Representatives to clear the way for Nicholas Biddle to step in, purchase the presidency, put the government, as one supporter exclaimed, "under the dominion of the Bank," and saddle the country with "a regularly organized Aristocracy." But Van Buren also had to patch up relations with the Democracy's northern hard-money wing. Although he had backed the Bank War and supported the use of coin in place of paper in minor transactions, Van Buren had angered New York's Loco Foco radicals by ignoring the proposals of William Leggett and others in favor of a so-called free banking system. The Loco Foco plan would have enacted a general incorporation law permitting any group to obtain a banking charter, but coupled with stringent state regulation of all banks. Van Buren's half-heartedness, along with his political alliances with the Tammany pols, whom the radicals despised, prompted the New Yorkers to withhold their endorsement. After attempting to straddle the issue, Van Buren finally decided, late in the campaign, to issue a ringing statement supporting the Specie Circular and to write a private letter (meant to be publicized) backing the deposit banks provided they were strictly regulated. Although he could not bring himself finally to support the Loco Focos outright (nor they him), his views were sufficiently radical to win the strong support of, among others, George Bancroft, Samuel Clesson Allen, William Leggett, and—in her return to radical politicking—Frances Wright. An old associate of Wright's and former contributor to the *Free Enquirer*, William Holland, ended up writing Van Buren's semiofficial campaign biography, hailing his subject as a proponent of "the most ultra democratic doctrines."[66]

Viewed from a certain angle, there was merit in Holland's claim. In 1836, the Democratic ticket included a presidential candidate who had endorsed some of the most radical economic doctrines of his day, and a vice presidential candidate who had endorsed those same doctrines while defending the separation of church and state—and also flaunted the nation's most fearsome racist taboos. Change the angle, however, and the Van Buren–Johnson ticket looked very different—the coupling of a cautious party man eager to mollify southern slaveholders and silence the abolitionists, with an actual slaveholder whose major claim to national fame was his dubious celebrity as the supposed killer of a feared and despised Indian. Both images contained part of the truth, which is precisely how the Democratic managers hoped their ticket would appear—persuading just enough voters to see just enough of what they wanted to see in Van Buren and Johnson, and then vote Democratic.

They succeeded, although not without some troubling political developments. In the popular vote, Van Buren outdistanced the combined total for his opponents, but only barely, by about twenty-five thousand votes out of 1.5 million cast. Van Buren's margin of victory in the Electoral College was much healthier, and the Democrats generally ran strong in state and local races, but there were disappointments. A close look at the state-by-state returns nationwide shows that the great majority of new voters who had joined the electorate since 1832 voted Whig. The Democracy had not lost its hold on its older supporters, but was having a very difficult time attracting younger ones, and voters who had previously abstained. Although Webster won only in Massachusetts, the cipher Harrison carried seven states, including at least one from every major region outside the South. Although Van Buren won most of the South and ran surprisingly well in Virginia, his margins in Mississippi and Louisiana were razor thin. Worse, he lost both Georgia and (to Jackson's disgust) Tennessee to Hugh Lawson White's "true Jacksonian" campaign. Even where he won, Van Buren's southern totals were feeble compared to Jackson's in 1828 and 1832. (The oligarchy of South Carolina, the last state whose legislature still picked presidential electors, cast its eleven votes in protest on behalf of the pro-nullifier North Carolinian, Willie P. Mangum.)[67]

And still the Jacksonian majority held, retaining both houses of Congress (including a nine-seat pickup in the Senate) and sending the evolving coalition and its experiment in economic policy into another term in the White House. On March 4, 1837, the outgoing president, looking sallow but serene, rode to the inauguration ceremonies at the Capitol alongside his handpicked successor. Jackson had a new reason to feel vindicated. In the 1834 elections, his supporters had won a bare majority in the Senate, and after a long struggle, Democrats led by Thomas Hart Benton finally succeeded, in January 1837, in having Jackson's censure officially expunged in bold black lettering from the Senate's official journal. With satisfaction, Jackson watched another of his handpicked men—Chief Justice Roger B. Taney, his replacement for the old Federalist, John Marshall, who died in 1835—administer the oath of office to the new president. Van Buren, in his inauguration speech, promised he would uphold the spirit of his predecessor and keep slavery out of national politics—and included a pledge to veto any bill authorizing abolition in the District of Columbia.[68]

The ceremony done, Jackson descended to his carriage, to an immense cheer from the throngs. If the nation was in greater turmoil than it had been eight years earlier, the transit of power was far more surefooted and self-assured than the inaugural melee of 1829. The displays that Washington insiders had found pitiable had been replaced by something more tested, more majestic. "I had seen the inauguration of many presidents," Senator Benton recalled, all of which "appeared to be as pageants, empty and soulless." Van Buren's installation, by contrast, "seemed to be a reality—a real scene."[69]

JACKSON'S FAREWELL

Early on inauguration day, Jackson issued his farewell message, an address brimming with gratitude and a sense of fulfillment at what his administration had achieved. Yet Jackson's valedictory, like George Washington's forty years earlier, also included words of foreboding. The war against the banking aristocracy begun with the destruction of the Second BUS was not over, Jackson warned. "The paper-money system and its natural associations—monopoly and exclusive privileges—have already struck their roots too deep in the soil," he said, "and it will require all your efforts to check its further growth and to eradicate the evil." Then there were the sectional battles, instigated by those who would "sow the seeds of discord between different parts of the United States . . . to excite the *South* against the *North* and the *North* against the *South*, and to force into the controversy the most delicate and exciting topics—topics upon which it is impossible that a large portion of the Union can ever speak without strong emotion."[70]

Having entered the presidency proclaiming the democratic idea that "*the majority is to govern,*" Jackson left it having witnessed how that idea brought not peace but further conflict, not the settling of arguments but their continuation alongside new arguments and rediscovered old ones. For Jackson, legislating the people's will and preserving the Constitution had come to mean advancing the battle against concentrated monied power while quieting the growing tumults over slavery. President Van Buren would follow his lead, only to discover that even Jackson's creative destruction and majoritarian reforms could neither fully describe, nor contain, the people's will.

15

THE POLITICS OF
HARD TIMES

Five weeks after Martin Van Buren's inauguration, the long-feared financial crash finally came. Commodity prices had skyrocketed over the winter of 1836–37, an inflationary boom fueled by foreign investment and worsened by two successive years of wheat crop failures. In Manhattan, a public meeting called by the Loco Focos in February to protest the runaway prices turned into a riot, as hungry workers plundered private storerooms filled with sacks of hoarded flour. While farmers failed to pay their bank debts, placing new pressures on overextended bankers, the decline of agricultural exports abroad threw the balance of trade against the United States. The imbalance, coupled with falling cotton prices, led British banks and creditors to demand repayment in hard currency from American borrowers.

On May 10, 1837, New York City's banks, having been stripped of much of their specie reserves in anticipation of the Whig-Calhounites' Deposit Act coming into effect, suspended the redemption of paper in gold or silver. Soon thereafter, nearly every bank in the country followed suit, causing prices and property values to tumble. In some places, bank failures and rising unemployment seemed to level the economy. "At no period of its history," one radical Democratic paper said of New York at month's end, "has there been as great a degree of general distress as there is at this day." The panic proved a prelude to more severe and widespread suffering. After a fifteen-month recovery beginning in 1838, the economy crashed again, causing a national depression that lasted three more years.[1]

The Panic of 1837 and ensuing depression, and how to deal with them, were the outstanding political quandaries of Van Buren's presidency. Yet the struggle over economic issues did not distract from fights on other fronts, above all over slavery. Amid rising sectional discord, Van Buren continued to try placating the South without giving in to the most militant pro-slavery forces. Following the panic, Van Buren turned more and more to hard-money economic policies, but he governed as if radicalism on economics required conservatism on slavery, in order to keep Jacksonian slaveholders in line and the Democrats in power. The political results were devastating for Jacksonian loyalists. Hamstrung over slavery issues and divided over economics, Van Buren's party found itself upholding an increasingly unstable conception of democracy. By 1840, opposed by a fully evolved Whig Party, it faced repudiation at the polls.

LOCO FOCOISM IN THE WHITE HOUSE

Jackson's Specie Circular, and his administration's larger hard-money experiment, became the immediate scapegoats for the economic disasters of 1837 and after, but Jackson's opponents were up in arms even before the panic struck. Immediately after Van Buren's installation, Senate Whigs offered new legislation to repeal the circular. Conservative Democrats, led by Nathaniel Tallmadge and William C. Rives (who had returned to the Senate in 1836), tried to persuade the new president to abandon his loyalties to Jackson. After the panic, businessmen remonstrated with Van Buren and swore to resist the circular, peaceably if possible, forcibly if necessary. Nicholas Biddle, more convinced than ever of his own greatness, added a suggestion that his Pennsylvania Bank of the United States be made a government bank of deposit, so that the wounds inflicted by Jackson might be healed. ("If *I* can forgive them," he said, "they may forgive me.") Yet as spring turned into summer, Van Buren buckled but did not break.[2]

Van Buren had three choices. He could renounce Jacksonian policy, rescind the Specie Circular, and propose the creation of a Third Bank of the United States—capitulating to the Whigs and restoring, institutionally, the status quo. He could rescind or modify the circular and sustain the deposit-bank system as it had existed, thereby moving closer to Tallmadge, Rives, and the Conservative Democrats—salvaging his Jacksonian label but rejecting Jackson's hard-money experiment. Or he could attempt the unprecedented by fighting for the divorce of the government's fiscal affairs from all private banks—what some radical Democrats and their supporters had begun demanding as "the absolute and unconditional SEPARATION OF BANK AND STATE." The majority of politicians, Democrats and Whigs, as well as virtually the entirety of large American business, would have preferred Van Buren to select either of the first two options. But as president, Van Buren mixed political pragmatism with a quiet but growing affinity for hard-money writers and radicals.[3]

William Gouge had broached the idea of an independent treasury or "sub-treasury" plan in his *History of Banking and Paper Money* in 1833. By cutting all connections with private banks and collecting and paying out its revenues in specie, he argued, the federal government could end its corrupting collaboration with private capital, rein in credit expansion by locking up most of the nation's specie, and thereby modulate the boom-and-bust cycle. Reformulated by Gouge's Philadelphia friend, the free-trade theorist Condy Raguet, the concept caught on briefly in 1835 with southern anti-BUS state-rights men, but the time was not ripe. The union leader John Windt and other former New York Working Men picked up the idea, and in July 1836, at the outset of the Specie Circular struggle, the *Evening Post* vigorously endorsed it. Thomas Hart Benton, who had first heard a rough version of the plan from John Randolph, outlined a two-stage process to the Senate in April 1836, involving removing the deposits from all banks and eventually excluding all paper money from government transactions. "The state of the paper system," Benton declared, had become "hideous and appalling, and those who [do] not mean to suffer by its catastrophe should fly from its embraces."[4]

The failures of 1837 turned the independent treasury idea into a politically practical proposal, as a substitute for the pet bank system. Gouge's energetic memoranda and pamphlets from inside the Treasury Department tried to per-suade Van Buren that the national welfare would be ruined unless the government's fiscal operations were affected "as little as possible by the doings of banks and speculators." Hard-money friends of Van Buren's, including the Loco Focos' ally Churchill Cambreleng and, from his deathbed, the venerable Old Republican Nathaniel Macon, wrote strong letters urging the president to stay the course. A freshet of polemics by Frances Wright, William Leggett, Theodore Sedgwick Jr., Theophilus Fisk, and other radicals pushed the subtreasury idea, as did public meetings in towns and cities across the country. One demonstration in Philadelphia—"projected and carried on entirely by the working classes," Henry Gilpin told Van Buren—drew an orderly but agitated crowd of twenty thousand, purportedly the largest the city had ever seen. Trade union leaders denounced the paper system, and a committee of Philadelphians soon produced a report that called for the government to cut its financial relations with the banks.[5]

Van Buren—a self-styled Jeffersonian but no radical, and protective as always of party unity—took the advice of his sober political friends more seriously than he did any Loco Foco rumblings. Only after the moderate John Brockenbrough, president of the Bank of Virginia, endorsed a watered-down version of the inde-pendent treasury as a means to liberate state banks from government regulation did Van Buren begin to rally his forces behind the idea. As it happened, Treasury Secretary Levi Woodbury had already placed a considerable portion of the fed-eral surplus in government vaults immediately after the crisis in May. (Woodbury was acting in compliance with the Deposit Act of 1836, which forbade depositing public money in banks that had suspended specie payments.) The effect was to take some of the exotic edge off the subtreasury plan. And when Van Buren prepared his version of the plan for delivery in September, he made sure to add features that pleased state bankers and might attract Conservative Democrats, including a proposal to issue new paper money in the form of federal Treasury bills. He also claimed he wanted to disentangle the economic crisis from "the passions and conflicts of party." Van Buren seemed to be on his old track, caution.[6]

To emphasize Van Buren's restraint, however, slights his growing conviction that some sort of hard-money program was required to salvage both his Jacksonian bona fides and the nation itself. Like the rest of his party, the president blamed the failures of Jackson's deposit bank policies on the irresponsible banks themselves, as well as on the obstructionist Whigs. After the panic, only a divorce of the federal treasury and the banks would suffice. Although some of his advisers counseled otherwise, Van Buren paid very close attention to Gouge, the author of the radicals' primer, as well as to close friends like Cambreleng and the Bucktail veteran and hard-money man, Benjamin F. Butler. He never sought to turn banking reform into a cover for deregulating the state banks, as some state bankers desired. Quite the opposite: by empowering managers of the subtreasury system to accumulate state bank notes and demand specie payment, Van Buren's plan promised significant regulation of all state banks, above and beyond the former pet deposit banks. Although he couched his proposals in the familiar Jeffersonian doctrines of limited government—themes that later readers, critics and admirers alike, have sometimes confused for conservative laissez-faire—Van Buren, like Jackson, took them to mean that the government should not be enlarged to serve the interests of a privileged and ambitious few. ("It is not [government's] legitimate object," he bluntly asserted, "to make men rich.")[7] Van Buren's conception of limited government did not preclude regulation for the public good, so long as government confined itself to the powers delegated by the Constitution.

Van Buren's message to a special session of Congress was lengthy but clear and direct, unburdened by the confusing verbosity that so often marred his public statements. Its stronger features included a sophisticated review of the panic's national and international origins, making points that economic historians would affirm more than a century later. The wording also displayed Van Buren's adeptness at making the dramatic sound routine, and the experimental sound like the most obvious affirmation of common sense. "[I]t is apparent that the events of the last few months," Van Buren said, calmly, "have greatly augmented the desire, long existing among the people of the United States, to separate the fiscal operations of the Government from those of individuals or corporations."

Apart from a fleeting reference to "the laboring classes," the address shunned the class-inflected bombast of Jackson's bank veto message. Compared to the soaring eloquence of Jackson's nullification proclamation, Van Buren's subtreasury message had all the moral and political fire of a bill of exchange. But it was Jacksonian in substance and uncompromising about the main issue at hand, divorcing the government from the banks.[8]

Whigs, Conservative Democrats, and the state bankers wailed, and the radical Democrats exulted. "He has identified himself wholly with the loco-focos—," the conservative *Boston Atlas* charged, "come forth a champion of the most destructive species of ultraism—and aimed at the vital interests of the country a blow, which if it [does] not recoil upon the aggressor, must be productive to the country of lasting mischief, perhaps of irretrievable anarchy." The new Conservative Democratic newspaper in Washington, the *Madisonian*, called Van Buren a convert to the wild-eyed radicalism of the original Working Men's parties. Hard-money Democratic officeholders sent letters of congratulations; Frances Wright hailed the plan as "the first practical, efficient, decisive realization of the Declaration of '76"; and the New York Loco Focos held a special meeting to congratulate the man they had distrusted for so long. Van Buren, having vindicated his self-image as a steadfast Jeffersonian, reveled in the praise and, without cutting his ties with moderates, reached out to the radicals. He sent a copy of the message to the New England Workie Theodore Sedgwick, asking for his opinion; Sedgwick replied warmly, calling it "unanswerable" and predicting that after "a great blow, a little thunder and lightning," the president would prevail. Van Buren soon befriended other radical writers and organizers, including a Free Enquirer-turned-Unitarian-turned-hard-money agitator in Boston, Orestes Brownson.[9]

The special session of Congress made quick work of approving the White House's uncontroversial relief proposals, above all a suspension of surplus distribution to the states and the issuing of ten million dollars in new Treasury notes. But the independent treasury bill sharply divided the Conservatives as well as the Whigs from the pro-administration Democrats. The *Madisonian* called the contest over the plan nothing less than "a battle between civilization and barbarism." Senator Tallmadge denounced Van Buren's effort as "a war upon the whole banking system." Although support for the administration in the Senate seemed just large enough to win approval, the House, hopelessly divided into a multitude of factions, looked like a booby-trapped battlefield.[10]

Suddenly, the wildcard of congressional politics, John C. Calhoun, commanded attention. After refusing to support either the Whigs or the Democrats in the 1836 elections, Calhoun had been thinking hard about how to strengthen his southern sectionalist political base. No longer, for the moment, a viable presidential candidate, he had subordinated his personal ambitions to defenses of slavery and nullifier doctrines—and into political maneuvering that, he hoped, would dominate the national government and sweep him back into contention for the White House. How, though, might his interests best be served in the wake of the panic? Many important southerners, like Waddy Thompson of South Carolina, had been making their peace with the Whigs, persuaded that what the wavering George McDuffie called "the wealth and intelligence of the northern and middle States" would best protect the South against the growing threat of "unbalanced Democracy" and the abolitionism that it spawned. Yet Calhoun's loathing of industrialism had led him to reject his earlier similar musings and to fear and detest northern Whiggery as a threat to the South. Sooner or later, he calculated, northern businessmen would demand high tariffs and internal improvements in exchange for any alliance with the planters.[11]

In Calhoun's view, the Democrats, now led by Jackson's second-rate sycophant Van Buren, presented better opportunities for manipulation. Calhoun would build on the earlier strategy of the pro-slavery Old Republicans: ally with northern Democrats; beat down the Yankee financiers and manufacturers; and then capture the Democracy, and the national government, for the South. And so, in October 1837, he decided not only to rejoin the Democratic Party and support the independent treasury bill but to add a tougher hard-money amendment, requiring that the Treasury accept only specie payments from state banks after 1840 and issue paper currency that would supplant bank notes. With the BUS dead, Calhoun had concluded, even before Van Buren's subtreasury message, that any formal connection between the federal government and the banks would now only augment sectional favoritism and federal consolidation. But he would take that principled conclusion an additional political step forward. Confident, he wrote, that Van Buren had been forced "to play directly into our hands," Calhoun aimed to deepen the schism between his old foe and the Conservatives, and seize the balance of power for himself and the nullifers. Van Buren, with his independent treasury, would deliver a fatal blow to his own supporters, the New York bankers, while giving the South "a fair opportunity to break the last of our commercial shackles"—and open a path to political supremacy for Calhoun and his supporters.[12]

As Tallmadge and the Conservatives would never back the subtreasury bill, pro-administration senators, commanded by the former Bucktail Silas Wright, immediately approved Calhoun's amendment, saying it was fully in line with administration policy. The amendment squeaked through; then the Senate narrowly approved the independent treasury. But the pro-treasury forces badly mismanaged things in the House, first by allowing Calhoun's foot soldier, Francis Pickens, to open debate on the bill's behalf (and deliver a harangue that, along the way, attacked Andrew Jackson and defended slavery), and then by permitting Churchill Cambreleng to mount a tactless tirade against the opposition that further alienated state bankers. The combined opposition—rallied by the Virginian Jacksonian-turned-Whig Henry A. Wise's slashing speech against the "Fanny Wright" campaign to destroy all banks—tabled the bill until the next congressional session in January.[13]

Over the next two years, the fight over the subtreasury plan polarized national politics by emboldening the Whigs, sending the Conservative Democrats into irreversible rebellion, and pushing mainstream Democrats as never before into an embrace of the party's eastern, pro-labor, hard-money wing. The subtreasury bill again passed the Senate in 1838 and early in 1839, but it failed in the House. During the second of these rematches, the Whigs and Conservatives eliminated Calhoun's specie amendment by winning over a number of regular Democrats, chiefly from the western states (where, apart from Benton and a radical minority, there was little enthusiasm for hard-money policies). Calhoun duly turned against the bill, as did Pickens and other congressional nullifiers, and the House did not even bring the measure to a vote. All the while, the Conservative *Madisonian*, no longer pretending any Democratic allegiance, carried on with its vitriolic propaganda campaign, publicizing the speeches of Wise and Clay as well as Tallmadge, and depicting Van Buren as Nero to Jackson's Caesar. Outwardly cheerful, the president began looking, to some supporters, like a used-up man, "too easy & passive & willing to let things take their own course," according to John Milton Niles of Connecticut.[14]

Thoroughly frustrated, many mainstream Democrats moved leftward, both in key eastern states like New York and Massachusetts and inside the administration. With patronage from Benjamin Butler, a new monthly, the *United States Magazine and Democratic Review*, appeared in Washington under the editorship of an energetic young radical, John L. O'Sullivan. (Dedicated to presenting the finest in American literary writing as well as political reporting, the *Review* also lashed out, in December 1838, at the "dishonest factiousness" of the subtreasury's opponents.) One hard-money radical after another was rewarded with either a federal job or a leadership post within the party—including (just before his premature death in 1839) William Leggett, his antislavery attacks forgiven, as well as Charles Douglas and the New York Loco Foco Moses Jaques. In July 1839, President Van Buren visited Manhattan (where a large portion of Tammany Hall had now embraced the radical program) and made a point of being seen mingling with the Loco Focos in their own haunts, including an evening at the Bowery Theater with Thomas Skidmore's former printer, Alexander Ming Jr., and Ming's wife. Not only the New York radicals but the entire Democratic Party now gained the nickname "Loco Foco"—a label that one meeting at Tammany Hall accepted, much as in "the brightest days of the illustrious Jefferson," the assembled declared, when the party had not objected to being called Democrats.[15]

The political costs of the Democrats' Loco Focoism—and of the effectiveness of Whig and Conservative attacks blaming the Van Buren administration for the hard times—began to become apparent in the 1837 elections. In New York, where Tallmadge and his Conservatives bolted and where Democratic Governor William Marcy, a reluctant backer of the subtreasury, remained cool to the radicals, the Whigs made stunning gains in local and statewide contests. Elsewhere, from Connecticut to Mississippi, the Whigs took command of state legislatures, committed to defending democracy and enterprise, and repealed Democratic hard-money and antibanking laws enacted over the previous two years. Hard-money loyalists were inclined to blame their losses on insufficient boldness by state leaders. ("What in hell is the difference between democratic principles this year and last year?" the New Yorker Preston King asked another hard-money Democrat, furious at Governor Marcy's vacillation.) Plainly, however, as long as the economy was depressed and the Conservative schism lasted, the Democrats' political position would continue to deteriorate—and the subtreasury plan would get nowhere.[16]

A reprieve from the economic difficulties came in part from some of the more enlightened leaders of American business—and with Nicholas Biddle once again making trouble. In midsummer 1837, bankers in New York, restive over the suspension of specie payments, proposed a general meeting to agree on practical steps toward resumption. When the gathering finally assembled in November, the delegates were divided between those like Albert Gallatin and the other New Yorkers for whom resumption was a straightforward economic necessity, and the Philadelphia and Boston delegations, led by Biddle, who wanted to continue the suspension, exploit the crisis, and demand restoration of a national bank. Biddle and his backers prevailed. The debacle of 1834 seemed to be repeating itself, with Biddle once again trying to blackmail his way to a political victory by playing havoc with the economy. New York's leading private financier Samuel Ward complained that too many bankers had become so intimidated by Biddle and scared by their apprehensions about the subtreasury that "like a frightened school boy they have become frightened of a shadow."[17]

Stymied at the national level, the New York bankers arranged for resumption of specie payments in their own state, to set an example to the rest of the nation. Biddle, as audacious as ever, issued a statement defending suspension on purely political grounds, and haughtily demanded that no general resumption begin until his Pennsylvania Bank of the United States was rechartered as a national institution. Late in June, he pressed the attack and boasted that the defeat of the independent treasury bill in the House had been "exclusively" the result of his bank's holding firm on suspension. But Biddle's latest game was nearly up. Exploiting his arrogance, the White House made overtures to other bankers, including an assurance that the Treasury would accept the notes of those institution that resumed specie payments. Because the federal and state governments were using specie as much as possible in their own transactions, gold and silver had begun reappearing in American markets. Aided by the Bank of England's shipping of one million pounds in gold to New York in the spring of 1838, arranged by Samuel Ward, it was enough to turn bankers and public alike against Biddle's proposals and resume specie payments in July.[18]

With the resumption came strong signs that the hard times were lifting, and for the ensuing fifteen months, the economic picture brightened. The Democracy's political situation duly improved. Although unable to prevent major statewide defeats in New York—including the election of William Henry Seward as governor—and significant losses in Connecticut and Mississippi, the Democrats carried six states in 1838 that they had lost the previous year, and held two others. In Massachusetts, the radical Democratic historian George Bancroft finally replaced David Henshaw as party boss, which paved the way for the election as governor, in 1839, of the perennial Democratic candidate Marcus Morton, a hard-money convert. (After a prolonged counting of the ballots, Morton was awarded exactly the number of votes required to win.) The Whigs, as expected, ran well in the congressional races nationwide in 1838, but fell short of winning their first House majority; Conservative Democrats lost ground in the House and the Democrats held the Senate.[19]

Thanks in part to some questionable dealings by Biddle's bank, enough leeway remained for Van Buren to hope that the independent treasury proposal might succeed in time for his reelection campaign in 1840. Gaining its new charter from the Pennsylvania legislature in 1836 had cost Biddle's institution nearly six million dollars, a steep price, but worth paying to survive. After the resumption of specie payments, several western state legislatures went on a borrowing binge, issuing bonds to pay for transportation improvements they expected would be serviced by future enhanced tax revenues. Biddle's bank led the way in aggressively marketing the state securities but badly overextended itself, and in 1839, when Biddle's and other institutions failed to meet their obligations to the borrowing states, the boom collapsed, forcing banks to close and nine states to default on their debts. Behind that disruption were additional dubious moves. Prior to the suspension of specie payments in 1837, Biddle borrowed heavily in Europe to try to corner the cotton market—just before cotton prices collapsed. Forced to draw on Pennsylvania Bank's credit until it completely evaporated, Biddle was suspected, in the spring of 1838, of attempting to raid the New York money market, which prompted Samuel Ward to negotiate the massive loan of bullion from the Bank of England. In ill health, Biddle resigned the bank's presidency in March 1839, but his successors continued his perilous policies. In early autumn, renewed financial difficulties prompted British banks to call in specie payments from the United States once again. The BUS was the first to resuspend specie payments on October 9, which sparked the rapid collapse of banks and the government defaults throughout the South and West. The latest panic plunged the nation into another, far deeper economic depression.[20]

The second collapse would in time further damage Van Buren's public standing. In the short term, however, the BUS's perceived role as the trigger for the latest crisis had a very different effect, reminding the public of Biddle's counterattacks of 1834 and his obstructionism after the bank crisis in 1837. "In every respect," the wizened ex-Biddle supporter Albert Gallatin, now in his late seventies, would say of Biddle's operation, "it has been a public nuisance . . . the principal, if not the sole, cause of the delay in resuming and of subsequent suspensions." Biddle's disgrace linked Van Buren once again in the public imagination with the hero of the Bank War, Andrew Jackson. More generally the collapse of 1839, which could not be blamed on the Specie Circular or any other government action, bolstered the Jacksonians' contentions that the paper-fueled banking system was fundamentally unsound.[21]

Despite the political turmoil and divisions that had hampered Van Buren during his first two years as president, the shift in public opinion gave renewed hope to the hard-money supporters of the subtreasury. But the fate of Van Buren's brand of Loco Focoism also depended on more tangled political realities in Washington. Above all, the White House was anxious over how Calhoun, his firebrand followers, and the other southerners in Congress would react. And events outside Congress, connected with slavery, would ensure that those reactions, along with Van Buren's political strategy, depended on much more than specie flows and the ups and downs of wholesale commodity prices.

Since the mid-1830s, continued agitation by the American Anti-Slavery Society and other northern abolitionists had hardened pro-slavery sentiments in the South. The tabling of abolitionist petitions to Congress under the gag rule did not calm the situation as Van Buren and other Democratic leaders had hoped it would. Once Calhoun had decided, in 1837, to return to the Democratic Party, pressure intensified on Van Buren to mollify him, along with the milder southern Democrats, over slavery. And in trying as hard as he did to calm the South, Van Buren handed fresh ammunition to antislavery northern Whigs, abolitionist radicals, and even some hard-money radical Democrats who were already offended by his friendliness to the slaveholders, and by his willingness to restrict Americans' rights to speak freely about slavery. The effect, ironically, was to reinvigorate an antislavery movement that was facing its own crisis.

ABOLITIONISM'S RECKONING

On April 28, 1836, in St. Louis, Francis McIntosh, a free black riverboat worker, was arrested and jailed on charges that he had killed a deputy sheriff and injured a second. A mob gathered, removed McIntosh from his cell, chained him to a large tree at the outskirts of town, and burned him to death. A grand jury was quickly impaneled, but on instructions of the presiding judge, one Luke E. Lawless, the jurors indicted no one. Near the end of his prepared remarks, Judge Lawless insinuated that the dead black McIntosh had been influenced by abolitionist doctrines, as "indicated by his peculiar language and demeanor," and he held up and read from a local antislavery newspaper, the St. Louis Observer, to prove his point. Lawless's words incited violence. On July 21, a large crowd smashed into the Observer's office, destroyed hundreds of dollars' worth of printing materials, and threw the pieces into the Mississippi River. The paper's editor, a thirty-two-year-old former seminarian named Elijah Lovejoy, immediately quit St. Louis but reestablished his operation in the town of Alton, across the river in the free state of Illinois.[22]

Lovejoy, a native of rural Maine, had come to the antislavery cause through his deep religious convictions. Raised in a devout household with his younger brother Owen (who would also become an abolitionist leader), he graduated first in his class from the Baptists' Waterville College, then traveled to St. Louis, where he established a school and became the copublisher of an anti-Jackson newspaper and a Sabbatarian reform activist. After having an intense religious experience in 1832, he returned East to complete ministerial training at the Theological Seminary of Princeton (later the Princeton Theological Seminary), the leading Presbyterian institution in the country. Then, in 1835, he doubled back to St. Louis to accept positions as Presbyterian pastor and editor of the Observer. Only peripherally perturbed by slavery, Lovejoy made his mark with slashing attacks on Roman Catholicism, and earned a deserved local reputation for religious bigotry. But living amid slavery in Missouri also stirred his conscience, and over the winter of 1835–36, he devoted increasing space in the Observer to antislavery articles and editorials. Lovejoy was not a Garrisonian immediatist, but the white citizens of St. Louis did not bother with fine distinctions and began hounding him as a promoter, in one vigilante committee's words, of "insurrection and anarchy, and ultimately, a disseverment of our prosperous Union."[23]

After moving to Alton, Lovejoy vowed that his new Alton Observer would chiefly discuss religious matters. Although they lived without slavery, Alton's white citizenry, typical of central and southern Illinois, despised abolitionist agitation. Yet gradually Lovejoy expanded both his antislavery editorializing and his antislavery activism, aided by his typesetter, a self-taught black, John Anderson, who had moved from St. Louis to Alton when he learned Lovejoy had relocated there. In mid-August 1837, Lovejoy signed a petition calling for a meeting in October in one of Alton's Presbyterian churches to organize a state antislavery society. Local anti-abolitionists, believing Lovejoy had betrayed them, mobbed and destroyed his press; Lovejoy obtained a new one, but another mob destroyed it before it could be removed from its crates. When the antislavery delegates finally met in Alton in October, they arranged for the delivery of yet another press, courtesy of the Ohio Anti-Slavery Society. In an impassioned speech before a hastily organized public meeting, Edward Beecher, son of the renowned Lyman Beecher, denied Lovejoy had any intention to harm the community, and insisted only on his American rights to "free discussion." But taking no chances, and lacking protection from town authorities, Lovejoy joined an ad hoc militia to protect himself and his new press once it arrived.[24]

As expected, a mob turned out and threw rocks and brickbats at the warehouse where the new press was sent. One rioter attempted to torch the warehouse's roof; a group of Lovejoy's defenders ran out of the building and fired shots into the crowd; one of the mob fell, mortally wounded. Berserk, the crowd advanced, and the incendiary climbed back up his ladder to the roof. Lovejoy stepped outside and aimed his pistol at the arsonist, but five shots instantly hit the editor in the chest. He managed to stagger back to the warehouse, where he quickly crumpled and died. The mob then completed what it had come to do, routing Lovejoy's small band and destroying the accursed antislavery machine.[25]

Elijah Lovejoy's martyrdom, the first murder of a white antislavery leader, shocked and emboldened the growing abolitionist movement, but its implications were much broader. For years, abolitionist meetings and speakers had been subject to physical attack. The abolitionist mails controversy and the congressional gag rule had raised charges that the South was trying to muzzle its critics. Yet never before had the issue of free speech arisen so dramatically. Lovejoy was, after all, an ordained minister. His major offense, prior to his appearance in Alton, had been to criticize a lawless lynching—and a lawless judge named Lawless who insisted on letting the lynchers go free. If Reverend Lovejoy's rights could be extinguished with impunity, and on pain of death, whose rights were then safe? Theodore Dwight Weld hammered the point home in an angry eulogy to Lovejoy:

> The empty name [of freedom] is everywhere,—*free* government, *free* men, *free* speech, *free* people, *free* schools, and *free* churches. Hollow counterfeits, all! FREE! It is the climax of irony, and its million echoes are hisses and jeers, even from the earth's ends. FREE! *Blot it out*. Words are the signs of *things*. The substance has gone! Let fools and madmen clutch at shadows.

What had begun in efforts to silence incendiary black agitators like David Walker and their white admirers like William Lloyd Garrison now looked like a lethal campaign to curtail free speech.[26]

The renewed repression had contradictory effects on the abolitionist movement. Anti-abolitionist violence evoked public sympathy in the North, as did the growing impression that southern officials, supported by pliable northern Democrats, were violating constitutionally protected freedoms. Those perceptions fed antisouthern feelings, which in turn helped spike the membership of abolitionist societies in 1837 and 1838. Yet the unremitting anti-abolitionist reaction and Congress's obduracy were also discouraging. By the time Elijah Lovejoy was given a hero's funeral in Alton, the American Anti-Slavery Society had been hard at work for nearly four years but had failed to free a single slave. No practical reform of the nation's laws seemed imminent. The only major constitutional change in the North coincided with the abolitionist efforts came in Pennsylvania in 1837–38, when a Democratic-dominated state constitutional convention eliminated voting rights for black men. The presidential election of 1836 offered no grounds for optimism. In the mainline northern Protestant churches, anti-abolitionists still prevailed, and even among evangelicals, abolitionists were in the minority. Among veteran field representatives and traveling speakers, the surge of rededication that followed the Lovejoy murder could not stem mounting frustration coupled with fatigue. The economic hardships after the Panic of 1837 drained the movement of vital funds as well as self-confidence.[27]

Philosophical divisions also plagued the AA-SS. Especially troublesome was the growing breach between, on one side, Garrison and his loyalists and, on the other, the society's evangelical funders and managers, led by Lewis and Arthur Tappan. The evangelicals had never felt entirely comfortable with abolitionism's symbolic leader. Although he had been raised a Baptist and spoke of sin and Christian ethics, Garrison had never joined a church or experienced a religious conversion. In the fall of 1836, Lewis Tappan arranged for Garrison and his family to travel to New York, all expenses paid, to attend a three-week training session for AA-SS agents, where they could talk over the state of the movement. Garrison hoped to persuade Tappan that he was not some "great stumbling-block" to the cause, and Tappan was reminded how much he liked and admired Garrison. Tappan was distressed to hear, however, that his guest now abjured family prayer and church attendance, and that he believed the regular clergy was spiritually useless.[28]

In the spring of 1837, Garrison took an even larger step away from the Tappans and toward the unorthodox netherworld of religious perfectionism when he became, briefly, a disciple of John Humphrey Noyes. A former student of Yale's Nathaniel Taylor, Noyes was one of thousands of northerners gripped by the Second Great Awakening whose spiritual journeys took them outside all orthodoxies and into a world of complete free will and total deliverance from sin. The perfectionists were particularly ubiquitous in New York's Burned-Over District. (Noyes eventually made Oneida his headquarters.) For Noyes, spiritual deliverance involved, among other practices, the downing of gin drinks in search of what he called "Gospel liberty," as well as a polygamous sexual arrangement that he called "complex marriage." Garrison accepted none of that, but he was captivated by Noyes's belief that sinful America would be destroyed by the Bible, once Americans renounced all of their corrupted institutions, including the federal government. This so-called come-outer impulse (based on the book of Revelation's command to sinners to "come out" of Babylon) brooked no compromise with sin, nor any connection with ungodly institutions. Garrison, impressed by Noyes's pacifism as well as his perfectionism, was soon reprinting one of Noyes's slogans in the *Liberator*: "*My hope of the millennium begins where Dr. Beecher's expires—viz*, AT THE OVERTHROW OF THIS NATION."[29]

Garrison's newfound apocalyptic anti-institutionalism fused well with his already highly developed sense of moral absolutism and caused increased consternation in antislavery's ranks, as when he criticized the murdered Elijah Lovejoy for raising a small armed militia. (Although Lovejoy, Garrison allowed, "was certainly a martyr—strictly speaking—he was not . . . a Christian martyr.") But the truly important shift concerned what came to be known as "the woman question." Beginning with Lucretia Mott's insistent interventions at the founding convention of the AA-SS, women had always played a large role in the everyday life of the movement, especially as organizers of petition campaigns. Garrison took particular care to include the voices of women, black and white, in the *Liberator*, including the formidable black orator and organizer Maria Stewart. But the idea that women should have a role as speakers on behalf of the AA-SS, let alone help govern the movement outside of their own separate organizations, was disturbing to some in the mainline and evangelical antislavery leadership and anathema to others.[30]

Ignoring complaints that he was promoting "Fanny Wright" heresies, Garrison strongly encouraged the women's work, above all the writings and speeches of Angelina and Sarah Grimké, South Carolina sisters who had moved north, converted to Quakerism, and joined the immediatist cause with Garrison as their mentor. By 1837, Garrison had added women's rights and pacifist nonresistance to the *Liberator* group's agenda for radical reform—a step the movement's conventional evangelicals denounced as at once a distraction from the movement's overriding cause and an endorsement of what one minister called "unnatural" presumptions about the sexes. Convinced that Garrison was injecting an impious "speculative antinomianism" into antislavery, Lewis Tappan and his allies braced themselves for a showdown over control of the AA-SS.[31]

The Garrisonian fracture was not the only source of disunity. Although black abolitionists remained loyal to the AA-SS, blacks' failure in general to rise higher than the ranks of the group's secondary leadership, and their feelings that the whites (except for Garrison) were patronizing them, caused constant tension. Among the AA-SS leaders, meanwhile, a battle was brewing between what might be called the moralist and the political factions—those who wanted the movement to adhere strictly to moral suasion and those who believed it was time to participate actively in mainstream electoral politics. Garrison and the come-outers would, of course, steer clear of immoral institutionalized politics; so would the Tappanite evangelicals, with their high-minded attachment to converting souls through moral argument. Yet by 1839, a growing minority of immediatist leaders was pushing for new experiments in political abolition. They included a major funder of the cause, Gerrit Smith, as well as the movement veterans Henry B. Stanton, James G. Birney, Alvan Stewart, Elizur Wright, and Joshua Leavitt. To ignore the electoral franchise, Birney charged, was "inconsistent with the duty of abolitionists under the constitution."[32]

While the abolitionists sorted out their differences, the focus of antislavery attention shifted to Washington—and to the persistent parliamentary attack on the gag rule undertaken by a small group of northern congressman led by the aging but feisty John Quincy Adams. Deeply depressed after his defeat by Jackson in 1828, Adams had recovered by indulging his appetite for political maneuvering, and in 1830, at the urging of his fellow National Republicans and with the support of the burgeoning Anti-Mason movement, he won a seat in Congress in a landslide. ("My election as President of the United States," he wrote in his diary, "was not half so gratifying to my inmost soul.") Thereafter, propelled in part by political calculation, in part by his liberal piety, and in part by his dislike of Henry Clay—whom he now regarded as imperious and untrustworthy—Adams became, in his own words, a "zealous Antimason."[33]

Anti-Masonry permitted Adams to find a political home free of the three groups whom he blamed for his own political woes and the nation's: old-line New England Federalists, especially in Boston (many Masons among them), who had regarded him as a traitor ever since he supported Thomas Jefferson's embargo; pro-Jackson slaveholders and their northern sympathizers (many Masons among them), who had turned him out of the presidency; and his long-time rivals for the leadership of the National Republicans, chief among them the Mason Henry Clay. Anti-Masonry fed Adams's distaste for political parties as corrupt vehicles for personal ambition. It also put him in contact with a kind of popular politics he had never before experienced—a democratic movement that, though commanded by political operatives such as Thurlow Weed, had been initiated by poor and middling farmers against the rich and privileged, and retained its demotic character. Adams described his involvement in the movement in some unintentionally amusing passages in his diary, including one relating his arrival in Boston by chaise from Quincy to attend an Anti-Mason convention in 1831—where he found that "of the aristocracy, not one" was present. It was not the sort of meeting the Massachusetts mandarin was used to attending, and it gave him a taste for the way, with tempered ardor, that ordinary men could influence politics for the better.[34]

By 1835, however, political Anti-Masonry was on its last legs, a victim of its own success once New England legislatures restricted the giving and taking of Masonic oaths and lodge membership plummeted. In Massachusetts, Daniel Webster reigned supreme over the new Whig Party, and when Webster crushed an Anti-Mason effort to elevate Adams to the Senate, some of Adams's supporters, including his son Charles Francis Adams, urged him to back Van Buren instead of Webster for the presidency. Unable to support Jackson's loyal successor, Adams remained neutral in 1836. Thereafter, realizing that Anti-Masonry had no political future, he, like most of his fellow Anti-Masons, joined the Whigs. Yet if he was a Whig in name, Adams had no intention of becoming a party man, or abandoning his reputation, enhanced with age, as a splendidly independent figure, now known (sometimes admiringly, sometimes ironically) as "Old Man Eloquent." He would take, as his special mission, overturning the gag rule.[35]

Prior to the 1830s, Adams had publicly displayed no desire to defend, let alone promote, the antislavery cause. His parents, and especially his mother, Abigail, had passed along to him their antislavery views. In 1820, during the debates over the Missouri crisis, Adams had some fascinating conversations with John C. Calhoun, after which he remarked in his diary on the perversity and hypocrisy of the slaveholders and noted that "[i]f the Union must be dissolved, slavery is precisely the question upon which it ought to break." Yet Adams, the nationalist, quietly endorsed the Missouri Compromise, adding to a long public record of seeming indifference on slavery and its spread. Nor did Adams think highly of the radical abolitionists, least of all Garrison and the Tappans, whom he regarded as fanatics. In 1831, Adams did obligingly present to the House fifteen petitions asking for the abolition of slavery and the slave trade in Washington. He also refrained from joining the anti-abolitionist chorus of Democrats and Whigs, and privately declared himself pleased that developments were "tending to universal emancipation." But as late as October 1835, Adams assured his constituents that he had no intention of getting mixed up in what he called the "Slave and Abolition whirligig." When new parcels of abolitionist petitions arrived in Washington in 1836, Adams berated the immediatists for engaging in tactics that would never win over a majority in the North and would only enrage the South.[36]

The gag rule, coming so soon after the abolitionist mails controversy, changed everything. Both J. H. Hammond's proposal and Henry Pinckney's milder one to disregard abolitionist petitions struck Adams as fundamental violations of Americans' rights and an effort by southern congressmen to turn the House into their own private debating society. During the closing arguments over the Pinckney resolution, Adams rose to explain his opposition, but before he could proceed, southerners including Henry Wise blocked him with demands to call the question. "Am I gagged or not?" Adams asked, thereby giving the resolution its name.[37]

Adams had only begun to fight. With the help of a handful of former Anti-Mason Whigs, he launched a hit-and-run campaign against the gag rule, trying to tie up the House in order to reopen debate over the matter. Careful never to say whether he thought slavery ought to be abolished, Adams rose on the floor virtually every day, always with a fresh abolitionist petition in hand, asking whether it fell under the gag rule's ban. He outdid himself on February 6, 1837, when he presented a petition signed by twenty-two persons "declaring themselves to be slaves." Waddy Thompson (earlier Ely Moore's antagonist) jumped to his feet, ripped into the Massachusetts madman, and proposed censuring Adams severely for his "gross disrespect to the House." It was bad enough for any Yankee to treat a petition from slaves as if slaves were citizens; even worse, from Thompson's perspective, the miscreant was a member of his own party, whose stunt reinforced southern Democratic claims that the Whigs were unreliable on slavery. "The sanctuary of age is not lightly to be violated," Thompson exclaimed, "but when that sanctuary is used to throw poisoned arrows, it ceases to be sacred."[38]

Other infuriated southerners lined up to pummel Adams verbally, charging him with inciting a slave insurrection and demanding that he at long last be censured. Then Adams sprung his trap—for the slaves' petition, he now told his colleagues, was actually a request by the petitioners that they continue to be held as slaves. Did an effort to help slaves stay bondsmen deserve censure? Adams asked sardonically. Chuckles rippled through the House. Thompson, embarrassed, denounced Adams anew for trying to turn his baiting of the South into a light amusement. Two more days of speeches followed. In his final address, Adams went in for the kill. Alluding to a threat by Thompson to have him indicted as an incendiary by a grand jury in Washington, he bid Thompson to educate himself about civil liberty, and asked him whether a congressman should be indicted, let alone censured, merely for presenting a petition. "If that, sir, is the law of South Carolina," he cuttingly observed, "I thank God I am not a citizen of South Carolina."[39]

Adams might as well have set off a bomb. (The transcript in the *Register of Debates* notes that "general agitation" followed his remark.) Not only had he made a laughingstock of the proud militant Thompson; not only had he made a mockery of the gag rule—Adams had focused the attention of the entire House on the slaveholders' willingness to limit free speech whenever, and wherever, they chose. A resolution condemning all House members who would present any petition from slaves then failed by a margin of 105 to 92, after which

Thompson's effort to censure Adams went down to a greater defeat, with even Henry F. Pinckney voting against the motion. The pro–gag rule coalition reasserted itself very quickly, to be sure. In December 1837 and at the same time next year, the House endorsed gag orders similar to Pinckney's original, with northern Democrats once again lining up to support their southern counterparts, and northern Whigs standing in opposition. But for a moment, John Quincy Adams had blasted apart the gentlemen's agreement to keep the slavery issue out of national debates.[40]

Two years later, the legal and political fallout from a shipboard rebellion by captive blacks brought Adams back to the center of antislavery politics, this time at the Supreme Court instead of the House, and in much closer connection with the abolitionists. On July 1, 1839, members of a cargo of fifty-three Africans (most of them from the Mende tribe) who were being held aboard the schooner *Amistad*, sailing from Havana, suddenly took over the ship, killing the captain and the cook. Most of the rebels had originally been part of a coffle of six hundred, shipped illegally from Lomboko on the west coast of Africa to Cuba. Bought by two speculators named Ruiz and Montes in Havana, they had been bound for the sugar plantations of Guanaja, on the other side of the island, when, under the leadership of a powerfully built man in his midtwenties named Sengbe Pieh (translated by one of the Spaniards as José Cinque), they slipped their chains.

Using as navigators Ruiz and Montes, whose lives they had spared, the rebels tried to change course for Africa. Sailing eastward by day but steered by the Spaniards at night in the opposite direction, the *Amistad* zigzagged around the Bahamas and farther northward. In late August, their supplies exhausted, the rebels caught sight of land and anchored the schooner at what turned out to be Culloden Point, just north of the settlement of Montauk on the eastern tip of Long Island. An American coast guard survey cutter spotted the ship, arrested the Africans, and towed the *Amistad* to New London, where U.S. District Judge Andrew Judson, a Democrat, ordered that the captives be tried in circuit court on charges of murder, mutiny, and piracy. Of the fifty-three Africans who had set out from Cuba, only forty-two had survived the mutiny and the haphazard trip north.[41]

As soon as he learned of the arrests, Lewis Tappan enlisted Joshua Leavitt and Simeon Jocelyn in a Friends of the Amistad Africans Committee, to extend what aid they could to the captives. Here was a cause, Tappan recognized, that could bolster the flagging immediatist movement by patching up the widening differences between moralists like himself and politicals like Leavitt, while also offering to the public a stirring example of the oppression of Africans. On September 6, Tappan visited the prisoners in their jail cells—"[t]heir demeanor is altogether quiet, kind, and orderly," he wrote—and, true to form, gave them a quick sermon on Providence that they had no way to comprehend. Undaunted, Tappan hired a group of Yale students to attend to the Africans' spiritual needs, and located, on the New York City docks, a cabin boy from a British African patrol ship who understood Mende dialect and could act as translator. Tappan also hired a team of three talented antislavery attorneys to work on freeing the Africans—the chief lawyer, Connecticut Whig Roger Sherman Baldwin, scion of two distinguished old Federalist families; Seth Staples from New York, an abolitionist who had founded the legal academy that would become the basis for Yale Law School; and, also from New York, the lawyer and editor Theodore Sedgwick III, an out-spoken hard-money Democrat, son of the Massachusetts class traitor and pro-Jackson radical Theodore Sedgwick Jr., and longtime colleague and friend of William Leggett.[42]

Together with Tappan and his committee, the legal team covered the political spectrum from evangelical radicalism to Whig respectability to hard-money Loco Focoism. To solidify that coalition, Tappan kept the Amistad committee's operations completely separate from those of the AA-SS, with its taint of antislav-ery extremism. Knowing that the facts of the case would speak for themselves, Tappan was able to gain broad public sympathy with a minimum of abolitionist rhetoric. Wealthy notables who normally shook their heads in dismay at the abo-litionists could feel a surge of liberal nobility in opening their hearts (and their purses) to help the wretched Africans. Ordinary northerners could feel sincere sympathy for the captives—and fury for the complacent federal officials who had jailed them. "Such base fraudulence—such *blood-hound* persecutions of poor defenceless strangers cast upon our shores," one Ohioan wrote to Tappan.[43]

International politics also loomed large at the Africans' trial. The Spanish gov-ernment insisted that, under existing treaty provisions, the United States had no right to try a case involving Spanish subjects only, arising from events that occurred on a Spanish ship on the open seas. Spain demanded the captives be summarily released to Spanish authorities in Cuba. President Van Buren and his cabinet basically agreed with the Spanish position, and but for the abolitionists' intervention might well have handed over the captives. But with his reelection campaign nearing, and the abolitionists making trouble, the president was eager not to appear to be giving in to a foreign power and abrogating due process, lest the affair inflame northern opinion. His secretary of state, John Forsyth, instructed the U.S. district attorney in Connecticut, a loyal Jacksonian named William Holabird, to take care that the Africans remain formally under the con-trol of the federal executive—but the abolitionists also got the hearing they wanted. Although Van Buren was fully prepared to return the captives to Cuba on his own, he hoped and expected that the courts would order him to do so, relieving him of political pressure.[44]

The legal arguments advanced by Baldwin, Staples, and Sedgwick sufficiently impressed Van Buren that in time he would order the State Department to release all its relevant documents on the case to the defense. But Secretary of State Forsyth, a Georgia slaveholder and state-rights extremist, was deeply involved in the case against the Africans, and he pressed hard for their conviction. After the circuit court, meeting in Hartford, ruled it lacked jurisdiction in the case, U.S. District Judge Judson ordered a new hearing, in his own court, to settle the Spaniards' outstanding property claims. Judson had overseen a high-profile conviction of the Connecticut abolitionist and schoolteacher Prudence Crandall six years earlier, and there was every reason to expect that he would be just as hostile to the abolitionists now. Forsyth assured the Spanish ambassador that the administration would immediately return the rebels once the federal district court had ruled.[45]

The trial to decide the captives' status commenced in New Haven, after a postponement, in January 1840, and turned on the testimony of Dr. Richard R. Madden, the British Commissioner of the Anglo-Spanish board in Havana in charge of suppressing the slave trade. Madden had volunteered his services to help the Africans, and in a sworn statement completed in November, he asserted that, according to Spanish treaty agreements with Great Britain, the captured Africans were not slaves but illegal immigrants who now had to be returned to their homelands. Ruiz and Montes had produced transportation passports with the captives' names in Spanish, seeming to show that they were actually Spanish subjects and slaves, but Madden proved that the documents were forgeries. U.S. Attorney Holabird tried to discredit Madden's testimony, both at the original deposition and at the rescheduled proceedings in January, but succeeded only in bearing out Madden's claims.[46]

While the trial was still in progress, President Van Buren, still confident of the outcome, assented to a secret executive order commanding the federal marshal, as soon as the proceedings ended, to deliver the prisoners to the schooner USS *Grampus*, which Secretary of the Navy James K. Paulding had directed to stand by in New Haven. As the abolitionists firmly and correctly suspected, the *Grampus* would whisk the Africans to Havana, and almost certain death, before their attorneys could file any appeal. But Judge Judson defied expectations by accepting the closing arguments of Baldwin and Sedgwick and ordering that the Africans be delivered back to Africa. "Bloody as may be their hands," he concluded, "they shall yet embrace their kindred."[47]

Van Buren was embarrassed by Judson's ruling—and would be all the more embarrassed over the coming weeks as word leaked out about his secret order, which allowed unfriendly northern newspapers to denounce him as a court-tampering tyrant, guilty of a "heartless violation of the inalienable rights of man." By declining to submit summarily to Spain's demands over the *Amistad* and placing the matter in the courts, Van Buren may have thought he had successfully checked the controversy. But Tappan and the abolitionists, by turning the case into a national cause, placed him in an awkward position: if he failed to do his utmost to secure the blacks' conviction, and if they were left unpunished, he would appear to be condoning slave insurrection—which would have ruined what chances he still had for reelection. The center would not hold: Van Buren, by intervening in the case as he did, looked as if he had gone out of his way to win over the southern slaveholders, which alienated northern opinion; and the pro-abolitionist *Amistad* decision strengthened the political hand of pro-slavery southerners led by Van Buren's nemesis, John C. Calhoun.[48]

Calhoun, unsatisfied by what he considered Pinckney's weak-kneed gag resolution, had worked tirelessly since rejoining the Democrats to push the party into toughening its stance against antislavery agitation. At the end of December 1837, he tendered to the Senate six resolutions aimed at protecting southern slavery. The first four restated Calhoun's version of the compact theory of the Constitution (contending that the individual states retained absolute sovereignty) and declared that all "open and systematic attacks" on slavery violated the spirit of that compact. All four passed by large margins. The fifth resolution, declaring the undesirability of any congressional effort to legislate on slavery in the District of Columbia or the territories, passed in amended form. Only the sixth resolution, declaring that any effort to prevent the annexation of new states or territories over the slavery issue would violate the rights of the slaveholding states, was tabled, mainly because the point was already pending in a resolution before the Senate calling for the annexation of Texas. Pro-administration Democrats were happy to approve what the Conservative Senator Rives mocked as "the *abstractions* invoked in Mr. Calhoun's resolutions" if it meant preserving party unity. But it came at the cost of appearing to follow Calhoun wherever he led them in order to protect President Van Buren—a man southern Democrats had begun to laud (and antislavery northerners begun to ridicule) as "a northern man with southern feelings."[49]

And still Calhoun would not stop. After withdrawing his support for the independent treasury bill early in 1839, he consolidated his political command in South Carolina while wasting no opportunity to show off his growing mastery of the national scene. In December 1839, the Calhounites in the House brusquely broke with the Democrats and helped elect as Speaker the Virginian R. M. T. Hunter—a nominal Whig who supported the subtreasury idea but was also a strong supporter of Calhoun's. Soon thereafter, intermediaries arranged for Calhoun to pay a formal visit to Van Buren at the White House—the two had not spoken to each other in eight years—and an icy truce was arranged. But there was never much faith that the truce would last, at least from Calhoun's end. The outcome of the *Amistad* trial seemed custom-made as a pretext for Calhoun to inflame sectional antagonisms anew, especially after he denounced how the

British had meddled in the affair and proposed Senate resolutions designed to deny rebel slaves on foreign ships any future protection from American courts.[50]

Calhoun and his allies were not the only Democrats about whom Van Buren had reason to worry in connection with the slavery issue and the *Amistad* affair. In the aftermath of the gag rule controversy, Van Buren's efforts at compromise had also alienated antislavery opinion within the eastern radical Democracy. Some northern labor leaders and hard-money advocates, notably Ely Moore, stood by the administration and denounced the abolitionist petition drives. A tiny number, most conspicuously Theophilus Fisk, went even further to praise racial slavery as a much kinder system for degraded blacks than wage labor was for whites. Many of the antislavery radicals—including Frances Wright, Robert Dale Owen, and others—temporarily subdued their attachments to the antislavery Paineite tradition in order to preserve unity against what they considered the greatest immediate danger, pro-bank Whiggery. Yet the presence of Theodore Sedgwick III on the *Amistad* defense team was one sign of the growing antislavery commitments in some radical Democratic circles. The acidulous editorials of William Leggett—whose attack on what he called Van Buren's truckling to the slaveholders in his inauguration address and whose declaration that he was an abolitionist had temporarily made him a pariah with party leaders—represented another. The Massachusetts self-described radical Democrat Marcus Morton, shortly after his election as governor, pronounced slavery "the greatest curse and most portentous evil which a righteous God ever inflicted upon a nation." In Washington, the leading hard-money Jacksonian Senator Thomas Morris of Ohio was the only senator, of either party, openly to denounce the gag rule and defend the abolitionists—a courageous stance that would cost him renomination and his good standing inside the Ohio Democracy. On the Senate floor, Morris popularized a phrase that would later resound in antislavery politics—"the slave power," by which he meant the tightening alliance between southern planters and northern pro-bank Whigs, "both looking to the same object—to live upon the unrequited labor of others."[51]

The Van Buren White House, preoccupied with the *Amistad* controversy, reasonably regarded the slaveholders as the greater immediate threat to its own self-preservation. Accordingly, the president, through Forsyth, directed U.S. Attorney Holabird to appeal Judge Judson's opinion, with the idea of sending it almost directly to the U.S. Supreme Court. Tappan, his committee, and the Africans were deeply disappointed. But as the court hearing date neared, yet another stroke of inspiration hit—that of adding Old Man Eloquent, John Quincy Adams, to the legal staff.[52]

Adams had already been aroused by the *Amistad* story. Shortly after Judge Judson's first ruling, he wrote a public letter defending the Africans' uprising to secure their "natural right to liberty," and lamenting the lack of compassion and

justice displayed by most federal officials. Adams had also helped the Friends of
the Amistad committee obtain State Department correspondence relevant to the
case. Although he would add little to the legal expertise of Baldwin and his associates, Tappan wrote, "his station, age, character, &c &c will give an importance
to his services in this cause not to be overlooked." Adams hesitated at first, still
wary of the abolitionists, but his outrage at the government's decision to appeal to
the Supreme Court overcame his misgivings, and he threw himself into studying
up on the case. Opening arguments were scheduled for February 22, Washington's Birthday—only ten days before either Martin Van Buren or his opponent in
the autumn election would be sworn in as president.[53]

Successful as he was in galvanizing opinion over the *Amistad* matter, Lewis
Tappan was having much greater difficulty holding together the AA-SS and the
larger radical abolitionist movement. At the society's annual convention in 1839,
the Garrisonians defeated efforts to condemn nonresistance and won the right of
women to vote. All through late 1839 and early 1840, Tappan, discouraged but
adamant, began laying the groundwork for a new antislavery organization. The
final showdown came at the AA-SS convention in New York in May 1840, when
the Garrisonians tried to elect the impressive come-outer woman Abby Kelley to
the group's business committee. Although the woman question was the trigger,
Tappan told Theodore Dwight Weld, the real battle was over what he called Garrison's wish to "make an experiment upon the public" by adding numerous new
radical reforms to the abolitionists' agenda. Amid jeering, cheering, and considerable plotting, the Garrison faction managed to elect Kelley, whereupon Tappan
and his men walked out and formed their own American & Foreign Anti-Slavery
Society. The breach had become a schism.[54]

Simultaneously, the tiny band of political abolitionists mistrusted by both
Tappan and Garrison had begun getting somewhere. The AA-SS had endorsed
certain kinds of political as well as moral action against slavery, as early as Garrison's original Declaration of Principles in 1833. Occasionally, immediatists had
backed a particular candidate whom they viewed as sufficiently stalwart, most
notably in 1834 when Garrison backed and voted for the Massachusetts abolitionist Democrat Amasa Walker in his unsuccessful race for Congress. But
before 1840, antislavery political activists largely confined themselves to circulating questionnaires among candidates, challenging them to take sides on the slavery issue, and vowing to vote for no one deemed unsuitable. Not surprisingly, the
tactic was ineffective. Abolitionist sympathizers held the balance of power in very
few places, and most party nominees, with no interest in being linked in any way
to the antislavery extremists, simply disregarded the circulars. Pushed by Garrison's deepening perfectionism, and by the disappointing results of 1836, the
hardcore immediatists became even less enamored of electoral politics with the
approach of the 1840 presidential elections—a contest in which no national can-

didate would be even remotely acceptable to them. Yet to a minority within the movement, the dire situation made it seem all the more urgent that they nominate candidates of their own.[55]

In January 1839, James G. Birney and Henry B. Stanton tried unsuccessfully to persuade the Massachusetts Anti-Slavery Society to reject Garrisonian nonresistance and take up direct political action. But the wrangling continued at abolitionist meetings and conventions across the North. In a series of small gatherings in 1839, Myron Holley of Rochester, the former head of the New York Anti-Mason Party, tried to coax AA-SS members into making independent nominations for 1840. In November, Holley and his allies held a convention in Warsaw, New York, and nominated Birney for president on a ticket with Francis Julius LeMoyne, the president of a small college in Pennsylvania. The effort flopped: both Birney and LeMoyne declined their nominations, and antislavery societies passed resolutions rejecting the entire enterprise. The following April, however, Holley, now with the backing of Gerrit Smith, assembled more than one hundred delegates in Albany, New York. The group renominated Birney (who, this time, accepted) but with a different running mate, a well-known Loco Foco Jacksonian abolitionist editor from Pennsylvania, Thomas Earle. With only four months left in the campaign, the political abolitionists began stumping under a variety of names, including one apparently invented by Gerrit Smith, the Liberty Party. While the Garrisonians fumed and the Tappans prepared for the denouement of the *Amistad* affair, the first political party expressly dedicated to eliminating slavery began testing the limits of American democracy.[56]

ANXIETY AMONG THE DEMOCRATS

One month after the political abolitionists named their national candidates, troubled delegates gathered at the Democratic presidential convention in Baltimore. The unanimous renomination of Martin Van Buren was a foregone conclusion, but there were bitter divisions in the ranks over whether to keep the clumsy, ungenteel Vice President Richard Johnson on the ticket. The eastern radicals still claimed the anti-Sabbatarian, hard-money man Johnson as their hero, and Van Buren wanted to keep him as well. But southern distaste over Johnson's combined sexual and racial improprieties had worsened since 1836, amid talk that he had entered into yet another illicit liaison with a mulatto woman, aged eighteen or nineteen, who was the sister of one of his previous consorts. (After a trip to Kentucky, Amos Kendall informed friends that Johnson was devoting "too much of his time to a young Delilah of about the complexion of Shakespears swarthy Othello.") Secretary of State John Forsyth, still embroiled in the *Amistad* affair, badly wanted the nomination but withdrew angrily when Van Buren, while taking a public stance of neutrality, would not give way on dumping Johnson, and decided to leave the decision up to state party leaders. Andrew Jackson's favorite, James K. Polk, never formally backed down but issued a letter saying he did not wish to be an obstacle to the party, which was taken as a withdrawal. Johnson remained on the ticket.[57]

Van Buren, having dodged a nasty brawl over the vice presidency, then received a party platform—the first such document in American history—that was completely to his liking, designed to unite all but the most recalcitrant Conservatives behind him. The platform promised "the most rigid economy" in federal expenditures in order to preserve the Republic; it denounced "all efforts by abolitionists or others, made to induce congress to interfere with questions of slavery"; and, above all, it called for "the separation of the moneys of the government from banking institutions."[58] But a coherent platform did not mean a unified party, and Van Buren was in deep political trouble.

The obvious source of the worries was the enduring political impact of the Panic of 1837, but the Democracy's difficulties ran deeper than that. All of the divisions and contradictions that began emerging during Jackson's second term, in the Bank War and in the controversies over the abolitionists, had worsened under Martin Van Buren. By sticking to Jackson's banking and currency policies and allying with the Loco Foco radicals, Van Buren had kept the faith with the core concepts of Jacksonian politics, but at the expense of further fracturing the party. If the administration, building on renewed resentment at the banks, at last pushed the independent treasury plan through Congress, the president's supporters could claim that he had courageously stayed the course against the Money Power. If the economy showed any signs of revival, as it had in 1838, Van Buren could also proclaim his economic stewardship. But there were no guarantees that any of this would happen.

The slavery issue was getting to be just as difficult. Like Jackson and the rest of the party's mainstream, Van Buren believed strongly in keeping slavery out of national politics, for the good of the Union as well as the party. But more than Jackson, the northern broker Van Buren had always been on his guard against losing southern slaveholders' support. Now just as the radical abolitionist movement seemed to have peaked, the *Amistad* affair widened northern antislavery sympathies and aggravated sectional enmities. Although he tried to walk a delicate line while placating the South, Van Buren wound up reinforcing his reputation as the ultimate southern sympathizer, even as his administration failed to win its case against the black rebels. With a small but vociferous number of northern Democrats expressing sharp antislavery views, and with Calhoun back in the party, implacable as ever and making new trouble, the Democrats were in a tightening sectional bind—one that might cost them valuable votes in a close election.

Van Buren's and the Democrats' political difficulties exposed, once again, the deepening contradictions and dilemmas of Jacksonian egalitarianism. The Democracy's chances in 1840 would turn on whether the party could keep sectional enmity to a minimum, appeal in different ways to different parts of the country, and withstand any prolongation of economic hard times. They would also depend on whether the Whigs could at last nominate a credible candidate with a credible program and mount a credible national campaign. And as the Democrats would learn to their dismay, standards of credibility and campaigning were changing swiftly in national politics—as were the definitions of democratic idealism.

16

WHIGS, DEMOCRATS, AND DEMOCRACY

In the spring of 1835, William Henry Seward, having quit the collapsing Anti-Masons for the Whigs, accurately predicted the outcome of the presidential elections a year later: "It is utterly impossible, I am convinced, to defeat Van Buren," he wrote to his collaborator Thurlow Weed. "The people are for him. Not so much for him as for the principle they suppose he represents. That principle is Democracy. . . . It is with them, the poor against the rich; and it is not to be disguised, that, since the last election, the array of parties has very strongly taken that character."[1]

Seward exaggerated Van Buren's invincibility—the 1836 election turned out to be surprisingly close—but he hit the crucial point: as long as the Whigs appeared to be the party of the rich and privileged, they would never win a national election. The difficulty was in part institutional—"Our party as at present organized," Weed had written in 1834, "is doomed to fight merely to be beaten"—but it was also intellectual, ideological, and sectional.[2] To win power, the Whigs would have to square themselves, finally, with democracy—and bridge the divisions among state-rights southerners, border-state moderates, northern conservatives, and antislavery Yankees. In 1840, they figured out how to do so, and completed a revolution of American conservatism that stunned the Van Buren Democrats.

THE REVOLUTION OF AMERICAN CONSERVATISM:
THE NEW-SCHOOL WHIGS

The absorption by the Whigs in the mid-1830s of some key northern Anti-Mason politicians, including Seward and Weed, was a crucial factor in the party's consolidation. Weed—who thought universal suffrage a curse but an inescapable political fact—brought with him a hardheaded mastery of popular flattery and insider manipulation, hammered out in the canal-town politics of the Burned-Over District. Weed's alter ego, Seward, was more of a crusader who envisaged government as a lever for commercial improvement and as a weapon to combat social ills, from crime in the cities to inadequate schooling in the countryside. Other former Anti-Masons—Thaddeus Stevens and Joseph Ritner in Pennsylvania, William Slade in Vermont—combined idealism and realism in varying degrees, at odds with patrician conservatives as well as what they perceived as the false democracy of the Jacksonians. Contrary to the high-toned Whigs, they would appeal to the voters to oust the Democrats in order to put government, as one sympathizer declared, "IN THE HANDS OF THE PEOPLE."[3]

Weed was also responsible for recruiting the liveliest voice among a new crop of Whig newspaper editors, Horace Greeley. The son of a Vermont farmer and day laborer, Greeley had tramped across New York and Pennsylvania as a journeyman printer before settling in Manhattan in 1831. Three years later, he began his own literary review, the *New Yorker*, whose occasional pieces in praise of Henry Clay and Whig economics alerted Weed to his talents. Nearsighted, tall, and haphazardly vague in appearance, but a warm reform enthusiast, Greeley thought of Whiggery as the people's cause that would confound Democratic hypocrisy and uplift the masses. (When Weed arranged for him to edit a new Whig weekly, Greeley called it the *Jeffersonian*.) Greeley's Boston counterpart, Richard Haughton, editor of the *Boston Atlas*, was as much a political strategist as a journalist. With Richard Hildreth, a brilliant young polymath and humanitarian reformer, as its chief editorial writer, the brash, accessible *Atlas* pitched the Whig cause while proclaiming itself in basic harmony with "the abstract ideas of government advanced by the Globe, the Advocate and the Bay State Democrat."[4]

By the late 1830s, other up-and-comers throughout the country were bringing energy and freshness to the party. In the Old Northwest and the newer western states, enterprising small towns produced a host of ambitious young Whigs from obscure backgrounds, attracted by the charisma of Henry Clay and the expansive promise of the American System—among them, in New Salem, Illinois, the young state legislator Abraham Lincoln. Some—including a pair of rural Ohio law partners, Joshua R. Giddings and Benjamin Franklin Wade, both sons of impoverished Connecticut families—burned with evangelical antislavery conviction. In the South, state-rights insurgencies by former Jacksonians swept capable young men from outside the planter elite into Whiggery, among them a Georgia country schoolmaster's son and follower of George Troup named Alexander Stephens. Scores of new anti-Jackson southern newspapers appeared, from the weekly *Washington Whig and Republican Gazette* in eastern Beaufort County, North Carolina, to the Vicksburg *Whig* in patrician black-belt Mississippi.

A democratization of Whig politics and ideology ensued, turning the party's earlier attacks on Jacksonian corruption and tyranny into a populist cause. The process did not unfold evenly in all parts of the country. In Massachusetts, where Jacksonianism only began to make inroads in state politics very late in the 1830s, established networks of family and business ties dominated the Whig leadership and ran the state party's affairs more like a private gentlemen's club than a modern party organization. Southern Whigs, who by the mid-1830s included most of the section's great planters, always evoked a more traditional, localist, patriarchal air than most of their northern counterparts, befitting the planters' increasingly unquestioned predominance over southern life. State-rights southern Whigs promised, above all, that they would be less compromising on slavery and the abolitionists than the Democrats. More nationalistic southern Whigs, especially in the great plantation districts, promised that their policies would restore economic stability and secure better markets for slaveholders and petty merchants alike. Yet even southern Whiggery learned to widen its appeal, proclaiming itself to white southerners of all classes as the true people's choice—devoted, one North Carolina paper declared, to "popular liberty"—while saving its worst condescension for outsiders, including unwashed Yankee Democrats like Ely Moore and, as ever, the abolitionists.[5]

North and South, Whigs worked hard to create a truly national party organization. Having not even held a national convention in 1836, they would elect delegates to nominate a single candidate for the 1840 race. At the local and state levels, especially in the North, Whig managers and organizers paid close attention to raising funds and building a party infrastructure, from ward and township meetings on up. Whig committees and conventions picked candidates, passed resolutions, sustained members' loyalties, and, on election days, got out the vote, just as the Democrats did. Never again would the Whigs complain, as one New York loyalist had in 1835, that the party lacked "plan, purpose or principle," and that its "imbecility" and organizational maladroitness deterred "the young and ambitious."[6]

A crucial shift in Whig ideology concerned the party's guiding assumptions about property and politics. The old Federalist prescription that property needed protection from the power of numbers had eroded badly, but it had not collapsed completely. The disdain for what John Randolph had called King Numbers still permeated the southern Tidewater elite. In the North, old-line conservatives like

New York's Chancellor James Kent and business leaders like Nicholas Biddle believed that democracy menaced property, and they held in contempt the efforts by the expanded ignorant electorate to make economic policy through their equally ignorant elected representatives. "I think," William Sullivan of Massachusetts lamented in the year of the bank veto and Jackson's reelection, "that our experiment of self-government approaches to a total failure."[7]

By the mid-1830s, American social realities and the force of democratic politics had rendered those assumptions obsolete—and, in national politics, self-defeating. In almost all of the states, poor white men had secured the vote, but private property had not been despoiled. Quite the opposite: the dynamic economy of the early republic had sufficiently widened opportunities so that ordinary freemen could at least hope to gain a measure of propertied security for themselves and their families through their own efforts. There were, of course, Americans, especially in the eastern cities, who found prosperity chimerical. The economic inequalities among the white male citizenry, North and South, were deep and growing. But these inequalities did not portend an uprising against property by the great masses of white Americans. Even at their most incendiary, neither the slaveholder Andrew Jackson nor the political professional Martin Van Buren was Thomas Skidmore. The illusion that they were—an illusion that recurred during the Bank War and the struggle over the subtreasury—had become such an encumbrance to those who sought the Democrats' overthrow that it made the Democrats appear unbeatable. Instead of resisting democracy in the name of protecting property, the new-school anti-Jacksonians now declared, better to embrace it and turn it against the Democracy.[8]

This change in thinking, most visible in the rhetoric of the younger new-school Whigs, could also be seen in the adaptations of older national figures, none more dramatically than Daniel Webster. Early in his career, the young Federalist Webster, although less old-fashioned than some, had held to conventional conservative ideas about property and power. "We have no experience that teaches us, that any other rights are safe, where property is not safe," he declared at the 1820 Massachusetts constitutional convention, and on that basis, he joined a successful counterattack on a liberalized suffrage. "There is not a more dangerous experiment," Webster insisted, "than to place property in the hands of one class, and political power in those of another." Yet even then, Webster recognized that, at least in Massachusetts, the great majority of citizens actually did hold property and had an interest in its preservation. By the 1830s, he came to understand that by appealing for an even broader diffusion of property—to be achieved by sound conservative business policies and not by destructive Jacksonian foolishness—the experiment of democracy might be rendered safe. The masses, instead of posing a threat to property, could, if approached correctly, be turned into great defenders of property.[9]

From this rejection of archaic Federalist politics followed a number of important consequences. The Whigs contended that in the United States all freemen shared a basic harmony of interests that had effectively banished the existence of classes. The older, tough-minded conservatism of John Adams, shared, in part, by James Madison and other Republicans, assumed that the clash between rich and poor would forever shape politics and government, even in the American republic. In the new conservative view, America was a great exception among nations, fundamentally different from Europe, where, as Webster remarked, there was "a clear and well defined line, between capital and labor." Thanks to America's abundance of land and wealth, its shortage of free labor, and its lack of hereditary aristocracy, the idea of the few and the many had been banished— and, contrary to the Democrats, rendered permanently antithetical to the genius of American politics. In America, rich and poor alike were workingmen, and all workingmen were capitalists, or at least incipient capitalists, ready to strike out on the road to wealth that was open to everyone. The Jacksonians and their labor radical friends understood nothing about this blessed nation, where expanding commerce and manufacturing, according to the *American Quarterly Review*, placed "within the reach of even the very poorest, a thousand comforts which were unknown to the rich in less civilized ages." What was good for the wealthy of the country was inevitably good for those of aspiring wealth, and what was bad was bad—worse for the aspirants than for the already affluent. "It is moneyed capital which makes business grow and thrive, gives employment to labor, and opens to it avenues to success in life . . . ," one Whig publicist observed. "The blow aimed at the moneyed capitalist, strikes over the head of the laborer, and is sure to hurt the latter more than the former."[10]

A second corollary was political: Jacksonian politicians, and not privileged businessmen, were the true oppressors of the people. In place of the monied aristocrats whom the Democrats disparaged, the Whigs substituted what they described as a new class of selfish elected officials and appointees, led by King Andrew I—connivers who had turned government into their private trough, robbing the people of their money as well as their power. Attacks on Jackson as a despot expanded into charges that the Democrats' economic policies were subterfuges to create an empire of influence and self-enrichment with the people's money, most notoriously in the pet banks. Since Jacksonian power was greatest in the executive branch, those subterfuges (the Whigs observed) proceeded as expansions of presidential power, designed, as Justice Joseph Story wrote to Harriet Martineau, "to concentrate in the executive department the whole power over the currency of the country." That power would then be used for the exclusive benefit of Jacksonian insiders and their political clients.[11]

The Jacksonians' alleged despotism led directly to another Whig theme: Jacksonian corruption. With the implementation of Jackson's spoils system, so the

DEMOCRACY ASCENDANT

1. Andrew Jackson campaign
engraving, 1828

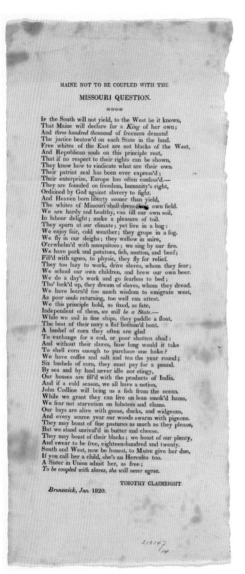

MAINE NOT TO BE COUPLED WITH THE

MISSOURI QUESTION.

IF the South will not yield, to the West be it known,
That Maine will declare for a *King* of her own;
And *three hundred thousand* of freemen demand
The justice bestow'd on each State in the land.
Free whites of the East are not blacks of the West,
And Republican souls on this principle rest,
That if no respect to their rights can be shown,
They know how to vindicate what are their own.
Their patriot zeal has been ever express'd;—
Their enterprize, Europe has often confess'd.—
They are founded on freedom, humanity's right,
Ordained by God against slavery to fight.
And Heaven born liberty sooner than yield,
The whites of Missouri shall dress their own field.
We are hardy and healthy, can till our own soil,
In labour delight; make a pleasure of toil.
They spurn at our climate; yet live in a bog:
We enjoy fair, cold weather; they grope in a fog.
We fly in our sleighs; they wallow in mire,
O'erwhelm'd with musquitoes; we sing by our fire.
We have pork and potatoes, fish, mutton, and beef;
Fill'd with agues, to physic, they fly for relief.
They too lazy to work, drive slaves, whom they fear;
We school our own children, and brew our own beer.
We do a day's work and go fearless to bed;
Tho' lock'd up, they dream of slaves, whom they dread.
We have learn'd too much wisdom to emigrate west,
As poor souls returning, too well can attest.
We this principle hold, as fixed, as fate,
Independent of them, *we will be a State.*—
While we sail in fine ships, they paddle a float,
The best of their navy a flat bottom'd boat.
A bushel of corn they often are glad
To exchange for a cod, or poor shotten shad:
And without their slaves, how long would it take
To shell corn enough to purchase one hake?
We have coffee and salt and tea the year round;
Six bushels of corn, they must pay for a pound.
By sea and by land never idle nor stingy,
Our houses are fill'd with the products of India.
And if a cold season, we all have a notion,
John Codline will bring us a fish from the ocean.
While we grant they can live on lean smok'd hams,
We fear not starvation on lobsters and clams.
Our bays are alive with geese, ducks, and widgeons,
And every scarce year our woods swarm with pigeons.
They may boast of fine pastures as much as they please,
But we stand unrival'd in butter and cheese.
They may boast of their blacks; we boast of our plenty,
And swear to be free, eighteen-hundred and twenty.
South and West, now be honest, to MAINE give her due,
If you call her a child, she's an Hercules too.
A Sister in Union admit her, as free;
To be coupled with slaves, she will never agree.

TIMOTHY CLAIMRIGHT.

Brunswick, Jan. 1820.

2. Northern broadside attacking the Missouri Compromise, 1820

3. Rufus King, 1819–20

4. Henry Clay, ca. 1818

6. Sequoyah, ca. 1828

5. Andrew Jackson, 1835

7. Virginia Constitutional Convention, 1829–30

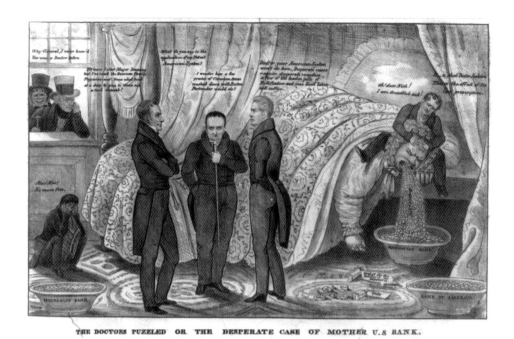

THE DOCTORS PUZZLED OR THE DESPERATE CASE OF MOTHER U.S BANK.

8. Antibank cartoon, ca. 1834–35. President Jackson at left, peeking through window; Henry Clay, Daniel Webster, and John C. Calhoun in the center; Nicholas Biddle on bed at right, holding the head of the symbolic monster bank

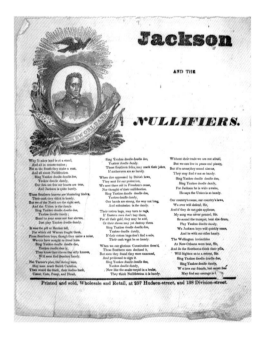

9. Antinullification broadside, 1832

10. John C. Calhoun, ca. 1832

11. William Lloyd Garrison, 1833   12. James Forten, ca. 1818

NEW METHOD OF ASSORTING THE MAIL, AS PRACTISED BY SOUTHERN SLAVE-HOLDERS, OR

ATTACK ON THE POST OFFICE, CHARLESTON, S.C.

13. Attack on abolitionist mailings, Charleston, South Carolina, 1835

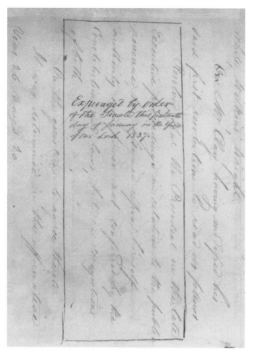

14. Expunged censure of Andrew Jackson in the *Senate Journal*, 1837

15. Charles Grandison Finney, ca. 1850

16. Texan battle flag flown at the Battle of San Jacinto, 1836

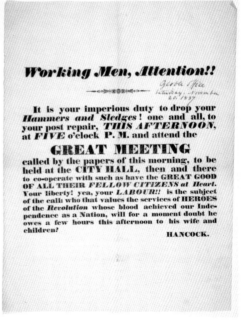

17. Labor broadside, 1837

18. Anti–Van Buren cartoon on the effects of the Panic, ca. 1838

19. Cartoon depicting Waddy Thompson intimidating John Quincy Adams over the gag rule, ca. 1839

20. William Leggett, ca. 1835

21. Whig campaign banner, 1840

22. Thurlow Weed, ca. 1861

23. Horace Greeley, between 1844 and 1860

argument went, the Democrats had replaced occasional malfeasance by corrupt individuals with a vast apparatus of systematic plunder of the people's money. The discovery of the Swartwout affair in 1838, in which the long-time Democratic collector of the New York port had absconded to Europe with more than one million dollars in public funds, reinforced these charges. The ironies of that scandal for Van Buren—who had sharply opposed Jackson's original appointment of Swartwout in 1829, and who later moved to replace him because of his opposition to the subtreasury plan and other White House policies—only intensified the president's and his party's embarrassment. The old democratic political categories got turned inside out, allowing Whigs like Greeley to claim the Jeffersonian legacy and charge that Van Buren headed a political racket that regarded government "as an agency mainly of corruption, oppression, and robbery."[12]

Democratic corruption was spiritual as well as material, the Whigs asserted. Playing off the stigma attached to freethinking radicals, Frances Wright above all, and the nativist fears of dissipated pro-Democratic immigrants, chiefly the Irish, Whig propagandists proclaimed their opponents dangerous to the very foundations of pious respectability and secure democratic government. If every Democrat was not an infidel, a libertine, or a drunk, the Whigs assured the upright, surely every infidel, libertine, and drunk was a Democrat. "Wherever you find a bitter, blasphemous Atheist and an enemy of Marriage, Morality, and Social Order," Greeley charged, "there you may be certain of one vote for Van Buren."[13]

For the Whigs to purport to represent the people, they had to talk more like the people, or how they thought the people talked. Some of the party's Federalist and National Republican predecessors had already experimented with popular campaigning, notably in the Federalists' short-lived Washington Benevolent Societies. Some Jeffersonians-turned-National Republicans, most famously the gregarious Henry Clay, were excellent treaters and braggers on the campaign stump—forms of public performance that long predated the democratic breakthroughs of the Jefferson era. Suddenly, in the mid-1830s, Whig "cracker-barrel" philosophers and down-home wits began appearing in print. The most successful of them was the transformed fictional Major Jack Downing. As invented by Seba Smith, the sage of Downingville was a humorous figure who poked fun at Jackson and his coterie. In the mid-1830s, however, numerous "new" Major Downings appeared—the most brilliant of them being the creation of Charles Davis, a close friend of Nicholas Biddle's and a director of the New York branch of the Second Bank of the United States. Davis's Downing was a Whig ideologue through and through, praising bankers as benevolent people who "in the nature of things" would "never do any thing agin the gineral prosperity of this country," and who were locked in a struggle against the true "*monied aristocracy*" of "politicians [who] manage to git hold of the mony of the people, and keep turnin it to their own account—. . . buy up a party with it." Better a government of enlightened businessmen than of politicians out "jest to git into office; and then, to keep themselves in office." The first modern conservative folk hero was born in a branch office of the Second BUS.[14]

There were other Whig populist heroes, some real, some imaginary, and some a combination of the two. David Crockett's emergence as a buck-skinned Whig celebrity was widely imitated. Whig favorites suddenly showed a fondness for manly, plebeian nicknames, including Tom "The Wagon Boy" Corwin, Henry "The Natick Cobbler" Wilson, and Elihu "The Learned Blacksmith" Burritt. Henry Clay, known widely as "Harry of the West," "The Great Compromiser," and even "Prince Hal," began to favor a name supposedly pinned on him in his youth, "Mill Boy of the Slashes"—a bit wordy but definitely down-home. On a more elevated level, the Whigs tried to match the Democrats' hard-money pamphlets with popular defenses of the credit system, the BUS, and high tariffs, the best of them written by Matthew Carey's son, Henry C. Carey.[15]

Binding together these new-school Whig themes—American classlessness and underlying social harmony, the oppression and corruption of Democratic government, Whig populism—was the doctrine of self-improvement and reform. Attacks on the Jacksonians' dishonesty and class-war demagogy could only carry the Whigs so far in reimagining America for the electorate. Even in the Whigs' classless pastorale, some citizens were better off than others, and despite rapid economic development, the curses of crime, pauperism, and drunkenness appeared to be growing worse, not better. How could these disparities and pathologies be explained? Not, the Whigs insisted, with sinister talk of systemic social inequalities, class warfare, or corrupt institutions (apart from those the Jacksonian politicians had inflicted). Rather, the problems were individual and moral and their solution lay in individual self-reform, or what Boston's eminent Whig Unitarian minister William Ellery Channing called "Elevation of the Soul"—an elevation that benign Whig government would help to encourage.[16]

Whig self-reform adapted ethical precepts from across the spectrum of post-Calvinist American Protestant belief, evoking the emotional revivalism of the Presbygationals and more proper of the southern evangelicals as well as Channing's rationalist Unitarianism. Their common theme, sacred and secular, was the all-surpassing importance of moral choice. The wealthy did not make the poor lazy and thriftless; the sober did not make drunkards drink; law-abiding, decent men and women did not make murderers murder, or thieves rob, or wife-beaters beat their wives. Rather, the lazy, the drunk, and the criminal chose wrongly, succumbed to sensuous temptation, and failed to exercise human faculties of self-control that could elevate their souls. What was at stake in the United States, the Whigs proclaimed, was nothing less than a battle over these self-evident facts—a momentous conflict between those who understood the basic moral conditions of human existence and those who rejected them. "We have, in truth, in the last eight or ten years, been in a continual state of moral war," the Tennessean John Bell said when he announced, in 1835, that he was joining the Whig Party. That war, as the Whigs depicted it, was essentially a democratic conflict, not between the privileged and the people or the wealthy and the poor, but between the righteous and the unrighteous.[17]

Self-reform in turn became the basis for an uplifting idealism that defined Whiggery as a spiritual cause as well as a political party. Later writers have mistaken this aspect of Whig ideology as a belief in the corrective, liberal, "positive" state, in stark contrast to a Democratic laissez-faire, backward-looking liberal "negative" state. In fact, like virtually all American political parties and movements, the Whigs and the Democrats blended aspects of both "positive" and "negative" government. In some spheres, notably with regard to the currency and the national bank, Whigs greatly preferred private to public power and tried to limit government regulation. They wanted to halt what they called the Democrats' "war on the currency of the country . . . on the merchants and mercantile interests"—a war they said was designed "to support the power of the federal government." But the Whigs did promote the uses of government to help direct and even coerce individuals toward what they considered personal improvement—the basis, as they saw it, for social and political progress. Materially, this program had already reached its apotheosis in Clay's American System, a coordinated plan of federal-supported commercial expansion anchored by a privately managed BUS. Morally, it led new-school Whigs in the late 1830s, most auspiciously the more liberal Whigs in New York, to call for increased state support of institutions that would help keep the young on the path of righteousness and help lead the fallen toward the elevation of their souls: public schools, benevolent societies, rehabilitative prisons, reformatories, and, for the truly unfortunate, insane asylums.[18]

"Of all the parties that have existed in the United States," John Quincy Adams's dyspeptic grandson Henry would later remark, "the famous Whig party was the most feeble in ideas." Given the subsequent intellectual history of other political parties, that judgment now seems severe. Whiggery did draw on some serious philosophical concepts, most of them derived from the Scottish so-called commonsense moral philosophers of the late eighteenth century, whose works were widely taught in American universities by the 1830s. In the area of economic thought, Henry Carey's pamphlets displayed a reasonably informed engagement with the writings of the political economists David Ricardo and Thomas Malthus—although, finally, Carey's vaunting of the harmony of interests and the protective tariff relied as much on moral as on economic logic.[19]

There was something of a Whig political and literary intelligentsia—mainly ministers and academics, under the leadership of cultural clerics and literary deacons. They included a few younger writers like the brash journalists Greeley and Hildreth, as well as others like Harvard's John Gorham Palfrey—at forty, the up-and-coming editor of the *North American Review* and later a courageous anti-slavery Whig congressman. In William Hickling Prescott, the Whigs could claim a lawyer-turned-historian whose scholarly reputation would eventually rank, for a time, near George Bancroft's. Southern Whigs produced the acclaimed novelist and congressman John Pendleton Kennedy, author of the picturesque *Swallow Barn* and, in 1844, of the pamphlet *A Defense of the Whigs*. Still, the Whig intelligentsia, even among the younger new-school Whigs, was meager in comparison to the Federalists and Jeffersonians before them—as well to the robust Jacksonians and those whom the Jacksonians attracted, including Orestes Brownson, Nathaniel Hawthorne, and a young New Yorker named Walter Whitman, among those whose work appeared in the *Democratic Review* during the *Review*'s early years. Harriet Martineau (whose work the *Review* also published) contended that although the Whigs embraced the men of learning and manners, the Democratic Party included "an accession small in number, but inestimable in power,—the men of genius."[20]

Yet if Whig ideology lacked intellectual sparkle and strenuousness, it drew on and abetted powerful impulses in the popular American mind. Intellectually ordinary, the evolving Whigs were culturally and ethically rich. The classical learning that pervaded Whig literature, art, and oratory—leading some to compare Daniel Webster to Demosthenes and Edward Everett to Cicero—was not simply intimidating; it had genuine prestige and allure, in an America where spoken rhetorical grandeur still carried weight in legislative debates and on occasions of state. Spiritually, the liberalization of Calvinist doctrine among mainline believers became a fulcrum for the Whiggish moralism expressed most famously by Channing. And the fires of the Second Great Awakening, in its Finneyite version, blazed fallow fields for northern Whig politics, with its emphasis on the exertion of individual will and self-control in the search for redemption, and its imperatives of Christian stewardship. Charles Finney steered clear of party politics in deference to saving souls, but by 1840, Lyman Beecher was prepared to campaign publicly for the Whig national ticket. Many leading new-school Whigs, such as Joshua R. Giddings, were devout New School evangelicals. Areas where the Finneyite revivals of the 1830s hit the hardest, notably in western New York and in Ohio's Western Reserve, were Whig electoral strongholds.[21]

Among more orthodox religious liberals and evangelicals alike arose the most compelling feature of new-school Whiggery, a broad Christian humanitarianism of the sort that had nourished the movements against Indian removal and, in the North, for the abolition of slavery. Just as post-Calvinist churchmen denounced human coercion and unbridled passion as unchristian, so they rejected everyday cruelties—the beating of children, wife abuse, the harsh treatment of convicts, and (according to some) the physical and mental torments of slavery—which other Americans took for granted as natural and even necessary forms of correction and social order. "The move toward a religion of the heart was a critical step away from the hard 'system' of Calvinism," the modern historian Elizabeth Clark put it succinctly, "and the revival meeting with its public prayer and testimony created a community of intense feeling."[22]

Whig humanitarianism was distinct from that of the Democratic labor radicals and hard-money men, with their abstract political and economic theories of inequality and their Enlightenment rationalist affinities. The Democrats saw farmers and workingmen as society's chief victims, oppressed by greedy and (often) perfectly pious monopolists. Whig humanitarians turned to a very different set of victims. With faith, sentiment, and empathy, they set about relieving the misery of battered wives, abused blacks, and others who suffered deliberately inflicted hardship and pain—all with the higher aim of building a good society of benevolent men and women united by an affectionate regard for the lowliest of God's creatures. Self-reform was the more didactic side of Whig moralism; Christian benevolence and stewardship reinforced that moralism with effusions of Christ's gospel, and tightened the connections between Whiggery and various compassionate causes. In the South, the impulse would inspire, alongside movements for temperance and other moral reforms, slaveholders' efforts to persuade other planters to be truly Christian masters, treat their slaves with holy forbearance, and bring the gospel to the slave quarters—all as a means to strengthen the slaveholders' regime. In the North, a similar benevolent impulse pushed a small but disproportionate number of Whigs into antislavery work. Most northern Whigs had no particular antislavery commitments (while conservative Whigs were among the most prominent anti-abolitionists), and not all antislavery advocates were Whigs. Nevertheless, new-school Whigs, especially the middling farmers and artisans in their ranks, were far more ubiquitous in the antislavery circles of the 1830s than were Jacksonian Democrats.[23]

Whig economics, as publicized by Henry Carey, also struck a nerve, especially after the Panic of 1837, among ordinary Americans enamored of a broad entrepreneurial ethos, sometimes labeled "middle class." The response was stronger in the free-labor North than in the slave South, but it arose in all sections. Over the decades since the American Revolution, with the collapse of old systems of deference, this ethos had practically become a version of the national creed, observed as a matter of principle if not always in practice—dignifying labor over affluent idleness, ennobling individual striving to make one's own way, glorifying humble efforts to improve opportunities for one's family by dint of hard work and delayed gratification. Early in the 1830s, the Jacksonians had turned that ethos to their advantage by mobilizing it, alongside labor-union discontent, against the politically privileged nonproducers. But after the Panic of 1837—which the Whigs blamed on the Democrats' class warfare and on the man they now mocked as Martin Van Ruin—the political advantage shifted, especially in appealing to younger small farmers, shopkeepers, and workingmen laid low by hard times. Having shed the old guard's stigma of social exclusivity, the Whigs were able to position themselves and their credit-driven economic policies as the true allies of labor and honest ambition, and to proclaim proudly, as one leading publicist would, that "[t]his is a country of *self-made men*, than which nothing better could be said of any state of society."[24]

This congeries of new-school Whig moral encomia and political polemics was completely in line with the well-being of business interests—northern and southern, insiders and outsiders alike—that had fallen on the political defensive during Jackson's presidency. Nicholas Biddle and his BUS may have been driven (and driven themselves) into disrepute, but the original friends of the bank, as well as the aggressive deregulating state bankers and the rest of the soft-money businessmen who despised the subtreasury plan and abandoned the Democracy, still formed one of Whiggery's chief political pillars. In the urban North as well as the plantation South, the overwhelming majority of the richest men were Whigs, and they contributed heavily to the party's coffers, sometimes ran for office, and exerted a pervasive influence on Whig policy at every level of government. No less than their National Republican forerunners, the new-school Whigs generally favored programs long championed by organized business, from government aid to internal improvements to the restoration of a national bank.[25]

There were ideological fault lines within Whiggery that, if left unattended, could ruin everything. Old-line party conservatives remained suspicious of the new-school Whigs, like William Henry Seward, whom they believed carried the idea of humanitarian reform too far. The evangelical antislavery of northern Whigs such as Joshua Giddings repelled Whig slaveholders as well as northern conservatives who wanted to lay all controversy over slavery to rest. As they themselves would soon discover, men like Seward and Giddings were unrepresentative of the Whig Party as a whole, and especially of its national leadership. (The same was true for the sworn enemy of the gag rule, John Quincy Adams, who, after Anti-Masonry's collapse, became a Whig by default.) But with the entry into the party of capable political managers such as Seward's cynical sideman, Thurlow Weed, there was good reason to believe that at the national level, the Whigs could stifle their differences and unite against the common Democratic foe without sacrificing their newfound democratic affinities.

If kept within their proper boundaries, the main lines of the democratized Whig ideology, far from threatening pro-business conservatism, greatly strengthened it, by releasing men of property and standing from persistent fears of democratic overthrow, by merging their interests with those of the great people, and by transforming their search for profit and power into a moral and patriotic impulse—and a politically effective democratic impulse. ("[W]e maintain that

the Whigs are THE Democrats, if there must be a party by that name . . . ,"
Henry Clay's publicist Calvin Colton would write. "Certainly they are the *true*
Democrats, if there be any such in the land.") As for the rest of the country,
democratized Whiggery gave another kind of hope—hope that the country
might be delivered from hard times, hope that prosperity might yet be regained
and enlarged, hope based on just enough of the realities of expansive American
life that it could seem plausible.[26]

LOG CABIN DEMOCRACY

The ascendancy of the new-school Whigs first became evident at the state level,
most powerfully in New York. Upon his election as governor in 1838, William
Seward transformed both the vocabulary and the programs that his constituents
and his Democratic opponents had come to expect from Whiggery. His first message to the state legislature was a lengthy document filled with activist calls for
reform and progress (in addition to vastly expanded internal improvements),
couched in epithets the Democrats normally hurled at the Whigs. "What is the
secret of aristocracy?" Seward asked. "It is that knowledge is power." Accordingly,
Seward proposed a large new public school program, including a new state
board of education, improved curricula for schools and colleges, and, for the rising tide of foreign immigrants to New York, equal education "with free toleration
of their peculiar creeds and instructions." He also called for improved
government-funded education for the state's black population, to help curb the
unusually high crime rate in black areas. It was a manifesto of new-school Whig
politics at their most liberal, promoting state aid to personal improvement without in any way disturbing—indeed, directly aiding—the state's vested economic
interests.[27]

A few months earlier, liberal Whigs in the New York legislature had affirmed
not only their allegiances to state bankers but also their cleverness in co-opting
the Democratic mantle of reform. Late in 1837, the long campaign for a free
banking law, led by William Leggett, the Loco Focos, and the hard-money wing
of the Albany Regency, seemed on the verge of victory. As proposed, the law
would repeal the existing restraining law on the establishment of private banks of
discount and deposit while imposing strict state regulations on the issue of paper
money. Too radical for Governor William Marcy and even for Van Buren, the
proposal had been the major source of division between Van Buren and the Loco
Focos in 1836—but the suspension of specie payments a year later greatly stimulated interest in the proposal, and early in 1838, Marcy endorsed it. Old-line
Whigs and Conservative Democrats rejected the plan out of hand. The pro-
Seward legislative Whigs, however, seized on it, struck out the offensive passages

about regulating paper money, and passed their rewritten version over Democratic objections. The new-schoolers had killed off hard-money reform, but had done so while looking as if they were the reformers.[28]

These new-school victories were too much for old-guard Whigs in New York and around the country. "My principles are too liberal, too philanthropic, if it not be vain to say so, for my party," Seward would later write privately, dismayed at how conservative Whigs refused to cede control of the new party without a fight. Seward, Weed, and the rest had wrongly abandoned Biddle and the BUS, the conservatives charged; they were unseemly in their solicitations of immigrants, especially the Irish Papists; they were positively dangerous with their friendliness to abolitionists and their proposals to educate degraded blacks. These new Whigs lacked gentility and high-mindedness; they were too crassly interested in the pursuit of power, too demagogic. They were, in fact, altogether too much like the Jacksonians. In 1839, Philip Hone, who had served as New York's mayor, expressed interest in running for office again but was turned away on the ground that no gentleman could possibly succeed any longer in Whig politics. "If they are right in what they say," Hone complained in his diary, "the party is not worth sustaining; better it would be that everything should go back to the dunghill of Democracy."[29]

Knowing that the Whig conservatives might well sink their own efforts to remold the party—and destroy a golden opportunity to capture the White House at last in 1840—the liberals and pragmatic new-schoolers set about eliminating from presidential contention the leading men of the party's National Republican establishment, especially those with conspicuous attachments to the unpopular Nicholas Biddle. First on the list was Daniel Webster. Hoping to unite New England and the North behind him, Webster in early 1837 announced his staunch opposition to a pending bill approving the annexation of Texas, declaring to one mass meeting that he would resist "anything that shall extend the slavery of the African race on this continent." After the panic, he advanced along a different line, blaming the Democrats' hard-money policies for the disaster and calling for the restoration of sound fiscal conservatism and the revival of the Bank of the United States. But Webster was more respected than he was loved by all but the crustiest of the Whig old guard, both in Congress and in the New England legislatures outside Massachusetts. When, in 1838, the new-school *Boston Atlas*, long one of Webster's chief supporters in the press, bitterly denounced him (along with Clay) as a favorite of the *"aristocratic Whigs"* and strongly endorsed the aging general and surprising vote getter from 1836, William Henry Harrison, Webster's candidacy took a nosedive from which it never recovered. Although he would not withdraw his name until the spring of 1839, Webster persisted chiefly out of jealousy, to see that his rival Clay would not succeed where he had failed.[30]

Clay still had strong hopes that he would not fail, despite his ties to Biddle.

Aware of how Texas annexation, abolitionism, and other matters connected to slavery were roiling just beneath the surface, and that his unfriendliness to Calhoun's pro-slavery resolutions of the previous congressional session was costing him southern support, Clay gave a major anti-abolitionist speech in the Senate in February 1839. The antislavery fanatics, he declared, were enemies to the Constitution, civil peace, and the antislavery cause they claimed to espouse—a cause which, Clay charged, they had set back by fifty years with their abstract incitements about good and evil. Although he proclaimed himself no friend to slavery—"[t]he searcher of all hearts knows that every pulsation of mine beats high and strong in the cause of civil liberty"—Clay charged that immediate emancipation would lead either to a war between the races, causing the extermination of one or the other, or to mongrelization and the ruination of both races. As a law-abiding American and as a white man, he had no choice but to defend the slaveholders' rights to hold their human property as they saw fit, and to sustain slavery as an inescapable exception to American liberty. The speech brought him closer than ever to the side of the pro-slavery state-rights men who formed the backbone of the Whig Party in the Deep South. Even John C. Calhoun, who understood perfectly Clay's underlying political motivations, flattered the Kentuckian on the Senate floor, claiming he had dealt abolitionism its death blow and commenced "a great epoch in our political history."[31]

The next summer, in order to shore up his northern support, Clay undertook a grand tour from Buffalo, across New York and into New England, then down to the elegant spa at Saratoga and after that Manhattan. "We never expect again," he told the faithful old-guard Virginian Benjamin Watkins Leigh, "to have such a great advantage in the contest." Huge, approving crowds and loud tributes greeted Clay at every stop along the way. At Saratoga—where the social season was in full swing, and where both President Van Buren and Thurlow Weed's new favorite, General Winfield Scott, were also plumping for votes—Clay gave a speech before a crowd of six thousand, the largest audience he had ever addressed, and whiled away the rest of his stay hobnobbing with Whig politicians. Among them was Weed, who broke the news that the triumphal tour was not all that it seemed, that although the Whig rank and file revered Clay's name and would always come out to him and cheer, his political support was fading, and he had better save face by withdrawing from the presidential contest. Preferring to believe his own eyes and ears instead of Weed's intelligence, Clay carried on to Albany and New York City, and then farther down the coast, and finally to the spa at White Sulphur Springs in western Virginia. He returned to his Kentucky estate, Ashland, hopeful that he would command a plurality of the delegates when the Whigs held their nominating convention in Harrisburg, Pennsylvania, the following December.[32]

All the while, Weed was personally supervising one of the most effective

poison-pen campaigns in American political history, attacking Clay as unelec-
table because his political record was too unambiguous. In New York, a chain-
letter scheme among local Whig leaders blew subtle and not so subtle anti-Clay
propaganda all around the state, and then as far west as Illinois, some of it suggesting that Clay was about to withdraw from the race. One Whig circular listed
a formidable coalition of voters who would never vote for Clay—including the
old Jackson men, most abolitionists, Anti-Masons, southern state-rights advocates, western squatters, and Irish immigrants—which precluded his winning
more than a state or two. A string of Whig defeats in state and local elections over
the summer and autumn of 1839 further persuaded party managers that almost
any candidate would be preferable to Prince Hal.[33]

In seeking a candidate with a wispier political background—or, better still, no
political background at all—the new-school Whig managers believed they were
reenacting what the Democrats had done so brilliantly in 1828. "The Whig party
were broken down by the popularity and non-committal character of old Jackson," one western New Yorker wrote, "and it is but fair to turn upon, and prostrate our opponents, with the . . . weapons, with which they beat us." In Ohio,
Indiana, and Pennsylvania, new-schoolers led by Thomas Corwin and the former
Anti-Mason Thaddeus Stevens pushed for Harrison. Weed and the New Yorkers,
unconvinced that the former general, at age sixty-six, could win, turned to General Scott, the colossal six-foot five-inch, three-hundred-pound commander who
proudly wore his full-dress uniform bedecked with medals everywhere he went.
The most capable officer in the American military, Scott had lately burnished his
reputation by bringing to a successful close a nasty if bloodless boundary-dispute
war between the state of Maine and the government of New Brunswick. Like
Jackson twelve years earlier, a supporter declared, "Scott's name will bring out
the hurra boys," who would then carry his massive frame into the White House.[34]

At the Harrisburg convention—the first national convention in the Whigs'
history—Clay's forces initially enjoyed a plurality, with solid support in a few of
the northern delegations as well as in the border states and the South, but his
position was precarious. Four slaveholding states, including South Carolina,
failed to send delegations, which undercut Clay's earlier efforts to court pro-
slavery opinion. That courtship, meanwhile, had alienated Weed and many
northerners, giving Clay little room in which to maneuver. Still twenty-five votes
shy of a majority, he only hoped that the pro-Scott and pro-Harrison supporters
in the middle states and New England might deadlock and finally turn to him.
Weed, chomping on his cigar and extroverted as ever, headed off that ploy by
peeling individual northern delegates away from Clay in backroom negotiations.
After several ballots, with Clay's support fading, Weed began coaxing some wobbly southern delegates to switch from Clay to Scott.[35]

Thaddeus Stevens, however, had in his possession a devastating secret weapon for undoing both Clay and Weed: a private letter from Scott to Francis Granger, the New York Whig who had run for vice president alongside both Harrison and Webster in 1836. In the letter, Scott had attempted to win over antislavery Whigs with hints that he was favorably disposed to the abolitionists. Stevens took the letter to the headquarters of the Virginia delegation, mingled with the delegates, and calmly dropped his time bomb on the floor, where it was sure to be found. Frightened that Clay's chances were doomed and even more frightened, now, that the evidently antislavery Scott would win, the Virginians bolted en masse for Harrison. Weed then packed away the Scott bandwagon and switched to Harrison, whom the convention nominated on the next ballot.

To complete the ticket, the convention eventually gave way to the southern delegations and settled on the anti-BUS, former Democratic state-rights stalwart, John Tyler, who had run with Hugh Lawson White in 1836. Although basically at odds with Clay's nationalist political principles, Tyler had reportedly wept over Clay's defeat. He brought to the ticket both the blessings of the party's old guard and sectional balance that the delegates expected would help Harrison greatly in the depression-wracked South. Harrison, himself a native Virginian and scion of a great Tidewater family, was, on that account alone, acceptable to the southern delegates. But the addition of Tyler made the ticket more than acceptable to southern Whigs, including those in two of the four states, Georgia and Tennessee, that had not bothered to send delegations to Harrisburg.

In Washington, at the hour of Harrison's victory, Clay anxiously awaited word at Brown's Hotel, drinking heavily, expecting to hear of Scott's success but hardly reconciled to it. As the alcohol supply dwindled, Clay launched into a stormy, vulgarity-rich monologue about his perfidious friends and devious enemies. Snapping to, he noticed two strangers in the room, dressed in black, who had come to meet him. "Gentlemen," Clay said, "for aught I know, from your cloth, you may be *parsons*, and shocked at my words. Let us take a glass of wine." He filled some glasses, then abruptly left the room, his visitors staring in shocked disbelief. ("That man can never be my political idol again," one of them said.) Clay walked across Pennsylvania Avenue to his boardinghouse, where he finally received word that Harrison, and not Scott, had bested him, prompting a fresh outburst of fist-shaking fury and self-pity. "My friends are not worth the powder and shot it would take to kill them! . . . If there were two Henry Clays, one of them would make the other President of the United States!" It would take several days for Clay to regain his grip and do the right thing, warmly endorsing the Harrison-Tyler ticket at a Whig campaign dinner in Tyler's honor back at Brown's Hotel.[36]

The Democrats, scornful of the opposition's mediocre nominee, tried to exploit Clay and his supporters' bitter disappointment—with disastrous results. Shortly after the convention, the pro–Van Buren *Baltimore Republican* baited the Whigs with an insult reportedly delivered by a Clay man against Harrison: "Give him a barrel of hard cider, and settle a pension of two thousand a year on him, and my word for it, he will sit the remainder of his days in his log cabin." The superannuated general—"Old Granny" Harrison, some Democrats called him—was simply too old, too befuddled, too undistinguished to be a credible president. But the insult played directly into the hands of Weed as well as the old-guard Whigs. Richard S. Elliott, a Harrisburg Whig editor, was one of the first to grasp fully the implications, in a postconvention conversation over some rare Madeira with the banker Thomas Elder at Elder's mansion on the Susquehanna. The Van Burenites' mockery could, the two figured out, become the Whigs' pride, projecting Harrison and his party as paragons of plain rustic virtue while condemning the Democrats (the possibilities grew richer with each sip of the Madeira) as scornful, out-of-touch nabob politicos. And so the Whigs' famous Log Cabin and Hard Cider campaign began, with an enormous Harrison transparency mounted in Harrisburg depicting a log cabin with a cider barrel by the door. New-school party managers were fully aware of political genius behind the ballyhoo. "The Log Cabin is the symbol of nothing that Van Burenism knows, feels, or can appreciate," Weed later explained to the readers of the *Albany Evening Journal*. "It tells of the hopes of the humble—of the privations of the poor—. . . it is the emblem of rights that the vain and insolent aristocracy of federal office-holders have . . . trampled upon."[37]

The Democrats, not taking this new Whig campaign symbolism at all seriously, entered the lists in their time-tested ways. Van Buren, outwardly unflustered as ever, did not reply to the volleys of personal attacks on him, preferring to have his supporters calmly restate his positions on the issues and leave it to the state and local Democratic campaign committees to stir up the faithful. His greatest boost came at the end of June 1840, when, after three years of dogged maneuvering and bargaining—and pushed hard by Van Buren following the bank collapse of the previous autumn—Congress finally passed an independent treasury bill. Hard-money Democratic radicals and their administration allies were ecstatic, all the more so because they thought their victory cleared the way for Van Buren's reelection. (The Massachusetts Democrat Robert Rantoul told the president that the new law would "purif[y] the political atmosphere" by finally destroying the "corrupt alliance between Bank & State.") Van Buren held off signing the bill until the Fourth of July, amid great celebrations of both American freedom and the independent treasury. Out on the campaign stump, Democrats hailed Van Buren as the new Thomas Jefferson and the subtreasury law as the second Declaration of Independence.[38]

Would it ring true? Months before July 4, it had become clear that economic depression had returned with a vengeance, that there would be no quick recovery, and that, though the fallout might win the subtreasury bill, Van Buren would bear an enormous political burden with the voters. Some radicals, notably John L. O'Sullivan, urged the administration to undertake even more direct efforts on behalf of the nation's hard-pressed wage earners. Van Buren complied by issuing, on March 31, an executive order establishing a ten-hour day for laborers on all public works with no reduction in pay. Although presented in the mildest possible way as a step toward ending "the inconvenience and dissatisfaction" that arose from having different work rules at different work places, Van Buren's order was a clear indication that his government would act on behalf of the nation's workers. New-school Whigs, caught off guard, complained that the order would have little positive effect and charged that it was, in any case, an unwarranted interference with the free market. The length of the workday, said the self-proclaimed champion of labor Horace Greeley, ought to be left to "mutual agreement" between workers and employers: "What have Governments and Presidents to do with it?" Shipyard workers thought differently. Looking back, a free black Washington Navy Yard hand named Michael Shiner wrote in his diary that "the Working Class of people of the United States Machanic and laboures ought to never forget the Hon ex president Van Buren for the ten hour sistom, . . . his name ought to be Recorded in evry Working Man heart."[39]

Otherwise, the Democrats hoisted their old banners emblazoned with slogans about defending the rights of labor against the paper-system aristocracy, and once again they celebrated their man as the anointed successor of Old Hickory. ("The *Paper Plague* affects us all," ran one broadside, "Its pains are past enduring;/Still we have hope in Jackson's robe,/Whilst it wraps around Van Buren"—the forced rhyme, loaded with a tired message, misfiring like a rusty musket.) Southern Democrats added their own twist, charging that the Bank Whigs wanted to violate state rights. Early in the campaign, Democrats remained confident that their old campaign weapons would suffice, and that the Whigs' demagogy about "Old Tippecanoe" Harrison, the heroic Indian fighter, would flop. "The Logg cabin hard cider and Coon humbugery is doing us a great service every where," Andrew Jackson wrote to Van Buren from his retirement at the Hermitage, "and none more so than in Tennessee." When the Whig chorus swelled ever louder, puzzled Van Buren men responded unavailingly with sweet reason. "The question is not whether Harrison drinks hard cider," William Cullen Bryant remonstrated. ". . . The question is what he and his party will do if they obtain the power." Bryant may have been right, but he missed the point by a mile.[40]

The Democratic side contributed the only intellectually forceful product of the 1840 campaign, an astonishing, rebellious essay by George Bancroft's discovery, Orestes Brownson, entitled "The Laboring Classes." A former associate of Frances Wright and the New York Working Men, Brownson had lurched between radical politics and religious exhortation in what his biographer has called "a pilgrim's progress," before winding up in Boston in the mid-1830s as the head of something he called the Society for Christian Union and Progress and as the editor of a little periodical, the *Boston Reformer*. After the Panic of 1837, the *Reformer* endorsed hard-money Loco Focoism in what Brownson described as the great contest between capital and labor. Bancroft, alerted to Brownson's polemical gifts, handed him a federal patronage job to cover the costs of establishing a larger journal, the *Boston Quarterly Review*. To the horror of Boston conservatives, Brownson's magazine, a local equivalent of O'Sullivan's *Democratic Review*, became a successful outlet for the radical Democracy and helped turn Brownson—a tall, striking man, not yet forty, who orated as forcefully as he wrote—into a political celebrity.[41]

"The Laboring Classes," formally a review of a brief book on Chartism by the famed British writer Thomas Carlyle, appeared in the *Boston Quarterly* just as the presidential campaign heated up. In part it was a biting restatement of the radical economic ideas that had become mainstream Democratic principles, directed against "the chiefs of the business community"—"nabobs, reveling in luxury," while "building miniature log cabins, shouting Harrison and 'hand cider.'" Some of the essay's fiercest diatribes pierced through the moral reformism typical of the new-school Whigs—"priests and pedagogues," Brownson called them, who "seek to reform without disturbing the social arrangements which render reform necessary." Brownson strongly endorsed the divorce of bank and state through the independent treasury system (enacted just after his article went to press). But Brownson also moved well beyond the radicalism of the hard-money Democracy, picking up themes developed earlier by the Free Enquirers, Thomas Skidmore, and the class-conscious trade unionists and reshaping them into a new manifesto of working-class revolution. Brownson demanded an abolition of the wage system, "to emancipate the proletaires, as the past had emancipated the slaves." (Perversely, Brownson also claimed that the wage system was a more efficient means of exploitation than the one oppressing southern slaves—whom, he failed to note, the past had hardly emancipated, and whose masters' defense of slavery were toughening.) He demanded the abolition of the corrupt existing churches and the rebirth of Christ's true gospel. Above all, he demanded the abolition of inheritance. Brownson had little faith that these changes could be won by elections or political parties. Only a cataclysmic final conflict—"a war," he wrote, "the like of which the world as yet has never witnessed," horrific yet unavoidable—would usher in the new just society, where labor and capital would be combined in the same individual and exploitation would cease.[42]

Based on his own volatile mixture of Workeyism, Loco Focoism, and Christianity, Orestes Brownson, in Boston, pushed the hard-money logic far beyond Jacksonian Democracy into a proletarian revolutionism every bit as startling as the one that Friedrich Engels and Karl Marx would proclaim in *The Communist*

Manifesto eight years later. Seeing an opportunity, even liberal Whig publicists and politicians grabbed hold of the essay and denounced it as the pluperfect statement of what Martin Van Buren and his friends intended to inflict on the ordinary citizens of the United States. Here was definitive proof, if any was really still needed, that Loco Focoism was "utterly subversive of all Rights of Property whatever," Horace Greeley said, determined to seize what honest men had worked so hard to earn. The clamor grew so loud that Secretary of the Treasury Woodbury desperately asked Bancroft in October why he had not yet removed Brownson from his government job.[43]

But the truly remarkable thing was that Bancroft, a contributor to Brownson's *Quarterly*, steadfastly refused to listen to Woodbury. Several Democratic papers, including Bryant's *Evening Post*, criticized what they called the campaign to censor Brownson far more than they did Brownson's outlandish ideas. Even as the election campaign drew to a close, Brownson remained a mainstay of the Massachusetts Democracy, stumping across the state for Van Buren and local Democratic candidates. Nothing approaching Brownson's revolution would be in the offing if the Democrats won the election, but the reaction by Bancroft, Bryant, and others to the attacks on him exposed the depth of the anti-Whig animus among considerable portions of the party—and how far to the left they had moved by 1840 on issues of labor and banking.[44]

In 1840, however, the new-school Whig campaigners carried much more weight with the public than defenses of the free-speech rights of a revolutionary intellectual. One facet of the Whigs' assault was to update the personal attacks on Van Buren, portraying him as a callous, aristocratic pervert. The smears of the president became increasingly baroque. One best-selling Whig campaign pamphlet—the reprint of a speech by Charles Ogle, an obscure Whig congressman from Pennsylvania, entitled "The Regal Splendor of the Presidential Palace"—accused Van Buren of living in said splendor and dining on fancy expensive delicacies prepared by a French chef, while hard-hit Americans went hungry. The electorate learned from Whig partisans that the degenerate widower Van Buren had instructed groundskeepers to build for him, in back of the Executive Mansion, a large mound in the shape of a female breast, topped by a carefully landscaped nipple. Van Buren, the Whigs cried, was a depraved executive autocrat who oppressed the people by day and who, by night, violated the sanctity of the people's house with extravagant debaucheries—joined, some whispered, by the disgusting Vice President Johnson and his Negro harem.[45]

The attacks on Van Buren's alleged dissipation reinforced the old Whig charges about presidential power run amok, but they also added spice to the new charges that he and the Democrats had ruined the economy with their bank and currency policies—charges that conveyed genuine principles about authentic issues. "Harrison and Prosperity or Van Buren and Ruin," ran the title of one

Whig pamphlet, which pretty much summed up the party's line of attack on the economic front: in times of contraction and low prices, currency inflation and eased credit seemed imperative. Some stump orators (notably, in Illinois, young Abraham Lincoln) called for the restoration of the BUS in order to supply needed credit for the common man. Others lashed out at the Democrats' restriction of paper money and at the subtreasury act, which Harrison vowed to repeal. Still others, especially in traditionally protectionist Pennsylvania, vaunted the protectionist tariff as the cure for hard times. In the South, however, the politics of slavery overshadowed the more orthodox economic issues. Whereas the anti-slavery elements among the northern Whigs pilloried Van Buren for supporting the gag rule, southern Whigs dismissed his anti-abolitionism, claiming that his despotic proclivities menaced their rights to hold slaves as well as the prosperity of the cotton economy. Harrison, by contrast, they deemed far safer on the slavery question as well as on economic policy, a son of Virginia who, according to the *Richmond Whig*, "breathes the most ardent and devoted attachment to the rights and institutions of the South."[46]

The Whigs, as ever, embedded their arguments about both economics and slavery in their arguments about politics and the Constitution, arguments that further confute later blanket descriptions of the Whigs as the party of active government and the Democrats the party of laissez-faire. Even the candidate, Harrison, normally limited to mouthing platitudes about liberty and log cabins, made it clear that the Whigs, and not the Democrats, were the party of restrained government, the true heirs of Jefferson and Madison. Instead of meddling with the economy and usurping power, the Whigs would undo the Jacksonians' mischief and then leave well enough alone. "The administration . . . now say to the people, 'You must not watch us, but you must watch the Whigs! Only do that, and all is safe!'" Harrison told a mass meeting in Indiana. "But that, my friends, is not the way. The old-fashioned Republican rule is to watch the Government. See that the Government does not acquire too much power. Keep a check on your rulers. Do this, and liberty is safe."[47]

The Whigs also applied more practical lessons from the Democrats' national campaigns. To Weed and the other party managers, establishing an effective national campaign organization was of equal importance as taking positions on issues. After the Harrisburg convention, an executive Whig committee set up shop in two rooms at the Washington city hall, which quickly became the national party's nerve center. Whig congressmen, making generous use of their franking privileges and the unpaid labor of loyal government workers, turned the place into a fountain of propaganda, largely financed at the public's expense. Down the chain of command, state committees, county committees, town committees, and the all-important local Tippecanoe Clubs geared up to oversee stump speaking, campaign festivities, patronage matters, and the crucial details about getting Whig voters to the polls. At Harrison's home in North Bend, Ohio, the national campaign supplied the general with his own personal committee— to shield him from troublesome correspondence, prepare whatever public remarks he might have to make, and otherwise ensure that he said or did nothing that might offend anyone. Campaign workers also hastily restored Harrison's commodious residence to look more like the log cabin it had originally been, in which Harrison had lived only briefly.[48]

The Whig campaigners showed great ingenuity in exploiting the broadened avenues of commerce and commercial culture and pitching their message into every cranny of American life. Log cabins turned up everywhere, in every imaginable form, as cheap trinkets, parade floats—and, in innumerable towns and cities, as actual edifices, surrounded by barrels of hard cider to treat all who cared to enter, often with a raccoon skin on the wall or even a live raccoon prowling the premises as a rustic finishing touch. Engravers and lithographers churned out endless streams of decorative vignettes and cartoons featuring Harrison as patriot-general, as farmer-citizen, as champion boxer. Medallions of brass and copper turned up like newly minted coins, with the log cabin on one side, Harrison on the other, and the motto, "He leaves the plow to save the country." Porcelain makers supplied campaign mugs and pitchers and platters of every grade to help voters eat, drink, and be merry in the unending presence of the Log Cabin campaign. One of the campaign's consumer items wound up permanently enriching the American vocabulary: the popularity of "Old Cabin Whiskey" (distributed for free along the Erie Canal) brought fame to its makers, the E.C. Booz Distillery of Philadelphia—thus, the birth of booze.

The partisan Whig press also played a crucial role, most successfully a new paper edited by Horace Greeley and named, naturally, the *Log Cabin*. Greeley, always at least two cuts above the average party hack or penny-paper sensationalist, filled his columns with some of the more earnest efforts at explaining new-school Whig political thought and programs, including William Ellery Channing's sermon on self-reform, "Essay on the Laboring Classes." But Greeley also made sure to include song lyrics and other gems of ready-made Whig literary and musical entertainment. (One Whig song stole the tune of an old Thomas Jefferson theme and ended with the words, "For HARRISON and LIBERTY!") Elsewhere these entertainments became as hard to miss as the Whigs' gewgaws. At the very moment that mass-produced pianos and sheet music were entering American parlors as markers of respectable middle-class taste, the Whigs came rushing after with their "Tippecanoe Song Sheets" and "Log Cabin Cotillions." Black-faced minstrel shows—a city-born entertainment, originally popular with young workingmen, that had swept the country in the 1830s—now featured players performing pro-Whig skits and caricatured Negro dialect ditties, to the accompaniment of banjoes and rat-a-tat bones sets. Glee clubs, urban and rural, and popular itinerant singers sang the Whigs' praises. Greeley's *Log Cabin* and the *Boston Atlas* tried to whip up a stir by announcing that Chang and Eng Bunker—the famed Siamese twins who had recently quit touring and retired to Wilkesboro, North Carolina—had most definitely decided to vote the Whig ticket.[49]

The Whigs also took to the political stump as never before. National figures joined in with gusto. Henry Clay, an excellent campaigner, regained his public dignity once he had recovered from his bitter loss, and managed to tell voters with a straight face that they had to choose between "the log cabin and the palace, between hard cider and champagne." The austere, godlike Daniel Webster got fully into the swing of things, dropping his classical cadences in favor of a more conversational and at times rip-snorting delivery. Not to be out-done, the erudite, elegant South Carolina editor and ex-congressman Hugh Swinton Legaré conducted a "slangwhanging" expedition through five states, declaring it unthinkable for southerners not to vote for "a man born and edu-cated in the South."[50]

Even the candidate made a historic breakthrough on the hustings. Perturbed by Democratic criticism of their efforts to keep Harrison under wraps—render-ing him "General Mum," Van Burenite papers snickered—the Whigs broke with campaign tradition and gave their candidate some formal public exposure. It began on July 6, with an unscheduled speech by Harrison on the steps of the National Hotel in Perrysburg, Ohio—the first approximation of a formal cam-paign speech ever delivered by an American presidential candidate. The old gen-eral turned out to be quite good at it, delivering some twenty-three speeches, each one more melodramatic and carefully crafted than the last. ("I am in favor of paper money," he declared in one public statement, which was an orthodox Whig sentiment; then he added straightaway, "I am not a Bank man," which was not.) Harrison milked his old soldiers' glory, timing his speeches to coincide with anniversaries of his military victories and always making sure to have some local old veteran from the War of 1812 totter up on stage beside him. In mid-speech, he would suddenly stop and ostentatiously take a few swigs from a barrel plainly marked "Hard Cider," throwing the audience into an uproar. As to substance, his addresses mainly took unterrified stances against monarchy in government and all unnecessary uses of the executive veto, and pledged he would serve only one term. Harrison showed his gray head to the people, said nothing too dangerous, and played wonderfully to the crowd.[51]

It was not merely theater: it was political theater, with several messages at once. With a combination of calculation and improvisation, the Whig campaign reformulated their broader economic, cultural, and moral precepts and pack-aged them for the voters. Appeals to labor, hard hit by the depression, were ubiq-uitous, not only in speeches and pamphlets but in banners and illuminations that freely borrowed trade union insignias—especially the familiar emblem of a brawny arm lifting a hammer—while praising Old Tip and the overarching harmony of economic interests. Evangelical Protestants could not only hear and read their local ministers extol Whig morality; they could read of how Lyman Beecher himself heartily endorsed Harrison's candidacy. The hard-cider motif, and all of the alcohol served up at the village-green log cabins, did pose a potential obstacle in winning over the pro-temperance evangelicals. But Whig strategists took care of that by releasing testimonials claiming that the party's efforts coaxed men away from taverns and distilled spirits toward loftier pastimes and less dangerous beverages, thereby rendering hard cider a temperance drink and the Whig log cabins halfway houses to sobriety. In a major campaign innovation, the Whig planners made sure to include women supporters by the tens of thousands, and feature them in their festivities—parading not as Fanny Wright feminists but as exemplars of the blossoming evangelical cult of domesticity who looked to General Harrison as their worthy protector. Here and there, women actually gave speeches; more typically, Whig advance men gathered the ladies together, supplied them with Harrison handkerchiefs for waving at the appropriate moments, and placed them conspicuously before the crowds. Obviously, there was no women's vote to be won, but wives and daughters could certainly exercise domestic moral suasion to help direct their men to attend the rallies and vote correctly on election day. The surviving evidence about their thoughts and perceptions suggests that Whig women were fully caught up in the politics as well as the theatrics of the campaign.[52]

The Whigs' ability to infuse these beliefs, values, and loyalties into giant rallies and processions, demotic and sometimes lighthearted spectacles, made the Log Cabin campaign so successful. Enormous contingents of pro-Harrison marchers gathered with torchlights behind their banners—"The Eleventh Ward Young Man's Whig Club," "Boot and Shoemakers for Old Tip"—and then set off, one after the other, along the designated route. In Cleveland, an industrious band of Whigs banged together an immense tin ball—a symbolic gibe at the Democrats—which they then pushed through towns and hamlets to a Whig convention and the state capital, Columbus, over a hundred miles away, cheered and sung to by the faithful:*

> As rolls the ball,
> Van's reign does fall,

---

* The ball-rollings were a joking reference to Thomas Hart Benton's speech when he began a campaign to expunge the Senate's censure of Jackson: "Solitary and alone, I set this ball in motion." Now the anything-but-solitary Whigs would get their own ball rolling—and roll it right over the Democrats.

And he may look
To Kinderhook.

After arriving in Columbus, the Clevelanders met up with another, even larger ball, covered in cowhide, which had been sent on a wagon by the Whigs of Muskingum County. Similar rollings occurred around the country. Even by the Democrats' systematic undercounts, the reported turnouts for these events and others were enormous, numbering upwards of a hundred thousand by the end of the campaign.[53]

As if these crushing events were not bad enough for the Democrats, the last-minute efforts of the political abolitionists were also irritating the Van Burenites in pockets of the North. Van Buren's support of the gag rule and involvement in the *Amistad* affair, and the abolitionists' charges that his complicity with the slaveholders ran even deeper, left him vulnerable. Although the Liberty Party men might have been counted on to draw support chiefly from Yankee Whigs, they seemed at times to be directing themselves chiefly toward dissident Democrats. Whig abolitionists—who scolded the Liberty men as sectarians and as the spoiler promoters of a "Van Buren trick"—stayed loyal to their party, joined the Tippecanoe Clubs, and left the Liberty men to appeal elsewhere. "They had nothing to fear for themselves," one Ohio Liberty man said of the Whigs, "and stumped it for Harrison, for weeks throwing out insinuations against the third party as an affair got up to help Van Buren."[54]

Both of the Liberty candidates, James Birney and Thomas Earle, had Democratic backgrounds, Earle with the hard-money Loco Focos. The Van Burenite editor of the *Albany Argus* became so fearful of the Liberty Party insurgents that he refused to follow instructions from higher-ups to deliver the usual Democratic attacks on abolitionism. Benjamin Butler had to calm Van Buren's fears that a local Democratic Party meeting in New York would favorably consider the abolitionist cause. In Massachusetts, western New York, and Ohio, Liberty Party committees included a healthy proportion of artisans, workers, and nominal Democrats who worked hard to bring Democratic voters into the fold. Their numbers, to be sure, were miniscule overall, and their political campaign was too quickly knocked together to make much of a difference. (In the final tally, the Liberty men would win, in the nonslaveholding states, barely seven thousand votes out of more than 1.7 million cast.) But as the electioneering wore on, the anxieties that pro-slavery forces had long caused Van Buren were complicated by antislavery anxieties that might only grow in the future, even if the Democrats squeaked out a victory. In some marginal northern districts, anger at the administration's placating of the slaveholders, endlessly stoked by the Liberty men, threatened to cost Van Buren valuable votes.[55]

By early autumn, it was obvious that a Democratic victory was impossible.

The Maine elections, held in September, brought a narrow Whig win—and with it the latest version of the most famous chorus of the 1840 campaign:

And have you heard to news from Maine
And what old Maine can do?
She went hell-bent for Governor Kent,
And Tippecanoe and Tyler too,
And Tippecanoe and Tyler too.

So went the nation. When the final results arrived, Harrison had won a respectable 53 percent of the popular vote and had humiliated Van Buren in the Electoral College by a margin of 234 to 60. The Whigs had won states in every section of the country; they had won all of the large states except Virginia; and they had captured both houses of Congress, gaining majorities that appeared impregnable. The results from the South were staggering: Louisiana, Mississippi, Georgia, North Carolina, and Tennessee, once the heartland of Jacksonian electoral success, had broken for Harrison, swayed by southern Whig arguments that their sound economic principles and zeal for state rights would protect slavery far better than the Yankee Loco Foco Van Buren and his corrupt coterie. And the northern states? All except New Hampshire and Illinois also voted for Harrison.[56]

Thurlow Weed and the new-schoolers, with energy, imagination, and all the luck they could ask for, had completed their masterpiece. Once the Whigs had rallied behind a single national candidate and mounted a spectacular campaign, they captured the electorate's imagination. More than 2.4 million voters, nearly a million more than in 1836, had surged to the polls, representing roughly 80 percent of those eligible to cast their ballots—by far the highest turnout ever in a presidential election, and a quantum leap from the figure of about 55 percent four years earlier. Democracy had spoken as never before— and democracy turned out to be Whig. Some alert Democrats saw what was happening as early as the summer. "[T]hey have at last learned from defeat the very act of victory!" the *Democratic Review* exclaimed. "We have taught them how to conquer us!"[57]

ANDREW JACKSON, JACKSONIAN DEMOCRACY, AND DEMOCRACY

"Corruption, bribery and fraud has been extended over the whole Union," Andrew Jackson howled after Harrison's victory. Jackson was burdened with financial difficulties once more, and dying, he said, as fast as he could get on with it. Like other Democrats, he had expected that the virtuous working masses would thwart the Whigs' campaign of gaiety and bunkum, in Tennessee as in the rest of the country. Rousing himself from his physical agonies, he had even ventured out of the Hermitage to give a speech in praise of Van Buren late in the canvass. But Harrison trounced Van Buren in Tennessee as he did nationwide (and pulverized him by a 5 to 1 margin in Jackson's own district), and now it looked as if the Whigs were in a position to destroy the independent treasury, restore the BUS, and then undo everything Jackson had achieved as president. Jackson could still muster his old faith in Providence as well as the people and look to the future. "The democracy of the U[n]ited States have been shamefully beaten," he consoled the defeated president, "*but I trust, not conquered.*" Yet the words rang hollow, with the insistent confidence of a fog-bound old campaigner.[58]

Jackson would live long enough to have a last laugh. Neither American democracy nor his own party—the Democracy—had been conquered in 1840. The Whig triumph raised questions, though, about how democratic the Democracy had been, still was, and would remain. More precisely: how had the Jacksonian ascendancy shaped, for better and for worse, the democratic impulses that had arisen out of the American Revolution and had evolved so furiously after 1815?

In its embryonic form, the Jackson Democracy was a political coalition produced chiefly by three crucial developments. The Panic of 1819 and subsequent depression shattered the overextended Republican Party that had led the nation to war against Britain and, at war's end, had promised new national development and prosperity. The coincident crisis over Missouri statehood produced arguments over the future of American slavery that threatened to rearrange the shattered political allegiances along sectional lines. The presidential election of 1824, instead of resolving these upheavals, ended in deadlock and an alleged corrupt bargain that, as far as Jackson and his supporters were concerned, was a virtual coup d'etat against the will of the electorate. In 1828, Jackson, running chiefly as the warrior-avenger against the plotters of 1824–25, John Quincy Adams and Henry Clay, took moderate and, to some, ambiguous stands on major issues like the tariff and internal improvements. But the promises that he did make to cleanse the Augean stables in Washington stirred planters, small farmers, and workingmen hit hard by the depression and wary of Adams and Clay's American System. They also attracted voters who feared that fights over slavery would tear the nation apart. With an electoral base that was strongest in the South and West, Jackson benefited greatly from the sophisticated political operations of his supporters in the middle states, above all the New Yorker Martin Van Buren, and swept to victory. "They believed him honest and patriotic," the veteran Washington politico Nathan Sargent later recalled of Jackson's supporters, "that he was a friend of the *people*, battling for them against corruption and extravagance, and opposed only by dishonest politicians."[59]

Jackson's winning coalition was not yet, however, the Jackson Democracy, which only emerged from the convulsive labors of Jackson's first term. The new president's comprehensive Indian removal policy reinforced, for a time, the allegiances of southern planters and small farmers, especially in states that contained the bulk of newly cleared land. But Jackson's bank veto and subsequent war with Nicholas Biddle alienated northern business interests (including the so-called Bank Democrats) as well as southern planters who saw the BUS as an anchor of financial stability. The nullification crisis, in turn, completed the schism that had begun with debates over the tariff and John C. Calhoun's fall from Jackson's political good graces, and that in time drove state-rights planters into the opposition. Although South Carolina wound up isolated from the other slaveholding states in 1833, sympathy for nullification and resentment of Jackson gripped a substantial portion of the southern planter elite—including "original" Jacksonians who, once the Indian removal issue was virtually settled, were repelled by both Jackson's democratic nationalism and his attack on the BUS. But Jackson threw down the gauntlet: "the tariff was only the pretext and disunion and a southern confederacy the real object," he observed immediately after the nullification crisis ended.[60] Nullification's defeat, along with Biddle's one year later, nearly completed the first important stage of the Democracy's formation, which would culminate under President Van Buren with the Conservative defections over the independent treasury.

What, then, was the Jackson Democracy in its mature form? One powerful interpretation, refuting earlier descriptions of Jacksonianism as a western movement, claims that the party actually owed more to eastern labor, and that the political conflict of the 1830s can be better understood in terms of classes than of sections. Other writers, asserting an entrepreneurial consensus over economic issues, have posited either that these conflicts were insubstantial clashes between rival "ins" and "outs," or that religion, ethnicity, and other cultural issues actually drove Jacksonian politics. Still others have charged that Jacksonian Democracy was an alliance of slaveholders and racist "northern men with southern feelings" dedicated to clearing out the Indians, expanding U.S. territory, and keeping the imperial republic safe for slavery. More recently, historians have revived the economic and class interpretation but without its eastern focus, depicting Jacksonianism as a movement of subsistence farmers and urban workers resisting the encroachments of capitalist development. Each view has something to recommend it, but all of them slight the dynamic and unstable character of the Democracy's rise and development, and the primacy of politics and political thinking in the conflicts of the era.[61]

Jacksonianism hardly began as an eastern movement concerned with labor, money, and banking, and some westerners remained vital loyalists. Support for Jackson in 1828 was far sturdier in the South and West than it was in the East. Through the 1830s and beyond, Jacksonian rhetoric always reserved a prized place for the noble independent farmer and the landed interest—what the neo-Jeffersonian Martin Van Buren called the great irreplaceable bulwark "against the political demoralizing and anti-republican tendency of the Hamiltonian policy."[62] Yeoman portions of the South and West generally stayed loyal to the Democrats in local and national elections through the 1830s and after. But the Democracy did evolve in ever closer association with eastern hard-money radicalism during the Bank War and its aftermath, merging Jackson's own antibanking views with those that arose out of the Workie and Loco Foco movements. Some western anti-BUS men—Thomas Hart Benton, Amos Kendall, Francis Blair—were also steadfast and influential hard-money Jacksonians for the duration of the 1830s. There is a case to be made that, apart from Jackson, these westerners, especially Kendall and Blair, exerted the most important pressure inside the administration to keep it on the hard-money path. Yet large numbers of anti-BUS westerners also deserted the party when the war on eastern privilege became a war on the paper system and speculation, including land speculation. And although many anti-BUS easterners did the same, eastern radicals supplied the intellectual and political firepower to support the removal of the deposits, the Specie Circular, and the subtreasury plan. If anyone was the intellectual architect of Jacksonian economic policy after 1832, it was the Philadelphia radical William Gouge.[63]

When, during Van Buren's presidency, the Whigs began labeling the Jacksonians as "Loco Focos," the attempted slur had merit. The meter as well as the rhymes of the Democrats' appeals may have slipped off-kilter by 1840, but their sentiments rang out clearly enough, as in one pro–Van Buren broadside:

> Then let the working class,
> As a congregated man,
> Behold an insidious enemy:
> For each *Banker* is a foe,
> And his aim is for our woe—
> He's the *canker-worm of liberty!*

The guarded Van Buren, long an ally of upstate New York bankers, would never go as far as the Loco Focos desired. But in his own careful way—praised by no less a radical than Frances Wright—Van Buren vindicated the core of hard-money radicalism. The rest of the Democracy, shorn of its Conservative wing, was increasingly a party dominated by the same ideas, advanced most coherently by eastern radicals with their roots in the old city democracy.[64]

The claim that these appeals betrayed an underlying entrepreneurial consensus with the Whigs stretches the idea of consensus beyond recognition. The Democrats favored private property, commercial growth, individual labor, and the personal accumulation of money, at which many of them excelled. None (apart from Brownson and whatever small coterie shared his ideas) were social revolutionaries of the sort that, in the last century, became widely considered the sine qua non of genuine radicalism. But the Democracy's economic radicalism, based on creating a hard-money currency regulated by the federal government, was predicated on a form of commerce and a way of life that were fundamentally at odds with the Whigs' credit-and-paper, boom-and-bust system—a system, Roger B. Taney complained, driven by "speculation and the desire of growing rich suddenly without labor" that had "made fearful inroads upon the patriotism and public spirit of what one called the higher classes of society." Whereas the Whigs savored the romance of risk and capitalist investment (where the greatest spoils belonged to the greatest victor), Democrats favored a more secure and egalitarian commercialism—not what the *Globe* called "a succession of throws of the die"—which they believed would distribute wealth more evenly while keeping political power in the hands of the majority of the citizenry. At stake in the politics of the 1830s, or so the participants believed, was which form of commerce would prevail.[65]

The depth of that conflict did not mean that Democrats and Whigs fought it out solely on class or on economic grounds, especially in the North. Like all successful parties, the Democrats and Whigs contained coalitions that included elements of all social classes. Economic interests—or voters' responses to the effects of rapid commercial growth, what some historians have called the "market revolution" of the era—were not the only interests in play. Part of the genius of new-school Whiggery was its ability to turn the Panic of 1837 against the Democrats while also describing political and economic issues culturally, reorienting debates along ethical and cultural lines that cut across differences of wealth and class. It was not merely a calculated sideshow: the "continual state of moral war" that the Whig John Bell described in 1835 tapped into a clash of ideologies far greater than any mere partisan subterfuge could invent. The Whigs' morality, in turn, attracted disproportionate numbers of Presbygational evangelicals, just as it consigned Irish Catholics (despite Seward's efforts in New York) and most of those masses who remained indifferent to religion to the Democrats. Class and economics were always central to Jacksonian politics, but the Whig revolution of conservatism encouraged voters to understand economic success and failure in cultural ways that reinforced the legitimacy of Whig economics. In the 1840s, that understanding, in polyglot northern polities like New York, would yield partisan voting returns that divided sharply along ethnic and (especially) religious lines.[66]

Race, slavery, and antislavery also shaped Jacksonianism. Jackson's anti-abolitionism (restated pointedly by Van Buren in his inauguration address) was a salient feature of the larger Democracy. The efforts by congressional Democrats and the White House to placate the party's southern wing without succumbing to the Calhounites became a running theme after 1833. Although this expediency, and toleration of "the Slave Power," alienated some northern Democrats, a minority of middling new-school Whigs appear to have greatly outnumbered the Jacksonians who gravitated to the abolitionists before 1840. Democrats, North and South, were friendlier than the Whigs to expansionist efforts that would widen opportunities for the spread of slavery. The propensity of Democratic leaders to see antislavery agitation in partisan terms led them to equate, falsely, political ambition and opportunism with genuine humanitarianism, much as they did in the fight over Indian removal—or as the antirestrictionist compromisers did during the Missouri crisis in 1819–21. To halt the abolitionist agitation and quiet southern counteragitation, both Jackson and Van Buren attacked the abolitionists' civil rights, in the mails and gag-rule controversies—and, in the latter, were resolutely opposed by a small group of House Whigs led by John Quincy Adams. Although Whigs and Democrats shared in the Negrophobia dominant among all whites in the 1830s, northern Democrats did take the lead in disenfranchising blacks (as in Pennsylvania in 1837–38), even as they celebrated the growing political participation of lower-class white men.

None of this, however, made the Jacksonians a pro-slavery party—or even, as one milder critic has argued, *functionally* pro-slavery"—fighting a proto-abolitionist Whig Party in order to protect a status quo that left the slaveholders the dominant class in American politics. The Jacksonians did not oppose interference with slavery where it existed, or obstruct the abolitionist efforts to arouse the South, because they wished to sustain the slaveholders as a national ruling class. They wanted, as the Whigs did, to keep slavery out of federal politics to protect constitutional order, national harmony, and party unity. Sustaining the slaveholders' power was the goal of Calhoun and others, who saw the planter class not as dominant but as beleaguered, and to whom the Jacksonians would never, after 1830, come close to measuring up. (The Jacksonians, by contrast, generally spoke of slavery as a misfortune that would eventually disappear.) As time passed, the most vociferous pro-slavery elements in the original Jacksonian coalition actually left the party—first the Calhounites, then the state-rights Whigs such as John Tyler, then the anti–Van Buren planters, and finally the southern bank Conservatives. When Calhoun temporarily rejoined the Democrats in 1838, he aimed chiefly to destroy it as it existed and remake it into a genuine slaveholders' party.[67]

Even the profound and sometimes vicious racism commonly found among northern Democrats was less uniform, less singular, and more complicated than it might appear. There were at least some important antislavery Democratic partisans, including William Leggett, whose radicalism also extended to race. And as the anti-abolitionist violence of the mid-1830s showed, conservative Whig gentlemen and nominal Democratic conservatives were just as drawn to hair-raising, inflammatory racist attacks on blacks as mainstream Democrats were. Even Democrats who led fights for black disenfranchisement were trying to sustain their egalitarian ideals against racist conservative hierarchy, in ways that now seem cruelly paradoxical and are difficult to comprehend. According to the Democracy's conception of citizenship, political equality was indistinguishable from social equality. And yet, pro-disenfranchisement Democrats argued, their Whig opponents were proposing political equality for black men without granting them social equality—to the Democrats, an absurdity that made a mockery of equal rights. "[Y]ou could not admit the blacks to a participation in the government of the country," one New York Democrat argued, "unless you put them on terms of social equality," something that neither the Whigs nor the Democrats intended to do. At the state constitutional convention of the new state of Michigan, another Democrat swore that he would oppose giving the vote to any blacks "until we consent to treat them as equal with us in all respects."[68] Only with the rise, very late in the decade, of the more liberal of the new-school Whigs such as Seward and Giddings did the opposition make any clear moves in the direction toward greater social tolerance of blacks—much to the consternation of more moderate and conservative northern Whigs and the horror of southern Whigs. Even then, mainstream northern Democratic racism was not the same thing as pro-slavery.

At bottom, the Jackson Democracy was chiefly what its proponents said it was—a political movement for, and largely supported by, those who considered themselves producers pitted against a nonproducer elite. Moral clashes, and the simmering disputes over abolitionism and slavery, helped further define the movement. Yet even these connections can mislead, for on all of these fronts, Democrats assumed that politics and government institutions remained the primary locus of power. Here was the key to Jacksonian politics: a belief that relatively small groups of self-interested men were out to destroy majority rule and, with it, the Constitution. The nonproducing few were able to oppress the productive many, the Democracy proclaimed, because of deliberate political corruptions that thwarted the great principle undergirding American government, popular sovereignty. The corrupt bargain of 1824–25 had negated the people's will and launched an administration awash in peculation and extravagance. The Second BUS had been granted enormous powers with no accountability to the people. The entire paper-and-credit system, unless properly reformed and regulated, created illegitimate authority at war with popular sovereignty and equal rights. The twisted doctrine of nullification proposed to allow a few designing men, under the pretext of opposing the tariff, to usurp powers delegated to the people's representatives by the Constitution—and then to permit those men, if challenged, to dissolve the Union. Abolitionists were deluded philanthropists, dupes of northern BUS aristocrats and southern nullifiers who wanted to create political havoc and destroy the Democracy. In all these cases and others, political abuses formed the matrix of oppression. Accordingly, the cure was political as well—above all, promulgating the central Jacksonian principle that the majority is to govern.

The Jacksonians hardly invented that democratic principle, nor did they initiate the expansion of democratic rights and power for ordinary white men that posterity too often associates purely with Andrew Jackson. But they greatly encouraged as well as benefited from that expansion, giving the politics forged earlier by the city and country democracies and then the Jefferson Republicans an unprecedented presence and power in national affairs. The Jacksonians' chief institutional innovation within the operations of government, apart from Jackson's rotation-in-office reform, was to vaunt the power of the executive—selected, as never before, by the ballots of ordinary voters and not (with the glaring exception of South Carolina) by state legislators—as the only branch of the national government chosen by the people at large. Jackson used that authority to the fullest extent granted him by the Constitution, turning a democratized version of Hamiltonian doctrines about an energetic executive toward goals that would have shocked Alexander Hamilton.

The destruction of the Second Bank of the United States and the creation of the independent treasury became the foremost of those goals—and, in attaining them, the Jacksonians made fundamental and lasting changes in the nation's political economy. At the time, and well over a century later, many observers misunderstood Jackson's and Van Buren's banking policies and the evolving hard-money Democracy. "Those who regard it in no higher aspect than a mere financial arrangement," John Niles declared in the Senate, "a question of temporary expediency, cannot appreciate the motive of those who consider it the first important stop in the reform of our wretched paper money system, on the one hand, and of our political institutions on the other." By ending Nicholas Biddle's privately controlled national bank, Whigs and Conservative Democrats predicted, Jackson and Van Buren threatened the nation with a revolution against property and a descent into barbarism. Instead came what Niles called "the entire separation and exclusion of the organized moneyed power from our political institutions," a final rejection of the Hamiltonian idea that the private banking and business community should have special powers in deciding economic policy.[69]

The Jacksonians' solutions would be tested over the decades to come, by pro-business forces and private corruption schemes, as well as by the ups and downs of a rapidly industrializing economy—ups and downs that no reform could completely quell. The decentralized arrangements that the Jacksonians inaugurated would eventually prove so unwieldy and ineffective that a later southern Democratic president, Woodrow Wilson, would help replace it with the Federal Reserve System. But never again would formal institutional control over banking and currency policy fall so far from the purview of the president and Congress—and, thus, the voters—as it had under Biddle's BUS. In the final analysis, it would be the government and its direct appointees, and not the business community, that would make the nation's decisions. Coupled with the Jacksonians' announced friendliness to labor, the reversal announced a momentous shift in concerns, with an increased wariness of the corrupting power of wealthy businessman and speculators, and a great receptivity for the view, expressed by William Gouge, that "[i]f any classes of the community deserve the favor of the government, in any country, they are the farmers, mechanics, and other hardworking men." If they did not invent democracy, the Jacksonians did make this way of thinking the basic credo of American liberal democracy.[70]

Jackson's emphatic presidential style affected American politics as well as government. By the end of his second term, Jackson had twice smashed and remade his cabinet, ostracized one vice president and handpicked his successor, hired and fired large batches of other civil servants at will, vetoed more legislation than all of his predecessors combined, destroyed nullification and the Second BUS—and seen a Senate resolution condemning him for constitutional misconduct officially expunged from the record. Thomas Jefferson had been an effective president, but Jackson transformed the office and its potential and made it the focus of national leadership based on boldly democratic premises unavailable to Jefferson. And although Jackson's performance as president would loom above his successors' for decades to come, his elevation of the presidency, coupled with the rise of a credible national opposition in the late 1830s, helped complete the process that turned presidential elections into quadrennial democratic frenzies. During the flush period of voting by eligible citizens between the 1790s and 1816, rates of participation in presidential contests generally lagged behind those for state and local offices. The "one-party" politics of the inaptly named Era of Good Feelings brought a general falling-off of participation, but when the pattern began to change in 1828, the nationwide turnout for the presidential election more than doubled, to 56.3 percent. There the figure stabilized until the battle over the reelection of Jackson's successor in 1840, when it jumped again to about 80 percent, a level that would be roughly sustained for the rest of the nineteenth century. The irony is that Jackson and the Jacksonians had made contests over the presidency, as well as the presidency itself, matter as never before, but the great surge of 1840 came on behalf of an anti-Jacksonian candidate and party pledged to curtailing presidential power.[71]

The Jacksonians also created the first mass democratic national political party in modern history—the institutional basis for mobilizing and then consolidating political loyalties and participation. Earlier approximations of mass parties had arisen over sharp ideological differences and devised effective means to spread their messages, get their supporters to the polls, and struggle over government policy at the local and national levels. More than the conventional historical wisdom on the "deferential-participant" politics of the era allows, there was a great deal of democracy in Jeffersonian Democracy. But to the founding generation, the idea of parties still remained tainted with associations to vicious factions that would corrupt and divide the republican commonwealth, and a great deal of power in national and state politics remained formally concentrated in the hands of small and constricted elites, concretized in the congressional nominating caucus.[72]

The Jacksonian party that emerged out of the collapse of the "one-party" period and the death of the caucus system dispensed with those fears and greatly enlarged on earlier forms of party organization. Elections were the crucial events for this new democracy, toward which all organizing efforts led. But elections were only the culmination of a continual effort to draw together the faithful. In place of the discarded nominating caucuses, the Jacksonians substituted a national network of committees, reaching up from the ward and township level to the quadrennial national convention, each a place where, at least in principle, the popular will would be determined and ratified. The political ferment continued almost year-round, with local committees calling regular meetings to approve local nominations, pass public resolutions, and mount elaborate processions. Sometimes, as in the Tammany Hall meeting that brought the Loco Foco schism in 1835, these party gatherings could get out of hand, further reinforcing conservative prejudices like Philip Hone's about "the dunghill of Democracy." But even at their most tumultuous, the Jacksonians could claim that more than any previous party or faction, they honored what New York's *Evening Post* called "[t]he democratic theory . . . that the people's voice is the supreme law."[73]

The Jacksonians did not, however, fully reconcile themselves to the idea of what later historians and social scientists would call a party system. Seeing themselves as the authentic legatees of the Jeffersonian Republicans, they assumed that if they did their work correctly, they would forever hold the opposing aristocratic party at bay. Far from regarding themselves as simply an electoral machine, they believed they were the constitutional party of the sovereign people. They were an organization, as Jacksonians ceaselessly reiterated, "of principles, not of men," in which active devotion to the party would sustain the classless Constitution. Lacking the private resources of the aristocrats of "associated wealth," the people had no choice but to organize as a party—virtually along military lines with ballot boxes as their weapons—to sustain their sovereignty. The few, in response, would be free to organize their own opposition party—a focus of competition that would make the Jacksonians' own political efforts more disciplined. But the Jacksonians never envisaged an operational contest between rival political organizations, or what the *Evening Post* called "the mere struggle of ambitious leaders for power." Instead, they expected a two-party system in which they, the party of popular sovereignty, would hold power more or less in perpetuity, unless, as Van Buren said, diminished zeal led to "the gradual abandonment of the principles it sustained."[74]

The politics of the 1830s proved how elusive Van Buren's party vision actually was—and how unstable the Democracy remained. Thanks, chiefly, to the new-school Whigs, the opposition not only improved on the Democracy's electioneering tools; it devised a contrasting democratic message that struck a deep nerve in the electorate that the Democrats did not even realize was there. And quite apart from Van Buren's defeat in 1840, the Democracy confronted internal difficulties and external challenges that majoritarian politics could not fully handle. The return of John C. Calhoun threatened to turn the party into a handmaiden for Calhoun's pro-slavery nullifier views. The appearance of the political abolitionists, although only a minor force in 1840, promised to prolong and intensify agitation over slavery. The stigma of the depression forced Democrats to think anew about the hard-money principles that had become a cornerstone of their democratic politics. So did the loss of both the White House and the Congress.

Larger ideological questions arose as well. How long could Democrats, in the name of preserving sectional harmony, back the gag rule and other attacks on free speech without fatally compromising their own ideals of equal rights? How long could the Democracy present itself as the party of the producing classes and still defend the interests of slaveholders—men whom some Democrats had begun regarding as nonproducers who lived, as Thomas Morris declared in the Senate, "upon the unrequited labor of others"? The very raising of those questions, meanwhile, caused consternation among southern Master Race Democrats, for whom the bondage of blacks had become a basic precondition for securing political equality among whites. How, in their eyes, could equality be preserved if the very foundation of equality came under question? How could democracy endure without slavery, or with slavery under assault?

The ironies of the Jacksonians' predicament were enormous—and, as far as the future of the Jackson Democracy was concerned, tragic. Their success in the 1830s had been so great that even when the opposition finally beat them, it was on their own democratic political terms that old-guard conservatives had abhorred. By decade's end, Whigs and Democrats alike could agree in principle with Jacksonian paeans to the people and majority rule. Two different intersectional, partisan versions of democracy had emerged, both propounded by diverse political coalitions. Yet by opening up popular politics and by enshrining the popular will, the Jacksonians also exposed the political system to new forms of agitation over precisely the issues they and the Whig Party leadership tried so hard to suppress. The first flickering of that new political agitation was the electoral debut of the Liberty Party in 1840. Over the years to come, the rising flame would consume both the Democracy and the Whigs—and ignite a democratic revolution more profound than anything discernible amid the torchlit furies of the Log Cabin campaign.

III.

SLAVERY AND THE CRISIS OF AMERICAN DEMOCRACY

17

WHIG DEBACLE, DEMOCRATIC CONFUSION

On March 1, 1841, in the vaulted Supreme Court hearing room at the Capitol just beneath the Senate chamber, seventy-four-year-old John Quincy Adams completed his eight-hour argument in defense of the *Amistad* rebels. The proceedings had been interrupted by the sudden death of Justice Philip Barbour, and by the time he resumed, Adams had been thinking about mortality and the departed great Americans of decades past.* His defense was more political than legal, charging the Van Buren administration with gross interference and moral indifference. Nearing the close of his statement, reverie and politics converged as Adams pointed to two framed copies of Jefferson's Declaration of Independence that hung in the room, in clear view of all the justices: "The moment you come, to the Declaration of Independence, that every man has a right to life and liberty, an inalienable right, this case is decided. I ask nothing more in behalf of these unfortunate men, than this Declaration." The maturing contradictions, for northerners, in the Jackson Democracy's professions of equality and its tolerance of slavery could not have been rendered more dramatically.[1]

Three days later, also at the Capitol, another Whig, the new president,

---

* The day before he finished his argument, Adams heard a sermon from the book of Revelation, to mark the closing of the congressional session. Although the minister was not, according to Adams, up to his task, Adams wrote out the verses in his diary, including Revelation 20:12: "And I saw the dead, small and great, stand before God; and the books were opened; and another book was opened, which is the book of life; and the dead were judged out of those things which were written in the books, according to their works." *JQAD*, 10: 434–5.

William Henry Harrison, delivered an inauguration address that was a fraction of the length of Adams's *Amistad* argument but seemed to go on forever. Speaking in a driving snowstorm for one hour and forty-five minutes—still the longest presidential inaugural speech in history—Harrison's billowing prolixity expounded little beyond a restatement of Whig precepts of a limited executive and his promise not to seek a second term, assurances that he would not overuse the veto power, and an opaque discussion of economic issues, hostile both to the independent treasury and to the revival of a national bank. It was a fitting commencement for a figurehead president (delivered to throngs of supporters in military finery and Tippecanoe Club gear) whose primary political virtue was his haziness and whose administration was already beset by rival Whig factions, each hoping to manipulate him and elect its own favorite in 1844.[2]

The contrast between the revitalized Adams's performance and Harrison's was stark. (Adams called the inauguration display "showy-shabby.") So was the difference in where the performances led. On March 9, the Supreme Court, in a 7 to 1 decision written by Justice Story, ruled in favor of the *Amistad* defense, declaring that the rebels had never been slaves and ordering them freed once and for all. The same day, and for weeks to come, Harrison, suffering from a severe cold since his swearing-in—he had declined to wear a topcoat despite the snowstorm—was beset by the locusts of Whig office seekers who had poured into Washington. Late in March, his illness was diagnosed as pleurisy. He recovered briefly (and one day slipped off to buy some household provisions at a nearby market), but suffered a relapse. Exactly one month after his inauguration, he died. A vice president of convenience, the state-rights, anti–national bank Virginian John Tyler, was suddenly the president, which plunged the Whig Party and the government into utter confusion.[3]

At the Hermitage, Andrew Jackson did not hide his delight at Harrison's demise. "A kind and overruling providence had interfered," he wrote to Francis Blair, "to prolong our glorious Union and happy republican system which Genl. Harrison and his cabinet was preparing to destroy under the dictation of that profligate demagogue, Henry Clay." Yet if Jackson's Democracy had been spared a fight to the finish, it would not be spared its own confusion. Most Democrats expected that, with Harrison dead, they would continue their struggle over economic issues, await what Martin Van Buren always called "the sober second thought of the people," and reinstall Van Buren with a new Democratic Congress in 1844. But John C. Calhoun—hard at work in his spare time writing what he called "a regular &, I think, I may say scientifick development of my views of gover[n]ment"—had different ideas.[4] So did many others, as growing popular unrest over slavery and democracy shook the Democracy to its core.

THE WHIGS IN DISARRAY

John Tyler—tall and refined, with an aquiline nose that reminded many of an ancient Roman statesman's—greeted Henry Clay graciously when the senator paid his first official visit in May. Tyler and Clay had long been political and personal friends, dating back to their alliance during the Missouri crisis twenty years earlier. Although their principles had since diverged widely, Tyler was considered a Clay man within his adoptive Whig Party. But lately Clay had been on a rampage, seeking to gather not just the Whigs but the entire federal government under his command on Capitol Hill, and the meeting with Tyler was bound to be difficult. The two men conversed in detail about the major current political issues, above all the rechartering of a new national bank, which Clay adamantly favored. Tyler demurred; Clay stood his ground; and the exasperated president finally lost his patience.

"Then, sir," Tyler snapped, "I wish you to understand this—that you and I were born in the same district; that we have fed upon the same food, and have breathed the same natal air. Go you now, then, Mr. Clay, to your end of the avenue, where stands the Capitol, and there perform your duty to the country as you shall think proper. So help me God, I shall do mine at this end of it as I shall think proper."[5]

After the Whig victories in 1840, Clay had determined that even if he was not president, he would run the government and shift power away from the executive branch and back to Capitol Hill. At last, the Whigs could undo President Jackson's supposed theft of Congress's power, but with Clay now eager to become a chieftain every bit as powerful as Jackson had been. Clay's legislative agenda—chartering another national bank, passing a land bill to provide revenues for internal improvements, sustaining a protective tariff—would, he expected, become the agenda for the whole Whig Party, and then the nation. Next would come what Clay considered urgent constitutional reforms: to limit the power of the presidential veto, limit presidential tenure to a single term, and bring the Treasury Department under the exclusive control of Congress.[6]

Clay was always aware that personal rivalries, especially with Daniel Webster, would complicate his plans. Harrison, offended by Clay's imperiousness, had named Webster secretary of state and appeared to favor Webster's friends over Clay's in selecting most of his cabinet. Yet the origins of Clay's new difficulties would prove, as ever, more political and ideological than personal—his failure, in this instance, to understand that his own view of proper Whig government was only one among many, and that even his iron will and disarming wit could not fully suppress the differences. The Whig Party, old Harrison Gray Otis advised Clay, was "a coalition of persons, brought together from the four ends of the earth." There were the Webster Whigs, conservative on economics and on abolitionism, but with some antislavery sympathies; there were the new-school Whigs, like Seward and Weed, uncomfortable with the Bank of the United States and with slaveholder domination; there were the northern Whigs like John Quincy Adams and his little anti–gag rule band, caught up in the slavery and abolition whirligig; and there were the slaveholder Whigs like Tyler and his fellow Virginians Abel Upshur and Henry A. Wise, supremely committed to southern state rights. If Clay failed to find, and then stick to, political ground that all factions could share (as they had during the Log Cabin enthusiasm), then, Otis warned, "the cossacks will be on you in one or two years." Otis was right.[7]

Tyler attempted to create a middle path between Clay's pro-BUS Whiggery and the hard-money radicalism that still dominated the Democracy. Although he had defected to the Whigs in 1835 over what he deemed Jackson's abuses of state rights—he had voted against the Force Bill in 1833—Tyler had always been an opponent of Biddle's BUS and had firmly supported Jackson's bank policies. His willingness to join the Whig ticket in 1840 led some to think that, as president, he could be persuaded to back the Whigs' measures—"including a Bank of the U.S.," Clay wrote hopefully upon hearing of Harrison's death.[8] But Tyler had a stubborn streak of his own. His row with Clay during their initial testy White House interview would degenerate during the summer of 1841 into an all-out war.

Clay had coaxed President Harrison, before his death, into calling a special summertime session of Congress because of the continuing economic depression and the possibility that the federal government would soon go bankrupt, but Clay also desired to pass as much of his program as quickly as he could and consolidate his rule. Working on a punishing daily schedule, he rammed through the Senate his first order of business, repeal of the independent treasury, and by the session's end, Tyler had signed the bill.[9] Other Clay-backed measures won approval after prolonged congressional haggling. Thanks to Tyler, however, Clay did not get his national bank, and after that defeat, the senator made sure that the president lost virtually all connection with the Whig Party.

The bank debacle unfolded in two stages. After close consultations with Secretary of the Treasury Thomas Ewing (a Webster ally), John C. Calhoun backed a carefully crafted administration bank bill with a section that provided for the establishment of branch offices, but only if the states where they were to be located formally approved. The requirement had been added to overcome Tyler's constitutional objections to the Second BUS. Clay would have none of it, declared the people wanted "a real old-fashioned Bank," and rewrote the bill. Eliminating the branching proposal proved politically impossible, so Clay concocted an awkward compromise, enabling the states to disallow branches only immediately after passage of the bank bill, but allowing the bank to overrule those objections whenever it became "necessary and proper" to establish a branch office. The contraption squeaked through the Senate, then passed the House in early August. On August 16, Tyler's veto arrived, objecting to the branching amendment as well the bank's proposed powers to discount notes. Hisses, boos, and groans rained down from the Senate gallery as the message was read. Clay sat at his desk, unperturbed; Thomas Hart Benton, who had joined a small delegation of Democrats at a well-lubricated White House celebration the night after Tyler announced his veto, turned to the galleries and shouted back at the "Bank ruffians."[10]

Tyler's veto was not his final word on the matter. Although he opposed any "old-fashioned" national bank, he could live with some sort of national fiscal institution so long as it passed constitutional muster. With an eye to running for president himself in 1844, and reluctant to be known as a simon-pure antibank man, he agreed to support yet another compromise bill, giving way on the branch office question but insisting that states have the power to disallow the branches' discounting of promissory notes. That bill, too, was destined to pass Congress, but by the time it did, Tyler had changed his mind once more.[11]

Clay, in responding to Tyler's veto of the original bill, could not help veering into sarcasm, referring to the president as "solitary and alone, shivering by the pitiless storm," with nary enough supporters to "compose a decent *corporal's guard.*" With friends like that, Tyler decided, he'd be better off rejoining the Democrats, or perhaps starting a third party to win the presidency. Besides, except for the estimable Webster, he had tired of his scheming, pro-BUS cabinet secretaries, and was looking for a way to get rid of them without conducting an ugly public purge. Reversing himself on the bank bill would surely drive them out. And so, in late August, Tyler informed the cabinet that he would not sign the bill and asked them to work for a postponement. "Never, never!" Clay replied when asked to withdraw the bill. "No, not if we stay here till Christmas." On September 9, Tyler announced his second veto. Within forty-eight hours, every cabinet member save Webster and Postmaster General Francis Granger had quit, and Granger resigned soon after. The special session of Congress ended with the Whigs thoroughly demoralized, but with Clay ready to rally the faithful once more. In a speech to the Whig caucus, he commended the members for their efforts and compared the president to Benedict Arnold: "Tyler is on his way to the Democratic camp. They may give him lodging in some outhouse, but they will never trust him. He will stand there, like Arnold in England, a monument of his own perfidy and disgrace."[12]

Clay would return for the next session of Congress, but fatigue and the effects of what may have been a mild heart attack sapped his will. On March 31, 1842, he resigned from the Senate and returned to Ashland, where he would rest in preparation for yet another try for the presidency in 1844. His spirit lingered in Congress, which passed a new protective tariff bill retaining the rates of the 1833

Compromise Tariff, just as Clay had hoped. (Tyler's veto of an earlier tariff bill led to the first serious presidential impeachment investigation in American history, led by John Quincy Adams, over alleged abuse of the veto power.) Clay's old rival Webster, meanwhile, stubbornly kept faith with the administration for as long as he could. In 1842, he concluded negotiations on a major treaty with British foreign secretary Lord Ashburton that resolved the Maine–New Brunswick border dispute and, for good measure, settled the entire length of the U.S.-Canadian border east of the Rocky Mountains, sparing the nation from what some feared was an inevitable third Anglo-American war. Reveling in an executive office—"[h]aving been without it all his life," George Bancroft observed, "he has a fondness for it, of which you can have no conception"— Webster happily (and injudiciously) attacked Clay's presidential prospects, thereby alienating his own virulently anti-Tyler state party. Webster feigned indifference, yet by 1843 Tyler had begun heeding southern Democratic counsels over a new project that Webster despised, the annexation of Texas. Finally, in May, Webster stepped down, severing the administration's last important tie to the Whigs.[13]

Hundreds of miles to the north, on his estate outside Kinderhook, New York, Martin Van Buren was gloating. With little experience but great common sense, he ran an excellent farm. He also indulged his love of entertaining guests with rich food and French champagne. More dubiously, Van Buren's admiration for European style extended to architecture, which would prompt him years later to deface the fine old Federalist-style mansion he had bought in 1839 by adding gingerbread frills and an Italianate tower. But in the early 1840s, pretension was crowded out by simple country elegance and pleasant conversation, much of it about politics. In his dining room, Van Buren hung portraits of Jefferson and Jackson, and here, and in his private study, he would talk over the Whigs' debacles and the deluge of letters supporting his return to office in 1844. The "eyes of the people" were reopening, he said, just as he had said they would.[14]

Early in 1842, Van Buren took a political tour of the South and West, from Charleston to New Orleans, up to Tennessee, and then, for the month of June, to the Old Northwest. The highlight was a sentimental visit to the Hermitage (Van Buren's first ever), where Jackson, though much reduced and hit by waves of chills and fever, gave him a delighted reception. Van Buren could not have known how at the time, but his journey looked to the future as well as the past. One evening, making his way from St. Louis to Chicago, he stopped in the town of Rochester, outside Springfield, Illinois. As usual, the local Democratic notables turned up to greet and entertain him, and they brought along a young Whig friend, now a former state representative, "Honest" Abe Lincoln. Lincoln had never liked Van Buren's mentor, and he had lately been gripped by a deep and prolonged melancholia that would chronically plague him the rest of his life. A night out would give him a chance to meet an ex-president and might even force him to relax. As it happened, perhaps to his surprise, he and the Little Magician Van Buren hit it off. Kindling to his company, Lincoln was in excellent form, spinning stories and telling jokes with the former president and his party until late at night. Van Buren went to bed aching from his laughter, and later remarked that he had never "spent so agreeable a night in his life."[15]

While Van Buren and Lincoln made merry, John C. Calhoun was plotting. Tyler's accession had frustrated Calhoun's hopes to manipulate the Democracy into becoming the party of southern state rights, with himself at the helm. Now the vindication of state rights lay in the hands of a nominal Whig, elected in a demagogic campaign that the South Carolina legislature had formally denounced as an insult to free men everywhere. The irony might have brought the hint of a smile even to Calhoun's thin lips, but he was never amused for long. In the Senate, Calhoun did what he could to resist Clay's nationalist onslaught while watching Clay and Tyler tear each other apart—a development that gave him hope so long as the South did not break en masse to support the president in 1844. Tyler would fight hard over the state-rights issues connected to the BUS, Calhoun cautioned, but he would be soft on the rest of the Whig program, which would be a disaster for the South. "I go for victory to my own cause, complete victory," he wrote one close associate on the day the special congressional session ended. "My principles now must triumph, or be defeated." The surest way to go for victory was to overtake Van Buren and run for president himself.[16]

The sight of his ancient enemy from New York living it up during his southern tour redoubled Calhoun's resolve. In his speeches to the Senate as well as in his outside political activities, Calhoun began his presidential quest with what for him amounted to a turn to the left, appealing to the Jacksonians' popular base outside the South. He quieted his pro-slavery views and spent most of his time attacking the monied interests that he claimed were still trying to impose Clay's American System. His most arresting effort came in response to one of Clay's impossible projects, a proposed constitutional amendment that would permit Congress to override presidential vetoes by simple majorities in both houses. In attacking the idea, Calhoun might have looked, to a careless viewer, like Andrew Jackson's twin, as he denounced efforts by Congress "to substitute the will of a majority of the people." Although he took the ground that the veto was essential as a check on majority rule—the reverse of Jackson's defense of the presidential veto—the real danger, Calhoun suggested, was Clay and the Whigs' effort to enact the American System, which could expand the illegitimate powers of the federal government. As far as Calhoun was concerned, the speech was virtually a restatement of his theories of nullification, "the premises," he wrote, "from which it irresistibly flows." But Francis Blair, who had denounced Calhoun bitterly in 1832 and 1833, could see only that Calhoun was attacking Clay and the forces of associated wealth, and he lauded the speech as one of the "ablest, most luminous, and unanswerable ever delivered on the nature of this Government."[17]

In the fall of 1842, Calhoun followed Clay's example and retired from the Senate to prepare for the presidential race. His chances, to his managers, looked good, especially if he could attract a reasonable hard-money northern Jacksonian—perhaps Levi Woodbury—to join his ticket. The mistaken belief that Calhoun had turned into a Jacksonian was so widespread that even the normally astute Amos Kendall tried to broker a rapprochement between Calhoun and Old Hickory, which for Calhoun was going much too far. The South Carolinian had strong contacts in New Hampshire and in Massachusetts (where, under Tyler's patronage, David Henshaw was making a political comeback), as well as in the South. To challenge Van Buren at his base, Calhoun tried with some success to make inroads within New York politics, especially in New York City, home to the most radical of those he once disparaged as the "more filthy" democrats. In a campaign managed by Joseph Scoville, a young Manhattan journalist, Calhoun reached out to two distinct constituencies: the city's established salt-water merchant elite, which hated the tariff nearly as much as the southern state-rights men did, and the city's working-class radicals, on the outs, despite some cooperation during the subtreasury struggle, with Van Buren's allies at Tammany Hall, and now aroused by Calhoun's attacks on the monied interests. Keeping up with changing working-class demographics, Calhoun also went out of his way to proclaim his Irish background and, suddenly a proud son of the Auld Sod, joined the New York Irish Immigrant Society.[18]

The one major force sidelined in national politics after Harrison's death was the new-school Whig leadership that had nominated and elected him. Clay had never been the new-schoolers' man (although many of the younger Whigs, such as Lincoln, admired him intensely), and the political misfit Tyler was impossible, a partisan ploy gone fatefully wrong. Thurlow Weed, courted by Tyler and counseling patience with the administration, traveled to Washington to see what soothing influence he might have, but for once even Weed's wizardry was not up to the task. Whig divisiveness in Washington, coupled with the continuation of hard times despite the great political shift of 1840, deeply depressed the party's voting base. Startling defeats in state elections in 1841, and even more devastating losses in the midterm congressional elections a year later, made it appear that the mighty Whig machine of the 1840 campaign had been built out of nothing more substantial than its own trinkets and illuminations. "The Whig Party now seems tota'y broken up and dismembered," one Whig official despaired, less than a year after the Log Cabin frenzy.[19] But these fears were overwrought. The Whigs' disarray would eventually redound to the benefit of Henry Clay, the one man who could undo the damage he himself had helped inflict and reunite the party's disparate elements. And inside the Democracy, new local and national battles over finances and political democracy, barely noticeable before 1842, were wreaking a different kind of havoc, favorable to the Whigs and with worrisome portents for the pro–Van Buren hard-money men, now known as Radicals.

Within a year of the Democratic downfall in 1840, the party faithful were back to the internecine bickering between Radicals and Conservatives that had sharpened in the struggle over the independent treasury. These renewed fights were conducted at the state and local level, chiefly in the North. The most important of them occurred in New York.

RADICALS, HUNKERS, AND CALHOUNITES

In the decade and a half since the completion of the Erie Canal, New York had fully earned its cognomen as the Empire State. Having commandeered the lion's share of commerce from the burgeoning commercial districts of the upper West, from the cotton plantations of the Deep South via New Orleans, and onward across the Atlantic, New York had become the preeminent mercantile and financial state in the Union. By 1840, New York City was the nation's most productive manufacturing center. Along the gigantic ditch connecting the Hudson River to Lake Erie, smaller industrial towns and cities were rising quickly to produce everything from milled flour to milled iron. The state's western rural counties, especially in the hinterlands of the canal towns, formed one of the leading commercial agricultural centers in the world. A new influx of immigrants from Ireland and Germany, settling in amid the old polyglot stock of Yankees, Dutch, and English, was making New York ethnically and religiously the most diverse state in the nation.[20]

One important effect of this growth was to complicate greatly New York's already complicated political scene, fracturing it into an ever-more confusing array of economic and social interests. With power and prestige so divided and so varied, politics was bound to be more turbulent than elsewhere in the country— and political movements from the bottom as well as the top of the system had greater opportunities to shake up the status quo. New York in the 1840s became a hotbed for the political permutations and combinations that would spread elsewhere, with portents for national politics as well. The tumult began with fights over the Erie Canal, the most important catalyst in New York's rise to power.

As early as 1827, the canal's immense profitability had permitted the state legislature to undertake the experiment of ending direct taxation and counting on the revenue from canal tolls to cover state expenditures. The plan proved overly optimistic. In 1835, backed by his comptroller Azariah Cutting Flagg, a flinty Jacksonian from the northernmost reaches of the state, Governor William Marcy announced that unless direct taxation was resumed, the state would slide into heavy debt. Marcy, who had been state comptroller himself in 1827 and had objected to the no-tax plan from the beginning, now pleaded with the legislature, insisting "that internal improvements cannot be long prosecuted on an extensive scale unless sustained by a wise system of finance." But Conservative Democrats friendly to Nathaniel P. Tallmadge joined with the Whigs in preferring debt to taxation, and in pledging the state's credit to extend the canal system even farther, thereby (they predicted) increasing revenues—an early version of what today is known as "borrow-and-spend" conservatism. In 1838, they passed a bill authorizing four million dollars in state borrowing for the canals. Marcy—whose views on canal construction had begun to moderate, and who would soon drift even closer to the Conservatives—did not veto it.[21]

Tensions among Democrats worsened during debates over the legalities of the specie suspension of 1837 (which the Conservatives backed strongly) and over a bill, that same year, to repeal a Radical-inspired law restricting the issue of small notes (a move the Radicals managed to forestall). Public meetings in Manhattan expressed outrage at the Conservatives' treachery over specie suspension, and pushed Radical demands ranging from the total eradication of the paper system to more moderate hard-money calls for "a well regulated credit system," including the Loco Foco free banking plan. But after the election of the new-school Whig William Seward as governor in 1838, to go along with a large Whig majority in the assembly elected the previous year, attention shifted back to the canal-funding issue.[22]

Governor Seward's ambitious agenda of liberal Whig reform quickly embroiled him in controversies with his own party's conservative wing as well as with Democrats. Old-guard Whigs and nativists disliked his humanitarian efforts, especially his alliance with New York City Catholic Bishop John Hughes to provide public funds for Catholic schooling. Democrats, meanwhile, hammered away at Seward's canal- and railroad-building proposals, as well as his support for a voter registry law (aimed, the Democrats claimed, to restrict poor and Irish voters) and allegations of systematic voter fraud by the Whigs in the 1839 elections. Seward won a second term in 1840, but his margin of victory was half of what it had been two years earlier. By the spring of 1841, discouraged, he had decided not to run again. Although Seward would, in his final message to the legislature, push for expansion of internal improvements, the only hope for their passage was that the Democrats might splinter and give the antitax, pro-development Conservatives the balance of power. Seward would not get his way, but divisions did appear inside the Democracy that proved deep and lasting.[23]

The Conservative faction came to be known as Hunkers, an obscure label that may have meant they were supposed to "hanker" after office. Their ostensible leader was, in fact, more of a moderate, William C. Bouck, an amiable commercial farmer and former canal commissioner who wore his hair in a peaked pompadour and was known as "Old White Hoss of Schoharie." Defeated by Seward in 1840, Bouck hoped to run again in 1842, with his measured canal-friendly brand of Democracy offering a third position between the Seward expansionists and the Radical Democrats. The Hunkers also counted on the former chief editor for the Albany Regency, Edwin Croswell of the *Albany Argus*; former Utica congressman and violent anti-abolitionist Samuel Beardsley; and Marcy's young protégé, Horatio Seymour, a banker's son from upstate. (Marcy by now had strong Hunker leanings, but he preferred to hold his formal allegiances close to his chest.) Without fully endorsing the Whigs' deficit-spending program, the Hunkers distinguished themselves from their Democratic opponents, the Radicals, by refusing to support a drastic retrenchment of internal improvements.[24]

New York Radical Democrats would in time receive their own nickname, the Barnburners, taken from Dutch tale about a farmer who chose to burn down his whole barn to destroy the rats. Led in the legislature by Michael Hoffman, an iron-willed, veteran hard-money Jacksonian and former congressman from Herkimer County, the Radicals introduced, in 1842, a "stop-and-tax" bill, imposing an immediate halt to all canal construction projects not deemed absolutely essential and raising new state revenues with a mild direct tax. After a heated debate, the bill passed the legislature and was enacted, reluctantly, by Seward. In support of these efforts, the Radicals mobilized most of what had been known as the Silas Wright wing of the old Albany Regency, including (besides Wright himself) Benjamin F. Butler, William Cullen Bryant, Azariah Flagg, and two rising young men, Van Buren's winsome, Yale-educated son, John, and Preston King, a lawyer from the same part of the state as Flagg, near the Canadian border. (The elder Van Buren, though bound by political necessity to stay above the fray and quite friendly with Bouck, was nevertheless unmistakably partial to the Radicals out of both family loyalty and political principle.)[25]

Although the Radicals carried their point in the legislature, the stop-and-tax measure nearly ripped the party in two at the Democrats' nominating convention in October. Compromising, the delegates nominated the Hunker Bouck for a second try at the governorship but adopted a Radical platform that proposed continued retrenchment, with an understanding that, if elected, Bouck would not obstruct the new retrenchment law. Bouck defeated an overrated, vainglorious Whig, Luther Bradish; the Democrats retained control of the legislature; and victory temporarily quieted intraparty fighting while leaving the Hunkers in control. The economy also cooperated with the Democrats, as the first signs of a gradual general recovery from the depression heightened the value of the state's bonds. Naturally, both the Conservatives and the Radicals claimed that their respective policies had improved the fiscal situation. But Bouck and the Hunker legislature seized the opportunity to initiate a scaled-down version of Seward's

internal-improvement drive. The passage of a new canal bill in 1844, shep-
herded through the legislature by the Conservative Horatio Seymour, left Hoff-
man, Flagg, and the Radical minority furious. Once again, the New York
Democracy was so divided, one veteran Democrat told Van Buren, that "at
Albany [t]here is not only no *harmony*, but no *cordiality* of feeling amongst our
Friends."[26]

The divisions in New York, although particularly sharp, were not unique. All
across the Northeast and West, equivalents of the Radical-Conservative fights
split the state Democratic parties, chiefly over banking issues. In Pennsylvania,
soft-money Democrats—abetted by Governor David R. Porter, a former iron-
maker and quiet Conservative sympathizer, and Porter's friend, Senator James
Buchanan—sustained an uneasy domination over the hard-money men, led by
three very different figures: Van Buren's former attorney general, Henry D.
Gilpin; the renegade son of Federalism and former Nicholas Biddle supporter,
Charles Ingersoll; and Thomas Earle, who in 1840 left the party to run with
James G. Birney on the Liberty Party ticket. In Ohio and points west to Missouri,
hard-money heroes such as Moses Dawson and Thomas Hart Benton held the
upper hand over the "softs." In the Southwest, a general revulsion against the
speculative boom mentality after 1837 produced the harshest hard-money reaction anywhere, which included the formal prohibition of commercial banking
with constitutional revisions in Louisiana and Arkansas and virtual prohibitions
in Alabama and Mississippi. (Somewhat paradoxically, Democrats in the Deep
South, where voters had repudiated Loco Foco ideas as late as 1840, were now
hailed by eastern hard-money radicals as the nation's leaders in the fight against
the banking and paper system.) Only in the Southeast, where the panic and
depression had been less wrenching, and where the banks were closely tied to
state funds for education and internal improvement, did a significant equivalent
of the militant hard-money Radicals fail to materialize.[27]

The implications of these fights were important—and ironic. At both the state
and national levels, the depression sparked by the Panic of 1837 had led voters to
repudiate the hard-money, antibanking Democrats, in favor of the pro-banking,
pro-improvement Whigs. Had President Harrison lived (and had he and Henry
Clay managed to keep their rivalry under control), some sort of Third Bank of
the United States would almost certainly have been established, and nationally
funded internal improvements would have received a great boost. Bolstered by
those successes, Whigs and Conservative Democrats in the states would have
been far stronger than they were. But the ascension of John Tyler and the disarray among the Whigs in Washington completely changed the political calculus—and Jacksonian-style fiscal retrenchment and hard-money radicalism
enjoyed a strong comeback. State governments, either through laws like New
York's "stop-and-tax" legislation or through new constitutional bans, took steps to

curtail and even outlaw initiatives basic to Whig political economy. The continuing hard times became a rationale for the kinds of economic programs that, in 1840, seemed to have been thoroughly disgraced. In a final irony, the one part of the country where the reversal was least pronounced was the Southeast, where Whig nationalism had long been weakest.

The Democracy's divisions over banking and internal improvements, which had additional implications for the presidential politics of 1844. Most hard-money Democrats strongly supported renominating Martin Van Buren. In New England, the Bancroft machine, including the old Workie Samuel Clesson Allen and the new governor Marcus Morton, was stalwartly pro–Van Buren. So were the New York Radicals, the Pennsylvania "hards," national hard-money leaders like Gilpin, Benton, and Dawson, and, in Washington, the surviving journalistic standard-bearer for true-blue Jacksonianism, Francis Blair. Conservative Democrats had far less attractive options. The most visible possible candidate, Jackson's former secretary of war, Lewis Cass, found himself (to his own surprise) being touted for the nomination late in 1842 by a combination of Pennsylvania protectionists and Ohio softs. As ponderous as he was vacuous, Cass chiefly had the virtue of availability, which led Philip Hone to remark, not completely disdainfully, that in this "he stands about on a par with General Harrison at the time of his nomination." Richard Mentor Johnson was also available, and he loudly proclaimed as much in a boisterous, saber-rattling western tour in 1843 that sapped some of Cass's support and enraged Andrew Jackson to the point where he was ready to read Johnson out of the Democratic Party. The New Yorker William Marcy, by now a Conservative in all but name, observed that Johnson was not only what he once was, "[i]t may be there was never so much of him as we were formerly led to suppose." The high-tariff centrist James Buchanan rounded out the Hunkers' short and lackluster list. Later, some Conservatives would work up support for Levi Woodbury.[28]

The most surprising development within the Democracy was a growing enthusiasm, among some of the most radical northeastern hard-money advocates, for, of all people, John C. Calhoun. The admixture of ideology and politics that fueled left-wing Calhounism arose from numerous sources. For some labor Jacksonians, the results of 1840 had been deeply disillusioning. Saving democracy, they now believed, required uniting the small disciplined group who understood what democracy really was, and upending the demagogic rule of capital by the most direct means necessary—which in 1842, after his own strange left-wing turn, seemed to be Calhoun. The perverse proposal that labor's redemption depended on the slaveholders' triumph must have unsettled some of the new Calhounites, who included at least some antislavery men. But the perversity was smoothed over by repeating the old Jacksonian claim that the abolitionists were just neo-Federalist aristocrats in disguise, and by picking up the pro-slavery ideologues' theme (a favorite of Calhoun's) that southern slaves were exploited far less severely than northern wage-earners. For the New Yorkers, the old animosities against Van Buren and Tammany Hall overcame the rapprochment over the independent treasury, and made Calhoun look more attractive. Above all, there was the lure of Calhoun as an antibusiness candidate, pledged to an official platform that included, *"No Debt—No Connection with Banks—Economy—Retrenchment—and a strict adherence to the Constitution."* Squint hard enough, and Calhoun might even look like a southern-style hard-money Radical, but without Van Burenism's taint on him.[29]

The largest clutches of left-wing Calhounites appeared in New York City. Some Barnburners and ex–Loco Focos would not, even now, accept the trimmer Van Buren. A Tammany Democrat loyal to the ex-president reported that Calhoun's supporters were confident that "the radical disaffected democrats" could "by judicious management be won for Mr. Calhoun." Leading the agitation was Fitzwilliam Byrdsall, the author of a partisan but informative history of the Loco Focos, whom he served as secretary. Byrdsall was among those in the northern pro-Calhoun ranks who thought slavery was being badly maligned in the North. In 1842, he established something called the Free-Trade Association, which was really a front for the Calhoun campaign, and among those he recruited were hard-core Loco Focos who had refused to rejoin the Democracy even after Van Buren issued his message on the independent treasury. The union leader John Commerford (who had signed an abolitionist petition in 1836) was selected as president, and other veteran Locos, including John Windt, assumed leading roles. George Henry Evans, who had left Manhattan for rural New Jersey and returned, also lent his support.[30]

The most exciting (and excitable) member of New York's pro-Calhoun left was a newcomer, the leader of the so-called shirtless or subterranean Democracy, Mike Walsh. Walsh was born in Ireland in 1810 and, as a toddler, emigrated to America with his father, a cabinetmaker and veteran of the United Irishman uprising of 1798. (A Protestant, Walsh always considered himself a "true American," though as an immigrant he detested nativism.) After apprenticing as an engraver and traveling across the South, he turned up as a journalist in New York at the end of the 1830s, first as a correspondent for the New York *Aurora* (where Walt Whitman was, for a time, his editor), then as editor of his own weeklies, the *Knickerbocker*, followed by, in 1843, the *Subterranean*. Aspiring to a position of power within the Democratic Party, Walsh also founded the Spartan Association, a combination political club and lower-class gang. Kept at a distance by the Tammany leadership, Walsh and his Spartans would storm party meetings, and to shouts of "Go it, Mike!," Walsh would launch into cocky tirades against corrupt office seekers and Tammany power brokers—those "who fawn upon us and call us the bone and sinew of the country . . . and who would use us until there was nothing but bone and sinews left of us." Like the Loco Foco diehards, Walsh reserved special sectarian hatred for Van Burenite Radicals such as Benjamin Butler, who, with their lying rhetoric about the few and the many, supposedly neutered radicalism and propped up wage slavery.[31]

Basking in his reputation as a favorite of the roughneck Bowery B'hoys, Walsh's social radicalism was as sincere as it was vitriolic. In his earliest speeches, he claimed the legacy of the Loco Focos and of William Leggett's war on "feudal corporations." The original rules of the Spartan Association mentioned political reforms such as the abolition of corporation charters as the group's major goals. Walsh's attacks on what he called "the slavery of wages" became increasingly pointed in the early 1840s, as did his attacks on Tammany politicians and those Whigs who worshiped moral reform "on the glutted altars of Mammon." Yet, though it would only become fully evident later in the decade, Walsh's economic radicalism was coupled with a racism that left him vulnerable to slaveholder politicians who in any way attacked northern capital. He greatly admired Tyler (and, in a personal letter to Walsh, Tyler returned the admiration), and he seemed to adore Calhoun, not because of any of Calhoun's ideas about democracy but because Calhoun attacked banks and was Van Buren's sworn enemy. Calhoun, in turn, was so anxious about securing a toehold outside South Carolina that, even more than Tyler, he was willing to flatter and encourage the shirtless democrat, a man he would later privately call the editor of "the organ of what may be called the lowest strata in the New York population."[32]

Calhoun developed closer ties with an uneasy radical who was better suited to his temperament, Orestes Brownson. For Brownson, the consummate rebel logician, the defeat of 1840 was worse than a political setback—it was a philosophical cataclysm. Previously, his skepticism about political democracy and universal suffrage had been based on his certainty that the ruling class would not give up its power without a violent fight. But the Log Cabin campaign showed that the people themselves could not be fully trusted to decide wisely, that they would eagerly hand their political birthright over to whatever threadbare pro-business demagogue came down the pike, so long as he claimed to be democratic. Majority rule could turn out to be tyrannical. Forced to rethink his politics entirely, he turned to Aristotle; more decisively, he turned to Calhoun, the only national statesman with a mind that Brownson respected. The two developed a warm correspondence in which Brownson sought advice on how he might, as he wrote in a despairing piece on the election, "come up with something worth having."[33]

As it happened, Calhoun, between congressional sessions, had begun writing his own summary view of politics, a work he called "Disquisition on Government." Here, Calhoun explained as fully as he ever would his idea of the concurrent majority. Given human imperfection, Calhoun posited, government was not a necessary evil (as the dewy-eyed optimist Jeffersonians believed), but a positive good required to restrain the masses. The majority, by these lights, had no claim to superior wisdom, only to superior force. History had shown that this majority was easily manipulated by the dominant economic force in any society, to prostrate all competing interests and establish its absolute rule. How, then, could that manipulative power be checked? For Calhoun, drawing his own logical conclusions from his nullification doctrines, it could only be done, as he had said in 1833, "by giving to each part [of society] the right of self-protection." Nullification had attempted to establish a mechanism for this protection but had failed. In the "Disquisition," Calhoun devised his alternative.[34]

"Power," Calhoun observed, "can only be resisted by power." He considered each sovereign state the embodiment, in national affairs, of a distinct political interest. And so, under his new theory, he would provide each state concurrent power in the making of national laws, and a veto over their execution. It might be viewed as a radical revision of the Articles of Confederation, which required a dissent from four of the thirteen states to annul a national law. Calhoun, writing at a time when there were twice as many states as there had been in 1778, would reduce that veto number, in perpetuity, to one. He declared, however, that he had borrowed not from some long-discarded federal plan but from the living, breathing elitist republican constitution of South Carolina. Alone of all the states, Calhoun believed, South Carolina had discovered the means to suppress majoritarian democracy while granting universal white manhood suffrage, thereby assuring that all of its citizens—low country and up-country, planter and merchant—had a say in government. Instead of a despotic "democracy," he had said four years earlier, South Carolina was "a republic, a commonwealth" that "protected the feebler interests"—"a far more popular government than if it had been based on the simple principle of the numerical majority." Calhoun wanted to nationalize the political structures of South Carolina, establishing a "Government of the people, in the true sense of the term," he wrote, "and not that of the mere majority, or the dominant interest."[35]

Here lay both the strength and the crippling weaknesses of Calhoun's scheme. His brilliant essential perception was that in modern societies, aggregations of whole interests and classes, and not individuals, had become the basic units of politics. Yet Calhoun was much more attentive to some interests than to others. Slaves, naturally, were excluded from any political consideration except as the property of their masters. But even as he was now flattering northern workers, Calhoun had remarkably little to say about or to southern nonslaveholders, the preponderance of the white South. He imagined, as he had told the Whig Horace Binney years earlier, that the republic rested on just two pillars, "a slave class and a property class, such white persons as were not within the property class being wholly ignored," except as incipient slaveholders. And while that may have been a reasonable simplification in South Carolina, it hardly fit the South as a whole, where political pressures from the yeomanry had created Master Race democratic polities far more egalitarian, for white men, than South Carolina's republic.[36]

Nor was eccentric South Carolina a reasonable model on which to build a national system of concurrent balanced interests. Peculiarities of geography, economics, and demography had conspired to create in South Carolina a coherent political elite that, if not monolithic, was certainly consensual. Interests in other states were far more complex and divided. Calhoun did not completely delude himself on this point, for he allowed that the conditions were far from ripe for his plan to succeed. But until a concurrent majority system could be established, he believed it was crucial to uphold in national politics one interest above all others, the strongest counterweight to majoritarian democracy, an interest that Calhoun now thought under siege—slavery. The northern masses had proved their stupidity in giving their oppressors consent to oppress them even further. Only the slaveholders had the intelligence and the will, as well as the material interest, to resist this hegemony and keep the northern capitalists at bay. Out of South Carolina's obsessions—and his own—with the tariff and the abolitionists, Calhoun had built a general theory of politics that, without prescribing slavery, provided a shield behind which the slaveholders could dwell securely.

To Brownson, all of this made perfect sense. Recent history proved, he believed, that the more that suffrage was expanded, the greater the power of the business class grew. Only a small minority of the voters was interested in the authentic liberation of labor from business rule and exploitation. Hence, the growing power of the federal government would always be wielded on behalf of the capitalists and against labor. It followed, Brownson argued, that the word *democracy* had to be forsaken in favor of the "old and legitimate appelation of REPUBLICAN," and that labor's surest allies would be the Calhounite South, united to establish "a rigid constitutional order" and check the power of capital. Since a considerable portion of the working class were dupes of the ruling class, it further followed that the enlightened few—including, of course, Brownson himself—would have to guide them to political wisdom. And to this task Brownson applied himself with his customary gusto in 1842 and 1843, writing pro-Calhoun newspaper editorials, churning out addresses for Calhoun public meetings, and considering, for a time, becoming the editor of a pro-Calhoun newspaper in New York City.[37]

The disarming appearance of remorseless logic can always obscure mere facts. Brownson's abstractions looked muscular and sounded plausible, except that they could not account for any number of basic political realities. How, for example, could Brownson explain that, in 1840, the major party of the great slaveholders and of strident pro-slavery state-rights leaders such as Henry A. Wise had been the Whigs—the party Brownson himself, in "The Laboring Classes," had denounced as the party of business? Much as he and Calhoun might have wished it so, neither Calhoun nor Calhoun's South Carolina represented slave-holders en masse in 1840, something that Calhoun at least recognized. Whig planters were more than happy to ally with northern capitalists, so long as the arrangement promised them sound and stable cotton prices and improved means to get their crop to market. Perhaps slaveholders were as susceptible to false consciousness as the workers who had voted Whig; perhaps, then, they were not such reliable anticapitalist allies of labor after all. In any event, Brownson's faith in the planter minority in protecting the good of the entire country looks more like a product of desperation than of logic. Although he instinctively recognized basic differences between workers and slaveholders (he called the first "democrats" and the second "anti-democrats"), he said nothing of substance about slavery itself, about how it contributed to "anti-democracy," and about why northern workers might regard it as a threat to their own dignity.[38]

There was far more to American politics than was ever dreamt of in Brownson's philosophy. By the end of 1844, Brownson himself would come to recognize this, as he quickly moved on to a philosophical system he at last found irrefutable, fastened to an organic order and religious faith beyond political uncertainty: the Roman Catholic Church. Calhoun, meanwhile, would continue his work as the self-appointed vanguard leader of the slaveholding South against the hated abolitionists and their apologists — a South that Calhoun loved but still thought was politically too soft on democracy outside of his great practical model, the people's republic of South Carolina.

The deepening divisions among Radicals, Hunkers, and Calhounites presented new challenges to Martin Van Buren and to the unity of the Democracy. As he traveled through the South in 1842, the former president had good reason to believe that he would also be the next president, given the Whigs' collapse. But the renewed clashes among Democrats over fiscal policy threatened to capsize Van Buren's candidacy in some crucial states, including New York. The Southeast was sorely lacking in the kinds of hard-money men who would form the backbone of his campaign. President Tyler might well exploit that weakness, launch a disruptive third-party bid, steal Virginia away from the Democrats, and throw all electoral calculations into chaos. Even worse, Calhoun might succeed in building a new version of the old coalition between the planters of the South and the plain republicans of the North, this time between South Carolina slaveholders and New York labor radicals (with Brownson pitching in up in Boston). All of these possibilities suggested that the Democratic national convention could become a logjam that would deny Van Buren the nomination.

Some of these matters would appear to be resolved by the outcome of yet another great fight at the state level in 1842 and 1843 — the final northern struggle for white manhood suffrage in the small but economically dynamic state of Rhode Island. The so-called war over Rhode Island's constitution has sometimes been portrayed as a comic opera conflict in a comic opera of a state, and it certainly had its absurd moments. But for those who followed into battle the Rhode Island rebel leader, one Thomas Dorr, and for those who bitterly opposed him, the conflict was a deadly serious test of democracy's meaning and democracy's future. Reactions to the Rhode Island events, in turn, destroyed Calhoun's quest for a slaveholder-labor alliance.

DEMOCRACY IN RHODE ISLAND: THE DORR WAR

There exists a daguerreotype portrait, attributed to the studio of Mathew Brady and dated between 1844 and 1854, of a frowning man with a forelock who is almost certainly Thomas Wilson Dorr. His suit, a bit tight in the shoulders, dignified and black, is that of a businessman or lawyer or political leader; nearly as black are the brows and shadowy bags around his eyes. The frown is enigmatic, projecting either defeat or determination, maybe both. The forelock could be an insouciant touch or just a matter of carelessness. It all fits with Dorr's career and personality. Some experts have demurred and said that the man in the picture is not Dorr but either the Whig orator and governor Edward Everett or the Prince Bonaparte. The claims are unlikely, but also oddly fitting, for there were bits of Everett and Bonaparte in Thomas Dorr as well.[39]

Dorr was born in Providence in 1805, the son of a wealthy Federalist family, and went on to graduate from Exeter and Harvard before studying law with the sturdiest pillar of the New York Federalist bar, Chancellor James Kent. Elected to the state's House of Representatives in 1834, he gravitated to a group of younger new-school Whigs, who shared liberal concerns about slavery issues and, even more, the state's continued governance under the colonial charter of 1663. Dorr was especially critical of the stiff property requirements for voting, and of the underlying social theory (still propounded by Kent) that justified it. "Enough has been said in vague and general terms, about '*unwholesome citizens*,' 'persons not to be *safely* trusted,' 'without property and vicious'—about 'protecting the *sound* part of the community against those who have nothing at stake in society' . . . ," Dorr declared. "Let those who use this language come out and say, if they will venture the assertion, *that the body of traders and mechanics, and professional men, and sons of landholders, are the base and corrupt persons who are aimed at in these sweeping denunciations*." In another state, Dorr might have ended up a liberal Whig, but there was no room for such heresies among the Whigs of Rhode Island. In 1837 Dorr formed his own heavily Democratic Constitutionalist Party and then defected in full to become head of the state's Democracy.[40]

Rhode Island's anomalous clinging to its colonial charter testified to the singular consolidated power of the state's old landed and mercantile elite, dating back to the eighteenth century. So jealous were Rhode Island's rulers of their peculiar privileges that they had refused to send a delegation to the constitutional convention in Philadelphia in 1787, and the state did not ratify the Constitution until 1790, the last of the original states to do so. But that tenacious order grew increasingly unstable as Rhode Island became a key manufacturing center, with a new working class that included thousands of Irish Catholic immigrants. The 1663 charter enfranchised only those who owned $134 in land or paid $7 in rent, which meant that by 1840 well over half of the adult male population could not vote, a proportion that was increasing as the number of factory workers swelled. Representation under the charter was severely malapportioned in favor of the older rural and seashore counties in the southern half of the state and at the expense of manufacturing towns like Pawtucket. The charter also lacked a bill of rights and other guarantees of personal liberties, and it failed to provide an independent judiciary. Popular agitation to replace it with a more liberal constitution had begun in 1817 (and was led, in the 1830s, by the ubiquitous workingman orator Seth Luther) but had always fizzled out because of the landowner legislature's adamance. In 1841, when agitation renewed with the emergence of a working class–based Rhode Island Suffrage Association, the reformers decided to bypass the legislature completely and proclaim their own constitution in the name of the sovereign people. At their head was Thomas Dorr.[41]

The insurgency quickly led to a crisis over who would govern Rhode Island. Dorr and the Suffrage Association called a state convention, based on what they claimed was the revolutionary "constituent power." The convention drafted a so-called People's Constitution establishing universal white manhood suffrage and an independent judiciary.[42] In December 1841, a referendum conducted through the state's town meetings ratified the Dorrite plan by an enormous margin. The legislature then called its own convention, which drafted its own so-called Freemen's constitution granting the most begrudging minor concessions on the franchise and none at all on legislative apportionment. The town meetings rejected it resoundingly in March 1842.[43]

On May 3, Dorr, who had been voted in as governor in elections held under the People's Constitution, started to organize his government in Providence and called for the new state legislature, already at work, to convene on July 4 at Sprague's Tavern in his hometown of Chepachet. The conservative pro-charter government held on fiercely, declared Dorr's regime illegitimate, and started arresting Dorrite leaders under newly enacted and highly punitive treason laws (measures that the reformers began denouncing as the "Algerine" laws, in reference to the tyrannical dey of Algiers). Dorr escaped to Washington, where he received an indifferent reception from government officials, and then journeyed to New York, where the Radical Democrats, including Ely Moore and Churchill C. Cambreleng, embraced him as the greatest hero of the day. Alexander Ming Jr., the old Loco Foco leader, offered to provide Dorr with an armed escort back to Providence; Levi Slamm, editor of the *New Era*, said he had hired a steamboat to carry a thousand citizen soldiers up to Rhode Island should the Tyler administration try to interfere against Dorr; and Mike Walsh, never to be outdone, promised to take along his shirtless Democrats and, if need be, personally lay Providence to waste on Dorr's behalf.[44]

Emboldened, Governor Dorr planned a military strike. At his side, providing continuity with the Workie and labor agitation of the past decade, was his organizational secretary, Seth Luther, but more important, he had pledges of support from most of the state's local militia companies. On the evening of May 17, Dorr and a force of 234 men stormed the Providence Arsenal, demanding control as the duly constituted government of Rhode Island. Backers of the Freemen's constitution, taking the name of the Law and Order Party, had occupied the arsenal and refused to hand it over to the rebels. When the Law and Order men would not budge, Dorr, near dawn, ordered two cannons wheeled forward and gave the order to fire; the cannon powder flashed but the cannons did not shoot, and the defenders stood their ground. Suddenly, all the bells of Providence began ringing the alarm, and an awakened citizenry stumbled into the streets, wondering what was happening. Dorr's men, beaten back and discouraged, returned home, and Dorr retreated to New York.[45]

A month later, Dorr returned to Rhode Island, accompanied by Walsh and a few of his Spartan Association roughnecks, planning to link up with a larger force in Chepachet. Entrenched atop Acote's Hill, the Dorrites learned of a large and well-equipped force headed their way in response to a general call to arms from the pro-charter governor Samuel King. After a brief standoff with King's troops, the rebels dispersed once more. Dorr left the state, discouraged by the Tyler administration's decision, at King's request, finally to send federal troops. A savage repression followed, as state officials declared martial law for six weeks, searched hundreds of homes, arrested hundreds of real and suspected Dorrites, and scattered sullen working-class crowds with live-round rifle fire. Among those jailed, on a charge of high treason, was Seth Luther, who spent a dispiriting few months writing an epic poem and finally tried, unsuccessfully, to escape by setting fire to the jailhouse. Recommitted to jail for arson, then released in 1843, he would return to his labor agitation and, in 1846, volunteer for service in the Mexican War—but judged insane, he instead wound up in the East Cambridge lunatic asylum in 1846 and would remain in Rhode Island and Vermont asylums until his death in 1863.[46]

The conservatives now devised a new draft constitution that combined significant reform with provisions that fractured the working-class electorate along ethnic and racial lines. Suffrage property requirements were drastically reduced to a token taxpaying requirement, bringing Rhode Island in line into conformity with most of the other states. Thomas Dorr's pleas to uproot the old stake-in-society principles had been largely heeded. But only native-born male taxpayers were included under the new liberalized rules. Naturalized immigrants had to meet the old charter's property requirements, as well as a new and lengthy residence requirement. As a result, virtually all of Rhode Island's rapidly growing Irish immigrant working class was disenfranchised. Regarding race, the new draft constitution incorporated a deft and divisive political payback to the state's relatively tiny proportion of black voters. Dorr himself was friendly to the abolitionists and defended equal rights for blacks. But during the Dorrite convention, reformers' fears of appearing too radical, coupled with the racist disdain shared by some delegates, led to the exclusion of blacks from voting under the supposedly radical People's Constitution. A number of black abolitionists who had been drawn to the cause immediately denounced the Dorrites, and black Rhode Islanders were thereafter conspicuous in their nonsupport of the reformers. In part out of gratitude, the new conservative constitution enfranchised black males who met the same minimal taxpaying requirements as native-born whites. The point was clear: blacks, supposedly, were more trustworthy citizens than naturalized Irishmen. Black voters rightly considered the constitution a great advance, whereas the Irish felt as if their wounds had been salted.[47]

Suppressed, exhausted, and divided against itself, the Dorrite movement collapsed, and the new constitution was approved (with most Dorrite voters abstaining) in November 1842. But Rhode Island's Law and Order Whigs were not quite finished wreaking their revenge. After the Chepachet fiasco, Thomas Dorr spent a year in wandering exile, living in nearby Democratic states whose governors refused to send him back to Rhode Island to face charges stemming from the rebellion. Once the new constitution was ratified, Dorr announced he would return home after the fall elections, which he did—only to be arrested shortly after his arrival in Providence under indictment for high treason. Four months later, a jury of twelve Whigs in Newport instantly found him guilty, and Dorr was sentenced to life imprisonment at hard labor in solitary confinement. In his incensed final remarks to the court, Dorr called the entire proceeding a travesty and, acting the hero, retorted that it "does not reach the man within."[48]

The spiteful severity directed at Dorr backfired. All of Dorr's old supporters, including Mike Walsh, protested both the trial and the sentence. Rhode Island Democrats and Dorr supporters, including the newly elected governor Charles Jackson, made obtaining Dorr's freedom their major political demand. In June 1845, after a year's imprisonment, Dorr was released by an act of a new Democratic-controlled legislature. Six years later, Dorr regained his political and civil rights, and three years after that, his treason conviction was voided. But it all came as cold comfort to the People's Governor and to his erstwhile supporters. In 1855, broken by his experiences, Dorr died at the age of forty-nine. The restrictions in the new Rhode Island Constitution of 1843 so demoralized the electorate that after a few years the state plunged into a profound political apathy.

The final important incident of the Dorr War did nothing to console the rebels. In 1842, during the Algerine law crackdown, a Rhode Island military official named Borden was ordered to arrest a Dorrite sympathizer named Luther. Luther sued Borden for breaking and entering, claiming that the government that had ordered the arrest had been supplanted when the People's Constitution was ratified. Article IV, Section 4 of the U.S. Constitution guaranteed to every state in the Union "a Republican Form of Government"; hence, the defense claimed, the Dorrite Constitution, replacing the manifestly unrepublican Charter of 1663, was fully legitimate. In effect, Luther's attorneys were reasserting the Dorrites' claim that the majority in any state had the right to overthrow its government and install a new one. The case wound its way to the U.S. Supreme Court, which in the landmark decision of *Luther v. Borden* in 1848 affirmed a lower-court ruling that Borden had not trespassed, and stated that the judiciary had no authority to offer a definition of a republican form of government. Luther's suit had acquired a strong political charge: Benjamin Hallett, the prominent Massachusetts Democrat, argued before the Court on Luther's behalf, while Senator Daniel Webster argued for Borden. And although Chief Justice Taney and the Court majority were evasive on the most explosive issue at hand, Borden's release strongly suggested that they had rejected the Dorrites's thinly veiled claims about the majority's right to revolution.[49]

The Dorr War was a striking, exceptional case in the history of American democratization before the Civil War. In no other state did a landed elite square off so sharply or so violently against a growing manufacturing working class and its liberal sympathizers. Elsewhere in the early industrializing North, the multiplicity of interests at the top of society and politics cracked open enough space for disenfranchised white men to win expanded political rights without resorting to firearms and revolutionary conventions. By comparison, tiny Rhode Island was more like Chartist Britain—indeed, in some ways, an even starker case than Britain—with an obstinate gentry that thought more like bygone ultra-Federalists than like Whigs, and fought to keep the industrial masses at bay before granting carefully calculated reform. Without question, the pro-charter conservatives were formally correct in claiming that the Dorrites' revolutionary majoritarianism threatened constitutional guarantees, and augured turning the will of the majority into merely the will of the strongest. Yet substantively, the Dorrites were also in the right, for they had been pushed into their rebellion by an atavistic ruling class that would brook no compromise until it was forced to do so. Without the uprising of 1842, it is impossible to imagine that the conservatives would have stopped stalling and proffered their constitution of 1843. Except for the exceptional rigidity and irresponsibility of Rhode Island's united rulers, constitutional reform could have come much earlier, with some faction of the old elite— led by someone like the young Whig Thomas Dorr—gaining the credit as friends of the people. That it had not was, in America, a strange story.

Unique though it was, the Dorr Rebellion had a significant impact on national politics. Although some Democratic leaders expressed private reservations about the rebels' conduct, most of them, as well as of the rank and file, thought the Dorrites had conducted a straightforward battle for democracy against aristocratic oppression. Shortly after Dorr's installation as governor, Senator Levi Woodbury sent him a private letter, counseling caution but stating emphatically that if his cause was unjust, then "the whole fabric of our American liberty rests on sand and stubble." Andrew Jackson, also in private, cheered the Dorrites' defense of majority rule. Martin Van Buren went further, publicly offering his "most hearty sympathy" for the Dorrites' labors. Francis Blair's *Globe* warned that any effort to suppress the Dorr government by force would be met with force. The same message came thundering from the Democratic governors who, during Dorr's exile in 1842 and 1843, refused to turn him over. "If the views of those who oppose the course, *be right*," New Hampshire Governor Henry Hubbard declared, "then, in my judgment, our revolution which was to secure to free men, just and equal rights . . . *has proved a solemn mockery.*"[50]

The Whigs were just as united in pronouncing Dorr a disloyal desperado. The most reactionary elements of the party's old guard, represented by Rhode Island's own Senator James F. Simmons, hailed the wisdom of the old charter's narrow property restrictions on suffrage, arguing they created "a feeling of cherished regard to home and to country." Other conservatives focused on Dorr's offenses against constitutional order and claims to majority sovereignty, likening the Dorrites (in the words of Connecticut's leading Whig paper) to "the Fanny Wrights, Robert Dale Owens, O.A. Brownsons, and their fellow laborers against the social system of our country." The most liberal of Whigs were no less condemnatory, recognizing the justice of expanding the suffrage but excoriating the rebels' methods. William Seward, while still New York's governor, flatly called the uprising "treason" and pledged to cooperate with Rhode Island officials should Dorr set foot in his state. Henry Clay, speaking on behalf of the broader Whig national coalition, called the events "a wanton defiance of established authority." Much as the rebellion blurred the factionalism within the Democracy, so it stimulated a primordial political unity among the Whigs.[51]

Coming amid the crack-ups of the Tyler years, the polarized reactions to the Dorr War reminded everyone that there truly were fundamental political differences between Democrats and Whigs. The reflexive return to partisan first principles, if only momentary, boded well for the preeminent established leadership of the national parties, and especially for Martin Van Buren and Henry Clay, preparing for the 1844 elections. It boded extremely ill for John C. Calhoun.

No one who had attended closely to Calhoun's writings and speeches could have doubted where he would stand on the Dorr War. For years, he had specifically criticized majoritarianism on the ground that it meant a mere majority might at its pleasure subvert the constitution. This is precisely what the Dorrites were attempting, and although Calhoun favored an expansion of the white male suffrage, he could never approve the Dorrite movement. Yet the rebellion also put Calhoun in a terrible bind, for if he were to denounce it openly, he would put at risk his fledgling alliance with northern labor, which firmly supported Dorr. Pro-Calhoun editors in New York demanded that he speak out, while his close southern political friends begged him to keep quiet lest he scuttle his own candidacy. Calhoun, at first, remained circumspect—although when Dorr visited Washington in search of support, Calhoun abruptly dressed him down in a private interview at Calhoun's boardinghouse. Finally, in July 1843, Calhoun publicly declared that the success of movements like the Dorrites' would be the "death-blow of constitutional democracy, to admit the right of the numerical majority, to alter or abolish constitutions at pleasure."[52]

Pro-Calhoun northerners now faced an even greater problem. Orestes Brownson had actually been something of a Dorrite, having addressed a meeting of the Rhode Island Suffrage Association, at Dorr's invitation, in 1841, and having written Dorr a letter of strong encouragement when Dorr was sworn in as governor a year later. Only later in 1842 did he change his mind, denouncing the Dorrites and ridiculing what he called "the virtue and intelligence of the people" as "all a humbug." Although a few other pro-labor Calhounites joined Brownson in his political line rectification (notably Theophilus Fisk, who had moved to Virginia and was editing a pro-Calhoun paper), others either ignored the matter or grew noticeably colder. Thereafter, all efforts by Calhoun's northern friends and loyalists to advance beyond their small beachheads were doomed.[53]

THE GLIMMERING OF NORMAL POLITICS

In January 1844—having lost a bid to obtain voting rules at the nominating convention favorable to his candidacy, and having watched his supporters in New York and elsewhere flounder—Calhoun publicly withdrew his name from consideration for the presidency.[54] By binding the Democracy ever closer to its majoritarian democratic ideals, the Dorr War had isolated him once again and demonstrated sharply that he was no democrat. Having suffered, then won a highly compromised victory, and then suffered again in Rhode Island, the Dorrites could claim that they had helped reconfigure national politics—a greater triumph, in some respects, than could ever have been achieved in a single state.

As the elections of 1844 neared, the major parties appeared to be pulling through the confusion in Washington, laying aside their factional divisions, and settling into their familiar partisan postures. Van Buren, although not the most exciting personality, would almost certainly be the Democratic presidential nominee, calling for a return to hard-money policies. Clay would most likely prevail among the Whigs, ending the aberrant interregnum of "His Accidency," John Tyler, and proclaiming the full enactment of the American System, including the establishment of the Third Bank of the United States. More clearly than ever, the nation would get to choose between the democratic commerce favored by the Democrats and the capitalist democracy favored by the Whigs.

But political normality would prove short-lived, when fate and John Tyler intervened to disrupt national politics once again in 1844. This new turn would transpire over slavery, territorial expansion, and the continuing activities of the antislavery movement. At the center of all the rearranging, ever on the alert, was the implacable John C. Calhoun. On the margins, but with a growing sense of purpose, were the equally implacable Liberty Party abolitionists, and the antislavery Whigs led by John Quincy Adams.

18

ANTISLAVERY, ANNEXATION, AND THE ADVENT OF YOUNG HICKORY

In 1840, the leaders of the fledgling Liberty Party assessed their showing in the presidential election with equanimity, even optimism. "The fewer we have now," Joshua Leavitt observed in his newspaper, the *Emancipator*, "the more we have to gain before we carry our point. 'That's all.'" The slaveholder Tyler's subsequent unexpected rise to the presidency, a disappointment to northern antislavery Whigs, reinforced the case for independent antislavery politics. By the end of 1841, the party's growing influence in antislavery districts caused the high-spirited Alvan Stewart to exult: "The matter is absolutely settled that we must abolish slavery, & as sure as the sun rises we shall in 5 or 6 years run over slavery at full gallop unless she pulls herself up & gets out of the way of Liberty's cavalry."[1] Stewart's ally Gerrit Smith speculated, two years later, that northern Whigs and Democrats would cut their party ties to the slaveholders and "identify themselves with our great doctrine of impartial and universal liberty"—a more reasonable, if premature forecast.[2]

Liberty Party activity alone, of course, would never be sufficient to convert sympathetic Whigs and Democrats and make slavery the central issue of national politics. The two major parties would have to divide from within, and the glimmering of political normality early in 1844 made that prospect seem unlikely. The normality would quickly dissipate, though, over the spring and summer, when pro-slavery forces attempted, once again, to bully the Democratic Party. At year's end, the collapse of the major parties over slavery still lay well in the future. But the crack-up had commenced.

ANTISLAVERY GOES POLITICAL

Lest anybody think it had given up, the Liberty Party held a convention in New York City only six months after the 1840 election, renominated James Birney for the presidency, and substituted the prominent former Jacksonian Thomas Morris for Thomas Earle in the vice presidential slot. The delegates then approved an ambitious plan of organization similar to those of the Democrats and Whigs. A national party committee would handle party matters between elections and oversee a chain of command leading down to state, county, district, city, town, and ward committees. The city and town committees would each keep a roll of voters who had pledged to back only abolitionist candidates. Two established newspapers with national audiences—Leavitt's *Emancipator* and, in Cincinnati, the continuation of Birney's *Philanthropist*, edited by Gamaliel Bailey—would spread the party's message.[3]

What that message ought to be was the subject of rich and sometimes sharp internal debate. The party's twin goals—to propagandize on behalf of abolition and to grapple for power within the political system—always caused divisions over how best to pursue the second without diluting the first. Some of the original Liberty Party leaders, including Thomas Earle, worried that by restricting itself to a "one-idea" antislavery program, the party would never gain credibility with the voters. The radical one-idea concept nevertheless prevailed, out of concerns that abandoning it might make the party look too much like a mere extension of one of the major parties, while exposing it to infiltration and co-optation.

Tensions remained over the party's political direction. Former Democrats and Democratic sympathizers, including the hard-money man Bailey and ex-Whig Ohio lawyer Salmon P. Chase, counseled drawing a distinction between the party's moral and political functions. While they proclaimed their hatred of slavery and racial inequality, they urged that the party bow to the Constitution's protection of slavery where it already existed, and confine itself to practical issues like the abolition of slavery in the District of Columbia and the territories. The point, as Thomas Morris said, was to achieve "the deliverance of the government from the control of the slave power"—luring Democrats and Whigs into the party and forcing a divorce of slavery and government akin to the Jacksonians' divorce of banking and government. Abolitionist evangelicals such as Joshua Leavitt, centered in the eastern states, countered that the effacement of universal abolition would cost the party its essential idealistic fervor. "What are we? . . . ," one Ohio Liberty man complained of the party's pragmatic turn. "We look upon it as a direct and bold attempt to sell the abolitionist . . . to one of the political parties, and we cry, Beware!!" The purists preferred to fight for the idea that the Constitution's provisions about habeas corpus, due process of law, and republican government overrode its compromises over slavery and rendered bondage illegal throughout the land.[4]

Through the mid-1840s, the pragmatic position held sway without causing any major splits in the party. Liberty men agreed to agitate over various issues that would hasten what they called the "de-nationalization of slavery." Congress could abolish slave labor on public works projects and in all federal facilities, including forts and navy yards, as well as in the District of Columbia. More important, by keeping slavery out of the federal territories, the government could halt the expansion widely deemed essential to slavery's survival, and accelerate slavery's total demise, without challenging the widely accepted claim that the Constitution protected slavery in the states where it already existed. "It is a more important object to prevent a million of human beings from being made slaves," argued the Milwaukee *American Freeman* (later the *Wisconsin Free Democrat*), "than it is to free an equal number who have already been half destroyed by being reared and long retained in the condition of slavery."[5]

These arguments directed attention to what Morris had called the Slave Power and at how it had twisted the nation's political institutions. The mails controversy, the gag rule, and the *Amistad* prosecution were only the most recent manifestations of the Slave Power's domination. Behind these events lay the Constitution's anomalous three-fifths clause, which, paradoxically, had become more oppressive with the rise of mass democratic parties. Without the added representation given the South under the clause, the gag rule almost certainly could not have survived. And because both the Whigs and the Democrats apportioned their national convention delegates on the basis of representation in the House, southern slaveholders exerted an inflated influence over party rules, platforms, and presidential nominations. That influence further augmented the Slave Power's ability to demand preference in federal appointments, from members of the cabinet down to the lowliest deputy postmaster. Even though they represented a tiny minority of the American population, the slaveholders and their northern lackeys could, it seemed, rule forever.[6]

In framing these arguments, the Liberty Party appealed directly to the Jacksonians' principles about majority rule and the illegitimacy of artificial combinations that thwarted it. In 1841, a Michigan Liberty paper sounded the theme urgently, pointing to the "overwhelming political ascendancy of the slave power." Slavery, the paper observed, was a moral excrescence—and it was also "an overwhelming political monopoly, in the hands of an oligarchy of 250,000 slaveholders, which by holding the balance of political power in the nation, has long rigidly controlled its offices, its finance and all its great interests, and has thus tyrannically subverted the constitutional liberties of more than 12,000,000 of nominal American freemen." Although hard-core Democrats would resist the idea that their beloved Jackson had bent to the Slave Power's control, the Liberty Party's reformulation of

Jacksonian ideas and rhetoric offered an antislavery idiom attractive to northern Jackson supporters. While they drew heavily on antislavery Whig alienation, the Liberty men also aimed to outdemocratize the Democrats.[7]

Because of local peculiarities in election procedures, the first significant Liberty Party victories occurred in New England. In Massachusetts, Liberty Party legislative candidates across the state drew just enough support in 1841 to prevent Whig or Democratic nominees from winning the absolute majority required by law, thereby leaving more than eighty seats in the state legislature unfilled. A year later, Liberty Party backers spoiled the election of nearly all of Massachusetts's congressional representatives and threw the gubernatorial election to the legislature. All across the North, Liberty Party support, although still small, grew steadily. State-by-state returns in 1841 showed a threefold increase over what the Birney-Earle ticket had received in 1840. A year later, the total jumped another 50 percent. At that rate, the Michigan editor Theodore Foster computed, the party would win 160,000 votes in 1844 and gain a huge majority in the nonslaveholding states by 1848.[8]

Where the Liberty men could not immediately grab the balance of power, they harassed vulnerable officeholders, invariably Whigs, in antislavery districts. The most famous case involved Joshua Giddings of Ohio. Giddings's district, in the Western Reserve around Ashtabula, recorded the largest support for the Liberty Party of any in the state, and the district also delivered the heaviest Whig majorities. Safe from any charges that they were aiding the Democrats, the Liberty men targeted the strongly antislavery Giddings, demanding that he defend his membership in a slaveholders' party. Gamaliel Bailey's *Philanthropist* hit Giddings hard for belonging to a party that upheld "capitalists, large manufacturers and farmers . . . and monied interests"—the Money Power as well as the Slave Power. The Liberty men also established an ably produced local weekly, and attracted Edward Wade, brother of Giddings's law partner, to run against him for Congress. Giddings insisted that the Whig Party offered the only practical vehicle for antislavery politics, and that the Whig leadership was quietly friendly to antislavery measures—an exaggeration that only harmed Giddings further by alarming southern Whigs as well as conservative downstate Ohio Whigs, who began to regard him as a dangerous man.[9]

Behind the scenes, the Liberty men exchanged the stick for the carrot. Even as he was lambasting Giddings and other antislavery Whigs for their subservience to the Slave Power, Bailey was writing privately to several of them, including John Quincy Adams, beseeching them to keep up their pressure on eliminating the gag rule, and offering his aid. Late in 1841, Joshua Leavitt, who had relocated to Washington as the *Emancipator's* capital correspondent, helped to organize an informal antislavery Whig caucus—a "select committee," he called it—which met at the boardinghouse of a Mrs. Ann Spriggs, across the street from the Capitol, where many of the younger men had taken up residence. Early in 1842, Theodore Dwight Weld joined the group, offering his services as a researcher. While pressing the antislavery Whigs from without, the Liberty men also did their best to ensure that the Whigs' national leadership would not excommunicate the party's antislavery wing, as Illinois's Democrats had eliminated Thomas Morris from the Senate in 1838.[10]

The presence of the Garrisonian Weld in the Whigs' small meetings signaled an additional important development—the softening of some hard-core abolitionists' objections to political abolitionism. In 1843, Lewis Tappan, influenced by both the suffrage agitation of the British Chartists and the parlous state of his American & Foreign Anti-Slavery Society, set aside his misgivings and endorsed the Liberty Party. ("Rallying under this banner will be bearing a testimony against the two great political parties," he wrote to Elizur Wright, "& encourage people to regard moral principle in their political act &c. &c.") Other abolitionists, like Weld, managed to shuttle easily between the different factions of the movement. Even William Lloyd Garrison—who called the ballot box "a proslavery argument," and who was rapidly coming to the disunionist conclusion that the U.S. Constitution was ineluctably pro-slavery—covered Liberty Party activities in the *Liberator*.[11]

Most striking were the connections between black abolitionists and the Liberty men. Black antislavery activists, dating back to the formation of the American Anti-Slavery Society in 1833, had always felt a special kinship and admiration for Garrison, the most prominent and immovable white foe of slavery and racism in the country. Dispiriting events in the North in the 1830s and early 1840s had deepened that respect, just as it deepened the blacks' alienation from the rest of white America. The reaffirmation of white-male-only suffrage, between 1830 and 1845, in Connecticut, Delaware, and New Jersey, the admission of Michigan on the same basis in 1837, and, most alarming of all, the wholesale disfranchisement of blacks in Pennsylvania in 1838 blasted black hopes about improving their situation through political action. ("We can never force our constituents to go peaceably to the polls, side by side with the negro," one Pennsylvania convention delegate declared.) The Dorrites' exclusion of blacks from their People's Constitution reinforced black antipathy to the Democracy. Throughout the North, an intensification of racial discrimination, in schooling, transportation, and other areas of public life, made the initial abolitionist hopes of the early 1830s seem naive.[12]

The Supreme Court's ruling in 1842 in the case of *Prigg v. Pennsylvania* reinforced the northern siege on black rights and antislavery. In 1826, the Pennsylvania legislature passed a "personal liberty law," forbidding state authorities from aiding in the capture and return of runaway slaves. Six years later, a slave named Margaret Morgan escaped with her children from their Maryland master and fled to Pennsylvania, where a slave catcher named Edward Prigg tracked them down and demanded they be handed over under the terms of the federal Fugitive Slave Act of 1792. The local constable refused, but Prigg seized them anyway, touching off a case that tested the constitutionality of the Pennsylvania law. Writing for the majority, Justice Story ruled that although states were not required to aid in the enforcement of the federal law, neither were they entitled to block that enforcement. In dissent, Justice Taney concurred on the law's unconstitutionality, but argued that individual masters were entitled to seize their human property wherever they might find it. For northern blacks and antislavery whites, the Court's split decision offered a choice between bad and even worse.[13]

The racist turn in northern laws pushed black activists to take an ever-greater concern in movements and organizations of their own for collective self-improvement and protection. The former included the black convention movement begun in the 1830s, as well as church groups, benevolent societies, and a plethora of local voluntary associations—like the vigilance committees already established in the seaboard cities to protect runaway slaves, and even free-born blacks, from being seized. Most famous of all was the New York Vigilance Committee and its secretary and general agent, David Ruggles. In 1837, two years after its formation, the New York committee reported that it had protected 335 persons from enslavement, and in time Ruggles himself would be credited with assisting in the escapes of upwards of one hundred slaves. Compared to such urgent matters, the idea of supporting a marginal, white-led third party in a period of black disenfranchisement could easily have looked like a distracting will-o'-the-wisp, and perhaps a dangerous one.[14]

Liberty Party leaders, however, purists and pragmatics alike, made clear from the start that they supported black rights throughout the country as well as the destruction of southern slavery. Northern oppression of blacks, they argued, was the sturdiest prop to the continued toleration of slavery by northern whites, and to what one Liberty convention called the "proslavery spirit" of the major parties. Negro heroes such as Toussaint L'Ouverture, Liberty men pointed out, proved that both races could produce valiant figures, and if there were not more blacks in that category at present, it was only because they were kept enthralled by ignorance and poverty. Party members became important advocates in numerous battles against northern racist laws and proscriptions, including discriminatory voting laws. Just as firmly as the Garrisonians, they repudiated the colonization movement as irredeemably racist, based on what one Liberty paper called the groundless assumption "that the blacks"—whose forefathers had helped secure American independence—"can never be so elevated as to enjoy their rights in this country."[15]

Thanks to this steadfastness, the Liberty Party, despite its sometimes patronizing tone, won wide and sometimes enthusiastic appreciation from northern black activists. The contrast, to blacks, between the Liberty men—who actually welcomed blacks into their ranks—and the Democrats and Whigs was obvious. The nation's leading black paper, Samuel Cornish's fiercely abolitionist *Colored American*, loudly trumpeted the party's virtues before the paper published its final issue in December 1841. The gifted ex-slave and minister Henry Highland Garnet took to the stump on behalf of Liberty Party candidates, as did the ex-slave abolitionist lecturer Henry Bibb. The National Convention of Colored Men, held in Buffalo in 1843, gave the party its overwhelming endorsement. The party even managed to gain the respect of an ex-slave who had begun making a name for himself as an uncompromising Garrisonian abolitionist—Frederick Douglass.[16]

Born Frederick Bailey in 1818 on Maryland's eastern shore, the son of a slave woman and unknown white father, Douglass had escaped from slavery in 1838, winding up in New York City, where he was taken in as one of David Ruggles's refugees (and married his betrothed, who escaped by prearranged plan shortly after he did). Moving to New Bedford, Massachusetts (where, to avoid detection, he took the name Douglass, after the hero of Sir Walter Scott's novel *The Lady of the Lake*), he found work as a common laborer and a ship's caulker and, upon reading the *Liberator*, became a quick convert to Garrison's cause. In 1839, Garrison published some of Douglass's anticolonizationist statements in the *Liberator*, and in April 1841, the two finally met when they both addressed the annual meeting of the Massachusetts chapter of the AA-SS. Impressed with the young man's bearing and sonority, Garrison immediately hired him as an AA-SS traveling lecturer, charged with telling audiences the story of his life and gathering up subscriptions to the *Liberator*.[17]

Douglass's powerful performances—there is no other word for them—were the finest example of what was to become the Garrisonians' most potent antislavery weapon in the 1840s, publicizing the testimony of escaped ex-slaves. For decades, southern slaveholders and their defenders had talked soothingly of slavery's mild, patriarchal hierarchy, so unlike the harsh free-labor system of the North. The fugitive slave lecturers were there to say it was all a grotesque lie, and nobody put truth to the lie better than Douglass. Introduced to his listeners as "a piece of property," or as "a graduate of that peculiar institution, with his diploma written on his back," Douglass would commence a horrifying recollection of his life as a slave—of the brutal beatings he had endured and seen inflicted on women, children, and elderly people, of the systematic "breeding" of female slaves, and more. He always reminded his listeners that his experiences in Maryland would seem idyllic to the vast majority of slaves in the cotton fields of the Deep South. The horror was not unrelieved: Douglass used wit and sarcasm to his advantage, taking special pleasure in telling how he beat up a "breaker" overseer named Covey, secure in the knowledge that Covey's pride would keep the embarrassing story under wraps. And while Douglass's words touched his listeners, his elegant manner and diction—still in formation, but already considerable—impressed upon them all the harder the basic human absurdity as well as the injustice of slavery.[18]

Douglass was an immediate hit on the Garrisonian circuit. In 1842, he traveled through New York and Massachusetts to lecture alongside Garrison himself. He also traveled to Rhode Island, where he denounced the Dorrites over black suffrage. The following year, he spoke before more than one hundred meetings in a tour that took him from New England through upstate New York, Ohio, and Indiana. In late July, he broke off from his travels to attend, with his fellow lecturer Charles Remond, the National Convention of Colored Men, and heard Garnet and others laud the Liberty Party. As a disciple of Garrison's, Douglass was bound to repudiate politics and insist that slavery had to be attacked as morally wrong, that it could be ended only by moral suasion. Yet the Buffalo convention was the first sizable gathering of black men Douglass had ever attended, and Garnet's forceful address impressed him (even though he delivered a sharp riposte). Without abandoning Garrison, at least for the moment, Douglass began defending the Liberty Party to antislavery audiences, on the ground that any and all attacks on slavery were worth supporting.[19]

Slowly but surely, the antislavery movement was investing its most consequential energies within the political realm. And those energies began making an impact in Washington—chiefly through the actions of the small knot of antislavery northern Whigs who had taken John Quincy Adams as their grand old man.

Aside from the dramatic *Amistad* affair, antislavery politics in Washington in the early 1840s focused on the continuing battle over the gag rule. In 1840, as the presidential campaign was getting started, southern Whigs led by Waddy Thompson and William Cost Johnson of Maryland, out to embarrass the Van Buren administration, passed a version of the rule much closer to James Hammond's severe original proposal than to the compromise measure Van Buren helped to maneuver through the House four years earlier. Under the new rule, antislavery petitions would not even be received. With the formerly united, pro–gag rule northern Democrats now split down the middle, the vote was nowhere near as decisive as that on the earlier, softer gag rule—but thanks to the extra seats given the South by the three-fifths rule, the revised "hard" gag rule squeaked through by a margin of 114 to 108.[20]

Adams and his coterie—above all Joshua Giddings, William Slade, and Seth Gates—remained undaunted. Early in the special congressional session of 1841, Adams and his allies managed on three separate occasions to have the newly installed hard gag rule voted down in the House—only to see the southern members, Whig and Democrat, regroup to demand a revote and reinstitute the rule. Six months later, on January 25, 1842, Adams pushed the matter to the wall. He had in his hand, he announced, a petition from one Benjamin Emerson and forty-five other citizens of Haverhill, Massachusetts, complaining of intolerable sectional imbalances in political power and praying for "measures peacefully to dissolve the Union." Adams moved that the petition be accepted and sent to committee, with instructions to inform the petitioners why their request ought not be granted.[21]

The reaction was a virtual reprise of the verbal brawl that Adams had instigated in 1838. One southern Whig demanded that the petition not only be rejected but publicly burned. Thomas Marshall, the Kentucky Whig and nephew of the late Chief Justice John Marshall, offered a resolution of censure, charging that Adams was complicit in "high treason." Adams, perhaps recalling his summation in the Amistad case a year earlier, asked the clerk to read the opening paragraphs of the Declaration of Independence, to remind his colleagues of the people's right to alter governments that denied their inalienable rights — then demanded the right to defend himself like any other American accused of a capital crime. Debate over the censure motion lasted several days, the high points coming when Henry A. Wise accused Adams of trying to foment disunion, and when Adams, taking advantage of the situation, accused the slaveholders of endangering every element of American liberty in order to suppress anything "that might not be pleasing to the members of the 'peculiar institution.'" Finally, as in 1838, the censure failed, though now with northern Democrats as well as Whigs voting to table the motion.[22] But the southerners' attack on the antislavery Whigs was not over. Having once again failed to bring down Old Man Eloquent, they set their sights on his young abettor, Joshua Giddings, who had recently offended southern honor over an incident eerily similar to the Amistad affair.

In late October 1841, the American brig Creole set sail from Hampton Roads, Virginia, bound for New Orleans, with a cargo of 135 slaves. Unlike the Amistad captives, the bondmen and women on the Creole were indubitably enslaved, and they were enslaved to Americans — chattel, by American law, being shipped southward in the fully legal coastal trade in slaves that operated between the southeastern seaports and New Orleans. On November 7, as the ship prepared to enter the harbor at Abaco Island in the Bahamas, a preorganized band of nineteen slaves, led by the ship's cook, Madison Washington, overpowered the crew and forced one of the white overseers to steer the ship to Nassau. One crew member and one slave were killed in the fighting, and when the Creole landed in the Bahamas on November 9, British colonial authorities arrested the nineteen rebels. The rest of the slaves were freed, partly at the insistence of locals who surrounded the brig with their small boats. The Creole finally arrived in New Orleans, slaveless, on December 2. The rebels were imprisoned in Nassau for five months, then also freed.[23]

Previously, when smaller American ships bearing slaves had wrecked or accidentally run aground on British shores, the local authorities had liberated the
slaves, under the 1833 British Emancipation Act that ended slavery in the
empire. But the decision to free summarily some of the *Creole*'s slaves, and then
lightly punish the others, touched off predictably impassioned reactions in the
United States. Southern newspapers denounced British interference with the
coastal trade in slaves. Northern abolitionist and evangelical papers called the rebels
saintly, above all the propitiously named Madison Washington, whom they
praised (fancifully) for ministering Christ-like to wounded members of the *Creole*'s crew. According to Elizur Wright, the rebellion was an act of God in the
truest sense. William Goodell, the Liberty Party leader, noted that the uprising
had occurred four years to the day after Elijah Lovejoy's martyrdom, which
could not have been a coincidence.[24]

The case would in time be settled diplomatically by Secretary of State Daniel
Webster, assisted by the British, as part of his treaty negotiations with Lord Ashburton (although compensation for the slaveowners only came in 1853). Well
before then, the *Creole* rebellion helped make Joshua Giddings into an antislavery hero. Ambitious, intrepid, and resourceful, Giddings exemplified the young
new-school men who had revitalized the Whig Party. Having pulled himself up
from next to nothing to become a lawyer in the Ohio Western Reserve, he had
entered politics in the early 1830s espousing the National Republican views of
his mentor and patron, Congressman Elisha Whittlesey. Financial difficulties
and a personal crisis of faith in 1837 pulled Giddings away from his nominal
Congregationalism and conventional Whiggery and into evangelical holy benevolence and abolitionism. Siding with the more politically oriented abolitionists—"the wisdom of providence is . . . manifestly to be seen in any subject"
debated in Congress, he later told a friend—he ran as a Whig and replaced
Whittlesey in the House when the older man retired in 1838. Arriving in Washington (where he had his first direct, devastating contact with the slave trade),
Giddings gravitated to John Quincy Adams and then to the small circle of young
antislavery Whigs headquartered at Mrs. Sprigg's. Giddings took up lodgings
there and aided in the battle against the gag rule, until the *Creole* case gave him
the opportunity to step forward on his own.[25]

Inspired by Adams, Giddings was determined, as he put it, to "spring" additional matters on the southern members, "when they think not of it." On February 28, a few days after the move to censure Adams failed, Giddings tried to
reintroduce the Haverhill remonstrance, and in early March, he helped beat
back an effort for compensation for slaves lost to the British during the War of
1812. Finally, on March 21, Giddings introduced nine resolutions, drafted earlier by Weld, asserting that the laws of slavery had no effect outside of the southern states, and that the *Creole* rebels were fully justified in their violent strike for

freedom. Isaac Holmes, a South Carolina Democrat, quickly arose and delivered a biting remark about fools rushing in where angels fear to tread. But revenge, and not mere bluster, was now on the southerners' agenda. In a maneuver led by Virginia Whig John Minor Botts and Ohio Democrat John Weller, Giddings's opponents sprang their own trap, demanding an instant vote on a motion censuring Giddings without giving Giddings the chance to reply as Adams had done so effectively. Giddings did try to defend himself the next day, but was ruled out of order, and the censure resolution passed by a margin of 125 to 69. Unlike in the Adams vote, virtually all of the northern Democrats turned against the younger, hotter antislavery Whig. Almost all of the southern Whigs also supported censure, splitting the party along sectional lines.[26]

Giddings curtly resigned his seat and returned home, determined to win reelection. Four years earlier, the Illinois legislature, still in control of the state's Senate selections, had been able to remove the unruly antislavery man Thomas Morris without consulting the voters. But the fate of Giddings's House seat could only be determined by the citizens of Ohio's fervently antislavery Sixteenth District—and so Giddings stood in the special election called for late April, expecting not simply to win but to turn the attack on him and the antislavery Whigs into a vindication for the antislavery cause. A Giddings victory, Seth Gates wrote, would be "of the very highest importance to the cause of freedom."[27]

Giddings received no aid whatsoever from Washington, either from the national Whig leadership in Congress or from the Whigs in his own state's House delegation. The largest Whig paper in the Western Reserve attacked him as a "firebrand" and urged Whittlesey to come out of retirement. But within Giddings's district, a combination of antislavery fervor and repugnance at having their elected representative chastised brought him overwhelming support. Every Whig paper in the district supported Giddings, as did the Liberty Party papers, as did Garrison's *Liberator*. Popular, nonpartisan conventions of local voters endorsed him and requested that he reintroduce his *Creole* resolutions in the House. The result was never in doubt, but the magnitude of Giddings's triumph—a 7,469 to 393 majority over a mocking Democrat—surprised even his friends.[28]

Giddings's triumph was of crucial significance in several ways. Once he returned to Washington, he was more passionate than ever in his antislavery floor speeches, attracting audiences eager to hear his fire and brimstone—and eliciting only occasional outbursts from southern members. Although the gag rule would not be formally voted down until December 1844, it had, as Giddings later related, "morally ceased to operate" after the moves to censure Adams and permanently remove Giddings failed. Killing the gag rule in turn dramatically increased the likelihood of additional sectional wrangling in Congress. When the pro-slavery stalwart Henry A. Wise told Giddings that his reelection was "the

greatest triumph ever achieved by a member of this House," he was both expressing his respect for Giddings's political fortitude and anticipating the opportunity
to reply in kind to the antislavery minority's attacks. Agitation over slavery, on
both sides, was now fair play.[29]

The manner of Giddings's victory was just as important as the fact that he
won. By taking his campaign back to the voters of the Sixteenth District of Ohio,
Giddings turned the affair into one of majority rule at odds with the Slave Power,
including its northern Whig allies. The special election in April 1842 left no
doubt that the voters wanted Giddings to represent them, in defiance of what the
political abolitionists had called the "pro-slavery spirit" of state and national leaders of both parties. Giddings's victory was, incontestably, a democratic victory. As
never before, antislavery radicals had successfully mobilized the principles of
majoritarian democracy and many of its techniques—campaign newspapers,
public conventions, the entire machinery of popular electioneering—while
attacking the great compromise over slavery on which the Democrats and Whigs
based their survival, and its constrictions of free speech and conscience. A special
election for a single congressional seat in Ohio cracked open a fearsome issue:
Could American democracy coexist with American slavery?

The Giddings affair also illuminated how even the lowliest of Americans, far
outside the broadened terrain of national politics, continued to shape the course
of political events. Giddings was on the lookout for some way to advance antislavery agitation beyond organizing yet again against the gag rule, but he found it
only after the *Creole* rebellion. Earlier black rebels and abolitionists had hammered at the contradictions between American slavery and American equality.
Their actions had pushed southern slaveholders to reply with their own arguments that there was no contradiction at all, that American democracy depended
on the existence of American slavery and white supremacy. Now, with the Giddings affair and the repeal of the gag rule, the conflict moved closer to becoming
a permanent issue in national politics. And at the bottom of these new developments was a rebellion led by a slave with a name suited to the ironies and importance of his impact—Madison Washington.

For Joshua Giddings's unfaithful Whig Party allies, the heightening of sectional tensions in Congress made it imperative that they find some compromise
middle ground in the 1844 campaign, a situation that further strengthened the
presidential aspirations of the Great Compromiser, Henry Clay. The same intersectional logic held true for the Democrats but would prove difficult for the
Democrats to heed. By early 1844, Martin Van Buren and the Radical Democrats controlled the party's nominating machinery—to the intense displeasure of
Calhounites and Hunkers alike, and to the trepidation of other Democrats who
feared that the uncharismatic Van Buren could never unite the party and win the
election. Calhoun's departure from the presidential race in January 1844

appeared to seal Van Buren's nomination. The New Yorker would, once again, have to find a way to placate the South if he were to defeat the Whigs' nominee, but Van Buren had been playing that game successfully for decades. The key question seemed to be whether candidate Van Buren could heal the divisions within the party over banking and internal improvements.[30]

Suddenly, only weeks after Calhoun's withdrawal, the entire political calculus changed. Deep inside the Tyler administration, the departure of Daniel Webster and the severing of the president's last surviving tie to the Whigs had already brought a sharp swerve in American foreign policy, under the new secretary of state, Calhoun's admirer, the conservative Abel Parker Upshur of Virginia. With Tyler's approval, Upshur had begun moving aggressively to promote the annexation of Texas, a polarizing policy that the president hoped might revive his own fading political hopes. Then, in February 1844, an accidental shipboard explosion accelerated a chain of events that would make Texas annexation the overriding issue in the fight for the Democratic nomination.

"A DEEP, DEEP, DEEP INTEREST": MANIFEST DESTINY AND TEXAS ANNEXATION

That Judge Upshur ended up in a position of great national importance in 1843 was one of the oddest elevations in the entire history of early American politics—and one of the sharper ironies of the Tyler presidency. Not that Upshur would have realized as much, for as far as he was concerned he had been born and bred to greatness. A native of Accomack County on Virginia's Eastern Shore, he had matriculated at Princeton (which threw him out for leading a student rebellion), then moved to Yale (where he failed to graduate), then studied law in Richmond with the superior Federalist William Wirt. Elected to the Virginia legislature in 1812 and to the post of commonwealth attorney in 1816, he served as a delegate to the state's constitutional convention of 1829–30, where he joined John Randolph and Benjamin Watkins Leigh in calling on his more wobbly colleagues to stand up against the western peasantry who, whatever their present disposition, might some day plunder the eastern slaveholders. After that moment of glory, Upshur withdrew to his Eastern Shore plantation and a seat on the Virginia Supreme Court. Inside his little world, he cut quite a figure, a large man with an imposing bald head, never without a malicious quip that his fellow squires thought the height of drollery. But that world was getting pushed aside, even in the Commonwealth of Virginia, by the vulgar Jackson Democracy and its contemptible agents like Thomas Ritchie.[31]

On the fringes of power, Upshur had time to write, and he was prolific, churning out political essays, reviews, pamphlets, and reams of private letters to, among others, his old friend Congressman John Tyler. Although he was formally a Whig (he bitterly opposed government regulation of banks), his principal views might best be described as orthodox Calhounite. Like his South Carolina hero, Upshur had little faith in the Whig Party as a vehicle for true conservatism, which upheld the virtuous rule of patrician whites over slaves and plebeian whites. The Whigs' victorious Log Cabin campaign only further depressed Upshur's hopes for himself as well as his country. After the election, he pathetically wrote to one associate that he "frequently had occasion to remark that for the last half of my life I have been almost something." Then, suddenly, Upshur's close friend Tyler was president; soon after, Tyler lost most of his cabinet and began casting about for loyal friends to stock a new one; and late in 1841, Judge Upshur traveled to Washington to take up his duties as Tyler's new secretary of the navy.[32]

Upshur's tenure at the Navy Department, which lasted less than two years, brought needed reorganization and modernization to the service, the construction of new sail and steam warships, and the establishment of both the Naval Observatory and the Hydrographic Office—a record of solid achievement that was all the more creditable given Upshur's lack of federal government experience. His efforts as a policy adviser were more frustrating. He certainly had the president's ear, perhaps more than any other person in Washington. And he had plenty of advice to give, about how Tyler could and should form a party of his own, "of which the St[ate] Rights Party may form a nucleus." But finding a way to launch the enterprise was next to impossible, given that Henry Clay (and, after Clay's departure, his supporters) were setting the Whig agenda at the other end of Pennsylvania Avenue. By the spring of 1843, Upshur sounded as if he had given up. Still, he did have ideas about one issue, the annexation of Texas, that might prove the galvanizing force he had been looking for—and, astonishingly, when Tyler named him to succeed the retiring Webster as secretary of state in June, Upshur suddenly had the power to press the issue forward.[33]

Texas annexation had long been a taboo subject for Whigs and Democrats alike. Ever since the formation of the independent Lone Star Republic in 1836, its new government had expressed interest in joining the United States. The newly elected Texas president, Sam Houston, backed the idea in his inaugural address in October, and in August 1837, a proposal favoring Texas annexation was laid before Congress. But the idea instantly ran into trouble in Washington. Although Jackson had been happy to recognize the new Texas Republic, annexing it as a state could well lead to war with Mexico, which both Jackson and Van Buren wanted to avoid. Moreover, northern antislavery opinion, riveted by Benjamin Lundy's account of the Texas revolution as a slaveholders' uprising, saw annexation as the latest southern subterfuge to augment slavery's control of the federal government. "[T]he whole people of the United States," John Quincy

Adams told the House, have "a deep, deep, deep interest in the matter." Adams was convinced that a very large portion of the citizenry, "dearly as they loved the Union, would prefer its total dissolution to the act of annexation of Texas." He proceeded to filibuster the annexation resolution for more than three weeks. In late August 1837, Secretary of State John Forsyth informed Texas officials that the effort would fail.[34]

Under Houston's successor, the Georgia émigré Mirabeau Buonaparte Lamar, Texas renounced annexation and turned inward, removing Indians by force, planning a state education system, and raising hopes that one day the Lone Star Republic would extend to the Pacific—all while its treasury virtually collapsed. There the annexation issue rested (even after Houston's return as president) until 1843, when rumors began feeding fears that the British government had designs on the floundering republic. "I anticipate an important movement in regard to Texas," Upshur wrote, months before he took over from Webster. Texas also had become ripe for reconquest by Mexico, which had never conceded its loss. The British, so the stories ran, would be happy to step in and prevent it, and get Mexico at last to recognize Texas's independence—so long as the Texans, respectful of the authority of Her Majesty's government, freed their slaves. From one angle, Upshur and other Tidewater conservatives reasoned, the British interference might be beneficial if it prevented the further draining away of eastern slaves westward and thereby helped the old-line eastern patricians to rebuild their former glory. But from another angle, the prospect of establishing a huge free territory (and potential haven for runaway slaves) on the borders of Louisiana and Arkansas was frightening.[35]

For Upshur, raising the specter of slavery besieged looked like the best way to break through the demagogy of low political party managers and initiate the great southern-led state-rights party. Prodded by word from Calhoun's right-hand man Duff Green, and then from Calhoun himself, that the British government, with assistance of British abolitionists, was on the verge of striking a deal with the Texans, Upshur pressed Tyler to secure the only practical check on Britain's ambitions, Texas annexation. By September, administration officials were engaged in secret talks with Sam Houston. On October 16, Upshur met with the Texas chargé d'affaires Isaac Van Zandt and began preliminary discussions toward negotiating an annexation treaty.[36]

The pursuit of Texas was bound to cause some sectional disagreements among the Whigs, but they were not nearly as sharp as those sparked by incidents like the Giddings censure. Since 1836, most old-guard and new-school northern Whigs had opposed annexation, some fearing a further expansion of slavery and southern power, others fearing that the nation was expanding too quickly ahead of the civilizing hand of moral progress and the American System, and still others hoping to make life more complicated for Webster's rival Clay. (Pro-

expansionist Democrats added charges that pro-business Whigs opposed westward expansion in order to create a glut in the eastern labor market and suppress
workers' wages.) Although some influential northern Whigs, above all Tyler's
minister to England, Edward Everett, strongly backed annexation, they were in
the decided minority. And if state-rights southern Whigs were more receptive to
Tyler's plans, a significant number of Whig planters, mainly in the older southeastern states, opposed them in order to halt the diffusion of the slave population—and what they feared was their imminent abandonment to their depleted
land and unpaid debts. Annexation's impact on the Democracy would be even
more complicated. Southern Democrats, as expected, generally lined up with
the administration, but the northern Democracy was deeply divided. Some leading New York Radicals took a dim view of annexation. Other northern Democrats loudly supported it, shouting new slogans about Manifest Destiny.[37]

The Manifest Destiny impulse fed off a mixture of crassness, truculence, and
high idealism. Without question, there were those who proclaimed America's
providential mission to expand as a eulogistic cover for speculation in land and
paper. But those were hardly the motives of John L. O'Sullivan, the writer who
coined the term, or the other writers, loosely referred to as Young America, in
and around O'Sullivan's *Democratic Review* (which had relocated from Washington to Manhattan over the winter of 1840–41). For O'Sullivan and his allies,
the expansionist imperative was essentially democratic—not simply in the old
Jeffersonian tradition of enlarging the empire of liberty, but in a supercharged
moral sense, stressing America's duties to spread democratic values and institutions to a world still dominated by monarchs and deformed by ignorant superstition. The grand national mission, O'Sullivan wrote as early as 1839, was to
spread four great freedoms around the globe: freedom of conscience, freedom of
person, freedom of trade, and what he called "universality of freedom and equality." The mission was even more precise closer to home, where, O'Sullivan
claimed six years later, America enjoyed "the right of our manifest destiny to
overspread and to possess the whole of the continent which Providence has given
us for the . . . great experiment of liberty."[38]

In retrospect, this posturing can look like the most arrogant form of imperial
bullying. Certainly it was arrogant, and Mexicans, including Mexican liberals,
had ample reason to consider it imperialist. But there was a deeply idealistic
democratic side to Manifest Destiny that, to be understood, requires an appreciation for the situation facing democrats around the world, and especially in
Britain and Europe, in the early 1840s. That situation was terrible. In Britain,
the Reform Bill of 1832 had left the vast majority of urban and rural workingmen
disenfranchised. Radicals from William Cobbett (who wrote an admiring brief
biography of Jackson) to the Chartists were struggling through one setback after
another, on the road to Chartism's collapse in 1848. In France, the hopeful revo-

lution of 1830 had produced a stockjobber monarchy that hesitated not at all to repress popular republican stirrings in blood—and that inspired, in Paris, Honoré Daumier's brilliant pictorial satires and indictments. In Ireland, Daniel O'Connell's nonviolent mass movement for repeal of the union with Britain was stirring great crowds, but getting nowhere fast against the obdurate ministry of Sir Robert Peel. Across the face of Europe, nationalist as well as democratic aspirations remained stifled by Metternichian reaction. In all of these places, but especially in England and Ireland, intellectuals and agitators looked to the United States for practical as well as spiritual inspiration—and, when the repression at home got too great, looked to the United States for asylum.[39]

Manifest Destiny was rooted in its proponents' allegiance to the beleaguered forces of democracy outside the United States. The name ascribed to and then embraced by the O'Sullivan circle, Young America, had been borrowed from the insurgent liberals of Giuseppe Mazzini's Young Italy, initiated in the 1830s. (There were, in time, many others in the international movement, including Young Germany, Young England, Young Ireland, Young France, Young Poland —and even, one writer tried to claim during the Dorr Rebellion, a Young Rhode Island.) Democracy, the expansionists asserted, was a universal value that should—and could—rule the world. "Why should not England be republican?" the *Democratic Review* queried in a typical article on the Chartists. "Are her lower classes unfit for the burden of government?" And what of Ireland, her lifeblood drained for centuries by the British monarchy: "[I]s Ireland incapable of entering upon the simple task of self-government, because for so long she has been unused to it?" What of the French, the Hungarians, the Italians, the much-abused Greeks?[40]

There were, of course, large omissions from this expansionist idealism: black slaves along with, as ever, displaced Indians. O'Sullivan and his admirers sharply denied that their intentions were pro-slavery. (On the Texas question, O'Sullivan agreed with southerners, most prominently Senator Robert J. Walker of Mississippi, who argued that annexation would lead to a dispersal of the slave population through the West and into Latin America, hasten slavery's demise, and leave behind an all-white United States—a rehashing of the old Jeffersonian "diffusion" idea.) But neither were they capable of expanding their democratic radicalism to endorse antislavery. Like the centrist mainstream of their party, the Manifest Destiny Democrats took an agnostic position on slavery. With regard to race, they candidly but clumsily evaded even considering the possibilities of equality between blacks and whites. "Strong as are our sympathies in behalf of liberty, universal liberty, in all applications of the principle not forbidden by great and manifest evils," O'Sullivan wrote in the *Democratic Review*, "we confess ourselves not prepared with any satisfactory solution of the great problem of which these questions present various aspects." After 1845, this moral indifference about slavery and race would leave the Young America movement and the slogans of Manifest Destiny vulnerable to capture by pro-slavery ideologues. But until then, Young America could electrify masses of northern Democrats, for whom enlarging on what O'Sullivan called the "gigantic boldness" of the American Revolution was the greatest idea in the world.[41]

O'Sullivan and Young America won support from a diverse collection of northern Radicals, Hunkers, and Calhounites, including Churchill Cambreleng and Mike Walsh. But there were other Democrats, including the flickering taper that was once Andrew Jackson, who desired Texas for defensive reasons, to block the unending treachery of Great Britain. For Jackson, the Texas maneuverings created the imminent danger of a British reconquest of America. With a base in Texas, Jackson predicted, the British would gather up hordes of Indians as well as slaves to attack the nation's borders, then send in their own troops to march on New Orleans and seize control of both the lower Mississippi Valley and the Gulf of Mexico. Reversing that course, even if successful, would spill oceans of American blood and cost untold fortunes. Texas, Jackson told Francis Blair in 1844, was "the important key to our future safety—take and lock the door against all danger of foreign influence."[42]

Contrary to both Young America and Jackson, however, a significant portion of the northern Democracy strongly objected to Texas annexation. Theodore Sedgwick III, the party's leading anti-annexation voice, had been writing antislavery Democratic pieces for the *Evening Post* for several years. In 1840—while he was working on the *Amistad* case and putting through the press a two-volume posthumous edition of William Leggett's collected writings—he sustained Leggett's Jacksonian abolitionism in terms that spoke directly to the Democracy: "Give us the real issue," he bellowed. "*Is Slavery a good or an evil to the free citizens of these States?*" Three years later, Sedgwick composed a fresh series of articles (which he eventually collected under the disarmingly calm title *Thoughts on the Proposed Annexation of Texas*) laying out the case that the admission of Texas to the Union was just "another name for '*the perpetuity of slavery*,'" which threatened the dignity of northern labor and thus democracy itself. Sedgwick's articles caused a stir among the New York Barnburners, which in turn reinforced Democratic antislavery opinion elsewhere. Silas Wright came out strongly against annexation, as did Wright's protégé, the one-time radical Jacksonian hotspur and now congressman from St. Lawrence County Preston King. They were joined by Marcus Morton of Massachusetts and another hard-money Radical Democrat, New Hampshire Senator John Parker Hale.[43]

Antislavery Democrats had long been a submerged element within the party, harassed by party officials and, in some cases, subdued by their own self-censorship in order to keep up a united front against the Whigs. By 1844, some had finally defected in disgust to the Liberty Party. Others had either died, fallen by the political wayside, or, like Nat Turner's defender George Henry Evans, embarked on the strange journey that took them temporarily into Calhounism. The fight over Texas, however, revived the antislavery intellectual strain with the Democracy, and it gave antislavery a new and potentially disruptive political urgency among party leaders. It was one thing for Sedgwick's Manhattan friends (including William Cullen Bryant) to oppose Texas annexation; it was quite another when the opposition came to include Silas Wright. Once Wright and other Radical worthies joined the anti-annexationists, questions inevitably arose about their boss and mentor, the Democracy's prospective presidential nominee, Martin Van Buren. Would Texas annexation enter into the campaign of 1844? If it did, how would the preternaturally cautious Van Buren handle it? And no matter how Van Buren acted, could a Democratic Party that included pro-slavery southerners, Manifest Destiny enthusiasts, and anti-annexationist northerners possibly unite as long as the Texas question was on everybody's mind?

Secretary of State Upshur was intent on forcing the issue, and he was not alone. At the end of 1843, Calhounites all across the South began exploiting Texas annexation to revive their man's fading presidential chances. Only "the immediate calling up of the Texas question," Calhoun's Maryland friend Virgil Maxcy wrote in December, could unite the South, weaken Henry Clay, and bring a true southern candidate to power. (Maxcy was already plotting with the South Carolina extremist Robert Barnwell Rhett on how to kill Van Buren's chances at the Democratic convention.) Upshur had a different script in mind: the South should nominate Calhoun as a third-party presidential candidate on a pro-annexation platform; that candidacy would throw the election into the House of Representatives; and the southern members, by refusing to vote for Van Buren, would at the very least hold the balance of power in selecting the next administration. Calhoun dampened speculation when he formally abandoned his quest for the Democratic nomination in January 1844, but he remained open to using Texas as a political bludgeon on behalf of the South and did not rule out a third-party presidential run. President Tyler, meanwhile, hoping to become the South's tribune, tried with his usual ineptness to get Van Buren out of the way by offering him a seat on the Supreme Court. Tyler's messenger brought back the derisive reply that Van Buren's nomination to the Court would give the nation "a broader, deeper, heartier, laugh than it ever had."[44]

On the diplomatic front, Upshur's steady labor was proving, tortuously, successful. He was well aware that gaining the two-thirds' majority in the Senate necessary to ratify any annexation treaty with Texas would be an uphill fight. The quicker he could conclude the treaty itself, the quicker he and his friends could go to work convincing Anglophilic southerners that the English emancipation threat had become an emergency. The southerners could then force the northern congressional Democrats to heel—or, failing in that, could form their own party along the lines Upshur favored and elect either Tyler or, even better, Calhoun as president. But getting a treaty out of the Texans proved difficult. President Sam Houston truly was interested in the British option and was pursuing it vigorously and openly. Only by applying all of the political pressure on Houston it could think of—including a plea from his old friend, Andrew Jackson—did the administration finally get him to come around. Finally, late in February 1844, Houston gave way.[45] But by the time news of Houston's agreement arrived in Washington, on March 5, Secretary Upshur was dead.

Six days earlier, Upshur had joined a large presidential party aboard the battleship USS *Princeton*, anchored in the Potomac. The *Princeton* was the pride of the fleet, carrying the largest naval gun ever built, called "The Peacemaker." The day's highlight was to be a demonstration firing of the massive weapon, but something went terribly wrong and instead it exploded, blasting the dignitaries and sailors on deck to pieces. Tyler's life was spared, but Upshur, along with Secretary of the Navy Thomas Gilmer, Calhoun's close friend Virgil Maxcy, and five others were killed, and nine persons, including Senator Thomas Hart Benton, were injured. The president, although stunned and grief-stricken, acted swiftly to shore up his shaken government. At his Fort Hill plantation, in the same mail that carried an eyewitness description of the tragedy from his son Patrick (who was nearly killed himself), John C. Calhoun received word that Tyler would nominate him as Upshur's successor.[46] Suddenly, the southern sectionalists' hero, who had figured so greatly in the plotting over Texas annexation, would be back in Washington as the chief officer of the cabinet, overseeing the entire Texas matter. And Martin Van Buren's renomination to the presidency was no longer a sure thing.

DIVIDED DEMOCRATS AND THE ELECTION OF 1844

Calhoun's accession augured little change in the broad lines of administration policy on Texas; indeed, Upshur's maneuverings had closely followed a letter of advice Calhoun had sent him six months earlier. But Calhoun's iron-willed personality and reignited political ambitions could not help but affect the tone of the annexation effort. On April 12, after only two weeks in office, Calhoun signed a treaty that would bring Texas into the Union as a territory—then added a political stinger in the form of an extraordinary letter to Richard Pakenham, the British minister to the United States. Two days before Upshur's death, Pakenham had forwarded Upshur a message from the British foreign minister, Lord Aberdeen, explaining that although his government supported the end of slavery throughout the world, it would support an independent Texas with or without slavery, a reassuring grace note that denied Britain was pursuing an abolitionist agenda. Calhoun, however, took offense at what he perceived as Aberdeen's moral smugness, and suggested to Pakenham undertaking an exchange of letters on slavery and emancipation. When Pakenham turned him down, Calhoun struck back with a long letter that defended not just annexation but American slavery.[47]

Calhoun had several motives for writing what soon became notorious as the Pakenham letter. At bottom he was following the same course he had outlined to Upshur the previous summer, though with an aggressiveness and moral indignation all his own. To Aberdeen's assertion that Britain had no intention of interfering with the internal affairs of Texas or the United States, Calhoun replied that Britain had in fact been interfering for a long time, always with the stated hope that slavery in both places would one day disappear. Unable to stop there, though, he added a long paternalistic defense of slavery based on the supposed inherent inferiority of blacks. In every state where slavery had been abolished, Calhoun claimed, blacks had sunk into wretchedness and depravity. Under slavery, blacks enjoyed levels of health and happiness on a par with any working population in the Western world—"and it may be added, that in no other condition or in any other country has the negro race ever attained so high an elevation in morals, intelligence or civilization" as in the slave South. British abolitionist philanthropy would consign freed slaves to misery, while throwing the rest of the world into confusion. Texas annexation—in Calhoun's formulation, an explicitly pro-slavery enterprise—would benefit all mankind.[48]

It is inconceivable that Calhoun did not comprehend his letter's political implications. Had he taken precautions to guarantee his remarks would not see print, his defense of slavery might be ascribed merely to his desire to upbraid Pakenham and Aberdeen. Instead, he sent the letter along with the other official documents pertaining to Texas to the Senate—the "Texas bombshell," Benton called it—thereby assuring that an antislavery senator would release it to the press (as Benjamin Tappan of Ohio swiftly did). Instantly, the letter became a public litmus test for national Democrats and Whigs: support Texas annexation and its pro-slavery rationale and alienate the North, or oppose it and forever lose the South. With one master stroke, Calhoun managed, in a presidential election year, to polarize national politics along sectional lines—the objective of all of his planning since at least 1833.[49]

Even before the release of the Pakenham letter, Van Buren had come under intense scrutiny over Texas. On March 20, a pro-annexationist Tennessee Democrat, Aaron Brown, published in Blair's *Globe* a letter that Brown had obtained a year earlier from Andrew Jackson supporting annexation. Immediately, Thomas Ritchie reprinted the letter in the *Richmond Enquirer*, accompanied by a warning that unless Van Buren followed Jackson's lead, he would ruin his chances to win their party's nomination. From every section of the country, Democratic leaders wrote to Van Buren making the same point. At the same time, the anti-annexationist Barnburners implored him, in Silas Wright's words, "to take boldly the side of truth and principle, [rather] than to temporize with a matter which may prove so vital to the perpetuity of our institutions." The release of Calhoun's Pakenham letter made the political cross-pressures on Van Buren almost unbearable.[50]

Van Buren responded by acting deliberately. Knowing that delay would be fatal, he decided to announce his position in reply to a letter he had received from Congressman William Hammett of Mississippi, but to keep on the safe side he sent a draft to his Regency friends for comments. When Benjamin Butler told him that he could imagine supporting annexation, provided Texas was admitted as a territory and not a state and provided Mexico consented, Van Buren sensed a possible compromise and dispatched Butler to the Hermitage to sound out Jackson. But before Butler could send back word from Tennessee, Van Buren changed his mind and decided to side as much as he could with truth and principle.[51]

Van Buren's reply to Hammett, dated April 20, was the most courageous act of his political career. Not that he failed to hedge his bets: in a vague concession to the South, he allowed that as president he would annex Texas if the people showed they strongly favored it. But the letter's thrust was strongly anti-annexation, criticizing Tyler for his secret and sudden negotiations and asserting that admitting Texas would be an act of aggression against Mexico—born of a "lust for power, with fraud and violence in the train" that would stain the nation's honor. After more than twenty years of doing all that he could to appease the slaveholders, Van Buren would appease them no longer. Without question, the letter was designed partly to solidify support among his Radical base. But in doing so, Van Buren knowingly courted the vehement hatred of the South, which had distrusted him in the best of times. Following, he said, "the path of duty," he would resist the expansion of slavery even if it meant jeopardizing his chances of winning the Democratic nomination.[52]

By coincidence, on the same day that Van Buren's letter appeared in the *Globe*, the *National Intelligencer* printed a letter from Henry Clay, also opposing annexation. Since retiring from the Senate, Clay had taken several tours around the country to build support for his presidential race. Reluctantly, he had given up on his quixotic quest for a new national bank. But the Texas issue struck him as a gigantic distraction from the real issues that remained: internal improvements, the tariff, and the rest of the American System. After the Pakenham letter appeared, Clay's political friends begged him to say nothing. He ignored them, arguing that annexation would inevitably lead to a costly and dishonorable war with Mexico over territory that a "considerable and respectable portion of the Confederacy" did not want to see brought into the Union anyway.[53]

Clay's so-called Raleigh letter (named after the place where he wrote it) took few of the political risks that Van Buren's letter to Hammett did. Clay had already, years earlier, made public his opposition to Texas annexation, so he had comparatively little to lose by reiterating it. Unlike Van Buren, he faced no formidable opposition from within his own party over Texas, and none was likely to arise before the Whigs held their nominating convention in early May, barely a week after the two letters appeared. Although some southern state-rights Whigs would oppose Clay's stance, his break with Tyler had already alienated them; northern Whigs would applaud him warmly. By contrast, Van Buren, by opposing annexation, held his Radical northern base, but repelled pro–Manifest Destiny northerners and infuriated southern Democrats. While Van Buren talked of doing his duty, Clay remained blandly confident that, for himself, going public was perfectly safe: "The public mind is too fixed on the Presidential question, the current is running too strong and impetuously to be now affected by Texas," he wrote to John J. Crittenden, who, aghast, had agreed to have the Raleigh letter published anyway.[54]

The Whig convention in Baltimore, which assembled on May 1, was a thoroughly joyous and exciting affair. The delegates unanimously approved Clay's nomination and then ratified a four-point unity platform that restated Clay's positions on the American System and did not even mention Texas. The one surprising development was the convention's selection of the venerable "Christian Statesman," Theodore Frelinghuysen of New Jersey, as Clay's running mate. More than most Whig leaders, Frelinghuysen, with his past opposition to Jackson's Indian removal policy and his solicitations for Yankee moral reform, might put off some southern voters. But his impeccable rectitude would also offset Clay's reputation for moral laxity and would reinforce the Whigs' chances in the evangelical strongholds of the middle states, above all New York. "The nomination of Mr. Frelinghuysen was no doubt unexpected by you," Clay wrote to Thurlow Weed, "as it certainly was by me. I think nevertheless it is a most judicious selection." Weed agreed.[55]

The Democratic convention met four weeks later, also in Baltimore, and was filled with sourness, division, and backroom recriminations. The timing of the meeting had been pushed back at the Calhounites' insistence in 1843, before their man withdrew, and the delay had a corrosive effect, allowing the delegates more than four weeks to absorb the implications of Van Buren's Hammett letter. The Democratic Richmond Junto had already denounced Van Buren over annexation; there was serious trouble brewing in the Tennessee delegation; and when the convention, prodded by Robert J. Walker of Mississippi, readopted the rule (first established in 1832 to benefit Van Buren) requiring a two-thirds' majority to win nomination, Van Buren's chances sharply dwindled. The Hunker-backed presidential hopefuls who had stayed the course—Lewis Cass,

James Buchanan, and Levi Woodbury—had once seemed doomed to win no more than the honorific designation as their respective states' favorite son. But now, Butler reported, pro-annexationists cooked up endless "plots and counter-parts," pledging to support one Hunker candidate or another in exchange for standing firm on the two-thirds rule. Van Buren's supporters, holding a majority of the delegates but not two-thirds of them, argued themselves white in the face to suspend the supermajority rule, to no avail. One inconclusive ballot followed another, and Van Buren's support collapsed piece by piece, as Vermont, Connecticut, Illinois, and finally Pennsylvania deserted him.[56]

On the eighth ballot, following a leaders' caucus involving Butler, George Bancroft, and a Tennessean, Gideon Pillow, the New Hampshire and Massachusetts delegations announced thirteen votes for a candidate new to the field who had the personal endorsement of Andrew Jackson: the pro-annexation ex-Speaker of the House of Representatives and former governor of Tennessee, James K. Polk. The Tennessee, Alabama, and Louisiana delegations followed suit (conventions at the time voted in geographical, not alphabetical order), and although the stalemate remained unresolved when the voting ended, a stampede had begun. In a hopeless fury, Samuel Young, New York's secretary of state and a Van Buren ally for decades, denounced the annexationists for denying the former president the nomination and demanded, one last time, a suspension of the two-thirds rule. Southern delegates tried to shout him down; fistfights broke out on the floor; and the New York delegates left the meeting room to caucus. When they returned, with the ninth ballot already started, Benjamin Butler, awash in tears, took the podium, officially withdrew Van Buren's name from consideration, called for party unity, and announced that he was switching his vote to Polk. The convention duly nominated the Tennessean in a unanimous vote.[57]

Mindful of the blow struck to sectional accord, the delegates tried to nominate Silas Wright for vice president. In Washington, Wright received word via the newly invented telegraph machine—and just as quickly, he wired back word declining the offer. To do otherwise, Wright believed, would have been a renunciation of both his personal loyalties and his highest principles. (The convention settled instead on the conservative Pennsylvanian George M. Dallas.) Later, Wright wrote Van Buren that, though defeated, they had upheld their individual honor and character as well as that of their state and party. Van Buren, for his part, vowed to stick by his position on Texas lest he look like exactly what his critics had long unfairly accused him of being, a trimmer, who adjusted his sails "to catch the passing breeze."[58]

What had the Democrats done? At first glance, they seemed to have succumbed to Calhoun's plotting and, by rejecting Van Buren, capitulated to the pro-slavery South. So thorough was the reversal, even southern Democrats reacted with dismay at what Justice Peter V. Daniel—a conservative pro-slavery

Virginian whom Van Buren had named to the Supreme Court—called the "self-ish avarice and ambition" of Calhoun and his henchmen. The outcome was actually more complicated, as the campaign to come would reveal. Above all, the party's aggressively pro-expansionist platform pressed not only for the annex-ation of Texas but for a favorable settlement of outstanding disputes over the Ore-gon border as well. Since 1842, westward migrants along the newly blazed Oregon Trail had swarmed into the fertile Willamette Valley and put increasing pressure on American authorities to secure the territory's borders as far north as the Russian-occupied area at latitude 54°40'. The Webster-Ashburton Treaty of 1842 had settled the U.S.-Canadian boundary only as far west as the Rockies, leaving the Oregon dispute open for agitation by westerners and Manifest Des-tiny propagandists, who raised the cry of "Fifty-four Forty or Fight!" In Baltimore, the Democrats linked the Oregon issue with Texas as "great American meas-ures." To the Whigs, it was mere sugarcoating of the bitter Texas pill; to Demo-crats, it was an effort to surmount sectionalism with democratic nationalist expansionism and to achieve equilibrium after what looked like the Cal-hounites' coup.[59]

James K. Polk was also an excellent choice to lead the Democrats out of their difficulties. Although he had benefited from Calhoun's plotting, he was not a Calhoun man. Less well known to the electorate than either Van Buren or Clay—prompting the Whigs to chant derisively, "Who is James K. Polk?"—he was well known in Washington as one of the most capable of the younger border-state Jacksonians, whose abilities had won him two terms as Speaker of the House of Representatives from 1835 to 1839. Polk had been a Democratic hero of the Bank War, serving as Jackson's congressional point man during the struggle over the removal of the deposits. Less prominent during the nullifica-tion controversy, he had nevertheless backed Jackson's Force Bill and denounced the South Carolina insurgency as heretical. On Texas, his support of annexation, like Jackson's, had to do with protecting the United States from British encroachments, and not the pro-slavery pretensions proclaimed by Cal-houn's Pakenham letter.[60]

In other respects, Polk embodied some of the spirit of the Jackson Democ-racy in its glory days, as carried forth by its younger generation. Born in 1795 in the North Carolina backcountry, the grandson of a blacksmith, he had worked hard to improve himself, graduating with honors from the newly established public University of North Carolina before turning to law and then to politics. A short, dignified, unfailingly courteous man with a high forehead and long swept-back hair, he was also an excellent party worker in the Van Burenite mold, known for his amazing skill at remembering names and faces. His person-ality was, to be sure, prim compared to Old Hickory's. A somewhat long-winded campaigner, known in Tennessee as "the Napoleon of the Stump," he had a formal, staid demeanor that served him poorly once the Whigs had mastered the demagogic arts. Still, Jackson himself, who had done more than anyone to initiate the boom that won Polk the nomination, saw him as a strong successor. Polk, combining the Young America nickname with his mentor's, became known as "Young Hickory."[61]

If any pro-annexationist could reach out to the Van Burenites, it was Polk. Apart from its plank on Oregon and Texas, Polk's platform was a straight Van Burenite Jacksonian document, calling for, among other things, restoration of the independent treasury. Polk pledged early in the campaign to serve only one term, giving Van Buren hope for 1848. Above all, Polk stood for annexation as an opportunity to expand not slavery but the freedom of American democratic institutions, coupled with the acquisition of more land for settlement by independent farmers who would not be forced to work for wages. Some committed antislavery Radicals considered Polk's nomination, Theodore Sedgwick III wrote, a "rascally fraud . . . a complete surrender by the Majority to the slaveholding Minority." But others—including Michael Hoffman, Silas Wright, and Churchill Cambreleng, who had served with Polk in the House—respected the candidate's record and concluded that if they could not have Van Buren, Polk was the next best man. Polk in turn worked closely with the Van Burenites to persuade Wright to leave the Senate and run for governor, in order to maximize the New York Democratic turnout. New York City Radicals, including Sedgwick and William Cullen Bryant, eventually composed a privately circulated letter that repudiated the Baltimore platform's annexationist plank and called for the defeat of pro-annexationist congressmen, but endorsed Polk for president. Van Buren himself wrote to friends who had threatened to boycott the election, and urged them strongly to back Polk and Dallas.[62]

Henry Clay reacted to Polk's candidacy with his usual nonchalant contempt for the opposition. "Are our Democratic friends serious in the nominations which they have made in Baltimore for President and Vice President?" he asked one associate. Yet Clay also knew that by naming Polk, the Democrats had wounded, perhaps mortally, the Whigs' electoral hopes in the South, where support for Texas annexation ran deepest. Only by carrying the border states along with New York, Pennsylvania, and New England would Clay's campaign stand a chance. With large blocs of voters in those states already committed one way or another, the surest strategy was to chip away at the margins, seeking to capture enough minor constituencies to add up to a majority. It was the same strategy that the Democrats would follow, making for a campaign that, in retrospect, looks jumbled and weirdly inconsistent.[63]

In the South, Democrats played racist politics and smeared Clay as a "niggar"-loving abolitionist, while in the North, they defamed him as a debauched, dueling, gambling, womanizing, irreligious hypocrite whose reversal on the bank issue proved he had no principles. They also pitched their nominees to particular local followings, having Polk hint preposterously, in a letter to a Philadelphian, that he favored "reasonable" tariff protection for domestic manufacturers, while they attacked the pious humanitarian Frelinghuysen as an anti-Catholic bigot and crypto-nativist enemy of the separation of church and state. To ensure the success of their southern strategy, the Democrats also muffled John Tyler. Still hopeful that he might ride the Texas issue to another four years as president, Tyler had his corporal's guard of supporters hold a third-party convention in Baltimore at the same time as the Democrats' meeting. Polk's surprise nomination ruined Tyler's plans, but the president continued his stumbling run through the early summer, until Democratic entreaties, including a respectful coaxing letter from Andrew Jackson, persuaded him to withdraw.[64]

The Whigs countered the Democratic attacks by revving up the Log Cabin electioneering machinery and redeploying it on behalf of the man they now celebrated as "Ol' Coon" Clay. They also attacked former House Speaker Polk as a political nobody who was, deep down, a dangerous Loco Foco radical. To mollify southern outrage at his Raleigh letter, Clay wrote two additional letters, both to Whig editors in Alabama, attempting to soften his stance on annexation, but succeeding only in looking like the prevaricator he had always accused Van Buren of being. ("Things look blue," Thurlow Weed wrote to Francis Granger after Clay's second missive appeared. "Ugly letter, that to Alabama.") With greater success, the Whigs linked up with a resurgent nativist anti-Catholic movement that was strongest in New York and Pennsylvania, and planted stories that as president Clay would tighten up immigration and naturalization laws. (Too late, Clay tried to distance himself from the nativists.)[65]

The Liberty Party campaign added to the confusion. Excited by the mere fact of their survival, the abolitionists greeted the Texas controversy as a godsend and concentrated their attack on Clay, the alleged antislavery candidate who, in their eyes, was as big a fraud as ever. Polk, they claimed, was "too small a man, too openly committed, body and soul to the Slave-Interest, to seduce any anti-slavery voter into his support." But Clay was a gifted leader whose northern managers were successfully depicting as someone "anti-slavery in his feelings." And so, Clay became the object of nasty abolitionist attacks. One notorious handbill, widely reprinted, by an abolitionist minister named Abel Brown, denounced Clay as a *Man Stealer, Slave-holder, and Murderer,* and accused him of "Selling Jesus Christ!" because he dealt in slaves. With the campaign to be decided at the electoral margins, Whig managers grew so concerned that, late in the campaign, they concocted a fraudulent letter that supposedly proved James Birney was secretly working in league with the Democrats, and circulated it in New York and Ohio.[66]

Polk won, narrowly. Clay held eleven states that Harrison had won in 1840:

Tennessee, Kentucky, and Ohio in the West; North Carolina, Maryland, Delaware, and New Jersey in the East; and, in New England, Connecticut, Rhode Island, Massachusetts, and Vermont. But Polk, the candidate of democratic (and not merely slave) expansionism, vastly increased the Democratic vote over the figures from 1840 in the Northwest and the middle Atlantic states, carried the entire Deep South as well as Virginia, won Pennsylvania for the Democrats, and, most important, carried New York by a scant 2,106 votes out of nearly one-half million cast. Had only a modest proportion of the Liberty Party's New York vote of nearly 16,000 gone instead to the Whigs, Henry Clay would have been elected president. Hurt by the Whigs' forged letter campaign, the abolitionists did less well overall than they had expected, winning only 2 percent of the vote nationwide. But they could claim that they had decided a presidential election — an outcome that sent new-school antislavery Whigs into paroxysms. "[T]he false representations of Birney, Leavitt & Co. that *Clay was as much for Annexation as Polk, and more likely to effect it, &c. &c.*," Horace Greeley's *New-York Daily Tribune* cried, "have carried all these votes obliquely in favor of Annexation, War, and eternal Slavery."[67]

Of course, things were not that simple. John Quincy Adams, a great maker of enemies' lists when provoked, better described the manifold reasons behind the Whigs' defeat, first and foremost the three-fifths clause that inflated Polk's electoral vote, but much more as well: "The partial associations of Native Americans, Irish Catholics, abolition societies, liberty party, the Pope of Rome, the Democracy of the sword, and the dotage of the ruffian" — Andrew Jackson — had undone Henry Clay. Adams's ire took him overboard, but his basic point was correct: in the 1844 presidential election, as in any close national race, numerous factors determined the outcome. Among those factors, which Whigs admitted only reluctantly, was that the orchestrated pandemonium of 1840 proved less effective the second time around, especially when mounted on behalf of genuinely substantive and thus controversial candidates. "Hurrah! Hurrah! The country's risin'/For Henry Clay and Frelinghuysen" sounded forced and tinny compared to the old roar for Tippecanoe and Tyler, too. In the crucial state of New York, the gubernatorial candidacy of anti-annexationist Silas Wright helped augment the Democratic totals, perhaps enough to swing the election. Overall, the northern Democrats' ability to get its voters to the polls, including new voters and a large number of Catholic immigrants offended by the Whigs' nativism, turned the electoral tide.[68]

The issues of annexation and slavery — interjected so methodically by Upshur and Tyler and then inflamed by Calhoun — had hovered over the election and shaped its larger significance. Without them, it is unclear whether Van Buren or Clay would have been the victor; but with them, it was perfectly clear that the sectional harmony crucial to both the Democratic and Whig Parties was coming under tremendous strain. The congressional results only worsened the strain, as the Democrats slightly increased their majority in the House and recaptured the Senate in spectacular fashion, turning a six-seat deficit into a twelve-seat majority and effectively wiping out the southern Whigs. To Adams, whose war against the gag rule had done so much to dissolve sectional comity, the result and the prospect looked grim, "sealing the fate of this nation, which nothing less than the interposition of Omnipotence can save."[69] But the Omnipotent moved in mysterious ways. The nation's fate would also hinge on the shifting political calculations and loyalties of the Van Burenite Radical Democrats, who had swallowed their pride and voted for Polk but still smoldered over the betrayals of 1844.

NORTHERN DEMOCRACY, SOUTHERN DEMOCRACY

On June 8, 1844, while the Democracy and the nation were recovering from the shock of Polk's nomination, the Senate rejected the Texas annexation treaty, 35 to 16. Only five northerners—two each from Pennsylvania and Illinois, and Levi Woodbury from New Hampshire—voted aye. Even after the fall elections, and the Democratic gains in the Senate, it remained highly unlikely that a two-thirds' majority could ever be won; in any case, that new body would not assemble until December 1845, which gave the skittish Sam Houston plenty of time to change his mind again. Tyler and Calhoun, determined to win their goal before leaving office, arrived at the alternative, albeit constitutionally dubious strategy, of immediately annexing Texas by joint congressional resolution, which would require a mere simple majority in both houses of Congress. The move would gain support from lame-duck southern Whigs who were eager to shed Democratic charges that they were soft on Texas. More important, it would achieve Texas annexation with the explicitly pro-slavery justification laid down by Calhoun instead of on the nationalist grounds favored by Polk. According to the White House plan, up to four new states—three of which were almost certain to be slave states—could eventually be carved out of the annexed territory and admitted to the Union.[70]

The proposal touched off a political scramble. In the House, southern Whigs attempted, unsuccessfully, to pass an annexation resolution they deemed even more favorable to the slaveholders' interests. In the Senate, Thomas Hart Benton, the only Democrat from a slaveholding state who had voted against annexation, offered his own plan, which would split the annexed Texas into two equal districts, one slave and one free, and require Mexico's consent. When his proposal failed, Benton offered a second that authorized the president to send a five-member commission to negotiate all the terms of annexation with the Texans.

With the support of the Radicals as well as Andrew Jackson, Benton's plan reconciled most northern Democrats to annexation. On February 27, six days before Polk's swearing-in, the Senate voted 27 to 25, along party lines, to admit Texas, leaving open the decision on what would become of the enormous new American dominion. The next day, on even stricter party lines, the House added its assent, which gave Tyler the option of signing the resolution or passing it on to his successor.[71]

Although laced with compromise, the annexation of Texas was the latest indignity for the Van Burenite northern Democrats. Once again, the southern minority had thrown a firebrand into national politics; once again, the northern majority had ended up giving way. Even worse for northern Democratic pride, antislavery Whigs seemed to have claimed the mantle of egalitarianism. The protracted fight over the gag rule, the Joshua Giddings affair, the Calhounite coup at the Democratic convention—all made the northern antislavery Whigs appear more consistent than the Democrats in championing the democratic rights of ordinary citizens. In Washington, the most inspired outcries to vindicate free speech and Jefferson's Declaration of Independence came not from any Jacksonian Radical but from the original object of the Jacksonians' ire, the newly revived John Quincy Adams. In the strange convulsions of American politics, the man who had forged the notoriously aristocratic corrupt bargain two decades earlier had become, in his resistance to the repressive southerners, a stalwart advocate of democracy.

Or, rather, of one version of democracy. In the Deep South and in the border slaveholding states, an alternative Master Race democracy remained strong in the 1840s, run at the state level almost entirely by slaveholders and dedicated to the proposition that white men's equality depended on black enslavement. Through the early 1840s, the intersectional alliances within the Whig and Democratic Parties had muted fundamental and growing contradictions between the two democracies, northern and southern. Now those alliances had been damaged, thanks to the political designs and will of southern extremists who were barely democrats at all, led by John C. Calhoun—their power suddenly increased far beyond their numbers by the advent of "His Accidency," John Tyler. How firmly the Calhounites could sustain their influence, over southern as well as national politics, would depend on how the issues connected with slavery and westward expansion played themselves out. In the short run, those matters depended on the presidency of James K. Polk.

19

THE BITTER FRUITS OF MANIFEST DESTINY

Goaded by John C. Calhoun, John Tyler would not depart the White House until he had squeezed the last bitter drops out of the Texas controversy. On the advice of Calhoun that delay might prove fatal, the outgoing president signed the joint congressional resolution on annexation three days before James K. Polk's inauguration. He then dispatched an envoy to Texas with orders to instruct the American diplomatic agent in Houston City, Jackson's nephew Andrew Jackson Donelson, to arrange for annexation on the pro-slavery terms favored by the House southern Whigs. Van Burenite Democrats complained that, at the last minute, Tyler had taken actions that should have been left to his successor. Polk conferred with his designated cabinet but mostly kept his own counsel, while putting the finishing touches on his inaugural address.[1]

In the address, Polk presented a full-throated defense of Manifest Destiny, celebrated the impending admission of Texas to the Union, and called America's claims to Oregon "'clear and unquestionable.'" Yet as George Bancroft remembered forty years later, Polk had much more on his mind. In a private meeting, Polk pledged to the politician-historian—whom he had just named to the cabinet as secretary of the navy—that he would gain four great measures during his four-year term: the settlement of the Oregon question; the reduction of the protectionist tariff of 1842; reestablishment of the independent treasury; and, astonishingly, the acquisition of California from Mexico. As for Texas, Polk would soon reveal that he, like Tyler and Calhoun, believed that the quicker the matter was concluded, the better. On March 10, Polk ordered Tyler's Texas envoy to offer annexation to the Texans according to Tyler's instructions. Thomas Hart Benton and his Radical allies immediately challenged Polk about repudiating his agreements to pursue Benton's plan. Polk claimed he had no idea what they were talking about: "if any such pledges were made," he said disingenuously, "it was in a total misconception of what I had said or meant."[2]

Other unsettling signs appeared throughout the transition and the early days of the new administration. In making his key appointments, Polk tried to satisfy all factions, but he tacked more heavily toward Hunker-style conservatives than even the most disappointed northern Radicals had feared. Having apparently agreed on the names of cabinet members with Jackson at the Hermitage, Polk tore up his list as soon as he got to Washington and had surveyed the political situation. Out of the running was the old hard-money veteran Amos Kendall, who had campaigned hard on his behalf. Out as well was Jackson's close friend Major William Lewis. Instead, Polk named a group that included the exasperating James Buchanan as secretary of state, Robert J. Walker of Mississippi as secretary of the Treasury, and the New York quasi-Hunker William Marcy as secretary of war. George Bancroft at the Navy Department was the one solid concession to the northern Radicals. Only the Calhounites received less than the Van Burenites.[3]

Even more outrageous to the Van Burenites was Polk's decision to remove Francis Blair from his editorship of the *Globe*. Polk feared, with reason, that because Blair had insulted so many important Democrats over the years, including Calhoun, he would now impair party unity. Polk also thought, again with reason, that Blair's political inclinations were dangerously close to Van Buren's. As Blair's replacement, Polk chose Thomas Ritchie of the *Richmond Enquirer*, who renamed the administration organ the *Union*. Andrew Jackson called the removal "the most unexpected thing I ever met with," and warned Polk that it might actually "result in injury to the perfect unity of the democracy." But Young Hickory seemed intent on remaking the Democracy to fit the political circumstances of a new age, one he hoped would quickly witness the growth of the United States into a transcontinental republic. Although the closeness of the electoral vote might have dictated that he proceed with caution, Polk would govern as if he had a magnificent popular mandate. He was determined, he wrote, "to be *myself* President of the U.S."[4]

Ten weeks later—his body bloated, his eyes sunk deep into his head—Andrew Jackson died. Toward the end, he wrote to another aging War of 1812 veteran of how "[t]rue virtue" could only reside "with the people, the great laboring and producing classes, that form the bone and sinew of our confederacy."[5] It was a fitting valedictory, the straight Jackson line of the 1830s, but now the line was snagged and tangled around issues of expansion and slavery that raised disturbing questions about both true virtue and the people. The Jacksonian revolution, and the revolution of conservatism that followed in its train, had run their course. New revolutions, already underway, would blast the old politics to pieces once Polk pushed the nation westward to California.

"A NEW AGE, A NEW DESTINY"

Polk was better than his word. Not only did he get his way on his four major measures; he largely completed his work during the first session of the Twenty-ninth Congress. In part, Polk's extraordinary diligence explained his efficiency. ("How he manages to perform so great an amount of labor as he accomplishes every twenty-four hours is a mystery too deep for our comprehension," one observer commented. "He is most justly entitled to the honorable appellation of *Workingman*.") His penchant for secrecy and disingenuousness, along with his audacity, helped him impose his will on a fractious, albeit heavily Democratic Congress. His greatest limitations—his lack of curiosity, his literal-mindedness—in some ways freed him to pursue his programs unburdened by the troubled moral imagination that afflicted other men. All of these qualities would enrage Polk's adversaries, not least within the Democratic Party, who came to regard him as not just misguided but mendacious. Yet while his critics fumed, Polk racked up one policy victory after another.[6]

Nothing indicated more clearly the passing of the Jacksonian era under Polk than the relative importance attached to domestic and foreign affairs. Jackson and Van Buren certainly had foreign policies; Jackson even came close to insti-gating a Franco-American war. But foreign affairs in the 1830s paled in impor-tance compared to the Bank War, nullification, Indian removal, and the Jacksonians' pursuit of reform. For the expansionist Young Hickory, hoping to spread the blessings of American democracy, widen the sphere for American set-tlement, and soothe sectional differences with a great patriotic endeavor, the agendas were reversed. Still, Polk did care deeply about his own domestic goals, and with the help of the large Democratic majorities in Congress, he reversed the policies of the Harrison-Tyler years.

Lowering the tariff posed the greatest political difficulties. In his inaugural address, Polk reiterated his earlier statements that he opposed "a tariff for protec-tion merely," and he suggested that some sort of "revenue limit" might be legis-lated to allow for incidental protection. During the following summer, Secretary of the Treasury Walker, overturning doubts that he was not up to his job, super-vised a massive survey of customs officials and importers in every major port, and ascertained the rates at which duties on particular items would bring maximum revenue without discouraging imports. Secretary of State Buchanan, the in-house spokesman for Pennsylvania's protectionist interests, urged major upward modifications on tariffs for iron, coal, and a few other items, but efforts at com-promise failed and Polk went to Congress with Walker's proposals.[7]

Along with eastern free traders, western congressmen, their districts now clamoring for foreign markets, strongly backed the Walker bill. Some antislav-ery Democrats and Whigs dissented, calling it, in John Niles's formulation, an act to "favour the slave labour of the south." But the sternest opposition came from the pro-tariff Pennsylvanians, who maneuvered this way and that in Congress, picking up support where they could about rates on specific items that they deemed too high or too low. Polk responded with a full political offensive, directing Ritchie's *Union* to chastise wayward Democrats, dispatching cabinet members to Capitol Hill to buttonhole waverers, and vowing not to let the congressional session end without a vote. Finally, at the end of July 1846—with Vice President Dallas casting a decisive tie-breaking ballot in the Senate—the Walker Tariff passed.[8]

The reestablishment of the independent treasury (or, as Polk preferred to call it, the "constitutional treasury") occasioned less struggle and excitement, a result of the Democrats' firm control of Congress but also proof positive that the Jackson–Van Buren era had ended. When the House took up the administration's bill in April 1846, Democratic congressmen demanded a hard-money amendment requiring that all payments to the government be made in gold and silver coin. Thus altered, the bill passed the House in a strict party-line vote. Immediately, consternation hit the nation's banking and financial circles, but it was nothing like the uprising of the 1830s. Although the old radical Benton–Van Buren forces raised suspicions of their own when the Senate amended the House bill, those objections were quickly stifled, and the measure passed the Senate, once again along strict party lines. A bill for the graduation of public land prices was the only major administration measure that failed to win congressional approval—and it fell short only because the House and Senate could not reconcile differences on various amendments.[9]

In foreign affairs, the Oregon boundary question was settled well before Congress adjourned, after a strange diplomatic dance with the British. Despite the expansionist bluster about "Fifty-four Forty," American settlement lay well to the south of the Russian border, and Polk was willing, like Tyler before him, to extend to the Pacific the forty-ninth-parallel border established east of the Rockies by the Webster-Ashburton treaty. The British insisted that the line be drawn at the Columbia River, leaving in dispute most of the present state of Washington. When Polk took office, he learned that the British were interested in a compromise devised by the outgoing American minister, Edward Everett, that would hand the bulk of the area below the forty-ninth parallel to the United States—a deal put in temporary jeopardy by Polk's belligerent inaugural address. The British minister in Washington, poorly informed about the situation, summarily rejected a renewed American offer to make the forty-ninth parallel the border. Considering himself insulted, Polk withdrew the proposal, demanded all of Oregon south of 54°40', and made menacing moves toward war. Polk's saber-rattling broke the impasse, and in June 1846, the two nations signed a treaty setting the boundary along the line that Everett had proposed a year earlier. After only fifteen months in office, Polk had reached half of his ambitious foreign policy goals.[10]

The other half, acquiring California, would take longer—but more than a month before the Oregon settlement was signed, Congress gave Polk the war with Mexico that his still-secret California project eventually required. As he entered office, the president could not be as candid in public about California as he had been with Bancroft. Yet he did make an issue of the Mexican government's continuing failure to recompense millions of dollars owed private Americans for various alleged seizures and spoliations of property. With Texas preparing to assent to annexation, Polk had the staging ground he needed to intimidate the Mexicans with the threat of armed conflict should peaceful pressure fail. Early in his presidency, Polk assured the Texans that he would support their most grandiose territorial claims, embracing the area from the Nueces River (the traditional Tejas border) to the Rio Grande, and following the latter northwest as far as the ancient settlements in the Mexican department of New Mexico. Then, in June 1845, the Washington *Union* let the troublesome word slip out in public: should the Mexicans resist the manifest destiny of the United States regarding the Texas border, a corps of American volunteers would invade and occupy Mexico, and "enable us not only to take California but to keep it."[11]

Polk followed up with what he called a peace initiative, but which was in fact an effort to bully Mexico into granting new territorial concessions and, failing in that, to persuade the American public of the need to go to war. Early in his term, Polk had secretly sent a diplomatic agent to Mexico City to begin negotiating additional American claims against Mexico. The Mexican government, under heavy pressure from its own war party, finally agreed to receive a formal emissary, and in September, Polk dispatched a Spanish-speaking, former Louisiana congressman and arch-expansionist, John Slidell. The *Union*, meanwhile, whipped up American public opinion by focusing on the "swaggering and gasconading" of the Mexican war party. And Polk, in response to reports about an impending Mexican invasion, backed up Slidell's mission in mid-October by ordering the U.S. Army under General Zachary Taylor to approach the Rio Grande.[12]

In November 1845, with Taylor's troops in no-man's-land, Slidell arrived at Vera Cruz bearing instructions from Secretary of State Buchanan to demand Mexican recognition of the Rio Grande boundary (giving the United States eastern New Mexico), the sale of the rest of New Mexico for three million dollars, and the sale of California for twenty-five million—all in exchange for American assumption of the outstanding private claims against the Mexican government. Already in crisis, the sitting government in Mexico City crumbled, and the war party took power. Polk immediately ordered Taylor's forces, who had not budged in October, to move all the way to the east bank of the Rio Grande, where they established a fortification with cannons aimed directly at the plaza of the Mexican border town of Matamoros. When the new Mexican government formally spurned Slidell on March 12, the White House had all the justification it thought necessary to declare war.[13]

Negotiations with the British over Oregon delayed matters, but five days after the Senate voted to approve the Oregon treaty, Polk asked Buchanan to begin drafting a war message to be sent to Congress. Slidell, taking his time traveling east to allow the Oregon matter to be settled, finally arrived in Washington on May 8; the next day, the cabinet approved Polk's plan to forward the war message to Capitol Hill. Four hours after the cabinet meeting ended, word arrived that a detachment of Americans had skirmished with Mexican cavalry on the Rio Grande, resulting in sixteen American casualties and forty-seven captured and adding emotionally charged patriotic gore to the outrage over Slidell's rejection. After a sharply curtailed debate in the House and a brief delay in the Senate, Congress overwhelmingly approved Polk's war bill on May 12 — not a formal declaration of war, but a recognition that, at Mexico's instigation, a state of war already existed.[14]

Massive displays of patriotic fervor followed the vote. Twenty thousand Philadelphians turned out for a pro-war rally. An even larger crowd assembled in New York to hear speeches and patriotic singing by, among others, the famed blackface minstrel George Washington Dixon. Newspapers around the country blared that the war, as the *New York Herald* put it, would "lay the foundation of a new age, a new destiny, affecting both this continent and the old continent of Europe." Northerners and southerners, Whigs and Democrats, all seemed caught up in the enthusiasm. (In Illinois, Abraham Lincoln, preparing for a congressional run on the Whig line, encouraged the nation's "citizen soldiery, to sustain her national character [and] secure our national rights" by volunteering to fight in Mexico.) Yet beneath the surface, there were grave misgivings about what would soon become known as Mr. Polk's War.[15]

The strongest dissent came from fourteen antislavery Whigs, led by John Quincy Adams and Joshua Giddings, who were the only House members to vote against the war bill. (Two Senate Whigs also voted nay.) All of the House dissenters except Adams and Giddings were little-known men, and they hailed from widely scattered constituencies that stretched from Maine to Ohio. All were considered "ultraists" on slavery issues. All believed that the war was an extension of the Slave Power's thinly veiled plot to extend its territory and power. Just as important, all were from districts that expected their representatives to take such ultraist positions or face political reprisals. The process that had begun with the Giddings affair two years earlier had gradually expanded beyond the antislavery redoubts of western New York and the Western Reserve of Ohio. There now existed a sectional Whig caucus consisting of men whose entire political raison d'être was to agitate over slavery at every turn — not a large caucus, but enough to stand as a beacon of conscience to antislavery northerners. In time, they would be joined by other Whigs who, though they voted for war, felt extremely uneasy doing so. Garrett Davis, representing Henry Clay's home district, exemplified these wary Whigs. Before the vote, Davis complained that the Democrats were rushing the bill through without sufficient consideration and debate, and that, though a state of "informal war" certainly existed, to blame Mexico was untrue: "It is our own president who began this war."[16]

The other most outspoken opponent of the war, surprisingly to some, was John C. Calhoun. Although gratified at the final acquisition of Texas, Calhoun (who returned to the Senate in 1845) dreaded the prospect that the United States might find itself at war with both Britain and Mexico over lands he deemed unfit for slavery. He was pleased by the Oregon treaty, and the settlement of the dispute short of war—a stance that brought him unlikely praise from some quintessential Yankee reformers, including Elihu Burritt, the outspoken Massachusetts antislavery and universal peace movement leader, and Arnold Buffum, a former principal lecturer for the American Anti-Slavery Society. Calhoun broke with Polk over Mexico, arguing that the full story of the skirmish on the Rio Grande had not been told, and that the administration's effort to evade a formal congressional declaration of war was unconstitutional. When the war vote finally came in the Senate, Calhoun along with two Whigs abstained. In the debate, Calhoun declared that he would no sooner vote for the war bill than "plunge a dagger into his own heart." Most of his political friends believed that, politically, it was his opposition that was lethal to his own political standing—"perfectly suicidal," one of them remarked.[17]

Most Democrats, including northern Radicals, initially backed the war, often with boisterous shouts affirming Manifest Destiny and national honor. "YES: Mexico must be thoroughly chastised—," the Radical Walt Whitman, now the editor of the *Brooklyn Daily Eagle*, wrote on the eve of the war bill's enactment. "We have reached a point in our intercourse with that country, when prompt and effectual demonstrations of force are enjoined upon us by every dictate of right and policy." Yet privately, Radical Democrats in Congress, already angry with Polk, were queasy over his latest maneuvers, and suspicious that the war had been manufactured to please expansionist slaveholders. "I am too sick of the miserable concern here to write or say anything about it . . . ," New York's Senator John Dix told Azariah Flagg. "I should not be surprised if the next accounts should show that there is no Mexican invasion of our soil." The war, Dix asserted, "was begun in fraud last winter and I think will end in disgrace." After reading the documents concerned with the Slidell mission, Francis Blair concluded that Polk "has got to lying in public as well as in private." Antislavery and anti-Polk discontent was even stronger among select groups of grassroots Democrats.[18]

The greatest Democratic antislavery convulsions, touched off by Texas annexation and intensified by the war with Mexico, occurred in New Hampshire. Home to the Jacksonian machine originally built by Isaac Hill, New Hampshire was, in national politics, the most reliably Democratic northeastern state. In every presidential election since 1832, it had broken for the Democrat. (In 1840, along with Illinois, it gave Martin Van Buren his only electoral votes from north of the Mason-Dixon Line.) The party's state chairman, Franklin Pierce, a former U.S. senator who had returned home in 1842 after renouncing an allegedly fierce drinking habit, commanded his troops with an iron hand. Early in 1845, the antislavery congressman John P. Hale upset party decorum by violating instructions from the state legislature and publicly condemning Texas annexation. Enraged, Pierce had Hale censured for "treachery" and arranged for his excommunication from the party at a special convention held in Concord in mid-February. Thrown off the Democratic ticket with the election for his seat less than a month away, Hale made tentative plans to move to New York City and practice law in partnership with Theodore Sedgwick III.[19]

Ten days after the convention, however, Hale's rank-and-file supporters, now organized as the Independent Democrats, assembled in Exeter to launch a reelection campaign. Liberty Party men and abolitionists throughout New England—including nonvoting Garrisonians—rallied to Hale's cause, and the irregular campaign gained enough votes to block his replacement on the Democratic ticket from winning the absolute majority required to win. Twice again in 1845 and once more in March 1846, there were fresh canvasses for the seat; each time Hale won enough votes to keep the seat open. Over the winter of 1845–46, Hale's group merged with New Hampshire's Liberty men and antislavery Whigs to form the New Hampshire Alliance, and swept to victory in the March 1846 legislative elections, gaining a large enough majority to elect an antislavery Whig as governor and to elect Hale as U.S. senator the following June. John Greenleaf Whittier, who had become antislavery's unofficial poet laureate, rejoiced in a brief ode, "New Hampshire,—1845": "Courage, then, Northern hearts!—Be firm, be true:/ What one brave State hath done, can ye not also do?"[20]

The Hale alliance was not interested simply in winning elections. One legislative resolution, drafted by Hale himself, condemned the Polk administration's war with Mexico as well as Texas annexation, and pledged the state's support for "every just and well-directed effort for the suppression and extermination of that terrible scourge of our race, human slavery." A second resolution called on New Hampshire's congressional delegation to demand abolition of slavery in the District of Columbia, exclusion of slavery from all federal territories, suppression of the domestic slave trade, and the prohibition of the admission of any new slave states. The Liberty Party program for the divorce of slavery and government had become the official policy of the Democratic state of New Hampshire.[21]

The New Hampshire uprising did not come as a complete surprise to the Van

Burenites. As early as 1840, when the Liberty Party made its modest debut, New York Democrats were concerned about the rise of antislavery sentiments among their own followers. Those concerns had redoubled in the ensuing five years. In February 1845, Van Buren himself had cautioned the Polk administration, in a letter to George Bancroft, that any further expansionist moves deemed favorable to slavery would force northern Democrats to choose between deserting their southern and western colleagues and facing "political suicide" back home. Holding their tongues during the war bill crisis, the Radicals asked Polk for guarantees during the early months of the fighting that the war would lead to no further acquisition of territory from Mexico. Polk, in his usual ambiguous way, placated them with assurances that he had no such designs.[22]

Meanwhile, the fighting in Mexico began in earnest. By August 1846, Taylor's troops had beaten Mexican forces back across the Rio Grande, occupied Matamoros, and then, after frustrating delays, moved upriver to a new staging ground in the little Mexican town of Camargo. To the north, another force of U.S. volunteers gathered at San Antonio de Bexar near the ruins of the Alamo; farther west, a force consisting mainly of Missouri volunteers secured the New Mexico settlement of Santa Fe without firing a shot and prepared to undertake a long march to Chihuahua. On the Pacific coast, American naval forces captured the ports of Monterey, Yerba Buena (San Francisco), Sonoma, and Los Angeles, as well as Nueva Helvetia, a fortified American settlement in the Sacramento River Valley owned by a Swiss emigrant named Johann Sutter.[23]

These victories, Polk hoped, would silence his carping critics, especially the antislavery northerners. Polk emphatically did not seek California to spread slavery and enlarge the slaveholders' political power. "Slavery," he would write, "was one of the questions adjusted in the compromises of the Constitution. It has, and can have no legitimate connection with the War with Mexico." On the contrary: in expanding American democracy to the Pacific, he wanted to supplant sectional jealousies with nationalist unity. Like Jackson (and unlike Calhoun), Polk had never presented any brief on behalf of slavery as a blessing, and he believed, in any event, that New Mexico and California would never prove hospitable to slavery. Rather, he expected his efforts to acquire new territory would unite men of goodwill in a national endeavor. Patriotism would overcome the designs of those he later described as "demagogues and ambitious politicians"—sectionalists who would pursue personal gain "even at the hazard of disturbing the harmony if not dissolving the Union itself." Polk's vision of Manifest Destiny was as an emollient on sectional discord, and not a sectional ploy.[24]

Polk's insistence on his nationalist goals badly aggravated what was becoming a huge and destructive political paradox—that efforts to eradicate sectionalism through expansion only inflamed sectional antagonisms. Responses to the war, pro and con, were based on clashing views of American government—about whether slavery's expansion did more to uphold the nation's supreme political values or erode them. To antislavery Whigs and Radical Democrats, Polk's spread-eagle nationalism looked increasingly like an apology for the South, and for those pro-slavery southern Democrats who saw the war as a means to extend the slaveholders' democracy. In this Polk's adversaries misjudged the president and went on to slander him as a willing tool of the Slave Power, charges that Polk understandably thought outrageous. Calhoun and his coterie certainly proved, in their opposition to the war, that pro-slavery and expansion were hardly synonymous, and the president despised the Calhounites' criticisms as much as he did the antislavery northerners. Yet Polk, with his cramped moral imagination, could never understand that the sectionalists, northern and southern, had their own views of patriotism and that they held those views as sincerely as he did. This lack of comprehension between Polk and his critics would in time widen the divisions within his own party, moving beyond the lingering political resentments from 1844 and later fights over appointments to more fateful matters about slavery and its spread.

The war fever of 1846 initially blurred those divisions. News of the early American military victories produced a rapid outpouring of books, pamphlets, illustrations, and newspaper dispatches, glorifying the bravery and sacrifice of America's gallant soldiers who were avenging the nation's honor on exotic battlefields that might as well have been in Mesopotamia as in northern Mexico. "[C]old must be the pulse, and throbless to all good thoughts . . . ," Walt Whitman wrote in the spring of 1847, "which cannot respond to the valorous emprise of our soldiers and commanders in Mexico."[25] Yet even as he wrote those words, Whitman, like many other northern Democrats, was having second thoughts about the administration's intentions. The Hale insurgency had planted doubts; even more consequential was a revolt in the House in the late summer of 1846, led by a band of antislavery Van Buren Democrats. That revolt would transform both the politics of the war and, in time, the politics of antislavery. It was rooted in state and local, as well as national events, dating back before the war began.

SLAVERY AND DEMOCRACY IN THE STATES

The conclusion of the Dorr Rebellion in Rhode Island did not end conflicts elsewhere over the basic structures of democratic government. Between 1844 and 1848, three new states, Texas, Iowa, and Wisconsin, adopted constitutions, while reformers either succeeded or campaigned hard in Connecticut, New York, Virginia, and Louisiana. (Florida, admitted as a state in 1845, adopted its territorial constitution drafted in 1838, which strongly endorsed slavery, provided for adult white male suffrage, and barred bankers, clergymen, and anyone who had participated in a duel from holding public office.) The general thrust of these movements, and other developments in state politics in the mid-1840s, advanced what had become a dialectic of democratic reform, in which changes at the local level had widening national implications, and vice versa. They also affirmed the growing divide between the South, largely committed to racist democracy with slavery as its foundation, and the North, committed to white male democracy and divided over black male participation but hostile to slavery.[26]

The new constitutions in the Southwest—Louisiana's revised document and the first Texas state constitution, both adopted in 1845—brought those states in line with the slaveholders' Master Race democracies of Alabama, Mississippi, and Arkansas. In Louisiana, the arrival of large numbers of small farmers in the northern and central portions of the state had put enormous pressure on the downstate Creole elite to revise the highly restrictive original constitution adopted in 1812. Elections, one reformer declared, had "become a sort of monopoly" under the existing charter, and that monopoly, radical Jacksonians charged with increasing fervor after 1837, propped up an artificial moneyed class headquartered in New Orleans. Calling itself the Red River Democracy, the reformers' movement, led by the lawyer and planter Solomon Downs of Ouachita Parish, broke through the Whigs' resistance in 1841 and compelled Governor André Bienvenu Roman to sign a resolution approving a convention to revise the existing organic law.[27]

The Louisiana convention, held in 1845, discarded the existing constitution and wrote a new one. The key change was the abolition of all property requirements for voting and officeholding—a reform, Downs assured the Whig delegates, that would not endanger the sanctity of private property and was essential to protect the dignity of white men in a slave society. ("There is no necessity, no true wisdom, in degrading the poorer classes and placing them on an equality with slaves, by denying them the most important privilege of freemen," Downs told the convention.) Other successful reforms, above all the abolition of monopolies and incorporated banks, infuriated Whig delegates, and in 1852, these stipulations would fall in another round of constitutional revision. But the principle of formal white male equality as a buttress to slavery was beyond discussion. The same principle was enshrined in the Texas constitution, based explicitly on both the draft Tejas constitution proposed at San Felipe in 1833 and the new Louisiana constitution.[28]

To the east, Virginia—still the least democratic southern polity outside South Carolina—felt some delayed aftershocks from its constitutional showdown of 1829–30. Representation was again the key issue. Despite the drastically reduced condition of its tobacco economy, Virginia's free population rose by nearly 10 percent between 1830 and 1840, with the largest increases occurring in the Shenandoah Valley and the counties west of the Alleghenies, where slavery was relatively unimportant. According to the 1840 census, the numbers of whites residing west of the Blue Ridge now exceeded those living east of the mountains by more than two thousand. The constitution of 1830 had provided for reapportionment in 1841 and every ten years thereafter, and in August 1841, a group of citizens in heavily Whig western Kanawha County, led by local Whig leaders, petitioned the legislature for the required adjustment. When the legislature ignored them, the old divisions reopened.[29]

The fight was chiefly sectional and not partisan. Pro-improvement Whigs who had come to dominate the western counties were more numerous than Democrats in the leadership of the reform movement. But eastern Whigs allied with eastern Democrats in resisting reapportionment. As in 1829 and 1830, only a few leading eastern Democrats, above all Thomas Ritchie, backed reform, as much to win the loyalty of Richmond workers as to appeal to western farmers; yet one of the leading western voices deploring the easterners' domination belonged to a young Democrat, John Letcher, the editor of the Lexington *Valley Star*. Along the sectional divide, reformers once again linked their cause to the Revolution, while assuring easterners that basing representation on the white population would do more to strengthen slavery than to weaken it. After the eastern-dominated state senate rejected reform in 1841–42 and 1842–43, the westerners escalated their rhetoric, charging that the easterners had made "slaves" of free western citizens, and threatening separation from the rest of the state if their demands were not met. In 1845, Governor James McDowell, a Democrat from Lexington, asked the legislature in his annual message to consider calling a constitutional convention, but the eastern planters killed reform yet again.[30]

By 1847, western Virginians had become so aggrieved that a few revived the antislavery ideas that had been defeated in the unsettling debates of 1832. The new controversy began modestly enough at a forum sponsored in Lexington by the Franklin Society and Library Company, a local organization that had begun as one of the late-forming Democratic-Republican societies in 1800 and was now devoted to literary uplift and political discussion. The topic—"Should the people of Western Virginia delay any longer steps to bring about a division of the state?"—drew several notable speakers, including Reverend Henry Ruffner, president of Washington College. Ruffner, a Whig slaveholder, caused a stir by linking his support for separation with his contention that slavery hurt the white population of the West and ought to be gradually eliminated, followed by the colonization of the freed blacks outside of the United States—a reprise of Thomas Jefferson Randolph's proposals fifteen years earlier. Shortly after the Lexington debate, a group of westerners, including John Letcher, asked Ruffner to expand his remarks into a pamphlet and to lay his "not only able but unanswerable" observations before the general public.[31]

Although Ruffner offered old arguments, he modified them with a Whiggish economic utilitarianism that was also appearing in northern antislavery newspapers and pamphlets. Slavery, Ruffner charged, not only propped up the artificial minority rule of the eastern planters; it was pernicious because it dishonored all labor and hampered economic development. Armed with the latest federal census statistics, Ruffner showed that based on all important indices—free population growth, agricultural productivity, commercial prosperity, the spread of common schools and public education—the slaveholding states lagged far behind the free states. "What has done this world of desolation? Not war; not pestilence," Ruffner declared, "not oppression of rulers, civil or ecclesiastical;— but *slavery*, a curse more destructive in its effects than all of them." In the impending struggle for her rights and prosperity, Ruffner concluded, western Virginia had to press beyond constitutional reform and get to the root of its oppression by completing slavery's gradual destruction. Yet while Ruffner's pamphlet gained wide circulation, it only won acceptance in the West. More than ever, Virginia consisted of two societies encompassed within a single border.[32]

While southern conventions and legislatures reinforced their commitment to slavery, some key northern legislatures affirmed a growing popular opposition to slavery. The most direct response, prior to the Hale Alliance uprising, was the enactment of personal liberty laws in the wake of the *Prigg* decision of 1842. The first of these laws, passed in Massachusetts in 1843, arose directly from a fugitive slave case. In October 1842, a fair-skinned runaway Virginia slave named George Latimer, who had reached the North with his wife, was arrested in Boston at the request of his owner, James Gray. The next day, a crowd of nearly three hundred angry blacks gathered at the county courthouse where Latimer was being held, to prevent his summary release into Gray's custody, thereby forcing the authorities to move Latimer to the city jail. Instantly, the case became a cause célèbre for the city's abolitionists, black and white. In November, a group of prominent whites (including William Ellery Channing's son, William Francis Channing) formed a Latimer Committee and founded a new newspaper, the *Latimer Journal and North Star*, to publicize Latimer's plight and "meet the urgency of the first enslavement in Boston."[33]

After a month of difficult negotiations with the state supreme court, the abolitionists succeeded in getting the charge against Latimer dropped and in gaining his manumission in exchange for a four-hundred-dollar fee, paid by a local black clergyman. But the most radical abolitionists, led by the Garrisonians, were not satisfied, and they demanded (according to the resolutions of one protest meeting) that Massachusetts never again "allow her soil to be polluted by the footprints of slavery." On November 19, an abolitionist convention assembled in Boston and approved the "Latimer and Great Massachusetts Petition," with three demands: a law forbidding all state officers from aiding in the capture or detention of any fugitive slave, a law forbidding the use of jails or any other public property for detaining fugitives, and amendments to the U.S. Constitution (the details left unspecified) that would "forever separate the people of Massachusetts from all connection with slavery." The Latimer Committee distributed thousands of copies of the petition to local postmasters and "every person who wishes to free Massachusetts."[34]

In February 1843, with the petition campaign in full swing and the Texas annexation issue heating up, John Quincy Adams's son, Charles Francis Adams, appeared at a large public meeting at Faneuil Hall and agreed to advocate the petition in the state legislature, where he was a member. The political outlook of this enlarged pro-petition movement, and of the report that it produced, was decidedly moderate compared to the Garrisonians', yet the joint committee that drafted the report preserved antislavery unity. More than sixty-five thousand persons in Massachusetts ended up signing the petition before Adams presented it and his personal liberty bill to the state legislature. In late March, the bill passed the lower house without debate and virtually without opposition. The next day, it passed the state senate by a vote of 25 to 3, and Governor Marcus Morton immediately signed it into law.[35]

By respecting the limits laid down by Justice Story and the Court majority in the *Prigg* decision, the Massachusetts Personal Liberty Law of 1843 struck a blow against slavery without in any way challenging the legitimacy of the U.S. Constitution. The law's practical effect was to place the burden for rounding up fugitive slaves on already overtaxed federal officials. Its political effect was to give fresh impetus to the political abolitionist movement. Not surprisingly, the New England legislatures reacted first: Vermont passed its own personal liberty law in 1843, New Hampshire (as an outgrowth of the Hale Alliance struggle) followed suit three years later, and Rhode Island did likewise in 1848. More strikingly, in Pennsylvania, where antiblack sentiment had led to wholesale black disenfranchisement in 1838, an intense petition campaign pushed the legislature into approving its own personal liberty law, even tougher than the Massachusetts version, in February 1847.[36]

Other northern states proved less liberal on issues connected to slavery and race through 1848. In 1845, Connecticut removed the minimal taxpaying suffrage requirement left over from its reforms of 1818, but sustained the disenfranchisement of blacks. Despite the Giddings uprising in the Western Reserve and the fervent activities of Salmon Chase and the Liberty Party elsewhere in the state, Ohio retained its notorious black codes dating back to 1804, as well as its disenfranchisement of blacks. Wisconsin, another site of growing antislavery activity, nevertheless barred blacks from voting under its new 1848 constitution, just as Iowa had under its new constitution two years earlier. By the end of 1848, black men could vote on the same basis as whites in only five northern states — one fewer than had been the case a decade earlier.[37] Still, even outside New England, the northern politics of democracy, race, and antislavery were neither simple nor static in the mid-1840s. Pennsylvania's personal liberty law was one example of movement. Far more complicated were constitutional debates that rocked New York, originating not in controversies over black rights but in factional politics and a rebellion by white tenant farmers.

Temporarily muted by the party's electoral successes in 1842, the fierce divisions among New York's Democrats soon reemerged, which led to calls for a complete overhaul of the state's constitution. Anticipating the end of the prolonged economic depression and a rise in canal revenues, the newly elected Hunker governor William Bouck caught the Radicals by surprise by proposing to spend surplus state monies on enlarging the Erie Canal and on two other pending canal projects—a direct violation of the platform on which he had run. Michael Hoffman, the Radical leader in the state legislature, was one of the few who had predicted Bouck's reversal, and he had vowed to push for a new state constitutional convention if new spending and borrowing were in the offing. "Monopoly may hiss and locality may yell," Hoffman wrote to Azariah Flagg shortly after Bouck's nomination, "but a convention of the people must be called to sit in judgment on the past and command the future." Soon thereafter, however, the Radicals' counteroffensive ran into complications caused by an upsurge of rural plebeian turmoil.[38]

The great Anti-Rent war that wracked New York in the 1840s was a social equivalent of the Dorr Rebellion, aimed at eliminating the antiquated remnants of the quasi-feudal leasehold tenure system that still governed large portions of the state. The epicenter of the uprising, the Manor of Rensselaerwyck, included the upper Hudson River Valley counties of Albany and Rensselaer, although in time the struggle moved farther south and west. In 1839, the longtime great landowner of Rensselaerwyck, Stephen Van Rensselaer III, died. Known as the "Good Patroon" because of his willingness to allow long overdue rents to go uncollected, Van Rensselaer left behind immense tracts of tenant-occupied land with their payments long in arrears. His heirs, less enamored of manorial paternalism, began demanding back payments and full compliance with the tenant-lease arrangements. The tenants immediately drafted an "Anti-Renters' Declaration of Independence" and began forcibly resisting landlord agents and sheriffs who attempted to serve writs on them.[39]

The Anti-Renters' campaign of intimidation and rent strikes continued on and off over the next five years, with no settlement forthcoming. Suddenly, in 1844, unrest flared, as resisters disguised as Indians preyed on any authority bold enough to enforce the hated tenure laws. Events reached a crisis in August 1845, when a crowd of Anti-Renters killed a deputy sheriff in Delaware County, prompting newly elected Radical Governor Wright to declare the entire county in a state of insurrection and have scores of Anti-Renters arrested and imprisoned. Normally, Radical Democrats, including Wright, could be expected to sympathize with the rebels, and the Whigs with the landowners, but the degeneration of the contest into violence under a Democratic governor and the attendant politics played havoc with expectations. Following the Delaware County killing, Bryant's *Evening Post* likened the Anti-Renters to the South Carolina nullifiers of 1832–33, and declared that "[a] free people cannot subsist in a state of violence and anarchy." Governor Wright refused to grant clemency to the men later convicted of the deputy's murder, and he told the state legislature to accede to none of the Anti-Renters' demands until farmers throughout the state laid down their arms. Angry tenant sympathizers—supported by a new land reform group called the National Reform Association, headed by the old Workie George Henry Evans—named independent Anti-Renter tickets in the state legislative elections in the fall of 1845, then bombarded the new legislature with requests to free the convicted men and abolish the existing land tenure system.[40]

Liberal new-school Whigs saw in the Anti-Rent agitation a political opportunity for themselves and for the state's disenfranchised blacks. Like the Democrats, New York's Whig Party remained badly divided between its progressives and conservatives. The majority Seward-Weed progressives, having expressed their sympathy for New York's black population in the struggles over state education and having pushed unsuccessfully to uphold a New York personal liberty law, wanted to expand the black electorate by revising the state constitution—thereby, they calculated, adding thousands of mostly Whig black voters to the election rolls and undercutting the Liberty Party's appeal. Horace Greeley, among others, made the case for black suffrage (and against the Democrats) on moral and democratic grounds: "On the one side," he wrote, "stand Equality, Reason, Justice, Democracy, Humanity; on the other are a base, slavery engendered prejudice and a blackguard clamor against "Niggers.'" Seward conceded, freely, that hardheaded motives were also at work, explaining to Gerrit Smith that "the obvious interests of the Whig party" dictated that it lead the way "for a convention to extend the Right of Suffrage." Whig conservatives, however, opposed any effort to make the party appear friendly to blacks, and preferred to strengthen the nativist connections they had forged in 1844.[41]

The Anti-Rent disturbances heightened the rift among the Whigs and gave the Seward progressives another constituency to cultivate. Whig conservatives despised the Anti-Renter movement as the latest example of home-grown Jacobinism, whose true aim, the stiff-necked Daniel D. Barnard declared in a long denunciation, was "the utter overthrow of all social order, and the ruin of the whole social fabric." But the Weed-Seward Whigs had long regarded the tenant-rent system as an obsolete anomaly and fetter on economic freedom, and they now thought they could win over traditionally Democratic voters in the disturbed counties who had been estranged by Governor Wright's opposition. Risking a party rupture, the liberal Whig press, preeminently Greeley's *Tribune*, took up the Anti-Renter cause, and the Sewardites suddenly found themselves in strange alliance with the pro-retrenchment Radicals, favoring the calling of a convention to draft a new state constitution. Expecting they could sustain their predominance within their own party, the Whig liberals hoped that Democratic factionalism over economic issues and over statewide patronage would clear a path to revising the 1821 constitution to their own advantage.[42]

The Whigs progressives failed, although not completely. Voters overwhelmingly approved a referendum calling for a new constitutional convention, but selected a body so heavily dominated by Radicals that the liberal Whigs had to change their strategy abruptly. Dropping their demands for equal black suffrage, Weed-Seward delegates quietly allied with the Hunkers, helping to moderate the more radical Democratic economic proposals at the convention while gaining the Hunkers' agreement to sit out the fall elections. Ultimately, the Radicals succeeded in democratizing the state court judiciary and placing some constitutional restrictions on canal funding; the Anti-Rent movement won a prohibition of the controversial land-contract system and of land leases over twelve years; and the Whigs, with their new links to the Hunker Democrats, put themselves in a strong position to defeat Silas Wright in the autumn election. The biggest losers were New York's blacks, who failed to gain any revision of the 1821 suffrage property qualifications, and who saw the old discrimination upheld in the autumn's popular referendum on the new constitution by a margin of greater than 2 to 1.[43]

Although the New York state convention did not expand black rights, the political fallout from it, especially the renewed division between Hunkers and Radicals (by now known as the Barnburners), helped aggravate the growing sectional discord in Washington and the nation at large. Over the summer of 1846, anger at the administration and at the South finally began to boil over among northern Democrats generally, and especially among the Van Burenites. On Capitol Hill, the Polk administration's willingness to compromise with Britain over Oregon but not with Mexico over Texas and California gnawed at northern Democrats. Polk's veto of a major river-and-harbor improvement bill in August 1846 convinced northwestern Democrats that the South had the president in its pocket. In Pennsylvania as well as New England, the rising popular sentiment behind resisting the South over the issue of fugitive slaves had made an impression on northern Democratic as well as Whig officials; so had the Hale uprising in firmly Democratic New Hampshire. And in New York, Barnburner Democrats found themselves suddenly embroiled in a desperate fight to reelect Silas Wright, fully aware that the Hunkers (with, they surmised, the backing of the White House) were now allied with the Whigs. As factional, partisan, and sectional pressures reached the bursting point, Radical Democrats throughout the North were coming to agree with the sturdy Connecticut Jacksonian Gideon

Welles that "[t]he time has come . . . when the Northern democracy should make a stand."[44]

That stand would take the form of a surprise effort by dissenting congressional Democrats to clarify the administration's aims in the war with Mexico with respect to slavery. Growing popular anxiety about Polk's ulterior motives played as great a role as factional calculations in persuading the northern dissidents to act; indeed, the two reinforced each other to the point where the northerners' political self-preservation now seemed to require a definitive challenge to both the South and the Polk administration. "[T]hroughout the entire northern portion of this country," one frustrated New York Radical congressman, Martin Grover, remarked early in 1847,

> it was the topic of conversation and discussion, and of earnest inves-
> tigation, what was to be the result of the war. The charge was iterated
> and reiterated that the war was undertaken on the part of the Admin-
> istration, aided by the South, for the purpose of extending the area of
> slavery. . . . I wished a declaration on that subject for the purpose of
> satisfying the northern mind: the northern mind was in doubt, was
> halting. . . . Satisfy the northern people—satisfy the people whom we
> represent—that we are not to extend the institution of slavery as the
> result of this war.[45]

By the time Grover offered these reflections, attempts to satisfy the northern mind had made a famous man out of a hitherto undistinguished freshman Democratic congressman from Pennsylvania.

"THE FIRST ELEMENT OF DEMOCRACY":
THE WILMOT PROVISO AND THE TRANSFORMATION
OF POLITICAL ANTISLAVERY

David Wilmot was, in his own humble way, every bit as devoted a Jacksonian Democrat as James K. Polk was. Born and raised in rural Bethany, Pennsylvania, he had studied law, resettled one hundred miles west in the town of Towanda in 1834, and become one of the most active Democrats in Bradford County. Wilmot supported hard money, the abolition of imprisonment for debt, the independent treasury—and, enthusiastically, the reelection of Martin Van Buren in 1840 and 1844. Elected to the House in the 1844 contest, he was the only mem-
ber of the Pennsylvania delegation to vote in favor of the Walker Tariff; with the rest of the Van Burenites, he went along with Texas annexation and voted in favor of the Mexico war bill.[46]

Wilmot looked as well as acted the part of a self-made man of the people, eternally vigilant about protecting the rights of labor. Unkempt in dress, his plump face distended by a chaw of tobacco that seemed permanently lodged in one cheek, he had the rough-hewn presence of a soldier in the army of unprepossessing Jacksonians that had been arriving in Congress since the 1830s—marked for dutiful service but not for distinction. His early career gave no indication that he would one day be regarded as an antislavery hero. That reputation began when he gravitated to a small group of restive antislavery Democrats informally headed by the New York Radical, Preston King.

King, who had arrived in Congress in 1843, was well suited politically and personally to unite the gathering insurgency. Although prone to periodic depression—a breakdown in 1838 had required his confinement in an asylum—King at his best was an outwardly calm and eminently sensible man, with a gift for influencing others and achieving consensus among like-minded colleagues. His record of hard-money Jacksonianism was beyond reproach among party loyalists, and his long-standing objections to southern influence in the party made him a natural leader among House antislavery Democrats. Gideon Welles later wrote that the modest and unsung King "more than . . . any other one man" deserved the credit for "boldly meeting the arrogant and imperious slaveholding oligarchy and organizing the party which eventually overthrew them." Thoroughly estranged from the Polk administration, King faced the additional pressure in the summer of 1846 to aid his mentor, Silas Wright, in Wright's difficult gubernatorial reelection campaign. Handled carefully, a measured Democratic strike in Congress against the Polk administration over the issue of slavery and the war would give tactical aid to Wright among antislavery New York voters and lift the burden of southern collaboration from the northern Democracy as a whole. Yet King himself, as Wright's acknowledged spokesman in Washington, could not be too assertive in public lest he make Wright look like the mastermind of a Democratic antislavery plot.[47]

King led a band of roughly a dozen kindred spirits, including his fellow New York Barnburners Timothy Jenkins, Martin Grover, and George Rathbun; Hannibal Hamlin of Maine; Jacob Brinkerhoff of Ohio; Paul Dillingham of Vermont; and James Thompson and David Wilmot of Pennsylvania. Quite apart from their politics, they had much in common. Most were younger men in their thirties. (King, at forty, was one of the older rebels, while Wilmot, thirty-two, was the youngest.) All were serving either their first or second term in the House. Several shared lodgings at Madam Masi's rooming house on Pennsylvania Avenue. None was interested in renouncing the war with Mexico or in burning all the northern Democrats' bridges to the South. (King, in particular, had hopes of gaining the presidential nomination in 1848 for Silas Wright, which would have been impossible without some southern support.) But as a group, they represented a junior cohort of Radicals, a full generation younger than Martin Van Buren and nearly two generations younger than the departed Jackson. Having come of political age after the Jackson Democracy had been formed, they were less reflexively beholden to the intersectional rules drawn up at the party's inception, less sensitive about a possible reprise of the Missouri crisis, and more capable of enlarging on the example of the antislavery Whigs.[48]

How and why Wilmot came to deliver the antislavery Democrats' signal blow remains obscure. Wilmot himself, in the glare of his sudden celebrity, later claimed that the idea was entirely his, although he conceded that he consulted beforehand with his friends. Jacob Brinkerhoff claimed that he, and not Wilmot, was the true author of the proposal, but that he allowed Wilmot to present it to Congress because his own antislavery views were so well known that he would have difficulty gaining the House floor to move the matter. More likely, several members, including Wilmot, came up with the idea independently and the proposal was hastily drafted by committee, with each of the drafters writing down a copy of the approved wording and agreeing that whoever got the first opportunity would have the honor of introducing it to the House. The lot fell to the unremarkable Wilmot.[49]

Polk provided the insurgents with their opening in August 1846 by asking Congress—on the eve of its adjournment, with many of its members having already departed—for a two-million-dollar appropriation for negotiations with Mexico. The request divulged that Polk planned to obtain additional territory, which he had been telling northern Democrats he had no intention of doing. Antislavery Whigs, delighted to be handed an election issue near the close of the congressional session, immediately pointed out the bill's not-so-hidden motive. Hugh White of New York demanded that, as a show of good faith, "gentlemen on the other side of the House" offer an amendment to the bill barring any extension of slavery into any newly acquired territory. Whether White was apprised of what the antislavery Democrats had planned, or whether he was merely taunting them, remains unclear. Either way, the Democrats were ready.[50]

Shortly after White delivered his challenge, with the House well into the evening session and with only a bare quorum present on the floor, one of the New York antislavery freshman Democrats, Bradford Ripley Wood, announced that he would not vote for the appropriation bill unless it was substantially amended "as proposed by the gentleman [Mr. Wilmot] from Pennsylvania." Wood then ceded his time to Wilmot, who, after some procedural interruptions, offered his amendment, its language based on the Northwest Ordinance of 1787, stipulating that "neither slavery nor involuntary servitude shall ever exist" in any territories acquired from Mexico as a result of the war. Pro-administration Democrats tried to have Wilmot ruled out of order, then tried to water down his amendment, but failed. The amendment—soon and forever after to be known as the Wilmot Proviso—passed 83 to 64, as did (more narrowly) the amended appropriations bill. Congress adjourned before the Senate could make a decision on the matter, temporarily shelving the administration proposal. But in January, soon after the new congressional session opened and the White House proposed a new and even larger appropriations bill, the antislavery Democrats' leader, Preston King (freed from his earlier constraints by Silas Wright's defeat for reelection), presented the Proviso once again, in an expanded form. Once again, the House passed it.[51]

The roll call on the original Proviso vote went unrecorded, but the results over the amended appropriations bill were startling. Virtually every northern Whig on hand supported the amended bill, while every southern Whig and Democrat opposed it. The most telling division occurred among the northern Democrats, fifty-two of whom supported the bill and only four of whom voted nay. The bonds of party had broken down. The House was almost perfectly divided along sectional lines, much as it had been during the Missouri crisis more than a quarter of a century earlier. Anti-administration, antislavery sentiments had spread through the entire congressional northern Democracy. Southern hard-liners took note, and as soon as the House passed the Proviso a second time, John C. Calhoun introduced in the Senate what amounted to an anti-Proviso: two resolutions denouncing any congressional law that would "make any discrimination between the States of this Union" or "deprive citizens of any of the States of this Union from emigrating, with their property, into any of the territories of the United States." The resolutions would never be debated or come up for a vote, but they offered the basis for later southern resistance.[52]

Outside of Congress, initial reaction to the Wilmot vote was mild. When the press mentioned the Proviso at all, it was as a mere procedural motion, covering an eventuality that had not yet come to pass. The administration's *Union* left the impression that it would happily accept the appropriations bill, with or without Wilmot's amendment. Apart from a few isolated cases, the Proviso appears to have had no effect on the 1846 congressional races (in which the Whigs regained, narrowly, the House majority), not even in Wilmot's successful reelection campaign.[53] Only after the second session of the Twenty-ninth Congress assembled—after four months of letting its purport sink in, and with the distractions of an impending election gone—did the Wilmot issue explode.

To understand that explosion, it is crucial to understand what the Wilmot Proviso was not, as well as what it was. It was not, by any means, either an antiwar or an anti-expansionist measure. Despite their misgivings about the war's origins and the hidden agenda of the slaveholders, the antislavery Democrats warmly supported Polk's war policies in 1847. David Wilmot himself, who considered California the rightful possession of the United States, declared his support for the "necessary and proper war" only minutes before he first moved his amendment. In this respect, the sectional solidarity between northern Whigs and Democrats was illusory. Antislavery liberal Whigs did rejoice at the Proviso as, in Horace Greeley's words, *"a solemn declaration of the United North against the further extension of Slavery."* But the antislavery Whigs, like the rest of their party, were opposed to any territorial conquest of Mexican lands and not just to the expansion of slavery. By the end of 1847, many moderate and conservative northern Whigs would find themselves backing off of the Wilmot Proviso and instead joining with southern Whigs under the slogan of "No Territory," a temporarily successful reassertion of intersectional party regularity over sectional loyalties.[54]

Neither was the Proviso a blow for the elevation and equality of blacks, as favored by the Liberty Party and some of the hard-core antislavery Whigs. Steeped in the Jacksonian tradition of protecting the rights of free labor, the antislavery Democrats made it clear that in trying to halt slavery's spread, they were chiefly interested in preventing the degradation and dishonor of white workingmen. "If slavery is not excluded by law," Preston King proclaimed when he reintroduced the Proviso in January 1847, "the presence of the slave will exclude the laboring white man." Unlike antislavery Whigs—who took more liberal stances on black rights and more conservative stances on economic policies—antislavery Democrats, radicals on economic matters, were primarily concerned with the future of white workers.[55]

Some Democrats' arguments also included the racist claim that by barring slavery from new territories, those territories could be kept lily-white. Jacob Brinkerhoff remarked at the height of the Proviso controversy that he had "selfishness enough greatly to prefer the welfare of my own race, and vindictiveness enough to wish to leave and keep upon the shoulders of the South the burden of the curse which they themselves created and courted"—the "curse" being a large black population. Wilmot took a similar view, declaring that he had "no morbid sympathy for the slave," and that the proposal bearing his name aimed to "preserve to free white labor a fair country, a rich inheritance" in the West, where "the sons of toil, of my own race and own color" could live free of blacks. The New York Barnburners had an especially baleful record of exploiting racial prejudice, having voted solidly against extending black suffrage at the 1846 state constitutional convention, and raised cries of "Nigger Party," "Amalgamation," and "Fried Wool" against the liberal Whigs who supported reform.[56]

Yet if racism abounded in their ranks, the antislavery Democrats were neither morally indifferent to black enslavement nor driven chiefly by racism. No matter how deep their Negrophobia, few if any accepted claims that racial differences justified slavery. "To hold a human being in bondage; to buy and sell his body," Radical John Van Buren stated, "was and must be repugnant to the ordinary sensibilities of every intelligent man." The Van Burenite *Seneca Observer*, in a typical Barnburner editorial, announced that it could not countenance a victory over

Mexico if the result "would be to deprive one human being of those rights which are his natural inheritance." In backing the Proviso, antislavery Democrats also picked up the widely held argument that by restricting slavery's spread, they were helping to ensure its eventual doom where it already existed—not in the lunatic manner favored by the most radical abolitionists, but within the limits of the U.S. Constitution. Lacking fresh lands to exploit, so the argument went, slave-based staple agriculture would eventually deplete the soil of the newer southern states just as it had along the seaboard—and then slavery would collapse under the weight of its own inefficiency. "What does the past teach us?" the political abolitionist Gamaliel Bailey's newspaper, the *National Era*, asked in 1847. "That slavery lives by *expansion*." Accordingly, antislavery Democrats reasoned, the Proviso's effort to quarantine slavery also was an effort to hasten slavery's abolition—or, as Wilmot declared in 1847, to "insure the redemption, at an early day, of the negro from his bondage and chains."[57]

The Democratic antislavery argument embodied in the Wilmot Proviso was above all an attack on the authority of the aristocratic Slave Power. At one level, the attack was factional, a settling of scores with southern Democrats going back at least to the Baltimore convention of 1844 and continuing through Polk's deceptions and perceived betrayals. But the outpouring of pent-up Democratic outrage in 1846 and after, inside and outside Washington, brought into the open far more than grudges over petty political matters and a thirst for revenge. The South, antislavery Democrats declared, was ruled by an oligarchy that would stop at nothing to get its way. That oligarchy degraded white labor while living off the labor of black slaves; it throttled free discussion of public matters in the North as well as the South; it retarded economic and mental progress; and now, insatiable as ever, it wanted still more territory "because," George Rathbun charged, "where slavery exists, the slave power prevails."[58]

In sum—and this was the Wilmot Democrats' crowning argument—slavery and the Slave Power were at war with democracy itself. Bradford Ripley Wood, the Radical who helped Wilmot introduce the Proviso, made the point cogently on the floor of the House in February 1847. "This is a national question," Wood observed.

> It is not a question of mere dollars and cents. It is not a mere political question. It is one in which the North has a higher and deeper stake than the South possibly can have. It is a question whether, in the government of the country, she shall be borne down by the influence of your slaveholding aristocratic institutions, that have not in them the first element of Democracy. It is a question whether this Republic shall be weakened, cramped, and degraded by an institution doomed of God and man. . . . Hug this institution to your own bosom, if you

choose, until it eats out your very vitals; but let it not blast, and blight, and curse, with the mildew of heaven, any other portion of God's heritage, save where, by leave of the Constitution, it now exists.[59]

Jacksonian antislavery arguments that, a decade earlier, were grounds for excommunication from the Democracy now galvanized virtually every northern Democrat in the House.

The rulers of South Carolina and their champion John C. Calhoun—who, now that American troops were under fire, had said he was prepared to give the war "a quiet but decided support"—responded swiftly. The Wilmot Proviso, the *Charleston Mercury* exclaimed, drew *"a line of political and social demarcation around the Slave States"* that would leave the South "on every side girt round with those who will continually excite our slaves to insubordination and revolt, which it would be folly to suppose would forever be resisted." Other southerners, Whig and Democratic, regarded the Proviso as more of a symbolic issue than a substantive one—a northern effort to insult and then humiliate the South by denying slaveholders rights that they actually did not intend to exercise. Calhoun dismissed the Proviso as an unconstitutional ploy to win over the small number of abolitionist voters who held the balance of power in many of the northern states. Still, Calhoun calculated that Wilmot's amendment might have its uses in finally realizing his dream of uniting southerners across party lines. "I am of the impression," he wrote, "that if the South acts as it ought, the Wilmot Proviso, instead of proving to be the means of successfully assailing us and our peculiar institution, may be made the occasion of successfully asserting our equality and rights by enabling us to force the issue on the North." By March 1847, Calhoun had launched a movement for southern rights and unity, which inspired anti-Proviso mass meetings across the South. One of these gatherings, in Lowndes County, Alabama, pledged to support no national candidate who favored the Proviso, noting that, on the subject of slavery, "among ourselves we know of no party distinctions and never will know any."[60]

In the North, the Proviso became a rallying point for diverse strands of antislavery opinion that augured the enlargement of political antislavery into a major force in national politics. Liberty Party men, recovering from their weaker-than-expected showing in 1844, took heart from the disruption of the Democracy and saw the Proviso's restrictionism as a powerful new weapon for denationalizing slavery. Among Democrats, rank-and-file support for the Proviso was so strong that even some pro-administration Hunkers felt it necessary to declare their repugnance for slavery (although they remained cool to the Proviso itself). Antislavery new-school Whigs, especially in Massachusetts—where they were coming to be known as "Conscience Whigs"—likewise regarded the Proviso as a boost, giving them needed ammunition against the still-predominant old-guard "Cotton Whigs," who counseled tact and restraint in dealing with their southern Whig allies. The Garrisonian radicals alone expressed skepticism about the Proviso as a political snare—a stance that raised further doubts about Garrisonian tactics in the mind of Frederick Douglass who, along with most black abolitionists, applauded Wilmot's amendment. Increasingly, antislavery northerners began contemplating building a northern democratic counter to what Calhoun was trying to create in the South.[61]

A GRAND PARTY OF FREEDOM?

At the end of 1846, while the political implications of Wilmot's Proviso were beginning to sink in, a young Massachusetts antislavery Whig, the lawyer Charles Sumner, predicted what he called "a new crystallization of parties, in which there shall be one grand Northern party of Freedom."[62] Something resembling that party would emerge in late 1847 and 1848. Mr. Polk's War, although begun with an outpouring of popular patriotism, was becoming a source of intense sectional division. The elements of an extraordinary democratic antislavery uprising were beginning to cohere.

The odds against the success of such an uprising remained formidable. Although the partisan bonds of the Jacksonian era had begun to fray, intersectional organizations and loyalties forged during the intense political conflicts of the 1830s and early 1840s were not easy to disrupt. The meager, if improved, Liberty Party turnout in 1844 suggested that third-party antislavery politics had yet to find anything approaching a northern mass base. Indeed, the outcome of the 1844 elections illustrated the perils of third-party politics, and the large possibility that any such effort in 1848 would elect the less desirable of the major-party candidates. The patriotic fervor surrounding the war carried over into 1847 and 1848, in curious counterpoint to the rising discontent, further limiting the appeal of sectional politics. But the struggles that the war provoked and that led to the fight over Wilmot's Proviso were also forcing a redefinition of what it meant to be a Democrat or a Whig—or an American. Those struggles would continue even after the nation's troops had returned from Mexico covered with glory, and after Polk had achieved his dream of a transcontinental republic.

20

WAR, SLAVERY, AND THE
AMERICAN 1848

Along with the War of 1812 and the Vietnam intervention, the war
against Mexico generated more dissent than any major military conflict
in U.S. history through the twentieth century. Yet unlike the other two,
the Mexican War was a rousing military success. The doubts and misgivings that
turned into repulsion arose not from American setbacks, but from American victories, culminating in the capture of Mexico City in September 1847. The result
was a schizophrenic experience on the home front, filled with both exhilarated
celebration of our troops and embittered criticism of the war and its goals.

The schizophrenia carried over into national politics. After David Wilmot
introduced his proviso, war and its immediate aftermath intensified factional discord and sectional divisions, leading to a burst of antislavery political activity that
created the Free Soil Party. Over the summer and early fall of 1848, as the Free
Soil revolt reached its peak, some of its leaders and supporters persuaded themselves that American politics was hurtling toward a crash. Given the frenzy that
surrounded the Free Soil effort, those assessments are understandable; antislavery politics would never be the same. But the immediate outcome of the American struggles of 1848 was the election to the White House of a southern Whig
war hero with no political record, hailed chiefly for his exploits against the cruel
Mexican foe. Cracks appeared in the nation's political system, but mainstream
party leaders, drawing on patriotic attachment to the Union as well as partisan
attachments, papered them over. Most voters appeared to reject sectional
schisms and favor moderation — at least for the moment.

"THE DEVIL'S THANKEE": VICTORY'S DIVISIVE GAINS

The American defeat of Mexico occurred in three separate theaters of operations. In late February 1847, Zachary Taylor's army won a bloody but decisive victory over a much larger force commanded by Santa Anna outside the hacienda of Buena Vista, near Monterrey. At virtually the same moment, Colonel Alexander Doniphan's Missouri volunteers, having occupied El Paso del Norte (what is now Ciudad Juárez), defeated a large Mexican army in Chihuahua. The victories effectively ended the north Mexican campaign. In California, despite the defeat of an American rebellion that declared a Bear Flag Republic, and despite powerful, temporarily successful uprisings by conquered Mexicans in Los Angeles, American force prevailed by the end of January 1847, leaving the leader of the Bear Flag rebels, the explorer John C. Frémont, to negotiate the Treaty of Cahuenga that secured Upper California for the United States.

The most important campaign, commanded by Winfield Scott, occurred in central Mexico and led to the fall of Mexico City. The plan, in the works after November 1846, involved approaching the capital from the Gulf Coast, along the same route Cortés took in his conquest of the Aztecs three hundred years earlier. Early in 1847, Scott assembled an invasion force on an island off the Mexican coast. Following several frustrating delays, he set off for the port city of Vera Cruz, and after a siege and bombardment of nearly three weeks, the city surrendered in late March. Scott immediately headed inland. Enduring ferocious combat at Cerro Gordo, San Antonio, Contreras, and Churubusco, the Americans finally stormed the fortress of Chapultepec, overlooking Mexico City, in mid-September. After brief engagements at the city's gates, Scott's army marched into the Main Plaza and hoisted the American flag above the National Palace, the so-called Halls of the Montezumas. A mopping-up operation ensued against refractories led by Santa Anna, but by the end of October, the Americans were digging in at Mexico City, to await the negotiation of a peace treaty. Inside of only eighteen months, Mr. Polk had won his war.[1]

The news of victory after victory set Americans agog—an effect made more stunning by the nation's expanding commercial culture. "People here are all in a state of delirium about the Mexican War. A military ardor pervades all ranks . . . and 'prenticeboys are running off to the wars by scores," the new literary celebrity Herman Melville wrote to his Democratic brother Gansevoort from a small town in upstate New York, early in the conflict. "Nothing is talked of but the 'Halls of the Montezumas.'" Melville had just published his first novel, *Typee*, a picturesque, sexually frank tale based on his experiences in the South Seas. He found the patriotic fervor confusing—though proud of the soldiers' valor, he thought the war was "nothing of itself"—and later wrote a series of satirical articles about

General Taylor, "Authentic Anecdotes of Old Zach," and a wild allegorical novel, *Mardi*, with a thinly veiled attack on John C. Calhoun.[2] But the preponderance of the nation's authors, songwriters, playwrights, illustrators, and editors enlisted in the war effort and helped deepen the public's delirium through 1847—enlarging the culture of mass celebration beyond anything Americans had ever known.

The aging James Fenimore Cooper—a critic of the war's management but a celebrator of its sublime uplift of American power—contributed a novel, *Jack Tier; or, The Florida Reef*, about the foiling of a traitorous plot to supply the oppressive Mexicans with gunpowder. George Lippard, an author of highly popular lurid Gothic romances, wrote the rhapsodic *Legends of Mexico: The Battles of Taylor* and a war novel, *'Bel of Prairie Eden*. The best the war could stimulate in the way of poetry, William Gilmore Simms's collection *Areytos: or, Songs of the South*, depicted the invading armies as latter-day chivalric knights. More typical were the blood-and-thunder novelettes churned out by Edward Zane Carroll Judson (later known as the father of the dime novel), and the patriotic lyrics and melodies of George Pope Morris, George Washington Dixon, and lesser-known composers (including such numbers as "General Taylor's Encampment Quickstep" and "The Rio Grande Quick March"). The public also sang adaptations of old patriotic tunes, including a rewrite of "Yankee Doodle" called "Uncle Sam's Song to Miss Texas," with the verse: "If Mexy, back'd by secret foes,/Still talks of taken you, gal,/Why we can lick them all, you know,/An' then annex 'em too, gal." Playwrights, actors' companies, and impresarios mounted several hastily written but grandly produced theatrical melodramas: Joseph C. Foster's "The Siege of Monterey" won rave reviews and played to capacity crowds at New York's Bowery Theater.[3]

War fever created a new American pantheon: democratic variants of the romantic great man described by the Scots poet and critic Thomas Carlyle in his widely read *Of Heroes and Hero Worship*, which had been published in 1841. Zachary Taylor best filled the bill. A career soldier but not a West Point graduate, Taylor had gained a modicum of fame as a resolute, even brutal Indian fighter during the War of 1812 and the second Seminole War (where he won his nickname, "Old Rough and Ready," for his unceremonious manner and his toughness under fire). Yet to most Americans, Taylor appeared to come out of nowhere in 1846, when Polk ordered him to lead his troops to the Rio Grande in the operation that led to war—and his quick victories in northern Mexico made him an instant idol of the new penny press. Admirers likened him to Alexander, Caesar, Napoleon, and (greatest of all) George Washington, and one journalist described him as "the American whom Carlyle would recognize as 'a hero' worthy of his pen's most eloquent recognition: THE MAN OF DUTY in an age of Self!" Talk started of making Taylor president. But there were other new action heroes, including the pompous yet effective Winfield Scott, gently mocked by his men as "Old Fuss and Feathers" but nevertheless the conqueror of Mexico City, and once again a possible presidential nominee. There were many smaller heroes as well, like Major General Samuel Ringgold and Captain George Lincoln, gloriously killed in action and symbolic of all the martyred dead.[4]

Curiously, most of the younger literary lights affiliated with the *Democratic Review* and Young America, previously so belligerent in support of Manifest Destiny and creating a new native literature, either said little about the war publicly or began openly expressing doubts. Nathaniel Hawthorne, who supported the war, wrote nothing of value about it. Walt Whitman tempered his initial enthusiasm after Wilmot introduced his Proviso, and took a strong Radical Democrat stance against allowing slavery into any newly annexed territory. The young writer who made the greatest popular reputation out of the war was not a Young American at all but the twenty-eight-year-old Boston abolitionist James Russell Lowell, whose antiwar dialect satire verses, collected as *The Biglow Papers*, lampooned the conflict as a crusade for slavery. "They jes want this Californy/ So's to lug new slave states in," Lowell's fictional Hosea Biglow proclaimed:

> To abuse ye, an' to scorn ye,
>   An' to plunder ye like sin,
>
> Aint it cute to see a Yankee
>   Take such everlastin' pains
> All to get the Devil's thankee,
>   Helpin' on 'em weld their chains?
> Wy, it's jest ez clear ez figgers,
>   Clear ez one an' one makes two,
> Chaps that make black slaves o' niggers
>   Want to make wite slaves o' you.

Beside the militarist clamor, antislavery sentiments like Biglow's (including, sometimes, his racism) intensified among northerners after 1846, eliciting predictable angry responses from the South—and creating political confusion in and out of the nation's capital.[5]

The politics of Wilmot's Proviso became the focus of conflict in Congress. President Polk had been injured and angered by the failure of his two-million-dollar appropriations bill after the House saddled it with the admendment. As soon as the new session of Congress assembled in December 1846, he went to work on muffling the slavery issue by lining up support from conservative Democrats including Michigan Senator Lewis Cass. But Preston King's introduction of an enlarged version of the Proviso, the House's affirmation of King's version, and

John C. Calhoun's angry resolutions in response seemed to rip the Democratic Party to shreds and forestall any future war appropriations. King's speech in January on the revised Proviso, criticized by some as a ploy to promote Silas Wright for the presidency, placed the New York Barnburners squarely behind the free-soil effort for the long haul. In the House, with the aid of other northerners, the Van Burenites defeated a proposal to extend the Missouri Compromise line of 36°30' that would have ensured the introduction of slavery into all of New Mexico and into Upper California as far north as San Luis Obispo. In Albany, at King's prompting, the Democratic-controlled legislature endorsed both annexation and congressional prohibition of slavery. By mid-February, similar resolutions had passed the legislatures of four other states, including Pennsylvania and Ohio, and five more states followed suit over the succeeding weeks and months. Calhoun could not have been more delighted. "You will see," Calhoun wrote to an associate, "that I have made up the issue between North and South. If we flinch we are gone, but if we stand fast on it, we shall triumph either by compelling the North to yield to our terms, or declaring our independence of them."[6]

The polarization of Van Burenites and Calhounites was complete, but with the help of Senator Cass, Polk managed to hold together the political center and get his way yet again. Cass, the old Jacksonian and anti–Van Buren Conservative, had backed the Wilmot amendment earlier on but had not been required to vote on it. Now, with his presidential aspirations still burning, he charged that the Proviso was causing needless sectional conflict and could prevent the acquisition of a single foot of Mexican territory. With help from the White House, Cass won over northern Democrats from Illinois and Indiana, as well as the Hunker Daniel S. Dickinson of New York, and the Senate approved the administration's unamended appropriations bill, 31 to 21. Sent back to the House, the bill finally passed without the Proviso on March 3, the very last day of the session, when seven northern Democrats changed their votes and six others abstained.[7]

Over the ninth-month interval between the close of the Twenty-ninth Congress and the opening of the Thirtieth, partisans in all camps of the Wilmot controversy tried to build support at the political grassroots. In July, President Polk undertook a goodwill tour of the northeastern states. Although he did not explicitly mention the territorial issue, he stressed the need for national harmony. "I would recommend in all parts of our beloved country," he told the Maine state legislature, "cultivation of that feeling of brotherhood and mutual regard between the North and the South, and the East and the West, without which we may not anticipate the perpetuity of our free institutions."[8] Polk did not need to add that he thought the chief offenders against brotherhood and mutual regard included David Wilmot, Preston King, and their presumed commander-in-chief, Silas Wright.

Sectional agitators also worked hard during the recess, sometimes achieving more success than met the eye. Calhoun's movement for southern unity ran into resistance from southern Democratic Party leaders who were willing to extend the Missouri Compromise demarcation to the Pacific and were wary of Calhoun's presidential aspirations. But Calhoun did gain support from important southern Whigs who appreciated his criticisms of the war as well as his stand on the territories. ("[T]he people of the South are now anxiously waiting to see what direction you will give it," Robert Toombs of Georgia, one of the leading Whig congressmen from the Deep South, told him.) And among ordinary southern Democrats, Calhoun's pro-slavery stance was increasingly popular outside his home state. In Virginia, for example, a Democratic faction known as "the Chivalry" won unanimous votes in both houses of the legislature in favor of resolutions based on Calhoun's anti-Wilmot proviso—resolutions henceforth called the "Platform of the South."[9]

Even more strikingly, in Alabama, a young rising Democratic star, the transplanted up-country South Carolinian William Lowndes Yancey, began exercising considerable influence inside the state party. In August 1846, even before Wilmot introduced his amendment, the mild-mannered but strong-willed Yancey, now certain that the northern Democracy was useless to the South, resigned from his House seat. Respecting no party at all and no interest other than slavery, Yancey moved about as he pleased. In the spring of 1847, he persuaded Alabama's Democrats to nominate the man he favored as governor and, later, to back the Platform of the South. After the election (with his man safely in office), Yancey dickered with state Whigs over whom to support for the presidency in 1848. "If this foul spirit of party which thus binds and divides and distracts the South can be broken, hail to him who shall do it," he proclaimed in one speech. Gradually, pro-slavery sectionalism that would surpass Calhoun's was gaining a wider purchase on southern minds.[10]

The political situation in the North was even more ominous, as the battle over slavery extention moved alarmed conservatives and moderates in both parties to restore soundness and caution. Among northern Whigs, divisions between antislavery men and conservatives deepened over how best to oppose the administration and terminate the war. At issue was the "No Territory" position hammered out in response to Wilmot's Proviso. To conservatives, who had initially supported the Proviso but who now had the 1848 elections in mind, "No Territory" looked like the only viable way to end the war, finesse the slavery issue, and preserve national party harmony. "We want no more territory, NEITHER WITH NOR WITHOUT THE WILMOT PROVISO," proclaimed the *Ohio State Journal*, which only months earlier had backed the Proviso. The antislavery Whig minority considered this a political as well as a moral evasion. Anything less than a ban on slavery, Joshua Giddings told the House, would encourage the slavocrats: "a revolution after the example of Texas will take place, and annexation to this Union, with a vast increase in the slave power in the councils of the nation, will be the result."[11]

The breach in the Whigs' ranks became particularly severe in Massachusetts, where the conservative so-called Cotton Whig faction (themselves split by a long-time feud between the allies of Daniel Webster and those of Abbott Lawrence) predominated over the minority antislavery Conscience Whigs. At the Whig state convention in 1846, Webster and Lawrence had paraded into the meeting hall for one session arm in arm, in a display of unity against the antislavery insurgents. A year later, however, the conservatives were divided over presidential politics—the Webster forces wanting to nominate their man, the Lawrence faction favoring Zachary Taylor—thereby handing Conscience Whigs the balance of power. Webster finally received the Conscience Whigs' backing, although it came so grudgingly that the prize was not worth the candle. But with that business done, Lawrence rallied the conservatives to defeat a resolution pledging all Whig candidates to support the Wilmot Proviso, thereby creating enormous bitterness among the minority. Soothing words from Webster at the convention's conclusion could not undo the damage. Never again would the Massachusetts antislavery men attend a Whig state convention.[12]

The fights between New York's antislavery Barnburner and conservative Hunker Democrats created an even more involved and fateful division. The entire history of the Polk administration had alienated the Barnburners from the White House and widened the old split in the New York Democracy. The Whigs' victory over Radical Governor Silas Wright in 1846—achieved, as even Polk angrily noted, with the malign connivance of the Hunkers—was a prelude to all-out war. By the spring and early summer of 1847, the undaunted congressional antislavery Democrats, including Preston King and David Wilmot, looked to Wright, the Hunkers' victim, as their candidate for the Democratic presidential nomination in 1848. So did a number of men in the pragmatic wing of the Liberty Party, including Salmon P. Chase, who promised Wright that the party would support him if he ran on a pro–Wilmot Proviso platform. A series of Democratic antislavery mass meetings in New York State, beginning in January, 1847, augured a convergence of Liberty men and dissident Barnburners.[13]

Wright was a shrewd as well as a popular choice for the antislavery forces. A charter member of Van Buren's Albany Regency, he had complete credibility as a professional politician who had always submerged his personal interests on behalf of the Democratic Party: honest, unselfish, and affable, if much too fond of alcohol. Wright also had strong antislavery credentials, dating back to his opposition to Texas annexation. His defeat in 1846, at the hands of the Whigs and the Hunkers—and, it was wrongly assumed, President Polk—had only elevated his stature among antislavery Democrats. After his loss, Wright returned to his plebeian rural origins in northern New York, quit drinking, and worked hard on his farm, with his public life, he thought, behind him. Apparently he was uninterested when, in 1847, his name began appearing atop newspaper mastheads as the people's choice for president. But none of it would matter, for in August, Wright keeled over from a heart attack and died, at age fifty-two.[14]

"Burnt out at last," Calhoun reveled when he heard of Wright's passing. Barnburners and other antislavery Democrats were disconsolate. "Ah, it has a crashing effect, still!" Walt Whitman wrote soon after hearing the news, adding that all Radical Democrats "were so identified with this man—relied so upon him in the future—were so accustomed to look upon him as our tower of strength, as a shield for righteous people—that we indeed feel pressed to the very earth by such an unexpected blow." The Barnburners were still grief-stricken when New York's Democrats gathered in Syracuse for their state convention two weeks later. Even without Wright's death, they would have fought hard with the Hunkers over state economic policy and national policy on slavery, but now the Barnburners also had a martyr. "The great chiefs of both factions were on the ground," the visiting Liberty Party abolitionist Henry B. Stanton observed, "and never was there a more fierce, bitter and relentless conflict between the Narragansetts and the Pequods than this memorable contest between the Barnburners and the Hunkers." A Barnburner delegate called on the convention to do justice to Silas Wright; a Hunker sneered in reply that it was too late, Wright was dead; whereupon another Barnburner leapt atop a table and declaimed that, though it might be too late to do Wright justice, "it is not too late to do justice to his assassins." The Hunkers, controlling a small majority of the delegates, defeated resolutions endorsing the Wilmot Proviso and seized the state party machinery. The embittered Barnburners left the convention and, led by John Van Buren, called for a meeting of their own in October in the nearby town of Herkimer.[15]

United in their outrage, the Barnburners differed over strategy and tactics. Many of the older heads, as well as Van Buren's sympathetic father, thought an overtly disloyal breakaway movement would prove self-defeating, and tried to head off the dissidents' meeting. But to the younger schismatics, all of the injuries since the 1844 national convention had begun to dissolve into a revolt against Polk, the Slave Power, and their Hunker servants. The events of August and September also touched an antislavery nerve among rank-and-file Barnburner Democrats that no call to party regularity could relieve. More than four thousand persons turned up in tiny Herkimer and gathered at the railroad station, the largest building in town. The old radical Jacksonian and Loco Foco sympathizer Churchill Cambreleng was brought in to lend a sense of continuity with the past, and named president of the assembly. David Wilmot proclaimed that the party's abiding mission was "to elevate man, to vindicate his rights, to secure his happiness"—a mission that "Slavery commands halt." The main speaker, John Van Buren, held the crowd rapt with his enthusiastic oratory—a skill his father had never commanded—and demanded no further extension of slavery, "in behalf of the free white laborers of the North and the South." The convention summarized the antislavery Democracy's outlook with a credo that would resound in American politics over the next dozen years: "Free Trade, Free Labor, Free Soil, Free Speech, and Free Men."[16]

"I know of no event in the History of Parties in this County, at all approaching, in sublimity & moment, the Herkimer Convention," Salmon Chase wrote to Charles Sumner. Regular Democrats, as well as older Barnburner sympathizers like Martin Van Buren, took a different view, as the party's division led directly to Whig triumphs in the fall election. (Pro-Herkimer Democrats, determined to defeat the Hunker candidate for governor, handed in spoiled ballots, inscribed "REMEMBER SILAS WRIGHT!") But as autumn gave way to winter, antislavery insurgents began pleading with old Van Buren to try once again for the presidency, this time on a pro–Wilmot Proviso platform. "You, Sir, are the only man left for us in the North, to whom we can look for advice," Wilmot wrote to the former president. Van Buren, who steadfastly refused publicly to endorse the Wilmot Proviso, kept Democrats guessing until late December, when he suddenly departed Lindenwald and took up quarters in New York City, at Julien's Hotel on Washington Square. There he would begin a new political venture.[17]

In Washington, debates over the war issue dragged on. The new Congress that assembled in December included an enlarged number of antislavery Whigs—part of the new Whig majority in the House of Representatives elected in 1846. These new arrivals were not as radical on the slavery issue as the Joshua Giddings hard core, but they were likely to raise uncomfortable partisan issues about Polk's handling of the war. Outside Washington, antislavery men in both parties were angrier than ever at their respective party establishments. Yet even in the North, conservative Democrats and conservative Whigs controlled the state parties' machinery, and as the presidential election year dawned, it seemed likely that they and their southern colleagues would control the national parties as well. Among antislavery men, there was no consensus on whether to fight the good fight from within or to take the politically risky course of allying with the Liberty men and forming a party of their own. And in the South, there remained the perpetual puzzlement over what John C. Calhoun would do, and what difference it would make.

THE AMERICAN 1848: BACKGROUND TO REVOLT

Revolutions tore across Europe in 1848, proclaiming a new age of liberal democracy—until reaction overtook the revolutionaries and installed a revised version of the post-Napoleonic conservative order. A similar, if far less violent dynamic unfolded in the United States. While Whigs viewed the European revolutions with dismay—"Poor France," Henry Clay said when he heard the news of the Paris uprising—Democrats of all factions hailed the demise of despotism and the vindication of the rights of man. Antislavery Democrats took the uprisings as a spur to their own labors. *"Shall we, in view of these struggles of all Europe, with our model before them,"* the Barnburner O. C. Gardiner wrote in one pamphlet, *"renounce the doctrine of our fathers, and the sentiments of the civilized world, that slavery is an evil?"*[18]

General Scott's victory at Mexico City had ended the military phase of the war, but the diplomatic phase that followed proved politically nearly as difficult. As long as the dispatches of military triumph had flowed in, patriotic fervor helped offset sectional divisions. But when weeks passed with no final treaty, political fights took precedence. Although vanquished on the field, the Mexican government refused to negotiate a settlement—suspicious, Polk's opponents claimed, that the administration now intended to swallow up most or even all of Mexico. "We should have had peace in September, but for the inexorable determination of the Executive to acquire a large slice of Mexico by conquest," Greeley's *Tribune* changed. Those charges gained credence in December when Polk, in his annual message, requested additional monies and troops to conclude the war, denounced the No Territory doctrine as an acknowledgment of American guilt, and claimed that the only alternative left to Mexico was "an adequate cession of territory" to the United States. Some took this to mean, despite Polk's explicit denials, that the "adequate cession" ought to be the entire country of Mexico.[19]

The "All Mexico" movement, which the president supposedly supported in secret, caught fire amid the frustrations of the autumn of 1847, and it assembled some strange bedfellows. Its leading proponents were the Manifest Destiny Democrats of the eastern penny press, who saw the total absorption of the foe as a blow for universal freedom. But a small number of antislavery advocates, led by Gamaliel Bailey, came up with their own version of the plan, whereby any or all of Mexico's nineteen states could voluntarily choose to join the United States. Like the antislavery Whigs, Bailey had denounced the war as unchristian and a threat to American democracy (although he ridiculed Whigs who criticized the conflict yet continued to vote in favor of war appropriations). Yet, Bailey also approved of the expansionist drive to acquire new territories, so long as it was done, as he put it, "by the natural process of colonization and assimilation." Now that Mexico was conquered, the United States had a duty to widen republicanism's ambit, and not leave its defeated foe in disarray. Above all, Bailey assumed that as the Mexican states had already abolished slavery, they would remain free states under the American flag, and send a large new crop of antislavery senators and representatives to Washington—a complete inversion of what most antiwar Whigs and abolitionists believed was the war's underlying evil motive.[20]

How much the All Mexico movement actually influenced the Polk administration is questionable, although within the cabinet both Secretary Buchanan
and Secretary Walker were known to be sympathetic. But the strong perception
that it had gained the initiative reinforced the Whig Party's solidarity across sectional lines. Among moderate and conservative northern Whigs, the idea, to
them repugnant, of grabbing all of Mexico, slave or free, strengthened support
for the No Territory position. Among southern Whigs, the All Mexico proposal
had the additional repellent aspect of adding new states that were unfit for slavery
and populated by antagonistic racial inferiors, unfit for enlightened free government. "Do you wish to be placed at the mercy of ten millions," one Georgia
Whig paper asked, "hostile to you, as enemies and conquerors, in the first place,
and as supporters of [slavery] in the next?" With their slender majority in the new
House, the Whigs could cause Polk significant political trouble if they unified
behind No Territory.[21]

The antiwar Whigs also had enough southern sectionalist allies to thwart a
few of Polk's grander initiatives. On January 4, 1848, Calhoun delivered a major
speech reiterating the defensive line strategy he had proposed a year earlier.
Going further with the war, he warned, would turn the United States into an
"imperial power" and would only compound the nation's racial difficulties. "I
protest against the incorporation of such a people," Calhoun observed of the
Indian and "mixed blood" Mexicans: "Ours is the government of the white
man." The alliance of Calhounites and Whigs blocked an administration appropriations bill to fund the raising of ten new regiments, and stymied the president's requests for twenty thousand new volunteers to fight the war and for duties
on coffee and tea to help pay for it.[22]

These anti-administration victories hardly signaled the rise of a unified and
all-powerful antiwar opposition. Even for the No Territory Whigs, the largest
group, articulating an agreed-upon policy proved easier than acting on it when
faced with practical choices. Most shared the view that Congress ought to reject
Polk's requests for more appropriations, but others, wanting to avoid looking
unsupportive of American troops, agreed to ordinary requests for supplies. Still
others, eager to end the war and fearing that Polk could successfully seize all of
Mexico no matter how much Congress objected, announced their willingness to
compromise and accept new territory short of what one editor called "the line
where indemnity ends and conquest begins," usually meaning New Mexico and
California. Divided among themselves, as well as against the pro-Wilmot minority, the No Territory Whigs had to fall back on whatever ingenious maneuvers
they could to embarrass the Polk administration and the Democrats.[23]

One of the most partisan of these Whig schemers was the ambitious ex-state
legislator from Illinois whom Martin Van Buren had run across in 1842: Abraham Lincoln. In 1846, Lincoln finally overcame his melancholia and won elec-

tion to Congress. The sole Whig representative from heavily Democratic (and heavily pro-war) Illinois, Lincoln went along with the administration's supply requests. But as if to prove his Whig bona fides, he also introduced a series of resolutions demanding that the administration provide evidence that the spot on which American blood was first shed over Texas was indeed on American soil. Lincoln pronounced Polk guilty of deception in getting the war started, and attacked him personally as "a bewildered, confounded, and miserably-perplexed man." His so-called spot resolutions earned their author the derisive nickname "Spotty" Lincoln but accomplished little else. After declining to run for reelection, he returned home to Springfield in 1849, the latest congressional one-term wonder.[24]

Suddenly, in late February, news arrived that a peace treaty had been concluded in Mexico and been sent to Polk for his consideration and agreement. The president's negotiator, Nicholas Trist, had accompanied Scott's army into Mexico City and, after being snubbed repeatedly by the Mexicans, received orders from Polk to return home. But Trist disobeyed, reopened talks with a newly elected Mexican regime, and, on February 2, signed a treaty in the village of Guadalupe Hidalgo, near the capital. Compared to what Polk had envisaged in 1845, the deal turned out to be a bargain: the United States would secure all of Texas above the Rio Grande and receive Upper California and New Mexico in exchange for $15 million plus American assumption of all outstanding private American claims against Mexico, which totaled about $3.25 million. Polk at first hesitated, unclear about the agreement's legitimacy, but after recognizing that Trist had negotiated under the terms originally set for him, and that any prolongation of the war would be even more politically disastrous, Polk sent the treaty to the Senate for ratification. A war begun under dubious circumstances would end with dubious authority.[25]

Senate approval of the treaty was not assured. Several members of the Foreign Relations Committee, of both parties, objected that Trist had had no powers to negotiate on behalf of the government once he had been recalled. Some Democrats thought the agreement gave the United States far too little territory; some Whigs, including the die-hard No Territory man Daniel Webster, thought it gave the United States far too much. But as secret deliberations continued, the prospect of finally ending the war overcame all other considerations. "The desire for peace," Calhoun wrote, "& not the approbation of its terms, induces the Senate to yield its consent." After two weeks of discussion, the Senate approved the treaty in a lopsided vote of 38 to 14 that cut across both partisan and sectional lines. The political press, although not uniformly pleased with the result, expressed relief that wonderful peace had returned.[26]

In antislavery circles, the relief was mixed with sorrow. On February 21, the same day the Senate received the treaty with Mexico, the House was debating one of the honorific resolutions of gratitude to the military that antiwar forces routinely voted against, but that always passed. Suddenly, Washington Hunt of New York interrupted the Speaker, and several members rushed over to the desk of eighty-year-old John Quincy Adams, who, after attempting to rise to make some remarks, had toppled nearly to the floor, his face flushed. Carried from the airless chamber into the Speaker's room, Adams lay, barely conscious, for two days. In a passing moment of alertness, he asked to have Henry Clay brought to him, and the old battlers bid each other a tearful goodbye. "This is the end of earth—I am composed," Adams is said to have murmured, and then he was dead.[27]

Adams had been the last link in American politics to the era of the American Revolution. In death, he received the public acclaim he had longed for, and never quite received, in his lifetime. Masses of Americans mourned him, both in the Capitol where he lay in state and alongside the railroad tracks over which his body returned to Boston, where thousands lined up to catch a glimpse of the funeral train. Thomas Hart Benton and Daniel Webster wrote tributes; Isaac Holmes of South Carolina, who had supported Adams's censure in 1842, put politics aside to mourn the passing of "the PATRIOT SAGE." (Henry A. Wise had already complimented Adams, backhandedly, as "the acutest, the astutest, the archest enemy of Southern slavery that ever existed.") Little of this would have been imaginable had Adams died before his return to Congress: it was Adams's second career, and his canny fight against the Slave Power, that brought him popular adulation. Although Old Man Eloquent Adams remained too set in his independent ways to endorse political abolitionism outright—or to give more than qualified support to the Wilmot Proviso—he had opened a path that younger antislavery politicians had followed and would follow over the years to come. They included three men present on the floor of the House when he was stricken: the political abolitionist Henry B. Stanton, the radical Whig Joshua Giddings, and the moderate Whig Abraham Lincoln.[28]

The conclusion of the Mexican War—celebrated on July 4, when President Polk formally declared the Treaty of Guadalupe Hidalgo in effect—ended debate over the extent of American expansion, but brought the slavery extension issue to the fore once again, now entangled in presidential politics. Either the national parties and their candidates would support the principles of the Wilmot Proviso or they would not—a matter some would raise insistently and others would do their utmost to evade.

Among the Democrats, who would hold their nominating convention first, attention focused on the badly divided New Yorkers. In February, the Barnburn-ers met in Utica to select their own slate of delegates to the Baltimore nominat-ing convention and adopt a pro–Wilmot Proviso platform. (The Hunkers had held their own meeting in late January.) Passions had cooled slightly since the

Herkimer convention, and to prove their party loyalty, the Barnburners dropped the demand that any Democratic presidential candidate support nonextension of slavery. But the growing insurgency had also won over some of the older Barnburners, above all Martin Van Buren. Later that winter, with the help of his son John and Samuel Tilden, Van Buren composed an address, soon to be known as the Barnburner Manifesto, to be read to the Democrats of the state legislature. Although it backed no national candidate, the document emphatically endorsed the Wilmot Proviso and insisted that the Barnburner delegation alone be seated at the Baltimore convention.[29]

At last, the elder Van Buren had taken an unequivocal stance on the extension of slavery. "Free labor and slave labor . . . cannot flourish under the same laws," the manifesto asserted. "The wealthy capitalists who own slaves disdain manual labor, and the whites who are compelled to submit to it . . . cannot act on terms of equality with the masters." If he still refused to allow his own name to be put forward as a pro-Wilmot candidate at the Democratic national convention, Van Buren was eager to put his hard-fought wisdom in service to the dissidents' cause. To his son John, he stressed the importance of blending firmness with common sense. A "single rash and unadvised step" would make them look "indifferent to the general success of the party," motivated by a desire "to revenge past injuries or indulge personal piques." If not admitted to the convention on a full and equal footing with the other delegates, he counseled, the Barnburners should depart the proceedings, making clear that they did so "upon the ground of opposition to the extension of Slavery to free Territories." If admitted, they should make their case to the convention, but be prepared to support whatever candidate won the nomination—unless it was the now intolerable James K. Polk. In late May, the Barnburners traveled to Baltimore full of Van Buren's advice. They would insist on their legitimacy as the sole voice of the New York Democracy and fight to uphold nonextension of slavery—two matters that were now one and the same.[30]

The convention, starting on May 22, could not have gone worse for the Barnburners. After a day of preliminaries, the delegates took up the Barnburners' and Hunkers' rival credentials claims, and the hall turned into a cacophonous confusion. First the credentials committee attempted summarily to award New York's seats to the Hunkers. Led by the Barnburners' bitter opponent, William Lowndes Yancey of Alabama—who may have feared such a precedent might some day be used against pro-slavery men—the convention allowed the Barnburners to make their case. For four hours, the delegates listened to each side. Yancey then moved a resolution that denounced the Barnburners as "factious Whigs in disguise and abolitionists" and awarded the seats to the Hunkers, but after a break for dinner, he withdrew his motion. Finally, the convention decided, by a tiny majority, to allow both delegations to be seated and cast New York's votes jointly. The next day, both sides refused the offer but resolutely held on to their seats in the convention hall.[31]

Unable to resolve the New York impasse, the delegates proceeded to the nominations. Polk, true to his original pledge, had decided not to try again, and the three top contenders were familiar: the conservatives James Buchanan and Lewis Cass, and the moderate Levi Woodbury. After an eight-ballot battle—with all of the New Yorkers looking on glumly—the nomination went to Cass, the uninspiring Michigander who had initially supported the Wilmot Proviso and then led the fight in Congress against it. Tumultuous applause greeted the announcement of Cass's triumph—then, suddenly, one of the sidelined Barnburner delegates, M. J. C. Smith, arose to speak. With the hall hushed, Smith denounced the convention and its candidate, and when he finished, all of the Barnburner delegates angrily walked out. They had not followed Van Buren's advice to the letter: by bolting the convention after the convention had selected its candidate, and not immediately upon being denied their full credentials, they invited accusations (as Van Buren had predicted) of an unpardonable breach of party decorum. Soon, however, the Barnburners and their allies would be planning an even larger rebellion—and Van Buren would wind up heading it.[32]

The loyalist Democrats completed their work by naming the anti-Wilmot military hero and former congressman William O. Butler of Kentucky as Cass's running mate, and by approving a platform that condemned those who would "induce Congress to interfere with questions of slavery, or to take incipient steps in relation thereto." This was not good enough for Yancey and the more militant pro-slavery southerners. Although mostly satisfied with the platform, they understood that Cass had endorsed an alternative to the Wilmot Proviso which had gained currency among northern moderate and conservative Democrats—the idea of "popular sovereignty," whereby, at some undetermined date, the inhabitants of a territory could decide for themselves whether slavery would be permitted. As the platform was unclear on the matter, Yancey moved an amendment that would have committed the party to the core idea of the Platform of the South, that all territories be opened to slaveholders and their property. The convention resoundingly defeated the motion, whereupon Yancey and another Alabaman along with the Florida delegation walked out amid loud jeers.[33]

Two weeks later, the Whigs opened their convention in Philadelphia. Both of the party's grand old men, Henry Clay and Daniel Webster, had announced for the nomination, but Webster enjoyed only the lukewarm endorsement of his own state's delegation and was nearly forgotten; and Clay, although still revered, was a two-time loser who remained suspect on all sides of the slavery question. The really exciting prospect to the party insiders was General Zachary Taylor. Apart from being the most celebrated man in America, Taylor owned slaves and a large Louisiana cotton plantation, which made him safe enough for the South, especially compared to the Yankee Democratic nominee, Lewis Cass. Taylor had also disagreed with Polk about the conduct of the war, and at one point asked to be relieved of his command, which softened his image among some northerners. Best of all, Taylor's own politics were so indistinct that on the eve of the presidential contest, it was not entirely clear which party he favored, making him an ideal figure in a divisive time. (When he finally chose the Whigs, he hastened to add that he was "not an ultra Whig," sustaining his useful ambiguity.) Taylor stood for national glory as opposed to sectional or partisan division. Indeed, more than Whig managers understood or would have preferred, Taylor, the professional soldier, would come to regard nonpartisanship as a fundamental principle, in government as well as in electioneering.[34]

Taylor's bandwagon of diverse supporters came to Philadelphia well prepared. (They included Abraham Lincoln who, though he worshipped Henry Clay, had decided Clay could never win.) A strong plurality went to Taylor on the first ballot, including several delegates previously pledged to Clay; two ballots later, Clay's forces nearly broke; on the fourth ballot, Taylor was nominated. After selecting the conservative New Yorker Millard Fillmore as Taylor's running mate, and not bothering to approve a platform, the convention adjourned. (After the fact, the Whigs issued a platitudinous simulacrum of a platform, affirming little more than that Taylor, "had he voted in 1844, would have voted the Whig ticket," and promising "Peace, Prosperity, and Union.") The antiwar and anti-annexation party had nominated the greatest hero of the war for the presidency of the United States.[35]

As Old Zach's energized supporters returned home to campaign, other Whigs stood aghast. Horace Greeley, a pro-Clay New York delegate, called the convention "a slaughterhouse of Whig principles." Fifteen other northern delegates and alternates asked a group of Ohio antislavery men led by Salmon Chase (who had already scheduled a Free Territory Convention in Columbus later in the month) to convene an additional anti-extension convention in Buffalo, New York, early in August, in order to forge some sort of merger. The Columbus meeting, one thousand strong, approved the idea, while all across the North, antislavery Whigs repudiated the Philadelphia convention. "This is the cup offered by the slaveholders for us to drink," one Ohio paper protested. "We loathe the sight."[36] The stage was nearly set for the Free Soil revolt.

"THE GREATEST QUESTION OF THE DAY": THE FREE SOIL REVOLT

Two weeks after Taylor's nomination, the New York Barnburners held their own meeting, once again in Utica. After their walkout at the Democratic convention, there was intense pressure on the rebels to curb their anger—or at least direct it solely against the New York Hunkers. But there were also great public outbursts of antislavery support. A large crowd greeted the mutinous Barnburner delegates at the Manhattan train station when they returned from Baltimore, whence the Barnburners went to City Hall Park to deliver defiant speeches before an even larger crowd of twelve thousand. "A clap of political thunder will be heard in this country next November that will make the propogandists of slavery shake like Belshazzar," exclaimed the old Regency man and Barnburner Samuel Young (the same man who had led the fight against black suffrage in 1821). A few days later, the delegation formally asked the New York party to repudiate Cass's nomination—"the price of the most abject subserviency to the slave power"—and then to select its own presidential candidate in Utica on June 22. The insurgency spread among Democrats in New York State, then throughout the North. Hundreds of Barnburners turned up in Utica, along with a small number of antislavery New York Whigs and about twenty antislavery Democratic representatives from Massachusetts, Connecticut, Ohio, Illinois, and Wisconsin. Letters and telegrams pledging support poured in from across the North. The delegates resolved to form what they called Jeffersonian Leagues to fight for "Free Soil and free principles."[37]

All that the movement lacked was a candidate. Benton turned the rebels down; so did New York's more conservative senator John Dix and (the unlikeliest selection) John Hale's persecutor in New Hampshire, Franklin Pierce. It was almost inevitable that the antislavery organizers would return to Martin Van Buren—and, to his friends' dismay, Van Buren seemed increasingly willing at least to leave the possibility open. Only Benjamin Butler of all the old Regency men encouraged Van Buren, envisaging a "northern Democratic party" that might "bring the despots & ingrates of the South & their obsequious satellites of the North, to their senses." ("I consider the prohibition of Slavery in the territories now free, the greatest question of the day," Butler wrote. "[A]s soon as the Mexican war is ended, it will be the only question . . . and fifty years hence, those who took a firm stand for the prohibition will be regarded as the greatest of public benefactors.") When asked to reconsider and allow his name to be put forward at Utica, Van Buren wrote two lengthy drafts before composing a nineteen-page reply. After claiming he did not wish to run, Van Buren called slavery inconsistent with the "principles of the Revolution," and declared that it should be kept out of the territories. Butler read the document to the Barnburners at Utica, who, swept away, inferred, correctly, that Van Buren actually would consent to run, and nominated him for president as a pro-Wilmot Democrat. Their platform defended the walkout in Baltimore, endorsed a number of traditional Democratic positions, upheld the Wilmot Proviso, and denounced slavery "as a great moral, social, and political evil—a relic of barbarism which must necessarily be swept away in the progress of Christian civilization."[38]

The Utica outcome was as disturbing to mainstream national Democrats as it was suspect to many antislavery veterans. President Polk called it "more threatening to the Union" than anything since the Hartford Convention. One southern Democrat attacked Van Buren's Utica letter as "the fierce war-cry of a new and formidable party," headed by a crafty politician reborn as "a bold, unscrupulous and vindictive demagogue." At the other end of the spectrum, Liberty men had strong misgivings about Van Buren from his days when he endorsed the gag rule, opposed abolition in the District of Columbia, and otherwise deferred to the slaveholders. Salmon P. Chase said he would have preferred John Van Buren to his father as the nominee. Others, including antislavery Whigs, sought assurances about Van Buren's sincerity.[39]

The momentum of the Utica meeting, however, pushed both political abolitionists and antislavery Whigs into the pro–Van Buren Democratic camp. John Parker Hale, who had received the Liberty Party's presidential endorsement the previous year, was willing to stand aside for the sake of unity. Preparatory to the grand antislavery meeting in Buffalo, now scheduled for August 9, the practical good sense of rallying behind Van Buren and the Barnburners began to dawn on political antislavery advocates. "[T]hings tend to Van Buren as our candidate," Charles Sumner remarked. "I am willing to take him. With him we can break the slavepower; that is our first aim." There was even a new name being bandied about as the antislavery label: either the Free Democracy or, even better, the Free Soil Party.[40]

Van Buren's decision to join a schism, let alone lead one, was obviously difficult, but it cannot be explained as an act of revenge, as many of his critics and later historians alleged. Van Buren's resentment of the Hunkers and the Polk administration, and his concerns over who would control both the state and national parties, had certainly worsened since 1844. The downfall of the now-martyred Silas Wright had been the last straw. But Van Buren's anger was controlled and purposeful, and it involved basic principles about slavery and antislavery as well as factional loyalties. If he was far from the most outspoken or radical of the Barnburners on the slavery-extension question, Van Buren had long been sympathetic to men like Theodore Sedgwick III and Silas Wright. His momentous letter on Texas annexation in 1844 was hardly calculated to advance his standing in the South, where he had always been suspect, and he had never renounced it. Van Buren's calm and measured correspondence in 1847 and 1848, and his steadily solidifying support for the principle of nonextension, betray no sense of vengefulness; indeed, he took pains to warn the younger Barnburners to avoid such impulses or even the appearance of them. Van Buren's intensely political side and his sense of principle had merged into a mistrust of the increasingly aggressive pro-slavery forces that had apparently grabbed the helm of the Democratic Party—forces, he told Francis Blair, that had "grossly humiliated" northern Democrats in order to expand slavery. Whereas in the 1830s, Van Buren had accommodated southern demands while trying to temper the Calhounite extremists, he now hoped that a show of force would knock some sense back into the southern Democrats and restore the balance of sectional forces on which the party had been built—after which it would be safe to rejoin the party he had helped to found. If pushing back the Slave Power was the only way to redeem the Democracy, then Van Buren was willing to lead the way.[41]

Other unexpected events accompanied the Barnburner revolt, including another democratic uprising in central New York—one very different from and far smaller than the Barnburners', but encouraged by the atmosphere of rebellion that pervaded the politics of 1848. Henry B. Stanton, the abolitionist and Liberty Party activist, kept in close touch with the antislavery Barnburners, whom he admired as the "Girondists of the Democracy." Stanton had attended the 1847 Syracuse convention as an interested spectator. He would go on to play a leading role at the Buffalo meeting in August 1848 and win a seat in the New York state senate as a Free Soiler in 1849. Also in 1848, he moved with his wife Elizabeth and their three sons from the clatter of Boston to the small, drab mill town of Seneca Falls, New York, in the heart of the reformist region that had successively spawned evangelical revivals, abolitionist campaigns, and utopian experiments—and was now roiled by the Barnburner insurgency.[42]

Elizabeth Cady Stanton, at age thirty-three, was an accomplished woman. The daughter of the prominent Federalist jurist, law teacher, and, eventually, state Supreme Court justice Daniel Cady, she had been educated at Emma Willard's pioneering Troy Female Seminary and had been well schooled informally in legal affairs by her father. Encounters with fugitive slaves while visiting the home of her wealthy cousin, Gerrit Smith, led Cady to the abolitionist movement, where she met Henry Stanton, whom she married (against her father's wishes) in 1840. It was a match of tireless reformers. Less than two weeks after their wedding, the couple embarked for London, where, along with other leading American abolitionists including William Lloyd Garrison, they attended a momentous World Anti-Slavery Congress—a meeting notable for the Americans' refusal to heed the convention rule separating male from female delegates with a curtain.[43]

Living on the outskirts of Boston, Henry and Elizabeth Stanton were at home in the most active abolitionist circles, which included the already legendary Philadelphia Quaker Garrisonian, Lucretia Mott, whom Elizabeth had befriended at the London congress in 1840. Yet while she participated in various lobbying efforts to reform laws discriminatory to women, Stanton stepped back from full-time engagement to attend to her growing family. The withdrawal brought enormous personal satisfactions, but also frustrations, which became intolerable after the move to isolated Seneca Falls. With her husband nearly always gone on his antislavery work, with three sons to look after and no house-hold help, Stanton began to suffer, she later recalled, from "mental hunger which, like an empty stomach, is very depressing." Overwhelmed, she retreated for a time to her parents' home in Johnstown. A daguerreotype of Stanton from these years shows an attractive, slightly disheveled young mother entwined with two of her sons—but with an arresting, searching stare.[44]

In July 1848, James and Lucretia Mott, on a journey through upstate New York, paid their annual summer visit to see Lucretia's sister Martha and Martha's husband, David Wright, in Auburn. A Quaker neighbor in nearby Waterloo, Jane Hunt, invited Lucretia and Martha to tea, with the happy news that Elizabeth Stanton, now living only a few miles down the road, would be joining them, along with another friend, Mary Ann McClintock. The table talk quickly turned to pol-itics—and to a promise that Stanton and Mott had made to each other, at the con-clusion of the London convention eight years earlier, to form a society to advocate the rights of women. Soon, Elizabeth was pouring out her personal dissatisfac-tions with such vehemence that, she later recalled, "I stirred myself, as well as the rest of the party, to do and dare anything." The next day, a notice appeared in the *Seneca County Courier*, announcing that a two-day Woman's Rights Convention would be held the following week at the Wesleyan Chapel in Seneca Falls, featur-ing a speech by none other than the celebrated Lucretia Mott.[45]

To the organizers' delighted surprise, upward of three hundred persons crowded the Seneca Falls chapel on the convention's first day. (Originally, the first session was supposed to be open to women only, but after a hasty caucus, the organizers decided to allow the men, including Mott's husband, to stay.) For two days, the participants were treated to a heady mixture of history, reportage, and satire on the oppressed status of women in the United States and around the world. Lucretia Mott, not surprisingly, dominated the proceedings. But Stanton and McClintock also addressed the convention, and Stanton, the lawyer's daugh-ter, had taken on the job of composing a declaration of sentiments. She wrote the document as a self-conscious adaptation of Jefferson's Declaration of Inde-pendence, altered to proclaim that all men and women were created equal—with the demand that women be accorded "the sacred right of elective franchise." The most celebrated man in attendance, Frederick Douglass, Mott's fellow Garrisonian, helped persuade the group to approve a suffrage resolution, which passed by a narrow margin. At the conclusion, Mott took the floor again to give a spirited address that lasted nearly an hour, exhorting women to press on with their fight. One hundred of those present, one-third of them men, signed Stanton's manifesto.[46]

The backlash was immediate. Conservative Whig newspapers served up par-ticularly savage commentary. "[A] dreadful revolt," the *Oneida Whig* pro-claimed, adding that the convention was "the most shocking and unnatural incident ever recorded in the history of womanity." At the *New York Herald*, James Gordon Bennett handled the story as if it were a farce, and took special pleasure in smearing Lucretia Mott as a misfit full of "old maidish crochets and socialist violations of Christian dignity." Only the antislavery press took the convention at all seriously.[47]

The Seneca Falls convention drew on more than the sudden inspiration of Mott, Stanton, and their friends. Legal reformism, free-thought radicalism, Quaker piety, and abolitionism all had an influence, and would create the foundations of the American women's rights movement for the next half century.[48] But the meeting was certainly connected closely, in spirit as well as timing, to the Barnburner revolt—an indication of how the rifts over slavery were opening up new democratic possibilities. The greatest common political identification of the participants at Seneca Falls—including eighteen of the twenty-six separate families with members who signed the Declaration of Sentiments—was with the emerging Free Soil alliance, including the most radical Barnburner Democrats, antislavery Whigs, and the pragmatic wing of the Liberty Party. It was not that most Free Soilers were also women's rights advocates. (If they had been, the meeting at Seneca Falls would have been far larger than it was.) Nor did Stanton, Mott, and the others act to advance the Barnburners' or the Liberty Party's political fortunes. Still, a highly disproportionate number of those who turned up at Seneca Falls were tied in one way or another to the Free Soil milieu. For them, as for Stanton, women's rights was a logical extension of the fight for liberty, equality, and independence being waged by the antislavery forces that, during the Seneca Falls convention, were preparing to take their stand three weeks later in Buffalo.[49]

The antislavery forces generated a mass movement in late June and July, proclaiming America's version of the revolution of 1848—a revolution fought not at the barricades but in convention halls, village greens, and city streets across the North. Less than a week after the Barnburners' Utica meeting, five thousand Conscience Whigs, along with a handful of Massachusetts Democrats, assembled in Worcester, listened to speeches attacking what Charles Sumner called the unholy alliance between "cotton planters and flesh mongers of Louisiana" and "cotton spinners and traffickers in New England," and selected six delegates to attend the upcoming Buffalo convention. Smaller antislavery meetings assembled throughout New England and New York, organized by Whigs and Democrats alike. Antislavery activity in the Northwest amazed observers. "We cannot find room for even brief notices of all the Free Soil meetings in Ohio," the *National Era* reported. "The people there seem to be cutting loose *en masse* from the old party organizations." In Indiana—previously cold to third-party antislavery politics—and in Michigan, statewide and local gatherings selected delegations to Buffalo and resolved to end all partisan differences in order to unite "for the one great cause of Free Soil and Free Labor." In Chicago, processions of antislavery Democrats and Whigs snaked through the city, chanting Martin Van Buren's name.[50]

The Buffalo National Free Soil Convention was multifarious and boisterous. Barnburners, Whigs, and Liberty men predominated, with a substantial portion of the latter two groups still uneasy about nominating Van Buren. But there were many other elements present, each holding some grievance against one or both of the major political parties: Democrats indifferent to the slavery issue but still rankled by Van Buren's snubbing in 1844; Clay Whigs furious at the nomination of Zachary Taylor; antislavery Whigs "breathing the spirit of the departed John Quincy Adams" (as Henry Stanton later put it); northwesterners, chiefly Democrats, angry at Polk's veto of river and harbor improvements; and land reformers allied with George Henry Evans, who now thought cheap homesteads were the workingman's salvation. Gathered beneath a massive tent erected in the city's public park, the army of political pilgrims, no fewer than twenty thousand persons, reminded observers of a gigantic religious revival.[51]

Among the crowds was a delegate from Brooklyn, the pro-Wilmot Democrat Walt Whitman, recently returned from an extended stay in New Orleans. Whitman's outspoken views on politics and slavery had cost him his job as editor of the *Brooklyn Daily Eagle*, whose owner was an unforgiving Hunker. They had also begun shaping his poetic imagination: "I go with the slaves of the earth equally with the masters," he wrote in his notebook in 1847, among the first recorded lines in what would become his mature style. But the poet was still in the middle of what Ralph Waldo Emerson would later call his "long foreground," and politics came first. Fired up by the mounting agitation and the Buffalo proceedings, Whitman would return to Brooklyn and begin editing a new paper he had started planning months earlier, in service to the cause: "Free Soilers! Radicals! Liberty Men! All whose throats are not rough enough to swallow Taylor or Cass! Come up and subscribe to the Daily Freeman!"[52]

The most politically awkward presence was a small group of black abolitionist leaders, including Charles Remond, Samuel Ringgold Ward, Henry Bibb, Henry Highland Garnet, and, most prominently, Frederick Douglass. Douglass had written a powerful autobiography, *Narrative of the Life of Frederick Douglass, An American Slave*, which became an immediate best-seller in 1845. After a two-year sojourn lecturing in Britain and Ireland, he settled with his wife, Anna, in Rochester, New York, an antislavery hotbed, and took up a new career as editor of the *North Star*, intended as a western equivalent of Garrison's *Liberator*. Throughout, Douglass remained, at least outwardly, a Garrisonian, upholding ideals of moral suasion and nonresistance that set him apart from Ward, Bibb, Garnet, and other black members of the Liberty Party. Yet Douglass was also in political and intellectual transition. Although wary of all party politicians—let alone one with hands as dirty as Martin Van Buren's—he attended the Buffalo gathering, curious to see how the invigorated antislavery political agitation would play itself out.[53]

Simply by showing up, Douglass and the other black leaders caused conster-nation—a sign of important racial divisions that distinguished the more Negro-phobic of the antislavery Democrats from the Liberty Party men and antislavery Whigs. Although the convention formally recognized and accepted Douglass and the others, the acceptance was not universal. One delegate later wrote that the Barnburners had not wanted Douglass admitted because "they didn't want a 'nigger' to talk to them." Others appear to have been willing to tolerate Doug-lass—who was, after all, famous—but not the other black men. Racist pro-Wilmot Democrats, who despised blacks as well as slavery, wanted to keep their Free Soil convention as lily-white as they hoped to keep the federal territories. It was a portent of the convention's eventual decision to avoid the question of black rights in its national platform, a retreat from the racial egalitarianism pro-pounded by the Liberty Party in 1840 and 1844.[54]

The most remarkable thing about the Buffalo meeting, however, was not its racism but its success in submerging political differences in the common cause—creating a program, heavily influenced by the antislavery Jacksonians' and prag-matic Liberty men's ideas, that the proud Douglass would regard as an imperfect but "noble step in the right direction." A torchlit rally in the park on the eve of the convention set the tone, as a dozen speakers called for a united effort against slav-ery and the Slave Power. "This Convention must be a self-sacrificing Conven-tion," one Barnburner speaker inveighed the next day at the convention's opening. "A crisis has arrived where old prejudices [have] got to be laid aside." With the turnout much larger than expected, Preston King devised a plan whereby each state delegation would appoint six delegates to form a committee of conferees, which would deliberate on the main issues before the convention and then refer their decision to the tented masses for ratification. The arrangement worked smoothly. Meeting behind closed doors at the Universalist Church, the conferees, chaired by Salmon Chase, appointed a subcommittee on resolutions, headed by Benjamin Butler. The main body of delegates settled in for long hours of militant speechmaking, presided over by the convention's permanent chair-man, Charles Francis Adams. (Among the speakers were Frederick Douglass and Henry Bibb, who overcame the racists' objections, received respectful applause, and wished the party well.) In time, the delegates would be asked to approve a platform, as drafted by the resolutions subcommittee and the conferees; then they would vote on the conferees' choice of national candidates.[55]

The platform, chiefly the work of Chase, Butler, and King, was an unambigu-ous call for the divorce of slavery and state. Its key plank demanded that the fed-eral government "relieve itself of all responsibility for the existence and continuance of slavery" wherever it possessed the constitutional authority to do so. This committed the new party to abolishing slavery in the District of Colum-bia as well as the territories, and to any additional action the antislavery men might decide was within the national government's purview—thereby pushing the Democratic delegates well beyond the terms of the Wilmot Proviso. The conferees added an assortment of other proposals, ranging from cheaper postal rates and a lower tariff to river and harbor improvements (the last thrown in to attract Whigs and western Democrats), but the party's main purpose was unmis-takable. The platform concluded with an abbreviated version of the Barnburn-ers' battle cry from the Herkimer meeting a year earlier: "We inscribe on our banner, 'Free Soil, Free Speech, Free Labor, and Free Men,' and under it will fight on, and fight ever, until a triumphant victory shall reward our exertions." The general assembly approved each plank in the platform with a roar.[56]

The choice of a presidential candidate presented greater difficulties. Some Liberty men and antislavery Whigs still could not stomach the idea of supporting Van Buren. (When Butler, in a speech extolling his friend, went on at length about the former president's skills as a farmer, a delegate interrupted: "D——n his turnips! What are his opinions about the abolition of slavery in the District of Columbia?") But a sense of greater purpose prevailed. "In common with my Whig associates, I had all along felt that I could not support Mr. Van Buren under any circumstances," George Julian of Indiana later recalled, "but the per-vading tone of earnestness in the Convention, and the growing spirit of political fraternity, had modified our views. We saw that several of the great leaders of the Liberty party were quite ready to meet the 'Barnburners' on common ground."[57]

The Barnburners' favorite candidate was just as ready to find common ground with the more radical political abolitionists, even if it meant giving up the Utica nomination and abandoning the Democratic Party, at least for this election. In a letter read to the committee of conferees by Benjamin Butler, Van Buren explained that although he had acquiesced in the Barnburners' nomination to help sustain "the ever faithful democracy of New York," the Buffalo convention was of far greater importance—greater, perhaps, than any before it "save, only, that which framed the Federal Constitution." Van Buren affirmed his dedication to keeping "human slavery . . . that great evil" out of the territories. (He would go on to reverse his old stance and pledge that he would sign a bill to abolish slavery in the District of Columbia.) And if, in the spirit of unity, delegates thought it better that he run solely as a Free Soiler, and not as a Democrat, he would hap-pily do so. Deafening cheers followed Butler's reading of the letter, and Van Buren was quickly nominated over the radicals' favorite John Hale, winning the support of about half the Whigs and a small but influential group of Liberty men including Salmon Chase and Henry Stanton. After a brief adjournment, the conferees named Charles Francis Adams, still grieving for his father, as Van Buren's running mate.[58]

The proposed ticket—uniting Andrew Jackson's right-hand man with the son of the man Jackson had overthrown—won the general assembly's approval with one more roar; then the assembled marched and celebrated in a torchlight parade, behind a giant banner:

'87 and '48
JEFFERSON AND VAN BUREN
No Compromise

The atmosphere of spiritual as well as political revival had converted even adamant radicals. Before the convention, Joshua Leavitt, the veteran evangelical, immediatist abolitionist, and Liberty Party man, contended dismissively that Van Buren was acting more "to avenge his old quarrel with the Hunkers than for sympathy for the cause" of free soil and antislavery. Near the convention's close, after Van Buren had won his majority, Leavitt obtained the floor and addressed the convention in a voice choked with emotion. "Mr. Chairman," he began, "this is the most solemn experience of my life. I feel as if in the immediate presence of the Divine Spirit." Then he moved that Van Buren's nomination be made unanimous, and concluded with a shout: "The Liberty party is not dead but TRANSLATED."[59]

Between them, Van Buren and Leavitt had aptly summarized the surpassing importance of the Free Soil convention. Although the new nominee flattered the delegates with his exaggerated comparison to the 1787 federal convention, he was correct to see the gathering as an important turn in American politics, the first deliberate effort to create from the grass roots, out of the disintegration of old party ties, a new political party that would seriously contend for the presidency. When Van Buren had helped cobble together the Jackson Democracy twenty years earlier, he operated from the top down; the Free Soil Party, by contrast, arose seemingly by spontaneous combustion amid the emergency over slavery in 1848. The Liberty Party had taken years to move beyond the political margins; in "translating" those efforts, the Free Soilers represented a wide-ranging political coalition from across the North, with a particularly heavy influx of pro-Wilmot Democrats. Nothing like it had been seen before, the product of a great shudder of popular revulsion and democratic organizing that united men who, all their lives, had opposed each other in politics. "The political table is now turning . . . ," one Ohio Free Soiler wrote, "and by a little effort now great changes can be wrought."[60]

Joshua Leavitt, meanwhile, although somewhat carried away by his enthusiasm, recognized correctly that the Free Soil Party had preserved the essentials of the Liberty Party's crusade, especially as it had been conducted by Salmon Chase, Gamaliel Bailey, and the pragmatic western political abolitionists. The new party did contain its share of open racists, who chiefly wanted to keep blacks out of the territories—although even they declared slavery a moral and political evil. Some spokesmen seemed to go out of their way to distance themselves from abolitionists of any variety. ("The question is not, whether black men are to be made free," one Barnburner bolter declared at the second Utica convention, "but whether we white men are to remain free.") The Free Soil platform's silence about fugitive slaves, the three-fifths clause, and racial discrimination diluted the egalitarian principles of the Liberty Party and hard-core antislavery Whigs—as, to many, did the party's nomination of Martin Van Buren. There would be those who, like William Goodell, believed that the Free Soilers betrayed political abolitionism by placing "its claim to liberty on the lowest possible ground, that of the non-extension of slavery." Many historians have agreed, and portrayed the Free Soil Party as an inglorious step backward for the antislavery movement, sacrificing the goal of black equality in a cynical effort to win votes.[61]

Leavitt and the majority of Liberty Party leaders and supporters knew better. By going beyond the Wilmot Proviso and calling for the complete divorce of slavery and the federal government, and by denouncing the moral enormity of black slavery, the Free Soil Party endorsed what had long been the primary objective of the Liberty men, and in a manner that might actually get masses of voters to listen. "It pledges the new party against the addition of any more Slave States, and to employ the Federal Government not to limit, localize, and discourage, but to abolish slavery wherever it has Constitutional power to do so," one political abolitionist said of the Buffalo platform. "This is all the Liberty party, as such, ever demanded." Whatever their constitutional scruples about interfering with the rights of slave states, observed Owen Lovejoy, brother of the abolitionist martyr Elijah Lovejoy, the two parties' "ultimate object is identical—the extinction of slavery." At those who said they could not abide the thought of voting for Martin Van Buren, Gamaliel Bailey leveled a stark retort: "It is folly to talk to us of the conduct of this man in 1836–40. You say it was subservient of slavery—grant it—what is his course now? . . . You stone Van Buren for his sins committed twelve years ago, though *you* yourself now fall far below the well-doing to which he has since attained!"[62]

Enthused by the drama of the Buffalo convention, the Free Soilers leapt into the 1848 campaign barely organized and short of time and money, but confident that their cause would sweep through the northern states. Huge majorities in the Western Reserve, Chase informed Van Buren, would swing Ohio into the Free Soil column. George Fogg, an ex-Democrat Free Soiler, thought New York would break for Van Buren, as would enough smaller northern states to throw the election into the House of Representatives. Even William Lloyd Garrison found himself caught up in the whirlwind. Although he thought the party's antiextension, pro-Wilmot position weaker than a spider's web, Garrison called it

"gratifying to see the old parties dissolving, 'like the baseless fabric of a vision,'"
and he duly reported on the Free Soilers' "eloquent appeals."[63]

"PARTY CONNEXIONS STILL RETAIN MUCH OF THEIR FORCE"

The Free Soil fever broke in November.

Early in the campaign, the Whig candidate, Zachary Taylor, began looking like a poor choice. By repeating professions about the weakness of his party ties, his campaign alienated genuine Whigs. Exasperated party managers finally prevailed on him to write a public letter stating that although he was not an "ultra" Whig, at least he was a "decided" one. It was sufficient to bring wary party members back into the fold, including antislavery men such as William Henry Seward, who were aghast at the possibility that Lewis Cass might be president. The Democrats hammered away at Taylor as two-faced and unprincipled. Cass also tried to square the circle of antislavery politics by promoting "popular sovereignty"—the somewhat vague, supposedly democratic solution that would allow the settlers in each territory to decide the slavery issue for themselves. (Taylor even more vaguely announced that he would leave the entire question up to Congress, while some of his northern supporters assured their constituents that he would never veto the Wilmot Proviso.) The Free Soilers, short on funds but long on enthusiasm, deployed dozens of "stumpers" who fanned out across the North to denounce Cass as a doughface and Taylor as a slaveholding political nonentity. The usual name-calling and campaign hoopla dominated the run-up to the election, although the electorate seemed, overall, less engaged than in the previous two elections.[64]

The Whig strategy worked. In part because of his military glory, but mainly on the strength of his being a large slaveholder, Taylor reversed the Whigs' southern setbacks in 1844, carried Georgia and Florida as well as his home state, Louisiana, and came within a whisker of winning Alabama and Mississippi. Overall, Taylor gained more than half of the total popular vote in the slave states. He also won convincingly in Pennsylvania and New Jersey. New York appeared to decide the election: by capturing more than one out of four New York voters and running second statewide, the Free Soilers took enough Democratic votes away from Lewis Cass to hand New York's thirty-six electoral votes to Taylor. Yet the Free Soilers also took enough votes away from Taylor in Ohio and, possibly, Indiana to give those states to Cass, virtually wiping out the New York advantage. Ultimately, Taylor's convincing victories in the upper South states of Kentucky, Tennessee, and North Carolina gave him the presidency.

The Van Buren–Adams ticket, meanwhile, won just 10 percent of the national popular vote and just 15 percent of the vote in the free states. The Free Soilers managed to best Cass in New York, Vermont, and Massachusetts, but failed to win a single electoral vote; in only one state, Vermont (and there just barely), did their popular vote come within 10 percentage points of doing so. Had the Free Soilers not run a presidential ticket, Taylor would probably have been elected anyway. As in Europe, it seemed the American 1848 had ended in the rebels' defeat.[65]

Why had the antislavery excitement produced what looked and felt to so many like an anticlimax? Nobody had expected the Van Buren–Adams ticket to prevail outright, but the outcome was still a letdown after the high hopes of August, when antislavery optimists had forecast a deadlocked election. Some Free Soilers who had come over from the Whigs or the Liberty Party blamed their disappointment on Van Buren's nomination, which certainly cost the party support in northeastern Ohio and other parts of greater New England. Yet the magnitude of the Free Soilers' presidential defeat cannot be explained so easily. (Nor did this explanation account for the Radical Democrats who voted Free Soil *because* Van Buren was the nominee.) Plainly, the frenzy at Buffalo unrealistically inflated expectations of the party's organizers, especially those like the exuberant Charles Sumner who had relatively little prior experience in national politics. As the election neared, Charles Francis Adams, who understood national politics well, arrived at more realistic expectations, later borne out by the result. "Enough is visible" to confirm, Adams wrote in mid-October, "that the people of the Free States are not yet roused so fully as they should be to the necessity of sustaining their principles."[66]

The party stumbled over obstacles that confront any third-party effort under the American constitutional system. Before the entry of the Free Soilers, the 1848 campaign had been a dreary affair, filled with the now-familiar spectacles staged by the party managers and focused on personal innuendo. After August, the Free Soilers enlivened the election—but at the cost of having the major parties blast them as dangerous zealots and enemies of the white man. George W. Julian later vividly recalled the abuse:

> I was subjected to a torrent of billingsgate which rivaled the fish market. Words were neither minced nor mollified, but made the vehicles of political wrath and the explosions of personal malice. The charge of abolitionism was flung at me everywhere. I was an "amalgamationist" and a "wooly head." I was branded as the "apostle of disunion" and the orator of "free dirt." It was a standing charge of the Whigs that I carried a lock of Frederick Douglass, to regale my senses with its aroma when I grew faint. . . . I was threatened with mob violence by my own neighbors.

In northern areas strongly influenced by antislavery ideas, Democrats stressed the Free Soilers' disloyalty; Whigs called the new party a bunch of Loco Foco radicals in disguise; and each party bid its old supporters not to waste their votes on a will-o'-the-wisp that would only help their old enemies. In other northern areas and in the slaveholding states (where the Van Buren ticket did not even appear on the ballot), the major parties tried to outdo each other in presenting their man as the eternal foe of Yankee "nigger"-loving heresy.[67]

On the flip side of these attacks, antislavery Whigs who might have been expected to join the Free Soil effort (and some who had appeared supportive early on) decided to stick with the Whig Party, chiefly because they saw in Old Zach a winner at last. Both leading and middle-level Whigs who either claimed to be or were viewed as being opposed to slavery's extension spurned and some-times harshly attacked the Van Buren–Adams ticket. Daniel Webster, Thurlow Weed, and Horace Greeley (who veered toward the Free Soilers but got pulled into line partly with a one-session replacement appointment to Congress), as well as less celebrated but highly effective campaigners like Thaddeus Stevens and Abraham Lincoln, all honored Whig unity and political self-preservation over the anti-extension principle in 1848. (Lincoln, a strong speaker, enthusiasti-cally stumped in antislavery areas in Massachusetts and Illinois, and said with a straight face that "the self-named 'Free Soil' party" was far behind the Whigs with regard to the Wilmot Proviso.) Except in Massachusetts and Ohio, Whig support for the Free Soilers was negligible. More than 80 percent of the Free Soil vote in New York, New Jersey, and Pennsylvania came from erstwhile Democrats, while at best only 10 percent came from the Whigs. If, from the vantage point of 1848, a seer had predicted that one of the major parties was doomed to collapse over slavery, the Democrats would have seemed the more likely of the two.[68]

Overall, the results bore out Charles Francis Adams's contention that "[p]arty connexions still retain much of their force." Outside New York, seat of the Barn-burner schism, the great preponderance of Democratic voters who went to the polls voted Democratic, and the great preponderance of Whigs voted Whig. Party identities born of the political clashes of the 1830s remained stubborn, as did fears of letting the other side prevail. To the extent that the major parties lost support in 1848, it was due more to absenteeism by an apathetic electorate who disliked all of the candidates than to defections. The most pronounced switching of parties in the country involved a surge to the Whigs in the Deep South states of Alabama and Mississippi, which the Democrats managed to win anyway; oth-erwise, the key to the outcome appears to have been that the Whigs did a better job of keeping their voters from staying at home than the Democrats did. The chief message from the voters was that most of them did not care for the sectional bitterness that at times seemed to have engulfed the nation's capital, and wanted a moderate solution to the issues connected with slavery.[69]

None of which meant, however, that the former status quo had been restored, or that the political dramas of 1848 had not affected the dynamics of American politics. Disappointment was not the same thing as repudiation. Martin Van Buren, overlooking his own inflated rhetoric of 1848, realized as much, and later expressed this sober second thought: "Everything was accomplished by the Free Soil movement that the most sanguine friend could hope for and much that there was no good reason to expect." The total vote for the Van Buren–Adams ticket marked a fivefold increase over the Liberty Party vote for Birney and Morris in 1844—a major advance for antislavery politics, even if it was smaller than the most fervent Free Soilers had expected. The Free Soilers also enjoyed some important victories in congressional contests as well as in races for local offices, electing eight men to the House and helping to elect four others in coalitions with antislavery Whigs. In 1849, an alliance of Democrats and Free Soilers in the Ohio legislature would select Salmon P. Chase for the U.S. Senate, where he would join sitting Senator John P. Hale, who had switched his affiliation to the Free Soil Party. (Simultaneously, Democratic state legislators switched their previous positions and helped finally abolish Ohio's notorious black codes.) In New York, Thurlow Weed brokered the election to the Senate of William Henry Seward—a Whig and not a Free Soiler, but a man of established antislavery convictions. More than ever, Congress would include northern members whose political careers were now linked to agitation over slavery. And, more than ever, erstwhile northern Democratic voters, by the tens of thousands, had voted for candidates of an avowedly antislavery party. The contradictions between equality and slavery that had begun hampering the old Jackson Democracy in the late 1830s were now splitting apart the northern Democracy.[70]

Nor had the election eliminated the sectionalist pro-slavery southerners as a force to be reckoned with in the future. The schismatic Alabaman William Lowndes Yancey, having been hooted out of the Democrats' Baltimore convention, did not fare much better thereafter, outside South Carolina, in trying to rally southerners behind pro-slavery principles; even the South Carolina legislature wound up handing the state's electoral votes to the Democratic ticket. Old Calhoun, now afflicted by the tuberculosis that would kill him, took a public stance of neutrality between what he said had become "two miserable factions." But in his personal correspondence, Calhoun's fury at the Democrats outweighed other considerations. "In my opinion, the best result, that can take place," he wrote from Washington in July, "is the defeat of Gen Cass, without our being responsible for it." Calhoun's wish came true—and in December, with the election safely over, he prevailed upon the South Carolina legislature to approve, unanimously, an ominous resolution, announcing its readiness "to cooperate with her sister states" in resisting any application of the Wilmot Proviso "at any and all hazards." In time, the lawmakers of Alabama, Virginia, Florida, and Missouri would endorse Calhoun's position.[71]

Above all, even if most voters seemed to favor moderation, after 1848 it was far from clear what a successful moderate program would look like with regard to the slavery and territorial issues. The composition of the new Thirty-first Congress—where Democrats held an eight-seat majority in the Senate, but where the House was evenly divided—gave no indication of what was to come. Each of the various compromise proposals that were making the rounds—ranging from the popular sovereignty idea, to keeping the territories free of slavery until the enactment of a positive law permitted its existence, to leaving the entire matter up to the Supreme Court—was open to clashing interpretations. Sectional animosities were swollen and sore. Although it had defeated the uprisings of 1848, the political center was fragile. And more than any other American, the responsibility for preserving it fell on an old soldier who had never even voted for president until he voted for himself—and who, more than anyone realized, was determined to be his own man.

21

POLITICAL TRUCE, UNEASY CONSEQUENCES

arly in January 1849, Henry Clay crossed paths with President-elect Taylor aboard a steamship at Baton Rouge. Clay was on his way to spend the winter in New Orleans, where, in February, he would learn that the Kentucky legislature had returned him to the U.S. Senate. At first Clay did not recognize the man who had defeated him for his party's presidential nomination. It was an understandable gaffe: the two did not know each other well at all, and the diminutive, poorly educated General Taylor emanated no authority off the battlefield. But Clay was embarrassed. After he found Taylor still on board, Clay extended his hand, saying that the general "had grown out of my recognition." Taylor was at least superficially gracious. "You can never grow out of mine," he replied, shaking Clay's hand vigorously. There the conversation politely but pointedly ended. Ten years after his struggles with William Henry Harrison and John Tyler, Clay would find himself back in Washington, dealing with an unfriendly Whig in the White House.[1]

Taylor's critics, including Clay, who considered him a dithering political figurehead, were in for a surprise. Not only did Taylor want to take charge of the government; he wanted to remake the Whig Party completely by throwing aside Clay's and Webster's "ultra" orthodoxies on economics and by luring Free Soil Whigs back into the fold. Having declared, long before his election, that he would never be "the slave of a party instead of the chief magistrate of the nation," Taylor patterned himself after another general-turned-president, George Washington, by attempting to govern above sordid partisan designs. But democracy had rendered the nonpartisan ideals of the Federalist era obsolete, so Taylor instead tried to build his own nationalistic, moderate party, soon to be known as the Taylor Republicans.[2]

Taylor surrounded himself mainly with unimaginative if unobjectionable men on whom he could rely for personal loyalty. (The major exceptions, in the cabinet, were the talented secretary of state, John Clayton of Delaware, and, in the new post of secretary of the interior, Thomas Ewing of Ohio.) Southern Whigs, presumably Taylor's political base, were conspicuously scarce in his inner counsels. Taylor replaced the staid old official Washington Whig paper, the *National Intelligencer*, with the *Republic*, geared to promoting his personal ambitions and his new party of no-party. Most alarmingly to Whig supporters, Taylor made little effort to ensure that government jobs went to party loyalists.[3]

Taylor also turned out to have strong views about territorial policy, a matter made even more urgent by a great unearthing in California. In January 1848, construction laborers were building a sawmill for Johann Sutter, the German-Swiss emigrant whose settlement near Sacramento, Nueva Helvetia, had been secured by American forces early in the war with Mexico. One of Sutter's men noticed gold flakes shimmering in the bed of the American River. News of the find quickly arrived in San Francisco, then headed eastward, and finally turned up in President Polk's final annual message, in a reference to the "extraordinary" California discoveries. The California gold rush was on. By the end of 1849, some eighty thousand Americans, a larger population than either of the states of Delaware and Florida, had arrived in what beckoned as the new El Dorado.[4]

Gold fever added to the pressure to bring California into the Union. The size of the area's new population foretold California's admission sooner rather than later; the roughneck lawlessness of the gold rush camps demanded the creation of some kind of accountable American authority; and the overwhelming dispro-portion of free-state emigrants to the region all but guaranteed that any new ter-ritorial or state constitution would exclude slavery. But if California demanded attention, so did the rest of the newly acquired Mexican cession, including an unusual American religious settlement over the western slope of the Wasatch Mountains, in the wasteland abutting Great Salt Lake.

The Church of Jesus Christ of Latter-day Saints was one of the most success-ful of the spiritual enthusiasms that swept through the Yankee Northeast in the 1820s and 1830s—and it was by far the most daring. In 1823, in Palmyra, New York, a young Vermont-born farmer named Joseph Smith Jr. received a visitation in his log cabin from the angel Moroni, who, after severe testing, led him to golden plates atop the hill Cumorah that translated into the Book of Mormon. After Prophet Smith guided a troop of followers westward to Ohio and later to Illinois (where a mob killed him in 1844), his command fell to an extraordinary organizer, Brigham Young, who completed the church's hegira to Salt Lake in 1847 and was named its second prophet. By 1849, thousands of other Mormon converts had settled in the region (the total would reach twenty thousand by 1852), holding to their American-inspired scripture and following the practices, above all polygamy, that had helped make them so despised back East. In his headquarters at Salt Lake, Young mapped out a sprawling new Mormon Zion, which he called Deseret, and began negotiating for control with the American government, which had formally obtained the land from Mexico shortly after Young and his pioneer Mormon party had settled there.[5]

President Polk, exhausted and prematurely aged—he would die three months after leaving office, probably of cholera—tried to persuade the lame-duck session of the Thirtieth Congress to admit California and New Mexico as territories and solve the slavery issue by extending the Missouri Compromise line of 36°30' to the Pacific. The proposal was dead on arrival at Capitol Hill. Antislavery members of the House reintroduced the Wilmot Proviso, drafted a constitution for California barring slavery, and passed a resolution calling for the abolition of the slave trade in Washington, D.C. Southerners fought back, some now warning of outright secession. A pro-slavery caucus asked Calhoun to draft a formal response, and Calhoun complied with his "Address of Southern Delegates in Congress to their Constituents." The address denounced a string of alleged northern abuses dating back to the Missouri crisis of 1819–21 and charged that the addition of new states without slavery would lead the North to force the South into total submission. Inspired by grand theories as well as changing political realities—he had completed his "Disquisition on Government" begun six years earlier and started working on an even longer manuscript about the American Constitution—Calhoun stopped short of disunionism but bid the South to unite on a "course of policy that may quietly and peaceably terminate this long conflict between the two sections."[6]

Calhoun's manifesto received a mixed response from southern congressmen—favorable from the great majority of Democrats, but hostile from Whigs who, as Alexander Stephens put it, felt "secure under General Taylor." The southern Whigs' confidence would soon disappear. Although a slaveholder and an expansionist, Taylor cared little about the introduction of slavery into the newly acquired territories, where, he believed, the institution would never take root. Taylor's nationalism, born of his lifelong military career, persuaded him that the southern insistence on slaveholders' rights was a divisive conceit that might destroy the Union in the name of legalistic abstractions. As much like a general as a politician, he planned an audacious field maneuver, proposing to bypass the territorial stage altogether (and thus render the Wilmot Proviso moot) and admit California and New Mexico directly as free states. Over objections at what one southern Democrat called his "monstrous trick and injustice," Taylor sent agents to Monterey and Santa Fe to urge settlers to begin drafting state constitutions. Sparsely settled New Mexico would be slow to act, but the Californians were at work even before Taylor's man arrived. In October 1849, California ratified a new state constitution barring slavery and, a month later, elected a governor and a legislature that petitioned Congress for statehood.[7]

By the time the Thirty-first Congress assembled in December 1849, Taylor's combination of nonpartisanship and nationalism had thoroughly demoralized Whig leaders of both sections and enraged southerners of both parties. Jefferson Davis, the former army officer and now a Democratic senator from Mississippi — and Taylor's son-in-law — denounced Taylor's territorial plans as the final step in destroying the balance of power between the sections. "If, by your legislation, you seek to drive us from the territories of California and New Mexico, purchased by the common blood and treasure of the whole people . . . ," the Georgia Whig Robert Toombs roared early in the new Congress's first session, "*I am for disunion.*" In October, a bipartisan meeting in Jackson, Mississippi, called for a southern rights convention to assemble in Nashville the following June "to devise and adopt some mode of resistance to northern aggression." Not surprisingly, southern Whigs took a terrible beating in the off-year state elections.[8]

Some old party loyalties and rivalries further complicated national politics, and to a degree they mitigated the sectional rancor. Although independent antislavery opinion remained strong in New England and northwestern areas, Barnburner Democrats, having made their point during the Free Soil revolt, largely returned to the Democratic Party. Some were confident they had taught the Slave Power a lesson; others were chastened by the Free Soilers' indifferent showing in the presidential tallies of 1848. "We can exercise more influence with our friends — with our own party — than we can standing outside as antagonists," one antislavery New York Democrat later observed. Important northern conservative Whigs, including Daniel Webster, were still allied with southern Whigs, who were gravitating to the idea of popular sovereignty detested by southern Democrats. Internal party splits in New York over patronage and slavery divided the Whigs between the old "progressive" forces of Thurlow Weed and newly elected Senator William Seward and the more conservative Whigs, now headed by Taylor's new vice president, former congressman Millard Fillmore. (Eventually, the latter would be nicknamed the "Silver Grays" after the hair color of one of their number, Francis Granger.) Caught in the crosswinds of party and section, the political system had broken down into a myriad of factions, no one of which held anything close to a working majority. Success would belong to those skilled parliamentarians, dedicated to keeping slavery out of national politics, who could fashion coalitions out of the confusion.[9]

THE EVASIVE TRUCE OF 1850

Two basic misconceptions have marred understanding of the congressional bargain known as the Compromise of 1850. The first stems from the familiar story of how the surviving disinterested wise men of the Senate, led by the Great Compromiser Henry Clay, stepped in one last time to broker national peace over slavery. In fact, the older heads, far from disinterested, stirred enormous conflict and left much of the difficult backroom work to younger men, whose motives were partisan as well as patriotic. Second, the very idea that the bargain was a compromise is misleading. A genuine compromise involves each side conceding something in order to reach an accord. What occurred in 1850 was very different: the passage of a series of separate laws, some of them purposefully evasive on crucial issues, with the majority of congressmen from one section voting in each case against the majority of congressmen from the other. The phrase "Compromise of 1850"—like the "Missouri Compromise" of 1820–21, which in many ways the deal resembled—has been so routinely repeated by generations of historians and schoolteachers that it is unlikely ever to be replaced. But the bargain was actually more of a balancing act, a truce that delayed, but could not prevent, even greater crises over slavery.[10]

The difficulties facing sectional and partisan peacemakers became obvious when the newly elected House of Representatives tried to pick a Speaker in December 1849. Although the Democrats held a marginal plurality of seats, the presence of twelve Free Soilers and one nativist member, along with divisions within the major parties, made a hash of partisan regularity. The Whigs put up their incumbent, an aristocratic but well-liked conservative Massachusetts Cotton Whig, Robert Winthrop. The Democrats countered with the planter Howell Cobb of Georgia, a genial veteran of the House (though only thirty-four years old) who had refused to sign Calhoun's "Address." After three weeks of jostling and more than sixty ballots, neither candidate had won the required absolute majority. Free Soil Whigs failed to back Winthrop because he had abandoned his initial support for the Wilmot Proviso; a half-dozen southern Whigs refused to support him because he once *had* supported the Proviso; and several southern Democrats deemed Cobb insufficiently reliable. "The house is not yet organized & parties are becoming inflamed," one diarist observed, with slavery issues disguising "the ambitious designs of demagogues." Finally, on the sixty-third ballot, the members agreed to abide by a mere plurality, and Cobb was elected Speaker by a margin of three votes. Cobb in turn named friendly moderate Democrats to the key chairmanships. But the chaos had hardly been resolved, and would break out anew once debate over the territorial question began in the Senate.[11]

President Taylor, unruffled by southern talk of disunion and the impending southern rights convention in Nashville, presented his territorial plan in a special message to Congress in January 1850, calling for California's admission to the Union as a free state at once, and New Mexico's admission as soon as it was ready. Having once blamed Yankee abolitionists and Free Soilers as the instigators of sectional divisions, he was now persuaded that the greatest fault lay with "intolerant and revolutionary" southerners, led by Jefferson Davis. Taylor's fury fed the southerners' own, which persuaded even skeptical northern congressmen that their threats of secession were deadly earnest and might well be made real at the Nashville meeting. Then, into the fray, in one last effort to placate the South, stepped Henry Clay.[12]

As ever, Clay had complicated motives. His desire to save the Union was sincere. Equally sincere was his desire to save the Whig Party by shoving aside the stubborn president and establishing his own dominance. On January 29, he presented his alternative to Taylor's plan in the form of eight resolutions, six of them paired as compromises between the North and South. In the first pair, Clay called for the admission of California as a free state and the organization of the remainder of the Mexican cession, including Brigham Young's Deseret, without "any restriction or condition on the subject of slavery." The second set resolved an existing boundary dispute between Texas and New Mexico in favor of the latter—a pro-northern position that would reduce the chance of a new slave state being carved out of Texas—while also assuming outstanding debts contracted by the Republic of Texas. Clay's third pair of resolutions tried to offset the resumed antislavery campaigns in the District of Columbia by appealing for abolition of the slave trade, but not slavery itself, inside the District. The seventh and eighth resolutions were pro-southern, denying congressional authority over the interstate slave trade and calling for a stiffened federal law for the recovery of fugitive slaves, in reaction to the personal liberty laws enacted by the northern states.[13]

Superficially, Clay's compromise tilted in favor of the South. Its rejection of the Wilmot Proviso principle was sufficient to enrage and permanently alienate the most committed antislavery northerners. When he first proposed his resolutions, Clay said he was asking the North to make the "more liberal and extensive concession." Yet beneath the surface, and at times explicitly, Clay, the Border South moderate, also repudiated what had become the political axioms of the Deep South: that slavery was a benevolent institution which deserved to expand along with the rest of the country, and that a belligerent Yankee minority had risen up to oppress the slaveholders. Much as he had in the debate over congressional powers during the Missouri crisis thirty years earlier, the Kentuckian was speaking heresy to pro-slavery hardliners. Once broken out of their "pairing" formula, Clay's proposals handed all of the truly important decisions about the territories—the admission of California and the adjustment of the New Mexico–Texas border—to the North. Although Clay opposed, on grounds of prudence, the abolition of slavery in the District of Columbia, he insisted that

Congress had the full power to do so if it chose—a sticking point with the South since the abolitionist petition campaigns of the mid-1830s. Even in the supposedly pro-southern fugitive slave proposal, Clay backed the guarantee of jury trials to decide on individual cases—a sop to the North that was certain to undermine any new process of returning runaways to their masters. In a five-hour follow-up speech commending his compromise, Clay not only failed to defend slavery; he charged that over the previous fifty years, the South had exercised a "preponderating influence" over national affairs and should now display forbearance and statesmanship before the citizenry and Almighty God.[14]

Clay's two greatest surviving colleagues presented lengthy replies in the Senate. On March 4, the dying John C. Calhoun sat at his desk, wrapped in flannels, his eyes blazing from behind pale and hollowed cheeks, as his friend Senator James Mason of Virginia, chief sponsor of the new bill on fugitive slaves, read aloud his prepared remarks. Here was hard-line pro-slavery incarnate, grim and unyielding. The primary reason for the current discord, Calhoun's text asserted, was Congress's long-standing and systematic promotion of national legislation favorable to the North. The Northwest Ordinance and then the Missouri Compromise had prevented the South from occupying vast new tracts of land. Tariffs and internal improvements had enriched northern business at the direct expense of the South. The oppression would end only if the North ceased its aggression. The South must have equal access to western territories; all criticism of slavery must cease; a new law had to be enacted providing for the swift return of runaway slaves to their owners; and the nation had to ratify a constitutional amendment that, according to Calhoun's vague description, would "restore to the South, in substance, the power she possessed of protecting herself before the equilibrium between the two sections was destroyed."[15]

Calhoun almost certainly envisaged, as the heart of any constitutional amendment, a proposal he had developed in his manuscript "Discourse on the Constitution and Government of the United States" (which, like his "Disquisition," would not be published until after his death) institutionalizing his concept of the concurrent majority by establishing two presidents, one northern and one southern, each with the power to veto congressional legislation. The proposal was as far-fetched as the rest of his speech was devious. One would never guess from Calhoun's syllogisms of oppression that he had supported not only the Missouri Compromise but also, early on and emphatically, the kinds of tariff and improvement legislation he now denounced as evil. One would never guess that anybody lived in the South except for slaves and slaveholders—and that the majority of white southerners, slaveless, were not barred from taking one bit of their property into the western territories. One would never guess that if any portion of the Union enjoyed an artificial subsidy of federal power, it was the slave states, whose representation in the House, the Electoral College, and the parties' national nominating conventions was greatly inflated thanks to the three-fifths clause—an arrangement which, in turn, had helped ensure that eight of the first twelve presidents of the United States, including the incumbent, were slaveholders. None of these evasions was new—but Calhoun's urgency and disunionist hints gave his remarks a foreboding power. The choice was simple, Calhoun said: were California admitted as a free state, either under Taylor's plan or Clay's, the southern states could no longer "remain honorably and safely in the Union."[16]

Four days later, Daniel Webster, delivered the nationalist address many expected of him. In a low even voice, Webster announced that he wished to speak "not as a Massachusetts man, not as a Northern man, but as an American." Having once opposed the Mexican War and supported the Wilmot Proviso, Webster changed his position, turning on the Proviso with special contempt as "the Wilmot"—a gratuitous measure, he now said, designed merely to "taunt or reproach" the South. For the Union to endure, such northern attacks must end, and some law was required to guarantee the return of fugitive slaves to their masters, just as the Constitution's framers had intended. Likewise, southerners had to appreciate the North's alarm at the gradual rise of pro-slavery views and cease their blustery talk of disunion. By the time Webster finished, it was not entirely clear whether he favored Taylor's territorial plan or Clay's compromise proposals—which may very well have been Webster's intention. But with that ambiguity, and coming so soon after Calhoun's effort to draw a line in the sand, Webster's speech bolstered the view that some sort of compromise was required to keep the nation from falling apart.[17]

Four days after Webster spoke, the freshman senator William Henry Seward presented the antislavery northerners' counterpoint to Calhoun's speech. Condemning out of hand Clay's compromise, and any such sectional deal, Seward attacked slavery as an oppressive and undemocratic institution—in "natural alliance with the aristocracy of the North, and with the aristocracy of Europe"— that should be hastened to its demise and not encouraged with craven bargaining. In Seward's view, Congress unquestionably had the constitutional power to exclude slavery from the territories. Even then, he continued, senators had to recognize that "there is a higher law than the Constitution," the law of nature's God, who had created all persons equal. Seward's claims were reprises of and variations on a theme antislavery northerners had advanced as early as the Missouri crisis in 1819 and 1820—that the egalitarian Declaration of Independence, with its invocation of the Creator, was the legal and moral basis of the Constitution. The bulk of Seward's speech concerned itself not with transcendent good and evil, but with a dense legalistic explication of why slavery was incompatible with the letter as well as the spirit of the Constitution, another familiar line of antislavery argument. Yet to some, Seward's reformulations of old contentions seemed to be asserting a new and unnerving radical claim, that the godly forces of antislavery were above the law. Reinforcing that impression was Seward's insistence that slavery was doomed, and that the only thing left to determine was the manner in which it would be destroyed—either peaceably, gradually, and with financial compensation under an intact Union, or violently, immediately, and utterly if the Union were dissolved.[18]

Reaction to Calhoun's, Webster's, and Seward's orations was instant. Hannibal Hamlin, the antislavery Maine Democrat, rose in the Senate to counter what he regarded as Calhoun's inflammatory speech. Many southerners praised Calhoun's fire and brimstone, although some, like former president John Tyler, considered it "too ultra." Calhoun found much to praise in Webster's speech, which he thought showed "a yielding on the part of the North" that would discredit Clay, but antislavery New Englanders condemned Webster as a turncoat factotum for the cotton-manufacturing aristocracy and its slave-mongering allies. (One enraged Yankee, John Greenleaf Whittier, dashed out an angry poem, "Ichabod," blaming Webster's fall on "the Tempter"; the Free Soil Whig Congressman Horace Mann read the work in full before the House of Representatives.) Seward's speech made the South howl; Clay denounced it as "wild, reckless, and abominable"; and President Taylor, already furious at Clay and Webster for what he saw as a concerted effort to undermine him, now unloaded his wrath at Seward, whom he had heretofore considered and consulted as an ally. Yet in the antislavery districts of New England and greater New England, Seward was suddenly a hero.[19]

While the speeches captivated the reading public, more mundane political efforts proceeded inside the Capitol's committee rooms. A special Senate committee, chaired by Clay, offered a long bill that incorporated several elements of Clay's proposed compromise: admission of California as a free state; the organization of two new territories, New Mexico and Utah (which had applied for admission in March), without reference to slavery; and a ten-million-dollar compensation to Texas in exchange for Texas's recognition of New Mexico's boundary claims. The committee's bill helped to dampen the radical disunionist fervor in the South, where the Nashville Convention—boycotted by Louisiana and North Carolina as well as most of the Border South states—transpired in June with only minor incident. Yet as debate over Clay's bill continued on into the summer, its chances for passage dwindled. Clay's prickly demeanor and his obvious distaste for the Taylor White House did not help his cause, but the major problems were arithmetical. With all of his prestige, Clay could muster only about one-third of the members of each house to support the measure (now mocked at by President Taylor as the "Omnibus"). Taylor and most northern Whigs stuck to the president's original plan of admitting California only, with no acquiescence in allowing New Mexico or the rest of the Mexican cession opened up to slavery. Whigs and Democrats from the Deep South would not agree to any bill that admitted California as a free state. Even if, by some parliamentary miracle, Clay were to find the necessary votes, it was no longer clear that the incensed Taylor would abide by his campaign promise not to exercise his veto power.

Matters worsened in late June when word arrived that a small convention in New Mexico had drafted and won ratification of a free-state constitution. Taylor immediately called for New Mexico's admission along with California's; southern outrage flared to new heights; and the state of Texas vowed to secure its claims to all of New Mexico east of the Rio Grande, by force if necessary. Taylor ordered the federal garrison at Santa Fe to prepare for combat. By early July, it looked as if civil war might break out, pitting the United States against southern volunteers determined to secure greater Texas for slavery.[20]

Fate intervened, as it had in 1841. On a blazing July 4, President Taylor spent much of the afternoon at the site of the unfinished Washington Monument, listening to patriotic speeches. Through the rest of the day and evening, he gorged himself on raw vegetables and cherries, washed down with pitchers of iced milk. The next day, he fell severely ill, and on July 9, he died of acute gastroenteritis. The ex-general who had become a southern Whig with northern feelings was suddenly replaced by a northern Whig with southern feelings, the conservative New Yorker Millard Fillmore.[21]

Fillmore's accession was the turning point in the crisis. Immediately, the new president defused the Texas–New Mexico conflict by laying aside New Mexico's application for statehood and throwing his support behind Clay's bill. Instead of obstruction from the White House, the Great Compromiser could now count on complete support, with the added advantage that the obstreperous Seward, Fillmore's foe in New York politics, would be rendered more marginal than ever. Yet Fillmore could not save Clay's proposals in their Omnibus form. After a month of Byzantine negotiations, the anticompromise blocs in the Senate, North and South, sent the bill down to defeat at the very end of July. Clay, depressed and feeling every one of his seventy-three years, withdrew to Newport, Rhode Island, to recover. Other, younger men stuck it out in sweltering Washington, determined to maneuver some sort of agreement through Congress. They were led by the thirty-seven-year-old senator from Illinois, Stephen A. Douglas.[22]

Personally and politically, Douglas epitomized the moderate to conservative nationalist Democratic politicians who had emerged in the North in the 1840s, at odds with Barnburner Jacksonian radicalism. Born in Vermont, he had moved to Illinois, where he prospered as a self-made lawyer and politician and married the daughter of a wealthy North Carolina planter (receiving, at his father-in-law's death, the title to a large and thriving Mississippi plantation). With ties to and sympathies for every section of the Union, Douglas believed that all sides were blowing the slavery issue out of proportion. A lifelong Democrat—he had gotten his start in politics as a teenager in Vermont, ripping down anti-Jackson hand-bills during the 1828 election—he had no truck with southern disunionist heresy, and he thought Wilmotism was an attack on the democratic rights of ter-ritorial settlers to determine their own form of government. Having rapidly ascended the political ladder by dint of his oratorical and backroom skills and his commanding presence (packed into a stumpy five-foot four-inch frame), the so-called Little Giant was chiefly interested in encouraging railroad construc-tion and other internal improvements—traditional Whig aims that Douglas and others now associated with Democratic expansionism. His chief vice (though in politics this could be a fraternal virtue) was a fondness for whiskey that, along with his Polkian addiction to hard work, would kill him before he reached the age of fifty.[23]

An implacable partisan infighter but with a cool political intelligence, Doug-las had never admired Clay's Omnibus strategy; indeed, Douglas remembered, as Clay seemed to have forgotten, how Clay himself had manufactured the Mis-souri Compromise thirty years earlier. The day after the large bill failed, Douglas began breaking it down into its parts and engineering their separate passage. The strategy was simple: start with the foundation of pro-compromise votes that did exist, and then add on sectional minorities large enough to pass each measure one by one. Northern Democrats and Whigs thus joined with border-state Whigs to approve the admission of California, the abolition of the slave trade in the Dis-trict of Columbia, and the adjustment of the Texas–New Mexico dispute along the lines Clay had originally proposed. Conservative and moderate northern Democrats joined with southern Democrats and Whigs to pass a new, stronger fugitive slave law (which would help recover long-gone as well as recent run-aways), and to organize New Mexico and Brigham Young's Deseret, now called Utah, without reference to slavery. Behind the scenes, President Fillmore pre-vailed on enough northerners to abstain from the floor votes on the latter two bills to ensure their passage. By the end of September, all of the measures had passed both congressional houses. President Fillmore would proudly declare that Congress had achieved "a final settlement" of sectional discord.[24]

Washington erupted in jubilation. Crowds chanted, "The Union Is Saved." The major government buildings were illuminated. According to one account, word spread that it was the duty of every patriot to get drunk. "[E]very face I meet is happy," wrote a friend of James Buchanan's. Happiest of all were the main pro-tagonists, above all Stephen Douglas, who had made a name for himself during the two months he had brokered the truce. "If any man has a right to be proud of the success of these measures," noted the defeated Jefferson Davis, "it is the Sen-ator from Illinois." Henry Clay, absent for most of the final heavy lifting, arrived back in Washington from his vacation in time to help pull the District of Colum-bia bill through the Senate and then bask in the adulation that came his way as the initiator of the bargain. "Let it always be said of old Hal," Douglas generously remarked, "that he fought a glorious & patriotic battle. No man was ever governed by higher & purer motives." Daniel Webster was elated and relieved. "I can now sleep anights," he wrote an associate (having long suffered intense bouts with insomnia). "We have gone thro' the most important crisis, which has occurred since the foundation of the Government; & what ever party may prevail, hereafter, the Union stands firm."[25]

Behind the intoxicated glow, there was reason enough for satisfaction among political moderates. The crisis of 1850 was real. Southern secessionist fervor had overtaken even mainstream politicians like Robert Toombs. William Seward's "higher law" antislavery enjoyed substantial popular support in the North. By late summer, the congressional impasse had defeated Henry Clay's best efforts, and its resolution required industry and finesse. That resolution would serve as a patriotic bulwark of antisectional politics for years to come, emboldening moderates in the North and South, shoring up the political center much as the Missouri Compromise had thirty years earlier.

But 1850 was not 1820, when the politics of antislavery had seemed to arrive out of nowhere. The Free Soiler Salmon Chase came closer to the truth than the revelers when he said that "the question of slavery in the territories has been avoided. It has not been settled." As part of the price of getting the Utah and New Mexico bills passed, Congress had consciously omitted including any stipulations about whether slavery would be permitted in these territories before they applied for statehood. The issue was instead left to the Supreme Court to decide—a decision that never came, as no relevant case ever arose out of either territory. In other portions of the as yet sparsely settled West, the evasions of 1850 would come back to haunt political leaders soon enough. Nor had the apparent triumph of pro-Union centrism in Congress halted the gradual erosion of the political system. The factionalism that plagued both parties now tended more than ever to run along alarming sectional lines. Slavery and its extension were, as ever, the core issues.[26]

Throughout the proceedings, the gaunt Calhoun, and then his ghost, haunted everyone. After showing up at the Senate one last time to hear Webster's nationalist oration, Calhoun died on March 31. Friends and even foes eulogized him as a brilliant leader of his cause. "[O]ne of the great lights of the Western world is extinguished," the conservative New York Whig Philip Hone, who disliked Calhoun's politics but admired the man, wrote in his diary. Southern moderates and Unionists were less charitable, calling his death, in one South Carolinian's words, "the interposition of God to save the country." Calhoun's old adversary Benjamin Perry said it was "fortunate for the country" and claimed that "the slavery question will now be settled." But Calhoun's passing did not lay the slavery question fully to rest any more than did the evasive truce of 1850. The spirit of Calhounism lived on, in an even more radical disunionist form, picked up by a new generation of unswervingly pro-slavery Deep South Democrats. "He is not dead sir,—he is not dead," said Thomas Hart Benton, who refused to speak at the official congressional obsequies. "There may be no vitality in his body, but there is in his doctrines."[27]

For the Calhounites and the more fiery southern disunionists, there was no question that the North's irresponsible form of democracy was ruining the country, just as there was no question among antislavery northerners that the Slave Power's perversion of democracy was ruining the country. William Yancey and his fellow extremists sounded less and less extreme to many southerners. Early in the post-truce session of Congress, a series of resolutions arrived from the Vermont legislature, calling slavery "a crime against humanity, and a sore evil in the body-politic," and denouncing "the so-called 'compromises of the Constitution.'" Jefferson Davis, appalled, announced that he had long trusted "in the intelligence and patriotism of the masses," but that now, in the North, demagogues and their dupes had "raised a storm which they cannot control . . . invoked a spirit which they cannot allay." Others went much further, to denounce democracy itself as the root of all evil, in need of responsible checks by responsible slaveholders. The Virginian Muscoe R. H. Garnett looked back with dismay at the general drift "in the direction of Democracy" across the nation for the previous fifty years. *Democracy, in its original philosophical sense,"* he wrote, *"is, indeed, incompatible with slavery, and the whole system of Southern society."* For the moment, moderates and Unionists had the upper hand in southern politics, both in Washington and at the state level. (A second disunionist Nashville Convention, held in November to denounce the truce, was even less well attended and effectual than the first.) But among slaveholders, especially in the Deep South, John Calhoun's shade was finally displacing Andrew Jackson's.[28]

Within two months of the settlement of 1850, the clash of southern and northern ideas of democracy would break out anew, over that portion of the truce called the Fugitive Slave Act. Once again, as in the 1820s and 1830s, Americans at the very bottom of political society would help instigate the conflict. Although its immediate effects did not dispel the flush of amity created by the truce of 1850, the conflict prefigured the truce's undoing.

THE POLITICS OF FUGITIVE SLAVES

On October 25, 1850, two slave-catchers named Hughes and Knight arrived in Boston to apprehend the fugitive slave cabinetmaker William Craft and his wife, Ellen, and bring them back into bondage in Georgia under the terms of the new

Fugitive Slave Law. The Crafts were antislavery celebrities. Two years earlier, using money that William had saved up from odd jobs as a hired-out slave, they had escaped from Macon, Georgia, to the North by train and steamboat, with Ellen (her hair cut short and her skin fair enough to pass for white) posing as a sickly planter, accompanied by a man-servant—her dark-skinned husband. The couple settled in Boston, amid other fugitive slaves, where the story of their audacious flight became, in the columns of Garrison's *Liberator*, the most famous runaway saga since Frederick Douglass's. The commotion surrounding the Crafts quickly caught the attention of their owner, who, as soon as the Fugitive Slave Act became law, sent his agents off to recapture them. The two slave-catchers, emboldened by the new requirements that compelled federal authorities and private citizens to assist them, swore that they would complete their mission even if they had to bring reinforcements from the South.[29]

Boston's abolitionists swung into action. An emergency meeting at the African Meeting House, in the black neighborhood on the back side of Beacon Hill, had already formed a group called the League of Freedom, pledged to protest the new Fugitive Slave Law, and ten days later, the group merged with Boston's revived, black-led Vigilance Committee. As soon as Hughes and Knight showed up, Ellen and William Craft went into hiding with the help of the Vigilance Committee—she winding up at the home of the Transcendentalist minister Theodore Parker, whose church the couple had joined, and he taking refuge at the home of a black abolitionist, Lewis Hayden. (The latter turned his place into a veritable fortress and promised to blow it sky-high rather than relinquish a single fugitive.) The Vigilance Committee, meanwhile, posted handbill descriptions of the "man stealers" all over the city, harassed and vilified them wherever they went, and had them detained on a charge of slander. After five days, the agents gave up and returned home.[30]

Although Hughes and Knight had departed, the local federal marshal still held a warrant for the Crafts' arrest, which he was now legally bound to execute. President Fillmore, enraged by the Bostonians' lawlessness, assured the Crafts' owner that he would have the pair apprehended, if need be by sending in federal troops. All the while, the veteran Garrisonian Samuel May, in contact with his English abolitionist friends, plotted out an escape route that took the Crafts to Portland, Maine, then to Halifax, Nova Scotia, and finally to Britain, where they connected with another well-known fugitive slave, William Wells Brown, and continued their antislavery work. Back in Boston, Theodore Parker sent a derisive note to Fillmore: "You cannot think that I am to stand by and see my own church carried off to slavery and do nothing to hinder such a wrong."[31]

The Craft affair was one of the first in a burst of spectacular episodes in late 1850 and 1851 involving resistance to the Fugitive Slave Law.[32] The following February, also in Boston, agents seized a runaway slave-turned-waiter, Frederick

Minkins, who had taken the name Shadrach, and rushed him to the federal courthouse, where he was held under the guard of some deputy federal marshals. Much as in the George Latimer drama eight years earlier, an angry crowd gathered—only this time, a group of black protesters overcame the marshals, snatched Shadrach, and spirited him to Canada. Conservative Bostonians called the incident an outrage, and at President Fillmore's insistence, local officials, including prominent Democrats, indicted and tried four blacks and four whites, but juries refused to convict any of them. Shortly thereafter, in April 1851, a show of force involving hundreds of U.S. troops as well as armed police deputized as federal marshals was sufficient to secure the reclamation of yet another fugitive in Boston, seventeen-year-old Thomas Sims. But later that same year, a runaway cooper in Syracuse, New York, named William Henry (familiarly known as Jerry) escaped across Lake Ontario and into Canada thanks to a plan devised by Samuel May and Gerrit Smith, who happened to be in the city attending an antislavery convention. A local grand jury duly indicted twelve blacks and twelve whites for rioting, but nine of the blacks had already fled to Canada. Only one person was convicted, a black man who died before he could appeal the verdict. Other rescues were reported in places as far-flung as Cincinnati and Ypsilanti, Michigan.[33]

The struggle reached a bloody crescendo on September 11, 1851, in the town of Christiana, Pennsylvania, near the Maryland border. Christiana was a Quaker settlement that welcomed fugitive slaves headed north, and reportedly two long-gone escapees were holed up there, hiding in the house of a free black. A posse consisting of a Maryland slaveholder, Edward Gorsuch, several of his relatives including his son, and three deputy marshals arrived in search of the pair and found them—surrounded by two dozen black men armed with clubs, corn cutters, and a few old muskets who were determined to send the slave-catchers packing. A pistol shot rang out, and in the melee, the slaveholder Gorsuch was killed and his son was severely wounded. The black resisters melted away into the countryside and their three leaders later turned up in Canada. "Civil War—The First Blow Struck," one Pennsylvania newspaper exclaimed.[34]

President Fillmore, still smarting from the Shadrach and Jerry fiascos, directed a large force of federal marines and marshals to Christiana. They hauled in nearly forty prisoners, more than thirty of them black. The administration, determined to end the northern resistance once and for all—and in blood—then had the arrested men indicted for treason, a capital offense, which led to the largest treason trial in all of American history. But by the time the government mounted its case, its high-handed strategy had backfired. Guilty as the accused might have been of riot or even murder, few could take seriously the idea that a band of a few dozen, poorly armed men, including several Christiana Quakers, had seriously intended to wage war on the United States of America. ("Blessed be God that our Union has survived the shock," one of the defense attorneys mocked.) After the first defendant was cleared, the government dropped its charges against the others.[35]

Various myths still cling to the fugitive slave disturbances of 1850–51. The greatest of them—originally propagated by irate southerners, and since given currency by Americans in search of abolitionist heroes—is the romantic image of what came to be known as the Underground Railroad. To hear some southerners at the time, one would imagine that the fugitive bondsmen presented a clear and present danger to the survival of slavery, abetted by a large and highly sophisticated conspiracy of northern whites who smuggled slaves to freedom. (One Virginia pamphleteer claimed that more than sixty thousand slaves had escaped to the North between 1810 and 1850, a figure Gamaliel Bailey called a "ridiculous perversion of facts.") In truth, the numbers of runaway slaves who were not returned to their masters within twelve months appear to have numbered several hundred annually, perhaps as many as a thousand, by the early 1850s—an embarrassment to southerners who claimed the slaves were perfectly content, but hardly enough to threaten a system of more than three million enslaved persons. Of the permanent runaways, a large number, possibly a majority, remained in the South, especially in coastal and river cities where they could blend in with free black populations. The preponderance of all runaways, especially in the Deep South, had no plan to escape completely from slavery, but would "steal away" from their masters for a short period of time, in anger at a rebuke, in respite from abuse, or simply in search of relief from backbreaking toil.[36]

A related myth is that the Fugitive Slave Law actually created an effective machinery for recapturing fleeing slaves. The law did have harsh, even draconian aspects. It brought a major expansion of federal authority to track down runaways—an ironic consequence insofar as it showed, more than ever, that even the most doctrinaire state-rights slaveholders were perfectly willing to invoke robust federal power to protect slavery. Various provisions in the law—including the denial of jury trials to the apprehended, and a clause giving federal commissioners a ten-dollar payment if the captive was remanded to his or her owner, but only five if the captive was set free—were plainly weighted toward the slavecatchers. Runaways who were seized were almost certain to be returned South. But relatively few were actually caught under the law, just over three hundred between 1850 and 1861—roughly 5 percent of all runaways during the period. For most slaveholders, the sheer cost of undertaking capture and prosecution in order to secure the return of an uncooperative slave hardly seemed worth it, either financially or psychologically. (It was estimated that the recovery of Thomas Sims cost his master three thousand dollars and the federal government more than five thousand dollars.) Some observers freely conceded that the real point of the law had never been to recapture slaves but to test the North's sincerity over the truce of 1850. "The number of slaves escaping from the South is inconsiderable," one Wilmington, Delaware, paper observed in 1851.[37]

Refutations of the myths surrounding the fugitive slaves can, however, themselves be exaggerated. The idea of the Underground Railroad certainly mattered, then and now, as a beacon of promise and possibility to slaves and free blacks, and of shame to slaveholders. Most successful runaways escaped in a haphazard manner, relying more on their own wits and planning than on other people's organizing—acts of extraordinary courage that may have done more than anything else to instill a hopeful endurance among southern slaves, and that later eulogies to (mostly white) abolitionists occluded. Some of the escapees, the most famous being the ex-Maryland slave Harriet Tubman—repeatedly and successfully dipped back down across the Mason-Dixon Line to help bring others to freedom. Neither "underground" nor secret, the black abolitionist vigilance committees, which had declined in the 1840s, sprang back to life after 1850, goaded by panic among northern blacks that now they were all, even the freeborn, more vulnerable than ever to being kidnapped into slavery. In Chicago, seven divisions of six men each took turns patrolling the city and "keep an eye out for interlopers." Blacks in New York passed resolutions condemning the Fugitive Slave Law and appointed a secret committee to assist runaways. Boston's Vigilance Committee, which played an important role in keeping Ellen and William Craft free, claimed a membership of two hundred. Far from Boston, some white abolitionists strategically well placed near the border slave states— most famously the Quaker Levi Coffin, first in Newport, Indiana, and later in nearby Cincinnati—rendered valuable assistance in hiding and dispatching northward large numbers of refugees. No vast, well-oiled conspiracy, the Underground Railroad did, nevertheless, exist as a loose congeries of determined resisters, with free blacks doing most of the work and taking most of the risks.[38]

The political and symbolic dynamics of the fugitive slave controversy were equally important. Of all the bills that made up the truce of 1850, the one on fugitive slaves stirred the least debate in the South. As originally proposed by Senator James Mason in January, it had appeared to some southerners as too weak, but by summer's end the dissenters managed to win tougher rules for the bill's enforcement. Not a single southern representative in Congress—Democratic or Whig, from the upper South or the Deep South, in either house—voted against the final proposal. For border-state men of both parties, it was the one issue in the compromise debates that truly hit home, as the vast majority of runaways came, not surprisingly, from areas neighboring the free states. For Deep South men, it was a grave matter of honor surpassing any economic considerations, an assertion of slaveholders' rights against Yankee extremists. "The loss of property is felt," Senator Mason would later remark, "the loss of honor is felt still more."[39]

The northern resistance, especially in William Lloyd Garrison's Boston, not surprisingly incensed the southern extremists, increasingly known as fire-eaters. ("[R]espect and enforce the Fugitive Slave Law as it stands," one pro-slavery editor warned the North. "If not, WE WILL LEAVE YOU!") But southern Unionists likewise took offense at the abolitionists' lawlessness. In several states, pro-Union southerners, following the example of the so-called Georgia Platform, passed by a special state convention in December 1850, pledged to abide by the 1850 truce as "a permanent adjustment of this sectional controversy," but only if the North also did its duty, including "a faithful execution of the *Fugitive Slave Law*." The embodiment of Border South Whig moderation, Henry Clay, charged that "except for the whiskey rebellion, there has been no instance in which there was so violent and forcible obstruction to the laws of the United States."[40]

The disturbances' impact on northerners was more complex. Radical immediatists gained the most within the antislavery camp. For more than a decade before the enactment of the Fugitive Slave Law, abolitionists, black and white, had been giving aid and comfort to escapees and then publicizing their travails—ranging from the famous story of Frederick Douglass to that of Henry "Box" Brown, who escaped Richmond ingeniously in 1849 by hiding in a small crate that was shipped to Philadelphia. Overshadowed by the political abolitionists, the Garrisonians made the most of the stream of runaways. "If Ohio is ever abolitionized," the immediatist leader Samuel May Jr. wrote, "it will be by fugitive slaves from Kentucky: their flight through the State, is the best lecture,—the pattering of their feet, that's the *talk*." The Fugitive Slave Law was an unintended political gift to the radicals, made more emphatic by their claim, now seemingly endorsed by William Seward—no abolitionist, but something of a fellow traveler—that a divine Higher Law could even take precedence over the Constitution.[41]

The controversy posed a conundrum, however, about the radical abolitionists' philosophy of nonresistance. Garrison never wavered in his pacifism; but to others, even before the affray at Christiana, the idea of throwing a human being back into bondage without a physical fight was too much to bear. Black abolitionists in particular became disenchanted with nonviolence. "The only way to make the Fugitive Slave Law a dead letter," Frederick Douglass snapped, "is to make half-a-dozen or more dead kidnappers." Newspapers in several places reported that local blacks were buying lethal weapons to protect themselves from the slave-catchers. Some white abolitionists, too, were persuaded that armed resistance was now in order. While Theodore Parker hid Ellen Craft from her would-be captors, he kept a loaded revolver at the ready on his desktop. More ominously, a still-obscure, Bible-reading wool merchant and abolitionist named John Brown, in Springfield, Massachusetts, organized under his command a small band of armed black resisters that he called the United States League of Gileadites.[42]

Among less radical antislavery northerners, the Fugitive Slave Law refocused attention on the Slave Power's alleged willingness to abrogate basic civil and democratic rights to get its way. The new law was not, to be sure, the first of its kind. The Constitution itself explicitly guaranteed to slaveholders the right to recover their fugitive property, under Article IV, Section 2. The Fugitive Slave Law of 1793 further guaranteed slaveholders' rights to cross state lines to do so. But enhancing those guarantees as it did, the new Fugitive Slave Law compelled ordinary northerners to participate in slave recoveries, on pain of fine and imprisonment, and placed heavy penalties on any found guilty of aiding runaway slaves—in effect turning the entire northern population, black and white, into one large slave patrol. By denying the fugitives jury trials, it attacked the most democratic aspect of American jurisprudence—one that, according to the lawyers who defended the fugitives, brazenly violated the Fifth Amendment's due process clause. The law carried across state lines, and by federal fiat, the full legitimacy of an institution still alive in the North in 1787, but since banned— restricting the prerogatives of the free states while edging toward declaring slavery a national, and not a local, institution. Why should federal power be extended, critics asked, to protect one special form of property to the exclusion of all others? Even if the idea of a fugitive slave law had constitutional legitimacy, did not this one go too far? The law's attacks on civil liberties and individual conscience, and its extraterritorial implications, seemed, at least momentarily, to awaken new concerns about northerners' rights. "The treason trials are making a great deal of talk here now," one of Joshua Giddings's associates wrote late in 1851, with reference to the Christiana affair, "and thousands are ready to listen who have long been indifferent."[43]

Antislavery advocates of all camps emphasized how the law was symptomatic of a moral as well as a political evil. Horace Greeley called it "a very bad investment for slaveholders" because it "produced a wide and powerful feeling among all classes averse to the institution itself." Official repression visited on white men as well as black men was bad enough: the sight of blacks who had lived in freedom for years being hauled in chains back into slavery also placed slavery's harsher realities in a glaring light, and punctured once again the slaveholders' argument that the slaves were content. "Our Temple of justice is a slave pen!" the Free Soil writer and lawyer Richard Henry Dana wrote during the Thomas Sims affair, adding that Massachusetts law had been silenced "before this fearful slave power wh. has got such entire control of the Union." In Concord, Ralph Waldo Emerson, infuriated by what he considered an immoral and therefore illegitimate law, wrote a lecture counseling disobedience. (In the one active election effort of his career, he delivered the lecture several times on behalf of John Gorham Palfrey's unsuccessful Free Soil congressional campaign in 1851.) "The Fugitive Slave Bill has especially been of positive service to the anti-slavery movement," Frederick Douglass claimed, because it at once dramatized the "horrible character of slavery toward the slave," exposed "the arrogant and overbearing spirit of the slave States toward the free States," and aroused a "spirit of manly resistance" among northern blacks.[44]

Despite all the drama, however, the antislavery forces made far less headway in the North than they hoped or expected. The majority of northerners regarded the Fugitive Slave Law, if only reluctantly, as the necessary price of sectional peace and regarded those who violated or obstructed it irresponsible troublemakers. "The law in question may be defective . . . ," one Illinois newspaper asserted, in a typical editorial. "But, so long as it shall remain on the Statute book of the United States, it will be the bounden duty of every good citizens to interpose no resistance to its execution." In the spring and summer of 1851, a counterreaction gained momentum, turning the fugitive slave controversy into a temporary victory for the forces of order and political stability. In Boston, Mayor John Prescott Bigelow (the Cotton Whig Abbott Lawrence's brother-in-law) allowed local police to be deputized as federal marshals during the Thomas Sims struggle, thereby assuring slaveholders and anti-abolitionists that the city's law-abiding gentlemen were still in charge of the city. In other northern cities, upright commercial associations and leaders of both major parties sponsored public meetings that drew huge crowds and passed resolutions supporting the Fugitive Slave Law. ("It is treason, treason, TREASON, and nothing else" to obstruct the law, a defiant Daniel Webster declared in Syracuse, considered an antislavery stronghold.)[45]

Evangelical as well as mainline Protestant clergymen denounced the agitation as, in the words of one Illinois minister, the product of "wicked principles" upheld by men "in rapid progress, in qualification, either for the penitentiary, or the lunatic asylum." One merchant frankly told the immediatist leader Samuel May that northern businessmen would not stand by and see their profits threatened by a sectional rupture: "We mean, sir, to put you abolitionists down, by fair means if we can, by foul means if we must." In 1851, the legislatures of Indiana and Iowa (followed, two years later, by Illinois) enacted laws barring the settlement of any blacks, slave or free, within their borders. Reflecting the racist sentiments of many southern whites who had migrated to the southernmost portions of these states, the laws were also intended to reassure the South that the presence of fugitive slaves would not be tolerated. So were a string of resolutions passed by the legislatures of Connecticut, Delaware, Illinois, Iowa, New Hampshire, and New Jersey, approving all of the measures enacted in 1850, including the law on fugitive slaves.[46]

The counterreaction worked. Even before the violence at Christiana in mid-September 1851, agitation against the Fugitive Slave Law had begun sputtering, and by midautumn, it was over. Moderates and Unionists rejoiced at the North's rejection of anarchic antislavery radicalism—a blow as well, as they saw it, against the disunionist southern hotheads. Sectional peace was holding, an elated Henry Clay announced in October; resistance was abating, "and the patriotic obligation of obeying the Constitution and the laws, made directly or indirectly by the people themselves, is now almost universally recognized and admitted." The fight had hardened the nerves of combative antislavery northerners and deepened their bitterness at the Slave Power. But on the surface, at least, it seemed as if the truce of 1850 was turning into a genuine compromise.[47]

"THOU JUST SPIRIT OF EQUALITY"

During the lull that followed the brief storm, two extraordinary novels appeared, both reflecting the debates of 1850 and the controversy over the Fugitive Slave Law—and affirming that literature can tell as much about underlying political realities as speeches, resolutions, and elections can. One novel had broadly Democratic origins; the other came from the heart of northern Whig evangelical antislavery. One was philosophical and demanding, doubting the existence of God and then pondering those doubts; the other was sometimes mawkishly sentimental and conveyed no doubt whatsoever that God not only existed but was a constant, redemptive presence. One was a complete commercial failure at the time but is now widely considered one of the greatest American novels; the other enjoyed the greatest commercial success of any work by an American writer in the nineteenth century, but is now thought of mainly for its historical interest. And both warned that no proclamations of compromise and nationalism could dispel the destructive forces that were overtaking the Union.

Herman Melville, disappointed at the critical failure of his political allegory *Mardi*, wrote a pair of potboiler novels to support his new family, then withdrew his household to Pittsfield, Massachusetts, in 1850, to be closer to his idol, Nathaniel Hawthorne, and to complete a romantic narrative he had begun about whaling. Against the backdrop of the compromise debates in Washington, Melville labored furiously over his manuscript as if in a trance, revising drastically even as he drafted it, enriching its language in Shakespearean cadences, and turning its details about whales and whalers into promptings for much darker and mysterious reflections. On September 10, 1851—the day before the Christiana riot—Melville sent the long-delayed manuscript to his British publisher, Richard Bentley, who published it in London five weeks later as *The Whale*. A month after that, the Harper Brothers' firm published the first American edition under *Moby-Dick; or The Whale*.[48]

Although still nominally a Democrat, Melville was no simple party man, and in its political implications, *Moby-Dick* was no simple moral fable. It was an assault on simple moral fables. (In apparent reply to abolitionists who would have northerners feel the oppressions of slavery, Melville has his odd narrator

Ishmael climb to rougher metaphysical ground: "Who ain't the slave?" he asks.) Instead, Melville spun a twisted yarn of the whaling ship, *Pequod*, evoking a Connecticut tribe massacred by the Puritans two centuries earlier. The ship's crew members came from all over the globe, and in their presence, Ishmael can invoke "thou just Spirit of Equality" and the "great democratic God . . . who didst pick up Andrew Jackson from the pebbles; who didst hurl him upon a war-horse; who didst thunder him higher than a throne!" Yet the *Pequod* is bound on no ordinary, orderly voyage of slaughtering whales but on a diabolical quest—ruled by a chewed-up, peg-legged monomaniac who brandishes a harpoon staffed with hickory, who draws power from his black, red, and brown harpooners, and who secures loyalty with a promised reward of a piece of gold nailed to the ship's main mast. The Quaker first mate Starbuck protests to the mad Captain Ahab, but Ahab is master and he presses on, smashing his quadrant, plowing into the Pacific. There the *Pequod*—a ship of the "old school" dating back to the Revolution, but now much changed with the acquisition of grisly trophies, its hull freshly sealed with caulked hemp from the compromiser Henry Clay's Kentucky—would be smashed to bits by its prey and swallowed up in a vortex.

There was no stable set of correspondences between Melville's characters and the nation's actual political leaders, although critics and historians have tried to find them. ("I had some vague idea while writing it, that the whole book was susceptible of an allegoric construction, & also that *parts* of it were," Melville said.)[49] The book contains no reference to fugitive slaves or the Fugitive Slave Law that would have been obvious to most readers, beyond the ambiguous person of the cabin-boy Pip, who may have been born free in Connecticut or may have been born a slave down South. ("[A] whale would sell for thirty times what you would, Pip, in Alabama," the second mate Stubb tells the boy after saving him from drowning when he leaps overboard. "Bear that in mind, and don't jump any more.") Melville moved by indirection. It is in the general ambience and pile-up of references that his prophecy of America's destruction, propelled by the politics of 1850–51, acquires its force. Yet *Moby-Dick*'s philosophical puzzles were not enough to impress readers and critics, who for the most part found the book impenetrable.* They were far more absorbed by another novel that had

---

* One who might not have was the Boston doorkeeper, bill-poster, and confidential agent of the city's Vigilance Committee, Austin Bearse, who used his sloop—which he launched six months after the book appeared, and named the *Moby Dick*—in at least one successful rescue of several captured fugitive slaves in 1853. As Melville invented the name Moby Dick, it is beyond dispute that Bearse named his craft after the book, although it is unclear whether Bearse actually read it. Bearse could have picked up the name from Richard Henry Dana Jr., a prominent member of the Vigilance Committee and a good friend of Melville's, with whom the author corresponded about the book during its composition, and who certainly did read it. At all events, Melville's white whale wound up symbolically embroiled in the fugitive slave controversy. See Bearse,

begun appearing in serialized form in Gamaliel Bailey's *National Era* in June 1851, and that would be published in book form, to a stupendous response, in March 1852.

Uncle Tom's Cabin; or Life Among the Lowly was not Harriet Beecher Stowe's first successful piece of writing. In the early 1830s, she won a short-story prize from the *Western Monthly Magazine* and eventually published a well-received collection of her stories. Later, she contributed regularly to more prominent periodicals, including the premier magazine of American Victorian womanhood, *Godey's Lady's Book*, and in 1850 alone, she published four antislavery pieces in the *National Era*. But if Stowe was an experienced professional author, nothing could have prepared her, or the public, for the success *Uncle Tom's Cabin* would enjoy. The daughter of renowned New England evangelical Lyman Beecher, she had accompanied her family to Cincinnati in 1832, when her father took up the presidency of the future abolitionist hotbed, Lane Seminary, and two years later she married Calvin Stowe, a professor of biblical literature at Lane. There, while mothering six children and writing stories to help supplement her husband's meager professorial income, Stowe was surrounded by evangelical antislavery enthusiasm, reinforced by the actual presence of slavery across the Ohio River in Kentucky—although, like her father, she was more tempered and even elitist in her Christian antislavery views than the immediatist radicals.[50]

Scenes of human torment—a family being separated at the auction block, escapees on the run uncertain of whom to trust—lodged in Stowe's imagination for future use. (If Melville's Ishmael claimed a whaling ship as his Yale College and his Harvard, Stowe had Lane Seminary and the ex-Lane man Theodore Dwight Weld's detailed exposé, *Slavery as It Is*.) But it took the Fugitive Slave Law—enacted after she had moved back to New England with her family—to inspire her greatest literary ambitions. "Now Hattie," her sister-in-law told her after Congress acted, "if I could use a pen as you can, I would write something that will make this whole nation feel what an accursed thing slavery is." This Stowe did, in her own trancelike state—induced, she would later say, by the Almighty, but helped along by the rigors of having to write late into the evening by candlelight, after her mothering and household chores were done.[51]

With its episodic construction and sudden, implausible plot twists, *Uncle Tom's Cabin* can be difficult to take seriously as literature. (Stowe herself, who never claimed great literary gifts, described it as merely a "series of sketches," and its original appearance in installment form may have marred its composition, as it did not the serialized writings of Balzac or Dickens.) As social analysis, beyond dramatizing slavery's moral horror, the book is saturated in the prejudices and

---

Reminiscences of Fugitive-Slave Law Days in Boston (Boston, 1880), 34–37; Sidney Kaplan, "The *Moby Dick* in the Service of the Underground Railroad," *Phylon*, 12 (1951): 173–6.

the idealism of Stowe's Yankee milieu. Stowe presented upper-class slaveholders—the tortured Arthur Shelby, the problematic, romantic Augustine St. Clair—as essentially kind, respectable men who want to do right but who are driven to misdeeds by financial misfortune or by ultimate failure in their search for God. The most upright white character of all, apart from the angelic Little Eva, is Shelby's deeply religious wife, Harriet, a model of Yankee female rectitude disguised as a plantation mistress. The darkest villains (other than St. Clair's wife, a symbol of self-centered southern womanhood driven mad by slavery) are godless, money-grubbing plebeian white men, above all the alcoholic transplanted Vermonter, Simon Legree—a tyrannical slave driver who, because he can never win the respect of his social betters, brutalizes his slaves and forces them to grovel in his presence. As for the slaves, the cruelest among them, Legree's assistants Sambo and Quimbo, are vessels of misery whose hearts are finally opened to Christ's love by the surpassing forgiveness and tender example of Uncle Tom. An antislavery novel above all else, *Uncle Tom's Cabin* can also be read as a temperance tract, an ode to evangelical womanhood, a witness of God's uplifting charity, and an appreciation of restrained Whiggish gentility.

None of the book's contrivances could detract from its transforming power. Previously, the testimony of escaped male slaves forced northern audiences to confront the horrors of captivity, yet projected with the manly, unforgiving bearing of a Joseph Cinque or a Frederick Douglass, often burning with contempt for their oppressors. Stowe's gripping scenes—of the quadroon slave Eliza Harris escaping across the ice floes in the Ohio River, or of the Christ-like Tom enduring and, finally succumbing under, Legree's savage beatings—deepened readers' sympathies by completely shifting the emotional focus. Stowe had her readers identify chiefly with defenseless mothers, little girls, and pious old men, whose unearned suffering and Christian redemption rendered their stories all the more moving—and rendered slavery all the crueler. More than that, by making the novel's slaves, above all Uncle Tom, the chief agents of Christ's redemption, Stowe broke through the racism of white America as no one, even the uncompromising Garrison, had done—a point too easily lost on some modern readers who can only see her portraits of black meekness and patience as racist caricature. The immense cultural resources of Whiggery in its Yankee evangelical, antislavery, self-reforming variant, raised to transcendent heights, drove the writing of *Uncle Tom's Cabin*. Together, they made Stowe's book the best-seller that *Moby-Dick* could never be in the 1850s. Fittingly, the most powerful Whig text of all time was neither a work of political philosophy, nor a speech, nor an official state paper, but a sentimental antislavery novel composed by one of the first daughters of the Second Great Awakening.

Uncle Tom's Cabin insisted that slavery was a national sin, to be eradicated only when Christ's love and higher law triumphed over men's customs, economics, and legislation. The connection with the Fugitive Slave Law controversy was direct, for the controversy destroyed once and for all any pretense that slavery was a purely sectional concern and that the North was not actively involved in slavery's perpetuation. It mattered not at all, in Stowe's ethical universe, if the number of fugitives tracked down was small: the moral stain and complicity in sin of just a handful of captures, or even one, could not be evaded. By making her novel's most hateful villain, Legree, a Yankee, Stowe chastised the nation, and not merely the South, for its depravity. (She did the same, more subtly, with the character of Ophelia, the oppressively prim and principled northern visitor to Kentucky who, lacking love, cringes at the idea of touching black sin.) And in the human conscience, Stowe found the surest instrument for erasing immoral laws. In an early chapter, an Ohio legislator named Bird—a sworn enemy of "these reckless Abolitionists"—arrives home having just cast a vote in favor of a state fugitive slave law. His pious wife upbraids him, and he scoffs at her political naïveté—yet when confronted with an actual, living, suffering runaway in the person of Eliza, Bird heeds his conscience and helps Eliza make her getaway. Stowe hoped to force her readers into making the same moral reckoning.

The magnitude of *Uncle Tom's Cabin*'s impact was and is difficult to gauge. Within a year of its release, the book version sold more than three hundred thousand copies in the United States—comparable to a sale of more than three million copies today. Countless other Americans were captivated by Stowe's "sketches" in the numerous stage adaptations of *Uncle Tom's Cabin* mounted quickly after the book's publication. Looking back, critics said reading it was a transforming experience. The book reviewer, writer, and Union army officer John William De Forest would, in 1868, proclaim it as close as anyone had ever come to writing "The Great American Novel" (despite its "very faulty plot"). In the South, where the book flew off the booksellers' shelves, critics vehemently denounced what they called its inaccuracies and fabrications, and described its author as a monster. Pro-slavery propagandists replied with several novels describing the misery of wage earners in the North, in contrast to the idyll of plantation slaves.[52]

Yet if the fugitive slave controversy and then Stowe's riveting book kept the slavery issue alive, their immediate political effects were muffled. Stowe, although deeply antislavery, had had little involvement in organized antislavery politics, and she strongly believed in the value of uplifting the bondsmen and in voluntary colonization. Garrisonians and other radical abolitionists found various gradualist themes in the book objectionable—above all, at story's end, the decision by its most rebellious protagonist, the ex-slave George Harris, to migrate to Liberia. At the other end of politics, the reaction against the antislavery resistance, spearheaded by officeholders and politicians determined to keep sectionalism at bay, dampened antislavery spirits. Outside Boston and a few other smaller northern cities, most northerners wanted to believe that the territorial and slavery issues had been resolved once and for all. In the South, Unionist moderates now held the political initiative in state politics, having staved off disunionist challenges in Georgia, Alabama, Mississippi, and even South Carolina. Northern Free Soilers tried to build on their revolt of 1848, sometimes in coalition with one of the major parties, but they found their influence dwindling drastically in the early 1850s. Pro-compromise mass meetings passed resolutions and deprecated extremism, as if the Union could be saved by an act of collective will. Melville's prophecy would take time to unfold, just as it would take fresh sectional struggles before Stowe's sermon sank in with northern voters.[53]

Mainstream party leaders remained confident that they could contain the slavery issue by adhering to the truce of 1850 and asserting the old partisan bonds that united Americans across the sectional divide. Thus encouraged, Democrats and Whigs alike approached the presidential election of 1852 with high hopes of victory. The Democrats would, in the end, succeed; the Whigs would fail badly. Yet both parties would also find themselves further entangled in what was becoming a brutal paradox: all efforts to shore up the political center eventually wound up worsening the clash between North and South.

LAST STAND OF THE OLD PARTIES

The Free Soil uprising of 1848 persuaded Salmon Chase that the antislavery insurgents could take over the northern Democratic Party. Old-line Hunkers, he believed, had learned a painful but valuable lesson from Lewis Cass's defeat. Now, cut off from national patronage, they would "cast a wistful eye toward the Buffalo platform," sever their ties with the South, and merge with the Free Soilers behind the "great cardinal doctrine of equal rights" once propounded by Jacksonian radicals.[54] Chase's hopes could not have been more misplaced. But that he held them at all bespoke not so much his own myopia as the confused state of antislavery politics during the Taylor and Fillmore presidencies.

What were the lessons of 1848 for the most dedicated members of the Free Soil Party? For some, notably Joshua Giddings, the result proved that both the Whigs and the Democrats were hopelessly corrupt, and that third-party efforts had to continue. Others, like Chase, came to a very different conclusion, that only by building broader coalitions could the antislavery men actually achieve power. "I fear that this world is not to be redeemed from its ten thousand self inflicted curses so easily as we flatter ourselves at the outset of any reform enterprise," Chase wrote to Charles Sumner. To win, antislavery advocates had to take a more realistic approach, and be "much in contact with the [political] machinery behind the scenes."[55]

Coalition efforts brought mixed results from 1849 through 1851. In Massachusetts, the Conscience Whig Charles Sumner, increasingly persuaded by radical Democratic economic ideas, helped arrange a Free Soil–Democratic alliance that elected him to the U.S. Senate. A similar coalition in Maine reelected Senator Hannibal Hamlin. But in the House, Free Soilers suffered a net loss of seven seats in the 1850 elections, which brought the defeat of, among others, Joshua Giddings's future son-in-law, the ex-Whig George W. Julian. In Ohio, the alliance of Free Soilers and Democrats that elected Chase to the Senate and ended Ohio's black code also embittered ex-Whig Free Soilers, who had hoped to win the Senate seat for Giddings. Even in places where the coalitions were successful, battles over patronage, partisan advantage, and personal ambitions kept the coalitions from winning anything close to what Chase had envisaged, while it sapped the more stubbornly independent Free Soilers of supporters and morale.[56]

The most telling effects of the coalition efforts appeared in New York, where prominent Barnburner Free Soilers began their drift back to the Democracy only weeks after the 1848 election was over. At first, the Barnburners—claiming they had revolutionized the party but needed to give the Hunkers time to adjust—remained zealous in their support of the Buffalo principles. Leading Hunkers (eager, for their own reasons, to complete a reunion) encouraged reconciliation by insisting that they, too, opposed the extension of slavery into the territories. By the late summer of 1849, however, the old factional differences over slavery reemerged. Under intense pressure, the two sides ran a joint state ticket but adopted a cautiously worded platform that allowed for "the free exercise of individual opinion" about slavery in territories "among members of the Democratic family." The Barnburners, hungry to reclaim party spoils from the Whigs, talked themselves into believing that they had not abandoned their principles, and that they were the Democratic dog wagging the Hunker tail, when it was the other way around. Only too late did thoroughgoing antislavery Democrats such as Preston King understand what had happened. In the aftermath of the truce of 1850, the now reunited New York Democracy formally repudiated the Wilmot Proviso and ran a mild conservative, Horatio Seymour, as its candidate for governor.[57]

Free Soil Democrats who had either rejoined the party or formed coalitions with it at the state level were just as confused and disorganized in national politics. Most of these antislavery Democrats had accepted the truce of 1850 as necessary for national peace. Yet as they looked to the presidential election of 1852, they recoiled at the idea of supporting any Democratic nominee who had formerly supported the expansion of slavery into the territories—the only kind of nominee the South would accept. The trouble was that the antislavery forces lacked a plausible alternative. Martin Van Buren, now seventy, had retired to Lindenwald and rejoined the Democracy, still antislavery in principle but persuaded that the sectional issues had been settled. Many Free Soilers were drawn to the old Jacksonian Thomas Hart Benton, still an active and influential presence in the Senate. But Benton's criticisms of the Slave Power and John C. Calhoun ("the prime mover and head contriver," Benton called him) had cost him dearly among Missouri's slaveholders, led by Benton's adamantly pro-slavery Democratic rival David Atchison, and Benton lost his Senate seat in 1850. Thereafter, Benton stuck to his declaration that he had no desire to be president. Other possibilities were floated—Benton suggested Justice Levi Woodbury, who was at least uncommitted on slavery—but none of the names mentioned raised much enthusiasm. (Woodbury died, anyway, in 1851, reducing the field to practically no one.)[58]

Antislavery Whigs likewise seemed to have lost their edge. The forestalling of the slavery issue in 1850 and the collapse of the resistance to the Fugitive Slave Law emboldened Cotton Whig conservatives to believe that they could now lead a common front of the sensible gentlemen of property, North and South, against all sectionalists—and particularly against the radical Free Soilers. One self-styled "Northern Conservative," writing in the Whigs' *American Review*, even courted southern Democrats. The erstwhile northern Democratic friends of the South, the writer charged, had declared war on "everything that is firm, established, and just." Differences remained between Whigs and southern Democrats, especially on economic issues, but the writer insisted that these could be ironed out once slaveholders understood that their interests would be better protected by Whigs than by "the hot, wild, reckless body that is organizing out of the loco-foco and abolition elements in the North and West." The alliance of the Money Power and the Slave Power that Thomas Morris had warned of a dozen years earlier was exactly what the more candid of the dominant northern Whig conservatives had in mind.[59]

As ever, some Whigs looked to Henry Clay as their standard-bearer, especially after his successful return to the Senate. If anyone could unite the splintering party, it was he. But Clay had never really recovered from the strain of his efforts in 1850. By the late spring of 1852, he was spitting up blood and suffering heavy chills. Old friends and adversaries stopped in for one last visit to his Washington hotel room. There he would die of tuberculosis at the end of June, barely a week after his party chose its presidential nominee.[60]

Daniel Webster, named by Fillmore for a second stint as secretary of state in 1850, had no less fire than ever in his ambition for the presidency—even though he, too, was silently wasting away. Encouraged by the Unionists' successes in the South, Webster spent much of 1851 trying to organize middle-of-the-road opinion in the northern states, beginning in New England. Building on his reputation from his Seventh of March speech, Webster hoped that a broad majority of pro-compromise, pro-Union moderates would carry him into the White House.

But Webster had rivals. The New York conservative President Fillmore, thanks to his vigorous enforcement of the Fugitive Slave Law, had become a favorite of southern Whigs. And poking their noses around Whig meetings were the friends of the also-ran general of 1840 and 1848, Winfield Scott—a Virginian but not a slaveholder, with no record on the truce of 1850, whose nationalist credentials some Whigs thought could rescue the party. Even antislavery Whigs like Horace Greeley seemed resigned to support the pretentious, officious Scott as the only available candidate who might win the votes of northern Whigs. "I suppose we must run Scott for President, and I hate it," Greeley wrote in February 1851.[61]

What was left of the independent Free Soil Party battled on. In September 1851, a convention of the Friends of Freedom met in Cleveland "to let the country know that we are not disbanded and do not intend to disband." The persistent delegates, led by Giddings, Julian, and Lewis Tappan, included former Liberty Party supporters who had balked at supporting Van Buren's nomination in 1848. While it unfurled once again the Free Soil banners, the meeting also passed resolutions condemning the Fugitive Slave Law, denounced both major parties as morally and politically bankrupt, and appointed a committee to arrange for the coming presidential campaign. The most radical delegates wanted to push even further and commit the group to abolition in all of the states, but the convention hemmed in that proposal at the last minute.[62]

As the battered remnants of the American 1848 struggled to survive, the politics of the European 1848 suddenly entered into domestic politics, with telling effects. In December 1851, Lajos Kossuth, the exiled hero of the failed Hungarian revolution, landed in New York to a tumultuous public response. A dazzling if diminutive figure, and a brilliant speaker, Kossuth embodied the spirit of European popular radicalism at war with reactionary monarchy. Dubbed the "noble Magyar," Kossuth elicited special warmth from spread-eagle, expansionist Democrats who had identified with Young America, but so great was the mass enthusiasm that elements from across the political spectrum (except for some southern Whigs and wary Hunkers) tried to align themselves with him. Daniel Webster retrieved a letter he had written to the Austrian ambassador late in 1850, refuting charges that the United States was improperly intervening in the Hungarian revolution, and upholding America's interest in "the movements and events of this remarkable age" that expanded popular constitutional rights. ("Webster has come out for Kossuth and must no longer be regarded as an 'Old Fogy,'" the *New York Herald* remarked.) William Seward, presumed by many to be backing Winfield Scott, along with other antislavery men went out of their way to praise Kossuth. President Fillmore's supporters arranged for an official invitation to the White House.[63]

The unanimity did not last. Kossuth demanded that the American government side with his cause and abandon official neutrality and nonintervention, which was bedrock American foreign policy. The more he did so—deciding, when rebuffed by Washington officialdom, to take his cause to the country in a public speaking tour—the more he wore out his welcome. Fillmore, seeing the danger Kossuth presented, rescinded the White House invitation. Southerners, meanwhile, became extremely nervous that Kossuth's agitation for self-determination and universal liberty implied condemnation of slavery and could stir up slave rebellions. Kossuth in fact took great precautions in his speeches to avoid the slavery question, a reticence which rankled the Garrisonian abolition-ists, but after 1850, any public mention of freedom in any context provoked dire inferences. In Washington, southerners led by Alexander Stephens made clear their displeasure at the Kossuth phenomenon. Under pressure from fellow south-erners, Senator Henry Foote withdrew a formal resolution he had introduced (at his ally Webster's suggestion) welcoming the revolutionary to the nation's capital. Most antislavery men, however, took delight in the Hungarian's appearances no matter how cautious his remarks on slavery: "Every speech [Kossuth] makes is the best kind of Abolition lecture," Benjamin Wade of Ohio remarked. The truce of 1850 was more fragile than mainstream party leaders wanted to admit. Efforts to remind Americans of the democratic political beliefs they supposedly held in common ran the risk of exposing how divided they actually were.[64]

At their national conventions in 1852, held a month before Kossuth returned to Europe, the Democrats and Whigs did their utmost to keep the divisions sub-merged. The Democrats met in Baltimore on June 1 and settled into a protracted four-way struggle among William Marcy (who had stepped back from the New York Hunkers and enjoyed the Barnburners' backing), Lewis Cass and Stephen Douglas (rival western proponents of popular sovereignty), and the southerners' favorite, the ever-malleable Pennsylvanian, James Buchanan. None of the north-erners except Buchanan was acceptable to the South; Buchanan was unaccept-able to the North; and for forty-eight ballots, the delegates deadlocked. Finally, the convention settled on the ex-senator and party stalwart, Franklin Pierce of New Hampshire. After declining an offer to serve as Polk's attorney general, Pierce had served with distinction in the Vera Cruz campaign during the Mexi-can War, then returned to private law practice in Concord, where he remained active in party affairs and warmly supported the truce of 1850. As a Yankee non-slaveholder from a traditionally Democratic state, a former doctrinaire Jacksonian (and antinullifier), and a military hero, Pierce was tolerable to northern dele-gates. As an outspoken antiabolitionist, nemesis of the Free Soiler John Hale, and pro-compromise candidate, Pierce looked even better to the southerners, including one South Carolina fire-eater who reflected that "a nomination so favorable to the South had not been anticipated."[65]

The Whigs convened two weeks later, also in Baltimore, for a marathon of their own, pitting General Scott against President Fillmore. (Webster's campaign, caught in the sectional switches, had faltered badly.) The contest was paradoxical: northern delegates, led by the New York Seward faction, backed the Virginian Scott, while southerners backed the New Yorker Fillmore, and many of the Whigs who had opposed the Mexican War now backed one of the top military commanders of that war, just as they had supported Zachary Taylor in 1848. The opposing forces agreed to a compromise over the so-called Compromise of 1850, by adopting a platform that called for "acquiescence in" the bargain as a final settlement of the slavery controversy. It took fifty-three ballots, and a last-minute defection of a handful of southern moderates, for Scott to win a narrow victory. Yet party unity was shaky, and it became all the shakier when the nominee's latitudinarian acceptance letter expressed only tepid support for the party's pro-truce platform. Immediately, nine southern Whig congressmen, including the influential Georgians Alexander Stephens and Robert Toombs, announced that they could not support Scott's election. Scott's nomination all but precluded the Whigs from running their usual pro-slavery campaign in the South.[66]

The most unified of the nominating conventions—though, in the short run, the least effective—was the Free Soilers', held in Pittsburgh in August. John P. Hale agreed to let his name be put forward, and he was nominated on a ticket with George Julian. Ohio delegates paraded around the convention hall carrying a banner declaring, "NO COMPROMISE WITH SLAVEHOLDERS OR DOUGHFACES"—an attack on the backsliding Barnburners. The convention adopted a platform that deepened the antislavery appeal of the Buffalo manifesto by denouncing slavery as "a sin against God and a crime against man," and dropping, by implication, disavowals of congressional interference with slavery where it existed. The delegates also repudiated the Fugitive Slave Law and called for official diplomatic recognition of the black republic of Haiti. Whereas Frederick Douglass had been treated gingerly at Buffalo, he was chosen a secretary at the Pittsburgh convention and took his seat to loud applause. And whereas Douglass had given grudging support to the Van Buren–Adams ticket in 1848, he exulted in the Hale-Julian campaign.[67]

On slavery questions, the new Free Soil platform marked a return to the spirit of the Liberty Party, but on other issues, it sounded even more strongly Democratic than the Buffalo platform had been. The intensification was signaled by the convention's official change in name from the Free Soil Party to the Free Democratic Party, and it turned up explicitly in the platform's policy program, which included one plank demanding "that the funds of the General Government be kept separate from the banking institutions" and another calling for strict construction of the federal Constitution (a blow against the Fugitive Slave Law). In part, the shift was tactical, since, following the major party conventions, Pierce the Democrat loomed as the greater of the two mainstream pro-slavery evils. Stressing Jacksonian affinities was one way to attack Pierce's northern base and, some Free Democrats hoped, deal the Democracy another national defeat that would push mainstream northern Democrats closer to antislavery. But the shift also bespoke the greater success Free Soilers had enjoyed in forging coalitions with Democrats than with Whigs after 1848, as well as the importance of Salmon P. Chase, Charles Sumner, John M. Niles, Gamaliel Bailey, and other pro-Democratic thinkers, including candidate Hale, in the political antislavery milieu. On matters of principle as well as pragmatics, the independents endorsed firm antislavery ideals while they promoted a general political orientation closer to that of radical Jacksonian Democracy than to Whiggery.[68]

There was an irony, though, to the Free Democrats' Jacksonianism, for by 1852 many of the ancient economic and constitutional issues that long divided mainstream Democrats and Whigs had become virtually irrelevant in local and national debates. President Polk, by reestablishing the independent treasury and obtaining the Walker Tariff, had killed off the Whig political economy of centralized, privately run national banking and government protection for the foreseeable future—and still, to the Whigs' vexation, the economy was soaring, aided by large treasury surpluses that ended up replenishing state banks' specie reserves, and fed by the California gold strikes and British investment in railroad stocks and bonds. The independent treasury system, neither a second Declaration of Independence nor a subversive catastrophe, had a usefully sobering effect on the economy by restricting the banks' power over the currency. The railroad boom, meanwhile, undercut old Jacksonian suspicions of government-supported internal improvements, especially when those improvements promised to aid their home districts. As the nation pushed westward to the Pacific Ocean, Democrats' ideals of expansionist Manifest Destiny demanded the kinds of projects, preeminently railroad construction, that required federal, state, and local government support. Whigs and Democrats would fight fiercely, especially in state legislatures, to ensure that their backers received the most pork from the barrel. But the denunciations of bank aristocrats or Loco Foco lunatics, although still heard from time to time to rouse the old party faithful, had become anachronistic rituals. "[Q]uestions of mere economy, those which pertain to banks, to internal improvements, or protective tariffs, no longer occupy the public mind," Joshua Giddings would observe a few years hence, but the effacement had been long under way.[69]

With the old party antagonisms softened, and with both the Democrats and the Whigs pledged to uphold the truce of 1850, the election of 1852 would turn on operational matters: which side could do the better job of holding together its strained intersectional coalition, vilifying the other party's candidate, and getting its own voters to the polls. The Whigs faced the more daunting task. The southern Whig defections that began after the struggle with Zachary Taylor and then the release of Scott's acceptance letter became a mass flight in the summer and early autumn. In the North, the Free Democrats' campaign promised to siphon off any antislavery vote Scott might receive with his equivocal stance on the 1850 bargain. Nativist Whigs, offended by Scott's decision to reject anti-immigrant appeals, organized separate tickets pledged to Daniel Webster in the mid-Atlantic states. In New York, embittered pro-Fillmore Silver Grays threatened further sabotage, while Sewardites backed Scott but not the party's platform. To rally their troops, the Whig managers stepped up their personal abuse of Pierce, mocking both his military career and, cruelly, his alcoholic past by dubbing him "the Hero of Many a Well Fought Bottle." (The Pierce forces countered more loftily with the best-known campaign biography in American history, written by the nominee's old friend from his student days at Bowdoin College, Nathaniel Hawthorne.) The Whigs also intensely courted Catholic voters and, with Fillmore's approval, sent Scott on an "official" tour of Ohio, Kentucky, Indiana, and New York, which allowed him to campaign in person without formally breaking the customary ban on overt presidential electioneering.[70]

No Whig maneuver could stave off disaster. In November, Scott carried only four states, Vermont, Massachusetts, Kentucky, and Tennessee (the last by a whisker), for a pitiable total of forty-two electoral votes. Of the twelve governorships at stake, the Whigs lost nine. In the House elections, Whig candidates won less than one-third of all contested races, representing a net loss of seventeen seats and giving the Democrats an unbreakable control of the lower chamber. Whig losses in state elections also threatened to worsen their minority status in the Senate, whose members were still selected by the state legislatures. Despite the enormous long-term political fallout from Texas annexation and the Mexican War, the nation once again faced the prospect of one-party Democratic rule of the federal government. "Was there ever such a deluge since Noah's time?" a despairing New York Whig asked William Seward.[71]

The damage done to the Whig Party, and to the national political system, in 1852 was severe, but it was not of biblical proportions. With his 1.4 million votes, Winfield Scott gained a larger popular total than any previous Whig candidate. Pierce's portion of the popular vote, 50.9 percent, was not exactly a landslide. The Whigs ran reasonably well in a number of important states, including New York, Pennsylvania, and Ohio. Above all, antislavery politics, so distracting to northern Whigs, had not recovered from the reassertion of political centrism that accompanied the bargain of 1850 and the reaction against the fugitive slave controversy. The Free Democrats won less than half the proportion of the total vote that the Free Soilers won four years earlier, ran well only in Massachusetts, Vermont, and Wisconsin, and barely made a difference in New York. Most Barnburners and other antislavery Democrats remained loyal to their old party and the uninspiring Pierce. The Whigs, although badly wounded, could read the returns—or, at least, the northern returns—and reasonably imagine they had survived to fight another day.

The results in the South, especially the lower South, were more worrisome. In 1848, General Taylor had won half the popular vote in the Deep South, carried six slaveholding states, nearly carried Alabama and Mississippi, and achieved what looked like a consolidation of southern Whiggery. Four years later, General Scott won only 35 percent of the popular vote in the Deep South and carried only two slaveholding states, Kentucky and Tennessee. Whig gubernatorial candidates went down to virtually universal defeat in the South, while the southern Whigs' ranks in the new Congress would be miniscule. Whig leaders and voters did not, to be sure, defect en masse to the Democrats; Whig losses owed more to abstentionism than to party-switching. But southern Whiggery, if not down and out, was on the ropes, with the loyalty of its voters more tenuous than ever. The 1852 elections marked the beginning of the creation of a nearly solid Democratic South.[72]

The southern results brought additional shifts in the locus of sectional power within the national parties. The collapse of southern Whiggery in congressional and state races in 1852 not only consolidated Democratic political hegemony in Washington; it made the South an even greater force within the Democratic Party—and the North an even greater force within what remained of the Whig Party. Democrats in Congress, more than ever, would find themselves unable to get much done without the support of their powerful southern bloc. The future of the Whig Party, if there was to be one, depended on which northern or border-state faction—pro-Fillmore Silver Grays, Cotton Whig Websterites, upper South moderates, or antislavery Conscience Whigs—could gain the political initiative. And on the future of the Whig Party would hang the future of American democracy.

THE WHIGS' LAST GASPS?

On October 24, 1852, at his home in Marshfield, Daniel Webster died, foreclosing the Cotton Whigs' fortunes. A lifetime of hard drinking—an addiction that had worsened in his later years—had rotted away his liver, but he actually died from the delayed effects of a fall he had suffered the previous spring. With Henry Clay dead in June, the last of the old Whig giants were gone. Between them, Clay and Webster, more than any other figures, had defined the combination of conservatism, nationalism, and capitalist developmentalism so central to the anti-Jacksonian opposition. Both had adapted to the new-school Whig innovations of the late 1830s; both had wanted desperately to be president; both were undone by a combination of poor judgment, bad luck, and, above all, the erosion of sectional harmony. Yet even when they were past their prime, both had stood up for a kind of Unionism that they deemed as essential for the nation's well-being as it was for their personal political fortunes. Those efforts, especially in 1850, calmed the country as much as was humanly possible. With them, the South Carolinian James Henry Hammond wrote in his diary, died "the last links of the chain of the Union," as well as the last great upholders of Whig moderation on slavery issues.[73]

The Union chain did not break, though, in 1852; neither did the Whig Party. The old partisan order—and the nation—had stood for one more round. The future of both hung on what kind of Democrat the new president, hailed by his admirers as "Young Hickory of the Granite Hills," turned out to be.

22

THE TRUCE COLLAPSES

Franklin Pierce entered the presidency mourning the death of his eleven-year-old son, Benjamin, who had been horribly killed two months earlier during a family trip when their railcar jumped its tracks and overturned. Pierce's pious wife, Jane, had never wanted her husband to return to the stresses and temptations of Washington, and she interpreted the tragedy as God's price for winning the presidency. She refused to attend the inauguration and withdrew into a seclusion at the White House that would last for the entirety of the Pierce administration. Her personable, determined, but also fragile husband, distracted by guilt and grief, inspired more apprehension than hope. Robert Toombs saw in poor Pierce "a man without claims or qualifications, surrounded by as dishonest and dirty a set of political gamesters as even Catiline ever assembled."[1]

Pierce's unexceptional inaugural address praised the Union, upheld Democratic orthodoxy on limiting federal power, and proclaimed that "the laws of 1850, commonly called the 'compromise measures,' are strictly constitutional and to be unhesitatingly carried into effect." The speech's most vigorous passages concerned territorial growth, which Pierce proclaimed a self-evident national imperative. "[T]he policy of my Administration will not be controlled by any timid forebodings of evil from expansion," he announced.[2] Along with his enforcement of the Fugitive Slave Law, Pierce's resolve to gain new territories, and to organize existing territories into states, would dominate his presidency—and blow the political system apart.

EMPIRES OF SLAVERY?:
FROM CUBA TO KANSAS-NEBRASKA

Pierce's most ambitious territorial design was on Cuba, which along with Brazil and the American South was the last great slave society in the Western Hemisphere. The idea of grabbing Cuba was not new. In 1848, after the signing of the Treaty of Guadalupe Hildalgo, President Polk disclosed his desire to acquire the island from Spain, a proposal endorsed by southern Democrats who wanted to enlarge the number of slave states and send as many as fifteen new pro-slavery representatives to the House and Senate. The Whig presidential victory that autumn ended the official planning, but not behind-the-scenes plotting. Led by a charismatic Cuban revolutionary patriot, Narciso López, pro-annexationists organized three unsuccessful invasion expeditions, the last of which, in 1851, led to López's capture by Spanish troops. Northern expansionists and southerners lamented the failures as a setback for anticolonial, democratic principles. Antislavery northerners condemned what Horace Greeley called "the Cuban foray" as "a crusade for the extension and consolidation of the Slave Power."[3]

The defeat of López's third so-called filibuster expedition (from the Spanish word *filibustero*, or "pirate") led to the execution by firing squad of fifty American mercenaries—and the garroting of López—in front of thousands of cheering Havanans. The killings touched off riots in New Orleans. For a time, a full-scale diplomatic crisis seemed imminent. The Fillmore administration, embarrassed by the affair, averted further conflict, and pro-slavery filibusterers started looking for a new president, friendlier to their cause, in 1852. With support from northern expansionists, they at first backed the nationalist Stephen A. Douglas. After Douglas's defeat for the Democratic nomination, they switched to Franklin Pierce. They celebrated the landslide in November under banners proclaiming "The Fruits of the late Democratic Victory—Pierce and Cuba."[4]

Among the most belligerent of the filibuster enthusiasts was the erstwhile Jacksonian radical and champion of Manifest Destiny, John L. O'Sullivan. O'Sullivan had sold the *Democratic Review* in 1846, but remained deeply interested in Democratic politics—raising doubts about Polk's drive to war and supporting his old Radical Democrat friends in the Free Soil campaign in 1848, but endorsing the annexation of Mexican land. After the war, O'Sullivan became fascinated with Cuba, an interest that turned into a fixation after his sister married a Creole planter who was also one of the founders of a rebel exile group, the Consejo de Gobierno Cubano, headquartered in New York. The 1848 revolutions in Europe also stirred O'Sullivan's antimonarchical soul. O'Sullivan lobbied Polk hard to purchase the island in 1848. He then gravitated to Narciso López's filibustering efforts, which landed him a federal indictment on charges that he had violated American neutrality laws. O'Sullivan was acquitted (several leading Barnburners, including John Van Buren, testified as character witnesses) and continued his agitation by returning as editor to the *Review*, persuaded that the political party that annexed Cuba would prove itself "the true American party, the party entrusted by God and Nature with the mission of American policy and destiny."[5]

O'Sullivan continued to think of himself as a radical, but his old friends flinched at his new jingoism. The original idea of Manifest Destiny rejected unprovoked war and armed conquest as repudiations of the worldwide spirit of liberty. It studiously avoided any endorsement of Calhounite pro-slavery heresy. But now Sullivan and the new *Review* (acquired in 1851 by a hotheaded Calhoun admirer, George Nicholas Sanders) had sunk into a strutting chauvinism, and seemed to be acting on behalf of land- and power-hungry slavocrats. Breaking ranks without breaking stride, O'Sullivan switched his targets and coarsened his rhetoric, in the service of a reborn Young America. The *Review* descended into shrill polemics against the "imbeciles" and "vile toads" who had the slightest misgivings about American expansionism. The Jacksonian heroes whose portraits and brief biographies had been regular features of the old *Review* now suffered denunciation as "old fogies." Only the spirit of revolutionary solidarity with Europe's oppressed had not fled. (The first issue of the new *Review* featured a celebration of Mazzini. Victor Hugo, in exile, would inscribe several novels to Sanders as his *concitoyen de la république universelle*.) But soon, even those ties would unravel, as southern Young Americans objected to Mazzini's and other Europeans' pointed condemnations of slavery. One by one, Democrats who had once identified with Young America, including David Dudley Field and Theodore Sedgwick III, dropped away, leaving O'Sullivan to consort with his new southern friends and aggressive northern expansionists like Stephen A. Douglas.[6]

President Pierce endorsed this belligerent new Young American spirit in his inaugural address, and he tried to advance it during his early months in office. His conservative Democratic cabinet (notable for its inclusion of the Hunker William Marcy as secretary of state, Jefferson Davis as secretary of war, and ex-Cotton Whig Caleb Cushing of Massachusetts as attorney general) was united in its pro-expansionist views. Pierce also appointed as his minister to Spain the hothead French émigré and filibuster supporter Pierre Soulé. Soulé received instructions that, although the United States would remain neutral, it fully expected Cuba's release, by invasion or revolution, from Spanish rule—and that, should events "excite revolutionary movements in that island," Cuban émigrés to America would undoubtedly be involved. Soulé soon began plotting with Spanish republican revolutionaries. Back home, the former Mississippi governor John A. Quitman, a fire-eater and backer of Narciso López's expeditions, began planning (apparently with Pierce's encouragement) yet another filibuster, greater than any yet attempted. Several influential southern leaders, including Alexander Stephens, supported the plan. By the spring of 1854, Quitman had recruited several thousand volunteer troops and, through Cuban exiles, contacted insurgents on the island.[7]

Quitman aborted his invasion plans when another, more urgent territorial issue distracted the administration. "The Nebraska question has sadly shattered our party in all the free states," Secretary of State Marcy wrote, "and deprived it of the strength which was needed & could have been more profitably used for the acquisition of Cuba." Early in 1853, Stephen Douglas had proposed to the Senate a House bill calling for the formal organization of the Nebraska Territory, which embraced most of the remaining portion of the Louisiana Purchase north of the Missouri Compromise line of 36°30'. Douglas's aim was to hasten the building of a transcontinental railroad. Instead, he threw national politics into the upheaval that the truce of 1850 had only delayed.[8]

The railroad had become an important factor in the nation's continuing economic development in the late 1840s and early 1850s, and the idea of a transcontinental line to California had long spellbound Manifest Destiny men. The acquisition of much wealth and prestige would turn on whether the new road ran across one of the proposed southern routes—where the required contiguous land mass had already been fully organized, thanks to the bargaining of 1850—or across the North. Douglas the expansionist had been pushing the idea of a Pacific railroad since his early days in Congress. Now he wanted desperately to get the remaining lands north of 36°30' organized, beginning with the area known as Nebraska, to secure the northern route, which he hoped would begin in Chicago. Southern representatives consequently had every reason to delay the organization of Nebraska, or to exact a terrible political price to allow it to proceed. And four hardline pro-southern senators—who shared quarters in a rented brick rowhouse on F Street and nicknamed themselves the F Street Mess—had virtual control over territorial organization: James M. Mason and Robert M. T. Hunter of Virginia (chairmen, respectively, of the Foreign Relations and Finance Committees), Andrew P. Butler of South Carolina (chairman of the Judiciary Committee), and David R. Atchison of Missouri (president pro tempore of the Senate). Atchison was especially important. The death of Pierce's vice president William R. King six weeks after taking office made him, under the existing rules of succession, next in line for the presidency. He was also among the Senate's most ardent defenders of slavery and southern rights.[9]

Democratic politics in Missouri had for some years revolved around the conflict between the bellicose Atchison and the antislavery Democrat Thomas Hart Benton. Apart from his detestation of the Calhounite influence in the Democratic Party, Benton (who had returned to Congress in 1852) wanted to halt the expansion of slavery and to keep the West, as far as possible, lily-white. Atchison feared that any restrictions on slavery's extension would spell the institution's eventual doom in Missouri. Surrounded by free soil, he supposed, Missouri would find itself under siege by the abolitionists, who would directly threaten the state's slave laws.[10]

Profane and provocative, Atchison had mixed feelings about the Nebraska question, as pro-railroad interests in St. Louis wanted to organize the territory in the hopes that their city might become the terminus of the transcontinental line. Reluctantly, he supported Douglas's Nebraska bill. At the same time, he vowed he would see Nebraska "sink in hell" before allowing it to bar slavery—and so, in effect, he also damned to oblivion the Missouri Compromise and any Nebraska bill that did not repeal it. Atchison's southern mess mates on F Street would not give even tepid support to Douglas's proposal.[11]

Douglas knew the score immediately. In March 1853, the House passed his Nebraska bill, but the Senate tabled it, with the senators from every state south of Missouri joining the majority. Lacking southern support, and especially the support of the F Street Mess, Douglas's efforts were doomed, but to accede to the South and repeal the Missouri Compromise would, as he put it, "raise a hell of a storm in the North." With hell on everybody's mind, Douglas introduced a new bill in January 1854 that tried to finesse the southerners' demands by allowing the residents of Nebraska to decide the slavery issue upon its admission as a state or as several states. But Douglas's fallback to supporting the popular sovereignty idea did not satisfy the southerners, who forced him to include a provision explicitly repealing the Missouri Compromise. To mitigate the expected northern reaction, Douglas's new bill organized two territories, Nebraska west of Iowa (which seemed to mark it for free soil), and Kansas west of Missouri (which seemed to mark it for slavery). The storm came anyway, and was no less hellish for Douglas's efforts to dodge and pacify.[12]

Even the eager northern expansionists at the White House had doubts about Douglas's bill, and the administration drafted an alternative that would have left the matter of slavery in the territories up to the Supreme Court. But the F Street Mess and Douglas, with the strong support of Secretary of War Davis, told Pierce that if he opposed Douglas's bill, he would lose the South. Not only did Pierce cave in to the pressure; he agreed to make support of what was now known as the Kansas-Nebraska Bill an absolute test of loyalty within the Democratic Party. The result was to provoke even further the northern Democrats, as well as Whigs, against what Thomas Hart Benton would call Douglas's "farrago of nullities, incongruities, and inconsistencies."[13]

In Congress, the remaining Free Soilers, now known as Free Democrats, and their closest allies were well prepared for the fight. As early as April 1853, the antislavery press warned that the Missouri Compromise might be endangered, and well before Douglas hammered his final bill into shape, efforts were underway to organize petition campaigns against it. Salmon Chase, Charles Sumner,

Joshua Giddings, and three other Free Democrats (including Gerrit Smith, who had been elected to the House) wrote a manifesto against the bill, designed to arouse antislavery opinion out of the quietude of the previous two years. First published the day after the Kansas-Nebraska Bill's formal introduction, in the moderately antislavery *New-York Daily Times* and in Gamaliel Bailey's *National Era*, "An Appeal of the Independent Democrats in Congress to the People of the United States" attacked slavery and Douglas's "atrocious plot" with the South and propounded the principles for a revival of antislavery politics.[14]

Sensing the breadth of the indignation against the bill, the authors of the "Appeal" reached out to northerners generally, as well as to every existing current of antislavery belief, with a blend of fierce demagogy and northern democratic idealism. The inflammatory conspiratorial language of the "Appeal" has too often overshadowed its substance, and how the authors braided together the different strands of antislavery opinion. Familiar Liberty and Free Soil Party arguments laid the foundations: that slavery was an abomination, and that the Founders had envisaged slavery's demise, only to have their intentions undermined by the Slave Power. The "Appeal" then enticed moderate Whigs by claiming that Douglas's handiwork threatened to destroy Henry Clay's statesmanship of 1820 and 1850. To attract wider Democratic constituencies, the manifesto charged that "immigrants from the Old World and free laborers from our own States" would be excluded from the new territories if the bill passed. The "Appeal" also addressed "Christians and Christian ministers" and reminded them that "their divine religion requires them to behold in every man a brother, and to labor for the advancement and regeneration of the human race."

The authors then presented their overarching theme: the crisis over the territories was a crisis of American democracy. The antislavery cause, the "Appeal" argued, had become the embodiment of "the dearest interests of freedom and the Union." Its opponents had described the antislavery men as reckless agitators, but the "Appeal" turned the tables: "Demagogues may tell you that the Union can be maintained only by submitting to the demands of slavery. We tell you that the Union can only be maintained by the full recognition of the just claims of freedom and man." If antislavery was the true nationalist cause, it was also the true democratic cause: "We entreat you to be mindful of that fundamental maxim of Democracy—EQUAL RIGHTS AND EXACT JUSTICE FOR ALL MEN. Do not submit to become agents in extending legalized oppression and systematized injustice over a vast territory yet exempt from these terrible evils." Old complaints about southern oligarchy became a powerful call to overthrow the despotic Slave Power.

The "Appeal" was a masterstroke of political strategy as well as powerful propaganda. The six authors plotted the timing of their manifesto as carefully as they did its language. (Just as Douglas was about to initiate the Senate debate over his bill, Salmon Chase nonchalantly asked for and received a temporary delay, purportedly to give him extra time to read the bill, but actually to give the *National Era* and the *Times* a few extra hours to get the "Appeal" printed.) By striking immediately, the Independent Democrats caught Douglas off guard and shifted the terms of debate onto their own ground. No longer could anybody pretend that the Kansas-Nebraska Bill was chiefly a railroad improvement project or a benign effort to bring new territories officially into the orderly national fold. It was a bill about slavery and democracy and would be contested as such.[15]

Over the next four months northern anti-Nebraska feeling, molded by the "Appeal," turned into a popular conflagration. Hundreds of local meetings sent petitions to Congress denouncing the "Nebraska infamy" and demanding the bill's defeat. Nine free-state legislatures either excoriated the measure or pointedly refused to endorse it. (Illinois lawmakers backed the bill only after Douglas and his friends and agents exerted intense pressure.) Even some inveterate Hunker Democrats joined the protests. "The Nebraska peace measure is working as might have been expected," one New Hampshire Democrat wrote to his brother, a close friend of President Pierce's, soon after the congressional debate ended. "Everybody almost is ready for a rebellion."[16]

Events outside Washington fortuitously deepened the crisis. In March, a hired-out slave named Anthony Burns, in his early twenties, escaped from his Virginia master, stowed away on a ship in Richmond, and arrived undetected in Boston. There, Burns found a job working in a black clothes dealer's shop on Brattle Street, not far from where the radical political writer David Walker had had his own clothing shop a quarter of a century earlier. Burns, like Walker, was deeply religious (the result, in Burns's case, of a Baptist revival that swept through his master's district in the mid-1840s), and like Walker, his religious piety shaped his hatred of slavery. ("Until my tenth year I did not care what became of me," he later recalled, "but soon after I began to learn that there is a Christ who came to make us free.") Soon after his arrival, he wrote to his brother to tell him of his deliverance, and took the pains to arrange to have the letter mailed from Canada—but he dated the letter at Boston. His master, Charles Suttle, intercepted the letter. In May, as debate over Douglas's bill reached its conclusion in Washington, Suttle set off for Boston to retrieve his human property under the Fugitive Slave Law.[17]

On the Senate floor, Stephen Douglas mounted an ingenious and disingenuous argument that the legislation of 1850, by opening up to popular sovereignty territory above and below the compromise line, had already nullified the Missouri Compromise. Antislavery northerners destroyed that claim by pointing out that the 1850 truce applied only to the Mexican cession and not to the Louisiana Purchase lands, and that everyone, including Douglas, understood so at the time. Douglas nevertheless prevailed in the Senate, with help from the White

House, by a wide margin. The situation was much more difficult in the House, where mainstream northern Democrats, feeling strong pressure from their home districts, worked up the nerve to resist their party's establishment. Every northern Whig representative voted against the bill (just as every northern Whig senator had)—and nearly half of the northern Democrats either voted nay or were paired against the measure. Tellingly, only two in five New York Democrats backed the bill, despite Douglas's fierce efforts to force them into line. Only because of the extra southern representation granted under the three-fifths clause did the bill pass on May 22, by a margin of 113 to 100. "Nebraska is through the House," the bill's southern Whig floor manager Alexander Stephens exulted. "I took the reins in my hand, applied whip and spur, and brought the 'wagon' out at eleven o'clock P.M. Glory enough for one day."[18]

Stephens's glory, however, spelled out his party's ruin. Many New York Silver Grays and other conservative northern Whigs had been offended by Douglas's measure, not for any antislavery reasons but on the conservative grounds that a compromise of more than thirty years' standing ought not to be destroyed. Yet by seizing the initiative with their "Appeal," the antislavery men crippled these northern conservatives' efforts to stake out their own political position, and they pushed southern Whigs into supporting Douglas lest they look like traitors to their section. The result was devastating to the Whig Party. "No man has . . . struggled as I have to preserve it as a national party," the conservative Connecticut Whig Truman Smith wrote at the end of January, but "I shall have nothing to do with any Southern Whig who joins Stephen A. Douglas in introducing into Congress & into the country another controversy on the subject of slavery." In the final tallies, a majority of southern Whigs, in both Houses, did exactly as Smith had feared. For all practical political purposes, the national Whig Party died on May 22, 1854, *aet.* 21 years.[19]

The Kansas-Nebraska Bill struggle also shattered the northern Democracy. "All democracy left the democratic party," the veteran Massachusetts labor Jacksonian Frederick Robinson later wrote of the reaction by anti-Nebraska Democrats, "and every true democrat that was too intelligent to be cheated by a name deserted its ranks." For some Democratic leaders, including Benton and Martin Van Buren, the ancient ties of party were strong enough to endure even their indignation over the repeal of the Missouri Compromise. But for many of the Barnburners and other antislavery Democrats—including William Cullen Bryant, Preston King, and David Wilmot—Kansas-Nebraska was the final insult; other angry old Jacksonians including Benjamin Butler and Francis Blair were coming to the same conclusion. The defections left the Democracy almost fully transformed into the party of the slaveholders, backed by a sharply reduced number of northern appeasers. Somewhere, John C. Calhoun's shade smiled. Two Yankees, Stephen A. Douglas and Franklin Pierce, under pressure from undaunted southerners, had turned the Democratic Party that Calhoun had long distrusted into a reasonable facsimile of the pro-slavery party he had spent two decades trying to create.[20]

The explosive denouement of Anthony Burns's story in Boston, beginning only two days after the Kansas-Nebraska Bill's passage, worsened the parties' disarray. On May 24, a deputy federal marshal arrested Burns on a false charge of robbery and incarcerated him under heavy guard in the federal courthouse. Boston's abolitionists responded much as they had in the earlier fugitive slave captures. A group of blacks met in the basement of Tremont Temple and decided to set Burns free. A much larger gathering at Faneuil Hall, largely of whites, denounced the "Virginia KIDNAPPER!," got word of the blacks' march on the courthouse, and dispersed, with hundreds rushing off to join in Burns's liberation. Armed with hatchets, pistols, and a battering ram, a small group of blacks led by the young white abolitionist minister Thomas Wentworth Higginson broke through the door, but were repulsed by club-swinging marshals. Someone fired a shot; then one of the deputies shrieked that he had been stabbed and he died several minutes later. Burns remained in custody.[21]

President Pierce reacted even more fiercely than Fillmore had in the Thomas Sims case in 1851, ordering Secretary of War Jefferson Davis to send marines, cavalry, and artillery to Boston, along with a federal revenue cutter that would await the inevitable order and return Burns to slavery. At one point, Burns's claimant, Charles Suttle, seemed willing to allow the abolitionists to purchase Burns's freedom, but the federal attorney insisted on enforcing the Fugitive Slave Law. Burns's legal defense, headed by Richard Henry Dana Jr., unavailingly tried to stall for time. Finally, on June 2—three days after President Pierce signed the Kansas-Nebraska Bill into law—federal troops marched the manacled captive through the streets of Boston to the wharfside. A throng estimated at fifty thousand persons witnessed the procession, their emotions shifting between sorrow and outrage. From inside buildings draped in funereal crepe came hisses and shouts of "Shame!" and "Kidnappers!" City church bells tolled a dirge. The scene shocked even conservative Bostonians. "When it was all over, and I was left alone in my office," wrote one old-line Whig, "I put my hands in my face and wept. I could do nothing less." In New York, a disgusted Walt Whitman, on the verge of his breakthrough as a poet, composed "A Boston Ballad": "How bright shine the cutlasses of the foremost troops!/Every man holds his revolver, marching stiff through Boston town."[22]

The Burns affair revived the fugitive slave frenzy and loudly punctuated the debates over Kansas-Nebraska. A federal grand jury indicted seven white and black abolitionists, including Higginson, for riot and incitement, but the government eventually dropped the cases, knowing that there was not a jury in Massachusetts that would vote for conviction. The New England states passed new

personal liberty laws at variance with federal law, as, eventually, did the legislatures of Ohio, Michigan, and Wisconsin. It was as if Anthony Burns had finally
completed Harriet Beecher Stowe's mission, arousing the northern majority
against slavery and the Slave Power—including, Dana wrote in his journal,
"[m]en who were hostile or unpleasant in 1851." To the delight of antislavery veterans, the outbursts over Kansas-Nebraska and Burns, coming one right after the
other, finally dissolved party allegiances. "Thank God," one Bostonian wrote to
Charles Sumner, "the chains that have bound the people to their old organizations, have been snapped assunder."[23]

Yet if the old organizations and loyalties had broken down, it was far from
clear what new political alliances would replace them. Would the antislavery
Whigs, as William Henry Seward and others now hoped, reemerge as a sectional
party to counter the slaveholder-dominated Democracy? If so, what would
become of the antislavery Democrats and of the old-line conservative northern
Whigs? What would become of the southern Whigs, some of whom had begun
drifting over to the Democracy, but others of whom, especially in the border
states, clung to their moderation on slavery issues? Much would depend on
events in the new territories now open to slavery, and especially in the territory of
Kansas. "Come on, then, gentlemen of the slave States," Seward bellowed three
days after the Kansas-Nebraska Bill passed the House. "Since there is no escaping your challenge, I accept it in behalf of the cause of freedom. We will engage
in competition for the virgin soil of Kansas, and God give the victory to the side
which is strongest in numbers as it is in right."[24] Discerning God's will would be
a gruesome business.

BLEEDING KANSAS, NATIVISM, AND
THE FORMATION OF THE REPUBLICAN PARTY

In February 1854, Eli Thayer, an educator, entrepreneur, and member of the
Massachusetts legislature, came up with the idea of forming a joint-stock company to promote the settlement of New Englanders in the proposed Kansas Ter-
ritory. Incorporated in April, and funded chiefly by the Whig manufacturer
Amos Lawrence, the Massachusetts Emigrant Aid Society (soon renamed the
New England Emigrant Aid Company) was a frankly profit-minded venture that
hoped to make a nice return by finding inexpensive group fares for sending New
Englanders west, and by then providing them with the means to begin construct-
ing their own towns and villages. (The first of the new towns would take
Lawrence's name as its own.) The company's social, political, and philanthropic
assumptions, however, came through clearly in its announced determination to
establish a Kansas newspaper as an "index of the love of freedom and of good

morals, which it is hoped may characterize the State now to be formed." By extending greater New England to the prairie, Thayer, Lawrence, and their investors appeared to intend, or at least to suppose, that Kansas would be free soil. By year's end, about 450 Emigrant Aid Company settlers had arrived at the site of Lawrence.[25]

The Yankees initially found themselves outnumbered by thousands of pro-slavery Missourians who had crossed the border and set down stakes. Few of the Missourians or emigrants from other slave states actually owned slaves, but they despised the New Englanders for what they saw as their air of moral superiority and their sickly love of blacks. Mocked as "pukes" and "border ruffians" by the free-staters, the pro-slavery men were determined to harass the abolitionists out of Kansas by any means necessary. ("We will be compelled to shoot, burn & hang, but the thing will soon be over," the ever violent Senator David Atchison predicted.) In November 1854, when the newly arrived territorial governor, Andrew Reeder, scheduled an election for a delegate to Congress, Atchison led an invasion force of more than one thousand Missourians to make sure that the pro-slavery candidate prevailed. With the help of seventeen hundred ballots later discovered to be bogus, Atchison's choice won the seat. In Kansas, it seemed, democratic power would grow out of the barrel of a gun.[26]

Back in the free North, a new antislavery political party, quickened by the Kansas-Nebraska fight, was struggling to be born. In the larger states of Pennsylvania, New York, and Massachusetts, where the tidal wave of 1852 had not completely wiped out the Whig Party, antislavery Whigs tried to pin the latest crisis on the Democrats. One party newspaper claimed that "the spreading of slavery over free territory is A LOCOFOCO MEASURE"; others, that northern Whig solidarity against the Kansas-Nebraska Bill had left the party stronger than it had been in years. William Seward and Thurlow Weed in New York were particularly insistent that the antislavery insurgency defer to the existing party of freedom—their own—and join it. Others, including Abraham Lincoln—deeply shocked by what Lincoln disparaged as "the spirit of Nebraska"—were less dogmatically partisan, but refrained, just yet, from abandoning their Whig loyalties.[27]

Anti-Nebraska Democrats, Free Democrats, and even some antislavery Whigs had other ideas. What was the point, Democrats and Free Democrats asked, to pledge allegiance to leaders of a party they had opposed for so long? For some antislavery Democrats, opposition to Whiggery had been the one last fiber attaching them to the Democracy. Why should they now genuflect to the Whig master manipulator Thurlow Weed? And what did Whiggery even amount to, now that the southern portion of the party had helped the Democrats destroy the Missouri Compromise? "I have ceased to expect wisdom from the Whig party," the liberal Whig editor Horace Greeley wrote to Schuyler Colfax early in 1853, before the Kansas-Nebraska fight pushed him over the edge.

"It is like the duelist whose brains *couldn't* have been injured by the bullet through his head—'cause if he had had any brains, he wouldn't have been in any such predicament." Only a new party combining all antislavery northerners, along the lines sketched out by the "Appeal of the Independent Democrats," would satisfy the growing insurgency.[28]

The anti-Nebraska fusion movement began taking shape three months before Douglas's bill actually passed. On February 22, Michigan's Free Democrats convened in Jackson and nominated a former Democrat for governor and two former Whigs for lesser offices. Six days later, antislavery Democrats and Whigs joined with Free Democrats in Ripon, Wisconsin, and resolved that, should the Kansas-Nebraska Bill pass, they would form a new "Republican" party (its name a tribute to the Jeffersonian Republican Party of old) to fight slavery's expansion. Larger state conventions, under various labels, named fusion slates. The most radical of them followed the Ripon example by calling themselves Republicans, and adopted resolutions based on the Free Soil platform of 1848 and the Free Democratic platform of 1852. More hesitant meetings (under titles such as "Union," "Fusion," "People's Party," "Independent," and "Anti-Administration") adopted narrower programs opposing repeal of the Missouri Compromise.[29]

The anti-Nebraska outrage was fearsome, but by the time the 1854 elections began in earnest, nothing approaching a coherent antislavery party was in place. Compounding the antislavery men's difficulties, the northern nativist impulse, long dormant within the Whig Party, had resurfaced as a conservative political alternative for disaffected voters.

Nativism—or, to be more precise, anti-Catholicism—had had a curious political career since the urban rioting and local anti-immigrant election campaigns of the 1830s. After 1845, the numbers of new immigrants skyrocketed, fed by people propelled from their homes by political unrest and agricultural disaster, and attracted to the United States by cheap steerage fares and a booming economy. The new immigrant wave of the 1840s and 1850s—nearly three million new arrivals between 1845 and 1854, representing the greatest proportional arrival of foreign-born in American history—was also markedly poorer and more Catholic than previous streams of newcomers. Roughly two in five of the immigrants came from famine-ravaged Ireland, and nearly as many came from distressed, heavily Catholic regions of Germany.[30]

Yet the cycles of migration and American political reaction seemed out of sync. The hard times of the late 1830s and early 1840s had inflamed ethnic and religious hatreds. Tensions between Protestant and Catholic workers degenerated into destructive and lethal rioting, most viciously in Philadelphia. In 1844, a nativist American Republican party, led by wealthy and middle-class evangelicals and by old-school Whigs, elected the wealthy publisher James Harper as mayor of New York City and won three congressional seats in Philadelphia. But then, just as the Irish famine immigration began, the nativist political movement stalled. In New York, the staunchly antinativist Seward Whigs reasserted control and cut off Whig support for the American Republicans. More broadly, recovery from the prolonged depression that had begun in the late 1830s alleviated the desperation in urban working-class districts; the war with Mexico (in which the pro-Catholic northern Democrats pushed for absorbing portions of a Catholic country into Protestant America) blurred ethnic and religious divisions; and anti-Catholic animus receded into more conventional channels within the Protestant churches and certain conservative precincts of the Whig Party. Among the latter was a New York fraternal group, the Order of United Americans, founded by a conservative Whig engraver and Harper supporter, Thomas R. Whitney.[31]

The sudden revival of nativism in the 1850s had political as well as social origins. The new immigrant wave reached its peak between 1850 and 1855, at a level five times greater than a decade earlier. (By 1855, an absolute majority of New York City's population had been born abroad, almost all of them recent arrivals from Ireland and Germany.) The fresh influx settled into urban immigrant districts that were already overcrowded and scraping by in an overstocked market for unskilled and casual labor. Crime rates and demands on public and private relief rose precipitously, which nativists blamed on the immigrants themselves — especially the Catholic Irish, spiritual captives of a church that, with its exculpatory rituals, supposedly encouraged dissolution. The immigrants' Catholicism, one nativist pamphleteer wrote in 1855, "had lowered the standard till it was beneath the average level of human nature."[32]

The fierce official Catholic reaction to these charges heightened the tensions. Most outspoken was New York's Archbishop John Hughes, Seward's ally during the school-funding controversies more than ten years earlier. Hughes not only refused to cower from the nativists' blasts; he conjured up their worst nightmares, declaring in one address that his church's great mission was "to convert the world, — including the inhabitants of the United States, — the people of the cities, and the people of the country . . . the Legislatures, the Senate, the Cabinet, the President, and all!" Hughes's defiance appeared in line with the crusading papacy of Pius IX (begun in 1846), which, with its staunch opposition to the European revolutions of 1848, made the Church among the most virulent opponents of liberalism and reform in the Western world. Hughes's and other prelates' equation of Free Soilers and abolitionists with the socialists and "Red Republicans" of Europe estranged him from American liberals, including Seward, but the sight of a new Church militant did even more to antagonize the established forces of conservative nativism.[33]

Divisions within American politics, and especially among the Whigs, also contributed to the nativist resurgence. The evangelical temperance movement begun in the 1820s had worked wonders through its combination of moral suasion and shaming. By 1850, alcohol had been virtually purged from northern middle-class homes where it had once been a mainstay. But the new immigrant Irish and German populations proved far less adaptable. To shut down the offensive saloons and *Biergartens* proliferating in northern cities, temperance advocates switched from coaxing to legal coercion. Their first breakthrough came with the passage in Maine of a strict prohibition law in 1851 (pushed by Portland's Whig mayor, the veteran total-abstinence campaigner Neal Dow). Over a dozen northern states adopted similar coercive laws over the next five years. The direct effects were uneven: nonenforcement of the prohibition laws was widespread; few who wanted to drink actually went dry; and in a quick counterreaction, most "Maine law" states repealed their antiliquor laws in the later 1850s. Still, the controversy reinforced the growing anxieties about the immigrant presence, just as it complicated divisions within the Whig Party. Whereas Democrats in the state legislatures generally opposed the temperance law drive, Whigs were divided between uncompromising "drys" and those who equivocated, still hoping to win over immigrant voters.[34]

The Whig divisions over nativism had worsened during the 1852 presidential campaign. With encouragement from the antinativist Seward, the Whig nominee, General Scott, tried to suppress the party's conservative legacy and court the Catholic vote. But eight years earlier, hoping to advance his political fortunes, Scott had published a letter (under the pseudonym "Americus") denouncing ignorant foreigners and their growing political influence, and demanding that naturalization be made contingent upon two years of military service. Scott's managers in 1852 tried to spin the "Americus" letter into a pro-immigrant declaration, but failed. Nor could they render credible Scott's vapid pronouncements during his "official" tour about how he simply loved "that rich Irish brogue." The result was doubly disastrous for Scott: repelled Irish Americans voted in droves for the colorless Democrat Pierce, while many conservative northern Whigs, offended by Scott's pro-immigrant appeals, sat out the election. For these conservatives, the clear political lesson was that the Whigs, and the nation, could be saved only by restricting the political rights of the papist Democratic hordes.[35]

By 1854, the anti-Catholic, antiliquor, and anti-immigrant zeal had produced a vast upsurge of organized nativism in the North, which contributed substantially to the Whig Party's collapse. Whitney's Order of United Americans (OUA)—with prominent New York Silver Gray Whigs including James Barker and Daniel Ullmann now in its leadership—claimed a membership of thirty thousand in New York State alone, as well as chapters in fifteen other states. In 1852, Barker and others began joining a smaller nativist organization, the Order of the Star Spangled Banner (OSSB), and incorporated it into the OUA to serve as a kind of political auxiliary, with Barker at the helm. Early in 1854, even before the Kansas-Nebraska Bill had been passed, Manhattan's leading Silver

Gray newspaper joined the OUA-OSSB fold, and by year's end, ex-President Fill-more, though disturbed by the most strident anti-Catholic nativists, was privately urging reluctant Whig conservatives to do the same. The energetic Barker, meanwhile, organized hundreds of OUA-OSSB lodges around the country, pledging to vote only for native-born Protestant candidates for public office. Members were instructed to handle any questions about the group's activities with the curt reply, "I know nothing." The phrase caught on, and according to reliable estimates, there were at least one million "Know-Nothings" at the move-ment's height—a formidable political power, especially in and around the immigrant-packed northern cities.[36]

As it edged into electoral politics, Know-Nothingism represented a rebirth of conservative Whiggery as an independent force, with a revamped program and a newfound, heterogeneous popular base. The movement's most prominent lead-ers were ex-Whig capitalists and other sectional conciliationists who had strongly backed the truce of 1850. Self-made businessmen like Harper were particularly conspicuous. The movement's mass following cut across class lines but consisted disproportionately of middle-aged and young urban men, in their thirties and for-ties, who worked in white-collar or skilled manufacturing jobs, or were successful small merchants or manufacturers: more petit bourgeois than working class. These were white natives who had escaped the debasements of early industrial-ization, who prided themselves on their elevation over the masses of sweatshop workers and day laborers—and who blamed the immigrants for the destruction of a fancied golden age before mass poverty, crime, and class strife. Nativist organizers reached out with particular skill to respectable, propertied, but anx-ious men at the border of middle-class life and just above it—men who came of age after the political struggles of the 1820s and 1830s and who pined for a sup-posedly pristine, preimmigrant past. It was this top-down populism—appealing to native skilled workingmen and shopkeepers as "the great bulwark of freedom and the foster-mother of liberty" while tapping into their social prejudices and insecurities—that primarily brought nativism its popular support. But it would also change the movement into a broader political coalition, focused less on Catholic immigrants than on corrupt politicians and the entire party status quo.[37]

Beneath nativism's original nostalgic rhetoric lay undemocratic aspirations of a kind that had been in abeyance in northern politics since the advent of the new-school Whigs in the later 1830s. Distrust of foreigners, and especially Catholics, had, of course, been a feature of American conservative thought dating back at least to the Federalists and the alien and sedition laws. But while it turned tradi-tional conservative disdain into an explicit attack on Catholic immigrants, nativist ideology also retrieved the broader old-line Federalist and early Whig contempt for partisan democratic politics—and, at times, for democracy itself.

Know-Nothings despised the established political parties as corrupt dispensers of patronage, interested more in gaining power and distributing spoils than in governing for the common welfare. Their own aim, as one Ohio nativist newspaper declared, was to "free our government from the . . . hordes of political leeches that are fattening their bloated carcasses in the people's money." The Democratic Party was the chief malefactor, having bought off its solid bloc of Catholic supporters with party jobs and drink and flattery. But the Know-Nothings' original mission to redeem the nation's politics advanced a deeper antidemocratic animus as well. "If democracy implies universal suffrage, or the right of all men to take part in the control of the State, without regard to the intelligence, the morals, or the principles of the man," OUA founder Thomas Whitney proclaimed, "I am no democrat." Whitney had a way of expressing nativism's political id, saying frankly what others tried to cloak, and he was also the revived movement's most prominent spokesman. By 1854, the proliferating Know-Nothing lodges were ready to pick up on Whitney's plan, which he had announced three years earlier, to establish a "great American party," a "conservative party, taking its cue from the doctrines set forth by the Order of United Americans."[38]

Hastily, they nominated their own candidates to run against the Democrats and the anti-Nebraska men. Yet as the movement grew, it absorbed voters of far less conservative views than Thomas Whitney and the OUA founders. Antislavery Democrats frustrated by the failures of their own fusion efforts in 1850 and 1851, but still suspicious of the Whigs; humble country farmers and shopkeepers resentful of the political power wielded by city machines and men of great wealth; voters simply fed up with mainline parties that had dropped their old ideological appeals and appeared to be nothing more than patronage and vote-gathering organizations—a diverse and contradictory array of alienated northerners found their way into nativism as an ill-defined reform party. Some came to nativism out of confusion and anger; others thought they could use the movement to achieve their own goals, described by one Massachusetts nativist as "a state government, not under control of powerful corporations, and a senator who would wake up the echoes of freedom in the Capitol of the nation."[39]

The point about freedom would prove crucial. In forming an alternative to the emerging antislavery fusionists, the Know-Nothings had to clarify their own views on slavery. In doing so, they articulated a vehemently anti-Nebraska position that has tricked some historians into believing the movement embodied the growing northern militancy over slavery and the Slave Power. To be sure, most nativists expressed a dislike of slavery as a backward institution, economically inferior to northern wage-labor capitalism—a blight, Whitney wrote, that discouraged "the development of great enterprises." As champions of the truce of 1850, Know-Nothing leaders were aghast at the needless provocations of the Kansas-Nebraska Act. Large numbers of Know-Nothings sincerely opposed the expansion of slavery, and the nativists' reputation as antislavery men as well as upholders of virtuous government helps explain the movement's eventual expansion into smaller towns and even rural areas where immigrants were scarce. On the other side of the divide, nativist-style contempt for Catholic immigrants was certainly an element in the thinking of many anti-Nebraska fusionists, especially in Whiggish evangelical districts.[40]

Yet there were limits to the nativist movement's antislavery commitments. Nativist leaders expressed little of the moral indignation at human bondage or at slavery's threats to democracy that propelled the Conscience Whigs, antislavery Democrats, and Free Democrats. Whitney, for one, sneered at "the attempts of Seward, Weed, Greeley, and Co., to engraft upon the Whig banner the doctrines of the abolitionists." To achieve sectional conciliation, nativist conservatives were prepared to yield a great deal to the slaveholders (including, in 1850, the Fugitive Slave Law), while they denounced Free Soilers as hateful dividers. What most concerned Whitney and others about the repeal of the Missouri Compromise was that it would feed sectional discord and give antislavery radicals additional fodder for their demagogy. Former Whig conservatives like Millard Fillmore drifted into Know-Nothingism more out of their desire to block the anti-Nebraska movement and buttress the Union than to attack Catholic immigrants. Like many of the more dedicated nativist leaders, they wanted to bury Kansas-Nebraska as a prelude to burying the slavery question once and for all—a question, one OUA leader would write in 1855, "so intrinsically difficult that wisdom and true conservatism dictate perfect silence upon it."[41]

More steadfast antislavery men immediately sensed the weaknesses in the Know-Nothings' antislavery views, and in any case regarded nativism as a distraction from the truly important issues. "Neither the Pope nor foreigners ever can govern the country or endanger its liberties," Horace Greeley's managing editor at the *Tribune*, Charles A. Dana, observed in 1854, "but the slavebreeders and slavetraders *do* govern it." Some even thought (confusing cause with effect) that the growth of political nativism was part of a Slave Power plot, "a well-timed scheme," George Julian later wrote, "to divide the people of the free states upon trifles and side issues, while the South remained a unit in defense of its great interest."[42] Few foresaw how the nativists would complicate the already confused northern political situation in 1854.

The overwhelming message of that year's election results was the thoroughness with which northern voters repudiated the badly divided Democrats. In 1852, the Pierce-King ticket had won all but two northern states; two years later, the Democrats held control of only two northern state legislatures. Northern Democratic congressional candidates took a drubbing, slashing the party's free-state delegation in the House from 93 to 22 (compared to 58 southern Democrats in the new Congress). Northern Democratic losses were especially heavy in districts where the incumbents, initially cool or even hostile to the Kansas-Nebraska Bill, finally voted for it. The antislavery forces—coming to be known simply as the Republicans—could count on holding about 100 of the 234 seats in the Thirty-fourth Congress. Yet the antislavery victory was not at all clear-cut. In some states, old partisan tensions within the antislavery coalition resurfaced quickly after the elections, with unsettling consequences. Notably, in the antislavery-dominated Illinois legislature, anti-Nebraska Democrats blocked Abraham Lincoln, still nominally a Whig, from gaining the necessary majority for election to the Senate, until Lincoln, to prevent the election of an organization Democrat, gave way to the antislavery Democrat Lyman Trumbull.[43]

More startling was the Know-Nothings' impressive showing, especially in New England and the middle Atlantic states. The most astounding nativist triumphs came in Massachusetts. A curious alliance of Cotton Whigs and Boston Irish Democrats had emerged in 1853 to defeat a referendum for a new state constitution that would have provided for, among other reforms, expanded rural representation. The constitutional struggle placed the anti-Nebraska men on the defensive and stirred up rural counties resentful at the immigrants' rising influence. Nativism suddenly caught fire, sweeping out of the western towns and consuming everything in its path. In a four-way race for governor, the Know-Nothing nominee, a hitherto obscure Boston merchant and former Webster Whig named Henry Gardner, won 63 percent of the vote. Nativists seized virtually unanimous control of the state legislature, and all of the state's members in the House of Representatives were now nativists. (They included the politically savvy Democratic congressman Nathaniel Banks of Waltham, a former factory worker and journalist known as "The Bobbin Boy," who defected to the Know-Nothings and was reelected.) The Democrats and the antislavery forces took a severe beating, but mainline Whiggery was reduced to the ultraconservative coterie who found the Know-Nothings demagogic. "Poor old Massachusetts!" Daniel Webster's former comrade Robert Winthrop moaned. "Who could have believed that the old Whig party would have been so thoroughly demoralized in so short a space of time?"[44]

Would the Know-Nothings surpass the antislavery fusionists as the major political opposition to the Democracy in the North? The odds seemed to favor them after the 1854 elections, but much would depend on the struggle in Kansas, which was fast verging on civil war. Not satisfied with their victory in the congressional delegate election in 1854, pro-slavery Missourians, egged on by David Atchison, prepared for future invasions and ballot-stuffing campaigns. Atchison and his allies were convinced—or at least claimed they were convinced—that Thayer and Lawrence's Emigrant Aid Company would eventually flood Kansas with tens of thousands of abolitionists. The charge was nonsense: at most, the company dispatched slightly more than fifteen hundred settlers by the end of 1855, and although free-soiler migrants were beginning to outnumber the slave-state Kansans, most of the new free-state advocates arrived from Ohio, Illinois, and Indiana, as well as from nonslaveholding areas in the southern border states. Far from bearing any "philanthropic" sympathies, these settlers wanted to keep slavery out of Kansas in part because they wanted the territory free of all blacks, slave and free. Without the provocations of the pro-slavery men, the northern majority probably would have made Kansas into a pro-Democratic free state. But fearing for the future of the peculiar institution in Missouri, and whipped up by the rise of the Republicans back East, the pro-slavery men continued to display what future governor John W. Geary described to President Pierce as "a virulent spirit of dogged determination to *force* slavery into this Territory."[45]

The territorial legislative elections in March 1855 turned into an even nastier and more corrupt proceeding than the delegate elections four months earlier. With Atchison once again the chief instigator, thousands of Missourians—some of them members of a new semisecret pro-slavery society, and many identified by a badge of hemp, the area's chief slave cash crop—poured over the border to vote illegally. "There are eleven hundred coming over from Platte County to vote," Atchison shamelessly exclaimed, "and if that ain't enough we can send five thousand—enough to kill every God-damned abolitionist in the Territory." There was no killing—although a group of about one thousand heavily armed Missourians did set up camp outside Lawrence on election eve—but there was plenty of intimidation, illegal vote counting, and other flagrant irregularities. The election, the prominent free-stater Charles Robinson reported, was "controlled entirely by Missourians" who had seized control of the polling places. The final count broke heavily in favor of the pro-slavery men, who elected thirty-six legislators to the free-soilers' three. Only later did a congressional investigation show that all save about 500 of the 5,427 pro-slavery votes counted had been cast illegally.[46]

Governor Reeder was unaware of the full scope of the fraud, but his initial sympathies for slavery had by now been destroyed by border ruffians' threats on his life if he tried to interfere. Reeder ordered new elections in one-third of the territory's election districts, and free-staters prevailed in most of them. But when the legislature met at Pawnee City in July, it scornfully seated the original pro-slavery winners. The lawmakers then passed a set of laws that incorporated Missouri's slave code and inflicted heavy penalties against anyone who spoke or wrote against slavery. Reeder journeyed east to inform the citizenry of the antidemocratic farce on the prairie and to beg President Pierce to intervene. "Kansas has been invaded, conquered, subjugated by an armed force from beyond her borders, led on by a fanatical spirit," he told one audience. Pierce greeted Reeder at the White House warmly, said that he approved of all he had done, and remarked that Kansas had caused him greater distress than anything since the death of his son. But the president went on to blame the Emigrant Aid

Company for the catastrophe and, at Atchison's urging, replaced Reeder with a less sensitive soul, the Hunker ex-governor of Ohio, Wilson Shannon. Shannon began implementing what northerners and Kansas free-soilers had begun calling the "bogus laws" passed by the territorial legislature.[47]

Pierce's fecklessness contributed to a crisis of political legitimacy. Free-staters—who, by the fall of 1855, represented a majority of settlers—flaunted the legislature's laws and freely accepted crates of new-model, breech-loading Sharps rifles sent out by sympathizers in New England. In September, a convention of "all the Free State elements of Kansas Territory" met at Big Springs near Lawrence, denounced the border ruffians and the territorial legislature, formed a free-state party, and nominated ex-Governor Reeder to Congress. A month later, the organized free-soilers reconvened in Topeka, drew up a territorial constitution that abolished slavery after July 4, 1857, and called their own elections for governor and a new legislature. The pro-slavery men, not surprisingly, boycotted the elections. Thereafter, Kansas had two governments, the official pro-slavery one (which had moved its seat to Lecompton, closer to the Missouri border) and the free-state one in Topeka. With both sides armed to the teeth, it seemed only a matter of time before combat commenced.[48]

The murder of Charles Dow, a pro–free-state settler, by a pro-slavery man on November 21 touched off a series of incidents that set the informal armies in motion. A force of Missourians, numbering well over twelve hundred men, crossed the border and tramped to the countryside outside of the Yankees' main stronghold in Lawrence, torching and pillaging farms in their path, with the eventual objective, one settler wrote, of burning down the city and driving out "all the *Dambd* Abilitionists." The Lawrence free-staters, a thousand strong, outfitted with their new rifles and a howitzer, and receiving a steady flow of reinforcements from the surrounding areas, dug in for a fight to the finish. Governor Shannon rushed to Lawrence and, with Atchison's help among the pro-slavery men, persuaded both sides to lay down their weapons. But Atchison's advice to the Missourians was more tactical than pacific. "If you attack Lawrence now, you attack as a mob," he told the irregular army, "and what would be the result? You could cause the election of an abolition President, and the ruin of the Democratic party. Wait a little. You cannot now destroy these people without losing more than you would gain."[49]

Free-staters and slave-staters alike held their fire for a few months, over a harsh and disabling winter. In the interim, they and the rest of the country would reflect hard and passionately on the struggle's importance and where it might lead. The northern press thundered against the official Kansas legislature, and publicized the Big Springs convention's resolution that the despotic lawmakers had "libeled the declaration of Independence, violated the constitutional bill of rights, and brought contempt and disgrace upon our republican institutions at home and abroad." Southerners insisted that any attempt to block the admission of Kansas over slavery would compel the Union's dissolution.[50] And while democracy seemed to dangle in the balance in Kansas, voters everywhere prepared for a national election with the major political parties in chaos.

1856: DRESS REHEARSAL FOR REVOLUTION

Among the most prominent northerners moved by the Kansas conflict was Reverend Henry Ward Beecher, the son of Lyman Beecher, brother of Harriet Beecher Stowe, and pastor of Brooklyn's Congregational Plymouth Church of the Pilgrims. Beecher opposed slavery, but, like his sister, he was not an abolitionist radical, and during the early stages of the Kansas controversy, he agonized over what a mere minister could do. During a trip through New England early in 1856, he discovered Yankee clergymen—including, to his lasting inspiration, his father—preaching against the Kansas outrages and backing a monster protest petition drive. In March, Beecher himself spoke at United Church in New Haven, where a group of sixty had formed an antislavery band bound for Kansas. Noting that previous northern settlers had traveled armed, Beecher said he hoped the present group would "lack for nothing." The aging Yale professor of chemistry Benjamin Silliman, a former slaveholder, immediately pledged twenty-five dollars toward the purchase of a Sharps rifle. United Church's pastor, Reverend Leonard Bacon, pledged the same, and soon Beecher, carried away by the spirit, declared that Plymouth Church would provide not twenty-five dollars but twenty-five rifles. In a few days, more than six hundred dollars was collected, and the rifles were shipped off (along with twenty-five copies of holy scripture) in a crate marked "Bibles." Beecher, back in Brooklyn, was embarrassed when critics called the rifle shipments "Beecher's Bibles" and his congregation "the Church of the Holy Rifle," but he stood by his claim that, in Kansas, "self-defense is a religious duty."[51]

In early March, the Topeka free-state government formally convened, and in mid-April, a special House committee arrived in the territory to investigate the charges of fraud in the previous year's elections. Witnesses told the congressmen one shocking tale after another; the spring brought fresh arrivals of northern settlers; pro-slavery tempers cracked. "Blood for Blood!" screamed one pro-slavery sheet, *Squatter Sovereignty*. "Let us purge ourselves of all abolition emissaries." Pro-slavery judge Samuel Lecompte convinced a grand jury to indict the entire Topeka government—"men who are dubbed governors . . . men who are dubbed all the various other dubs"—on charges of high treason. The local federal marshal falsely claimed that various free-staters forcibly resisted being served with papers, and called on the law-abiding citizens of Kansas to gather in Lecompton to form a deputized posse that would help the militia round up the miscreants. Lawrence was an obvious target, as several of the free-state officials lived there and the grand jury had brought additional indictments against the town's two antislavery newspapers and the Free State Hotel. Atchison's Missourians took the hint and joined the encampment at Lecompton.[52]

On May 21, the pro-slavery force of between five and eight hundred men, dragging with them four six-pounder brass cannons, lay siege to Lawrence. Reluctant to resist the federal government's authority, the free-staters stood aside, and the pro-slavery men went on a rampage, burning homes, ransacking shops, and smashing to bits the antislavery newspaper presses. By the time the marauding ended, the Free State Hotel was a smoldering ruin, and the home and farm of the free-state governor, Dr. Charles Robinson, had been torched. Atop the gutted offices of the *Herald of Freedom* flew a bright red flag with a star in its center, the slogan "Southern Rights" inscribed on one side and "South Carolina" on the other. Reporters on the scene from Republican newspapers wrote dispatches about "the Sack of Lawrence." The pro-slavery press in Kansas and in the South told a very different story: "Glorious Triumph of the Law and Order Party Over Fanaticism in Kansas," ran the headline of the Lecompton *Union*.[53]

On the day before Lawrence fell, Charles Sumner concluded a two-day speech in the Senate that he would later entitle "The Crime Against Kansas." Sumner knew nothing of what was about to transpire out West, but he was already furious. For months, Congress had been debating rival bills admitting Kansas as a state, either with the Topeka constitution or with a new constitution to be drafted under the auspices of the Lecompton government. Since southern Democrats controlled the Senate and northern Republicans controlled the House, neither side could prevail. Instead, speakers used the floors of Congress as soapboxes, to score points against their opponents. Finally, Sumner could take no more of the southerners' defense of the pro-slavery Kansans. "I shall make the most thorough & complete speech in my life," he wrote to Salmon Chase. "My soul is wrung by this outrage, & I shall pour it forth."[54]

"The Crime Against Kansas," delivered to a packed Senate gallery, was an overblown effort at classical oratory — carefully rehearsed, at times pompous and pedantic, but also unforgiving in its denunciations of slavery and the Slave Power. The alleged crime that was its centerpiece was "the rape of a virgin territory, compelling it to the hateful embrace of slavery," for which Sumner held the entire Pierce administration guilty of complicity. Squired by the Sancho Panza of Slavery, Stephen Douglas, the rapists had set loose assassins and thugs in Kansas — "[h]irelings, picked from the drunken spew and vomit of an uneasy civilization" — and established a fraudulent legislature that passed a slave code unsurpassed in "its complex completely of wickedness." Sumner defended the Emigrant Aid Company as a group of sober conservative businessmen, and com-

mended William Henry Seward's bill for the admission of Kansas as the only reasonable response to the Slave Power's attacks on God and the Constitution. Yet
despite its flashes of polemical brilliance, there was nothing new in the substance of Sumner's speech, while its heavy ballast of historical references,
extended metaphors, and gratuitous classical allusions at times threatened to
capsize it.[55]

Sumner's performance did manage two feats. As if to shame his Democratic
opponents, he reached back to recent history and explained how the ideas of
Jacksonian Democracy favored a free Kansas, not a slave Kansas. He drew a parallel between the Topeka free-state constitution and the case of Michigan,
where, in the mid-1830s, a popular convention, working at odds with an existing
territorial legislature, drafted a constitution for statehood—which Jackson and
the Democrats (including then-Congressman Franklin Pierce) accepted. The
true principle of democratic popular sovereignty could not be clearer than as
expounded by Thomas Hart Benton during the Michigan controversy twenty
years earlier: "The sovereign power to govern themselves was in the majority, and
they could not be divested of it." The most intense opposition to this claim, Sumner noted, came from John C. Calhoun, who supported legalistic authority over
the people, but Jackson and the Democrats overcame him. Yet two decades later,
Sumner declared, the nation was supposed to reject the majority's will and
respect "the fantastic tricks now witnessed in Kansas" instead of legitimate
democracy. "No such madness prevailed under Andrew Jackson," Sumner
declared, while glaring at some of Jackson's leading acolytes and would-be successors, including Stephen Douglas.[56]

Sumner also insulted the Slave Power, personified by the white-maned South
Carolina senator Andrew P. Butler of the F Street Mess, in the vilest possible
terms. Butler had given a speech that denounced the free-staters as fanatics, and
Sumner, early in "The Crime Against Kansas," attacked Butler as Don Quixote to
Douglas's Sancho Panza, tilting against antislavery "with such ebullition of ani-
mosity" that he had to be shown up for who he really was. And so Sumner exposed
him as an old man "who has chosen a mistress to whom he has made his vows,
and who . . . though polluted in the sight of the world, is chaste in his sight—I
mean the harlot Slavery." The next day, Sumner singled out Butler once again, as
one who had discharged "the loose expectoration of his speech" in defense of
South Carolina, a state wallowing in its "shameful imbecility from slavery." Cass
and Douglas immediately launched counterattacks on Sumner's insults. Republican newspapers, although pleased by the speech's substance, thought its rhetoric
excessive and counterproductive. For southerners, Sumner had committed an
unpardonable offense that deserved the meanest sort of punishment.[57]

Two days later, Sumner was sitting at his desk on the Senate floor after
adjournment, attending to his correspondence and franking copies of his contro-

versial speech. Out of nowhere, he heard a voice address him, and he looked up to see a tall man whom he did not recognize looming directly above. "I have read your speech twice over carefully," said the stranger. "It is a libel on South Carolina, and Mr. Butler, who is a relative of mine." As he spoke these last words, the man crashed a hollow gold-headed cane across Sumner's head, which knocked Sumner blind, then hit him again and again, until Sumner (his legs trapped beneath his desk, which was bolted to the floor) rose with such force that he wrenched the desk from its moorings. Still the blows rained down, twenty or more, snapping the cane into pieces, until Sumner lurched forward and fell to the floor senseless, his head gushing blood. A few senators tried to stop the assault but were held at bay by another cane-wielder, one of two men who had accompanied the assailant into the chamber. Other senators, including Douglas and Robert Toombs, watched in silence (Toombs with complete approval) and offered no assistance to their colleague. Finally, Ambrose Murray, an antislavery Whig congressman who happened to be there, seized the assailant. Sumner's friends helped the victim to his feet and guided him to a sofa in the Senate lobby.[58]

The attacker turned out to be the second-term congressman Preston Brooks, a South Carolina cousin of Butler's. (His accomplices were Congressmen Laurence Keitt, also of South Carolina, and Henry Edmundson of Virginia.) A staunch pro-slavery Democrat, Brooks had already declared that the fate of the South would be decided in Kansas, but now, honor as well as interest demanded instant vengeance. ("I went to work very deliberately . . . ," Brooks later said in a speech to the House, "and speculated somewhat as to whether I should employ a horsewhip or a cowhide.") The severity of the attack, and Brooks's pride in it, incensed even those northerners who had bridled at Sumner's excessive address. "Has it come to this," the old Jacksonian William Cullen Bryant asked in the *Evening Post*, "that we must speak with bated breath in the presence of our Southern masters? . . . Are we too, slaves, slaves for life, a target for their brutal blows, when we do not comport ourselves to please them?"[59]

Southern celebrations of Brooks and his deed deepened the shock. "Our approbation, at least, is entire and unreserved," the *Richmond Enquirer* announced. "We consider the act good in conception, better in execution, and best of all in consequences. The vulgar Abolitionists in the Senate are getting above themselves. . . . They must be lashed into submission." Brooks claimed that his admirers were begging for fragments of his cane "as *sacred relicts*." The House voted to expel him, but the southern members blocked the required two-thirds' majority. Brooks, defiant, resigned nevertheless and returned to South Carolina, determined to win vindication through reelection (which he would). The only punishment he would ever receive was a three-hundred-dollar fine assessed by a local court. Sumner, traumatized mentally and physically, would not return to steady work in the Senate for another four years. During his convalescence, the Massachusetts legislature reelected him, turning his repaired, empty desk in the Senate into a silent protest against the Slave Power's savagery.[60]

News of "Bleeding Sumner" hit "Bleeding Kansas" hard, especially coming so soon after the attack on Lawrence. A reliable witness said that one free-stater, in particular, went "crazy—*crazy*" upon hearing of Sumner's caning—the would-be guerrilla warrior John Brown. Brown, aged fifty-five and the father of twenty children, had left behind the quiet strains of wool growing and merchandising back in Springfield, Massachusetts, to become an avenger against slavery. His League of Gileadites, organized during the fugitive slave controversy, had come to nothing, as had had a plan, backed by Gerrit Smith, to establish a colony for free blacks in the Adirondack Mountains of New York. In the summer of 1855, Brown followed six of his sons to Osawatomie, a small settlement near Pottawatomie Creek in eastern Kansas. The sons had come to make a new life for themselves; Brown became more interested in fighting slavery. He was named captain of the Pottawatomie Rifles company of the free-stater Liberty Guards, and in May, he and his men were among the antislavery forces who rushed to the aid of besieged Lawrence, only to learn en route that the town had been leveled. A day later came word of Brooks's attack on Sumner.[61]

"Something must be done to show these barbarians that we, too, have rights," Brown declaimed—and he conceived a plan of retaliation for the caning of Sumner and the murders of free-staters over the previous year. On the night of May 24–25, Brown, four of his sons, and three other men, carrying broadswords, ambushed the farm of James Doyle, an anti–free-stater but not a slaveholder. They dragged Doyle and his two grown sons from their house and hacked them to pieces, sparing Doyle's wife and fourteen-year-old son. Then the band moved to the Wilkinson farm and abducted and killed the law-and-order man Allen Wilkinson before ending their attacks at the home of James Harris, where they split the skull of another pro-slavery partisan, William Sherman. Brown and his sons eluded capture; pro-slavery men destroyed the Brown homestead; and the massacre, combined with the Lawrence affair, touched off escalated violence all across the settled portions of the territory. Two hundred men (including Brown's son Frederick) died in the renewed combat. Brown himself fought on uncaptured until the autumn, when he headed back East to raise money to provide fresh supplies, hard cash, and more Sharps rifles to the Kansas warriors. "You know what I have done in Kansas . . . ," he cryptically told a group of abolitionist sympathizers in New York. "I have no other purpose but to serve the cause of liberty."[62]

Northern reaction to Brown's atrocities was divided. While some antislavery editors idolized him as "Old Osawatomie Brown," others looked away. Stories even began circulating that Brown had not been involved, or had acted in self-defense.[63] Brown, for his own part, would become cleverly evasive whenever questioned about what had happened along Pottawatomie Creek. In any event, dispatches about the subsequent bloodshed in Kansas soon enough overshadowed Brown's massacre. And by summer's end, when the prairie fighting temporarily died down, public attention had switched to the confusing presidential campaign.

"A VICTORIOUS DEFEAT": THE 1856 ELECTIONS AND THE CONSOLIDATION OF THE REPUBLICANS

The most surprising development in national politics during the Kansas excitement had been the precipitous decline of the Know-Nothing movement. The resurgence of the slavery issue played some role in diverting attention away from nativism, and so, too, did a sudden diminution of immigration after 1855—especially from Ireland, whose ruined population was nearly depleted of migrants. But the chief causes of the Know-Nothings' difficulties were internal to the movement and involved sectional issues.[64]

In part, the nativists were the victims of their own success and ambition. After the party's strong showing in 1854, Know-Nothing organizers believed they could look southward and build a national party, as the antislavery men could never do. The nativists' greatest appeal was in the Border South among former Whigs who abjured the disunionist southern Democracy, but there was also substantial nativist sentiment in southern cities, where the immigrant presence had grown. In 1855, Know-Nothings won a large majority of seats in the Maryland house of delegates, took control of the Tennessee legislature, ran well in Kentucky, and, overall, performed better than the Whigs had in any election since 1848. Some nativists were persuaded that with an enlarged vote in the South in 1856, their party could actually win the presidency for ex-President Fillmore, who was by now a Know-Nothing devotee.[65]

Instead of nationalizing nativism, however, the Know-Nothings' expansion caused an implosion. In June 1855, newly christened as the American Party, the Know-Nothings met in Philadelphia to draft their platform—and sectional divisions cracked wide open. Some northern statewide conventions had already adopted antislavery resolutions, while others had deferred to the South. New Englanders, led by newly elected Massachusetts Governor Henry Gardner, insisted on pragmatic grounds that without some sort of renunciation of the Kansas-Nebraska Act, the party would be doomed east of the Hudson. Southern delegates, joined by the conservative New York Silver Grays and the Californians, repudiated any such move as sectional and un-American. Able to agree about tightening naturalization laws and otherwise fighting the "aggressive policy and corrupting tendencies" of Roman Catholicism, the delegates split over slavery. When a majority report from the platform committee upholding Kansas-Nebraska passed the convention, a large majority of the northerners, including all of the New England and the Old Northwest delegations, formally repudiated the platform and boycotted the rest of the proceedings. The division was dually ruinous, not only pitting northerners against southerners but also dividing northern conservative Unionists in New York and the other middle Atlantic states against the rest of the northern nativists.[66]

A second factor was also spoiling the Know-Nothings' prospects: the manipulative efforts by antislavery men in the party who were either fed up with appeasing the South or had intended all along to capture the movement for the antislavery cause. The Massachusetts Know-Nothings, and their most outspoken antislavery leader, newly elected Senator Henry F. Wilson, exemplified what was happening. A former journeyman cordwainer from Natick, born in poverty, Wilson had risen to become a shoe manufacturer, entered politics as a new school Whig, and in 1848 helped to form the Free Soil Party. In 1854, when conservative Massachusetts Whigs, still certain they could dominate the state's politics, refused to fuse with the emerging Republicans, Wilson won the anti-Nebraska nomination for governor in 1854. Yet Wilson, whose background made him thoroughly familiar with the popular nativist milieu, sensed the Know-Nothing upheaval that was about to overtake the state's politics, and he signed up with the nativists, hoping to win their nomination as well.[67]

Not wanting to appear creatures of the free-soilers, the Know-Nothings spurned Wilson and chose instead Henry Gardner. But Wilson was not done. Knowing that the nativists could not afford to ignore the antislavery vote, he agreed to drop out of the governor's race and support Gardner if the nativist leaders would support him for the U.S. Senate seat soon to be vacated by Edward Everett, who had decided to retire. Some antislavery leaders accused Wilson of betrayal, but at least one old-line Whig conservative, Robert Winthrop, figured out his real intentions and how they had changed the political calculus. "Our K.N. lodges," he wrote a friend, "have been controlled by the most desperate sort of Free Soil adventurers." The newly elected Know-Nothing legislature elected Wilson to the Senate, where he paid little attention to nativist issues and became a stalwart Republican. In the House, the former Democrat Nathaniel Banks, elected to a second term as a Know-Nothing, likewise threw in his lot with the Republicans. (The House Republicans, in turn, elevated Banks to the Speakership of the new Congress after a taxing two-month struggle early in 1856.) The new Massachusetts legislature, more antislavery than nativist, also adopted a resolution condemning the Kansas-Nebraska Act, approved a new personal liberty law, and added a law banning racial segregation in the state's public schools—the first of its kind in the nation.[68]

In February 1856, the American Party met, once again in Philadelphia, to nominate its national ticket—and once again failed to mend its divisions over slavery. One Virginia delegate declared that the northern wing of the party was composed of abolitionists, that the party was a failure, and that the convention might as well disband. He exaggerated—there was still a strong complement of anti-abolitionist northern conservatives in the party—but every effort to finesse the slavery issue backfired. The convention adopted a prolix new plank that endorsed popular sovereignty in the territories, but was so confusing, one delegate remarked, that the election would be over before the people figured out what it meant. The convention nominated Millard Fillmore for president, the southerners' and New York Silver Grays' favorite, but totally unacceptable to New England and the Old Northwest. The northern malcontents withdrew, issued a protest demanding the repeal of Kansas-Nebraska, and called for a new convention of what would become known as the North American Party. The bolters agreed to meet in New York just prior to the scheduled Republican Party's Philadelphia convention in early June.[69]

The North American Party's stated objective was to nominate an antislavery nativist in the hopes that the Republicans, holding their first national convention, would feel the pressure to choose the same man. But the stealthy antislavery men had different plans: instead of converting the Republican Party to nativism, they would convert the North American Party, such as it was, to the Republicans. Their plotting centered on the new House Speaker, Nathaniel Banks, who had been careful to keep up good relations with his Know-Nothing backers. A strong contender for the North American presidential nomination, Banks allowed his name to be put forward, but with the quiet intention of standing down as soon as the Republicans named their ticket, and supporting the Republican candidates. The plan worked like a charm. The North Americans (with Thurlow Weed, Preston King, and other Republicans hanging around, quietly meeting with delegates) nominated Banks—and then the Republican Party took center stage.[70]

The Republicans had been organizing their gathering since the previous Christmas, when a small group of influential antislavery fusionists met at the home of the old Jacksonian warhorse, Francis Blair, just outside of Washington. The planners included Nathaniel Banks, Charles Sumner (Brooks's attack on him still five months in the future), Preston King, Salmon Chase, and Gamaliel Bailey—all men with either strong past Democratic links like Blair or Democratic affinities. They discussed the names of prospective nominees—including Blair's favorite, the California explorer and Bear Republic hero John C. Frémont—but left the matter to rest until a larger informal national meeting to be held early in the new year. The second meeting, held in Pittsburgh in late February, gathered antislavery radicals and moderates from across the North and from five slave border states as well, to plan for a nominating convention and draft a party platform. The meeting's tone and the platform it approved were pur-

posefully temperate—firm on issues that united the disparate antislavery movement like Kansas-Nebraska, but circumspect on others, including nativism and
the Fugitive Slave Law. ("There is not a single warm and living position, taken
by the Republican party," Frederick Douglass complained, "except freedom for
Kansas.") The more radical delegates, like the now aging Joshua Giddings,
checked their chagrin and prepared for the truly important national nominating
convention, scheduled to open in Philadelphia on June 17.[71]

In the interim, the sack of Lawrence and the attack on Sumner hardened the
antislavery men's views, and ensured that the Philadelphia convention would be
forceful. The platform committee, chaired by David Wilmot, produced a document that, without offending moderates, sounded radical, by reaching back to
the Buffalo Free Soilers, citing the egalitarian principles of the Declaration of
Independence, and denouncing slavery along with Mormon polygamy as "twin
relics of barbarism." The platform also stressed the obliteration of legally protected rights in Kansas and arraigned the Pierce administration for committing
an impeachable "high crime against the Constitution, the Union, and humanity" by permitting the Kansas outrages. Ultimately, however, the convention's
work would be judged on whom it nominated for the presidency. Two men—
William Henry Seward and Salmon P. Chase—loomed largest, yet neither was
acceptable to important constituencies, including the antislavery nativists. Far
better was Blair's original choice, John C. Frémont.[72]

Raven-haired, adventuresome, and charismatic, Frémont had earned his
romantic heroic nickname, "The Pathfinder," with his exploits mapping the Oregon Trail, the Sierra Nevadas, and the Pacific coast in the 1840s. His marriage to
Jessie Benton, daughter of Thomas Hart Benton and a formidable person in her
own right, made him more acceptable to ex-Democrats, and conservative
Republicans liked the fact that he had been born and raised in Georgia. Frémont's support for a free-soil California in 1850 and his opposition to his father-
in-law's enemy, David Atchison, over Kansas established his antislavery bona
fides. But Frémont had no strong previous party allegiances and had played no
direct political role during the previous six years, which spared him the complaints that dogged Chase and Seward. He won the nomination decisively on the
first ballot. After naming the New Jersey ex-Whig William Dayton as Frémont's
running mate to pacify its conservative wing, the party took to the hustings
enthusiastically, under an updated version of the Free Soil slogan of 1848: "Free
Speech, Free Press, Free Men, Free Labor, Free Territory, and Fremont." The
convention, one antislavery Indiana newspaper later exulted, had "organized the
Republican party—a FREE SOIL PARTY in the fullest sense of the term, gave it a
Free Soil baptism, and a Free Soil Platform, and sent it forth."[73]

As expected, the North American nominee Banks abandoned his candidacy
and supported Frémont. Some angry northern nativists, chiefly in New York,

ended up supporting Fillmore—an unsatisfying move given that Fillmore had
become a tribune for staggered southern Whigs and some Silver Gray northerners more interested in Unionism than nativism. But the biggest losers in the wake
of the Republicans' absorption of the North Americans were the old-line conservative northern Whigs, including Robert Winthrop, Rufus Choate, and assorted
other ex-Websterites, Cotton Whigs, and patricians. The heirs to a Federalist
political tradition that had once ruled the nation, these men, on the political
defensive for decades, had been rendered obsolete in 1856. Some, like Choate, a
founder of the Massachusetts Whig Party, joined with Webster's and Henry
Clay's sons in switching to the Democrats, hoping to kill off the Republican fanatics and believing that the slaveholders' party now embodied the last vestiges of
respect for property, order, and the Union. "Whig principles!" Choate exclaimed.
"I go to the Democrats to find them. They have assumed our principles, one
after another, till there is little difference between us." Other conservative Whigs
(now derided as "Old Fogeys"), unwilling to ally with the one-time party of Jackson, decided to back Fillmore, not out of any sudden enthusiasm for nativism
but to warm themselves around the dying embers of conservative Whiggery.[74]

Pro-administration northern Democrats were also mightily troubled. The
Pierce White House, alternating between inertness and pro-slavery complicity
over Kansas, had tried to revive the aggressive expansionism that had been President Pierce's strongest original commitment. Redoubling efforts to obtain Cuba,
Pierce had reauthorized Minister Pierre Soulé in 1854 to approach the Spanish
government with a deal and, if spurned, to direct the effort "to detach that island
from the Spanish dominion." The hotheaded Soulé assembled the American
ministers to Britain and France, James Buchanan and John Young Mason, in the
Belgian city of Ostend and had them sign a memorandum stating that if Spain
balked, then "by every law, human and Divine, we shall be justified in wresting
it from Spain." News of the so-called Ostend Manifesto leaked to the press and
raised such a row in Congress that the stunned White House finally forced Soulé
to resign.[75]

Undeterred, Soulé linked up with the American man of fortune, William
Walker, who took control of rebel armies in far-off Nicaragua in 1855, defeated
the standing government, and appointed himself de facto dictator. Walker
opened the country to southern slaveholders and quickly received diplomatic
recognition from the Pierce administration. Celebrated by southern newspapers
as "the grey-eyed man of destiny," Walker would eventually fall out with Pierce,
lose his revolutionary regime, and wind up executed in 1860 by a Honduran firing squad, but the episode came as one more reminder of how Manifest Destiny
had decayed into pro-slavery adventurism. With the blessings of the American
government, a self-proclaimed American liberator had promised to bring slavery
back to Central America. "[A] barbarous people can never become civilized

without the salutary apprenticeship which slavery secured," one New Orleans paper asserted, in support of Walker's project.[76]

With freedom on the run from Kansas to Nicaragua, northern Democrats, having been soundly rejected in 1854, were splintered into rival factions, some dating back to the aftermath of the Free Soil revolt. The most bitter and confusing divisions arose, as ever, in New York, where the so-called Hard Shell Hunkers, longtime fierce opponents of the antislavery Democrats, had turned against the Pierce White House over lack of patronage consideration, which they believed had gone instead to their Soft Shell Hunker rivals. The returns in 1855 were devastating, plunging the northern Democrats' numbers in Congress into a trough in which they would stay for twenty years. The violence in Kansas and on the Senate floor in 1856 left what remained of the northern Democracy reeling—mocked, in a retrieval of John Randolph's old phrase, as the Doughface Democracy. Pierce became the emblem of the Doughface disaster. The president's own former secretary, B. B. French, wrote that he "is in rather bad odor, and will stink worse yet before the 4th of March next. The Kansas outrages are all imputable to him, and if he is not called to answer for them here, 'In Hell they'll roast him like a herring.'"[77]

The situation was exactly the reverse for southern Democrats. One by one, the leaders of southern Whiggery outside of the border states had defected, Robert Toombs as early as 1853, his Georgia colleague Alexander Stephens in the wake of Kansas-Nebraska. And in bastions of patrician domination, Master Race democracy finally made breakthroughs that enhanced the Democrats' political prospects while augmenting the slaveholders' power. In Virginia, the mercurial, furiously pro-slavery, sometime Whig Henry A. Wise had led a redrafting of the commonwealth's constitution in 1851 that finally wiped away the old freehold suffrage, provided for popular election of the governor, and more fairly apportioned the lower house of the legislature. Failure to reform the old regime, Wise persuaded his colleagues, would endanger slavery itself by alienating the mass of white freemen: "Will you dare say," he asked the convention, "that you will balance 94,000 free white population, with all their interests, moral, intellectual and political, with their police and arms-bearing responsibilities, with a million even of your black serfs?" Southern-style democracy, its hegemony in the hands of the slaveholders, would not threaten the peculiar institution but strengthen it by tightening the bonds of racial solidarity. Five years later, in the spring of 1856, Wise made good on his predictions by coming out of political retirement to run for governor as a pro-slavery Democrat—and, with his convincing victory, to stall the momentum of crypto-Whig Know-Nothingism in the upper South. Wise's triumph, Pierce wrote to Douglas, "has put a new face upon the prospects of the Democratic Party."[78]

Pierce and Douglas came to the Democratic nominating convention in

Cincinnati as rivals for the presidential nomination, sharing support from southern delegates grateful for their aggressive roles in the Kansas-Nebraska turmoil. Yet while Pierce also had backing from his native New England, it was not enough to gain a majority, and Douglas, outside Illinois, was reviled for having caused the northern Democracy's tribulations. That left the candidate with the best organization on the convention floor: James Buchanan of Pennsylvania. Few delegates could remember a time when the sixty-five-year-old Buchanan had not played some part either in government or in the party. His public service dated back to the War of 1812, when he fought as a volunteer in the defense of Baltimore; thereafter, he had won five elections to the House, three to the Senate, and served as minister to Russia under Jackson, secretary of state under Polk, and minister to Great Britain under Pierce. A tall, heavy, large-headed bachelor, he cut a dashing enough figure until he spoke, when his high-pitched voice (which Henry Clay used to mock in Senate debate) gave added currency to rumors that he lacked virility. He also had a defect in one eye that caused him to tilt his head slightly forward and sideways in conversation, which some regarded as a sign of intensity and others as a sign of deceit. Above all, Buchanan had the reputation of a dutiful and able public servant, a conservative who never allowed great principles to obstruct his political career. "[H]e was, assuredly, . . . a cautious, circumspect and sagacious man, amply endowed with . . . clear perceptions of self-interest and of duties as connected with it," recalled Martin Van Buren, a connoisseur of caution.[79]

Buchanan also had the advantage of having been largely out of the political line of fire over the previous four years. As minister to Britain, he had signed on to Soulé's inflammatory Ostend Manifesto, but unlike Pierce or Douglas he bore no stigma in the public mind from the struggle over Kansas. He was a political powerhouse in his native Pennsylvania, a swing state. Although lackluster, he seemed a safe and acceptable option compared to either Pierce, Douglas, or any Republican nominee—unobjectionable to the North and the South, and therefore a potential winner. Even Frémont's father-in-law, Thomas Hart Benton, found Buchanan suitable enough, "[n]ever a leading man in any high sense, but eminently a man of peace." After more than a dozen ballots at the convention, Pierce and Douglas withdrew, and on the seventeenth ballot, Buchanan was nominated. The delegates gave him a platform that endorsed popular sovereignty, denounced the Republicans as inciters of treason, and tried to stir up what was left of the old Jacksonian fervor, including one plank opposing the creation of a national bank.[80]

As Frémont could expect virtually no support in the slaveholding states, the southern campaign became a battle between Buchanan and Fillmore. Given the Democrats' sectional strength, Buchanan's victory there was a foregone conclusion. In the North, the Republicans had a lock on New England, Michigan, and

Wisconsin. Thus, the national contest came down to the battle between Frémont and Buchanan in a few key free states. Buchanan only needed to carry Pennsylvania and one other toss-up state to win the election. But in New York, Pennsylvania, and Illinois, the numerous conservative pro-Fillmore Whigs were potential electoral wild cards, and Ohio, Indiana, and New Jersey, each of which had voted Democratic in 1852, were now closely divided between Democrats and Republicans.

Not since 1840 had the nation witnessed the kind of riotous, impassioned electioneering that the Frémont Republicans mounted. The shock of the Kansas-Nebraska Act, and the rush of spectacular events earlier in 1856, along with the Pierce administration's apparent siding with the South, excited antislavery sentiment to a fever pitch. Pro-Frémont Wide-Awake Clubs appeared across the North, leading mass parades and carrying banners espousing the Republican cause. Pamphlets, books, and popular songsheets (including one ditty based on the minstrel-song writer Stephen Foster's "Camptown Races") flooded the market, celebrating The Pathfinder and excoriating his Democratic opponent, "The Old Public Functionary" Buchanan. Yet the boisterous Frémont campaign also had a moral seriousness and sense of impending cataclysm that the Whigs' Log Cabin campaign of 1840 had completely lacked. John Greenleaf Whittier wrote fervently of how, finally, the time had come, "When Good and Evil, as for final strife,/ Close vast and dim on Armageddon's plain." Writers who normally refrained from political speechmaking, including the stage-shy William Cullen Bryant, turned out in support of Frémont. The more practiced antislavery stump-speakers—Chase, Giddings, Hale—seemed to be everywhere at once. Abraham Lincoln—pushed by his more radical law partner William Herndon to drop his Whig label at last and join the Republicans—delivered ninety-odd speeches for Frémont.[81]

In the swing states of the lower North, the Republicans had to fend off Democratic charges that they were out to destroy the Union and impose racial equality. (One group of Indiana Democrats organized a parade featuring young girls in white dresses holding banners that read "Fathers, Save us from nigger husbands.") To the claims about their disunionism, the Republicans responded much as the authors of the "Appeal of the Independent Democrats" had two years earlier, arguing that it was the southern bullies, always threatening secession, who actually denigrated the Union. In reply to the racist attacks, Republicans, notably the ex-Democrats among them, fell on the defensive, sometimes claiming that their true intention was to save white labor from having to compete with black labor. That maneuver in turn alienated abolitionists including William Lloyd Garrison, who denounced the Republicans as "a complexional party, exclusively for white men, not for all men."[82]

Frémont's supporters also raised their own powerful charges, that the Democrats wanted to subvert American democracy in favor of an aristocracy based on human bondage. A Frémont victory, one meeting in Buffalo proclaimed, would guarantee "for our country a government of the people, instead of a government by an oligarchy; a government maintaining before the world the rights of men rather than the privileges of masters." As their prime example, the Republicans needed to look no farther than Kansas. Even voters who had tolerated southern demands for state rights were appalled by the Kansas events and switched to the Republicans. "[H]ad the Slave Power been less *aggressively insolent*, I would have been content to see it extend . . . ," one former Democrat wrote a friend, "but when it seeks to extend its sway by fire & sword, I am ready to say hold, enough!"[83]

The Democrats' advantages were their superior campaign organization and huge campaign war chest, raised by well-placed supporters in New York, Philadelphia, and the South. Much of the money went into producing tracts, carefully aimed at the voters in the battleground states. Party speakers everywhere received copies of the *Democratic Handbook*, which laid out the strategy: attack the Republicans as Know-Nothings (to shore up the Catholic immigrant vote), as "Black Republicans" (to exploit racial animosities), and as disunionists (to appeal to moderate and conservative ex-Whigs). Personal criticism of Frémont was tailored to particular local constituencies. (Northwest Democrats bandied about a charge that Frémont was a closet Catholic, which hurt the Republicans in some pockets of evangelical piety.) Above all, the Democrats harped on the Unionist issue in deftly contradictory ways. In the North, they warned that the wild-eyed Republican fanatics intended to dissolve the Union; in the South, they promised that if the wild-eyed Republican fanatics were elected, southerners would be forced to choose, as a leading Louisianan declared, "immediate, absolute, eternal separation." Either way, Democrats could claim, a Frémont victory would seal the nation's doom.[84]

As expected, Buchanan swept the South and Frémont won New England, Michigan, and Wisconsin. The antislavery voters in the northern portions of New York and Ohio turned out large enough majorities to carry those states for the Republicans as well. But the Democrats ran well in Pennsylvania, New Jersey, Illinois, and Indiana, topping the Republican vote by margins that, in the first two states, came close to 20 percentage points—and deciding the election. Buchanan's electoral vote total, although far reduced from Pierce's landslide four years earlier, was a comfortable 174 to the Republicans' 114 (with Fillmore carrying only Maryland's 8 votes). The Democrats also reclaimed the majority in the House of Representatives. Still, Republicans greeted the results as highly encouraging. "We are beaten," said Senator William Pitt Fessenden of Maine, "but we have frightened the rascals awfully. They cannot help seeing what their doom must inevitably be, unless they abandon their unrighteous ways."[85]

A closer look at the presidential returns bears out Fessenden's optimism. In only two of the crucial lower North states did Buchanan win a bare majority of the popular vote — 50.4 percent in Indiana and 50.1 percent in his home state of Pennsylvania. In both of those states, as well as in New Jersey and Illinois (where he won, respectively, 47.2 and 44.1 percent of the vote), unexpected large turnouts for the American Party accounted for the margins between the Democrats and Republicans. Although the American Party died in its very first national election, there still turned out to be a considerable old Whig vote in the lower North — Unionists intimidated by charges of Republican radicalism, yet not willing to go all the way and vote for the Democrats. (Fillmore also showed unexpected strength in the border slave states as well as in Louisiana, an indication of persisting political divisions within the seemingly solid Democratic South.) Although enough to win Buchanan the White House, the outcome was hardly a resounding endorsement of the northern Democrats. In every free state outside New England, the Democracy's vote declined from what it had been in 1852, including a drop of nearly 20 percentage points in New York. Meanwhile, the Republican Party had polled 1.3 million votes and carried eleven of the sixteen free states, in an election that saw northern turnout rise to more than 80 percent of the eligible voters — by any measure a stunning debut.[86]

Still, if the Republican campaign had ended in what one of Charles Sumner's correspondents called "a victorious defeat," Democrats had sufficient reason to refuse seeing their victory as pyrrhic. They had retained the White House; they now controlled the Congress; and the Supreme Court, under Roger Brooke Taney, seemed favorable to their political views. Of the two great parties of the Jacksonian years, the Whigs, and not themselves, had disintegrated, leaving the Democracy standing as the only authentically national political party. Hard-line southern Democrats were especially elated, to the point of cockiness. Their threats of disunion had, they thought, once again been heeded. The Yankee fanatics had once again been laid low. If some southerners wished that the party had stuck by Pierce, the proven breaker of abolitionist mischief, there was every reason to believe that Buchanan would be just as noble, would eradicate Douglas's weak-kneed popular sovereignty doctrine, and would protect slavery in the territories — and thereby make southern secession unnecessary. "Mr. Buchanan and the Northern Democracy," one Virginia Democrat reflected after the election, "are dependent on the South. If we can succeed in Kansas, deep down the Tariff, shake off our Commercial dependence on the North and add a little more slave territory, we may yet live free men under the Stars and Strip[e]s."[87]

"ON THE TIP-TOE OF REVOLUTION":
THE REPUBLICANS AND NORTHERN DEMOCRACY

Early in the 1856 canvass, a Buffalo Republican wrote to William Seward that it appeared as if public opinion was "on the tip-toe of Revolution." A staggered Republican journalist was more emphatic: "the process now going on in the politics of the United States," he wrote, "is a *Revolution*." By November, such pronouncements seemed overblown. Despite all of the turmoil, and despite the Republicans' consolidation, the American government would look, in 1857, much as it had in 1854, with the southern-dominated Democratic Party in charge. The events of 1856 were instead a dress rehearsal for revolution. The revolutionary process was well underway, and by year's end, a crucial part of the process had been largely completed—the formation of a coherent Republican political ideology.[88]

The Republican Party, like all successful American political parties, was a ragtag coalition. At its heart were the antislavery Whigs, antislavery Democrats, and Free Democrats who had begun abandoning the established parties long before 1854. In the wake of Kansas-Nebraska, that core was joined by Whigs and Democrats who could no longer stomach what they considered the aggression of the aristocratic, pro-slavery South in the wake of Bleeding Kansas and Bleeding Sumner. The new antislavery recruits came from all classes, from urban as well as rural areas, and (though less plentiful in New Jersey and Pennsylvania and the southern portions of Indiana and Illinois) from every northern state. The Republican coalition included former reformist Whigs and former reformist Democrats, immigrants (especially Germans) and nativists, old Liberty Party egalitarians and old Barnburner and midwestern racists. All shared the conviction that slavery had become a blight on the nation—a relic of barbarism that, if allowed to spread, would block the advance of free labor, squelch American prosperity, and degrade the status of the vast majority of ordinary American citizens. Republican leaders proclaimed the virtues of northern free-labor society, which, they asserted, were under siege by the slaveholders and the Democratic Party—"[i]ts Democracy . . . a lie, a cheat, and a delusion," one Republican editor declared. Above all else, they presented the Slave Power as a forceful and growing threat, "an aristocratic oligarchy" which would force "the twenty millions of freemen [to] surrender their dearest privileges at the ipse dixit of 347,000 slaveholders."[89]

The testimony of two very different Republicans—veteran partisans from clashing political backgrounds—illuminates how the party's democratic ideology merged aspects of radical Jacksonianism and the more liberal strands of new-school Whiggery from the 1830s. Francis Blair was a comparative newcomer and moderate within the Republicans' ranks, and at age sixty-five, his career as the consummate Jacksonian polemicist was largely behind him. But in the wake of Kansas-Nebraska, some of the old brimstone of his days at the *Globe* erupted. In a letter addressed to a public meeting in New York, which he entitled *A Voice from the Grave of Jackson!*, Blair lit into his old party for abandoning the democratic principles it had vindicated in 1832 and 1833. "To use a homely phrase," he exclaimed, "*the Democracy has been 'sold out'* to Mr. Calhoun's nullifying party." There was no question, in Blair's mind, that Jackson, were he alive, would have stood up to the "perfect Southern phalanx" that now threatened disunion; the only question, he wrote, was whether "the Nullifiers who have thus usurped the name and organization of the Democratic party, but who have no principles in common with it, shall be allowed to carry out their designs in such disguise." The "spurious Democracy," Blair charged, had "perfected its system in the Kansas act, and made it their test"—and against it, "I, as a Democrat of the Jefferson, Jackson, and Van Buren school, enter my protest."[90]

The ex-Whig Charles Francis Adams, son of John Quincy Adams, had a much longer history than Blair in antislavery politics, though by 1856 he, too, was a moderate among Republicans. His temperament was much milder than the old Jacksonian Blair's. But Adams also blamed the crisis chiefly on the self-preserving tenacity of a small elite, which had rejected the axioms of "the great apostle of modern democracy, Thomas Jefferson." Adams calmly explained to a New York audience that "[t]his slave power consists, in fact, of about three hundred and fifty thousand active men"—a tiny minority that commanded fifteen states directly, materially affected five or six more, and, through its "numerous friends and dependents" elsewhere, controlled the national government. To sustain their power and "what they consider [their] property," against "the prevailing tendencies of the age" and "a large body of their own countrymen," these men found it impossible to escape "adopting a system of policy aggressive upon the rights of the freemen." The influence of the Slave Power was pervasive and unrelenting: "It never relaxes in its vigilance over public events. It never is turned aside by the temptation of an incidental purpose." At stake, Adams said, was the fate of free institutions and the rights of freemen as well as slaves.[91]

Republican spokesmen and supporters repeated the theme constantly—that an oligarchic enormity had disfigured the Constitution and perverted the very word *democracy* into a cover for its own domination. Genuine democracy, according to these formulations, was a peculiar feature of free societies. At issue, as William Seward explained on the campaign trail, was "an ancient and eternal conflict . . . between the system of free labor, with equal and universal suffrage, free speech, free thought, and free action, and the system of slave labor, with unequal franchises secured by arbitrary, oppressive, and tyrannical laws." The conflict between true and sham democracy could no longer be stilled or postponed by compromise, Seward contended: "The slaveholders can never be content without dominion, which abridges the freedom as well as circumscribes the domain of the non-slaveholding freemen." Slavery was incontrovertibly aristocratic, both where it held sway and where it wished to do so. But the future was democratic and the Republican Party was devoted to preparing for it, against a Democratic Party that had thoroughly betrayed its name.[92]

As Seward remarked, the events of the mid-1850s threw into sharp relief how two different democracies, shaped by slavery, had arisen within the same nation. Although some southern franchises and systems of representation were, in fact, more equal than others, slaveholders, and normally wealthy slaveholders, held a commanding power in the courts and legislatures throughout the South. By contrast, power was more dispersed in most of the North, where ordinary farmers and even wage earners not only voted but also held state offices. Southern politics could brook no open criticism of slavery for fear of destabilizing the system; northerners were free to write and say whatever they wanted about any political subject. In Kansas, upholders of southern-style popular sovereignty had flagrantly rigged elections, violently seized control of polling places, and turned democracy into a mockery—and had gained federal sanction from a doughface Democrat bullied into compliance by Slave Power congressmen and cabinet members. When an elected northern Republican had the temerity to call the bullies to account, one of them cut him down and beat him mercilessly on the floor of the U.S. Senate.[93]

The Republicans demanded a rebirth of American politics, to break, once and for all, the slaveholders' stranglehold over the nation's political institutions and to hasten tyrannical slavery's demise. And it was precisely as revolutionaries that the slaveholders regarded their new sectional foe. Who were these Yankees, they asked, to challenge the duly constituted authorities in Kansas? Who were they to preach democracy to states where every white man could vote, just like in the North? Who were they to declaim against slavery, what the *Richmond Enquirer* called "a social system as old as the world, universal as man"? One Alabama newspaper editor said exactly who they were: "a conglomeration of greasy mechanics, filthy operatives, smallfisted farmers, and moonstruck theorists." To conserve all that was natural, moral, Christian, and orderly in America, these degraded radicals had to be put down now, put down hard, put down once and for all.[94]

What remained to be seen, after the 1856 elections, was the shape that the southern counterrevolution would take, and whether the new administration, with its party in control of the entire federal apparatus, would back it. And in this, the proponents of the southern-style slaveholders' democracy could count on the sympathies of a significant number of northerners: ex-Whig hard-line conservatives; seaport merchants tied to the cotton trade; Catholic workers (especially Irish immigrants) offended by the Republicans' nativist tinge and empathy for black slaves; and farmers and small townsmen all across the lower North who preferred Stephen Douglas's version of popular sovereignty and white supremacy to the prospect of disunion and "Black Republican" rule.

Buchanan's ascendancy boded well for the forces of resistance in the southern Democracy—and it boded even better when the new president began selecting a heavily pro-southern cabinet. But that final conservative effort would end up wrecking what was left of the Democratic Party, and then it would wreck the nation. It began with a momentous judicial ruling about an obscure Missouri slave, Dred Scott, who a decade earlier, with his wife, Harriet, had begun fighting for his freedom.

23

A NIGHTMARE BROODS
OVER SOCIETY

As he walked to the crowded podium at the Capitol to deliver his inauguration speech and take the oath of office, President-elect James Buchanan stopped to have a brief private conversation with the man who would swear him in, Chief Justice Roger Brooke Taney. Everyone toward the front of the throng below could see the two huddle together. Buchanan then told the nation that a case pending before the Supreme Court would settle the outstanding issues regarding slavery and the territories. He bid all good Americans to submit "cheerfully" to the decision "whatever [it] may be."[1]

Two days later, Taney and the court majority rendered their stern pro-slavery ruling in *Dred Scott v. Sandford*. Republicans immediately speculated that Buchanan, at the inauguration, had known precisely how the case would turn out because Taney had just tipped him off. Over the months to come, the conjectures hardened into a conviction that a long-maturing Slave Power conspiracy lay behind the case, the Court's ruling, and Buchanan's remarks. The "whisperings" at the Capitol, William Seward told the Senate, had allowed the new president to sound impartial and magnanimous, when in fact he knew that the Court was about to hang "the millstone of slavery" on Kansas—and, potentially, clear the way to force slavery on every state and territory in the Union.[2]

Seward's case against Buchanan was speculative and circumstantial. Yet there was unquestionably an affinity between pro-slavery southerners and the new administration, which confirmed a decade-long trend toward slavery's expansion. And, although the evidence would remain hidden for decades, there actually was improper collusion in the matter of *Dred Scott*. Weeks prior to his swearing-in, Buchanan started receiving covert reports from his fellow Pennsylvanian, Justice Robert C. Grier, about the Court's internal debates, and Buchanan, secretly alerted by pro-slavery Justice James Catron, pressed Grier to side with the pro-slavery majority. Well before inauguration day, Buchanan was fully apprised of how the Court would rule, and in his address he disingenuously undertook an advance campaign to get the nation to accept it. Seward and the Republicans knew nothing of the contacts, and never would, but the gist of their accusations about the new president and the *Dred Scott* decision turns out to have been true.[3]

Buchanan's prediction that the ruling would at last settle the sectional battle proved just as hapless as Millard Fillmore's similar prediction about the truce of 1850. To southern Democrats and their northern allies, that failure would be shocking. Although the principles of judicial review and supremacy had not yet been fully established in American law, there was a widespread presumption that the Supreme Court should be respected as the most informed arbiter on constitutional issues. As the pro-administration Washington *Union* observed, with measured cheer, "the judgement of the highest tribunal in the land" stood "elevated above the schemes of party politics, and shielded alike from the effects of sudden passion and of popular prejudice." Failure to comply with *Dred Scott*, the leading New York doughface newspaper claimed, would amount to an endorsement of "rebellion, treason, and revolution." But instead of commanding respect, the *Dred Scott* decision thoroughly discredited the Taney Court among Republicans and persuaded them more than ever that the dictatorial Slave Power needed to be eradicated.[4]

Once again, a much-hailed final settlement of the nation's sectional rift worsened the rift. The middle ground, still sought by Douglas Democrats, conciliatory northern Whigs, and southern Unionists, crumbled into dust; the Buchanan administration exacerbated the situation; and the Republican Party, the intended political victim of the Court's ruling in *Dred Scott*, grew stronger in response. As if the battles over slavery were not bad enough, the nation was rocked, in the summer of 1857, by a financial panic that briefly augured a general economic collapse—and that snapped the boom mentality that had captivated political leaders for more than a decade. "A nightmare broods over society . . . ," one northerner remarked in the wake of the panic. "God alone foresees the history of the next six months." The economy proved more resilient than was feared, but for the Union the nightmare was just beginning.[5]

"TIMES NOW ARE NOT AS THEY WERE": THE POLITICS OF *DRED SCOTT V. SANDFORD*

Of all the black Americans who achieved prominence in the fight over slavery, Dred Scott is among the most enigmatic. We know what he looked like thanks to daguerreotypes made in the last year of his life—although his expression, some-where between bemused and startled, raises as many questions about him as it answers. Other sources show that he was probably born in Virginia in the late 1790s, that he was slight in stature, and that he was illiterate. A St. Louis newspa-per claimed, in 1857, that, although unlettered, Scott was "not ignorant" and that he commanded a "strong common sense." Along with his wife, he was plainly resolute about gaining their freedom, a determination possibly reinforced by the congregation of St. Louis's antislavery Second African Baptist Church, where Harriet Scott attended services in the mid-1840s—and which was pastored by the martyred Elijah Lovejoy's former typesetter, now Reverend John Ander-son.* It is likely that Harriet had as much or even more to do with instigating the suit than her husband. Otherwise, the circumstances of Dred Scott's fame have left him a cipher—and at times an almost incidental participant in the events for-ever linked with his name.[6]

Scott's whereabouts between 1830 and 1846—the key facts in his case—are known precisely. In 1830, Scott's Virginia owner, Peter Blow, resettled his family and his six slaves to St. Louis. Within two years, both Blow and his wife died. (Their children stayed in the city and married into prominent families.) At some point before 1833, either Peter Blow or his children sold Scott to an army sur-geon named John Emerson, who took him from Missouri to posts in Illinois and at Fort Snelling in the newly created Wisconsin Territory. While at Fort Snelling, Scott married Harriet Robinson, a teenage slave who was also Emerson's prop-erty. Over the next six years, the Scotts returned to St. Louis (where they lived in the custody of Emerson's wife) and spent time with their master in Louisiana and Iowa, before winding up, after Emerson's death, in St. Louis once again, inher-ited by Emerson's widow and working as hired-out slaves. (During these travels, Harriet had given birth to a daughter in free territory.) Finally, on April 6, 1846, Dred and Harriet filed separate petitions at the St. Louis District Court, charging Emerson's widow, the former Isabella Sanford, with false imprisonment, and claiming their freedom on the basis of their previous residency in Illinois and Wisconsin Territory. Members of the Blow family provided the couple with legal and financial assistance.[7]

The Scotts had a strong case. For decades, Missouri courts had ruled that

---

* Anderson was in Alton when the mob killed Lovejoy in 1837. Grief-stricken, he returned to St. Louis, where he took up a Baptist ministry, claiming that Lovejoy's martyrdom had been his spiritual inspiration. Although not an outspoken abolitionist, Reverend Anderson was known quietly to give slaves seeking their freedom needed moral and financial support—an invitation to extreme danger in St. Louis in the mid-1840s. It is difficult to imagine that he did not have some influence in instigating the Dred Scott case, through his parishioner, Harriet Scott. See Kenneth C. Kaufman, *Dred Scott's Advocate: A Biography of Roswell M. Field* (Columbia, MO, 1996), 135–48.

slaves taken by their masters to free states were automatically emancipated. Although the Scotts lost at their first trial on a technicality—there was no record to prove that Mrs. Emerson actually held them as slaves—a much-delayed second trial, held in 1850, clarified the record. On instructions from the judge, the jury found for the plaintiffs. Mrs. Emerson's lawyers appealed, and the state supreme court agreed to hear the case, leaving no hint that it would fail to sustain its earlier rulings on such matters. But by the time the appeal came up for argument, the membership of the court had become marginally more pro-slavery, and the reaction to the truce of 1850 and the fugitive slave controversy had persuaded the court's majority, in the name of sectional peace, to overturn precedent. In March 1852, the court ruled against the Scotts, on the grounds that Missouri was not bound to recognize the laws of slavery of any other state or territory. "Times now are not as they were, when the former decisions on this subject were made," noted the majority decision, written by a pro-slavery Democrat.[8]

Fortuitously—and for reasons that remain murky—Irene Emerson's brother, a wealthy New York businessman named John Sanford, then claimed ownership of the Scotts. The shift allowed the Scotts' lawyer, the Vermont-born antislavery Missourian Roswell Field, to take the matter into federal court. Field wanted to test federal law on residency and freedom. Although the Missouri Circuit Court agreed to hear the case—thus recognizing that Scott was a U.S. citizen—the jury, in mid-1854, affirmed the Missouri high court's decision. By then, it was a foregone conclusion that the dispute would wind up before the U.S. Supreme Court, providing the Court with an opportunity to resolve numerous troublesome constitutional issues about slavery in the territories.[9]

Knowing that the case had become too high profile for him to handle, Field arranged for Francis Blair's son, Montgomery, a well-connected, pro-Benton, free-soil Missouri Democrat, to argue in Washington on Dred Scott's behalf. (Blair was later joined by George T. Curtis, a more conservative Massachusetts constitutional expert and the brother of Supreme Court Justice Benjamin Curtis.) Sanford engaged the services of Missouri's pro-slavery Whig senator, Henry Geyer, and a respected Unionist Whig and former attorney general, Reverdy Johnson. After some delay, the justices heard the case in February 1856 and allowed four days for argument, an exceptionally protracted span. The justices then held the matter over for reargument in the 1856–57 term, possibly to avoid having to render a decision until after the presidential election. Although it was still unknown to the broad American public, Court insiders now understood the case had acquired explosive potential.

The justices confronted three large questions. First, was Scott, as a black man, legally a citizen of Missouri and a citizen of the United States, and thus entitled to bring a suit against anybody? Second, was the Missouri Compromise constitutionally valid in prohibiting slavery north of 36°30', including Wisconsin Terri-

SLAVERY AND THE CRISIS OF AMERICAN DEMOCRACY

1. Lincoln-Hamlin campaign banner, 1860

2. Thomas Wilson Dorr, between
1844 and 1854

4. Polling booth in New York City, 1844

BULLETIN.

BY TELEGRAPH TO "UNION," WASHINGTON.

To the Editor of the Union :

NEW ORLEANS, Sept. 26, 1847.

SIR : The J. L. Day arrived here last evening from
Vera Cruz. The news by her is important. The details
are meagre, and something uncertain. The main points
are, that the armistice has been concluded, without a treaty
of peace ; and, after a considerable amount of hard fighting, the city of Mexico was captured, and our troops
entered. Gen. Bravo was killed. Santa Anna was wounded, and has retired with his shattered forces to Guadalupe,
about twelve miles from the city. The entrance to the
city was on the 16th. The reports are that Scott lost from
1,000 to 1,700 men, killed and wounded.

Respectfully, yours, &c.

3. War bulletin, 1847

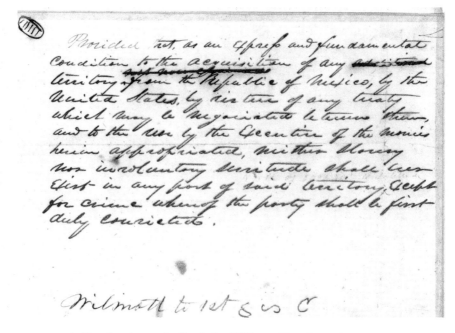

5. Handwritten draft of the Wilmot Proviso, 1846

6. Free Soil Party campaign
engraving, 1848

7. Elizabeth Cady Stanton with her sons
Henry and Daniel, ca. 1848

8. The United States Capitol, ca. 1846

9. Henry Clay, between 1850 and 1852

10. Daniel Webster, between
1845 and 1849

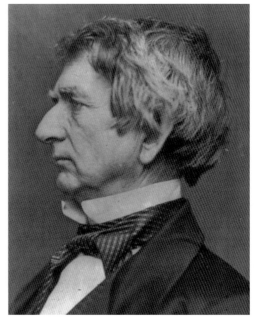

11. William Henry Seward, 1860

12. John C. Calhoun, ca. 1849

13. Fugitive Slave Law abolitionist convention, Cazenovia, New York, 1850. Seated at the table, on the left, is Frederick Douglass; standing above him, hand outstretched, is Gerrit Smith

14. John Brown, ca. 1847

15. Anthony Burns, ca. 1854

16. The caning of Charles Sumner, 1856

17. Dred Scott, ca. 1857

18. William Lowndes Yancey, ca. 1860

19. Robert Barnwell Rhett, ca. 1860

20. Alabama infantry flag, 1860

22. Wide-Awake Club and Band,
Mohawk, New York, 1860

21. Abraham Lincoln, 1857

23. The inauguration of President Abraham Lincoln, March 4, 1861

tory? Finally, had the Scotts' prolonged residence in a free state and a free territory earned them their freedom? Early in its deliberations, the Court appeared to
be converging on a minimalist strategy by seizing on the last of these questions
and ruling according to the precedent of its 1851 decision in the case of *Strader
v. Graham*. Under *Strader*, individual states had complete power to decide for
themselves if a slave who had lived in the North had been thereby freed. By
applying that logic to *Scott v. Sandford*, the Court could summarily reject the
Scotts' claims without having to touch any of the other delicate constitutional
issues. In mid-February, the justices voted to follow precisely that course and
gave Justice Samuel Nelson the job of writing the decision.

The compromise quickly came unstuck. The Court's five southern justices,
including Chief Justice Taney, had hoped to hand down an expansive decision
that declared the Missouri Compromise unconstitutional and banned any congressional interference with slavery in the territories. They agreed to the evasive
minimalist strategy only to ensure that the two northern Democratic justices,
Grier of Pennsylvania and Nelson of New York, would join the majority. In late
February, however, word circulated inside the Court that the other two northern
justices, Curtis of Massachusetts and the aging ex-Jacksonian-turned-Republican,
John McLean, planned to issue dissents that would declare congressional prohibitions of slavery in the territories constitutional and affirm the citizenship of blacks.
The southerners hastily approved a motion that gave Taney the task of writing a
majority opinion covering every outstanding issue. All the majority needed was for
one northern Democrat to sign on in order to give the comprehensive ruling
some bisectional protective coloration. Under pressure from President-elect
Buchanan, Justice Grier consented; Justice Nelson, initially hesitant, also signed
on; by early March, the Scotts' fate was sealed by a 7 to 2 margin.[10]

Taney wrote a decision as imposing as any John Marshall might have imagined—ironically, given that Andrew Jackson's old confidant could not have been
more ideologically unlike his Federalist predecessor. Taney's twenty-eight-year
tenure as chief justice had been notable for some early decisions, above all his
1837 ruling in *Charles River Bridge Company v. Warren*, which had eroded the
powers of special corporate charters that the Marshall Court had held beyond
reproach. (Justice Joseph Storey thought Taney's opinion in the *Charles River
Bridge* case so outrageous that he nearly resigned from the Court.) But beginning with the fugitive slave ruling in *Prigg v. Pennsylvania* in 1842, Taney's reputation became increasingly associated with defending slavery against northern
troublemakers. Although he himself had sold off the slaves he had inherited
from his Maryland tobacco-planter family, Taney believed that the integrity of
southern life (which he revered) depended on slavery's survival. He privately
railed against the "northern aggression" that he believed was out to slit slavery's
throat. His four fellow southerners on the Court, Democrats all, shared his out-

rage. With their concurrence, Taney would attempt, at last, to place the full power and majesty of the Court behind the most resolute of pro-slavery views.[11]

Reading his lengthy decision aloud in the crowded, dusky Court chamber, Taney, ill and a fortnight shy of eighty, spoke for two hours in a voice so tremulous that at times he could barely be heard—but his words were anything but feeble. Contending that Negroes had not been among the sovereign people who framed and ratified the Constitution—that they had, in fact, been held "so far inferior, that they had no rights which the white man was bound to respect"—Taney rejected the proposition that blacks, slave or free, were American citizens. In a few sentences, he then dismissed the assertion that Scott's residence in either the free state of Illinois or Wisconsin Territory made him free, even if Wisconsin were constitutionally deemed free soil. Finally, and at length, Taney rejected the claim that Wisconsin Territory had *ever* been free, on the shaky legal ground that the Fifth Amendment's protection of property superseded Congress's constitutional power to "make all needful rules and regulations" for the territories. Mere rules and regulations, Taney claimed, were not laws. Thus, he concluded, the already repealed Missouri Compromise had been unconstitutional all along, the Douglasite concept of popular sovereignty was equally unconstitutional, and slaveholders had the right to bring their slaves into whatever territory they pleased.[12]

Taney's was the first Court ruling since *Marbury* to strike down (albeit retrospectively) an important federal law—a turning point in the rise of the doctrine of judicial supremacy that has since become a deep assumption in American politics and law. Taney's ruling was also filled with historical falsehoods and legal irrelevancies, a point that Justices McLean and Curtis were not shy in making in their dissents. When the Constitution was ratified, free black men had enjoyed many legal rights, including, in all but three states, the right to vote.* Black voters had participated in the ratification process. That made them citizens not simply of their respective states but of the United States as well, under Article IV, Section 2 of the Constitution, which stipulated that "[t]he citizens of each state shall be entitled to all privileges and immunities of citizens of the several states." Concerning Congress's powers over slavery in the territories, numerous Framers—including later congressmen as well as Presidents Washington and Madison—had overseen congressional exclusion of slavery from various territories and raised no constitutional objections. Taney's assertions about the Missouri Compromise

---

* In 1790, free black men could vote on equal terms with whites in New Hampshire, Massachusetts, Rhode Island, Connecticut, New York, New Jersey, Pennsylvania, Delaware, Maryland, and North Carolina. Free black men were enfranchised in the new states of Kentucky in 1792 and Tennessee in 1796, although the right was removed in Kentucky in 1799 and in Tennessee in 1834. See Alexander Keyssar, *The Right to Vote: The Contested History of Democracy in the United States* (New York, 2000), Table A.3, 336–41.

were utterly moot, as the powers of territorial governments regarding slavery were not at issue in Dred Scott's suit. Finally, to prevent a slaveholder from taking his slave into a territory did not deprive him of his property. If it did, what might prevent slaveholders from in the future asserting their Fifth Amendment rights and settling with their slaves in free states as well as in the territories?[13]

Armed with McLean's and Curtis's dissents, Republicans denounced the decision as a politicized abomination, lacking precedent or standing. Much of their argument rested on the contention that Taney's opinion in *Scott* was "not binding in law and conscience"—and, in another turn of the screw, that the ruling consisted of *obiter dicta*, having no pertinence to the case at hand, and was thus irrelevant—a charge that, with respect to the Missouri Compromise, was certainly valid. "[F]ive slaveholders and two doughfaces," Horace Greeley's *New-York Daily Tribune* sneered, had handed down a decision "entitled to just as much moral weight as would be the judgement of a majority of those congregated in any Washington bar-room." Republican legislatures in several states, including New York, passed resolutions that attacked the Court for intruding on state rights.[14]

Most of the remaining loyal northern Democrats reflexively supported the decision, but there were those who considered it too much to bear. "I feel quite mortified for the course of this Tawny Lion of Gen. Jackson—it is a great drawback on his fame," one New York Democrat wrote. In the Old Northwest states, some Democratic newspapers endorsed the Republican view that the decision was part of a conspiracy to elevate slavery nationwide. Thomas Hart Benton, in retirement, fired off a reply to Taney that ran to nearly two hundred pages (including appendices) denouncing the decision as an affront to the Constitution. Even Democrats, led by Stephen A. Douglas, who initially backed the Court came to understand that it had nullified their precarious doctrine of popular sovereignty. In a speech three months after the ruling, Douglas attempted to square the circle by claiming that although the slaveholders' right to property in slaves remained inviolate, it would prove "worthless" unless buttressed by "appropriate police regulations and local legislation" enacted by the territory's residents. For the moment, Douglas and his allies could retrieve this bit of middle ground. But what if *Douglas* was correct? Could the slaveholders, some proslavery Democrats wondered, fully protect their constitutional rights in the territories without additional federal legislation? Was Congress, declared by the Court as powerless to bar slavery in the territories, now compelled to pass new laws *guaranteeing* slavery in the territories—or even in all of the states?[15]

At every point, Taney's decision raised questions and portents that heightened sectional tensions. Above all, it solidified the Republicans' claims that the Court had become a cog in a great conspiracy intent on nationalizing slavery. The fear turned up in private correspondence as well as in campaign speeches: if a slave could be brought into a free territory and his condition of bondage be left intact, what would then prevent Congress from foisting on the free states toleration of slavery within their own borders? Already, a case entitled *Lemmon v. The People* was wending its way through the New York courts, testing whether slaves brought temporarily to New York City were, as state law stipulated, freed persons. How would the Taney Court rule if it were to receive that case on appeal? Given *Dred Scott*, could it fail to overturn New York's freedom laws? What then would be left to prevent a slaveholder from "temporarily" enjoying his right to human property in a free state for months, or for years—or forever?[16]

For the main participants in the *Dred Scott* case, who had almost been forgotten amid the tumult, ensuing events brought poignancy as well as paradox. Two months after the ruling, John Sanford, who had fought for his purported property to the end, died in a New York City insane asylum. Title to the Scotts reverted to his brother-in-law, a Massachusetts Republican congressman named Calvin Chaffee who had married Irene Emerson—and who would soon resign his seat, forced out by the anger created by his unfortunate link to the case. Chaffee transferred title to Taylor Blow of St. Louis, the youngest son of Dred Scott's deceased original owner, who, as a Missouri citizen, had the power to manumit the Scotts. On May 26, 1857, the Scotts finally gained their freedom. Dred landed a job as a hotel porter, while Harriet took in laundry. Dred also became a minor local celebrity, fit to get his picture made at the daguerreotypist's—but his enjoyment was brief. On September 17, 1858, he died, in his early sixties, of tuberculosis. Within four years, both Harriet and their elder daughter Eliza also died. Irene Emerson Chaffee, the original defendant in the suit, lived on in a decent obscurity until 1903.[17]

For the rest of the country, the decision deepened the crisis of American democracy. Pro-slavery southerners hailed Taney for vindicating the Constitution and slavery. "Southern opinion upon the subject of southern slavery . . . is now the supreme law of the land . . . ," the Augusta, Georgia, *Constitutionalist* declared, "and opposition to southern opinion upon this subject is now opposition to the Constitution, and morally treason against the Government." For antislavery northerners, the decision proved that an entire branch of the federal government had fallen into the Slave Power's clutches. Taney's opinion, according to the Ohio Republican state convention, was "anti-constitutional, antirepublican, anti-democratic, incompatible with State rights, and destructive of personal security." Justice Curtis, disgusted, resigned from the Supreme Court in September, on the transparent pretext that his salary was insufficient. Designed, as one New Orleans newspaper put it, to place "the whole basis of the Black Republican organization under the ban of law," the ruling backfired, reinforcing Republican resolve to win the White House in 1860, appoint new justices to the Court, and wipe away Taney's stain.[18]

Among the northerners most exercised by the decision was the once-reluctant Republican of Illinois, Abraham Lincoln. A year later, Lincoln would make *Dred Scott* the chief issue in his campaign to unseat the man he considered the chief northern tool of the Slave Power, Stephen A. Douglas. But Lincoln's attack on *Scott*—and the worsening of sectional animosities—also reflected intervening events in Kansas and Washington.

"GENERAL JACKSON IS DEAD, SIR"

Once the initial astonishment at Taney's opinion had passed, it was unclear how *Dred Scott* would affect the inflamed political situation. For free blacks, certainly, the decision had dire implications. Yet unlike the Fugitive Slave Law or the Kansas-Nebraska Act, it did not demand immediate federal enforcement or force any reassessment among the chief political factions. For pro-slavery and antislavery partisans, the ruling did more to affirm existing views than to change any minds. Even Stephen Douglas, his principle of popular sovereignty now exploded, found ways, temporarily, to give the impression that the northern and southern Democracy remained united in principle. Fresh disturbances in Kansas soon destroyed such wishful thinking.

During the summer and fall of 1856, the situation in Kansas had seemed to improve dramatically. In August, President Pierce accepted the resignation of the disgraced territorial governor Wilson Shannon and replaced him with a no-nonsense Democrat, John W. Geary. Although unfriendly to the abolitionists, Geary, a fearsome man who stood six feet five inches tall, believed in law and order more than he did in protecting slavery. A hero of the Mexican War, he had enlarged his reputation for toughness as San Francisco's first mayor in the early 1850s, when he personally led the suppression of the city's endemic violent lawlessness. Directed to stop the Kansas border war, he did so inside of two months, skillfully deploying federal troops, disbanding the rival "armies," and showing no quarter to either side. Yet only four months later, on the day of Buchanan's inauguration in 1857, Geary quit his post over continuing abuses by the official proslavery legislature. First the pro-slavery men refused to consider his request to soften the harsh slave code that Governor Shannon had signed into law. Then they passed a new bill calling for a constitutional convention the following June, with the territory's flagrantly pro-slavery county sheriffs to oversee the election of delegates. The approved constitution would go into effect without any popular referendum. Stunned by the bill's audacity, Geary vetoed it, only to have it passed over his veto by what he would soon be calling the "felon legislature" in Lecompton. It was too much even for the formidable enforcer to bear.[19]

Determined that Kansas would not break him the way it had broken Pierce,

President Buchanan persuaded former Treasury Secretary Robert J. Walker of Mississippi to succeed Geary, with assurances that the administration desired a fair electoral outcome. Walker, a close friend of Stephen Douglas's (with whom he met in Chicago on his way to Kansas), was more of a partisan Democratic realist than a sectionalist. Surveying the territory's electorate, he estimated, accurately, that although most of the voters were Democrats, the majority were non-Yankee free-staters who wished to keep slavery out of Kansas in order to keep blacks out of Kansas. The only way to admit Kansas expeditiously as a safe Democratic state, Walker concluded, was to approve a free constitution. Accordingly, upon his arrival in Kansas in May, he tried to dissuade free-staters from their plans to boycott the imminent convention delegate elections. Coming after years of bushwhacking and bogus elections, Walker's appeals were useless. Pro-slavery men won every seat in the convention, which was scheduled to assemble in Lecompton in September.[20]

Walker would end up just as sickened as Geary. A strict Jacksonian, he insisted that any state constitution be subject to a public referendum, which provoked an outcry from pro-slavery men in Kansas and Washington alike. In October, Walker threw out blatantly fraudulent returns from yet another legislative election and certified a free-state majority, prompting Jefferson Davis, Alexander Stephens, Robert Toombs, and other southern Democratic leaders to denounce him. (Some southerners also began expressing misgivings about Buchanan as, in one Georgian's words, Walker's "master who lives in the White House.") Finally, Walker squared off against the dubiously selected Lecompton constitutional convention. Declaring the rights of slaveowners to their human property as inviolable, the delegates' new constitution prohibited any future amendment abridging those rights. Ignoring Walker's warnings, the convention sent their constitution directly to Congress, accompanied by a petition for statehood.[21]

Walker's complaints, and northern Democratic opposition on Capitol Hill, blocked the statehood maneuver, and in early November, the Lecompton convention acceded to a referendum to choose between a "constitution with slavery" and a "constitution with no slavery." But the choice turned out to be meaningless, since the "no slavery" version guaranteed the ownership of slaves already in the territory—in effect prohibiting the future importation of slaves while formally preserving slavery. The convention also gave oversight of the referendum to the same officials who had conducted the offensive convention delegate elections in June—an open invitation to rig the process. Northern Democrats as well as Republicans saw through the tricks and denounced them. Governor Walker called the convention's supposed compromise "a vile fraud, a bare counterfeit," and expressed certainty that President Buchanan would reject it. But Buchanan went along with the Lecompton arrangement, pleading that if he did not, the South would secede. Walker departed Kansas forever, to derisive pro-slavery charges that he had betrayed the cause and joined the blackest ranks of the "Black Republicans."[22]

The Lecompton constitution controversy finally made Stephen Douglas snap. Douglas still wanted to be president, and he knew that if he were to swallow hard and support the pro-slavery Kansas legislature, the southern Democracy would probably support his nomination in 1860. But he knew equally well that doing so would ruin his chances in the North. The source of the difficulty, he concluded, was Buchanan. Bullied by the South, the president had betrayed his repeated claims that he wanted fair elections in Kansas. A consultation in Chicago with his friend Robert Walker helped convince Douglas that the only way to dissociate the national Democrats from southern extremism and stave off defeat by the Republicans was to force Buchanan to change course. On December 3, Douglas marched into the White House to assail the "trickery and juggling" of the Lecompton men and to try to get the president to listen to angry reason.[23]

Buchanan frostily received the senator and heard him out. At stake, in their meeting, were the battered remnants and legacy of what had once been the Jackson Democracy—now, increasingly, the slavocrats' Democracy. The latest events in Kansas, Douglas charged, had made a mockery of popular sovereignty. If Buchanan persisted, he warned, the Democratic Party in the North was doomed. To prevent that, Douglas, said, he would break with the administration and head the anti-Lecompton forces in Congress. Buchanan, the old functionary and quasi-Hunker, still lived in the mental universe of the 1830s and 1840s, when appeasing the South was paramount to keeping the Democracy in power. Douglas, for all of his own loyalties to the past, understood that times and men had changed. "Mr. Douglas," Buchanan responded smugly to Douglas's threat, "I desire you to remember that no Democrat ever yet differed from an administration of his own choice without being crushed." As if likening himself to Old Hickory, Buchanan told Douglas to "[b]eware the fate of Tallmadge and Rives," the party disloyalists of another era. "Mr. President," Douglas shot back, "I wish you to remember that General Jackson is dead, sir."*

The proceedings in Kansas followed a now-familiar course. In December, free-state voters stayed home during the sham referendum, and the "constitution with slavery" won overwhelming approval. (Leaving nothing to chance, pro-slavery men cast nearly three thousand fraudulent ballots.) The new free-state legislature would not let the vote stand and scheduled its own referendum on the

---

* Buchanan's memory was selective: John C. Calhoun, whose legacy the president now appeared to be advancing, defied Andrew Jackson and, although defeated in 1833 over nullification, was not "crushed." Buchanan also underestimated Douglas, who was a far more formidable political leader than either Nathaniel Tallmadge or William C. Rives.

constitution for two weeks later, in which voters could choose between the "with slavery" and "no slavery" versions or reject them both. Now it was the pro-slavery men's turn, once again, to boycott—and the result, as expected, was a nearly unanimous vote against both of the Lecompton constitutions. Immediately, southern politicians and officeholders pressured the White House to accept the first vote and send the pro-slavery constitution to Congress for its approval. Buchanan crumpled. Declaring the free-soil advocates "in a state of rebellion against the government," he pointed to *Dred Scott* as the ultimate confirmation that "slavery exists in Kansas by virtue of the Constitution of the United States," and concluded that "Kansas is therefore at this moment as much a slave state as Georgia or South Carolina."[24]

Douglas proved as good as his word and threw every ounce of his strength into opposing Kansas statehood under the Lecompton constitution. Working sixteen hours a day, the Little Giant pushed himself to the center of every verbal fray on the Senate floor. ("The South never made a greater mistake than in provoking his opposition," the freshman Republican Senator James Dixon of Connecticut observed. "He will prove a terrible foe.") The urgency of his arguments sometimes made him sound heretical. On the final day of debate, Douglas objected to what he called an "authoritative" editorial in the Washington *Union*, which had declared property in slaves a natural right. "The attempt now," he asserted, "to establish the doctrine that a free State has no power to prohibit slavery . . . that slavery is national and not local, that it goes everywhere under the Constitution of the United States, and yet is higher than the Constitution . . . will not be tolerated." Without once mentioning *Dred Scott*, Taney, or Buchanan, Douglas had come dangerously close to sustaining the Republican charge that a plot was afoot to nationalize slavery.[25]

Douglas's fury did not change a single vote in the Senate, which approved Kansas's admission as a slave state, 33 to 25. In the House, where the result was less certain, the debate led to violence. At two in the morning during one House session, the South Carolinian Laurence Keitt—one of Preston Brooks's accomplices in the attack on Charles Sumner—called another member a "damned Black Republican puppy," which touched off a donnybrook involving upwards of thirty congressmen. (Alexander Stephens, the floor manager for the pro-Lecompton side, claimed that had weapons been present, there would have been serious bloodshed.) Finally, after a week of nail-biting procedural votes and despite heavy administration lobbying, the Lecompton bill failed, by a margin of 120 to 112.[26]

Congress's rejection of the Lecompton constitution did not bring peace to Kansas. Undaunted, the Buchanan administration attempted one last ploy—a kind of mass bribe—with a new referendum that would expand the size of the normal land grant to be offered settlers upon the territory's admission to statehood. No less transparent than any of the earlier pro-slavery schemes, this one went down to a resounding defeat in August 1858. By then, portions of Kansas had returned to open warfare. In the most spectacular incident, in May 1858—apparently timed to coincide with the second anniversary of the Pottawatomie atrocity—a group of slave-staters descended on the cabins of several free-staters, shot five of the residents to death, and wounded four others. Old John Brown, shuttling between fund-raising back East and hell-raising in Kansas, retaliated by taking his terrorists into Missouri, attacking two slaveholders and killing one, and carrying their horses and eleven liberated slaves up to Canada.[27]

In Washington, however, the death of the Lecompton scheme looked like a turning of the political tide in Kansas. (Those perceptions would later prove accurate. After defeating the Lecompton plan once and for all, free-state Kansans would organize a Republican Party and control a new constitutional convention elected in 1859. Kansas would finally be admitted to the Union as a free state in January 1861.) Republicans rejoiced—as did the pro-Douglas, anti-Lecompton northern Democrats, who had provided twenty-two vital votes against the bill. "The agony is over," wrote one, "and thank God the right has triumphed!" Up on Manhattan, 120 guns fired off the Battery in an enormous celebration, one for every vote against the accursed constitution.[28]

THE PANIC OF 1857: DEPRESSION, LABOR, AND SECTIONAL POLITICS

New Yorkers had additional reason to rejoice in the early spring of 1858—the lifting of a brief economic depression, sparked by the financial panic over the late summer and fall of 1857. The turmoil caused by the downturn had been mild compared to the civil war in Kansas. But it had been real enough, adding the specter of class warfare to the crisis over slavery, and forcing Democrats and Republicans in some key electoral battlegrounds to respond.

The origins of the crisis, as in 1837, were both foreign and domestic. The decade from 1847 to 1857 had witnessed a vast expansion of industrial development and railroad construction, funded largely by British and European investors and accelerated by the influx of newly mined California gold. In 1856–57, a sudden sell-off of American securities abroad, caused by a rise in foreign interest rates prompted by the Crimean War, depressed the value of American stocks and bonds. The war's elimination of Russian grain from the European market also fed a rapid rise in American grain exports and a speculation boom in western land. As American paper values sank and the land speculation bubble grew, investors turned jittery, looking for the smallest signal for them to liquidate their assets. An isolated episode in late August—the suspension of specie payments by the New York branch of an important Ohio bank, after one of its cashiers embezzled its funds—proved the trigger. Investors pulled their money out of banks; banks were forced to call in loans; and overextended businessmen, especially in the North and West, went under in droves. By mid-October, virtually every bank in the nation had suspended specie payments, and the fearsome phrase "hard times" appeared everywhere. "As to the hard times, it has wrought wonders—banks breaking and failures of many persons, business stopping, and labourers thrown out of employment," one Indianapolis resident related. Stephen Foster, no stranger to penury despite the popularity of his songs, authored a grim new composition: "'Tis a dirge that is murmured around the lowly grave,/Oh! hard times come again no more."[29]

The depression hit New York City especially hard. "[B]ands of men paraded in a menacing manner through the streets of the city demanding work or bread," the British consul reported to his superiors. Local relief agencies were swamped during the fall and winter; unemployment, especially among the poorest classes of day laborers and sweatshop workers, skyrocketed; and on November 10, soldiers and marines under the command of Winfield Scott had to be dispatched to lower Broadway and Wall Street to keep a large and angry crowd from breaking into the U.S. Customs House and the subtreasury and stealing the twenty million dollars in their vaults. Similar if less spectacular unrest unfolded in smaller northern and western cities. Trade union organizing picked up its pace, and through the following year labor unrest continued in textile towns and railroad camps from New England to Pennsylvania.[30]

The panic focused attention on the plight of northern wage-earners as nothing had since the economic collapse of 1837, but the rediscovered working class was very different from its Jacksonian forerunner. The proliferation of large textile mills and elaborate put-out clothing operations in New England had turned the pastoral dreams of an industrial utopia into a grimmer reality of stretched-out hours and tightened pay. Increasingly, the industrial labor force consisted not of farm daughters in temporary jobs but families resigned to being mill workers for life. The immigrant waves after 1845 had, in turn, profoundly changed working-class demographics, creating a workforce in the large cities and in the mining and railroad camps that consisted overwhelmingly of newcomers (above all Irish and German Catholics) and their children. That remaking deeply affected labor politics in the 1840s and 1850s, leading to the disturbances of 1857, which had important implications for national politics.[31]

There had been some continuities in between the labor movements of the Jacksonian period and those of the succeeding twenty years, but the most important activities involved newly arrived immigrants as well as natives in innovative efforts. Unskilled day laborers and craft workers built unions, cooperatives, and protective associations. Smaller, more radical political associations, like the

Befreigundsbund, a secret revolutionary society founded in 1847 by the German émigré Wilhelm Weitling, arose in the immigrant neighborhoods. The new organizations attempted to create unity among skilled and unskilled workers, efforts that bore fruit in 1850 with the formation, in New York, of the national Industrial Congress. Although internal factional warfare soon divided the Congress, individual craft and laborers' unions persisted and led a wave of strikes in 1853–54, halted only by a brief financial panic (a prelude to 1857) in late 1854 and 1855.[32]

Accompanying these union activities were various broader efforts at labor reform, preeminently the land reform movement headed by the former Working Men's Party leader George Henry Evans. Evans, exhausted, had retreated from his Manhattan base to the New Jersey countryside in 1835. When he returned to radical agitation in 1841, he was a thorough convert to the proposition that the wage slave would be freed only if he could obtain a patch of land. Followers of various utopian writers (including Albert Brisbane, the leading American champion of the French visionary Charles Fourier), as well as of British Chartist land reformers, found their way into Evans's fold. Constituted as the National Reform Association, the land reformers invented a snappy slogan, "Vote Yourself A Farm!," encouraged local movements like the New York state Anti-Renters, and developed blueprints for neo-Jeffersonian townships to be built out West—the building blocks of an America of free and independent labor.[33]

While they spoke of equality and economic justice, these new labor movements had developed renewed tensions with the antislavery movement. A strong sense of rapport did arise in many quarters, especially in New England where urban skilled workers, factory hands, and trade unionists had been active abolitionists since the 1830s. In Boston as well as smaller cities, workingmen's mass meetings condemned southern aggression, and labor organizers helped elect Free Soil Democrats to local and national office in the early 1850s. William Lloyd Garrison's *Liberator* enthusiastically covered these developments and supported trade union strikes by journeymen (including journeymen printers) over wages. But there were also labor leaders (including Evans, who always hated slavery and preached racial equality, and who denounced anti-abolitionists) who came to regard the slavery issue as, at best, secondary to the emancipation of northern labor. "[R]eform should begin at our own firesides . . . ," Evans declared, "and philanthropists, if they would have an influence, must no longer confine themselves to *color*." Others argued that the living conditions for northern wage workers were no better and maybe worse than those of southern slaves—precisely the argument that slaveholders used to defend their system. Although workingmen's denunciations of "white slavery" always implied a hatred of all bondage—"the sin of slavery," one New Hampshire anti-abolitionist labor paper called it—they could also suggest that whites deserved better consideration from society than blacks. Antislavery radicals responded that no matter how just the workingmen's cause, equating northern labor's conditions with slavery was, as Garrison wrote, like "magnifying mole-hills into mountains, and reducing mountains to the size of mole-hills."[34]

Alienation from the antislavery movement was particularly severe among the newly arrived Irish immigrant workers packed inside the slums of Boston, New York, and Philadelphia. The Irish sometimes found themselves in sharp competition with blacks for jobs at the nether end of the big-city workforce, and they feared that an end to slavery would only bring more blacks north. Antislavery also carried with it, many Irish believed, all the nativist prejudices of Yankee Protestantism—regarding papist Celts as a lower form of life, uncomprehending of the suffering the Irish had endured during the Famine years and after, magnanimous when it came to faraway black slaves but indifferent, even hostile, to the new immigrants. To be held by some in even greater contempt than blacks, in a nation whose highest tribunal had declared that blacks had no rights the white man was bound to respect, provoked sharp ethnic and class resentments among the Irish against abolitionists and Republicans—and an even more lethal hatred of blacks. The Irish were not monolithic: in the dance halls of the poorest slums, in some trade unions, and in private life, there was abundant evidence of toleration, cooperation, and even deep affection between blacks and Irish immigrants. But in the swirl of insecurity and resentment that buffeted Irish American working-class life in the 1850s, two conservative pillars loomed to many newcomers as the safest sanctuaries: the Catholic Church and the southern-dominated (and immigrant-friendly) Democratic Party. The Democrats, in particular (like the conservative anti-abolitionists of the 1830s), exploited and enlarged Irish working-class racism with the crudest kinds of Negrophobic propaganda.[35]

The panic of 1857 and ensuing depression strengthened those political realities. In the eastern cities, local Democratic politicos leapt into the breach and came to the immediate aid of the unemployed. Leading the way was New York City's mayor, Fernando Wood, a strong-arming, pro-southern conservative with a penchant for public works and civic reform. Wood called himself a man of honor, protector of the poor, and "true friend of the Irish." He churned the political waters early in 1857 when, in trying to stave off the imposition of a Maine-style liquor law in Manhattan and preserve home rule of the city's police force, he helped provoke several days of mob violence. After the panic hit, he devised a bold relief plan in which the city would provide food and coal to the poor and hire the unemployed to work on a string of public improvement projects, including construction of the new Central Park. The city's Common Council blocked Wood's proposal (although the park commissioners eventually hired thousands of jobless men), and a fusion movement of anti-Wood Tammanyites, Republicans, and Know-Nothings, alarmed at Wood's identification with what one patrician called "the *canaille*," unseated the mayor in a close election in November. To the city's polyglot labor movement, and its masses of immigrant workers, the maverick Wood stood prouder and taller than ever.[36]

Republicans responded to the panic by taking very different positions aimed at aiding workingmen. In March 1857, the Democratic Congress had enacted some additional downward revisions of the Walker Tariff of 1846—and to protectionist-minded Republicans, notably Horace Greeley, there was a direct link between the changes and the economic distress. The pro-tariff argument was especially effective in Pennsylvania, where, supposedly, iron companies had been undercut by British iron imports unleashed by the recent tariff reductions. In making their pitch, Republicans revived the old Whig doctrine of the harmony of interests, calling protection for the iron masters a boon for their workers as well. A higher tariff, Greeley's *Tribune* declared, would employ thousands "who have languished for months in unwilling idleness." The campaign would help spike the Pennsylvania Republicans' totals in the autumn 1858 congressional elections, bringing them an unanticipated and highly encouraging rout of the Democrats.[37]

Congressional Republicans also pushed hard for three extant land-grant proposals that they presented as pro-labor: a homestead bill to guarantee cheap land for settlers, a Pacific railroad bill, and a bill offering grants to the states to found publicly funded agricultural and mechanical colleges. The provenance of these efforts was complex. The homestead and school land-grant bills drew on the ideas of Evans's National Reform Association. The transcontinental railroad bill was, in part, an effort to complete the project that had prompted Stephen Douglas to propose the Kansas-Nebraska Bill, but to do so under Republican auspices. All three measures were designed to appeal to working-class Democrats around the country, especially in the Old Northwest. After the panic, Republicans expanded their claims, offering the bills as the means to rescue workingmen and their families from the latest economic catastrophe. Cheap land in particular, Gamaliel Bailey wrote, would "secure to all our large cities a safety-drain," elevate living standards, and promote social order for both the homesteaders and the working men who stayed behind.[38]

The panic had additional cultural effects in the North, including an outpouring of revivalist religion more fervent than any seen since the 1830s. Whether or not the prayers worked, the depression lifted much more quickly than anticipated, thanks largely to resupplies of gold from California and Europe. New York banks resumed specie payments as early as December 1857, and the rest of the nation's banking system was back on its feet within months. Factories reopened; wages were restored to their former levels; and the jobless began finding work again. "There was never a more severe crisis nor a more rapid recovery," the London *Economist* observed. Although the suffering had been great, the social upheaval it had caused had been relatively short-lived and largely nonviolent.[39]

Despite its brevity, the downturn had immediate political effects. By strengthening the connections between immigrant workers and the Democratic Party, it solidified an important constituency of the dwindling northern Democracy, especially in the key state of New York—one that was as hostile to blacks as it was to Yankee Republicans. The depression also exacerbated sectional divisions in national politics. The impetus given to the Republican tariff and land-grant proposals raised new complaints from the South about the arrogant, plundering North. Successful in killing the railroad bill, the southerners could not prevent sectional majorities from passing a land-grant college bill in 1859 and, in the succeeding session, a homestead bill, but President Buchanan vetoed both, further infuriating the Republican rank and file.

The panic also reinforced a growing confidence among southern slaveholders that their way of life and ideas about politics were far superior to the northern free-labor democracy. In sharp contrast to the depression of 1837–43, the downturn of 1857–58 was mainly a northern phenomenon. Relatively untouched by overinvestment in railroad construction and by overspeculation in stocks, bonds, and western lands, the plantation cotton economy suffered only slightly and rebounded quickly once demand from the North and Britain resumed. At first, the panic caused southerners to wail at the latest disaster brought upon them and the nation by greedy Yankee bankers and capitalists, but their outrage soon gave way to smugness. The region's very backwardness with respect to industrial and financial development had spared it from the worst. To numerous slaveholder politicians, this was a sign of southern social and political superiority.[40]

That case was put most famously early in 1858 by John C. Calhoun's ex-protégé, James H. Hammond. In a speech to the Senate during the Lecompton struggle but also attuned to the panic, Hammond compared the current conditions of the two sections: "Cotton is king. . . . Who can doubt, that has looked at recent events, that cotton is supreme? . . . We have poured in among you one million six hundred thousand bales of cotton just at the moment to save you from destruction." If cotton was king, Hammond contended, slavery made it possible. "[T]he greatest strength of the South arises from the harmony of her social and political institutions. This harmony gives her a frame of society, the best in the world, and an extent of political freedom, combined with entire security, such as no other people ever enjoyed upon the face of the earth." Hammond emphasized that slavery produced the fairest and most secure form of political democracy. "In all social systems," he said, "there must be a class to do the mean duties, to perform the drudgery of life . . . It constitutes the very mud-sills of society, and of political government." For Hammond, the South's respect for the self-evident supremacy of all whites over all blacks stood in shining contrast to the absurd democracy of the North: "Your slaves are white, of your own race; you are brothers of one blood. They are your equals in natural endowment of intellect, and they feel galled by their degradation. Our slaves do not vote. We give them no political power. Yours do vote, and being the majority, they are the depositories of all your political power. If they knew the tremendous secret, that the ballot-box is stronger than an army with bayonets, and could combine, where would you be?"[41]

Hammond had no particular empathy for the "galled" proletarians of the North. The lessons of his class analysis were those of a landed gentleman: either the rulers in the North could emulate the South by giving all "mean duties" to enslaved and politically powerless blacks, or they would run the risk of expropriation by their own enfranchised white slaves. The offensiveness of Hammond's claims, both to the dignity of labor and to Yankee democracy, was not lost on northerners. Hammond's speech, Horace Greeley wrote, expressed "the sentiment of all aristocracies, and simply assert[s] the old proposition that the few were made to rule, and the many to be governed." But those implications were of less immediate importance to national politics than Hammond's confident view that the South had built the greatest society in history, and with the greatest government—"satisfied, content, happy, harmonious, and prosperous." It was a view long in gestation. It formed the foundations of a self-conscious southern democracy, fundamentally at odds with the northern democracy. And it was becoming increasingly ubiquitous among southerners, despite the abiding divisions and anxieties that afflicted the region's rulers.[42]

DIXIE DEMOCRACY

On the evening of March 4, 1859, at New York's Mechanics' Hall, Dan Emmett, a five-string banjo player for the enormously popular blackface Bryant Minstrels, introduced a catchy new "walk-around" song about an adulterous weaver named Willum. A native of central Ohio, Emmett was an accomplished songwriter— credited with, among other compositions, "Turkey in the Straw" and "Ol' Dan Tucker"—and he was an expert performer in the googly-eyed, part-contemptuous, part-envious blackface style that set young northern workingmen to roaring. Emmett had kept the tune in his suitcase for years, and some writers have speculated that he first picked it up from free black musicians. The song's hastily written lyrics—with the refrain, "In Dixie Land I'll took my stand/To lib and die in Dixie"—were an unexceptional mixture of nonsense and contrived nostalgia typical of the northern minstrel genre. What made the song special, like all of Emmett's best work, was its rousing melody. Thus, from a corked-up Yankee pretending to be a slave—singing about a "gay deceiver" before a New

York audience of "greasy mechanics"—came what was destined to be filched and transformed, to Dan Emmett's horror, into the best-known pro-slavery southern nationalist anthem.[43]

The appropriated, wishful, and self-ratifying qualities of the emerging cult of the South and southern nationalism cannot belie the genuine outrage and bitterness of the later 1850s. Nor can they belie the intellection and shared ethical assumptions, rooted in slavery, that helped make the improvised seem natural and all-embracing. The polarizing sectionalism in national affairs and the demise of southern Whiggery pushed southern political leaders toward an appearance of utter unity. But the political realities of the slave South remained, as they had always been, fraught with internal divisions and fears. Differences that might seem just noticeable to outsiders were difficult and contentious to clear-eyed southerners. Those differences owed as much to the mixed character of southern political institutions as they did to variations in class, geography, and traditional loyalties. Ironically, they would reinforce the plausibility of those in the fire-eater wing of southern politics who argued that, short of an assertion of solidarity and secession from the Union, slavery was doomed—an argument that initially resistant southern democrats came to share.

The aristocratic republic of South Carolina remained the seat of southern reaction but also a perplexity—matching, more closely than any other state, the undemocratic South conjured up by the Republicans, yet defying standard images of the Cotton Kingdom. The short-staple cotton economy of the South Carolina up-country still supported an elegant slaveholder elite, but both the land and its owners were showing signs of wear and tear. After supporting two generations of cotton planters, the soil was losing its nutrients, and many of the scions of the original fortune hunters had pushed on to the rich black soils of Alabama and Mississippi. Surrounding the great estates like John C. Calhoun's Fort Hill (its slaves and white-columned mansion house sold by Calhoun's cash-poor widow to their son, Andrew, at her husband's death) were the vacant houses and weed-covered lawns of plantations abandoned for better prospects out West. The planters who remained regarded themselves as refined patriarchs, more interested in making a life than merely in making a living. Yet as they sipped their brandy and smoked their Spanish cigars, their voluble self-satisfaction betrayed an unnerving suspicion that time was running out.[44]

Low-country South Carolina elite life, centered in Charleston, was more rarefied and showy but also fraying at the edges. In stark contrast to the nouveau riche southwest, the rice and long-staple cotton plantations of malarial coastal Carolina had an almost antiquated look, worked on by masses of dark-skinned African slaves (who outnumbered whites by ratios five times higher than in Alabama) commanded by semiresident masters and their overseers. Charleston, where the low-country planters and their families took refuge all summer and whenever else they could, was gay and cosmopolitan, closer in spirit to London than to Boston. Yet for all of the learning and wealth on conspicuous display along the Battery where the Ashley and Cooper Rivers met, Charleston also had a slightly outdated air, its reputation as the self-styled Athens of America no longer what it once was, its skyline still dominated by the colonial spire of St. Michael's Episcopal Church, built from the designs of Sir Christopher Wren. An English visitor observed that Charleston's street names—King Street, Queen Street—were markers of a "polished and aristocratic" upper class that had "reminiscences of the 'old country' and is proud of them." "We like the old things—," William Grayson, the poet, ex-congressman, and chief customs collector in Charleston, remarked, "old books, old friends, old and fixed relations between employer and employed."[45]

The state's politics were even more antiquated, but they showed little sign of fatigue. In the 1850s, as ever, a singularly united class of slaveholders ruled South Carolina through the omnipotent state legislature in Columbia. The legislature appointed the governor (who was replaced every two years and lacked the power of veto); it also picked the lieutenant governor, attorney general, state military commanders, court clerks, justices of the peace, sheriffs, and all presidential electors. Through gross malapportionment, the interests of the low-country squirearchy and its backcountry allies reigned supreme and unchecked. With statewide elections virtually nonexistent, political parties never really took root in South Carolina. Partyless politics in turn shielded local leaders from opposition while dampening popular interest and participation.[46]

The system did not go completely untested. After the Virginia constitutional revision of 1851, democrats from the rugged, northernmost counties that brushed the Blue Ridge, where slavery was scarce, demanded similar reforms. South Carolina's government, wrote one angry pamphleteer, existed "to guard and secure the interests of the large rice and cotton planters. The interests of men who have to work with their hands are entirely unprotected." That autumn, defiant ultra-sectionalists, infuriated at the terms of the national truce of 1850 and at the collapse of the Nashville Convention movement, pushed for a secession convention in a rare statewide vote—and huge majorities in the mountain districts helped send the disunionists down to a crushing defeat. It was enough to cause the Beaufort grandee William Henry Trescot to predict that in South Carolina, democracy—a word, he said, that "has betrayed the South"—would kill slavery. But with the legislature firmly in control, only the most trivial alteration of election laws ensued from the brief mountain uprising. Although pragmatic anti-extremists might momentarily hold sway, they endangered neither slavery nor the state's peculiar oligarchy.[47]

Unreconstructed South Carolina nourished the most extravagant forms of pro-slavery reaction, exemplified by Robert Barnwell Rhett. Born Robert Barnwell Smith in Beaufort in 1800, Rhett had changed his last name in 1837 to honor an ancestor who had been British governor-general of the Bahamas and to pump up his own aristocratic lineage. (Completing the makeover, he also preferred to be called Barnwell instead of his commonplace first name.) Overcoming an interrupted formal education, he had begun his career as a lawyer, thrown himself into the most radical currents of the nullification movement in 1832–33, then climbed the political ladder from state attorney general to the U.S. Senate, where in 1850 he filled the vacancy left by John C. Calhoun's death. Although closely associated with the Great Nullifier, Rhett had always been more fiery, less interested in political ideas than in political action. (In his reverential eulogy to Calhoun, he could not help noting that the departed had "pursued principles too exclusively.") Rhett would pursue power for the South in order to turn principles into reality, and by 1850 he had decided that the only path left open was resistance and disunion. Efforts at compromise, he told the Nashville Convention, merely inspired "the Northern people with the belief that we value a union with them more than we value the institution of slavery." Slaveholders, he proclaimed, "must rule themselves or perish."[48]

Although dejected by the surge of southern moderation during the early 1850s (which led him to resign from the Senate in 1852), Rhett never wavered. After the Republicans' strong national showing in 1856, he wrote an open letter to Governor James H. Adams, charging that a "complete revolution" by the antislavery North had transformed the federal government into "a sheer despotism," and that the only honorable course was for the South to seize its "glorious destiny" as "a great free and independent people!" The following year, Rhett obtained control of the old Calhounite newspaper, the *Charleston Mercury*, when his son bought it and installed himself as editor. In a purely tactical move, Rhett then modulated his tone, reentered the national Democratic Party, which he had abandoned years before, and began praising such figures as James Hammond and Jefferson Davis—southern rights stalwarts whom he had long criticized as unreliable party hacks. His unannounced aim was to capture the Democracy from within and use it to complete what he would soon be calling the South's "high mission"—to create a magnificent independent slaveholders' republic larger in territory than all of Europe, producing the world's most valuable commodity, cotton.[49]

"Rhettism" won over such luminaries as congressmen Laurence Keitt and William Porcher Miles (the latter an ex-mayor of Charleston). Elsewhere in the South, ex-Carolinians, and out-of-staters with close spiritual and political ties to Carolina politics, expounded their own versions of disunionist extremism. Edmund Ruffin of Virginia, thrice appointed South Carolina commissioner of agriculture, made a considerable reputation beginning in the 1820s as a proponent of scientific land reclamation, but he earned popular acclaim only in the

1850s when he abandoned his earlier doubts about slavery, laid aside his work on calcareous manures, and began expounding on southern greatness and disunion. In Alabama, William Lowndes Yancey, the up-country South Carolina-born lawyer and scourge of the northern Democracy, formed, at Ruffin's suggestion, the pro-secession League of United Southerners—a group, Yancey announced, that would crush "the mere political tricksters, who now make the slavery question subordinate to the Parties." In Texas, a young firebrand émigré from a wealthy up-country South Carolina family, Louis Trezevant Wigfall, emerged as the major political rival to the old Jacksonian and Unionist Sam Houston. There were important pro-slavery extremists from outside the Carolina connection, most conspicuously the startling Virginia scribbler George Fitzhugh, a down-at-the-heels descendant of an old Commonwealth family who declared slavery "the natural and normal condition of society." But South Carolinians and ex-Carolinians dominated the fire-eaters' ranks.[50]

Philosophically as well as politically, the fire-eaters stepped beyond the nullifier hero, Calhoun. ("I think Mr Rhett the logical extension of Mr Calhoun," William Trescot observed in 1858.) For Calhoun, liberty and equality meant the preservation of slaveholders' rights. His attacks on democracy—or what, in his unpublished "Disquisition on Government," he carefully called "absolute democracy"—amounted to an attack on majoritarian government and the reign of what John Randolph had called King Numbers. Until the last months of his life, Calhoun had always thought of interposition and nullification as the means to secure southern rights short of disunion, and even in 1850, when he talked more about secession, his mind was full of ideas about radical reforms that might yet keep the South within the Union. The later pro-slavery extremists went further, aiming at nothing less than secession, vaunting liberty as the prerogative of the naturally superior few, and rejecting the concepts of equality and democracy altogether. Man, Calhoun's old ally William Harper came to observe in 1852, was "born to subjection," and civilization rested on the enforcement of inequality. Self-government through universal suffrage, another South Carolinian wrote, was "the most pernicious humbug of the age." No society, wrote yet another, had ever "commenced the march of social movement" as "a mass of unarticulated democracy." For the Rhettist militants, the racial inequality of southern slavery reinforced their belief in the inequality of all mankind. They wanted to establish their own government as a pure slaveholders' republic untainted by the egalitarian foolishness of the age.[51]

The Virginian Fitzhugh confronted the matter with clarity and audacity in a direct attack on Thomas Jefferson. "Men are not," he declared, "born entitled to equal rights!" Jefferson, with his palaver about how the mass of men had not been created to be ridden like horses by other men, was utterly wrong: "[I]t would be far nearer the truth to say, 'that some were born with saddles on their backs, and others booted and spurred to ride them' . . . they need the reins, the bit, and the spur." Few would go as far as Fitzhugh and claim that most whites as well as blacks were best fitted for slavery. But in the fire-eater mind, racial slavery was the cornerstone of a society that permitted the best men to rule over all the rest in virtuous harmony.[52]

It all sounded slightly daft to most southern slaveholders. In the border states, where Unionism remained strong and where pro-slavery, though dominant, was still more equivocal than elsewhere, Rhettism seemed treasonous. Among Deep South planters, it was an affront to white solidarity. On certain essentials, most slaveholders could agree: slavery created an economy, society, and polity superior to the crass and cutthroat North; slavery was a benevolent, Christian institution which uplifted the slaves from the barbarism of their African ancestors; and the Yankees were determined to destroy all order, grace, and conservatism. But the transit from defending slavery to attacking some of the fundamental principles of 1776 seemed, outside South Carolina and among its extremist sons and admirers elsewhere, driven by unreal syllogisms. "Mr. Rhett is the most consistent of politicians," one Petersburg, Virginia, newspaper remarked in 1852. "He pushes his doctrines to their legitimate conclusions. He is rigidly logical, but remarkably impractical. He is something of a fanatic withal." And that was a friendly assessment. Farther west and south, the class-based, aristocratic, disunionist arguments clashed with ingrained white egalitarian assumptions. "Nowhere in this broad Union but in the slaveholding states," Albert Gallatin Brown of Mississippi proclaimed, "is there a living breathing, exemplification of the beautiful sentiment, that all men are equal." Brown immediately stipulated that by *men*, he meant "of course, white men," but with that vital exception, his own state and most others embraced the idea, enshrined in the opening passage of Mississippi's Declaration of Rights, that "all freemen, when they form a social compact, are equal in rights."[53]

Master Race democracy of such an intense variety perforce insisted on black inferiority and on the indispensability of slavery to sustain white equality. Here, variations on the "mud-sills" theory propounded by James Hammond in 1858 largely displaced the antidemocratic conceits of the most reactionary fire-eaters. All blacks, supposedly, were the moral, intellectual, and biological inferiors of all whites. Blacks were thus suited for servile drudgery without in any way demeaning their God-given limited capacities. By freeing superior whites from the mind-numbing tasks required of any society, slavery permitted the cultivation of a wise and advanced social leadership, not least in politics. But slavery also permitted the poorest white man to share social and civil privileges with his rich white neighbor, and to feel that basic political equality—"inspired," one pro-slavery man wrote, "with the just pride of a freeman, a sovereign." In the North, the exploited poor were held in contempt; in the South, the lowly white man enjoyed esteem and a basic equality with the richest planter. And slavery made it all possible, one Alabama convention declared, "by dispensing with grades and castes" among the free, "thereby preserv[ing] republican institutions."[54]

These democratic defenses of slavery were shot through with their own contradictions. Did not the majority of slaveholders, working on small estates with fewer than five slaves, at least occasionally labor in the fields alongside their property? Did not the vast majority of white southerners, the nonslaveholders, lead lives full of hard labor and mental drudgery? Given the facts of life as opposed to the slaveholder's idyll, how truly egalitarian was southern slavery and the slaveholders' democracy for whites? Although white adult male suffrage was now universal, and men of humble attainment often filled local and county offices, did the slaveholders—and usually large slaveholders—not completely dominate the southern state legislatures, courts, and congressional delegations? How could slavery be justified on the basis of race when the actual labor performed by the great preponderance of whites and blacks was so similar? Master Race democrats blinded themselves to these questions, fixed on beliefs neatly summarized by the *Richmond Enquirer* in 1856: "[F]reedom is not possible without slavery."[55]

Southern racist egalitarianism promoted an attachment to national political parties as well as to slavery. Outside South Carolina, southern Whigs and southern Democrats had long fought fiercely in local and statewide elections over which party would do the most to fend off the abolitionists. After the collapse of the Whigs in 1854, leaders of the southern Democracy remained assured that their command over the national party was so complete, they could have their way without leaving the Union. Contrary to the extremists who, like Yancey, believed that intersectional parties "preyed upon the vitals of the South" and deadened resistance to the Northern aggressor, southern Democrats believed that they had already achieved, within the Democracy, the Calhounite dream of a national party of slavery. Disunionists were not simply irrelevant; with their divisive antics in state politics and their attacks on solid, state-rights southern Democrats, they were a hindrance to southern domination of national affairs, which, at least through 1857, seemed to be growing ever stronger.[56]

The clash between national Democrats and the fire-eater minority chronically disturbed southern politics. "As to the Rhetts, Yanceys &c.," the Louisiana Democrat John Slidell told Howell Cobb in 1852, "the sooner we get rid of them the better." Five years later, the venerable Democratic *Richmond Enquirer* attacked the "idle twaddle" of the extremist secessionists who seemed to consider themselves the "anointed defenders" of the South and slavery. The paper went on to single out the Rhetts' *Charleston Mercury* for its "editorial ravings" and "hopeless insanity." The Milledgeville, Georgia, *Federal Union*, having long criticized those who "wish to arouse the South by ringing in her ears the notes of preparation for battle," berated the fire-eaters' "excessive sensitiveness" on the subject of Southern rights. With a different kind of conservatism, the South's national Democrats insisted that the old ways really were best, that backroom deals, subcommittee struggles, and smoke-and-spitoon caucuses had served the South well—and that slavery was safe so long as the South could rely on what the *Federal Union* called "the magnanimity, good sense and prudence" of northern Democrats.[57]

The divisions between fire-eaters and national Democrats were not, however, ineluctable. Some Deep South Democrats, including the Mississippians Albert Gallatin Brown and Jefferson Davis, flirted with extremist ideas. Even Robert Toombs of Georgia, a strong proponent of guarded moderation and Unionism after the truce of 1850, had been riled at times into embracing disunionism. The two sides could be pulled closer together by shared fears of Yankee aggression, as well by the chronic fears of slave insurrection and any signs of southern yeoman disloyalty to the slaveholders' regime. The last of these had flared up repeatedly in the border states, especially Kentucky, where, in 1845 and after, Henry Clay's antislavery cousin, Cassius Marcellus Clay, tried to stir the nonslaveholders out of their slumbers, and where, as recently as 1850, emancipationists had used the occasion of a state constitutional convention to push, albeit unsuccessfully, for slavery's gradual elimination. The fears flared again in 1857.[58]

"Non-slaveholders of the South! farmers, mechanics and workingmen, we take this occasion to assure you that the slaveholders, the arrant demagogues whom you have elected to offices of honor and profit, have hoodwinked you, trifled with you, and used you as mere consummation of their wicked designs." So read *The Impending Crisis of the South: How to Meet It*, a new book published in New York but written by a North Carolinian of yeoman stock, one Hinton Rowan Helper. Soon the book was enjoying a respectable sale. More alarmingly, antislavery northern editors and orators, alerted by a lengthy and enthusiastic review in the *New-York Daily Tribune*, began spreading Helper's incendiary message. Might Helper's book prove that the southern nonslaveholders were not really as trustworthy and pro-slavery as the racist egalitarians assumed? Might Rhett and the aristocrats have been correct all along about the white lower classes of the South as well as the North?[59]

Helper was an odd and determined fellow. Born and raised in rural Davie County, North Carolina, near the Appalachian foothills, the son of a poor blacksmith, farmer, and slaveholder, he had been educated at Mocksville Academy and, upon graduating in 1848, had moved down the road to Salisbury, where he found a job working for a storekeeper. Restless, he journeyed to New York in 1850, where he boarded a ship bound for San Francisco and the gold rush. After three disappointing years trying to strike it rich, he returned home to write an embittered narrative of his California experiences, *Land of Gold*, as a warning to any would-be prospectors. But as Helper surveyed the depressed condition of the Carolina backcountry, his mind turned to writing an embittered book about the

South and what he would call "the bloodhounds of slavery." After moving to Baltimore, he completed a new manuscript two years later, but no southern firm would touch it, and so Helper went to New York once more. He finally acquired the services of a small publisher, A. B. Burdick, on Nassau Street.[60]

The book was a mixture of roaring polemics and plodding statistics. Its basic argument was that slavery lay "at the root of all the shame, poverty, ignorance, tyranny, and imbecility of the South." Far from respecting the nonslaveholders as equals, Helper charged, slaveholders intentionally kept the ordinary folk ignorant by denying them a basic public education, thereby reducing their own tax burdens while making it all the easier to sustain their own political power over a semiliterate electorate. A tiny aristocracy—some three hundred thousand slaveholders out of some six million white southerners—ruled over what they fatuously called a democracy. "Slave-driving Democrats" regularly committed legislative outrages to keep the poor and middling white man down. Blacks, along with Indians and Chinese, were certainly inferior to whites, and Helper put no store by the insipid racial sentimentalism that he ascribed to the abolitionists. ("Yankee wives," he wrote, with Harriet Beecher Stowe clearly in mind, had provided "the fictions of slavery; men should give the facts.") Helper hated slavery in part because it contaminated a pure white America. But he also considered human bondage a moral abomination, and he wrote at length about how great southerners of the past had said as much. He then piled on row upon row of statistics culled from the 1850 federal census to prove that the South lagged far behind the North economically, socially, and intellectually—all because slavery degraded labor and left a despised people to wallow in material and mental poverty. The book concluded with an eleven-point program for emancipation without compensation to the masters, coupled with the resettlement of the freed blacks to Africa.[61]

Much of Helper's racist emancipationism had been anticipated in earlier border-state and backcountry diatribes against the slaveholders. But Helper attacked the underlying myths of southern democracy with an unprecedented clarity and harshness—and he collaborated with a Yankee publisher. In the poisonous climate of 1857, that was sufficient to get the book noticed and to require its refutation. In his "mud-sills" speech early in 1858, James Hammond went out of his way to impugn Helper's statistics (without deigning to mention Helper's name) as taken from "trashy census books, all of which is perfect nonsense." Book-length rebuttals appeared under titles like *Helper's Impending Crisis Dissected* and *Review and Refutation*. Finally, taking no chances, several southern states made it a crime to circulate *The Impending Crisis*—laws that eventually led to at least two indictments. In North Carolina, anyone caught distributing the book faced a public whipping and a year in jail for the first offense, and hanging if caught again.[62]

The attack on Helper's book only brought the book more attention—and seemed to confirm Helper's criticisms of the stunted southern democracy. By the late 1850s, every southern state save Kentucky had passed some sort of legislation infringing upon freedom of speech and of the press, to curtail the distribution of antislavery works. The chief motivation behind these laws was to stave off incitements to slave insurrection—fears which, despite the long peace that followed Nat Turner's rampage, loomed ever larger to slaveholders with the rise of the Republicans. To slaveholder democrats and antidemocrats alike, the abridgements were perfectly rational responses to Yankee aggression. Antislavery northerners regarded them as further proof that slavery and democracy could not coexist. To Republicans, the ban on *The Impending Crisis* marked the latest escalation in the struggle over free speech that stretched back to the 1830s. It also gave at least some of them the impression that the South was filled with whites who (as one young Pennsylvanian wrote) were "emancipationists at heart, and free-soilers secretly"—and that the oligarchic Slave Power was more vulnerable than ever.[63]

By thus emboldening the Republicans, the controversy over *The Impending Crisis* drew the slaveholders closer together. Southern Democrats remained at least cautiously confident that Helper himself was an eccentric who would gain little support from the yeoman South. Fire-eaters were less sanguine. But nobody could deny that the "Black Republican" fanatics had emerged as the major opposition to the Democrats in the North—and that Helper was aiding their cause. As their exploitation of *The Impending Crisis* showed, those fanatics posed a clear and present danger to the stability of Dixie democracy. If they were ever to seize federal power—which, if they won the White House in 1860, they would take an enormous step toward completing—then in most of the South, the slaveholders' disagreements would dissolve, the fire-eaters would gain momentum, and secession would be the agenda.

What remained to be seen was whether the northern Democracy, rattled by the Lecompton tumult, could pull itself together and preserve its tenuous southern alliance, and whether the Republicans could unite behind a plausible presidential ticket. For clues, the nation turned its attention, during the summer and early fall of 1858, to a sensational election in Illinois.

POPULAR SOVEREIGNTY AND THE COMMON RIGHT OF HUMANITY: THE LINCOLN-DOUGLAS CAMPAIGN

As he approached his reelection campaign in 1858, Senator Stephen A. Douglas knew he would be in the fight of his political life. His break with the Buchanan administration over Lecompton had been costly. President Buchanan knew that

Douglas held him in contempt personally as well as politically, and to many southern Democrats, Douglas's defiance showed the senator's utter unreliability. A militant southern clique within Buchanan's cabinet, consisting of Howell Cobb, John Floyd of Virginia, and Jacob Thompson of North Carolina, pressed for a purge of the recusant. In May, the pro-administration *Union* announced that Douglas would henceforth be treated as a pariah. Quietly, Douglas's foes within the party, including his detractors in Illinois, helped arrange for a separate slate of pro-administration legislative candidates in the 1858 canvass in order to kick him out of the Senate—even if it meant electing a Republican in his stead.[64]

Douglas, who still longed to be president, did what he could to be conciliatory. He would not repudiate his revolt over Lecompton—doing so would be political suicide in the North—but he hoped to bring about a general agreement among the national Democrats over a diluted form of popular sovereignty, and to convince all sides to let bygones be bygones. In that effort, he had some important southern pro-slavery allies of his own in Washington, including Vice President John C. Breckinridge of Kentucky, Robert Toombs and Alexander Stephens of Georgia, and the ever-voluble Governor Henry A. Wise of Virginia. Douglas's home-state supporters, meanwhile, were convinced that, thanks to his fame and their financial resources, they could defeat the administration threat in Illinois and force the national party to come to its senses. Returning home to start his campaign in early July, Douglas affirmed his attachment to popular sovereignty, berated his vengeful Democratic foes as well as the Republicans, and vowed "to fight that allied army wherever I meet them." But Douglas had an additional problem. Three weeks earlier, a Republican convention in Springfield had nominated the opponent he feared above all others.[65]

At age forty-nine, Abraham Lincoln enjoyed only modest renown outside Illinois, in marked contrast with the lightning-rod Democrat Douglas. Apart from political aficionados who recalled the one-term congressman, "Spotty" Lincoln, most Americans had little to go on about the man. Lincoln had certainly evolved in the 1850s. After returning home from Washington, he emerged, alongside his partner William H. Herndon, as one of the most skilled and respected lawyers in the western states and won the clientage of various large railroad and business corporations. The shocks and aftershocks of Kansas-Nebraska rudely reawakened his political interests and pushed him into the Republican Party. Yet while Lincoln's ambition remained, as Herndon would later recall, a "little engine that knew no rest," his political hopes had been thwarted more often than they had been fulfilled. President Zachary Taylor had rejected his application to be commissioner of the General Land Office in 1849; Lincoln was offered instead the governorship of Oregon Territory, a booby prize he wisely declined. Although he had gained a certain stature when he graciously gave way to Lyman Trumbull in the state legislature's selection of Illinois's junior U.S. senator in 1854, Lincoln had still been the loser.[66]

More arresting than Lincoln's political résumé was his persona. Standing six feet four inches tall, a gigantic height for the time, thin but muscular, with a craggy face, outsized, slightly jugged ears, and striking gray eyes, he looked an ungainly popular leader—but a leader nevertheless. His background and early experiences—as the grandson of a migrating Virginia country democrat murdered by Indians in Kentucky, as the son of an uneducated, log-cabin farmer who had taken the family up to Indiana, as a young Illinois store clerk, ferryboat hand, and indifferent militiaman—were hardly extraordinary. But Lincoln's ability to connect those experiences to politics in simple prose, by turns humorous and icily logical, was rare. His speaking style, in the courtroom and on the political stump, was to begin in perfect stillness (his hands clasped behind his back), followed by emphatic head jerks, his semikempt hair flying, as he kindled to his argument, followed by waves of indignation, all punctuated with a sudden glowing gravitas. His tenor voice was sometimes shrill, even "unpleasant," his law partner Herndon reported, especially at the start of his speeches, but he learned how to hurl his remarks hard enough to reach to the farthest reaches of the crowd. The combination was quirky but arresting enough that both the Whigs and later the Frémont Republicans had made ample use of Lincoln's talents in their presidential campaigns.[67]

Even more dangerous, from Douglas's standpoint, was Lincoln's mixture of seemingly preternatural moderation, hard-nosed political realism, and sincere conviction. Having entered politics as a new-school Whig, Lincoln's first political hero had been Henry Clay, and at least until 1854, his views on national issues connected with slavery ran much closer to Clay's than to those of Whig radicals like Joshua Giddings. (In a eulogy to Clay, delivered in Springfield in 1852, Lincoln's most striking remark was his ringing endorsement of the American Colonization Society.) His switch from guarded support to vocal opposition over the Mexican War, though not exceptional among northern Whigs, did require some political courage for a congressman from central Illinois. Otherwise, whenever Lincoln had had to choose between political alternatives—including, in 1848, siding with Zachary Taylor for the Whig presidential nomination—he usually took the more moderate, even safe political course. After he joined the Republicans, the Kentucky-born Lincoln eschewed polemics against the South, supported the Fugitive Slave Law, and remained open to the possibility of sectional reconciliation over slavery. Douglas would find it difficult to portray him as a crusading fanatic.[68]

Yet neither could Lincoln be dismissed as merely a clever lawyer and political striver. For all of his restraint, his hatred of slavery ran deep, as did his certainty that Douglas's revised position on popular sovereignty was politically dangerous and morally bankrupt. The Kansas-Nebraska controversy had, for Lincoln, changed everything. Although still formally a Whig, he campaigned hard in 1854 for anti-Nebraska candidates—and twice confronted Senator Douglas. He forthrightly denounced "the monstrous injustice of slavery itself" and cited all of the by-now-familiar claims that the Founding Fathers had intended to see it eventually disappear. "The spirit of seventy-six and the spirit of Nebraska, are utter antagonisms," he declared in one widely publicized reply to Douglas at Peoria. "Let us re-adopt the Declaration of Independence, and with it, the practices, and policy, which harmonize with it." Although repeated acts of political compromise had permitted slavery to coexist with freedom, the thrust of American policy, he insisted, had been to confine slavery and prepare for its extinction, not to expand it. The great "moral wrong and injustice" of Douglas's Kansas-Nebraska Act was that it reversed that process and placed the accursed institution "on the high road to extension and perpetuity."[69]

Three years later, the *Dred Scott* decision redoubled Lincoln's fury—and, once again, he directed it against Douglas, in a speech delivered in Springfield. Carefully noting that he favored no outright resistance to Taney's ruling, Lincoln proclaimed that the decision was "based on assumed historical facts which are not really true," and thus was not truly binding, as Douglas supposed it was. In the past, he noted, the Supreme Court had overruled its mistaken decisions, "and we shall do what we can to have it to over-rule this." Lincoln then quoted from Andrew Jackson's Bank Veto message on the duty of each public servant to support the Constitution "'*as he understands it.*'" He also quoted, once again, from the Declaration of Independence, charging that its egalitarian words, in 1776, were "held sacred by all, and thought to include all," and calling it "a stumbling block to those who in after times might seek to turn a free people back into the hateful paths of despotism." Taney and Douglas—the self-professed carriers of the Jeffersonian and Jacksonian traditions—had actually betrayed those traditions.[70]

Lincoln returned to these lines of argument in his campaign for the Senate against Douglas in 1858, but he also sharpened them to fit the requirements of a rough-and-tumble political campaign. In retrospect, the contest has been viewed as a series of high-minded debates over grand American political principles. The impression is true but incomplete. Although the candidates engaged some of the most difficult and abiding problems of American democracy, the campaign, like any other, was a political fight in which each side sought to exploit the weaknesses of the other for maximum advantage. Douglas's political difficulties within his own party, after *Dred Scott* and Lecompton, could not have been more obvious. Lincoln thought hard for weeks prior to the state Republican convention about how he could divide Douglas even farther from pro-administration Democrats while stirring up his own Republican supporters. By the time he gave his first speech of the campaign, immediately following his nomination, he had found the words he needed.[71]

Addressing a jacketless, sweating crowd inside the state Capitol, Lincoln opened with his main point. For five years, he charged, the federal government had followed an avowed policy of ending agitation over slavery, only to stir that agitation even more: "In *my* opinion, it *will* not cease until a *crisis* shall have been reached, and passed. 'A house divided against itself cannot stand.' I believe this government cannot endure, permanently half *slave* and half *free*. I do not expect the Union to be *dissolved*—I do not expect the house to *fall*—but I *do* expect it will cease to be divided. It will become *all* one thing, or *all* the other." Lincoln left no doubt that he also expected freedom would prevail against slavery and its northern abettors like Stephen A. Douglas.

What would forever after be known as Lincoln's "House Divided" speech was both a political preemptive strike and a call for fresh Republican boldness. Its main objectives were to destroy Douglas's benign view of the *Dred Scott* decision and to link Douglas to the grand designs of the Slave Power. First, Lincoln charged, Douglas's Kansas-Nebraska Act opened the national domain to slavery; then the Democrats interpreted the 1856 elections as a mandate to inflict slavery on Kansas; then Taney prohibited Congress and local legislatures from barring slavery in any territory. Reflecting the conspiratorial thinking that was abroad in Republican circles, Lincoln claimed that it was "impossible not to *believe* that Stephen and Franklin and Roger and James all understood one another from the beginning." The next step, Lincoln suggested, would be a Supreme Court decision prohibiting states as well as territories from keeping slavery outside their borders. And Lincoln would fight such an outcome with all his might—unlike the "*caged* and *toothless*" incumbent.[72]

Lincoln's personal attack was demagogic, not least because it slighted Douglas's principled break with the administration over Lecompton. Yet its political value lay not so much in smearing Douglas as in forcing him, even before he had begun his campaign, onto his shakiest ground. Anything less than a stout defense by Douglas of his diluted popular sovereignty idea would rattle moderate Illinois voters who had admired his break with Buchanan. But that defense would further inflame pro-administration Democrats, especially in the southern portions of the state, and it would all but foreclose any chance of Douglas's winning his party's presidential nomination in 1860. For exposing his flank to Lincoln's offensive, Douglas had no one to blame but himself and his past entanglements with the Slave Power, and Lincoln intended to make him pay for it. At the same time, Lincoln wanted to rouse the Republican base and Democrats of goodwill with the stark image of a house divided that he believed, to the depths of his soul, was accurate. After *Dred Scott*, he had decided, it was no longer possible to rest the Republican case solely on the prohibition of slavery in the territories, as some of the more cautious Republicans preferred. It was now imperative to state candidly that halting slavery's expansion was one way to put slavery "in the course of ulti-mate extinction"—a prerequisite for preserving American freedom.[73]

Douglas saw vulnerabilities in Lincoln's position. In his homecoming speech in Chicago on July 6 (delivered after he had sportingly shaken hands with his opponent, who sat just behind him), Douglas avoided any mention of his quarrel with Buchanan but still attacked the Lecompton constitution as a "monstrosity." He then defined his differences with Lincoln. Why could the United States, a diverse nation in so many respects, not tolerate both slavery and freedom? What evidence was there to support Lincoln's assertions that the nation was bound to be all slave or all free? The Founding Fathers whom Lincoln quoted so blithely believed no such thing. On the contrary: "The framers of the Constitution well understood that each locality, having separate and distinct interests, required sep-arate and distinct laws, domestic institutions, and police regulations adapted to its own wants and its own condition." Lincoln's rash declarations about slavery and freedom portended certain war between the North and the South; Douglas preferred peace. Lincoln, furthermore, had refused to abide by the authority of the highest court in the land—a refusal, Douglas charged, that arose from Lin-coln's nauseating belief in racial equality as well as in abolition. Pugnacious as ever, Douglas would reject the extremism of the Lecompton supporters and of the "Black Republicans" alike, and sustain the proven American principles of Union, expansion, and democracy—above all the latter, "the right of the people in each state and territory to decide for themselves."[74]

Lincoln, the underdog, took to following Douglas along the campaign trail, and in late July he proposed that they debate each other formally all across the state. Knowing how formidable Lincoln would be, but never one to back down from a challenge, Douglas cut Lincoln's suggested list of nine debates to seven. In a staggered schedule, the candidates would appear in easily accessible towns from the Wisconsin border down to the southernmost counties known collec-tively as "Egypt." Public interest, in and out of Illinois, was intense by the time the two met for the first contest in Ottawa, on August 21. Thence began one of the most stirring pieces of sustained political theater in all of American history. Trainloads of supporters traveled to the debate towns in banner-bedecked passen-ger cars, accompanied by brass bands. Local farmers and shopkeepers clogged the roads surrounding the debating grounds with their horses, wagons, and bug-gies. Newspaper reporters took down the verbal cuts and thrusts on the podiums and instantly relayed the news by telegraph to the rest of the nation. (The New-York Daily Tribune, along with numerous Illinois papers, printed verbatim tran-scripts, while reporters from Charleston and New Orleans, as well as from all over the North, covered the events.) In the middle of it all were the principals, both experienced debaters—one an absurdly tall, leathery shambler whose stovepipe hat and ill-fitting coat made him look all the odder, but who never lost his self-control; the other an exquisitely tailored bulldog who emanated prestige as well as stamina, but who had a tendency to bark his words and, if pushed too hard, to snarl.

The reporters in the crowd were swept up in the show, and described the seven contests as packed with suspense and revelation, like champion prize-fights. And so the Lincoln-Douglas debates have become lodged in the national memory. In fact, the candidates said little of substance that they had not already said before the debates began. Lincoln mainly stuck to the themes of his "House Divided" speech, asserted that Douglas had departed from the designs of the Founding Fathers, and repeated that the nation could not forever stand half slave and half free. Douglas countered that the Founders (including the slaveholder Jefferson) had left the establishment of slavery up to the individual states, that Lincoln's talk of slavery's ultimate extinction was "revolutionary" and would ensure civil war, and that his distortions of American political principles were driven by the monstrous heresy that "the Almighty . . . intended the negro to be the equal of the white man."[75]

Even the debates' supposed apex, during the second clash at Freeport, repli-cated well-established positions. Under the rules of this particular debate, the candidates were permitted to direct questions at each other, and Lincoln asked Douglas whether the people of any territory could "in any lawful way" exclude slavery if they wished to do so. Lincoln knew exactly what Douglas's reply would be, since Douglas had in effect been giving it in public speeches for more than a year—that a territory's citizens could, in accordance with *Dred Scott*, exclude slavery since, in the absence of supporting local laws from a territorial legislature, slavery could not exist. Republican newspapers hyped the exchange as a devastat-ing body blow by Lincoln, and ever since, Douglas's enunciation of the so-called Freeport Doctrine has been remembered as a pivotal moment not just in the debates but in American history. But Lincoln's question merely recapitulated his efforts to strike at the contradiction between *Dred Scott* and popular sovereignty and thereby divide the Democratic vote. Douglas's reply would have been remarkable only if it had been any different from what it was.[76]

If either candidate was thrown on the defensive during the debates, it was Lin-coln, over the questions of racial equality and abolition. Douglas repeatedly charged, most ferociously in the central and southern portions of the state, that Lincoln's objections to *Dred Scott* arose from his unstated wish to confer full cit-izenship on the Negro. While his partisans cheered, Douglas hammered away, inviting all those who wished to see emancipated blacks flood into Illinois and become citizens equal with whites to vote for Lincoln and the "Black Republi-cans." Douglas even claimed (at the Jonesboro debate, deep in "Egypt") that he had spotted a carriage at Freeport, driven by its white owner, carrying "Fred

Douglass, the Negro" who was "sitting inside with the white lady and her daughter," all part of the Republican coterie that "advocated negro citizenship and negro equality, putting the white man and the negro on the same basis under the law." ("Never, never," the crowd shouted.) Lincoln tried humorously to deflect the attacks. "I do not understand that because I do not want a negro woman for a slave I must necessarily want her for a wife," he jested at the next debate in Charleston, but Douglas's barbs hit their mark. Lincoln was reduced to explaining that he opposed equal rights for free blacks, and that physical differences "will for ever forbid the two races living together on terms of social and political equality." Likewise, when Douglas alleged that Lincoln's "House Divided" statements were just a cover for his disunionist, abolitionist designs, Lincoln responded, weakly, that he had no plan for slavery's elimination, only a certainty that it would one day occur.[77]

The peril, for the moderate Lincoln, was that Douglas would push him to endorse prevalent racial prejudices to the point where he would antagonize more radical Republicans. No less than his opponent, the Democrat knew how to play wedge-issue politics. But in the concluding debate, in the downstate town of Alton (where a mob had killed Elijah Lovejoy more than twenty years before), Lincoln eloquently regained the offensive. Whether he wanted to "make war between the free and the slave States" or introduce "a perfect social and political equality between the white and black races," Lincoln declared, were "false issues, upon which Judge Douglas has tried to force the controversy." The real issue was whether slavery should be viewed as wrong: "That is the issue that will continue in this country when these poor tongues of Judge Douglas and myself shall be silent. It is the eternal struggle between these two principles—right and wrong—throughout the world. They are the two principles that have stood face to face from the beginning of time; and will ever continue to struggle. The one is the common right of humanity, and the other the divine right of kings. It is the same principle in whatever shape it develops itself. It is the same spirit that says, 'You work and toil and earn bread, and I'll eat it.'" Loud applause interrupted Lincoln's remarks, followed by cheers at his conclusion. Douglas replied that the enemies of popular sovereignty were the real Tories, to more rousing cheers; and with that the debates ended.[78]

In the balloting less than three weeks later, Lincoln's side narrowly won the most votes, but Douglas's side won the election. The geographical split was pronounced: Democrats swept virtually all of the southern counties and Republicans virtually all of the northern counties. The legislature had not, however, yet been reapportioned to account for the rising numbers of voters in the pro-Republican counties, and, by a quirk, most of the seats not up for election in 1858 were held by Democrats. As a result, although Republican candidates statewide won about four thousand more votes than the Democrats (out of roughly a quarter-million cast), the Democrats held a clear majority in the legislature and Douglas was thereby reelected to the Senate. For Douglas, it was a major vindication, not only because he had defeated Lincoln but because only a handful of voters, about five thousand in all, had supported the pro-administration Democratic candidates. In his first electoral test since the Lecompton schism, Douglas had affirmed his position as a leader—perhaps *the* leader—of the northern Democrats, and fortified his bid for the presidential nomination in 1860.[79]

Yet who won the debates? The historical consensus favors Lincoln, although that conclusion is colored by hindsight. Certainly Douglas's views on the Founding Fathers and slavery had merit. No matter what the Northwest Ordinance said, slavery had been permitted to expand beyond the limits of its existence in 1787 into areas where it could flourish. Prior to the Missouri crisis, challenges to the rights of new southern states and territories to decide for themselves about slavery got nowhere. At the end of his life, Thomas Jefferson had explicitly opposed the antislavery agitation that led to the Missouri Compromise. Nor was Lincoln always the more high-minded or persuasive debater. Although Douglas cheapened the political currency with his misrepresentations and racist pandering, Lincoln's jibes about "Franklin and Stephen and Roger and James" and his purposeful effacement of the differences between Douglas and the Buchanan administration were hardly fair. His refusal to engage in any discussion of how he foresaw emancipation, although politically wise and necessary, also left an air of vagueness hanging over his arguments. Lincoln never lost his wit or his parables, and always had his claque, but Douglas's fierce style appears (from the reports of the cheering and shouting) to have played better to the crowds.

Still, merely by holding his own against the renowned incumbent, Lincoln won a huge personal triumph. And on the issues that mattered and were coming to matter, Lincoln got the better of his opponent, especially when his sentiments were read in cold print—an achievement that, although no substitute for actual victory, counted for a great deal. Douglas, his popular sovereignty solution ripped apart by the Taney Court, offered no shred of convincing evidence that unfriendly local legislation alone could halt slavery's expansion. The Court, after all, had ruled that Dred Scott was a slave even during his residence in a territory that lacked pro-slavery policing regulations. "[T]here is vigor enough in slavery to plant itself in a new country even against unfriendly legislation," Lincoln concluded during the debate at Jonesboro; Douglas never provided a persuasive rebuttal. More obliquely, but also importantly, the fact that the debates barely made mention of tariffs, banks, internal improvements, or anything other than slavery sustained Lincoln's basic contention that slavery was the one great issue that had divided the country and continued to divide it, despite repeated assertions that the issue had been settled.[80]

Above all, Lincoln captured the moral high ground without sacrificing his moderate standing within the Republican Party. If he would not endorse the radical idea that the black man was his perfect equal, he did insist that the black man was entitled to freedom—and with it the rights to life, liberty, and the pursuit of happiness. As Lincoln put it in the first debate, "[I]n the right to eat the bread, without leave of anybody else, which his own hand earns, *he is my equal and the equal of Judge Douglas, and the equal of every living man.*"[81] Among Republicans, it was a principled yet hardly outlandish sentiment, but Lincoln's insistence on proclaiming it in the face of racist invective arraigned Douglas's view of "equality" as mean and morally bankrupt. In doing so, Lincoln proved that a centrist western Republican could forcefully clarify the fundamental differences between his own party and the northern Democrats. He thereby began turning himself, despite his loss, from a provincial party leader into a national party hero.

The theatrics of the Lincoln-Douglas debates, and the intense coverage they received in the press, also created a new political reality which overwhelmed the fact that both candidates were largely repeating themselves. Although a crucial Senate seat was in play, both sides knew that even larger stakes were involved, and they conducted the debates accordingly, with the hope of influencing elections elsewhere and setting the stage for 1860. For the pro-Douglas Democrats, the Illinois contest was crucial to halting the Republicans' momentum and to establishing that they, and not the toadies of the Buchanan administration, were in charge of the northern Democracy, without alienating reasonable southern Democrats. For the Republicans, it was a matter of building on their stunning victories in 1856 and enlarging their attacks on a Slave Power that, in their eyes, had confirmed it would stop at nothing to enlarge its despotism. And here, Lincoln may have understood the new campaign realities better than his opponent, delivering speeches and ripostes that, as read in the newspapers around the country rather than heard by the local campaign crowds, carried greater moral and logical weight.

Lincoln's party was certainly the greater beneficiary. Outside Illinois, the Republicans, capitalizing on *Dred Scott* and Lecompton, succeeded beyond their wildest expectations in 1858. Democratic congressional candidates lost in droves, handing control of the House of Representatives to the Republicans. In the lower northern battleground states that had carried Buchanan to victory two years earlier, the Republicans won 52 percent of the vote, an increase that augured extremely well for 1860. The Douglas Democracy did secure its home base, including victories in five of Illinois's nine congressional elections, despite opposition from the administration—success that offered strong clues about where, between Douglas and Buchanan, the northern Democrats' best political interests lay. Yet even Douglas's victorious campaign was a mixed blessing for the

Democracy and, in time, for Douglas. By the summer after his defeat, Lincoln was back on the stump, invited to speak on behalf of Republican candidates in Ohio and Wisconsin. In time, cheap editions of the complete text of the instantly famous Lincoln-Douglas debates appeared—edited and corrected by Lincoln himself, issued by the Ohio Republican Committee, and publicized by, among other newspapers, Greeley's *Tribune*. Growing numbers of Republicans were determined to see their new hero Lincoln have another go at Stephen Douglas— but this time for the presidency.[82]

"ANOTHER EXPLOSION WILL SOON COME"

Abraham Lincoln knew how volatile the political situation remained late in 1858. The *Dred Scott* decision, the continuing war in Kansas, and the Democrats' division over Lecompton had deepened the sectional divide, amplified the differences between northern and southern democracy, and made slavery and its expansion the overriding issue in national politics. The Republican victories in 1858 outside Illinois ensured that brutal new struggles would precede the 1860 elections, although Lincoln could only guess at where and how they would arise. "The fight must go on," he wrote to a consoling supporter shortly after his defeat. "Douglas had the ingenuity to be supported in the late contest both as the best means to *break down*, and to *uphold* the Slave interest. No ingenuity can keep those antagonistic elements in harmony long. Another explosion will soon come."[83]

Eight months later, a man calling himself Isaac Smith rented a small, secluded Maryland farm near the Virginia border from the heirs of a doctor named Booth Kennedy. All summer long, men, white and black, arrived at the place, at least once carrying heavy crates labeled "Hardware and Castings." A daughter and daughter-in-law of the mysterious Smith, both aged sixteen, did the men's cooking and cleaning and kept on the lookout for any prying neighbors. Suddenly, in September, the young women vanished, and the men began their final phase of preparations. Smith's visitors turned out to be a ragtag army; Smith turned out to be John Brown.[84]

24

THE FAITH THAT
RIGHT MAKES MIGHT

The years from 1859 to 1861 marked the fortieth anniversary of the Missouri crisis, and brought the final defining of the two American democracies. In the South, hard-line pro-slavery politics had come to prevail, and disunionism was gaining momentum. For the most intense of the fire-eaters, the conflict loomed over the legitimacy of democracy itself. "It is obvious that two distinct and antagonistic forms of society have met for the contest upon the arena of this Union," wrote the South Carolinian L. W. Spratt:

> The one assumes that all men are equal and that equality is right, and, forming upon that theory, is straining its members to the horizontal plain of a democracy. The other assumes that all men are not equal, that equality is not right, therefore, and forming upon this theory, is taking upon itself the rounded form of a social aristocracy.

More mainstream southerners prized political equality for white men, but insisted that true democracy required the mudsill system of racial slavery. And the more southern slavery seemed endangered, from within and without, the more the pro-slavery Master Race democrats converged with the planter aristocrats against the alien Yankee democracy.[1]

In the North, the few surviving antislavery veterans of the Missouri crisis, including Marcus Morton, as well as older leaders of the Republican Party, could look back at the previous four decades with enormous satisfaction. The political antislavery movement had grown far beyond the temporary alliance of northern

Jeffersonian Republicans and surviving Federalists that backed James Tallmadge in 1819. The moral and constitutional arguments against slavery's extension raised by Tallmadge and others had been sustained and enlarged. Salmon P. Chase remarked with astonished gratitude that the good old doctrine—"denationalization of slavery entire"—was now seriously contending for national power. "The feeble cause I espoused at Cincinnati in 1832," Henry B. Stanton later recalled, had come to rest "on the broad shoulders of a strong party which was marching on to victory." After the crack-up of the southern-dominated Democratic Party over Lecompton, that victory looked increasingly certain—and with it, the consolidation of a revolutionized northern democracy that would vindicate the Declaration of Independence by checking and, in time, overthrowing the Slave Power.[2]

Uncompromising radical abolitionists, preeminently William Lloyd Garrison, took a more ambivalent view of developments since the Missouri crisis. The radicals could, with justice, claim they had changed the terms of antislavery politics by renouncing gradualism and colonization in the 1830s. The antislavery views advanced by the Liberty men and upheld by the Republicans had certainly been formed in the crucible of the American Anti-Slavery Society's early campaigns. But the radicals of the 1850s also berated more conventional antislavery advocates for their toleration of anything short of speedy emancipation and full racial equality. On July 4, 1854, Garrison, in response to the Kansas-Nebraska Act and the Anthony Burns affair, publicly burned a copy of the Constitution, which the Republicans had pledged to uphold, calling it a pact made in Hell with the Devil. Among some hard-core radical abolitionists like Parker Pillsbury and Abby Kelley Foster and her husband Stephen, idealism curdled into sectarianism. Pillsbury called the Republicans' watered-down antislavery "more dangerous to the cause of liberty" than the Democrats' forthright oppression. Wendell Phillips, the brightest new radical star, scrutinized the rising antislavery politician Abraham Lincoln and denounced him as a "huckster" and "The Slave-Hound of Illinois."[3]

In their frustration, the radical abolitionists also confronted anew their dedication to nonviolence. The warfare in Kansas had further weakened the hold of pacifism, even among some of Garrison's friends and loyalists. Gerrit Smith, who had been an officer in the American Peace Society, declared that the Kansas crisis had prepared him "and ten thousand other peace men" to have the Slave Power not just repulsed with violence "but pursued even unto death with violence." In November 1856, Thomas Wentworth Higginson, who had led the attack to free Anthony Burns, devised plans for a fighting force drawn from all of the northern states "for resisting the U.S. Government in Kanzas, and sustaining such resistance everywhere else." A year later, Higginson's supporters met in Cleveland and adopted a resolution extolling slave uprisings. The politics of insurrection would take precedence over fruitless efforts at moral suasion and over the hopelessly compromised politics of democracy.[4]

To the consternation of Republicans, the new militant mood among the radicals had come to condone and even design violent efforts to overthrow the Slave Power—efforts, the Republicans feared, that would discredit their own democratic resistance and return the Democrats to power in 1860. But Higginson and his frantic friends alone could not get plans for insurrection off the ground. An experienced killer would carry the war directly into the American Egypt.

JOHN BROWN AND THE POLITICS OF INSURRECTION

John Brown never had to break with any previous commitment to nonviolence. Born in Torrington, Connecticut, in 1800 and raised chiefly in Ohio, he had been trained by his devout parents in the old Congregational Calvinism, with its adherence to predestination and divine intervention. Other antislavery activists had been moved by the evangelical promise of spiritual rebirth in Christ's merciful bosom. Brown, as comfortable in the Old Testament as the New, worshipped an angrier God and the Jesus of Matthew 10:34, who came not to send peace but a sword. As Brown grew older—wandering through Ohio, Pennsylvania, and upstate New York, following up one business failure with another—his hatred of slavery and his projected kinship with abused blacks hardened. Finally, in Kansas, he killed his first Philistines. To some who met him, the unforgiving, hatchet-faced Brown, with his fondness for speaking in pseudo-biblical epigrams, was plainly a crazy man, laboring under religious delusions. To his admirers, he was a reborn Cromwell, a Puritan who would dare to do God's will when others merely talked about it.[5]

On Washington's Birthday in 1858, Brown met with Smith at the latter's grand estate in Peterboro, New York. They were joined by Franklin B. Sanborn, a young Harvard graduate, schoolteacher, and protégé of Ralph Waldo Emerson who had been helping Brown in his fund-raising activities for more than a year, and, possibly, by Captain Charles Stuart, an Anglo-American abolitionist. Brown laid out a plan for an attack on the South at some undisclosed spot, which would touch off a gigantic slave rebellion. To their protests that the proposal was mad— "an amazing proposition,—desperate in its character . . . ," Sanborn later wrote, "of most uncertain result"—Brown replied that he would carry on with or without their support. Awed by Brown's self confidence, and by the possibility that even if the plan failed, it might hasten a civil war, Smith and Sanborn agreed to help. With four other abolitionist radicals—Higginson, Parker, the physician and reformer Samuel Gridley Howe, and George L. Stearns, an affluent pipe manufacturer—they formed a secret advisory and fund-raising committee. Over the coming months, Brown and the so-called Secret Six quietly informed other radicals, including Frederick Douglass, of the plot.[6]

Brown had become fascinated with the guerrilla tactics of the Spanish resisters against Napoleon's armies during the Peninsular War. His plan centered on a raid into mountainous western Virginia, followed by a hit-and-run campaign that would extend into Tennessee and the Deep South, picking up rebel slaves along the way. He expected that free blacks would, from the start, compose a large contingent in his band, and serve as further encouragement for the slaves to rise up. In early May, before his final journey to Kansas, Brown and eleven white men arrived at a community of former slaves in Chatham, Ontario, near Detroit, and secretly met with a group of more than thirty. Brown announced that he had completed a plan of action, and the assembled approved it along with the constitution for a provisional freedmen's republic. They also named Brown the new government's commander-in-chief, granting him unchecked powers to wage war. Brown left with the impression that blacks from Canada would join him en masse. "Had a good Abolition convention," he wrote to his family. He arranged to have plenty of copies of the provisional government plan printed up for when he made his strike.[7]

After a year more of preparation, Brown was ready to go in the summer of 1859. Yet once his recruits had assembled at the rented Kennedy farm in Maryland (and received pikes and rifles in disguised crates), Brown's "army" amounted to a pitiful twenty-one soldiers, only five of them black. With radical free blacks backing away from the venture and some members of the Secret Six growing jittery, Brown appealed to Frederick Douglass, an old friend in the antislavery struggle, to join him. More than anyone, Douglass would legitimize that venture among free blacks, and he would be the ideal organizer of the slaves whom Brown expected would swarm to join in after the first blow had been struck. But at a secret meeting of the two in August at a quarry in Chambersburg, Pennsylvania, Douglass refused. Brown had determined that his guerrilla war would begin with an assault on the federal armory in Harpers Ferry—a plan that Douglass warned was suicidal and "would array the whole country against us." Brown carried on anyway, deeply disappointed at Douglass's demurral and at the failure of his other black supporters to show up for slavery's Armageddon. He hoped that the slaves living in and around his target would prove more receptive and steadfast.[8]

Douglass's military instincts proved sound. Harpers Ferry, five miles from the Kennedy farm, was situated on a tip of land formed by the Potomac and Shenandoah rivers and surrounded by imposing cliffs—a "perfect steel-trap" as Douglass called it. Once inside the town, Brown's little force would be easy prey for a counterattack, which is exactly what transpired. On the evening of October 16, Brown's men marched out and easily captured the armory by overcoming its single watchman, and collected several dozen hostages. Brown had sent out a two-man patrol to spread the alarm and free slaves at the neighboring plantation of a distant descendant of George Washington; then he sat with his men and waited for the rebels to arrive. He had made no previous contacts with those neighboring slaves to prepare them; he had planned no escape route out of Harpers Ferry; and, even less explicably, he held a midnight train bound for Baltimore hostage for a few hours, but then allowed it to proceed—and bring word to a hostile outside world about what was happening in Harpers Ferry. The haphazardness of Brown's behavior suggests that by the time the raid began, he had realized it would be futile. But it is just as likely that he simply threw the dice and hoped that the slaves would join him—prepared, if they did not, to exchange the role of avenging commander-in-chief for that of martyr.[9]

Less than a day and a half after it began, the raid was crushed. Brown's raiders did round up a number of slaves, but most appeared unmoved by what was happening and did not join in the fighting. Armed townsmen, not content to wait for the Virginia and Maryland militia, fired on Brown's volunteers, picking off eight of them while losing three men of their own. Brown, his surviving guerrillas, and some prisoners retreated inside a small but sturdy brick-walled fire-engine house. After nightfall, a company of federal marines, commanded by Colonel Robert E. Lee and Lieutenant J. E. B. Stuart, joined the militiamen on the scene and prepared for the final assault, using a battering ram and their bayonets in order to avoid killing innocent hostages. When the fighting ended, Brown, wounded in action, was taken captive. The combat had killed ten raiders (including two of Brown's sons), four townsmen (including the black baggage-handler at the railroad station, mistaken for a watchman), and one marine. Seven of Brown's men escaped, although two were later captured. One of the freed slaves was killed; the others were returned to bondage.

Defeated, Brown had a second drama to perform, which would prove perhaps more important than the first. In his jail cell in Charles Town, charged with treason, Brown recovered from his wounds, wrote letters, and gave interviews with an impressive solemnity. In his courtroom testimony, he claimed he had not intended to raise an insurrection against the United States, but only to arm oppressed slaves—a hair-splitting defense that made no impact on the judge and jury. (Having brought along copies of the provisional government proclamation from the Chatham meeting along with his war maps, all later discovered by his captors, Brown certainly looked like an insurrectionist.) But with his dignity and his uncowering remarks about slavery, he became a public sensation, and he saved his best for last. In his closing speech before being sentenced to hang, Brown eloquently appealed to the laws of God and expressed contentment that, in a just cause, he would "mingle my blood further with the blood of my children and with the blood of millions in this slave country." On the morning of his execution, December 2, he wrote out with a steady hand his final prophecy, that "the crimes of this *guilty, land: will* never be purged *away*; but with Blood. I had *as I now think: vainly* flattered myself that without *very much* bloodshed; it might be done."[10]

Governor Henry A. Wise, fearing an effort to free the prisoner, ordered fifteen hundred soldiers to Charles Town, which only heightened the tension. (Among the troops was John Wilkes Booth, a well-known actor who had enlisted in the Richmond Grays militia with the sole intention of seeing Brown die. Others in the hanging-day throng included the fire-eater Edmund Ruffin and Thomas J. Jackson of the Virginia Military Institute, who would one day earn the nickname "Stonewall.") Brown, taken to the gallows in a wagon, stared out over the Blue Ridge Mountains and remarked, "This *is* a beautiful country." After the deed was done and while John Brown's body dangled, a Virginia colonel intoned, "So perish all such enemies of Virginia! All such enemies of the Union! All foes of the human race!"[11]

Southern reactions to the affair were varied, and swerved, within a matter of weeks, from alarm to reassurance to fury. While Brown's men exchanged gunfire with the citizenry of Harpers Ferry, exhilarated crowds lined the railroad tracks from Baltimore to Harpers Ferry to cheer the federal forces on their way. Then a wave of hysteria hit the slaveholding states. Early reports about the Brown raid and the captured materials suggested that the long-feared moment of reckoning had arrived, and that Brown's crimes in Kansas had been a mere prelude to massive uprisings on southern plantations. Well into the autumn, reports circulated about imagined black rebellions and about whole armies of abolitionists marching southward as reinforcements. Vigilance committees sprang to life; the South Carolina legislature passed several measures further restricting slave movement and augmenting military preparations. But when the rumors faded, and it became clear that no massive movement of slaves had joined Brown's insurrection or any other, relieved southerners momentarily calmed down. The insurrectionists represented only a small number of monomaniac Yankees. Some claimed that the events had actually vindicated slavery by proving that slaves everywhere were loyal and content. The raid itself, one Richmond paper had observed early on, was "a miserably weak and contemptible affair." Edmund Ruffin, who considered Brown an atrocious criminal and thorough fanatic, conceded that he was also "a very brave & able man." If the abolitionists would realize that the slaves were content, cease their mad plotting, and put their abundant energies to good use, there would be perfect peace in the valley. Only after the convict's execution, when northerners began their apotheosis of John Brown, did southern outrage revive.[12]

Northern opinion passed through its own evolution. Initially, the acts shocked even some radical abolitionists—"misguided, wild, and apparently insane," Garrison said, though, as with David Walker and Nat Turner thirty years earlier, he would not renounce the guerrillas. But Brown's moving gallantry in defeat quickly led to the rise of a virtual religious cult of the man in antislavery circles. At the hour of his hanging, northern church bells tolled from Boston to Chicago. Ministers preached special sermons on Brown's sacrifice; mass meetings bowed their head in worshipful silence. Well before execution day, New England abolitionists and intellectuals were already beside themselves: Henry David Thoreau wrote "A Plea for Captain Brown" and called him "a transcendentalist above all, a man of ideas and principles," and Ralph Waldo Emerson predicted that Brown would "make the gallows glorious like the cross." In New York, William Cullen Bryant said that Brown's name would go down in history "among those of its martyrs and heroes." The Boston patrician Charles Eliot Norton observed that "[t]he heart of the people was fairly reached, and an impression has been made upon it which will be permanent and produce results long hence." Illustrators churned out portraits of Brown and his exploits; hagiographies flew off northern presses. As the train bearing Brown's body to his last homestead in upstate New York pulled into Philadelphia, a gathering of free blacks greeted it, in a gesture of respect to the fallen hero.[13]

The Christian imagery in so many of the northern outbursts revealed the emotional power of Brown's elevation. (It may also have reflected the impact, especially in New England, of the religious revival of 1857 and 1858.) In his letters from the Charles Town jail, Brown himself encouraged comparisons between his fate and Christ's sacrifice, although he sometimes imagined himself as Peter taking a sword from Christ rather than as Christ Himself. Northern orators and ministers picked up the Christ comparison: Charles Town suddenly became Calvary; and Brown's execution would, supposedly, achieve the salvation of the enslaved and the nation's redemption. Yet unlike Charles Sumner, who had also suffered and been likened to Jesus, Brown could only be honored as an enraged savior, a killer as well as a victim. The switch from extolling Sumner to extolling Brown betokened a shift in radical antislavery sensibilities, following the Southern outrages that had begun in Kansas. Instead of holy meekness, the new mood projected manly fury, sending not peace but a sword.[14]

Henry David Thoreau, the erstwhile theorist of nonviolent civil disobedience, summed up the new attitude in secular as well as biblical terms. "[T]here are at least as many as two or three individuals to a town throughout the North who think much as the present speaker does about [Brown] and his enterprise," Thoreau told the citizens of Concord. ". . . We aspire to be something more than stupid and timid chattels, pretending to read history and our Bibles, but desecrating every house and every day we breathe in." All of the speeches of the supposedly noble Republicans put together, he charged, "do not match for manly directness and force, and for simple truth, the few casual remarks of crazy John Brown, on the floor of the Harper's Ferry engine-house." The true day of reckoning really was coming, Thoreau warned the slaveholders, and slavery would be no more: "We shall then be at liberty to weep for Captain Brown. Then, and not till then, we will take our revenge."[15]

Talk of avenging the crackpot killer and traitor infuriated white southerners even more than Brown's raid had. How, one Baltimore newspaper asked, could the South any longer "live under a government, a majority of whose subjects or citizens regard John Brown as a martyr and Christian hero?" To allay fears that Brown's sympathizers came even close to a northern majority, northern conservatives and businessmen sponsored their own public meetings condemning Brown and any who would trample on the Constitution. Democrats, North and South, tried to tie Brown around the neck of the Republican Party, singling out William Henry Seward—widely considered the most radical Republican—as Brown's instigator. Alarmed Republicans hastily distanced themselves from Brown. Seward announced his approval of the execution. Abraham Lincoln, more sensitive to the new militant mood, said that although Brown "agreed with us in thinking slavery wrong," this alone "cannot excuse violence, bloodshed and treason." Drawing similar distinctions between Brown's motives and his actions helped Republicans win several important victories in the off-year 1859 elections. But to the white South, expressions of even a modicum of sympathy with Brown's purposes affirmed their worst fears about Republicans and northerners generally.[16]

What, then, was John Brown's achievement and significance? Tested against his original plans, his final attack was full of unintended consequences. Although rightly labeled, then and now, as a terrorist for his Kansas muders— John Wilkes Booth called him a "terrorizer"—Brown aimed at Harpers Ferry not to wreak terror but to ignite a revolution, and he failed. In that failure, Brown had succeeded, first, in shocking the South, but then in allowing white southerners to affirm that their slaves were perfectly content—the farthest thing from what he had hoped to do. Northern free blacks, who had long been the combative mainstays of abolitionism, showed little interest in joining a doomed mission, no matter how much they admired its leader's courage. Nor did Brown, a white man, stir the loyalty of the slaves his men temporarily freed. The paradoxes played out in national politics. By putting the perceived radical Republicans such as Seward on the defensive, Brown's attacks gave further political credibility to more moderate men within the party like Lincoln—an encouragement of restraint that Brown did not foresee and would have detested, but that would eventually strengthen the Republicans' political hand.[17]

Most of these ironic ramifications were far from evident over the winter of 1859–60, when the Harpers Ferry attack stirred up nothing but strife. Above all, southern outrage at Brown's glorification created a pervasive mood of panic and fury at the end of 1859 that brought on what the British consul in Charleston,

John Bunch, likened to a reign of terror. New military companies and vigilance committees sprang up to resist an expected abolitionist onslaught. Fresh reports of slave uprisings and abolitionist terrorism arose at the least sign of trouble, and sometimes at no sign at all. Southern state legislatures appropriated new funds for military preparations and expressed solidarity with their sister slaveholding states. The lawmakers of Louisiana considered a proposal affirming that if any Republican were elected president, it would be reason enough to dissolve the Union. There were numerous reports of random, unprovoked violence against northerners, including several confirmed lynchings.[18]

These shocking scenes reinforced northerners' dismay at the slaveholders' democracy and greatly encouraged the southern fire-eater minority. Looking back, Herman Melville, who, disheartened at his continued failing career, had turned to poetry but still claimed no prophecy, would find in Brown's dangling body a portent:

> Hidden in the cap
>   Is the anguish none can draw;
> So your future veils its face,
>   Shenandoah!
> But the streaming beard is shown
>   (Weird John Brown),
> The meteor of the war.

Throughout 1859, disunionists had been hatching and acting on plots of their own, to win over less strong-willed pro-slavery Democrats and destroy whatever chances a northerner like Stephen Douglas might have of winning the Democratic presidential nomination. After Brown's attack, and over the following winter, secessionist efforts accelerated. "If you can only urge our Carolina view in such a manner as to imbue Virginia with it . . . ," Barnwell Rhett's ally Porcher Miles wrote to the Charleston lawyer and educator Christopher Memminger in early January, "we may soon hope to find the fruits of your addresses in . . . a Southern Confederacy." Thus began the political struggle of 1860.[19]

THE REVOLUTION OF 1860 AND
THE POLITICS OF DEMOCRACY

Memminger's mission was to persuade the Virginia legislature to send delegates to a fire-eater convention, planned by the South Carolina militants, which would discuss how best to protect slaveholders' rights and property—a not so thinly veiled appeal for disunion. "[T]here must be new terms established," he would tell the Virginians, "or a Southern Confederacy is our only hope of safety." Memminger spoke for three and a half hours and impressed his audience, but he failed to persuade—"Virginia is not prepared to do anything"—as his allies failed to do elsewhere. Only Mississippi heeded the fire-eaters' convention call: the rest of the South, despite the John Brown hysteria, still held out hope that slavery could be vindicated without dissolving the Union. Temporarily frustrated, the disunionists moved on to the next stage of their campaign.[20]

Southern belligerence gravitated to two causes: reopening the African slave trade and enacting a federal slave code to guarantee slavery's protection in all national territories. After its initial law of 1807 forbidding the importation of Africans, Congress had acted unsteadily, sometimes reinforcing the ban with fresh legislation, but sometimes pulling back from efforts to enforce it. Proposals to end the ban completely began in the early 1850s in South Carolina, as an effort to begin reversing all of the federal restrictions on slave trading that had begun during the presidency of Thomas Jefferson. Advocates knew all too well that the exclusions of slavery from the territories, from the Missouri Compromise's 36°30' line through the Wilmot Proviso, had as its implicit goal ending slavery. The same, they argued, held true for federal laws restricting the supply of slaves dating back to 1807, which had had the additional effect of stigmatizing slave labor as a form of plunder. After the Kansas-Nebraska Act's repeal of the Missouri Compromise, pro-slave traders became more frankly expansionist, insisting, as one of their spokesman asserted, that to survive, "[s]lavery must spread in power and area," which required fresh supplies of Africans. The dashed dreams of the pro-slavery filibusterers returned as a planters' utopian vision of a reborn New World slavery.[21]

By 1859, the argument had broadened to include the claim that, with more slaves available, slavery would be made more efficient and profitable, while ordinary southern farmers would enjoy widened opportunities to be slaveholders. Hierarchical fire-eaters were learning how to both overcome concerns about a restive yeomanry and appeal to Master Race democrats. "Remove the restrictions upon the Slave Trade," wrote one Georgia yeoman (or a writer who claimed to be a yeoman), "and where is there a poor man in the South who could not soon become a slaveholder[?]" In 1859, the annual meeting of the Southern Commercial Convention voted to demand the repeal of all state and federal laws restricting the international slave trade. Soon after, a new organization appeared, the African Resupply Association, headed by an influential economic improver and budding southern nationalist, the Charleston-raised James D. B. De Bow of *De Bow's Review* (George Fitzhugh's chief literary forum and the most widely circulated southern periodical). William Yancey, not surprisingly, favored reopening the slave trade, but so did Alexander Stephens and Jefferson Davis. The latter charged in July 1859 that an 1820 law declaring overseas slave trading a capital crime had been enacted "under the false plea of humanity" and was an insult both to the South and to the U.S. Constitution.[22]

The demand for a federal slave code arose directly out of *Dred Scott* and Stephen Douglas's revision of the popular sovereignty idea, although it had long been implicit in southern demands for equal access to the territories. For Senator Albert Gallatin Brown (now leaning heavily to the fire-eaters), it was a matter of upholding transcendent right, as affirmed by the Taney Court, against the meddling of a territorial majority. "What I want to know," Brown inquired of the Senate in February 1859, "is whether you will interpose against power and in favor of right; or whether you will stand by . . . refusing to interpose your authority to overthrow the unconstitutional and tyrannical acts of your creature—the Territorial Legislature." In a July 4 speech, Barnwell Rhett declared that without a federal slave code the South would secede. Yancey, using the Montgomery *Advertiser* as his mouthpiece, said much the same.[23]

To judge from the reactions of other southern leaders, and much of the southern press, the fire-eaters' political offensive did not convert the mass of voters. "Is there any sane man living in the broad land," the *Montgomery Confederation* asked, "who believes that the laws prohibiting the African slave trade can be repealed?" Senator James Hammond, who wavered on the fire-eaters' campaigns, wrote his friend William Gilmore Simms that the slave code demand was "as absurd to ask for as a railroad to the moon (and everybody knows it)." Yet the fire-eaters were gradually gaining momentum, especially in the Deep South. In 1857, Rhett had long emphasized the disunionists' need to cultivate capable and established leaders with popular influence. By the summer of 1859, armed with their new issues, they had won the sympathies of several Democratic eminences, including Jefferson Davis, Howell Cobb, and John Slidell. The Deep South fire-eaters also fared well at the polls. In the autumn state elections, one disunionist won the governor's race in Mississippi and another was reelected governor in Alabama. The governor of South Carolina, William Henry Gist, was already working hand in glove with the Rhett-Ruffin-Yancey forces. The upholders of southern aristocracy were gaining power through the southern democratic ballot box.[24]

The fire-eaters' next goal was to disrupt the Democratic Party, the last intersectional redoubt blocking their path. In September 1859, a weary President Buchanan affirmed his decision, announced in his inauguration address, not to seek reelection. The worst possible result, from the southern disunionists' standpoint, would be for the party to turn to another northern Democrat in 1860—worst of all Stephen A. Douglas, his prospects brightened by his victory over Abraham Lincoln. If Douglas ran with the backing of southern Democrats, he might actually win the election, thereby severely setting back the secessionist cause. If he did not—and if a southerner ran—a Republican would probably win enough northern electoral votes to win the White House, and thereby (dis-unionists calculated) trigger secession. The first step was to ensure that the Democratic ticket in 1860 firmly endorsed hard-line positions on the slave trade and the slave code. Late in 1859, Albert Gallatin Brown made it plain: "The South will demand . . . a platform explicitly declaring that slave property is enti-tled in the Territories and on the high seas to the same protection given to any other and every other species of property and failing to get it she will retire from the Convention."[25]

The struggles among the sectional and intraparty factions carried over to the new Congress in December. Selection of the Speaker of the House had been an arduous process for several sessions, and the two-month battle that commenced in December 1859, only days after John Brown's execution, would prove nastier still. The proximate cause of the turmoil was not Brown's raid, but Hinton Helper's *The Impending Crisis*. Earlier in the year, Republican publicists, spear-headed by the old Jacksonian Francis Blair, had compiled a shortened, slightly toned-down version of Helper's work and distributed it by the tens of thousands around the country. Over sixty Republican congressmen signed a circular endorsing the book, among them the moderate former Whig John Sherman of Ohio—the man whom the Republican caucus, back in the majority, favored for Speaker. Guilt by association with *The Impending Crisis* was enough to block Sherman's elevation, on ballot after ballot. The rhetoric on both sides in both the House and Senate became so vicious, James Hammond remarked, that "the only persons who do not have a revolver and a knife are those who have two revolvers." After forty-four ballots, but before any shooting started, Sherman with-drew in favor of a bland Republican New Jerseyan who had supported the Fugi-tive Slave Act in 1850 and whom the upper South deemed safe enough.[26]

Thereafter, inside and outside Congress, hard-liners and their sympathizers raised the stakes and exerted enormous pressure on southern Democrats. On January 18, 1860, Albert Gallatin Brown laid before the Senate resolutions call-ing for a territorial slave code to protect "property recognized by the Constitu-tion of the United States." Two weeks later, Jefferson Davis presented an even more elaborate set of proposals, backing a slave code while also pronouncing all interference with slavery by any state government as well as the federal govern-ment a breach of the Constitution. In March, the Democratic Senate caucus approved Davis's resolutions, and pushed by the southern cabinet faction headed by Treasury Secretary Cobb, the Buchanan administration did the same. The Alabama Democratic Convention, which Yancey and his allies took over, voted to bolt from the party's national convention unless the platform sup-ported a territorial slave code. The other Deep South Democratic organizations quickly followed suit.[27]

In 1856 at Cincinnati, the Democratic National Committee, hoping to provide "an incentive to Union," selected Charleston over New York for its convention site in 1860. Hard to get to (the rail journey from Washington required ten changes of train), and lacking adequate accommodations for a national convention, Charleston was an unfortunate choice—and by late April 1860, it had become a disastrous one, especially for Stephen Douglas. By the flickering of gaslights, as sweltering northern delegates crammed into their overpriced hotel rooms, fire-eater orators addressed the street crowds, demanding honor and threatening disunion. Douglas men, headquartered at Hibernian Hall, were aghast at the hatred that their mere presence provoked among the southern delegates. The scenes so frightened the ex-Whig and staunch southern sympathizer Caleb Cushing that he decided to work for the nomination of some northern candidate—perhaps, he thought, ex-President Pierce would do—as a compromise between Douglas and one of the more hard-line southern favorites like Jefferson Davis.[28]

Push came to shove over the platform. In the platform committee, where each state had one vote, a 17 to 16 majority supported a plank on the slave code similar to the Davis resolutions approved earlier by the Senate Democrats. Yancey, a superb speaker, led the floor fight for the majority report, proclaiming slavery a positive good and warning the northerners of the "great heaving volcano of passion and crime" that would erupt if they insisted on imposing their will. But the North, holding a three-fifths' majority of delegates in the general convention, could not be denied, and after two days of fierce tussling, the convention adopted the minority plank, which reaffirmed the 1856 convention's endorsement of popular sovereignty. Fifty southern delegates, led by the Alabamans, immediately walked out; those who remained denied Douglas the two-thirds' majority of the original delegate count of 304 required for nomination. After fifty-seven ballots, the delegates gave up and scheduled a second convention to meet six weeks later in the less combustible city of Baltimore.[29]

The rescheduling merely delayed the inevitable rupture. Douglas enjoyed some support in the South, from unswerving Unionists such as Benjamin Perry of South Carolina and from moderate ex-Whigs like Alexander Stephens (who had recently tempered his views). In June, the Douglas men in the Deep South named state delegations to the Baltimore convention. But Douglas's southern foes, adopting what Stephens called a "rule or ruin" strategy, also showed up in Baltimore, and when the delegates approved a credentials committee report awarding seats to both pro-Douglas and anti-Douglas men, the Deep South recalcitrants walked out, joined by most of the border-state delegates and a small group of pro-slavery northerners. The schismatics immediately reconvened in Richmond and named Douglas's erstwhile friend, Vice President John C. Breckinridge, as their presidential candidate. The northern rump of the Democracy joylessly nominated Douglas. Once he had recovered from a drunken rage, the nominee said with more hope than assurance that he thought the bolters would see the light and return to the party before it was too late to save the Union.[30]

Apart from Douglas's wishful scenario, there was one other possible way to prevent a Republican victory. If northern and border-state conservatives drew substantial numbers of votes away from the Republicans and the southern extremists, they might throw the election into a fractured House of Representatives, which in turn could elevate a sane compromise candidate to the White House. Toward that end, a group calling itself the Constitutional Union Party began organizing late in 1859, and a few days after the Democrats' Charleston debacle ended, the new party held its own nominating convention in Baltimore. Hopes for the enterprise ran high early on, within its own ranks if nowhere else. The core membership consisted of border-state ex-Whigs who, running as an opposition movement against the southern Democrats, had registered some impressive victories in 1858 and 1859. They were joined by some of the most venerable former old-line northern conservative Whigs, including Edward Everett, Amos Lawrence, and Robert C. Winthrop. The Constitutional Unionists' political program was simple: banish the slavery question from national affairs and uphold the Union. If high-toned respectability and good intentions had been reliable predictors of electoral success, the forces of sectional compromise—faintly echoing the old nationalist moderation of Henry Clay—might have immediately established themselves as a major force.[31]

But the party had the vices of its virtues, and other vices as well. Many of its most prominent members—above all its most active promoter, seventy-year-old John Crittenden of Kentucky—were so aged and august that they gave the party the air of an over-the-hill gentlemen's club. Although pledged to end sectional strife, the party was beset by tensions that pitted southern ex–Know-Nothings against northern and border-state ex-Whigs. (The former wanted to nominate Sam Houston for the presidency, but the northern and border-state men prevailed and selected the ex-Whig Unionist slaveholder John Bell of Tennessee, age sixty-three, alongside the vice presidential nominee, Edward Everett, age sixty-six.) However noble, the party's brief pledge "to *recognize* no political principle other than *the Constitution of the Country, the Union of the States, and the Enforcement of the Laws*," sounded at once pious, evasive, and antediluvian. Finally, the party's success would hinge on the outcome of the Republican convention in Chicago, scheduled to commence a few days after the Constitutional Unionists' convention ended. If the Republicans nominated one of their radical leaders—above all William Henry Seward—then the Whig gentlemen might stand a chance of winning over timid Republican sympathizers. If the Republicans nominated a moderate, the Constitutional Unionists would almost certainly prove irrelevant.[32]

The early odds strongly favored Seward. Although never as extreme as his opponents described him, Seward personified the evolution of the reformist, new-school liberal Whiggery of the late 1830s and 1840s into Republicanism. His stands in favor of black education and against nativism had forever marked him as more egalitarian than most of his Whig colleagues. His uncompromising antislavery position long predated the Kansas-Nebraska controversy, and it had only hardened over the years. With his unfussy, at times rumpled dress, his addiction to cigars, and his outgoing manner, Seward defied the stereotype of starchy Whig propriety. He also had an impressive political operation at his disposal, headed by his eternally loyal wire-puller, Thurlow Weed. Over the months before the convention, Weed's lieutenants were everywhere, soliciting funds for Seward's campaign and rounding up public support from figures as different as Nathaniel Banks (now governor of Massachusetts) and Archbishop John Hughes.[33]

The political intelligence that came back to Seward and Weed was unsettling. Support for Seward in New England as well as New York was solid, but elsewhere Republican leaders found him troubling. In the mid-Atlantic and Old Northwest states, Seward's radical reputation on slavery and race alienated the party's more conservative ex-Whigs and racist ex-Democrats. In those same states, his repudiation of nativism would make it difficult for the Republicans to attract ex-Whig Native Americans, who had voted in such surprisingly large numbers for Millard Fillmore in 1856. Although his home state had named a delegation pledged firmly to him, intraparty feuding over the years had made enemies out of influential New Yorkers, above all Horace Greeley of the widely read *New-York Daily Tribune*. Seward also had a whiff of corruption about him, made stronger by the recent awarding of lucrative franchise grants by the New York legislature to his political friends. A string of stunning Washington scandals involving Democratic graft and bribery under Pierce and Buchanan was just coming fully to light, and the Republicans planned to exploit them in the fall campaign. Nominating the suspect Seward would make that more difficult.[34]

But who could stop Seward and Weed? Republican managers from the lower North preferred four candidates with strong regional appeal: Governor Salmon P. Chase, the ex–Free Soiler from Ohio; Senator Simon Cameron of Pennsylvania, a former state adjutant general who had risen through the ranks first as a Democrat, then as a Know-Nothing; Edward Bates of Missouri, an aging ex-Whig backed by the Blair family, Horace Greeley, and various border-state delegates; and the great debater from Illinois, Abraham Lincoln. Chase was the best known but was deemed by some, even within his own state delegation, as too radical. Cameron could win his crucial home state, but his party-switching career and his fondness for dispensing patronage made him seem unprincipled. Bates had his imposing supporters, but he was also nearing seventy, had once been a slaveholder, and in 1856 had supported Fillmore and the Know-Nothings. Lincoln, although impressive in person, had not won an election since 1846.[35]

Lincoln alone, however, had taken important steps before the convention to improve his chances. Although he lacked an experienced top political manager like Weed, he assembled an extremely talented group of political advisers, all from Illinois, including circuit court judge David B. Davis, Norman Judd, the chairman of the Illinois Republican Party, and Joseph Medill, co-owner of the *Chicago Tribune*. In 1859, Lincoln delivered political speeches all across the midwestern states, and he followed that up in February 1860 with a major address at New York's Cooper Institute and a speaking tour of New England. Without seriously threatening Seward's northeastern base, Lincoln's appearances won over a few Republicans completely, and established him as a viable alternative to Seward should the New Yorker's drive for the nomination falter. More important in the long run, his performance at the Cooper Institute laid out a powerful case not just for himself but for the Republican Party.[36]

The previous September, Douglas had published an essay in *Harper's New Monthly Magazine* that, while candidly describing the rifts within the Democracy over the territories, attempted to vindicate popular sovereignty yet again with a labored discussion of federal and local law. Lincoln prepared his Cooper Institute speech as a rebuttal to Douglas, citing from the historical record to prove (once again) that the Framers had given Congress the power to bar slavery in the territories, and that the founding generation had marked slavery for extinction. Less than a week before Lincoln's scheduled address, Seward announced that he would deliver a major speech of his own on the Senate floor, formally to propose the admission of Kansas as a free state but with the obvious intention of laying out his claim on the Republican nomination. Lincoln's speech was bound to be compared to Seward's, and Lincoln knew it. Lincoln also knew that his New York audience would include dozens of influential Republican supporters and the most important press corps in the country.[37]

Inside the cavernous, subterranean Great Hall of Peter Cooper's two-year-old institute, Lincoln put on a show that superbly conveyed his peculiar combination of political moderation and moral firmness about slavery. The first half of the speech, directed against Douglas's article, provided a point-by-point refutation that was far better informed and reasoned than Douglas's original. But it was in the second half, ostensibly directed at the South, that Lincoln bowled over his distinguished audience. In a calm and even conciliatory way, he declared the southern people just and reasonable, repudiated John Brown, and emphatically urged Republicans to show restraint in the face of southern provocations. Yet he would not concede an inch on the main points in contention. At bottom, he declared (his momentum building), the raging controversy was a moral issue — whether slavery was right or wrong. Despite what he called the "sophisticated contrivances" of the Douglas men, there was no middle ground. Could men of good conscience stand by while those who thought slavery good tried to bring it to places where it had never been? "If our sense of duty forbids this," Lincoln declared in a rousing peroration, "then let us stand by our duty fearlessly and effectively. . . . LET US HAVE FAITH THAT RIGHT MAKES MIGHT."[38]

When Lincoln finished, the Great Hall rang with exultation. The first newspaper reviews singled out his riveting speaking style as an unexpected sensation. ("No man," the *Tribune*'s rapturous reporter wrote, "ever before made such an impression on his first appeal to a New York audience.") But the words mattered as well, and although Seward's speech two days later also won effusive praise, Lincoln's was easily its match. In the short run, Seward's remarks — delivered on the floor of the U.S. Senate by a long-time national leader — garnered even more publicity and affirmed Seward as the front-runner for the Republican nomination. But with his Cooper Institute address and subsequent speaking tour of New England, Lincoln began in earnest his effort to overtake him.[39]

Chicago proved as fortunate a choice of convention site for Lincoln's supporters as Charleston had proved catastrophic for Douglas's. Although Seward and Weed sent trainloads of supporters westward, well supplied with liquor, to cheer their man on, Lincoln had an entire city at his disposal for volunteers to pack the galleries. Amid the raucousness of the convention's hotels and spacious meeting hall (built especially for the occasion and dubbed "The Wigwam"), Lincoln's political team went to work, first to secure enough first-ballot votes to deny Seward an instant victory, then to gain enough second-ballot commitments to turn the tide. Who promised what to whom in the way of patronage remains unclear. Although Lincoln had righteously told his managers to make no binding commitments, there is no reason to believe that Davis, Judd, & Co. took him seriously. Lincoln's side also wielded a powerful practical argument: Seward would lose the lower North and thus, probably, the election; Lincoln would carry the lower North and become the nation's sixteenth president. And so Lincoln's side made special work of cajoling delegates from the battleground states. Indiana's decision to join with Illinois and support Lincoln on the first ballot was a signal victory for Lincoln's negotiators, as was Pennsylvania's agreement to abandon Cameron after the first ballot and give most of its votes to Lincoln.[40]

Lincoln's strategy succeeded brilliantly. On the first ballot, Seward held a commanding lead but fell well short of the simple majority required to nominate, while Lincoln ran a strong second. On the next ballot, the bulk of the Pennsylvania delegation and a number of New Englanders defected to Lincoln, and Seward's lead melted to a mere three and one-half votes. With that, the gallery crowd of ten thousand, the vast majority of them Lincoln supporters, let loose a roar of anticipation. When the third ballot was totaled up, Lincoln was only a vote and a half from winning a majority — and when the Ohio delegation added four more votes for Lincoln, the noise literally shook the Wigwam's wooden rafters, the entire scene gripped, one reporter wrote, "with the energy of insanity." To assure party unity, the convention nominated for vice president Hannibal Hamlin, a former Democrat from Maine and a friend of Seward's. It had already approved a platform that condemned John Brown; opposed nativist changes in the naturalization laws; backed a homestead act, federal aid to internal improvements, and an upward adjustment of tariff rates; and, quoting the Declaration of Independence, asserted that the normal condition of all American territories was and always had been freedom.[41]

The enthusiasm of the May convention sustained the Republicans for the rest of the campaign. As if in response to southern truculence, thousands joined the revived "Wide Awake" Clubs and marched in pseudomilitary regalia. To applause and laughter, one of Lincoln's supporters had hailed his nomination in Chicago by calling him "the man who knows how to split rails and maul [D]emocrats"— and fence rails became the popular emblem of "The Railsplitter." Although Lincoln followed the custom of not appearing publicly—he passed the summer receiving callers at the governor's room in the State House in Springfield— Republican leaders, including the disappointed Seward, campaigned hard. Governor Edwin D. Morgan of New York, chairman of the party's national committee, commanded the most efficient electioneering machine in the field.[42]

With New England secure for Lincoln, and with their antislavery credentials unimpeachable to all except the most radical abolitionists, the Republicans paid special attention to attracting voters in the lower North and the West by stressing ancillary issues. The Buchanan administration scandals, stoked in June by the release of a large and damning report by a special House investigating committee, allowed Republicans everywhere to position themselves as the party of reform. In the western states, party spokesmen played up the homestead issue. In protection-friendly Pennsylvania, they dwelt on the tariff, which they presented chiefly as a pro-labor measure designed to shield workingmen's wages against competition from the "pauper labor" of Europe. Although the Irish working-class vote seemed well out of reach, the national committee worked hard to win over German immigrants. Headed by the radical émigré from the 1848 revolutions, Carl Schurz, German-speaking Republicans proclaimed Lincoln the true workingman's candidate in a string of German-language party newspapers—among them the *Illinois Staats-Anzeiger*, a small but lively sheet in Springfield that Lincoln himself had purchased in 1859 and handed over to a reliable Republican immigrant editor.[43]

The campaigns of the pro-Breckinridge southern Democrats and the Constitutional Unionists were, by comparison, lackluster. Managed, essentially, out of the White House, the Breckinridge campaign could never quite decide whether its chief aim was to win the election or lambaste Stephen Douglas. Any serious chance that the southern schismatics would see the light and reunite with the pro-Douglas men, as Douglas had hopefully predicted, died early on. ("They do well to call us bolters," the pro-slavery New York Hunker Daniel Dickerson declaimed, "for we intend to bolt the door fast against all hucksters, auctioneers, and jobbers.") The sectional tensions evident at the Constitutional Unionists' convention resurfaced, as several of the party's southern leaders crumpled under fire-eater pressure and endorsed the call for a federal slave code, which in turn prompted some of the party's northerners to desert and announce for Lincoln. Late in the campaign, Jefferson Davis, probably with the White House's support, tried to broker a deal whereby Breckinridge, Bell, and Douglas would withdraw in favor of a pro-southern Unionist, but Douglas spurned the offer as impractical and said that, in any case, he would rather see Lincoln elected than collaborate with the southerners who had tried to destroy him.[44]

Douglas campaigned furiously and courageously, both for himself and the Union. Although his health was nearly ruined by alcohol abuse and overwork, the Little Giant defied convention and campaigned in every region of the country, save only the Pacific West. At the outset, he offered himself to the voters as the only genuinely national candidate who could prevent the horror of secession. In late summer, when, to his surprise, he was virtually certain that Lincoln would win, he shifted gears and took his campaign southward—less in the hopes of overcoming Breckinridge than to confront what he was now convinced was a southern plot to stage a coup d'état in November or December. In the crucial border states, he warned darkly of what the Deep South extremists had in mind, and evoked the spirit of Andrew Jackson, declaring that the next president should treat all attempts at disunion "as Old Hickory treated the Nullifiers in 1832." If elected, he vowed, he would hang all disunionists "higher than Haman." After a speaking tour of the friendlier Old Northwest, he then plunged deep into Georgia and Alabama, encouraged by friends like Alexander Stephens and drawing larger crowds than expected. Near the campaign's end, Douglas stood on the steps of the State Capitol in Montgomery at midday and, facing down rowdies who tried to disrupt his speech, delivered a powerful attack on secession. A politician to his marrow, Douglas managed to become become a stump-speaking statesman.[45]

Not all of Douglas's campaigning was so lofty. In Illinois and the rest of the Old Northwest—where voter enthusiasm for him ran highest—Douglas and his supporters returned to his tactics of 1858 and baited the Republicans as champions of black equality. His supporters elsewhere were even nastier. In New York, where radical Republicans had placed a doomed equal male suffrage referendum on the ballot, pro-Douglas Democrats tried to label their opponents as advocates of "Amalgamation" and "Nigger Equality." A float in one Manhattan Democratic parade carried effigies of Horace Greeley and a "good looking nigger wench, whom he caressed with all the affection of a true Republican." Tapping into the racism and economic insecurity of Irish workers, as well as into their distrust of Republican Puritans, the pro-southern *New York Herald* claimed that "if Lincoln is elected you will have to compete with the labor of four million emancipated Negroes."[46]

The racist attacks, mingled with charges that Lincoln's election would guarantee secession, caused the Republicans some headaches. If the national Breckinridge and Douglas forces were almost inalterably at odds, there was room for tactical alliances among northern Douglas Democrats, Constitutional Unionists, and unaffiliated ex-Whig conservatives. Here and there, particularly in New York and Pennsylvania, even Breckinridge and Douglas electors managed to bury the hatchet and dickered over forming a fusion ticket. Douglas repudiated any links with Breckinridge but he encouraged merging with the Bell forces, and for a time, it looked as if the alliances might prove just strong enough to affect the outcome—not least in New York City, where leading bankers and merchants had forged a united antisecession opposition. Could Manhattan's large anti-Republican Irish and silk-stocking vote knock New York out of the Lincoln column and throw the election into the House, where under the one-state, one-vote rule, Lincoln might well lose? How would the attacks of a combined opposition to Lincoln play in the closely divided lower North? Apart from the fusion threat, how could the Republicans respond to the Democrats' inflammatory racial charges and secure the lower North without alienating their antislavery base?[47]

The Lincoln campaign had to come to terms with its basic political identity. Republican spokesmen in toss-up districts tried to deflect the wedge issues by describing themselves as a white man's party and by reemphasizing issues like the tariff, internal improvements, and Democratic corruption. Some alarmed conservative Republicans even begged Lincoln to issue a public statement to appease the South and renounce racial egalitarianism. But here Lincoln drew the line. His "conservative views and intentions" had long been crystal clear: although dedicated to slavery's extinction by halting its spread, he intended no direct interference with slavery in the states or the Fugitive Slave Law. What could be gained from stating this yet again? ("Why do not uneasy men *read* what I have already said? and what our *platform* says," Lincoln wrote to one alarmed supporter.) Southerners who hated him and his party were not likely to be converted. Courting uncertain northerners with soothing words, Lincoln wrote, would only permit "*bad* men . . . to fix upon me the character of timidity and cowardice." Better to stay the course—not, he said, "merely on *punctilio* and pluck," but on principles that were as plain as day.[48]

Whatever suspense remained about the outcome evaporated in the small hours of the morning after election day, when word flashed along the telegraph lines that Lincoln had carried New York by a large majority. In the final tally,

Lincoln won every free state except New Jersey (where his vote was large enough to earn him a share of the state's electoral votes), which was sufficient to give him a sizable triumph in the Electoral College. Although the Republican ticket won only 40 percent of the popular vote nationwide, it won 54 percent of the northern vote. Had all the northern votes for Douglas, Breckinridge, and Bell been combined for one candidate, Lincoln would still have won the election. Crowds cheered the result—in the secessionist South as well as in the antislavery North. "A party founded on the single sentiment . . . of hatred of African slavery," the *Richmond Semi-Weekly Examiner* reported, "is now the controlling power."[49]

Overall, the election showed how polarized the sections had become over the slavery issue. Only one candidate, Stephen Douglas, won any appreciable support in all regions of the country, the last faint echo of the intersectional Jacksonian party system—yet Douglas managed narrowly to win the popular vote in only two states, New Jersey and Missouri. A large majority, 58 percent, of the popular vote backed either Lincoln or Breckinridge, the candidates with the least compromising views on the slavery question. That polarization in turn marked the collapse of old-line Whig conservatism in the North. In only three free states— Massachusetts, Vermont, and California—did the Constitutional Unionists receive more than 3 percent of the popular vote.

Some portions of the respective sections were more estranged than others. Aided, perhaps, by Douglas's pro-Union tour, the Constitutional Unionists carried the Border South states of Virginia, Kentucky, and Bell's native Tennessee, came within a whisker of winning Maryland, and ran well in North Carolina and Georgia. Even in the secessionist hotbed of Alabama, the Constitutional Unionists ran strong in the northernmost yeoman counties and won nearly one-third of the vote statewide. In Louisiana, the combined Bell-Douglas total was far *greater* than the vote for Breckinridge. The Republican victory in the North was similarly uneven. In New England and the upper Northwest, Lincoln's victory was gargantuan. But the Republicans barely carried 50 percent of the vote in Illinois and Indiana, and won an unimpressive 52 percent in Ohio. If Republicanism had become a virtual political religion in much of the North, in some areas—Illinois's "Egypt" counties, the Butternut areas of southern Ohio, the city of New York—it was anathema.

Still, on the election's crucial issue, the expansion of slavery, the nation was split in two. If northerners disagreed about the efficacy of Douglas's popular sovereignty idea, the returns showed them thoroughly united about the necessity to halt slavery's unchecked spread—and to resist forcefully any southern effort to secede. If southerners disagreed about secession, they were nearly unanimous in their repudiation of the northern candidates and of slavery's restriction, whether by "Black Republican" fiat or Douglas's obnoxious popular sovereignty plan. The political reality of 1860 was incontrovertible: a sharply divided nation had, by wholly constitutional means, decided in the North's favor. Charles Francis Adams could hardly believe it: "There is now scarcely a shadow of a doubt that the great revolution has actually taken place," he wrote in his diary, "and that the country has once and for all thrown off the domination of the Slaveholders."[50]

"THE DEMOCRATIC PROCLIVITIES OF THE AGE"

The election of 1860 had ended exactly as Adams and his fellow Republicans had hoped but could only have dreamed of four years earlier. No less pleased, though, were the southern fire-eaters. As Adams considered the magnitude of Lincoln's victory, southern militants took the next step toward creating their slaveholders' republic.

The election campaign had aggravated the fears provoked by what southerners perceived as the North's embrace of John Brown. Pro-Breckinridge newspapers were filled with unconfirmed reports of arson and rape by slaves, along with notices about shady Yankees seen moving about the countryside. A string of suspicious fires in Texas, all of which broke out at about the same time, convinced some southerners that a huge insurrection plot was building—timed, it was said, to coincide with Christmas. Here and there, vigilantes assaulted and, on occasion, lynched alleged evildoers, including two suspicious men in Texas found to be holding copies of Helper's *Impending Crisis*. In every district of South Carolina, a semisecret organization of self-described "minute men" pledged to take up arms and march to Washington to prevent Lincoln's inauguration, and the volunteers began drilling and wearing blue cockades in their hats, the emblem of nullification during the crisis of 1832–33.[51]

The slaves, by their very presence, also contributed to the pervasive sense of dread. Despite every effort by slaveholders and southern legislatures to cordon off the South from incendiary talk and reading materials, the slaves, even in the interior regions, appear to have learned a great deal about what was occurring, through the "grapevine way" that transmitted overheard talk and rumor to the slave quarters. As Booker T. Washington, then a young Virginia slave, later recalled, the slaves were remarkably informed "about the great National questions that were agitating the country." Word of John Brown's raid had been impossible to suppress; now, slaves from central Georgia to northeast Texas were hearing that a man named Lincoln would soon be president and set them all free. At least some of the rumors of slave revolts appear to have originated with the slaves themselves, in an effort to scare local whites. And the masters knew they were sitting atop a powder keg.[52]

But the greatest fears, far from hysterical, had been building for years, and were finally realized on election day. These fears were not confined to fire-eater extremists or jumpy vigilantes. Over the long, hot, and drought-ridden summer of 1860—which killed off much of the cotton crop and made the South a literal tinder box—even temperate southern slaveholders stood horrified at the impending electoral victory of northern-style democracy and its ramifications. "The democratic proclivities of the age pervade our whole country—," one ex-Whig Unionist North Carolinian despaired, "nothing can arrest our downward tendency to absolute Government." The absolutism they feared most meant policies geared to eventual emancipation, and its genius was Abraham Lincoln.[53]

25

THE ILIAD OF
ALL OUR WOES

The fire-eaters of South Carolina quickly made good on their secessionist threats. "[T]he revolution of 1860 has commenced," the *Charleston Mercury* bellowed as soon as Lincoln's victory was official. "On every lip is the stern cry la liberta!'" The grand drama had arrived, and Charleston would play its crucial part, "as becomes her intelligence, her stake and her civilization." In liberty's name, and slavery's, the southern reaction was massing, to strike back at the North and secede from the Union before Lincoln could even take office.[1]

Lincoln himself was hopeful, even confident, the secessionists would fail. They had badly misrepresented him, he said. He was not a radical abolitionist. He would not eradicate slavery immediately. Soon enough, the sensible people of the South would see through the extremists' lies, abide by the democratic results of 1860, and remain true to the Union. "Disunionists *per se*, are now in hot haste to get out of the Union," Lincoln wrote, ". . . With such '*Now, or never*' is the maxim."[2]

The president-elect was utterly mistaken. His election, the culmination of the long-building crisis of American democracy, instantly turned many Deep South moderates and even erstwhile Unionists into secessionists. No misrepresentation was necessary to show that he and his Republicans wanted to put slavery on the road to extinction, which was enough to make him a tyrant in Dixie. There were differences among southerners, to be sure, about how secession ought to proceed, and in Lincoln's native Border South, his assumptions about Unionist sentiment had considerable merit. But from South Carolina southward, and then westward to Texas, the main question was now not whether to secede but when and how. And by the time he began composing his inauguration speech, Lincoln found himself forced to find the right words to address a nation ripped asunder.[3]

SECESSION, SLAVERY, AND THE POLITICS OF COUNTERREVOLUTION

South Carolina, predictably, instigated secession. On November 5, the legislature met in Columbia to name the state's presidential electors, in accordance with the state's uniquely archaic system. The fire-eater governor William Gist duly informed the members that, in view of the impending Republican victory, they ought to stay in session and, if Lincoln won, call a state convention to consider disunion. On November 9, the secession convention bill passed, scheduling the election of delegates for January 8 with the convention to assemble a week later. The two-month wait would leave enough time to determine the desires of other states. But the Charleston hard-liners would brook no delay, and following a large protest meeting, the legislature moved the election back to December 6 and the opening of the convention to December 17. On December 20, the convention unanimously approved an ordinance (drafted by a committee that included Barnwell Rhett) tersely announcing that "the union now subsisting between South Carolina and other States, under the name of the 'United States of America,' is hereby dissolved." Over the next week, the convention approved two longer declarations justifying secession, one by Rhett, the other by the somewhat more moderate Christopher Memminger, both explicit in their defense of slavery. Rhett denounced how the American republic had degenerated into a "consolidated Democracy."[4]

South Carolina's alacrity surprised neither friends nor foes of secession. (Upon hearing of the ordinance, the staunch, lonely South Carolina Unionist James Petigru is reported to have remarked that his state was "too small for a republic, but too large for an insane asylum.") But the swiftness with which the rest of the Deep South followed suit was breathtaking. On November 29, the Mississippi legislature passed its own secession convention bill, and on January 9, the Mississippi convention approved, by a huge margin, an ordinance similar to South Carolina's. The next day, Florida seceded, and the day after that so did Alabama, followed by Georgia on January 19, Louisiana on January 26, and Texas on February 1. "The time is now come," one delegate from Mobile told his state's convention, "and Alabama must make her selection, either to secede from the Union . . . [or] submit to a system of policy on the part of the Federal Government that, in a short time, will compel her to abolish African Slavery."[5]

The upper South and border states resisted the trend; indeed, Unionists in Maryland, Virginia, North Carolina, Tennessee, Missouri, and Arkansas mounted a successful, explicitly antisecession counteroffensive during the early months of 1861. One former Tennessee governor told his disunionist Alabama cousin that the cotton states had no legitimate grounds for separating from the federal government, and warned that his state and Kentucky would never be "dragged into a rebellion that their whole population utterly disapproved." With larger nonslaveholder white populations than in lower Dixie, and with a stronger persistent Whig political organization (which produced the victorious turnouts for the Constitutional Unionists in 1860), the upper South contradicted militant proclamations about an imminent united southern nation. This gave hope to northerners (like the Kentucky-born Lincoln) that secession was a chimera, and emboldened those who believed that the slaveholders' democracy could be overturned by the white yeomanry and even by slaveholders who remained ambivalent about human bondage.[6]

The Unionist counteroffensive, however, also had sharp limits. Portions of some of the most politically important reluctant states, especially the so-called Southside counties of Virginia and the Democratic plantation districts of North Carolina, seethed with southern rights discontent. And although the border-state Unionists included a large number of nonplanters—who, in places, even expressed antislavery opinions—their leaders came out of the same elite of comfortable slaveholders who dominated politics throughout the South. For these upper South gentlemen, secession, far from a necessity, looked suicidal for slavery, handing the northern Republicans the grounds for destroying the institution even where it existed. The Union, they believed, gave infinitely greater protection to slavery than some fancied and untested new confederacy. Yet if they were willing to allow a formal ban on slavery's expansion in northern territories where they believed slavery would never flourish, all but the most flexible Unionist slaveholders also wanted to provide what one Virginian called "explicit *protection* of slavery" in the form of a federal code, to cover territories south of the old 36°30' Missouri Compromise line. If their hostility to secession obstructed the spread of disunionism, their allegiance to the Union extended only so far as it would preserve, protect, defend, and extend the slaveholders' democracy.[7]

The Deep South's allegiance to slavery led to more pessimistic conclusions now that the Republicans had won the presidency. "Our people are calmly and fully determined never to submit to Lincoln's administration, or to any Compromise with the Northern States," one Alabaman observed. The Deep South's solidarity confounded the Republican moderates' thinking about southern loyalty to the Union, and has puzzled historians ever since. Even in the cotton kingdom, the fire-eaters appeared, at first, to face considerable opposition. Outside of South Carolina and Texas, a substantial number of voters—at least 40 percent of the total—cast their ballots for convention delegate candidates who expressed reservations about the suddenness of secession, or about having their state secede independently of others. Support for the most extreme disunionists dwindled remarkably in those Deep South counties inhabited chiefly by nonslaveholders, as well as in traditionally Whig wealthy cotton counties and urban areas with strong commercial links to the North. In the conventions, opponents of immediate secession called into question not merely the fire-eaters' accelerated program but the legitimacy of the conventions themselves. In Alabama, for example, the convention was nearly evenly divided between supporters and opponents of immediate secession. On the third day of debate, Nicholas J. Davis of Huntsville, directly challenged the disunionists' leader, William Lowndes Yancey, by claiming that the convention was irregular, and that a plebiscite was the only proper way to ascertain the public's sentiment on so grave a matter as secession. Yancey, on the verge of his greatest victory and apoplectic at any sign of resistance, charged that resistance to secession was treason to Alabama. Davis shot back that the secessionists were acting like Tories, out "to coerce an unwilling people." Should Yancey treat those who opposed him as enemies of the people, Davis exclaimed, they would "meet him at the first of our mountains, and there with his own selected weapons, hand to hand, and face to face, settle the question of the sovereignty of the people."[8]

These divisions led some writers to describe secession in the Deep South as a coup d'état by the fire-eaters, who pulled an unwilling white citizenry out of the Union. There is certainly reason to think the extreme disunionists in various states either helped rig the outcome of the convention elections or misled the public about the strength they enjoyed. The secessionists' victory in Louisiana—where the Unionist vote had been strong in 1860, and the actual vote count was suppressed for months—was particularly dubious. In Alabama, the heavy vote for immediate secession in Mobile and Auranga Counties, strongholds for Douglas and Bell only two months earlier, raised eyebrows. The holding of elections and conventions as quickly as possible, and a marked decline in turnout in the convention delegate elections compared to the presidential elections, looked like the products of extremist threats. "In South Carolina the people have little to do in politics but choose their own masters," one outraged Alabaman wrote. "And outside of South Carolina in the Cotton States politicians are trying the experiment of getting along without the people."[9]

Yet these assessments slighted the slaveholders' long-standing domination of the very terms of debate within the Dixie democracy—and the popular revulsion that swept through the Deep South after Lincoln's election. Even in Alabama, where doubts about immediate secession ran high, slaveholders were elected to the state conventions out of all proportion to their numbers in the population, and tended to take a more militant posture than the nonslaveholders. More important, the hard reality of the Republican victory, and the threat it posed to the slaveholders' democracy, changed Deep South skeptics into secessionists. The prominent Mobile, Alabama, editor John Forsyth Jr.—son of Martin Van Buren's meddlesome secretary of state and a resolute Douglas man in 1860—typified the shift. With Douglas's defeat, Forsyth concluded, "the cause of the Union was lost," and he started to resign himself to secession and civil war lest the South be "stripped of 25 hundred millions of slave property & to have loose among us 4,000,000 of freed blacks." All across the Deep South, a pro-Douglas Georgia newspaper observed, "[t]he hopelessness of preserving the Union has made disunionists, since the election, of thousands of Conservative and Union men."[10]

The Deep South debates over secession were mainly about means, not ends. In the secession conventions, the major fault line was never between Unionists and disunionists, but between two groups of disunionists: the conditional secessionists (sometimes called, a bit confusingly, "cooperationists") and the immediate secessionists. Conditional secessionists wanted to slow the chain reaction of state-by-state secessions. Some of them thought it wiser to organize a united southern confederacy first; others wanted to deliver a list of impossible demands to Lincoln and then secede; and still others truly wished to test Lincoln's claims to moderation and await an overt act against the South before dissolving the Union. Although their ranks included a few leaders of great stature, including Alexander Stephens, few of the conditional secessionists had much faith that secession was avoidable, and virtually none thought that secession was illegitimate. Some refused to assent when secession finally came—residents of one Alabama county burned Yancey in effigy—but the great majority signed on quickly thereafter, either out of localist loyalty or determination to resist any Yankee interference. "I shall vote against the ordinance," Nicholas Davis told the Alabama convention. "But if Alabama shall need the strong arm of her valorous sons to sustain her . . . I say for myself and for my constituents—and I dare say for all North Alabama—that I and they will be cheerfully ready to take our part in the conflict." Stephens, who had argued for months that slavery was safer inside the Union than outside, backed the new sovereign state of Georgia as soon as it declared its independence.[11]

More telling was a philosophical division within the disunionist camp over the constitutional theory of secession. The division was not sharply expressed in 1860 and 1861, in part because the immediate secessionists tried to soften it, in part because some major figures blew back and forth about it, and in part because the audacity of secession overwhelmed other considerations. But the division was real, and it conformed to the preexisting division between hard-core Rhettists and the majority of slaveholder Master Race democrats.[12]

Fire-eater secessionists held the militant view that secession was perfectly legal and represented nothing radical. The core of their argument was the state-rights compact theory of the Union as it had been developed by John C. Calhoun and then made operative by the fire-eaters in the 1850s. The states, so the argument went, existed before the Union. The Constitution did not alter the states' powers and prerogatives as autonomous governments. By seceding, the states were merely reasserting the total sovereignty they had exerted in creating the Union in the first place. That assertion had been necessitated by a revolution undertaken by northern Republicans, who had abrogated the original constitutional agreement that left slavery undisturbed. "I am a secessionist and not a revolutionist," William Yancey explained. The Republicans, Barnwell Rhett concurred, were "the practical revolutionists and hatchers of trouble," opposed to the true southern conservatives. "We are not revolutionists," the pro–fire-eater editor James D. B. De Bow declared. The southern states, one secessionist leader announced, had left the Union "to preserve their old institutions" from "a revolution [that] threatened to destroy their social system."[13]

Embodied in the militant fire-eater argument was a thorough repudiation of Jeffersonian politics, especially about equality and natural rights, in favor of what its proponents upheld as the natural differences among men. The new slaveholders' republic would stand as a living refutation of Jefferson's harebrained egalitarian doctrines, and of the anarchic vulgarities that had emanated from them and degraded the North. Fire-eater anti-Jeffersonianism did not, however, fully persuade the majority in the disunionist camp, including some like Jefferson Davis who had long been among the most forceful advocates of southern rights. The southern states, on this other view, had no more constitutional right to secede from the Union than the original colonies had to separate themselves from the British Empire. Instead, these secessionists draped themselves in the Jeffersonian natural right to revolution. Senator Alfred Iverson of Georgia put the matter squarely just before he departed Washington for good, insisting that although no state had the right to secede, "each State has the right of revolution, which all admit," when placed under burdens "so onerous that it cannot bear them." By this logic, the Republicans were the Tories, enlarging and then abusing the powers of the central government to strangle the liberties of the revolutionary southern patriots. Secession was a replay of the American Revolution, a new War of Southern Independence that aimed to vindicate, not repudiate, the struggles of the founding generation. Resisting "an unbridled majority, the most odious and least responsible form of despotism," Jefferson Davis intoned, echoing Calhoun, would "renew such sacrifices as our fathers made to the holy cause of constitutional liberty."[14]

Where the two versions of secessionism firmly agreed, forging the ideological foundations of the Confederacy, was over the defense of a polity based on slavery and an insistence on preserving the slaveholders' liberty against northern despotism. Decades later, in what has turned out to be one of the most consequential acts of falsification in American history, secessionist leaders tried to deny this crucial fact. In a long, self-justifying memoir, Jefferson Davis asserted that "the existence of African servitude was in no wise the cause of the conflict, but only an incident." Secession, he said, was really prompted by sectional rivalry, political ambition, and the passions, prejudices, and sympathies fomented by the North. Alexander Stephens, the reluctant secessionist, put the matter in familiar but highly abstracted constitutional terms, as a battle not over "the policy or impolicy of African Subordination," but "between the supporters of a strictly Federative Government on the one side, and a thoroughly National one, on the other." Davis, Stephens, and others wanted their readers to believe that secession was the culmination of a political contest rooted in the clash between Federalists and Anti-Federalists in the 1780s, a clash that just happened to become attached to slavery.[15]

It was all very different in 1860 and 1861, when the state secession conventions and secessionist leaders justified leaving the Union. There were, of course, southerners in the Unionist minority who claimed to support secession for reasons that had little or nothing to do with slavery. "I care nothing for the 'Peculiar institution,'" one wrote, "but I cant stand the idea of being domineered over by a set of Hypocritical scoundrels such as Sumner, Seward, Wilson, Hale, etc., etc." But for those who effected secession, including those in Davis's and Stephens's home states, slavery and the attacks on it by the northern democracy were the fundamental issues—and they declared as much to a candid world. The South Carolina convention's "Declaration of the Immediate Causes" was matter-of-fact: "an increasing hostility on the part of the non-slaveholding States to the institution of slavery" had led the North to assume "the right of deciding upon the propriety of our domestic institutions." Now that the free states had "denounced as sinful the institution of slavery" and encouraged slave runaways and "servile insurrection," they had released South Carolina from her obligation to the Union. "Our position is thoroughly identified with the institution of slavery," the Mississippi convention declared, "the greatest material interest in the world." (The Mississippians mentioned no other cause for secession.) The Georgia convention emphasized above all "the subject of African slavery," and the Texas secessionists declared themselves the defenders of "a commonwealth holding, maintaining and protecting the institution known as negro slavery— the servitude of the African to the white race within her limits." Even more moderate heads in the Deep South fully agreed: the fight to extend slavery, one cooperationist delegate to the Alabama convention asserted, was "'the Iliad of all our woes.'"[16]

Alexander Stephens was no less direct in an extemporaneous speech he gave in Savannah two months after Georgia seceded. "The prevailing ideas entertained by [Jefferson] and most of the leading statesmen at the time of the formation of the old constitution," Stephens remarked, "were that the enslavement of the African was in violation of the laws of nature; that it was wrong in *principle*, socially, morally, and politically. It was an evil they knew not well how to deal with, but the general opinion of the men of that day was that, somehow or other in the order of Providence, the institution would be evanescent and pass away." But that cherished idea of Jefferson and the Founders was fundamentally mistaken:

> Our new government is founded upon exactly the opposite idea; its foundations are laid, its corner-stone rests upon the great truth, that the negro is not equal to the white man; that slavery—subordination to the superior race—is his natural and normal condition. . . . This, our new government, is the first, in the history of the world, based upon this great physical, philosophical, and moral truth. . . . It is upon this, as I have stated, our social fabric is firmly planted; and I cannot permit myself to doubt the ultimate success of a full recognition of this principle throughout the civilized and enlightened world.

"Slavery, so called," as Stephens later termed it, was not incidental to secession; it was the summum bonum that united the secessionist cause.[17]

Building a polity based on slavery did leave open questions about the loyalties of the nonslaveholding white majority. Helper's *Impending Crisis* had alarmed slaveholders sufficiently to cause them to suppress the book, lest it delude and arouse the yeomanry. Lincoln actually picked up more than twenty-five thousand votes in slaveholding border states, a tiny proportion of the total but disturbing enough to edgy extremists.* Even more disturbing was the concentration of anti–fire-eater opinion in up-country districts with few slaveholders, especially noticeable in Georgia and Alabama. Leaving nothing to chance, the secessionists propagandized the interests of slaveholders and nonslaveholders as, in James De Bow's words, "in the present sectional controversy identical." First, they rebutted the charge that the slaveholders represented a privileged minority of white southerners. Most slaveholders, they noted (correctly), owned fewer than five slaves. Even in the largest slaveholding states, the proportion of landowners in the total free population was higher than in several New England states. And although, as De Bow conceded, "a very large class" of southern whites owned no slaves, they profited directly from slavery by providing goods and services to those

---

* Lincoln's name did not appear on the ballot in ten slaveholding states. He won a smattering of votes in Kentucky and Virginia, nearly four thousand votes in Delaware, as well as more than seventeen thousand votes in Missouri—roughly 10 percent of the state total—mainly in German-speaking districts in and around St. Louis.

who did. In many cases the nonslaveholders were themselves incipient masters waiting only for their chance to accumulate sufficient funds to purchase a bondsman. "This, with ordinary frugality, can in general be accomplished in a few years," De Bow wrote, "and is a process continually going on"—a slaveholders' version of the Yankee theme of prudent upward mobility, as well of the overriding social harmony of interests.[18]

Above all, the secessionists appealed to the nonslaveholders' white supremacist pride and fears, as well as to their local loyalties. Georgia's hotspur secessionist Joseph Brown—a humbly born, up-country ex-Democrat, nicknamed "The Ploughman"—made the racist argument with plebeian pungency, proclaiming that slavery "is the poor man's best Government." Abolition would eradicate this happiest of estates for the poor, and create particular hardships for nonslaveholders. "[T]he slaveholders, in the main, will escape the degrading equality which must result by emigration," De Bow wrote; the poor white, however, would "be compelled to remain and endure the degradation . . . unless, as is to be supposed, he would prefer to suffer death instead." Apocalyptic visions dominated the slaveholders' warnings about immediate emancipation followed by white submission of the most shameful sort. Beyond slavery and race, nonslaveholders, like many a hesitant planter secessionist, were also determined to resist any northern effort to crush secession by force, and to uphold what Nicholas J. Davis—William Yancey's harsh critic at the Alabama convention—called the South's "honor or the rights of her citizens."[19]

Sealing the unity among slaveholders and nonslaveholders was the rush of militance that came with the final cast of the die. Alexander Stephens, before Georgia seceded, called it a kind of madness in which the people became "wild with passion and frenzy, doing they know not what." It was actually more of a catharsis—a release of outraged emotion that had been building for more than a decade, and had been exacerbated by the "reign of terror" that followed the trauma of Harpers Ferry, but now had focus and purpose. At mass gatherings in Charleston and Savannah and New Orleans, in country towns where new volunteer companies and vigilance committees of old men and young lined up on dirt roads, there appeared improvised and not so improvised elements of allegiance to a nation that did not yet exist: irregular uniforms; flags of numerous designs; heart-pumping songs, adapted from stage tunes, whose lyrics shouted, "Hurrah! Hurrah/For Southern rights hurrah!" In the wake of the threatening triumph of "Black Republicanism," southern nationalism began becoming something real.[20]

The calculating politics and the emotionalism reached a crescendo in Montgomery in early February, when thirty-seven delegates from six of the seceded Deep South states assembled to draft a national constitution and establish a provisional government. A festive air surrounded the convention, which grew more intense as the deliberations continued. (After hearing a band play "Dixie," Jefferson Davis's wife, Varina, suggested that the song be adopted as the Confederacy's anthem.) But the delegates also worked with great seriousness and efficiency. Within four days, they adopted a preliminary constitution for the provisional government of the Confederate States of America. The next day, they unanimously chose Jefferson Davis as president of the provisional government and scheduled popular elections for the autumn. The convention then unanimously chose Alexander Stephens as vice president and set about debating a permanent Confederate constitution, which it finally approved on March 11.[21]

On the evening of February 16, Davis arrived in Montgomery from his Mississippi plantation and gave a fiery impromptu speech, promising that all who opposed the new Confederacy would "smell Southern powder and feel Southern steel." Yet for the most part, the new government projected as moderate an image as possible, both to keep the ranks in Montgomery solid and to appeal to the upper South states still undecided about secession. Among the delegates, several leading fire-eaters, including Barnwell Rhett and Laurence Keitt, recoiled at the restraint and harbored doubts about the stalwartness of men like Davis and Stephens. Davis, after all, although pro-secession and at times something of a fire-eater fellow traveler, had participated in congressional efforts to defuse the crisis only weeks earlier. But friends persuaded the fire-eaters to suppress their distrust, lest they frighten off Virginia and other hesitant slave states. ("The man and the hour have met," Yancey famously declared to the crowds, with forced friendliness, after he had accompanied the newly arrived Davis to his hotel.) With the crucial support, sent from Richmond, of leading Virginia pro-secessionists, Davis had emerged as the best man, broadly acceptable for his strong record on southern rights and secession, his long military record, and his experience in the Senate and as secretary of state. Stephens's elevation to the vice presidency was both a sop to the Georgia delegation, disappointed that a Georgian did not get the presidency, and an affirmation of the new government's efforts to project calm reasonableness.[22]

Davis's inaugural address, delivered two days after his arrival, reached out for a broad southern base. The new president asserted that the new government harbored no aggressive intent and issued a warm invitation to any states that might wish to join. Above all—and no doubt to the suppressed outrage of the fire-eaters—Davis explicitly linked the Confederacy to certain ideas and words of Thomas Jefferson, including the "inalienable" right to revolution. "Our present political position has been achieved in a manner unprecedented in the history of nations," he intoned. "It illustrates the American idea that governments rest upon the consent of the governed, and that it is the right of the people to alter or abolish them at will whenever they become destructive of the ends for which they were established." In establishing a new government, the convention, he said, promised a permanent constitution "differing only from that of our fathers in so far as it is explanatory of their well-known intent." Secession was a perfectly American revolution.[23]

Yet if Davis's words were soothing, nothing could disguise the Confederacy's overriding purpose, dear to Rhettist aristocrats and southern Master Race democrats alike: to create a republican government formally based on racial slavery. The new permanent constitution's scattered departures from the text of the U.S. Constitution left no doubt on these matters. The preamble, following the opening phrase, "We, the people," omitted the reference to creating "a more perfect Union"—a line that suggested that the Union was older than the Constitution—and eliminated the clause committing the government "to promote the general Welfare." It then explicitly endorsed the Calhounite compact theory of state sovereignty, proclaiming that each state was "acting in its sovereign and independent character." The rest of the document contained none of the semantic evasions about slavery (or, as the new constitution sometimes called it, "negro slavery") so carefully worked out by the Framers in 1787. In deference to Britain (whose official recognition the new government craved) and the Border South (which enjoyed a virtual monopoly on selling slaves to the lower South), the constitution prohibited the importation of slaves from abroad. But it protected the interstate slave trade and guaranteed the existence of slavery in any new territories the Confederacy might obtain. One departure from the U.S. Constitution stood out above all: Article I, Section 9, which stated that "[n]o . . . law impairing or denying the right of property in negro slaves shall be passed."[24]

In other ways, the convention designed a central government with minimal powers, except with respect to protecting slavery and the slaveholders' supremacy. The Confederate plan at once weakened the executive branch (by limiting the president to a single six-year term) and strengthened it in order to curb congressional fiscal excesses (by giving the president a line-item veto over appropriations bills and by giving cabinet officers nonvoting seats in Congress). The constitution made difficult central government expenditures on anything other than national defense and delivering the mail. With a few notable exceptions about river and harbor projects (which planters needed to get their cotton safely shipped), government aid to "internal improvement intended to facilitate commerce" was banned. All congressional appropriations required a two-thirds' supermajority in both the House and the Senate. A tariff was permitted for raising revenue but not for protecting home industries, although the provision was worded so vaguely that the distinction would have to be worked out by later Confederate congresses. The constitution's suffrage and representation provisions basically replicated those in the U.S. Constitution, leaving broad latitude to the states, but with one exception—a formal exclusion, from both state and national elections, of all persons of foreign birth not citizens of the Confederacy. Suspicious outsiders would have no formal political voice.[25]

The convention and its constitution codified what most secessionists meant when they spoke of liberty—the liberty of whites to own black slaves and take them wherever they chose, with only minimal obligations to the central government. With that core conviction, the southern reaction of 1860–61 brought about what would in time represent a momentous shift in American politics, away from the hierarchical conservatism of Federalism and old-line Whiggery, now all but vanished, and toward a southern hierarchical conservatism, based on the presumptions of white supremacy, the supreme political power of local elites, and the proclaimed virtues of "small government." But that long-term shift was not on Americans' minds in 1861: the fate of the country was. On Jefferson Davis fell the burden of forging a new nation out of seven sovereign states—and, if possible, expanding that nation to include as many additional slave states as possible. On Abraham Lincoln fell the task of stopping that expansion cold and deflating the secessionist movement.

"THIS GREAT TRIBUNAL, THE AMERICAN PEOPLE"

Lincoln departed Springfield for Washington on the same day, February 11, that Davis departed Mississippi for Montgomery. Northern majority opinion had already lined up solidly behind Lincoln's position (identical to Andrew Jackson's in 1832) that the Union was older than any of the states, that secession was anarchy, and that in this current crisis hung the fate of constitutional democracy. The foremost principle animating the Union, Lincoln would reflect, "is the necessity of proving that popular government is not an absurdity," and on this point, even the outgoing President James Buchanan seemed to agree. Although sharply critical of the North for starting the slavery agitation, Buchanan had startled his southern patrons by declaring, in his final annual message in early December, that secession over Lincoln's election was illegitimate and that the Union's dissolution "would be quoted as conclusive proof that man is unfit for self-government." Yet if the outgoing president opposed disunion, he also believed that, under the Constitution, he lacked any powers to prevent it. With Lincoln not due to take office until March 4, 1861, and with members of the cabinet and the lame-duck Congress from the Deep South departing after their states seceded, the federal government was rudderless and adrift.[26]

Buchanan did offer a compromise of sorts in his final address, whereby the northerners would cease criticizing slavery, support a constitutional amendment protecting slavery in all territories, and approve of renewed efforts to secure Cuba. Republicans instantly saw through this as capitulation. Some pledged to break secession even if it meant reducing the South to rubble. At all events, the Republicans argued, the government had to enforce the laws of the United

States, including the collection of customs duties in southern ports, and stand up to the rebels just as President Jackson had to the nullifiers. ("Oh, for one hour of Jackson!" the Springfield *Republican* exclaimed.) Other Republicans, including Horace Greeley, declared that if the Union could be saved only by surrendering Republican principles, it would be better simply to let the South go and let it fester in its own backwardness. (Radical abolitionists, including William Lloyd Garrison and Frederick Douglass, agreed.) Still others, fearful that bellicosity would provoke the upper South to secede, tried to fashion a congressional compromise less one-sided than Buchanan's.[27]

The most promising compromise plan emerged from the special Senate Committee of Thirteen in early December, before any state had seceded. Established to sift through the numerous compromises coming out of Congress, the committee included some of the ablest and influential men from all sides, among them William Henry Seward, Benjamin Wade, Stephen Douglas, Jefferson Davis, and Robert Toombs. Chief credit for crafting the committee's compromise proposal belonged to John Crittenden of Kentucky, the aging ex-Whig and, lately, prominent Constitutional Unionist. The plan called for a series of irrevocable amendments to the Constitution, the most important of which would revive the old Missouri Compromise line at 36°30', extend it all the way to the Pacific, ban slavery in all territories to its North, and protect slavery in territories (including any territories gained in the future) to its South. Although less offensive to Republicans than Buchanan's suggestions, the so-called Crittenden compromise was still one-sided. Yet some powerful Republican business interests were worried that secession might touch off a financial panic far worse than that of 1857, and they endorsed the idea. So did Thurlow Weed and (in more muffled ways) William Henry Seward.[28]

In Springfield, President-elect Lincoln broke his determined silence in order to help kill the plan. The ironies of the situation were large. Seward, the supposed radical, was playing the conciliator, to the consternation of Republican radicals like Joshua Giddings and Charles Sumner. ("God damn you, Seward," one senator told him, "you've betrayed your principles and your party; we've followed your lead long enough.") It was left to Lincoln the moderate, whose political fortunes the insurrectionist John Brown had inadvertently improved, to stand by Republican principles. The Crittenden plan, Lincoln wrote to a few influential Republicans—most pointedly Seward and Weed—"would lose us everything we gained in the election," reawaken the South's lust for Cuba, and put the nation once again "on the high-road to a slave empire." More important, the plan repudiated the basic Republican proposition that slavery's expansion should be halted everywhere. At Lincoln's urging, all five Republicans on the committee voted against the compromise, and with Toombs and Davis also opposed, the measure failed. Crittenden brought the plan to the Senate floor anyway, but by the time it came to a vote in mid-January, senators from states that had seceded or were about to secede abstained, and the remaining Republican majority defeated it.[29]

Other compromise schemes made the rounds in January and early February—although with one Deep South state after another declaring secession, efforts at mediation increasingly looked like stalling maneuvers until Lincoln could formally take over. The House counterpart to the Senate's special committee offered two measures that avoided violating Republican fundamentals and gained Lincoln's passive support: a resolution in support of the Fugitive Slave Law (which eventually passed on February 27) and a constitutional amendment prohibiting federal interference with slavery in the states (which also passed, much more narrowly, the following day). Seward also supported a self-described "peace convention," called by the Virginia legislature, that met in Washington on the same day that the Confederate convention opened in Montgomery. Chaired by the seventy-one-year-old former president John Tyler, the assembly looked even more antique than the Constitutional Union Party. After three weeks of deliberations, it offered a revised version of the Crittenden compromise, limiting the extension of the Missouri Compromise to the existing territories, and requiring majority votes of senators from both the free and the slave states before adding any new territories. The idea got nowhere.[30]

Lincoln, while keeping tabs on these discussions and bolstering the Republican faith, applied all of his political skills to appointing his cabinet and preparing for his inauguration. Keeping his fractious Republican rivals in line—especially Seward, who believed that he should have been elected president—was extremely difficult. On the principle of keeping one's friends close and one's rivals even closer, Lincoln chose Seward as secretary of state, Edward Bates as attorney general, Simon Cameron as secretary of war, and Salmon Chase as secretary of the Treasury. When Seward objected to Chase's selection and threatened to withdraw, Lincoln persuaded him to stay. More unfortunate was Lincoln's decision to turn his journey to Washington into a twelve-day railroad tour of northern towns and cities. Not wanting to add fuel to the fire, Lincoln addressed the trackside crowds with platitudinous speeches which raised concerns that he really was the unexceptional provincial his critics had always claimed. As the train headed south, recurring reports about planned assassination attempts gained more credibility, compelling a sudden change of schedule that left the president-elect to arrive in Washington secretly and ignominiously in the predawn hours of February 23—"like a thief in the night," he ruefully remarked.[31]

The situation in the capital was dismal. Since the election nearly four months earlier, almost half of the slaveholding states had seceded from the Union, formed their own country, and begun seizing federal property within their own borders. No clear policy had been established about the collection of customs duties in ports where the new Confederacy now claimed full authority, or about the disposition of what federal assets remained in Union hands—most auspiciously, Fort Sumter, perched on a man-made island in Charleston harbor. Yet Lincoln had some cause for hope. After buckling in the immediate aftermath of the presidential elections, Unionists had made a strong comeback in the Border South. Virginia and Missouri, as well as Arkansas, had elected Unionist majorities to their state conventions called to consider secession. Given the choice over calling a convention, voters in North Carolina (by a narrow margin) and Tennessee (by a four-to-one majority) rejected the idea. Lincoln's repudiation of the Crittenden compromise and the failure of the Virginia peace conference had somewhat undermined "conditional Unionist" sentiment in the upper South. Much like the conditional secessionists of the cotton states, large numbers of antisecessionists elsewhere would consider any armed intervention by the federal government an act of invasion. But short of taking any overt military action against the South, Lincoln still had some room in which to operate, and he thought that his inaugural address could well determine the outcome. With input from Seward and from a close Illinois adviser, Orville Browning, Lincoln tried to compose a message that would help preserve the Union without abdicating his duty to assert federal authority. At the very last minute, he revised his text, on Seward's advice, to emphasize conciliation.[32]

March 4 dawned cold and gloomy in Washington, but a crowd estimated at twenty-five thousand turned up at the Capitol for the inauguration ceremonies, and bright sunshine broke through at noon, just as President Lincoln began his speech. Looking stately beneath a newly grown beard, Lincoln reversed the usual order and began the ceremonies by taking the oath of office from a man he considered an arch fiend (the feeling was mutual), Chief Justice Roger Brooke Taney. Then, with an eloquence that announced the lifting of the Pierce-Buchanan era's rhetorical fog, Lincoln developed a series of points and counterpoints about slavery and the Constitution, and defended the democracy that the southern disunionists had spurned and traduced.

As president, he said, he would refuse "directly or indirectly, to interfere with the institution of slavery in the States where it exists," but he would not countenance secession. He would enforce the constitutional obligation to return fugitive slaves, but he would also "hold, occupy, and possess the property and places belonging to the government, and . . . collect the duties and imposts." He would not deny "the very high respect and consideration" due Supreme Court rulings on constitutional questions (did Taney squirm at this obvious reference to *Dred Scott?*), but he would not allow "erroneous" decisions and their "evil effect" to fix irrevocably "the policy of the government upon vital questions, affecting the whole people." In a moving peroration, Lincoln pleaded with his native Border

South and men of patriotic goodwill everywhere. "I am loth to close," he said. "We are not enemies, but friends. We must not be enemies. Though passion may have strained, it must not break our bonds of affection. The mystic chords of memory, stretching from every battle-field, and patriot grave, to every living heart and hearthstone, all over this broad land, will yet swell the chorus of the Union, when again touched, as surely they will be, by the better angels of our nature."[33]

The speech was a blend of political cunning and bedrock idealism, a style of leadership that Lincoln had been mastering since 1858. On the crucial matter of reasserting the government's authority over forts, customs houses, mints, and armories appropriated by the Confederates, he remained purposefully vague. Anything more specific could easily be regarded as a provocation, which would undermine his efforts to keep the Border South from seceding. A shrewd court-room and political strategist thrown into a national crisis, Lincoln understood that what he needed above all else was time, time to get his White House in order, to persuade the persuadable of his moderation, and, if possible, to permit the secession fever finally to break. He made the point explicitly in his address: "Nothing valuable can be lost by taking time."

Yet Lincoln did not rely simply on temporizing and artful ambiguity. The speech's evocations of the Union and "the better angels of our nature" were as lofty an appeal to nationalist principles as any since the days of Webster and Jackson. And above and beyond the slavery issue, Lincoln unflinchingly defended certain basic ideals of freedom and democratic government, which he asserted he had been elected to vindicate. There was, he said, a single "substantial dispute" in the sectional crisis: "[o]ne section of our country believes slavery is *right*, and ought to be extended, while the other believes it is *wrong*, and ought not to be extended." There could be no doubt about where Lincoln stood, and where his administration would stand, on that fundamental moral question. But regardless of that, the only just and legitimate way to settle the matter, Lincoln insisted (with a direct echo of Thomas Jefferson's first inaugural address), was through a deliberate democratic decision by the nation's citizenry:

> Why should there not be a patient confidence in the ultimate justice of the people? Is there any better, or equal hope, in the world? In our present differences, is either party without faith of being in the right? If the Almighty Ruler of nations, with his eternal truth and justice, be on your side of the North, or on yours of the South, that truth, and that justice, will surely prevail, by the judgment of this great tribunal, the American people.

The future of American democracy, the best hope in the world, would rise or fall on whether secession—"the essence of anarchy"—succeeded or failed.

Reactions to the address encouraged the new president. Not surprisingly, most Republicans applauded its mixture of moderation and adamancy, while Confederates and their supporters denounced it, either as an outright declaration of civil war—"couched in the cool, unimpassioned, deliberate language of the fanatic," the *Richmond Enquirer* claimed—or as a cleverly Delphic contrivance, "concealing dark designs, iniquitous and flagitious." But anxious Wall Street Republicans, and even some northern Democrats, who had pushed for concilia- tion found the speech reassuring. (One Wall Streeter named H. D. Faulkner reported to Lincoln that he heard almost unanimous praise from his friends, ranging from a Breckinridge Democrat who called the speech "first rate . . . and full of faith" to an old Silver Gray who thought it "splendid.") Moderates in the upper South worried over its lack of specifics, but hailed what the *Spectator* of Staunton, Virginia, called its "frank and conciliatory" tone. Contrary to the secessionists' diatribes, they insisted, Lincoln's speech was *"not a war message"* and was "not unfriendly to the South."[34]

More than Lincoln knew, however, time was running out. On inauguration day, Buchanan's departing secretary of war, Joseph Holt, received an alarming dispatch, dated February 28, from Major Robert Anderson, commander of the federal forces at Fort Sumter. Holt quietly put it aside for the incoming adminis- tration. Anderson reported it would take a force of at least twenty thousand troops to fight their way into Charleston harbor and relieve the weary garrison. The Union, it seemed, could evacuate Sumter—repudiating Lincoln's vows on the Capitol steps—or it could initiate a war with a massive and bloody show of force that was bound to unite the entire South and divide the North.[35]

The next morning, Lincoln walked into his White House office for his first full day's work as president and found Major Anderson's dispatch lying on his desk.

THE SLAVEHOLDERS' REBELLION

The back-and-forth scheming over Fort Sumter lasted for six weeks and pitted Lincoln against members of his own cabinet as well as against Jefferson Davis. Winfield Scott, now general-in-chief of the U.S. Army, told Lincoln and his advisers that there were not enough ships and men available to save Sumter and that the fort ought to be evacuated. All but Treasury Secretary Salmon Chase (who favored relieving the fort if it could be done without risking war) and Post- master General Montgomery Blair (who wanted to hold the fort under any cir- cumstances) agreed with Scott. Secretary of State Seward, carrying over both his conciliatory strategy with the South and his ambition to undermine Lincoln's authority, secretly advised a group of Confederate commissioners that the government would indeed abandon Sumter. Such an act of generosity and goodwill, Seward reasoned, would impress the Border South and encourage Unionists within the seceded states.[36]

Northern newspapers, including some that were pro-Democratic, expressed outrage when reports of Sumter's imminent evacuation leaked out. Lincoln, under pressure, agreed with Blair that any display of charity over Sumter would only look like a sign of weakness and embolden the rebels. His position hardened after Blair's father, the old Jacksonian Francis Blair, paid a personal visit to tell him, heatedly, that a surrender of Sumter would be "virtually a surrender of the Union" and might even constitute treason. But the impasse within the White House only broke on March 28, when General Scott, overplaying his hand, urged the evacuation of both Fort Sumter and Fort Pickens in Pensacola Bay, and cited the political arguments favored by Seward as well as military considerations. Montgomery Blair accused the general of "playing politician," and most of the cabinet swung over in favor of resupplying Sumter.[37]

Seward, isolated, switched his ground and told Lincoln that the abandonment of Sumter linked with a defense of Pickens would change the focus of the showdown from slavery to Union. After personally ordering a large ship bound for Sumter diverted to Pickens, the secretary of state sent an astonishing note to Lincoln, demanding, in effect, that he, Seward, be given command over the situation. Lincoln rejected the suggestions firmly, but not wanting to antagonize Seward and lose his services, he kept the exchange private. On April 4, at the chastened Seward's prompting, Lincoln met with a Virginia Unionist to discuss a deal whereby Sumter would be abandoned in exchange for adjournment of the Virginia secession convention. The meeting was fruitless, and Lincoln ordered that the Sumter resupply mission commence.[38]

Plans for that mission had been evolving for weeks. Now, instead of trying to reinforce Sumter with an all-out assault, the Union would send unarmed supply boats out to the fort, with warships standing by in case shooting started. If the Confederates tried to halt the mission, they would bear the burden of having started hostilities—and if they did not, the Union would win a great symbolic victory. On April 6, Lincoln dispatched an envoy to Charleston to inform Governor Francis Pickens of the impending resupply effort, stating that if the mission was allowed to proceed unharmed, "no effort to throw in men, arms, or ammunition will be made, without further notice, [except] in case of an attack on the Fort."[39]

The focus now shifted to Jefferson Davis's provisional presidential office in Montgomery. Weeks earlier, Davis had placed the newly commissioned Confederate General Pierre G. T. Beauregard in command of the thousands of militia in Charleston and of the harbor defense works that menaced the Yankee fort. On March 9, Beauregard received orders to prevent Sumter's resupply, on the premise that, once strengthened, the Union forces would rain ruin on

Charleston. But now Lincoln had undercut that rationale with his humanitarian supply-boat scheme.

Like Lincoln, Davis was under tremendous pressure to act. The weeks of waiting had taken their toll, leading some southern newspapers to denounce the new government's "do-nothing" policy and to despair for southern independence. Veteran fire-eaters were especially vociferous, arguing that a show of military might was essential to the Confederate cause. Virginia secessionists told their Charleston allies that the surest way to bring the Old Dominion and the rest of the border states into the fold would be to strike a blow. "The shedding of blood," the extremist eminence Edmund Ruffin, now living in Charleston, wrote in his diary, "will serve to change many voters in the hesitating states, from the submission or procrastinating ranks, to the zealous for immediate secession." It mattered little which side fired the first shot, so long as the shot was fired. If only South Carolina and the Davis government would vindicate the South's honor, then all of the slaveholding states would rally to the Confederate banner.[40]

The fire-eaters' predictions would prove accurate soon enough. Informed of Lincoln's resupply mission, Davis interpreted it as an attempt to relieve Fort Sumter by force. He at once drafted orders to Beauregard, instructing him to demand the fort's immediate surrender and, if Major Anderson refused, to reduce it. On April 9, Davis's cabinet endorsed the order; two days later, Anderson, as expected, turned Beauregard down, remarking in passing that if help did not arrive within a few days, he and his men would be starved out. Taking Anderson's remark as confirmation that the Yankee reinforcements would be arriving soon, Davis and Beauregard moved quickly. Final orders were telegraphed from Montgomery: confirm Anderson's commitment to abandon Sumter or else attack the fort. During the night of April 11–12, the Confederate forces moved into battle position. Anderson attempted to stall for time by telling Beauregard's aides that he would leave on April 15, but only if the Confederates agreed to a host of conditions. At 3:20 A.M. on April 12, the aides informed Anderson that his reply was insufficient and that Beauregard's mortars would open fire in one hour's time. Then the aides returned to their boat and went directly to one of the surrounding Confederate batteries on Fort Johnson, at the tip of James Island.

Might this showdown have been prevented or at least forestalled? With full knowledge of all that followed the events at Fort Sumter, Americans have sought to find some point where events might have taken a different course, and affix blame accordingly. Do not Lincoln and his Republican allies bear responsibility for defeating the Crittenden compromise, thereby ensuring secession by the Deep South? Had Alexander Stephens and other moderates taken a stronger and better-organized stand against disunion, might the fire-eater juggernaut have been slowed or even halted? If true statesmen, on the order of Clay and Webster, had been in command of events instead of sectional politicians, would not the Union have been saved once again?

Like most counterfactual inquiries, these questions are based on premises easily distorted by hindsight. Over the winter of 1860–61, few Americans had the slightest conception of the mass butchery that would follow secession. The more truculent southerners asserted that the pencil-necked mongrel Yankees would not put up a real fight, and that if they tried to, they would be quickly vanquished with little loss of life. "You may slap a Yankee in the face and he'll go off and sue you," one politician claimed, "but he wont fight!" South Carolina's Senator James Chesnut, husband of the subsequently famous diarist Mary Chesnut, said that he would personally drink all of the blood that would be shed as a result of secession. Northerners were no less certain that, by the grace of God, any war against the backward South would be short and glorious. (One exception, Harriet Beecher Stowe, foresaw that the millennial *"last* struggle for liberty" would be "a long pull.") With this sense of what in retrospect looks almost like blitheness about the consequences of secession and of resisting it, there is little wonder that the pro-compromise forces did not exert more influence.[41]

In any case, by 1861, no effort at compromise could have long bridged the chasm in the American political soul. That chasm was deep before 1856, when the Republicans with their revolutionary antislavery ideology emerged as the chief opposition to the pro-Nebraska Democrats and their southern allies. Subsequent polarizing events—*Dred Scott*, the struggle over Lecompton, the Democrats' sectional debacles—flowed directly from the Republicans' rise. So long as the Republicans expanded their following and stayed true to their basic principles—that slavery was morally wrong, that it was an oligarchic system that perverted democracy, and that its expansion had to be halted—the ultimate clash between North and South was unavoidable. In Abraham Lincoln, the party found a leader who would prove both popular and principled. Once Lincoln was elected president, there was, for the Deep South, no turning back from secession, which was well under way before any compromise proposals arose.

Fittingly, the crisis came down to a stand-off in Charleston, spiritual capital of the slaveholders' cause in its purest form, where for more than thirty years the ideals proclaimed by John C. Calhoun had evolved into ideals of the Confederacy. And, fittingly, a well-known survivor of roughly Calhoun's own generation was on the scene. In 1823, as a young Virginia state senator, Edmund Ruffin had refused to support Calhoun for the presidency, as Calhoun was too much the nationalist. Only in succeeding years did the South Carolinian, in Ruffin's eyes, see the light and emerge as a great spokesman for southern rights and slavery. At Calhoun's death in 1850, Ruffin joined with younger pro-slavery extremists who picked up the torch, and he emerged as one of the elder statesmen of the secessionist movement. In 1861, the glorious moment come round at last—Ruffin enlisted, at age sixty-seven, as a private in a Charleston militia company, the Palmetto Guards. At 4:30 on the morning of April 12, he stood at the east mortar battery of Fort Johnson, unmistakable with his long white mane, his homespun suit with a fresh insignia, and his hat with a rebel blue cockade. General Beauregard had selected the Palmettos to fire the first shot at Sumter, and the company in turn handed the honors over to Ruffin, who was "highly gratified by the compliment, & delighted to perform the service—which I did." Ruffin's shell exploded on Sumter's parapet; nearby Confederate batteries let loose their fire; and the War of the Rebellion had begun.[42]

EPILOGUE

On the morning of June 17, 1865, Edmund Ruffin sat in his study at his Virginia estate, Redmoor, placed the muzzle of his loaded rifle into his mouth and, with the aid of a forked stick, forced the trigger.

After the attack on Fort Sumter pushed reluctant Virginia to secede from the Union, Ruffin had happily returned home to watch the war. But now all of the Confederate armies had surrendered; one of Ruffin's sons had been killed in action; Union soldiers had pillaged Ruffin's plantations; and all of his slaves had run away forever. Ruffin's health was failing, and he was nearly deaf—but worst of all, he wrote in his diary, he himself had been rendered, with the Union's victory, "a helpless & hopeless slave, under the irresistible oppression of the most unscrupulous, vile, & abhorred of rulers." For weeks, he had struggled with the Bible and finally concluded that suicide, unlike murder, was no sin. After writing out instructions to his family that his body be buried in hallowed South Carolina, he rose from his breakfast table, walked upstairs, and rigged his rifle.[1]

Unexpected visitors at the front door interrupted him, and Ruffin waited until they left. After making one last diary entry, he resumed his final task—but though the firing cap exploded, the bullet remained in its chamber. Hearing the noise, his daughter-in-law frantically fetched her husband, and the two dashed upstairs, as another shot rang out. Inside the study, they found Ruffin, his head blown to pieces, the rest of him seated bolt upright in his chair.

The final words in his diary read, "And now, with my latest writing & utterance, & with what will be near to my last breath, I here repeat, & would willingly proclaim, my unmitigated hatred to Yankee rule—to all political, social, & business connection with Yankees, & to the perfidious, malignant, & vile Yankee race. Edmund Ruffin sen. Kept waiting by successive visitors to my son, until their departure at 12.15 P.M." The man who had fired the first shot of the rebellion had fired the symbolic last shot as well.[2]

The gruesome war that killed the Confederacy settled some of the basic issues that attended the rise of American democracy. Slavery was abolished. Secession was disgraced. A southern rural vision of formally equal and independent white men, their equality and independence made possible by the bondage of blacks, was destroyed. So was another, older southern vision, of superior, aristocratic slaveholders ruling virtuously and wisely over a grateful people, slave and free, black and white. The free-labor North with its very different democracy—denounced by southerners on the eve of the war as a motley throng of infidels, free lovers, and panderers who insisted that "equality is the right of man" and believed government should be run by "the heels" instead of "the head of the society"—had won the Second American Revolution. Out of that revolution emerged a transformed nation, no longer referred to as the Union or, as in common prewar parlance, in the plural sense—the United States *are*—but in the singular—the United States *is*. That is what President Lincoln had promised in his address at Gettysburg in 1863, when he said that the war would bring "a new birth of freedom" to a "nation, conceived in Liberty, and dedicated to the proposition that all men are created equal."[3]

The paradox, of course, is that this second revolution, as well as part of the effort to halt it, had been inspired by the words of a southern slaveholder who had helped lead the first revolution. As he transformed himself from a Henry Clay Whig to a Republican to a national leader, Lincoln found himself pulled more than ever to the ideas and the figure of Thomas Jefferson. "All honor to Jefferson," he wrote in 1859, who in the midst of the War for Independence had had the "coolness, forecast, and capacity" to introduce the great truth of equality, "applicable to all men and all times," that would forever stand as "a rebuke and a stumbling block to . . . re-appearing tyranny and oppression." For all of his inconsistencies and hypocrisies, Jefferson had not only pronounced what Lincoln called "the definitions and axioms of free society," but, in the 1790s and after, had put them into practice, winning over, encouraging, and giving a measure of real political influence to the city and country democracies that had emerged out of the American Revolution.[4]

That Jefferson also won over so many of his fellow slaveholding planters, with his Declaration of Independence later cited by Jefferson Davis, has confused later writers, and persuaded some that the protection of slavery was the hidden motive behind Jeffersonian democracy. But as the historian and biographer James Parton observed in 1867, Jefferson was no defender of slavery, and the paradox surrounding his politics was really a fateful ambiguity: "The Southern aristocrat saw in Jefferson the sovereignty of his State; the 'smutched artificer' of the North gloried in Jefferson as the champion of the rights of man." Parton was too constrictive. Some of those "smutched artificers" were southern whites who fought the "aristocrats" for widened political rights, just as some were blacks, slave and free, who fought to end American bondage. Females and males would champion the rights of woman as well as man. These Americans, taking Jefferson at his word, would expand the principles and practices of political democracy beyond what even Jefferson had envisaged.[5]

Still, Parton's basic point holds. By the 1840s and 1850s, two distinctive democracies, northern and southern, had finally arisen out of the strivings of the city and country democrats of the infant republic. The southern democracy enshrined slavery as the basis for white men's political equality (except for those disunionists who recoiled at any sort of equality). In national politics, southern democrats proclaimed (when it was convenient) what they called the Jeffersonian idea of state sovereignty, but only as filtered through the writings of Jefferson's factional adversaries, the Old Republicans, through the refractory writings of schismatic Federalists, and then through the pro-slavery stalwart John C. Calhoun. The northern democrats thought slavery a moral abomination that denied the basic humanity of blacks and whose expansion threatened white men's political equality (to say nothing, as free blacks and a minority of whites charged, of full political equality for all men). They stood, forthrightly, for Jeffersonian ideas about the rights of man, including free speech, which southern democrats perforce had to curtail.

Neither of these democracies was fully formed at the nation's founding. Federalism's defeat at the hands of the Jeffersonian Republicans, along with a myriad of reform efforts at the state and local level, undid many of the prevailing hierarchical political assumptions that had survived the eighteenth century. Thereafter, the largest vehicle for expanding democracy became the flawed Jackson Democracy. Organized as a movement of reform to eliminate a perceived recrudescence of privilege, the Jacksonians combined the evolving city and country democracies into a national political force. They also created a new kind of political party, more egalitarian in its institutions and its ideals than any that had preceded it, unabashed in its disciplined pursuit of power, dedicated to securing the sovereignty that, as its chief architect Martin Van Buren observed, "belongs inalienably to the people." Yet Jackson and Van Buren's Democracy had its contradictions as well, which brought, initially, the great mass of southern planters into its ranks. Out of that revived coalition of "Southern aristocrats" and "smutched artificers"—what Van Buren called the alliance of planters and "plain republicans"—the Jacksonians believed that the "monarchical spirit" of established, monied privilege could be subdued.[6]

Tensions within the original Jackson coalition quickly undermined its unity, leading to the departure of Calhoun and the nullifiers, and to the defection of northern conservatives and wealthy southern planters over Jackson's banking and currency policies. Yet the Jacksonians were hardly consistent egalitarians, nor did they encompass all of the democratic impulses that were breaking out in the 1830s. Above all, in order to preserve the spirit of the Missouri Compromise and their party's intersectional unity, the Jacksonians joined in the attack on the radical abolitionists and bent over backward to placate southern outrage, short of disunion, at attacks on slavery. The strategy was partly successful, but it could neither prevent a small number of northern antislavery Democrats from bolting the party in disgust, nor halt the defection of more southern planters once the Yankee Van Buren became the Democracy's standard-bearer. Nor could it halt the emergence of a new-style Whig opposition more reconciled to political democracy than old-guard conservatives, and adept at turning the programs of government-supported economic development that Jacksonians had held constitutionally suspect into manifestos for the common man. In the North, these new-school Whigs, combining secular humanitarianism and the moral imperatives of the Second Great Awakening, leaned more heavily than the Jacksonians to antislavery politics and to various crusades for moral reform.

Two factors—the expansionist pursuit of Jefferson's empire of liberty, and the extraordinary continued growth of plantation slavery thanks to the cotton revolution—upset the Democratic and Whig Parties that had formed by 1840, and hastened the growth of the antagonistic northern and southern democracies. Americans experienced the crack-up primarily as a political crisis, about whether slavery would be allowed to interfere with democratic rights—or, alternatively, whether northern tyranny would be allowed to interfere with southern democracy. Over those questions, which encompassed clashes over northern free labor and southern slavery, the political system began falling apart in the mid-1840s. First the Wilmot Proviso and the Free Soil revolt temporarily split the Democracy; then the Whig Party collapsed under the weight of sectional discord; and finally a new northern Republican coalition emerged—its name borrowed from Jefferson's old party—consisting of northern antislavery Whigs, Free Soil Democrats, and the long-beleaguered political abolitionists. After the demise of what remained of the Jackson Democracy over the struggles in Kansas in the late 1850s, Americans' differences became so profound that they could not be settled at the ballot box, but only on the battlefield.

Before his election in 1860, Lincoln looked back over this history to the time of the Federalists and Jeffersonians and likened it to a brawl between two drunks, in which one man manages to fight his way into the greatcoat of the other, and vice versa: "If the two leading parties of this day are really identical with the two in the days of Jefferson and Adams, they have performed about the same feat as the two drunken men." Like the old-line Federalists, and unlike the party of its supposed founder Jefferson, he explained, "the so-called democracy of to-day" — meaning the slaveholder-dominated Democratic Party — "hold the *liberty* of one man to be absolutely nothing, when in conflict with another man's right of *property*." On the contrary, he explained, Republicans "are for both the *man* and the *dollar*; but in cases in conflict, the man *before* the dollar" — devoted, as Jefferson was, "to the *personal* rights of men, holding the rights of *property* to be secondary only, and greatly inferior."

Lincoln then turned to the politics of his own time and observed that it would be difficult "to save the principles of Jefferson from total overthrow in this nation" when slaveholders and their apologists either pronounced them "glittering generalities" and "self-evident lies," or argued that they applied only to "superior races." These expressions had the same objective: "supplanting the principles of free government, and restoring those of classification, caste, and legitimacy. They would delight a convocation of crowned heads, plotting against the people. They are the van-guard — the miners, and sappers — of returning despotism. We must repulse them, or they will subjugate us."[7] Lincoln did repulse them, and saved Jefferson's principles as he saw them — though at the cost of more than six hundred thousand American lives.

How would the victors define and implement democracy, now that secession and slavery were crushed and the South's peculiar democracy lay in ruins? Lincoln was murdered before he could make his own thinking plain and test it against hard realities. Other Americans, North and South, pressed ahead with their own solutions.

One democratic proposal came from Garrison Frazier, a black Baptist preacher in Georgia, who had been a slave for sixty years before he purchased his freedom for a thousand dollars in 1857. At an official meeting with Secretary of War Edwin Stanton and General William Tecumseh Sherman in Savannah, after the city was safely in Union hands, Frazier, speaking on behalf of a group of twenty prominent local blacks, replied to questions about bondage, freedom, the past, and the future. What was slavery? "[R]eceiving by *irresistible power*, the work of another man, and not by his *consent*," Frazier said. And freedom? Frazier defined it as "placing us where we could reap the fruit of our own labor, take care of ourselves and assist the Government in maintaining our freedom." The minister unhesitatingly called the South "the aggressor" in the war, given that "President Lincoln was elected President by the majority of the United States, which guaranteed him the right of holding that office and exercising that right over the whole United States," after which "the South rebelled." Frazier concluded that the best way to ensure the ex-slaves' freedom was "to have land, and turn it and till it by our own labor."[8]

Hundreds of miles to the North, a now largely forgotten Jacksonian-era labor leader read Frazier's remarks in a newspaper and heartily approved—and hinted at the links between the stripling democracy of the 1820s and 1830s and the politics of the postwar era. William Heighton had been the pivotal intellectual and political leader in the transformation of Philadelphia's old city democracy into an independent but broadly pro-Jackson labor movement. He had disappeared in the early 1830s, only to resurface in 1865, living across the Delaware River in rural Elmer, New Jersey. There the abolitionist and former member of John Brown's Secret Six, George L. Stearns, tracked him down and asked for his ideas about "the reconstruction of the social and political institutions of the Rebel States." Stearns immediately published Heighton's reply (alongside remarks by Wendell Phillips, Frederick Douglass, and other radical antislavery leaders) in a pamphlet entitled *The Equality of All Men before the Law Claimed and Defended.*[9]

Heighton, now in his midsixties, had retained his old radical fire. He still railed against "money rule" and "MONOPOLIES," and the slavery of wages, and he upheld the doctrine that all "[a]ll human beings have an *equal* right" to life, liberty, and "*property* in the common elements of nature—light, air, water, and the land." Yet Heighton also saw the connections between those older ideas and the challenge of what he, like others, had begun calling "reconstruction." Noting Garrison Frazier's "uncommon shrewdness and good sense," Heighton laid out a two-step plan for rebuilding southern democracy. First, fair and universal elections: "[a] corrupt use of the ballot-box is not Democracy, but an aristocracy (money rule) of the most odious kind." Second, the redistribution of land: "[t]he landed estates . . . of all the prominent and active rebels, the great chiefs, should be confiscated and broken up," a portion of it given to their heirs, and "an equal homestead should be apportioned to each colored family." The ex-slaves deserved the land, having cleared and improved it by their own labor, Heighton asserted. More than that, "[i]mmense landed estates in a few hands (baronies) the world over, are death to Democracy. If three or four men own a whole country, they will be its governors . . . even under republican forms."[10]

Heighton's updating of his Jacksonian labor radicalism as Reconstruction radicalism was but one democratic response to the postwar political situation. The Confederacy's defeat cracked open all sorts of ideas about how equality might best be expanded—or curtailed—in the new era, especially in the North. For Elizabeth Cady Stanton, an active Lincoln Republican in 1860, and her widening circle of allies, it was a signal to press harder for the cause that Stanton had helped ignite at Seneca Falls in 1848, in the cauldron of the Free Soil revolt. ("Suffice it, therefore, to say," the veteran radical abolitionist Lydia Maria Child would write, "either the theory of our government is *false*, or women have a right to vote.") For a Massachusetts machinist, antislavery campaigner, and trade unionist named Ira Steward, his newfound ally Wendell Phillips, and organized wage earners across the North, it was time to undertake the creation of a new labor movement, based on the charge that "something of slavery" persisted in the rapidly industrializing North. Opponents of these and other northern stirrings recoiled with horror at a democracy that seemed to be boiling over, and they began challenging, in essays, editorials, and proposed legislation, the most basic of democratic principles. Charles Francis Adams's son, Charles Jr., would sneer in 1869, in an article heavy with hostility toward the lowly, that "Universal Suffrage can only mean in plain English the government of ignorance and vice."[11]

For the immediate future, the problems of southern Reconstruction were paramount—and deeply divisive. William Heighton's anti-aristocratic radicalism was one legacy of the old Jacksonian movement. So was the obstructionism of Andrew Johnson, an ex-cobbler and true-blue yeoman Democrat from East Tennessee who would prove that while he despised the planter oligarchy, he despised the freedmen even more. Among the ascendant northern Republicans, the fractiousness that Lincoln had handled so masterfully reasserted itself under President Johnson, dividing radicals like Thaddeus Stevens (who favored land distribution) against a panoply of northern moderates and conservatives. Within the South, alongside a small new class of black political and social leaders, old-line Whigs—men who had never fully adjusted to the democratizing trends of the prewar era—grabbed the mantle of Unionism, loyalty, and leadership. And everywhere in the fallen Confederacy there were southern whites, ex-slaveholders and ordinary farmers alike, who were no more reconciled to the new order than Edmund Ruffin had been, but who carried on anyway, in sullen detachment or in night-riding fury, vowing one day to redeem the South from Yankee "Black Republican" rule. "I hates the Yankee nation/And everything they do," ran one popular song ostensibly written by an ex-Confederate, "I hates the Declaration/Of Independence too/I hates the glorious Union—'Tis dripping with our blood/ And I hates their striped banner,/I fit it all I could."[12]

The collision of hopes and despairs that marked the development of American democracy after 1865 would take decades to settle, and in some respects, they remain unsettled 140 years later. Not long after the war ended, an aborted trial dramatized—and a photograph survives to illustrate—the enormous challenges that lay ahead.

On May 10, 1865, Jefferson Davis was captured by U.S. Army forces near Irwinsville in southern Georgia, as he tried to flee to Texas. Imprisoned under military guard at Fort Monroe in Virginia, Davis faced a charge of treason for levying war against the United States, but the government decided he would have to be tried by a civil court. After nearly four years of indecision and delay (two of which Davis spent behind bars), the case was finally dropped. Davis, who had wanted to use the trial to justify secession, would live for another twenty years, enough time for him to complete and publish his two-volume recollection, *The Rise and Fall of the Confederate Government*. Here, in what is still the most influential presidential memoir in American history, Davis blamed many others (but himself not at all) for the Confederacy's defeat and established the myth that slavery had nothing to do with secession—a crucial part of the larger, then-emerging myth of the Lost Cause.[13]

Jefferson Davis got his say, though not his trial. Yet the federal court in Virginia had made full preparations for that trial, to the point of empanelling thirteen men to decide the case—twelve petit jurors plus one alternate, all respectable citizens of the Commonwealth of Virginia. Seven were black. Even today, the picture that was made of the twelve proud men startles, inspires, provokes.[14] It affirms that the revolution caused by the rise of American democracy had created realities and possibilities scarcely imaginable five years earlier. Would those new realities endure and those possibilities flourish? On the outcome relied the fate of what Thomas Jefferson and Abraham Lincoln had called the world's best hope.

NOTES

In direct quotations, I have kept the original spelling and punctuation as often as possible, to preserve the peculiar flavor of my subjects' writing. For example, where Thomas Jefferson wrote "it's" instead of "its" when "its" is proper modern usage (as he habitually did) or where Andrew Jackson spelled "corroded" as "coroded," I have allowed Jefferson's and Jackson's versions to stand. Here and there, to clarify obscure passages, I have corrected the original, as marked in brackets. Primary materials quoted from printed editions follow the editors' style.

ABBREVIATIONS USED IN NOTES

AC—*Annals of Congress*

AHR—*American Historical Review*

ANB—John A. Garraty and Mark Carnes, eds. *American National Biography* (New York, 1999)

CAJ—John Spencer Bassett, ed., *Correspondence of Andrew Jackson* (Washington, DC, 1926–35)

CG—*Congressional Globe*

CWAL—Roy P. Basler, ed., *The Collected Works of Abraham Lincoln* (New Brunswick, NJ, 1953)

DR—*The United States Magazine and Democratic Review*

HL—Huntington Library, San Marino, CA

HSP—Historical Society of Pennsylvania

HU—Houghton Library, Harvard University

JAH—*Journal of American History*

JER—*Journal of the Early Republic*

JQAD—Charles Francis Adams, ed., *Memoirs of John Quincy Adams, Comprising Portions of His Diary from 1795 to 1848* (Philadelphia, 1874–77)

JSH—*Journal of Southern History*

LC—Library of Congress

LoV—Library of Virginia (formerly Virginia State Library)

MHS—Massachusetts Historical Society

NA—National Archives

NWR — *Niles' Weekly Register*

NYPL — New York Public Library

N-YHS — New-York Historical Society

PAH — Harold C. Syrett and Jacob E. Cooke, eds., *The Papers of Alexander Hamilton* (New York, 1967–87)

PAJ — Sam B. Smith, Harriet Chappell Owsley, et al., eds., *The Papers of Andrew Jackson* (Knoxville, TN, 1980–)

PHC — John F. Hopkins et al., eds., *The Papers of Henry Clay* (Lexington, KY, 1959–92)

PJCC — Robert L. Meriwether et al., eds., *The Papers of John C. Calhoun* (Columbia, SC, 1959–2003)

PJM — William T. Hutchinson and William M.E. Rachal, eds., *The Papers of James Madison* (Chicago, 1962–91).

PJMP — Robert A. Rutland et al., *The Papers of James Madison: Presidential Series* (Charlottesville, 1984–)

PTJ — Julian P. Boyd et al., eds., *The Papers of Thomas Jefferson* (Princeton, NJ, 1950–)

PU — Princeton University Library

Richardson — James D. Richardson, ed., *A Compilation of the Messages and Papers of the Presidents* (1897; Washington, DC, 1910)

RD — *Register of Debates in Congress*

S & I — Arthur M. Schlesinger Jr. and Fred L. Israel, eds., *History of American Presidential Elections, 1789–1968* (1971; New York, 1985)

SPCP — John Niven, ed., *Salmon P. Chase Papers: Microform Edition* (Frederick, MD, 1987).

Thorpe — Francis N. Thorpe, *The Federal and State Constitutions: Colonial Charters and Other Organic Laws of the States, Territories, and Colonies Now or Heretofore Forming the United States of America* (Washington, DC, 1909)

TJC — Thomas Jefferson Papers, Library of Congress

VBP — Martin Van Buren Papers, Library of Congress

WMQ — *William and Mary Quarterly*, 3rd series

PREFACE

1. Cabot to Timothy Pickering, Feb. 14, 1804, in Henry Adams, ed., *Documents Relating to New England Federalism, 1800–1815* (Boston, 1877), 346.

2. James Otis, *The Rights of the British Colonies Asserted and Proved* (Boston, 1764), 12.

3. Dixon Ryan Fox, *The Decline of Aristocracy in the Politics of New York, 1801–1840* (New York, 1919); J. Franklin Jameson, *The American Revolution Considered as a Social Movement* (Princeton, 1926); Henry Adams, *History of the United States during the Administrations of Thomas Jefferson and James Madison* (1889–91; New York, 1986); Charles A. Beard and Mary R. Beard, *The Rise of American Civilization* (New York, 1927); Frederick Jackson Turner, *The United States, 1830–1860: The Nation and Its Sections* (New York, 1935); Arthur M. Schlesinger Jr., *The Age of Jackson* (Boston, 1945) (quotation on 522); Richard Hofstadter, *The Idea of a Party System: The Rise of Legitimate Opposition in the United States, 1780–1840* (Berkeley, 1969); Gordon S. Wood, *The Radicalism of the American Revolution* (New York, 1992).

4. See, above all, Charles Sellers's formidable *Market Revolution: Jacksonian America, 1815–1846* (New York, 1991).

5. On the background to this mental universe, with enormous implications for understanding nineteenth-century politics, see Gordon S. Wood, "Conspiracy and the Paranoid Style: Causality and Deceit in the Eighteenth Century," *WMQ*, 39 (1982): 401–41. The literature on the republican ideology Wood describes is due in no small part to the influence of Wood's *Creation of the American Republic* (Chapel Hill, 1969). For a stimulating study of the ideology's persistence into the 1830s, see Major L. Wilson, "The Country versus the Court: A Republican Consensus and Party Debate in the Bank War," *JER*, 15 (1995): 619–47. I by no means wish to imply that American political thinking did not change

between 1787 and 1840. The rise of American democracy was, in fact, the most crucial change of all. But I also see democracy developing within the context of older ways of thinking that persisted long after 1787 and that marked ideas all across the mainstream political spectrum. Indeed, there is persuasive evidence that the older patterns persisted long after 1860. For an important account of these and related matters in later nineteenth- and early-twentieth-century politics, see Richard L. McCormick, "The Discovery That Business Corrupts Politics: A Reappraisal of the Origins of Progressivism," in *The Party Period and Public Policy: American Politics from the Age of Jackson to the Progressive Era* (New York, 1986), 311–56.

PROLOGUE

1. Harry R. Warfel, ed., *Letters of Noah Webster* (New York, 1953), 449. A fine brief assessment of Webster's politics appears in Joseph J. Ellis, *After the Revolution: Portraits of Early American Culture* (New York, 1979), 161–212 (description of Webster on porch quoted on 161).
2. Emily Ellsworth Ford Skeel, ed., *Notes on the Life of Noah Webster* (New York, 1912), 2: 351–3; Noah Webster, *Letter to the Hon. Daniel Webster, on the Political Affairs of the United States* (Philadelphia, 1837); Warfel, *Letters*, 478–504, 511–2.
3. William Kent, *Memoirs and Letters of James Kent, LL.D.* (Boston, 1898), 218; John Theodore Horton, *James Kent: A Study in Conservatism* (New York, 1939), 318; Hone, *The Diary of Philip Hone*, Allan Nevins, ed. (New York, 1936), 122–3, 141 David M. Saunders to William A. Graham, Apr. 26, 1834, in J. G. De Roulhac Hamilton, ed., *The Papers of William Alexander Graham* (Raleigh, 1957–92), 1: 310.
4. Horton, *Kent*, 318; Jackson to Francis Blair, Aug. 22, 1836, Andrew Jackson Papers, LC.
5. On reconfigurations of what he calls the "fiction" of popular sovereignty, see Edmund S. Morgan, *Inventing the People: The Rise of Popular Sovereignty in Britain and America* (New York, 1988). An important aspect of the history of American democracy, on contests over voting rights, is now less mysterious than it was: see Alexander Keyssar, *The Right to Vote: The Contested History of Democracy in the United States* (New York, 2000), esp. 1–76.
6. For an overview of antidemocratic presumptions in early modern England, see Christopher Hill, "The Many-Headed Monster," in *Change and Continuity in Seventeenth-Century England* (Cambridge, MA, 1975), 181–204.
7. Lilburne, *The Upright Mans Vindication* (London, 1653), 15. See also Christopher Hill, *The World Turned Upside Down: Radical Ideas during the English Revolution* (New York, 1972); idem, *The Experience of Defeat: Milton and Some Contemporaries* (New York, 1984); Richard L. Greaves, *Deliver Us from Evil: The Radical Underground in Britain, 1660–1663* (New York, 1986); idem, *Enemies under His Feet: Radicals and Nonconformists in Britain, 1663–1677* (Stanford, 1990); idem, *Secrets of the People: British Radicals from the Popish Plot to the Revolution of 1688–89* (Stanford, 1992); Kathleen Wilson, *The Sense of the People: Politics, Culture, and Imperialism in England, 1715–1785* (Cambridge, UK, 1995).
8. Williams, "The Bloudy Tenent of Persecution" (1644), in *Publications of the Narragansett Club*, 1st ser., 3 (1867): 249; Billerica Town Records, June 6, 1774, Town Hall, Billerica, MA; J. R. Pole, *Political Representation in England and the Origins of the American Republic* (London, 1966), 514 (quotation); Eric Foner, *Tom Paine and Revolutionary America* (New York, 1976), 76–77. See also Alfred F. Young, "English Plebeian Culture and Eighteenth-Century American Radicalism," in Margaret C. Jacob and James Jacob, eds., *The Origins of Anglo-American Radicalism* (London, 1984), 185–212, esp. 194–200, 204; Ronald Schultz, *The Republic of Labor: Philadelphia Artisans and the Politics of Class, 1720–1830* (New York, 1993), 27–28. British politics did produce important democratic stirrings in the 1760s in connection with the agitation surrounding John Wilkes, which in turn influenced American events. See Pauline Maier, *From Resistance to Revolution:*

Colonial Radicals and the Development of American Opposition to Britain, 1765–1776 (New York, 1972), esp. 163–9.

9. *Rivington's New York Loyal Gazette*, Nov. 1, 1777 (referring specifically to Massachusetts). For the most systematic portrayals of colonial America as a middling democracy, see Robert E. Brown, *Middle-Class Democracy and the Revolution in Massachusetts, 1691–1780* (Ithaca, NY, 1955); Robert E. Brown and B. Katherine Brown, *Virginia, 1705–1786: Democracy or Aristocracy?* (East Lansing, MI, 1964).

10. Adams and Washington quoted in Gordon S. Wood, *The Radicalism of the American Revolution* (New York, 1992), 27. The evidence of lower rates of voter eligibility, and the broader controversy about democracy in the colonial era, are fairly summarized in Robert J. Dinkin, *Voting in Provincial America* (Westport, CT, 1977), esp. 40–49; but see also Pole, *Political Representation in England*, esp. 136–48; Gary B. Nash, *The Urban Crucible: Social Change, Political Consciousness, and the Origins of the American Revolution* (Cambridge, MA, 1979), esp. 63, 266, 351. Alexander Keyssar estimates that the overall proportion of adult white males eligible to vote on the eve of the Revolution was "probably less than 60 percent," and points out that while colonial Massachusetts and Virginia passed laws reducing property requirements, in several other colonies (including ever-contradictory Virginia) requirements became more stringent. He also notes that various exclusionary laws barring Catholics, blacks, mulattoes, and Indians from the polls came chiefly in the eighteenth century. Keyssar, *Right to Vote*, 7. On New England town meetings and the context of consensus, see Michael Zuckerman, "The Social Context of Democracy in Massachusetts," *WMQ*, 25 (1968): 523–44; idem, *Peaceable Kingdoms: New England Towns in the Eighteenth Century* (New York, 1970); although on the latter's overstatements, see John M. Murrin, "Review Essay," *History and Theory*, 11 (1972): 245–54. Interestingly, the two authors have seemed to switch positions in recent debates, with Zuckerman virtually denying the existence of social deference among the lower orders in colonial America, and Murrin taking a more measured view. See "Deference and Defiance in Early America: A Round Table," *JAH*, 85 (1998): 13–97. On the intensification of monarchical presumptions and institutions in the pre-Revolutionary colonies, and their subsequent downfall, see Gary J. Kornblith and John M. Murrin, "The Making and Unmaking of an American Ruling Class," in Alfred F. Young, ed., *Beyond the American Revolution: Explorations in the History of American Radicalism*, (De Kalb, IL, 1993), 28–65.

11. [William Smith], *A True and Important State of the Province of Pennsylvania* (Philadelphia, 1759), 9; A Gentleman [John Adams], *Thoughts on Government* (Philadelphia, 1776), 26; John Adams to James Warren, Apr. 22, 1776, in "Warren-Adams Letters, Being Chiefly a Correspondence among John Adams, Samuel Adams, and James Warren," *Collections of the Massachusetts Historical Society*, 72–73 (1917–25): 1: 234; Paine, *Rights of Man* (1791–92; Harmondsworth, 1969), 202. See also Roy N. Lokken, "The Concept of Democracy in Colonial Political Thought," *WMQ*, 16 (1959): 568–80.

12. William Borden, "An Address to the Inhabitants of North Carolina and an Address to the Burgesses of North Carolina," in William K. Boyd, ed., *Some Eighteenth Century Tracts Concerning North Carolina* (Raleigh, 1927), 69; Rev. John Davenport, quoted in Lokken, "Concept," 578. See also, e.g., Pole, *Political Representation*, 149, on the deceptiveness of popular elections in Virginia: "The role of the electorate was severely circumscribed. The voters were called into action to elect a new House of Burgesses in the colonial period about once every three years; they knew little of the issues, had practically no opportunity to read political debates, and were very rarely called upon to make decisions that would determine between alternative policies. They formed an essentially deferential electorate who willingly acknowledged the leadership and authority of the gentry."

13. Highlights of the large literature on mobs and crowds in eighteenth-century America, arguing from different points of view, include Jesse Lemisch, "Jack Tar in the Streets: Merchant Seamen in the Politics of Revolutionary America," *WMQ*, 25 (1968): 371–407; Jesse Lemisch and John K. Alexander, "The White Oaks, Jack Tar, and the Concept of the 'Inarticulate,'" *WMQ*, 29 (1972): 109–42; Gordon S. Wood, *The Creation of the American*

Republic, 1776–1787 (Chapel Hill, 1969), esp. 319–28 (quotation on 321); Pauline Maier, "Popular Uprisings and Civil Authority in Eighteenth-Century America," *WMQ*, 27 (1970), 3–35; Dirk Hoerder, *Crowd Action in Revolutionary Massachusetts, 1765–1780* (New York, 1977); Paul A. Gilje, *The Road to Mobocracy: Popular Disorder in New York City, 1763–1834* (Chapel Hill, 1987).

14. [John Joachim Zubly], *An Humble Enquiry into the Nature of the Dependency of the American Colonies* (n.p. [Charleston, SC], 1769), 22. On concepts of representation and the Revolution, see Wood, *Creation*, 162–96; John Philip Reid, *The Concept of Representation in the Age of the American Revolution* (Chicago, 1989), esp. 43–62.

15. Blackstone, *Commentaries on the Laws of England* (London, 1765), 1: 165; Jefferson to Edward Pendleton, Aug. 27, 1776, in *PTJ*, 1: 503–4.

16. Adams to James Sullivan, May 26, 1776, in Charles Francis Adams, ed., *The Works of John Adams* (Boston, 1850–56), 9: 375–8.

17. *The People the Best Governors, or, a Plan of Government Founded on the Just Principles of Natural Freedom* (n.p., 1776), 13.

18. Charles de Secondat, Baron de Montesquieu, *The Spirit of the Laws*, Thomas Nugent, trans. (London, 1750), 1: Book II, 7; *Massachusetts Gazette*, Jan. 22, 1788; *New-York Gazette; and the Weekly Mercury*, June 17, 1776.

19. An American [Charles Inglis], *The Interest of America Impartially Stated, In Certain Strictures on a Pamphlet Intitled Common Sense* (Philadelphia, 1776), 18; Madison, "Vices of the Political System of the United States," in *PJM*, 9: 345–58; Wilson, *The Substance of a Speech delivered by James Wilson, Esq., Explanatory of the General Principles of the Proposed Federal Constitution* (Philadelphia, 1787), 10; J. B. McMaster and Frederick D. Stone, eds., *Pennsylvania and the Federal Constitution, 1787–1788* (Philadelphia, 1888), 231, 344.

20. Webster, *An American Selection of Lessons in Reading and Speaking* (Philadelphia, 1789), 214.

CHAPTER ONE:
AMERICAN DEMOCRACY IN A REVOLUTIONARY AGE

1. See J. Paul Selsam, *The Pennsylvania Constitution of 1776: A Study in Revolutionary Democracy* (Philadelphia, 1936); Robert L. Brunhouse, *The Counter-Revolution in Pennsylvania, 1776–1790* (Harrisburg, 1942), 18–52; Gordon S. Wood, *The Creation of the American Republic, 1776–1787* (Chapel Hill, 1969), 83–90; Eric Foner, *Tom Paine and Revolutionary America* (New York, 1976), 118–34; Richard A. Ryerson, *The Revolution Is Now Begun: The Radical Committees of Philadelphia, 1765–1776,* (Philadelphia, 1978), 240–3; Leonard W. Larabee et al., eds., *The Papers of Benjamin Franklin* (New Haven, 1959–), 22: 512–5; Edmund S. Morgan, *Benjamin Franklin* (New York, 2002), 231–41. On Franklin's political transformations and the limits of his egalitarianism, see Gordon S. Wood, *The Americanization of Benjamin Franklin* (New York, 2004)

2. One other Pennsylvanian was a delegate to all three assemblies, James Bayard Smith, an Irish immigrant surveyor and lawyer from York. George Clymer and George Ross were delegates to the Continental Congress and the State Convention, but not to the Provincial Congress. Franklin did not attend the Provincial Conference meetings in June, which is not surprising given his age, the pro forma nature of most of the Conference's work that week, and the press of business leading up to Congress's declaration of independence. Among the Convention's first acts was to elect him its president in a unanimous vote. See *The Proceedings Relative to Calling the Conventions of 1776 and 1790* (Harrisburg, 1825), 35–36, 45–46, 65–66.

3. The extent of Franklin's involvement remains in dispute, mainly because the Convention kept skimpy records. He certainly played a strong advisory role and offered important editorial changes to the constitution's opening Declaration of Rights. Some scholars claim he

did little more; others suggest that he, along with the radical James Cannon and, perhaps, George Bryan, was a coauthor. Without question, Franklin thought highly of the new plan, did not contradict those who said he had written it, and defended the constitution until his death in 1790. The historians who are most emphatic that he was not the father of the Pennsylvania Constitution insist, nevertheless, that he had reason to consider himself its "godfather." See Larabee et al., eds., *Papers*, 22: 515, 528–33. On Cannon's involvement, see Foner, *Tom Paine*, 131.

4. Allison to Robert [unknown], Aug. 20, 1776, reprinted in *Pennsylvania Magazine of History and Biography*, 28 (1904): 379. A delegate from Bedford County was even more contemptuous of his colleagues, complaining that "not a sixth part of us ever read a word" about government and politics. Foner, *Tom Paine*, 131.

5. J. Hector St. John [de Crèvecoeur], *Letters from an American Farmer* (1782; New York, 1957), 20–21. Crèvecoeur—whose true name was Michel-Guillaume-Jean de Crèvecoeur—had been a naturalized citizen since 1764. He spent his first twenty-four years in France, Britain, and Canada, the last twenty-four years of his life in Europe, and about fifteen of the intervening years in America.

6. Logan, *Five Letters Addressed to the Yeomanry of the United States* (Philadelphia, 1792). This account of the yeomanry is based on nearly three decades of work on eighteenth-century American agriculture by, among others, Christopher Clark, James A. Henretta, Michael Merrill, and Winifred Barr Rothenberg. For an excellent summary, see also Allan Kulikoff, "The Transition to Capitalism in Rural America," WMQ, 46 (1989): 120–44. For divergent interpretations, see Merrill, "Putting 'Capitalism' in Its Place: A Review of the Recent Literature," WMQ, 52 (1995): 312–26; Gordon S. Wood, "The Enemy Is Us: Democratic Capitalism in the Early Republic," *JER*, 16 (1996): 293–308.

7. James T. Lemon, *The Best Poor Man's Country: A Geographical Study of Southeastern Pennsylvania* (New York, 1972), xiii.

8. "Are you so uninfluenced by justice, and so blinded by self-interest, as to not discern the force of equity, 'tho it is thus glaringly obvious?" one antidebtor Massachusetts man wrote in response to a petition for debtor relief in 1781. *Boston Gazette and Country Journal*, May 28, 1781.

9. See Marvin L. Michael Kay, "The North Carolina Regulation, 1766–1776: A Class Conflict," in Alfred F. Young, ed., *The American Revolution: Explorations in the History of American Radicalism* (De Kalb, IL, 1976), 73–106; A. Roger Ekirch, "The North Carolina Regulators on Liberty and Corruption," *Perspectives in American History*, 11 (1977–78): 191–256; idem, "'A New Government of Liberty': Hermon Husband's Vision of Backcountry North Carolina, 1755," WMQ, 34 (1977): 632–46; idem, *"Poor Carolina": Politics and Society in Colonial North Carolina* (Chapel Hill, 1981); Alden T. Vaughan, "Frontier Banditti and the Indians: The Paxton Boys' Legacy, 1765–1775," *Pennsylvania History*, 51 (1984): 1–29; George William Franz, "Paxton: A Study of Community Structure and Mobility in the Colonial Pennsylvania Backcountry" (Ph.D. dissert., Rutgers University, 1974); James Kirby Martin, "The Return of the Paxton Boys and the Historical State of the Pennsylvania Frontier, 1764–1774," *Pennsylvania History*, 38 (1971): 117–33; Richard Maxwell Brown, *The South Carolina Regulators* (Cambridge, MA, 1963). For overviews, see Alan Taylor, "Agrarian Independence: Northern Land Rioters after the Revolution," in Alfred F. Young, ed., *Beyond the American Revolution: Explorations in the History of American Radicalism* (De Kalb, IL, 1993), 222–45; Eric Hinderaker and Peter C. Mancall, *At the Edge of Empire: The British Backcountry in British North America* (Baltimore, 2003), 125–83; Stephen Aron, "Pigs and Hunters: 'Rights in the Woods' on the Trans-Appalachian Frontier," in Andrew R. L. Cayton and Fredrika J. Teute, eds., *Contact Points: American Frontiers from the Mohawk Valley to the Mississippi, 1750–1830* (Chapel Hill, 1998), 175–204. On specific uprisings, see Sung Bok Kim, *Landlord and Tenant in Colonial New York: Manorial Society, 1664–1775* (Chapel Hill, 1978), 281–345; Alan Taylor, *Liberty Men and Great Proprietors: The Revolutionary Settlement on the Maine Frontier, 1760–1820* (Chapel Hill, 1990). On Indian-settler relations and the complex story of

the hatreds they spawned, see Peter Silver's forthcoming book, *Transforming Fear: Indian War and the Reinvention of European Identities in Eighteenth-Century America*, based on his 2001 Ph.D. dissertation at Yale.

10. William L. Saunders, ed., *The Colonial Records of North Carolina* (Raleigh, 1886–90), 8: 75–80. Typical of the many hundreds of Virginia missives that arrived in Richmond was one in 1779 signed by forty-four "freeholders and other inhabitants of the County of Rocking-ham" asking for repeal of a recent law placing an additional tax of a bushel of grain on every tithable person. A drought had ruined grain crops; a great part of what little corn remained had to be laid aside to fatten hogs; and while the poor farmer suffered acutely ("where is this man to get his additional tax of a bushel of grain?"), even "those of more happy circum-stances must feel the effects." Among the complaining signers was one Abraham Lincoln, whose Kentucky-born grandson would be his namesake. Legislative Petitions, Rockingham County, #434-a, LoV. For an astute analysis, see Ruth Bogin, "Petitioning and the New Moral Economy of Post-Revolutionary America," *WMQ*, 45 (1988): 391–425.

11. From the 1760s to the 1780s, the proportion of farmers seated in the lower houses in New Hampshire, New York, and New Jersey rose from one-fourth to more than half the total. See Jackson Turner Main, "Government by the People: The American Revolution and the Democratization of the Legislatures," *WMQ*, 23 (1966): 391–407.

12. See Robert J. Taylor, *Western Massachusetts in the Revolution* (Providence, 1954), 75–102; also Richard W. Hale Jr., "The American Revolution in Western Massachusetts," *New England Historical and Genealogical Register*, 129 (1975): 325–34. On related move-ments in western New Hampshire in the 1770s, see Wood, *Creation*, 287–8.

13. Petition of Pittsfield, Dec. 26, 1775, Petition of Pittsfield, May 1776, in Robert J. Taylor, ed., *Massachusetts: Colony to Commonwealth* (Chapel Hill, 1961), 18, 28. The second petition called the plan to adopt a new constitution without popular consent "the rankest kind of Toryism, the self-same Monster we are now fighting against." On Allen, see Frank Anthony DeSorbo, "The Reverend Thomas Allen and Revolutionary Politics in Western Massachusetts" (Ph.D. dissert., New York University, 1995); Theodore M. Hammett, "Rev-olutionary Ideology in Massachusetts: Thomas Allen's 'Vindication' of the Berkshire Con-stitutionalists, 1778," *WMQ*, 33 (1976): 514–27.

14. Oscar Handlin and Mary Flug Handlin, *The Popular Sources of Political Authority: Docu-ments on the Massachusetts Constitution of 1780* (Cambridge, MA, 1966), 267, 430. The new constitution failed to include the insurgents' demands for appointive judgeships as well as for universal manhood suffrage. In 1782, crowds of yeoman in western Massachu-setts and northern Connecticut rallied to the cause of a preacher, Samuel Ely, who had been jailed for allegedly threatening a local judge. Four years later came Shays' Rebellion. See Taylor, *Western Massachusetts*, 112–3, 116–7.

15. "Attleborough" [George Brock], "To the Yeomanry of Massachusetts," *Independent Chron-icle* [Boston], Aug. 31, 1786; John Montgomery to James Wilson, Mar. 2, 1788, in Merrill Jensen et al., eds., *The Documentary History, of the Ratification of the Constitution* (Madi-son, WI, 1976–) 2: 705. On the fear of "lordships" before the Revolution, see Richard L. Bushman, *King and People in Provincial Massachusetts* (Chapel Hill, 1985), 198–206.

16. Madison to William Bradford, Apr. 1, 1774, in *PJM*, 1: 112. See Rhys Isaac, *The Transfor-mation of Virginia, 1740–1790* (Chapel Hill, 1982), esp. 58–80, 161–80; Stephen A. Marini, *Radical Sects of Revolutionary New England* (Cambridge, MA, 1982); Nathan O. Hatch, *The Democratization of American Christianity* (New Haven, 1989); Ruth Bloch, *Visionary Republic: Millennial Themes in American Thought, 1756–1800* (New York, 1985); Susan Juster, *Doomsayers: Anglo-American Prophecy in the Age of Revolution* (Philadelphia, 2003). According to figures gathered by Marini for the whole country, the number of Anglican congregations declined between 1760 and 1790 from just over three hundred to fewer than two hundred. By contrast, the number of Baptist congregations grew over the same period from about one hundred to more than eight hundred, while the number of Methodist congregations grew from zero to more than seven hundred. Nomi-nally Congregationalist and Presbyterian churches showed strong if more modest growth.

17. Handlin and Handlin, *Popular Sources*, 634.
18. Jefferson to Thomas Mann Randolph Jr., May 6, 1793, in *PTJ*, 25: 668.
19. According to historical statistics as reconstructed by the U.S. Bureau of the Census, just over 200,000 persons lived in "urban areas" in 1790, defined as settlements with 2,500 or more residents, out of a total population of over 3.7 million. *Historical Statistics of the United States: Colonial Times to 1970* (Washington, DC, 1975), Part 1: 12. Of this "city-dwelling" population, between 100,000 and 150,000 persons (upwards of 75 percent of the total) lived in and around one of the five major seaports: Boston, New York, Philadelphia, Baltimore, and Charleston. The best general study of American cities in this period is Gary B. Nash, *The Urban Crucible: Social Change, Political Consciousness, and the Origins of the American Revolution* (Cambridge, MA, 1979); also Edwin G. Burrows and Mike Wallace, *Gotham: A History of New York City to 1898* (New York, 1999), 191–264; Thomas M. Doerflinger, *Vigorous Spirit of Enterprise: Merchants and Economic Development in Revolutionary Philadelphia* (Chapel Hill, 1986); Gary Lawson Browne, *Baltimore in the Nation, 1789–1861* (Chapel Hill, 1980); George C. Rogers, *Charleston in the Age of the Pinckneys* (Norman, OK, 1969).
20. Burrows and Wallace, *Gotham*, 183, 187–90; Sean Wilentz, *Chants Democratic: New York City & the Rise of the American Working Class, 1788–1850* (New York, 1984), 24–35; Sharon V. Salinger, "Artisans, Journeymen, and the Transformation of Labor in Late Eighteenth-Century Philadelphia," *WMQ*, 40 (1983): 62–84. In general, see Jacob Price, "Economic Function and the Growth of American Port Towns in the 18th Century," *Perspectives in American History*, 8 (1974): esp. 131–7, 184–5; Richard Oestreicher, "The Counted and the Uncounted: The Occupational Structure of Early American Cities, 1790–1810," *Journal of Social History*, 28 (1994): 351–61.
21. Nash, *Urban Crucible*, 325; Richard B. Morris, *Government and Labor in Early America* (New York, 1946), 196.
22. Nash, *Urban Crucible*, 76–101; idem, "The Transformation of Urban Politics, 1700–1764," in *Race, Class, and Politics: Essays on American Colonial and Revolutionary Society* (Urbana, IL, 1986), 140–70.
23. "A Brother Chip," *Pennsylvania Chronicle*, Sep. 27, 1770; Nash, *Urban Crucible*, 376 (quotation); Gordon S. Wood, *The Radicalism of the American Revolution* (New York, 1992), 245.
24. Bernard Mason, *The Road to Independence: The Revolutionary Movement in New York, 1773–1777* (Lexington, KY, 1966), esp. 27–41, 134–77; Alfred F. Young, *The Democratic Republicans of New York: The Origins, 1763–1797* (Chapel Hill, 1967), 3–32; Burrows and Wallace, *Gotham*, 226–9; Charles G. Steffen, *The Mechanics of Baltimore: Workers and Politics in the Age of Revolution, 1763–1812* (Urbana, IL, 1984), 53–80; Richard Walsh, *Charleston's Sons of Liberty, A Study of the Artisans, 1763–1789* (Columbia, SC, 1959), 26–87.
25. Ryerson, *Revolution Is Now Begun*, 25–115; Nash, *Urban Crucible*, 376–80; Ronald Schultz, *The Republic of Labor: Philadelphia Artisans and the Politics of Class, 1720–1830* (New York, 1993), 33.
26. Ryerson, *Revolution Is Now Begun*, 214–6 (quotation on 215); Adams quoted in David Freeman Hawke, "Dr. Thomas Young—'Eternal Fisher in Troubled Waters': Notes for a Biography," *New-York Historical Society Quarterly*, 54 (1970): 8. Apart from the voluminous literature on Paine, see Brooke Hindle, *David Rittenhouse* (Princeton, 1964); David Freeman Hawke, *In the Midst of a Revolution: The Politics of Confontation in Colonial America* (Philadelphia, 1961); idem, *Benjamin Rush: Revolutionary Gadfly* (Indianapolis, 1967); Pauline Maier, "Reason and Revolution: The Radicalism of Dr. Thomas Young," *American Quarterly*, 28 (1976): 229–49; A. M. Stackhouse, *Col. Timothy Matlack: Patriot and Soldier* (n.p., 1910). In general on the Philadelphia radicals, see also Foner, *Tom Paine*, 108–18.
27. Paine, *Common Sense* (1776; London, 1976), 72, 78. See Foner, *Tom Paine*, 71–106; John Keane, *Tom Paine: A Political Life* (Boston, 1995), esp. 108–37.

28. Joseph Shippen to ?, Jan. 15, 1776, quoted in Elisha P. Douglass, *Rebels and Democrats: The Struggle for Equal Political Rights and Majority Rule during the American Revolution* (Chapel Hill, 1955), 253; Paine, *Common Sense*, 65; Adams quoted in Foner, *Tom Paine*, xviii; Adams, *Thoughts on Government: Applicable to the Present State of the American Colonies* (Philadelphia, 1776); *Pennsylvania Gazette*, Feb. 28, 1776.

29. See Ryerson, *Revolution Is Now Begun*, 117–47; Steven Rosswurm, *Arms, Country, and Class: The Philadelphia Militia and the "Lower Sort" during the American Revolution* (New Brunswick, NJ, 1987), esp. 49–227 (quotation on 158).

30. *Proceedings . . . 1776 and 1790*, 39; Foner, *Tom Paine*, 129. On the Philadelphia convention, see the sources cited in note 1.

31. On Pennsylvania politics after 1776, see Brunhouse, *Counter-Revolution*, 53–221. See Rush, *Observations Upon the Present Government of Pennsylvania: In Four Letters to the People of Pennsylvania* (Philadelphia, 1777), esp. 7–9. The democratic coalition also divided against itself over wartime price controls, violence against suspected food monopolizers, and the establishment of the Philadelphia-based Bank of North America (favored by city democrats, including Paine, but opposed by the backcountry). See esp. Foner, *Tom Paine*, 145–209. The discarded 1776 Pennsylvania Constitution did have a sort of country afterlife, thanks to the radical Dr. Thomas Young, whose influence helped make it a model for Vermont's democratic constitution when the Green Mountain State obtained its independence in 1791. See Hawke, "Young," 28; Gary J. Aichele, "Making the Vermont Constitution: 1777–1824," *Vermont History*, 56 (1988): 166–90.

32. Young, *Democratic Republicans*, 31, 201–3 (quotation on 202); Burrows and Wallace, *Gotham*, 266–7.

33. Robert Parker Smith et al., "Farmers in Amherst and Others in Hillsborough Co. [NH], Feb. 1783," [Walter Brewster], "A Mechanic, not yet a Free-Man," *Norwich Packet*, Sep. 8, 1791, both quoted in Bogin, "Petitioning," 423.

34. *New-York Journal*, July 8, 1795. Four years later, a meeting of the Tammany Society toasted "The mechanic arts—May they . . . find a passage from Erie to Ontario, and lead Champlain in triumph to the bosom of the deep." *New-York Journal*, July 6, 1799.

35. Jonathan Elliot, *The Debates in the Several State Conventions on the Adoption of the Federal Constitution* (1836–45; Philadelphia, 1901), 2: 102. On evangelicalism in the major cities before 1815, see Richard Carwardine, *Transatlantic Revivalism: Popular Evangelicalism in Britain and America, 1790–1865* (Westport, CT, 1978), 11–12. On evangelicalism and the city democrats, see Foner, *Tom Paine*, 111–8. As Foner points out, during the Revolutionary era, the evangelicals and deist radicals' common emphasis on individual conscience and their shared millenarian streak at times brought them closer together than might be assumed. Also see David P. Jaffee, "The Village Enlightenment in New England, 1760–1820," *WMQ*, 47 (1990): 327–46; Michael Merrill and Sean Wilentz, "William Manning and the Invention of American Politics," in *The Key of Liberty: The Life and Democratic Writings of William Manning, "A Labourer," 1747–1814* (Cambridge, MA, 1993), esp. 39–59.

36. The immense literature on democracy and the Revolution stretches back almost as far as the event itself, and runs the full gamut from works that celebrate and that denigrate the patriots' egalitarian achievements. For provocative studies that trace scholarly trends in recent decades, see Merrill Jensen, "Democracy and the American Revolution," *Huntington Library Quarterly*, 20 (1956–57): 321–42; Richard Buel, "Democracy and the American Revolution: A Frame of Reference," *WMQ*, 21 (1964): 165–90; Bernard Bailyn, *Ideological Origins of the American Revolution* (New York, 1967), esp. 230–319; Thomas J. Archdeacon, "American Historians and the American Revolution: A Bicentennial Overview," *Wisconsin Magazine of History*, 63 (1980): 278–98; Wood, *Radicalism of the American Revolution*; Linda K. Kerber, "The Revolutionary Generation: Ideology, Politics and Culture in the Early Republic," in Eric Foner, ed., *The New American History* (1990; Philadelphia, 1997), 31–59.

37. "The Free Republican" [Benjamin Lincoln], in *Independent Chronicle*, Dec. 22, 1785.

Georgia, New Hampshire, North Carolina (for lower-house elections), Pennsylvania, and South Carolina established taxpaying requirements. Of the eleven original states that wrote new state constitutions, six had property requirements for officeholders higher than the suffrage property requirements. These stipulations ranged, upward, from Massachusetts (£1,000 freehold for governor, £300 freehold for senators, and £100 freehold for members of the House of Representatives) to South Carolina (£10,000 freehold for governor and £2,000 freehold for senators). Thorpe, 3: 1897–98, 1900, 6: 3258–59, 3262. For different interpretations of these matters, see Alexander Keyssar, *The Right to Vote: The Contested History of Democracy in the United States* (New York, 2001), 9–11, 24–25; Wood, *Creation*, 127–73, 197–222; Willi Paul Adams, *The First American Constitutions: Republican Ideology and the Making of the State Constitutions*, Rita Kimber and Robert Kimber, trans. (Chapel Hill, 1980), 196–217; Marc W. Kruman, *Between Authority and Liberty: State Constitution Making in Revolutionary America* (Chapel Hill, 1997), 87–108, 131–54. The fourteenth state, Vermont, upon achieving its independence from New York in 1791, adopted a constitution—drafted in 1786 and based on the Pennsylvania Constitution of 1776—that eliminated all property requirements. See esp. Michael A. Bellisles, *Revolutionary Outlaw: Ethan Allen and the Struggle for Independence on the Early American Frontier* (Charlottesville, 1993), 47, 136–41, 161–3, 258–60; Aichele, "Making."

38. On the Revolution in New York, see Young, *Democratic Republicans*, 3–109. On Loyalism and the suffrage, see Kruman, *Between Authority and Liberty*, 98–103. More generally, see Gary J. Kornblith and John M. Murrin, "The Making and Unmaking of an American Ruling Class," in Young, *Beyond the American Revolution*, 27–79, and the voluminous literature cited therein.

39. On the changes described in this paragraph and the next, see Kruman, *Between Authority and Liberty*, 65–81, 92–98; J. R. Pole, "Suffrage and Representation in Maryland from 1776 to 1810: A Statistical Note and Some Reflections," in Joel H. Silbey and Samuel T. McSeveney, eds., *Voters, Parties, and Elections: Quantitative Essays in the History of American Voting Behavior* (Lexington, MA, 1972), 62–63; Charles G. Steffen, *The Mechanics of Baltimore: Workers and Politics in the Age of Revolution, 1763–1812* (Urbana, IL, 1984), 61–64; Keyssar, *Right to Vote*, 16–17; Wood, *Creation*, 143–50, 170 (quotation). Free black men were permitted to vote on the same terms as whites in ten states in 1787, as they had been in ten colonies on the eve of independence. Discussion also arose during the Revolution about enfranchising propertied married women, and one state, New Jersey, actually did so. See Judith Apter Kinghoffer and Lois Elkins, "The Petticoat Electors: Women's Suffrage in New Jersey, 1776–1807," *JER*, 12 (1992): 159–94.

40. Jackson Turner Main, "Government by the People: The American Revolution and the Democratization of the State Legislatures," *WMQ*, 23 (1966): 391–407 (quotation on 406); idem, *The Upper House in Revolutionary America* (Madison, WI, 1967), 136, 157. Based on his close study of six state legislatures, Main concluded that whereas only one-fifth of the pre-Revolutionary legislators were middling yeomen and artisans, the proportion roughly doubled, on average, after the Revolution. See Jack P. Greene, "Legislative Turnover in British America, 1696 to 1775: A Quantitative Analysis," *WMQ*, 38 (1981): 422–63. On annual elections, see Kruman, *Between Authority and Liberty*, 81–86.

41. "Spartanus," "The Interest of America," *New-York Journal, or the General Advertiser*, May 30, June 13, 20, 1776; "The Considerate Freeman," *Pennsylvania Packet*, Nov. 26, 1776; *The People the Best Governors, or, a Plan of Government Founded on the Just Principles of Natural Freedom* (n.p., 1776); "A Faithful Friend to His Country," *Independent Chronicle*, Aug. 7, 1777. See also Harry A. Cushing, ed., *The Writings of Samuel Adams* (New York, 1904–08), 3: 244. The broadest survey of popular democratic thought in the Revolution remains Douglass, *Rebels and Democrats*. A different interpretation appears in Wood, *Radicalism*.

42. Pendleton to Jefferson, Aug. 10, 1776, in *PTJ*, 1: 480.

43. Peale painted numerous versions of this portrait, with different backgrounds. The rendering discussed here is owned by Princeton University.

44. Force, comp., *American Archives*, 4th ser., 1: 312.

45. See David P. Szatmary, *Shays' Rebellion: The Making of an Agrarian Insurrection* (Amherst, MA, 1980); Leonard L. Richards, *Shays' Rebellion: The Revolution's Final Battle* (Philadelphia, 2002). See also Richard D. Brown, "Shays' Rebellion and the Ratification of the Federal Constitution in Massachusetts," in Richard Beeman et al., eds., *Beyond Confederation: Origins of the Constitution and American National Identity* (Chapel Hill, 1987), 113–27. On similar, chronic disturbances in rural Pennsylvania that continued through the 1790s, see Terry Bouton, "A Road Closed: Rural Insurgency in Post-Revolutionary Pennsylvania," *JAH*, 87 (2000): 855–87.

46. Merrill and Wilentz, eds., *Key of Liberty*, 165.

47. Madison to George Washington, Dec. 9, 1785, in *PJM*, 8: 439.

48. Max Farrand, ed., *The Records of the Federal Constitution of 1787* (1937; New Haven, 1966), 1: 51; Hamilton to Robert R. Livingston, Aug. 13, 1783, in *PAH*, 3: 43.

49. Farrand, ed., *Records*, 1: 282–301. The quotations are from Robert Yates's transcription of Hamilton's speech. Hamilton absented himself from most of the remaining debates, returned to sign the final draft of the Constitution despite his deep misgivings about it, then defended it powerfully as one of the chief authors of *The Federalist* papers.

50. Numerous works have appeared since 1787 indicting the Constitution as essentially undemocratic or even antidemocratic, including, recently, Robert A. Dahl's pessimistic *How Democratic Is the American Constitution?* (New Haven, 2002).

51. Clinton Rossiter, ed., *The Federalist Papers* (1787–88; New York, 1961), 322; *Independent Gazeteer* [Philadelphia], Nov. 6, 1787. Compare esp. Main, *Upper House*, 216–29; Wood, *Creation*, 519–64. The Constitution's provisions for the Electoral College system carried these more democratic features into the selection of the executive, by stipulating that should no candidate receive a majority of the electors' votes, the decision would fall to the House of Representatives, the most clearly democratic element in the federal structure, with each state delegation granted one vote. In the era before the rise of national political parties, the Framers generally assumed that few figures if any (apart from George Washington) could gain the fame and reputation required for such an electoral majority, and that the House would normally end up selecting the president. See Jack N. Rakove, *Original Meanings: Politics and Ideas in the Making of the Constitution* (New York, 1996), 89–90, 264–8.

52. Jonathan Elliot, *Debates on the Adoption of the Federal Constitution, in the Convention Held at Philadelphia, in 1787* (Philadelphia, 1859), 5: 385–9; and Farrand, ed., *Records*, 2: 201–11, provide different transcriptions of the suffrage debates, from which this account draws.

53. On the origins and implications of the convention's decision to acquire, in Madison's words, "not merely the assent of the Legislatures, but the ratification of the people themselves," see Wood, *Creation*, 532–6 (quotation on 532); Rakove, *Original Meanings*, 94–130.

54. See Arthur Zilversmit, *The First Emancipation: The Abolition of Slavery in the North* (Chicago, 1967).

55. Farrand, *Records*, 2: 417; Elliot, *Debates*, 4: 286. For a concise corrective to the common anachronistic readings of these compromises, see also Rakove, *Original Meanings*, 73–74.

56. Elliot, *Debates*, 2: 102, 246–7. Melancton Smith, no ideologue, did eventually switch sides at the New York convention, persuaded more by Madison's arguments in favor of the Constitution than Hamilton's. As a credible critic of the document's potential dangers, he played a major role in achieving ratification in New York, possibly greater than Hamilton's. See Robin Brooks, "Alexander Hamilton, Melancton Smith, and the Ratification of the Constitution in New York," *WMQ*, 24 (1967): 339–58. See also Robert Allen Rutland, *The Birth of the Bill of Rights, 1776–1791* (Chapel Hill, 1955); Helen C. Veit et al., *Creating the Bill of Rights: The Documentary Record from the First Federal Congress* (Baltimore, 1991);

Kenneth R. Bowling, "A 'Tub to a Whale': The Founding Fathers and the Adoption of the Federal Bill of Rights," *JER*, 8 (1998): 223–51; Sean Wilentz, "The Power of the Powerless," *New Republic*, Dec. 23, 30, 1991, pp. 32–40; Rakove, *Original Meanings*, 288–338; Akhil Reed Amar, *The Bill of Rights: Creation and Reconstruction* (New Haven, 1998).

57. Elliot, *Debates*, 2: 227. In New York, all adult males were permitted to vote for delegates to the state's ratifying convention, and in Connecticut, all men eligible to vote in town meetings. In the other states, the suffrage was opened to all those eligible to vote for representatives in the lower house of the legislature (or, in Pennsylvania and Georgia, for representatives to the state's unicameral legislature). As Charles Beard pointed out long ago, the actual turnout for the state convention elections, overall, appears to have been far lower than the number of those eligible to vote. But the fact remained, crucial to the Constitution's legitimacy, that the Framers had recognized, as Madison said, that "the people were in fact, the fountain of all power." Beard, *An Economic Interpretation of the Constitution of the United States* (1913; New York, 1962), 239–52; Farrand, *Records*, 2: 92–94.

58. Morris to Washington, Oct. 30, 1787, in Jensen et al., eds., *Documentary History*, 2: 206–7; Mason, "Objections to the Constitution of Government formed by the Convention" (1787), in Herbert J. Storing, ed., *The Complete Anti-Federalist* (Chicago, 1981), 2: 13. Also see Saul Cornell, *The Other Founders: Anti-Federalism & the Dissenting Tradition in America, 1788–1828* (Chapel Hill, 1999).

59. Elliot, *Debates*, 2: 102; [Petrekin], *The Government of Nature Delineated or An Exact Picture of the New Federal Constitution by Arisocrotis* (1788), in Storing, ed., *Complete Anti-Federalist*, 3: 196–213 (quotations on 197–8). On Petrekin, see Cornell, *Other Founders*, 46–48, 107–9, 216–7.

60. Elliot, *Debates*, 2: 247–8; Stephen A. Marini, "Religion, Politics, and Ratification," in Ronald Hoffman and Peter J. Albert, eds., *Religion in a Revolutionary Age* (Charlottesville, 1994), 184–217.

61. *New-York Packet*, Aug. 5, 1788; Whitfield Bell Jr., "The Federalist Processions of 1788," *New-York Historical Society Quarterly*, 46 (1962): 5–39; *Independent Gazetteer*, Oct. 17, 1787.

62. Cornell, *Other Founders*, 109–20; Bouton, "Road Closed," 878–85; Joan Wells Cowan, *Kentucky in the New Republic: The Process of Constitution Making* (Lexington, KY, 1979), 1–11; Thomas Perkins Abernathy, *From Frontier to Plantation in Tennessee: A Study in Frontier Democracy* (Chapel Hill, 1932), 115–43. As the Tennessee experience showed, the common desire for independence hardly reconciled all sides in the new states. William Blount, the premier Tennessee speculator and political power, was originally a Federalist who wanted to create a new constitutional order based as closely as possible on North Carolina's. He switched over to the Republican side when national Federalists opposed Tennessee statehood. Country democrats, led by the Revolutionary veteran John Sevier, both opposed Blount's ascendancy and pushed for more liberal constitutional provisions, some of which they won (including popular election of the governor), but for the most part the more conservative forces prevailed.

63. The best of many versions of Franklin's famous final speech to the Pennsylvania convention on Sept. 17, 1787, is the handwritten manuscript included in the CD-ROM edition of Franklin's papers, produced by The Papers of Benjamin Franklin at Yale University, 45:u161. On Franklin's tortured thinking about slavery and his gradual move into antislavery, see also David Waldstreicher, *Runaway America: Benjamin Franklin, Slavery, and the American Revolution* (New York, 2004).

64. Quotations in Keith Arbour, "Benjamin Franklin as Weird Sister: William Cobbett and Federalist Philadelphia's Fears of Democracy," in Doran Ben-Atar and Barbara Oberg, eds., *Federalists Reconsidered* (Charlottesville, 1998), 180, 190, 192. The latter quotations are from the British émigré William Cobbett, Franklin's most virulent traducer, but as Arbour shows, Cobbett's anti-Franklin sentiments were more widely shared in the mid-1790s. See also Larry E. Tise, *The American Counterrevolution: A Retreat from Liberty, 1783–1800* (Mechanicsburg, PA, 1998).

65. Farrand, *Records*, 1: 153.
66. See Jack N. Rakove, "The Structure of Politics at the Accession of George Washington," in Richard Beeman et al., eds., *Beyond Confederation: Origins of the Constitution and American National Identity* (Chapel Hill, 1987), 261–94 (quotation on 269).

CHAPTER TWO: THE REPUBLICAN INTEREST AND THE SELF-CREATED DEMOCRACY

1. *National Gazette* [Philadelphia], Apr. 13, 1793; *Aurora General Advertiser* [Philadelphia], Mar. 10, 1794. In November 1794, Bache changed his newspaper's title to the *Aurora General Advertiser*, better known simply as the *Aurora*, which would remain a leading democratic paper until 1822. These documents, along with many others cited, are conveniently collected in Philip S. Foner, ed., *The Democratic-Republican Societies, 1790–1800: A Documentary Sourcebook of Constitutions, Declarations, Addresses, Resolutions, and Toasts* (Westport, CT, 1976), 54, 57. Several leaders of the German society, including Michael Leib, also joined the larger Philadelphia group. Muhlenberg, a member of the First Congress, would be reelected to the Third and Sixth Congresses.
2. No full-scale study of the societies has appeared since Eugene Perry Link's *Democratic-Republican Societies, 1790–1800* (New York, 1942) (quotation on 174). See also Matthew Schoenbachler, "Republicanism in the Age of Democratic Revolution: The Democratic-Republican Societies of the 1790's," *JER*, 18 (1998): 237–62. Recent studies of the Philadelphia society include Albrecht Koschnick, "The Democratic Societies of Philadelphia and the Limits of the American Public Sphere, Circa 1793–1795," *WMQ*, 58 (2001): 615–36; Jeffrey Alan Davis, "The Democratic-Republican Societies of Pennsylvania, 1793–1796 (Ph.D. dissert., Washington State University, 1996). On the other clubs, see Eugene P. Link, "The Democratic Societies of the Carolinas," *North Carolina Historical Review*, 18 (1942): 259–77; Judah Adelson, "The Vermont Democratic-Republican Societies and the French Revolution," *Vermont History*, 32 (1964): 3–23; Michael Kennedy, "Le Club Jacobin de Charleston en Caroline du Sud (1792–1795)," *Revue d'histoire moderne et contemporaine*, 24 (1977): 420–38; Marco M. Sioli, "The Democratic-Republican Societies at the End of the Eighteenth Century: The Western Pennsylvania Experience," *Pennsylvania History*, 60 (1993): 288–304; Jeffrey A. Davis, "Guarding the Republican Interest: The Western Pennsylvania Democratic Societies and the Excise Tax," *Pennsylvania History*, 67 (2000): 43–62. The actual number of societies is uncertain, as many more have been discovered since Link wrote his book. Schoenbachler, "Republicanism," 237, says that more than fifty appeared between 1793 and 1800, a reasonable baseline. At least two clubs, both in South Carolina, honored specific men as well as broad ideals: the Madisonian Society of Greenville and the Franklin or Republican Society of Pendleton. Link, *Democratic-Republican Societies*, 14.
3. Kenneth R. Bowling and Helen E. Veit, eds., *The Diary of William Maclay and Other Notes on Senate Debates, March 4, 1789–March 3, 1791* (Baltimore, 1988), 26.
4. Adrienne Koch, *Jefferson and Madison: The Great Collaboration* (New York, 1950). See Dumas Malone's *Jefferson and His Time* (New York, 1948–81); Irving Brant's *James Madison* (Indianapolis, 1941–68); along with the modern editions of the Jefferson and Madison papers cited elsewhere. Excellent biographies based on more recent scholarship include Merrill Peterson, *Thomas Jefferson and the New Nation* (New York, 1970); Noble E. Cunningham, *In Pursuit of Reason: The Life of Thomas Jefferson* (Baton Rouge, 1987); Ralph Ketchum, *James Madison: A Biography* (New York, 1971); Robert A. Rutland, *James Madison: Founding Father* (New York, 1987); Lance Banning, *The Sacred Fire of Liberty: James Madison and the Founding of the Federal Republic* (Ithaca, NY, 1995). For a stimulating comparison, including Hamilton, see James H. Read, *Power Versus Liberty: Madison, Hamilton, and Jefferson* (Charlottesville, 2000).
5. Jefferson to Madison, Feb. 6, 1788, in *PTJ*, 7: 569–70.

6. Jefferson to Madison, Jan. 30, 1787, in *PTJ*, 11: 93.
7. Clinton Rossiter, ed., *The Federalist Papers* (1787–88; New York, 1961), 103.
8. Rossiter, ed., *Federalist Papers*, 188. A discerning discussion of Hamilton's political economy appears in Stanley Elkins and Eric L. McKitrick, *The Age of Federalism: The Early American Republic, 1788–1800* (New York, 1993), 92–131.
9. Hamilton to Robert Morris, Apr. 30, 1781, in *PAH*, 2: 604–35.
10. Hamilton, "Report Relative to a Provision for the Support of Public Credit, January 9, 1790," in Jacob E. Cooke, ed., *The Reports of Alexander Hamilton* (New York, 1964), 4. This oft-quoted phrase actually referred to the debt run up during the Revolution, but Hamilton quickly moved on to discuss the benefits of peace-time debt as well, and in similar terms.
11. Madison to Edward Carrington, March 14, 1790, in *PJM*, 13: 104.
12. See Jacob E. Cooke, "The Compromise of 1790," *WMQ*, 27 (1970): 523–45; Kenneth R. Bowling, "Dinner at Jefferson's: A Note on Jacob E. Cooke's 'Compromise of 1790,'" *WMQ*, 28 (1971): 629–48; Norman K. Risjord, "The Compromise of 1790: New Evidence on the Dinner Table Bargain," *WMQ*, 33 (1976): 309–14.
13. Jefferson to James Monroe, June 20, 1790, in *PTJ*, 18: 536–7; "Opinion on the Constitutionality of the Bill for Establishing a National Bank, February 15, 1791," in *PTJ*, 19: 275–82. See also Thomas Jefferson to George Washington, May 23, 1792, in *PTJ*, 23: 535–41.
14. *AC*, 1st Congress, 2nd session, 1755, 3rd session, 2012. Nine of the 13 members in favor of Madison's proposal were Virginians; 18 of 28 southerners voted against the assumption bill. On the bank bill, northerners voted in favor by 33 to 1, while southerners voted 19 to 6 in opposition. The six pro-bank southerners included William L. Smith of South Carolina, who would emerge as the most pro-slavery voice in Congress. (The sole northerner to vote against the bank bill was the country democrat and lawyer Jonathan Grout from Massachusetts.) On the two occasions when the First Congress debated proposals concerning slavery and the slave trade, the congressmen from South Carolina and Georgia stood solidly—and angrily—united, whereas Madison and some of the other Virginians who opposed Hamilton's projects initially voted in the majority with the northerners; *AC*, 1st Congress, 2nd session, 1182–91, 1197–205, 1450–73, 1523. See also chapter 7.
15. "Report on Retaliation Against Britain [Oct. 1, 1781]," in *PJM*, 3: 271. See Herbert E. Sloan, *Principle and Interest: Thomas Jefferson and the Problem of Debt* (New York, 1995). The phrase about the public debt was linked to Hamilton in the *New-York Daily Gazette*, Feb. 10, 1790. In fact, Hamilton wrote in his report on public credit that a properly funded debt would be "a national blessing," a phrase he had used as early as 1781. See Elkins and McKitrick, *Age of Federalism*, 776 n. 80.
16. *AC*, 1st Congress, 3rd session, 1941.
17. See Gerald Stourzh, *Alexander Hamilton and the Idea of Republican Government* (Stanford, 1970). On Jeffersonian political economy, see Drew R. McCoy, *The Elusive Republic: Political Economy in Jeffersonian America* (New York, 1980).
18. Thomas Jefferson, *Notes on the State of Virginia*, William Peden, ed. (Chapel Hill, 1954), 164–5; Jefferson to Madison, Oct. 28, 1785, in *PTJ*, 8: 682. Jefferson wrote *Notes* for private circulation in 1783 and 1784. Published privately in 1784, it was reprinted first in French in 1786, and in English a year later.
19. [Madison], "Republican Distribution of Citizens," *National Gazette*, Mar. 5, 1792.
20. [Madison], "Parties," *National Gazette*, Jan. 23, 1792; idem, "Spirit of Governments," *National Gazette*, Feb. 20, 1792. Hamilton charged that Madison's opposition to the public credit report was "a perfidious desertion of the principles which he [Madison] was solemnly pledged to defend." Hamilton quoted in John C. Miller, *The Federalist Era, 1789–1801* (New York, 1960), 41.
21. Bowling and Veit, eds., *Diary of William Maclay*, 377.
22. Jefferson to Philip Freneau, Feb. 28, 1791, in *PTJ*, 19: 351.
23. Jefferson to Thomas Mann Randolph Jr., May 15, 1791, in *PTJ*, 20: 416. The best biography of Freneau remains Jacob Axelrad, *Philip Freneau: Champion of Democracy* (Austin,

1967). See also Jeffrey L. Pasley, "'The Tyranny of Printers': Newspaper Politics in the Early Republic (Charlottesville, 2001), 51–78; Noble E. Cunningham Jr., The Jeffersonian Republicans: The Formation of Party Organization, 1789–1801 (Chapel Hill, 1957), 13–19; Paul Starr, The Creation of the Media: Political Origins of Modern Communications (New York, 2004), 71–82.

24. Madison to Mann Page Jr., Aug. 1791, in PJM, 14: 72.

25. Jefferson to Thomas Mann Randolph Jr., May 15, 1791, in PTJ, 20: 416.

26. Historians have long disagreed over the extent to which Jefferson and Madison engaged in political discussions during their northern journey. Federalists called the trip a "passionate courtship" of the northern leaders and claimed that Jefferson and Madison consorted with former Shaysite rebels. Those extreme partisan charges were mostly false. But the most exacting study concludes that although the latter portion of the trip was probably void of politics, the first leg, in New York City, certainly was political. Alfred F. Young, The Democratic Republicans of New York: The Origins, 1763–1797 (Chapel Hill, 1967), 194–201. On the Federalist reaction, see Robert Troup to Alexander Hamilton, June 15, 1791, Nathaniel Hazard to Alexander Hamilton, Nov. 25, 1791, in PAH, 8: 478–9, 9: 529–37.

27. [Madison], "A Candid State of Parties," National Gazette, Sept. 26, 1792.

28. Cunningham, Jeffersonian Republicans, 33–45; Young, Democratic Republicans, 277–303. In New York, a hard-fought statewide contest for governor in the spring of 1792 pitted John Jay (sympathetic to the administration) against the incumbent, George Clinton (sympathetic to the Republicans). But both sides rejected party and relied instead on coteries of prominent men to sway the voters. In Pennsylvania, that same year, the opposition tried mightily to craft an independent, statewide slate of presidential electors, but wound up offering the voters a list that shared seven of its thirteen candidates with the Federalists.

29. Jefferson to Jonathan B. Smith, Apr. 26, 1791, Jefferson to George Washington, May 8, 1791, Jefferson to John Adams, July 17, 1791, in PTJ, 20: 290–2, 302–3; Worthington Chauncey Ford, ed., Writings of John Quincy Adams (New York, 1913–17), 1: 65–110. For a judicious assessment of the entire controversy, see PTJ, 20: 268–90. See also Joyce Appleby, "The Adams-Jefferson Rupture and the First French Translation of John Adams' Defence," AHR, 73 (1968): 1084–91. Beckley, an émigré from London, had arrived in Virginia as an indentured servant in 1769, and, thanks to his clerical skills, rose to independence as an official record keeper. Madison arranged his appointment to the House post in 1790. See Jeffrey L. Pasley, "'A Journeyman, Either in Law or Politics': John Beckley and the Social Origins of Political Campaigning," JER, 16 (1996) 536–43.

30. See Jacob Katz Cogan, "The Reynolds Affair and the Politics of Character," JER, 16 (1996): 389–418.

31. See Young, Democratic Republicans, 304–23; James Roger Sharp, American Politics in the Early Republic: The New Nation in Crisis (New Haven, 1993), 57–58; John Ferling, Adams vs. Jefferson: The Tumultuous Election of 1800 (New York, 2004), 58.

32. [Madison], "A Candid State of Parties," National Gazette, Sept. 26, 1792.

33. Taylor, A Definition of Parties; or, The Effects of the Paper System Considered (Philadelphia, 1794), 14. Although published in 1794, the manuscript circulated widely well before then among leading Virginia Republicans, including Madison, Monroe, and Jefferson, who gave it their approval. Sharp, American Politics, 61. In Pennsylvania, for example, even following the Republicans' considerable efforts after 1794, only about 25 percent of those eligible to vote would do so in the presidential elections in 1796—considerable less than the 31 to 33 percent turnout for the virtually uncontested gubernatorial elections of 1790 and 1796. See Elkins and McKitrick, Age of Federalism, 521.

34. Taylor, An Enquiry into the Principles and Tendency of Certain Measures (Philadelphia, 1794), 49, 54–55; Axelrad, Freneau, 262–74. On the Virginians' concern about "the great mass of society who are generally uninformed," see also James Monroe to Thomas Jefferson, July 17, 1792, in PTJ, 24: 236–7. Direct election of U.S. senators would not be secured until 1913.

35. Jefferson to James Madison, Aug. 3, 1793, in *PTJ*, 26: 606. See Harry Ammon, *The Genet Mission* (New York, 1973); Eugene R. Sheridan, "The Recall of Edmond Charles Genet: A Study in Transatlantic Politics and Diplomacy," *Diplomatic History*, 18 (1994): 463–83. As Sheridan shows, Genet fell afoul of the French Jacobins—who came to power during his mission and considered him a counterrevolutionary—as well as of the Washington administration. Realizing that Genet would be guillotined if he were recalled, Washington eventually allowed him to stay in America, where he settled and married the daughter of the New York Republican (and eventual vice president of the United States) George Clinton.

36. *American Daily Advertiser* [Philadelphia], May 20, Dec. 21, 1793; Foner, ed., *Democratic-Republican Societies*, 7; *New-York Journal*, Jan. 18, 1794; Link, *Democratic-Republican Societies*, 139.

37. Seth Ames, ed., *The Works of Fisher Ames* (Boston, 1854), 2: 150. That some critics tried, falsely, to portray the societies as exotic imports from abroad does not mean that foreign influences were irrelevant—though those influences were themselves partly inspired by previous American examples. There is considerable evidence, for example, that the American societies, at least in the seaports, were well aware of the activities of the Paine-influenced London Corresponding Society (founded in 1792), widely regarded as the pioneering modern proponent of English working-class democratic reform, and much closer in its politics to the American societies than the Jacobin Club of Paris. In 1794, the Democratic Society of Pennsylvania denounced the repression directed against the LCS by the William Pitt ministry. Minutes, Democratic Society of Pennsylvania, July 12, 1794, HSP. One of the chief defenders of the societies, the émigré Philadelphia editor William Duane, had himself been active in the LCS. The connections merely affirm that the Americans remained fully attuned to the wider world of Atlantic democratic radicalism after 1787, as described in (among other works) R. R. Palmer, *The Age of the Democratic Revolution: A Political History of Europe and America, 1760–1800* (Princeton, 1959–64). On the LCS, see E. P. Thompson, *The Making of the English Working Class* (1963; Harmondsworth, 1968), esp. 111–203.

38. *New-York Journal*, June 11, Aug. 31, 1790. A strong example of rural restiveness is William Manning, "Some Proposals for Making Restitution to the Original Creditors of Government" (1790), in Michael Merrill and Sean Wilentz, eds., *The Key of Liberty: The Life and Democratic Writings of William Manning, "A Laborer," 1747–1814* (Cambridge, MA, 1993).

39. Quotation in Young, *Democratic Republicans*, 201; see also Sean Wilentz, *Chants Democratic: New York City & the Rise of the American Working Class* (New York, 1984), 38–39.

40. Democratic Society of New York, *Circular [to the Democratic Society of Philadelphia]*(New York, 1794), 6. For continued resentment among club members of Hamilton's financial measures before 1793, see e.g., Democratic Society of the Borough of Norfolk, "Address to Friends and Fellow Citizens, June 9, 1794," *Virginia Gazette and Richmond and Manchester Advertiser* [Richmond], July 3, 1794; T[unis] Wortman, *An Oration on the Influence of Social Institution Upon Human Morals and Happiness* (New York, 1796), 29; *Pittsburgh Gazette*, May 17, 1794, quoted in Foner, ed., *Democratic-Republican Societies*, 133; *American Daily Advertiser*, July 10, 1795. On Hamilton's program as a product of "foreign climes," meaning British and Tory influence, see, e.g., Democratic Society of the Borough of Norfolk, "Address to Friends and Fellow Citizens, June 9, 1794," *Virginia Gazette and Richmond and Manchester Advertiser*, July 3, 1794, quoted in Foner, ed., *Democratic-Republican Societies*, 349–50.

41. Democratic Society of Pennsylvania, Minutes, Oct. 9, 1794, HSP.

42. The Franklin or Republican Society of backcountry Pendleton, South Carolina, claimed 400 members. If that figure is accurate, the Philadelphia group, with 315 members, was the second largest in the country. Most of the societies were much smaller, with memberships numbering one or two dozen. Foner, ed., *Democratic-Republican Societies*, 7.

43. Among the less well-remembered intellectuals in the group was William Thornton, physi-

cian, linguist, antislavery organizer, architect, fellow of the American Philosophical Society, and member of the Pennsylvania Democratic Society, who thanked heaven that he lived "in this Age of Revolution, in this Age of Light and Reason." In his devotion to the French republic, Thornton sent the French "hints" on effective weaponry, including plans for fragmentation bombs made of volcanic rock and for a harpoon-like contraption that (Thornton contended) would retrieve fleeing ships. Thornton would become Thomas Jefferson's original choice to design the capitol building in the new federal city along the Potomac. Thornton to the Citizen President of France, June 12, 1794, in C. M. Harris, ed., *Papers of William Thornton: Volume One, 1781–1802* (Charlottesville, 1995), 278. Thornton's "hints" are included in folios 163 and 164 of the William Thornton Papers, LC. On the radical intellectuals, see, in addition to the works cited in note 40, Jeffrey A. Smith, *Franklin and Bache: Envisioning the Enlightened Republic* (New York, 1990); James D. Tagg, *Benjamin Franklin Bache and the Philadelphia Aurora* (Philadelphia, 1991), esp. 1–170. On veteran Revolutionary radical leaders who joined clubs in other cities, see Link, *Democratic-Republican Societies*, 98–99.

44. Ronald Baumann, in an analysis of the membership's occupations, concluded that it was composed of men "who were very mobile, commercial minded, and status conscious." Citing Baumann, and referring to a handful of the Democratic Society's leaders, Elkins and McKitrick argue it consisted chiefly of upwardly mobile entrepreneurs and not the humbler orders, as Eugene P. Link argued in 1942 in *Democratic-Republican Societies*, 91. Yet the most painstaking study of the society's membership, using tax lists as well as occupational listings, shows that the preponderance of the rank and file, although skilled and not from the very bottom rungs of society, was far from affluent, and that Link came closer to the mark than his critics. See Andrew Bechman, "Sentinels of Liberty: The Democratic Society of Pennsylvania, 1793–1796" (senior thesis, Princeton University, 1980). Compare Ronald M. Baumann, "The Democratic-Republicans of Philadelphia: The Origins, 1776–1797" (Ph.D. dissert., Pennsylvania State University, 1970) (quotation on 430); Elkins and McKitrick, *Age of Federalism*, 457–8. The New York society, which numbered about two hundred members, likewise seems to have included largely professionals and merchants among its leaders, but with a much humbler rank and file dominated by middling artisans of indifferent wealth and status. See Wilentz, *Chants Democratic*, 68; Edwin G. Burrows and Mike Wallace, eds., *Gotham: A History of New York City to 1898* (New York, 1999), 322–3. See also Schoenbachler, "Republicanism," 241–3, which finds similar patterns in societies located in Vermont, Delaware, and Kentucky.

45. Democratic Society of Pennsylvania, Minutes, May 1, 1794, HSP; *New-York Journal*, May 25, 1794; *Independent Chronicle* [Boston], Jan. 5, 1795. Francophilia was not restricted to the northern cities. The Charleston Democratic Club, an outpost of egalitarianism in Anglophilic South Carolina, successfully petitioned to be officially adopted by the Jacobin Club in Paris; on one occasion, the club's members toasted the guillotine as the proper remedy for "all tyrants, plunderers and funding speculators." Charleston Democratic Club petition quoted in Henry F. May, *The Enlightenment in America* (New York, 1976), 245.

46. *Independent Chronicle*, Jan. 5, 1795; *Principles, Articles, and Regulations, Agreed Upon by the Members of the Democratic Society in Philadelphia, May 30th, 1793* (Philadelphia, 1793), 6–8; *Constitution of the Democratic Society of the City of New-York* (New York, 1794), 5–15. From another angle, of course, the positions of the Jacobins and the Democratic-Republicans were actually the reverse of each other, with the Jacobins promulgating centralized power under their terror-backed reign of virtue and the Americans resisting what they considered Hamiltonian abuses of government centralization.

47. "Address to the Patriotic Societies through the United States," in Democratic Society of Pennsylvania, Minutes, Oct. 9, 1794, HSP. On the rise of the radical editors of the 1790s, see Kim Tousley Phillips, "William Duane, Revolutionary Editor" (Ph.D. dissert., University of California at Berkeley, 1968), 4–100; Tagg, *Bache*; Pasley, *"Tyranny of Printers,"* esp. 1–79, 176–229.

48. *North Carolina Gazette* [New Bern], Apr. 19, 1794, quoted in Foner, ed., *Democratic-Republican Societies*, 11. The fullest philosophical and political defense of these freedoms by a society leader appeared in a treatise published shortly after most of the societies had folded: Tunis Wortman, *A Treatise Concerning Political Enquiry and the Freedom of the Press* (New York, 1800).

49. *New-York Journal*, July 8, 1795; Link, *Democratic-Republican Societies*, 156–74; Foner, ed., *Democratic-Republican Societies*, 13–15.

50. *Independent Chronicle*, Mar. 30, 1795; *New-York Journal*, May 31, 1794.

51. *Independent Chronicle*, Mar. 30, 1795. On the parades and festivals as attacks on deference, see also Simon P. Newman, *Parades and the Politics of the Street: Festive Culture in the Early American Republic* (Philadelphia, 1997); David Waldstreicher, *In the Midst of Perpetual Fetes: The Making of American Nationalism* (Chapel Hill, 1997).

52. Wortman, *Oration*, 24–25, 30. Similar thoughts of a harmonious, prosperous, postaristocratic world were shared by liberal writers as far-flung as James Madison, Joel Barlow, and Immanuel Kant, despite their basic differences on other matters. (Wortman, for example, was probably a deist and had a highly optimistic view of human nature, much closer to Jefferson's than to Madison's.) The Massachusetts country democrat (and orthodox Calvinist) William Manning wrote along the same lines in the later 1790s. For further discussion, see Merrill and Wilentz, eds., *Key of Liberty*, 66–67; Ruth H. Bloch, *Visionary Republic: Millennial Themes in American Thought, 1756–1800* (Cambridge, UK, 1985), esp. 194–201.

53. *Principles, Articles, and Regulations . . . of the Democratic Society in Philadelphia*, 5; *Aurora*, Oct. 17, 1795; Link, *Democratic-Republican Societies*, 132 n. 20; Young, *Democratic Republicans*, 560. See also Cunningham, *Jeffersonian Republicans*, 62–66; Noble E. Cunningham Jr., "John Beckley: An Early American Party Manager," *WMQ*, 13 (1956): 40–52; Edmund Berkeley and Dorothy Smith Berkeley, *John Beckley: Zealous Partisan in a Nation Divided* (Philadelphia, 1973), esp. 104–31; Jeffrey L. Pasley, "'A Journeyman'"; Democratic Society of Pennsylvania, Minutes, May 1, 1794, HSP.

54. Madison to Jefferson, Dec. 21, 1794, in *PTJ*, 8: 220–1; *New-York Journal*, Mar. 1, 8, 12, 15, 1794; Young, *Democratic Republicans*, 373–5. The young lawyer and Princeton graduate Edward Livingston did indeed defeat his opponent, in his first election to the Congress. See William B. Hatcher, *Edward Livingston: Jeffersonian Republican and Jacksonian Democrat* (Baton Rouge, 1940), 28–34.

55. *New-York Journal*, June 18, 1794. William Miller, "First Fruits of Republican Organization: Political Aspect of the Congressional Elections of 1794," *Pennsylvania Magazine of History and Biography*, 63 (1939): 118–43.

56. Wolcott quoted in Foner, ed., *Democratic-Republican Societies*, 24; Ammon, *Genet Mission*, 133–46. See also "A Federal Republican," *New-York Journal*, June 18, 1794.

57. Cobbett, *A Little Plain English Addressed to the People of the United States* (Philadelphia, 1795), 70; "Acquiline Nimble Chops, Democrat," *Democracy: An Epic Poem* (New York, 1794).

58. Republican Society at the Mouth of Yough, Constitution, Article I, Section 8, in *Pittsburgh Gazette*, June 28, 1794. Rural societies also showed less interest in many of the broad humanitarian reforms advocated by city democrats. Regarding cruel and unusual punishments, for example, one Vermont society member, a county sheriff, declared he believed in "whipping criminals 'til blood ran." William Slade quoted in Link, *Democratic-Republican Societies*, 152.

59. *Kentucky Gazette*, Aug. 31, 1793; "The Remonstrance of Citizens West of the Allegheny Mountains," in Foner, ed., *Democratic-Republican Societies*, 367; Republican Society at the Mouth of Yough, Constitution, Article I, Section 10, in *Pittsburgh Gazette*, June 28, 1794. The Kentuckians' fractiousness reached the point where, in late 1793, they threatened to secede from the Union unless the federal government procured from Spain undisturbed navigation of the Mississippi River to New Orleans.

60. Link, *Democratic-Republican Societies*, 153–4; Jasper Dwight [William Duane], *A Letter*

to George Washington, President of the United States (Philadelphia, 1796), 47–48. A well-known cartoon attacking the societies, "A Peep Into the Antifederal Club," dated New York City, 1793, featured a grinning crouching black man among the democratic faithful. Engraving at Free Library of Pennsylvania. A toast calling for the "speedy abolition of every species of slavery throughout America" was drunk in New York in November 1794—though at a gathering of the largely pro-opposition Tammany Society, and not of the New York Democratic Society. See Aurora, Nov. 29, 1794.

61. PAH, 12: 308–9; Gazette of the United States, Sept. 1, 5, 1792. On these early agitations, see Thomas P. Slaughter, The Whiskey Rebellion: Frontier Epilogue to the American Revolution (New York, 1986), esp. 109–24.
62. Slaughter, Whiskey Rebellion, 125–89.
63. Democratic Society, New York, Circular, 10; Hugh H. Brackenridge, Incidents of the Insurrection in the Western Parts of Pennsylvania in the Year 1794 (Philadelphia, 1795), 2: 18; Pittsburgh Gazette, Jan. 24, 1795.
64. Slaughter, Whiskey Rebellion, 205–28, also 276 n. 27.
65. Edmund Randolph to George Washington, Oct. 11, 1794, in Jared Sparks, ed., The Writings of George Washington (Boston, 1836), 10: 443. Some of the radicals of the Pennsylvania Democratic Society were so incensed at the rebels that they offered a resolution (proposed by Michael Leib) charging that "so far from entitling them to the patronage of Democrats, [violence] will merit the proscription of every friend of equal liberty." Although the society eventually passed a much milder reprimand, a substantial number of members, including Leib and his brother, actually volunteered to help suppress the uprising. How many society men joined the fight against the rebels is unclear, although the German Republican Society, voicing its approval, claimed that members of the Democratic Society had been "among the foremost" in marching west and "could have made a quorum in the field." Democratic Society of Pennsylvania, Minutes, Sept. 11, 1794, HSP; Phillips, "William Duane," 104–7; Philadelphia Gazette and Universal Daily Advertiser, Dec. 29, 1794.
66. Richardson, 1: 153–9 (quotations on 153, 155); Washington to Henry Lee, Aug. 26, 1794, in Sparks, Writings of George Washington, 10: 429–30. Edmund Randolph to Alexander Hamilton, Henry Knox, and William Bradford, Apr. 14, 1794, in PAH, 16: 259–60. The last of these contains a remonstrance from the Democratic Society of Washington County, on which Hamilton wrote a suggestion that it be forwarded to the attorney general for possible prosecution. Federalists outside of Philadelphia applauded the repression. One of Hamilton's Virginia friends demanded nothing less than "a radical extirpation" of the "Democratic societies, British debtors & other Factions" who presumed to speak for the people. Edward Carrington to Alexander Hamilton, Aug. 25, 1794, in PAH, 17: 138–9.
67. Minor quoted in Link, Democratic-Republican Societies, 194; Aurora, Jan. 26, March 21, 1795. On the Tammany affray, see the reports reprinted in Foner, ed., Democratic-Republican Societies, 205–16.
68. AC, 3rd Congress, 2nd session, 920–32 (quotation on 923).
69. Madison to James Monroe, Dec. 4, 1794, in PJM, 15: 406–7. See also Madison to Thomas Jefferson, Nov. 30, 1794, in PTJ, 28: 213.
70. AC, 3rd Congress, 2nd session, 908–9, 934–5.
71. Independent Chronicle, Jan. 16, 1794; Pennsylvania Gazette, Dec. 29, 1794.
72. General Advertiser, May 10, 1794. See Jerald A. Combs, The Jay Treaty: Political Battleground of the Founding Fathers (Berkeley, 1970), 159–70. On the matter of Jay's appointment and the violation of the separation of powers, the Democratic Society in Wythe County, Virginia, offered a typical critique: "What is despotism? Is it not a union of executive, legislative, and judicial authorities in the same hands? . . . Your Chief Justice has been appointed to an executive office, by the head of that branch of Government; In that capacity he is to make treaties: Those treaties are your supreme law?—and of this supreme law he is supreme Judge!!! What has become of your constitution & liberties?" American Daily Advertiser, Aug. 2, 1794.

73. *New-York Journal*, July 22, 1795; *New York Argus*, July 20, 1795. The *Argus*, edited by the city democrat Thomas Greenleaf, printed the fullest contemporary account of the New York town-meeting affair; for different interpretations, see Young, *Democratic Republicans*, 449–54; Joanne Freeman, *Affairs of Honor: National Politics in the New Republic* (New Haven, 2001), xiii–xxiv. Young doubts that Hamilton was stoned, although he credits reports that the crowd pulled him down and dragged him through the gutter. The Senate did not permit any member of the public to attend its sessions until compelled to do so, under Republican pressure, in February 1794. In 1795, the Senate finally added a public gallery but conducted its debates over the Jay Treaty behind closed doors. See Gerald L. Grotta, "Philip Freneau's Crusade for Open Sessions of the U.S. Senate," *Journalism Quarterly*, 48 (1971): 667–71.

74. *City Gazette* [Charleston], Oct. 28, 1795.

75. An exception that proved the rule was the antitreaty speech delivered to the Democratic Society of Canaan in Columbia County, New York, in Foner, ed., *Democratic-Republican Societies*, 246–52.

76. Combs, *Jay Treaty*, 171–88 (quotation on 184).

77. Paul A. W. Wallace, *The Muhlenbergs of Pennsylvania* (1950; Freeport, NY, 1970), 284–8. Never again nominated to any elective office, Muhlenberg would die of a stroke five years later, at age fifty-one. The sources on the Polly story are, alas, silent on whether Muhlenberg's vote allowed the wedding to go forward.

78. *American Mercury* [Hartford], Jan. 25, 1796; *Gazette of the United States*, Sept. 1, 1796.

79. *Farmer's Library* [Fairhaven, VT], Feb. 17, 1794; *New-York Journal*, Mar. 8, May 31, 1794; *Independent Chronicle*, Jan. 3, 1793. Ironically, the New Yorker relied on the authority of the Tory Samuel Johnson's famous dictionary in equating a republic with a democracy. See also Aleine Austin, *Matthew Lyon: "New Man" of the Democratic Revolution, 1749–1822* (University Park, PA, 1981).

80. "To the People of the United States Approving the Conduct of the President of the United States, January 19, 1795," *New-York Journal*, Jan. 21, 1794; Chipman to Alexander Hamilton, June 9, 1794, in *PAH*, 16: 465–70 (quotations on 468). On the controversy that followed the Tammany pro-Federalists' declaration, see *Daily Advertiser* [New York], Feb. 9, 1795; *New-York Journal*, Feb. 18, 1795.

81. Madison to James Monroe, Dec. 4, 1794, in *PJM*, 15: 406.

CHAPTER THREE: THE MAKING OF JEFFERSONIAN DEMOCRACY

1. Jefferson to Edmund Randolph, Feb. 3, 1794, Jefferson to Horatio Gates, Feb. 3, 1794, in *PTJ*, 28: 14–5. See also Jefferson to James Madison, June 9, 1793, in *PTJ*, 26: 239–41.

2. James Monroe to Thomas Jefferson, Mar. 16, 1794, James Madison to Thomas Jefferson, Apr. 28, 1794, Jefferson to Monroe, Apr. 24, 1794, to Madison, Dec. 28, 1794 (quotation), in *PTJ*, 28: 42, 55, 62–63, 228.

3. Jefferson to Thomas Mann Randolph, Aug. 11, 1795, in *PTJ*, 28: 434–5; Jefferson to Philip Mazzei, Apr. 24, 1796, in *PTJ*, 29: 73–88, which includes a full account of how the text of the Mazzei letter became public knowledge.

4. *Aurora General Advertiser* [Philadelphia] [hereafter *Aurora*], Sept. 13, 1796. In order to prevent a riot of state favorite-son candidacies, the Framers had stipulated that each presidential elector would cast two votes. The winner of the most votes would become president, and the runner-up would be elected vice president. In the crowded field of other candidates in 1796, Adams's purported running mate, Thomas Pinckney, received nine fewer electoral votes than Jefferson, while twenty-four electoral votes went to a scattering of other Federalists, including Oliver Ellsworth and John Jay. Two electors, one in North Carolina, the other in Virginia, voted for George Washington, despite the president's decision to retire. There is some scholarly disagreement about how formal the con-

gressional Republicans' deliberations were in 1796, although certainly some sort of meeting or meetings took place. Four years later, both the congressional Republicans and the Federalists held recognized nominating caucuses, although in secret. See William G. Morgan, "The Origins and Development of the Congressional Nominating Caucus," *Proceedings of the American Philosophical Society*, 113 (1969): 184–96.

5. James Roger Sharp, *American Politics in the Early Republic: The New Nation in Crisis* (New Haven, 1993), 138–62; and John Ferling, *Adams vs. Jefferson: The Tumultuous Election of 1800* (New York, 2004), 83–98, provide succinct accounts of the 1796 elections as they do of national politics generally in the 1790s. See also Stanley Elkins and Eric L. McKitrick, *The Age of Federalism: The Early American Republic, 1788–1800* (New York, 1993), 513–28; Page Smith, "Election of 1796," in S & I, 1: 59–98; Joanne Freeman, "The Presidential Election of 1796," in Richard Alan Ryerson, ed., *John Adams and the Founding of the Republic* (Boston, 2001), 142–70.

6. "Public Notice" [1796], Broadside, HSP. Harry Marlin Tinkcom, *The Republicans and Federalists in Pennsylvania, 1790–1801: A Study in National Stimulus and Local Response* (Harrisburg, 1950), 159–74, is the basic account of the 1796 elections in Pennsylvania, but see also Noble E. Cunningham, *The Jeffersonian Republicans: The Formation of Party Organization, 1789–1801* (Chapel Hill, 1957), 107–8; Elkins and McKitrick, *Age of Federalism*, 521. Beckley proved an exceptionally shrewd campaign manager. In the months before the election, the Federalist-controlled Pennsylvania legislature revised the state election laws to have presidential electors chosen by a statewide vote instead of by districts. A statewide contest, they believed, would undermine the Republicans' strength in various localities. Under instructions from Beckley, however, the Republican assembly caucus nominated a slate of electors with as many notable names as it could muster—then kept the list secret, lest the Federalists catch on. The Federalists duly nominated a list of names somewhat less recognizable across the state and immediately found themselves at a disadvantage. To punish him for his partisan successes, the new Federalist majority fired Beckley from his position as clerk of the House of Representatives, but he remained a stalwart Republican organizer. In 1802, President Jefferson appointed him as the first librarian of Congress and returned him to his post as clerk of the House. Beckley, who deserved and had hoped for a more influential and lucrative appointment, died disappointed and heavily in debt in 1807.

7. *Aurora*, Nov. 1, 1796. On the campaign in New York, see Alfred F. Young, *The Democratic Republicans of New York: The Origins, 1763–1797* (Chapel Hill, 1967), 546–51. For concise accounts of Hamilton's alleged scheme, see Sharp, *American Politics*, 146–9; Ferling, *Adams vs. Jefferson*, 87–89. Anti-administration forces had won a House majority in the Third Congress (1793–95), which they enlarged in the Fourth, only to lose their advantage in the 1796 elections.

8. Adams to Tristram Dalton, Jan. 19, 1797, quoted in Sharp, *American Politics*, 160; Jefferson to Rutledge, Dec. 27, 1796, Jefferson to Madison, Jan. 1, 1797, in *PTJ*, 29: 232, 248. Adams later claimed that he would have ruined his presidency at the start had he not agreed to reappoint Washington's cabinet members. Jefferson knew better, remarking that Adams had surrounded himself with Hamilton's acolytes, "only a little less hostile to him than to me." Jefferson to Elbridge Gerry, May 13, 1797, in *PTJ*, 29: 362. For a brief time, even Bache's *Aurora* tried to build support for Adams, whom Bache regarded as far more acceptable than Hamilton and the ultra-Federalists. Arthur Sherr, "'Vox Populi' versus the Patriot President: Benjamin Franklin Bache's Philadelphia *Aurora* and John Adams (1797)," *Pennsylvania History*, 62 (1995): 503–51. Hamilton was more sardonic about the situation: "Our Jacobins say they are well pleased," he wrote, "and that the *Lion* & the *Lamb* are to lie down together." Hamilton to Rufus King, Feb. 15, 1797, in *PAH*, 20: 515–6.

9. See John Ferling, *John Adams: A Life* (Knoxville, 1992); also Page Smith, *John Adams* (New York, 1962); Joseph Ellis, *Passionate Sage: The Character and Life of John Adams* (New York, 1993).

10. Adams quoted in Elkins and McKitrick, *Age of Federalism*, 532.
11. "An American Citizen" [John Adams], *Discourses on Davila. A Series of Papers on Political History* (1790; Boston, 1805), 87–88; Adams, *A Defence of the Constitutions of the United States of America* (1787–88), in Charles F. Adams, ed., *The Works of John Adams* (Boston, 1850–56), 6: 185. Adams's thinking continued to evolve; see Adams to Jefferson, Nov. 15, 1813, TJC. For an illuminating analysis, see Gordon S. Wood, *The Creation of the American Republic, 1776–1787* (Chapel Hill, 1969), 574–80.
12. Jefferson to Thomas Pinckney, May 29, 1797, in *PTJ*, 29: 404–6. The most thorough account of these events is William Stinchcombe, *The XYZ Affair* (Westport, CT, 1980); see also Alexander DeConde, *The Quasi-War: The Politics and Diplomacy of the Undeclared War with France, 1791–1801* (New York, 1966), 36–73.
13. There was also a "W" involved in the negotiations, an Englishman named Nicholas Hubbard who was a partner in an Amsterdam bank. The power of patriotism and, in other contexts, Protestant fervor to mobilize a powerful plebeian conservatism has received far too little attention from early American historians, who often seem to assume that the lower and middling orders of the late eighteenth century were steadfast Republicans. For a useful comparative point of departure, see Linda Colley, *Britons: Forging the Nation, 1707–1837* (New Haven, 1992).
14. Hamilton to Rufus King, June 6, 1798, in *PAH*, 21: 490. See Richard H. Kohn, *Eagle and Sword: The Federalists and the Creation of the Military Establishment in America, 1783–1802* (New York, 1975), 193–273; James Morton Smith, *Freedom's Fetters: The Alien and Sedition Laws and American Civil Liberties* (Ithaca, NY, 1956), 3–155; Douglas M. Bradburn, "'True Americans' and 'Hordes of Foreigners': Nationalism, Ethnicity, and the Problem of Citizenship in the United States, 1789–1800," *Historical Reflections*, 29 (2003): 19–41. Years later, Adams would try to blame the alien and sedition acts chiefly on Hamilton's influence. In fact, although Hamilton strongly supported repressive measures, and eventually took a direct hand in suppressing individual Republican printers, he also worried that excessive zeal would make martyrs of the Republicans, and behind the scenes he tried toning down early drafts of the proposed Sedition Law that he found "highly exceptional": "Let us not establish a tyranny," he wrote to Oliver Wolcott, "Energy is a different thing from violence." Hamilton to Oliver Wolcott Jr., June 29, 1798, in *PAH*, 21: 522. Once the law was passed, he became a vigorous advocate for its enforcement. See James Morton Smith, "Alexander Hamilton, the Alien Law, and Seditious Libels," *Review of Politics*, 16 (1954): 305–33. As for Adams, although he did not propose the new bills or play any part in their passage, neither he nor most other leading Federalists made any effort to oppose them, either before or after Congress had acted. The major exception was John Marshall: see Albert Beveridge, *The Life of John Marshall* (Boston, 1916–19), 2: 389.
15. Jefferson to James Madison, Apr. 26, 1798, to John Taylor, June 4, 1798, in *PTJ*, 30: 300, 389. Republican fears were fully justified. Early in 1799, Hamilton, claiming that Jefferson and Madison were engaged in "a regular conspiracy to overthrow the government," was pushing hard for raising military force against the Virginia Republican leadership. See Hamilton to Theodore Sedgwick, Feb. 2, 1799, in *PAH*, 22: 452–4.
16. The basic facts appear in Sharp, *American Politics*, 187–207. See also Dumas Malone, *Jefferson and His Time* (New York, 1958–81), 3: 395–409, for a more benign interpretation; Elkins and McKitrick, *Age of Federalism*, 719–26, for a tougher one. On the composition of the resolves, see *PTJ*, 30: 529–35; *PJM*, 17: 199–206, 303–7. On protests of the laws, see *Aurora*, July 11, 14, 1798; James Morton Smith, "The Grass Roots Origin of the Kentucky Resolutions," *WMQ*, 27 (1970): 221–45. To say that Jefferson and Madison acted out of a sense of crisis is not at all to deny that they and other Virginians—above all, John Taylor— had not long feared a consolidation of federal power. It is to insist, however, that the sense of crisis was real, and not merely a pretext for asserting long-held doctrines. Compare K. R. Constantine Gutzman, "The Virginia and Kentucky Resolutions Reconsidered: 'An Appeal to the *Real* Laws of Our Country,'" *JSH*, 66 (2000): 473–96.

17. Jefferson's draft and his fair copy, both composed before Oct. 4, 1798, appear in *PTJ*, 30: 536–49. Madison, although supportive, was disquieted from the start by Jefferson's stance and urged moderation, especially on the question of the state legislatures' powers to intervene on constitutional issues. See Madison to Jefferson, Dec. 29, 1798, in *PTJ*, 30: 606. John Taylor, Jefferson's ally, suggested as a "provisional project" that special state conventions nullify federal laws, but Jefferson was unwilling to go that far. See Taylor to Thomas Jefferson, Dec. 11, 1798, in *PTJ*, 30: 601–2.

18. Resolutions Adopted by the Kentucky General Assembly, in *PTJ*, 30: 550–6; Jonathan Elliot, *The Debates in the Several State Conventions on the Adoption of the Federal Constitution* (1836–45; Philadelphia, 1901), 4: 528–80 (quotation on 535). See also the old but still informative article by Frank M. Anderson, "Contemporary Opinion of the Virginia and Kentucky Resolutions," *AHR*, 5 (1899–1900): 45–63, 225–52. Breckinridge's softening of Jefferson's language was in part aimed at reconciling the document with resolutions passed by numerous Kentucky counties, most of which he had written and which called for congressional repeal of the offensive acts. See Smith, "Grass Roots."

19. For detailed discussion of these cases, see Smith, *Freedom's Fetters*, 221–306, 334–417; Jeffrey L. Pasley, *"The Tyranny of Printers": Newspaper Politics in the Early American Republic* (Charlottesville, 2001), 105–31; Michael Durey, *Transatlantic Radicals and the Early American Republic* (Lawrence, KS, 1997), 251–7; David A. Wilson, *United Irishmen, United States: Immigrant Radicals in the Early Republic* (Ithaca, NY, 1998), 36–57.

20. AC, 6th Congress, 1st session, 111; Smith, *Freedom's Fetters*, 279–98; Kim Tousley Phillips, "William Duane, Revolutionary Editor" (Ph.D. dissert., University of California at Berkeley, 1968), 76–91.

21. Smith, *Freedom's Fetters*, 221–46, 390–8; Young, *Democratic Republicans*, 456–7, 508–20. On Peck, see Alan Taylor, *William Cooper's Town: Power and Persuasion on the Frontier of the Early American Republic* (New York, 1995), esp. 241–9, 267–91; Sherman Williams, "Jedidiah [*sic*] Peck, the Father of the State Public School System of the State of New York," *New York State Historical Association Quarterly Journal*, 1 (1920): 219–40. The charges against Peck were eventually dropped and in 1800, now a leading organizer of New York's upstate Republicans, he was reelected to the legislature.

22. *Aurora*, Oct. 12, 1799; Smith, *Freedom's Fetters*, 257–74. Brown, a common laborer, Revolutionary veteran, and itinerant political speaker, had visited more than eighty Massachusetts towns over the previous two years, railing against the Federalists and, more generally, against "those lazy rascals that have invented every means that the Devil had put in their hands to destroy the labouring part of the Community." See *Independent Chronicle* [Boston], June 17, 1799.

23. See Arthur Zilversmit, *The First Emancipation: The Abolition of Slavery in the North* (Chicago, 1967), 169–200. There is a familiar argument that the New York Federalists favored abolition while the Republicans opposed it. Zilversmit's close analysis of the legislative votes in 1799, however, shows that the Republicans split evenly over the bill in the senate and overwhelmingly supported it in the assembly, in a proportion slightly greater than the Federalists. For Jeffersonian antislavery opinion, see *The Argus; or Greenleaf's New Daily Advertiser* [New York], Jan. 23, Feb. 3, 6, 1796. On suffrage law changes, see Chilton Williamson, *American Suffrage from Property to Democracy, 1760–1860* (Princeton, 1960), 124

24. Phineas Hedges, M.D., *An Oration Delivered Before the Republican Society, of Ulster County, and Other Citizens* (Goshen, NY, 1795), 13; Rachel N. Klein, *The Unification of a Slave State: The Rise of the Planter Class in the South Carolina Backcountry, 1760–1808* (Chapel Hill, 1990), 142–7; *American Museum*, Dec. 1790, 282; Williamson, *American Suffrage*, 138–44; Scaevola [Henry Clay], "To the Electors of Fayette County, April 16, 1798," "To the Citizens of Fayette [Feb. 1799]," in *PHC*, 1: 3–8, 10–14; Joan Wells Cowan, *Kentucky in the New Republic: The Process of Constitution Making* (Lexington, KY, 1979), 69–161; Steven Aron, *How the West Was Lost: The Transformation of Kentucky from Daniel Boone to Henry Clay* (Baltimore, 1996), 82–102. See also Rosemarie Zagarri,

"Representation and the Removal of State Capitals, 1776–1812," *JAH*, 74 (1988): 1239–56.

25. William Heth to Alexander Hamilton, Jan. 14, 1799, in *PAH*, 22: 413–6. On the stockpiling of arms in Virginia, see ibid., and Heth's letter of Jan. 18, 1799, in *PAH*, 22: 422–4; Sharp, *American Politics*, 203–6. For an assessment of popular support for the Federalists during the war scare, see Thomas M. Ray, "'Not One Cent for Tribute': The Public Addresses and American Popular Reaction to the XYZ Affair, 1798–1799," *JER*, 3 (1983): 389–412. On the Federalist election triumphs, see the qualifying findings in John W. Kuehl, "Southern Reaction to the XYZ Affair: An Incident in the Emergence of American Nationalism," *Register of the Kentucky Historical Society*, 70 (1972): 21–49; idem, "The XYZ Affair and American Nationalism: Republican Victories in the Middle Atlantic States," *Maryland Historical Magazine*, 67 (1972): 1–20. On the Fries Rebellion, see Robert H. Churchill, "Popular Nullification, Fries' Rebellion, and the Waning of Radical Republicanism, 1798–1801," *Pennsylvania History*, 67 (2000): 105–40; Terry Bouton, "'No Wonder the Times Were Troublesome': The Origins of Fries' Rebellion," *Pennsylvania History*, 67 (2000): 21–42; Peter Levine, "The Fries Rebellion: Social Violence and the Politics of the New Nation," *Pennsylvania History*, 40 (1973): 241–58.

26. On Adams's mood, see esp. Theodore Segwick's report on a meeting with the president, in Sedgwick to Alexander Hamilton, Feb. 7, 1799, in *PAH*, 22: 469–72 (quotation on 471). On Adams's meetings with Elbridge Gerry and George Logan, see Ferling, *Adams vs. Jefferson*, 118–9.

27. Hamilton to Rufus King, Jan. 5, 1800, in *PAH*, 24: 168.

28. James Nicholson Statement, Dec. 26, 1803, DeWitt Clinton Papers, Columbia University; Cunningham, *Jeffersonian Republicans*, 147–66 (quotation on 149).

29. See Milton Lomask, *Aaron Burr: The Years from Princeton to Vice President, 1756–1805* (New York), 1–255; Mary-Jo Kline, ed., *Political Correspondence and Public Papers of Aaron Burr* (Princeton, 1983), liii–lxx, 3–282.

30. Jefferson to James Madison, Mar. 3, 1800, TJC.

31. James Nicholson to Albert Gallatin, in Henry Adams, *The Life of Albert Gallatin* (1879; Philadelphia, 1880), 241; Cunningham, *Jeffersonian Republicans*, 176–85; Elkins and McKitrick, *Age of Federalism*, 733. According to Matthew Davis, Burr spent the last day of the three-day voting period "at the poll of the Seventh Ward"—a workingman's district thought vulnerable to Federalist strong-arming—for "Ten Hours, without intermission." Davis to Albert Gallatin, May 1, 1800, Gallatin Papers, N-YHS.

32. James McHenry to John McHenry, May 20, 1800, in George Gibbs, ed., *Memoirs of the Administrations of George Washington and John Adams, Edited from the Papers of Oliver Wolcott* (New York, 1846), 2: 347; Albert Gallatin to his wife, May 12, 1800, in Adams, *Life of Albert Gallatin*, 243. On these developments, see Elkins and McKitrick, *Age of Federalism*, 732–6; Sharp, *American Politics*, 233–40.

33. Monroe to Jefferson, Apr. 22, 1800, Monroe to Brigadier General Matthews, March 17, 1802, quoted in Douglas R. Egerton, *Gabriel's Rebellion: The Virginia Slave Conspiracies of 1800 and 1802* (Chapel Hill, 1993), 47, 49; but see also James Sidbury, *Ploughshares into Swords: Race, Rebellion, and Identity in Gabriel's Virginia* (New York, 1997). On American slave rebellions elsewhere, see Sylvia R. Frey, *Water from the Rock: Black Resistance in a Revolutionary Age* (Princeton, 1991).

34. Monroe, "Message to the Virginia Legislature, December 5, 1800," in Stanislaus Murray Hamilton, ed., *The Writings of James Monroe* (New York, 1898–1903), 3: 234–44; Egerton, *Gabriel's Rebellion*, 18–33. By Gabriel's lights, certain fair-minded whites—including Quakers, Methodists, and Frenchmen—would sympathize with a slave revolt; certainly, he believed, free blacks and mulattoes would support the insurgency once it began; and he told more than one of his confederates that he hoped "poor white people" would also join. As divisions between Richmond's mostly Federalist merchants and mostly Republican artisans had widened with the approach of the 1800 elections, the time seemed ripe for a black-led rebellion from below. Gabriel would lead that rebellion carrying a flag inscribed

with the words "death or Liberty," reversing Patrick Henry's enduring Revolutionary phrase delivered from a Richmond pulpit. See ibid., 31–32, 51. The trial testimony and related material on the rebellion are in the Executive Papers and the Gabriel's Insurrection, Military Papers, LoV.

35. Egerton, *Gabriel's Rebellion*, 50–68.

36. Ibid., 69–115.

37. *Virginia Herald* [Fredricksburg], Sept. 19, 1800; Adams quoted in Linda K. Kerber, *Federalists in Dissent: Imagery and Ideology in Jeffersonian America* (Ithaca, NY, 1970), 50; *Boston Gazette*, Oct. 9, 23, 1800; Egerton, *Gabriel's Rebellion*, 103–4. See also *Gazette of the United States* [Philadelphia], Sept. 13, 1800, which claimed that the rebellion had apparently been organized "*on the true French plan.*" Despite Monroe's efforts, news of the Frenchmen's involvement leaked out anyway, but Republicans were able to portray it as unconfirmed rumor, spread by malevolent Federalists.

38. *Aurora*, Sept. 24, 26, 1800; Jefferson to Monroe, Sept. 20, 1800, TJC.

39. On the elections of 1800 and 1801, see also James Horn, Jan Lewis, and Peter Onuf, eds., *The Revolution of 1800: Democracy, Race, and the New Republic* (Charlottesville, 2002).

40. *Letter from Alexander Hamilton Concerning the Public Conduct and Character of John Adams, Esq., President of the United States* (New York, 1800), 190; Wolcott to Fisher Ames, Aug. 10, 1800, in Gibbs, ed., *Memoirs,* 2: 401.

41. *Aurora*, May 19, 1800; *Gazette of the United* States, May 28, 1800. An excellent summary of the 1800 campaign's rhetoric appears in Ferling, *Adams vs. Jefferson,* 134–61.

42. Jefferson to Thomas Mann Randolph, Nov. 30, 1800, in *Collections of the Massachusetts Historical Society,* 7th ser., 1 (1890), 78. On voter turnout, see J. R. Pole, *Political Representation in England and the Origins of the American Republic* (Berkeley, 1971), 543–64.

43. See Andrew J. Bethea, *The Contribution of Charles Pinckney to the Formation of the American Union* (Richmond, 1937) for some useful information on Pinckney's early career. On his involvement in 1800, see Marvin R. Zahniser, *Charles Cotesworth Pinckney: Founding Father* (Chapel Hill, 1967), 224–33; also Cunningham, *Jefferson Republicans,* 231–6.

44. Monroe to John Drayton, Oct. 21, 1800, in Hamilton, ed., *Writings of James Monroe,* 3: 217; Pinckney to Thomas Jefferson, Nov. 22, Dec. 2, 1800, TJC.

45. "I believe we may consider the election as now decided . . . ," Jefferson wrote to Thomas Mann Randolph in mid-December. "It was intended that one vote [in South Carolina] should be thrown away from Col Burr. It is believed Georgia will withhold from him one or two. The votes will stand probably T.J. 73, Burr about 70, Mr. Adams 65. Pinckney probably lower than that." Jefferson to T M Randolph, Dec. 12, 1800, in *Collections of the Massachusetts Historical Society,* 7th ser., 1 (1890), 80.

46. Gallatin, "Plan," in Henry Adams, ed., *The Writings of Albert Gallatin* (Philadelphia, 1879), 1: 18–23; Jefferson to James Monroe, Feb. 15, 1801, TJC.

47. There are various interpretations of Burr's behavior in late 1800 and early 1801. For a judicious account, somewhat more favorable to Burr than mine, see Lomask, *Burr,* 268–95.

48. Sharp, *American Politics,* 259–62 (quotation on 260).

49. For Jefferson's account of these transactions, see Jefferson, "The Anas," Apr. 15, 1806, in Paul Leicester Ford, ed., *The Works of Thomas Jefferson* (New York, 1904), 1: 393. See also Morton Borden, *The Federalism of James A. Bayard* (New York, 1955), esp. 89–95.

50. Adams to Benjamin Stoddert, Mar. 31, 1801, in Adams, ed., *Works of John Adams,* 9: 582.

51. The best contemporary description of inauguration day is in the *National Intelligencer* [Washington], Mar. 6, 1801, but see also Margaret Bayard Smith, *The First Forty Years in Washington Society,* Gaillard Hunt, ed. (New York, 1906), 22–27. Having not been sure whether he would be elected, Jefferson did not move into the president's house for another two weeks, and conducted business in a parlor at his boardinghouse, Conrad and McMunn's. There were joyous celebrations of the event in other cities; see, e.g., on the grand Philadelphia parade, *Gazette of the United States,* Feb. 18, Mar. 5, 11, 1801.

52. Richardson, 1: 310.

53. Ibid.; Hamilton, "Address to the Electors of the State of New York," Mar. 21, 1801, in

PAH, 25: 365. For Jefferson's rendering of "republicans" and "federalists," see "Draft of First Inaugural," Mar. 4, 1801, TJC. Jefferson's exact meaning remains ambiguous because he often resorted to lowercase in his drafts.

54. Richardson, 1: 310.

55. Ibid., 311.

56. Jefferson to Levi Lincoln, Oct. 25, 1802, Jefferson to Joseph Priestley, Mar. 21, 1801, Jefferson to Spencer Roane, Sept. 6, 1819, Jefferson to Walter Jones, Mar. 31, 1801, TJC; *Aurora*, Jan. 4, 1801. See also Jefferson to Levi Lincoln, July 11, 1801, Jefferson to William Killem, Oct., 1802, TJC.

57. In Maryland and North Carolina, where selection of electors was by district, Adams won a combined total of twelve electoral votes, even though Jefferson carried the overall popular vote in both states. In Kentucky, where the same rules applied, Jefferson carried every district, and hence all of the state's four electoral votes.

58. New England Federalists would soon begin charging that the three-fifths clause was the main factor responsible for Jefferson's victory. Numerous later studies have repeated the charge, most recently Garry Wills, "*Negro President*": *Jefferson and the Slave Power* (Boston, 2003). In fact, the surviving evidence shows that the Republicans won about 52 percent of the votes cast in state and national elections in 1800, and this total does not include the returns from Kentucky, Tennessee, and Georgia, where Jefferson and the Republicans almost certainly won tremendous victories. Although Adams fell victim to the three-fifths clause, his own electoral vote was artificially enlarged by election law manipulation in Massachusetts as well as Pennsylvania. Without those advantages, Adams almost certainly would have lost even had there been no three-fifths clause, and even if he had not been awarded electoral votes from the pro-Jefferson states of New Jersey, Maryland, and North Carolina. In any event, there is no substance to the claim that Adams won a popular victory that was thwarted by the Constitution's favoritism to the slaveholding states. See Ferling, *Adams vs. Jefferson*, 168–9.

59. Jefferson to Francis Hopkinson, Mar. 13, 1789, in *PTJ*, 14: 650. Compare Jefferson's alarmed exhortation to partisan politics and "systematic energies & sacrifices" in his letter to James Madison, Feb. 5, 1799, in *PTJ*, 31: 10.

CHAPTER FOUR: JEFFERSON'S TWO PRESIDENCIES

1. Marshall quoted in Jean Edward Smith, *John Marshall: Definer of a Nation* (New York, 1996), 11; Jefferson to Madison, Nov. 26, 1795, in *PTJ*, 28: 539. Important interpretive narratives of Jefferson's administrations, apart from Henry Adams's classic *History of the United States during the Administrations of Thomas Jefferson and James Madison* (1889–91; New York, 1986), vol. 1, include Dumas Malone, *Jefferson and His Time* (New York, 1958–81), vols. 4, 5; Merrill Peterson, *Thomas Jefferson and the New Nation* (New York, 1970), 652–921; Forrest McDonald, *The Presidency of Thomas Jefferson* (Lawrence, KS, 1976); Joyce Appleby, *Thomas Jefferson* (New York, 2003).

2. Marshall to C. C. Pinckney, Mar. 4, 1804, reprinted in *AHR*, 53 (1948): 518–20; Margaret Bayard Smith, *The First Forty Years of Washington Society*, Gaillard Hunt, ed. (New York, 1906), 25.

3. Thomas McKean to Uriah Tracy, Jan. 14, 1804, McKean Papers, HSP.

4. Henry Lee to Rufus King, June 18, 1801, in Charles R. King, ed., *The Life and Correspondence of Rufus King* (New York, 1894–1900), 3: 475–6 (quotation on 475).

5. Richardson 1: 319. Although Brown was not officially pardoned until March 12, Jefferson and his cabinet reached the decision to do so earlier. Jefferson also personally paid part of Brown's fine. See James Morton Smith, *Freedom's Fetters: The Alien and Sedition Laws and American Civil Liberties* (Ithaca, NY, 1956), 268–9, 303–6.

6. Gallatin to Thomas Jefferson, Nov. 16, 1801, TJC.

7. Jefferson to David Denniton and James Cheetham, June 6, 1801, TJC.

8. Elias Shippen et al. to Jefferson, June 18, 1801, Jefferson to Elias Shippen and others, July 12, 1801, TJC.

9. Jefferson to Pierre du Pont de Nemours, Apr. 24, 1816, to Elias Shippen and others, July 12, 1801, TJC. On Jefferson's replacement policies, see Leonard D. White, *The Jeffersonians: A Study in Administrative History, 1801–1829* (New York, 1951), 347–68; Sidney H. Aronson, *Status and Kinship in the Higher Civil Service: Standards of Selection in the Administrations of John Adams, Thomas Jefferson, and Andrew Jackson* (Cambridge, MA, 1964), 3–22 passim.

10. Richardson, 1: 319. On the Jeffersonians' political struggle over the courts, see Richard E. Ellis, *The Jeffersonian Crisis: Courts and Politics in the Young Republic* (New York, 1971).

11. Jefferson to John Dickinson, Dec. 19, 1801, TJC.

12. Chase to William Paterson, Apr. 6, 1802, Samuel Chase Manuscripts, N-YHS; Ellis, *Jeffersonian Crisis*, 36–52.

13. Jefferson to Pierre S. du Pont de Nemours, Jan. 18, 1802, TJC.

14. "Prudence seems to be more necessary than anything else . . . ," wrote New York's archconservative Gouverneur Morris. "*Nil desperandum.*" The conservative Federalist Fisher Ames of Massachusetts, an acrid antidemocrat when so moved, said invective would be counterproductive: "Even when bad measures occur, much temperance will be requisite." Anne Carey Morris, ed., *Diary and Letters of Gouverneur Morris* (London, 1889), 2: 383; Ames to Theodore Dwight, Mar. 19, 1801, in Seth Ames, ed., *Works of Fisher Ames* (Boston, 1854), 1: 293. See also Linda K. Kerber, *Federalists in Dissent: Imagery and Ideology in Jeffersonian America* (Ithaca, NY, 1970).

15. On Federalist fears that some of their number were going too far, see Cabot to Oliver Wolcott, Aug. 3, 1801, in Henry Cabot Lodge, ed., *Life and Letters of George Cabot* (Boston, 1877), 321. On impeachment, see *Connecticut Courant* [Hartford], Nov. 2, 1801.

16. Jefferson to Thomas Cooper, July 9, 1802, in Paul Leicester Ford, ed., *The Writings of Thomas Jefferson* (New York, 1905), 10: 450–1.

17. Theodore Sedgwick to Rufus King, Feb. 20, 1802, in King, ed., *Life*, 4: 74.

18. Randolph to Joseph Nicholson, Jan. 1, 1801, quoted in Henry Adams, *John Randolph* (1882; Armonk, NY, 1996), 47; Jefferson to DeWitt Clinton, Dec. 2, 1803, TJC. On Burr's first year as vice president, see Milton Lomask, *Aaron Burr* (New York, 1979–82), 1: 296–307; Malone, *Jefferson and His Time* (1948–81), 4: 88–89. See also Russell Kirk, *John Randolph of Roanoke* (1951; Indianapolis, 1978); Norman K. Risjord, *The Old Republicans: Southern Conservatism in the Age of Jefferson* (New York, 1965); Robert Dawidoff, *The Education of John Randolph* (New York, 1979); William Cabell Bruce, *John Randolph of Roanoke* (New York, 1922).

19. In addition to the books and articles cited in chapter 1 notes 13 and 26, see Lyman H. Butterfield, "Elder John Leland, Jeffersonian Itinerant," *Proceedings of the American Antiquarian Society*, New Series, 62: (1952): 155–242; Sidney Kaplan, "'Honestus' and the Annihilation of the Lawyers," *South Atlantic Quarterly*, 48 (1949): 401–20; Ellis, *Jeffersonian Crisis*, 113–14, 208–9, 159–71, 208, 218–9, 222–3; Kim Tousley Phillips, "William Duane, Revolutionary Editor" (Ph.D. dissert., University of California at Berkeley, 1968), 101–234; Andrew Shankman, "Malcontents and Tertium Quids: The Battle to Define Democracy in Jeffersonian Philadelphia," *JER*, 19 (1999): 43–72.

20. *Aurora*, Mar. 31, 1803; Jefferson to Albert Gallatin, Mar. 28, 1803, TJC. AC, 7th Congress, 1st session, 426. The northern congressmen voted 44 to 8 against the Nicholson bill, which was defeated 46 to 43. Michael Leib was a singular exception in voting for it, although later he would vote consistently against the South on issues related to slavery. In many respects, the terms of the Nicholson bill, and the sharp sectional response it elicited, foreshadowed the controversy over the Fugitive Slave Act half a century later. On the differences between the northern democrats and the planter ideologues on economic and political issues, see Ellis, *Jeffersonian Crisis*, 234–5; Andrew Shankman, "Democracy in Pennsylvania: Political, Social, and Economic Arguments in the Jeffersonian Party, 1790–1820" (Ph.D. dissert., Princeton University, 1997), esp. chap. 5.

21. Gallatin to Thomas Jefferson, Aug. 10, 1801, in Henry Adams, ed., *The Writings of Albert Gallatin* (Philadelphia, 1879), 1: 33.
22. Madison to Nicholas Trist, May 1832, in Gaillard Hunt, ed., *The Writings of James Madison* (New York, 1900–10), 9: 479.
23. Jefferson to Albert Gallatin, Aug. 14, 1801, in Adams, ed., *Writings*, 1: 37; Jefferson to Thomas Paine, Mar. 18, 1801, in Ford, ed., *Writings*, 9: 212–4: Jefferson to James Madison, Aug. 16, 1803, TJC. On the public outburst over Jefferson's overtures to Paine, see, e.g., *The Visitor* [New Haven], Jan. 11, 1803.
24. Bayard to Alexander Hamilton, Apr. 25, 1802, in *PAH*, 25: 613–4.
25. Jefferson to Lord Buchan, July 10, 1803, TJC. On the diplomatic background to the Louisiana Purchase, its negotiation, and completion, see Alexander DeConde, *This Affair of Louisiana* (1976; Baton Rouge, 1979); on the larger implications, Jon Kukla, *A Wilderness So Immense: The Louisiana Purchase and the Destiny of America* (New York, 2003).
26. Jefferson to James Madison, Feb. 12, 1799, in *PTJ*, 31: 29–30; Pichon to Talleyrand, July 22, 1801, quoted in Malone, *Jefferson*, 4: 252. Also see Tim Mathewson, "Jefferson and Haiti," *JSH*, 61 (1995): 209–48; idem, "Jefferson and the Non-Recognition of Haiti," *Proceedings of the American Philosophical Society*, 140 (1996): 22–48.
27. Pichon to Talleyrand, Jan. 28, 1803, quoted in Malone, *Jefferson*, 4: 292.
28. Livingston quoted in Kukla, *Wilderness*, 281.
29. The report that a restless Bonaparte, in an unguarded moment, cursed the entire transatlantic project—"Damn sugar, damn coffee, damn colonies"—may be apocryphal, but without question by late winter he had shifted his ambitions to Egypt. See E. Wilson Lyon, *Louisiana in French Diplomacy, 1759–1804* (Norman, OK, 1934), 194.
30. *National Intelligencer* [Washington], July 8, 1803; Jefferson to Sir John Sinclair, June 30, 1803, TJC.
31. *Columbian Centinel* [Boston], July 13, 1803; King to Christopher Gore, July 10, 1803, in King, ed., *Life*, 4: 286.
32. Paine to Thomas Jefferson, Sept. 23, 1803, TJC. Jefferson's reasoning can be traced in Jefferson to John Breckinridge, Aug. 12, 1803, Jefferson to James Madison, Aug. 25, 1803, Jefferson to Wilson Cary Nicholas, Sept. 7, 1803 (quotation), TJC.
33. On Pickering and the secession plot, see Pickering to Richard Peters, Dec. 24, 1803, Pickering to George Cabot, Jan. 29, 1804, Pickering to Rufus King, Mar. 4, 1804, Roger Griswold to Oliver Wolcott, Mar. 11, 1804, in Henry Adams, ed., *Documents Relating to New England Federalism, 1800–1815* (Boston, 1877), 338–53 (quotation on 341).
34. On the expedition, two recent works stand out: Stephen Ambrose, *Undaunted Courage: Meriwether Lewis, Thomas Jefferson, and the Opening of the American West* (New York, 1996); Landon Y. Jones, *William Clark and the Shaping of the West* (New York, 2004), esp. 114–79.
35. Jefferson to Meriwether Lewis, Jan. 13, 1804, TJC. "Their bitterness," Jefferson added about the Federalists, "increases with the diminution of their numbers and despair of a resurrection."
36. AC, 7th Congress, 1st session, 650; George Cabot to Oliver Wolcott, Dec. 20, 1802, in Lodge, ed., *Life and Letters*, 328–9.
37. *Marbury v. Madison*, 5 U.S. (1 Cranch), 137. On *Marbury v. Madison*, see Ellis, *Jeffersonian Crisis*, 65–68; Larry D. Kramer, *The People Themselves: Popular Constitutionalism and Judicial Review* (New York, 2004), 114–27.
38. Peterson, *Jefferson*, 699.
39. *Washington Federalist* [Georgetown], Mar. 14, 1803.
40. Cabot to Timothy Pickering, Feb. 14, 1804, Pickering to Rufus King, Mar. 4, 1804, in Adams, ed., *Documents*, 346, 351.
41. Pickering to Rufus King, Mar. 4, 1804, in Adams, ed., *Documents*, 352; John Quincy Adams, "Reply to the Appeal of the Massachusetts Federalists" [1829], in ibid., 148. On the Federalists' ridicule of the Jeffersonians as slaveholding democrats, and the strategic political impetus behind much Federalist "antislavery," see Kerber, *Federalists*, 23–66.

42. Pickering to Rufus King, Mar. 4, 1804, in Adams, ed., *Documents*, 351–2; Lomask, *Burr*, 331–44. On Burr's failed governor's race, see also the editorial note in Mary-Jo Kline, ed., *The Political Correspondence and Public Papers of Aaron Burr* (Princeton, 1983), 2: 827–42. On Burr's dickering over the presidency, see also Rufus King, "Memorandum of a Conversation between Burr and Griswold," Apr. 5, 1804, in ibid., 862–5.

43. Gallatin to Thomas Jefferson, July 18, 1804, in Adams, ed., *Writings*, 1: 201. For a balanced account of the duel and the events preceding it, see Arnold A. Rogow, *A Fatal Friendship: Alexander Hamilton and Aaron Burr* (New York, 1998), which quotes the psycho-biographer Nathan Schachner on Hamilton's "pathologic" hatred of Burr (228). See also Harold C. Syrett and Jean G. Cooke, eds., *Interview in Weehawken: The Burr-Hamilton Duel, as Told in Original Documents* (Middletown, CT, 1960); Kline, ed., *Burr*, 2: 876–83; Joanne B. Freeman, "Dueling as Politics: Reinterpreting the Burr-Hamilton Duel," *WMQ*, 53 (1996): 289–318.

44. Adams to John Adams, Nov. 1804, in Ford, ed., *Writings*, 3: 81; Jefferson quoted in Peterson, *Jefferson*, 800. In March, several Federalist papers urged Pinckney and King to run, but thereafter the party kept silent. In October, the Federalist Boston *Columbian Centinel* announced that the Federalists' position was that "the proper personages to be voted for as President will be the inquiry of the electors after they have been chosen." *Columbian Centinel*, Oct. 3, 1804. Manning Dauer's assessment of the election concludes that the Federalists' high-mindedness probably contributed to their loss of Massachusetts. See Dauer, "The Election of 1804," in S & I, 1: 159–82.

45. Latrobe quoted in Chilton Williamson, *American Suffrage from Property to Democracy, 1760–1860* (Princeton, 1960), 209.

46. *Scioto Gazette*, July 17, 1802; *Western Spy*, Aug. 21, 1802; Jared Mansfield to William Lyon Jr., Feb. 20, 1804, quoted in Donald J. Ratcliffe, *Party Spirit in a Frontier Republic: Democratic Politics in Ohio, 1793–1821* (Columbus, OH, 1998), 70, 107. Ratcliffe's deeply researched study corrects earlier historians' misimpressions of minimal partisanship in early Ohio politics, and thoroughly overturns what Ratcliffe calls "the myth of gentry control." Other new states in the Old Northwest could use similar reexamination. In Indiana, for example, one group of relocated southerners wrote to the territorial governor William Henry Harrison that freehold voting requirements favored the wealthy and were "subversive of the liberties of the Citizens and tending to throw too great a weight in the Scale of wealth." "Petition of the Vincennes Convention, December 28, 1802," Indiana Historical Society, *Collections*, 7 (1922): 62–67 (quotation on 66). Indianans also secured democratic reforms of voting procedures, including establishing the township rather than the county as the polling unit statewide. See J. D. Barnhart, "The Democratization of Indiana Territory," *Indiana Magazine of History*, 43 (1947): 1–21. On party organization in Ohio, see also Noble E. Cunningham, *The Jeffersonian Republicans in Power: Party Operations, 1801–1809* (Chapel Hill, 1963), 196–200.

47. Thorpe, 3: 1265, 1278; 5: 2901–13; 6: 3414–25.

48. *The Palladium* [Frankfort, KY], Dec. 11, 1801. On the Kentucky struggles, see John Howard Parks, *Felix Grundy: Champion of Democracy* (Baton Rouge, 1940), 7–18; Ellis, *Jeffersonian Crisis*, 139–56; Steven Aron, *How the West Was Lost: The Transformation of Kentucky from Daniel Boone to Henry Clay* (Baltimore, 1996), 156–9.

49. *The Hornet* [Frederick, MD], 1 (1802) no. 47; J. R. Pole, "Suffrage and Representation in Maryland from 1776 to 1810: A Statistical Note and Some Reflections," in Joel H. Silbey and Samuel T. McSeveney, eds., *Voters, Parties, and Elections: Quantitative Essays in the History of American Popular Voting Behavior* (Lexington, MA, 1972), 61–71; Charles G. Steffen, *The Mechanics of Baltimore: Workers and Politics in the Age of Revolution, 1763–1812* (Urbana, IL, 1984), 121; L. Mark Renzulli Jr., *Maryland: The Federalist Years* (Cranbury, NJ, 1972), 211–27; Rachel N. Klein, *Unification of a Slave State: The Rise of the Planter Class in the South Carolina Backcountry, 1760–1808* (Chapel Hill, 1990), 262–8; Lacy K. Ford Jr., *Origins of Southern Radicalism: The South Carolina Upcountry, 1800–1860* (New York, 1988), esp. 99–113. On the influence of the writings of Paine and

other radical reformers, British and American, on Charleston's persisting city democracy, see *Carolina Gazette* [Charleston], June 17, 1808; *Times* [Charleston], Jan. 18, 1809.

50. *Watch-Tower* [New York], June 17, 1801; Ames to Oliver Wolcott, Nov. 4, 1796, Oliver Wolcott Papers, Connecticut Historical Society. On the structure of Connecticut politics in these years, see Richard J. Purcell, *Connecticut in Transition: 1175–1818* (1918; Middletown, CT, 1963), 113–45. On reform stirrings before 1800, see also J. Hammond Trumbull, *Historical Notes on the Constitutions of Connecticut and on the Constitutional Convention of 1818* (Hartford, 1901), 13–22. On political reform and Republican activities after 1800, see Purcell, 23–35; William A. Robinson, *Jeffersonian Democracy in New England* (New Haven, 1916), 39–41; Williamson, *American Suffrage*, 164–72; Cunningham, *Republicans in Power*, 125–32; Andrew Siegel, "'Steady Habits' Under Siege: The Defense of Federalism in Jeffersonian Connecticut," in Doran Ben-Atar and Barbara B. Oberg, eds., *Federalists Reconsidered* (Charlottesville, 1998), 198–224.

51. *Connecticut Courant* [Hartford], Aug. 4, Sept. 1, 29, 1800, Aug. 16, 1802; Abraham Bishop, *An Oration on the Extent and Power of Political Delusion* (Newark, NJ, 1800), 53; idem, *Oration Delivered in Wallingford on the 11th of March, 1801, before the Republicans of the State of Connecticut* (New Haven, 1801); idem, *Oration, in honor of the election of President Jefferson, and the peaceable acquisition of Louisiana* (n.p. [New Haven], 1804); Cunningham, *Republicans in Power*, 124–32. See David Waldstreicher and Stephen R. Grossbart, "Abraham Bishop's Vocation; or, The Mediation of American Politics," *JER*, 18 (1998): 617–57; Franklin B. Dexter, "Abraham Bishop of Connecticut and His Writings," *Proceedings of the Massachusetts Historical Society*, 2nd ser., 19 (1905), 190–9. Bishop was an outspoken abolitionist. See Tim Matthewson, "Abraham Bishop, 'The Rights of Black Men,' and the American Reaction to the Haitian Revolution," *Journal of Negro History*, 67 (1982): 148–54. Bishop's pro-Jefferson father, Samuel, was the focus of the famous New Haven collectorship battle in 1801. Polemical Federalist responses to Bishop included David Daggett, *Three Letters to Abraham Bishop, Esq.* (Hartford, 1800); Noah Webster, *A Rod for the Fool's Back* (New Haven, 1800).

52. Bishop, *Oration, in honor of the election of President Jefferson*, 9–10, 16; *American Mercury* [Hartford], Apr. 28, 1803; *Connecticut Republican Magazine*, 1 (1802): 155; Williamson, *American Suffrage*, 172. On the Stand Up Law and its operations, see Trumbull, *Historical Notes*, 39–40; Purcell, *Connecticut*, 139–40. In 1802, Connecticut Republicans introduced a bill that would have granted suffrage to all adult male taxpayers—and the Federalist majority tried to stifle debate with ostentatious "coughing, sneezing [and] shuffling of feet." The bill went down to resounding defeat, along almost strictly party lines. See *American Mercury*, Nov. 18, 1802; *Connecticut Journal*, Nov. 24, 1802; *The Visitor* [New Haven], Jan. 11, 1803.

53. *Independent Chronicle* [Boston], Feb. 24, 1808. On Massachusetts politics and the growth of Jeffersonian Republicanism, see Robinson, *Jeffersonian Democracy*, 57–75; Cunningham, *Republicans in Power*, 133–42; Paul Goodman, *The Democratic-Republicans of Massachusetts* (Cambridge, MA, 1964), esp. 128–53. Federalists predictably denounced their opponents' committees as wicked innovations, yet by 1804 they had established a statewide committee system of their own, nearly identical to the Republicans', with the signal exception of refusing to call mass meetings and conventions of the party's supporters.

54. The Republicans' criticisms carried weight, for in the privacy of their personal correspondence, Massachusetts Federalists did not hide their belief that, as Fisher Ames wrote to Christopher Gore in 1803, "[w]e may need the state tribunals as sanctuaries when Jacobinism comes to rob or slay." Ames to Christopher Gore, Feb. 24, 1803, in Ames, ed., *Works of Fisher Ames*, 1: 321. On the Massachusetts judiciary struggles, see Ellis, *Jeffersonian Crisis*, 184–229. On Sedgwick, see Richard E. Welch Jr., *Theodore Sedgwick, Federalist: A Political Portrait* (Middletown, CT, 1965), 239–52, although the book concentrates on Sedgwick's career before 1801.

55. See, e.g., *Pittsfield Sun*, Dec. 19, 1803.

56. Leland quoted in Ellis, *Jeffersonian Crisis*, 199; W. W. Story, ed., *Life and Letters of Joseph Story* (Boston, 1851) 1: 128. Austin, a ropemaker, first made his political mark in the 1780s under the pen name "Honestus," excoriating the legal profession in the columns of the Boston *Independent Chronicle* (edited by his good friend and future victim of the Sedition Law, Abijiah Adams). See Austin, *Observations on the Pernicious Practice of the Law* (Boston, 1819). On Story, see R. Kent Newmyer, *Supreme Court Justice Joseph Story: Statesman of the Old Republic* (Chapel Hill, 1985), 56–58.

57. *Pittsfield Sun*, quoted in *Independent Chronicle* [Boston], Jan. 15, 19, 1807.

58. *American Citizen* [New York], Jan. 10, Mar. 2, 31, 1801; Howard B. Rock, *Artisans of the New Republic: The Tradesmen of New York City in the Age of Jefferson* (New York, 1979), 50–51.

59. See Judith A. Klinghoffer and Lois Elkin, "The 'Petticoat Electors': Women's Suffrage in New Jersey," *JER* (1992): 161–93; J. R. Pole, "The Suffrage in New Jersey: 1790–1807," *Proceedings of the New Jersey Historical Society*, 71 (1953): 39–61.

60. This period in Pennsylvania political history has been singularly well covered: Sanford W. Higginbotham, *The Keystone of the Democratic Arch: Pennsylvania Politics, 1800–1816* (Harrisburg, 1952); Russell J. Ferguson, *Early Western Pennsylvania Politics* (Pittsburgh, 1938), 176–209; Cunningham, *Republicans in Power*, 156–66, 213–20; Ellis, *Jeffersonian Crisis*, 157–83; G. S. Rowe, *Embattled Bench: The Pennsylvania Supreme Court and the Forging of a Democratic Society, 1684–1809* (Newark, DE, 1994), 253–90; Andrew Shankman, *Crucible of American Democracy: The Struggle to Fuse Egalitarianism and Capitalism in Jeffersonian Pennsylvania* (Lawrence, KS, 2004).

61. See *Evening Post* [Philadelphia], Feb. 21, 1804. On the moderate Republicans, see Higginbotham, *Keystone*, 11, 19; James H. Peeling, "Governor McKean and the Pennsylvania Jacobins (1799–1808)," *Pennsylvania Magazine of History and Biography*, 54 (1930): 320–54; John M. Coleman, *Thomas McKean, Forgotten Leader of the Revolution* (Rockaway, NJ, 1975); G. S. Rowe, *Thomas McKean: The Shaping of an American Republicanism* (Boulder, 1978); Raymond Walters Jr., *Alexander James Dallas, Lawyer, Politician, Financier, 1759–1817* (Philadelphia, 1943), 1–146.

62. *Aurora*, Sept. 7, 1803. On Leib, Duane, and the Philadelphia democrats, see Shankman, "Malcontents and Tertium Quids," 43–64; Ellis, *Jeffersonian Crisis*, 159–60.

63. On the leading Clodhopper Democrats, see Higginbotham, *Keystone*, 50–51, 81–82, 136–7; Shankman, *Crucible*, 89–95. On McKean's derisive remarks, see *Aurora*, Mar. 29, 1805. McKean later admitted that he had described the country democrats as "clodpoles" and "ignoramuses" who wished to overthrow the state constitution. *Aurora*, June 3, 1805.

64. *Pennsylvania Archives*, 4th ser. (Harrisburg, 1900), 4: 460–1; Alexander Addison, *Rise & Progress of Revolution* (Whitehall, PA, 1801); McKean to Thomas Jefferson, Feb. 7, 1803, TJC; *Constitution of the Democratic Society of Friends of the People* (Philadelphia, 1805). On the impeachments, the rise of the Pennsylvania Quids, and the democratic coalition, see also Ellis, *Jeffersonian Crisis*, 160–70 (quotation on 161); Higginbotham, *Keystone*, 49–75; Cunningham, *Republicans in Power*, 162–3; Rowe, *Embattled*, 264–9; Shankman, *Crucible*, 96–125. Duane's *Aurora* appears to have invented the term Tertium Quid: see *Aurora*, May 19, 1804.

65. Paine, "To the Citizens of Pennsylvania on the Proposal for Calling a Convention, Aug. 1805," in *The Political Writings of Thomas Paine* (New York), 1: 439–55; Ellis, *Jeffersonian Crisis*, 174–81 (quotations on 178); Gallatin to Jean Badolet, Oct. 25, 1805, in Henry Adams, *The Life of Albert Gallatin* (Philadelphia, 1879), 331; *Aurora*, Sept. 1, 1807; Shankman, *Crucible*, 127–72; Higginbotham, *Keystone*, 77–176.

66. On changes in the selection methods of presidential electors, see Series Y 1–26, in U.S. Bureau of the Census, *Historical Statistics of the United States, Colonial Times to 1970* (Washington, DC, 1975), 2: 1071.

67. Jefferson to John Tyler, Mar. 29, 1805, TJC.

68. On the Pickering impeachment, see Lynn Turner, "The Impeachment of John Pickering," *AHR*, 54 (1949): 485–507; Ellis, *Jeffersonian Crisis*, 69–75.

69. AC, 8th Congress, 2nd session, 674–76 (quotations on 675); Jefferson to Joseph Nicholson, May 13, 1803, TJC. For different viewpoints on the Chase impeachment, see Keith Whittington, "Reconstructing the Federal Judiciary: The Chase Impeachment and the Constitution," *Studies in American Political Development*, 9 (1995): 55–116; Jane Shaffer Elsmere, *Justice Samuel Chase* (Muncie, IN, 1980), 159–306; Jerry W. Knudson, "The Jeffersonian Assault on the Federal Judiciary, 1802–1805: Political Forces and Press Reaction," *American Journal of Legal History*, 14 (1970): 55–75; Ellis, *Jeffersonian Crisis*, 76–82, 96–107. On Chase's enforcement of the alien and sedition laws, and the responses, see Elsmere, *Chase*, 114–36; Smith, *Freedom's Fetters*, 267–8, 324–7, 335.

70. Jefferson to John Nicholson, May 13, 1803, TJC; AC, 8th Congress, 2nd session, 669.

71. In 1795, a group of speculators had bribed a fabulously corrupt Georgia state legislature into selling off, for a song, some 35 million acres of Indian land known as the Yazoo territory (what is today the states of Alabama and Mississippi). A year later, irate Georgia voters elected a new legislature, which in turn negated the deal—but not before much of the Yazoo land had been sold (and, in some cases, resold and sold again) to northern investors, who knew nothing of the fraud involved. The Jefferson administration inherited the mess and appeared to have resolved it in 1802, getting Georgia to relinquish all claims to the Yazoo territory while agreeing to find some satisfaction for all of the traduced northern purchasers. A special presidential commission decided that the federal government should reserve 5 million acres of land for the claimants. But as soon as the commission announced its plan in February 1804, Randolph rose yet again to denounce the Yazoo compromise and the corrupt administration that had produced it. The executive, he charged, was attempting to twist government to favor northern speculators in ways fearfully injurious to Georgia's sovereignty and the principles of state rights. "On other occasions we have heard much of party spirit and the rights of minorities," he told the House. "But this is one of those occasions where the tocsin of party spirit and an overruling majority will not answer the purpose in view." AC, 8th Congress, 2nd session, 1109. See Peter C. McGrath, *Yazoo: Law and Politics in the New Republic* (Providence, 1966).

72. Samuel Taggart to the Rev. John Taylor, Dec. 3, 1804, Feb. 18, 1805, in George Haunes, ed., "Letters of Samuel Taggart," *Proceedings of the American Antiquarian Society*, New Series, 33 (1923), 134–41, 158–9; Ellis, *Jeffersonian Crisis*, 76–82, 91–95.

73. JQAD, 2: 359.

74. The northern Federalist *Evening Post*, founded by Hamilton four years earlier, remarked acidly that whereas formerly courts arraigned murderers before the judge, "now we behold the Judge arraigned before the murderer." *Evening Post* [New York], Feb. 6, 1805. On Burr's handling of the trial, see Ellis, *Jeffersonian Crisis*, 105–6.

75. See the different interpretations in Thomas P. Abernethy, *The Burr Conspiracy* (New York, 1954); Smelser, *Democratic Republic*, 111–24; Buckner F. Melton Jr., *Aaron Burr: Conspiracy to Treason* (New York, 2001); Kline, ed., *Burr*, 2: 919–1039.

76. Burr to Andrew Jackson, Mar. 24, 1806, in Kline, ed., *Burr*, 2: 957.

77. Albert Gallatin described Wilkinson as an "extravagant and needy" man. Gallatin to Thomas Jefferson, Feb. 12, 1806, TJC. On Burr's trial, see the brief and lively account in Smelser, *Democratic Republicans*, 119–23.

78. On the *Chesapeake* affair and the background to it, see Bradford Perkins, *Prologue to War: England and the United States, 1805–1812* (Berkeley, 1961), 1–148. Three of the four men seized were black; one was soon after convicted of desertion and hanged in Canada.

79. Jefferson to Thomas Mann Randolph Jr., July 13, 1807, Yale University Library; Jefferson to John Taylor, Aug. 1, 1807, Washburn Collection, MHS.

80. Jefferson to Thomas Cooper, Feb. 18, 1806, MHS. Gallatin, though he thought the plan badly mistaken, ended up backing Jefferson and managed the embargo bill through Congress. See Richard Mannix, "Gallatin, Jefferson, and the Embargo of 1808," *Diplomatic History*, 3 (1979): 151–72.

81. Jefferson to Albert Gallatin, Dec. 3, 1807, in Adams, ed., *Writings*, 1: 367; *Independent Chronicle*, Aug. 15, 1808; Jefferson to Thomas Mann Randolph Jr., Jan. 2, 1809, TJC. For

a sharp interpretation of Jeffersonian foreign policy, see Robert W. Tucker and David C. Henderson, *Empire of Liberty: The Statecraft of Thomas Jefferson* (New York, 1990), esp. 180–228. For a judicious interpretation of the embargo, see Burton Spivak, *Jefferson's English Crisis: Commerce, Embargo, and the Republican Revolution* (Charlottesville, 1979) (quotation on 204). Leonard Levy, *Jefferson and Civil Liberties: The Darker Side* (Cambridge, MA, 1964), 138–9, condemns the embargo and, even more, Jefferson's efforts to enforce it as "the most repressive and unconstitutional legislation ever enacted by Congress in peacetime." For a less strident account of the domestic crackdown and the protests against it, see Malone, *Jefferson*, 5: 583–604.

82. Jefferson to John Taylor, Jan. 6, 1808, Washburn Collection, MHS. See also Jefferson to James Madison, Mar. 11, 1808, TJC.

83. On the embargo's economic impact, see Peterson, *Jefferson*, 892–4. For a study of the shipping records of Providence, Rhode Island, showing that, overall, coastal arivals and departures actually increased, see William Jeffrey Bolster, "The Impact of Jefferson's Embargo on Coastal Commerce," *Log of Mystic Seaport*, 37 (1986): 111–23.

84. Glenn S. Gordinier, "Autonomy, Politics, and Embargo in New London, Connecticut, 1807–1809," *American Neptune*, 52 (1992): 180–6; Douglas Lamar Jones, "'The Caprice of Juries': The Enforcement of the Jeffersonian Embargo in Massachusetts," *American Journal of Legal History*, 24 (1980): 307–30; Joshua M. Smith, "Murder on Isle au Haut: Violence and Jefferson's Embargo in Coastal Maine, 1807–1809," *Maine History*, 39 (2000): 17–39; Harvey Strum, "Smuggling in Maine during the Embargo and the War of 1812," *Colby Library Quarterly*, 19 (1983): 90–97; Edward Brynn, "Vermont and the British Emporium," *Vermont History*, 45 (1977): 5–30; H. Nicholar Muller, "Smuggling into Canada: How the Champlain Valley Defied Jefferson's Embargo," *Vermont History*, 38 (1970), 5–21. Of the sixty-five Massachusetts cases heard by juries, only twelve ended in convictions. By contrast, of the seventy cases heard by federal Judge John Davis, forty-six ended in convictions.

85. See Jack McLaughlin, *To His Excellency Thomas Jefferson: Letters to a President* (New York, 1991), 14–38 (quotation on 27).

86. Bryant, "The Embargo, or Sketches of Our Times," quoted in Malone, *Jefferson*, 5: 606; John Langdon to Thomas Jefferson, May 14, 1808, Plumer to Thomas Jefferson, July 22, 1808, TJC. Bryant would later call his bit of juvenilia a "foolish thing." Smelser, *Democratic Republic*, 175. The Hemings story, still a cause célèbre today, is by no means an absolutely settled truth, although I find most convincing both the reasoning and the humane, realistic interpretation in Annette Gordon-Reed, *Thomas Jefferson and Sally Hemings: An American Controversy* (Charlottesville, 1997).

87. Jefferson to Thomas Mann Randolph, Feb. 7, 1808, in Ford, ed., *Writings*, 9: 244.

88. For details on the election, see Irving Brant, "Election of 1808," in S & I, 1: 185–246.

89. Jefferson to Levi Lincoln, Nov. 13, 1808, TJC. George Clinton received six electoral votes, all from New York, and retained the vice presidency.

90. Jefferson to Pierre du Pont de Nemours, Mar. 2, 1809, TJC.

91. For more extended remarks on the current literature about Jefferson, see Sean Wilentz, "Life, Liberty, and the Pursuit of Thomas Jefferson," *New Republic*, Mar. 10, 1997, 32–42; idem, "The Details of Greatness," *New Republic*, Mar. 29, 2004, 27–35.

92. Jefferson to W. A. Burwell, Jan. 28, 1805, HL. Although he eventually questioned his own startling observations about black inferiority, as once expressed in his *Notes on the State of Virginia* in 1785, Jefferson's initial concern about the black revolutionaries of Saint Domingue, his eventual indifference to their fate, and his refusal to recognize Haiti's achievement of independence in 1804 underscored his fundamental pessimism about black-white relations in the New World.

93. Jefferson to John Holmes, Apr. 22, 1820, TJC; Richardson, 1: 396; Matthew E. Mason, "Slavery Overshadowed: Congress Debates Outlawing the Atlantic Slave Trade to the United States, 1806–1807," *JER*, 20 (2000): 59–81. Just before he left the presidency, Jefferson wrote Henri Gregoire, admitting his earlier views on blacks were limited and that,

in any case, did not in any way touch on the question of equal rights. "Because Sir Isaac Newton was superior to others in understanding, he was not therefore lord of the person or property of others." It was little enough to commend Jefferson to blacks, now or then, but his racism was not as thoroughgoing as some writers have claimed. Jefferson to Henri Gregoire, Feb. 25, 1809, in Ford, ed., *Writings*, 11: 99–100. There is a large and contentious literature on Jefferson's views and actions concerning slavery, and on the "necessarily evil" argument in general. Put a little too simply, the historians divide between those who take Jefferson and others at their word (and contrast them with the early pro-slavery advocates of the Deep South) and those who consider Jefferson and others like him deep hypocrites, whose antislavery pronouncements paid lip service to the Enlightenment spirit of the age but lacked conviction and substance, in part because (as in Jefferson's case) so many continued to own slaves and in part because the three-fifths clause aided the Republicans politically. See William W. Freehling, "The Founding Fathers and Slavery," *AHR*, 77 (1972): 81–93; John Chester Miller, *The Wolf by the Ears: Thomas Jefferson and Slavery* (New York, 1977); on the harsher side, see Robert McColley, *Slavery and Jeffersonian Virginia* (1964; Urbana, IL, 1973); Drew Gilpin Faust, ed., *The Ideology of Slavery: Proslavery Thought in the Antebellum South, 1830–1860* (Baton Rouge, 1981); Paul Finkelman, "Jefferson and Slavery: Treason against the Hopes of the World," in Peter S. Onuf, ed., *Jeffersonian Legacies* (Charlottesville, 1992); idem, *Slavery and the Founders: Race and Liberty in the Age of Jefferson* (Armonk, NY, 1996).

94. AC, 5th Congress, 2nd session, 1306; Matthewson, "Abraham Bishop," 153.
95. Jefferson to Horatio Gates, Feb. 21, 1798, in *PTJ*, 30: 124; Jefferson to John Melish, Jan. 13, 1813, TJC; Lawrence A. Peskin, "How the Republicans Learned to Love Manufacturing: The First Parties and the 'New Economy,'" *JER*, 22 (2002): 589–615.
96. See Randolph's letter, written under the pseudonym "Decius," in *Richmond Enquirer*, Aug. 15, 1806.
97. Bishop, *Oration on the Extent and Power of Political Delusion*, 45–46.
98. For figures, see Jeffrey L. Pasley, "The Cheese and the Worms: Popular Political Culture and Participatory Democracy in the Early American Republic," in Pasley et al., eds., *Beyond the Founders: New Approaches to the Political History of the Early Republic* (Chapel Hill, 2004), 45–49; J. R. Pole, *Political Representation in England and the Origins of the American Republic* (London, 1966), 545–6, 553, 563. According to Pole, 24 percent of free adult males in Virginia voted for president in 1800, compared to 16 percent in 1808. Pasley's recent study draws on figures collected by the First Democratization Project at the American Antiquarian Society, which affirm that participation rates were generally much higher between 1800 and 1816 than many historians have presumed.
99. For a related review on the state of democratic changes as of 1809, as seen through the lens of party organization, see Cunningham, *Republicans in Power*, 299–305.
100. Adams to Louise Catherine Adams, Mar. 5, 1809, in Worthington Chauncy Ford, ed., *The Writings of John Quincy Adams* (New York, 1913–17), 3: 289.

CHAPTER FIVE: NATIONALISM AND THE WAR OF 1812

1. On Madison's presidency, in addition to the relevant volumes in Irving Brant, *James Madison* (Indianapolis, 1941–61), see Robert Rutland, *The Presidency of James Madison* (Lawrence, KS, 1990); Garry Wills, *James Madison* (New York, 2002).
2. On the Olmstead case, see Sanford W. Higginbotham, *The Keystone in the Democratic Arch: Pennsylvania Politics, 1800–1816* (Harrisburg, 1952), 183–98; Brant, *James Madison*, 4: 28–30; Kim Tousley Phillips, "William Duane, Revolutionary Editor" (Ph.D. dissert., University of California at Berkeley, 1968), 268–79; Margaret Ruth Reilly Kelly, "State Rebellion, States' Rights, and Personal Politics: Pennsylvania and the Olmstead Case (*United States v. Peters*)" (Ph.D. dissert., State University of New York at Buffalo, 2000).

3. Snyder to James Madison, Apr. 6, 1809, Madison to Simon Snyder, Apr. 13, 1809, *PJMP*, 1: 105, 114.

4. See Bradford Perkins, *Prologue to War: England and the United States, 1805–1812* (Berkeley, 1961), 184–437; J. C. A. Stagg, *Mr. Madison's War: Politics, Diplomacy, and Warfare in the Early American Republic, 1783–1830* (Princeton, 1983), 3–120.

5. Duane to Joseph Carrington Cabell, June 6, 1811, quoted in Stagg, *Mr. Madison's War*, 51 n. 12. On the factionalism early in Madison's first term, see ibid., 48–58; Higginbotham, *Keystone*, 151–61. The leaders of the "Invisibles" or "Malcontents" — alienated moderates from the upper South — included Wilson Cary Nicholas and William Branch Giles of Virginia and the brothers Robert and Samuel Smith of Maryland.

6. Stagg, *Mr. Madison's War*, 51. Gallatin's (and Madison's) other Jeffersonian critics followed "a more ambiguous course on the issue of foreign policy." Ibid., 50–52.

7. "The book called the federalist," John Taylor of Caroline wrote of Madison's writings, "is full of federalism." Taylor to Wilson Cary Nicholas, Feb. 5, 1808, in Norman K. Risjord, *The Old Republicans: Southern Conservatives in the Age of Jefferson* (New York, 1965), 35.

8. See Robert V. Remini, *Henry Clay: Statesman for the Union* (New York, 1991), 1–31; Merrill D. Peterson, *The Great Triumvirate: Webster, Clay, and Calhoun* (New York, 1987), 1–18.

9. Everett Somerville Brown, ed., *William Plumer's Memorandum of Proceedings in the United States Senate, 1803–1807* (New York, 1923), 608; *JQAD*, 1: 444; Clay to [James Monroe], Nov. 13, 1810, in *PHC* 1: 498.

10. On Clay and the killing of the bank bill, see Clay's speech to the Senate, *AC*, 11th Congress, 3rd session, 209–19 (quotation on 213); Remini, *Clay*, 68–71.

11. *AC*, 11th Congress, 2nd session, 579–82 (quotation on 581).

12. See Charles M. Wiltse, *John C. Calhoun* (Indianapolis, 1944–51); John Niven, *John C. Calhoun and the Price of Union: A Biography* (Baton Rouge, 1988); Irving H. Bartlett, *John C. Calhoun: A Biography* (New York, 1993); see also Peterson, *Great Triumvirate*, 18–27.

13. South Carolina House of Representatives Journal, Nov. 25, 1800, quoted in Rachel N. Klein, *The Unification of a Slave State: The Rise of the Planter Class in the South Carolina Backcountry, 1760–1808* (Chapel Hill, 1990), 108–305 (quotation on 247). On the peculiarities of South Carolina society and politics, see James M. Banner, "The Problem of South Carolina," in Stanley Elkins and Eric McKitrick, eds., *The Hofstadter Aegis: A Memorial* (New York, 1974), 60–93; Lacy K. Ford, *Origins of Southern Radicalism: The South Carolina Upcountry, 1800–1860* (New York, 1988), 44–144.

14. On Waddell's school, see Klein, *Unification*, 243; Wiltse, *Calhoun*, 1: 28–29. In addition to Calhoun, such future Palmetto political notables as John H. Petigru, Hugh Swinton Legaré, and George McDuffie studied with Waddell.

15. Calhoun to Floride Colhoun, Oct. 1, 1807, in *PJCC*, 1: 38.

16. Calhoun to James Macbride, Feb. 16 [17?], 1812, in *PJCC*, 1: 90; *AC*, 12th Congress, 1st session, 476–83 (quotation on 479).

17. On divisions within the new House, see Marshall Smelser, *The Democratic Republic, 1801–1815* (New York, 1968), 208–9. On the defeat of Grundy's Green River revolt in Kentucky, see Stephen Aron, *How the West Was Lost: The Transformation of Kentucky from Daniel Boone to Henry Clay* (Baltimore, 1996), 150–69. On Porter, see J. C. A. Stagg, "Between Black Rock and a Hard Place: Peter B. Porter's Plan for an American Invasion of Canada in 1812," *JER*, 19 (1999): 385–422.

18. Calhoun quoted in Wiltse, *Calhoun*, 1: 105.

19. Richardson, 1: 479.

20. Logan Esarey, ed., *Governor's Messages and Letters of William Henry Harrison, 1800–1811* (Indianapolis, 1922), 1: 223, 490; Jefferson to Henry Dearborn, Aug. 12, 28 (quotation), 1807, *TJC*. For a concise account of Indian-government relations from Jefferson's presidency to the War of 1812, see Reginald Horsman, *Expansion and Indian Policy: 1783–1812* (1967; Norman, OK, 1992), 104–73; but see also Gregory Evans Dowd, *A Spir-*

ited Resistance: The North American Indian Struggle for Unity, 1745–1815 (Baltimore, 1992); Stagg, *Mr. Madison's War*, 177–87.

21. See Horsman, *Expansion*; U.S. Bureau of the Census, *Statistical Abstract of the United States* (Washington, DC, 1982–83), 6; Anthony F. C. Wallace, *The Death and Rebirth of the Seneca* (New York, 1970), esp. 149–236; James H. Merrell, "Declarations of Independence: Indian-White Relations in the New Nation," in Jack P. Greene, ed., *The American Revolution: Its Character and Limits* (New York, 1987), 197–223.

22. Jefferson to Benjamin Hawkins, Feb. 18, 1803, Jefferson to William H. Harrison, Feb. 27, 1803, TJC. For a highly critical interpretation of Jefferson's policies regarding the Indians, see Anthony F. C. Wallace, *Jefferson and the Indians: The Tragic Fate of the First Americans* (Cambridge, MA, 1999). See also Bernard W. Sheehan, *Seeds of Extinction: Jeffersonian Philanthropy and the American Indian* (Chapel Hill, 1973), which, although alive to the paradoxes of Jefferson's Indian policies, insists that Harrison was merely carrying out Jefferson's wishes in his aggressive moves to obtain more land. See also Robert M. Owens, "Jeffersonian Benevolence on the Ground: The Indian Land Cession Treaties of William Henry Harrison," *JER*, 22 (2003): 405–35.

23. Chief Blackbeard quoted in John Sugden, *Tecumseh: A Life* (New York, 1998), 108. The Greenville Treaty had included a provision, at the Indians' insistence, stating that their new lands would be held in common—but under Jefferson, some American officials, including Harrison, negotiated directly with the chief users of certain tracts, a divide-and-conquer strategy that provoked intense divisions among the tribes. On Harrison's treaty-making as a direct extension of Jefferson's Indian policies, see Owens, "Jeffersonian Benevolence." See also Dorothy Burne Goebel, *William Henry Harrison: A Political Biography* (Indianapolis, 1926); Freeman Cleaves, *Old Tippecanoe: William Henry Harrison and His Time* (New York, 1939).

24. For the best recounting of the Prophet's visions and early preaching, see R. David Edmunds, *The Shawnee Prophet* (Lincoln, NE, 1983), 28–41. Among the Prophet's sternest injunctions was for Indian women to cease cohabitating and having sexual contact with white men, a sign of how intermingled whites and Indians had become on the further reaches of white incursion.

25. Dowd, *Spirited Resistance*, 123–29; Sugden, *Tecumseh*, 117–21 (quotation on 117). Dowd observes that Lalawethika's visions, although strongly antisettler, showed some Christian influences, proving that purism on either side of the cultural divide was impossible. See also Edmunds, *Shawnee Prophet*, 40.

26. Sugden, *Tecumseh*, 13–110.

27. Ibid., 127–30.

28. Alexander McKee quoted in ibid., 157; Jefferson to Henry Dearborn, Aug. 28, 1807, TJC.

29. Esarey, ed., *Governor's Messages*, 1: 299, 302, 321; Edmunds, *Shawnee Prophet*, 67–93; Sugden, *Tecumseh*, 166–74. On Prophetstown, see also Timothy D. Willig, "Prophetstown on the Wabash: The Native Spiritual Defense of the Old Northwest," *Michigan Historical Review*, 23 (1997): 115–58.

30. Sugden, *Tecumseh*, 174–225; but compare Dowd, *Spirited Resistance*, 139–42, which persuasively argues that although Tecumseh took the lead in organizing the pantribal alliance, Tenskwatawa and the religious aspects of the brothers' movement remained strong, at least until the Battle of Tippecanoe.

31. Esarey, ed., *Governor's Messages*, 1: 548.

32. For descriptions of the Battle of Tippecanoe, see Sugden, *Tecumseh*, 228–36; also Richard G. Carlson, ed., "George P. Peters' Version of the Battle of Tippecanoe (November 7, 1811)," *Vermont History*, 45 (1977), 38–43. Harrison's offensive required some preliminary political maneuvering—and chicanery—in Washington. President Madison, concerned about the looming war with Britain, had directed that peace be preserved with the Indians and that Harrison be barred from advancing beyond the boundary of the Wabash purchase line. Harrison, eager to hit Prophetstown—which lay fifty miles beyond the purchase line—directed himself instead to Secretary of War William Eustis, an amiable

incompetent held over from the Jefferson administration. Madison happened to be away from the capital visiting his Virginia plantation, Montpelier, and so Eustis took it upon himself to send authorizations permitting Harrison to cross the boundary should circumstances require it. See Brant, *Madison*, 284–7; Stagg, *Mr. Madison's War*, 183–6.

33. These eruptions, known as the New Madrid earthquakes, have been estimated as the most severe in the modern history of North America. For a general account, see Wayne John Viitanen, "The Winter the Mississippi Ran Backwards: The Impact of the New Madrid, Missouri, Earthquake of 1811–12 on Life and Letters in the Mississippi Valley" (Ph.D. dissert., Southern Illinois University at Carbondale, 1972). For the quakes' effects on the Indians, see Sugden, *Tecumseh*, 249–51.

34. Sugden, *Tecumseh*, 252–7; Thomas Worthington quoted in Stagg, *Mr. Madison's War*, 188.

35. Richardson, 1: 481–2 (quotation on 482); Sugden, *Tecumseh*, 260–75; Stagg, *Mr. Madison's War*, 188–90.

36. NWR, Dec. 7, 1811. On the political, diplomatic, and military history of the coming of the War of 1812, and the war itself, see Donald R. Hickey, *The War of 1812: A Forgotten Conflict* (Urbana, 1989).

37. Historians' charges against Madison as an inept, confused, and manipulated president date back to Henry Adams's classic history of Madison's administration. These generally echo the opinion of the Massachusetts Federalist Samuel Taggart, that unlike the "cunning" Jefferson, Madison was "a mere puppet or a cypher managed by some chiefs of the faction who are behind the curtain." George Hames, ed. "Letters of Samuel Taggart," *Proceedings of the American Antiquarian Society*, New Series, 33 (1923), 3: 347–48.

38. AC, 12th Congress, 1st session, 1388; Madison to Thomas Jefferson, Apr. 3, 1812, *PJMP*, 4: 285–9 (quotation on 287). Jefferson agreed with Madison and wrote back that although he preferred peace, the presumptuous British were making peace impossible. Madison did come to look both conniving and gullible to some in the months before war began, when his administration fell into spending fifty thousand dollars for a set of reports worth far less on alleged Federalist perfidy, proferred by a Canadian, one John Henry, and his accomplice, a mysterious French swindler who called himself the Count de Crillon. A Federalist ex-army officer, Henry had been working in the pay of British-Canadian authorities, with whom he had grown disgruntled. Some Federalists charged the entire affair was a cheap trick to rile anti-British sentiment. Yet the administration seized upon the scandal as proof of British meddling in American affairs. Compare the account in Samuel Eliot Morison, *By Land and by Sea: Essays and Addresses* (New York, 1953), 265–86.

39. Madison quotation in Richardson, 1: 489. For analyses of the congressional debate and votes over going to war, see Roland L. Hatzenbuehler, "Party Unity and the Decision for War in the House of Representatives, 1812," WMQ, 29 (1972): 367–90; Stagg, *Mr. Madison's War*, 110–5.

40. On these ultimately anticlimactic events, see Perkins, *Prologue*, 300–41.

41. *Columbian Centinel* [Boston], July 25, Nov. 4, 1807; Pickering to Edward Pennington, July 12, 1812, in Henry Adams, ed., *Documents Relating to New England Federalism, 1800–1815* (Boston, 1877), 388; AC, 12th Congress, 1st session, 1385. John Quincy Adams, having broken with the Federalists in 1808, called the impressment of Americans "an authorized system of kidnapping upon the ocean," and considered it such a blow against national honor that it justified war. See Adams, "Reply to the Appeal," in Adams, ed., *Documents*, 178.

42. For an astute analysis of the economic factors in the voting patterns, see Smelser, *Democratic Republic*, 216–8. On other political and partisan factors, see Hatzenbuehler, "Party Unity"; Reginald Horsman, "Who Were the War Hawks?" *Indiana Magazine of History*, 60 (1964): 121–36; Stagg, *Mr. Madison's War*, 110–7. Pennsylvania, sixteen of whose eighteen representatives voted for war, was the crucial pro-war state outside the South and West. Cultural differences overlapped with economics. Congressional antiwar sentiment was concentrated in the mercantile lower New England states (Massachusetts, Rhode

Island, and Connecticut), as well as in portions of New York and New Jersey populated chiefly by Yankee migrants. Several Republican as well as Federalist representatives from these heavily Congregational and English-stock districts, saturated with the more traditional hierarchical ideals of ordered liberty, opposed the war—in marked contrast to the pro-war tendencies of the more heavily Scots-Irish Presbyterian and evangelical southern backcountry, Quaker and German Pennsylvania, and Virginia (aside from the Shenandoah Valley, where the Old Republicans held sway).

43. AC, 12th Congress, 1st session, 297; Monroe to Col. John Taylor, June 13, 1812, Monroe Papers, LC. One of the most fervent pro-war city democrats, William Duane, volunteered for military service at the age of fifty-two. See chapter 6, pp. 210–1.

44. Adams to John Adams, July 13, 1812, to Abigail Adams, Aug. 10, 1812, in Worthington C. Ford, ed., The Writings of John Quincy Adams (New York, 1913–17), 4: 372, 388. For contrasting views of the war's ideological origins, see Roger Brown, The Republic in Peril: 1812 (New York, 1964); Stephen Watts, The Republic Reborn: War and the Making of Liberal America, 1790–1820 (Baltimore, 1987).

45. Democratic Press, Jan. 28, 1812. On the political jockeying in early 1812, see Higginbotham, Keystone, 256–8.

46. Aurora, Oct. 24, 1812. See Evan Cornog, The Birth of Empire: DeWitt Clinton and the American Experience, 1769–1828 (New York, 1998), 88–103.

47. Calhoun to James Mcbride, Dec. 25, 1812, in PJCC, 1: 146. On the military history of the entire conflict, see Reginald Horsman, War of 1812 (New York, 1969); Harry L. Coles, The War of 1812 (Chicago, 1965); Hickey, War of 1812.

48. On Federalist organizing and electioneering efforts—and the spread of the so-called Washington Benevolent Societies after 1808—see esp. David Hackett Fischer, The Revolution of American Conservatism: The Federalist Party in the Era of Jeffersonian Democracy (New York, 1965), 73–129.

49. Van Buren, The Autobiography of Martin Van Buren, John C. Fitzpatrick, ed. 1920; (New York, 1969), 1: 37. Van Buren later confessed that "we all acted in great error" by opposing a wartime president "in the absence of any act to show his incompetency." Ibid. The best biographies of Van Buren are John Niven, Martin Van Buren: The Romantic Age of American Politics (New York, 1983); Donald B. Cole, Martin Van Buren and the American Political System (Princeton, 1984). See also Cornog, Empire, 96–97.

50. Higginbotham, Keystone, 256–69 (quotation on 260). Compare Staggs, Mr. Madison's War, 118, which argues that Clinton's victory "seemed remote" as soon as war was declared in June.

51. Fisher, Revolution, passim. On the 1812 results, as well as on the election campaign, see Norman K. Risjord, "Election of 1812," in S & I, 1: 249–96.

52. AC, 13th Congress, 2nd session, 943–4.

53. On the campaign leading up to Perry's victory, and the consequences, see David Curtis Skaggs and Gerard T. Altoff, A Signal Victory: The Lake Erie Campaign, 1812–1813 (Annapolis, 1997); Robert J. Dodge, Battle of Lake Erie (Fostoria, OH, 1967).

54. On the battle and its significance, see Marshall Smelser, "Tecumseh, Harrison, and the War of 1812," Indiana Magazine of History, 65 (1969): 25–44; John Sugden, Tecumseh's Last Stand (Norman, OK, 1985).

55. George Robert Gleig, A Narrative of the Campaigns of the British Army at Washington and New Orleans (1826; London, 1827), 134–5; Anthony S. Pitch, Washington Is Burning: The British Invasion of 1814 (Annapolis, 1998), 8–152. Madison traveled on to a tavern at Montgomery Courthouse in Maryland, then returned to the burned-out city on August 27 after the British had withdrawn, determined to show that the American government was still functioning. He and Dolley would never again live in the Executive Mansion. The Patent Office was spared at the behest of the old Democratic-Republican inventor, architect, and part-time weapons designer William Thornton, for many years past the nation's chief patent officer, on the grounds that its contents belonged to all humanity and not just to the citizens of the United States. Burning them, Thornton said, would earn the attackers the same condemnation that the Turks had received from the civilized world when

they destroyed the library at Alexandria. See ibid., 134–35; Smelser, *Democratic Republic*, 269.

56. On the negotiations at Ghent, see the unsurpassed accounts in Bradford Perkins, *Castlereagh and Adams: England and the United States, 1812–1832* (Berkeley, 1964), 37–127; George Dangerfield, *The Era of Good Feelings* (New York, 1952), 63–91, as well as *JQAD*, 2: 603–62, 3: 3–144; *PHC*, 1: 852–1013.

57. On one violent incident, the beating of a Republican congressman in Boston, see James M. Banner Jr., *To The Hartford Convention: The Federalists and the Origins of Party Politics in Massachusetts, 1789–1815* (New York, 1970), 308. Outside New England, fierce Republican mobs attacked Federalists, notably in Baltimore shortly after the war began. See Frank A. Cassell, "The Great Baltimore Riot of 1812," *Maryland Historical Magazine*, 70 (1975): 241–59. In Connecticut, antiwar sentiment ran high among Connecticut River Valley farmers as well as seacoast traders. Although Abraham Bishop's Republican organization survived, Federalist fervor foreclosed any revival of the defeated constitutional reform movement of 1802. Rhode Island, essentially governed by the terms of the royal charter of 1663, retained its restrictive voting laws and its inequitable distribution of representatives, despite the rise of an abortive reform movement in 1811 dedicated to securing what one Rhode Island Republican called "a free suffrage for the people." The state also remained firmly Federalist. *Rhode Island Republican*, May 29, 1811; Richard J. Purcell, *Connecticut in Transition, 1775–1818* (1918; Middletown, CT, 1963), 183–5.

58. Strong quoted in Banner, *Hartford Convention*, 306–7; Memorial of the Town of Wendell, 1814, Senate Documents 4820/39, Massachusetts Archives, quoted in ibid., 317.

59. William Baylies, *An Oration, Pronounced at Middleborough. . . . July 4, 1808* (Middleborough, MA, 1808), 23; Higginson to Timothy Pickering, Nov. 22, 1803, Pickering Manuscripts, MHS. On divisions, see Dawes to Noah Webster, June 25, 1812, Webster Manuscripts, NYPL; Dwight to Timothy Pitkin, Jan. 9, 1815, quoted in Banner, *Hartford Convention*, 345. In 1805, following Jefferson's triumphant reelection and shortly before the Jeffersonians captured control of the Massachusetts legislature, Ames moaned, "We are sliding down into the mire of a democracy, which pollutes the morals of its citizens before it swallows up their liberties." Seven years later, his opinion had not improved. Ames, "Political Thoughts," *Monthly Anthology*, 2 (1805), 556. For a measured but powerful delineation of Massachusetts Federalist conservatism, see Banner, *Hartford Convention*, esp. 53–83, 122–67.

60. For contrasting accounts, see Banner, *Hartford Convention*, 104–9; Linda K. Kerber, *Federalists in Dissent: Imagery and Ideology in Jeffersonian America* (Ithaca, NY, 1970), esp. 50–66; John Kyle Dale, "The Federalist Press and Slavery in the Age of Jefferson," *Historian*, 65 (2003): 1303–29; Matthew Mason, "'Nothing Is Better Calculated to Excite Divisions': Federalist Agitation against Slave Representation during the War of 1812," *New England Quarterly*, 75 (2002): 531–61. For a somewhat overstated examination of proslavery views among the Federalists, see Larry E. Tise, *Proslavery: A History of the Defense of Slavery in America, 1701–1840* (Athens, GA, 1987).

61. Morse, *A Discourse Delivered at the African Meeting House . . . July 14, 1808* (n.p., n.d. [1808]), 18. The Yankee Federalist worldview became, if anything, increasingly hierarchical after 1800, even as some of the more practical-minded Federalists updated their electioneering and organizing tactics. See, e.g., George Cabot to Timothy Pickering, Feb. 14, 1804, in Henry Cabot Lodge, *Life and Letters of George Cabot* (Boston, 1878), 344. Most of those who could not abide the party's Anglomane conservatism—preeminently John Quincy Adams—simply cut their political ties with Federalism.

62. Legislative Petitions, Bath County, 1815, LoV; J. R. Pole, "Representation and Authority in Virginia from the Revolution to Reform," *JSH*, 24 (1958): 34; *Columbian Register* [New Haven], Nov. 2, 1816. For a clearheaded assessment of the strengths and weaknesses of the militias' performance in combat, see C. Edward Skeen, *Citizen Soldiers in the War of 1812* (Lexington, KY, 1999).

63. *Columbian Centinel*, Oct. 12, 1814.

64. Noah Webster, *A Collection of Papers on Political, Literary and Moral Subjects* (New York,

1843), 311–4; Edmund Quincy, *Life of Josiah Quincy of Massachusetts* (Boston, 1867), 358; Banner, *Hartford Convention*, 321–6.

65. The convention's resolutions appear in full, alongside the complete convention journal, in Theodore Dwight, *History of the Hartford Convention* (New York, 1833), 552–79.

66. Banner, *Hartford Convention*, 343–8 (quotation on 346).

67. Clay quoted in *JQAD*, 3: 101.

68. Ibid., 101–2.

69. The most thorough study of Jackson is Robert V. Remini's three-volume biography, of which the first volume, *Andrew Jackson and the Course of American Empire, 1767–1821* (New York, 1977), is the most relevant to the period under discussion here. Also see James Parton, *Life of Andrew Jackson* (New York, 1860).

70. Vincent Nolte, *Fifty Years in Both Hemispheres; or, Reminiscences of the Life of a Former Merchant* (New York, 1854), 209–10 (quotation). See also Alexander Walker, *Jackson and New Orleans* (New York, 1856), 150; Arsene Lacarrière Latour, *Historical Memoir of the War in West Florida and Louisiana in 1814–15* (1816; Gainesville, FL, 1999), 68–69; Robin Reilly, *The British at the Gates: The New Orleans Campaign in the War of 1812* (New York, 1974); Robert V. Remini, *The Battle of New Orleans* (New York, 1999).

71. Jackson quoted in Marquis James, *Andrew Jackson: The Border Captain* (Indianapolis, 1933), 31.

72. The most elaborate and provocative psychobiography of Jackson is Michael Paul Rogin, *Fathers and Children: Andrew Jackson and the Subjugation of the American Indian* (New York, 1975). Some of Rogin's themes recur in Andrew Burstein, *The Passions of Andrew Jackson* (New York, 2003).

73. Jackson, "Division Orders, Mar. 7, 1812," in *CAJ*, 1: 220–3 (quotation on 221).

74. "Message to the Troops, October 24, 1813," in ibid., 337–8; Jackson to Willie Blount, Nov. 4, 1813, in ibid., 1: 341; Crockett, *The Life of Davy Crockett by Himself*, Curtis C. Davis, ed. (New York, 1955), 46. Accounts of the death toll of militiamen and civilians at Fort Mims vary from 250 to 400. See also Karl Davis, "'Remember Fort Mims': Reinterpreting the Origins of the Creek War," *JER*, 22 (2000): 611–36.

75. Jackson to Rachel Jackson, Aug. 15, 1814, quoted in Remini, *Course of American Empire*, 233.

76. See Jane Lucas De Grummond, *The Baratarians and the Battle of New Orleans* (Baton Rouge, 1961). On the 1811 insurrection, see James H. Dorman, "The Persistent Specter: Slave Rebellion in Territorial Louisiana," *Louisiana History*, 18 (1977): 389–404; Thomas Marshall Thompson, "National Newspaper and Legislative Reactions to Louisiana's Deslondes Slave Revolt of 1811," *Louisiana History*, 33 (1992): 5–29. In the aftermath of the Louisiana insurrection, several southern state legislatures strengthened their militias and passed new slave control laws, confirming and even increasing the pervasive sense of anxiety.

77. Jackson to W. Allen, quoted in Remini, *Course of American Empire*, 254.

78. Jackson quoted in Parton, *Jackson*, 2: 208.

79. Andrew Jackson to Robert Hays, Feb. 9, 1815, in *CAJ*, 2: 162. On the celebrations, see Remini, *Course of American Empire*, 292–5.

80. Otis to Mrs. Harrison Gray Otis, Feb. 22, 1815, Harrison Gray Otis Papers, MHS.

81. Story to Nathaniel Williams, Feb. 22, 1815, in William W. Story, ed., *Life and Letters of Joseph Story* (Boston, 1851), 1: 254.

82. Among the more generous appraisals are Horsman, *War of 1812*; John K. Mahon, *The War of 1812* (Tallahassee, 1972). Adams's view was more ironic, seeing in the war's outcome the Jeffersonians' final repudiation of their old republican values.

83. Adams to Louisa Adams, Dec. 23, 1814, in Ford, *Writings*, 5: 246; Bayard to R. Bayard, Dec. 26, 1814, in Elizabeth Donnon, ed., "The Papers of James A. Bayard, 1796–1815," *Annual Report of the American Historical Association for the Year 1913* (Washington, DC, 1915), 2: 366.

84. Story to Williams, in Story, ed., *Life and Letters*, 1: 254.

85. On increased voting participation, see J. R. Pole, *Political Representation in England and the Origins of the American Republic* (London, 1966); Richard P. McCormick, "New Perspectives on Jacksonian Politics," *AHR*, 65 (1960): 292. The latter finds that of the seventeen states admitted to the Union by 1815, seven enjoyed their highest voter turnouts in the first quarter of the nineteenth century between 1809 and 1815: New Hampshire, Vermont, Massachusetts, Rhode Island, New York, Georgia, and Louisiana (the last only admitted to statehood in 1812).
86. Cabot to Rufus King, July 30, 1801, Rufus King Papers, N-YHS.

CHAPTER SIX: THE ERA OF BAD FEELINGS

1. Richardson, 1: 547–54.
2. Gallatin to Matthew Lyon, May 17, 1816, in Henry Adams, ed., *The Writings of Albert Gallatin* (Philadelphia, 1879), 1: 700.
3. John Taylor, *An Inquiry into the Principles and Policy of the Government of the United States* (1814; New Haven, 1950).
4. Although the most sustained and consequential democratic movements between 1815 and 1819 emerged at the state and local level, there were signs of increasing public restiveness about alleged corruption and privilege at the national level as well. Above all, Congress's decision to vote itself a pay hike in 1816, perceived as a salary grab, brought a storm of protests around the country—and retribution at the polls. Federalist losses were particularly heavy, with only nine of the party's representatives carrying over from one Congress to the next, but both parties took a beating. Chastened, the lame-duck session of the Fourteenth Congress repealed the compensation law and left the entire matter of congressional salaries to its successor. See C. Edward Skeen, "*Vox Populi, Vox Dei*: The Compensation Act of 1816 and the Rise of Popular Politics," *JER*, 6 (1986): 353–74.
5. Richardson, 2: 579; *Columbian Centinel* [Boston], July 12, 1817.
6. Richard J. Purcell, *Connecticut in Transition, 1775–1818* (1918; Middletown, CT, 1963), 188. For a sympathetic but critical appraisal of Connecticut Federalist politics and ideology after 1800, see Andrew Siegel, "'Steady Habits' under Siege: The Defense of Federalism in Jeffersonian Connecticut," in Doran Ben-Atar and Barbara B. Oberg, eds., *Federalists Reconsidered* (Charlottesville, 1998), 198–224. See also John Hastings Chatfield, "'Already We Are a Fallen Country': The Politics and Ideology of Connecticut Federalism, 1797–1812" (Ph.D. dissert., Columbia University, 1986).
7. John Leland, *A Blow at the Root* (New London, 1801), 1–28; idem, "The High Flying Churchman Stript of His Legal Robe," in *Connecticut Dissenters' Strong Box* (New London, 1802), 17; John J. Reardon, "Religious and Other Factors in the Defeat of the 'Standing Order' in Connecticut 1800–1818," *Historical Magazine of the Protestant Episcopal Church*, 30 (1961): 93–110.
8. *American Mercury* [Hartford], Oct. 24, 1811, quoting *The Democrat*. On early Connecticut manufacturing in 1818 (though biased toward minimizing its importance), see Grace Pierpont Fuller, *An Introduction to the History of Connecticut as a Manufacturing State* (Northampton, MA, 1915), 13–29. On Republican affinities with "the new professional and commercial interests," see William F. Willingham, "Grass Roots Politics in Windham, Connecticut, during the Jeffersonian Era," *JER*, 1 (1981); 127–48. On Federalist support for manufacturing, see Siegel, "'Steady Habits,'" 222.
9. *American Mercury* [Hartford], Oct. 25, 1815, quoting *American Watchman*; George H. Richards, *The Politics of Connecticut, addressed to Honest Men of all Parties, by a Federalist Republican* (Hartford, 1817), 26.
10. The best account of these events and the reformers' subsequent triumph remains Purcell, *Connecticut*, 211–64, but see also J. Hammond Trumbull, *Historical Notes on the Constitutions of Connecticut and on the Constitutional Convention of 1818* (Hartford, 1901), 32–62.

11. On Wolcott, *American Mercury*, Feb. 26, 1801. See also Purcell, *Connecticut*, 211–2. For a different view of the convergence of Federalists and Republicans, see Siegel "'Steady Habits,'" 221–3.
12. *American Mercury* [Hartford], Jan. 27, 1818; Richards, *Politics*; Purcell, *Connecticut*, 231–2. On Ingersoll, a prominent Episcopalian, see Trumbull, *Historical Notes*, 37–38.
13. Reverend Thomas Robbins, *Diary*, I. N. Tarbox, ed. (Boston, 1886–87), 1: 748.
14. John Niles quoted in Trumbull, *Historical Notes*, 59. The convention votes are recorded in *Journal of the Proceedings of the Convention of Delegates Convened at Hartford, August 26th, 1818* (Hartford, 1873), 7–72, although without transcriptions of the debates. Transcriptions do appear in the *Connecticut Courant* [Hartford], Sept. 8, 15, 22, 1818. See also J. Hammond Trumbull, *Historical Notes on the Constitutions of Connecticut, 1639–1818* (Hartford, 1901), 51–62; Simeon E. Baldwin, "The Three Constitutions in Connecticut," *Papers of the New Haven Colony Historical Association*, 5 (1894): 179–246; Purcell, *Connecticut*, 238–58.
15. On black disenfranchisement in Connecticut, see James Truslow Adams, "Disenfranchisement of Negroes in New England," *AHR*, 30 (1925): 543–7 (quotation on 546); Leon Litwack, *North of Slavery: The Negro in the Free States, 1790–1860* (Chicago, 1961), 75, 79.
16. *Connecticut Courant*, Sept. 22, 1818.
17. *Journal of the Proceedings*, 90–91.
18. Purcell, *Connecticut*, 258–61 (quotation on 261, n. 49); *Journal of the Proceedings*, 93–94; Trumbull, *Historical Notes*, 56–57.
19. Edmund Quincy, *Life of Josiah Quincy of Massachusetts* (Boston, 1869), 374–5; Matthew H. Crocker, *The Magic of the Many: Josiah Quincy and the Rise of Mass Politics in Boston 1800–1830* (Amherst, MA, 1999), 11 (quotation). On Massachusetts politics after 1815, see Ronald P. Formisano, *The Transformation of Political Culture: Massachusetts, 1790s–1840s* (New York, 1983), 117–27; Harlow W. Sheidley, *Sectional Nationalism: Massachusetts Conservative Leaders and the Transformation of America, 1815–1836* (Boston, 1998); William F. Hartford, *Money, Morals, and Politics: Massachusetts in the Age of the Boston Associates* (Boston, 2001), esp. 32–64. On Quincy's life and political activities, see Robert A. McCaughey, *Josiah Quincy 1772–1864: The Last Federalist* (Cambridge, MA, 1974), esp. 96–131. On the old-line Federalist resistance and the Quincy faction's success, see Harlow Walker Sheidley, "Preserving 'The Old Fabrick': The Massachusetts Conservative Elite and the Constitutional Convention of 1820–21," *Proceedings of the Massachusetts Historical Society*, 103 (1991): 114–37; Crocker, *Magic of the Many*, 34–35. The best account of Buckingham and the Boston "Middling Interest" is in Gary J. Kornblith, "Becoming Joseph T. Buckingham: The Artisanal Struggle for Independence in Early-Nineteenth-Century Boston," in Howard B. Rock et al., eds. *American Artisans: Crafting Social Identity, 1750–1850* (Baltimore, 1995), 123–34. After 1820, Quincy's popularity would head a popular insurgency that swept him into office as Boston's mayor and foreshadowed the final collapse of Massachusetts Federalism. See chapter 9, n. 2; Crocker, *Magic of the Many*, 24–96; McCaughey, *Quincy*, 96–113.
20. *Journal of Debates and Proceedings in the Convention of Delegates, Chosen to Revise the Constitution of Massachusetts* (Boston, 1853), 277–9, 304–21 (quotations on 278, 312).
21. Joseph Story to Jeremiah Mason, Jan. 21, 1821, Oliver Papers, MHS. On the tactics employed to head off radical reform, see Merrill Peterson, ed., *Democracy, Liberty and Property: The State Constitutional Conventions of the 1820's* (Indianapolis, 1966), 6–7; Sheidley, "Preserving 'The Old Fabrick.'" Of the fourteen amendments proffered to the voters for approval, five, including the minor adjustments to the provisions on religion, failed to win a majority—largely, it appears from the patterns of the state returns, because they offered too little change, not too much. Over the following decade, the religious establishment became increasingly impossible to sustain, as the number of churches and sects in the state grew. In 1833, working under the rules of the 1820 revised constitution, the legislature put up for public approval an amendment very similar to the one that failed in 1820, and it won by a majority of 10 to 1.

22. *New England Galaxy*, Jan. 5, 1821; Daniel Webster to Jeremiah Mason, Jan. 12, 1821, in Charles M. Wiltse, ed., *The Papers of Daniel Webster: Correspondence, 1798–1824* (Hanover, NH, 1974–89) 1: 280.

23. *Albany Argus*, June 24, 1817, Aug. 21, 1818, Feb. 9, June 1 (quotation), 1821; *American* [New York], Feb. 15, 1821; *National Advocate* [New York], June 21, 30, July 9, 1821.

24. The classic account is Jabez D. Hammond, *The History of Political Parties in the State of New-York* (Albany, 1842), 1: 451–7; but see also Jerome Mushkat, *Tammany: The Evolution of a Political Machine, 1789–1865* (Syracuse, NY, 1971), 56–74.

25. Donald B. Cole, *Martin Van Buren and the American Political System* (Princeton, 1984), 50–52; Evan Cornog, *The Birth of Empire: DeWitt Clinton and the American Experience, 1769–1828* (New York, 1998), 127–44. On the Bucktails' political ideology, see esp. Michael Wallace, "Changing Concepts of Party in the United States: New York, 1815–1828," *AHR*, 74 (1968): 453–91 (quotations on 458, 483).

26. *New-York Statesman* [Albany], Feb. 20, 1821; Peterson, ed., *Democracy*, 125–30; Cole, *Van Buren*, 61–67. Voting on the convention referendum was opened to male taxpayers, militiamen, and all who worked on the public roads.

27. Peterson, ed., *Democracy*, 130–2; Cole, *Van Buren*, 67–68. The pro-Bucktail faction included some anti-Clintonian Federalists who had supported the War of 1812, such as the former Massachusetts senator Rufus King—the "high mindeds"—who had been recruited by Van Buren.

28. The convention proceedings were immediately printed as L. H. Clarke, ed., *Report of the Debates and Proceedings of the Convention of the State of New-York* (New York, 1821). A much fuller version appeared soon after as Nathaniel Carter and William L. Stone, eds., *Reports of the Proceedings and Debates of the Convention of 1821* (Albany, 1821). I have relied here on the latter. On the votes on the key points of contention, see Peterson, ed., *Democracy*, 270. See also John A. Casais, "The New York State Constitutional Convention of 1821 and Its Aftermath" (Ph.D. dissert., Columbia, 1967); Cole, *Van Buren*, 67–82.

29. According to the figures gathered in the 1820 federal census, New York's total black population of 39,367 was nearly twice that of all of the New England states combined. Of the 10,088 slaves counted in New York, slightly more than half (5,188) were male.

30. Carter and Stone, eds., *Reports*, 178–83 (quotation on 178). Earlier constitutional conventions in Maryland, Connecticut, and Massachusetts had also restricted the vote either to state or U.S. citizens, as would, in coming years, the states of Vermont (1828) and Virginia (1830). New Jersey had completed the same change in its statutory revision of voting laws in 1807. The constitutions of new states admitted after 1815 would also limit voting to citizens. "By the Jacksonian era," Alexander Keyssar writes, "aliens were barred from the polls nearly everywhere." Under federal law, foreign-born white males who met a five-year residency requirement were entitled to become U.S. citizens three years after announcing their intention of doing so. Of course, it would be much easier for ineligible white aliens to skirt the 1821 ban than it would be for blacks—despite another regulation, approved by the 1821 convention, that demanded voters provide "proper proofs" of their eligibility. In practice, if not in the letter of the law, the restriction of black voting would prove more severe than of white aliens. See Keyssar, *The Right to Vote: The Contested History of Democracy in the United States* (New York, 2001), 32–33. More effective means to restrict immigrant voting would be imposed in New York and elsewhere only with the rise of a powerful nativist movement in the 1830s and 1840s.

31. Carter and Stone, eds., *Reports*, 401–27 (quotation on 407).

32. Ibid., 186, 191, 226.

33. Ibid., 181, 190 (quotation), 191 (quotation). The conservatives who favored property restrictions across the board and who also voted to ban black suffrage were Robert Rose, Richard Van Horne, and John W. Woods. They were joined by the chief justice of the New York Supreme Court, Ambrose Spencer, a Republican who, although favorably inclined to other democratic proposals, initially took a hard line on the suffrage. He later changed

his position somewhat, voting against the $250 freehold restriction for blacks on the grounds that it discriminated against those nonfreeholders with substantial leaseholds or personal wealth. Ibid., 376.

34. Ibid., 376. On the vote to reinstate black suffrage, 9 of 25 identified Bucktail radicals, including Clarke, joined with the 63 to 59 majority. Only 3, again including Clarke, voted with the minority against the freehold requirement for blacks. Ibid., 202, 377. Eighteen moderate Bucktails, most of them from rural upstate districts, also voted against the freehold requirement.

35. Ibid., 353.

36. Ibid., 226. For the interpretation of the convention's outcome as partisan and essentially conservative, see Lee Benson, *The Concept of Jacksonian Democracy: New York as a Test Case* (Princeton, 1961), 7–9. On the operational and political influences, see especially Wallace, "Changing Concepts." These interpretations are an overreaction to an older literature, epitomized by Dixon Ryan Fox's *Decline of Aristocracy in the Politics of New York, 1801–1840* (New York, 1919), 229–70; to a lesser extent, Arthur M. Schlesinger Jr., *The Age of Jackson* (Boston, 1945), 48.

37. Carter and Stone, eds., *Reports*, 221; Van Buren to Rufus King, Jan. 14, 1821, King Papers, N-YHS.

38. Van Buren to Rufus King, Oct. 28, 1821, in Charles R. King, ed., *The Life and Correspondence of Rufus King* (New York, 1894–1900), 6: 422. On the effects of the new voting laws on the size of the New York electorate, see Richard P. McCormick, "Suffrage Classes and Party Allegiance: A Study in Voter Behavior," *Mississippi Valley Historical Review*, 46 (1959): 397–410.

39. *Columbian* quoted in *American Mercury*, Oct. 21, 1817; *Worcester Spy* quoted in Chilton Williamson, *American Suffrage from Property to Democracy, 1760–1860* (Princeton, 1960), 210. Thorpe, 1: 89–114, 2: 972–85, 1057–73, 4: 2032–48.

40. J. Mills Thornton III, *Politics and Power in a Slave Society: Alabama, 1800–1860* (Baton Rouge, 1978), 11–13 (quotation on 13); Charles S. Sydnor, *A Gentleman of the Old Natchez Region: Benjamin L. C. Wailes* (Durham, NC, 1938), 27; Clarence E. Carter, ed., *The Territorial Papers of the United States* (Washington, DC, 1934), 6: 526, 7: 240–2, 526, 8: 111–2; John D. Barnhart and Donald F. Carmony, *Indiana: From Frontier to Industrial Commonwealth* (New York, 1954), 1: 110–1; AC, 11th Congress, 3rd session, 1347–8.

41. In general on these points, see Keyssar, *Right to Vote*, 38.

42. *Journal of the Convention of the Alabama Territory begun July 5, 1819* (Huntsville, AL, 1819), esp. 20–36; *Republican* [Huntsville, AL], July 22, Aug. 5, 12, 1819; Malcolm C. McMillan, *Constitutional Development in Alabama, 1798–1901: A Study in Politics, the Negro, and Sectionalism* (Chapel Hill, 1955), 3–46.

43. *Journal of the Convention of the Indiana Territory: Begun and Held in the Town of Corydon* (Louisville, KY, 1816); Charles Kettleborough, *Constitution Making in Indiana: A Source Book of Constitutional Documents with Historical Introduction and Critical Notes* (Indianapolis, 1916), 1: xv–xxii, 65–133; Barnhart and Carmony, *Indiana*, 1: 151–60; Jacob Piatt Dunn, *Indiana and Indianans: A History of Aboriginal and Territorial Indiana and the Century of Statehood* (Chicago and New York, 1919), 1: 295–313; Andrew R. L. Cayton, *Frontier Indiana* (Bloomington, IN, 1996), 228–60.

44. *Journal of the Convention of the Indiana Territory*, 38; Kettleborough, *Constitution Making*, xvi; Cayton, *Frontier Illinois*, 228–33; Emma Lou Thornbrough, *The Negro in Indiana before 1900: A Study of a Minority* (Indianapolis, 1957), 23–24; "Journal of the Illinois Constitutional Convention, 1818," *Journal of the Illinois State Historical Society*, 5 (1913): 355–424; Legislative Reference Bureau, *Constitutional Conventions in Illinois* (Springfield, 1918), 9–12; N. Dwight Harris, *The History of Negro Servitude in Illinois and of the Slavery Agitation in That State 1719–1864* (Chicago, 1904), 6–49; Robert M. Sutton, "Edward Coles and the Constitutional Crisis in Illinois, 1822–1824," *Illinois Historical Journal*, 82 (1989): 33–46; James Simeone, *Democracy and Slavery in Frontier Illinois: The Bottomland Republic* (DeKalb, IL, 2000), esp. 68–165. Edward Coles, elected governor of

Illinois in 1822, urged the end of the indenture system and the black codes, and for legislation protecting free blacks. Pro-slavery men in the state General Assembly responded by calling for a constitutional convention that would legalize bondage. In a popular referendum, Coles and the anticonvention forces won a solid victory, but the indenture system and black codes remained intact.

45. Printed copies of the petition can be found in the legislative petitions from several counties in 1815 held at the LoV in Richmond. On these events, see William G. Shade, *Democratizing the Old Dominion: Virginia and the Second Party System, 1824–1861* (Charlottesville, 1996), 57–59; but also J. A. C. Chandler, *Representation in Virginia* (Baltimore, 1896), 23–26; idem, *The History of Suffrage in Virginia* (Baltimore, 1901), 9–28; J. R. Pole, "Representation and Authority in Virginia from the Revolution to Reform," *JSH*, 24 (1958): 16–50; Williamson, *American Suffrage*, 226–7.

46. Archibald Stuart to William Wirt, Aug. 25, 1816, quoted in Shade, *Democratizing*, 58–59; Pole, "Representation," 34–36.

47. H. Tompkinson [Samuel Kercheval] to Thomas Jefferson, June 13, 1816, Jefferson to H. Tompkinson [Samuel Kercheval], July 12, 1816, TJC. Jefferson did manage, against Kercheval's wishes, to prevent the letter from being published, but not before it had been widely distributed, hand-to-hand, among reformers in Winchester County. Dumas Malone, *Jefferson and His Time* (New York, 1948–81), 6: 350. See also Jefferson to John Taylor, May 28, 1816, TJC.

48. *Proceedings and Debates of the Virginia Convention of 1829–30* (Richmond, 1830), 533.

49. William F. Wickham to Littleton W. Tazewell, May 2, 1817, quoted in Dickson D. Bruce Jr., *The Rhetoric of Conservatism: The Virginia Convention of 1829–30 and the Conservative Tradition in the South* (San Marino, CA, 1982), 22; Shade, *Democratizing*, 59.

50. In 1789, ten of the original thirteen states had significant property requirements for voting, whereas only three—Georgia, South Carolina, and Virginia—restricted the franchise to white men, and only three—Georgia, Pennsylvania, and South Carolina—had any kind of citizenship requirement. Of the twenty-four states in the Union in 1825, six—Maine, New Hampshire, Vermont, Massachusetts, Pennsylvania, and Tennessee—had no significant property bars or racial exclusions, and fifteen—Connecticut, New York, New Jersey, Delaware, Maryland, South Carolina, Georgia, Ohio, Louisiana, Indiana, Illinois, Kentucky, Mississippi, Alabama, and Missouri—had no significant property requirements for white men but either restricted or outlawed black voting. Virginia had significant property restrictions and banned black voting. Rhode Island and North Carolina had significant property restrictions for whites but did not ban black voting. See the summaries in Keyssar, *Right to Vote*, Appendix, 328–42.

51. William Wirt, *Letters of the British Spy* (1803; Baltimore, 1813), 109. See Harry Ammon, *James Monroe: The Quest for National Identity* (1971; Charlottesville, 1990), 352–545.

52. Biddle to B. Henry, Nov. 27, 1816, draft, Nicholas Biddle Papers, LC; Rush to Charles J. Ingersoll, Jan. 4, 1817, Ingersoll Papers, HSP.

53. King to ?, Jan. 3, 1818, in King, ed., *Life*, 6: 95.

54. On the failed national bank recharter efforts, see Bray Hammond, *Banks and Politics in America from the Revolution to the Civil War* (Princeton, 1957), 209–26 (quotation on 210).

55. Raymond Walters Jr., *Alexander James Dallas: Lawyer-Politician-Financier, 1759–1817* (Philadelphia, 1943), 160–200 (quotation on 186); idem, *Albert Gallatin: Jeffersonian Financier and Diplomat* (New York, 1957), 215–9, 254–60, 294–5; Hammond, *Banks and Politics*, 213, 226–53. Opposition to the bank bill in 1816 came chiefly from Federalists, led by Daniel Webster, who, though they approved of a national bank in principle, could not overcome their partisan suspicions that *this* bank would do more to benefit the Republican Party than it would to benefit the nation.

56. Monroe to James Madison, May 4, 1815, cited in Ammon, *Monroe*, 341.

57. Calhoun quoted in M. St. Clair Drake and D. A. Hall, eds., *Legislative and Documentary History of the Bank of the United States* (Washington, D.C. 1832), 528.

58. See Hammond, *Banks and Politics*, 252–62, 274–6.

59. Astor to Albert Gallatin, Mar. 3, 1817, Mar. 14, 1818, Albert Gallatin Papers, N-YHS.

60. On the panic, its origins, and the Second Bank of the United States, see Hammond, *Banks and Politics*, 251–62; George Dangerfield, *The Era of Good Feelings* (New York, 1952), 175–96; Murray N. Rothbard, *The Panic of 1819: Reactions and Policies* (New York, 1962), esp. 1–24. In Kentucky alone, the legislature chartered forty-six new banks, each empowered to issue $25,000 in paper money with no specie restrictions. See Sandra F. Van-Burkleo, "'The Paws of Banks': The Origins and Significance of Kentucky's Decision to Tax Federal Bankers, 1818–1820," *JER*, 9 (1989): 462. On declining commodity prices, see Arthur Harrison Cole, *Wholesale Commodity Prices in the United States, 1700–1861* (Cambridge, MA, 1938), 135, 156, 179, 185. See also Clyde Haulman, "Virginia Commodity Prices during the Panic of 1819," *JER*, 22 (2002): 675–88.

61. Jones quoted in Hammond, *Banks and Politics*, 253.

62. For a revisionist assessment that finds the state banks in Pennsylvania not as culpable as most historians have claimed they were in feeding the speculative bubble, see Robert M. Blackson, "Pennsylvania Banks and the Panic of 1819: A Reinterpretation," *JER*, 9 (1989): 335–58.

63. Biddle quoted in Hammond, *Banks and Politics*, 261; William Gouge, *A Short History of Paper Money and Banking in the United States* (n.p., 1833), 2: 109–10 Cheves's historical reputation rose during the twentieth century, in part because important scholars came to rely heavily on his own, highly self-serving narrative of the events, published in 1822. For a corrective, based on a closer look at the BUS's actual reserve ratios and excess reserves, see Edwin J. Perkins, "Langdon Cheves and the Panic of 1819: A Reassessment," *Journal of Economic History*, 44 (1983): 455–61. It would appear that Gouge, in 1833, came closer to the truth than Cheves's later admirers.

64. *JQAD*, 4: 382–3. On the impact of the panic and ensuing depression, see Samuel H. Rezneck, "The Depression of 1819–1822: A Social History," *AHR*, 39 (1933), 28–47; Rothbard, *Panic*, 14–16; Dorothy B. Dorsey, "The Panic of 1819 in Missouri," *Missouri Historical Review*, 29 (1935): 79–91; Thomas H. Greer, "Economic and Social Effects of the Panic of 1819 in the Old Northwest," *Indiana Magazine of History*, 44 (1948): 227–43; James A. Kehl, *Ill-Feeling in the Era of Good Feeling: Western Pennsylvania Political Battles, 1815–1825* (Pittsburgh, 1956); Andrew R. L. Cayton, "The Fragmentation of a 'Great Family': The Panic of 1819 and the Rise of the Middling Interest in Boston, 1818–1822," *JER*, 2 (1982): 143–67; J. David Lehman, "Explaining Hard Times: Political Economy and the Panic of 1819 in Philadelphia" (Ph.D. dissert., University of California at Los Angeles, 1992); Sarah Kidd, "'To Be Harrassed by My Creditors Is Worse than Death': Cultural Implications of the Panic of 1819," *Maryland Historical Magazine*, 95 (2000): 160–89; idem, "The Search for Moral Order: The Panic of 1819 and the Culture of the Early American Republic" (Ph.D. dissert., University of Missouri, 2002).

65. James Flint, *Letters from America*, Reuben Gold Thwaites, ed. (Cleveland, 1904), 224–6; Jefferson to Wilson Cary Nicholas, Aug. 11, 1819, TJC; Rothbard, *Panic*, 140. On the origins and development of Jefferson's opposition to bank credit and paper notes, see Donald F. Swanson, "'Bank-Notes Will Be as Oak Leaves': Thomas Jefferson on Paper Money," *Virginia Magazine of History and Biography*, 101 (1993): 37–52.

66. Richardson, 1: 623, 630, 642 (quotation); United States Treasury Department, *Reports of the Secretary of the Treasury of the United States* (Washington, DC, 1837), 2: 481–525.

67. Benton quoted in Rezneck, "Depression," 33; Rothbard, *Panic*, 24–111.

68. For a useful survey on the emergence of paper-money and hard-money arguments in the aftermath of the panic, see Rothbard, *Panic*, 57–111, 136–58.

69. On the rise of Philadelphia's diverse early manufacturing economy, see Bruce Laurie, *Working People of Philadelphia, 1800–1850* (Philadelphia, 1980), 3–30. See also Diane Lindstrom, *Economic Development in the Philadelphia Region* (New York, 1978).

70. Robert Wellford quoted in Ronald Schultz, *The Republic of Labor: Philadelphia Artisans and the Politics of Class, 1720–1830* (New York, 1993), 171. See Ian M. G. Quimby, "The

Cordwainers' Protest: A Crisis in Labor Relations," *Winterthur Portfolio*, 3 (1967): 83–101; Sean Wilentz, *Chants Democratic: New York City and the Rise of the American Working Class, 1788–1850* (New York, 1984), 107–42.

71. *Aurora*, Nov. 27, 1805, Jan. 9, 1807. On Duane during the period before 1815, see Kim Tousley Phillips, "William Duane, Revolutionary Editor" (Ph.D. dissert., University of California at Berkeley, 1968), 288–407.

72. Kim T. Phillips, "William Duane, Philadelphia's Democratic Republicans, and the Origins of Modern Politics," *Pennsylvania Magazine of History and Biography*, 101 (1977): 383–7; Schultz, *Republic of Labor*, 191–2.

73. *Aurora*, July 31, 1817; Klein, *Pennsylvania Politics*, 96–112; Kim T. Phillips, "Democrats of the Old School in the Era of Good Feelings," *Pennsylvania Magazine of History of Biography*, 95 (1971): 371–5; idem, "The Pennsylvania Origins of the Jackson Movement," *Political Science Quarterly*, 91 (1976): 491–3; Jamie Karmel, "The Market Moment: Banking and Politics in Jeffersonian Pennsylvania, 1810–1815," *Pennsylvania History*, 70 (2003): 55–80.

74. Simpson, writing as "Brutus," in *Aurora*, June 24, Nov. 26 (quotation), 29, 1819; Phillips, "Duane, Revolutionary Editor," 435–89; Pennsylvania General Assembly, *Journal of the Thirtieth House of Representatives of the Commonwealth of Pennsylvania* (Harrisburg, 1819–20), 476–88; Rothbard, *Panic*, 39–40, 72–76, 165, 171; Schultz, *Republic of Labor*, 196–8 (quotations on 197, 198). Both Rothbard and Schultz misidentify William Duane, and not his son, as the assemblyman and author of the panic investigation report.

75. *Aurora*, Jan. 4, 1816. See also *Aurora*, July 31, 1817. On Duane's shifting thoughts about banking and currency, see Phillips, "Duane, Revolutionary Editor," 474–80.

76. Reginald C. McGrane, ed., *The Correspondence of Nicholas Biddle Dealing with National Affairs, 1807–1844* (Boston, 1919), 14–15; Klein, *Pennsylvania Politics*, 132–49; Phillips, "Pennsylvania Origins," 494; Schultz, *Republic of Labor*, 209–10. Biddle, a former Federalist and a member of the Second BUS's board of directors, was also a member in good standing of the New School or Family Party, which proudly ran him for Congress in 1818 and 1820. Old School refusal to vote for anyone officially connected to the bank led to Biddle's crushing defeat both times, after which he lost interest in elective office. In 1823, he was named president of the Second BUS. See Thomas P. Govan, *Nicholas Biddle: Nationalist and Public Banker, 1786–1844* (Chicago, 1959), 1–77; Phillips, "Democrats," 374.

77. *McCulloch v. The State of Maryland et al*, 4 Wheat. 316 (1819). The irony was that this was the very BUS branch whose directors were looting the bank to the tune of millions. The McCulloch named on the docket was the Baltimore branch's cashier, James E. McCulloch, who profited handsomely from the deception. Ohio continued to enforce its law and levy taxes, in defiance of the *McCulloch* decision, until the Court cut down that law as well, in *Osborn v. Bank of the United States*, 22 U.S. 738 (1824).

78. John Taylor, *Construction Construed and Constitutions Vindicated* (Richmond, 1820), 298, 321.

79. *Aurora*, Mar. 16, 18, Apr. 7, 1819.

80. See Charles G. Sellers Jr., "Banking and Politics in Jackson's Tennessee," *Mississippi Valley Historical Review*, 61 (1954): 61–84 (quotations on 69). See also John Howard Parks, *Felix Grundy, Champion of Democracy* (Baton Rouge, 1949), 101–21; Rothbard, *Panic*, 90–97 (quotation on 94).

81. On Carroll, see Thomas Perkins Abernethy, *From Frontier to Plantation in Tennessee* (Chapel Hill, 1932), 231–8; Sellers, "Banking and Politics," 71–75.

82. Pennsylvania General Assembly, *Journal of the Thirtieth Senate of the Commonwealth of Pennsylvania* (Harrisburg, 1819–20), 221–36, 311–37.

83. Hammond, *Banks and Politics*, 274, 281.

84. Jefferson to John Adams, Nov. 7, 1819, TJC. Adams not only agreed with Jefferson; he had gone so far as to write a friendly letter to his old political foe John Taylor of Caroline in which he denounced banks, blamed them for the depression, and called paper money val-

ued higher than specie a "theft." John Adams to John Taylor, Mar. 12, 1819, in Charles F. Adams, ed., *Works of John Adams* (Boston, 1856), 10: 375.

CHAPTER SEVEN: SLAVERY, COMPROMISE, AND DEMOCRATIC POLITICS

1. AC, 1st Congress, 2nd session, 1224–5. On the persistence of the slavery issue after 1787, see Donald Robinson, *Slavery in the Structure of American Politics, 1765–1820* (1971; New York, 1979), 248–423. On the early antislavery petitions and their reception, see Richard S. Newman, "Prelude to the Gag Rule: Southern Reaction to Antislavery Petitions in the First Federal Congress," *JER*, 16 (1996): 571–99. More generally, see above all David Brion Davis, *The Problem of Slavery in the Age of Revolution, 1770–1823* (Ithaca, NY, 1975).
2. AC, 1st Congress, 1st session, 352; 2nd session, 1503–14 (quotations on 1505, 1509).
3. AC, 2nd Congress, 2nd session, 861; 5th Congress, 2nd session, 1308; 8th Congress, 1st session, 242. In the 48 to 7 House vote approving the fugitive slave bill, Fisher Ames, Elias Boudinot, and James Hillhouse were among the leading Federalists to vote aye; only five northerners and only one important Federalist, the abolitionist George Thatcher, voted with the minority. Apart from Thatcher, who raised the proposal, Gallatin and Joseph Varnum, a Massachusetts Republican, were the only congressmen to speak up on behalf of restricting slavery in Mississippi in 1798, and it went down to a heavy defeat. In the vote on the Hillhouse amendment barring slavery in the Louisiana Territory six years later, the preponderance of votes in favor came from northern Republicans, while decisive votes in opposition were cast by the then-Federalist John Quincy Adams and the arch-Federalist Timothy Pickering of Massachusetts. AC, 8th Congress, 1st session, 242–4.
4. Jefferson, *Notes on the State of Virginia* William E. Peden, ed. (New York, 1954), 162–63. There is considerable dispute among historians about how to interpret the burst of manumissions after the Revolution—between those who minimize its importance and those who stress the genuine moral awakening experienced, if only gradually, by such prominent slaveholders as George Washington. The point to stress is that the tone did change between 1800 and 1820, making antislavery sentiments even more tenuous among slaveholders throughout the South. See Robert McColley, *Slavery and Jeffersonian Virginia* (1964; Urbana, IL, 1973), esp. 111–62; Henry Wiecek, *An Imperfect God: George Washington, His Slaves, and the Creation of America* (New York, 2003). On the congressional struggle in 1790, see Robinson, *Structure*, 302–12. Of the House floor leader for compromise, Robinson (312) writes, "Having initially supported the investigation of Congressional powers over slavery and the slave trade, Madison quickly sensed that opinions were so profoundly divided that the mere discussion of them constituted a serious threat to the union." Thus, the political threats and anxieties that helped shape the federal convention in 1787 persisted in the First Congress—and well beyond. See Newman, "Prelude"; Stuart Knee, "The Quaker Petitions of 1790: A Challenge to the Democracy of Early America," *Slavery and Abolition*, 6 (1985): 151–9.
5. For a recent analysis of the economic and political factors behind American slavery's renaissance, see Adam Rothman, "The Expansion of Slavery in the Deep South, 1790–1820" (Ph.D. dissert., Columbia University, 2000).
6. AC, 9th Congress, 2nd session, 238.
7. AC, 8th Congress, 2nd session, 995–6. On the decline of southern Federalism after 1800, see James H. Broussard, *The Southern Federalists, 1800–1816* (Baton Rouge, 1978), 43–91. On northern Republican support for the South over details concerning the abolition of the Atlantic slave trade, see AC, 9th Congress, 2nd session, 264–65; Matthew B. Mason, "Slavery Overshadowed: Congress Debates Outlawing the Atlantic Slave Trade to the United States, 1806–1807," *JER*, 20 (2000):67–68. On the other hand, the prime mover in Congress for the slave trade ban was the Vermont Republican Senator Stephen Row Bradley.

8. The number of Virginia slaves sold to the internal slave trade nearly doubled over the first decade of the nineteenth century, and doubled again before 1820. On slave sales and prices, see Michael Tadman, *Speculators and Slaves: Masters, Trades, and Slaves in the Old South* (Madison, WI, 1989).

9. Tallmadge's decision to leave the House has never adequately been explained, although the death of his son early in 1819 no doubt played a part. (He proposed his famous amendments having just returned to Washington from the boy's funeral.) On Tallmadge, see the useful summary in *ANB*, 21: 280–1; also Tallmadge to John W. Taylor, Apr. 4, Sept. 14, 1819, Dec. 4, 1820, John W. Taylor Papers, N-YHS. The most thorough narrative of the Missouri crisis remains Glover Moore, *The Missouri Controversy, 1819–1821* (Lexington, KY, 1953), although many of its interpretations have lost their force over the decades since its publication. See also Shaw Livermore Jr., *The Twilight of Federalism: The Disintegration of the Federalist Party, 1815–1830* (Princeton, 1962), 88–112; Richard H. Brown, "The Missouri Crisis, Slavery, and the Politics of Jacksonianism," *South Atlantic Quarterly*, 65 (1966): 55–72; Don E. Fehrenbacher, "The Missouri Controversy and the Sources of Southern Separatism," *Southern Review*, 14 (1978): 653–67; Ronald C. Woolsey, "The West Becomes a Problem: The Missouri Controversy and Slavery Expansion as the Southern Dilemma," *Missouri Historical Review*, 77 (1983): 409–32; William W. Freehling, *The Road to Disunion: Secessionists at Bay, 1776–1854* (New York, 1990), 144–61; Robert Pierce Forbes, "Slavery and the Meaning of America, 1819–1837" (Ph.D. dissert., Yale University, 1994); Leonard L. Richards, *The Slave Power: The Free North and Southern Domination* (Baton Rouge, 2000), esp. 52–82; Joshua Michael Zeitz, "The Missouri Compromise Reconsidered: The Rhetoric of Free Labor and the Emergence of the Free Labor Synthesis," *JER*, 20 (2000): 447–85. On Taylor, see Edward K. Spann, "John W. Taylor, The Reluctant Partisan, 1784–1854" (Ph.D. dissert., New York University, 1957). Some of the material in this discussion appears in condensed form, but with additional documentation, in Sean Wilentz, "Jeffersonian Democracy and the Origins of Political Antislavery in the United States: The Missouri Crisis Revisited," *Journal of the Historical Society*, 4 (2004): 375–401.

10. For a summary of the Illinois controversy and its strong impact on Tallmadge, see Richards, *Slave Power*, 72–75.

11. In the course of the debates over Tallmadge's amendments, pro-slavery spokesmen—notably the Missouri delegate John Scott—would claim a stronger precedent, charging that the third article of the 1803 Louisiana Purchase treaty with France prevented Congress from barring slavery from any state carved out of Purchase lands. The argument cut no ice with Tallmadge and his allies, who found no such guarantee in the treaty's somewhat vague language, and who argued that, in any case, Congress had the overriding constitutional power to admit states on whatever terms it pleased. For Scott's argument, see *AC*, 15th Congress, 2nd session, 1195–203.

12. *AC*, 15th Congress, 2nd session, 1214–5, 1438; Salma Hale to William Plumer, Feb. 21, 1819, quoted in Moore, *Missouri Controversy*, 49. Tallmadge's amendments would have brought to Missouri a restricted version of New York's gradual emancipation law, limited to slaves born henceforth in Missouri. In addition to the two Illinois senators, two other free-state Republicans and one Federalist—the conservative mainstay Harrison Gray Otis of Massachusetts—voted to admit slavery to Missouri. Otis later switched positions, under the influence of Rufus King.

13. King to Mrs. Giles, Mar. 1820, in Charles R. King, ed., *The Life and Correspondence of Rufus King* (New York, 1894–1900), 6: 324–5; *NWR*, Dec. 4, 1819. King's later speeches on Missouri were more forthright in denouncing slavery as an evil. See summaries in ibid. On King's shifting emphasis during the Missouri crisis, see also Robert Ernst, *Rufus King: American Federalist* (Chapel Hill, 1968), 369–75. The ablest pro-restriction speech of the entire crisis by a Federalist actually came not from King but from the Pennsylvanian John Sergeant—a brilliant defense of Congress's constitutional powers to restrict slavery in new states. Even John Randolph was moved to congratulate Sergeant after the speech, telling

him *"Never speak again! Never speak again, sir!"* AC, 16th Congress, 1st session, 1172–216; Moore, *Missouri Controversy*, 96.

14. Jefferson to Henry Dearborn, Aug. 17, 1821, Jefferson to W. T. Barry, July 2, 1822, TJC; Jackson to Andrew Jackson Donelson [Apr. 16 (?), 1820], in *CAJ*, 3: 21; John Taylor, *Construction Construed and Constitutions Vindicated* (Richmond, 1820), 291–314; *JQAD*, 4: 529. Like Jefferson, Henry Clay and the more hard-line pro-slavery Richmond editor Thomas Ritchie suspected a Federalist plot. See Clay to Leslie Combs, Feb. 5, 1820, in *PHC*, 2: 774; *Richmond Enquirer*, Feb. 17, 1820; Brown, "Missouri Crisis," 59–61. Although most northern Federalists backed restriction, they were hardly monolithic on the issue; indeed, early in the controversy, they were slightly less supportive than northern Republicans. On the first House vote over the Tallmadge amendment banning the extension of slavery into Missouri in 1819, 78.6 percent of the northern Federalists (N=28) voted in favor, in contrast to 83.1 percent of the northern Republicans (N=77). Early in 1820, the antislavery Republican congressman William Darlington scoffed at the idea that he was the dupe of "political jugglers" who were using the Missouri debates to revive the Federalists. "From my earliest youth, upwards, I have been a democratic republican; and I leave it to those who have once belonged to the aforesaid expiring party, if there be any such here, to develop the schemes of the jugglers. I have never been in their secrets; but I cannot help observing, that I see gentlemen who are avowed members of that unfortunate party, zealously engaged in the ranks of our opponents, in endeavors to defeat the amendment." AC, 16th Congress, 1st session, 1374. John Quincy Adams wrote in his diary of his sympathies for the restrictionists, but as secretary of state, he decided it proper to guard his views, and he went along with efforts to reach a settlement. Privately, however, he astutely noted the growing political contradictions between Jeffersonian ideals and slavery: "The seeds of the Declaration of Independence are yet maturing. The harvest will be what [Benjamin] West, the painter, calls the terrible sublime." *JQAD*, 1:492–93.

15. AC, 15th Congress, 2nd session, 1179–84, 1191–3, 1195; 16th Congress, 1st session, 1466–89; 16th Congress, 2nd session, 1007–15. Hemphill, although listed by some sources as a Federalist in 1820, had already undertaken a migration into the Republican Party (in Pennsylvania, he aligned himself with the Old School country democrat Simon Snyder) that would in time lead him into the Jacksonian camp. On Wendover's pro-Jefferson, artisan republican politics, see P[eter] H. Wendover, *National Deliverance: An Oration Delivered in the New Dutch Church in the City of New York on the Fourth of July, 1806* (New York, 1806). On Morton, see Jonathan H. Earle, *Jacksonian Antislavery and the Politics of Free Soil* (Chapel Hill, 2004), 103–22. Fuller is best known as the father of the extraordinary Margaret Fuller; see Charles Capper, *Margaret Fuller, an American Romantic Life: The Private Years* (New York, 1992), 8–15. One of the few accounts of the Missouri crisis to take the ideas of the antislavery Jeffersonians in Congress seriously (though it lumps together Clintonians and regulars) is Major L. Wilson, *Space, Time, and Freedom: The Quest for Nationality and the Irrepressible Conflict 1815–1861* (Westport, CT, [1974]), 22–48, to which my own interpretation is indebted.

16. AC, 15th Congress, 2nd session, 1181, 1184. See also AC, 15th Congress, 2nd session, 1192; 16th Congress, 1st session, 1114, 1134,1300, 1376, 1396–7, 1426–7, 1467. To be sure, not all Republican antislavery pro-restrictionists shared egalitarian views on race. See, for example, Ezra C. Gross of New York's suggestion that were slavery to expand, the rapid increase of the black population would be "an earnest of the future extinction of the whole European race." AC, 16th Congress, 1st session, 1244. Yet even Gross's comments were delivered in passing and were not fundamental to his basic point, that slavery was a moral and political evil that should not be permitted to spread.

Southerners understandably claimed that the antislavery Republicans' "guarantee" clause argument meant that the southern slave states were in violation of the Constitution unless and until they abolished slavery. The antislavery response, offered most cogently by Timothy Fuller, was that Article I, Section 9 (on the slave trade) and Article IV, Section 2 (on fugitive slaves) of the federal Constitution "effectually recognized" the existence of slavery, but only in those states where slavery existed in 1787 "until they should think proper to meliorate their condition." By these lights, freedom was the rule, slavery the exception. See *AC*, 15th Congress, 2nd session, 1181–2.

17. *AC*, 15th Congress, 2nd session, 1192; 16th Congress, 1st session, 1116, 1437–8. Plumer, among others, also maintained that the Framers considered the Constitution "as guarding effectively against [slavery's] introduction into the new States."

18. *AC*, 5th Congress, 2nd session, 1307; 16th Congress, 1st session, 337, 1395, 1397. For similar arguments in connection with the emancipation fight in New York State, see *New York Argus*, Jan. 26, Feb. 3, 6, 1796. On the growing restiveness about the three-fifths clause as undemocratic, see Freehling, *Road to Disunion*, 147–48.

19. *AC*, 16th Congress, 1st session, 1377.

20. *AC*, 15th Congress, 2nd session, 1174.

21. *AC*, 15th Congress, 2nd session, 1200. The gist of Clay's opening remarks can be gleaned from the responses by John Taylor and Timothy Fuller in ibid., 1170–84.

22. *AC*, 16th Congress, 1st session, 1024.

23. *AC*, 16th Congress, 1st session, 1384, 1391. For diffusionist arguments, in addition to Tyler's speech, see the summary of Clay's speech and Philip C. Barbour's of Virginia in *AC*, 15th Congress, 2nd session, 1174–75, 1184–91. See also the columns of the Monroe administration's quasi-official organ, the *National Intelligencer*. "The question," it argued, "concerns only the diffusion of the concentration of the slaves now in the county." Jan. 29, 1820.

24. Clay to J. Sloane, Aug. 12, 1823, quoted in Robert V. Remini, *Henry Clay: Statesman for the Union* (New York, 1991), 180; *AC*, 16th Congress, 1st session, 1384. On the early American Colonization Society, see P. J. Staudenraus, *The African Colonization Movement, 1816–1865* (New York, 1961), 23–81.

25. *AC*, 15th Congress, 2nd session, 1436; 16th Congress, 1st session, 225, 227–8. See also Charles Pinckney's speech in *AC*, 16th Congress, 1st session, 1310–29.

26. *AC*, 16th Congress, 1st session, 259–75. This William Smith should not be confused with the pro-slavery Federalist William Loughton Smith, who died in 1812.

27. Tallmadge to John Taylor, Dec. 4, 1820, John Taylor Papers, N-YHS.

28. Plumer to William Plumer Jr., Jan. 31, 1820, Plumer Letterbooks, LC; *Aurora*, Nov. 23, 1819; *New York Post*, Feb. 10, 1821. The ancient, gouty Federalist humanitarian Elias Boudinot, a leader of the protests, wrote to his nephew that the agitation "seems to have run like a flaming fire thro our middle States, and causes great anxiety." Boudinot to Elias E. Boudinot, Nov. 27, 1819, Boudinot Papers, Stimson Deposit, PU. On the northern "Free Missouri" meetings, see also (though it overstates the Federalist influence) Moore, *Missouri Controversy*, 65–83.

29. *Baltimore Patriot & Mercantile Advertiser*, Feb. 17, 1820, quoted in Charles S. Sydnor, *The Development of Southern Sectionalism, 1819–1848* (Baton Rouge, 1948), 131; *AC*, 16th Congress, 1st session, 99.

30. *AC*, 16th Congress, 1st session, 841; Moore, *Missouri Controversy*, 84–100. The idea of banning slavery north of 36°30' had originated in a proposal forwarded by the antislavery leader John W. Taylor following the defeat of his effort to bar slavery in Arkansas Territory. Taylor ended up withdrawing his motion, but the idea soon revived as the heart of the Missouri bargain. The irony is that Taylor had designated the line—the southern boundary of what would be the new state of Missouri—with the idea that Missouri would be admitted as a free state. In its new formulation, slavery would be banned everywhere in the Louisiana Purchase lands north of 36°30' with the anomalous *exception* of Missouri. See *AC*, 15th Congress, 2nd session, 1280–2.

31. *AC*, 16th Congress, 1st session, 428, 1409–10, 1567.

32. Holmes to William G. King, Mar. 2, 12 (quotation), 1820, John Holmes Papers, Maine Historical Society; Moore, *Missouri Controversy*, 100–28. My thanks to Michael McManus for bringing the Holmes correspondence to my attention.

33. Plumer to William Plumer, Feb. 26, 1820, in Everett Somerville Brown, ed., *The Missouri*

Compromises and Presidential Politics, 1820–1825, from the Letters of William Plumer, Junior, Representative from New Hampshire (St. Louis, 1926), 13; Charles M. Wiltse, *John C. Calhoun* (Indianapolis, 1944–51) 1: 191–97, 219–21. For a corrective to the traditional view that Monroe was utterly passive during the crisis, see Harry Ammon, *James Monroe: The Quest for National Identity* (1971; Charlottesville, 1990), 450–5. On Biddle's involvement, see Moore, *Missouri Controversy*, 163–4 (quotation on 163). On Monroe's wielding of patronage and favors, especially among New York Bucktails, against Clinton, see Solomon Nadler, "The Green Bag: James Madison and the Fall of DeWitt Clinton," *New-York Historical Society Quarterly*, 59 (1975): 204–14.

34. Stokes to Governor John Branch, quoted in Moore, *Missouri Controversy*, 114. According to a Pittsburgh newspaper report, Randolph claimed that the pro-slavery side had so terrified the northern defectors that "[t]hey were scared of their own dough faces." He was probably referring to a game where children placed wet dough on their faces and frightened themselves and their friends by looking in a mirror. See *Statesman* [Pittsburgh], Apr. 26, 1820, cited in ibid., 104.

35. AC, 16th Congress, 1st session, Jan. 26, 1820, 943–4. For a similar appraisal of Van Buren's anti-Clintonian view of the Missouri crisis, see Donald B. Cole, *Martin Van Buren and the American Political System*, (Princeton, 1984), 57–62. On the "lukewarm" views of the Bucktails about restriction, see William Plumer Jr. to William Plumer, Apr. 17, 1820, in Brown, ed., *Missouri Compromises*, 16. On Monroe, patronage, and the Bucktails, see Nadler, "The Green Bag."

36. In all, of the thirty-four Republicans who voted for one of the original Tallmadge amendments in 1819 and who were still in office a year later, one voted for opening Missouri to slavery and one absented himself. The northern tally for restriction remained the same in 1820 as it had been in 1819: eighty-seven votes, of whom an even larger number than before were northern Republicans. Northern supporters for compromise in 1820 included two Massachusetts Republicans from the district of Maine, who were eager to gain Maine's admission to the Union; four conservative holdovers from the previous Congress (two Federalists, two Republicans) who had voted against the original Tallmadge amendments; one representative who had absented himself in 1819; and six additional members, all but one of them freshman and only four of whom were Republicans. Of the twenty-one New York Republicans in the House, seventeen voted for restriction in 1820, as did four out of five New York Federalists—roughly the same proportions in each party. See Wilentz, "Jeffersonian Democracy," esp. 389–91.

37. Clay quoted in Remini, *Clay*, 192. For contrasting narratives of the second Missouri Compromise, see Moore, *Missouri Controversy*, 129–69, and George Dangerfield, *The Era of Good Feelings* (New York, 1952), 233–43.

38. Jefferson to John Holmes, Apr. 22, 1820, TJC. For a reassessment of Jefferson's fears of disunion, see Stuart Leibiger, "Thomas Jefferson and the Missouri Crisis: An Alternative Interpretation," *JER*, 17 (1997): 121–30.

39. Macon quoted in Moore, *Missouri Controversy*, 109. On the 1822 results, see Wilentz, "Jeffersonian Democracy," 390–1.

40. For the most thorough account of Joseph Vesey and the early life of Telemaque, see John Lofton, *Denmark Vesey's Revolt: The Slave Plot That Lit a Fuse to Fort Sumter* (1964; Kent, OH, 1983), 5–36; also Douglas R. Egerton, *He Shall Go Free: The Lives of Denmark Vesey* (Madison, WI, 1999); David Robertson, *Denmark Vesey* (New York, 1999), 11–40. The new name "Denmark" may have been a corruption of "Telemaque" and may have referred to the Danish-controlled island where he was reared. The basic primary sources for almost all of this scholarship on the Vesey affair include the vexingly ambiguous or highly contestable official printed account, Lionel H. Kennedy and Thomas Parker, *An Official Report of the Trial of Sundry Negroes, Charged with an Attempt to Raise an Insurrection in the State of South Carolina* (1822; Boston, 1970); and James Hamilton Jr., *Negro Plot, An Account of the Late Intended Insurrection Among a Portion of the Blacks of the City of Charleston, South Carolina* (Charleston, 1822). The narrative here is based on all of these

sources, as well as what appears to be the manuscript transcript of the inquiries covered in the official report, "Evidence Document B," Records of the General Assembly, Nov. 28, 1822, Governors' Messages, 1328, South Carolina Department of Archives and History.

41. In all, charges were considered against 131 blacks, slave and free, of whom 93 were put on trial. Of the latter, 35 were convicted and executed, while 31 were convicted and sentenced to be transported out of state at their owners' expense, usually to plantations farther south and west. Another 11 men who were acquitted were deemed so dangerous by Charleston authorities that they were also transported. Five slaves who testified against the convicted men were set free. See Lofton, *Denmark Vesey's Revolt*, 173–5. For a biographical record of all of those executed, see Robertson, *Denmark Vesey*, 155–65.

42. Richard C. Wade first claimed that the plot amounted to little more than "loose talk among aggrieved and bitter men," in his "The Vesey Plot: A Reconsideration," *JSH*, 30, (1964): 143–61. Subsequent scholarship has generally supported Lofton's interpretation in *Denmark Vesey's Revolt* that a genuine conspiracy was underway. Yet even among these historians there is no consensus about the actual extent of the conspiracy. See William W. Freehling, *Prelude to Civil War: The Nullification Controversy in South Carolina, 1816–1836* (New York, 1965), 53–61; idem, *Road to Disunion*, 79–82; Sterling Stuckey, "Remembering Denmark Vesey—Agitator or Insurrectionist?" *Negro Digest*, 15 (1966): 28–41; Robert Starobin, "Denmark Vesey's Slave Conspiracy of 1822: A Study in Rebellion and Repression," in John Bracey et al., eds., *American Slavery: The Question of Resistance* (Belmont, CA, 1971), 142–55. Most recently, Michael P. Johnson, relying on the manuscript court transcripts, has revived Wade's line of argument, but his view has in turn been criticized by still other historians who insist that the alleged rebels' testimony cannot be dismissed as coerced falsehood. See Johnson, "Denmark Vesey and His Co-Conspirators," *WMQ*, 58 (2001): 915–76, and the responses in *WMQ*, 59 (2002): 135–202.

43. Kennedy and Parker, *Official Report*, 87–88; Holland, *A Refutation of the Calumnies Circulated Against the Southern and Western States, Respecting the Institution and Existence of Slavery Among Them* (Charleston, 1822), 86. Purcell, who barely spoke at his own trial, is supposed to have made his confession to James Hamilton moments before his execution—circumstances that cast doubt on its veracity. But appearing in the official report, his supposed remarks seemed true enough to readers in 1822. And quite apart from Vesey's possible use of King's pamphlet, there is ample evidence that blacks were both aware of and took an intense interest in the Missouri crisis. Blacks in Washington filled the congressional galleries during the debates. Word undoubtedly spread through a grapevine hidden to whites (and most historians); subsequent black abolitionists, including David Walker, would take note of the debates and King's contributions. See "Evidence Document B," 204, 227; Moore, *Missouri Controversy*, 91.

44. On Adams's early career, see Samuel Flagg Bemis, *John Quincy Adams and the Foundations of American Foreign Policy* (New York, 1965), 3–468; but see also Paul C. Nagel, *John Quincy Adams: A Public Life, A Private Life* (New York, 1997), 3–267. Adams's abrupt resignation in 1808 came after the Federalist-controlled Massachusetts legislature named a replacement for him six months ahead of schedule.

45. *JQAD*, 5: 315; Erastus Root to Martin Van Buren, Jan. 3, 1823, VBP. See Chase C. Mooney, *William H. Crawford, 1772–1834* (Lexington, KY, 1974), 1–248. Crawford also carried a sense of entitlement, having been unofficially assured of the nomination by Monroe's friends when he refrained from challenging the Virginian in 1816.

46. Van Buren to Charles Dudley, Jan. 10, 1822, in Catharina V. R. Bonney, *A Legacy of Historical Gleanings* (Albany, 1875), 1: 382; Mooney, *Crawford*, 289; Cole, *Van Buren*, 104–10.

47. Mooney, *Crawford*, 212–48; Wiltse, *Calhoun* 1: 211–46; Irving H. Bartlett, *John C. Calhoun: A Biography* (New York, 1993), 105–15.

48. *AC*, 18th Congress, 1st session, 1962–2001 (quotation on 1978).

49. *JQAD*, 5: 258.

50. On Jackson's controversial actions in Florida and his career through 1822, see Robert V. Remini, *Andrew Jackson and the Course of American Empire, 1767–1822* (New York, 1977), 298–424.

51. On all of these events, see Charles Sellers, "Banking and Politics in Jackson's Tennessee, 1817–1827," *Mississippi Valley Historical Review,* 41 (1954): 79–81; idem, "Jackson Men with Feet of Clay," *AHR,* 62 (1957): 537–51; Murray N. Rothbard, *The Panic of 1819: Reactions and Policies* (New York, 1962), 94–96. On Jackson's opposition to the Tennessee loan office as both unconstitutional and "prohibited by the principles of general Justice to the people," see Jackson to William B. Lewis, July 15, 16 (quotation), 1820, in *Bulletin of the New York Public Library,* 4 (1900): 162, 189–91.

52. On Simpson's admiration of Jackson, and Jackson's growing popularity among Old School Pennsylvania Democrats, urban and rural, see Kim T. Phillips, "The Pennsylvania Origins of the Jackson Movement," *Political Science Quarterly,* 91 (1976): 497, 499–502. On the early maneuvers in Pennsylvania, which led Calhoun to believe, he wrote, that his prospects were "firm as a rock," see Philip Shriver Klein, *Pennsylvania Politics, 1817–1832: A Game without Rules* (Philadelphia, 1940), 150–7. See also Herman Halperin, "Pro-Jackson Sentiment in Pennsylvania, 1820–1828," *Pennsylvania Magazine of History and Biography,* 50 (1926): 193–240.

53. *Columbian Observer* [Philadelphia], Apr. 6, May 4, 1822, Sept. 12, 1823. Kim Tousley Phillips, "William Duane, Revolutionary Editor" (Ph.D. dissert., University of California at Berkeley, 1968), 528–83 (quotations on 569, 576); idem, "Pennsylvania Origins," 494–9, 502–8; George McDuffie to Charles Fisher, Jan. 13, 1823, quoted in Sellers, "Jackson Men," 546; Klein, *Pennsylvania Politics,* 158–66. In May 1822, Simpson's paper announced—two months prematurely—that the Tennessee legislature had nominated Jackson for president. Two months later, Simpson personally pledged his loyalty to Jackson, noting his own proud service at New Orleans. By August, Jackson was a gratified subscriber to the *Columbian Observer;* Jackson's close advisers William B. Lewis and John Eaton contributed important articles and sent advice; and Jackson refused to interfere when asked to tone down Simpson's writings, much as Thomas Jefferson had refused to meddle with William Duane twenty years earlier. See *Columbian Observer,* May 4, 1822; Simpson to Andrew Jackson, July 5, 1823, Andrew Jackson Papers, LC; Phillips, "Duane, Revolutionary Editor," 566; idem, "Pennsylvania Origins," 497.

54. Plumer to William Plumer, Dec. 2, 1823, in Brown, ed., *Missouri Compromises,* 84–85. According to Plumer, Adams explained that Jackson "would administer the government with perfect integrity & disinterestedness, free from all bargains, compromises, coalitions, or corruption—& this, he added, with great emphasis, is more than I can say of either Crawford, Calhoun, Clay, or Clinton." It would prove, in a year's time, one of the most ironic assessments in the era's political history.

55. *AC,* 13th Congress, 2nd session, 843; William Plumer to William Plumer Jr., Apr. 24, 1820, in Brown, ed., *Missouri Compromises,* 50–51. For early criticisms of the caucus system, see, e.g., *Aurora,* Feb. 19, 1800.

56. King to C. King, Jan. 1, 1824, in King, ed., *Life,* 6: 544. Mooney, *Crawford,* 249–68, gives an excellent account of the machinations behind the last congressional caucus and the surrounding debate about the caucus system, but see also Cole, *Van Buren,* 124–6. Rufus King went on to endorse the calling of conventions as the best-available method for choosing national candidates. King to C. King, Mar. 23, 1824, in King, ed., *Life,* 6: 557. On the early operations of the congressional caucus system and its subsequent development and decline, see also Noble E. Cunningham Jr., *The Jeffersonian Republicans in Power: Party Operations, 1801–1809* (Chapel Hill, 1963), 101–24; William G. Morgan, "The Origins and Development of the Congressional Nominating Caucus," *American Philosophical Society Proceedings,* 113 (1969): 184–96; idem, "The Decline of the Congressional Nominating Caucus," *Tennessee Historical Quarterly,* 24 (1965): 245–55; Mosei Ostrogorski, "The Rise and Fall of the Nominating Caucus, Legislative and Congressional," *AHR,* 5 (1900): 252–83.

57. Robert P. Hay, "The Case for Andrew Jackson in 1824: John Eaton's 'Wyoming' Letters,"

Tennessee Historical Quarterly, 29 (1970): 139–51; Jackson to L. H. Coleman, Apr. 26, 1824, to William S. Fulton, July 4, 1824, in *PAJ*, 5: 398, 426.

58. Jackson to William Lewis, May 24, 1824, quoted in Remini, *Course of American Freedom*, 68; Jackson to L. H. Coleman, Apr. 26, 1824, in *PAJ*, 5:399. Clay's reported remark appears in Remini, *Course of American Freedom*, 70.

59. William Plumer Jr. to William Plumer, Dec. 2, 1823, in Brown, ed., *Missouri Compromises*, 85. On a visit to Monticello, Daniel Webster and George Ticknor found Thomas Jefferson deeply ill-disposed to the popular general, whom, they claimed, he considered a man of "terrible" passions, a warrior with little respect for law and constitutions. "Notes of Mr. Jefferson's Conversation 1824 at Monticello," in Charles M. Wiltse, ed., *The Papers of Daniel Webster: Correspondence* (Hanover, NH, 1974–86), 1: 375–6. The notes were written in Ticknor's hand, and their veracity is dubious.

60. NWR, Mar. 20, 1824, 39; *Mercantile Advertiser* [Mobile, AL], Jan. 8, 1824. For further elaboration of this point, see by Paul C. Nagel, "The Election of 1824: A Reconsideration Based on Newspaper Opinion," *JSH*, 26 (1960): 315–29.

61. George M. Dallas to William Darlington, Jan. 27, 1824, quoted in Klein, *Pennsylvania Politics*, 158. See also Philips, "Pennsylvania Origins," 504; S & I, 1: 399; Melba Porter Hay, "1824," in Arthur M. Schlesinger Jr., *Running for President: The Candidates and Their Images* (New York, 1994), esp. 1: 94.

62. For the most detailed account of New York politics in this period and the rise of the People's Party, see Craig Hanyan with Mary Hanyan, *De Witt Clinton and the Rise of the People's Men* (Montreal, 1996), esp. 3–148; but also Cole, *Van Buren*, 126–8; Evan Cornog, *The Birth of Empire: DeWitt Clinton and the American Experience, 1769–1828* (New York, 1998), 145–57. The Hanyans provide abundant evidence to show that, for all of its populist rhetoric and trappings, the People's Party wound up electing a legislature that had far stronger connections to the state's social and economic elites than the previous Bucktail legislatures.

63. Cornog, *Empire*, 145–57.

64. Van Buren, *Autobiography of Martin Van Buren*, John C. Fitzpatrick, ed. (1920; New York, 1970) 1: 143–6 (quotations on 144); Cole, *Van Buren*, 129–33.

65. Cole, *Van Buren*, 134–6 (quotation on 136), offers a clear explication of these extremely confusing events. Within a year, old Skinner was dead and soon forgotten outside of the taproom lore of Albany politics. Van Buren, who had merely suffered through a terrible season, would never again overlook the importance of seeking, and then following, the will of the majority.

66. Ibid., 136–7.

67. *Westmoreland Republican* [Pennsylvania] quoting *Lancaster Journal*, Dec. 6, 1822, quoted in Phillips, "Pennsylvania Origins," 502.

68. *JQAD*, 5: 128–9.

69. Jonathan Roberts to Matthew Roberts, Mar. 5, 7, 9, 1824, quoted in Phillips, "Pennsylvania Origins," 507.

70. In Ohio, where he expected to run well, Clay won the state legislature's nomination only after a bitter struggle, and narrowly edged Jackson in the popular vote in the general election. One politician from the antislavery eastern part of the state observed, during the nomination fight, that "[w]ere it not the recollection of the Missouri question, there would scarcely be a dissenting voice to Clay's nomination." Support for Adams from New England migrants and Quakers offended by the opening of Missouri to slavery appears to have cut heavily into Clay's vote. See Donald J. Ratcliffe, "The Role of Voters and Issues in Party Formation: Ohio, 1824," *JAH*, 59 (1973): 847–70 (quotation on 851).

71. John C. Spencer to Albert H. Tracy, May 28, 1821, Albert Tracy Papers, New York State Library.

72. NWR, March 20, 1824, 39–40.

73. Thomas Hart Benton, *Thirty Years' View; or, a History of the Working of the American Government for Thirty Years, from 1820 to 1850* (New York, 1854–56), 1: 47.

CHAPTER EIGHT: THE POLITICS OF MORAL IMPROVEMENT

1. Clay to Francis Preston Blair, Jan. 8, 1825, in *PHC*, 4: 9.
2. William Plumer Jr. to William Plumer, Jan. 20, 1825, in Everett Somerville Brown, ed., *The Missouri Compromises and Presidential Politics, 1820–1825* (St. Louis, 1926), 133. See also Clay to Richard Bache, Feb. 17, 1824, in *PHC*, 3: 645. On the Adams-Clay entente, and more generally on the jockeying in Congress, see, apart from the Clay papers and Adams's diary, Charles Grier Sellers Jr., "Jackson Men with Feet of Clay," *AHR*, 62 (1957): 537–51; James F. Hopkins, "Election of 1824," in S & I, 1: 349–408; Robert V. Remini, *Henry Clay: Statesman for the Union* (New York, 1991), 251–72; Merrill D. Peterson, *The Great Triumvirate: Webster, Clay, and Calhoun* (New York, 1987), 126–31.
3. *Columbian Observer* [Philadelphia], Jan. 28, Feb. 2, 1825; *National Intelligencer* [Washington], Jan. 31, 1825.
4. Kremer, a country storekeeper back home—and nephew of the Clodhopper ex-governor, Simon Snyder—liked to appear on the floor of the House dressed in a leopard-skin coat. Much of the congressional leadership considered him a backbench bumpkin, unworthy of Clay's notice. See, e.g., Daniel Webster to Ezekiel Webster, Feb. 4, 1825, in Charles M. Wiltse, ed., *The Papers of Daniel Webster: Correspondence* (Hanover, NH, 1974–86), 2: 20. Adams thought Kremer was drunk the night he wrote the letter and did not know what he was saying. *JQAD*, 6: 495–7. Jackson, on the contrary, would always regard him, gratefully, as "honest George Kreamer." Jackson to [Stephen] Simpson, Nov. 23, 1825, in *PAJ*, 6: 123. On the widespread disapproval of Clay's original challenge, and the delicate position Clay had to adopt regarding his accuser, see William Plumer Jr. to William Plumer, Feb. 6, 1825, in Brown, ed., *Missouri Compromises*, 136–7. There were widespread and credible suspicions at the time that the actual writer of the Kremer letter was Samuel Ingham, a leading New School Pennsylvanian long hostile to Stephen Simpson but now supporting Jackson. See James Parton, *Life of Andrew Jackson* (New York, 1860), 3: 102–20.
5. *JQAD*, 6: 501.
6. Jackson to William B. Lewis, Feb. 14, 1825, in *PAJ*, 6: 29–30.
7. On the ideological as well as political logic of an Adams-Clay alliance, see Remini, *Clay*, 253–4. Various historians have endorsed Clay's appraisal, calling the connection, in Richard Hofstadter's words, a "necessary statesmanlike understanding." Hofstadter, *The Idea of a Party System: The Rise of Legitimate Opposition in the United States, 1780–1840* (Berkeley, 1969), 232.
8. *JQAD*, 7: 98.
9. Ibid., 6: 518–9; Clay to James Brown, May 9, 1825, in *PHC*, 4: 336; Jackson to Samuel Swartwout, Feb. 22, 1825, in *PAJ*, 6: 42; Robert V. Remini, *Andrew Jackson and the Course of American Freedom, 1822–1832* (New York, 1981), 105–6. Jackson's acceptance appears in his farewell address upon resigning his Senate seat. "To the Tennessee Legislature," Oct. 12, 1825, in *CAJ*, 3: 293–6 (quotation on 294). Calhoun interpreted the events leading up to Adams's selection much as Jackson did, although with less personal animus. See Calhoun to J. G. Swift, Mar. 10, 1825, in *PJCC*, 10: 9–10.
10. Adams to John Quincy Adams, Apr. 23, 1794, Adams Papers, MHS. For the best recent biography of Adams, emphasizing his private difficulties, see Paul C. Nagel, *John Quincy Adams: A Public Life, A Private Life* (New York, 1997); also the perceptive chapter on Adams in Daniel Walker Howe, *The Political Culture of the American Whigs* (Chicago, 1979), 43–68. The standard works remain Samuel Flagg Bemis, *John Quincy Adams and the Foundations of American Foreign Policy* (New York, 1949); and Bemis, *John Quincy Adams and the Union* (New York, 1956).
11. Adams quoted in Nagel, *Adams*, 259; *JQAD*, 6: 539–40, 7: 21–22, 97–98, 200–1 (quotations on 22, 200), 8: 41 (quotation).
12. Adams, *An Oration Delivered at Newburyport* (Newburyport, MA, 1837), 54. A useful pose in certain official diplomatic situations, Adams's austere mask did not, he knew, endear him to most people—which only caused him to worry all the more that his political adver-

saries maligned him as a "gloomy misanthropist" and "an unsocial savage." Adams quoted in Nagel, *Adams*, 246; *JQAD*, 6: 413.

13. Edward Waldo Emerson and Waldo Emerson Forbes, eds., *Journals of Ralph Waldo Emerson* (Cambridge, MA, 1909–14), 6: 349; Adams quoted in Howe, *Political Culture*, 47. Adams always acknowledged his intensely political side. In 1811, he declined President Madison's offer of a seat on the Supreme Court because, he wrote privately, "I am . . . and always shall be too much of a political partizan for a Judge." Adams to Thomas Boylston Adams, Apr. 10, 1811, Adams Papers, MHS.

14. Richardson, 2: 878.

15. Ibid., 2: 877, 882.

16. Ibid., 862–3, 882. The concepts of the "positive" and "negative" state distinguish between governments and policies that advance liberty through intervention in social and economic life, and those that do so through restraint of government power. The terms are closely related to Isaiah Berlin's distinction between "positive liberty" and "negative liberty," in his "Two Concepts of Liberty: An Inaugural Lecture Delivered before the University of Oxford, on 31 October 1958" (Oxford, 1959). They entered into the discussion of the Jacksonian era in Lee Benson, *The Concept of Jacksonian Democracy: New York as a Test Case* (Princeton, 1961), esp. 109, which argues that the National Republicans and Whigs came much closer to being forerunners to modern New Deal liberalism than their Jacksonian opponents did. Although useful as a heuristic, the distinction too often ignores that virtually all American political parties and movements have favored a blend of "positive" and "negative" government.

17. The southern concerns about Adams's antislavery were as yet overwrought, given that Adams had supported the Missouri Compromise and showed no eagerness to threaten the Union with sectional appeals. Yet Adams also made it increasingly plain to his southern friends—who still included his vice president, John C. Calhoun—that he disapproved of slavery and feared it would eventually rip the Union asunder. See Chandra Miller, "'Title Page to a Great Tragic Volume': The Impact of the Missouri Crisis on Slavery, Race, and Republicanism in the Thought of John Quincy Adams and John C. Calhoun," *Missouri Historical Review*, 94 (2000): 365–88.

18. Richardson, 2: 882; *JQAD*, 7: 62–65, 77–78; 185.

19. Charles Wilson Hackett, "The Development of John Quincy Adams's Policy with Respect to an American Confederation and the Panama Congress, 1822–1825," *Hispanic-American Historical Review*, 8 (1928): 496–525; Richardson, 2: 868. On Adams's early involvement in plans for the Panama Congress, see *JQAD*, 6: 536–7. On the Adams administration's Latin America policies and the Panama Congress debacle, see also Bemis, *Adams and the Foundations*, 536–65.

20. John H. Marable to Andrew Jackson, Apr. 3, 1826, in *PAJ*, 6: 161; *RD*, 19th Congress, 1st session, 389–404 (quotations on 401, 403); Remini, *Clay*, 293–5; Peterson, *Great Triumvirate*, 142. Two years after the fact, Adams had occasion to describe Randolph's attack on him in Congress: Randolph, drunk on porter, launched into "raving balderdash in the meridian of Wapping" and reviled "the absent and the present, the living and the dead." Calhoun refused to interfere, Adams claimed, because he was not the object of Randolph's remarks and because he was afraid of the Virginian. See *JQAD*, 7: 433. The actual author of the letter insulting Calhoun was Philip Fendall, a friend of Clay's who was later appointed State Department clerk.

21. Calhoun to Joseph G. Swift, Sept. 2, 1825, in *PJCC*, 10: 10. On Adams's policies, see *JQAD*, 7: 89–92; Richardson, 2: 939; Michael D. Green, *The Politics of Indian Removal: Creek Government and Society in Crisis* (Lincoln, NE, 1982), 98–140, which offers a clear explication of the Creek removal from all perspectives, especially the Creeks'. On Georgia politics, see Ulrich Bonnell Phillips, *Georgia and State Rights* (Washington, DC, 1902); Paul Murray, "Economic Sectionalism in Georgia Politics, 1825–1855," *JSH*, 10 (1944): 293–307; idem, "Party Organization on Georgia Politics, 1825–1853," *Georgia Historical Quarterly*, 29: (1945): 196–209; Richard P. McCormick, *The Second American Party Sys-*

tem: Party Formation in the Jacksonian Era (Chapel Hill, 1966), 236–46; Donald A. DeBats, *Elites and Masses: Political Structure, Communication, and Behavior in Antebellum Georgia* (New York, 1990), 15–83. See also Edward J. Harden, *The Life of George M. Troup* (Savannah, 1859), 3–171.

22. *JQAD*, 7: 90.
23. Quotation in Harden, *Troup*, 485; NWR, Sept. 10, 1825; Richardson, 2: 936–9. Troup claimed that questions of sovereignty were open to negotiation between the federal government and the states, but was vague about how such negotiations might be conducted. He adamantly refused to recognize the authority of the U.S. Supreme Court to decide such matters, on the grounds that because the Court was a branch of the federal government, it was a party to any case it would be asked to decide. See Harden, *Troup*, 489–92.
24. Quotation in Harden, *Troup*, 485.
25. Jackson to Edward G. W. Butler, July 25, 1825, in *PAJ* 6: 94; to Butler, Jan. 24, 1826, to John H. Eaton, Feb. 8, 1827, in *CAJ*, 3: 288, 342. In his letter to Eaton about the administration's "absurd" threats, Jackson made clear that he thought Adams's situation hopeless, as the regular army would "be eat up" before it even arrived in Georgia, and the southern and western militias "will never arm in such a cause." He also said that Congress and the judiciary—"not the bayonette"—should properly settle the matter. Jackson's disdain for Troup dated back to 1819, when Jackson supported Troup's archrival in Georgia, the country democrat John Clark, in part because Clark had promised to clamp down on evasions of the overseas slave trade—violations Jackson called "the illegal and inhuman traffic of the poor african." Jackson to John Clark, Nov. 23, 1819, in *CAJ*, 2: 442.
26. See Eli W. Caruthers, *A Sketch of the Life and Character of the Rev. David Caldwell, D.D.* (Greensboro, NC, 1842); Ethel Stevens Arnett, *David Caldwell* (Greensboro, NC, 1976); Paul K. Conkin, *Cane Ridge: America's Pentecost* (Madison, WI, 1990), 43–45.
27. The fullest contemporary descriptions of the Cane Ridge revival appear in Anonymous, *Increase of Piety, or the Revival of Religion in the United States* (Philadelphia, 1802) (quotation on 53), but see also Conkin, *Cane Ridge*, 64–114. On McGready and the Logan County revivals, see ibid., 53–59.
28. Porter quoted in Robert Baird, *Religion in America; or, An Account of the Origin, Relation to the State, and Present Condition of the Evangelical Churches in the United States* (New York, 1856), 403. See Annabelle S. Wenzke, *Timothy Dwight (1752–1817)* (Lewiston, NY, 1989), 41–53; John R. Fitzmaier, *New England's Moral Legislator: Timothy Dwight, 1752–1817* (Bloomington, IN, 1998), 53–78; Charles Roy Keller, *The Second Great Awakening in Connecticut* (New Haven, 1942), esp. 36–69.
29. There is no thorough general history of the Second Great Awakening, but see two pioneering works about its larger social and political impact: William G. McLoughlin, *Revivals, Awakenings, and Reform: An Essay on Religion and Social Change in America, 1607–1977* (Chicago, 1978), 98–140; Donald G. Mathews, "The Second Great Awakening as an Organizing Process, 1780–1830: An Hypothesis," *American Quarterly*, 21 (1969): 23–43. For an exceptionally lucid and thorough account of the contradictory theological currents at play, in and out of the evangelical churches, see Mark A. Noll, *America's God: From Jonathan Edwards to Abraham Lincoln* (New York, 2002), 159–421.
30. On the southern revivals and their background, the key interpretive works are Donald G. Mathews, *Religion in the Old South* (Chicago, 1977); John B. Boles, *The Great Revival, 1787–1805: The Origins of the Southern Evangelical Mind* (Lexington, KY, 1972); Robert M. Calhoon, *Evangelicals and Conservatives in the Early South, 1740–1861* (Columbia, SC, 1988); Christine Leigh Heyrman, *Southern Cross: The Beginnings of the Bible Belt* (New York, 1997).
31. Diary of William McKendree, Sept. 18, 1790, quoted in Matthews, *Religion*, 62.
32. Matthews, *Religion*, 68–69 (quotation on 68); Conkin, *Cane Ridge*, 91; Heyrman, *Southern Cross*, 46.
33. Furman to W. E. Bailey, Dec. 18, 1848, quoted in Matthews, *Religion*, 136; idem, *Slavery and Methodism: A Chapter in American Morality, 1780–1845* (Princeton, 1965), 28–29;

Mitchell Snay, "American Thought and Southern Distinctiveness: The Southern Clergy and the Sanctification of Slavery," *Civil War History* 35 (1989): 311–28; Eugene D. Genovese and Elizabeth Fox-Genovese, "The Religious Ideals of Southern Slave Society," *Georgia Historical Quarterly*, 70 (1986): 1–16; Anne C. Loveland, *Southern Evangelicals and the Social Order, 1800–1860* (Baton Rouge, 1980).

34. The history of religion among southern blacks, and its shifting connections with white religious belief, is a large subject with an abundant literature, and with subtleties too intricate for full explication here. On eighteenth-century mixtures of West and Central African beliefs with Christianity—and the close relations between white and black evangelicals, especially Baptists—see Albert J. Raboteau, *Slave Religion: The "Inivisible Institution" in the Antebellum South* (New York, 1978), 4–35; Mechal Sobel, *Trabelin' On: The Slave Journey to an Afro-Baptist Faith* (Westport, CT, 1979), esp. 5–48. On nineteenth-century slave religion, in addition to the above works, see C. Eric Lincoln and Lawrence H. Mamiya, *The Black Church in the Afro-American Experience* (Durham, NC, 1990), 21–30, 47–68; Eugene D. Genovese, *Roll, Jordan, Roll: The World the Slaves Made* (New York, 1975), esp. 162–284. On the political functions of black churches, see Sylvia Frey, *Water from the Rock: Black Resistance in a Revolutionary Age* (Princeton, 1991), 183–93; Steven Hahn, *A Nation under Our Feet: Black Political Struggles in the Rural South from Slavery to the Great Migration* (Cambridge, MA, 2003), 43–51.

35. Lyman Beecher, *Autobiography* (1864–65; Cambridge, MA, 1961), 1: 66, 344, 392–406. See Douglas A. Sweeney, *Nathaniel Taylor, New Haven Theology, and the Legacy of Jonathan Edwards* (New York, 2003).

36. Beecher, *The Practicality of Suppressing Vice by Means of Societies Instituted for That Purpose* (New London, 1804), 19. See also three very different but useful studies: Vincent Harding, *A Certain Magnificence: Lyman Beecher and the Transformation of American Protestantism, 1775–1863* (Brooklyn, 1991); Stephen H. Snyder, *Lyman Beecher and His Children: The Transformation of a Religious Tradition* (Brooklyn, 1991); James W. Fraser, *Pedagogue for God's Kingdom: Lyman Beecher and the Second Great Awakening* (Lanham, MD, 1985).

37. Beecher, *Autobiography and Correspondence of Lyman Beecher*, Charles Beecher, ed., (New York, 1864), I, 261.

38. Ely, *On Duty of Christian Freemen to Elect Christian Rulers* (Philadelphia, 1828), 11–13. On the Presbygationals' efforts and others, see Charles I. Foster, *An Errand of Mercy: The Evangelical United Front, 1790–1837* (Chapel Hill, 1960), esp. 3–179.

39. The most thoughtful appraisal of the Sabbatarian movement of the 1820s is Richard R. John, "Taking Sabbatarianism Seriously: The Postal System, the Sabbath, and the Transformation of American Political Culture," *JER*, 10 (1990): 517–67; but see also Bertram Wyatt-Brown, "Prelude to Abolitionism: Sabbatarian Politics and the Rise of the Second Party System," *JAH*, 58 1971: 316–41 (quotation on 328).

40. Bissell quoted in Wyatt-Brown, "Prelude," 330.

41. The story of Morgan's abduction and the subsequent furor has been told several times, most recently in Paul Goodman, *Towards a Christian Republic: Antimasonry and the Great Transition in New England, 1826–1836* (New York, 1988), 3–19. Other important studies of Anti-Masonry include Charles P. McCarthy, "The Antimasonic Party: A Study in Political Antimasonry in the United States, 1827–1840," *Annual Report of the American Historical Association for 1901* (Washington, DC, 1902), vol. 1; David M. Ludlum, *Social Ferment in Vermont, 1791–1850* (New York, 1939), 86–133; Whitney R. Cross, *The Burned-over District: The Social and Intellectual History of Enthusiastic Religion in Western New York, 1800–1850* (Ithaca, NY, 1950), 113–25; Lee Benson, *The Concept of Jacksonian Democracy: New York as a Test Case* (Princeton, 1961), 11–28; Michael F. Holt, "The Antimasonic and Know-Nothing Parties," in Arthur M. Schlesinger Jr., *History of U.S. Political Parties* (New York, 1973), 1: 583–9; Ronald P. Formisano and Kathleen S. Kutolowski, "Antimasonry and Masonry: The Genesis of Protest, 1826–1827," *American*

Quarterly, 29 (1977): 139–65; William Preston Vaughan, *The Antimasonic Party in the United States, 1826–1843* (Lexington, KY, 1983); Kathleen Smith Kutolowski, "Antimasonry Reexamined: Social Bases of the Grass-Roots Party," *JAH*, 71 (1984): 269–93; Robert O. Rupp, "Parties and the Public Good: Political Antimasonry in New York Reconsidered," *JER*, 8 (1988): 253–79. Above all, see Donald J. Ratcliffe, "Antimasonry and Partisanship in Greater New England, 1826–1836," *JER*, 15 (1995): 199–239. Ratcliffe's reexamination links Anti-Masonry's political origins to earlier national and statewide political events, especially the rise of New York's Clintonian People's Party and the 1824 Adams presidential campaign. "Antimasonry," he writes perceptively, "was Jacksonian Democracy, in a sense, for those who could not stand Jackson."

42. Thurlow Weed, *Autobiography of Thurlow Weed*, Harriet A. Weed., ed. (Boston, 1883), 319. Alleged Morgan sightings occurred around the country and abroad, as far away as Turkey, throughout the winter, spring, and summer of 1827.

43. Glyndon G. Van Deusen, *Thurlow Weed: Wizard of the Lobby* (Boston, 1947), 41–42. On Van Buren and Anti-Masonry in 1827, see John Niven, *Martin Van Buren, The Romantic Age of American Politics* (New York, 1983), 186–93.

44. See Richard Hofstadter, *The Paranoid Style in American Politics and Other Essays* (New York, 1965), esp. 14–18; David B. Davis, "Some Themes of Countersubversion: An Analysis of Anti-Masonic, Anti-Catholic, and Anti-Mormon Literature," *Mississippi Valley Historical Review*, 47 (1960): 205–24. Both Hofstadter's and Davis's essays take care to distinguish the style of politics they describe from a kind of mass-induced insanity. For a related analysis, see Seymour Martin Lipset and Earl Raab, *The Politics of Unreason: Right-Wing Extremism in America, 1790–1970* (New York, 1970), 39–49. On the eighteenth-century versions of the moralistic style discussed here (which persisted into the nineteenth century), see the valuable corrective in Gordon S. Wood, "Conspiracy and the Paranoid Style: Causality and Deceit in the Eighteenth Century," *WMQ*, 39 (1982): 401–41.

45. Thomas S. Webb, *The Freemason's Monitor; or Illustrations of Masonry* (Salem, MA, 1821), 34. The best interpretive history of early Freemasonry in the United States is a local study, Dorothy Ann Lipson, *Freemasonry in Federalist Connecticut, 1789–1835* (Princeton, 1977); but see also John L. Brooke, *The Heart of the Commonwealth: Society and Political Culture in Worcester, Massachusetts, 1713–1861* (Cambridge, 1989), 242–7, 320–9; idem, "Ancient Lodges and Self-Created Societies: Voluntary Association and the Public Sphere in the Early Republic," in Ronald Hoffman and Peter J. Albert, eds., *Launching the "Extended Republic": The Federalist Era* (Charlottesville, 1996), 273–377.

46. Quotation in Paul E. Johnson, *A Shopkeeper's Millennium: Society and Revivals in Rochester, New York, 1815–1837* (New York, 1978), 67. The Masons' self-regard often exceeded the usual fraternal exuberance. "In almost every place where power is important," one Connecticut Mason boasted in 1825, the lodges assembled "men of rank, wealth, order, and talent." See Formisano and Kutolowski, "Antimasonry," 144; *Albany Evening Journal*, Nov. 12, 1830; Brooke, *Heart*, 243–51.

47. Quotation in Goodman, *Christian Republic*, 83.

48. Van Deusen, *Weed*, 25. Van Deusen's remains the best biography, but it should be supplemented with Weed's autobiography.

49. Van Deusen, *Weed*, 43–46.

50. Glyndon G. Van Deusen, *William Henry Seward* (New York, 1967), 3–11 (quotations on 11). See also John M. Taylor, *William Henry Seward: Lincoln's Right Hand* (New York, 1991).

51. On the persistence of these problems elsewhere as Anti-Masonry spread, see Michael F. Holt, *The Rise and Fall of the American Whig Party: Jacksonian Politics and the Onset of the Civil War* (New York, 1999), 13–14 (quotation on 14); Ronald P. Formisano, *The Transformation of Political Culture: Massachusetts Parties, 1790s–1840s* (New York, 1983), 209–10.

52. E. D. Barber, *An Address, Delivered before the Rutland County Antimasonic Convention*

(Castleton, VT, 1831), 7. On the importance of these political themes throughout the Anti-Masonic upsurge, see Goodman, *Christian Republic*, 20–33.

53. On Ely and Adams, see chapter 10, p. 322.

CHAPTER NINE: THE ARISTOCRACY AND DEMOCRACY OF AMERICA

1. Jackson to John Branch, Mar. 3, 1826, quoted in Robert V. Remini, *Andrew Jackson and the Course of American Freedom, 1822–1832* (New York, 1981), 110. See also Jackson to John C. Calhoun, [July 18, 1826], in *PAJ*, 6: 187–8.

2. *Mechanics' Free Press* [Philadelphia], Apr. 17, 1830. On the continuing and sometimes baffling factional struggles in Pennsylvania after 1824, see Philip Shriver Klein, *Pennsylvania Politics, 1817–1832: A Game without Rules* (Harrisburg, 1940), 188–227.

    The Working Men's Party should not be confused with the more moderate so-called Middling Interest reform movements that had appeared elsewhere earlier in the decade most conspicuously in Boston, and that mobilized successful artisans. After the disappointing Massachusetts Constitutional Convention in 1821, Josiah Quincy, Joseph Bucking-ham, and their allies enjoyed a string of victories in Boston, overhauling the city's charter, installing Quincy as mayor in 1823, and consolidating their control over the city's politics. The renegade Boston patrician-populist Quincy served four years, pursuing an ambitious program to expand public services and improve municipal efficiency. But then the old-line Brahmins were able to reelect Quincy's predecessor, Federalist stalwart Harrison Gray Otis, and roll back what the touchy old-liners had talked themselves into believing was "the triumph of a revolutionary movement." A similar movement in Baltimore overthrew the city's patrician Republican machine in 1823, but found itself out on its ear at the next election. See Matthew H. Crocker, *The Magic of the Many: Josiah Quincy and the Rise of Mass Politics in Boston, 1800–1830* (Amherst, MA, 1999), 61–148; Andrew R. L. Cayton, "The Fragmentation of a 'Great Family': The Panic of 1819 and the Rise of the Middling Interest in Boston, 1818–1822," *JER*, 2 (1982): 143–67; Gary L. Browne, *Baltimore in the Nation: 1789–1861* (Chapel Hill, 1980), 103–4, 106–13.

3. Weed, *Autobiography of Thurlow Weed*, Harriet A. Weed, ed. (Boston, 1883), 58; Sean Wilentz, *Chants Democratic: New York City & the Rise of the American Working Class, 1788–1850* (New York, 1984), 58. For a useful account of urban early industrialization, see Bruce Laurie, *Artisans into Workers: Labor in Nineteenth-Century America* (New York, 1989), 15–46. William Duane and his son, William Duane Jr., took an active interest in the Working Men's Party, and Stephen Simpson was one of its leaders. Some of the new party's demands and proposals—including public funding for free elementary schools, abolishing imprisonment for debt, and, above all, curbing bank charters—had already been raised by the Duanites and Old School Democrats, in some cases decades earlier.

4. There are several informative studies of the origins and history of the Working Men's Party: John R. Commons et al., *History of Labour in the United States* (1918; New York, 1966), 1: 185–230; Leonard Bernstein, "The Working People of Philadelphia from Colonial Times to the General Strike of 1835," *Pennsylvania Magazine of History and Biography*, 74 (1950): 322–39; Louis H. Arky, "The Mechanics' Union of Trade Associations and the Formation of the Philadelphia Workingmen's Movement," *Pennsylvania Magazine of History and Biography*, 76 (1952): 142–76; Edward Pessen, *Most Uncommon Jacksonians: The Radical Leaders of the Early Labor Movement* (Albany, NY, 1967), 3–51; Bruce Laurie, *Working People of Philadelphia, 1800–1850* (Philadelphia, 1980), 67–83; idem, *Artisans into Workers*, 67–72; Ronald Schultz, *The Republic of Labor: Philadelphia Artisans and the Politics of Class, 1720–1830* (New York, 1993), 211–33. Arky, "Mechanics' Union," 152, emphasizes that the organizers of the Mechanics' Union of Trade Associations had been laying plans since 1826, and that its formal emer-

gence during the carpenters' strike was a coincidence. See also *Mechanics' Free Press*, Oct. 11, 1828.

5. *Mechanics' Free Press*, Sept. 27, 1828, Mar. 21, 1829, William Heighton, *Address to the Members of the Trade Societies and to the Working Classes Generally* (Philadelphia, 1827), 34–35. The MUTA manifesto was reprinted in the *Mechanics' Free Press*, Oct. 25, 1828.

6. On Heighton, see Arky, "Mechanics' Union," 144; David Harris, *Socialist Origins in the United States: American Forerunners of Marx* (Assen, The Netherlands, 1967), 82–90.

7. John Gray, *A Lecture on Human Happiness* (Philadelphia, 1825), 26–27, 68. Ignored in Britain, Gray's lecture was reprinted in at least three inexpensive editions in Philadelphia alone. In 1828, the *Mechanics' Free Press* reprinted it in serialized form. On Gray's influence, specifically on Heighton, see Arky, "Mechanics' Union," 145–7; Laurie, *Working People*, 77; Schultz, *Republic*, 214. On the labor theory of value and its various adaptations, see Wilentz, *Chants Democratic*, 157–68.

8. Heighton, *Address to the Members of Trade Societies*, 31, 37. See also idem, *An Address Delivered Before the Mechanics and Working Classes Generally, in the City and County of Philadelphia* (Philadelphia, 1827); [idem], *The Principles of Aristocratic Legislation* (Philadelphia, 1828).

9. Heighton, *Address to the Members of Trade Societies*, 31, 37. See Gray, *Lecture*, 5–6.

10. On religious unorthodoxy and the Philadelphia artisan milieu, see Laurie, *Working People*, 68–81; Schultz, *Republic*, 225–8. On Bache and the freethinkers, see James Tagg, *Benjamin Franklin Bache and the Philadelphia Aurora* (Philadelphia, 1991), 282; more generally, Jeffrey Alan Smith, *Franklin and Bache: Envisioning the Enlightened Republic* (New York, 1990). Similar currents appeared in other seaports; see, e.g., Wilentz, *Chants Democratic*, 78–79, 153–7.

11. Winchester, *The Outcasts Comforted, A Sermon Delivered at the University in Philadelphia, January 4, 1782* (Philadelphia, 1782), 7. On the plebeian Universalists in Philadelphia, see Laurie, *Working People*, 69–75; Schultz, *Republic*, 131–2, 225–6.

12. *Mechanics' Free Press*, Aug. 16, 1828. For a typical example of Heighton's attacks on dissipation, see ibid., Aug. 23, 1828.

13. See William Nisbet Chambers, *Old Bullion Benton, Senator from the New West: Thomas Hart Benton, 1782–1858* (Boston, 1956), 3–126; Elbert Smith, *Magnificent Missourian: The Life of Thomas Hart Benton* (Philadelphia, 1958), 12–102.

14. Chambers, *Old Bullion*, 109, 116–31.

15. NWR, Nov. 29, Dec. 13, 27, 1823, Jan. 3, 1824. The best collection of contemporary materials on the Kentucky court struggle is contained in George Robertson, *Scrap Book on Law, Politics, Men and Times* (Lexington, KY, 1885). Robertson, a former congressman, was one of the ablest leaders of the antirelief faction. Key secondary sources, apart from those cited below, are; Murray Rothbard, "The Frankfort Resolutions and the Panic of 1819," *Register of the Kentucky Historical Society*, 61 (1963): 214–9; Frank Mathias, "The Turbulent Years of Kentucky Politics, 1820–1850" (Ph.D. dissert., University of Kentucky, 1966), esp. 19–65; idem, "The Relief and Court Struggle: Half Way House to Populism," *Register of the Kentucky Historical Society*, 81 (1973): 154–76; Stephen W. Fackler, "John Rowan and the Demise of Jeffersonian Republicanism in Kentucky," *Register of the Kentucky Historical Society*, 78 (1980): 1–26; Paul E. Goutrich III, "A Pivotal Decision: The 1824 Gubernatorial Election in Kentucky," *Filson Club Historical Quarterly*, 56 (1982): 14–29. See also Sandra F. VanBurkleo, "'That Our Pure Republican Principles Might Not Wither': Kentucky's Relief Crisis and the Pursuit of 'Moral Justice,' 1818–1826" (Ph.D. dissert., University of Minnesota, 1988).

16. See William Stickney, ed., *Autobiography of Amos Kendall* (Boston and New York, 1872); Lynn LaDue Marshall, "The Early Career of Amos Kendall: The Making of a Jacksonian" (Ph.D. dissert., University of California at Berkeley, 1962); Donald B. Cole, *A Jackson Man: Amos Kendall and the Rise of American Democracy* (Baton Rouge, 2004), 9–94. On Kendall and the Clays, see also Robert V. Remini, *Henry Clay: Statesman for the Union* (New York, 1991), 200–3.

17. *Argus of Western America* [Frankfort, KY], Feb. 15, July 5, 1821, Aug. 2, 1826. For similar attacks on both the Bank of the United States and banks generally, see *Kentucky Gazette*, Mar. 17, Apr. 14, Nov. 16, 1820, Sept. 6, 1821.

18. Blair to Henry Clay, Oct. 3, 1827, in *PHC*, 6: 1106–7 (quotation on 1107). On Blair's early life through the Relief War, see Elbert B. Smith, *Francis Preston Blair* (New York, 1980), 1–25.

19. *Kentucky Reporter*, Aug. 1, 1825; *Argus of Western America*, Feb. 22, 1822; Robertson, *Scrap Book*, 92–94; Arndt D. Stickles, *The Critical Court Struggle in Kentucky, 1819–1829* (n.p. [Bloomington, IN], 1929), 66, 88, 91, 98–99; Lynn L. Marshall, "The Genesis of Grass-Roots Democracy in Kentucky," *Mid-America*, 47 (1965): 276; Dale Maurice Royalty, "Banking, Politics, and the Commonwealth of Kentucky, 1800–1825" (Ph.D. dissert., University of Kentucky, 1972), 318–23; Smith, *Blair*, 21–23.

    When the new court finally met early in 1825, it had a docket of about one hundred pending suits but lacked the files and records necessary to try them, which remained in the possession of the old court's clerk, one Achilles Sneed. Sneed refused to turn them over and was found in contempt and fined by the new court, but he died, suddenly, with his fine still outstanding. Meanwhile, the new court twice dispatched Francis Blair and a posse of several others to snatch the papers from Sneed's office, most of which (after forcible entries) they managed to obtain. The old court duly held Blair in contempt, but Blair stood fast, put the records under lock and key, and rendered all but moot efforts by either court to adjudicate standing cases. Later, when the crisis deepened, Blair placed his office under armed guard and warned that anyone coming to seize the records would be shot on sight. On the Sneed affair and its consequences, see Stickles, *Court Struggle*, 69, 79; Smith, *Blair*, 20–21.

20. More than half of the state's counties shifted their support from one side to the other between 1824 and 1826; only twenty counties, one-fourth of the total, remained loyal to the antirelief and Old Court parties in each election. According to Frank F. Mathias, the outcome of the court battle consolidated opposition to the Bluegrass elite and badly undermined Henry Clay's statewide political base. See Mathias, "Henry Clay and His Kentucky Power Base," *Register of the Kentucky Historical Society*, 78 (1980): 127. A close analysis of the Kentucky voting returns also shows that the pro-relief and New Court Party voters backed Jackson in 1824 and, even more, in 1828. See Marshall, "Grass-Roots," 275–87.

21. Jackson to Andrew Jackson Donelson, July 5, 1822, in *CAJ* 3: 167. Jackson also disapproved of the Relief men's creation of a Commonwealth Bank. Those New Court leaders who had once been aligned with Clay were likewise wary of Jackson. Kendall, whose views on banking and currency were closer to Jackson's than to those of many of his Kentucky allies, distrusted what he regarded as the general's tyrannical disposition. As late as 1826, he insisted that, if given a choice between Jackson and Adams in 1828, he planned to stay neutral. See *Argus of Western America*, Feb. 10, 1820, May 2, 1822, June 11, 1819, Apr. 4, 1822; Cote, *Jackson Man*, 69, 71, 95.

22. Troup quoted in Richard B. Latner, *The Presidency of Andrew Jackson: White House Politics, 1829–1837* (Athens, GA, 1979), 13.

23. William W. Freehling, *Prelude to Civil War: The Nullification Controversy in South Carolina, 1816–1836* (New York, 1966), Appendix A, 361–2; *Charleston Courier*, Aug. 23, 1830; Charles S. Sydnor, *The Development of Southern Sectionalism, 1819–1848* (Baton Rouge, 1948), 180–1; Thomas Cooper to Gulian C. Verplanck, May 15, 182, Verplanck Papers, N-YHS. Recent econometric scholarship has found that overproduction in a volatile market, currency contraction, and a cotton-boom psychology had more to do with the planters' woes than the tariff, especially in the backcountry. See Gavin Wright, *The Political Economy of the Cotton South* (New York, 1978), 131.

24. Edward Brown, *Notes on the Origin and Necessity of Slavery* (Charleston, 1826), 6. On the post-Vesey crackdown in South Carolina and its repercussions, see Freehling, *Prelude*, 108–16.

25. Smith quoted in Freehling, *Prelude*, 118. Smith's resolutions of 1825 were a restatement of a set of resolutions proposed by his fellow low-country lawmaker, Stephen Miller, the year before. On Smith and the rise of state-rights extremism in South Carolina, see ibid., 97–121; Lacy K. Ford, *Origins of Southern Radicalism: The South Carolina Upcountry, 1800–1860* (New York, 1988), 113–25.

26. AC, 18th Congress, 1st session, 1072; Benjamin F. Perry, *Reminiscences of Public Men* (Philadelphia, 1883), 80–83 (quotation on 80); Calhoun to James Monroe, June 23, 1826, in *PJCC*, 10: 132–5, (quotation on 134). Calhoun's political motivations were, as they would continue to be, based on principle as well as self-interest. On Calhoun's alienation from the expansive nationalism in President Adams's first annual message, see Calhoun to J. G. Swift, Dec. 11, 1825, Swift Papers, NYPL. Also see Chandra Miller, "'Title Page to a Great Tragic Volume': The Impact of the Missouri Crisis on Slavery, Race, and Republicanism in the Thought of John C. Calhoun and John Quincy Adams," *Missouri Historical Review*, 94 (2000): 365–88.

27. Richardson, 2: 44–58; *JQAD*, 7: 383. Adams, torn as ever between gloom and competitiveness, consoled himself with the conviction that the electorate would eventually regain its senses and, in 1832, replace the violent ignoramus Jackson with Henry Clay.

28. On Henshaw in the 1820s, see the lively account by the original Jacksonian (and later harsh critic) John Barton Derby, *Political Reminiscences* (Boston, 1835), esp. 16–33. See also Ronald P. Formisano, *The Transformation of Political Culture: Massachusetts Parties, 1790s–1840s* (New York, 1983), 192–6, 247–8. The Lyman faction kept its distance from Henshaw, and the two groups barely cooperated. Jackson was elated by the merest semblance of a New England campaign on his behalf. "[E]ven in Boston, the former hotbed of Federalism has had a meeting," he wrote John Coffee, astonished. Jackson to John Coffee, Sept. 25, 1826, in *CAJ*, 3: 314.

29. Houston to Andrew Jackson, Jan. 1827, in *PAJ*, 6: 270.

30. *JQAD*, 7: 111; Donald B. Cole, *Martin Van Buren and the American Political System* (Princeton, 1984), 142–51.

31. Van Buren to Ritchie, Jan. 13, 1827, VBP. Van Buren's letter did urge strong consideration of calling a national nominating convention in lieu of the old congressional caucus—a move, Van Buren argued, that would prove embarrassing to President Adams (who would never consent to a convention nomination for himself) and encourage the nomination of Jackson as something more than a military hero. Yet even if Van Buren had learned his lesson from the pro-Crawford caucus debacle of 1824, he was, he wrote, "not tenacious whether we have a congressional caucus or a general convention." Historians both sympathetic to and highly critical of Van Buren have long focused on this letter. See Robert V. Remini, *Martin Van Buren and the Making of the Democratic Party* (1959; New York, 1970), 130–3; Richard H. Brown, "The Missouri Crisis, Slavery, and the Politics of Jacksonianism," *South Atlantic Quarterly*, 65 (1966): 55–70. On another tack, see Richard Hofstadter, *The Idea of a Party System: The Rise of Legitimate Opposition in the United States, 1780–1840* (Berkeley, 1969), 212–71. For a useful corrective, see Gerald Leonard, *The Invention of Party Politics: Federalism, Popular Sovereignty, and Constitutional Development in Jacksonian Illinois* (Chapel Hill, 2002), 18–50. See also Sean Wilentz, "Jeffersonian Democracy and the Origins of Political Antislavery: The Missouri Crisis Revisited," *Journal of the Historical Society*, 4 (2004): 375–401.

32. Jefferson to W. T. Barry, July 2, 1822, TJC.

33. Jabez Hammond to Martin Van Buren, May 23, 1827, VBP; Hamilton, *Reminiscences of James A. Hamilton* (New York, 1869), 67–72 (quotation on 68).

34. Cole, *Van Buren*, 152–3, 159–60; Smith, *Blair*, 32–33. Kendall needed the loan in order to pay off numerous debts, including one being pressed by his former employer, Henry Clay. The affair, and other political solicitations on Kendall's behalf, can be traced through Van Buren's correspondence; see esp. Richard Mentor Johnson to Van Buren, Sept. 22, 1827, Van Buren to Kendall, Nov. 10, 1827, VBP. Kendall's account appears in Stickney, ed., *Autobiography*, 269–76.

35. See Murray N. Rothbard, *The Panic of 1819: Responses and Policies* (New York, 1962), 159–80; Norval Neil Luxon, *Niles' Weekly Register, Newsmagazine of the Nineteenth Century* (Baton Rouge, 1947); Earl L. Bradsher, *Matthew Carey, Editor, Author and Publisher: A Study in American Literary Development* (New York, 1912). On Raymond, see Paul K. Conkin, *Prophets of Prosperity: America's First Political Economists* (Bloomington, IN, 1980), 77–107.

36. Raymond, *The Elements of Political Economy* (Baltimore, 1823), 1: 35, 2: 13.

37. NWR, Aug. 11, 1827. The Harrisburg meeting was the culmination of state meetings held earlier in New England, New York, New Jersey, Delaware, Maryland, Virginia, Ohio, and Kentucky. See Mary W. M. Hargreaves, *The Presidency of John Quincy Adams* (Lawrence, KS, 1985), 194.

38. Cooper to Martin Van Buren, July 5, 1827, VBP; RD, 19th Congress, 2nd session, 496. See also Cooper's follow-up letter to Van Buren, dated July 31, 1827, VBP. Van Buren later claimed, implausibly, that he missed the vote because he had promised a friend he would join him on a visit to the congressional cemetery. Van Buren, *The Autobiography of Martin Van Buren*, John C. Fitzpatrick, ed. (1920; New York, 1969), 1: 169. On the South Carolina protests, see Manisha Sinha, *The Counterrevolution of Slavery: Politics and Ideology in Antebellum South Carolina* (Chapel Hill, 2000), 18–19.

39. RD, 20th Congress, 1st session, 2472. For able contrasting accounts of the political calculations and maneuvering that lay behind the Tariff of 1828, see George Dangerfield, *The Era of Good Feelings* (New York, 1952), 396–414; Remini, *Van Buren*, 170–85; Cole, *Van Buren*, 162–9; Hargreaves, *Adams*, 192–7; Merrill D. Peterson, *The Great Triumvirate: Webster, Clay, and Calhoun* (New York, 1987), 159–61. The traditional interpretation long held that Van Buren originally introduced, through Wright, a bill he knew would fail, thereby securing the support of the West (who would blame the failure on the pro-Adams Northeast) and the South (who would credit the Jacksonians for defeating the measure). Supposedly, the bill's unexpected success then forced Van Buren to switch his position, praising Jackson as a successful protectionist in the West and as a defeated but undaunted antitariff man in the South.

40. Smith quoted in Peterson, *Great Triumvirate*, 160.

41. Calhoun to Micah Sterling, May 15, 1828, in *PJCC*, 10: 384–5. On the caucuses and protests, see NWR, June 14, July 19, 1828; *Charleston Courier*, Nov. 2, 22, 1828; *Charleston Mercury*, Nov. 10, 1828.

42. On Calhoun's thinking over the summer and early fall of 1828, see Irving H. Bartlett, *John C. Calhoun: A Biography* (New York, 1993), 146–9; on the intellectual and political background, see also John Niven, *John C. Calhoun and the Price of the Union* (Baton Rouge, 1988), 158–63. A year earlier, in reaction to the Harrisburg protectionist convention, Calhoun had privately embraced the idea that would later be known as nullification, observing that the "despotism" imposed by one section on another "admits of but one effectual remedy, a veto on the part of the local interest, or under our system, on the part of the States." Calhoun to Littleton Walker Tazewell, Aug. 25, 1827, in *PJCC*, 10: 300–2 (quotation on 301).

43. On Jackson's chronic poor health, see Remini, *Course of American Freedom*, 1–3, 91–92.

44. Van Buren to Andrew Jackson, Sept. 14, 1827, John Eaton to Andrew Jackson, Jan. 21, 1828, in *CAJ*, 3: 382, 390. On the New Orleans commemorations, see the accounts in NWR, Feb. 8, 1828; James Parton, *Life of Andrew Jackson* (New York, 1860), 3: 38–40.

45. See, e.g., Jackson to James B. Ray, Feb. 28, 1828, in *National Intelligencer* [Washington], Apr. 29, 1828: "I pray you, sir, respectfully, to state to the Senate of Indiana, that my opinions, at present, are precisely what they were in 1823 and '24 . . . when I voted for the present tariff and appropriations of internal improvements." Ray was the governor of Indiana.

46. Amos Kendall to Francis Blair, Feb. 3, Mar. 7, 1829, Blair-Lee Papers, PU; "To the Tennessee Legislature," Oct. 12, 1825, Jackson to John Coffee, Sept. 25, 1826, in *CAJ*, 3: 294–5, 314; *Crawford Messenger* [Pennsylvania], Mar. 24, 1831, quoted in Klein, *Pennsyl-*

vania Politics, 345–6; Remini, *Clay*, 317–8. Under Jackson's proposed amendment, both he and Clay would have been ineligible to run for president in 1824.

47. Jackson to John C. Calhoun, [July 18, 1826], to Thomas P. Moore, July 1826, in *PAJ*, 6: 187, 194.

48. See Robert V. Remini, *The Election of Andrew Jackson* (New York, 1963), 51–120.

49. Ibid., 77.

50. Ibid., 77; Klein, *Pennsylvania*, 228–51. Samuel Ingham, long suspected as one of the forces behind George Kremer's corrupt-bargain allegation in 1825, also contributed anti-Adams polemics to Duff Green's *Telegraph* and played a large role in reviving and expanding the corrupt-bargain charge.

51. Gulian Verplanck to Jesse Hoyt, Jan. 22, 1828, in William L. Mackenzie, *The Life and Times of Martin Van Buren* (Boston, 1846), 202; *Evening Post* [New York], Oct. 28, 1828.

52. Nathaniel Williams to John W. Taylor, Sept. 24, 1828, Taylor Papers, N-YHS. See Remini, *Election*, 121–65.

53. Van Deusen, *Weed*, 47–48. Horace Secrist, "The Anti-Auction Movement and the New York Workingmen's Party of 1829," *Transactions of the Wisconsin Academy of Science, Arts and Letters*, 17 (1914): 149–66, contains the fullest secondary account of the New York City events, but see Wilentz, *Chants Democratic*, 150–1. The 1828 anti-auction effort is well covered in the *Evening Post*, Oct. 14, 16, 17, 21, 31, 1828. On Philadelphia, see Remini, *Election*, 144.

54. Clay to Daniel Webster, Aug. 19, Oct. 25, Nov. 8, 1827, in *PHC*, 6: 929 (quotation), 1187, 1243–4. Webster agreed, telling Clay that Hammond's sheet was "certainly ably & vigorously conducted." Webster to Clay, Sept. 8, 1827, in *PHC*, 5: 1084. Confronted by John Eaton about his "fact-finding tour" and connection to Hammond, Clay denied any wrongdoing and then wrote Hammond, "I have now no recollection that the case of Mrs. Jackson formed any topic of conversation between us," which reads like an epistolary nudge and wink. Clay to Charles Hammond, Dec. 23, 1826, in *PHC*, 5: 1023–4. For a sharp elucidation of the larger cultural patterns and prejudices surrounding the scandalmongering, see Norma Basch, "Marriage, Morals, and Politics in the Election of 1828," *JAH*, 80 (1993): 890–918. As the events of the late 1990s suggest, the cultural cleavages revealed in 1828 remain very much a part of our politics—and open to manipulation on a scale undreamed of by Charles Hammond and Henry Clay.

55. The nastier attacks struck some political managers as counterproductive. Sent copies of the "Coffin Handbill," along with another piece of anti-Jackson propaganda, Thurlow Weed decided they would do more harm than good and kept the material under lock and key in his printing office. Although denounced by Adams's friends as a traitor, Weed later claimed vindication when Adams carried western New York by comfortable majorities. Weed, ed., *Autobiography*, 308–9. On the themes evoked by both sides, see John William Ward, *Andrew Jackson, Symbol for an Age* (New York, 1955), 46–78, as well as Basch, "Marriage," esp. 895–6.

56. Jefferson to John Adams, Oct. 28, 1813, TJC.

57. Jackson to John Coffee, May 12, 1828, in *PAJ*, 6: 458; Edward [Edmund?] P. Gaines to Andrew Jackson, n.d., quoted in Remini, *Election*, 190.

58. Remini, *Election*, 181–6.

59. The final results from the key states were as follows:

States	Popular Vote		Electoral Vote	
	Jackson	Adams	Jackson	Adams
New York	140,763	135,413	20	16
Ohio	67,597	63,396	16	—
Kentucky	39,397	31,460	14	—

Figures from S&I, 2: 492.

60. Jackson to John Coffee, Nov. 24, 1828, quoted in Remini, *Course of American Freedom*, 149; Parton, *Jackson*, 3: 159.

61. For voting returns, in addition to S&I, 2: 492, see Charles Sellers, *The Market Revolution: Jacksonian America, 1815–1846* (New York, 1991), 299–300; Wilentz, *Chants Democratic,* 408; Marshall, "Grass-Roots," 275–87.
62. Abraham Lincoln, "Speech at Springfield, Illinois, June 16, 1858," in *CWAL*, 2: 461.

CHAPTER TEN: THE JACKSON ERA: UNEASY BEGINNINGS

1. Margaret Bayard Smith, *The First Forty Years of Washington Society*, Gaillard Hunt, ed. (New York, 1906), 293–4; Joseph Story to Mrs. Joseph Story, Mar. 7, 1829, in William W. Story, ed., *Life and Letters of Joseph Story* (Boston, 1851), 1: 563.
2. Richardson, 2: 1001. This description is based chiefly on the eyewitness accounts gathered in James Parton, *Life of Andrew Jackson* (New York, 1860), 3: 164–73. See also Edwin A. Miles, "The First People's Inauguration," *Tennessee Historical Quarterly*, 37 (1978): 293–307. For a more baleful description, see Richard R. John, *Spreading the News: The American Postal System from Franklin to Morse* (Cambridge, MA, 1995), 212–3.
3. Smith, *First Forty Years*, 284. Other reports were less perturbed, including the claim by one pro-Adams newspaper that the day passed peacefully and that "the Sovereign People" were no more than "a little uproarious" at the White House. *National Intelligencer* [Washington], Mar. 6, 1829. Part of the problem seems to have been that the White House — which had planned a plain republican affair with spiked orange punch and an orderly reception line — badly miscalculated the numbers that would turn out.
4. The upright New York patrician Philip Hone decided to see Wright — "this female Tom Paine" — at the Masonic Hall for himself, and found her doctrines subversive of "our fundamental principles of morality." Yet, he admitted, "I found the room so full that I remained but a short time." Hone, *The Diary of Philip Hone, 1828–1851*, Allan Nevins, ed. (New York, 1936), 9–10. See Celia Morris Eckhardt, *Fanny Wright: Rebel in America* (Cambridge, MA, 1984); Peter P. Hinks, *To Awaken My Afflicted Brethren: David Walker and the Problem of Antebellum Slave Resistance* (University Park, PA, 1997), 1–90; Sean Wilentz, ed., *David Walker's Appeal* (New York, 1995), vii–xxiii.
5. Jackson to John C. McLemore, Apr. 1829, in *CAJ*, 4: 21; *NWR*, June 6, 1829, 235–40. For more on the scandals, see Donald B. Cole, *The Presidency of Andrew Jackson* (Lawrence, KS, 1993), 40–41, which argues that although the amounts embezzled were not unusually high, they were substantial enough to provide the incoming Jacksonians with an immediate sense of vindication. Watkins was eventually convicted, fined, and sentenced to nine months' imprisonment. Unable to pay his fine, which Jackson refused to remit, he wound up spending more than three and a half years behind bars. Cole, *A Jackson Man: Amos Kendall and the Rise of American Democracy* (Baton Rouge, 2004), 130.
6. Richardson, 2: 1012. For a selection of contemporary sources on incumbent officeholders' fears, see Parton, *Jackson*, 3: 206–27. On the early historiography on rotation and the spoils system, and the tempering of early hostile interpretations, see William F. Mugleston, "Andrew Jackson and the Spoils System: A Historiographical Survey," *Mid-America*, 59 (1977): 117–25.
7. Hoyt to Martin Van Buren, Mar. 21, 1829, in William L. Mackenzie, *The Life and Opinions of Benj'n Franklin Butler . . . and Jesse Hoyt* (Boston, 1845), 51–52 (quotation); David Petrekin to Martin Van Buren, Nov. 18, 1836, VBP. On Van Buren's early difficulties with Jackson's patronage moves, see Donald B. Cole, *Martin Van Buren and the American Political System* (Princeton, 1984), 191–7.
8. Richardson, 2: 1012. See also Jackson's draft for his first annual message, in which he wrote that "[t]he government of the U. States was one of experiment; opening for the contemplation of new and untried principles," and that "as the science of our government is improved" and imperfections exposed, continual reform was "imperative." The 1824 result was, as ever, at the top of his thoughts. "For a single individual of the House of Representatives to give a decision in behalf of a million people," he wrote, "which frequently

may be done . . . can seldom fail to excite suspicion jealousy, and distrust in the minds of a people vigilant, and attentive to the maintenance of their own rights." Jackson had not merely paid lip service to "reform" in 1828: he wanted to achieve it. *CAJ*, 4: 98–99.

9. Bentham to Andrew Jackson, Apr. 26, 1830, in Bentham, *The Works of Jeremy Bentham* (Edinburgh, 1843), 11: 40. Bentham would later write even more enthusiastically that after hearing Jackson's first annual message, he had come to the conclusion that "in politics and legislation I do not think there was a single topic in which we appeared to differ." Bentham also observed that he thought the Senate a "Superfluous" institution — an outlandish sentiment that, on purely political grounds, Jackson would later have reason to appreciate. Bentham to Jackson, June 14, 1830, in *CAJ*, 4: 146–50. On Jackson's highminded view of rotation, see also Jackson to Susan Decatur, Apr. 2, 1829, in *CAJ*, 4: 21–22; Jackson, "Fragment of a Letter of 1831 [?]," in *CAJ*, 6: 504. Rotation and term limitation were only two of Jackson's reformist hobby horses during his early presidency, all of them products of his determination to restore public faith in and control over the government. In letters, private memoranda, and public addresses, Jackson proposed new safeguards for the popular will. The most direct reflections of 1825 were his ideas that the House should have no role in selecting presidents if no candidate received an electoral majority, and that cabinet members should be constitutionally barred from succeeding to the presidency. More interesting was his proposal to abolish the Electoral College and substitute direct election of the president — although, he added, with a possible regulation "to preserve to each state its present relative weight in the election." Yet with the scandals that broke so quickly after Jackson took power, along with the need to satisfy his own loyalists, rotation in office became the one experiment that actually took hold. Richardson, 2: 1010–2 (quotation on 1011).

10. Ritchie to Martin Van Buren, Mar. 27, 1829, VBP; Leonard White, *The Jacksonians: A Study in Administrative History, 1829–1861* (New York, 1954), 300–25; Cole, *Presidency*, 42–43. For a case study of the Jacksonians' use of federal patronage of the local press through job work, see Elizabeth Snapp, "Government Patronage of the Press in St. Louis, 1829–1832," *Missouri Historical Review*, 74 (1980): 190–216. The initial fears of the Adams men apparently drove some of them mad. One Adams appointee, a War Office clerk, desperate at his impending removal and loss of income, reportedly "cut his throat from ear to ear," while another went "raving distracted." See *JQAD*, 8: 144; *National Intelligencer*, May 9, 1829. See Sidney Aronson, *Status and Kinship in the Higher Civil Service, Standards of Selection in the Administrations of John Adams, Thomas Jefferson, and Andrew Jackson* (Cambridge, MA, 1964), which toppled the traditional idea that Jackson's presidency brought a dramatic democratization of "elite" federal appointments, but also confirmed that, even at the upper levels of the civil service, his appointments expanded the trend, begun under Thomas Jefferson, toward broadening the social base of appointments.

11. *RD*, 22nd Congress, 1st session, 1325–37.

12. On the Barry scandals, and the deleterious effects of Jackson's patronage policies at the Post Office, see John, *Spreading the News*, 200–56 (quotation on 242). On the unhappier consequences of rotation generally during Jackson's administration and over the ensuing quarter-century, see White, *Jacksonians*, 325–46. Jackson's faith in Swartwout stemmed from the latter's defense of Jackson over his alleged involvement with the Burr conspiracy in 1807. On the Swartwout appointment and the ensuing scandal from differing perspectives, see Robert V. Remini, *Andrew Jackson and the Course of American Freedom, 1832–1845* (New York, 1981), 198–9; Cole, *Van Buren*, 192–4, 337–40; Jerome Mushkat, *Tammany: The Evolution of a Political Machine, 1789–1865* (Syracuse, NY, 1971), 188–9.

13. After an official investigation in 1835, Jackson replaced William Barry with Amos Kendall, who proved a superb administrator. The Post Office Act of 1836, supported by the administration, corrected many of the flaws in the system that had undermined its integrity. Samuel Swartwout kept his larceny well hidden until after Jackson left office — making Jackson, in this instance, more of a trusting victim than a conniving spoilsman.

14. [Margaret Eaton], *The Autobiography of Peggy Eaton* (New York, 1932), 5. Eaton dictated

this self-serving but useful memoir in 1873. The most recent narrative of the Eaton affair is John F. Marszalek, *The Petticoat Affair: Manners, Mutiny, and Sex in Andrew Jackson's White House* (New York, 1997); but see also Richard B. Latner, "The Eaton Affair Reconsidered," *Tennessee Historical Quarterly*, 36 (1977): 330–51; Kirstin E. Wood, "'One Woman So Dangerous to Public Morals': Gender and Power in the Eaton Affair," *JER*, 17 (1997): 237–75; Catherine Allgor, *Parlor Politics: In Which the Ladies of Washington Help Build a City and a Government* (Charlottesville, 2000), 190–238.

15. Jackson to Rachel Jackson, Dec. 21, 1823, Mar. 19, 27, Apr. 5, 1824, in *CAJ*, 3: 217–8, 238–41, 244; Parton, *Jackson*, 3: 203–5.

16. "Reply to John Eaton's Address," published in *Messenger*, [Pendleton, SC] Oct. 19, 1831, in *PJCC*, 11: 447; Jackson to John C. McLemore, Nov. 24, 1829, in *PAJ*, 4: 88–89. Why Jackson settled on Calhoun as the culprit is unclear, although Richard Latner suggests that he might have been persuaded by James Eaton and William Lewis, as well as by his advisor James A. Hamilton, all of whom disliked the vice president. Latner also argues that the animus against Eaton was fed by hostility to his closeness to Van Buren among antitariff southerners wary of the New Yorker, including Attorney General John Berrien and Navy Secretary John Branch. Treasury Secretary Samuel Ingham was an exception, a northerner but (with his wife) one of the Calhouns' closest personal friends in Washington. See Richard B. Latner, *The Presidency of Andrew Jackson: White House Politics, 1829–1837* (Athens, GA, 1979), 62–66.

17. *JQAD*, 8: 184–5. For Kendall's view, see Kendall to Francis Blair, Mar. 7, 1829, Blair-Lee Papers, PU.

18. Van Buren, *Autobiography of Martin Van Buren*, John C. Fitzpatrick, ed. (1920; New York, 1969), 2: 340–65; Smith, *First Forty Years*, 310; Jackson to John Overton, Dec. 31, 1829, in *CAJ*, 4: 109.

19. Richard Hofstadter, *The American Political Tradition and the Men Who Made It* (1948; New York, 1973), 73.

20. Calhoun's draft and final text of the *South Carolina Exposition and Protest* appear in *PJCC*, 10: 442–539 (quotation on 490).

21. *PJCC*, 10, 511. On the political and intellectual origins of nullification, see esp. George C. Rogers Jr., "South Carolina Federalists and the Origins of the Nullification Movement," *South Carolina Historical Magazine*, 71 (1970): 17–32; but see also Gordon Wood, *The Radicalism of the American Revolution* (New York, 1992), 268; Manisha Sinha, *The Counterrevolution of Slavery: Politics and Ideology in Antebellum South Carolina* (Chapel Hill, 2000), 20–26; W. Kirk Wood, "In Defense of the Republic: John C. Calhoun and State Interposition in South Carolina, 1776–1833," *Southern Studies*, 10 (2002): 9–48.

22. *RD*, 21st Congress, 1st session, 58–80, 92–93. Calhoun is alleged to have passed notes to Hayne during the encounter, a point historians have disputed. See Robert V. Remini, *Daniel Webster, the Man and His Time* (New York, 1997), 321 n. 25. Three days after the inauguration, Amos Kendall wrote that Jackson had purposely excluded any South Carolinian from the cabinet because of the state's reaction to the tariff fights in 1828 and the legislature's approval of the *Exposition and Protest*. Kendall to Francis P. Blair, Mar. 7, 1829, Blair-Lee Papers, PU.

23. The best secondary account of this oft-described confrontation is in Remini, *Course of American Freedom*, 233–6. For contrasting newspaper reports, see *United States Telegraph*, Apr. 17, 1830; *National Intelligencer*, Apr. 20, 1830. Soon after, Jackson explained his actions to Amos Kendall, remarking that he was a principled Jeffersonian and that "many of the sentiments uttered at the dinner were such as Jefferson abhorred." Kendall to Francis Blair, Apr. 25, 1830, Blair-Lee Papers, PU. On Calhoun, Jackson, and their early disagreements over the tariff, see also Richard E. Ellis, *The Union at Risk: Jacksonian Democracy, States' Rights, and the Nullification Crisis* (New York, 1987), 53–54. The best summary of Jacksonian thinking at this stage of the nullification controversy appears in Senator Edward Livingston's speech in reply to both Hayne and Webster. Livingston charged Webster with going too far in the direction of a consolidated

nationalism, and allowed for secession under certain extreme circumstances, but flatly repudiated nullification as without authority and a direct threat to the Union. "[T]he people," he said, "would not submit to consolidation, nor suffer disunion." *RD*, 21st Congress, 1st session, 247–72 (quotation on 272). This was the same Edward Livingston who had been a New York Democratic Society member and successful Jeffersonian congressional candidate in 1794, and who moved to New Orleans in 1804. See William B. Hatcher, *Edward Livingston, Jeffersonian Republican and Jacksonian Democrat* (Baton Rouge, 1940), 348–51.

24. Jackson to Ezra Stiles Ely, Mar. 28, 1829, in Parton, *Jackson*, 3: 186–91 (quotation on 191). See also Jackson to Ely, Apr. 10, 1829, in ibid., 192–5. The complete postal committee report is reprinted in Joseph Blau, ed., *Social Theories of Jacksonian Democracy* (Indianapolis, 1954), 274–81 (quotation on 275). For a shrewd assessment of the report and the anti-Sabbatarian reaction as anticlerical but not irreligious, see John, *Spreading the News*, 199–200. On Ely and the 1828 campaign, see Bertram Wyatt-Brown, "Prelude to Abolitionism: Sabbatarian Politics and the Rise of the Second Party System," *JAH*, 58 (1971): 325–9. Even before the inauguration, Ely began injecting himself into Jackson's administration, telling him to eschew Sunday travel and be a "Christian ruler of a Christian people." Ely to Andrew Jackson, Jan. 28, 1829, in *CAJ*, 4: 3–4. Early in 1830, Ely's correspondence with Jackson dwindled down to nothing.

25. Contrasting accounts of the struggle over the Cherokees, as of Jackson's Indian removal policies in general, appear in Ronald N. Satz, *American Indian Policy in the Jacksonian Era* (Lincoln, NE, 1975), esp. 9–125; Francis Paul Prucha, *The Great Father: The United States and the American Indians* (Lincoln, NE, 1984), 1: 214–42. On the Georgia events, see also David Williams, *The Georgia Gold Rush: Twenty-Niners, Cherokees, and Gold Fever* (Columbia, SC, 1993).

26. On religious missions among the Cherokee, see William McLoughlin, *Cherokees and Missionaries, 1789–1839* (New Haven, 1984); idem, *Cherokee Renascence in the New Republic* (Princeton, 1986), 228–410; John A. Andrew III, *From Revivals to Removal: Jeremiah Evarts, the Cherokee Nation, and the Search for the Soul of America* (Athens, GA, 1992). For Jackson's earliest presidential pronouncements on Indian removal—a topic he did not mention in his inaugural address—see *NWR*, June 13, 1829. See also Cole, *Presidency*, 69.

27. Van Buren, *Autobiography*, 1: 288–90 (quotation on 288). On the protest movement and its prefiguring of later benevolent reform efforts, see the excellent study by Mary Hershberger, "Mobilizing Women, Anticipating Abolition: The Struggle against Indian Removal in the 1830s," *JAH*, 86 (1999): 15–40 (quotation on 17). George Cheever would go on to become a prominent abolitionist as well as a leader in the fight to abolish capital punishment.

28. The text of the Indian Removal Bill appears in Francis Paul Prucha, ed., *Documents of American Indian Policy* (Lincoln, NE, 1975), 52–53. On Jackson's involvement in stacking the Indian affairs committees, see Cole, *Presidency*, 71.

29. *RD*, 21st Congress, 1st session, 309–20 (quotation on 312). In the Senate, where the bill passed 28 to 19, the Jacksonians voted unanimously in favor, apart from one member who was absent; the opposition voted 19 to 3 against the bill. *RD*, 21st Congress, 1st session, 383. See Robert Eels, *Forgotten Saint: The Life of Theodore Frelinghuysen, A Case Study of Christian Leadership* (Lanham, MD, 1987), esp. 20–24.

30. See Mary Elizabeth Young, *Redskins, Ruffleshirts, and Rednecks: Indian Allotments in Alabama and Mississippi 1830–1860* (Norman, OK, 1961); and the harsher accounts in Michael P. Rogin, *Fathers and Children: Andrew Jackson and the Subjugation of the American Indian* (New York, 1975); James C. Curtis, *Andrew Jackson and the Search for Vindication* (Boston, 1976). For a subsequent study blaming Jackson's racism as the chief source of his "metaphysics of genocide," see Ronald T. Takaki, *Iron Cages: Race and Culture in Nineteenth-Century America* (New York, 1979), esp. 100–7. The most stalwart defenses of Jackson appear in Francis Paul Prucha, "Andrew Jackson's Indian Policy: A Reassessment,"

JAH, 56 (1969): 527–39; Robert V. Remini, *Andrew Jackson and His Indian Wars* (New York, 2001), 206–81.

31. Jackson to James Gadsden, Oct. 12, 1829, in *CAJ*, 4: 81; *JQAD*, 7: 89–90. For Jackson's earlier views on the "absurdity" of Indian claims to sovereignty, see Jackson to John C. Calhoun, Jan. 18, 1821, in *CAJ*, 3: 36–38. Clay was not alone among Jackson's adversaries in suddenly embracing the Indians' cause. See Marshall Foletta, *Coming to Terms with Democracy: Federalist Intellectuals and the Shaping of American Culture* (Charlottesville, 2001), 185–7. On the childless Jacksons' adoption of the Creek child Lyncoya, who survived the Battle of Tallushatchee, its sad denouement, and the boy's sudden death of tuberculosis in 1828 at age sixteen, see Remini, *Course of American Freedom*, 3–4, 66, 144.

32. Richardson, 2: 1083. An early formulation of Jackson's views on the constitutional aspects of Indian removal appeared in a set of instructions, signed by Secretary of War Eaton, to Generals William Carroll and John Coffee, whom Jackson sent on a mission to the Creeks and Cherokees in May 1829 to try and secure the Indians' voluntary relocation: Senate Documents, 21st Congress, 1st session, Document 1, Serial 160. On Jackson's pessimistic realism—"He knew the white man, and he knew the red man, and he knew how each was accustomed to treat each other"—as well as his desire to keep the Indians from being overrun by predatory whites, see the remarks of Indian Commissioner Henry Schoolcraft in Parton, *Jackson*, 3: 280.

33. *RD*, 21st Congress, 1st session, 1132. Together, the respective tallies resemble the early votes over the Tallmadge amendments during the Missouri crisis in 1819, with partisan allegiances holding strong in the Senate but sectional cleavages dividing the House. The pro-removal, pro-slavery Thomas Ritchie noticed this at the time, warning that continued northern resistance to Cherokee removal might provoke "another Missouri Question." See *RD*, 21st Congress, 1st session, 383, 1133; *Richmond Enquirer*, Feb. 26, 1830, Mar. 8, 1832. Historians differ on the political implications of the votes. See Charles Sellers, *The Market Revolution: Jacksonian America, 1815–1846* (New York, 1991), 311; Cole, *Presidency*, 73–74. On the New Yorkers and Van Buren—who candidly called the bill a "southern measure" and wished the issue would go away—see Van Buren, *Autobiography*, 1: 293–4; Leonard L. Richards, *The Slave Power: The Free North and Southern Domination* (Baton Rouge, 2000), 125–7.

34. See Jackson's draft for his first annual message, in *CAJ*, 4: 103–4, as well as the final address, Richardson, 2: 1005–25 (quotation on 1021). The removal bill appropriated a miserly $500,000 for the Indians' "support and subsistence" for the first year after removal. For an excellent assessment of this inflammatory issue, see Ronald N. Satz, "Rhetoric versus Reality: The Indian Policy of Andrew Jackson," in William L. Anderson, ed., *Cherokee Removal: Before and After* (Athens, GA, 1991), 29–54. For the toll exacted along the Trail of Tears—normally listed as between two thousand and four thousand of the sixteen thousand Cherokee removed—see Russell Thornton, "The Demography of the Trail of Tears: A New Estimate of Cherokee Population Losses," in ibid., 75–95. By 1840, about seventy thousand Indians were removed to what is now Oklahoma.

35. *Globe* [Washington], Feb. 26, 1831. See also Van Buren, *Autobiography*, 1: 288.

36. *RD*, 22nd Congress, 1st session, 650. See Pamela L. Baker, "The Washington National Road Bill and the Struggle to Adopt a Federal System for Internal Improvement," *JER*, 22 (2002): 437–64.

37. On the background and behind-the-scenes maneuvering over the Maysville bill, see Carlton Jackson, "The Internal Improvement Vetoes of Andrew Jackson," *Tennessee Historical Quarterly*, 25 (1966): 268–72.

38. Richardson, 2: 1046–56 (quotation on 1053). For Jackson's thinking in preparation for the veto, see "Notes for the Maysville Road Veto [May 19–26 ?, 1830], in *PAJ*, 4: 137–9. Jackson was particularly eager to fight what he called "flagitious Legislation arising from combinations if you will vote with me I will vote with you so disgraceful to our country." Contrary to the impression that Jackson was hostile to internal improvements, his two administrations would wind up spending more on federal projects—in excess of ten mil-

lion dollars—than all previous administrations combined. The greatest expenditures were on lighthouse building and maintenance and on river and harbor improvements, but Jackson was also partial to road-building projects in the federal territories, the construction of military and post roads, and (despite serious reservations) further work on completion of the Cumberland or National Road. For the conclusion that Jackson's internal-improvement policy was "effective and fairly consistent," and represented "a carefully thought out and reasonable response to a very complicated issue," see Ellis, *Union*, 24–25.

39. Jackson to John Coffee, June 14, 1830, in *CAJ*, 4: 146.

CHAPTER ELEVEN: RADICAL DEMOCRACIES

1. Peter P. Hinks, *To Awaken My Afflicted Brethren: David Walker and the Problem of Antebellum Slave Resistance* (University Park, PA, 1997), 1–90, 116–72, 213 (quotation); Sean Wilentz, ed., *David Walker's Appeal* (New York, 1995), xix. Hinks finds persuasive evidence that Walker died of natural causes.

2. Ralph Waldo Emerson, "New England Reformers" (1844), in Brooks Atkinson, ed., *The Selected Writings of Ralph Waldo Emerson* (1950; New York, 2000), 403–4.

3. On the American Colonization Society, see P. J. Staudenraus, *The African Colonization Movement, 1816–1865* (New York, 1961), but see also Douglas Egerton, "'Its Origin Is Not a Little Curious': A New Look at the American Colonization Society," *JER*, 5 (1985): 462–80, which emphasizes the fear of slave uprisings as the key motive behind the group's formation.

4. Clay, "Speech at Organization of the American Colonization Society," in *PHC*, 2: 263–4 (quotations on 263). See also "Motions and Speech at Meeting of American Colonization Society, January 1, 1818," in ibid., 420–2.

5. NWR, Nov. 27, 1819; *Freedom's Journal* [New York], Mar. 30, May 18, June 8, July 6, Sept. 4, 1827; Benjamin Quarles, *Black Abolitionists* (New York), 4–8; C. Peter Ripley, ed., *The Black Abolitionist Papers* (Chapel Hill, 1985–92), 3: 6; Julie Winch, *Philadelphia's Black Elite: Activism, Accommodation, and the Struggle for Autonomy, 1787–1848* (Philadelphia, 1988), 35–38. The connections between black resistance to colonization and Indian removal deserve additional research, but see Hinks, *To Awaken My Afflicted Brethren*, 123–34. See also Mary Hershberger, "Mobilizing Women, Anticipating Abolition: The Struggle against Indian Removal in the 1830s," *JAH*, 86 (1999), 35–40, on the Indian removal struggle's importance in shaping the anticolonizationist views of Benjamin Lundy, William Lloyd Garrison, and other prominent white abolitionists.

6. William G. Nell quoted in Ripley, ed., *Black Abolitionist Papers*, 6. For a fine overview of free blacks in the North, including their importance to antislavery activities, see James Oliver Horton and Lois E. Horton, *In Hope of Liberty: Culture, Community, and Protest among Northern Free Blacks, 1700–1860* (New York, 1997), 77–236; idem, *Black Bostonians: Family Life and Community Struggle in the Antebellum North* (New York, 1979); Leonard P. Curry, *The Free Black in Urban America, 1800–1850* (Chicago, 1981); George A. Levesque, *Black Boston: African American Life and Culture in Urban America, 1750–1860* (New York, 1994); Donald M. Jacobs, ed., *Courage and Conscience: Black and White Abolitionists in Boston* (Bloomington, IN, 1993); Shane White, *Somewhat More Independent: The End of Slavery in New York City, 1770–1810* (Athens, GA, 1991); Leslie M. Harris, *In the Shadow of Slavery: African Americans in New York City, 1626–1863* (Chicago, 2003); Gary B. Nash, *Forging Freedom: The Formation of Philadelphia's Black Community, 1720–1840* (Cambridge, MA, 1988); Winch, *Philadelphia's Black Elite*; idem, *Gentleman of Color: The Life of James Forten* (New York, 2002).

7. Hinks, *To Awaken My Afflicted Brethren*, 63–115; Quarles, *Black Abolitionists*, 16; *Freedom's Journal*, Oct. 3, 24, 1828. Among Walker's more important Boston associates were the hairdressers Walker Lewis and John Hilton, the Baptist minister Thomas Paul, and the tailor William Guion Nell.

8. On the possible links between Walker's *Appeal* and Young's *Manifesto*, see Hinks, *To Awaken My Afflicted Brethren*, 180–1. A more likely source, especially for Walker's historical arguments, were the newspapers, including *Freedom's Journal*. In addition to Hinks's study, see Bruce Dain, *A Hideous Monster of the Mind: American Race Theory in the Early Republic* (Cambridge, MA, 2002), esp. 139–48. Plainly, Walker had been thinking about his themes for years. In an address to the Massachusetts General Colored Association at the end of 1828, he developed arguments—the need for blacks to participate even more actively in antislavery activities, and "to try every scheme that we think will have a tendency to facilitate our salvation, and leave the final result to . . . God"—that, in retrospect, anticipated the *Appeal*. See Wilentz, ed., *Walker's Appeal*, 79–83 (quotation on 81).

9. Wilentz, ed., *Walker's Appeal*, 1, 15.

10. Ibid., 70.

11. Ibid., 3.

12. On the alarm and repression that followed the discovery of the *Appeal*, see Clement Eaton, "A Dangerous Pamphlet in the Old South," *JSH*, 2 (1936): 323–34; Hinks, *To Awaken My Afflicted Brethren*, 116–72.

13. On Bourne and Heyrick, see John W. Christie and Dwight L. Dumond, *George Bourne and* The Book and Slavery Irreconcilable (Wilmington, DE, 1969). On the weakness of the southern antislavery movement, see Gordon E. Finnie, "The Antislavery Movement in the Upper South before 1840," *JSH*, 35 (1969): 319–42; but see also Lowell H. Harrison, *The Antislavery Movement in Kentucky* (Lexington, KY, 1978); Jeffrey Brooke Allen, "The South's 'Northern Refutation' of Slavery: Pre-1830 Kentucky as a Test Case," *Southern Studies*, 20 (1981): 351–60. For interesting closer looks at specific areas, lasting past 1830, see Durwood Dunn, *An Abolitionist in the Appalachian South: Ezekiel Birdseye on Slavery, Capitalism, and Separate Statehood in East Tennessee, 1841–46* (Knoxville, 1997); Caitlin Annette Fitz, "'Impoverishing Her Soil, Corrupting Her Morals': Pragmatism and Principle in Tennessee's Antislavery Movement before 1835" (senior thesis, Princeton University, 2002).

14. Merton L. Dillon, *Benjamin Lundy and the Struggle for Negro Freedom* (Urbana, IL, 1966), 1–120. Embree's career, which deserves a full-scale scholarly work, can best be studied in the large collection of his papers held by the HSP.

15. For examples of Lundy's heated rhetoric, see *Genius of Universal Emancipation* [Boston], Jan. 1822, pp. 102–3, July 1822, p. 12, Oct. 1822, p. 49, May 1823, p. 163, June 1823, p. 171. For Walker's remarks, see Wilentz, ed., *Walker's Appeal*, 81.

16. *National Philanthropist* [Boston], Jan. 18, 1828. Two modern biographies of Garrison stand out: John L. Thomas, *The Liberator: William Lloyd Garrison, A Biography* (Boston, 1963); Henry Mayer, *All on Fire: William Lloyd Garrison and the Abolition of Slavery* (New York, 1998).

17. The fullest available text of the Park Street address is in *National Philanthropist*, July 22, 29, 1829.

18. *Liberator* [Boston], Jan. 1, 1831. Ten days after the Park Street gathering, Garrison attended what had become an annual Boston black festival honoring Great Britain's abolition of the slave trade in 1807, and was shaken when the audience protested a white temperance speaker's claim that southern slaves were not yet fully prepared, morally and intellectually, for emancipation. On Garrison's earliest-known contacts with Boston's black abolitionists, and the possibility that they were not in fact the first, see Mayer, *All on Fire*, 68–69. The man who was widely regarded as David Walker's son was named Edwin Garrison Walker, a strong sign that the elder Walker was at least aware of William Lloyd Garrison before his own death in August 1830. The younger Walker went on to become a leading figure in black Boston politics. Walker's most painstaking biographer concludes that there is "a strong possibility" that he was Walker's son. Hinks, *To Awaken My Brethren*, Appendix E, 270. The similarities between Garrison's Park Street address and Walker's *Appeal*, especially in their attacks on the unrepublican hypocrisy and in particular of Jefferson's *Notes*, also strongly suggest the two men influenced each other. Did Walker—hard at work com-

posing the first edition of his pamphlet—borrow from Garrison's speech? Or might Garrison have taken his cues in part from Walker, in some unrecorded conversation? Like Walker's possible links with Vesey, the matter must remain conjectural. On Garrison's crucial ties with blacks, in both Baltimore and Boston, see also Paul Goodman, *Of One Blood: Abolitionism and the Origins of Racial Equality* (Berkeley, 1998), 41–44.

19. Garrison, *A Brief Sketch of the Trial of William Lloyd Garrison for an Alleged Libel on Francis Todd of Newburyport, Mass.* (1830; Boston, 1834). Lundy, who was not even in Baltimore when the offending column ran, was also indicted, but got his case severed from Garrison's and passed over to an indefinite continuance.

20. *Liberator*, Jan. 1, 1831.

21. Garrison, *An Address delivered before the Free People of Color, in Philadelphia, New York, & Other Cities during the Month of June, 1831* (Boston, 1831); *Liberator*, Jan. 8, 1831. In its first months, the *Liberator* included more than ten column inches of reports and letters about Walker's *Appeal*. Mayer, *All on Fire*, 115. For a more skeptical view of Garrison's preoccupation with Walker as an artful effort to appeal to black readers, see Donald M. Jacobs, "David Walker and William Lloyd Garrison: Racial Cooperation and the Shaping of Boston Abolition," in Jacobs, ed., *Courage and Conscience*, 1–20. On the *Liberator's* close ties to black readers, subscribers, and agents, in and out of Boston, see Quarles, *Black Abolitionists*, 19–21; Mayer, *All on Fire*, 109–16.

22. *Genius of Universal Emancipation*, Nov. 8, 1828.

23. Garrison proudly reprinted some of the attacks; see, e.g., *Liberator*, Jan. 15, 29, Feb. 26, Aug. 20, 1831.

24. Kenneth S. Greenberg, ed., *The Confessions of Nat Turner and Related Documents* (Boston, 1996), 45. Greenberg's edition, one of several, includes the complete text of Turner's famously problematic *Confessions* (as transcribed by Thomas R. Gray) as well as a useful compendium of related contemporary material. One month after the uprising, the antislavery writer Samuel Warner published a narrative of the events, calling Turner's actions "nefarious" but attacking slavery as the root of the problem. Warner, *Authentic and Partial Narrative of the Tragical Scene Which Was Witnessed in Southampton County (Virginia) On Monday the 22nd of August Last* (New York, 1831). Highlights of the large literature on Turner and the rebellion include Henry Irving Trangle, ed., *The Southampton Slave Revolt of 1831: A Compilation of Source Material* (Amherst, MA, 1971); Stephen B. Oates, *The Fires of Jubilee: Nat Turner's Fierce Rebellion* (New York, 1975); Kenneth S. Greenberg, ed., *Nat Turner: A Slave Rebellion in History and Memory* (New York, 2003); Scot French, *The Rebellious Slave: Nat Turner in American Memory* (Boston, 2004).

25. Greenberg, ed., *Confessions*, 46, 47–48.

26. I have drawn this narrative from the sources collected in Trangle, ed., *Southampton Slave Revolt*, and the account in Oates, *Fires*, 35–126.

27. *Constitutional Whig* [Richmond], Sept. 3, 1831.

28. *National Intelligencer* [Washington], Sept. 15, 1831; Mayer, *All on Fire*, 121–3. Conservative northern newspapers also turned on the abolitionists: see, e.g., the fervently pro-colonization and antiblack *Morning Courier and Enquirer* [New York], Oct. 3, 1831.

29. *Liberator*, Sept. 3, 1831.

30. Hammond quoted in Chilton Williamson, *American Suffrage from Property to Democracy, 1760–1860* (Princeton, 1960), 157; Thorpe, 1: 114–15; 4: 2049–63.

31. On the political geography of Virginia and the constitutional debates of 1829 and 1830, see William G. Shade, *Democratizing the Old Dominion: Virginia and the Second Party System, 1824–1861* (Charlottesville, 1996), 1–49; Dickson D. Bruce Jr., *The Rhetoric of Conservatism: The Virginia Convention of 1829–30 and the Conservative Tradition in the South* (San Marino, CA, 1982); William Freehling, *The Road to Disunion: Secessionists at Bay, 1776–1854* (New York, 1989), 162–77.

32. NWR, Apr. 14, 1829; *Richmond Enquirer*, Feb. 14, 1829; *Constitutional Whig*, July 25, Aug. 4, Sept. 25, Nov. 24, 1829.

33. Shade, *Democratizing*, 61–64; Bruce, *Rhetoric*, 22, 31–69 passim. According to Bruce's

findings, all thirty-six Tidewater delegates were either strong or moderate conservatives. The Piedmont representatives were more varied, with fourteen tending toward conservatism and eleven tending toward reform. The valley and western delegates overwhelmingly favored reform, but their grossly disproportional small numbers kept them at a strong disadvantage. Abel Upshur, one of the foremost defenders of the conservative position on most issues, was among those with divided views, adamant about sustaining unequal representation but supportive of reforming the franchise regulations. Thomas Jefferson, two years before his death, had weighed in yet again shortly before the second Staunton Convention, supporting sweeping reform and democratic rule, calling the existing constitution a denial of "equal political rights" and a "usurpation of the minority over the majority." See Jefferson to John Hampden Pleasants, Apr. 19, 1824, TJC, later printed in NWR, May 25, 1824. Jefferson's authority would be both upheld and challenged at the constitutional convention.

34. Hugh Blair Grigsby quoted in Merrill Peterson, ed., *Democracy, Liberty, and Property: The State Constitutional Conventions of the 1820s* (Indianapolis, 1966), 331. On Doddridge, a western lawyer of humble origins, see also Bruce, *Rhetoric*, 56–57.

35. *Proceedings and Debates of the Virginia Convention of 1829–30* (Richmond, 1830), 70. On the Burkean connections, see Bruce, *Rhetoric*, esp. 166–7. Reformers could also be just as frank about the underlying issues. As Chapman Johnson remarked, "We are engaged . . . in a contest for power—disguise it as you will—call it a discussion of the rights of man, natural or social . . . all our scholastic learning and political wisdom, are but the arms employed in a contest, which involves the great and agitating question, whether the sceptre shall pass away from Judah, or to the lawgiver from between her feet." *Proceedings*, 257.

36. Ibid., 75, 282–3.

37. Ibid., 76, 151, 158, 160, 316.

38. Ibid., 78, 364, 382, 411. For powerful defenses of the reformers' natural rights position, see also the speeches by the valley reformer John R. Cooke and by Philip Doddrige, early in the proceedings. Ibid., esp. 53–62, 85–88.

39. Shade, *Democratizing*, 64–77, which aptly calls the new constitution "antediluvian, even in terms of its own times" (70).

40. On the vote, see Peterson, *Democracy, Liberty, and Property*, 444–5; Shade, *Democratizing*, 59. Heavy votes in favor of the new constitution came from the Piedmont and Shenandoah Valley, which had gained the most from the convention's minimal reforms.

41. *The Speech of Thomas J. Randolph in the House of Delegates . . . on the Subject of Slavery* (Richmond, 1832), quotation on 9. The most thorough study of the Virginia slavery debates is Alison Goodyear Freehling, *Drift toward Dissolution: The Virginia Slavery Debate of 1831–32* (Baton Rouge, 1982); but see also Freehling, *Road to Disunion*, 178–96.

42. *Richmond Enquirer*, Jan. 12, 19, 1832; *Constitutional Whig*, Jan. 19, 1832; *The Speech of James McDowell, Jr. (of Rockbridge) in the House of Delegates . . . on the Slavery Question* (Richmond, 1832), 21. See also *The Speech of William H. Brodnax (of Dinwiddie) . . . in the House of Delegates* (Richmond, 1832), 25–26. Brodnax had been the commanding officer of the state troops that marched against Nat Turner. In November 1831, Governor Floyd, a western slaveholder who cautiously responded to the Turner uprising, began taking circumspect steps toward advancing emancipation, while the legislature, responding as well to some Quaker remonstrances, appointed a special committee to look into the status and future of the state's slaves and free blacks—which in time prompted the larger legislative debate. See Freehling, *Drift*, 122–9.

43. *The Speech of Charles Jas. Faulkner (of Berkeley) in the House of Delegates . . . with Respect to Her Slave Population* (Richmond, 1832), 9–10; *Richmond Enquirer*, Feb. 14, 1832; *Constitutional Whig*, Feb. 16, Mar. 16, 28, 1832; Leigh quoted in Freehling, *Road to Disunion*, 185.

44. On the vote and its aftermath, see Freehling, *Drift*, 160–7.

45. Thomas R. Dew, *Review of the Debate in the Virginia Legislature of 1831 and 1832* (n.p., n.d. [1832]).

46. See *Constitutional Whig*, Jan. 21 (quotation), 24, 26, 28, 1832.

47. In 1810, the entire nation claimed only forty-six settlements with populations greater than 2,500 (the vast majority of them in the North) and none with a population greater than 100,000. By 1830, the numbers of northern towns and cities had doubled. Manhattan alone claimed more than 200,000 inhabitants, with Baltimore and Philadelphia at 80,000 each. Many of the fastest-growing northern cities were inland settlements, including Cincinnati (ranking eighth largest in the nation); Pittsburgh (seventeenth); Troy, New York (nineteenth); and Rochester, New York (twenty-fifth). Series A 43–56, in U.S. Bureau of the Census, *Historical Statistics of the United States from Colonial Times to 1970* (Washington, DC, 1975), 1: 11.

48. George G. Foster, *New York Naked* (New York, [1852]), 149. In addition to Sean Wilentz, *Chants Democratic: New York City & the Rise of the American Working Class, 1788–1850* (New York, 1984), 107–42, 257–71, see the brilliantly detailed account of antebellum New York in Edwin G. Burrows and Mike Wallace, *Gotham: A History of New York City to 1898* (New York, 1999), 429–863.

49. James Boardman, *America and the Americans* (London, 1833), 131; Michel Chevalier, *Society, Manners and Politics in the United States* (Boston, 1839), 143. See also Paul E. Johnson, *A Shopkeeper's Millennium: Society and Revivals in Rochester, New York, 1815–1837* (New York, 1978); Thomas Dublin, *Women at Work: The Transformation of Work and Community in Lowell, Massachusetts, 1826–1860* (New York, 1979); Barbara Tucker, *Samuel Slater and the Origins of the American Textile Industry, 1790–1860* (New York, 1984). On an early, smaller industrial community that nevertheless faced many of the tensions discussed here, see Anthony F. C. Wallace, *Rockdale: The Growth of an American Village in the Early Industrial Revolution* (New York, 1978).

50. John Pintard to Eliza Noel Pintard Davidson, Sept. 10, 1819, in *Letters from John Pintard to His Daughter, Eliza Noel Pintard Davidson, 1816–1833* (New York, 1940), 1: 217.

51. Finney, *Memoirs of Rev. Charles G. Finney* (New York, 1876), 24. See also Keith Hardman, *Charles Grandison Finney, 1792–1875: Revivalist and Reformer* (Syracuse, NY, 1987).

52. Charles G. Finney, *Lectures on Revivals of Religion* (New York, 1835), esp. 9–44 (quotation on 13), 232–55.

53. Ibid., 16.

54. Finney, *Memoirs*, 285–6; Henry B. Stanton, *Random Recollections* (1885; New York, 1887), 40–42. The best study of the Rochester revivals is Johnson, *Shopkeeper's Millennium*.

55. On revivalism and the rise of northern domesticity, see above all Mary P. Ryan, *Cradle of the Middle Class: The Family in Oneida County, New York, 1790–1865* (New York, 1981). Nancy A. Hewitt, *Women's Activism and Social Change: Rochester, New York, 1822–1872* (Ithaca, NY, 1984), also focuses on women and domestic reform, but more on Quakers and holiness sects in western New York.

56. Finney, *Lectures*, 406. On Finney's New York efforts, see Hardman, *Finney*, 239–92, 301–23.

57. Celia Morris Eckhardt, *Fanny Wright: Rebel in America* (Cambridge, MA, 1984), 168–206; Wilentz, *Chants Democratic*, 77–87, 176–82.

58. *Free Enquirer* [New York], Mar. 4, Apr. 15, May 6, 20, 27, Nov. 7, 1829, May 1, 1830.

59. Thomas Skidmore, *The Rights of Man to Property!* (New York, 1829), 81. For Skidmore's views on tariffs, see 80, 271–82. See also Edward Pessen, "Thomas Skidmore: Agrarian Reformer in the Early American Labor Movement," *New York History*, 25 (1954): 280–94; Wilentz, *Chants Democratic*, 183–4.

60. Skidmore, *Rights of Man to Property*, 334, 369.

61. Ibid., 386.

62. [Thomas Skidmore], *Political Essays* (New York, n.d. [1831]), 22.

63. *Commercial Advertiser* [New York], Apr. 25, 1829; *Morning Courier and Enquirer*, Apr. 25, 1829. On these events, and the 1829 Working Men's campaign and its aftermath, see Wilentz, *Chants Democratic*, 190–211.

64. *Working Man's Advocate* [New York], Dec. 25, 1829; *Evening Journal* [New York], Dec. 12, 28, 30, 1829.

65. *Evening Journal*, Dec. 30, 1829.

66. *Mechanics' Free Press*, Aug. 23, Oct. 17, 1829 (quotation); *American Sentinel* [Philadelphia], Oct. 13, 1830. See also *Mechanics' Free Press*, Oct. 31, 1829. On the demise of the party, see Leonard Bernstein, "The Working People of Philadelphia from Colonial Times to the General Strike of 1835," *Pennsylvania Magazine of History and Biography*, 74 (1950): 332–3; Ronald Schultz, *The Republic of Labor: Philadelphia Artisans and the Politics of Class, 1720–1830* (New York, 1993), 232–3.

67. *Delaware Free Press*, Aug. 14, 1830; Edward Pessen, "La Première Presse du Travail: Origine, Role, Idéologie," in Jacques Godechot, ed., *La presse ouvrière, 1819–1850* (La Roche-sur-Yon, 1966), 43–67.

68. *Mechanics' Free Press*, Aug. 23, 1828; *Working Man's Advocate*, Oct. 31, 1829; *Farmers', Mechanics', and Workingmen's Advocate* [Albany], Dec. 29, 1830; *Free Enquirer*, May 22, Sept. 25, 1830.

69. *Mechanics' Free Press*, Mar. 21, Apr. 25, 1829.

70. "Statement of Andrew J. Donelson," Nov. 10, 1830, in *CAJ*, 4: 204–5; "Jackson's Memorandum on Biddle's Letter," [Nov.?] 1829, in *CAJ*, 4: 84 n. 1. Jackson and Simpson's friendship survived, for the moment, despite Jackson's exasperation at what he considered Simpson's overly aggressive search for a patronage job, and Simpson's various dissatisfactions with the administration. See, in addition to Donelson's statement, Jackson to Stephen Simpson, June 27, 1829, in *CAJ*, 4: 48–49. For a shrewd contemporary analysis of the evolving connections between the Working Men and the Jackson Democrats, see Hobart Berrian, *A Brief Sketch of the Origin and Rise of the Workingmen's Party in the City of New York* (Washington, n.d. [1840]).

71. Cambreleng to Jesse Hoyt, Feb. 6, 1832, in William McKenzie, *Lives and Opinions of Benj'n Franklin Butler and Jesse Hoyt* (Boston, 1845), 100.

CHAPTER TWELVE: 1832: JACKSON'S CRUCIAL YEAR

1. Jackson to John C. Calhoun, May 30, 1830, Jackson to John Coffee, Dec. 6, 1830, in *CAJ*, 4: 141, 212.

2. Kendall to Francis P. Blair, Oct. 2, 1830, Blair-Lee Papers, PU. On the foundation and early operations of the *Globe*, see Elbert Smith, *Francis Preston Blair* (New York, 1980), 45–61; Robert V. Remini, *Andrew Jackson and the Course of American Freedom* (New York, 1981), 291–9; Donald B. Cole, *A Jackson Man: Amos Kendall and the Rise of American Democracy* (Baton Rouge, 2004), 144–8. On Jackson's decision to hire Blair, see Michael W. Singletary, "The New Editorial Voice for Andrew Jackson: Happenstance or Plan?" *Journalism Quarterly*, 53 (1976): 672–8.

3. Henry Storrs to Abraham Van Vechten, Feb. 22, 1831, quoted in Remini, *Course of American Freedom*, 310. On the cabinet reorganization, see the concise and judicious account in Donald B. Cole, *The Presidency of Andrew Jackson* (Lawrence, KS, 1993), 84–91. Margaret Eaton, allowing no perceived slight to go unpunished, treated Jackson icily after her husband was removed, leaving Jackson scratching his head in wonder. After a round of public insults by Samuel Ingham, Eaton demanded satisfaction and allegedly stalked his former colleague; Ingham fled Washington for his life. Eaton, accompanied by Margaret, then took up his appointment as governor of Florida Territory, conclusively ending the "Eaton malaria."

4. On Jackson's early suspicions of banks and the paper money system, see Jackson to Joseph

Saul, May 12, 1815, in *CAJ*, 2, 207–8; Jackson to William B. Lewis, July 16, 1820, in *Bulletin of the New York Public Library*, 4 (1900): 189; Jackson to John C. Calhoun, Sept. 15, 1820, in *CAJ*, 3: 32–33; Jackson to John Coffee, Aug. 26, 1821, quoted in Remini, *Course of American Freedom*, 46; Jackson to John Donelson, Sept. 3, 1821, in *CAJ*, 3: 117. On the suspicions about the BUS branches in the 1828 election, see Robert V. Remini, *Andrew Jackson and the Bank War* (New York, 1967), 50–51. On the continuing claims that the Kentucky BUS branches were providing funds to Jackson's political opponents, see, e.g., Francis P. Blair to Andrew Jackson, Aug. 17, 1830, in *CAJ*, 4: 174.

5. Felix Grundy to Andrew Jackson, May 22, Nov. 22, 1829, Jackson to James K. Polk, Dec. 23, 1833, in *CAJ*, 4: 37, 83, 5: 236. The best concise account of the Bank War, at once partial to Jackson and too narrow in its rendering of Jackson's political thinking, remains Remini, *Bank War*. For a stimulating and more recent interpretation, critical of both Jackson and BUS President Nicholas Biddle, see Edwin J. Perkins, "Lost Opportunities for Compromise in the Bank War: A Reassessment of Jackson's Veto Message," *Business History Review*, 61 (1987): 531–50.

6. Hamilton to Andrew Jackson, Jan. 4, 1830, Andrew Jackson to Moses Dawson, July 17, 1830, Jackson to Hugh Lawson White, Apr. 29, 1831, *CAJ*, 4: 111–4 (quotation on 113), 161–2 (quotation on 162), 271–2 (quotations on 272).

7. Hamilton to Andrew Jackson, Jan. 4, 1830, Andrew Jackson to Dawson, July 17, 1830, "Memorandum on the Bank in View of Veto" [July 1832], in *CAJ*, 4: 111–4, 161–2, 458–9 (quotations on 458). On the various plans discussed early in Jackson's administration, see also Remini, *Bank War*, 59–63. Many contemporaries—and Jackson's biographer James Parton—cited an incident involving a plot by the New Hampshire Jacksonian leader Isaac Hill and others to depose the head of the BUS's mismanaged branch in Portsmouth as the instigation for the Bank War. Although the episode, along with Jackson's certainty that other bank branches had aided Adams in 1828, contributed to the unfolding events, it is an exaggeration to see either of them as the start of the affair, especially in view of Jackson's longstanding hostility to the BUS. See ibid., 49–56.

8. Richardson, 2: 1025, 1091–2; Jackson to White, Apr. 29, 1831, in *CAJ*, 4: 272. On Van Buren's caution, see Hamilton, *Reminiscences of James A. Hamilton* (New York, 1869), 149–50.

9. Ingham to Andrew Jackson, Nov. 26, 27, 1829, Berrien to Andrew Jackson, Nov. 27, 1829, in *CAJ*, 4: 92–95; Jackson to James A. Hamilton, Dec. 12, 1831, in Hamilton, *Reminiscences*, 234.

10. Kendall to Francis P. Blair, Mar. 1, 1830, Blair-Lee Papers, PU; *Globe* [Washington], Apr. 25, 1831. See Carl B. Swisher, *Roger B. Taney* (New York, 1936), 1–159.

11. *RD*, 21st Congress, 2nd session, 46–78 (quotations on 74–75); *Globe*, Feb. 5, 1831.

12. *Working Man's Advocate* [New York], Dec. 18, 29, 1830; *Free Trade Advocate* [Philadelphia], May 9, 16, 1831. Stephen Simpson, after a personal falling-out with Jackson, broke with the president over the Bank War, but remained hostile to banks and bankers in general, defended his radical interpretation of the labor theory of value, and thought the BUS needed major reforms. See Stephen Simpson, *The Working Man's Manual: A New Theory of Political Economy, on the Principle of Production the Source of Wealth* (Philadelphia, 1831); Jackson, "Charges Against the Bank, September 1833 [?]," in *CAJ*, 5: 175; Edward M. Pessen, *Most Uncommon Jacksonians: The Radical Leaders of the Early Labor Movement* (Albany, 1967), 77–78; Philip Shriver Klein, *Pennsylvania Politics, 1817–1832: A Game without Rules* (Philadelphia, 1940), 345–6.

13. [David Henshaw], *Remarks Upon the Bank of the United States* (Boston, 1831); John Barton Derby, *Political Reminiscences* (Boston, 1835), esp. 78–86 (quotation on 86). Derby, an original Jacksonian, favored killing the rechartering of the BUS, and its replacement with another institution, but later soured on Jackson and his patron Henshaw. Thus, his engaging acerbic memoirs need to be read with care. Various bankers in New York City had similar ideas about establishing a new bank in Manhattan. During his brief tenure as New York's governor, Martin Van Buren had helped establish a Safety

Fund system to regulate and to protect the credit and solvency of state banks. New York City bankers, suspicious of Van Buren and his Albany friends, did not back the idea as country banks did. On the Safety Fund, see Cole, *Van Buren*, 177; Frank Otto Gattell, "Sober Second Thoughts on Van Buren, the Albany Regency, and the Wall Street Conspiracy," *JAH*, 53 (1966): 19–40. Gattell, in particular, upsets the idea endorsed by some contemporaries and later historians that the Bank War was an effort, led in part by Van Buren, to shift the center of banking power from Philadelphia to Manhattan. Although some New York City bankers hoped for as much, Van Buren's main ties were to banks outside Manhattan. Those interests, and Van Buren's political friends with state bank ties, were divided over the BUS issue, with some favoring recharter and some opposed. See Cole, *Presidency*, 97.

14. Alexis de Tocqueville, *Democracy in America* (1835–40; New York, 1969), 1: 389. Thomas Hart Benton later rebutted Tocqueville directly, charging that the attack on the BUS was based on genuine concerns about constitutionality and banking and not on "base or personal motives" or "feelings of revenge." Benton, *Thirty Years View; or, A History of the Working of the American Government for Thirty Years, from 1820 to 1850* (New York, 1854–56), 1: 228. The outstanding, if at times polemical, work in the anti-Jackson vein is Bray Hammond, *Banks and Politics in America from the Revolution to the Civil War* (Princeton, 1957). For refutations, see Gattell, "Second Thoughts," and, above all, John M. McFaul, *The Politics of Jacksonian Finance* (Ithaca, NY, 1972), esp. 1–15.

15. Charles Biddle later wrote that he was surprised when, without his knowledge, he was elected as one of the original officers of the Democratic Society, as he had played no role in its formation and "most of my friends were Federalists, and some of them violent ones." Biddle, *Autobiography of Charles Biddle* (Philadelphia, 1883), 252.

16. J. S. Buckingham, *America, Historical, Statistic, and Descriptive* (London, 1841), 2: 214. Thomas P. Govan, *Nicholas Biddle: Nationalist and Public Banker, 1786–1844* (Chicago, 1959), remains the best biography.

17. On the operations of the Second BUS, see Ralph C. H. Catterall, *The Second Bank of the United States* (Chicago, 1903), esp. 10–21; more generally on the Bank War, see Walter Buckingham Smith, *Economic Aspect of the Second Bank of the United States* (Cambridge, MA, 1953), 147–220.

18. Biddle to Thomas Swann, Mar. 17, 1824, in Senate Documents, 23rd Congress, 2nd session, no. 17, 297–8. Under Biddle's aegis, the bank returned annual profits to its shareholders of 8 to 10 percent of the par value of their stock, a handsome rate of return at the time.

19. Biddle Memorandum, n.d. [1829], Biddle Papers, LC. For additional remarks by Jackson, before and after, affirming his hatred of all banks, see Charles G. Sellers Jr., "Banking and Politics in Jackson's Tennessee," *Mississippi Valley Historical Review*, 61 (1954): 77.

20. Benton quoted in Hammond, *Banks and Politics*, 400; RD, 21st Congress, 1st session, Appendix, 103. On the *Globe*'s bribery allegations, see Remini, *Bank War*, 97. Daniel Webster was the most notorious of Biddle's alleged placemen, but the *Globe* charged that there were many others, including Senator Poindexter of Mississippi, who received a $10,000 loan after he backed the bank's rechartering, and Josiah Johnson of Louisiana, who received $36,000. See Edwin Miles, "Andrew Jackson and Senator John Poindexter," *JSH*, 26 (1958): 59. On Biddle and newspaper editors, see Arthur M. Schlesinger Jr., *The Age of Jackson* (Boston, 1945); 86–87 n. 22. James L. Crouthamel, "Did the Second Bank of the United States Bribe the Press?" *Journalism Quarterly*, 36 (1959): 35–44.

21. Cambreleng to Jesse Hoyt, Dec. 29, 1831, in William L. Mackenzie, *The Life and Times of Martin Van Buren* (Boston, 1846), 230. *Globe*, Dec. 9, 12, 17, 19, 1831, provides a survey of hostile reactions to McLane's report. On the foiled anti-Blair plot, see Cole, *Jackson Man*, 161–2. McLane's strategy of rapprochement collapsed completely when Biddle decided to go along with the effort to obtain an early rechartering of the BUS, a move McLane foresaw would be disastrous. See John A. Munroe, *Louis McLane: Federalist and Jacksonian* (New Brunswick, 1973), 302–23.

22. "Address of the National Republican Convention," Dec. 1831, in S & I, 2: 553–66 (quotation on 562). On the Anti-Masons' failure to ally with the National Republicans, see E. Malcolm Carroll, *Origins of the Whig Party* (Durham, NC, 1925), 48–53; Michael F. Holt, *The Rise and Fall of the American Whig Party: Jacksonian Politics and the Onset of the Civil War* (New York, 1999), 12–15.

23. Henry Clay to Nicholas Biddle, Dec. 15, 1831, Daniel Webster to Nicholas Biddle, Dec. 18, 1831, in Reginald C. McGrane, ed., *The Correspondence of Nicholas Biddle Dealing with National Affairs, 1807–1844* (Boston, 1919), 142, 145–6; Samuel Smith to William C. Rives, Jan. 3, 1832, quoted in Munroe, *McLane*, 321 (quotation).

24. *RD*, 22nd Congress, 1st session, 968. Biddle did a good job with his petition campaign, gathering almost two hundred memorials, compared to only eight antibank petitions drummed up by the administration in reply. On the campaign, see Jean Alexander Wilburn, *Biddle's Bank: The Crucial Years* (New York, 1967).

25. Benton, *Thirty Years View*, 1: 219; Carl B. Swisher, ed., "Roger B. Taney's 'Bank War Manuscript'," *Maryland Historical Magazine*, 53 (1958): 223 (quotation). Upon hearing that Calhoun had cast the deciding vote on Van Buren, Jackson swore vengeance. The aging John Randolph of Roanoke, who shared many of Calhoun's views but considered him an unprincipled and contemptible schemer, fed the president's outrage: "Calhoun, by this time, must be in Hell. . . . He is self-mutilated like the Fanatic that emasculated himself." Randolph to Andrew Jackson, Mar. 28, 1832, in *CAJ*, 4: 429. In the votes on rechartering, the opposition proved more united than the Jacksonians, but outside of the exceptional pro-Pennsylvania delegation, party lines mainly prevailed. In the Senate, for example, excluding the Pennsylvanians, Jacksonians voted 20 to 4 against rechartering, while the opposition voted unanimously for it. Sectional divisions were less pronounced among Jackson's supporters than some studies have suggested. Again excepting the Pennsylvanians, the Jacksonian votes against rechartering came from two slave-state senators and two free-state senators (the latter from Illinois and Indiana), while northern Jacksonians voted against rechartering by a margin of 5 to 2. See Cole, *Presidency*, 103.

26. Van Buren, *The Autobiography of Martin Van Buren*, John C. Fitzpatrick, ed. (1920; New York, 1969), II, 625; Lynn L. Marshall, "The Authorship of Jackson's Bank Veto Message," *Mississippi Valley Historical Review*, 50 (1963): 466–77, argues persuasively that Kendall was the chief author. Without question, Kendall wrote the first draft, conceived its most famous egalitarian passages, and wrote most of the revisions. There is also evidence that Taney, who provided Kendall with a detailed memorandum, influenced both the tone and the arguments of the key middle section on constitutional matters. For differing views on the involvement of Taney and Kendall, see Swisher, ed., "'Bank War Manuscript,'" 103–30, 215–37; Remini, *Course of American Freedom*, 365–6; Cole, *Jackson Man*, 165–72.

27. Richardson, 2: 1139–54 (quotations on 1139, 1140).

28. Ibid., 2: 1144. On the constitutional issues, see also Jackson to Thomas Hart Benton [June ? 1832], in *CAJ*, 4: 446. As Richard Ellis notes, even the sections in the veto message on foreign ownership of bank stock, sometimes derided by historians as merely base appeals to nationalist emotions, were rooted in Jackson's constitutionalism. The bank bill included a provision that allowed individual states to tax that portion of bank stock held by their own citizens. Yet the extent of foreign stock ownership, Jackson pointed out, rendered the provision meaningless; moreover, since most of the remaining stock was owned by easterners, it gave unfair advantages to some states rather than others. Richard E. Ellis, *The Union at Risk: Jacksonian Democracy, States' Rights, and the Nullification Crisis* (New York, 1987), 39.

29. Richardson, 2: 1153.

30. Ibid. On the economic and fiscal aspects of the veto message, see also Peter Temin, *The Jacksonian Economy* (New York, 1969), 28–44. On early fears that Jackson would simply kill the bank, see Warden Pope to Andrew Jackson, June 19, 1831, in *CAJ*, 4: 296–9. In his memorandum regarding the veto, Jackson wrote of his willingness to approve a bank of deposit of exchange, with no exclusive privileges "except for meritorious services per-

formed." He also suggested that should Congress want to establish a bank like the BUS, it should submit a constitutional amendment to the states—a dare based on his presumption that no such amendment would ever win ratification. By omitting these elements, the veto message did not in any way depart from Jackson's principles—but in sticking strictly to the task at hand of refusing to approve the new BUS charter, it helped set the stage for an enormous escalation of the Bank War. "Memorandum," in *CAJ*, 4: 458.

31. *National Intelligencer* [Washington], Nov. 22, 1834; *RD*, 22nd Congress, 1st session, 1221–40 (quotations on 1240, 1267, 1270); Biddle to Henry Clay, Aug. 1, 1832, in *PHC*, 8: 556. The reduced margin in the vote resulted from the absence of six senators from various parts of the country who had voted in favor of rechartering: five National Republicans and one Jacksonian, Samuel Smith of Maryland. One Jacksonian who had opposed rechartering, Mahlon Dickerson of New Jersey, did not participate in the vote over the veto.

32. *Morning Courier and Enquirer* [New York], Aug. 24, 27, 1832. Another pro-BUS New Yorker, Congressman Gulian C. Verplanck, found himself unceremoniously dumped from the Tammany ticket as punishment for his House vote in favor of rechartering. Robert William July, *The Essential New Yorker: Gulian Crommelin Verplanck* (Durham, NC, 1951), 176–9; Schlesinger, *Age of Jackson*, 92–93.

33. Clay quoted in Merrill D. Peterson, *The Great Triumvirate: Webster, Clay, and Calhoun* (New York, 1987), 208; *Boston Daily Advertiser and Patriot*, Oct. 10, 1832, quoted in Remini, *Bank War*, 101. On the National Republicans and the Anti-Masons, see Holt, *Rise and Fall*, 14–15.

34. Quotations in *Globe*, Oct. 13, 1832; S & I, 2: 509; Richard B. Kielbowicz, "Party Press Cohesiveness: Jacksonian Newspapers, 1832," *Journalism Quarterly*, 60 (1983): 518–21. On the Jacksonians' electioneering tactics as well as their opponents', see Robert V. Remini, "1832," in Arthur M. Schlesinger Jr., ed., *Running for President: The Candidates and Their Images* (New York, 1994), 1: 121–9. On the cholera epidemic, see Charles E. Rosenberg, *The Cholera Years: The United States in 1832, 1849, and 1866* (Chicago, 1962), 13–98.

35. Martin Van Buren to Andrew Donelson, Aug. 26, 1832, VBP; Weed, *Autobiography of Thurlow Weed*, Harriet A. Weed, ed. (Boston, 1883), 371–3. Later, when the Bank War escalated, pro-BUS leaders, including Henry Clay, claimed unpersuasively that the bank veto had had little or nothing to do with Jackson's landslide, and that many or even most of his confused supporters actually favored the BUS. Not surprisingly, these assertions got their widest circulation in a book funded and published by Nicholas Biddle. See T. F. Gordon, *The War on the Bank of the United States* (Philadelphia, 1834), esp. 113, 115.

36. On the 1832 campaign and results, see esp. S & I, 2: 493–574. The situation was especially ominous in two key states: New York (where the Anti-Masons swept the evangelical Burned-Over District in the western counties, and where Jackson won statewide by only a slender majority) and Pennsylvania (where the Jacksonians lost ten House seats, chiefly over the bank and Indian removal).

37. On these developments, see William J. Cooper, *The South and the Politics of Slavery, 1828–1856* (Baton Rouge, 1978), 16–22.

38. The most thorough studies of the nullification crisis, with clashing interpretations, are William W. Freehling, *Prelude to Civil War: The Nullification Crisis in South Carolina, 1816–1836* (New York, 1966); Ellis, *Union At Risk*. For contrasting views of the crisis in the context of South Carolina politics, see James M. Banner, "The Problem of South Carolina," in Stanley Elkins and Eric McKitrick, eds., *The Hofstadter Aegis: A Memorial* (New York, 1974), 60–93; Lacy K. Ford, *Origins of Southern Radicalism: The South Carolina Upcountry, 1800–1860* (New York, 1988), esp. 99–144; Stephanie McCurry, *Masters of Small Worlds: Yeoman Households, Gender Relations, and the Political Culture of the South Carolina Low Country* (New York, 1995), 234–76; Manisha Sinha, *The Counterrevolution of Slavery: Politics and Ideology in Antebellum South Carolina* (Chapel Hill, 2000), 33–61. See also Merrill D. Peterson, *Olive Branch and Sword: The Compromise of 1833* (Baton Rouge, 1982).

39. James Hamilton Jr. quoted in William W. Freehling, *The Road to Disunion: Secessionists at Bay, 1776–1854* (New York, 1990), 274; Calhoun to Virgil Maxcy, Sept. 11, 1830, in *PJCC*, 11: 229.

40. Legaré quoted in Freehling, *Prelude*, 208. Other low-country aristocrats who opposed nullification included Joel Poinsett, Daniel R. Huger, James L. Petigru, and Langdon Cheves. William Smith, having pushed Calhoun toward Radicalism and supported the *Exposition and Protest*, backed off from the nullifiers in 1832. Opposition to nullification was also strong among nonslaveholding yeomen in the state's upper Piedmont as well as among some backcountry planters. The latter divisions conformed to patterns elsewhere in the South, but because South Carolina's isolated, mountainous regions were comparatively small, these elements, as ever, were less of a political force than in other states. See Ford, *Origins*, 122. On the nullifiers' theme of resistance to centralized authority as a backward-looking, republican legacy of the Revolution, see ibid., 125–6. On the nullifiers' pseudodemocratic mobilization, see James Brewer Stewart, "'A Great Talking and Eating Machine': Patriarchy, Mobilization, and the Dynamics of Nullification in South Carolina," *Civil War History*, 27 (1981): 197–220.

41. On South Carolina's growing social, economic, and cultural peculiarity, see Freehling, *Road to Disunion*, 213–70. According to the 1830 federal census, slaves comprised 54.2 percent of South Carolina's total population. Only Louisiana (50.8 percent slaves) came close to that figure. In the four largest low-country South Carolina parishes—Beaufort, Charleston, Colleton, and Georgetown—slaves comprised 77.4 percent of the total population. On racial fear as the major force driving nullification, see idem, *Prelude*, esp. 258–9.

42. On Calhoun's political thinking and initially awkward relations with the more radical nullifiers, see Freehling, *Prelude*, 221–7 (quotation on 223); Ellis, *Union*, 64–65. But see also, Ford, *Origins*, 123–5, which minimizes the divisions between radical and moderate nullifiers and emphasizes Calhoun's immense power over South Carolina politics.

43. Calhoun to Nathan Towson, Sept. 11, 1830, in *PJCC*, 11: 230–1.

44. The Fort Hill Letter appears as Calhoun to [Frederick W.] Symmes, July 26, 1831, in *PJCC*, 11: 413–40 (quotations on 415, 418, 428). Symmes was the editor of the Pendleton, South Carolina, *Messenger*, where the letter was first published.

45. Jackson to John Coffee, July 17, 1832, in *CAJ*, 4: 462. In 1822, Governor Hamilton, then mayor of Charleston, had been the prime mover in instigating the crackdown on the suspected rebels in the Vesey affair.

46. On the nullifiers' popular organizing and the 1832 campaign in South Carolina, see esp. Freehling, *Prelude*, 235–59; Ford, *Origins*, 130–41; Sinha, *Counterrevolution*, 36–44 (quotations on 34, 35).

47. For different but complementary interpretations of the voting returns, see Freehling, *Prelude*, 254–9; Sinha, *Counterrevolution*, 44–48, which also includes a compilation of the vote by parish (45). As with any county-wide voting tabulations, the outcomes defy simple interpretation. In the parishes of Georgetown, Williamsburg, and Sumter, for example—plantation areas where more than half the population was black—the nullifiers won, overall, only 55.9 percent of the vote, considerably less than their total statewide. In Williamsburg, both sides appear to have won exactly the same number of votes. On the other hand, the Pendleton parish, well outside the strongest plantation belt, broke for nullification by a margin of 2 to 1. Many factors, including personal influence—John C. Calhoun's Fort Hill plantation was in Pendleton parish—affected the vote. In general, however, the nullifiers appear to have won their greatest support from slaveholders statewide and from nonslaveholders in overwhelmingly slaveholding areas.

48. "Ordinance of Secession," in *State Papers on Nullification: Including the Public Acts of the Convention of the People of the State of South Carolina* (Boston, 1834), 28–31. See also the militant "Address to the American People," drafted by Calhoun and revised by George McDuffie, and approved by the convention, in ibid., 57–71.

49. Richardson, 2: 1160–2. On Jackson's evolving views about the protective tariff, see Ellis, *Union*, 41–46.

50. James Parton, *Life of Andrew Jackson* (New York, 1860), 3: 465–7; Cambreleng to Martin Van Buren, Dec. 10 [?], 1832, VBP. For a hint at Jackson's direct involvement in drafting the message, see his note to Edward Livingston suggesting a new conclusion, much of which Livingston did add to the text in somewhat toned-down language. "To Edward Livingston [Dec. 1832]," in *CAJ*, 4: 484–95. According to Parton's account, when the drafting of the Nullification Proclamation was complete, Major Lewis asked Jackson if he might not want to omit the portions that would be most objectionable to the nullifiers. Jackson refused: "Those are my views," he said, "and I will not change them, or strike them out." William Freehling goes further than most recent historians in recognizing Jackson's constancy, noting that "[t]here was no *intellectual* inconsistency" between Jackson's annual message and his proclamation, but Freehling finally succumbs to the conventional wisdom by calling the latter an "ultranationalist" document with an "emotional nationalism" that ended up advancing the economic policies of Henry Clay and his National Republican (later Whig) allies. Freehling, *Prelude*, 294.

51. Richardson, 2: 1203–19. Jackson had prefigured his defense of the protective tariff's constitutionality, as a delegated power that enabled the people "to foster their own industry," in his second annual message. Richardson, 2: 1086.

52. Ibid., 2: 1207–9.

53. Ibid., 2: 1205. Jackson did elide Jefferson's draft of the Kentucky Resolutions, with its explicit mention of "nullification," as well as the more tempered resolutions adopted by the Virginia and Kentucky legislatures in 1798. Jefferson's draft had been discovered and published earlier in 1832, despite an embarrassed James Madison's efforts to suppress it. Jackson might have pointed out that Jefferson's and Madison's resolutions, unlike the South Carolina ordinance, were at least founded on what he called in his proclamation "the indefeasible right of resisting acts which are plainly unconstitutional and too oppressive to be endured." He also might have argued that Jefferson and Madison, as they saw it, were trying to protect the rights of the majority, not curtail them. Instead, wisely for the sake of his argument, he chose not to mention the Kentucky and Virginia Resolutions at all. See ibid., 2: 1204; Merrill Peterson, *The Jefferson Image in the American Mind* (New York, 1960), 36–66; Ellis, *Union*, 86–88.

54. Richardson, 2: 1206, 1211.

55. Clay to Francis Brooke, Dec. 12, 1832, *PHC*, 8: 603; Cole, *Presidency*, 161.

56. Jackson to James Hamilton Jr., June 29, 1828, in *CAJ*, 3: 411. Other Democrats, including some strong southern state-rights men, sensibly considered nullification's connections to Federalism much stronger than those to Jeffersonian state-rights ideas. Thomas Ritchie, for example, although critical of Jackson's proclamation, repeatedly compared nullification to the Federalist disunionism of 1804 and 1814. See esp. George C. Rogers Jr., "South Carolina Federalists and the Origins of the Nullification Movement," *South Carolina Historical Magazine*, 71 (1970): 17–32.

57. Richardson, 2: 1209. Blair's *Globe* defended the consistency of Jackson's state-rights and nationalist views on similar grounds; see esp. *Globe*, Jan. 8, 1833. When the *Globe* later reviewed the affair in language more acceptable to state-rights men, Jackson called the explication superfluous "folly" and repeated that the proclamation expressed his views exactly. *Globe*, Sept. 27, 1833; Jackson to Martin Van Buren, Sept. 29, 1833, in *CAJ*, 5: 212.

58. Jackson to Martin Van Buren, Jan. 13, 25, Feb. 20, 1833, Van Buren to Andrew Jackson, Dec. 27, 1832, in *CAJ*, 4: 506–8, 5: 2–4, 12–13, 19–21 (quotation on 5: 3). Jackson, during the summer's break at the Hermitage, told Martin Van Buren that he had heard one of Calhoun's best former friends say that "for his nullfycation doctrines," Calhoun "ought to be hung as a traitor to the liberties of his country." Jackson to Martin Van Buren, Aug. 30, 1832, in ibid., 4: 470. Jackson was probably referring to some remarks by Governor William Carroll. On other formulations of majoritarian nationalism prior to the nullification crisis, particularly James Madison's, and on Madison's influence on Jackson's thinking in 1832, see Ellis, *Union*, 9–11, 86–87.

59. Cole, *Presidency*, 166; Paul H. Bergeron, ed., "A Tennessean Blasts Calhoun and Nullification," *Tennessee Historical Quarterly*, 26 (1967): 383–6. Compare Ellis, *Union*, 159–60.
60. Jackson to Joel R. Poinsett, Jan. 24, 1833, in *CAJ*, 5: 11: Sinha, *Counterrevolution*, 53–54. On two of the southern states most sympathetic to Jackson, see Lucie Robertson Bridgeforth, "Missisipy's Response to Nullification, 1833," *Journal of Mississippi History*, 45 (1983): 1–22; Paul H. Bergeron, "Tennessee's Response to the Nullification Crisis," *JSH*, 39 (1973): 23–44.
61. Joel R. Poinsett to Andrew Jackson, Oct. 16, Nov. 16, 29, Dec. 17, 1832, Jan. 16, 19, 20, 22, 24, 30, Feb. 7, 9, 22, 1833, Jackson to Lewis Cass, Dec. 17, 1832, in *CAJ*, 4: 481–2, 486–8, 491–2, 501–2, 5: 6–10, 13–17, 21–22; Floyd quoted in Sinha, *Counterrevolution*, 53.
62. *RD*, 22nd Congress, 2nd session, 100–3, 519–53 (quotation on 538). On the Force Bill Message, see Freehling, *Prelude*, 184–6; but also Ellis, *Union*, 94–95, which finds the message much more belligerent and threatening.
63. Calhoun to W[illiam] C. Preston, n.d., [ca. Feb. 3, 1833], in *PJCC*, 12: 38.
64. *RD*, 22nd Congress, 2nd session, 575.
65. The best rendering of the Calhoun-Webster confrontation appears in Charles M. Wiltse, *John C. Calhoun* (Indianapolis, 1944–51), 2: 189–95 (quotation on 194). Excellent contrasting accounts of the negotiations that led to the compromise of 1833 and the eventual rescinding of nullification appear in Freehling, *Prelude*, 286–97; Ellis, *Union*, 158–77; Sinha, *Counterrevolution*, 54–56. Nathan Appleton, the manufacturer and House member from Massachusetts who was close to the negotiations, claimed that "[i]t was arranged" for the compromise tariff and the Force Bill to "go through side by side." See Cole, *Presidency*, 173–4. The more candid of the hard-core nullifiers remarked that the gesture of repealing the Force Bill was faintly ridiculous. George McDuffie facetiously asked the convention how it proposed to nullify the military portions of the bill, as "the army and navy of the United States required something more than an ordinance to nullify them." McDuffie quoted in Freehling, *Prelude*, 296.
66. Ellis, *Union*, 102–60, 178–98 (quotations on 159, 194).
67. Richard E. Ellis makes the strongest case that the nullifiers won, in ibid., esp. 178–82, claiming that Jackson "had backed down or been defeated on the most important points." On the collapse of South Carolina Unionism, see ibid., 180–81; Freehling, *Prelude*, 354: Sinha, *Counterrevolution*, 59–60 (quotation on 60).
68. Jackson to Andrew J. Crawford, May 1, 1833, in *CAJ*, 5: 72.
69. Ibid.; *Globe*, Aug. 4, 1832.
70. Calhoun to Virgil Maxcy, Sept. 11, 1830, in *PJCC*, 11: 2291; *Speeches Delivered in the Convention of the State of South Carolina* (Charleston, 1833), 25–26; *Globe*, Apr. 5, 12, 20, 25 (quotation), 1833.
71. Richardson, 2: 1222–4.
72. Marc Friedlaender and L. H. Butterfield, eds., *Diary of Charles Francis Adams* (Cambridge, MA, 1964–), 5: 106.
73. Wirt to John T. Lomax, Nov. 15, 1832, quoted in Remini, *Course of American Freedom*, 391–2.

CHAPTER THIRTEEN: BANKS, ABOLITIONISTS, AND THE EQUAL RIGHTS DEMOCRACY

1. *JQAD*, 8: 546–7; Josiah Quincy [Jr.], *Figures of the Past from the Leaves of Old Journals* (Boston, 1883), 352; James Parton, *Life of Andrew Jackson* (New York, 1860), 3: 492.
2. Parton, *Jackson*, 3: 493. On Jackson's northern tour, his physical agonies, and his second term, see Robert V. Remini, *Andrew Jackson and the Course of American Democracy, 1833–1845* (New York, 1984), 61–83; Donald B. Cole, *The Presidency of Andrew Jackson* (Lawrence, KS, 1993), 183–267. The Rip Raps, at Hampton Roads, was home, ironically,

to what was then known as Fort Calhoun, an as yet uncompleted fortification named in honor of former Secretary of War John C. Calhoun.

3. Calhoun to Christopher Vandeventer, Mar. 25, 1833, in *PJCC*, 11: 145.
4. Jackson to Martin Van Buren, Sept. 8, 1833, in *CAJ*, 5: 183.
5. Jackson, "Memorandum on the Bank in View of Veto [July 1832]," in *CAJ*, 4: 458–9.
6. Jackson to James K. Polk, Dec. 16, 1832, in *CAJ*, 4: 501. See also James Hamilton to Andrew Jackson, Feb. 28, 1833, in ibid., 5: 22–23, in which Hamilton laid out the theory that the Bank of the United States planned to gain its recharter by triggering a panic. According to James Parton, Jackson made up his mind to remove the deposits early in 1833 during a conversation with Blair, in which the latter complained that Biddle was using public funds "to frustrate the people's will." Parton, *Jackson*, 3: 500. That account may be fanciful, but Kendall later wrote that he and Blair "persistently urged" Jackson to remove the deposits. Kendall also claimed that Vice President Van Buren was staunchly opposed to removal until persuaded otherwise by Kendall's arguments. Secretary of the Treasury Louis McLane, who strongly opposed the move, offered a different account, suggesting that Van Buren was more persuaded by Jackson's intransigence than by Kendall's reasoning. On these divisions, the active role played by Blair and (especially) Kendall, and Jackson's decision to go ahead, see Robert V. Remini, *Andrew Jackson and the Bank War: A Study in the Growth of Presidential Power* (New York, 1967), 111–5; Donald B. Cole, *A Jackson Man: Amos Kendall and the Rise of American Democracy* (Baton Rouge, 2004), 177–92. More generally, on Kendall's and Blair's powerful influence within the administration on the banking and nullification issues, see Richard B. Latner, "A New Look at Jacksonian Politics," *JAH*, 61 (1975): 943–69.
7. Hamilton, *Reminiscences of James A. Hamilton* (New York, 1869), 253.
8. Kendall to Andrew Jackson, Mar. 20, 1833, in *CAJ*, 5: 41–44 (quotation on 44); Kendall to John M. Niles, Oct. 2, 1833, John M. Niles Papers, Connecticut Historical Society. One Baltimore state banker reported to an associate that receiving a portion of the federal deposits would bring a profit of between twenty and thirty thousand dollars a year. Frank Otto Gatell, "Spoils of the Bank War: Political Bias in the Selection of Pet Banks," *AHR*, 70 (1964): 36.
9. Biddle quoted in Gatell, "Spoils," 57; Kendall to Jackson, Mar. 20, 1833, in *CAJ*, 5: 43. On the mixture of political and personal calculations that governed the initial choice of state deposit banks, see Gatell, "Spoils," 35–58. Gatell shows that there is virtually no substance to the charges that the transferred funds ended up in the hands of local Democratic organizations. He also points out that, even after the chartering of the Second BUS in 1816, some federal funds went to state banks in areas where there were no BUS branches.
10. Kendall to Jackson, Mar. 20, 1833, Jackson to Martin Van Buren, Sept. 8, 1833, in *CAJ*, 5: 43, 183. For a corrective of narrowly partisan interpretations of the deposit removal, see Major L. Wilson, "The Country Versus the Court: A Republican Consensus and Party Debate in the Bank War," *JER*, 15 (1995): 619–47.
11. Government Bank Directors to Andrew Jackson, Aug. 19, 1833, Draft of Cabinet Paper, Sept. 18, 1833, in *CAJ*, 5: 160–5, 192–203 (quotations on 193–4); Richardson, 3: 1224–38. In the new cabinet shakeup, Jackson replaced Edward Livingston as secretary of state with Treasury Secretary Louis McLane (substituting Duane in place of McLane), and sent Livingston off to serve as the American minister to France. Livingston had tired of Washington and expressed a desire for the reposting—which Jackson was more than happy to arrange, given Livingston's partiality to the BUS. There is no evidence, however, to support some historians' charges that Jackson engineered the reshuffling in order to find someone friendlier than McLane to removing the government deposits in the BUS. Fortune, not calculation, dominated these events. See the account in Remini, *Course of American Democracy*, 45–59. Compare to Bray Hammond, *Banks and Politics in America, from the Revolution to the Civil War* (Princeton, 1957), 413; Thomas P. Govan, *Nicholas Biddle: Nationalist and Public Banker, 1786–1844* (Chicago, 1959), 227.

12. Jackson to Martin Van Buren, Sept. 22, 1833, in *CAJ*, 5: 206. The elder William Duane traveled to Washington to urge his son to take another course "more satisfactory to the Prest," but arrived too late to salvage the situation. *CAJ*, 5: 205 n. 2. Hard-money antibank Jacksonians were pleased by Duane's removal, an opinion amply reflected in Arthur M. Schlesinger Jr., *The Age of Jackson* (Boston, 1945), 100–2. For a much more critical view of Jackson's "poor management and inept executive leadership," which often marred his personnel decisions, see Remini, *Course of American Democracy*, 104. With Taney designated to run the Treasury Department, Jackson named the Bucktail leader Benjamin Butler, Van Buren's former Albany law partner, as his new attorney general, which helped overcome Van Buren's squeamishness about the Bank War.

13. Jacob P. Meerman, "The Climax of the Bank War: Biddle's Contraction," *Journal of Political Economy*, 71 (1963): 381; Walter B. Smith, *Economic Aspects of the Second Bank of the United States* (Cambridge, MA, 1953), 47, 50. Gatell, "Spoils," 57, finds that the mocking term "pets" entered the vocabulary of opposition critics barely a week after the removal order went into effect.

14. The seven initial pet banks were those Kendall recommended at the end of the summer of 1833. By December 1835, the number would rise to twenty-nine, and by June 1836 to thirty-three. Harry N. Scheiber, "The Pet Banks in Jacksonian Politics and Finance, 1833–1841," *Journal of Economic History*, 23 (1963): 197.

15. Hone, *The Diary of Philip Hone, 1828–1851*, Bayard Tuckerman, ed. (New York, 1889), 1: 184; Biddle to Robert Lenox, July 30, Oct. 1, 1833, to Daniel Webster, Aug. 13, 1833, to J. G. Watmough, Feb. 8, 1834, to Joseph Hopkinson, Feb. 21, 1834, all in Reginald C. McGrane, ed., *The Correspondence of Nicholas Biddle Dealing with National Affairs, 1807–1844* (Boston, 1919), 212–3, 214–6, 221, 222; Biddle to William Appleton, Jan. 27, 1834, quoted in Remini, *Bank War*, 126–7. On Biddle's contraction, which cut the bank's assets and demand liabilities by more than one-fifth, see also Meerman, "Climax," 378–88.

16. *RD*, 23rd Congress, 1st session, 59, 442; Story to Judge [S. P.] Fay, Feb. 18, 1834, in William W. Story, ed., *Life and Letters of Joseph Story* (Boston, 1851), 2: 154.

17. Kendall, *Autobiography of Amos Kendall* (Boston, 1872), 416; Samuel Bell to Joseph Blount, Feb. 27, 1834, quoted in Remini, *Bank War*, 131.

18. *RD*, 23rd Congress, 1st session, 206–23 (quotation on 221); Green quoted in Robert V. Remini, *Henry Clay: Statesman for the Union* (New York, 1991), 445. See also Charles M. Wiltse, *John C. Calhoun* (Indianapolis, 1944–51), 2: 42, 205–8, 219–20.

19. *RD*, 23rd Congress, 1st session, 2450; Theodore Sedgwick Jr., ed., *A Collection of the Political Writings of William Leggett* (New York, 1840), 1: 68. The remark by the Jacksonian congressman Samuel Beardsley terrified pro-BUS conservatives and gave them, they thought, a powerful slogan; they began emblazoning "PERISH CREDIT, PERISH COMMERCE" on antiadministration tokens and circulars.

20. Parton, *Jackson*, 3: 548–50; Everett quoted in Schlesinger, *Age of Jackson*, 110–1.

21. *RD*, 23rd Congress, 1st session, 58–94 (quotation on 58). "To you, then, sir," Clay stormed at Van Buren amid one of his denunciations, ". . . I make the appeal. . . . Go to [the president] and tell him, without exaggeration, but in the language of truth and sincerity, the actual condition of his bleeding country." Van Buren listened intently, waited until Clay was finished, strode, menacingly, over to the senator—and calmly asked if he might have a pinch of his excellent snuff, puncturing Clay's posturing at least for a day. *RD*, 23rd Congress, 1st session, 97–139, 831–2 (quotation on 831); Thomas Hart Benton, *Thirty Years' View; or, a History of the Working of the American Government for Thirty Years, from 1820 to 1850* (New York, 1856–59), 1: 420; Henry B. Stanton, *Random Recollections* (1886; New York, 1887), 205–6. Morbid coincidences darkened the already ominous climate. Amid its normal business, the Senate paused to hear announcements of the deaths of General Lafayette, William Wirt, John Randolph, and Charles Carroll, the last surviving signer of the Declaration of Independence. While he was reading the announcement on Randolph, Virginia Congressman James Boudin suddenly dropped dead. Soon after, the sole

antinullifier representative from South Carolina committed suicide. See Remini, *Course of American Democracy*, 142 (quotation).

22. Richardson, 2: 1288–312 (quotations on 1309, 1311, 1312).

23. *RD*, 23rd Congress, 1st session, 1336–40, 1373–87 (quotations on 1336, 1376); Erskine Eichelberger to Henry Clay, Feb. 22, 1834, in *PHC*, 8: 700. The Virginia Tidewater conservative Benjamin Watkins Leigh summed up what passed for the conventional wisdom, telling the Senate that "[u]ntil the President developed the faculties of the executive power, all men thought it inferior to the legislative." *RD*, 23rd Congress, 1st session, 1375.

24. The *Journal of Commerce*'s criticisms were so startling that Blair's Washington *Globe* saw fit to reprint them and consider the *Journal* an ally; see *Globe*, Nov. 30, 1833.

25. Appleton and others to the Board of Directors of the United States Branch bank at Boston, June 21, 1834, Appleton to Nicholas Biddle, July 1834, Nathan Appleton Papers, MHS. Best known as a manufacturer and guiding spirit of the Boston Associates, Appleton also had interests and knowledge in banking. See Frances W. Gregory, *Nathan Appleton: Merchant and Entrepreneur, 1779–1861* (Charlottesville, 1975), esp. 280–3. Appleton had served in Congress in 1831–33 and would return there briefly in 1842.

26. James Van Alen to Martin Van Buren, Jan. 27, 1834, VBP. On the effects of Biddle's contraction, see Meerman, "Climax," 381–5; Peter Temin, *The Jacksonian Economy* (New York, 1969), 59–68.

27. Nicholas Biddle, *An Address delivered before the Alumni Association of Nassau-Hall, on the Day of the Annual Commencement of the College of New Jersey, September 30, 1835* (1835; Philadelphia, 1836), 22–23. When Biddle refused to testify before the House committee, Taney, Kendall, and Blair pressed for his indictment for contempt, but were restrained by House Democrats who had done private business with the BUS and who feared that a full revelation of the bank's papers might prove personally embarrassing. As Biddle remarked, it would be ironic indeed if he were jailed "by the votes of members of Congress because I would not give up to their enemies their confidential letters." See Remini, *Bank War*, 167. Although Biddle later retired to a splendid estate on the Delaware River and played one last fleeting role in national politics, he would die in 1844 a broken man, mocked even by his former supporters as a wicked fellow who had once headed a "corruptly managed" bank. *Whig Almanac* [1843] quoted in Schlesinger, *Age of Jackson*, 395.

28. Clay to Nicholas Biddle, Feb. 2, 1834, in *PHC*, 8: 694.

29. Richardson, 2: 1312; Alexander Coffin to Henry Clay, May 12, 1834, in *PHC*, 2: 383–4. On the opposition's abandonment of the BUS in 1834 and the political ramifications, see John McFaul, *The Politics of Jacksonian Finance* (Ithaca, NY, 1972), 75–77. On the opposition's arguments as a conservative pro-business smoke screen, the most influential statement is Schlesinger, *Age of Jackson*, esp. 105–11.

30. *Raleigh Register* [North Carolina], June 10, 1834, quoted in Michael Holt, *The Rise and Fall of the American Whig Party: Jacksonian Politics and the Onset of the Civil War* (New York, 1999), 29–32 (quotation on 29). As Holt explains, the use of the name "Whigs," sometimes credited to Philip Hone, is of uncertain origin, but had spread widely by mid-1834.

31. *National Intelligencer* [Washington], Apr. 29, 1834; Brothers, *The United States of North America as They Are; Not as They Are Generally Described: Being a Cure for Radicalism* (London, 1840), 261.

32. *Commercial Advertiser* [New York], Oct. 3, 1833. The only local newspapers of note to express sympathy for Garrison on free-speech grounds were the Tappan brothers' *Journal of Commerce* [New York], Oct. 3, 1833, and George Henry Evans's *Working Man's Advocate*, Oct. 5, 1833. Deeply opposed over labor issues, evangelical abolitionist businessmen and working-class radicals could agree on repudiating anti-abolitionist violence. On Garrison's trip to Britain and his frightening return to the United States, see Henry Mayer, *All on Fire: William Lloyd Garrison and the Abolition of Slavery* (New York, 1998), 150–67.

33. T. R. Sullivan, *Letters Against the Immediate Abolition of Slavery; Addressed to the Free Blacks of the Non-Slaveholding States* (Boston, 1835), 23. An excellent recent study of the

American Anti-Slavery Society and its radical ideology is Paul Goodman, *Of One Blood: Abolitionism and the Origins of Racial Equality* (Berkeley, CA, 1998).

34. *Liberator* [Boston], Dec. 14, 1833; Mayer, *All on Fire*, 134–8, 173–7.

35. Mayer, *All on Fire*, 174–5; Bertram Wyatt-Brown, *Lewis Tappan and the Evangelical War against Slavery* (Cleveland, 1969), 107–9.

36. On AA-SS fund-raising and propaganda efforts, see Benjamin Quarles, "Sources of Abolitionist Income," *Mississippi Valley Historical Review*, 32 (1945): 63–76.

37. See Lawrence T. Lesick, *The Lane Rebels: Evangelicalism and Antislavery in Antebellum America* (Metuchen, NJ, 1980), esp. 116–66; Robert Abzug, *Passionate Liberator: Theodore Dwight Weld and the Dilemmas of Reform* (New York, 1980), 3–122; Betty Fladeland, *James Gillespie Birney: Slaveholder to Abolitionist* (Ithaca, NY, 1955), 75–155. For the Lane rebellion's bracing effects on other abolitionists, see Wyatt-Brown, *Tappan*, 126–29; Mayer, *All on Fire*, 189–91.

38. *Cincinnati Journal*, May 30, 1834; Wyatt-Brown, *Tappan*, 126–48; Abzug, *Weld*, 123–49. On Weld's lecturing after leaving Lane, see also Vernon L. Volpe, "Theodore Dwight Weld's Antislavery Mission in Ohio," *Ohio History*, 100 (1991): 5–18.

39. Child to Theodore Dwight Weld, July 10, 1880, quoted in Deborah Pickman Clifford, *Crusader for Freedom: A Life of Lydia Maria Child* (Boston, 1992), 98. See also Lawrence J. Friedman, *Gregarious Saints: Self and Community in American Abolitionism, 1830–1870* (New Rochelle, NY, 1982); Donald M. Scott, "Antislavery as a Sacred Vocation," in Lewis Perry and Michael Fellman, eds., *Antislavery Reconsidered: New Perspectives on the Abolitionists* (Baton Rouge, 1979), 51–74; Robert H. Abzug, *Cosmos Crumbling: American Reform and the Religious Imagination* (New York, 1994).

40. *Sunday Morning News* [New York] quoted in John B. Jentz, "The Antislavery Constituency in Jacksonian New York City," *Civil War History*, 27 (1981): 120; *Emancipator*, July 21, 1836.

41. On the missed connections, see Eric Foner, "Abolitionism and the Labor Movement," in *Ideology and Politics in the Age of the Civil War* (New York, 1980), 57–76. See also the less nuanced accounts in Alexander Saxton, *The Rise and Fall of the White Republic: Class, Politics and Mass Culture in Nineteenth-Century America* (New York, 1990); David Roediger, *The Wages of Whiteness: Race and the Making of the American Working Class* (New York, 1991). On this point, and on the abolitionists' membership base, see Goodman, *Of One Blood*, esp. 139–60.

42. *Emancipator*, Aug. 25, 1836; Jentz, "Antislavery Constituency," 101–22; Edward Magdol, *The Antislavery Rank and File: A Social Profile of the Abolitionist Constituency* (New York, 1986), esp. 61–100; Goodman, *Of One Blood*, 137–72.

43. Sarah L. Forten to Angelina E. Grimké, Apr. 15, 1837, in C. Peter Ripley, *The Black Abolitionist Papers* (Chapel Hill, 1985–92), 3: 222.

44. Leonard L. Richards, *"Gentlemen of Property and Standing": Anti-Abolition Mobs in Jacksonian America* (New York, 1970); Theodore M. Hammett, "Two Mobs of Jacksonian Boston: Ideology and Interest," *JAH*, 62 (1976): 843–68.

45. Sullivan, *Letters*, 18. On the variety of motivations driving different kinds of mobs, see Richards, "Gentlemen," esp. 82–103; Sean Wilentz, *Chants Democratic: New York City & the Rise of the American Working Class, 1788–1850* (New York, 1984), 263–6.

46. Richards, "Gentlemen," 92–100, 131–50; *Evening Post* [New York], July 22, 1834; *National Intelligencer*, Sept. 15, 30, 1831, July 24, Aug. 5, 1835.

47. *Globe*, Aug. 22, 29, 1835.

48. For the basic narrative and different interpretations of the abolitionist mails controversy, see Bertram Wyatt-Brown, "The Abolitionists' Postal Campaign of 1835," *Journal of Negro History*, 50 (1965): 227–38; William W. Freehling, *Prelude to Civil War, The Nullification Controversy in South Carolina, 1816–1836* (New York, 1966), 340–53; Remini, *Course of American Democracy*, 258–63; Richard R. John, *Spreading the News: The American Postal Service from Franklin to Morse* (Cambridge, MA, 1995), 257–83; Cole, *Jackson Man*, 199–202.

49. Kendall to Alfred Huger, Aug. 5, 1835, *NWR*, Aug. 22, 1835; Jackson to Amos Kendall, Aug. 9, 1835, in *CAJ*, 5: 360.
50. Richardson, 2: 1394–95 (quotation on 1395).
51. On Forsyth, see John, *Spreading the News*, 278–9; Cole, *Jackson Man*, 201. Without question, many northern Democrats openly approved of the mob attacks as, in the words of Senator Silas Wright of New York, "evidences of the correct state of public opinion." Most Jacksonian Democratic politicians detested the abolitionists and were determined to placate the South, especially with a presidential election in the offing, and some of their local leaders helped coordinate the disruptions. (The head of the Utica mob was the conservative Van Burenite Democratic congressman, Samuel Beardsley.) But it is important to remember that anti-abolitionism was a bipartisan affair—and that since the Democracy, unlike the opposition, was organized as an intersectional party in 1835, it felt far greater political pressure to mollify the South. It is likewise important to remember that at least some northern Democrats sympathized more with the abolitionists than with their attackers. Beginning with the mails controversy, their numbers would grow—the first important episode in the fitful rise of Jacksonian antislavery that would eventually help destroy the Jackson Democracy. See Richards, *Gentlemen*, esp. 85–92, 134–50; Howard Alexander Morrison, "A Closer Look at Utica's Anti-Abolitionist Mob," *New York History*, 62 (1981): 64–79. On Calhoun and the nullifiers' reaction, and the subsequent struggle in Congress, see Freehling, *Prelude*, 346–8.
52. On the Post Office Act, see John, *Spreading the News*, 247–8. Initially, Jacksonian leaders opposed the bill, not because of the abolitionist uproar but out of fear that the Whigs might use it, along with the Barry scandals, against Van Buren's election effort in 1836. Eventually the reform bill won over bipartisan support as the only practical means to repair the postal system's reputation. The main architects of the bill were two northern Whigs, Hiland Hall and George N. Briggs, and the anti-BUS New York Democrat, Abijah Mann.
53. *JQAD*, 9: 254; *National Intelligencer*, July 24, Aug. 5, 1835.
54. *Evening Post*, Aug. 12, 14, 15, 22 (quotation), 1835; *Standard and Democrat* [Utica], quoted in Richards, "*Gentlemen*," 87. The *Evening Post* editorial was written by the radical Jacksonian William Leggett, at the time a forthright opponent of those he called the "fanatical" abolitionists, but he would later change his mind. A year before the mails controversy, Leggett harshly attacked the anti-abolitionist mobs and the journalists who incited them: "Let them be fired upon, if they dare collect together again to prosecute their nefarious designs." *Evening Post*, July 12, 1834.
55. *Emancipator*, Nov. 14, 1836, quoted in Wyatt-Brown, *Tappan*, 162.
56. *RD*, 24th Congress, 1st session, 2678, 3429.
57. Ibid., 3434, 3439; A Reporter, "Glances at Congress," *DR*, 1 (1837): 75–76; *Globe*, June 27, 1836. See Walter E. Hugins, "Ely Moore: The Case History of a Jacksonian Labor Leader," *Political Science Quarterly*, 65 (1950): 105–25; Wilentz, *Chants Democratic*, 225–6. Moore, age thirty-seven at the time he collapsed, lived another twenty-four years and died as registrar at the United States Land Office in Lecompton, Kansas, in 1860.
58. *National Trades' Union* [New York], Dec. 27, 1834. On the trade unionism of the 1830s, see Edward Pessen, *Most Uncommon Jacksonians: Radical Leaders of the Early Labor Movement* (New York, 1967), esp. 80–99; Bruce Laurie, *Working People of Philadelphia* (Philadelphia, 1980), 85–104; idem, *Artisans into Workers: Labor in Nineteenth-Century America* (New York, 1989), 83–91; Wilentz, *Chants Democratic*, 219–54.
59. *National Trades' Union*, Sept. 27, 1834; *Pennsylvanian*, n.d., quoted in John R. Commons et al., *History of Labour in the United States* (New York, 1918–35), 1: 385.
60. *Working Man's Advocate* [New York], Nov. 30, 1833.
61. *Union* [New York], Apr. 28, 1836. On continuities in leadership, see Pessen, *Most Uncommon Jacksonians*, 82–86; Wilentz, *Chants Democratic*, 223–5.
62. John Finch, *Rise and Progress of the General Trades' Union of the City of New York* (New

York, 1833), 10 (quotation), 16–17, 23; *National Trades' Union*, Oct. 24, 1835, Mar. 5, 1836; *Man* [New York], June 16, 1835; *Union*, June 2, 1836.

63. *Working Man's Advocate*, Sept. 20, 1834. *Man* quoted in Wilentz, *Chants Democratic*, 252.

64. Wilentz, *Chants Democratic*, 248–53; *Man*, Apr. 15, 22, 1834. In New York, the tailors' union did not formally admit women (who had been uniting and striking since the mid-1820s) to their ranks, but they did vow to use "all honorable means" to help them. Women in the sweated branches of the trade had been organizing and striking on their own since the mid-1820s, and after 1830 they did so again, joined by independent groups of women shoe-binders, bookbinders, umbrella makers, and others.

65. *Union*, Apr. 21, June 2, 23, 1836; Laurie, *Working People*, 90–91.

66. Commons et al., *History of Labour*, 1: 401–12; Wilentz, *Chants Democratic*, 289–91.

67. John R. Commons et al., *Documentary History of American Industrial Society* (Cleveland, 1910–11), 5: 317–8; *Union*, June 20, 24, 27, 28, 1836; *Evening Post*, June 14, 1836; *Journal of Commerce*, June 18, 1836; Wilentz, *Chants Democratic*, 291–4. After the demonstrations, unionists began hatching plans to call a convention later in the summer that would consider forming "a separate and distinct party, around which the laboring classes and their friends can rally with confidence."

68. Quotation in Wilentz, *Chants Democratic*, 233. On the harsh conditions for the canal-diggers that bred a kind of guerrilla warfare along the Chesapeake & Ohio Canal, see Peter Way, *Common Labour: Workers and the Digging of North American Canals, 1780–1860* (Cambridge, MA, 1993), esp. 200–28.

69. *Union*, June 8, 1836; Charles Douglas quoted in Commons et al., *Documentary History*, 6: 213; *National Trades' Union*, Sept. 20, 1834.

70. On the founding of the New England Association of Farmers, Mechanics, and Other Workingmen, see *New England Artisan*, Oct. 11, 1832. Both Douglas and the association deserve more intense study, but see Pessen, *Most Uncommon Jacksonians*, esp. 90–91; Ronald P. Formisano, *The Transformation of Political Culture: Massachusetts Parties, 1790s–1840s* (New York, 1983), 222–44; as well as Schlesinger, *Age of Jackson*, 148–58. See also Louis Hartz, "Seth Luther: Working Class Rebel," *New England Quarterly*, 13 (1940): 408–18. Arthur B. Darling, "The Workingmen's Party in Massachusetts, 1833–1834," *AHR*, (1923): 81–86, stresses the rural base of the Workies' support in Massachusetts, but see Formisano, *Transformation*, 238–44.

71. Schlesinger, *Age of Jackson*, 151–2 (quotation on 152); Allen, *An Address Delivered at Northampton before the Hampshire, Franklin & Hampden Agricultural Society, October 27, 1830* (n.p., 1830), 19. On the younger Sedgwick, who, along with his radical son, deserves more extended study, see Schlesinger, *Age of Jackson*, 154–5, 187–9.

72. *Boston Courier*, Oct. 22, 1834. See also Bancroft's address to the public in *Northampton Courier*, Oct. 29, 1834. For the most informative single work on Bancroft, see M. A. DeWolfe Howe, *The Life and Letters of George Bancroft* (New York, 1908); but see also the contrasting interpretations in Russel B. Nye, *George Bancroft, Brahmin Rebel* (New York, 1944); Lilian Handlin, *George Bancroft: The Intellectual as Democrat* (New York, 1984). On Bancroft's place in Massachusetts politics, and the radical shifts within the Massachusetts Democracy, see Schlesinger, *Age of Jackson*, 159–76; Formisano, *Transformation*, 250–61.

73. *Globe*, Dec. 13, 1832; *Boston Courier*, Oct. 1, 1833 (quotation); *New England Artisan*, Oct. 2, 10, 1833; Schlesinger, *Age of Jackson*, 170–6, 254 (quotation on 176). For a harsher view of the Working Men's alliance with the Democrats, see Formisano, *Transformation*, 238–67.

74. J. M. Morse, *A Neglected Period of Connecticut's History, 1818–1850* (New Haven, 1932), 62–63, 286–300; John Niven, *Gideon Welles: Lincoln's Secretary of the Navy* (New York, 1973), esp. 119–66; Schlesinger, *Age of Jackson*, 203–5. Muhlenberg was a nephew of Peter Muhlenberg, one of the founders of the first Democratic-Republican Society in 1793.

75. See Carl N. Degler, "The Locofocos: Urban Agrarians," *Journal of Economic History*, 16

(1956): 322–33; Leo Hershkowitz, "The Loco Foco Party of New York: Its Origins and Career, 1835–1837," *New-York Historical Society Quarterly*, 46 (1962): 305–29; Jerome Mushkat, *Tammany: The Evolution of a Political Machine, 1789–1865* (Syracuse, NY, 1971), 158–84. The contemporary "official" history, F[itzwilliam] Byrdsall, *The History of the Loco-Foco or Equal Rights Party* (New York, 1842), contains much valuable documentation.

76. *Working Man's Advocate*, Nov. 7, 1835; Byrdsall, *History*, 23–28.
77. Byrdsall, *History*, 37, 44–99; Schlesinger, *Age of Jackson*, 198–9; Mushkat, *Tammany*, 169–73.
78. See Sean Wilentz, "Jacksonian Abolitionist: The Conversion of William Leggett," in John Patrick Diggins, ed., *The Liberal Persuasion: Arthur Schlesinger, Jr., and the Challenge of the American Past* (Princeton, 1997), 84–106, as well as the works described therein on 102 n. 1.
79. *Evening Post*, Dec. 6, 1834, in Sedgwick, ed., *Political Writings*, 1: 109; Byrdsall, *History*, 26; Wilentz, "Conversion," 90–102. See also Goodman, *Of One Blood*, 167–72.
80. *Globe*, Apr. 16, 1835. "If we cannot get a better class of men into the legislature," John A. Dix wrote to Van Buren amid the conservative Democrats' bank charter–granting frenzy, "the sooner we go into the minority the better." Dix to Martin Van Buren, June 7, 1836, VBP. For contrasting interpretations of the Chesapeake & Ohio violence and Jackson's response, see Richard B. Morris, "Andrew Jackson, Strikebreaker," *AHR*, 55 (1949): 54–68; Remini, *Course of American Democracy*, 129. On Jackson and the ten-hour day in Philadelphia, see ibid., 340–1.

CHAPTER FOURTEEN: *"THE REPUBLIC HAS DEGENERATED INTO A DEMOCRACY"*

.1. *Richmond Whig* quoted in *Globe* [Washington], Aug. 22, 1834.
2. Ronald N. Satz, *American Indian Policy in the Jacksonian Era* (Lincoln, NE, 1975), 97.
3. Cecil Eby, *"That Disgraceful Affair": The Black Hawk War* (New York, 1973); John K. Mahon, *History of the Second Seminole War, 1836–1842* (Gainesville, FL, 1967); John Missall and Mary Lou Missall, *The Seminole Wars: America's Longest Indian Conflict* (Gainesville, FL, 2004). Between 450 and 600 of Black Hawk's followers were killed, while the losses of American soldiers and civilians numbered exactly 72. Among the Illinois militiamen on active duty was a twenty-three-year-old store clerk, Abraham Lincoln, whose unit elected him captain but who saw no combat. Mocking military pretension, Lincoln later wryly called himself a war hero who "had a good many bloody struggles with the musquetoes." "Speech in the U.S. House of Representatives on the Presidential Question. July 27, 1848," in *CWAL*, 1: 510. By contrast, in charge of showily transporting Black Hawk, at the end of the fighting, from Wisconsin to St. Louis was a spit-and-polished second lieutenant and West Point graduate, two years Lincoln's junior, who had spent most of the war on leave. His name was Jefferson Davis.
4. Mary Elizabeth Young, *Redskins, Ruffleshirts, and Rednecks: Indian Allotments in Alabama and Mississippi, 1830–1860* (Norman, OK, 1961), 47–98; Satz, *Indian Policy*, 66–87.
5. *Cherokee Nation v. State of Georgia*, 5 Peters 1 (1831); Van Buren, *Autobiography of Martin Van Buren* (1920; New York, 1973), 1: 292. On the Cherokees' struggle, see Mary E. Young, "Indian Removal and the Attack on Tribal Autonomy: The Cherokee Case," in John Mahon, ed., *Indians of the Lower South: Past and Present* (Pensacola, FL, 1975), 125–42; idem, "The Exercise of Sovereignty in Cherokee Georgia," *JER*, 10 (1990): 43–63; William G. McLoughlin, *Cherokees and Missionaries, 1789–1839* (New Haven, 1984); idem, *Cherokee Renascence in the New Republic* (Princeton, 1986), 428–47; John A. Andrew III, *From Revivals to Removal: Jeremiah Evarts, the Cherokee Nation, and the Search for the Soul of America* (Athens, GA, 1992).

6. *Worcester v. Georgia*, 31 U.S. 515 (1832), 561.
7. On the settlement of the immediate crisis and its political context, see Edwin Miles, "After John Marshall's Decision: *Worcester v. Georgia* and the Nullification Crisis," *JSH*, 39 (1973): 519–44.
8. Major Ridge and John Ridge to Andrew Jackson, June 20, 1836, quoted in Donald B. Cole, *The Presidency of Andrew Jackson* (Lawrence, KS, 1993), 116. On Ross's career, including the "Christmas trick" of the New Echota treaty, see Gary E. Moulton, *John Ross, Cherokee Chief* (Athens, GA, 1978). In 1839, the Ridges were separately assassinated in an orchestrated plot by antitreaty partisans.
9. The paradoxes mounted: in pursuing his aim to lessen federal costs, Jackson tried to keep expenses for Indian removal to a minimum, which compounded the suffering for the hungry, disease-ridden Indians headed west. Yet between treaty-making and the wars with Black Hawk and with the Indians, Jackson's Indian policy helped spike overall federal expenditures during his final year in office to more than twice the figure for John Quincy Adams's final year. See Cole, *Presidency*, 117.
10. Porter, described by his biographer as the epitome of an aristocratic Whig planter, argued that the resettled tribes might well "stir up a war which would carry blood and desolation from the Mississippi to the Sabine." See Wendell Holmes Stephenson, *Alexander Porter: Whig Planter of Old Louisiana* (Baton Rouge, 1934), esp. 59–61 (quotation on 60).
11. *RD*, 23rd Congress, 1st session, 1645.
12. When the Senate tried to limit ladies' access to the badly overcrowded gallery, Calhoun immediately interpreted it as part of a devious Jacksonian plot to keep the public from knowing what the White House and its congressional pawns were doing. See Irving H. Bartlett, *John C. Calhoun: A Biography* (New York, 1993), 213.
13. *United States Telegraph* [Washington], June 18, 1833; Horace Binney to Dr. [Francis] Lieber, Jan. 5, 1861, in Charles C. Binney, *The Life of Horace Binney, with Selections from His Letters* (Philadelphia, 1903), 313–6 (quotations on 314); *RD*, 24th Congress, 1st session, 201. See also *Charleston Mercury*, Oct. 21, 1833.
14. Michael F. Holt, *The Rise and Fall of the American Whig Party: Jacksonian Politics and the Onset of the Civil War* (New York, 1999), 20–21, 34–36 (quotation on 35); Arthur B. Cole, *The Whig Party in the South* (Washington, DC, 1913), 3–38.
15. These generalizations are based largely on numerous state and local studies of southern politics, nicely summarized in Harry L. Watson, "Conflict and Collaboration: Yeomen, Slaveholders, and Politics in the Antebellum South," *Social History*, 10 (1985): 273–98 (quotation on 293). See also Morton Rothstein, "The Antebellum South as a Dual Economy: A Tentative Hypothesis," *Agricultural History*, 41 (1967): 373–82; Charles G. Sellers Jr., "Who Were the Southern Whigs?" *AHR*, 69 (1954): 335–46. The divisions over class and commerce replicated themselves within different subregions. In mountainous, Whig-dominated East Tennessee, for example, the Whigs' base consisted of wealthier commercial farmers who resided in places with relatively easy access to markets, whereas the Democrats attracted poorer, more remote subsistence farmers. See John H. Shroeder, "The Market Revolution and Party Preference in East Tennessee: Spatial Patterns of Partisanship in the 1840 Presidential Election," *Appalachian Journal*, 25 (1997): 8–29.
16. Harold J. Counihan, "The North Carolina Constitutional Convention of 1835: A Study in Jacksonian Democracy," *North Carolina Historical Review*, 46 (1969): 335–64; Chase C. Moody, "The Question of Slavery and the Free Negro in the Tennessee Constitutional Convention of 1834," *JSH*, 11 (1946): 487–509; Thorpe, 6: 3434.
17. Arthur P. Hayne, "The Slave Question," appended to Hayne to Jackson, Nov. 11, 1835, Jackson Papers, LC; William J. Cooper, *Liberty and Slavery: Southern Politics to 1860* (New York, 1983), 170–91 (quotation on 187). On the social and economic as well as political bonds fostered between planters and poor farmers, see also Samuel C. Hyde Jr., "Mechanisms of Planter Power in Eastern Louisiana's Piney Woods, 1810–1860," *Louisiana History*, 39 (1998): 19–44.
18. See Edwin A. Miles, "Franklin E. Plummer: Piney Woods Spokesman of the Jackson Era,"

Journal of Mississippi History, 14 (1952): 11–34. For a sample of Plummer's rhetoric, see *RD*, 23rd Congress, 1st session, 4832–4.

19. Constance Rourke, *Davy Crockett* (New York, 1937), 128–9; Matthew St. Clair Clark, *Life and Adventures of Colonel David Crockett of West Tennessee* (Cincinnati, 1833); Crockett to Charles Schultz, Dec. 25, 1834, quoted in Arthur M. Schlesinger Jr., *The Age of Jackson* (Boston, 1945), 279. See also James Atkins Shackford, *Davy Crockett, the Man and the Legend* (1956; Chapel Hill, 1986); M. J. Heale, "The Role of the Frontier in Jacksonian Politics: David Crockett and the Myth of the Self-Made Man," *Western Historical Quarterly*, 4 (1973): 405–23; Michael A. Lofaro and Joe Cummings, *Crockett at Two Hundred: New Perspectives on the Man and the Myth* (Knoxville, TN, 1989).

20. On the Texas Revolution, see Eugene C. Barker, *The Life of Stephen F. Austin, Founder of Texas, 1793–1836: A Chapter in the Westward Expansion of the Anglo American People* (Austin, 1949); supplemented with John H. Jenkins, ed., *The Papers of the Texas Revolution, 1835–1836* (Austin, 1973); Paul D. Lack, *The Texas Revolutionary Experience: A Political and Social History, 1835–1836* (College Station, TX, 1992). On the Alamo, see Richard Bruce Winders, *Sacrificed at the Alamo: Tragedy and Triumph in the Texas Revolution* (Abilene, 2004).

21. José Enrique de la Peña, *With Santa Anna in Texas: A Personal Narrative of the Revolution*, Carmen Perry, trans. (College Station, TX, 1975), 42.

22. Ibid., 51–54. The exact manner of Crockett's death remains in dispute, although efforts to discredit de la Peña's diary account as a forgery have largely been laid to rest.

23. In addition to the publicly announced agreement, the interim Texan authorities concluded a second, secret Velasco Treaty with Santa Anna in which he agreed to attempt to gain Mexico's official recognition of the new government.

24. *Globe*, May 17, 1836.

25. [Benjamin Lundy], *War in Texas; A Review of the Facts and Circumstances* (1836; Philadelphia, 1837), 3; Merton L. Dillon, *Benjamin Lundy and the Struggle for Negro Freedom* (Urbana, IL, 1966), 221–4. On Jackson's handling of the Texas question, see John M. Belohlavek, *"Let the Eagle Soar!": The Foreign Policy of Andrew Jackson* (Lincoln, NE, 1985), 218–38; Robert V. Remini, *Andrew Jackson and the Course of American Democracy, 1833–1845* (New York, 1984), 347–68.

26. Harriet Martineau, *Retrospect of Western Travel* (London, 1838), 1: 161. On the assassination attempt, see James Parton, *Life of Andrew Jackson* (New York, 1860), 3: 582–4; Remini, *Course of American Democracy*, 227–30; Richard C. Rohrs, "Partisan Politics and the Attempted Assassination of Andrew Jackson," *JER*, 1 (1981): 149–63.

27. *Evening Post* [New York], Feb. 4, 1835.

28. On the Coinage Act, see John McFaul, *The Politics of Jacksonian Finance* (Ithaca, NY, 1972), esp. 115–6. On the French crisis, and more generally on Jackson's foreign policy, see Belohlavek, "Eagle," 90–126; Remini, *Course of American Democracy*, 193–21, 274–92.

29. Taney to Andrew Jackson, Oct. 12, 1834, Andrew Jackson Papers, LC; Richardson, 2: 1326; *Globe*, Jan. 13, 1835.

30. On Butler's plan and the continuing search for a "Third Bank" solution, see Robert V. Remini, *Andrew Jackson and the Bank War* (New York, 1967), 131–4 (quotation on 132).

31. Ibid., 173; Schlesinger, *Age of Jackson*, 218; Richard Hofstadter, *The American Political Tradition and the Men Who Made It* (1948; New York, 1973), 78. On changing historical trends, see Larry Schweikart, "U.S. Commercial Banking: A Historiographical Survey," *Business History Review*, 65 (1991): 606–61. In addition to Remini, *Bank War*, and McFaul, *Jacksonian Finance*, see the differing interpretations in several other studies of banking and policy during the Jackson era, including Hugh Rockoff, "Money, Prices, and Banks in the Jacksonian Era," in Robert Fogel and Stanley Engerman, eds., *The Reinterpretation of American Economic History* (New York, 1971): 448–58; idem, *The Free Banking Era: A Reexamination* (New York, 1975); James Roger Sharp, *The Jacksonians Versus the Banks: Jacksonian Politics in the States after the Panic of 1837* (New York, 1970);

William G. Shade, *Banks or No Banks? The Money Issue in Western Politics, 1832–1865* (Detroit, 1972); David Martin, "Metallism, Small Notes, and Jackson's War with the B.U.S.," *Explorations in Economic History*, 11 (1974): 227–47; Richard Timberlake, *The Origins of Central Banking in the United States* (Cambridge, MA, 1978); Edwin J. Perkins, "Lost Opportunities for Compromise in the Bank War: A Reassessment of Jackson's Veto Message," *Business History Review*, 61 (1987): 531–50; Larry Schweikart, "Jacksonian Ideology, Currency Control, and 'Central' Banking: A Reappraisal," *Historian*, 51 (1988): 78–102.

32. *Evening Post*, Nov. 21, 1834; *DR*, 1 (1837): 6. O'Sullivan went even further: "A strong and active democratic government, in the common sense of the term, is an evil, differing only in degree and mode of operation, and not in nature, from a strong despotism." Ibid. Much of the misunderstanding arises from a confusion over Jacksonian means and ends. The lightly governed, democratic society that the Jacksonians saw as their ideal was a goal, but not always, as they discovered, the best means to that goal. Even O'Sullivan, who tended more than most to portray government itself as the source of society's difficulties, described democracy this way, as "that great result, to which mankind is to be guided down the long vista of future years by the democratic principle" of majoritarian rule. The means to achieving that end usually involved sharply reducing (although not eliminating) the involvement of the federal government, as with the restriction of government-supported internal improvements to national projects. But sometimes, undoing what O'Sullivan called "the anti-democratic, or *aristocratic* principle"—that the many were unfit for self-government—required asserting federal power within the sharply drawn limits of the Constitution. Ibid., 4, 8.

33. After stifling any direct discussion of their hard-money proclivities in the bank veto message, Jackson and his advisors did allow that, once he had been reelected, the president's main objective was to confine the use of banknotes to large-scale commerce so that "a metallic currency [would] be ensured for the common purposes of life." But if Jackson had long held hard-money ideas, the fall-out from the Bank War consolidated them. Jackson quoted in NWR, Mar. 1, 1834.

34. Gouge, *A Short History of Paper Money and Banking in the United States* (1833; New York, 1968). There is no adequate study of Gouge's life, ideas, and influence, but see Paul Conkin, *Prophets of Prosperity: America's First Political Economists* (Bloomington, IN, 1980), 207–15. For examples of Jacksonian enthusiasm over Gouge's work, see *Evening Post*, Sept. 15, 1834, June 29, 1837; Theodore Sedgwick Jr., ed., *A Collection of the Political Writings of William Leggett* (New York, 1840), 1: 96.

35. *Evening Post*, Aug. 6, 1834; *Globe*, Mar. 29 (quotation), Oct. 1, 1834.

36. RD, 23rd Congress, 1st session, 1092–3; Theophilus Fisk, *The Banking Bubble Burst; or the Mammoth Corruptions of the Paper Money System Relieved by Bleeding* (Charleston, 1837), 72; *Globe*, Nov. 16, 1833. As Gouge put it, "Such privileges as the Banks possess, ought neither to be sold nor to be given away, by a republican legislature, to any men or any body of men. A control over the whole of the cash and credit of the community, is a power as despotic in its nature as any possessed by the nobility of Germany," Gouge, *Paper Money*, Part I, 53.

37. *St. Lawrence Republican Extra* [New York], July 1837.

38. On McVickar and Phillips, see Conkin, *Prophets*, 111–4, 178–88. The Reverend Potter's best-known work on political economy was *Political Economy: Its Objects, Uses, and Principles* (New York, 1841), which drew on essays and articles he had written in the 1830s.

39. Harry N. Scheiber, "The Pet Banks in Jacksonian Politics and Finance, 1833–1841," *Journal of Economic History*, 23 (1963): 197–214 (quotation on 208); McFaul, *Jacksonian Finance*, 143–77.

40. *Globe*, May 23, June 10 (quotation), 1835. On the inflation, and especially its international origins, see Peter Temin, *The Jacksonian Economy* (New York, 1969), 59–112; for a different view, see Stanley Engerman, "A Note on the Economic Consequence of the Second Bank of the United States," *Journal of Political Economy*, 78 (1970), 725–8.

41. Schieber, "Pet Banks," 197–214 (quotation on 208).
42. Levi Woodbury, "Report from the Secretary of the Treasury, December 6, 1836," included in *RD*, 24th Congress, 2nd session, Appendix, 80; *RD*, ibid., 610.
43. Jackson to Francis Blair, Sept. 6, 1837, in *CAJ*, 5: 508–9; Lee to Martin Van Buren, Aug. 14, 1837, VBP. On the political machinations that led to White's nomination, see Charles Sellers, *James K. Polk, Jacksonian, 1793–1843* (Princeton, 1957), 253–62.
44. Cole, *Presidency*, 233–4; McFaul, *Jacksonian Finance*, 130–8; Schieber, "Pet Banks," 202–6 (quotation on 202). For a fine study of land policy and politics in the 1820s and 1830s, leading to the Deposit Act, see Daniel Feller, *The Public Lands in Jacksonian Politics* (Madison, WI, 1984). An earlier version of the distribution bill passed the Congress during the nullification crisis debates in 1833, but Jackson promptly vetoed it.
45. *Globe*, Nov. 9, 1836; *RD*, 24th Congress, 1st session, 1255.
46. Nathan Sargent, *Public Men and Events* (Philadelphia, 1875), 1: 321; Richardson, 2: 1467 (quotation), 1501–2.
47. Peter L. Rousseau, "Jacksonian Monetary Policy, Specie Flows, and the Panic of 1837," *Journal of Economic History*, 62 (2002): 457–88, contains a review of the literature and fresh findings, but see also Temin, *Jacksonian Economy*, 120–36. Traditional interpretations of the panic's origins include Reginald C. McGrane, *The Panic of 1837: Some Financial Problems of the Jacksonian Era* (1924; Chicago, 1965).
48. Jackson to Amos Kendall, Nov. 24, 1836, in *CAJ*, 5: 438–9 (quotation on 439).
49. "Speech at the Woodford Festival, Versailles, Kentucky, July 26, 1836," in *PHC*, 8: 861.
50. Weed to William Henry Seward, Apr. 13, 1835, William Henry Seward Papers, University of Rochester.
51. *JQAD*, 9: 276; Donald B. Cole, *Martin Van Buren and the American Political System* (Princeton, 1984), 258.
52. Van Buren to Andrew Jackson, Jan. 9, 1833, VBP; Charles W. March, *Reminiscences of Congress* (New York, 1850), 276.
53. *Charleston Mercury*, Apr. 10, 20, 1835; Van Buren quoted in Cole, *Van Buren*, 261. On disaffection from Van Buren elsewhere in the South, see, e.g., Derek Hackett, "The Days of This Republic Will Be Numbered: Abolition, Slavery, and the Presidential Election of 1836," *Louisiana Studies*, 15 (1976), 131–60; Richard P. McCormick, *The Second American Party System: Party Formation in the Jacksonian Era* (Chapel Hill, 1966), esp. 250–1, 338–40. For a hostile assessment of Van Buren in the 1836 election, see William G. Shade, "'The Most Delicate and Exciting Troubles': Martin Van Buren, Slavery, and the Election of 1836," *JER*, 18 (1998): 459–84.
54. *Free Enquirer* [New York], Feb. 9, 1833; *NWR*, Feb. 1, 1834.
55. John Catron to Andrew Jackson, Mar. 21, 1835, in *CAJ*, 5: 331. See Thomas Brown, "The Miscegenation of Richard Mentor Johnson as an Issue in the National Election Campaign of 1835–1836," *Civil War History*, 39 (1993): 5–30; Robert Bolt, "Vice President Richard M. Johnson of Kentucky: Hero of the Thames—Or the Great Amalgamator?," *Register of the Kentucky Historical Society*, 75 (1977): 191–203.
56. Weed to Frances Granger, Nov. 23, 1834, quoted in Holt, *Rise and Fall*, 40. For an excellent corrective of traditional interpretations that see the Whigs as more of a national party than they really were in 1836, and suggest the multicandidate effort was a carefully thought-out master plan, see Richard P. McCormick, "Was There a 'Whig Strategy' in 1836?," *JER*, 4 (1984): 47–70.
57. On the Whig campaign, see Holt, *Rise and Fall*, 37–45. The best coverage of the White campaign appears in Cooper, *Politics*, 74–97. On Harrison in 1819, see Murray N. Rothbard, *The Panic of 1819: Reactions and Policies* (New York, 1962), 151–2. More happily for his northern Whig supporters, Harrison had fairly consistently supported high tariffs—but now, in the aftermath of the nullification crisis, he tempered his views and announced his support for the compromise tariff of 1833. One Chillicothe, Ohio, editor thought the sound and spelling of Harrison's name recommended him as much as anything: "The very fact that his name ends in *on*, is of great importance. The popular men have had such

names. There was Washington, Jefferson, Madison and Jackson. Why not Harrison?" See Freeman Cleaves, *Old Tippecanoe; William Henry Harrison and His Time* (New York, 1939), 306–9; NWR, Sept. 10, 23–24, Nov. 5, 1836; Daniel Feller, "1836," in Arthur M. Schlesinger Jr., *Running for President: The Candidates and Their Images* (New York, 1994), 2: 137.

58. New York State Whig Convention, "Resolutions and Address," Feb. 4, 1836, reprinted in Arthur M. Schlesinger Jr., *History of U.S. Political Parties* (New York, 1973), 1: 391–6 (quotations on 391, 395).

59. *Evening Post*, Nov. 2, 1836; David Crockett, *The Life of Martin Van Buren* (1835; New York, 1845), 13; Nathaniel Beverley Tucker, *The Partisan Leader; A Tale of the Future* (1836; Chapel Hill, 1971). The book purportedly by Crockett also impugned Van Buren's virility, charging (80–81) that he laced himself up in corsets "such as women in a town wear," and that but for his whiskers, "it would be difficult to say, from his personal appearance, whether he was man or woman."

60. See Cole, *Van Buren*, 266–7; Feller, "1836," 135.

61. Cole, *Van Buren*, 269; Ray Allen Billington, *The Protestant Crusade, 1800–1860: A Study of the Origins of American Nativism* (New York, 1938), 32–117.

62. Crockett, *Martin Van Buren*, 71–75 (quotation on 73); Steven Hahn, *A Nation under Our Feet: Black Political Struggles in the Rural South from Slavery to the Great Migration* (Cambridge, MA, 2003), 59.

63. Cole, *Van Buren*, 270–2 (quotation on 270); *Globe*, Sept. 30, 1835.

64. Van Buren to Nathaniel Macon, Feb. 13, 1836, quoted in Cole, *Van Buren*, 272. On the politics of the gag rule and the divisions it exposed between Calhounites and other southerners, see William W. Freehling, *The Road to Disunion: Secessionists at Bay, 1776–1854* (New York, 1990), 308–36. More generally, see William Lee Miller, *Arguing about Slavery: The Great Battle in the United States Congress* (New York, 1996).

65. *RD*, 24th Congress, 1st session, 4028–32, 4050–4; *Charleston Mercury*, Sept. 8, 1836. Only Daniel Wardswell of Mansville, north of Syracuse, and in the last of his three congressional terms, broke with his fellow New York Democrats over the gag rule. Northern Whigs who voted against the rule included the stiff-necked anti-abolitionist conservative Caleb Cushing of Massachusetts as well as antislavery and anti-Jacksonian stalwarts like William Slade of Vermont.

66. James Walker to James K. Polk, Sept. 7, 1836, in Herbert Weaver, et al., eds., *Correspondence of James K. Polk* (Nashville, 1975–), 3: 717; William M. Holland, *The Life and Political Opinions of Martin Van Buren, Vice President of the United States* (1835; Hartford, 1836), 363. After trying, unavailingly, to patch up the Loco Foco sectarian schism in New York, Frances Wright campaigned hard for Van Buren, addressing, as ever, mixed audiences of men and women, but confining her remarks to politics. See the account in Celia Morris Eckhardt, *Fanny Wright: Rebel in America* (Cambridge, MA, 1984), 242–55, which takes Wright to task for slighting slavery. On the New England radicals, see *Boston Post*, Oct. 29, 1836. Leggett was warier of Van Buren than other radical writers, taking especially strong exception to his anti-abolitionism. Always critical, Leggett would nevertheless support Van Buren as, he later wrote, "the instrument chosen by the democracy of the country to carry into effect democratic principles in the administration of the federal government." *Plaindealer* [New York], May 6, 1837.

67. On the 1836 returns, see the excellent analyses in Joel H. Silbey, "The Election of 1836," in S & I, 2: 595–600; Holt, *Rise and Fall*, 45–59.

68. Richardson, 2: 1530–3, 3: 1534–7; on the campaign to expunge the censure, see Cole, *Presidency*, 250, 252–4, 264–6.

69. Thomas Hart Benton, *Thirty Years' View; or, A History of the Working of the American Government for Thirty years from 1820 to 1850* (New York, 1854–56), 1: 735.

70. Richardson, 2: 1511–27 (quotations on 1514, 1525).

CHAPTER FIFTEEN: THE POLITICS OF HARD TIMES

1. *New Era* [New York], May 35, 1837. On the Flour Riot, and its political repercussions, see F[itzwilliam] Byrdsall, *History of the Loco-Foco or Equal Rights Party* (New York, 1842), 99–113. On the panic's economic origins, see Peter Temin, *The Jacksonian Economy* (New York, 1969), 113–71; Peter L. Rousseau, "Jacksonian Monetary Policy, Specie Flows, and the Panic of 1837," *Journal of Economic History*, 62 (2002): 457–88. On the broader social impact, see Samuel Rezneck, "The Social History of an American Depression, 1837–1843," *AHR*, 60 (1935): 662–87, a useful work in need of updating. On the interesting case of St. Louis, where the panic led to a spurt of militant trade unionism, see Gary M. Fink, "The Paradoxical Experience of St. Louis Labor during the Depression of 1837," *Missouri Historical Society Bulletin*, 26 (1969): 53–63. On all of these events, and on Van Buren's presidency in general, see Major L. Wilson, *The Presidency of Martin Van Buren* (Lawrence, KS, 1984); Ted Widmer, *Martin Van Buren* (New York, 2005), which appeared while this book was in press.
2. *Journal of Commerce* [New York], May 2, 1837; Henry D. Gilpin to Martin Van Buren, May 22, 1837, VBP. The pressure on the untested new president to back down was intense: "every mail brings me bundles of letters, and memorials from our friends in favor of rescinding the Treasury order," he told Jackson, Van Buren to Andrew Jackson, Mar. 1837, VBP.
3. *Evening Post* [New York], July 19, 1836. For clashing interpretations of the depth of Van Buren's conversion to hard-money doctrines, see Arthur M. Schlesinger Jr., *The Age of Jackson* (Boston, 1945), esp. 222; Wilson, *Presidency*, esp. 53, 58.
4. William Gouge, *A Short History of Banking and Paper Money in the United States* (Philadelphia, 1833), Part I, 111–3; *Working Man's Advocate* [New York], Feb. 15, 1834; *Evening Post*, July 19, 1836; *RD*, 24th Congress, 1st session, 1255.
5. [William Gouge], "Probable Consequences of the Repeal of the Treasury Circular, March 19, 1837," VBP; idem, *Inquiry into the Expedience of Dispensing with Bank Agency and Bank Paper in the Fiscal Concerns of the United States* (Philadelphia, 1837), 39 (quotation); Henry D. Gilpin to Martin Van Buren, May 15, 21, 1837, Cambreleng to Martin Van Buren, Aug. 2, 1837, Macon to Martin Van Buren, June 18, 1837, VBP; Celia Morris Eckhardt, *Fanny Wright: Rebel in America* (Cambridge, MA, 1984), 258–65; *Plaindealer* [New York], July 22, 1837; Theophilus Fisk, *The Banking Bubble Burst; or the Mammoth Corruptions of the Paper Money System Relieved by Bleeding* (Charleston, 1837), 75–77; *Globe* [Washington], May 17, 18, 1837.
6. Richardson, 3: 1542. Donald B. Cole, *Martin Van Buren and the American Political System* (Princeton, 1984), 285–316, offers a balanced appraisal of Van Buren's response to the panic.
7. Richardson, 3: 1561.
8. Richardson, 3: 1541–63 (quotation on 1545).
9. *Boston Atlas* quoted in Arthur M. Schlesinger Jr., *The Age of Jackson* (Boston, 1945), 237; *Madisonian* [Washington], Jan. 30, Mar. 8, 1838; Frances Wright, *What Is the Matter?* (New York, 1838), 15–16; Sedgwick to Martin Van Buren, Sept. 11, 1837, VBP. Sedgwick reported that his radical son Theodore, "who is not a little hypercritical in such affairs," also approved and "writes with great enthusiasm about the message."
10. *Madisonian*, Nov. 7, 1837; *RD*, 25th Congress, 1st session, 171.
11. *Globe*, Dec. 25, 1834.
12. Calhoun to James Edward Colhoun, Sept. 7, 1837, in *PJCC*, 13: 535–6.
13. *RD*, 25th Congress, 1st session, 1380–97, 1614–82. Other subtreasury proponents performed better, including Ely Moore. Ibid., 1587–1614.
14. *Madisonian*, Mar. 6, 1838, Aug. 14, 29, 1839; Cole, *Van Buren*, 330–41; Niles quoted in Wilson, *Presidency*, 114.
15. "The Coming Session," *DR*, 4 (1838): 291–9 (quotation on 296); Hone, *The Diary of Philip Hone, 1828–1851*, Bayard Tuckerman, ed. (New York, 1889), 1: 365–6; *A Voice*

from Old Tammany! Meeting of the People! (New York, 1838), 10; Schlesinger, *Age of Jackson*, 261–2. Philip Hone, who paid a courtesy call while the president was in New York, could not quite believe that Van Buren had chosen such low political company—but, he wrote, "as he had avowed that this visit was for his own political friends, and he has consigned himself to the worst part of that clique, it is well to let them retain possession of him." On the formation and early days of the *Democratic Review*, see Edward L. Widmer, *Young America: The Flowering of Democracy in New York City* (New York, 1999), 34–39. The martyred Leggett, in life the scourge of Tammany Hall, would be honored with a commemorative bust in the hall's Long Room, where the Loco Foco revolt had begun in 1835. "Tammany Hall has come round to the *Evening Post*," the *Democratic Review* remarked tartly, "not the *Evening Post* returned to Tammany Hall." "The Duty of the Democratic Party," *DR*, 6 (1839): 442.

16. King to Azariah C. Flagg, Nov. 22, 1837, Azariah Cutting Flagg Papers, NYPL. Only in Pennsylvania, where popular distrust of the Whigs' connections to Nicholas Biddle persisted, did the Democrats salvage an important victory. See Michael F. Holt, *The Rise and Fall of the American Whig Party: Jacksonian Politics and the Onset of the Civil War* (New York, 1999), 60–88. Hard-money reformers also faced stiffened resistance in the state legislatures, but they won some measured victories in establishing specie reserves and a harder currency. See James Roger Sharp, *The Jacksonians Versus the Banks: Politics in the States after the Panic of 1837* (New York, 1970).

17. Ward to Nathan Appleton, Feb. 7, 1837, Nathan Appleton Papers, MHS.

18. Biddle to John Quincy Adams, Apr. 5, 1838, in *National Intelligencer*, Apr. 11, 1838; Biddle to S. Jaudon, June 29, 1838, in Reginald C. McGrane, ed., *The Correspondence of Nicholas Biddle Dealing with National Affairs, 1807–1844* (Boston, 1919), 315 (quotation). On the international aspects of the recovery and subsequent crash, see Temin, *Jacksonian Economy*, 148–71. On the Van Buren administration's moves, see Wilson, *Presidency*, 107–8.

19. On the connections between the election returns and the shifting economy, see Holt, *Rise and Fall*, 71–76. But for the failure of an effort by New Jersey's Whig governor to award to his party, on a technicality, all of the state's six House seats, the Whigs would have won a slim House majority in 1838. See Wilson, *Presidency*, 138.

20. On Biddle's late policies and on the international causes of the 1839 collapse, see Bray Hammond, *Banks and Politics in America, from the Revolution to the Civil War* (Princeton, 1957), 467–542; Temin, *Jacksonian Economy*, 148–55. See, above all, John J. Wallis, "What Caused the Crisis of 1839?," National Bureau of Economic Research, Working Paper H0133 (2001).

21. Albert Gallatin, *Suggestions on the Banks and Currency of the Several States, in Reference Principally to the Suspension of Specie Payments* (New York, 1841), 45.

22. *Missouri Republican*, May 26, 1836. On the McIntosh lynching and the attack on Lovejoy, see Merton L. Dillon, *Elijah P. Lovejoy, Abolitionist Editor* (Urbana, IL, 1961), 81–93.

23. *Missouri Republican*, Oct. 27, Nov. 7, 1835; Dillon, *Lovejoy*, 1–93.

24. Edward Beecher, *Narrative of Riots at Alton: In Connection with the Death of Rev. Elijah P. Lovejoy* (Alton, 1838), 50–51. Beecher's account gives an effective description of the mounting tension in Alton during and after the antislavery convention. See also Leonard L. Richards, *"Gentlemen of Property and Standing": Anti-Abolition Mobs in Jacksonian America* (New York, 1970), 92–93, 110–1.

25. Dillon, *Lovejoy*, 159–70. Lovejoy's typesetter, John Anderson, was in Alton the night of the murder, and he returned in sorrow to St. Louis—where, nine years later, he may have played an influential role in an even more consequential fight over slavery. See chapter 23, p. 709.

26. Weld to S. Webb and Wm. H. Scott, Jan. 3, 1838, in Gilbert H. Barnes and Dwight L. Dumond, *Letters of Theodore Dwight Weld, Angelina Grimké Weld, and Sarah Grimké, 1822–1844* (New York, 1934), 2: 511.

27. Two years earlier, the constitutional convention for the new state of Michigan, likewise

controlled by Democrats, also excluded blacks from the franchise. See Leon F. Litwack, *North of Slavery: The Negro in the Free States, 1790–1860* (Chicago, 1961), 74–75, 84–86, 91–93; Thorpe, 5: 3108. The evangelical abolitionist editor Joshua Leavitt was one of many cases of burn-out. Heavily in debt, politically discouraged, he told his friend Theodore Dwight Weld that he was "a good deal worn down" and considering returning to the ministry. See Weld to James Birney, July 10, 1837, in Dwight L. Dumond, ed., *Letters of James Gillespie Birney, 1831–1857* (New York, 1938), 1: 394–5.

28. Bertram Wyatt-Brown, *Lewis Tappan and the Evangelical War against Slavery* (Cleveland, 1969), 186 (quotation); Henry Mayer, *All on Fire: William Lloyd Garrison and the Abolition of Slavery* (New York, 1998), 230–1. According to Garrison, he and Tappan "harmoniously agreed to differ." It was also at the New York sessions that Garrison first met Sarah and Angelina Grimké, the subjects of a growing controversy between the editor and Tappan.

29. *Liberator* [Boston], June 30, 1837; Wyatt-Brown, *Tappan*, 186–7; Mayer, *All on Fire*, 224–6.

30. Garrison quoted in Mayer, *All on Fire*, 237. On the mixed response to Lovejoy among other nonresistants, including Benjamin Lundy and the Grimké sisters, see Dillon, *Lovejoy*, 177. For an assessment of Garrison that makes "the woman question" a key measure of his radicalism, see Aileen S. Kraditor, *Means and Ends in American Abolitionism: Garrison and His Critics on Strategy and Tactics, 1834–1850* (New York, 1969). On Garrison's early inclusion of women, see Mayer, *All on Fire*, 133. On rank-and-file women's activities in the American Anti-Slavery Society and other abolitionist organizations, see above all Julie Roy Jeffrey, *The Great Silent Army of Abolitionism: Ordinary Women in the Antislavery Movement* (Chapel Hill, 1998).

31. For the attacks on Garrison's perfectionism and Garrison's replies, see *Liberator*, Aug. 11, 18, 25, Sept. 1, 8, 1837.

32. *Emancipator* [New York], May 2, 1839. On racial tensions within abolitionism, see, e.g., C. Peter Ripley, ed., *The Black Abolitionist Papers* (Chapel Hill, 1991), 3: 20–23; but see also James Oliver Horton and Lois E. Horton, *In Hope of Liberty: Culture, Community, and Protest among Northern Free Blacks, 1700–1860* (New York, 1997), esp. 219–20, for more successful efforts to overcome the racial divisions. Historians' emphasis on the covert and sometimes overt racism of all but a few white abolitionists, a feature of the revisionist scholarly literature from the 1960s, has come under reexamination, as more is learned of the contacts between white and black abolitionists. On the older revisionist literature, see the books discussed in C. Vann Woodward, *American Counterpoint: Slavery and Racism in the North-South Dialogue* (Boston, 1971), 140–62; but compare Horton and Horton, *In Hope of Liberty*; Paul Goodman, *Of One Blood: Abolitionism and the Origins of Racial Equality* (Berkeley, CA, 1998), esp. 54–68. The tensions were certainly there, but so too was a determination to overcome them.

33. *JQAD*, 8: 247; Adams to Edward Ingersoll, Sept. 21, 1831, in Adams, *Letters on the Masonic Institution* (Boston, 1847), 14.

34. *JQAD*, 8: 379. At the Anti-Mason convention in 1831, Adams found that there was as yet "scarcely any popular feeling on the subject of Anti-Masonry," wanting "an application of a blister upon the bosom of the public." That would soon change.

35. Paul Goodman, *Towards a Christian Republic: Antimasonry and the Great Transition in New England, 1826–1836* (New York, 1988), 238–9. On Adams's early career in the House and his turn to agitating over the gag rule, see also Leonard L. Richards, *The Life and Times of Congressman John Quincy Adams* (New York, 1986), 3–112.

36. *JQAD*, 5: 12; Adams to Dr. Benjamin Waterhouse, Oct. 15, 1835, quoted in Richards, *Life and Times*, 110.

37. *RD*, 24th Congress, 1st session, 4030.

38. *RD*, 24th Congress, 2nd session, 1587–91.

39. Ibid., 1594–6, 1679.

40. Ibid., 1684–5; William W. Freehling, *The Road to Disunion: Secessionists at Bay, 1776–1854* (New York, 1990), 344–5.

41. On the *Amistad* uprising, and its immediate consequences, see above all Howard Jones, *Mutiny on the* Amistad: *The Saga of a Slave Revolt and Its Impact on American Abolition, Law, and Diplomacy* (New York, 1987), 14–30. Ruiz had bought all forty-nine of the adult male slaves in the original cargo; Montes claimed four young children, three of them girls.

42. *Emancipator*, Sept. 12, 19, 1839: Jones, *Mutiny*, 39–40; Wyatt-Brown, *Tappan*, 207–8. The precocious and energetic Sedgwick had worked side by side with Leggett at the *Evening Post* since 1834, one year after he was admitted to the New York bar at age twenty-two—and he contributed numerous hard-money and antimonopoly pieces thereafter under the pen name "Veto." He would often step in as editor when the sickly Leggett could not work. The compiler of a two-volume, posthumous collection of his friend's writings, Sedgwick, more than any other figure, embodied Leggett's Jacksonian abolitionism. See Jonathan Earle, *Jacksonian Antislavery and the Politics of Free Soil, 1824–1854* (Chapel Hill, 2004), 52–54.

43. "Reverdy Johnsting" to Tappan, Apr. 3, 1841, quoted in Wyatt-Brown, *Tappan*, 209.

44. Jones, *Mutiny*, 47–62.

45. Lewis Tappan to Benjamin Tappan, Apr. 24, 1840, annotated by Aaron Vail, VBP; Jones, *Mutiny*, 56–62, 96–98. Tappan, hoping to keep the affair roiling, arranged to have Ruiz and Montes arrested in New York City, where they had taken up temporary residence, on charges of false imprisonment and cruelty. New York's fierce anti-abolitionist press then demanded Tappan's imprisonment for false arrest. But although the anti-abolitionist attacks, so successful at arousing public opinion in the past, undermined some of the abolitionists' moderate support, they made little difference to the outcome. Even Van Buren's intimate advisor, Benjamin Butler, now the district attorney for New York and generally friendly to the Cubans, refused the White House request to free them summarily, although he did give the men advice and counsel—a thoroughly inappropriate interference by the administration in a state legal matter. Montes, no martyr, quietly raised bail and returned to Cuba; Ruiz soon did the same; neither man appeared at the final proceedings in the case. On the effects of these developments, compare the accounts in Wyatt-Brown, *Tappan*, 208–9, and Jones, *Mutiny*, 86–94. The defense also charged, with reason, that the documents provided by the State Department had been doctored, but could not conclusively prove the claim.

46. Jones, *Mutiny*, 95–135. Sengbe Pieh—or "Cinque"—also made a powerful impression in the courtroom in January, testifying through a translator about how he and the other Africans had been kidnapped into slavery. At one point, he arose and shouted in broken English, "Give us free! Give us free!"

47. *Commercial Advertiser* [New York], Jan. 15, 1840; *Liberator*, Jan. 24, 1840. On the *Grampus* order and its ramifications, see Jones, *Mutiny*, 112–9.

48. *Hartford Courant*, Feb. 10, 1840. Unfortunately, Van Buren said nothing at all about the *Amistad* affair in his autobiography, and little of value on the matter appears in his papers. But plainly, by giving Secretary Forsyth direction on the case, and with his own interference both in the trial of the two Cubans and in the dispatching of the *Grampus*, Van Buren signaled that he was chiefly concerned about his own political scalp—and that he feared political retribution from the slaveholders far more than from the abolitionists.

49. CG, 25th Congress, 2nd session, 55; W. C. Rives to Governor [David] Campbell, Jan. 24, 1838, quoted in Irving H. Bartlett, *John C. Calhoun: A Biography* (New York, 1993), 241.

50. Jones, *Mutiny*, 184–5. Calhoun's resolutions, supported by the administration and later approved by the Senate, declared that any ship on a legal voyage in the high seas was under the sole jurisdiction of the country whose flag it flew, and that, if forced into a foreign port, all persons and property aboard remained under that jurisdiction.

51. NWR, Dec. 1, 1838; CG, 25th Congress, 3rd session, Appendix, 167–75 (quotation on 168). On Leggett, and on the first appearance of the broader antislavery Democracy, see Sean Wilentz, "Jacksonian Abolitionist: The Conversion of William Leggett," in John Patrick Diggins, ed., *The Liberal Persuasion: Arthur Schlesinger, Jr., and the Challenge of the American Past* (Princeton, 1997), 84–106; and idem, "Slavery, Antislavery, and Jack-

sonian Democracy," in Melvyn Stokes and Stephen Conway, eds., *The Market Revolution in America: Social, Political, and Religious Expressions, 1800–1880* (Charlottesville, 1996), 202–23. On Morris, see John A. Neuenschwander, "Senator Thomas Morris: Antagonist of the South, 1836–1839," *Cincinnati Historical Society Bulletin,* 32 (1974): 123–39; Earle, *Jacksonian Antislavery,* 37–48. Morris first used the term *slave power* in a speech to the Senate in April 1836, delivered in opposition to Calhoun's bill to bar "incendiary materials" from the mails. Until then, the idea had been bandied about by abolitionists such as James G. Birney; it was Morris who first brought it into national debates. It received even greater exposure three years later when Morris, following his excommunication from the Ohio Democratic Party, gave his last lengthy speech to the Senate (quoted here) which newspapers throughout the North reprinted. At that point, the phrase became permanently lodged in national debates.

52. Jones, *Mutiny,* 140–3; Wyatt-Brown, *Tappan,* 212. As Jones notes (142), "It is impossible to be sure of the guiding principle in Van Buren's thinking" when he ordered the appeal. Inside the cabinet, Secretary Forsyth was more involved in pushing the *Amistad* matter than was Attorney General Henry D. Gilpin, who would wind up arguing the government's case in Washington. The Spanish connection to the affair gave Forsyth his leverage, and it was on the basis of Spanish demands that Gilpin later turned away a last-ditch effort by John Quincy Adams to halt the appeal. By leaning to Forsyth, Van Buren almost surely had political expediency as well as international concerns in mind, much as Jones suggests. *JQAD,* 10: 361–2, 372–3. Adams replaced Sedgwick and Staples, who had left the team after Judson's ruling.

53. Tappan to Roger S. Baldwin, Oct. 28, 1840, quoted in Wyatt-Brown, *Tappan,* 212; *JQAD,* 10: 358.

54. Tappan to Theodore Dwight Weld, May 26, 1840, in Barnes and Dumond, eds., *Letters,* 2: 836. For accounts of the split from different perspectives, see Wyatt-Brown, *Tappan,* 185–204; Mayer, *All on Fire,* 261–84; Kraditor, *Means and Ends,* esp. 39–140; Ronald G. Walters, *The Antislavery Appeal: American Abolitionism after 1830* (Baltimore, 1978), 3–18.

55. On Garrison's early political endorsements, see, e.g., *Liberator,* Dec. 20, 1834, Oct. 29, Nov. 6, 1836.

56. See Richard H. Sewell, *Ballots for Freedom: Antislavery Politics in the United States, 1837–1860* (New York, 1976), 3–74.

57. Cole, *Van Buren,* 357–8 (quotation on 357). Van Buren, pressed hard by Jackson, told his patron that he had no choice but to take a position of "rigid neutrality." But by allowing the states to settle the issue, Van Buren virtually assured Johnson's renomination. See Van Buren to Andrew Jackson, n.d. [Apr. 1840], in *CAJ,* 6: 55–56.

58. The platform appears in S & I, 2: 691–2.

CHAPTER SIXTEEN: WHIGS, DEMOCRATS, AND DEMOCRACY

1. Seward to Thurlow Weed, Apr. 12, 1835, in Seward, *William H. Seward: An Autobiography* (New York, 1891), 1: 257–8.

2. Weed to Francis Granger, Nov. 23, 1834, quoted in E. Malcolm Carroll, *The Origins of the Whig Party* (Durham, NC, 1925), 219.

3. Harriet A. Weed, ed., *Autobiography of Thurlow Weed* (Boston, 1883), 90; *Daily Advertiser* [New York], Mar. 21, 1834 (quotation). There were several roads out of Anti-Masonry, with very different political destinations. In New England, some prominent Anti-Masons, notably the notorious opportunist Benjamin Hallett of Massachusetts, became Democrats. Other Anti-Masons, including Myron Holley, became active political abolitionists. But it was within Whiggery that the Anti-Masons' populist ideals and organizing methods had the greatest impact. See Paul Goodman, *Towards a Christian Republic: Antimasonry and the Great Transition in New England, 1826–1836* (New York, 1988), 138–9, 215; Michael

F. Holt, *The Rise and Fall of the American Whig Party: Jacksonian Politics and the Onset of the Civil War* (New York, 1999), 28–32, 52–55.

4. *Boston Atlas*, quoted in Arthur M. Schlesinger Jr., *The Age of Jackson* (Boston, 1945), 289. The best biographies of Greeley are, on politics, Glyndon Van Deusen, *Horace Greeley, Nineteenth-Century Crusader* (Philadelphia, 1953); on journalism, Lurton D. Ingersoll, *The Life of Horace Greeley* (New York, 1974); but see also Jeter A. Isley, *Horace Greeley and the Republican Party, 1853–1861: A Study of the New York Tribune* (1947; Princeton, 1965). On Hildreth, who deserves more study, see Arthur M. Schlesinger Jr., "The Problem of Richard Hildreth," *New England Quarterly*, 13 (1940), 223–45; Donald E. Emerson, *Richard Hildreth* (Baltimore, 1946).

5. On the Massachusetts Whigs, see Ronald P. Formisano, *The Transformation of Political Culture: Massachusetts Parties, 1790s–1840s* (New York, 1983), 268–301; Robert F. Dalzell Jr., *Daniel Webster and the Trial of American Nationalism, 1843–1852* (Boston, 1973), 59–97. On the evolution of southern Whiggery, see Arthur C. Cole, *The Whig Party in the South* (Washington, 1913); Charles Sellers, "Who Were the Southern Whigs?," *AHR*, 54 (1954): 335–46; Richard P. McCormick, *The Second American Party System: Party Formation in the Jacksonian Era* (Chapel Hill, 1966), 176–254, 287–303, 310–20; William J. Cooper Jr., *The South and the Politics of Slavery, 1828–1856* (Baton Rouge, 1978), 28–29, 38–97 (quotation on 28); J. Mills Thornton III, *Politics and Power in a Slave Society: Alabama, 1800–1860* (Baton Rouge, 1978), 36–37, 116–62; Harry L. Watson, *Jacksonian Politics and Community Conflict: The Emergence of the Second Party System in Cumberland County, North Carolina* (Baton Rouge, 1981), 202–5, 208–13, 258–61, 271–81; Marc Kruman, *Parties and Politics in North Carolina, 1836–1865* (Baton Rouge, 1983), 3–54.

6. Albert H. Tracy to William Henry Seward, Apr. 14, 1835, William H. Seward Papers, University of Rochester. On improved Whig organization, see also McCormick, *Party System*, esp. 346–56; Holt, *Rise and Fall*, 113.

7. Sullivan to Nathan Appleton, Feb. 29, 1832, Nathan Appleton Papers, MHS.

8. On the rising economic inequality of the period, see Jeffrey G. Williamson and Peter Lindert, *American Inequality: A Macroeconomic History* (New York, 1980), 36–46, 67–75.

9. *Journal of the Debates and Proceedings of the Convention of Delegates, Chosen to Revise the Constitution of Massachusetts* (Boston, 1853), 286.

10. *CG*, 25th Congress, 2nd session, Appendix, 633; *American Quarterly Review*, 24 (1832): 306; [Calvin Colton], *The Junius Tracts* (New York, 1844), 110. Jeffersonians and Jacksonians, to be sure, held to their own version of America's exceptional character, based on the absence of aristocracy and the abundance of land. But whereas the Democrats promoted that idea as a warning against the power of associated wealth, the Whigs came to uphold it as a denial that there was such a thing as associated wealth in America, and that the Democrats' warnings were sheer demagogy. See Rush Welter, *The Mind of America, 1820–1860* (New York, 1975), 105–28.

11. Story to Harriet Martineau, Jan. 19, 1839, in William W. Story ed., *Life and Letters of Joseph Story* (Boston, 1851), 2: 308.

12. *New-York Daily Tribune*, Nov. 29, 1845, quoted in Holt, *Rise and Fall*, 70. As Holt points out, although Greeley wrote these words in 1845, they beautifully capture "the ideological chasm that opened between the rival parties after 1837."

13. *Log Cabin* [New York], Sept. 5, 1840.

14. [Charles A. Davis], *Letters of J. Downing, Major* (New York, 1834), 227–8. On Charles Davis and Major Downing, see Henry Ladd Smith, "The Two Major Downings: Rivalry in Political Satire," *Journalism Quarterly*, 41 (1964): 74–78. On the origins of public campaign styles and how democratic electioneering borrowed many techniques from an earlier, more deferential political era, see Andrew W. Robertson, "Voting Rites and Voting Acts: Electioneering Ritual, 1790–1820," in Jeffrey L. Pasley et al., eds., *Beyond the Founders: New Approaches to the Political History of the Early Republic* (Chapel Hill, 2004), 57–78.

15. Henry C. Carey, *Principles of Political Economy. Part the First: On the Production and Distribution of Wealth* (Philadelphia, 1837). On the origins of Clay's "Mill Boy" nickname and its usefulness in cultivating the myth that he was born into poverty, see Robert V. Remini, *Henry Clay: Statesman of the Union* (New York, 1991), 5.

16. William Ellery Channing, *Lectures on the Elevation of the Labouring Portion of the Community* (Boston, 1840), 15.

17. John Bell, May 23, 1835, quoted in Daniel Walker Howe, *The Political Culture of the American Whigs* (Chicago, 1979), 32.

18. [Colton], *Junius Tracts*, 3; *New York American* quoted in *Cincinnati Daily Gazette*, Jan. 17, 1837. For a sympathetic account of Whig reform, see Howe, *Political Culture*, 37–39, among many other studies.

19. Henry Adams, *Life of Albert Gallatin* (Philadelphia, 1879), 635. Even the *North American Review*, arbiter of Whig intellectual merit, found Carey's first major work, *Principles of Political Economy*, a shallow and unoriginal disappointment, filled with "zigzags and dark passages." See "Political Economy," *North American Review*, 48 (1838): 73–90 (quotation on 76). On the influence on the Whigs of eighteenth-century Scottish moral philosophy and faculty psychology, with its belief that an innate moral sense could overcome unruly passions, see Howe, *Political Culture*, esp. 23–32. Whigs also received intellectual sustenance and comfort from writers across the Atlantic who were trying to solve the riddle of American democracy. The most brilliant of them—more brilliant than anyone the Whigs themselves produced—was the liberal French aristocrat Alexis de Tocqueville, the first of whose two epigrammatic volumes on *Democracy in America* won praise from an otherwise highly critical essayist in the *Democratic Review* as the work of "a really profound and vigorous thinker." "European Views of American Democracy," *DR*, 1 (1837): 91–107; 2 (1838): 337–57 (quotation on 337).

20. Harriet Martineau, *Society in America* (London, 1837), 1: 13–14. See Frank Otto Gattell, *John Gorham Palfrey and the New England Conscience* (Cambridge, MA, 1963), 78–107; Charles H. Bohner, *John Pendleton Kennedy: Gentleman from Baltimore* (Baltimore, 1961). Henry David Thoreau dismissed the *North American Review* as "a venerable cobweb," and Edgar Allan Poe wrote that its editors and contributors should be hanged. For a more sympathetic view of the *Review* and its efforts to adapt to changing realities after 1815, see Marshall Foletta, *Coming to Terms with Democracy: Federalist Intellectuals and the Shaping of American Culture* (Charlottesville, 2001) (quotations on 9). Among the older but still vigorous writers who appeared in the *Democratic Review* were William Cullen Bryant and James Fenimore Cooper.

21. Howe, *Political Culture*, 26–27, 150–80.

22. See Elizabeth B. Clark, "'The Sacred Rights of the Weak': Pain, Sympathy, and the Culture of Individual Rights in Antebellum America," *JAH*, 82 (1995): 463–93 (quotation on 477); James Essig, *The Bonds of Wickedness: American Evangelicals against Slavery, 1770–1808* (Philadelphia, 1982); Daniel Walker Howe, *The Unitarian Conscience: Harvard Moral Philosophy 1805–1861* (Cambridge, MA, 1970). For a fine case study of a reform movement informed by both Enlightenment ideals and Whiggish reform conscience, see Louis P. Masur, *Rites of Execution: Capital Punishment and the Transformation of American Culture, 1776–1865* (New York, 1989). Also in connection with the abolitionists, see Ronald G. Walters, *The Antislavery Appeal: American Abolitionism after 1830* (New York, 1978), esp. 54–69.

23. On the complexities of southern paternalist religious reform, see, among many fine studies, Erskine Clarke, *Wreasalin' Jacob: A Portrait of Religion in Antebellum Georgia and the Carolina Low Country* (1979; Tuscaloosa, 2000). On the compatibility of southern evangelical spirituality and pro-slavery, see Eugene D. Genovese, "Religious and Economic Thought in the Pro-Slavery Argument," *Essays in Business and Economic History*, 15 (1997): 1–9; Mitchell Snay, *Gospel of Disunion: Religion and Separatism in the Antebellum South* (New York, 1993); Drew Gilpin Faust, "Evangelicalism and the Meaning of the Proslavery Argument: The Reverend Thornton Stringfellow of Virginia," *Virginia Maga-*

zine of History and Biography, 85 (1977): 1–17. On the most successful of the moral reform crusades in the South, on and off the plantations, see Stanley K. Schultz, "Temperance Reform in the Antebellum South: Social Control and Urban Order," *South Atlantic Quarterly*, 83 (1984), 323–39. On the broader themes of politics and moral progress in the slaveholders' ideology, see Eugene D. Genovese, *The Slaveholders' Dilemma: Freedom and Progress in Southern Conservative Thought, 1820–1860* (Columbia, SC, 1992). The links between northern Whiggery and antislavery are emphasized in Howe, *Political Culture*, esp. 9, 31, 37, 168–79. It is important to note that middling, new-school Whigs, rather than old-line wealthy conservatives, appear to have predominated in the antislavery cause—and that after 1840 the political abolitionists connected with the Liberty Party gravitated toward Free Soil and Democratic social and economic planks. See Edward Magdol, *The Anti-Slavery Rank and File: A Social Profile of the Abolitionist Constituency* (Westport, CT, 1986), 105. Daniel Walker Howe's assertion that "[t]here was more debate over slavery within the Whig party than within the Democratic party" might hold true until 1844 (in part because the Democrats were the only truly national party until 1840), but the claim is itself debatable at various points thereafter. See Howe, *Political Culture*, 37.

24. [Colton], *Junius Tracts*, 111. Howe, *Political Culture*, 96–122, includes a full discussion of Whig entrepreneurialism.

25. On the Whigs and the wealthy, see, in addition to the studies cited in n. 5, Frank Otto Gattell, "Money and Party in Jacksonian America: A Quantitative Analysis," *Political Science Quarterly*, 72 (1967): 235–52; Robert Rich, "'A Wilderness of Whigs': The Wealthy Men of Boston," *Journal of Social History*, 4 (1971): 263–76. In some areas, new-school Whigs failed to expand the party's base or shift its ideology. In New Hampshire, this failure would keep the party in the minority; in Rhode Island, it would lead to the Dorr War of the 1840s. See Steven P. McGiffen, "Ideology and the Failure of the Whig Party in New Hampshire," *New England Quarterly*, 59 (1986): 387–40; and chapter 17, pp. 539–45.

26. [Colton], *Junius Tracts*, 89. Historians, persuaded by some brilliant essays by Marvin Meyers, have sometimes overgeneralized that the Whigs spoke to the hopes of the American people while the Jacksonians spoke to their fears. See Meyers, *The Jacksonian Persuasion: Politics and Belief* (Stanford, 1957). In fact, under Jackson, it was the Democrats who took by far the more optimistic tack, energized by the prospect of grand reform, propelled by the doctrine of majority rule, and projecting a bright new future free of privilege and gross class injustice. The emerging Whigs were the pessimists, all but certain that the republic was sliding into an abyss of fiery ruin, as portrayed in all its sublime classical grandeur by the pro-Whig artist Thomas Cole's apocalyptic series, "The Course of Empire." Only in the later 1830s did the Whigs learn to think and to speak as optimists, while portraying the Democrats as the harbingers of doom and gloom and the false prophets of class warfare.

27. Charles Z. Lincoln, ed., *Messages from the Governors, Comprising Executive Communications to the Legislature and Other Papers Relating to Legislation* (Albany, 1909), 3: 706–47, 946–7; Glyndon G. Van Deusen, *William Henry Seward* (New York, 1967) (quotations on 57).

28. On the twists and turns, see James Roger Sharp, *The Jacksonians versus the Banks: Politics in the States after the Panic of 1837* (New York, 1970), 301–5.

29. Seward to Christopher Morgan, June 10, 1841, in Seward, *Autobiography*, 1: 547; Hone, *The Diary of Philip Hone, 1828–1851*, Bayard Tuckerman, ed. (New York, 1889), 1: 427. On the continuing controversies over Seward's support of public funding for Catholic schools, see Van Deusen, *Seward*, 67–71.

30. The *Boston Atlas* editorials, written by Richard Hildreth, appeared on Sept. 14, 17, 20, 29, Oct. 1, 11, Nov. 19, 20, 1838. On the machinations among the Whig rivals for the nomination, see Holt, *Rise and Fall*, 90–101.

31. CG, 25th Congress, 3rd session, Appendix, 354–9 (quotation on 359); ibid., 25th Congress, 3rd session, 167. Privately, Calhoun, who had his own priorities, said what he really thought: "He has chopped round on it. He had no choice. . . . His speech is far from sound

on many points, but he has said enough to offend mortally the abolitionists, which will do much to divide the north & consolidate us." Calhoun to Armistead Burt, Feb. 17, 1839, in *PJCC*, 14: 555.

32. The best account is Remini, *Clay*, 532–44 (quotation on 533).

33. Robert Gray Gunderson, *The Log-Cabin Campaign* (Lexington, KY, 1957), 45–46; Holt, *Rise and Fall*, 100. The New York circular is quoted in full in Merrill D. Peterson, *The Great Triumvirate: Webster, Clay, and Calhoun* (New York, 1987), 290.

34. Both quotations from M. Bradley to Thurlow Weed, Aug. 29, 1839, quoted in Gunderson, *Log-Cabin Campaign*, 52.

35. The following account of the Harrisburg convention relies chiefly on Gunderson, *Log-Cabin Campaign*, 57–66; Holt, *Rise and Fall*, 101–5. The official proceedings appear in Arthur M. Schlesinger Jr., ed., *History of U.S. Political Parties* (New York, 1973), 1: 401–10.

36. This anecdote originally appeared in the memoir of the Virginia state-rights Whig Henry A. Wise, *Seven Decades of the Union, The Humanities and Materialism* (Philadelphia, 1872), 170–2. Although the story is in keeping with Clay's character, Wise, Clay's old enemy and writing thirty years after the fact, may have embellished the details. See Remini, *Clay*, 555 n. 31.

37. *Baltimore Republican*, Dec. 11, 1839; Richard S. Elliott, *Notes Taken in Sixty Years* (Boston, 1884), 120–2; *Albany Evening Journal*, quoted in *Log Cabin*, May 23, 1840. Other Whigs were catching on to the rich possibilities of the log cabin symbol simultaneously and independently of Elliot and Elder; see Gunderson, *Log-Cabin Campaign*, 74–75.

38. Rantoul to Van Buren, July 13, 1840, VBP; Donald B. Cole, *Martin Van Buren and the American Political System* (Princeton, 1984), 360.

39. Richardson, 3: 1819; *Log Cabin*, May 30, 1840; Michael Shiner Diary, May 30, 1840, LC, quoted in Schlesinger, *Age of Jackson*, 266. Compare with Cole, *Van Buren*, 367–8.

40. "The Producer's Election Hymn, or an Address to Poor Men," (n.p., 1840), VBP; Jackson to Martin Van Buren, July 31, 1840, in *CAJ*, 6: 68; *Evening Post*, Mar. 10, 1840.

41. Brownson, "The Laboring Classes," *Boston Quarterly Review*, 3 (1840): 358–95. Brown's own account of his rise to notoriety appears in his memoir, "The Convert; Or, Leaves from My Experience," in Henry F. Brownson, ed., *The Works of Orestes A. Brownson* (Detroit, 1884), 5: 50–121; but see also Arthur M. Schlesinger Jr., *Orestes A. Brownson: A Pilgrim's Progress* (Boston, 1939), 28–111.

42. Brownson, "Laboring Classes," 363, 370, 374, 394–5. Among the "priests and pedagogues" Brownson singled out for criticism was William Ellery Channing.

43. *Log Cabin*, Aug. 1, 1840; Woodbury quoted in Schlesinger, *Brownson*, 101.

44. *Evening Post*, July 17, Aug. 8, Oct. 2, 7, 1840; *Boston Post*, Oct. 6, 12, 22, 23, 31, 1840.

45. Charles Ogle, *The Regal Splendor of the President's Palace* (Boston, 1840). On Ogle's conniving with the Pennsylvania Whig leader Thaddeus Stevens, see Gunderson, *Log-Cabin*, 101. In fact, testimony from both Democratic and Whig visitors to the White House affirmed that the place had become badly run down over the years, displaying, at best, an unostentatious comfort that was combined, here and there, with downright shabbiness, all of it covered by a leaky roof. See Cole, *Van Buren*, 345.

46. *Richmond Whig*, Mar. 24, 1840. On the Whig campaign, see Gunderson, *Log-Cabin*, passim; Holt, *Rise and Fall*, 105–11. On the campaign in the South, see also Cooper, *Politics of Slavery*, 132–48.

47. A. B. Norton, ed., *The Great Revolution of 1840: Reminiscences of the Log Cabin and Hard Cider Campaign* (Mount Vernon, OH, 1888), 185.

48. For many of the details in this and the ensuing six paragraphs, see Gunderson, *Log-Cabin Campaign*, 122–218; Sean Wilentz, "1840," in Arthur M. Schlesinger Jr., ed., *Running for President: The Candidates and Their Images* (New York, 1994), 1: 145–53.

49. *Log Cabin*, May 9, 13, Oct. 3, 1840; *Boston Atlas*, Nov. 26, 1840.

50. Clay quoted in Gunderson, *Log-Cabin*, 185; Cooper, *Politics of Slavery*, 136–7 (quotation

on 136). "Instead of expatiating upon Sparta and Lycurgus," the *Globe* reported, "the eloquent H.S. Legaré discourses right sturdily about 'gammon,' and 'scare crow,' and 'scape goat.'" *Globe* [Washington], Aug. 13, 1840.

51.   *Ohio State Journal* [Columbus], June 9, 1840.
52.   See Elizabeth R. Varon, "Tippecanoe and Ladies, Too: White Women and Party Politics in Antebellum Virginia," *JAH*, 82 (1995): 494–521; John M. Sacher, "'The Ladies Are Moving Everywhere': Louisiana Women and Antebellum Politics," *Louisiana History*, 42 (2001): 439–57; Ronald J. Zboray and Mary Saracino Zboray, "Whig Women, Politics and Culture in the Campaign of 1840: Three Perspectives from Massachusetts," *JER*, 17 (1997): 277–315; Gunderson, *Log-Cabin*, esp. 135–9, 143–4. By the time of the 1844 election, Whig women would speak regularly at party rallies and hold their own meetings. On evangelicals' identification with Harrison, see Richard Carwardine, "Evangelicals, Whigs and the Election of William Henry Harrison," *Journal of American Studies*, 17 (1983): 47–75.
53.   Schlesinger, *Age of Jackson*, 291–2; Gunderson, *Log-Cabin*, 129–30.
54.   *Philanthropist* [Cincinnati], Nov. 25, 1840; *Emancipator* [New York], Dec. 9, 1840.
55.   Cole, *Van Buren*, 361–2; Richard H. Sewell, *Ballots for Freedom: Antislavery Politics in the United States, 1837–1860* (New York, 1976), 74–79; Alan M. Kraut, "The Forgotten Reformers: A Profile of Third Party Abolitionists in Antebellum New York," in Lewis Perry and Michael Fellman, eds., *Antislavery Reconsidered: New Perspectives on the Abolitionists* (Baton Rouge, 1979), 119–48; Reinhard O. Johnson, "The Liberty Party in Massachusetts, 1840–1848: Antislavery Third Party Politics in the Bay State," *Civil War History*, 28 (1982): 237–65. Both John Niven and Donald Cole argue that the *Amistad* affair may have contributed greatly to Van Buren's loss of six northern states he had carried in 1836, including New York. See Niven, *Martin Van Buren: The Romantic Age of American Politics* (New York, 1983), 471; Cole, *Van Buren*, 373. On the Democratic Liberty Party constituency — one that would grow in years to come — see also Magdol, *Antislavery Rank and File*, 102–8.
56.   S & I, 2: 684–90.
57.   "The War of the Five Campaigns, "*DR*, 7 (1840): 475–89 (quotation on 486).
58.   Jackson to Martin Van Buren, Nov. 12, 24, 1840, in *CAJ* 6: 82, 83. During the campaign, Jackson had predicted that Van Buren would carry every state south and west of the Potomac, except perhaps Kentucky. Jackson to Martin Van Buren, July 31, 1840, in ibid., 68.
59.   Nathan Sargent, *Public Men and Events* (Philadelphia, 1875), 1: 347.
60.   Jackson to Reverend Andrew J. Crawford, May 1, 1833, in *CAJ*, 5: 72.
61.   The key general studies include Schlesinger, *Age of Jackson*; Bray Hammond, *Banks and Politics in America, from the Revolution to the Civil War* (Princeton, 1957); Richard Hofstadter, *The American Political Tradition and the Men Who Made It* (1948; New York, 1973); Edward Pessen, *Jacksonian America: Society, Personality, and Politics* (Homewood, IL, 1978); Robert H. Wiebe, *The Opening of American Society: From the Adoption of the Constitution to the Eve of Disunion* (New York, 1984); Alexander Saxton, *The Rise and Fall of the White Republic: Class Politics, and Mass Culture in Nineteenth-Century America* (New York, 1990); Harry L. Watson, *Liberty and Power: The Politics of Jacksonian America* (New York, 1990); Charles Sellers, *The Market Revolution: Jacksonian America, 1815–1846* (New York, 1991); Daniel Feller, *The Jacksonian Promise: America, 1815–1840* (Baltimore, 1995).
62.   Van Buren, *Inquiry into the Origins and Course of Political Parties in the United States* (New York, 1867), 230.
63.   For a forceful account of the western radicals' influence, see Richard B. Latner, "A New Look at Jacksonian Politics," *JAH, 61* (1975): 943–69.
64.   "The Producer's Election Hymn," 1840, VBP.
65.   Taney to Andrew Jackson, Oct. 18, 1843, in *CAJ*, 6: 235; *Globe*, July 1, 1839. Feller, *Jacksonian Promise*, offers a sophisticated updating of the consensus interpretation, arguing that Whigs and Democrats shared in the era's "spirit of improvement" but provided alter-

native means of advancing it. I remain more impressed by the evidence of the profound differences between those alternatives.

66. In this sense, the academic current known as the "ethnocultural" school of political history, pioneered by Benson, *Concept*, is still very useful in helping to explain northern political divisions, especially at the state and local level. Studies of southern politics, where the voters were relatively homogeneous, consistently show that "ethnocultural" factors played a much smaller role in the slave states. For an incisive appreciation and critique, see Richard L. McCormick, *The Party Period and Public Policy: American Politics from the Age of Jackson to the Progressive Era* (New York, 1986), 29–63.

67. See, e.g., *Albany Argus*, Nov. 1, 1833, which, confronting the claims that slavery was beneficial, denounced them as "the creed of nullification and of its desperate leader, Mr. Calhoun." Had Van Buren and the Democrats been pro-slavery, they would have seized a golden opportunity and named a conventional state-rights southerner to the national ticket, and not the northern Radicals' favorite, Richard Mentor Johnson — the slaveholder Democrat most likely to repel southern slaveholders. Among the more influential works calling the Jacksonians pro-slavery and the Whig Party much more sensitive on issues of race and slavery is Pessen, *Jacksonian America*, esp. 214–5, 233, 246–7, 322. On "functional" pro-slavery, see John Ashworth, *Slavery, Capitalism, and Politics in the Antebellum Republic*. Vol. 1: *Commerce and Compromise, 1820–1850* (New York, 1995), 337. On northern Jacksonians as not simply anti-abolitionist but actively pro-slavery — arguing chiefly from the writings of unrepresentative figures such as James Kirke Paulding — see above all Saxton, *Rise and Fall*. For a thoughtful assessment of these issues, see John M. McFaul, "Expediency vs. Morality: Jacksonian Politics and Slavery," *JAH*, 62 (1975): 24–39.

68. Bishop Perkins quoted in Ashworth, *Slavery*, 343.

69. *CG*, 25th Congress, 3rd session, Appendix, 85.

70. William M. Gouge, *An Inquiry into the Expediency of Dispensing with Bank Agency and Bank Papers in Fiscal Concerns of the United States* (Philadelphia, 1837), 27–28.

71. There is still a great deal to be discovered about voting participation and results in the early republic, especially before 1824, about which valuable information is currently being compiled by the First Democratization Project at the American Antiquarian Society, under the directorship of Philip J. Lampi. In at least some states where elections were highly contested, participation in presidential elections before 1815 rivaled and even surpassed that of the Jacksonian era and after. Significantly, though, the highest statewide turnouts before 1815, which appear to have ranged between roughly 40 and 80 percent, were almost always in gubernatorial and legislative elections. The major exception, Virginia, had its highest pre-1815 turnout in the presidential election of 1800, when only about one-quarter of the eligible voters actually voted. By contrast, in eighteen of the twenty-three states admitted to the Union before 1824, the turnout in the 1840 presidential election exceeded that recorded for *any* election before 1824. See Richard P. McCormick, "New Perspectives on Jacksonian Politics," *AHR*, 65 (1960): 288–301.

72. The reference is to the illuminating article by Ronald P. Formisano, "Deferential-Participant Politics: The Early Republic's Political Culture," *American Political Science Review*, 68 (1974): 473–87.

73. Quotation in Mary P. Ryan, *Civic Wars: Democracy and Public Life in the American City of the Nineteenth Century* (Berkeley, CA, 1997), 112.

74. *Evening Post*, Nov. 21, 1834; Van Buren, *Autobiography of Martin Van Buren*, John C. Fitzpatrick, ed. (1920; New York, 1973), 1: 303. Van Buren was referring specifically to party developments under President James Monroe. For a strong reassessment of Van Buren's thinking on political parties, see Gerald Leonard, *The Invention of Party Politics: Federalism, Sovereignty, and Constitutional Development in Jacksonian Illinois* (Chapel Hill, 2002), esp. 3–50.

CHAPTER SEVENTEEN: WHIG DEBACLE, DEMOCRATIC CONFUSION

1. *Argument of John Quincy Adams before the Supreme Court of the United States in the Case of the United States Appellants, vs. Cinque, and Others, Africans* (New York, 1841), 89.
2. Richardson, 3: 1860–76.
3. *JQAD*, 10: 439; Howard Jones, *Mutiny on the* Amistad: *The Saga of a Slave Revolt and Its Impact on American Abolition, Law, and Diplomacy* (New York, 1987), 188–94; *U.S. v. The Libellants and Claimants of the Schooner Amistad*, 40 U.S. 518 (1841); Norma Lois Peterson, *The Presidencies of William Henry Harrison and John Tyler* (Lawrence, KS, 1989), 31–43. With Barbour dead, only eight justices voted. Justice Henry Baldwin of Pennsylvania, now a firm Jacksonian, was the sole dissenter, but he did not write an opinion. The Court's ruling did not require the federal government to transport the freed men to Africa. Lewis Tappan duly raised funds by putting some of the Africans (including Sengbe Plehe) on public display to demonstrate their English-language skills, read from the Bible, and tell of their plight. In November 1841, the surviving Africans boarded a chartered ship, and they arrived in Sierra Leone two months later.
4. Jackson to Francis Blair, Apr. 19, 1841, in *CAJ*, 6: 105; Calhoun to Orestes Brownson, Oct. 31, 1841, in *PJCC*, 15: 801.
5. The encounter is described in Lyon G. Tyler, *The Letters and Times of the Tylers* (Richmond, 1884–1992), 33–34. See also Oliver P. Chitwood, *John Tyler: Champion of the Old South* (New York, 1984); Robert J. Morgan, *A Whig Embattled: The Presidency under John Tyler* (Hamden, CT, 1974); Peterson, *Presidencies*; Dan Monroe, *The Republican Vision of John Tyler* (College Station, TX, 2003).
6. On Clay's intentions and actions under Harrison and Tyler, see the appraisals in Merrill Peterson, *The Great Triumvirate: Webster, Clay, and Calhoun* (New York, 1987), 297–318; Robert V. Remini, *Henry Clay: Statesman for the Union* (New York, 1991), 578–99; Michael F. Holt, *The Rise and Fall of the American Whig Party: Jacksonian Politics and the Onset of the Civil War* (New York, 1999), 127–40.
7. Otis to Henry Clay, Dec. 16, 1840, in *PHC*, 9: 465.
8. Clay to John L. Lawrence, Apr. 13, 1841, in ibid., 519.
9. Whigs rejoiced and accompanied a mock casket labeled "The Sub Treasury" in a grand procession down Pennsylvania Avenue from the Capitol, past the White House, where they saluted the president, before winding up at Clay's boardinghouse some fifteen blocks away—as if to pay tribute to the man they considered their party's real leader. Ben: Perley Poore, *Perley's Reminiscences of Sixty Years in the National Metropolis* (Philadelphia, 1886), 1: 271–2.
10. *CG*, 27th Congress, 1st session, 354–5; *New-York Daily Tribune*, Aug. 19, 1841; Thomas Hart Benton, *Thirty Years' View; or, a History of the Working of American Government for Thirty Years, from 1820 to 1850* (New York, 1854–65), 2: 350–3.
11. The protracted maneuvers over the bank bills are well explained in Peterson, *Presidencies*, 57–84.
12. *CG*, 27th Congress, 1st session, 404; Appendix, 364–6, 368–9; "To the Whig Caucus," Sept. 13, 1841, in *PHC*, 9: 608–9.
13. Bancroft to Martin Van Buren, Feb. 21, 1842, quoted in Robert V. Remini, *Daniel Webster: The Man and His Time* (New York, 1997), 570. On the treaty and Webster's departure from the cabinet, see ibid., 535–86; Peterson, *Triumvirate*, 318–34.
14. Van Buren quoted in Donald B. Cole, *Martin Van Buren and the American Political System* (Princeton, 1984), 384. On the scenes of Van Buren's retirement at his Lindenwald estate, see ibid., 381–4; John Niven, *Martin Van Buren: The Romantic Age of American Politics* (New York, 1983), 495–7, 545.
15. On the southern tour, see Cole, *Van Buren*, 384–6; Niven, *Van Buren*, 488–94. The story of Van Buren's encounter with Lincoln appears in Mentor L. Williams, ed., "A Tour of Illinois in 1842," *Journal of the Illinois State Historical Society*, 42 (1949): 292–4.

16. Calhoun to Virgil Maxcy, Sept. 13, 1841, in *PJCC*, 15: 773.

17. *CG*, 27th Congress, 2nd session, 266 (quotation); Appendix, 164–8 (quotations on 168); Calhoun to Anna Maria Calhoun Clemson, Mar. 20, 1842, in *PJCC*, 16: 204.

18. Irving Bartlett, *John C. Calhoun: A Biography* (New York, 1993), 300–1.

19. David Lambert to Willie P. Mangum, Oct. 14, 1841, in Henry Thomas Shanks, ed., *Papers of Willie Person Mangum* (Raleigh, 1950–56), 3: 244–6 (quotation on 245); Glyndon G. Van Deusen, *Thurlow Weed: Wizard of the Lobby* (Boston, 1947), 122.

20. For an overview, see Edwin G. Burrows and Mike Wallace, *Gotham: A History of New York City to 1898* (New York, 1999), 429–645.

21. Charles Z. Lincoln, ed., *Messages from the Governors, Comprising Executive Communications to the Legislature and Other Papers Relating to Legislation* (Albany, 1909), 3: 545; L. Ray Gunn, *The Decline of Authority: Public Economic Policy and Political Development in New York, 1800–1860* (Ithaca, NY, 1988), 159–61; Herbert D. A. Donovan, *The Barnburners: A Study of the Internal Movements in the Political History of New York State and of the Resulting Changes in Political Affiliation, 1830–1852* (New York, 1925), 21–22.

22. *NWR*, May 27, Aug. 12, 1837 (quotation). On banking issues in New York, see esp. James Roger Sharp, *The Jacksonians versus the Banks: Politics in the States after the Panic of 1837* (New York, 1970), 297–305.

23. Glyndon G. Van Deusen, *William Henry Seward* (New York, 1967), 55–86.

24. Donovan, *Barnburners*, 20. Donovan reports that the term *Hunkers* may have derived from the Dutch word *honk*, meaning "post" or "station," connoting the Conservatives' supposed immobility about reforms. Ibid., 33.

25. Ibid., 23–25; Gunn, *Decline*, 151–66; Cole, *Van Buren*, 386–7. For a description of Hoffman, an impressive figure with an expert command of state finances, see Henry B. Stanton, *Random Recollections* (1886; New York, 1887), 85. On Hoffman's politics, see James A. Henretta, "The Strange Birth of Liberal America: Michael Hoffman and the New York Constitutional Convention of 1846," *New York History*, 77 (1996): 151–76.

26. Jacob Gould to Martin Van Buren, Apr. 13, 1844, VBP. For a detailed account of the patronage and personal issues that contributed to the fights in New York, see Donovan, *Barnburners*, 34–51.

27. Sharp, *Jacksonians*, 55–109, 123–210, 274–96.

28. Hone, *The Diary of Philip Hone, 1828–1851*, Bayard Tuckerman, ed. (New York, 1889), 2: 163; Marcy to Martin Van Buren, Nov. 1, 1843, VBP. Although Blair, as editor of the *Globe*, had to keep up appearances of neutrality, he praised Van Buren with special warmth, and every Democrat knew where he stood. See Elbert B. Smith, *Francis Preston Blair* (New York, 1980), 147. Hone, for his part, said that if Clay could not be elected, "I do not know that I shall not be prepared to hurrah for Cass." But amid the mess of the Tyler presidency, Hone also said he would support "[a]nybody but Calhoun, even Van Buren."

29. Michael A. Bernstein, "Northern Labor Finds a Southern Champion: A Note on the Radical Democracy, 1839–1848," in William Pencak and Conrad Wright, eds., *New York and the Rise of American Capitalism: Economic Development and Social and Political History of an American State, 1780–1870* (New York, 1989), 147–67; Arthur M. Schlesinger Jr., *The Age of Jackson* (Boston, 1945), 407 (quotation).

30. *Subterranean and Working Man's Advocate* [New York], Nov. 9, 1844; Bernstein, "Northern Labor," 160–2. Bernstein suggests that among the veteran New York labor reformers, Byrdsall had by far the closest political affinities for Calhoun. The two continued their correspondence for years after 1844. The other old Loco Focos, as well as Evans, seem to have had a fleeting fascination, driven by their search for any Democratic candidate other than Martin Van Buren.

31. Sean Wilentz, *Chants Democratic: New York City & the Rise of the American Working Class* (New York, 1984), 326–35 (quotation on 328).

32. Walsh, *Sketches of the Speeches and Writings of Michael Walsh* (New York, 1843), 13–16; John Tyler to Michael Walsh, Feb. 16, 1843, Michael Walsh Papers, N-YHS; Calhoun to Anna Maria Calhoun Clemson, Mar. 23, 1846, in *PJCC*, 22: 748.

33. *Evening Post* [New York], Dec. 5, 1840.
34. *RD*, 22nd Congress, 2nd session, 519–53 (quotation on 543). The text of the "Disquisition," as published in 1851, after Calhoun's death, appears in *PJCC*, 28: 1–68.
35. *PJCC*, 28: 13; *RD*, 24th Congress, 2nd session, 303–4.
36. Binney to Dr. [Francis] Lieber, Jan. 5, 1861, in Charles Chauncey Binney, *The Life of Horace Binney with Selections from His Letters* (Philadelphia, 1903), 314.
37. Brownson in *Boston Quarterly Review*, 5 (1842): 89–90. See also Brownson, "Democracy and Liberty," *DR*, 12 (1843), 374–87. To the latter, John O'Sullivan added a long rebuttal, lamenting that Brownson had lost "so much more than we did" because of the 1840 elections: "his good humor with his party, and his confidence in the principle of self-government." On Brownson's campaign work for Calhoun, see Arthur M. Schlesinger Jr., *Orestes A. Brownson: A Pilgrim's Progress* (Boston, 1939), 160–2.
38. Brownson in *Boston Quarterly Review*, 4 (1841): 86.
39. On Dorr and the Dorr War, see Arthur May Mowry, *The Dorr War, or, the Constitutional Struggle in Rhode Island* (Providence, 1901); Peter J. Coleman, *The Transformation of Rhode Island, 1790–1860* (Providence, 1963), 274–94; Marvin E. Gettleman, *The Dorr Rebellion: A Study in American Radicalism, 1833–1849* (New York, 1973); George M. Dennison, *The Dorr War: Republicanism on Trial, 1831–1861* (Lexington, KY, 1976).
40. [Dorr], *An Address to the People of Rhode-Island, from the Convention Assembled at Providence* (Providence, 1834), 56. On Dorr's antislavery and antiracist views, his connections to abolitionists including James G. Birney, and his support of the American Anti-Slavery Society, see Dennison, *Dorr War*, 22.
41. On early reform movements and the formation of the Rhode Island Suffrage Association, see Mowry, *Dorr War*, 8–55; Coleman, *Transformation*, 218–74. On Luther's involvement in suffrage agitation, including the Dorrite movement, see Louis Hartz, "Seth Luther: Working-Class Rebel," *New England Quarterly*, 13 (1940): 406–9.
42. The early organizing by the Suffrage Association can be followed in the reform paper *New Age* [Providence], from January through July 1841; see above all June 3, 25, 1841. The complete text of the People's Constitution appears in Mowry, *Dorr War*, 322–46. Among the interesting features of the agitation was the heavy involvement of women in support and fund-raising efforts. See Ronald P. Formisano, "The Role of Women in the Dorr Rebellion," *Rhode Island History*, 51 (1993): 88–104.
43. On the returns for the 1842 referendum, see Coleman, *Transformation*, 276, which shows the state roughly—but only roughly—divided between its more populous, urban northern counties, opposed to the legislature's proposed constitution, and the more conservative rural and maritime counties to the South.
44. *New York American*, June 9, 1842; *NWR*, May 21, 1842; *Subterranean* [New York], June 21, 1845.
45. Among the arsenal's defenders, placing political principles above family, were Dorr's conservative father, Sullivan Dorr, and his uncle, Crawford Allen, the proprietors of a major cotton-mill complex in Woonsocket.
46. On Luther's sad end, see Hartz, "Luther," 409–10; Carl Gersuny, "Seth Luther: The Road from Chepachet," *Rhode Island History*, 33 (1974): 47–55.
47. Among the black leaders who denounced the Dorrites was an ex-slave Garrisonian named Frederick Douglass. See Douglass, *Life and Times of Frederick Douglass: His Early Life as a Slave, His Escape from Bondage, and His Complete History* (1892; New York, 1962), 220–1. In addition to excluding the Irish, the new draft constitution limited voting in all towns and cities on matters affecting taxation and financial policies to property owners, further undercutting reform.
48. F. H. Green, *Might and Right: By a Rhode Islander* (1843; Providence, 1844), 333–7.
49. *Luther v. Borden*, 48 U.S. 1 (How.), 1849. On the case, see Michael A. Conron, "Law, Politics, and Chief Justice Taney: A Reconsideration of the *Luther v. Borden* Decision," *American Journal of Legal History*, 11 (1967): 377–88; Dennison, *Dorr War*, 140–92; Remini, *Webster*, 640–1. On the hidebound political and legal ideology of the Rhode Island con-

servatives, see William M. Wiecek, "A Peculiar Conservatism and the Dorr Rebellion: Constitutional Clash in Jacksonian America," *American Journal of Legal History*, 22 (1978): 237–53.

50. For quotations, see John B. Rae, "Democrats and the Dorr Rebellion," *New England Quarterly*, 9 (1936), 476–83; John Ashworth, *"Agrarians" and "Aristocrats": Party Political Ideology in the United States, 1837–1846* (Cambridge, 1983), 226–7. Some Democratic leaders, although sympathetic to the Dorrites, disapproved of their conduct and their revolutionary principles of majority rule. "Their affairs there are in confusion," George Bancroft wrote to Van Buren, "and offer no safe ground for practical statesmanship." Bancroft to Martin Van Buren [Oct. 1843], quoted in Schlesinger, *Age of Jackson*, 416. Most radical and even moderate Democrats, however, would remain more shocked at the standing government's actions than at the Dorrites'. Later elevated to the Supreme Court, Woodbury dissented from the majority opinion in *Luther v. Borden*, taking special exception to the official repression.

51. *National Intelligencer* [Washington], May 24, 1842; *Hartford Courant*, July 2, 1842; *Albany Evening Journal*, Oct. 29, 1844; Clay quoted in Gettleman, *Dorr Rebellion*, 165.

52. Calhoun to William Smith, July 3, 1845, in Richard K. Crallé, *The Works of John C. Calhoun* (New York, 1883), 6: 229.

53. Brownson, "Democracy and Liberty," *DR*, 12 (1843), 375. On Brownson's early support of Dorr, see Schlesinger, *Age of Jackson*, 417.

54. Bartlett, *Calhoun*, 304–5.

CHAPTER EIGHTEEN: ANTISLAVERY, ANNEXATION, AND THE ADVENT OF YOUNG HICKORY

1. *Emancipator* [New York], Nov. 12, 1840; Stewart to Samuel Webb, Nov. 13, 1841, quoted in Richard H. Sewell, *Ballots for Freedom: Antislavery Politics in the United States 1837–1860* (New York, 1976), 82. On the Liberty Party's early development, in addition to Sewell's excellent study, see Theodore Clarke Smith, *The Liberty and Free Soil Parties in the Northwest* (1897; New York, 1967), 27–120; Vernon L. Volpe, *Forlorn Hope of Freedom: The Liberty Party in the Old Northwest, 1838–1848* (Kent, OH, 1990), 34–79.

2. Smith to Abby Kelley, July 24, 1843, in Sewell, *Ballots*, 84.

3. *Emancipator*, May 20, 27, 1841. On Bailey's early antislavery career and assumption of the editorship of the *Philanthropist*, see Stanley Harrold, *Gamaliel Bailey and Antislavery Union* (Kent, OH, 1986), 1–24. In 1843, the party also began publishing brief tracts summarizing its message, along with two dozen struggling but energetic new sheets begun between 1840 and 1844.

4. Harrold, *Bailey*, 25–69; Morris quoted in Sewell, *Ballots*, 90; Leavitt to Salmon P. Chase, Dec. 6, 1842, in *SPCP*; *Philanthropist*, March 16, 1842.

5. *American Freeman* [Milwaukee], June 1, 1844.

6. On the realities of the Slave Power, far more critical of Van Buren and the Democrats than of the Whigs for sustaining it, see Leonard L. Richards, *The Slave Power: The Free North and Southern Domination, 1780–1860* (Baton Rouge, 2000), esp. 107–33.

7. *Signal of Liberty* [Ann Arbor], Sept. 15, Oct. 13, 1841. On the Democratic themes in political abolitionism, see also Sean Wilentz, "Slavery, Antislavery, and Jacksonian Democracy," in Melvyn Stokes and Stephen Conway, eds., *The Market Revolution in America: Social, Political, and Religious Expressions, 1800–1880* (Charlottesville, 1996), 202–23; above all, Jonathan H. Earle, *Jacksonian Antislavery and the Politics of Free Soil* (Chapel Hill, 2004).

8. *Signal of Liberty*, Dec. 26, 1842.

9. James Brewer Stewart, *Joshua R. Giddings and the Tactics of Radical Politics* (Cleveland, 1970), 95–98; Harrold, *Bailey*, 41–54 (quotation on 54).

10. Stewart, *Giddings*, 69–71 (quotation on 70); Hugh Davis, *Joshua Leavitt: Evangelical Abolitionist* (Baton Rouge, 1990), 188–9.

11. Tappan quoted in Bertram Wyatt-Brown, *Lewis Tappan and the Evangelical War against Slavery* (Cleveland, 1969), 269; Davis, *Leavitt*, 189–90, 269; Garrison quoted in Henry Mayer, *All on Fire: William Lloyd Garrison and the Abolition of Slavery* (New York, 1998), 326.

12. *Proceedings and Debates of the Convention of the Commonwealth of Pennsylvania, To Propose Amendments to the Constitution* (Harrisburg, 1837–39), 9: 328. On the northern crackdown on black political and civil rights, see Leon Litwack, *North of Slavery: The Negro in the Free States, 1790–1860* (Chicago, 1961), esp. 64–152.

13. *Prigg v. Commonwealth of Pennsylvania*, 41 U.S. 539 (Pet.) 1842. On the legal and political background to the case, and the case itself, see Thomas D. Morris, *Free Men All: The Personal Liberty Laws of the North, 1780–1861* (Baltimore, 1974), 42–106.

14. *Herald of Freedom* [Concord, MA], Mar. 8, 1839; Larry Gara, *The Liberty Line: The Legend of the Underground Railroad* (Lexington, KY, 1961), 101–2; Benjamin Quarles, *Black Abolitionists* (New York, 1969), 90–115, 143–67; James Oliver Horton and Lois E. Horton, *In Hope of Liberty: Culture, Community, and Protest among Northern Free Blacks* (New York, 1997), 229–30. Ruggles had been a familiar figure in black antislavery circles since the early 1830s, and in 1838, he expanded his established bookselling operation by starting up the nation's first black magazine, the *Mirror of Liberty*. But his greatest renown came with his vigilance work, hiding and protecting endangered blacks and providing them with legal assistance.

15. *Proceedings of the Great Convention of the Friends of Freedom in the Eastern and Middle States, Held in Boston, October 1, 2, & 3, 1845* (Lowell, MA, 1845), 18; *Liberty Standard* [Hallowell, ME], Dec. 7, 1842.

16. On blacks and the Liberty Party, see Quarles, *Black Abolitionists*, 183–5; Sewell, *Ballots*, 95–101. There were elements of patronizing prejudice in the Liberty Party, just as there were in the American Anti-Slavery Society. To say that blacks could be elevated to enjoy their American rights might easily be taken to mean that they still had a long way to go before they deserved full equality. Thomas Morris had once opposed black suffrage in Ohio, although by the early 1840s he apparently had changed his mind. In an embarrassing incident, causing what one Liberty paper called "ill-concealed mortification," the Michigan Liberty Party state convention in 1843 refused to allow two black delegates to participate in making nominations because they were not legal voters. Yet shortly thereafter, at a national Liberty Party conclave, also held in Buffalo, Henry Highland Garnet and another black leader, Samuel Ringgold Ward, delivered formal addresses, while a black New York minister, Charles B. Ray, acted as one of the convention secretaries.

17. The best biography is William S. McFeely, *Frederick Douglass* (New York, 1991); but see also Benjamin Quarles, *Frederick Douglass* (Englewood Cliffs, NJ, 1968).

18. On Douglass's early antislavery speeches, see McFeely, *Douglass*, 83–103.

19. Ibid., 104–14; Sewell, *Ballots*, 101.

20. On the politics of the "hard" gag rule, see William W. Freehling, *The Road to Disunion: Secessionists at Bay, 1776–1854* (New York, 1990), 345–50. Thompson, a state-rights Whig and pro-slavery man of long standing, based his efforts on bedrock principle; Johnson was a more nationalist southern Whig, who "to escape from the charge of being an abolitionist," John Quincy Adams observed, "is obliged to take an overcharge of zeal against the right of petition." *JQAD*, 10: 204. On Adams and the continuing fight against the gag rule, see also Leonard L. Richards, *The Life and Times of Congressman John Quincy Adams* (New York, 1986), 139–45.

21. CG, 27th Congress, 2nd session, 168.

22. Ibid., 168–77, 179–84, 186–95, 197–203, 203–15 (quotations on 208).

23. The most thorough account is George Hendrick and Willene Hendrick, *The Creole Mutiny: A Tale of Revolt aboard a Slave Ship* (Chicago, 2003); but see also Howard Jones, "The Peculiar Institution and National Honor: The Case of the *Creole* Slave Revolt," *Civil*

War History, 21 (1975): 28–56; Edward D. Jervey and C. Edward Huber, "The Creole Affair," *Journal of Negro History*, 65 (1980): 196–211.

24. Frederick Douglass contributed a novella, "The Heroic Slave," some years later; see Hendrick and Hendrick, *Creole Mutiny*, 128–37. See also Jones, "Peculiar Institution," 37; Roy E. Finkenbine, "The Symbolism of Black Mutiny: Black Abolitionist Responses to the *Amistad* and *Creole* Incidents," in Jane Hathaway, ed., *Rebellion, Repressions, and Reinvention: Mutiny in Comparative Perspective* (Westport, CT, 2001), 233–52.

25. Stewart, *Giddings*, 3–70 (quotation on 31). On the settlement of the *Creole* case, see Jones, "Peculiar Institution," 39–47.

26. Stewart, *Giddings*, 70–74; CG, 27th Congress, 2nd session, 308.

27. Gates to James G. Birney, Mar. 24, 1842, in Dwight L. Dumond, ed., *Letters of James Gillespie Birney, 1831–1857* (New York, 1938), 2: 688.

28. Stewart, *Giddings*, 74–76 (quotation on 74).

29. Quotations in ibid., 76, 78.

30. Concerns about Van Buren's ability to unite the Democracy heightened in 1843, when the Whigs, with all of their difficulties in Washington, won an impressive number of state and local races, including state elections in Massachusetts, Maryland, Virginia, North Carolina, Georgia, Kentucky, and Tennessee. Even the pro–Van Buren New York *Evening Post* was worried, arguing that although the Hunkers were the great malefactors, the fall elections showed "how loosely [the Democracy] is organized, and with how little mutual understanding its different portions have acted." See Michael A. Morrison, "Martin Van Buren, the Democracy, and the Partisan Politics of Texas Annexation," *JSH*, 61 (1995): 700–9 (quotation on 700).

31. *Proceedings and Debates of the Virginia State Convention of 1829–30* (Richmond, 1830), esp. 65–79. See Claude H. Hall, *Abel Parker Upshur: Conservative Virginian, 1790–1844* (Madison, WI, 1963), which is especially strong on Upshur's career before 1840.

32. Upshur quoted in Freehling, *Road to Disunion*, 390.

33. Upshur quoted in ibid., 391.

34. CG, 25th Congress, 1st session, 24.

35. Upshur to Beverly Tucker, Mar. 13, 1843, quoted in Freehling, *Road to Disunion*, 392.

36. The best account of these maneuverings, and of the Calhoun-Upshur connection, is Frederick Merk, *Slavery and the Annexation of Texas* (New York, 1972), 3–82; but see also Freehling, *Road to Disunion*, 394–8.

37. On Whig opposition to expansion and annexation, see esp. Frederick Merk, *Manifest Destiny and Mission in American History: A Reinterpretation* (New York, 1963), esp. 39–40. Michael A. Morrison, "Westward the Curse of Empire: Texas Annexation and the American Whig Party," *JER*, 10 (1990): 221–49.

38. "The Great Nation of Futurity," *DR*, 6 (1839): 430; "Annexation," *DR*, 17 (1845): 5. The most thorough and useful studies of Manifest Destiny remain Albert K. Weinstein, *Manifest Destiny: A Study of Nationalist Expansionism in American History* (Baltimore, 1935); Merk, *Manifest Destiny and Mission*. Harsher and less subtle—but provocative— assessments include Reginald Horsman, *Race and Manifest Destiny: The Origins of American Racial Anglo-Saxonism* (Cambridge, MA, 1981); Thomas R. Hietala, *Manifest Design: Anxious Aggrandizement in Jacksonian America* (Ithaca, NY, 1983); Anders Stephanson, *Manifest Destiny: American Expansionism and the Empire of Right* (New York, 1995). On the pro-democratic, pro-expansionist intelligentsia, centered in New York City, Edward L. Widmer, *Young America: The Flowering of Democracy in New York City* (New York, 1999), is superb. On related democratic themes elsewhere, see Norman A. Tuturow, *Texas Annexation and the Mexican War: A Study of the Old Northwest* (Palo Alto, 1978).

39. The full history of America's image among radicals and liberals in Britain and Europe remains to be written, but there are interesting beginnings in Joseph Rossi, *The Image of America in Mazzini's Writings* (Madison, WI, 1954); Ray Boston, *British Chartists in America* (New York, 1971).

40. "English Chartism and English Credit," *DR*, 8 (1840): 179–93 (quotation on 184–5); Widmer, *Young America*, 58–59.
41. "Introduction," *DR*, 1 (1837), 9; "Annexation," *DR*, 17 (1845), 8.
42. Jackson to Francis Blair, May 11, 1844, in *CAJ*, 6: 286.
43. *Evening Post* [New York], Feb. 20, 1840; Sedgwick, *Thoughts on the Proposed Annexation of Texas* (New York, 1844), 34–35; Wright to Martin Van Buren, Apr. 8, 1844, VBP; Richard H. Sewell, *John Parker Hale and the Politics of Abolition* (Cambridge, MA, 1965), 48. On Sedgwick, and on Hale's gradual conversion to antislavery in the early 1840s, see Earle, *Jacksonian Antislavery*, 52–54, 83–85.
44. Maxcy to John C. Calhoun, Dec. 3, 10, 1843, in *PJCC*, 17: 586 (quotation), 599–603; Silas Wright to Martin Van Buren, Jan. 2, 1844, VBP; John Arthur Garraty, *Silas Wright* (New York, 1949), 235–6.
45. For the details, see Freehling, *Road to Disunion*, 402–6.
46. On the *Princeton* disaster, see Hall, *Upshur*, 209–13.
47. Calhoun's letter to Pakenham, Apr. 15, 1844, in *PJCC*, 18: 273–8. On the political background to the Pakenham affair, see, above all, Charles Grier Sellers, *James K. Polk, Continentalist, 1843–46* (Princeton, 1966), 56–61. On the politics of annexation and the election of 1844, see esp. Merk, *Slavery*, 83–100.
48. Calhoun to Edward Pakenham, Apr. 15, 1844, in *PJCC*, 18: 277.
49. Benton quoted in Sellers, *Polk, Continentalist*, 59. On Tappan, see Daniel Feller, "Brother in Arms: Benjamin Tappan and the Antislavery Democracy," *JAH*, 88 (2001): 48–74.
50. *Globe* [Washington], Mar. 20, 1844; *Richmond Enquirer*, Mar. 22, 1844; Wright to Martin Van Buren, Apr. 11, 1844, VBP. While Azariah Flagg urged Van Buren to oppose annexation, George Bancroft, Levi Woodbury, and various southern Democrats counseled him to support it. Donald B. Cole, *Martin Van Buren and the American Political System* (Princeton, 1984), 392.
51. Butler to Martin Van Buren, Mar. 29, Apr. 6, 29, 1844, VBP.
52. Van Buren to William H. Hammett, Apr. 20, 1844. Francis Blair published the letter in the *Globe*, Apr. 27.
53. *National Intelligencer* [Washington], Apr. 27, 1844.
54. Clay to John J. Crittenden, Apr. 21, 1844, quoted in Peterson, *Triumvirate*, 360.
55. Clay to Thurlow Weed, May 6, 1844, quoted in Remini, *Clay*, 645. The Whig platform appears in S & I, 2: 807.
56. Butler to Martin Van Buren, May 27, 1844, VBP. An accessible selection from the official transcript, "Proceedings of the Democratic National Convention, Baltimore, May 27–30, 1844," appears in S & I, 2: 829–52. See also Sellers, *Polk, Continentalist*, 85–107.
57. "Proceedings," 841–9; John L. O'Sullivan to Martin Van Buren, May 29, 1844, Benjamin Butler to Martin Van Buren, May 31, 1844, VBP; Sellers, *Polk, Continentalist*, 96–98; Cole, *Van Buren*, 397.
58. Van Buren to Amos Kendall, June 12, 1844, VBP; Garraty, *Silas Wright*, 279–86.
59. Daniel to Martin Van Buren, June 11, 1844, VBP; S & I, 2: 851.
60. For a shrewd, if highly partisan, assessment of why Polk's nomination was "necessary to the salvation of the party," see *Globe*, June 26, 1844.
61. The indispensable biography remains Charles Grier Sellers, *James K. Polk, Jacksonian, 1795–1843* (Princeton, 1957). Elected governor of Tennessee in 1839, Polk, like every Democrat, had to answer to charges that Jackson's and Van Buren's policies had ruined the economy. In 1841, he was decisively defeated for reelection by a young, wisecracking, first-term Whig state legislator named James Chamberlain Jones, dubbed "Lean Jimmy" Jones, because, though six feet tall, he weighed only 125 pounds.
62. Sedgwick to Charles Sumner, June 9, 1844, Charles Sumner Papers, HU; Wright to Benjamin Butler, June 8, 1844, Wright-Butler Papers, NYPL; Jabez D. Hammond, *Life and Times of Silas Wright, Late Governor of the State of New York* (Syracuse, NY, 1848), 412, 499–500. Until the 1844 convention, Polk still considered himself a Van Burenite, and would have happily run for vice president with Van Buren at the head of the ticket. See

also Sellers, *Polk, Continentalist*, 103. On Polk's politics and the reassertion of Democratic unity after the party's convention, see also Morrison, "Martin Van Buren," 711–5.

63. Clay to Willie Mangum, June 7, 1844, in *PHC*, 10: 66. The official Whig paper in Washington crowed that Polk's nomination "may be considered as the dying gasp, the last breath, of the 'Democratic' party." *National Intelligencer*, May 20, 1844.

64. On the Democratic campaign, see the detailed accounts in Sellers, *Polk, Continentalist*, 108–61; Michael F. Holt, *The Rise and Fall of the American Whig Party: Jacksonian Politics and the Onset of the Civil War* (New York, 1999), 187–94. On Tyler's short-lived campaign and Jackson's successful effort to get him to withdraw, see Robert J. Morgan, *A Whig Embattled: The Presidency under John Tyler* (Hamden, CT, 1974), 171–2; Robert V. Remini, *Andrew Jackson and the Course of American Democracy, 1833–1845* (New York, 1989) 504–5.

65. Weed to Granger, Sept. 3, 1844, quoted in Holt, *Rise and Fall*, 186. On the Whig campaign, see ibid., 176–94; Remini, *Clay*, 647–67.

66. *Philanthropist*, Sept. 11, 1844; *Morning Courier and Enquirer* [New York], Aug. 23, 1842; *New-York Daily Tribune*, Oct. 10, 19, 26, Nov. 2, 1844.

67. *New-York Daily Tribune*, Nov. 11, 1844. The Liberty Party vote may also have deprived Clay of victory in Indiana and Michigan.

68. *JQAD*, 12: 110. For an exacting and expert analysis of the 1844 returns, see Holt, *Rise and Fall*, 194–207. See also Morrison, "Martin Van Buren," 721–4; Vernon L. Volpe, "The Liberty Party and Polk's Election, 1844," *Historian*, 53 (1991): 691–710. Volpe notes other factors that contributed to the outcome, including Polk's wooing of pro-protectionists in Pennsylvania and Clay's vacillation on Texas, which cost him southern votes.

69. *JQAD*, 12: 110.

70. *CG*, 28th Congress, 1st session, 652. On the congressional maneuverings, see Merk, *Slavery and Annexation*, 101–81; Freehling, *Road to Disunion*, 440–8.

71. *CG*, 28th Congress, 2nd session, 362, 372. Jackson predicted that, by resisting Tyler and Upshur but achieving annexation, Benton would "be hailed again by the democracy of the U. States as their champion & leader." Jackson quoted in Remini, *Course of American Democracy*, 510.

CHAPTER NINETEEN: THE BITTER FRUITS OF MANIFEST DESTINY

1. See Norma Lois Peterson, *The Presidencies of William Henry Harrison and John Tyler* (Lawrence, KS, 1989), 251–9.

2. Richardson, 3: 2231; Milo Milton Quaife, ed., *The Diary of James K. Polk during His Presidency, 1845 to 1849* (Chicago, 1910), 4: 42. Bancroft wrote several slightly differing accounts of his conversation with Polk. This version follows the one presented in Charles Grier Sellers, *James K. Polk, Continentalist, 1843–1846* (Princeton, 1966), 213.

3. See Sellers, *Polk, Continentalist*, 167–212.

4. Jackson to Francis P. Blair, Apr. 9, 1845, to James K. Polk, Apr. 11, 1845, in *CAJ*, 6: 395, 399; Polk to Cave Johnson, Dec. 21, 1844, in "Letters of James K. Polk to Cave Johnson, 1833–1848," *Tennessee Historical Magazine*, 1 (1915): 254.

5. Jackson to Jesse Duncan Elliott, Mar. 27, 1845, in *CAJ*, 6: 391.

6. *Madisonian* [Washington], Apr. 7, 1845.

7. Richardson, 3: 2229; Sellers, *Polk, Continentalist*, 324–30.

8. Niles to Martin Van Buren, Aug. 8, 1846, VBP; Sellers, *Polk, Continentalist*, 451–68. One of the selective opponents, a young East Tennessean and doctrinaire Jacksonian named Andrew Johnson, protested the proposed high tariffs on tea and coffee for showing favoritism to "the wealthy man . . . who sits at home behind his bank counter, and realizes his hundreds and thousands from speculating, stockjobbing and shaving." Johnson pro-

posed instead an annual tax on bank stock, bonds, money at interest, capital invested in manufacturing, and gold and silver plate. CG, 29th Congress, 1st session, 10011–3.

9. CG, 29th Congress, 1st session, 595; Sellers, *Polk, Continentalist*, 468–71. Twelve old-line Conservatives, remnants of the old Tallmadge-Rives faction, initially opposed the measure but quickly gave way. Congress also passed the Public Warehouse Act, which allowed importers to stockpile goods in bad times without paying duties until market conditions improved (another blow to protectionism), and Polk vetoed an expensive river-and-harbors bill, supported by Midwestern Democrats.

10. Sellers, *Polk, Continentalist*, 357–97.

11. *Union* [Washington], June 6, 1845; Sellers, *Polk, Continentalist*, 213–30.

12. *Union*, Oct. 2, 1845; Sellers, *Polk, Continentalist*, 259–66. Simultaneously, Polk directed American naval forces in the Pacific to seize San Francisco, in the event that war with Mexico commenced.

13. Sellers, *Polk, Continentalist*, 398–404.

14. Ibid., 404–9; Richardson, 4: 449–50; CG, 29th Congress, 1st session, 795–804, 810.

15. *New York Herald*, May 21, 1846; *Sangamo Journal* [Illinois], June 4, 1846, quoted in Donald W. Riddle, *Lincoln Runs for Congress* (New Brunswick, NJ, 1948), 170.

16. CG, 29th Congress, 1st session, 794. On the antislavery, antiwar Whigs, see John H. Schroeder, *Mr. Polk's War: American Opposition and Dissent, 1846–1848* (Madison, WI, 1973), 29–32.

17. Irving Bartlett, *John C. Calhoun: A Biography* (New York, 1993), 334; CG, 29th Congress, 1st session, 796; R. M. Saunders to James K. Polk, May 14, 1846, James K. Polk Papers, LC. On the Calhounites and the debate on going to war, see Sellers, *Polk, Continentalist*, 416–21. On the broader misgivings about the war among Calhounites and South Carolinians generally, see Ernest McPherson Lander Jr., *Reluctant Imperialists: Calhoun, the South Carolinians, and the Mexican War* (Baton Rouge, 1980).

18. *Brooklyn Daily Eagle*, May 11, 1846, in Walt Whitman, *The Gathering of the Forces*, Cleveland Rogers and John Black, eds. (New York, 1920), 1: 240; Dix to Azariah Flagg, May 15, 1846, Azariah Cutting Flagg Papers, NYPL; E. B. Lee to S. P. Lee, May 17, 1846, Blair-Lee Papers, PU. On growing northern Democratic restiveness over the war, see also Jonathan H. Earle, *Jacksonian Democracy and the Politics of Free Soil, 1824–1854* (Chapel Hill, 2004), 66–68.

19. Richard H. Sewell, *John P. Hale and the Politics of Abolition* (Cambridge, MA, 1965), 52–59; Earle, *Jacksonian Antislavery*, 78–102. On the New Hampshire Democracy, see Donald B. Cole, *Jacksonian Democracy in New Hampshire, 1800–1851* (Cambridge, MA, 1970), esp. 216–33.

20. Sewell, *Hale*, 59–85; Stanley Harrold, *Gamaliel Bailey and Antislavery Union* (Kent, OH, 1986), 74–75; *Poems by John G. Whittier* (Boston, 1850), 182.

21. Sewell, *Hale*, 84; idem, *Ballots for Freedom: Antislavery Politics in the United States 1837–1860* (New York, 1976), (quotation, 129).

22. Van Buren to George Bancroft, Feb. 15, 1845, "Van-Buren-Bancroft Correspondence, 1830–1845," MHS *Proceedings*, 42 (1909): 439.

23. A reliable and engaging account of the military action, from the standpoints of both opposing armies, appears in John S. D. Eisenhower, *So Far from God: The U.S. War with Mexico, 1846–1848* (New York, 1989), see 98–232.

24. Quaife, ed., *Diary*, 2: 305, 5: 251.

25. *Brooklyn Daily Eagle*, Apr. 16, 1847, in Whitman, *Gathering*, 1: 85.

26. Thorpe, 2: 673–4. On the state conventions of the 1840s, see also Laura J. Scalia, *America's Jeffersonian Experiment: Remaking State Constitutions, 1820–1850* (De Kalb, IL, 1999)

27. *Proceedings and Debates of the Convention of Louisiana. Which Assembled in the City of New Orleans, January 14, 184[5]* (New Orleans, 1845), 105. The best review of constitutional developments in Louisiana in these decades remains Roger W. Shugg, *Origins of Class Struggle in Louisiana: A Social History of White Farmers and Laborers during Slavery and After, 1840–1875* (Baton Rouge, 1939), 121–56; see also Thomas F. Ruffin, "The

Common Man Fights Back," *North Louisiana Historical Association Journal,* 7 (1976): 91–95, on methods used by small-property holders to gain the vote prior to 1845.

28. *Proceedings . . . Louisiana,* 116; Thorpe, 6: 3520–68.

29. The best study of Virginia reform and its troubles after 1830 is William G. Shade, *Democratizing the Old Dominion: Virginia and the Second Party System, 1824–1861* (Charlottesville, 1996), esp. 262–92.

30. The Democratic and Whig appeals can be followed, respectively, in *Valley Star* [Lexington], July 17, 1845, Feb. 5, 1846; *Lexington Gazette,* June 26, 1845, Feb. 12, 1846. See F. N. Boney, *John Letcher of Virginia; The Story of Virginia's Civil War Governor* (University, AL, 1966), esp. 36–52. The Whigs were prominent in the western counties chiefly because popular interest in gaining new roads and schools attracted voters to the party of Henry Clay. Thus, Whigs were particularly conspicuous in the ranks of the reformers, most notably a veteran of the 1829–30 constitutional convention, Samuel McDowell Moore. Still, the argument that the reform movement "continued to be primarily sectional rather than partisan" is persuasive. See Shade, *Old Dominion,* 266.

31. The story of the debate, and of its effects, is well told in William Gleason Bean, "The Ruffner Pamphlet of 1847: An Antislavery Aspect of Virginia Sectionalism," *Virginia Magazine of History and Biography,* 61 (1958): 260–82. Ruffner was an interesting independent-minded provincial intellectual, of a kind still common enough in the South (and especially the upper South) in the 1840s. He had distinguished himself sufficiently as a theologian to be awarded an honorary degree from Princeton, but he also wrote works in other veins, including a novel, *Judith Bensaddi: A Tale,* published in 1839—an early sympathetic treatment of the condition of the Jews in America, replete with vivid descriptions of the wild beauty of Rockbridge County. A dark-eyed man with an impressive high forehead, Ruffner commanded great respect at the Franklin Society's gatherings. That he had inherited a country estate, including slaves, from his father gave his arguments about emancipation added credibility. He pointedly signed the pamphlet that grew out of his Franklin Society remarks "A Slaveholder." On the Franklin Society, see Charles W. Turner, "The Franklin Society, 1800–1891," *Virginia Magazine of History and Biography,* 66 (1958): 432–47.

32. Henry Ruffner, *Address to the People of West Virginia* (Lexington, 1847), (quotation, 11).

33. *Latimer Journal and North Star,* Nov. 11, 1842. On the legal and political aspects of the Latimer case, see Thomas D. Morris, *Free Men All: The Personal Liberty Laws of the North, 1780–1861* (Baltimore, 1974), 109–17.

34. *Liberator* [Boston], Nov. 4, 1842; "The Latimer and Great Massachusetts Petition" (1842), Adams Family Papers, MHS.

35. Martin B. Duberman, *Charles Francis Adams, 1807–1886* (Boston, 1961), 81; *Latimer Journal and North Star,* May 10, 1843; Morris, *Free Men All,* 114.

36. Morris, *Free Men All,* 117–9; Sewell, *Ballots,* 129. In certain technical respects, the new Massachusetts and Pennsylvania laws were actually stiffer than the earlier state law that *Prigg* overturned, which had allowed for some limited involvement of state officials in adjudicating fugitive slave claims—involvement that the new laws banned.

37. Thorpe 1: 549, 2: 1125, 7: 4080–1. Three of the exceptional states that allowed blacks to vote—Massachusetts, Vermont, and New Hampshire—were among the four that passed personal liberty laws before 1848. Ohio's revised Constitution of 1851 would sustain the white male suffrage. Ibid., 5: 2924.

38. Hoffman to Azariah Flagg, Aug. 3, 1842, Azariah Cutting Flagg Papers, NYPL. When the battle over Bouck's canal-funding plans ended in stalemate, the pro-Radical *Evening Post* launched a highly coordinated agitation campaign, which produced the State Association for Constitutional Reform, with Hoffman as its president. Hoffman spelled out a ten-point reform program, including sharp restriction of the legislature's powers over debt and expenditure. The proposals' popular impact was great enough to force Governor Bouck to adopt a far more conciliatory tone in his second annual message, in which he positioned himself roughly midway between the Hunkers and the Radicals on internal improve-

ments. Bouck would be ousted anyway in the 1844 election, replaced by the Radical Silas Wright. On these and related events, see Herbert D. A. Donovan, *The Barnburners: A Study of the Internal Movements in the Political History of New York State and of the Resulting Changes in Political Affiliation, 1830–1852* (New York, 1925), 35–58; L. Ray Gunn, *The Decline of Authority: Public Economic Policy and Political Development in New York State, 1800–1860* (Ithaca, NY, 1988), 170–97; Charles W. McCurdy, *The Anti-Rent Era in New York Law and Politics, 1839–1865* (Chapel Hill, 2001), 121–7.

39. The best accounts are Reeve Huston, *Land and Freedom: Rural Society, Popular Protest, and Party Politics in Antebellum New York* (New York, 2000), esp. 87–194; McCurdy, *Anti-Rent Era*, esp. 128–316; but see also Earle, *Jacksonian Politics*, 35–37, 58–62, on the links among the Anti-Rent wars, land reform ideology, and the rise of antislavery Free Soil politics.

40. *Evening Post*, Dec. 18, 23 (quotation), 1844. On Evans and the land reformers, see Sean Wilentz, *Chants Democratic: New York City & the Rise of the American Working Class, 1788–1850* (New York, 1984), 335–43.

41. *New-York Daily Tribune*, Apr. 21, 1846; Seward to Gerrit Smith, Jan. 21, 1845, William Henry Seward Papers, University of Rochester.

42. Daniel Dewey Barnard, "The Anti-Rent Movement and Outbreak in New York," *American Whig Review*, 2 (1845): 577–98 (quotation on 596); *New-York Daily Tribune*, Aug. 11, Sept. 6, 1845.

43. The twists and turns can be traced in S. Croswell and R. Sutton, *Debates and Proceedings in the New York Convention for the Revision of the Constitution* (Albany, 1846). See also Gunn, *Decline*, 170–97, and McCurdy, *Anti-Rent Era*, 200–4, 207–12, which stress the restrictions placed on state borrowing and spending and the decline of Whig political authority. On race and suffrage, see Phyllis Field, *The Politics of Race in New York: The Struggle for Black Suffrage in the Civil War Era* (Ithaca, NY, 1982), 43–79.

44. Welles to Martin Van Buren, July 28, 1846, VBP.

45. *CG*, 29th Congress, 2nd session, 136.

46. Charles Buxton Going, *David Wilmot, Free-Soiler: A Biography of the Great Advocate of the Wilmot Proviso* (New York, 1924), remains the standard biography. On the politics of the Wilmot Proviso, see above all Eric Foner, "The Wilmot Proviso Revisited," *JAH*, 56 (1969); Chaplain W. Morrison, *Democratic Politics and Sectionalism: The Wilmot Proviso Controversy* (Chapel Hill, 1967); Earle, *Jacksonian Antislavery*, 1–4, 123–43.

47. Howard K. Beale, ed., *Diary of Gideon Welles* (New York, 1960), 2: 386. King lacks a modern biography.

48. On the antislavery Democrats, see also Foner, "Wilmot Proviso," 263 n. 6, 264–73.

49. *Proceedings of the Herkimer Mass Convention of October 26, 1847* (Albany, 1847), 12; Charles Eugene Hamlin, *The Life and Times of Hannibal Hamlin* (Cambridge, MA, 1899), 156–7; Foner, "Wilmot Proviso," 264.

50. *CG*, 29th Congress, 1st session, 1213–4 (quotation on 1214).

51. Ibid., 1217–8 (quotation on 1217); *CG*, 29th Congress, 2nd session, 114–5, 425.

52. *CG*, 29th Congress, 1st session, 1218; ibid., 29th Congress, 2nd session, 453–5. According to the *New-York Weekly Tribune*, six northern representatives voted against the Proviso; Jacob Brinkerhoff later said that only three did. See Morrison, *Democratic Politics*, 182 n. 86. The amended bill passed 87 to 64.

53. *Union*, Aug. 12, 1846; Morrison, *Democratic Politics*, 21–22; Going, *Wilmot*, 154–5. John Quincy Adams wholly supported the Proviso's objectives but regarded the measure as premature, since no determination had yet been made about whether the territories in question even belonged to the United States. *CG*, 29th Congress, 1st session, 1215–6. In his diary, Adams mentioned the Proviso's introduction only briefly and in passing. See *JQAD*, 12: 270.

54. *CG*, 29th Congress, 1st session, 1214; *New-York Daily Tribune*, Aug. 12, 1846.

55. *CG*, 29th Congress, 2nd session, 114.

56. Brinkerhoff to Salmon P. Chase, Nov. 22, 1847, in *SPCP*; *CG*, 29th Congress, 2nd ses-

sion, Appendix, 317; *New-York Daily Tribune*, Jan. 12, 1852; Harrold, *Bailey*, 94–108. Wilmot was even harsher in private: "By God, sir," he exclaimed to one associate, "men born and nursed by white women are not going to be ruled by men who were brought up on the milk of some damn Negro wench!" Going, *Wilmot*, 174–5 n. 9.

57. "Sketch of the Remarks of John Van Buren" (Oct. 26, 1847), in O. C. Gardiner, *The Great Issue; or, the Three Presidential Candidates* (New York, 1848), 62–72 (quotation on 64); *Seneca Observer* quoted in Sewell, *Ballots*, 175; *National Era* [Washington], Feb. 4, 1847; *Albany Atlas*, Nov. 9, 1847. For a more extended discussion, see Sean Wilentz, "Slavery, Antislavery, and Jacksonian Democracy," in Melvyn Stokes and Stephen Conway, eds., *The Market Revolution in America: Social, Political, and Religious Expressions, 1800–1880* (Charlottesville, 1996), esp. 213–7.

58. *CG*, 29th Congress, 2nd session, Appendix, 180.

59. Ibid., 345. Wood's speech, overlooked by historians, contains a particularly thorough and pointed summation of the chief Democratic antislavery themes, which would become the ideological foundations of the Free Soil and then the Republican Parties. A founder of the New York Republican Party in 1856, Wood would serve as minister to Denmark under the Lincoln administration.

60. Calhoun quoted in Bartlett, *Calhoun*, 337; *Charleston Mercury*, Aug. 16, 1847; Calhoun to Percy Walker, Oct. 23, 1847, *PJCC*, 24: 616–20; *Tri-Weekly Flag and Advertiser* [Montgomery, AL], Apr. 24, 1847. On southern reactions, see also Morrison, *Democratic Politics*, 38–51; William W. Freehling, *The Road to Disunion: Secessionists at Bay, 1776–1854* (New York, 1990), 459–74.

61. Sewell, *Ballots*, 131–51; William S. McFeely, *Frederick Douglass* (New York, 1991), 156–7.

62. Sumner to Salmon P. Chase, Dec. 12, 1846, in *SPCP*.

CHAPTER TWENTY: WAR, SLAVERY, AND THE AMERICAN 1848

1. John S. D. Eisenhower, *So Far from God: The U.S. War with Mexico, 1846–1848* (New York, 1989), 166–342.

2. Melville to Gansevoort Melville, quoted in Hershel Parker, *Herman Melville: A Biography* (Baltimore, 1996–2002), 1: 421.

3. Cooper, *Jack Tier; or, The Florida Reef* (New York, 1848); Lippard, *Legends of Mexico* (Philadelphia, 1847); idem, *'Bel of Prairie Eden* (Boston, 1848); Sims, *Areytos: or, Songs of the South* (Charleston, 1846). On popular cultural responses to the war, as well as the literary work, see Robert W. Johannsen, *To the Halls of the Montezumas: The Mexican War in the American Imagination* (New York, 1985), 175–240.

4. *Literary World*, 1 (1847): 582; Johannsen, *Halls*, 108–43.

5. Whitman, *The Gathering of the Forces*, Cleveland Rogers and John Black, eds., (New York, 1920), 2: 197–228; Homer Wilbur, ed. [James Russell Lowell], *The Biglow Papers* (Boston, 1848), 6–7.

6. *Albany Atlas*, Jan. 16, 27, Feb. 1, 1847; *CG*, 30th Congress, 1st session, Appendix, 680. Calhoun quoted in Chaplain W. Morrison, *Democratic Politics and Sectionalism: The Wilmot Proviso Controversy* (Chapel Hill, 1967), 35.

7. *CG*, 29th Congress, 2nd session, 573.

8. *New Hampshire Patriot and Star Gazette*, July 15, 1847.

9. Toombs to John C. Calhoun, Apr. 30, 1847, in *PJCC*, 24: 339–40 (quotation on 340). On the southern rights movement, see Morrison, *Democratic Politics*, 38–51; William W. Freehling, *The Road to Disunion: Secessionists at Bay, 1776–1854* (New York, 1990), 475–9.

10. *Tri-Weekly Flag and Advertiser* [Montgomery, AL], May 8, July 22, 1847. See John Irvin Selman, "William Lowndes Yancey: Alabama Fire-Eater" (Ph.D. dissert., Mississippi State University, 1998); John Witherspoon DuBose, *The Life and Times of William Lowndes*

Yancey (Birmingham, AL, 1892). On Alabama politics through 1848, see above all J. Mills Thornton III, *Politics and Power in a Slave Society: 1800–1860* (Baton Rouge, 1978), 165–82.

11. *Ohio State Journal*, Apr. 3, 1847; *CG*, 29th Congress, 2nd session, Appendix, 404.
12. The most complete account, through the 1848 election, is in Kinley J. Brauer, *Cotton versus Conscience: Massachusetts Whig Politics and Southwestern Expansion, 1843–1848* (Lexington, KY, 1967), 180–94, 207–45; but see also Frank Otto Gattell, "Conscience and Judgment: The Bolt of the Massachusetts Conscience Whigs," *Historian*, 21 (1958): 18–45.
13. Herbert D. A. Donovan, *The Barnburners: A Study of the Internal Movements in the Political History of New York State and of the Resulting Changes in Political Affiliation, 1830–1852* (New York, 1925), 76–83. On Chase's support of Wright, see Chase to Preston King, July 15, 1847, in *SPCP*. On all these matters, leading up to the New Yorkers' participation in the Free Soil revolt in 1848, the best account is now Jonathan H. Earle, *Jacksonian Antislavery and the Politics of Free Soil, 1824–1854* (Chapel Hill, 2004), 62–77.
14. John Garraty, *Silas Wright* (New York, 1949), 389–409.
15. Calhoun quoted in Arthur M. Schlesinger Jr., *The Age of Jackson* (Boston, 1945), 458; Whitman, *Gathering of the Forces*, 2: 185; Henry B. Stanton, *Random Recollections* (1886; New York, 1887), 159–60; *New York Herald*, Oct. 6, 1847.
16. The major speeches at Herkimer are reproduced in O. C. Gardiner, *The Great Issue; or, the Three Presidential Candidates* (New York, 1848), 49–72 (quotations on 52, 62). Van Buren's quotation is from the convention's official address to the Democratic electors of New York, which he wrote.
17. Chase to Charles Sumner, Dec. 2, 1847, in *SPCP*; Wilmot to Martin Van Buren, Oct. 6, 1847, Van Buren to David Wilmot, Oct. 22, 1847, Van Buren to Campbell P. White, Nov. 29, 1847, VBP; Schlesinger, *Age of Jackson*, 461; Donald B. Cole, *Martin Van Buren and the American Political System* (Princeton, 1984), 411. On Van Buren's changing views about slavery issues, see also Daniel Feller, "A Brother in Arms: Benjamin Tappan and the Antislavery Democracy," *JAH*, 88 (2001): 64–65.
18. Clay to Christopher Hughes Jr., Mar. 19, 1848, quoted in Robert V. Remini, *Henry Clay: Statesman for the Union* (New York, 1991), 701; Gardiner, *Great Issue*, 21. Antislavery forces took special encouragement from the abolition of colonial slavery by decree of the revolutionary French Second Republic in late April. The best studies of the Free Soil revolt and its background are Joseph G. Rayback, *Free Soil: The Election of 1848* (Lexington, KY, 1970); Frederick J. Blue, *The Free Soilers: Third Party Politics, 1848–54* (Urbana, IL, 1973); John Mayfield, *Rehearsal for Reconstruction: Free Soil and the Politics of Antislavery* (Port Washington, 1980).
19. *New-York Daily Tribune*, Nov. 16, 1847; Richardson, 4: 2387.
20. *National Era* [Washington], Aug. 19, 1847; Stanley Harrold, *Gamaliel Bailey and Antislavery Union* (Kent, OH, 1986), 76–80, 94–97 (quotation on 79). On the All Mexico movement, see John D. P. Fuller, *The Movement for the Acquisition of All Mexico, 1846–1848* (Baltimore, 1936); above all, Frederick Merk, *Manifest Destiny and Mission in American History: A Reinterpretation* (New York, 1963), 107–43.
21. *Daily Chronicle and Sentinel* [Augusta], Oct. 25, 1847. The racist anti-expansionist view was not limited to Whigs in the Deep South. The Whig Senator John Clayton of Delaware told his colleagues that absorbing Mexico would only add eight million persons of "a colored population, having no feelings in common with us," who would almost certainly be antislavery. *CG*, 30th Congress, 1st session, Appendix, 75.
22. Ibid., 49–53 (quotation on 51).
23. *Picayune* [New Orleans], Feb. 7, 1848, quoted in Merk, *Manifest Destiny and Mission*, 154.
24. *CG*, 30th Congress, 1st session, Appendix, 93–95 (quotation on 95).
25. Merk, *Manifest Destiny and Mission*, 180–8.
26. Calhoun to T[homas] G. Clemson, Mar. 7,1948, in *PJCC*, 25: 231.

27. *CG*, 30th Congress, 1st session, 381; Leonard L. Richards, *The Life and Times of Congressman John Quincy Adams* (New York, 1986), 202–3.

28. *CG*, 30th Congress, 1st session, 386, 388; Wise quoted in Paul C. Nagel, *John Quincy Adams: A Public Life, A Private Life* (New York, 1997), 386. Stanton had met with Adams just before his collapse and was still on the floor of the House as an official guest. For his eyewitness account, see Stanton, *Random Recollections*, 158–9.

29. Donovan, *Barnburners*, 98–101; Gardiner, *Great Issue*, 72–96; "Address of the Democratic Members of the Legislature of the State of New York," Apr. 12, 1848, VBP.

30. "Address of the Democratic Members"; Van Buren to John Van Buren, May 3, 1848, VBP. See also Joseph G. Rayback, "Martin Van Buren's Desire for Revenge in the Campaign of 1848," *Mississippi Valley Historical Review*, 40 (1954): 707–16; idem, *Free Soil*, 177–81. Compare Cole, *Van Buren*, 411, which is skeptical about the depth of Van Buren's antislavery beliefs and sees his advice that of "the same old canny politician, still a party man."

31. The Democratic convention proceedings appear in NWR, Aug. 2, Nov. 22, 29, 1848.

32. On the Barnburners at Baltimore, see Stanton, *Random Recollections*, 161.

33. Yancey's resolution won the solid support of the South Carolina, Florida, Georgia, Alabama, and Arkansas delegations and scattered support from Maryland, Kentucky, and Tennessee.

34. The Whig convention proceedings appear in NWR, Nov. 29, Dec. 6, 1848. On the convention and the complicated intrigues leading to it, see also Michael F. Holt, *The Rise and Fall of the American Whig Party: Jacksonian Politics and the Onset of the Civil War* (New York, 1999), 284–330.

35. S & I, 3: 901–2 (quotations on 901).

36. *New-York Daily Tribune*, July 1, 1848; *True Democrat* [Cleveland], June 10, 1848.

37. Stanton, *Random Recollections*, 80 (quotation), *Albany Atlas*, June 2, 1848; Gardiner, *Great Issue*, 107–37; see also NWR, Dec. 13, 20, 1848; Rayback, *Free Soil*, 201–8; Earle, *Jacksonian Antislavery*, 77.

38. Butler to Martin Van Buren, May 29 (quotation), 30 (quotation), 31, 1848, VBP; NWR, Dec. 13, 20, 1848; Gardiner, *Great Issue*, 110–6, 118–20; Rayback, *Free Soil*, 208–12. In a bow to westerners and a slap at Polk, the platform also called for federal aid for river and harbor improvements.

39. Milo Milton Quaife, ed., *The Diary of James K. Polk during His Presidency, 1845–1849* (Chicago, 1910), 3: 502; J[oseph] W. Lesesne to John C. Calhoun, July 5, 1848, in *PJCC*, 25: 564–8 (quotations on 566); Chase to John Van Buren, June 19, 1848, cited in Cole, *Van Buren*, 414.

40. Richard H. Sewell, *Ballots for Freedom: Antislavery Politics in the United States, 1837–1860* (New York, 1976), 154–6; Sumner to John Greenleaf Whittier, July 12, 1848, quoted in Cole, *Van Buren*, 414; Blue, *Free Soilers*, 169 n. 34.

41. Van Buren to Francis Blair, June 22, 1848, Blair Family Papers, LC. Part of the confusion over Van Buren's motives stems from his critics' conflation of the abolitionism and slavery extension issues. It was not inconsistent, as they suggest it was, for Van Buren to oppose the abolitionists in the 1830s and also to oppose slavery's expansion in the 1840s. For months before the Utica convention, his letters showed a predisposition toward anti-extension ideas, and the Barnburner Manifesto, which he chiefly authored, stood among the most powerful and carefully reasoned defenses of the Wilmot Proviso. That he came, in the altered political climate of 1848, also to change his old position about abolishing slavery in the District of Columbia is much more easily explained by the evolution of his political thinking than by some alleged deeper thirst for revenge, for which there is no documentary evidence. See Rayback, "Revenge."

42. Stanton, *Random Recollections*, 160.

43. See Elisabeth Griffith, *In Her Own Right: The Life of Elizabeth Cady Stanton* (New York, 1984), 3–39.

44. Stanton, *Eighty Years and More: Reminiscences, 1815–1897* (1898; New York, 1971), 147; Griffith, *In Her Own Right*, 39–50.

45. Stanton, *Reminiscences*, 148; Griffith, *In Her Own Right*, 47–61.

46. Griffith, *In Her Own Right*, 56. Mott, the nonresistant Garrisonian, at first thought the suffrage passage "ridiculous," but later supported it.

47. *Oneida Whig*, Aug. 1, 1848; Elizabeth Cady Stanton, Susan B. Anthony, et al., *The History of Women Suffrage* (New York, 1881–86), 1: 804–5. On William Lloyd Garrison's support for the movement, see Henry Mayer, *All on Fire: William Lloyd Garrison and the Abolition of Slavery* (New York, 1998), 390.

48. During the 1846 New York constitutional convention, at least three petitions from female citizens had arrived asking for women's suffrage. In April 1848, three months before the Seneca Falls gathering, another petition campaign, undertaken more than a decade earlier by a freethinking Owenite Polish émigré and friend of Frances Wright's, Ernestine Potowski Rose, had finally won the passage of the New York Married Woman's Property Act. The first comprehensive legislation of its kind in the nation, the act gave wives control over property they had owned before marriage, which heretofore had automatically gone to their husbands. (Both Stanton and Paulina Wright Davis, another future feminist leader, who in 1849 would marry an antislavery Democrat, had actively supported Rose's campaign.) As soon as the Seneca Falls meeting concluded, the organizers were planning a follow-up meeting in Rochester two weeks later, which would in turn pave the way for the first National Woman's Rights Convention at Worcester in 1850. At the Worcester meeting and at successive national conventions, such feminist pioneers as Lucy Stone and Susan B. Anthony would join with Mott, Stanton, Rose, and Davis. The convergence of intellectual and ideological currents at Seneca Falls is beautifully covered in Judith Wellman, *The Road to Seneca Falls: Elizabeth Cady Stanton and the First Woman's Rights Convention* (Urbana, IL, 2004). See also Lori Ginzburg, *Women and the Work of Benevolence: Morality, Politics, and Class in the Nineteenth Century* (New Haven, 1990), 11–32; Jacob Katz Cogan and Lori D. Ginsburg, "1846 Petition for Woman's Suffrage, New York State Constitutional Convention," *Signs*, 22 (1997): 427–39; Ellen Carol Dubois, *Feminism and Suffrage: The Emergence of an Independent Women's Movement in America, 1848–1869* (Ithaca, NY, 1978), 21–52; Nancy Isenberg, *Sex and Citizenship in Antebellum America* (Chapel Hill, 1998).

49. On the participants at Seneca Falls and the Free Soil milieu, see Judith Wellman, "The Seneca Falls Women's Rights Convention: A Study of Social Networks," *Journal of Women's History*, 3 (1991): 9–37. Henry Stanton was among the male Free Soilers unsettled by the meeting's radical tone. As soon as he learned that his wife planned to demand the franchise, he left town; in his memoirs, he noted uneasily how his wife's fame "in another department" had come to overshadow her antislavery work. Griffith, *In Her Own Right*, 55; Stanton, *Random Recollections*, 68.

50. Sumner, *The Works of Charles Sumner* (Boston, 1873), 2: 75–88; Gattell, "Conscience"; *National Era*, July 20, 1848; Rayback, *Free Soil*, 212–5 (quotation on 214).

51. Stanton, *Random Recollections*, 163. The official proceedings appear as Oliver Dyer, *Phonographic Report of the Proceedings of the National Free Soil Convention* (Buffalo, 1848); but see also the accounts in Rayback, *Free Soil*, 223–30; Sewell, *Ballots*, 156–65; Earle, *Jacksonian Antislavery*, 159–62.

52. Betsy Erkkila, *Whitman the Political Poet* (New York, 1989), 51–53; David S. Reynolds, *Walt Whitman's America: A Cultural Biography* (New York, 1995), 120–7.

53. William S. McFeely, *Frederick Douglass* (New York, 1991), 114–8, 156–8; Sewell, *Ballots*, 160.

54. *Reunion of the Free Soilers of 1848 at Downer Landing, Hingham, Mass., August 9, 1877* (Boston, 1877), 43; *North Star* [Rochester], Aug. 11, 25, Sept. 10, 22, Nov. 24, 1848. Douglass wavered and for a time backed a splinter candidacy by the abolitionist Gerrit Smith, but he eventually stuck by the Free Soilers because they had a much better chance of success. He would later revise his thoughts yet again and complain about the Free Soilers' half-heartedness; see ibid. Jan. 12, Mar. 25, 1849. Other blacks, notably Samuel Ward, rejected the Free Soilers and backed Smith. A gathering of free black activists in Cleve-

land in September praised the party for increasing interest in antislavery, but also criticized it for setting too low a standard and stopped short of an endorsement. See Howard H. Bell, "The National Negro Convention, 1848," *Ohio Historical Quarterly*, 67 (1958): 357–68; Charles H. Wesley, "The Participation of Negroes in Antislavery Political Parties," *Journal of Negro History*, 29 (1944), 53; Earle, *Jacksonian Antislavery*, 168.

55. Dyer, *Phonographic Report*, 4; Stanton, *Random Recollections*, 162.

56. Dyer, *Phonographic Report*, 19–20; Gardiner, *Great Issue*, 138–40. The Free Soil platform is also reprinted in S & I, 3: 902–5.

57. Stanton, *Random Recollections*, 164; George W. Julian, *Political Recollections, 1840–1872* (Chicago, 1884), 58–9.

58. Van Buren to Benjamin Butler and others, Aug. 22, 1848, VBP; NWR, Aug. 16, 1848; Martin B. Duberman, *Charles Francis Adams, 1807–1886* (Boston, 1961), 150–1.

59. Leavitt to Joshua Giddings, July 6, 1848, quoted in Blue, *Free Soilers*, 80; NWR, Sept. 27, 1848; Julian, *Political Recollections*, 59–61; Rayback, *Free Soil*, 229–30; Sewell, *Ballots*, 158. The banner's reference to 1787 alluded to the Northwest Ordinance, not the Federal Constitutional Convention. After the convention, Leavitt wrote that he was getting his "steam up to the highest pitch (below the bursting point) in favor of *Van Buren & Adams*," and that, having visited the Free Soilers "'glorious old man,'" was convinced he would "be with us to the last battle against the Slave Power." Leavitt to Salmon P. Chase, Aug. 21, 1848, in SPCP. The Anti-Masonic Party, which had emerged over a three-year period out of the Burned-Over District, was the closest thing to the Free Soilers, serving as a sectional precursor to the new-school Whig Party much as the Free Soilers would prove a precursor to the Republican Party. The Anti-Masons also proved a more persistent independent force in state politics than the Free Soilers. But even the Anti-Masonic excitement of the late 1820s and early 1830s could not match the ebullitions of 1848. The profusion of state-rights, workingmen's, and other parties of the 1830s had been locally based, and they were quickly absorbed into larger mainstream coalitions.

60. Valentine Nicholson to Van Buren, Aug. 14, 1848, VBP.

61. Gardiner, *Great Issue*, 108. Gerrit Smith called the Buffalo meeting "an anti-abolition Convention," because it failed to deny any rights of existing slaveholders to own human property. Goodell and Smith quoted in Sewell, *Ballots*, 163. This more sectarian view regarding the Free Soilers' (and especially the Barnburners') shortcomings seems to have become the prevailing interpretation among American historians. See Alexander Saxton, *The Rise and Fall of the White Republic: Class Politics and Mass Culture in Nineteenth Century America* (London, 1990), esp. 142–54; Eric Foner, "Politics and Prejudice: The Free Soil Party and the Negro, 1849–1852," *Journal of Negro History*, 50 (1965): 239–56; idem, "Racial Attitudes of the New York Free Soilers," *New York History*, 46 (1965): 311–29. The major exception is Sewell, *Ballots*, 160. Usually neglected is how, like the party itself, some of its most offensively racist ex-Democrats, including David Wilmot, always pronounced *slavery* a moral evil—an ethical stance that transcended keeping blacks out of the western territories, recognized the basic humanity of blacks, and set its proponents well apart from mainstream Democrats and conservative Whigs. On this point, see also Sean Wilentz, "Slavery, Antislavery, and Jacksonian Democracy," in Melvyn Stokes and Stephen Conway, eds., *The Market Revolution in America: Social, Political, and Religious Expressions, 1800–1880* (Charlottesville, 1996), esp. 213–4; Earle, *Jacksonian Antislavery*, 161–2.

62. *American Freeman* [Milwaukee], Aug. 23, 1848; Sewell, *Ballots*, 159; *National Era*, Aug. 24, 31, 1848. See also Cole, *Van Buren*, 416; Harrold, *Bailey*, 120–3.

63. *Liberator*, May 26, July 14, 1848 (quotation).

64. For strong accounts of the campaigning in 1848, see Rayback, *Free Soil*, 231–78; Gil Troy, "1848," in Arthur M. Schlesinger Jr., ed, *Running for President: The Candidates and Their Images* (New York, 1994), 1: 185–203. Some recent historians have focused on the antiblack themes in some Free Soilers' rhetoric, but have elided how by far the most consistent and vicious racist campaigning came from Whigs and Democrats attacking the

Free Soilers. For balanced correctives, see Sewell, *Ballots*, 173–5; Earle, *Jacksonian Antislavery*, 167–8.

65. The returns are expertly analyzed in Rayback, *Free Soil*, 278–87; Holt, *Rise and Fall*, 356–82; Earle, *Jacksonian Antislavery*, 169–80.

66. Charles Francis Adams Diary, Oct. 13, 1848, MHS. On disappointment among Free Soilers at "the smallness of our vote," see Salmon P. Chase to Mrs. Chase, Nov. 14, 1848, in *SPCP*.

67. Julian, *Political Recollections*, 65–66.

68. Glyndon Van Deusen, *Horace Greeley, Nineteenth-Century Crusader* (Philadelphia, 1953), 121–3; Rayback, *Free Soil*, 244–7; Blue, *Free Soilers*, 112–7 (quotation on 115). Overall, the Whigs retained more than 98 percent of their support from 1844; the Democrats, only about 85 percent. Those figures, in turn, reflected the different degrees to which the slavery controversy was affecting the parties' respective cohesion. Although Taylor's nomination led to a furious reaction among both antislavery Whigs and pro-Clay Whigs, the rift in the Democracy, dating back to 1844, was much more severe. Thanks to vigorous Whig efforts to mobilize their constituencies, most of the pro-Clay men, for whom antislavery was at best a secondary commitment, found their way back into the Whig Party. With the South leaning pro-Whig in marked contrast to 1844, the result was devastating for the Democrats. In 1848, the Democracy paid a far higher price for its internal divisions over slavery and extension than the Whigs did.

69. Adams to Seth Gates, Oct. 1, 1848, quoted in Blue, *Free Soilers*, 133. With participation rates by eligible voters plummeting, the actual number of voters nationwide rose only marginally in 1848 compared to 1844; in five states—Alabama, Connecticut, North Carolina, Rhode Island, and Vermont—the absolute number of voters actually fell.

70. Van Buren to Francis Blair, Dec. 11, 1848, Blair Family Papers, LC. Blair had already said as much to Van Buren; Blair to Martin Van Buren, Nov. 30, 1848, VBP. For other hopeful conclusions among Free Soilers, see Charles Sumner to Salmon P. Chase, Nov. 16, 1848, in *SPCP*; *New-York Daily Tribune*, Nov. 18, 1848. The eight Free Soil congressmen, including former Democrats and former Whigs, would be Charles Allen (MA), Charles Durkee (WI), Joshua Giddings (OH), George Julian (IN), Preston King (NY), Joseph Moseley Root (OH), Amos Tuck (NH), and David Wilmot (PA). The coalition Free Soil–Whig representatives would be Walter Booth (CT), John W. Howe (PA), Horace Mann (MA), and William Sprague (MI). See Blue, *Free Soilers*, 137. See also ibid., 138–9, on Free Soil success at winning local offices in New York, Massachusetts, and Ohio.

71. Calhoun to H. W. Comer, July 9, 1848, Calhoun to J[oseph] W. Lesesne, July 15, 1848, in *PJCC*, 25: 578, 590; Merrill D. Peterson, *The Great Triumvirate: Webster, Clay, and Calhoun* (New York, 1987), 447.

CHAPTER TWENTY-ONE: POLITICAL TRUCE, UNEASY CONSEQUENCES

1. Various accounts of the exchange are reported in Holman Hamilton, *Zachary Taylor: Soldier in the White House* (Indianapolis, 1951), 141. For Clay's version, see Henry Clay to Thomas B. Stevenson, Jan. 31, 1849, in *PHC*, 4: 584.

2. Taylor to Robert C. Wood, Sept. 27, 1847, in *Letters of Zachary Taylor from the Battlefields of the Mexican War* (Rochester, NY, 1908), 134. The most current and reliable account of Taylor's presidency is in Elbert B. Smith, *The Presidencies of Zachary Taylor and Millard Fillmore* (Lawrence, KS, 1988) esp. 25–42, 49–68.

3. One government job that did change hands, the position of revenue surveyor at the customhouse in Salem, Massachusetts, was taken away from its Democratic incumbent, Nathaniel Hawthorne—a move that, in the opening pages of *The Scarlet Letter*, would become the most important patronage incident in American literary history.

4. Richardson, 4: 2486. Malcolm J. Rohrbough, *Days of Gold: The California Gold Rush and*

the American Nation (Berkeley, 1997), is the best study of the discovery and its immediate social impact across the country.

5. There is a huge and contentious historical literature on the origins and early history of the Mormons, well distilled in Claudia L. Bushman and Richard L. Bushman, *Building the Kingdom: The History of Mormons in America* (New York, 2001), 1–74. On the political aspects from 1847 to the Civil War, see also Leonard J. Arrington and Davis Bitton, *The Mormon Experience: A History of the Latter-day Saints* (New York, 1979), esp. 109–26, 161–84; Norman F. Furness, *The Mormon Conflict, 1850–1859* (New Haven, 1960).

6. Calhoun, "The Address of Southern Delegates in Congress to their Constituents, January 22, 1849," in *PJCC*, 26: 225–44 (quotation on 242).

7. Stephens to John J. Crittenden, Jan. 17, 1849, *Richmond Enquirer*, Nov. 30, 1849, quoted in William J. Cooper, *The South and the Politics of Slavery 1828–1856* (New York, 1978), 271, 278.

8. *CG*, 31st Congress, 1st session, 28; Thelma Jennings, *The Nashville Convention: Southern Movement for Unity, 1848–1851* (Memphis, 1980), 3–79 (quotation on 7); Michael F. Holt, *The Rise and Fall of the American Whig Party: Jacksonian Politics and the Onset of the Civil War* (New York, 1999), 449–51. Davis was briefly married to Taylor's daughter, Sarah, until her sudden death from malaria in 1835. According to one of Taylor's biographers, the president's statement, in a speech in Pennsylvania in August, that "the people of the North need have no apprehension of the further extension of slavery," was widely misinterpreted in the South as a covert endorsement of the Proviso. Hamilton, *Taylor*, 225.

9. Arphaxed Loomis quoted in Herbert Donovan, *The Barnburners: A Study of the Internal Movements in the Political History of New York State and of the Resulting Changes in Political Affiliation, 1830–1852* (New York, 1925), 113; Holt, *Rise and Fall*, 433–5, 506. On persistent independent Free Soilism in the immediate aftermath of the 1848 elections, see *National Era* [Washington], Mar. 22, Apr. 19, May 3, Aug. 30, Sept. 6, 1849.

10. The standard study of the truce remains Holman Hamilton, *Prologue to Conflict: The Crisis and Compromise of 1850* (Lexington, KY, 1964). My own view has been strongly influenced by David M. Potter, *The Impending Crisis, 1848–1861* (New York, 1976), 90–120, and William W. Freehling, *The Road to Disunion: Secessionists at Bay, 1776–1854* (New York, 1990), 487–510, both of which prefer the more formal term *armistice* to *truce*.

11. Sidney G. Fisher Diary, Dec. 16, 1849, HSP.

12. Richardson, 4: 2564–8; Thurlow Weed Barnes, *Memoir of Thurlow Weed* (Boston, 1884), 177.

13. *CG*, 31st Congress, 1st session, 244–52 (quotation on 244).

14. Ibid., 246; Appendix, 126–7 (quotation on 126).

15. *CG*, 31st Congress, 1st session, 451–5, (quotation on 455).

16. Calhoun, "A Discourse on the Constitution and Government of the United States," in *PJCC*, 27: 227–34; *CG*, 31st Congress, 1st session, 455.

17. *CG*, 31st Congress, 1st session, Appendix, 269–76 (quotation on 269).

18. *CG*, 31st Congress, 1st session, 260–9 (quotations on 265, 268).

19. Ibid., Appendix, 242–8; Tyler quoted in Hamilton, *Prologue*, 74; Robert V. Remini, *Daniel Webster: The Man and His Times* (New York, 1997), 677–8; Allan Nevins, *The Ordeal of the Union* (New York, 1947), 1: 301–2 (quotation on 301). Seward's more cautious political managers also read the speech as a radical manifesto on government and God's laws, and thought he had gone too far. Thurlow Weed told him that he read the speech "with a heavy heart." Weed to William Henry Seward, Mar. 14, 1850, Seward Papers, University of Rochester. Horace Greeley thought the speech was brilliant. See *New-York Daily Tribune*, Mar. 19, 1850.

20. Hamilton, *Prologue*, 95–104; Thelma Jennings, *The Nashville Convention: Southern Movement for Unity, 1848–51* (Memphis, 1980), 135–66.

21. Smith, *Presidencies*, 156–7. See Robert J. Rayback, *Millard Fillmore: Biography of a President* (Buffalo, 1959), 1–191.

22. Hamilton, *Prologue*, 107–17.

23. See above all the sympathetic and authoritative biography by Robert Johannsen, *Stephen A. Douglas* (New York, 1973), 3–303.

24. Richardson, 5: 2629; Hamilton, *Prologue*, 191–200. On the fugitive slave bill, later to become of surpassing importance, only about one in five northern members of Congress (34 out of 154) voted for the measure, a signal of future distress. Thirty-two members absented themselves, including the chief northern compromiser Stephen Douglas, William Seward (who was said to be ill), and, more surprisingly, the Free Soiler John P. Hale.

25. *New York Herald*, Sept. 10, 1850; J. M. Foltz to James Buchanan, Sept. 8, 1850, quoted in Nevins, *Ordeal*, 1: 343; CG, 31st Congress, 1st session, 1830; Douglas quoted in Remini, *Clay*, 761; Webster to Peter Harvey, Oct. 2, 1850, in Charles M. Wiltse, ed., *The Papers of Daniel Webster: Correspondence* (Hanover, NH, 1974–86), 7: 155.

26. CG, 31st Congress, 1st session, 1859.

27. Hone, *The Diary of Philip Hone, 1828–1851*, Bayard Tuckerman, ed. (New York, 1889), 2: 378; Perry and William Preston quoted in Jennings, *Nashville Convention*, 53–54; Benton quoted in John Wentworth, *Congressional Reminiscences* (Chicago, 1882), 23–24.

28. CG, 31st Congress, 1st session, 137; M. R. H. Garnett to William H. Trescott, May 3, 1851, in Henry O'Reilly, *Origin and Objects of the Slaveholders' Conspiracy against Democratic Principles* (New York, 1862), 10–11. On the southern reactions to the truce, the second Nashville Convention, and the collapse of the disunionist movement, see Jennings, *Nashville Convention*, 187–211.

29. William Craft published his narrative of the escape as *Running a Thousand Miles for Freedom; or The Escape of William and Ellen Craft from Slavery* (London, 1860). See also *Liberator* [Boston], Apr. 6, 1849; Larry Gara, *The Liberty Line: The Legend of the Underground Railroad* (Lexington, KY, 1967), 48–49; R. J. M. Blackett, "The Odyssey of William and Ellen Craft," in *Beating against the Barriers: Biographical Essays in Nineteenth-Century Afro-American History* (Baton Rouge, 1986), 87–108; Barbara McCaskill, " 'Yours Very Truly': Ellen Craft—The Fugitive as Text and Artifact," *African American Review* 28 (1994): 509–29.

30. On Parker, see Michael Fellman, "Theodore Parker and the Abolitionist Role in the 1850s," *JAH*, 61 (1974): 666–84. Fellman illuminates Parker's place in the rise of what might be called post-Garrisonian abolitionism—radical in its hatred of slavery, but increasingly dubious of nonresistance, and racist in its view of blacks and other non-Anglo-Saxons. On Parker's intellectual development before 1850, see Dean Grodzins, *American Heretic: Theodore Parker and Transcendentalism* (Chapel Hill, 2002).

31. Parker to Millard Fillmore, Nov. 21, 1850, in John Weiss, ed., *Life and Correspondence of Theodore Parker* (New York, 1864), 2: 101–2.

32. A month earlier, the fugitive freedman James Hamlet was arrested in Manhattan, in the first case brought under the new Fugitive Slave Law. The arrest sparked large demonstrations. After failing to free Hamlet through the courts, Lewis Tappan raised eight hundred dollars to purchase him from his Baltimore mistress, and Hamlet was returned to his wife and children. In early October, another fugitive was arrested in Detroit, and a crowd of armed blacks threatened to free him. Federal troops kept the man in custody until local abolitionists bought his freedom for five hundred dollars. See Stanley W. Campbell, *The Slave Catchers: Enforcement of the Fugitive Slave Law, 1850–1860* (Chapel Hill, 1970), 115.

33. [James W. Stone], *Trial of Thomas Sims on an Issue of Personal Liberty* (Boston, 1851); Thomas Wentworth Higginson, *Cheerful Yesterdays* (Boston, 1898), 135–40; Gara, *Liberty Line*, 107–12; Campbell, *Slave Catchers*, 117–21; Gary Collison, *Shadrach Minkins: From Fugitive Slave to Citizen* (Cambridge, MA, 1997), esp. 110–65. Minkins settled in Montreal, where he briefly ran a restaurant, then lived out his freedom as a barber. The strangest sight in the cases connected with the Minkins escape, according to Richard Henry Dana Jr., was that of the Jacksonian opportunist Benjamin Hallett—"the Dorr-ite, the slangwhanging radical"—serving as federal prosecutor and becoming "the fiercest &

most despotic engine of power." Robert F. Lucid, ed., *The Journal of Richard Henry Dana, Jr.* (Cambridge, MA, 1968), 2: 414. Daniel Webster personally led the unsuccessful prosecution of those accused of helping Minkins escape, which embittered him and further dimmed his reputation among antislavery Whigs. See Gary Collison, "'This Flagitious Offense': Daniel Webster and the Shadrach Rescue Cases, 1851–1852." *New England Quarterly*, 68 (1995): 609–25.

34. Quotation in James M. McPherson, *Battle Cry of Freedom: The Civil War Era* (New York, 1988), 85. For different renderings of the affair, see Jonathan Katz, *Resistance at Christiana: The Fugitive Slave Rebellion, Christiana, Pennsylvania, September 11, 1851: A Documentary Account* (New York, 1974); Thomas P. Slaughter, *Bloody Dawn: The Christiana Riot and Racial Violence in the Antebellum North* (New York, 1991), 3–138.

35. The trial transcript appears as James J. Robbins, *Report of the Trial of Castner Hanway for Treason* (Philadelphia, 1852), 109 (quotation). See also Paul Finkelman, "The Treason Trial of Castner Hanway," in Michal R. Belknap, ed., *American Political Trials* (Westport, CT, 1981), 79–100. The State Department tried to extradite the alleged ringleaders— William Parker, Alexander Pinckney, and Abraham Johnson—but Canadian authorities refused to comply.

36. *National Era*, Aug. 22, 1850, June 19, 1851. On the extent and the complexities of slave flight, see Gara, *Liberty Line*, 19–41; above all, the brilliant and humane account in Eugene D. Genovese, *Roll, Jordan, Roll: The World the Slaves Made* (New York, 1975), 648–57. On the Underground Railroad, see also Charles L. Blockston, *The Underground Railroad* (New York, 1987).

37. *Delaware State Journal* [Wilmington], Apr. 1, 1851; Gara, *Liberty Line*, 114–42. The best calculations show that only one in ten of runaways apprehended either escaped or was set free, usually over mistaken identity.

38. Catherine Clinton, *Harriet Tubman: The Road to Freedom* (New York, 2004); Jean McMahon Humez, *Harriet Tubman: The Life and Life Stories* (Madison, WI, 2003); and Kate Clifford Larson, *Bound for the Promised Land: Harriet Tubman, Portrait of an American Hero* (New York, 2004), are the latest appraisals of Tubman, their titles indicative of their approaches. On Coffin, see his *Reminiscences of Levi Coffin, the Reputed President of the Underground Railroad* (1876; New York, 1971). On the black protests and vigilance committees, see Austin Bearse, *Reminiscences of Fugitive-Slave Law Days in Boston* (Boston, 1880); Benjamin Quarles, *Black Abolitionists* (New York, 1969), 200–3; more generally, Gara, *Liberty Line*, 101–7.

39. CG, 36th Congress, 2nd session, 56.

40. *North Carolina Standard* [Raleigh],Nov. 13, 1850, quoted in Avery O.Craven, *The Growth of Southern Nationalism, 1848–1861* (Baton Rouge, 1953), 103; *Debates and Proceedings of the Georgia Convention, 1850* (Milledgeville, GA, 1850), 8–9; CG, 31st Congress, 2nd session, Appendix, 322. On the toughening of Mason's original bill, see Campbell, *Slave Catchers*, 15–23.

41. May quoted in Gara, *Liberty Line*, 115. On Brown, see the reissue of his *Narrative of the Life of Henry Box Brown* (1849; New York, 2002).

42. Douglass quotation in John W. Blassingame, ed., *The Frederick Douglass Papers: Series One, Speeches, Debates, and Interviews* (New Haven, 1982–92), 2: 277; Stephen B. Oates, *To Purge This Land with Blood: A Biography of John Brown* (1970; Amherst, 1984), 72–75. Brown's reference was to Judges 7:3: "Whoever is fearful and afraid, let him return and depart early from Mount Gilead." See also Jane H. Pease and William H. Pease, "Confrontation and Abolition in the 1850's," *JAH*, 58 (1972): 923–37.

43. Oliver Johnson to Joshua Giddings, Dec. 31, 1852, quoted in Gara, *Liberty Line*, 135.

44. Greeley and Douglas quoted in Gara, *Liberty Line*, 131; Lucid, ed., *Journal of Richard Henry Dana, Jr.*, 2: 424; Leonard G. Gougeon, "Emerson and the Campaign of 1851," *Historical Journal of Massachusetts*, 16 (1988): 20–23.

45. Campbell, *Slave Catchers*, 49–79 (quotation on 59–60); *The Writings and Speeches of Daniel Webster* (Boston, 1903), 13: 408–21 (quotation on 419). On Webster and the polit-

ical background to the backlash, see also David D. Van Tassel, "Gentlemen of Property and Standing: Compromise Sentiment in Boston in 1850," *New England Quarterly*, 23 (1950): 307–19. On the limits of antislavery opinion even in Syracuse, see Monique Patenaude Roach, "The Rescue of William 'Jerry' Henry: Anti-Slavery and Racism in the Burned-Over District," *New York History*, 82 (2001): 135–54.

46. Campbell, *Slave Catchers*, 55–75 (quotations on 67, 72). "The most serious obstacle to the progress of the antislavery cause was the conduct of the clergy and churches of our country," Samuel May later remarked. May, *Some Recollections of Our Antislavery Conflict* (Boston, 1869), 127.

47. *New-York Weekly Tribune*, Oct. 25, 1851.

48. Hershel Parker, *Herman Melville: A Biography* (1996–2002), 1: 739–854.

49. Melville to Sophia Hawthorne, Jan. 8, 1852, quoted in Parker, *Melville*, 2: 3.

50. See Joan Hedrick's splendid biography, *Harriet Beecher Stowe: A Life* (New York, 1994), 3–201; Barbara A. White, *The Beecher Sisters* (New Haven, 2003), 1–52.

51. Isabella Jones Beecher to Harriet Beecher Stowe, quoted in Hedrick, *Stowe*, 207. According to one of her children, Stowe, upon hearing this letter read aloud in the parlor, arose and declared, "I will write something. I will if I live." Too much ought not to be made of this legendary melodramatic scene. Stowe had already been writing fiction in angry response to the Fugitive Slave Law, and she had been bidding others—including her brother, the famous minister Henry Ward Beecher—to take a stand. Isabella Beecher's letter may have been a catalyst, but Stowe was on the way to writing something bigger than she ever had attempted by the time the letter arrived. Just how big it would be was beyond any possible prediction. See ibid., 202–17.

52. John William De Forest, "The Great American Novel," *Nation*, Jan. 9, 1868, 27–29 (quotation on 28); Stephen A Hirsch, "Uncle Tomitudes: The Popular Reaction to Uncle Tom's Cabin," *Studies in the American Renaissance*, n.v. (1978): 303–30.

53. Despite his misgivings, however, William Lloyd Garrison told Stowe he was glad she had written the book. On Stowe and Garrison, and Stowe's more elitist Christian antislavery beliefs, see Hedrick, *Stowe*, 251–2. As late as 1857, William Seward would remark that the effects of the truce of 1850 had "brought on a demoralization over the whole country from which even New England has not yet adequately recovered." Seward to Cornelius Coles, Sept. 8, 1857, William Henry Seward Papers, University of Rochester. On the resurgence of southern political moderation, see James L. Huston, "Southerners against Secession: The Arguments of the Constitutional Unionists in 1850–51," *Civil War History*, 46 (2000): 281–99.

54. Chase to James H. Smith, May 8, 1849, in *SPCP*.

55. Chase to Charles Sumner, Sept. 15, 1849, in *SPCP*.

56. On the fusion efforts, see especially Richard H. Sewell, *Ballots for Freedom: Antislavery Politics in the United States, 1837–1860* (New York, 1976), 202–30. Other efforts at consolidation, most often with Democrats, unfolded in Wisconsin, Indiana, Illinois, Iowa, Vermont, New Hampshire, and Maine. Further factional squabbling led Chase's Ohio Free Democrats to name Giddings's former law partner (and now bitter rival), the antislavery man Benjamin F. Wade, to the state's other Senate seat.

57. *National Era*, Sept. 27, 1849; Donovan, *Barnburners*, 110–6; Sewell, *Ballots*, 223–9. Free Soilers outside New York had little patience for the retreating Barnburners. "The 'democratic party' is the ruling notion with them," Richard Henry Dana Jr. wrote, "& slavery is subordinate." Lucid, ed., *Diary of Richard Henry Dana, Jr.*, 1: 390.

58. *Speech of the Hon Thos. H. Benton, Delivered at the Capitol at Jefferson City, May 26, 1849* (St. Louis, n.d. [1849]), 6.

59. "A Word to Southern Democrats. By a Northern Conservative," *American Review*, 4 (1849): 190–9 (quotations on 194).

60. Robert V. Remini, *Henry Clay: Statesman for the Union* (New York, 1991), 780–1.

61. Greeley to Schuyler Colfax, Feb. 12, 1851, Greeley-Colfax Correspondence, Horace

Greeley Papers, NYPL. On Whig political developments, see Remini, *Clay*, 762–81; idem, *Webster*, 722–40; Holt, *Rise and Fall*, 673–89.

62. *National Era*, Oct. 2, 9, 1851; James Brewer Stewart, *Joshua Giddings and the Tactics of Radical Politics* (New York, 1970), 201–5; Stanley Harrold, *Gamaliel Bailey and Antislavery Union* (Kent, OH, 1986), 149.

63. *New York Herald*, Jan. 15, 1852; John H. Kolmos, *Kossuth in America, 1851–1852* (Buffalo, 1973), 75–94.

64. Wade to Milton Surliff, Jan. 2, 1852, quoted in Sewell, *Ballots*, 235; Kolmos, *Kossuth*, 97–167. Garrison accused Kossuth of dodging the slavery issue "to secure the favor of a slaveholding and slave-breeding people." *Liberator* quoted in John L. Thomas, *The Liberator: William Lloyd Garrison, a Biography* (Boston, 1963), 371.

65. Cooper, *South and the Politics of Slavery*, 334 (quotation). The key portions of the convention transcript as well as the Democratic platform appear in S & I, 3: 951–3, 958–68. See Roy Franklin Nichols, *Franklin Pierce: Young Hickory of the Granite Hills* (1931; Philadelphia, 1958), 3–196.

66. S & I, 3: 956–7 (quotation on 957); Holt, *Rise and Fall*, 712–25. The language of Scott's letter was strongly influenced, it appears, by Horace Greeley and other pro-Scott northerners. Toombs returned to Washington from the convention and denounced Scott as the tool of the northern Free Soil Whigs, "untrustworthy men most active . . . in promoting section strife and discord." CG, 31st Congress, 1st session, Appendix, 818. See also William E. Gienapp, "The Whig Party, the Compromise of 1850, and the Nomination of Winfield Scott," *Presidential Studies Quarterly*, 14 (1984): 399–415.

67. *National Era*, Aug. 19, 1852; Schuyler C. Marshall, "The Free Democratic Convention of 1852," *Pennsylvania History*, 22 (1955): 146–67; S & I, 2: 953–6 (quotation on 954); Sewell, *Ballots*, 244–7; Stewart, *Giddings*, 214–6; Harrold, *Bailey*, 152–4; Martin Duberman, *Charles Francis Adams, 1807–1886* (Stanford, CA, 1960), 181–2.

68. S & I, 2: 954, 955. Gamaliel Bailey wanted an even more Jacksonian-style platform, especially over free trade. See Harrold, *Bailey*, 152–3.

69. CG, 35th Congress, 1st session, Appendix, 65. On the convergence of the parties at the national level, see Joel H. Silbey, *The Shrine of Party: Congressional Voting Behavior, 1841–1852* (Pittsburgh, 1967), 121–36. At the state level, see Harry N. Scheiber, "Urban Rivalry and Internal Improvements in the Old Northwest, 1820–1860," *Ohio History*, 71 (1962): 227–39; Herbert Ershkowitz and William G. Shade, "Consensus or Conflict? Political Behavior in the State Legislatures during the Jacksonian Era," *JAH*, 58 (1971): 591–621; Peter Levine, *The Behavior of State Legislative Parties in the Jacksonian Era: New Jersey, 1829–1844* (Rutherford, NJ, 1977), esp. 91–235; Marc W. Kruman, *Parties and Politics in North Carolina, 1836–1865* (Baton Rouge, 1983), 55–85. See also Holt, *Rise and Fall*, 684–9, which confirms these findings for several additional states. This convergence should not be taken to mean that a smooth consensus over economic development had arisen throughout American society. Especially in the rural South, it appears, the convergence left many voters unsettled—and open to appeals from politicians who promised a break with politics as usual. See above all J. Mills Thornton III, *Politics and Power in a Slave Society: Alabama, 1800–1860* (Baton Rouge, 1978), 267–342. A similar dynamic to the one that Thornton ties to the rise of secessionism may have unfolded in the North, and helped shape the emergence of both political nativism and the Republican Party in the mid-1850s—a topic in need of further investigation.

70. Nevins, *Ordeal*, 2: 41; Nathaniel Hawthorne, *Life of Franklin Pierce* (Boston, 1852); Holt, *Rise and Fall*, 726–51. For a different interpretation of the election, which stresses religious and ethnic issues above all, see William E. Gienapp, *The Origins of the Republican Party, 1852–1856* (New York, 1987), 13–35. On the Whigs' disintegration in their strongest Deep South state, see John M. Sacher, "The Sudden Collapse of the Louisiana Whig Party," *JSH*, 65 (1999): 221–48. Hawthorne, knowing that the strains of a campaign and, even worse, the presidency would badly afflict his friend, also expressed sympathetic con-

cern: "Frank, I pity you! Indeed, I do, from the bottom of my heart!" Maunsell B. Field, *Memories of Many Men and of Some Women* (London, 1874), 160.

71. Henry Raymond to William Henry Seward, Nov. 6, 1852, Seward Papers, University of Rochester; S & I, 3: 103.

72. There were mitigating factors for the Whigs, even in the most lopsided southern returns. Scott had not run as a proud slaveholding son of the South, which cost him votes. The southern voters who rejected Scott did not apparently vote for the Democrats (whose overall southern vote, with a Yankee at the head of the ticket, also declined). Instead, most of the dissatisfied southern Whigs—more than 40 percent of its total from four years earlier—stayed home. Still, southern Whiggery was a shell of what it had been only four years earlier. On the returns as a whole, see Holt, *Rise and Fall*, 756–62.

73. Remini, *Webster*, 756–63 (quotation on 762).

CHAPTER TWENTY-TWO: THE TRUCE COLLAPSES

1. Toombs to John J. Crittenden, Dec. 5, 1852, quoted in Allan Nevins, *The Ordeal of the Union* (New York, 1947), 2: 41. On the train accident, see Roy Franklin Nichols, *Franklin Pierce: Young Hickory of the Granite Hills* (1931; Philadelphia, 1958), 224–36. Benny, as the boy was known, had been the Pierces' only surviving child; an older son had died at birth, and a second had perished of typhus at age four. On Pierce's presidency, see above all Larry Gara, *The Presidency of Franklin Pierce* (Lawrence, KS, 1991).

2. Richardson, 4: 2731, 2735.

3. *New York Tribune*, Aug. 27, 1851. On filibustering, the older study by Basil Rauch, *American Interests in Cuba, 1848–1852* (New York, 1948), should now be supplemented with Charles H. Brown, *Agents of Manifest Destiny: The Lives and Times of the Filibusterers* (Chapel Hill, 1980); Robert E. May, *Manifest Destiny's Underworld: Filibustering in Antebellum America* (Chapel Hill, 2002). On early escapades, see ibid., 1–18; John Hope Franklin, "The Southern Expansionists of 1846," *JSH*, 25 (1959): 323–38. See also Tom Chaffin, *Fatal Glory: Narciso López and the First Clandestine U.S. War against Cuba* (Charlottesville, 1996); from the Cuban as well as the U.S. perspective, Louis Perez, *Cuba and the United States: Ties of Singular Intimacy* (1990; Athens, GA, 1997), 29–50.

4. Brown, *Agents*, 67–108 (quotation on 105).

5. Edward L. Widmer, *Young America, the Flowering of Democracy in New York City* (New York, 1999), 185–209 (quotation on 187); May, *Underworld*, 112–6, 126–7.

6. "Mazzini-Young Europe," *DR*, 30 (1852): 41–52. On Sanders and the transformation of the *Review*, see Widmer, *Young America*, 189–92. The *Review's* literary department virtually disappeared after it ran its last book review of note, an obtuse pan of *Moby-Dick* as a work of "bad rhetoric, involved syntax, stilted sentiment and incoherent English." *DR*, 30 (1852): 93.

7. William L. Marcy to Pierre Soulé, July 23, 1853, in William R. Manning, ed., *Diplomatic Correspondence of the United States: Inter-American Affairs, 1831–1860* (Washington, 1932–39), 11: 160–6, (quotation on 162). See Amos Aschbach Ettinger, *The Mission to Spain of Pierre Soulé, 1853–1855* (New Haven, 1932); J. Preston Moore, "Pierre Soulé: Southern Expansionist and Promoter," *JSH*, (1955): 203–23; May, *Underworld*, 131–40; idem, *John A. Quitman: Old South Crusader* (Baton Rouge, 1985), esp. 236–95.

8. Robert E. May, *The Southern Dream of a Caribbean Empire, 1854–1861* (Baton Rouge, 1973), 60 (quotation).

9. Robert Johannsen, *Stephen A. Douglas* (New York, 1973), 304–400. Historical argument over the Kansas-Nebraska debate has, in its contentiousness, at times mimicked the debate itself. The narrative and interpretation here are indebted to Nevins, *Ordeal*, 2: 88–121; Roy F. Nichols, "The Kansas-Nebraska Act: A Century of Historiography," *Mississippi Valley Historical Review*, 43 (1956): 187–212; Johannsen, *Douglas*, 374–434; David Potter, *The Impending Crisis, 1848–1861* (New York, 1976), 145–76; James M. McPherson, *Bat-*

tle Cry of Freedom: The Civil War Era (New York, 1988), 121–9; Michael F. Holt, *The Rise and Fall of the American Whig Party: Jacksonian Politics and the Onset of the Civil War* (New York, 1999), 804–35.

10. See William E. Parrish, *David Rice Atchison of Missouri: Border Politician* (Columbia, MO, 1961), esp. 110–210. On the early struggles between Atchison and Benton, which cost Benton his Senate seat, see also William Nisbet Chambers, *Old Bullion Benton: Senator from the New West* (Boston, 1956), 341–3, 355–77.

11. Nevins, *Ordeal*, 2: 93 (quotation).

12. CG, 32nd Congress, 2nd session, 1117; Douglas quoted in Nevins, *Ordeal*, 2: 96. Douglas may have envisaged as early as November 1852 a bill that would repeal the Missouri Compromise. See his letter to Partemas Taylor Turnley, Nov. 30, 1852, in Robert Johannsen, ed., *The Letters of Stephen A. Douglas* (Urbana, IL, 1961), 255. The authenticity of that letter, however, remains in dispute. On the Senate vote to table Douglas's original bill in 1853, all of the leading antislavery northerners, including Charles Sumner, William Seward, and Salmon Chase, along with the majority of New Englanders, abstained; the antislavery New York Whig Hamilton Fish voted with the southerners against Douglas. From the start, Douglas knew that his best chances of passing a Nebraska bill lay in building a Senate coalition of northwesterners and southerners.

13. CG, 33rd Congress, 1st session, Appendix, 559.

14. *National Era* [Washington], Jan. 24, 1854. For contrasting interpretations of the "Appeal," none of which quite takes its full measure, see Nevins, *Ordeal*, 2: 111–3; Eric Foner, *Free Soil, Free Labor, Free Men: The Ideology of the Republican Party before the Civil War* (New York, 1970), 94–95; Potter, *Impending Crisis*, 162–5; Richard H. Sewell, *Ballots for Freedom: Antislavery Politics in the United States, 1837–1860* (New York, 1976), 255–7. Salmon Chase, who claimed that at least half a million copies of the "Appeal" were circulated, called its publication the turning point in rallying the North against Douglas's bill. If Chase, in character, somewhat exaggerated its immediate popular impact, the importance of the "Appeal" in polarizing the debate over Douglas's bill along sectional lines was enormous. See Chase to John P. Bigelow, Sept. 23, 1854, John P. Bigelow Papers, HU.

15. CG, 33rd Congress, 1st session, 239; Potter, *Impending Crisis*, 163.

16. H. F. French to B. B. French, May 30, 1854, quoted in Sewell, *Ballots*, 257. Had more state legislatures been in session, it is likely that the official protests would have been even wider.

17. *Liberator* [Boston], May 9, 1855; Stanley W. Campbell, *The Slave Catchers: Enforcement of the Fugitive Slave Law, 1850–1860* (Chapel Hill, 1970), 124–32; Jane H. Pease and William H. Pease, *The Fugitive Slave Law and Anthony Burns: A Problem in Law Enforcement* (Philadelphia, 1975), 28–29; also Albert J. Von Frank, *The Trials of Anthony Burns: Freedom and Slavery in Emerson's Boston* (Cambridge, MA, 1998).

18. CG, 33rd Congress, first session, 1254; Stephens quoted in Nevins, *Ordeal*, 2: 156. The northern Democrats voted narrowly in favor of the bill, 44 to 42; southerners, Whigs and Democrats combined, voted in favor, 69 to 9.

19. Smith to John Wilson, Jan. 31, 1854, quoted in Holt, *Rise and Fall*, 818. Nine southern Whig senators and thirteen southern Whigs in the House voted for the bill. Smith, in disgust, resigned his Senate seat.

20. Robinson, *Address to the Voters of the Fifth Congressional District* (n.p., n.d. [1862]), 11. See also *Evening Post* [New York], May 15, 1854; Francis P. Blair Sr. to Martin Van Buren, Aug. 24, 1854, Benjamin Butler to Martin Van Buren, Dec. 2, 1854, VBP; Preston King to Gideon Welles, Oct. 21, 1854, Gideon Welles Papers, Connecticut Historical Society. Van Buren thought the Kansas-Nebraska Act odious and, as he recalled, "mourned over its adoption." Yet he would later back down and, in 1856, support both the act and the Democratic Party, despising the Republicans as a purely sectional party and clinging to his old insistence that only the Democrats could "maintain party cohesions between men of the free and slave states." Van Buren, *Inquiry into the Origin and Course of Political Parties in*

the United States (New York, 1867), 355; Donald B. Cole, *Martin Van Buren and the American Political System* (Princeton, 1984), 423–4.

21. *National Intelligencer* [Washington], May 29, 1854; Thomas Wentworth Higginson, *Cheerful Yesterdays* (Boston, 1899), 153–4; Pease and Pease, *Burns*, 28–33.

22. George S. Hillard to Francis Lieber, June 2, 1854, quoted in Nevins, *Ordeal*, 2: 152–3; Pease and Pease, *Burns*, 38–48; Whitman, "A Boston Ballad (1854)," in *Walt Whitman: Complete Poetry and Collected Prose*, Justin Kaplan, ed. (New York, 1982), 404. Burns's friends eventually bought him his freedom from a speculating North Carolina slave trader for fourteen hundred dollars, and Burns returned to Boston (though part of the way he traveled under the armed protection of the slave trader). After two years of study at Oberlin College, paid for with the proceeds of a biography, Burns served as a minister, first in Indianapolis, then in a small Canadian settlement near Lake Ontario, where he died in 1862, at age twenty-eight.

23. Robert F. Lucid, ed., *The Journal of Richard Henry Dana, Jr.* (Cambridge, MA, 1968), 2: 638; John B. Allen to Charles Sumner, June 5, 1854, Charles Sumner Papers, HU; Thomas D. Morris, *Free Men All: The Personal Liberty Laws of the North, 1780–1861* (Baltimore, 1974), 167–85.

24. CG, 33rd Congress, 1st session, Appendix, 769.

25. *Nebraska and Kansas Report of the Committee of the Massachusetts Emigrant Society with the Act of Incorporation and Other Documents* (Boston, 1854), 7. On the Emigrant Aid Company, see Louise Barry, "The New England Emigrant Aid Company Parties of 1855," *Kansas Historical Quarterly*, 12 (1943): 227–68; Nevins, *Ordeal*, 2: 307–11; Samuel A. Johnson, *The Battle Cry of Freedom: The New England Emigrant Aid Company in the Kansas Crusade* (Lawrence, KS, 1954), 3–91; James A. Rawley, *Race and Politics: "Bleeding Kansas" and the Coming of the Civil War* (Philadelphia, 1969), 84–85.

26. Atchison to Jefferson Davis, Sept. 24, 1854, David Rice Atchison Papers, University of Missouri. The pro-slavery men's precaution was probably unnecessary given the balance of forces among the actual settlers at the time the election was held. A territorial census in 1855 found only 242 bondmen in all of Kansas, and confirmed that three-fifths of the eligible voters came from Missouri and other slave states. See McPherson, *Battle Cry*, 146.

27. *Dover Enquirer* [NH], Feb. 21, 1854; Lincoln, "Speech at Peoria, Illinois, October 16, 1854," in CWAL, 2: 275; Nevins, *Ordeal*, 2: 316–7; William E. Gienapp, *The Origins of the Republican Party, 1852–1856* (New York, 1987), 147–8; Holt, *Rise and Fall*, 836.

28. Greeley to Schuyler Colfax, Jan. 18, 1853, Greeley-Colfax Correspondence, Horace Greeley Papers, NYPL.

29. Gienapp, *Origins*, 103–66, presents the most detailed state-by-state examination of the strengths and weaknesses of the fusion effort, but for different views of the movement, see Nevins, *Ordeal*, 2: 316–23; McPherson, *Battle Cry*, 126–30.

30. On the immigration of the 1840s and 1850s, including the relevant statistics, see Marcus Lee Hansen, *The Atlantic Migration, 1607–1860* (Cambridge, MA, 1940), 242–306; Maldwyn Allen Jones, *American Immigration* (Chicago, 1960), 92–116; Kerby A. Miller, *Emigrants and Exiles: Ireland and the Irish Exodus to North America* (New York, 1985), 280–344; Hasia R. Diner, *Erin's Daughters in America: Irish Immigrant Women in the Nineteenth Century* (Baltimore, 1983); Tyler Anbinder, *Nativism and Slavery: The Northern Know-Nothings and the Politics of the 1850s* (New York, 1992), 3–8. Between 1845 and 1854, no fewer than 1.2 million Irish immigrants arrived in the United States.

31. Anbinder, *Nativism*, 9–15; Michael Feldberg, *The Philadelphia Riots of 1844: A Study in Ethnic Conflict* (Westport, CT, 1975); Leo Heshkowitz, "The Native American Democratic Association in New York City, 1835–1836," *New-York Historical Society Quarterly*, 46 (1962): 41–59; Ira M. Leonard, "The Rise and Fall of the American Republican Party in New York City," *New-York Historical Society Quarterly*, 50 (1966): 151–92; Sean Wilentz, *Chants Democratic: New York City & the Rise of the American Working Class, 1788–1850* (New York, 1984), 315–34. On Whitney and the Order of United Americans,

see above all Bruce Levine, "Conservatism, Nativism, and Slavery: Thomas R. Whitney and the Origins of the Know-Nothing Party," *JAH*, 88 (2001): 455–88.

32. Robert Ernst, *Immigrant Life in New York City, 1825–1863* (New York, 1949), 214–7; J. Wayne Laurens, *The Crisis; or, The Enemies of America Unmasked* (Philadelphia, 1855), quoted in Levine, "Nativism." 468.

33. John Hughes, *The Decline of Protestantism and Its Cause. A Lecture: Delivered in St. Patrick's Cathedral, on Sunday Evening, November 10, 1850* (New York, 1850), 26. On the conservative Roman Catholic reactions over the slavery issue, see Walter G. Sharrow, "Northern Catholic Intellectuals and the Coming of the Civil War," *New-York Historical Society Quarterly*, 58 (1974): 35–56. While Hughes frightened and antagonized sensitive American Protestants, the fortuitous arrival and extended American tour of papal nuncio Gaetano Bedini, a ruthless antirevolutionary, in 1853 created an anti-Catholic sensation. The furor is well covered in Anbinder, *Nativism*, 24–30.

34. See esp. Ian R. Tyrell, *Sobering Up: From Temperance to Prohibition in Antebellum America, 1800–1860* (Westport, CT, 1979); W. J. Rorabaugh, *The Alcoholic Republic: An American Tradition* (New York, 1976). On temperance and the Whigs, see Gienapp, *Origins*, 44–60; Holt, *Rise and Fall*, esp. 689–92.

35. On Scott and the "Americus" disaster in the 1852 campaign, see Potter, *Impending Crisis*, 245 (quotation); Holt, *Rise and Fall*, 730. A high-church Episcopalian who had had his daughters educated in a Catholic convent, and was sometimes accused of being a crypto-Roman Catholic, Scott had principled reasons to repudiate nativism, but his clumsy efforts to do so in the campaign were utterly unconvincing.

36. Anbinder, *Nativism*, 20–51, gives the most thorough recent account, but see also Levine, "Nativism."

37. Samuel C. Busey, *Immigration: Its Evils and Consequences* (New York, 1856), quoted in Levine, "Nativism", 475; Anbinder, *Nativism*, 31–43; Mark Voss-Hubbard, *Beyond Party: Cultures of Antipartyism in Northern Politics before the Civil War* (Baltimore, 2002), 109–17. For different views over the social complexion of the northern nativist movement, see, e.g., Michael F. Holt, "The Politics of Impatience: The Origins of Know Nothingism," *JAH*, 60 (1973): 309–31; Ronald P. Formisano, *The Birth of Mass Political Parties: Michigan, 1827–1861* (Princeton, 1971), 239–65; James L. Hutson, "Economic Change and Political Realignment in Antebellum Pennsylvania," *Pennsylvania Magazine of History and Biography*, 113 (1989): 347–95; Robert D. Parment, "Connecticut's Know-Nothings: A Profile," *Connecticut Historical Society Bulletin*, 31 (1966): 84–90; Dale Baum, *The Civil War Party System: The Case of Massachusetts, 1848–1876* (Chapel Hill, 1984), 27–28; John R. Mulkern, *The Know-Nothing Party in Massachusetts: The Rise and Fall of a People's Movement* (Boston, 1990). On less conservative and more plebeian forms of working-class nativism that evolved alongside the Order of United Americans, emphasized some of its themes, but displayed an uneasiness with the more prominent nativist groups — and was later effaced — see Wilentz, *Chants Democratic*, 343–6.

38. On Know-Nothing ideology, see above all the contrasting discussions in Anbinder, *Nativism*, 103–26 (quotation on 123); Levine, "Nativism" (quotations on 466, 480); Voss-Hubbard, *Beyond Party*, 105–40.

39. Henry Wilson quoted in Baum, *Party System*, 28.

40. Quotation in Levine, "Nativism," 477. On nativist thinking in antislavery circles, see the balanced appraisal in Foner, *Free Soil*, 226–60. Foner usefully distinguishes between the broad cultural nativism, in which many antislavery northerners shared, and the more pointed political nativism pushed by the Know-Nothings.

41. Quotations in Levine, "Nativism," 478, 481.

42. Dana quoted in Foner, *Free Soil*, 234; George Julian, *Political Recollections, 1840–1872* (Chicago, 1884), 141–2.

43. On Kansas-Nebraska and Democratic losses, see Leonard L. Richards, *The Slave Power: The Free North and Southern Domination, 1780–1860* (Baton Rouge, 2000), 190, 193–4.

On the Illinois intrigues, see Nevins, *Ordeal*, 2: 393–5; Don Fehrenbacher, *Prelude to Greatness: Lincoln in the 1850s* (Stanford, 1962), 34–38.

44. Robert C. Winthrop to John H. Clifford, Nov. 16, 1854, quoted in Holt, *Rise and Fall*, 893; Mulkern, *Know-Nothing*, 61–86; Anbinder, *Nativism*, 52–102. Elsewhere, the nativists ran well in New York (winning four congressional seats and cooperating in the victories of seven other candidates) and in Pennsylvania (supporting the triumphant Whig candidate for governor and winning the mayoral election in Philadelphia). They could claim some sort of significant victory in every other state where they had time to organize. On the Massachusetts constitution battle, see Kevin Sweeny, "Rum, Romanism, Representation, and Reform: Coalition Politics in Massachusetts, 1847–1853," *Civil War History*, 22 (1976): 116–37.

45. John W. Geary to Franklin Pierce, Dec. 22, 1856, quoted in Nevins, *Ordeal*, 2: 381.

46. Charles Robinson to Eli Thayer, Apr. 2, 1855, Eli Thayer Collection, Kansas State Historical Society; Don W. Wilson, *Governor Charles Robinson of Kansas* (Lawrence, KS, 1975), 17–35. The fullest account of these proceedings is the official report by the committee, headed by William A. Howard of Michigan, to investigate the voting irregularities; see 34th Congress, 1st session, House Report No. 200 (quotation on 357).

47. 34th Congress, 1st session, House Report No. 200, 937 (quotation); Nevins, *Ordeal*, 2: 384–90; Nichols, *Pierce*, 407–18.

48. "Free State Convention!" broadside, Kansas State Historical Society; Nevins, *Ordeal*, 2: 390–3, 408–9. A former-pro-Douglasite-turned-free-stater named Jim Lane attempted, first at Big Springs, to commit the antislavery forces to the removal of all blacks and mulattoes as well as slaves, but Reeder and his supporters prevailed, and the abolition provision passed the Topeka convention by a tally of 21 to 11. "Journal, Topeka Constitutional Convention, November 9, 1855, Afternoon session," Kansas State Historical Society.

49. Hiram Hill to "Dear Brother," Dec. 7, 1855, Hiram Hill Collection, Kansas State Historical Society; Leverett W. Spring, *Kansas: The Prelude to the War for the Union* (Boston, 1890), 97, 98. On the so-called Wakarusa War, named after a creek near Lawrence, that culminated in the aborted attack, see also Nevins, *Ordeal*, 2: 409–11.

50. Quotation in R. G. Elliott, "The Big Springs Convention," Kansas State Historical Society, *Transactions* 8 (1904): 362–77 (quotation on 376).

51. *Independent* [New York], Mar. 7, 1856; *New-York Daily Tribune*, Apr. 9, 1856; Paxton Hibben, *Henry Ward Beecher: An American Portrait* (New York, 1927), 159.

52. *Squatter Sovereignty* [Kansas], May 6, 8, 13, 20, 1856; Nevins, *Ordeal*, 2: 433–5.

53. *Union* [Lecompton], May 24, 1856. On the "Sack of Lawrence" and its impact, see Nevins, *Ordeal*, 2: 435–6; Rawley, *Race and Politics*, 129–34.

54. Sumner to Salmon Chase, May 15, 1856, in *SPCP*. For accounts of Sumner's preparation and his speech, generally unfriendly to Sumner's harshness, see Nevins, *Ordeal*, 2: 441–3; David H. Donald, *Charles Sumner and the Coming of the Civil War* (New York, 1960), 278–89. Neither take notice of Sumner's remarks about political democracy.

55. *CG*, 34th Congress, 1st session, Appendix, 529–43 (quotations on 530, 534, 535). The speech also appears in Sumner, *The Works of Charles Sumner* (Boston, 1873), 4: 125–48.

56. *CG*, 34th Congress, 1st session, Appendix, 540–2 (quotations on 542).

57. Ibid., 530, 543, 544–6. Horace Greeley departed from other Republican editors, declaring that the speech had added "a cubit to [Sumner's] stature." *New-York Daily Tribune*, May 20, 1856. On other responses, see Donald, *Sumner*, 288–9.

58. The attack is well described in Donald, *Sumner*, 289–97.

59. *CG*, 34th Congress, 1st session, 832; *Evening Post*, May 23, 1856. The *New-York Daily Tribune* ran a lengthy maudlin verse by one of Theodore Parker's parishioners, Julia Ward Howe, the wife of the reformer and fierce abolitionist Samuel Gridley Howe: "SUMNER, the task thou hast chosen was thine for its fitness./Never was a paschal victim more stainlessly offered,—/Never on milder brow gleamed the crown of the martyr." See Sumner, *Works*, 4: 325–6.

60. *Richmond Enquirer*, June 2, 1856; Donald, *Sumner*, 297–8; McPherson, *Battle Cry*, 151.

Reelected to both the Thirty-fourth and Thirty-fifth Congresses, Brooks would die from the croup in January 1857 at age thirty-eight. The Georgia legislature immediately renamed a county in his honor, which remains Brooks County to this day. The best review of the immediate reactions to and repercussion of the Sumner affair is William E. Gienapp, "The Crime against Sumner: The Caning of Charles Sumner and the Rise of the Republican Party," *Civil War History*, 25 (1979): 218–45. Gienapp persuasively shows that the attack on Sumner and the southern response greatly enlarged the Republican Party's appeal. I find more strained his argument that this appeal had little to do with revulsion against slavery, but was instead directed at what Gienapp regards as a symbolic intellectual and cultural construct, the Slave Power—as if the concept of the Slave Power was somehow imaginable without slavery at its foundation. In addition to Larry Gara, "Slavery and the Slave Power: A Crucial Distinction," *Civil War History*, 15 (1969): 5–18, see Gienapp's fuller arguments in "The Republican Party and the Slave Power," in Robert H. Abzug and Stephen Maizlish, eds., *New Perspectives on Race and Slavery in America* (Lexington, KY, 1986), 51–78; Gienapp, *Origins*, 76–77, 357–65. As Gienapp himself recognized, the vast majority of northerners "disliked the institution of slavery in the abstract and had no great desire to see it expand." Ibid., 76. Concerning the mid-1850s, this is to put the matter too mildly. The Sumner affair helped crystallize that dislike for many voters who had heretofore rejected antislavery politics.

61. Salmon Brown, "John Brown and His Sons in Kansas Territory," *Indiana Magazine of History*, 21 (1935): 142–50; Stephen B. Oates, *To Purge This Land with Blood: A Biography of John Brown* (1970; Amherst, MA, 1984), 51–125, 129 (quotation). As Oates notes, there are several conflicting interpretations of Brown's state of mind in the summer of 1856, and of whether the attack on Sumner played a role in causing his subsequent actions. I am persuaded by Oates's argument that a desire for retaliation had a great deal to do with moving Brown to murder. See ibid., 384–5 n. 3.

62. Ibid., 126–205 (quotations on 129, 193). Although it is not as persuasive as Oates's book, see the rich and rambling account in James C. Malin, *John Brown and the Legend of Fifty-six* (Philadelphia, 1942), which concentrates on this period in Brown's life and debunks many of the more heroic or exculpatory depictions of the Pottawatomie affair.

63. See Nevins, *Ordeal*, 2: 475–6.

64. Although mainly concerned with the North, Anbinder, *Nativism*, 162–245, offers the most useful account of political nativism's decline, but see also Voss-Hubbard, *Beyond Party*, 178–216.

65. W. Darrell Overdyke, *The Know-Nothing Party in the South* (Baton Rouge, 1950), esp. 16–33, 73–126, 198–239; James H. Broussard, "Some Determinants of Know-Nothing Electoral Strength in the South," *Louisiana History*, 7 (1966): 5–20; Jean H. Baker, *Ambivalent American: The Know-Nothing Party in Maryland* (Baltimore, 1977); Holt, *Rise and Fall*, 932–9; Ira Berlin and Herbert G. Gutman, "Natives and Immigrants, Free Men and Slaves: Urban Workingmen in the Antebellum American South," *AHR*, 88 (1983): 1175–200. Although partly based in the southern coastal and river port cities (where gang warfare between working-class nativists and immigrants rivaled the ethnic rioting that resurged in the North), the preponderance of southern Know-Nothing support came from displaced Whig planters. On Fillmore's secret Know-Nothing membership, see Gienapp, *Origins*, 260 n. 76.

66. *National Intelligencer*, May 8, 1855; Nevins, *Ordeal*, 2: 399–400; Anbinder, *Nativism*, 165–72. On southern nativists and the 1856 election, see Overdyke, *Know-Nothing*, 127–55.

67. Anbinder, *Nativism*, 89–90. On Wilson, one of the most capable politicians of his day, see also Richard H. Abbott, *Cobbler in Congress: The Life of Henry Wilson, 1812–1875* (Lexington, KY, 1972); Ernest A. McKay, *Henry Wilson, Practical Radical: A Portrait of a Politician* (Port Washington, NY, 1971). Wilson would later express embarrassment for his connection with nativism but justified it on pragmatic grounds, claiming that large numbers of antislavery men "saw that the demolition of the Whig and Democratic parties by

the American party might produce a political chaos out of which a new and better creation might spring." Wilson quoted in Voss-Hubbard, *Beyond Party*, 179.

68. Winthrop to John P. Kennedy, Oct. 27, 1854, quoted in Nevins, *Ordeal*, 2: 343; Baum, *Party System*, 24–48; Gienapp, *Origins*, 133–9; Mulkern, *Know-Nothings*, 97–99; Anbinder, *Nativism*, 91. Another Massachusetts ex–Free Soiler, nativist lawyer Anson Burlingame, won a seat in the House as a nominal Know-Nothing in 1854.

69. *New York Herald*, Feb. 19, 20, 21, 1856; Gienapp, *Origins*, 259–64; Anbinder, *Nativism*, 206–9.

70. *New York Herald*, June 13, 14, 15, 1856; Anbinder, *Nativism*, 215–7.

71. Sewell, *Ballots*, 277–9; Gienapp, *Origins*, 250–9; Julian, *Political Recollections*, 147–50; Leonard H. Bernstein, "Convention in Pittsburgh: The Story of the National Founding of a New Party," *Western Pennsylvania Historical Magazine*, 49 (1966): 289–300; *Frederick Douglass's Paper* [Rochester, NY], Apr. 25, 1856. By August, Douglass had changed his mind and, after a dalliance with his friend Gerrit Smith's secretarian Radical Abolitionist Party, supported the Republican ticket. Ibid., Aug. 15, 1856. William Seward declined an invitation to attend the Silver Spring meeting, on the dubious grounds that he made a rule of staying away from "plans or schemes of political action." Seward to Francis P. Blair Sr., Dec. 29, 1855, Blair-Lee Papers, PU.

72. S & I, 2: 1039–41 (quotations on 1040, 1041). The fullest account of the Republican convention and the machinations that led to Frémont's nomination appears in Gienapp, *Origins*, 305–46.

73. Useful recent studies of Frémont include Ferol Egan, *Frémont: Explorer for a Restless Nation* (New York, 1977); Tom Chaffin, *Pathfinder: John Charles Frémont and the Course of American Empire* (New York, 2002); but on politics see also Allan Nevins, *Fremont: Pathmarker of the West* (1928; New York, 1992). *Indiana True Republican*, Sept. 2, 1858.

74. Joseph Neilson, *Memories of Rufus Choate* (Boston, 1884), 350–1; Anbinder, *Nativism*, 217–9, 226–33. Among the prominent Whig conservatives who finally endorsed Fillmore in 1856 were Robert Winthrop and Edward Everett.

75. Manning, ed., *Diplomatic Correspondence*, 11: 175–8, 193–4; May, *Southern Dream*, 67–71.

76. On Walker, see C. Stanley Urban, "The Ideology of Southern Imperialism: New Orleans and the Caribbean, 1845–1860," *Louisiana Historical Quarterly*, 29 (1956): 48–73 (quotation on 66); Albert Z. Carr, *The World and William Walker* (New York, 1963); May, *Southern Dream*, 77–135; Brown, *Agents*, 174–93, 267–467.

77. B. B. French to H. F. French, May 29, 1856, French Papers, LC. On the Democratic divisions in New York, see Gienapp, *Origins*, 147–50; Walter L. Ferree, "The New York Democracy: Division and Reunion, 1847–1852" (Ph.D. dissert., University of Pennsylvania, 1953).

78. William G. Bishop, *Register of the Debates and Proceedings of the Virginia Reform Convention* (Richmond, 1851), Appendix, 5–6; Pierce to Stephen A. Douglas, May 28, 1855, quoted in Nevins, *Ordeal*, 2: 398. On Wise's reasoning and maneuvering, see Craig Simpson, "Political Compromise and the Protection of Slavery: Henry A. Wise and the Virginia Constitutional Convention of 1850–51," *Virginia Magazine of History and Biography*, 83 (1975): 387–405; also William W. Freehling, *The Road to Disunion: Secessionists at Bay, 1776–1854* (New York, 1990), 511–5. In North Carolina, a similar campaign for constitutional revision in the late 1840s and 1850s led to the toppling of the persisting freehold requirement in voting for the upper legislative house, a reform finally approved by a three-to-one majority in a popular referendum in 1857. Henry Wise's North Carolina reform counterpart was pro-slavery Democratic Governor David S. Reid, who was elected in 1850 promising to eliminate the property requirement and proclaiming that the "elective franchise is the dearest right of an American citizen." Reform was less successful, as ever, in South Carolina. Yet even in Columbia, the neo-Calhounite radicals temporarily lost the political initiative to more moderate (though assuredly pro-slavery) reform Democrats led by James L. Orr. The effect of all these efforts to embrace nonslaveholders was to check

the most extreme of the fire-eaters, who shared Calhoun's mistrust of democracy and the established political parties. They also strengthened the Democrats against the nationalist ex-Whig Americans in the South—and made the pro-slavery southerners all the more powerful within the counsels of the Democratic Party. On the politics of constitution revision in North Carolina, see Paul Apperson Reid, *Gubernatorial Campaigns and Administrations of David S. Reid* (Cullowhee, NC, 1953); John Spencer Bassett, "Suffrage in the State of North Carolina, 1776–1861," *American Historical Association Annual Report for 1895* (Washington, DC, 1896), 281–4 (quotation on 281); Marc W. Kruman, *Parties and Politics in North Carolina, 1836–1865* (Baton Rouge, 1983), 86–103; Thomas E. Jeffrey, *State Politics and National Politics: North Carolina, 1815–1861* (Athens, GA, 1989), esp. 205–18, 241; idem, "'Free Suffrage' Revisited: Party Politics and Constitutional Reform in Antebellum North Carolina," *North Carolina Historical Review*, 59 (1982): 24–38; Alexander Keyssar, *The Right to Vote: The Contested History of Democracy in the United States* (New York, 2000), 41.

79. Van Buren, *Autobiography of Martin Van Buren* (1920; New York, 1973), 2: 496. The best biography of Buchanan remains Philip S. Klein, *President James Buchanan: A Biography* (University Park, PA, 1962); but see also Elbert B. Smith, *The Presidency of James Buchanan* (Lawrence, KS, 1975), 11–16; Michael J. Birkner, ed., *James Buchanan and the Political Crisis of the 1850s* (Selinsgrove, PA, 1996), esp. 17–67.

80. Benton quoted in Smith, *Presidency*, 5. On the Democratic convention, see Roy F. Nichols, *The Disruption of American Democracy* (1948; New York, 1962), 28–32.

81. Whittier, "What of the Day?" (1856), in Whittier, *Anti-Slavery Poems: Songs of Labor and Reform* (Boston, 1888), 192. On the electioneering in 1856, see Nevins, *Ordeal*, 2: 487–505; Nichols, *Disruption*, 17–62; Gienapp, *Origins*, 375–411.

82. Quotations in Rawley, *Race and Politics*, 151, 167.

83. Quotations from Michael F. Holt, *The Political Crisis of the 1850s* (New York, 1978), 197; McPherson, *Battle Cry*, 160.

84. John Slidell quoted in Nevins, *Ordeal*, 2: 496.

85. Fessenden quoted in Sewell, *Ballots*, 291.

86. S & I, 3: 1094. On the Fillmore campaign, its successes, and its far greater failures, see Anbinder, *Nativism*, 220–45. Outside Maryland, Fillmore ran strongest in Louisiana (48.3 percent), Tennessee (47.8 percent), and Kentucky (47.4 percent). A shift of a few thousand votes in these states to Fillmore would have thrown the election into the House of Representatives. In the free states, Fillmore voters—though not Fillmore or the American Party—would hold the balance of power in future elections in Pennsylvania, New Jersey, Indiana, Illinois, and California, a matter of abiding concern to the Republicans.

87. W. H. Furness to Charles Sumner, Nov. 9, 1856, Charles Sumner Papers, HU; quotation in Rawley, *Race and Politics*, 172.

88. Quotations in Hendrik Booraem V, *The Formation of the Republican Party in New York: Politics and Conscience in the Antebellum North* (New York, 1983), 190; S & I, 3: 1031.

89. *New Bedford Mercury*, quoted in *The Republican Scrap Book* (Boston, 1856), 35.

90. Blair, *A Voice from the Grave of Jackson! Letter from Francis P. Blair to a Public Meeting in New York, held April 29, 1856* (New York, 1856), 1, 3, 8, 11.

91. Charles Francis Adams, *What Makes Slavery a Matter of National Concern? A Lecture Delivered, By Invitation, at New York, January 30, and at Syracuse, February 1, 1855* (Boston, 1855), 19–20, 27–8.

92. Seward, *The Parties of the Day. Speech of William H. Seward at Auburn, October 21, 1856* (Washington, DC,1857), in Joel H. Silbey, *The American Party Battle: Election Campaign Pamphlets, 1828–1876* (Cambridge, MA, 1999), 73–74. See also Seward, *The Slaveholding Class Dominant in the Republic. Speech of William H. Seward, October 2, 1856* (Washington, DC,1857). On a similar address, given a year earlier, Richard Henry Dana wrote, "Seward's speech at Albany, on the 'privileged classes', the oligarchy of Slavery, has been the key note of the New Party." Lucid, ed., *Journal of Richard Henry Dana, Jr.*, 2: 681.

93. On northern officeholding, see, e.g., Horace B. Davis, "The Occupations of Massachu-

setts Legislators, 1790–1950," *New England Quarterly*, 24 (1951): 89–100; Rodney O. Davis, "The People in Miniature: The Illinois General Assembly, 1818–1848," *Illinois Historical Journal*, 81 (1988): 95–108. On the South, see chapter 14, pp. 431–2, and chapter 23, pp. 725–34.

94. *Richmond Enquirer and Muscogee Herald* [AL] in *London Times*, Oct. 28, 1856, quoted in Nevins, *Ordeal*, 2: 516.

CHAPTER TWENTY-THREE: A NIGHTMARE BROODS OVER SOCIETY

1. Richardson, 4: 2962.
2. *CG*, 35th Congress, 1st session, 939–45 (quotations on 941).
3. Don E. Fehrenbacher, *The Dred Scott Case: Its Significance in American Law and Politics* (New York, 1978), 311–3. Fehrenbacher's book remains by far the most thorough account of the legal and political issues, but see also two useful collections of sources and commentary: Stanley I. Kutler, *The Dred Scott Decision: Law or Politics?* (Boston, 1967); Paul Finkelman, *Dred Scott v. Sandford: A Brief History with Documents* (Boston, 1997). See also Walter Ehrlich, *They Have No Rights: Dred Scott's Struggle for Freedom* (Westport, CT, 1979). The contacts between Buchanan and Grier went undiscovered for nearly seventy years. See Philip Auchampaugh, "James Buchanan, the Court, and the Dred Scott Case," *Tennessee Historical Magazine*, 9 (1926): 231–40. For press speculation and predictions at the time, see *New York Express*, Jan. 5, 1857; *New-York Daily Tribune*, Mar. 5, 1857; *Commercial Advertiser* [New York], Mar. 5, 1857.
4. *Daily Union* [Washington], Mar. 12, 1857; *New York Herald*, Mar. 8, 1857. The northern conservative mercantile press agreed with the southerners and doughface Democrats, claiming that the case had been "decided on authority which admits of no appeal or question, and which few will presume to dispute." *Journal of Commerce* [New York], Mar. 11, 1857.
5. Peter Lesley to Lydia Maria Child, Oct. 11, 1857, quoted in James L. Huston, *The Panic of 1857 and the Coming of the Civil War* (Baton Rouge, 1987), 25. For an older but still extremely useful narrative of the Democratic Party's crack-up, more sympathetic to Buchanan and his administration, see Roy F. Nichols, *The Disruption of American Democracy* (1948; New York, 1962), esp. 17–364.
6. *Evening News* [St. Louis], Apr. 3, 1857; Fehrenbacher, *Scott*, 240; Ehrlich, *Rights*, 9–40. On Harriet Scott, see also Lea VanderVelde and Sandhya Subramanian, "Mrs. Dred Scott," *Yale Law Journal*, 106 (1997): 1033–122.
7. For detailed accounts of the Scotts' travels and legal actions before the case reached the Supreme Court, see Fehrenbacher, *Scott*, 239–83; Ehrlich, *Rights*, 16–88. A Supreme Court clerk mistranscribed "Sanford" as "Sandford" on the case docket—hence, the misnomer in the official record.
8. *Scott v. Emerson*, 15 Missouri 576, 582.
9. Kaufman, *Dred Scott's Advocate*, esp. 162–228.
10. Both McLean and Curtis are in need of modern biographies, but see Francis P. Weisenburger, *The Life of John McLean: A Politician on the United States Supreme Court* (Columbus, OH, 1937), 188–210; Benjamin R. Curtis, *A Memoir of Benjamin Robbins Curtis, LL.D., With Some of His Professional and Miscellaneous Writings* (Boston, 1879); Stuart Alan Streichler, "Justice Curtis and the Constitution in the Civil War Era" (Ph.D. dissert., Johns Hopkins University, 1996).
11. For a concise account of Taney and the Taney Court, see R. Kent Newmyer, *The Supreme Court under Marshall and Taney* (Arlington Heights, IL, 1968), 89–146; also Arthur Bester, "The American Civil War as a Constitutional Crisis," *AHR*, 69 (1964): 327–52; Paul Finkelman, "Hooted Down the Pages of History: Reconsidering the Greatness of Chief Justice Taney," *Journal of Supreme Court History*, 18 (1994): 83–102. On the other

southern justices, see Robert Saunders Jr., *John Archibald Campbell: Southern Moderate, 1811–1889* (Tuscalooa, AL, 1997), esp. 124–35; John Paul Frank, *Justice Daniel Dissenting: A Biography of Peter V. Daniel, 1784–1860* (Cambridge, MA, 1964), esp. 243–58; and (despite its blatant hostility to the abolitionists) Alexander A. Lawrence, *James Moore Wayne: Southern Unionist* (Chapel Hill, 1943), 139–79.

12. Taney's opinion, the concurring opinions, and the dissents appear in *Dred Scott v. Sandford*, 19 Howard 393 (1857). A useful and accessible selection appears in Finkelman, ed., *Scott*, 55–126. On the scene at the Court, see Allan Nevins, *The Emergence of Lincoln* (New York, 1951), 1: 101–2; Fehrenbacher, *Scott*, 315–6. On the question of citizenship, Taney recognized that individual states could give state citizenship to blacks. But he insisted that since blacks were not part of the national "family" under the Constitution, black state citizenship was irrelevant in the rest of the Union, regardless of the Constitution's so-called comity clause (Article IV, Section 1), which guarantees that any state's "public Acts, Records, and judicial Proceedings" must be given "Full Faith and Credit" in all other states. After so ruling on black citizenship, the chief justice could have dismissed the rest of the case on the grounds that Scott had no standing to file a suit. But Taney insisted that because the Missouri circuit court had ruled on all aspects of the case, he and his Court would do so as well.

13. For a discussion of the issues of judicial supremacy in the case, see Keith Whittington, "The Road Not Taken: Dred Scott, Judicial Authority, and Political Questions," *Journal of Politics*, 63 (2001): 365–91. Whittington points to a more constrained and reasonable version of judicial review contained in Justice Curtis's dissent, which would have allowed for important realms of constitutional politics outside the judiciary.

14. *New-York Daily Tribune*, Mar. 7 (quotation), 26, 1857; Fehrenbacher, *Scott*, 431–7. Connecticut, Maine, Pennsylvania, and Ohio also passed resolutions against the decision. See also *Evening Post* [New York], Mar. 7, 1857; *Chicago Tribune*, Mar. 12, 17, 19, 1857.

15. Quotation in Richard H. Sewell, *Ballots for Freedom: Antislavery Politics in the United States, 1837–1860* (New York, 1976), 301; Benton, *Historical and Legal Examination of That Part of the Dred Scott Decision Which Declares the Unconstitutionality of the Missouri Compromise* (New York, 1857); Douglas, *Kansas, Utah, and the Dred Scott Decision. Remarks of Hon. Stephen A. Douglas, Delivered in the State House at Springfield, Illinois, on 12th of June, 1857* (n.p., n.d. [1857]).

16. On the *Lemmon* case and its ramifications, see Paul Finkelman, *An Imperfect Union: Slavery, Federalism, and Comity* (Chapel Hill, 1981), 296–312.

17. Fehrenbacher, *Scott*, 468–70; Ehrlich, *Rights*, 179–84.

18. Quotations in Fehrenbacher, *Scott*, 418, 419, 435.

19. Geary quoted in Rawley, *Race and Politics*, 179. Ironically, it is possible that Geary's silencing of the Kansas troubles on the eve of the presidential election contributed to James Buchanan's election. On Geary's pacification of Kansas, see above all the account by his secretary, John H. Gihon, *Geary and Kansas* (Philadelphia, 1857). See also Harry Marlin Tinckom, *John White Geary: Soldier-Statesman, 1819–1873* (Philadelphia, 1940), esp. 58–98.

20. James P. Shenton, *Robert James Walker: A Politician from Jackson to Lincoln* (New York, 1961), esp. 150–74, is the best study of Walker's governorship.

21. Thomas W. Thomas to Alexander Stephens, June 15, 1857, in Ulrich Bonnell Phillips, ed., "The Correspondence of Robert Toombs, Alexander H. Stephens, and Howell Cobb," *Annual Report of the American Historical Association for the Year 1911* (Washington, DC, 1911), 2: 401.

22. Walker quoted in James M. McPherson, *Battle Cry of Freedom: The Civil War Era* (New York, 1988), 165.

23. On Douglas's outrage and his confrontation with Buchanan, see Robert W. Johannsen, *Stephen A. Douglas* (New York, 1973), 581–6.

24. Richardson, 4: 3010.

25. James Dixon to Gideon Welles, Mar. 17, 1858, Welles Papers, LC; *CG*, 35th Congress, 1st

session, Appendix, 200. The congressional struggle over the Lecompton constitution is covered in detail in Nevins, *Emergence*, 1: 256–301; but see also Rawley, *Race and Politics*, 223–56; Johannsen, *Douglas*, 576–613.

26. CG, 35th Congress, 1st session, 603, 1264–5, 1437–8; *New-York Weekly Tribune*, Feb. 13, 1857; Rawley, *Race and Politics*, 239–40; Nevins, *Emergence*, 1: 296.

27. McPherson, *Battle Cry*, 168–9; Stephen B. Oates, *To Purge This Land with Blood: A Biography of John Brown* (1970; Amherst, MA, 1984), 181–273.

28. Nevins, *Emergence*, 1: 288, 296; McPherson, *Battle Cry*, 168 (quotation).

29. Charles W. Calomiris and Larry Schweikart, "The Panic of 1857: Origins, Transmission, and Containment," *Journal of Economic History*, 51 (1994): 807–34; Peter Temin, "The Panic of 1857," *Intermountain Economic Review*, 6 (1972): 1–12; George W. Van Vleck, *The Panic of 1857: An Analytical Study* (New York, 1943); Huston, *Panic of 1857*, esp. 14–34; David Spring to James S. Griffing, Apr. 7, 1858, in *Private Letters: The Correspondence of Rev. James F. Griffing and John August Goodrich*, at www.griffingweb.com; "Hard Times Come Again No More. By Stephen C. Foster" (1857), Broadside, American Song Sheets Collection, LC. The wreck off Cape Hatteras, in September, of the SS *Central America*, which was carrying two million dollars in gold from San Francisco to the eastern banks, redoubled the panic wave on Wall Street. On the gradual spread of the panic from businessmen to masses of small-account holders, including immigrants, see Cormac Ó Gráda and Eugene N. White, "The Panics of 1854 and 1857: A View from the Emigrant Industrial Savings Bank," *Journal of Economic History*, 63 (2003): 213–40.

30. Sean Wilentz, *Chants Democratic: New York City & the Rise of the American Working Class, 1788–1850* (New York, 1984), 395 (quotation), Edwin G. Burrows and Mike Wallace, *Gotham: A History of New York City to 1898* (New York, 1999), 842–52; Huston, *Panic of 1857*, 25–28.

31. Oscar Handlin, *Boston's Immigrants, 1790–1865: A Study in Acculturation* (1941; New York, 1968); Thomas Dublin, *Women at Work: The Transformation of Work and Community in Lowell, Massachusetts, 1826–1860* (New York, 1979), 145–64; Wilentz, *Chants Democratic*, 349–56; Amy Bridges, *A City in the Republic: Antebellum New York and the Origins of Machine Politics* (New York, 1984); Bruce Laurie, *Artisans into Workers: Labor in Nineteenth-Century America* (New York, 1989), 103–4, 122.

32. The New England Workingmen's Association (NEWA; successor to Charles Douglas's similarly named Jacksonian organization) established its own newspaper, the *Voice of Industry*, in the 1840s and undertook massive petition campaigns to secure a ten-hour workday for factory hands and artisan wage earners. In Lowell, female factory operatives, led by a redoubtable organizer, Sarah Bagley, formed their own Lowell Female Labor Reform Association, and allied with the NEWA. See Dublin, *Women at Work*, 108–31, 198–207; Laurie, *Artisans*, esp. 74–112; Wilentz, *Chants Democratic*, 363–89. See Carl Wittke, *The Utopian Communist: A Biography of Wilhelm Weitling* (Baton Rouge, 1950).

33. On Evans and the land reformers, see Wilentz, *Chants Democratic*, 335–43; Reeve Huston, *Land and Freedom: Rural Society, Popular Protest, and Party Politics in Antebellum New York* (New York, 2000), 137–45, 168–72; Jonathan H. Earle, *Jacksonian Antislavery and the Politics of Free Soil* (Chapel Hill, 2004), 58–62. This so-called agrarian argument had already appeared during the union wars of the 1830s, when New York labor leader John Commerford declared in 1834 that, apart from union strikes, distribution of cheap public lands was "the great outlet of relief in view" for hard-pressed workers. *Working Man's Advocate* [New York], Sept. 19, 1835.

34. *Liberator*, Mar. 19, 1847, May 26, Dec. 15, 1848; *Radical* [New York], Mar. 1841; Eric Foner, *Ideology and Politics in the Era of the Civil War* (New York, 1980), 59 (quotation). Paul Goodman, *Of One Blood: Abolitionism and the Origins of Racial Equality* (Berkeley, 1998), 137–75, nicely traces the continuing and often overlooked collaboration between much of the labor movement and antislavery. The erstwhile "shirtless Democrat" and one-time Calhounite Mike Walsh became the most prominent and pugnacious exponent of northern labor's contempt for the antislavery cause. See CG, 33rd Congress, 1st session,

1232; Robert Ernst, "The One and Only Mike Walsh," *New-York Historical Society Quarterly*, 36 (1952): 60–61; Wilentz, *Chants Democratic*, 333.

35. The conventional and by no means wholly discredited view on Irish-black relations appears in such works as Robert Ernst, *Immigrant Life in New York City, 1825–1863* (New York, 1949), 105, 173; Carl Wittke, *The Irish in America* (Baton Rouge, 1956); Phyllis Field, *The Politics of Race in New York: The Struggle for Black Suffrage in the Civil War Era* (Ithaca, NY, 1982). For a valuable corrective, see Graham Hodges, "'Desirable Companions and Lovers': Irish and African Americans in the Sixth Ward," in Ronald H. Baylor and Timothy J. Meagher, eds., *The New York Irish* (Baltimore, 1996), 107–24. David Roediger, *The Wages of Whiteness: Race and the Making of the American Working Class* (New York, 1991), esp. 65–92, sketches this working-class racism, but also exaggerates its uniformity among northern workers generally, as well as among the Irish. On the Democrats' purposeful exploitation of racism, see Jean H. Baker, *Affairs of Party: The Political Culture of Northern Democrats in the Mid-Nineteenth Century* (Ithaca, NY, 1983), esp. 212–58.

36. Burrows and Wallace, *Gotham*, 831–41, 847–51 (quotations on 831, 850); Huston, *Panic of 1857*, 25–27; Bridges, *City*, 113–24, 146–61.

37. *New-York Daily Tribune*, Oct. 22, 1857; Huston, *Panic of 1857*, 139–72. Huston demonstrates that the tariff issue also played well for the Republicans in New Jersey, another closely contested swing state.

38. *National Era* [Washington], Nov. 12, 1857, quoted in Huston, *Panic of 1857*, 103. See also Helene S. Zahler, *Eastern Workingmen and National Land Policy, 1829–1862* (New York, 1941), 127–76.

39. *Economist* [London], Jan. 2, 1858. On the 1857 revivals, whose effects would long outlast the financial panic, see Timothy L. Smith, *Revivalism and Social Reform: American Protestantism on the Eve of the Civil War* (New York, 1857); above all, Kathryn Teresa Long, *The Revival of 1857–58: Interpreting an American Religious Awakening* (New York, 1998).

40. On the regional disparities, see Huston, *Panic of 1857*, 33–34, 60–65.

41. *CG*, 35th Congress, 1st session, 959–62 (quotations on 961–2).

42. Ibid., 962; *New-York Daily Tribune*, Mar. 11, 1858.

43. "I Wish I Was in Dixie's Land" (New York, 1860); Hans Nathan, *Dan Emmett and the Rise of Early Negro Minstrelsy* (Norman, OK, 1962), esp. 243–75. Blackface minstrelsy has come in for intensive analysis as a manifestation of race hatred, hidden admiration, or something far more complicated. The most rewarding recent works are Eric Lott, *Love and Theft: Blackface Minstrelsy and the American Working Class* (New York, 1993); Dale Cockrell, *Demons of Disorder: Early Blackface Minstrels and Their World* (Cambridge, 1997); but see also the classic interpretation by Constance Rourke, *American Humor: A Study of the National Character* (1931; New York, 2004), 70–90. The disputed claims about "Dixie's" black origins appear in Howard L. Sacks and Judith Rose Sacks, *Way Up North in Dixie: A Black Family's Claim to the Confederate Anthem* (Washington, DC, 1993).

44. William W. Freehling offers a fine sketch of the South Carolina slaveholders' different milieux, based on diaries, letters, and travelers' accounts, in *The Road to Disunion: Secessionists at Bay, 1776–1854* (New York, 1990), 28–30. On the up-country, see also Lacy K. Ford, *Origins of Southern Radicalism: The South Carolina Upcountry, 1800–1860* (New York, 1988), 44–95.

45. Charles Mackay, *Life and Liberty in America; or, Sketches of a Tour in the United States and Canada, in 1857-8* (London, 1859) 1: 307; William J. Grayson, *Letters of Curtius* (Charleston, 1851), 8.

46. Representation in South Carolina was based on a ratio of white population to taxes paid; accordingly, one contemporary estimated, low-country districts, home to one-fifth of the state's whites, controlled 40 percent of the lower house and 50 percent of the state senate. The disparity led to complaints from the underrepresented parishes that they were ruled by the "barons of the low country." See Chauncey Samuel Boucher, "Sectionalism, Rep-

resentation, and the Electoral Question in Antebellum South Carolina," *Washington University Studies*, 4 (1916): 3–62, esp. 39–41; Ford, *Origins*, 282 (quotation).

47. Trescott to M. R. H. Garnett, Mar. 14, 1851, quoted in Freehling, *Road to Disunion*, 515. On the persisting political divisions within South Carolina, see Ford, *Origins*, 281–307.

48. *The Death and Funeral Ceremonies of John Caldwell Calhoun* (Columbia, SC, 1850), 164; *Charleston Mercury*, June 20, 1850. See the superb biography by William C. Davis, *Rhett: The Turbulent Life and Times of a Fire-Eater* (Columbia, SC, 2001).

49. *Charleston Mercury*, Nov. 10, 1856, July 7, 1859.

50. "Except for an occasional Carolinian," one New Orleans editor reported in 1850, "there is not a disunionist in Louisiana." *Louisiana Spectator* [New Orleans], Aug. 30, 1850. On all of these figures, including Rhett, see the excellent biographical essays in Eric H. Walther, *The Fire-Eaters* (Baton Rouge, 1992).

51. Trescott to J. H. Hammond, Dec. 5, 1858, quoted in Walther, *Fire-Eaters*, 149; Harper, "Harper's Memoir on Slavery," in *The Pro-Slavery Argument as Maintained by the Most Distinguished Writers of the Southern States* (Charleston, 1852), 6–19; David Gavin quoted in Manisha Sinha, *The Counterrevolution of Slavery: Politics and Ideology in Antebellum North Carolina* (Chapel Hill, 2000), 225; L. W. Spratt, "Report on the Slave Trade," *De Bow's Review*, 24 (1858): 475. The secular, antidemocratic, pro-slavery argument found reinforcement in scriptural defenses of slavery and attacks on the infidel egalitarian Thomas Jefferson. For one striking example out of many, see Thornton Stringfellow, "The Bible Argument: or, Slavery in the Light of Divine Revelation," in E. N. Elliott, *Cotton Is King and Pro-Slavery Arguments* (Augusta, GA., 1860), esp. 503–4. There is a large literature on pro-slavery theology, but see above all Eugene D. Genovese, *"Slavery Ordained of God": The Southern Slaveholders' View of Biblical History and Politics* (Gettysburg, 1985); Eugene D. Genovese and Elizabeth Fox-Genovese, "The Religious Ideals of Southern Slave Society," *Georgia Historical Quarterly*, 70 (1986): 1–16.

52. Fitzhugh, *Sociology for the South, or the Failure of Free Society* (New York, n.d. [1854]), 179. For an earlier, remarkably similar attack on Jeffersonian egalitarianism, see William Porcher Miles, *An Address Delivered Before the Alumni Association of the College of Charleston, on Commencement Day, March 30th, 1852* (Charleston, SC, 1852), 21–25. For contrasting views of Fitzhugh's work as the scribblings of an interesting oddball or, alternatively, the logical conclusion of slaveholders' thinking, see Fitzhugh, *Cannibals All! Or, Slaves Without Masters*, C. Vann Woodward, ed. (Cambridge, MA, 1960), vii–xxxix; Eugene D. Genovese, *The World the Slaveholders Made: Two Essays in Interpretation* (New York, 1969), 118–244.

53. *Democrat* [Petersburg] quoted in *Charleston Mercury*, May 15, 1852; Brown quoted in John Ashworth, *Slavery, Capitalism, and the Politics of the Antebellum Republic: Vol. I: Commerce and Compromise, 1820–1850* (Cambridge, 1995), 216; Thorpe, 4: 2049.

54. George S. Sawyer, *Southern Institutes; or, An Inquiry into the Origin and Early Prevalence of Slavery and the Slave-Trade* (Philadelphia, 1859), 374; *Resolutions of the Montgomery Southern Rights Convention of March 1852*, quoted in J. Mills Thornton III, *Politics and Power in a Slave Society: Alabama, 1800–1860* (Baton Rouge, 1978), 206–7. The biological defense of slavery received increasing attention in the late 1850s, thanks to popularization of new "scientific" confirmations of the claim by writers such as the distinguished Alabama physician and researcher, Josiah C. Nott.

55. *Richmond Enquirer*, Apr. 15, 1856. On southern officeholding, see above all two studies by Ralph A. Wooster: *The People in Power: Courthouse and Statehouse in the Lower South, 1850–1860* (Knoxville, 1969), and *Politicans, Planters, and Plain Folk: Courthouse and Statehouse in the Upper South, 1850–1860* (Knoxville, 1975). See also the voluminous literature cited in Edward M. Pessen, "How Different from Each Other Were the Antebellum North and South?," *AHR*, 85 (1980): 1138 n. 62. For a broader assessment of class and politics in the slave South, see Eugene D. Genovese, "Yeoman Farmers in a Slaveholders' Democracy," *Agricultural History*, 49 (1975): 331–42.

56. Yancey to Joel E. Matthews and others, May 10, 1851, quoted in Walther, *Fire-Eaters*, 63.

57. Slidell to Howell Cobb, Jan. 28, 1852, in Phillips, ed., "Stephens, Toombs, Cobb Correspondence," 275–6; *Richmond Enquirer*, Mar. 27, July 17, 21, Aug. 7, Sept. 4, 27, 1857; *Federal Union* [Milledgeville, GA] Mar. 28, 1854, May 5, Nov. 5, 1857.

58. On Cassius Clay's agitation, and on the broader antislavery currents in Kentucky, see David L. Smiley, *Lion of White Hall: The Life of Cassius M. Clay* (Madison, WI, 1962), 80–111; Freehling, *Road to Disunion*, 462–74; Richard Sears, *The Kentucky Abolitionists in the Midst of Slavery, 1854–1864: Exiles for Freedom* (Lewiston, NY, 1993), 1–298; Harold D. Tallant, *Evil Necessity: Slavery and Political Culture in Antebellum Kentucky* (Lexington, KY, 2003).

59. Helper, *The Impending Crisis of the South: How to Meet It* (New York, 1860), 120.

60. Ibid., 328. See Hugh C. Bailey, *Hinton Rowan Helper, Abolitionist-Racist* (University, AL, 1965).

61. Helper, *Impending Crisis*, v–vi, 153, 169.

62. CG, 35th Congress, 1st session, 961; Samuel M. Wolfe, *Helper's Impending Crisis Dissected* (Philadelphia, 1860); Gilbert J. Beebe, *A Review and Refutation of Helper's "Impending Crisis"* (Middletown, NY, 1860); Louis Schade, *A Book for the "Impending Crisis"! Appeal to the Common Sense and Patriotism of the People of the United States. "Helperism" Annihilated! The "Irrepressible Conflict" and Its Consequences!* (Washington, 1860); Clement Eaton, *The Freedom-Of-Thought Struggle in the Old South* (Durham, 1940), 139–42, 213, 244–5.

63. Charlton T. Lewis to Horace Greeley, July 23, 1854, Greeley Papers, NYPL.

64. *Daily Union* [Washington], May 27, 1858; Johannsen, *Douglas*, 645–55.

65. Johannsen, *Douglas*, 655–6; *Chicago Times*, July 10, 11, 1858. The full text of Douglas's speech also appears in Paul M. Angle, ed., *Created Equal? The Complete Lincoln-Douglas Debates of 1858* (Chicago, 1958), 12–25 (quotation on 24).

66. W. H. Herndon and J. W. Weik, *Herndon's Life of Lincoln*, Paul M. Angle, ed. (1889; New York, 1949), 304. Out of the huge biographical literature on Lincoln, I have found most useful, in addition to *Herndon's Life*, the classic works of John G. Nicolay and John Hay, *Abraham Lincoln: A History* (New York, 1890); Albert J. Beveridge, *Abraham Lincoln* (Boston, 1928); Stephen B. Oates, *With Malice toward None: The Life of Abraham Lincoln* (New York, 1977); David H. Donald, *Lincoln* (New York, 1995).

67. There are numerous contemporary descriptions of Lincoln's appearance and speaking style, but one of the best appears in Herndon and Weik, *Herndon's Life of Lincoln*, 2: 384, 406–8. On the structure of both Lincoln's and Douglas's stump rhetoric and their respective debating tricks and techniques, see Lionel Crocker, ed., *An Analysis of Lincoln and Douglas as Public Speakers and Debaters* (Springfield, IL, 1968), 5–182, 473–539.

68. Lincoln, "Eulogy on Henry Clay, July 6, 1852," in CWAL, 2: 131–2.

69. Lincoln, "Speech at Peoria, Illinois, October 16, 1854," in CWAL, 2: 247–83. Lincoln would later write that his law business "had almost superseded the thought of politics in [my] mind," when the repeal of the Missouri Compromise mightily disturbed him. "Autobiography Written for John Scripps, ca. June, 1860," in CWAL, 4: 67.

70. Lincoln, "Speech at Springfield, Illinois, June 26, 1857," in CWAL, 2: 398–410 (quotations on 401, 402, 406).

71. Among the stimulating assessments of the issues in the debates, and the candidates' handling of them, are David Zarefsky, *Lincoln, Douglas, and Slavery: In the Crucible of Public Debate* (Chicago, 1990); Harry V. Jaffa, *The Crisis of the House Divided: An Interpretation of the Issues in the Lincoln-Douglas Debates* (1959; Chicago, 1982). Useful accounts of the spectacle as well as the substance of the campaign appear in Nevins, *Emergence*, 1: 374–99; Don Fehrenbacher, *Prelude to Greatness: Lincoln in the 1850:* (Stanford, 1962), 48–142; Saul Sigelschiffer, *American Conscience: The Drama of the Lincoln-Douglas Debates* (New York, 1973).

72. Lincoln, "Speech at Springfield, Illinois, June 16, 1858," in CWAL, 2: 461–9 (quotations on 461, 466, 467).

73. Ibid., 461. Lincoln was also concerned about earlier efforts by eastern Republicans,

including Horace Greeley, to persuade the Illinois party to support Douglas with the hope of deepening the Democratic divisions over Lecompton. For details, see Fehrenbacher, *Prelude*, 48–69.

74. *Chicago Times*, July 11, 1858; Angle, ed., *Created Equal?*, 17, 19, 24.
75. Angle, ed., *Created Equal?*, 109, 112. Aside from Angle's, there are several collections of transcriptions of the Lincoln-Douglas debates, each with differing claims to exactness. See also *CWAL*, 3: 1–325; Robert W. Johannsen, ed., *The Lincoln-Douglas Debates of 1858* (New York, 1965); Harold Holzer, ed., *The Lincoln-Douglas Debates: The First Complete, Unexpurgated Text* (New York, 1993).
76. Angle, ed., *Created Equal?*, 138–76 (quotation on 143–4).
77. Ibid., 195–6, 235.
78. Ibid., 390, 393.
79. Nevins, *Emergence*, 1: 396–8; Fehrenbacher, *Prelude*, 114–20.
80. Angle, ed., *Created Equal?*, 218.
81. Ibid., 117.
82. Nevins, *Emergence*, 1: 400–4; Fehrenbacher, *Prelude*, 144–6.
83. Lincoln to Henry Asbury, Nov. 19, 1858, in *CWAL*, 3: 339.
84. Oates, *Purge*, 274–82.

CHAPTER TWENTY-FOUR: THE FAITH THAT RIGHT MAKES MIGHT

1. Spratt, "Report on the Slave Trade," *De Bow's Review*, 24 (1858): 473–74.
2. S & I, 2: 801; James Brewer Stewart, *Joshua Giddings and the Tactics of Radical Politics* (New York, 1970), 240 (quotation); Richard H. Sewell, *Ballots for Freedom: Antislavery Politics in the United States, 1837–1860* (New York, 1976) 285 (quotation); Henry B. Stanton, *Random Recollections* (1886; New York, 1887), 185. Stanton's memoir explicitly invoked the Missouri crisis, calling it the beginning of "the revolt," and claimed that the speeches of James Tallmadge, John W. Taylor, and Rufus King in Congress were "as strong in argument, as splendid in diction" as any antislavery utterances before 1865. Ibid., 164–5. See also Gamaliel Bailey in *National Era* [Washington], June 26, 1856. Astonishment did not completely banish skepticism among the political abolitionists—and perhaps contributed to it. Chase, for example, doubted that the majority of Republicans actually "understood what broad principles they were announcing." But that mattered less than the fact that the party had stood firm. George Julian despised the "scurvy pack of politicians" who ran the Indiana Republican Party, but was more than satisfied because the party's program embraced "the whole anti-slavery doctrine." Julian to Salmon P. Chase, July 22, 1856, in *SPCP*.
3. *National Anti-Slavery Standard* [Washington], Mar. 31, 1860; *Liberator* [Boston], June 8, 1860; Phillips quoted in James M. McPherson, *The Struggle for Equality: Abolitionists and the Negro in the Civil War and Reconstruction* (Princeton, 1964), 12, 27. Garrison took a more hopeful view of Lincoln than other radicals did, in part because his friend (and Lincoln's law partner) William Herndon, as well as Charles Sumner, assured him about Lincoln's antislavery bona fides. Herndon was a subscriber to the *Liberator*, meaning that Lincoln was the only candidate ever to have Garrison's latest blasts turn up regularly in his law office. On Garrison and the 1860 election, see Henry Mayer, *All on Fire: William Lloyd Garrison and the Abolition of Slavery* (New York, 1998), esp. 504–14. The "Slave Hound" label arose from a case in Illinois where Lincoln helped in the legal return of a runaway slave under the Fugitive Slave Law. By the close of the 1860 campaign, Phillips would support Lincoln's election.
4. Smith quoted in Mabee Carleton, *Black Freedom: The Nonviolent Abolitionists from 1830 through the Civil War* (New York, 1970), 318; Higginson quoted in Allan Nevins, *The Emergence of Lincoln* (New York, 1951), 2: 21.

5. See, e.g., F. B. Sanborn, *Recollections of Seventy Years* (Boston, 1909), 1: 83: "Like Cromwell, whom in certain rare qualities he much resembled, he had 'cleared his mind of cant': the hollow formulas of scholars, priests and politicians had little force with Brown. He had a purpose, knew what it was, and meant to achieve it." On Brown at the time of the Harpers Ferry attack, and his subsequent apotheosis, see Stephen Oates, *To Purge This Land with Blood: A Biography of John Brown* (1970; Amherst, 1984), 229–361 passim; and Merrill D. Peterson, *John Brown: The Legend Revisited* (Charlottesville, 2002); also David S. Reynolds, *John Brown, Abolitionist: The Man Who Killed Slavery, Sparked the Civil War, and Seeded Civil Rights* (New York, 2005), which appeared while this book was in press.

6. Sanborn, *Recollections*, 1: 145. On Brown's benefactors, see also Edward Renehan Jr., *The Secret Six: The True Story of the Men Who Conspired with John Brown* (New York, 1995).

7. Oates, *Purge*, 242–7; Benjamin Quarles, *Allies for Freedom: Blacks and John Brown* (New York, 1974), 43–51 (quotation on 51).

8. *Life and Times of Frederick Douglass, Written by Himself* (1892; New York, 1962), 317–20. On the Brown-Douglass encounter and Brown's other efforts to recruit blacks, see Quarles, *Allies*, 63–91.

9. The details of the Harpers Ferry raid are well presented in Oates, *Purge*, 274–306. The raiding party succeeded in capturing George Washington's sword and pistol, when they took over Lewis Washington's plantation. Brown had wanted to use the relics as weapons, as his version of poetic justice.

10. *New York Herald*, Nov. 3, 1859; John Brown ms. note dated Dec. 2, 1859, Chicago Historical Society; Oates, *Purge*, 307–52.

11. Quotation in Nevins, *Emergence*, 2: 97; Oates, *Purge*, 322, 351 (quotation).

12. *Richmond Dispatch*, Oct. 20, 1859; William Kauffman Scarborough, ed., *The Diary of Edmund Ruffin* (Baton Rouge, 1972), 1: 350. See also Stephen A. Channing, *Crisis of Fear: Secession in South Carolina* (New York, 1970), 17–57; James M. McPherson, *Battle Cry of Freedom: The Civil War Era* (New York, 1988), 207–8; Peter Wallenstein, "Incendiaries All: Southern Politics and the Harpers Ferry Raid," in Paul Finkelman, ed., *His Soul Goes Marching On: Responses to John Brown and the Harpers Ferry Raid* (Charlottesville, 1995), 149–73.

13. *Liberator*, Oct. 21, 28, 1858; Thoreau, "A Plea for Captain Brown," in H. S. Salt, ed., *Anti-Slavery and Reform Papers by Henry D. Thoreau* (London, 1890), 51–81 (quotation on 55); Emerson quoted in Oates, *Purge*, 318; Bryant quoted in Nevins, *Emergence*, 2: 99; Norton, *Letters of Charles Eliot Norton* (Boston, 1913), 1: 197–8. Brown's apotheosis came too late for some of his supporters. Three of the Secret Six, now certain they had been exposed, fled into Canada soon after the raid; Gerrit Smith suffered a nervous breakdown and had to be confined to the Utica asylum. On the northern reactions, see Peterson, *Brown*, 15–17, 22–27; Paul Finkelman, "Manufacturing Martyrdom: The Antislavery Response to John's Brown Raid"; Daniel C. Littlefield, "Blacks, John Brown, and a Theory of Manhood"; Wendy Hamand Venet, "'Cry Aloud and Spare Not': Northern Antislavery Women and John Brown's Raid," all in Finkelman, *Soul*, 41–115.

14. Oates, *Purge*, 337–51. One version of the later immortal Union army marching song, "John Brown's Body," assigned him yet another biblical role: "John Brown was John the Baptist of the Christ we are to see/Christ who of the bondsmen shall the Liberator be." See the posting, "History of 'John Brown's Body,'" Public Broadcasting System, www.pbs.org/wgbh/amex/brown/sfeature/song.html/. On the song's peculiar origins, see Sarah Vowell, "John Brown's Body," in Sean Wilentz and Greil Marcus, eds., *The Rose & the Briar: Death, Love, Liberty and the American Ballad* (New York, 2004), 81–89. The connection between Brown's apotheosis and the revivals of 1857–58 cries out for more attention, especially given the prominence of New England abolitionists and antislavery advocates in the revivals and the rugged, masculine themes that they cultivated. For some suggestive remarks, see Kathryn Teresa Long, *The Revival of 1857–58: Interpreting an American Religious Awakening* (New York, 1998), 93–95, 110–4.

15. Thoreau, "A Plea," 58, 68, 81.

16. Oswald Garrison Villard, *John Brown, 1800–1859: A Biography Fifty Years After* (New York, 1910), 568, 564; Lincoln, "Speech at Leavenworth, Kansas, December 3, 1859," in *CWAL*, 3: 502. Seward's radical reputation had been augmented by his famous "Irreconcilable Conflict" speech during the 1858 campaign, in which he declared that the conflict between slavery and freedom could not be forestalled or suppressed. Glyndon Van Deusen, *William Henry Seward* (New York, 1967), 193–4. Lincoln, taking a practical look at the 1859 elections and beyond, also described the Democratic attacks on Republicans over Brown as an "electioneering dodge." "Second Speech at Leavenworth, Kansas, December 5, 1859," in *CWAL*, 3: 503.

17. Booth quoted in Reynolds, *John Brown*, 396.

18. On the "reign of terror" in the South, see Ollinger Crenshaw, *The Slave States in the Presidential Election of 1860* (Baltimore, 1945), 89–111; Nevins, *Emergence*, 2: 107–10; McPherson, *Battle Cry*, 212–3. From Mississippi, one slaveholder wrote to his brother, "In the heart of the planting states we have a foretaste of what Northern brother-hood means, in almost daily conflagrations & in discover of poison, knives & pistols distributed among our slaves by emissaries sent out for the purpose by openly organized associations. I suppose there cannot be found in all the planting States territory ten miles Square in which the foot prints of one or more of these miscreants have not been discovered." There were just enough isolated incidents involving the murder of masters and discovery of arms to feed the panic, though even in these cases it is often difficult to separate fact from fancy. Ollinger Crenshaw likened the hysteria to the famous "great fear" that swept rural France during the summer of 1789. R. S. Holt to Joseph Holt, Nov. 9, 1860, quoted in Crenshaw, *Slave States*, 106.

19. Melville, "The Portent (1859.)," in *Battle-Pieces and Aspects of the War* (New York, 1866), 11; Miles to Christopher Memminger, Jan. 10, 1860, quoted in Eric H. Walther, *The Fire-Eaters* (Baton Rouge, 1992), 288.

20. Memminger to William Porcher Miles, Dec. 27, 1859, quoted in Channing, *Crisis*, 18; Memminger to Miles, Jan. 30, 1860, quoted in Walther, *Fire-Eaters*, 288. The full text of Memminger's speech appears as Christopher Gustavus Memminger, *Address of the Hon. C.G. Memminger, Special Commissioner from the State of South Carolina before the Assembled Authorities of the State of Virginia, January 19, 1860* (Richmond, n.d. [1860]). On the Memminger mission, see also Channing, *Crisis*, 112–27.

21. On the slave trade campaign, see Ronald T. Takaki, *Pro-Slavery Crusade: The Agitation to Reopen the African Slave Trade* (New York, 1971); Manisha Sinha, *The Counterrevolution of Slavery: Ideology and Politics in Antebellum South Carolina* (Chapel Hill, 2000), 125–86 (quotation on 127).

22. *Dispatch* [Augusta] in *Daily News* [Savannah], Jan. 27, 1859, quoted in Takaki, *Pro-Slavery Crusade*, 67; Davis quoted in Nevins, *Emergence*, 2: 33. See also *CG*, 36th Congress, 1st session, 2303–4. When rebuffed by Congress, some southern hard-liners broke the law and tried to import slaves anyway. The most important case, involving the schooner *Wanderer*, led to the arrest, trial, and acquittal of its owner, Charles A. L. Lamar—an incident that further inflamed sectional passions. See Takaki, *Pro-Slavery Crusade*, 201–13. De Bow, the former editor of the *Southern Quarterly Review*, moved from Charleston to New Orleans in 1846, and immediately established what would become *De Bow's Review*.

23. *CG*, 35th Congress, 2nd session, 1242; *Charleston Mercury*, July 7, 1859.

24. *Montgomery Confederation* quoted in *Constitution* [Washington], Aug. 3, 1859; Hammond to W. G. Simms, Apr. 22, 1859, in Nevins, *Emergence*, 2: 39.

25. Brown quoted in Nevins, *Emergence*, 2: 176.

26. *John Sherman's Recollections of Forty Years in the House, Senate, and Cabinet: An Autobiography* (Chicago, 1895), 1: 168–80; Hammond quoted in Nevins, *Emergence*, 2: 121–2 (quotation on 121); *CG*, 36th Congress, 1st session, 650. Sherman recalled that the southern uproar over the Republicans' condensed Helper pamphlet "seemed so ludicrous that we regarded it as a manufactured frenzy."

27. CG, 36th Congress, 1st session, 494, 658, 1490; J. Mills Thornton III, *Politics and Power in a Slave Society: Alabama, 1800–1860* (Baton Rouge, 1978), 384–9.

28. Claude M. Fuess, *The Life of Caleb Cushing* (New York, 1923), 2: 247. The editor and reporter Murat Halstead of the Cincinnati *Commercial* brilliantly evoked both the atmosphere and the political maueverings in Charleston. See Murat Halstead, *Caucuses of 1860. A History of the National Political Conventions of the Current Campaign* (Columbus, 1860); for a more accessible version, see William B. Hesseltine, ed., *Three against Lincoln: Murat Halstead Reports the Caucuses of 1860* (Baton Rouge, 1960), esp. 3–110. See also Roy F. Nichols, *The Disruption of American Democracy* (1948; New York, 1962), 288–308. The transcript appears as *Proceedings of the National Democratic Convention: Convened at Charleston, S.C., April 23, 1860* (Washington, 1860).

29. *Proceedings*, 40; Hesseltine, ed., *Three*, 52–3; *Charleston Courier*, Apr. 30, 1860.

30. Stephens quoted in McPherson, *Battle Cry*, 215; Robert Johannsen, *Stephen A. Douglas* (New York, 1973), 759–60. On the Baltimore and Richmond gatherings, see also Hesseltine, ed., *Three*, 185–278; Nichols, *Disruption*, 308–20.

31. On the Constitutional Unionists, see Albert Dennis Kirwan, *John J. Crittenden: The Struggle for the Union* (1962; Westport, CT, 1974), 346–65; John V. Mering, "The Slave-State Constitutional Unionists and the Politics of Consensus," *JSH*, 43 (1977), 395–410. On the convention, see Hesseltine, ed., *Three*, 138–40.

32. Hesseltine, ed., *Three*, 140; S & I, 2: 1127.

33. Glyndon G. Van Deusen, *William Henry Seward* (New York, 1967), 211–24. Two years before his "higher law" speech opposing Clay's truce of 1850, Seward had been rash enough to say that "slavery must be abolished and you and I must do it"—a statement his congressional adversaries, including Stephen Douglas, never let him forget.

34. On the Buchanan and New York scandals and their effects on the politics of 1860, see Mark W. Summers, *The Plundering Generation: Corruption and the Crisis of the Union, 1849–1861* (New York, 1987), 239–80.

35. Nevins, *Emergence*, 2: 233–9.

36. On Lincoln's preparations for 1860, see the useful older studies by William E. Baringer, *Lincoln's Rise to Power* (Boston, 1937); Don E. Fehrenbacher, *Prelude to Greatness: Lincoln in the 1850s* (Stanford, 1962), 143–61; and also, now, Harold Holzer, *Lincoln at Cooper Union: The Speech That Made Abraham Lincoln President* (New York, 2004), 7–54.

37. Stephen A. Douglas, "The Dividing Line Between Federal and Local Authority," *Harper's New Monthly Magazine*, 19 (1859): 519–37; Holzer, *Cooper Union*, 5–118. Recent interpreters have argued inaccurately that at the Cooper Institute (later renamed "Cooper Union"), Lincoln began invoking the rhetoric of the Founders, especially the Declaration of Independence, as a symbolic pillar of the Republican Party. Supposedly he did the same, as president, to save the Union. See above all Garry Wills, *Lincoln at Gettysburg: The Words That Remade America* (New York, 1992). But the basic theme was practically a cliché in political antislavery rhetoric in 1860, dating back to when Lincoln was a stripling Whig politician. Lincoln deployed it expertly, but he hardly invented it.

38. Lincoln, "Address at Cooper Institute, New York City, February 27, 1860," in CWAL, 3: 522–50 (quotation on 550).

39. *New-York Daily Tribune*, Feb. 28, 1860; Holzer, *Cooper Union*, 149–205.

40. There are splendid accounts of the Chicago convention in Hesseltine, ed., *Three*, 141–77; Nevins, *Emergence*, 2: 229–60. The official transcript appears as *Proceedings of the National Republican Convention* (n.p., n.d. [1860]).

41. Hesseltine, ed., *Three*, 171; S & I, 3: 1124–7.

42. *Proceedings . . . Republican Convention*, 109. There are informative accounts of the 1860 campaign in Emerson D. Fite, *The Presidential Campaign of 1860* (New York, 1911); Nevins, *Emergence*, 2: 272–86; James A. Rawley, *Edwin D. Morgan, 1811–1883: A Merchant in Politics* (New York, 1955), 103–20; Elting Morison, "Election of 1860," in S & I, 3: 1097–152; McPherson, *Battle Cry*, 221–33. The image of Lincoln as "The Railsplitter" appears to have first gained public notice at the state Republican convention in Decatur a

week before the Chicago convention, when Lincoln's old friend John Hanks appeared with another friend, carrying two weather-beaten planks they claimed had been made by Hanks and Lincoln in 1830. Their banner proclaimed Lincoln "The Rail Candidate For President in 1860." See Nevins, *Emergence*, 2: 245; Mark Plummer, "Lincoln and the Rail-Splitter Election," *Lincoln Herald*, 101 (1999): 111–6.

43. Contract with Theodore Canisius, May [30?], 1859, Lincoln to Frederick C. W. Koehnle, July 11, 1859, in *CWAL*, 3: 383, 391. On the much-disputed importance of the German vote in the 1860 election, see William E. Gienapp, "Who Voted For Lincoln?," in John Thomas, ed., *Abraham Lincoln and the American Political Tradition* (Amherst, MA, 1980), 50–97. Despite Lincoln's best efforts, the immigrant vote in Springfield would break heavily Democratic in 1860, and he only narrowly carried his hometown.

44. *New-York Weekly Tribune*, Aug. 11, 1860; Johannsen, *Douglas*, 792.

45. *New-York Weekly Tribune*, Sept. 8, 1860; *New York Herald*, Sept. 17, 1860; Johannsen, *Douglas*, 774–807.

46. *New York Herald*, Oct. 24, Nov. 5, 6 (quotations), 1860; Phyllis Field, *The Politics of Race in New York: The Struggle for Black Suffrage in the Civil War Era* (Ithaca, NY, 1982), 114–46. As Field shows, the effort by New York Democrats to turn the suffrage referendum to their advantage failed, as many conservative Republicans simply chose not to vote at all on the referendum but did vote for Lincoln.

47. On the various fusion schemes, see Johannsen, *Douglas*, 792–3.

48. Lincoln to George D. Prentice, Oct. 29, 1860, in *CWAL*, 4: 134–5.

49. *Richmond Semi-Weekly Examiner*, Nov. 9, 1860, in Dwight L. Dumond, ed., *Southern Editorials on Secession* (New York, 1931), 223; S & I, 3: 1152.

50. Charles Francis Adams Diary, Nov. 7, 1860, Adams Papers, MHS.

51. Clement Eaton, "Mob Violence in the Old South," *Mississippi Valley Historical Review*, 29 (1942): 351–71; Fite, *Campaign*, 229–30; Crenshaw, *Slave States*, 89–112, 301–2.

52. On the slave "grapevine" and possible instigations in 1860, see Steven Hahn, *A Nation under Our Feet: Black Political Struggles in the Rural South from Slavery to the Great Migration* (Cambridge, MA, 2003), 13–14, 65–68 (quotation on 68).

53. J. G. de Roulhac Hamilton, ed., *The Papers of Thomas Ruffin* (Raleigh, NC, 1918–20), 3: 85. Ruffin, the former longtime chief justice of the North Carolina state supreme court, opposed nullification in 1832–33 and secession in 1860, but went on to vote for his state's ordinance of secession in 1861.

CHAPTER TWENTY-FIVE: THE ILIAD OF ALL OUR WOES

1. *Charleston Mercury*, Nov. 8, 1860.

2. "Passage Written for Lyman Trumbull's Speech at Springfield Illinois, Nov. 20, 1860," in *CWAL*, 4: 142.

3. There is a large and contentious literature about secession in the Deep South, much of it focused on whether disunion came as a result of a conspiracy or a popular upsurge. I have found especially useful Dwight L. Dumond, *The Secessionist Movement, 1860–1861* (New York, 1931); Lee Rainwater, *Mississippi: Storm Center of Secession, 1856–1861* (Baton Rouge, 1938), esp. 121–225; Ralph A. Wooster, "The Secession of the Lower South: An Examination of Changing Interpretations," *Civil War History*, 7 (1961): 117–27; idem, *The Secession Conventions of the South* (Princeton, 1962), esp. 11–135; William J. Donnelly, "Conspiracy or Popular Movement: The Historiography of Southern Support for Secession," *North Carolina Historical Review*, 42 (1965): 70–84; Stephen A. Channing, *Crisis of Fear: Secession in South Carolina* (New York, 1970); William L. Barney, *The Secessionist Impulse: Alabama and Mississippi in 1860* (Princeton, 1974); Michael P. Johnson, *Toward a Patriarchal Republic: The Secession of Georgia* (Baton Rouge, 1977); J. Mills Thornton III, *Politics and Power in a Slave Society: Alabama, 1800–1860* (Baton Rouge, 1978), 342–461.

4. *Journal of the Convention of the People of South Carolina Held in 1860, 1861, and 1862* (Columbia, SC, 1862), 43–45, 75–77. Memminger's declaration focused on recent grievances, above all the election of a Republican president hostile to the South. Rhett cast the conflict in larger terms, as the culmination of the South's decades-long struggle for independence and self-rule dating back to the Revolution and the ratification of the Constitution. For contrasting interpretations of these events see Channing, *Crisis of Fear*, 252–84; Lacy K. Ford, *Origins of Southern Radicalism: The South Carolina Upcountry, 1800–1860* (New York, 1988), 338–73.

5. E. S. Dargan in William R. Smith, *The History and Debates of the Convention and People of Alabama* (Montgomery, 1861), 94. Petigru's oft-cited remark, reportedly delivered to a group of secessionists and which fits his blunt style and politics, may be apocryphal. But he did write, in despair, to a fellow South Carolina Unionist leader, "Why should one put himself to the pains of speaking to the insane if he has not the power of commanding a straight jacket for them." James L. Petigru to B. F. Perry, Dec. 8, 1860, quoted in Ford, *Origins*, 371.

6. See esp. Daniel W. Crofts, *Reluctant Confederates: Upper South Unionists in the Secessionist Crisis* (Chapel Hill, 1989), xvi (quotation).

7. Alexander Rives quoted in ibid., 210. The less adamant Unionists were willing to abandon the southern rights demand for a positive slave code, but only in exchange for a constitutional amendment barring federal interference with the right to hold slaves in territories south of 36°30'.

8. William Clark quoted in ibid., xv–xvi; Smith, *History*, 73–74 (quotations on 74); Wooster, *Secession Conventions*, 28–29, 41–48, 51–52, 62–66, 68, 76–79, 82–84, 95–100, 104, 115–20; James M. McPherson, *Battle Cry of Freedom: The Civil War Era* (New York, 1988), 238. In the Alabama convention, fifty-four delegates were immediate secessionists and forty-six were "cooperationists," the latter coming mainly from the northern yeoman counties. For a more detailed and nuanced examination of the Alabama secession convention, and its connections to previous party and factional divisions, see Thornton, *Power*, 343–461.

9. *Picayune* [New Orleans], Feb. 17, Mar. 18, 1861; Roger W. Shugg, *Origins of Class Struggle in Louisiana: A Social History of White Farmers and Laborers during Slavery and After, 1840–1875* (Baton Rouge, 1939), 161–6; Thomas M. Peters to Andrew Johnson, Jan. 15, 1861, quoted in Allan Nevins, *The Emergence of Lincoln* (New York, 1951), 2: 424. A close study of the Louisiana returns dispels the claims of outright fraud and confirms that the immediate secessionists prevailed, but also shows that the outcome was closer than the secessionists would have liked and that their backers misreported numbers to make their victory seem even larger than it was. See Charles B. Dew, "Who Won the Secession Election in Louisiana?," *JSH*, 36 (1970): 18–32.

10. Forsyth to Stephen A. Douglas, Dec. 28, 1860, quoted in Johannsen, *Douglas*, 808–9; *Augusta Constitutionalist*, Nov. 16, 1860, in Dwight L. Dumond, *Southern Editorials on Secession* (New York, 1931), 242–7 (quotation on 246). See also Lonnie A. Burnett, "The 'Disturber' of the Democracy: John Forsyth and the Election of 1860," *Gulf States Historical Review*, 17 (2001): 6–35. In Alabama, 79 percent of the convention delegates were slaveholders, the overwhelming majority of whom (84.8 percent) owned ten slaves or more. Nearly half (43.4 percent) of the cooperationist delegates were either nonslaveholders or slaveholders with fewer than ten slaves. See Wooster, *Secession Conventions*, 56.

11. Smith, *History*, 110; Thomas E. Schott, *Alexander Stephens: A Biography* (Baton Rouge, 1988), 305–23.

12. The distinction, like many differences in political thinking, was not always clear-cut. At times, especially when it was politically convenient, the fire-eaters could present themselves as revolutionaries, and southern Democrats like Jefferson Davis could sound like perfect conservatives, claiming that secession was called a revolution only "by abuse of language." Sometimes purposefully, sometimes out of confusion, some leading secessionists moved back and forth—or straddled both positions at once. The lines of divergence

described here should be regarded as strong tendencies more than as hard and fast schools of thought. See Davis, "Inaugural Address of the President of the Provisional Government," Feb. 18, 1861, in Dunbar Rowland, ed., *Jefferson Davis, Constitutionalist: His Letters, Papers and Speeches* (Jackson, MS, 1923), 5: 50.

13. *Montgomery Confederation*, Sept. 22, 1858, quoted in Eric H. Walther, *The Fire-Eaters* (Baton Rouge, 1992), 71; *Charleston Mercury*, June 7, 1860; *De Bow's Review*, 33 (1862): 44; McPherson, *Battle Cry*, 245 (quotation).

14. CG, 36th Congress, 2nd session, 11; Davis "Inaugural Address," Feb. 22, 1861, in Rowland, *Davis*, 5: 202. Some southerners returned to the symbolism of the 1790s, wearing old-fashioned cockades in their hats (colored blue, this time, the color favored by the nullifiers in 1832–33), and sang songs with titles like "The Southern Marseillaise." More often, the revolution-minded slaveholders had 1776 and not 1789 in mind. Even William Lowndes Yancey bowed before the rhetorical power of these American revolutionary themes: in the battle to secure secession, he wrote, "the nomenclature of the Revolution of 1776 will have to be revived." See James Oakes, *The Ruling Race: A History of American Slaveholders* (New York, 1982), 239–42 (quotation on 239).

15. Davis, *The Rise and Fall of the Confederate Government* (New York, 1881), 1: 80, Alexander H. Stephens, *A Constitutional View of the Late War Between the States* (Philadelphia, 1868), 1: 12.

16. R. N. Hemphill to William R. Hemphill, Dec. 14, 1860, quoted in Channing, *Crisis*, 289; "Declaration of the Immediate Causes Which Induce and Justify the Secession of South Carolina from the Federal Union," in J. A. May and J. R. Faunt, *South Carolina Secedes* (Columbia, SC, 1960), 79–80; "A Declaration of the Immediate Causes which Induce and Justify the Secession of the State of Mississippi from the Federal Union," in *Journal of the State Convention and Ordinances and Resolutions Adopted in January, 1861* (Jackson, MI, 1861), 86; *Journal of the Public and Secret Proceedings of the Convention of the People of Georgia* (Milledgeville, GA, 1861), 104; "A Declaration of the Causes Which Impel the State of Texas to Secede from the Federal Union," in Ernest William Winkler, ed., *Journal of the Secession Convention in Texas, 1861* (Austin, 1912), 61; Smith, *History*, 81. South Carolina, Mississippi, Georgia, and Texas were the only four states to issue explanatory documents beyond their pro-forma ordinances of secession.

17. Stephens's "corner-stone" speech appears in Henry Cleveland, *Alexander H. Stephens in Public and Private: With Letters and Speeches, Before, During, and Since the War* (Philadelphia, 1866), 717–29 (quotation on 721–2).

18. De Bow, "The Non-Slaveholders of the South: Their Interest in the Present Sectional Controversy Identical with That of the Slaveholders," *De Bow's Review*, 30 (1861): 67–77 (quotations on 67, 68, 74). Secessionist efforts to ensure the nonslaveholders' loyalties antedated Lincoln's election, provoked in part by the controversy over Helper's *Impending Crisis*. Commonly, though, these efforts simply asserted, as one Kentucky editor put it, that "the strongest pro-slavery men in this State are those who do not even own one dollar of slave property," and that impressions to the contrary were abolitionist fantasies, meant "to array one class of our citizens against the other." With the secession crisis, the matter became too important to be left to bland affirmations. See *Kentucky Statesman* [Lexington], Oct. 5, 1860, in Dumond, ed., *Southern Editorials*, 173–5.

19. Brown quoted in Steven Hahn, *The Roots of Southern Populism: Yeoman Farmers and the Transformation of the Georgia Upcountry, 1850–1890* (New York, 1983), 86–87; De Bow, "Non-Slaveholders," 75; Russell, *History*, 110.

20. Quotation in Richard Malcom Johnston and William Hand Browne, *Life of Alexander Stephens* (Philadelphia, 1878), 370. The "madness" Stephens describes had something in common with what Charles Royster has called the "rage militaire" that broke out among American patriots after the first blows of the Revolution. See Charles Royster, *A Revolutionary People at War: The Continental Army and American Character, 1775–1783* (New York, 1979), 25–53. The quoted lines are from "The Bonnie Blue Flag," Broadside, n.p., n.d., Nineteenth-Century American Songsheets Collection, LC. The song, based on the

flag raised atop the Mississippi statehouse following secession, was second only in popularity to "Dixie" as the anthem of southern nationalism. It was written early in 1861 by Harry McCarthy, an English-born veteran entertainer who based the tune on an old popular Irish song, "The Irish Jaunting Car."

21. For descriptions of the Montgomery Convention, see E. Merton Coulter, *The Confederate States of America 1861–65* (Baton Rouge, 1950), 19–35; Emory M. Thomas, *The Confederate Nation, 1861–1865* (New York, 1979), 57–66; William C. Davis, *"A Government of Our Own": The Making of the Confederacy* (New York, 1994).

22. "Arrival of President Davis at Montgomery—His Speech," in Rowland, *Davis*, 5: 48.

23. Davis, "Inaugural Address of the President of the Provisional Government," Feb. 18, 1861, in ibid., 50, 52.

24. The text of the Confederate Constitution appears in Thomas, *Confederate*, 307–22.

25. Rhett and other fire-eaters fought the slave trade provision and otherwise tried to make the constitution even more to their liking, but they failed. "The Constitution has been adopted by an overwhelming majority against Rhett & Company, Slave traders, Free traders, fire eaters, and extremists," James H. Hammond happily reported in early April, "and I suppose this is the end of them." Having engineered secession, the fire-eaters were relegated to the margins. But they would remain an affliction to Jefferson Davis's government for as long as the Confederacy lasted. Hammond to J. D. Ashmore, Apr. 8, 1861, quoted in William C. Davis, *Rhett: The Turbulent Life and Times of a Fire-Eater* (Columbia SC, 2001) 461. The separate Deep South states completed ratification of the Confederate constitution between March 12 and April 22.

26. Tyler E. Dennett, *Lincoln and the Civil War in the Diaries and Letters of John Hay* (1939; New York, 1988), 19; Richardson, 5: 3157–65, 3168 (quotation). On Lincoln and the details of the secession crisis, another topic with a voluminous scholarly literature, see above all David M. Potter, *Lincoln and His Party in the Secession Crisis* (1942; Baton Rouge, 1995); Kenneth M. Stampp, *And the War Came: The North and the Secession Crisis* (Baton Rouge, 1950); Nevins, *Emergence*, 2: 362–413, 436–71. For a judicious and more recent interpretation, see McPherson, *Battle Cry*, 246–74.

27. Richardson, 5: 3168–70; *Republican* [Springfield, IL], Dec. 17, 1860; *New-York Daily Tribune*, Nov. 9, 1860; Henry Mayer, *All on Fire: William Lloyd Garrison and the Abolition of Slavery* (New York, 1998), 516. The evocations of Jackson varied. While antislavery and some pro-Douglas editors alike pushed Lincoln to act more like the "vigorous and defiant" Jackson, some of the more conservative Democrats saw Jackson's legacy differently. "The sword of the old Hero of New Orleans might have leapt from its scabbard in this conflict," the *Daily Chicago Times* said, "but it would never have glittered in the ranks of the Abolitionists." For the first view, see *Cincinnati Daily Commercial*, Nov. 15, 1860 (quotation); *Wisconsin Daily State Journal* [Madison], Nov. 17, 1860; *Sioux City Register*, Dec. 1, 1860; and for the second, *Circleville Watchman* [OH], Nov. 23, 1860; *Daily Chicago Times*, Dec. 7, 1860; *Cincinnati Daily Enquirer*, Dec. 27, 1860, Feb. 10, 1861, all in Harold Cecil Perkins, ed., *Northern Editorials on Secession* (New York, 1942), 1: 111, 169, 181, 216, 270, 429, 2: 991.

28. The text of the amendment compromise appears in *CG*, 36th Congress, 2nd session, 114. See also Albert Dennis Kirwan, *John J. Crittenden: The Struggle for the Union* (1962; Westport, CT, 1974), 391–421. Some southern sympathizers—notably New York's Fernando Wood, now the city's mayor—made noises about starting their own secession movement and turning Manhattan and some surrounding counties into an independent nation and free port, what an enthusiastic George Fitzhugh instantly dubbed "the Republic of New-York." The plan died, although many of New York's pro-southern merchants and Irish Democrats would remain a thorn in the North's side for years to come. See Fitzhugh, "The Republic of New-York," *De Bow's Review*, 30 (1861): 181–7; more generally, William C. Wright, *The Secession Movement in the Middle Atlantic States* (Rutherford, NJ, 1973).

29. Glyndon Van Deusen, *William Henry Seward* (New York, 1967), 249; Lincoln to Thurlow

Weed, Dec. 17, 1860, to William H. Seward, Feb. 1, 1861, in *CWAL*, 4: 154, 183; *CG*, 36th Congress, 2nd session, 409.

30. On the peace convention, see Robert G. Gunderson, *Old Gentleman's Convention: The Washington Peace Conference of 1861* (Madison, WI 1961); Jesse L. Keene, *The Peace Convention of 1861* (Tuscaloosa, 1961). The Senate rejected the revised version of the Crittenden compromise by a vote of 28 to 7, while the House did not even bother to bring it up for final consideration. *CG*, 36th Congress, 2nd session, 1254–5.

31. McPherson, *Battle Cry*, 260–2 (quotation on 262).

32. Crofts, *Reluctant Confederates*, exhaustively studies the conflicts over secession in the Border South, focusing on Virginia, Tennessee, and North Carolina. The process of drafting and revising Lincoln's inaugural address, including Seward's and Browning's suggested revisions, can be tracked in the text and notes in *CWAL*, 4: 249–62. Both advisers softened the language of Lincoln's first draft, adding much of the purposeful ambiguity and conciliatory language that appeared in the final speech.

33. The final text of the address appears in *CWAL*, 4: 262–71. On the scene at the inauguration, see *New York Herald*, Mar. 5, 1861; *New-York Daily Tribune*, Mar. 5, 1861; Nevins, *Emergence*, 2: 457–8.

34. *Richmond Enquirer*, Mar. 5, 1861; T. W. MacMahon, *Cause and Contrast: An Essay on the American Crisis* (Richmond, 1862), 137; Faulkner to Abraham Lincoln, Mar. 5, 1861, Abraham Lincoln Papers, LC; *Staunton Spectator* [Virginia], Mar. 5, 1861; *North Carolina Standard*, Mar. 9, 1861, *Nashville Republican Banner*, Mar. 14, 1861, quoted in Crofts, *Reluctant Confederates*, 260.

35. Nevins, *Emergence*, 2: 461–2.

36. On the events of March and early April 1865, I have relied especially on Stampp, *And the War Came*; Allan Nevins, *The War for the Union* (New York, 1959), 1: 6–70; Richard N. Current, *Lincoln and the First Shot* (Philadelphia, 1963); David M. Potter, *The Impending Crisis, 1848–1861* (New York, 1976), 555–83; McPherson, *Battle Cry*, 264–74.

37. Perkins, ed., *Northern Editorials*, 2: 699–703; Elbert B. Smith, *Francis Preston Blair* (New York, 1980), 270–1, 275–6.

38. The text of Seward's memorandum, entitled simply "Some thoughts for the President's consideration," appears in *CWAL*, 4: 317–8. Lincoln drafted a reply (ibid., 316–7) in which he noted Seward's assertion that the president must hand responsibility to "some member" of his cabinet. "I remark," Lincoln's letter read, "that if this must be done, *I* must do it." It is highly probable that Lincoln left the letter undelivered and rebuked the secretary of state in person and in private. On the unsuccessful meeting with the Virginian, John Baldwin, see William C. Harris, "The Southern Unionist Critique of the Civil War," *Civil War History*, 31 (1985): 50–51.

39. Lincoln to Robert S. Chew, Apr. 6, 1861, in *CWAL*, 4: 323–4 (quotation on 323).

40. William Kauffman Scarborough., ed., *The Diary of Edmund Ruffin* (Baton Rouge, 1972–89), 1: 542.

41. E. J. Arthur [?] quoted in Nevins, *Emergence*, 2: 335; Coulter, *Confederate States*, 15; Stowe, "Getting Ready for a Gale," *Independent* [New York], Apr. 25, 1861, 1.

42. Scarborough, ed., *Diary of Edmund Ruffin*, 2: 588.

EPILOGUE

1. William Kauffman Scarborough, ed. *The Diary of Edmund Ruffin* (Baton Rouge, 1972–89), 3: 895. The Virginia convention, motivated in part by Lincoln's military call-up after Fort Sumter, approved a secession ordinance on April 17, 1861, which was ratified by popular referendum on May 23. Virginia's decision helped persuade other reluctant southerners to join the cause, including Robert E. Lee, who had earlier called slavery "a moral and social evil" and opposed secession. The remaining three Confederate states—Arkansas, Tennessee, and North Carolina—seceded in May. The western counties of Vir-

ginia, under Union military control, in turn seceded from Virginia, beginning with a state-hood referendum in October 1861 that eventuated in the admission of the new state of West Virginia to the Union on June 20, 1863. See Daniel W. Crofts, *Reluctant Confederates: Upper South Unionists in the Secession Crisis* (Chapel Hill, 1989), 308–52; James M. McPherson, *Battle Cry of Freedom: The Civil War Era* (New York, 1988), 276–307.

2. Scarborough, ed., *Diary of Edmund Ruffin*, 3: 949–50. The last entry is dated June 18, but Scarborough determines that the event occurred on the previous day.

3. L.W. Spratt in *Southern Literary Messenger*, 32 (1861): 243–4; *CWAH*, 7: 23. Spratt's piece, delivered in the form of a letter, was an updated version of his earlier essay on reopening the slave trade. The *Messenger* hailed it as a masterpiece for its "just conception of the elemental causes which have excited such intense disturbances in national politics during the last forty years, and which have culminated in the formation of a new Confederacy." For similar denunciations of northern government and society, see William H. Russell, *The Civil War in America* (Boston, 1861), 44–45; J. Hamley Smith to Alexander Stephens, Apr. 3, 1860, quoted in Allan Nevins, *The Emergence of Lincoln* (New York, 1951), 2: 330.

4. Lincoln to Henry L. Pierce and Others, Apr. 6, 1859, in *CWAL*, 3: 376.

5. James Parton, *Famous Americans of Recent Times* (Boston, 1867), 191.

6. Van Buren, *Inquiry into the Origin and Course of Political Parties in the United States* (New York, 1867), 12.

7. Lincoln to Pierce, Apr. 6, 1859, in *CWAL*, 3: 374–5.

8. On the Savannah meeting, see "Colloquy with Colored Ministers," *Journal of Negro History*, 16 (1931), 88–94; Eric Foner, *Reconstruction: America's Unfinished Revolution* (New York, 1988), 70–71. The transcript of Frazier's words is most accessible in Ira Berlin et al., *Free at Last: A Documentary History of Slavery, Freedom, and the Civil War* (New York, 1992), 310–8.

9. Heighton, "Reconstruction: A Letter from William Heighton to George L. Stearns," in [Stearns, ed.], *The Equality of All Men before the Law Claimed and Defended* (Boston, 1865), 42–43.

10. Ibid. Heighton apparently retained his radical Universalist religious beliefs as well, writing of "the Creator's gift to all human beings of equal rights to the development and culture of body, mind, and moral nature."

11. Melanie Susan Gustafson, *Women and the Republican Party, 1854–1924* (Urbana, IL, 2001), 7–8; Lydia Maria Child to Charles Sumner, July 9, 1872, Charles Sumner Papers, HU; David Roediger, "Ira Steward and the Anti-Slavery Origins of American Eight-Hour Theory," *Labor History*, 27 (1986), 410–26 (quotation on 424); Adams, "The Protection of the Ballot in National Elections," *Journal of Social Science*, 1 (1869): 108–9.

12. "O I'm a Good Old Rebel," n.d. [ca. 1865], in Richard Crawford, ed., *The Civil War Songbook* (New York, 1977), 71–2 (quotation on 72). On the variegated politics of Reconstruction, see, among numerous studies, Kenneth M. Stampp, *The Era of Reconstruction, 1865–1877* (New York, 1965); Foner, *Reconstruction*.

13. William C. Davis, *An Honorable Defeat: The Last Days of the Confederate Government* (New York, 2001), 286–312, 384–96 passim.

14. The second man from the left in the front row of the photograph is Joseph Cox. Born free in 1833, Cox was a Richmond blacksmith who also worked as a bartender and day laborer, and for a time was a storekeeper. An activist in Republican Party politics after the war, he served as a delegate to the Virginia constitutional convention of 1867–68, where he joined with the moderates in opposing the widespread disenfranchisement and property expropriation of ex-Confederates. A vice president of the Richmond meeting of the Colored National Labor Union in 1870, Cox worked to bring white moderates into the Republican Party and blacks into Richmond city government. At his death in 1880, three thousand blacks marched in his funeral procession. See Eric Foner, *Freedom's Lawmakers: A Directory of Black Officeholders during Reconstruction* (1993; Baton Rouge, 1996), 52.

ACKNOWLEDGMENTS

I am deeply grateful to the John Simon Guggenheim Memorial Foundation and the American Council of Learned Societies for their financial support. An intellectually challenging fellowship year at the Woodrow Wilson International Center for Scholars in 1998–99 transformed my understanding of American democracy, for which I am indebted to the Center and its excellent staff. I am equally indebted to the Princeton University Research Board, the Shelby Cullom Davis Center for Historical Studies, and the Princeton University History Department for their generosity over many years.

Gerald Howard, then of W. W. Norton & Company, showed faith in this book and its author when he signed me up long ago, and he remains a steadfast ally. At Norton, I have been blessed to work with Drake McFeely, a friend for more than two decades and a wise editor, who also possesses the patience and fortitude of a saint. His assistant, Brendan Curry, offered me his energy, encouragement, and shrewd expertise. Mary Babcock's superb copyediting improved my prose and pushed me to omit large amounts of extraneous material. Thanks go as well to Starling Lawrence and Jeannie Luciano for their support. During the final stages, Nancy Palmquist, Anna Oler, Gina Webster, Don Rifkin, Bill Rusin, Louise Brockett, Elizabeth Riley, Sally Anne McCartin, and their staffs performed splendidly in turning out the finished book.

Tom Wallace of T.C. Wallace, Ltd., and Andrew Wylie of the Wylie Agency handled business matters with sagacity and efficiency.

Judith Ferszt, the manager of the Program in American Studies at Princeton, has helped me in matters large and small nearly every day for the past dozen years, and given me the gifts of her singular intelligence and good cheer.

Amanda Ameer and Samantha Williamson put in many hard hours checking footnotes and quotations.

Numerous friends, loved ones, colleagues, students, teachers, librarians, research assistants, technical wizards, counselors, and confessors have helped me beyond measure, in everything from suggesting sources, locating documents, and reading drafts to making allowances for my exasperating distraction. To praise them here as they deserve would add many more pages to an already long book. I have thanked them, and will continue to thank them, personally. Above all, thanks go to my beloved and forbearing family, who make me wish I could have been a poet instead of a historian and said it all much better and quicker.

The dedication is a toast to essential companions and decades of companionship—and to decades more, through thick and thin.

CREDITS

DEMOCRACY ASCENDANT

1. Library of Congress
2. Library of Congress
3. National Portrait Gallery, Smithsonian Institution / Art Resource, NY
4. Library of Congress
5. Picture History
6. The Granger Collection, New York
7. Virginia Historical Society, Richmond, Virginia
8. Library of Congress
9. Library of Congress
10. *John C. Calhoun (1782–1850)*, 1838, by Rembrandt Peale (1778–1860), oil on canvas, Gibbes Museum of Art / Carolina Art Association, 1959.23.01
11. National Portrait Gallery, Smithsonian Institution / Art Resource, NY
12. The Historical Society of Pennsylvania (HSP) James Forten, Leon Gardiner Collection
13. Library of Congress
14. National Archives and Records Administration
15. Oberlin College Archives, Oberlin, Ohio
16. State Preservation Board, Austin, Texas
17. Library of Congress
18. Library of Congress
19. Library of Congress
20. Courtesy of the author
21. Ross County Historical Society, Chillicothe, Ohio
22. The Granger Collection, New York
23. Library of Congress

SLAVERY AND THE CRISIS OF AMERICAN DEMOCRACY

1. The Granger Collection, New York
2. Library of Congress
3. Library of Congress
4. The Granger Collection, New York
5. Picture History
6. The Granger Collection, New York
7. Coline Jenkins / Elizabeth Cady Stanton Trust
8. Library of Congress
9. Library of Congress
10. Library of Congress
11. Library of Congress
12. The Granger Collection, New York
13. The Granger Collection, New York
14. National Portrait Gallery, Smithsonian Institution / Art Resource, NY
15. Library of Congress
16. Library of Congress
17. Picture History
18. Library of Congress
19. Library of Congress
20. Alabama Department of Archives and History, Montgomery, Alabama
21. Library of Congress
22. Picture History
23. Library of Congress

INDEX

Page numbers beginning with 797 refer to notes.